Queen Elizabeth

THE QUEENS OF ENGLAND AND THEIR TIMES.

FROM
MATILDA, QUEEN OF WILLIAM THE CONQUEROR,
TO
ADELAIDE, QUEEN OF WILLIAM THE FOURTH.

BY
FRANCIS LANCELOTT, ESQ.
AUTHOR OF "AUSTRALIA AS IT IS," "THE PILGRIM FATHERS," &c. &c.

IN TWO VOLUMES.
VOL. II.

NEW YORK:
D. APPLETON AND COMPANY,
346 & 348 BROADWAY.
M DCCC LVIII.

THE

QUEENS OF ENGLAND

AND THEIR TIMES.

ELIZABETH, SECOND QUEEN REGNANT.

CHAPTER I.

Elizabeth's birth—Parentage—Christening—Infancy—Early misfortunes—Letter from her governess—Attends the christening of Edward the Sixth—Resides with him—Precociousness—Friendship with Anne of Cleves; with Katherine Howard; with Katherine Parr—Restored to her right of succession—Futile overtures for her marriage with Philip of Spain.

THE illustrious Elizabeth, daughter of King Henry the Eighth by the beautiful and unfortunate Queen Anne Boleyn, was born on Sunday, the seventh of September, 1533, between three and four in the afternoon, at the royal palace of Greenwich. Although the King had earnestly hoped that the babe would prove a son, he stifled his disappointment. *Te Deum* was sung, and bonfires blazed, in honour of her birth; and preparations were made for her christening, which, on the tenth of September, was celebrated with extraordinary pomp and splendour. On that day, the lord mayor, with the aldermen and council of the city of London, in their robes and chains, took to their barges at one in the afternoon, and rowed to Greenwich, where they found assembled lords, knights, and gentlemen, in great numbers. The walls between Greenwich Palace and the Convent of the Grey Friars were hung with tapestry, and the way strewn with green rushes; the Friars' church, of which not a vestige now remains, was also hung with rich tapestry. The fount was of silver; it was placed in the middle of the church, raised three steps high, the steps being covered with fine cloth, surmounted by a square canopy of crimson satin, fringed with gold, enclosed by a rail covered with red ray, and guarded by several gentlemen with aprons and towels about their necks. Between the quire and body of the church a closet was erected, with a pan of fire in it, that the child might be dismantled for the ceremony without taking cold. When all these things were ready, the child was brought into the hall of the palace, and the procession proceeded to the

Grey Friars' church. The citizens led the way, two and two; then followed gentlemen esquires, chaplains. After them the aldermen, then the mayor by himself, then the privy council in robes, then the gentlemen of the King's chapel in copes, then barons, bishops, earls, then the Earl of Essex, bearing the gilt covered basin; after him the Marquis of Exeter, with a taper of virgin wax, followed by the Earl of Dorset, bearing the salt, and the Lady Mary of Norfolk, bearing the chrism, which was very rich with pearls and precious stones; lastly, came the Dowager Duchess of Norfolk, bearing in her arms the royal infant, wrapped in a mantle of purple velvet, having a long train furred with ermine, which was borne by the Countess of Kent, assisted by the Earls of Wiltshire and Derby. The Duchess was supported on the right side by the Duke of Norfolk, with his marshal's rod, and on the left by the Duke of Suffolk—the only dukes then existing in the peerage of England —and a rich canopy was borne over the babe by the Lords Rochford, Hussey, and William and Thomas Howard. At the church door the child was received by the Bishop of London, who performed the ceremony, and a grand cavalcade of bishops and mitred abbots. The sponsors were Archbishop Cranmer, the Dowager Duchess of Norfolk, and the Marchioness of Dorset. The future Queen was carried to the fount, and, with the ceremony of the Catholic church, christened Elizabeth, after her grandmother, Elizabeth of York; and that done, Garter King-at-Arms cried aloud, "God, of his infinite goodness, send prosperous life, and long, to the high and mighty Princess of England, Elizabeth!" then the trumpets sounded, the Princess was carried up to the altar, the Gospel read over her, and she was confirmed by Archbishop Cranmer, and presented with the following gifts:—A standing cup of gold by Cranmer; a similar cup, fretted with pearls, by the Duchess of Norfolk; three gilt bowls, pounced, with covers, by the Marchioness of Dorset; and three standard bowls, graven and gilt, with covers, by the Marchioness of Exeter. Then, after wafers, comfits, and ipocras had been served in abundance, the procession returned to the palace, in the same order as it had set out, excepting that the Earl of Worcester, Lord Thomas Howard, the Lord Fitzwalter, and Sir John Dudley, preceded by trumpeters, carried the gifts of the sponsors before the Princess. Five hundred staff torches, carried by the yeomen of the guard and the King's servants, lit up the way homeward; and twenty gentlemen, bearing large wax flambeaux, walked on each side of the Princess, who was carried to the Queen's chamber door, when a flourish of trumpets sounded, and the procession dispersed.

Elizabeth passed the first six weeks of her existence at Greenwich; the Lady Margaret Bryan was appointed governess to her; in December she was removed to Hatfield, where she resided till the subsequent April, when she was conveyed to the Bishop of Winchester's palace at Chelsea. She was created Princess of Wales when three months old, and weaned in her thirteenth month with extraordinary ceremony. About this time a futile attempt was made to betroth her to the Duke D'Angoulême, the third son of Francis the First of France. In compliance with the act of Parliament, passed in March, 1534, which pronounced the marriage between Henry the Eighth and Katherine of Arragon unlawful and null, and that between him and Anne Boleyn lawful and valid, Elizabeth was honoured as heiress presumptive, and the Princess Mary forced to yield precedence to her, and to dwell under the same roof with her, more like a bondmaid than a sister and a princess. But this unjust elevation was of short continuance. The divorce and tragic death of Anne Boleyn rendered Elizabeth motherless in her third year, and placed her in a situation at once precarious and embarrassing. On the day immediately succeeding the Queen's death, the King, with the most unblushing effrontery, was publicly married to Jane Seymour; and shortly afterwards an act of Parliament was passed, illegitimatizing Elizabeth, and settling the succession to the throne on the offspring of Henry VIII. by his present Queen.

The following interesting letter from the governess of Elizabeth, Lady Bryan, to Mr. Secretary Cromwell, will afford an idea of the neglect and contempt to which she was for a period exposed:—

"My Lord,

"When your Lordship was last here, it pleased you to say that I should not mistrust the King's Grace nor your Lordship, which word was more comfort to me than I can write, as God knoweth. And now it boldeth me to shew you my poor mind. My Lord, when the Lady Mary's Grace was born, it pleased the King's Grace to appoint me lady mistress, and make me a Baroness; and so I have been, and am so still, to the children his Grace have had since. Now it is so, my Lady Elizabeth is put from that degree she was before, and what degree she is at now I know not, but by hearsay; therefore, I know not how to order her, nor myself, nor none of hers that I have the rule of, that is, her woman and her groomes: beseeching you to be good Lord to my Lady, and to all hers, and that she may have some raiment, for she hath neither gown, nor kirtel, nor petticoat, nor no manner of linen for smocks, nor kerchiefs, nor sleeves, nor rails, nor body-stitchet, nor handkerchiefs, nor mufferlers, nor biggens. All this her Grace must take, I have driven off as long as I can, that, by my troth, I cannot drive it no longer; beseeching you, my Lord, that ye will see that her Grace may have that is needful for her, as my trust is ye will do; beseeching you, my own good Lord, that I may know from your writing how I shall order myself, and what is the King's Grace's pleasure and yours that I shall do, in everything and whatsoever it shall please the King's Grace or your Lordship to command me at all times, I shall fulfill it to the best of my power.

"My Lord, Mr. Shelton sayes, he is master of this house; what fashion that shall be, I cannot tell, for I have not seen it before. My Lord, ye be so honourable yourself, and every man reporteth your Lordship loveth honour, that I trust your Lordship will see this house honourably ordered, howsomever it hath been aforetime; and, if it please you, that I may know what your order is, and if it be not performed, I shall certify to your Lordship of it, for I fear me it will be hardly now performed; for if the head of . . . . knew what honour meaneth, it would be the better ordered, if not, it will be hard to bring it to pass. My Lord, Master Shelton would have the Lady Elizabeth to dine and sup every day at the board of estate. Alas! my Lord, it is not meet for a child of her age to keep such a rule yet. I promise you, my Lord, I dare not take it upon me to keep her Grace in health if she keep that rule, for there she shall see divers meat, and fruits, and wine, which would be hard for me to refrain her Grace from it. Ye know, my Lord, there is no place of correction there, and she is yet too young to correct greatly. I know well, if she be there, I shall not bring her up to the King's Grace's honour, nor hers, nor to her health, nor my poor honesty; wherefore, I shew your Lordship this my discharge, beseeching you, my Lord, that my Lady may have a mess of meat to her own longing, with a good dish or two that is meet for her Grace to eat of, and the reversion of the mess shall satisfy all her women, a gentleman usher, and a groom, which being eleven persons on her side, sure I am it will be (into right little) as great profit to the King's Grace this way as the other way, for if all this should be set abroad, they must have three or four messes of meat, where this one mess shall suffice them all, with bread and drink. According as my Lady Mary's Grace had before, and to be ordered in all things as her Grace was before; God knoweth my Lady hath great pain with her great teeth, and they come very slowly forth, and causeth me to suffer her Grace to have her will more than I would, I trust to God her teeth were well grafte to have her Grace after another fashion than she is yet, so as, I trust, the King's Grace shall have great comfort in her Grace, for she is as toward a child, and as gentle of conditions as ever I knew one in my life, Jesu preserve her Grace. And as for a day or two at a time, or whensoever it shall please the King's Grace to have her set abroad, I trust so to endeavour me that she shall so do as shall be to the King's honour and hers, and then after to take her ease again.

"I think Master Shelton will not be content with this; he may not know it is my desire, but that it is the King's pleasure and yours it should be so. Good, my Lord, have my Lady's Grace and us, her poor servants, in your remembrance, and your Lordship shall have our hearty prayers by the grace of Jesu. O, ever preserve your Lordship with long life, and as much honour as your noble heart can desire! From Hunsdon, with the evil hand of her that is your daily bed-woman, MARGET BRYAN."

"I beseech you, my own good Lord, be not miscontent that I am so bold to write thus to your Lordship; but, I take God to my judge, I do it of true heart, and for my discharge; beseeching you accept my good mind."

"To the right noble and my singular good Lord, my Lord Privy Seal, be this delivered."

This letter, an evidence of the minute details on which the first minister of the state was expected in those days to bestow his attention, rendered it apparent that the Lady Bryan and Mr. Shelton, the chief officers at Hunsdon, where Elizabeth then resided, each desired to bring up the Princess after their own notion. However, we may presume that the reasonable request of Lady Bryan was granted, for we hear no more of the vexatious dispute, and are assured that much of the greatness of Elizabeth, as a Queen, was due to Lady Bryan's judicious training and education, combined with the adversity which at once bastardized her, and deprived her of the injurious magnificence and adulation which, ere she could lisp, had been showered upon her as the heiress to the throne.

The first public ceremony in which Elizabeth took part, was the christening of Edward the Sixth. She was just four years old when, borne in the arms of the Earl of Hertford, brother to the Queen, Jane Seymour, she carried the chrism for her new-born half-brother, and on returning, walked with infant dignity in the procession, the Princess Mary leading her by the hand, and the Lady Herbert bearing her train. For some time after Prince Edward's birth, Elizabeth was permitted to reside under the same roof with him. Between the brother and sister a sincere affection sprang up, and the day Edward was two years old the Princess made him a birth-day present of "a shyrte of cam'yke of *her owne woorkynge*." She had then just entered the seventh year of her age, and was remarkably attractive and precocious. Wriothesley says, "when he visited her in December, 1539, she enquired after the King's welfare with as great gravity as if she had been forty years old;" and he adds, "if she be no worse educated than she then appeared to me, she will prove an honour and a blessing to her father, whom the Lord long preserve."

With Henry the Eighth's fourth wife, Anne of Cleves, Elizabeth formed an ardent friendship. The first letter, said to have been written by the Princess, was a compliment to that august lady on her marriage. The original is lost, but the following is a copy, modernized in phraseology as well as orthography:—

"MADAM,

"I am anxiously desirous to see your Majesty, but as the King, my father, has commanded me not to leave my house for the present, I cannot as yet gratify my wish. In the meantime I beg of your Grace to accept this my written devotion and respects to you as my Queen and my mother. My youth prevents me from doing more than heartily felicitating you on your marriage, and sincerely wishing that your good will for me equals my zeal for your service."

By one of the terms of her divorce, Anne of Cleves was granted permission to see Elizabeth as often as she wished, provided that the Princess did not address her as Queen. Katherine Howard, who was sincerely attached to the youthful Elizabeth, anxiously desired to remove from her the brand of illegitimacy. After that unhappy Queen had suffered on the block, Elizabeth resided for some time with her sister Mary at Havering Bower. Soon after the birth of the unfortunate Mary, Queen of Scots, Henry formed the project of uniting the whole island under one crown, by the marriage of that infant Queen with his son Prince Edward. As a further means of securing this important object, he, in the autumn of 1543, offered the hand of Elizabeth to the Earl of Arran, who then laid claim to the regency of Scotland. Thus early were blended the interests and happiness of two princesses, whose celebrated rivalry and illustrious character were destined to endure, until the life of one was sacrificed to the jealousy and hatred of the other. The Kings of France and England eagerly contended for the hand of the youthful Mary: while that of Elizabeth was offered to a Scottish Earl, of equivocal birth and indifferent reputation. Yet so little was the Scottish Earl flattered by the offer, that he actually declined the honour, and the future Queen of England remained unbetrothed!

Katherine Parr, the last and one of the best of Henry the Eighth's wives, was a great admirer of Elizabeth. She caused her to be present at her royal marriage, and when the Princess, in her twelfth year, deeply offended her father by committing an offence, the nature of which has not been handed down to us, she interceded in her behalf with the royal tyrant; an act of motherly kindness, which evidently proved succcessful,* and which Elizabeth acknowledged in the subjoined epistle.

"Inimical fortune, envious of all good and ever revolving human affairs, has deprived me for a whole year of your most illustrious presence; and not thus content, has yet robbed me of the same good, which thing would be intolerable to me, did I not hope to enjoy it very soon. And in this my will, I well know that the clemency of your Highness has had as much care and solicitude for my health as the King's Majesty himself, by which thing I am not only turned to serve you, but also to revere you with filial love; since I understand that your most illustrious Highness has not forgotten me every time you have written to the King's Majesty, which, indeed, it was my duty to have requested from you; for, heretofore, I have not dared to write to him. Wherefore, I now humbly pray your excellent Highness, that when you write to his Majesty, you will condescend to recommend me to him, praying ever for his sweet benediction, and similarly entreating our Lord God to send him best success, and the obtaining victory over his enemies; so that your Highness and I may, as soon as possible, rejoice in his happy return. No less, I pray God that he will preserve your most illustrious Highness, to whose Grace, humbly kissing your hands, I offer and recommend me,

"Your most obedient daughter,
And most faithful servant,
"Elizabeth."

"From St. James's, this thirty-first of July."

This year, 1544, Henry the Eighth restored Elizabeth to her right of succession; and, although the act which pronounced her illegitimate remained *for ever unrepealed*, she was, nevertheless, universally recognised as a Princess Royal of England; and so completely was the divorce forgotten, that in 1546, when France, Spain, and England, had concluded a treaty of peace, proposals were made for the marriage of Elizabeth with Philip, Prince of Spain, that same Philip, afterwards her brother-in-law, her friend and protector in adversity; then a second time her suitor, and afterwards her bitterest enemy.

* Henry the Eighth, in his letter to Katherine of September the eighth, says: "We pray you to give in our name, one hearty blessing to all our children." Elizabeth, we therefore may presume, was forgiven by her father before he went to France. See memoirs of Katherine Parr, page 445.

CHAPTER II.

Death of Henry the Eighth—Lord Seymour marries the Queen Dowager—His improprieties with Elizabeth—He offers her marriage on the death of the Queen Dowager—He is arrested—Elizabeth is placed under restraint—Their conduct investigated—Confession of Mrs. Ashley and Parry—Elizabeth's behaviour—Her letter to the Protector, asserting her innocence—Seymour attainted—Elizabeth appeals in behalf of Mrs. Ashley and Parry—Seymour beheaded—Harrington's sonnet to his memory—Elizabeth's learning—Correspondence with Edward the Sixth—Restored to royal favour—Futile efforts to marry her to the Prince of Denmark—Quarrels with Northumberland—King Edward wills the Crown to Jane Gray—Extracts from Elizabeth's Household Book.

HE demise of Henry the Eighth, which happened on the twenty-eighth of January 1547, materially affected the situation and prospects of Elizabeth. By the testament of Henry, the houses of Parliament were empowered to regulate the government of the country during the minority of his son, now Edward the Sixth, and to arrange the order of succession to the crown. The Act of Parliament was confirmed, by which his two daughters, Mary and Elizabeth, were restored to their rights. In his will, Henry bequeathed to each of them a pension of three thousand pounds, with a marriage portion of ten thousand pounds, on condition of their not marrying without the consent of such of his executors as should then be alive. Sixteen persons were appointed, who were to exercise, in common, the royal functions, until the young King should reach the age of eighteen. The Earl of Hertford, the brother of Lady Jane Seymour, who now assumed the title of Duke of Somerset, was declared Protector of the realm, and Governor of the King's person. His brother, Lord Seymour, of Sudeley, was created Lord High Admiral. Immediately after the death of Henry, the Admiral proffered Elizabeth his hand in marriage. By the advice of Katherine Parr, the Princess, then in her fourteenth year, declined the offer. But, to her annoyance, only five days after this refusal, Lord Seymour was the accepted lover of the Queen Dowager Katherine; and a few weeks afterwards, their marriage was privately solemnized. The impropriety and haste of this marriage so offended the Princess Mary, that she wrote to Elizabeth, requesting her to leave the home of Katherine Parr, where she at that time abode, and come and dwell with her; but Elizabeth being too wise to put a public affront on the King's adored uncle, who was then intriguing to supersede the Protector Somerset, declined to accept Mary's invitation, on the plea that she could not withdraw herself from the Queen, who had shown her so much kindness, without appearing ungrateful.

The youthful Elizabeth had been, previous to the death of her father, entrusted to the care and protection of the Queen Dowager, with whom she resided, either at Chelsea, or the more sylvan retreat of Hanworth. It thus happened, that after the Queen's marriage with Seymour, the Princess found herself domesticated under the roof of the Lord High Admiral, and consequently she soon became an object of his marked attention. Neither respect for her exalted rank, nor a sense of the deep responsibility attached to the office of guardian, with which the circumstance of his marriage with the Queen Dowager invested him, were sufficient to restrain him from a certain freedom of behaviour towards Elizabeth, which no limits of propriety could justify. On some occasions the Princess endeavoured to repel his rudeness by such expedients as her youthful inexperience suggested; but her governess and attendants, gained over and intimidated, were guilty of a treacherous neglect of their duty, and even the Queen Dowager herself was deficient in delicacy and due caution, until the improprieties detailed in the memoirs of Katherine Parr excited her jealousy, when a quarrel ensued between the royal step-mother and step-daughter; which, although it did not destroy the friendship subsisting between them, terminated in their immediate and final separation.

About a week before Whitsuntide, in 1548, Elizabeth removed with her governess, Mrs. Katherine Ashley, who was related by marriage to Anne Boleyn, and with the rest of her ladies and officers of state, from the home and guardianship of Katherine Parr to Cheston, and subsequently to Hatfield and Ashridge. In September the Queen Dowager died in child-bed, and very soon afterwards the Lord Admiral aspired to the hand of Elizabeth herself, who, after the death of her stepmother, was left, at the critical age of fifteen, without a paternal adviser to follow the dictates of her own maidenly will, and the pernicious counsels of her wily governess and of her intriguing cofferer, Thomas Parry, in both of whom her confidence was unlimited. Seymour having gained over these notable agents, and through them opened a direct correspondence with Elizabeth, his iniquitous designs prospered for some time according to his desires. Although he was twenty years her senior, Elizabeth loved him; and, as she afterwards acknowledged, would have married him, if the consent of the royal executors, required by law, could be obtained. But this being impossible whilst Somerset was at the head of affairs, he plotted against the government, and on the sixteenth of January was arrested and committed to the Tower on a charge of high treason, and a few days afterwards Elizabeth was placed under restraint.

The confessions of Mrs. Ashley and of the man Parry before the Privy Council, contain all that is known of the conduct of the Lord High Admiral towards the Princess Elizabeth, during the life-time of the Queen Dowager. These authentic documents have been fortunately preserved, and furnish some very singular traits of the early character of their royal mistress. They cast upon Mrs. Ashley the double imputation, of having permitted such behaviour to pass before her eyes as she certainly ought not to have endured for a moment, and of having disclosed particulars to Parry, which reflected the utmost disgrace on herself, the Lord High Admiral, and the Princess Elizabeth. And so far was the Princess from resenting anything that Mrs. Ashley had either done or confessed, that she continued to patronize her in the highest degree, and after her accession to the throne promoted her husband to a high and lucrative office:—a circumstance which certainly affords strong suspicion, that there were some important secrets in her possession, respecting later transactions between the Princess and Seymour, which she had but too faithfully kept. It may, however, be urged, in palliation of the liberties which she accused the Admiral of taking, and the Princess of tolerating, that Elizabeth had barely completed her fourteenth year, at the period when this intercourse took place. Experience, nevertheless, proves, that, even at that early age, young ladies, educated in all the learning and accomplishments of the great, are not to be trusted with impunity in the society of the vicious and profligate.

Elizabeth refused the Lord High Admiral permission to visit her after he became a widower, on account of the general belief that she was likely to become his wife; and no trace was at this period found of any correspondence between them; yet Harrington afterwards suffered an imprisonment, for having delivered to her a letter from Seymour. The partiality of the Princess betrayed itself, by many involuntary tokens, in presence of her attendants, who were thus encouraged to entertain her with accounts of the attachment of the Lord High Admiral, and to enquire whether, if the consent of the council could be obtained, she would consent to admit his addresses. The Admiral proceeded with caution equal to that of Elizabeth.

The Protector, with the hope of criminating his brother, rather than of clearing the Princess, sent Sir Robert Tyrwhitt to her residence at Hatfield, empowered to examine her on the whole matter; and his papers inform us of some interesting facts. When, by means of a spurious letter, he had led her to believe that both Mrs. Ashley and her cofferer, Parry, were committed to the tower, "her Grace was," he says, "marvellously abashed, and did weep very tenderly a long time, demanding whether they had confessed any thing or not." Sending for Sir Robert soon after, the Princess related several circumstances which she had forgotten to mention, when the master of the household and master Denny came from the Protector to examine her. "After all this," continues Sir Robert, "I did require of the Lady Elizabeth to consider her honour, and the peril that might ensue, for she was as yet but a subject; and I farther declared what a woman Mrs. Ashley was, with a strong assurance, that if she would open or reveal every thing herself, all the evil and shame should be ascribed to her and her associates, and her youth considered, both with the King's Majesty, your Grace's, and the whole council. But in no way would she, by Mrs. Ashley, or the cofferer, confess any practice concerning my Lord Admiral; and yet I do see in her face that she is guilty, and plainly perceive that she will yet abide more storms ere she accuse Mrs. Ashley. Upon sudden news, that the master of the household and Master Denny were arrived at the gate, the cofferer went hastily to his chamber, and said to his wife—'I would I had never been born, for I am undone,' and wrung his hands, and cast away his chain from his neck, and his rings from his fingers. This is confessed by his own servant, and there are divers witnesses of the same."

Again, on the following day, Sir Robert Tyrwhitt writes to the Duke of Somerset, that all he has yet gotten from the Princess was by gentle persuasion, whereby he began to grow with her in credit; "for I do assure your Grace she hath a good wit, and nothing is obtained from her but by great policy." He afterwards states to the Duke his opinion that there had been some secret promise between the Princess, Mrs. Ashley, and the cofferer, never to confess till death; "and if this be so," he remarks, "it will never be got out of her but either by the King's Majesty or else by your Grace." On another occasion, Sir Robert tried her with feigned intelligence of Parry's having confessed; on which she called him "False wretch," and said "it was a serious matter for him to make such a promise and to break it." Sir Robert, with all his pains, was unable to elicit a single fact of decisive importance, as to the alleged illicit intercourse of Lord Seymour with the Princess Elizabeth; but that there was in the connection between them a great deal more than met the public eye, there can be no question. In a letter from Elizabeth herself to the Duke of Somerset, she admits "that she did indeed send her cofferer to speak with the Lord High Admiral, but on no other business than to recommend to him one of her chaplains, and to request him to use his interest that she might have Durham Palace for her London house; that Parry, on his return, informed her, that the Admiral said she could not have Durham Palace, which was wanted for a mint, but offered her his own house for the time of her being in London; and that Parry then inquired of her, whether, if the council would consent to her marrying the Admiral, she would herself be willing? That she refused to answer this question, demanding, who bade him ask it? He said, no one; but from the Admiral's inquiries, as to what she spent in her house, and whether she had got her patents for certain lands signed, and other questions of a like nature, he thought he was rather given that way than otherwise." She denies that her governess ever advised her to marry the Admiral without the consent of the council; but relates the hints which Mrs. Ashley had thrown out, of his attachment to her, and the artful attempts made by her to discover how she stood affected towards such a connection with that personage. In conclusion, Elizabeth remarks, with great spirit—"Master Tyrwhitt and others have told me, that there goeth rumours abroad which greatly affect both my honour and honesty (which above all things I esteem); amongst these, that I am in the Tower, and with child by my Lord Admiral. My Lord, these are shameful slanders, for which, besides the desire I have to see the King's Majesty, I shall most humbly desire your Lordship, that I may come to the court after your first determination, that I may shew myself there as I am."

In Parry's confession, he relates what passed between himself and the Lord High Admiral, when he waited upon him by command of the Princess, and alludes to the earnest manner in which the Admiral had urged "her endeavouring to procure, by way of exchange, certain crown lands which had been the Queen's, and which were adjacent to his own; from which he inferred, that he wanted to have both them and the Princess for himself. That the Admiral said he wished the Princess to go to the Duchess of Somerset, and by her means make suit to the Protector for the lands, and for a town house, and to entertain her Grace for the furtherance thereof. That when he repeated this to the Princess, she would not at first believe that he had ever uttered such words, or could wish her so to do; but on his declaring that it was true, she seemed to be angry that she should be driven to make such suits, and said, 'In faith I will not go there, nor begin to flatter now.'" That Parry had repeated his visits to the Lord High Admiral oftener than was at first acknowledged, either by Elizabeth or himself, is clearly indicated by a confession afterwards addressed to the Protector by the Princess; but even with this confession, Sir Robert Tyrwhitt declares himself unsatisfied as to the real nature of this mysterious connection. Parry was afterwards rewarded for his fidelity to Elizabeth, who made him comptroller of the royal household, an office which he held till his death.

Mrs. Ashley, in consequence of the part she played in this affair of the Admiral, was removed from her situation of governess to the Princess, and Lady Tyrwhitt, the wife of Sir Robert, succeeded in her place. On this occasion, the behaviour of Elizabeth is thus described in a letter from Sir Robert Tyrwhitt to the Protector:—

"Pleaseth your Grace to be informed, that after my wife's repair hither, she declared to the Lady Elizabeth, that she was called before your Grace and the council, and had a rebuke; that she had not taken upon herself the office to see her well governed, in the lieu of Mrs. Ashley. The answer of the Lady Elizabeth was, that Mrs. Ashley was her mistress, and that she had not so demeaned herself, that the council should now need to put any other mistress in her place. Whereunto my wife replied, seeing she did allow Mrs. Ashley to be her mistress, she need not be ashamed to have any honest woman in her stead. She took the matter so heavily to heart, that she wept all that night, and sighed all the next day, till she received your letter; and then she sent for me, and asked me whether it was best for her to write to you again or not: I said, if she would make answer that she would follow the advice of your letter, I thought she had better write; but in the end I perceived that she was very loth to have a governess; and to avoid the same, she said, the world would note her to be a great offender, having so hastily a governess appointed her. And after all, she fully hopes to recover her old mistress again. The love she yet beareth her is greatly to be wondered at. I told her, if she would but consider her honour, and the sequel thereof, she would, considering her years, make suit to your Grace to have one sent, rather than delay being without one for an hour. She cannot digest such advice in any way; but if I should speak my mind, it were more meet she should have two than one. She would in any wise write to your Grace, wherein I offered her my advice, which she would in no wise follow, but write her own will and pleasure. She beginneth now a little to droop, by reason she heareth that my Lord Admiral's houses are all dispersed. And my wife telleth me that she cannot hear him *discommended*, but she is ready to make answer therein; and so she hath not been accustomed to do, unless Mrs. Ashley were touched, whereunto she was very ready to make answer vehemently."

Instead of addressing to Somerset the sentiments desired by the crafty Tyrwhitt, Elizabeth, in the subjoined cautious epistle, urged the Protector and the council to endeavour to stop the scandalous reports in circulation against her.

"My Lord,

"Having received your Lordship's letters, I perceive in them your good will towards me, because you declare to me plainly your mind in this thing, and again, for that you would not wish that I should do anything that should not seem good unto the council, for which thing I give you most hearty thanks. And whereas, I do understand that you do take in evil part the letters that I did write unto your Lordship, I am very sorry that you should take them so, for my mind was to declare unto you plainly as I thought in that thing, which I did also the more willingly, because (as I write to you) you desired me to be plain with you in all things; and as concerning that point that you write, that I seem to stand in my own wit, in being so well assured of my own self, I did assure me of myself no more than I trust the truth shall try; and to say that which I knew of myself, I did not think should have displeased the council or your Grace. And surely, the cause why that I was sorry that there should be any such about me, was because that I thought the people will say that I deserved throughout my lewd demeanour to have such a one, and not that I mislike anything that your Lordship or the council shall think good, for I know that you and the council are charged with me; or that I take upon me to rule myself, for I know they are most deceived that trusteth most in themselves, wherefore I trust you shall never find that fault in me, to the which thing I do not see that your Grace has made any direct answer at this time, and seeing they make so evil reports already, shall be but a increasing of their evil tounges. Howbeit you did write, that if I would bring forth any that had reported it, you and the council would see it redrest, which thing, though I can easily do it, I would be loath to do it, for because it is my own cause, and again that should be but a abridging of an evil name of me, that am glad to ponesse [punish] them, and so get the evil will of the people, which thing I would be loath to have; but if it must seem good unto your Lordship, and the rest of the council, to send forth a proclamation into the countries, that they refrain their tounges, declaring how the tales be but lies, it should make both the people think that you and the council have great regard that no such rumours should be spread of any of the King's majesty's sisters as I am, though unworthy; and also I should think myself to receive such friendship at your hands as you have promised me, although your Lordship hath shewed me great already; howbeit I am ashamed to ask it any more, because I see you are not so well-minded thereunto. And as concerning that you say, that I give folks occasion to think, in refusing the good to uphold the evil, I am not of so simple understanding, nor would I that your Grace should have so evil opinion of me, that I have so little respect to my own honesty that I would maintain it if I had sufficient promise of the same, and so your Grace shall prove me when it comes to the point; and thus I bid you farewell, desiring God always to assist you in all your affaires.

"Written in haste from Hatfeild, this 21st February.

"Your assured Friend, to my little
"power,
"ELIZABETH.

"To my very good Lord, my Lord Protector."

The bill of attainder against Lord Seymour, of Sudeley, passed the Lords on the 4th of March, 1549: the clandestine courtship of Elizabeth formed one of the articles against him; and as the Princess feared that the imprisoned governess, Mrs. Ashley, and her husband, would be involved in his fall, she addressed the subjoined appeal to Somerset in their behalf.

"My Lord,

"I have a request to make unto your Grace, which fear has made me omit till this time for two causes, the one because I saw that my request for the rumours which were spread abroad of me took so little place, which thing when I considered I thought I should little profit in any other suit; howbeit now I understand that there is a proclamation for them, (for the which I give your Grace and the rest of the council most humble thanks) I am bolder to speake for another thing, and the other was because peradventure your Lordship and the rest of the council will think that I favour her evil doings for whom I shall speake for, which is Katharine Ashley, that it would please your Grace and the rest of the council to be good unto her, which thing I do not to favour her in any evil, (for that I would be sorry to do), but for this consideration which follow, the which hope doth teach me in saying that I ought not to doubt but that your Grace and the rest of the council will think that I do it for the other considerations. First, because she hath been with me a long time and many years, and hath taken great labour and pain in bringing me up in learning and honest, and therefore I ought of very duty speak for her, for Saint Gregory sayeth that we are more bound to them that bringeth us up well than to our parents, for our parents do that which is natural for them, that is, bringing us into this world, but our bringers-up is to cause us to live well in it; the second is, because I think that whatsoever she hath done in my Lord Admiral's matter, as concerning the marriage of me, she did it because knowing him to be one of the council, she thought he would not go about any such thing without he had the council's consent thereunto, for I have heard her many times say that she would not have me marry in any place without your Grace's and the council's consent: the third cause is because that it shall and doth make men thinke that I am not clear of the deed myself, but that it is pardoned in me because of my youth, because that she I loved so well is in such a place, thus hope prevailing more with me than fear, hath won the battel, and I have at this time gone forth with it, which I pray God be taken no other ways than it is meant.

"Written in haste from Hatfield, this 7th day of March. Also, if I may be so bold, not offending, I beseech your Grace and the rest of the council, to be good to Master Ashley, her husband, which because he is my kinsman I would be glad he should do well.

"Your assured Friend, to my
"little power,
"Elizabeth.

"To my very good Lord, my Lord Protector."

When Elizabeth was informed by one of Somerset's creatures of the decapitation of Seymour, which took place on the twentieth of March, she had the presence of mind to conceal her emotion, and with apparent sang froid remarked, "this day died a man with much wit and little judgment." This was the first of those fortunate escapes with which the singular and eventful life of Elizabeth so remarkably abounds. Her attachment to Seymour was the earliest and strongest impression of a tender nature which her heart was destined to receive, and although her characteristic caution would doubtless have restrained her from forming an irrevocable engagement, it might not have been in her power much longer to recede with honour, or even with safety, had the designs of Seymour proved successful.

Another faithful adherent of the youthful Elizabeth, at this period, was a gentleman in the service of the Lord Admiral, of the name of Harrington. He was repeatedly examined by the council respecting his master's intercourse with the Princess; but he revealed no secret of importance. He was subsequently taken by Elizabeth into her own household, and treated with distinguished favour. Indeed, so convinced was this gentleman, who was a man of talents, of her tenderness for the memory of a lover, that several years after her accession to the throne, he ventured to present his royal mistress with a portrait of the Admiral, under which was inscribed the following sonnet to his memory:

"Of person rare, strong limb, and manly shape,
By nature framed to serve on sea or land;
In friendship firm, in good state or ill hap,
In peace head-wise, in war-skill great, bold hand
On horse or foot, in peril or in play,
None could excel, though many did essay.
A subject true to King, a servant great,
Friend to God's truth, and foe to Rome's deceit;
Sumptuous abroad, for honour of the land,
Temp'rate at home, yet kept great state with stay,
And noble house, that fed more mouths with meat.
Then soon advanced on higher steps to stand,
Yet against nature, reason, and just laws,
His blood was spilt, guiltless, without just cause."

The unhappy fate of the Lord High Admiral Seymour, and the disgrace and danger in which Elizabeth had herself been involved, in consequence of her intercourse with that nobleman, afforded the young Princess a severe but useful lesson; and during the remainder of her brother's reign, she conducted herself with that extreme caution becoming her exalted station. Her time was now more agreeably spent in prosecuting her youthful studies, under the able superintendence of her learned preceptor, the celebrated Roger Ascham. The letters of this distinguished scholar, addressed to the rector of the University of Strasburgh, in 1550, abound with anecdotes of his royal pupil, of whose proficiency he was justly proud. We select the following interesting passages:—

"Never was the nobility of England more learned than at present. Our illustrious King Edward, in talent, industry, perseverance and erudition, surpasses both his own years and the belief of men. Numberless honourable ladies of the present time surpass the daughters of Sir Thomas More in every kind of learning. But amongst them all, my illustrious mistress, the lady Elizabeth, shines like a star, excelling them more by the splendour of her virtues and her learning, than by the glory of her birth. In the variety of her commendable qualities, I am less perplexed to find matter for the highest panegyric, than to circumscribe that panegyric within just bounds. Yet I shall mention nothing respecting her but what has come under my own observation.

"For two years she pursued the study of Greek and Latin under my tuition; but the foundations of her knowledge in both languages were laid by the diligent instructions of William Grindal, my late beloved friend, and seven years my pupil in classical learning at Cambridge. After some years, when through her native genius, aided by the efforts of so excellent a master, she had made a great progress in learning, and Grindal, by his merit and the favour of his mistress, might have aspired to high dignities, he was snatched away by a sudden illness, leaving a greater blank of himself in the court than I remember any other to have done these many years.—I was appointed to succeed him in his office, and the work which he had so happily begun, without my assistance indeed, but not without some counsels of mine, I diligently laboured to complete. Now, however, released from the throng of a court, and restored to the felicity of my former learned leisure, I enjoy, through the bounty of the King, an honourable appointment in this university.

"The lady Elizabeth hath accomplished her sixteenth year; and so much solidity of understanding, such courtesy united with dignity, have never been observed at so early an age. She has the most ardent love of true religion, and of the best kind of literature. The constitution of her mind is exempt from female weakness, and she is endued with a masculine power of application. No apprehension can be quicker than hers—no memory more retentive. French and Italian she speaks like English; Latin with fluency, propriety, and judgment; she also spoke Greek with me, frequently, willingly, and moderately well. Nothing can be more elegant than her handwriting, whether in the Greek or Roman character. In music she is very skilful, but does not greatly delight. With respect to personal decoration, she greatly prefers a simple elegance to show and splendour, so despising the outward adorning of plaiting the hair, and of wearing of gold, that in the whole manner of her life she rather resembles Hippolita than Phœdra.

"She read with me almost the whole of Cicero, and a great part of Livy: from these two authors, indeed, her knowledge of the Latin language has been almost exclusively derived. The beginning of the day was always devoted by her to the New Testament, in Greek, after which, she read select portions of Isocrates, and the tragedies of Sophocles, which I judged best adapted to supply her tongue with the purest diction, her mind with the most excellent precepts, and her exalted station with a defence against the utmost power of fortune. For her religious instruction, she drew first from the fountains of Scripture, and afterwards from St. Cyprian, the 'Common Places' of Melancthon, and similar works, which convey pure doctrine in elegant language. In every kind of writing, she easily detected any ill-adapted or far-fetched expression. She could not bear those feeble imitators of Erasmus, who bind the Latin language in the fetters of miserable proverbs; on the other hand, she approved a style chaste in its propriety, and beautiful by perspicuity; and she greatly admired metaphors, when not too violent, and antitheses, when just and happily opposed. By a diligent attention to these particulars, her ears became so practised and so nice, that there was nothing in Greek, Latin, or English, prose or verse, which, according to its merits or defects, she did not either reject with disgust, or receive with the highest delight."

Fox says, "that one of her schoolmasters informed a friend of his, that he learned every day more of her than she of him. 'I teach her words,' quoth he, 'and she me things. I think she is the best-disposèd lady in all Europe: she has a singular wit, and a marvellous meek stomach.'"

Elizabeth, on account of her improprieties with the Admiral, had fallen into disgrace, and was not permitted to enter the royal presence; but Edward, although held in thrall by the Protector, longed to behold his offending sister," and Elizabeth, aware of the fact, addressed to him the following interesting letter, preserved in the royal archives:—

"Like as a shipman in stormy weather plucks down the sails, tarrying for better wind, so did I, most noble King, in my unfortunate chance, on Thursday, pluck down the high sails of my joy and comfort, and do trust one day that, as troublesome waves have repulsed me backward, so a gentle wind will bring me forward to my haven. Two chief occasions moved me much, and grieved me greatly; the one, for that I doubted your Majesty's health; the others, because, for all my long tarrying, I went without that I came for. Of the first, I am relieved in part, both that I understood of your health, and also that your Majesty's lodging is far from my Lord Marquis's chamber. Of my other grief I am not eased; but the best is, that whatsoever other folks will suspect, I intend not to fear your Grace's goodwill, which, as I know that I never deserved to forfeit, so I trust it will stick by me; for if your Grace's advice that I should return, whose will is a commandment, had not been, I would not have made the half of my way the end of my journey. And thus, as one desirous to hear of your Majesty's health, though unfortunate to see it, I shall pray God for ever to preserve you. From Hatfield, this present Saturday.

"Your Majesty's humble sister to command,

"Elizabeth."

"To the King's most excellent Majesty."

In reply, Edward sent to Elizabeth for her portrait, which she forwarded him, with the following pedantic epistle:

"Like as the rich man that daily gathereth riches to riches, and to one bag of money layeth a great store till it come to infinite; so methinks your Majesty, not being sufficed with so many benefits and gentleness shewed to me afore this time, doth now increase them, in asking and desiring, where you may bid and command: requiring a thing not worthy the desiring for itself, but made worthy for your Highness's request—my picture, I mean; in which, if the inward good mind towards your Grace might as well be declared as the outward face and countenance shall be seen, I would not have tarried the commandment, but prevented it; nor have been the last to grant, but the first to offer it. For the face, I grant, I might well blush to offer, but the mind I shall never be ashamed to present. But though from the grace of the picture, the colours may fade by time, may give by weather, may be spotted by chance; yet the other, nor time with her swift wings shall overtake, nor the misty clouds with their lowering may darken, nor chance with her slippery foot may overthrow.

"Of this also—yet the proof could not be great, because the occasions have been so small; notwithstanding, as a dog hath its day, so may I perchance have time to declare it in deeds, which now I do write them but in words. And further, I shall humbly beseech your Majesty, that when you shall look on my picture, you will vouchsafe to think, that as you have but the outward shadow of the body before you, so my inward mind wisheth that the body itself were oftener in your presence. Howbeit, because both my so being, I think, could do your Majesty little pleasure, though myself great good; and again, because I see not as yet the time agreeing thereunto, I shall learn to follow this saying of Horace—

'*Feras non culpes, quod vitari non potest.*'

And thus I will (troubling your Majesty I fear) end, with my most humble thanks, beseeching God long to preserve you to his honour, to your comfort, to the realm's profit, and to my joy.

"Your Majesty's most humble sister and servant,

"ELIZABETH."

"From Hatfield, this fifteenth day of May."

Elizabeth was evidently not long in regaining her influence with the King; for we find, in Strype's Memorials, a striking instance of the high consideration which she enjoyed at the court of her brother, as well as the state which she at this period assumed in her appearance before the public:—

"London, March 17th, 1551.

"The Lady Elizabeth, the King's sister, rode this day through London unto St. James's, the King's palace, with a great company of lords, knights, and gentlemen; and after her, a great company of ladies and gentlemen on horseback—about two hundred. On the nineteenth, she came from St. James's, through the park to the court; the way from the park-gate unto the court spread with fine sand. She was attended with a very honourable confluence of noble and worshipful persons of both sexes, and received with much ceremony at the court gate."

The talents of the young Princess, her vivacity, her proficiency in all these classical attainments to which the young King was himself devoted, endeared her exceedingly to her brother, who was wont to call her—in allusion to the sobriety of dress and manners by which she was then distinguished—his "Sweet sister Temperance." On the part of Elizabeth, his affection was responded to by every mark of sisterly affection, joined to those delicate attentions, and that respectful demeanour, which his rank entitled him to receive.

With respect to her learning, after she ascended the throne, Roger Ascham roundly asserts that there were not four men in England, distinguished either in the church or the state, who understood more Greek than her Majesty. And, as an instance of her proficiency in other tongues, he mentions that he was once present at court when she gave answers, at the same interview, to three ambassadors—the imperial German, the French, and the Swedish—in Italian, in French, and in Latin—and all this fluently, without confusion, and to the purpose.

It was now deemed expedient for the King to seek an alliance with the King of Denmark, Christian the Third—an able and enlightened prince, who had recently acquired the respect of the whole Protestant body, by establishing the Reformation in his dominions. An agent was accordingly dispatched to the court of Copenhagen, to solicit a marriage between the Prince Royal of Denmark and the Princess Elizabeth. But this negotiation proved fruitless, in consequence of the reluctance to the connection manifested by Elizabeth herself.

The Princess never could be prevailed upon to give the slightest encouragement to the addresses of any foreign prince, whilst she herself was still in the light of a subject: she was too well convinced that, to accept such an alliance, would be the means of sending her out of the kingdom, and thus hazard the right of her succession to the throne of England. Edward the Sixth, thus disappointed in his views, lost no time in offering his own hand in marriage to the infant daughter of Henry the Second of France --a contract, however, which he did not live to carry into effect.

Elizabeth was too discreet to take part in the struggle between the Somerset and Warwick factions; and when Somerset, a condemned prisoner in the Tower, supplicated her to urge the King to spare his life, she, in answer, coolly assured him that she had no power to do anything in his behalf, as the ruling faction prevented her from entering the royal presence. Yet her credit with Edward must then have been considerable, since she openly asserted her claims to Durham House, which Somerset had unjustly deprived her of, and which Warwick, who had just been created Duke of Northumberland, had the presumption to retain. She even appealed to the Lord Chancellor—a step she was too politic to take, without being first assured of the friendship of her royal brother.

Immediately, Northumberland, to bolster up his own power, conceived the traitorous design of causing the claims of the Princess Mary and Elizabeth to be set aside in favour of his daughter-in-law, the unfortunate Lady Jane Gray, who had been married to his son, Lord Guildford Dudley. He endeavoured to estrange, by every means, the love of the death-sick young Edward the Sixth from his sisters; and he succeeded in completely excluding Elizabeth from the presence of the dying King. Latimer and Ridley furthered his dangerous project by preaching in favour of passing over the daughters of Henry the Eighth, on the ground that they might endanger the Protestant institutions of the realm, by marrying Popish princes, although it was well known that Elizabeth, who was sincerely attached to the reformed religion, had rejected a foreign alliance. But at this momentous period the voice of Elizabeth's friends at court was silenced, and, indeed, if the assertions of some writers are to be believed, she had but one sincere friend there, and that was the crafty Cecil.

Elizabeth resided at Hatfield during the last month of Edward the Sixth's reign. Her household book for the first of October, of the fifth of Edward the Sixth, to the last of September, in the sixth year of that Monarch, is still extant, in the possession of Lord Strangford. "It is entitled," says Mr. Ellis,* "The Accompte of Thomas Parry, esquyer, Conferor, [cofferer] to the righte excellent Princesse, the Ladie Elizabeth, her Grace, the King's Majestie's most honorable Sister." Every page is signed at the bottom in the Princess's own hand. The sum total of receipts, including the "remayne of the preceding year," amounts to five thousand seven hundred and ninety one pounds one shilling and three-pence farthing, with the third part of a farthing. The payments are entered under the heads of "Bakehouse and Pantry, Butrey and Cellar, Spicery and Chaundrey, Kitchen and Larder, the Acatryes, Pultry, Squillerie, Sawcerye, Wood-yard, Stable, Wages, Lyveries and Almes, Chamber and Robes, and Reparacions." The total of payments within the time of the account, amounted to three thousand six hundred and twenty-nine pounds eighteen shilhings and eight-pence three farthings; leaving for the wants of the next year, one thousand five hundred and seven pounds, one half-penny, a half-farthing, and a third part of a farthing; which sum is stated to have been "delivered

* Royal Letters, vol. ii. p. 210.

into her Grace's hands, upon the determination of this account. The expenses of the house amounted to three thousand nine hundred and thirty-eight pounds eighteen shillings and seven-pence. But deductions for the "hides, felles, and intrails of the cattle supplied, two hundred and seven pounds three shillings and eight-pence half-penny." The entries in the Bakehouse and Pantry are chiefly for wheat. Under the Butrey and Cellar great quantities of beer are entered, with "swete wine, Raynish wine, and Gascoigne wine." In the Spicery and Chaundery, nothing occurs worthy of note. In the Kitchen and Larder, fresh-water fish are frequently entered. Board wages for servants are continually mentioned. Lamprey-pies are once entered as a present. John Taylor was paid for making the "Torne-broches' [turnspits] coats, nine shillings and two-pence." In the Wood-yard rushes occur, in the Stable "horsbrede." The wages of household servants for a quarter of a year amounted to eighty-two pounds seventeen shillings and eight-pence. The liveries of velvet coats for thirteen, gentlemen, at forty shillings the coat amounted to twenty-six pounds. The liveries of the yeomen to seventy-eight pounds eighteen shillings; given in alms, seven pounds fifteen shillings and eight-pence at "sondrie times to poore men and womene." Amongst the entries of the chamber and robes, are the following. "Paid to John Spithonius, the seventeenth of May, for books, and to Mr. Allin for a bible, twenty-seven shillings and four-pence. Paid to Edmund Allin for a bible, twenty shillings. Paid the third of November, to the keeper of Hertford jail, for fees of John Wingfield, being in ward, thirteen shillings and fourpence. Paid the fourteenth of December to Blanch Parry, for her half year's annuity, one hundred shillings; and to Blanche Courtnaye for the like, sixty-six shillings and eight-pence. Paid the fourteenth of December, at the christening of Mistress Pendred's child, as by warrant doth appear, one shilling. Paid in rewards unto sundry persons at St. James, her Grace then being there, viz., the King's footman, forty shillings; the under-keeper of St. James's ten shillings, the gardener five shillings; to one Russell, groom of the King's great chamber, ten shillings; John Forman, ten shillings; to the wardrobe, forty shillings; the violins, forty shillings; a Frenchman, that gave a book to her Grace, ten shillings; the keeper of the park gate of St. James's, ten shillings; Mr. Standford's servant, twenty shillings; the Lord Russell's minstrels, ten shillings. In the whole, as by warrant appeareth, nine pounds fifteen shillings. Paid in rewards, to sundry persons, the tenth of August, viz., to Farmor, that played on the lute, thirty shillings; to Mr. Ashfeild's servant, with two prize oxen, and ten muttons, twenty shillings; More, the harper, thirty shillings; to him that made her Grace a table oı walnut tree, forty-four shillings and nine pence; and to Mrs. Cock's servant, who brought her Grace a sturgeon, six and eight-pence."

CHAPTER III.

Death of Edward the Sixth—Lady Jane Grey—Accession of Mary—Elizabeth's hypocritical profession of the Popish Faith—Takes part in Mary's Coronation—Is set up as a rival to the Crown—Breach between her and Mary, widened by the rival factions—Refuses to marry the Prince of Piedmont—Implicated in the Wyatt Rebellion—Sent for to Court—Imprisoned in the Tower—Severely treated—Gardiner's attempt to take her life—Removed to Richmond—The Duke of Savoy offered her in marriage—Removed to Woodstock—Still treated with rigour—Sent for to Court—Is forgiven, and restored to Royal favour—Philip's efforts to marry her to the Duke of Savoy—Spends Christmas at Court—Proceeds to Hatfield—Renewed offer of marriage—Magnificent entertainments—Proposals of Eric of Sweden—Her dislike of marriage—Mary bequeaths the Crown to her—Her dying request to her—She vows that she is a Catholic—Affects surprise when informed of Mary's demise.

THE long-anticipated death of Edward the Sixth took place at Greenwich, on the sixth of July, 1553. It was hastened by the unskilful treatment of a female empiric, to whose care the royal patient had been improperly confided; and coming, as it did, upon Northumberland somewhat by surprise, compelled him to act with a degree of precipitation, injurious to his crafty designs. Several preparatory measures were yet to be adopted, particularly the important one of securing the persons of the two princesses, Mary and Elizabeth. Accordingly he ordered the death of the King to be carefully concealed, whilst he wrote letters in the name of Edward the Sixth, requiring the immediate attendance of his sisters at court. How far the stratagem succeeded with Mary, and her subsequent proceedings, have already been detailed. The more wary Elizabeth, informed, it is supposed by Cecil, of the treachery hatching at court, remained tranquil at her residence in Hertfordshire.

The Duke of Northumberland soon after despatched messengers to Elizabeth, apprizing her of the accession of Lady Jane Grey to the throne, and proposing to her the alternative of resigning her own title, in consideration of a sum of money and certain lands to be assigned for her benefit. Elizabeth prudently and firmly replied, that her eldest sister, Mary, was the first to be treated with, during whose lifetime she, for her part, had no right or title to renounce. Whilst Mary asserted her rights by an appeal to arms, Elizabeth, confined to her house by a sickness, most probably feigned, merely avoided taking part in the struggle for the crown. She did not, as some historians state, raise troops in aid of Mary. But although, during this eventful crisis, she no more supported Mary than Lady Jane, the moment the contest was at an end, and the news of her sister's victory had reached her, she forgot her indisposition, and hastened in state, to meet and court the favour of the conqueror. At the head of one thousand persons, on horseback, many of whom were ladies, she met her sister Mary at Wanstead, where she first paid homage to her as Queen. When Mary made her triumphal entry into London, she rode by her side. In personal appearance and manners, she had the advantage of Mary. She was but twenty, about half the age of the Queen, and without pretensions to extraordinary beauty, she could boast of a tall, portly, graceful figure, evenly chiselled features, large blue eyes, a fine but rather sallow complexion, and delicate hands, the elegant symmetry of which she was proud to display on every possible occasion. She also condescended to court popularity by all those arts of which her after-conduct proved her to be a perfect mistress.

But a few weeks after Mary had been proclaimed Queen, the partizans of the opposing religions succeeded in exciting her jealous ill-will against her sister Elizabeth. When Mary made known her intention of restoring the mass and other Catholic rituals, the Protestants took the alarm; fixed their hopes on the constancy of Elizabeth, who had already won for herself the good will of the people generally, and openly declared that she might be placed upon the throne with as little difficulty as Mary had been. On this account Mary was advised to place her sister under arrest. But this unjust, unpopular measure, she refused to consent to; and to at once gratify her own religious prejudices, and weaken the power of the reformers, she endeavoured, by entreaties, promises, threats, to withdraw her royal sister from the Protestant to the Catholic Church. Elizabeth firmly resisted every attempt, till she found that her repugnance was attributed not to motives of conscience, but to the persuasions of factions; when, demanding an audience with the Queen, she, on her knees, and with tearful eyes, excused her past obstinacy, on the plea that she had never practised, nor been taught, any other than the reformed religion, and employed Mary to furnish her with proper books and instructors, that she might learn her error, and embrace the religion of her fathers. In a week her defection from the Protestant Church was effected; policy induced her to make a hypocritical profession of the Catholic faith, and, as a show of sincerity, to attend mass on the eighth of September, and to shortly afterwards write to the Emperor, for permission to purchase in Flanders a chalice, cross, and other ecclesiastical ornaments for a Catholic chapel, she was about to open in her own house. By this and other dissimulation, Elizabeth succeeded for a time in retaining her influence at court. Mary, evidently believing in her sincerity, treated her, in public and private, with extraordinary kindness. In the splendid procession of her Majesty from the Tower to Whitehall, previously to her coronation, in October, 1553, the royal carriage, sumptuously covered with cloth of tissue, and drawn by six horses with similar trappings, was immediately followed by another, likewise drawn by six horses, and covered with cloth of silver, in which sat the Princess Elizabeth and the Lady Anne of Cleves, the former of whom assisted in this ceremony as the Queen's sister, and the latter not as the widow, but as the adopted sister of Henry the Eighth.

At the coronation banquet, Elizabeth dined at the same table with the Queen —an honour conferred on none else but Anne of Cleves. She was prayed for by Dr. Harpfield, as the Queen's sister, and generally recognized as heiress presumptive to the throne. She, however, enjoyed this state of felicity for little more than a month. The act passed by Mary's first Parliament, legitimizing the Queen, in effect, though not in words, bastardized Elizabeth, and so wounded her pride, that she requested permission to remove from court—a request which was refused, and followed by a temporary estrangement between the royal sisters. Intrigue was now rife at court, independent of the religious partizans. The King of France, in the hope of obtaining the whole sovereignty of the Britannic isles for his daughter-in-law, Mary Queen of Scots, resolved to ruin Queen Mary by setting up Elizabeth as her rival, and afterwards to destroy the Princess herself. With this view, the unprincipled French ambassador, Noailles, devised, and supported with supplies of arms and money, an attempt to depose Mary in favour of Elizabeth, who was to be married to Courtney, Earl of Devonshire. Whilst this conspiracy was hatching, Elizabeth, who, in all probability, tacitly countenanced it, again requested permission to retire to one of her seats in the country. Leave was granted, and the day fixed for her departure, when the representations of Renaud, the Spanish ambassador, that she was deeply implicated in the plots against the government, so incensed the Queen and the privy council against her, that she was ordered not to leave the palace, and, in the end, confined to her own chamber, and surrounded by spies, who reported her every movement to the privy council. The peril of her position daily increased. Mary deeply mortified her by permitting the Countess of Lennox and the Duchess of Suffolk, the representatives of her aunts, the Scottish and French Queens, to take precedence of her; and, at length, Renaud openly charged Noailles with paying her nocturnal visits, with treasonable designs; but, fortunately for Elizabeth, she explained away the charges against her, and Mary, despite the opposition of Renaud and others, forgave her, granted her permission to depart, and, on the sixth of December, dismissed her with tokens of affection, and a present of a double set of large and valuable pearls. She retired to her mansion at Ashridge, in Bucks, where she had scarcely arrived when she was annoyed by an offer of the hand of the Prince of Piedmont in marriage, and a renewal of the matrimonial proposals in favour of the King of Denmark's son; both of these offers she promptly negatived; and she also refused Noailles' request, that she would unite herself openly with the conspirators, whose plot was scarcely arranged, when the fears or simplicity of Courtney induced him to impart the whole secret to Gardiner, whilst the privy council intercepted letters to Elizabeth, in ciphers; from the French King, offering her money, and urging her to seek an asylum in France; from the French ambassador, advising her to throw off the mask, and openly espouse their cause, and from Wyatt, Sir James Crofts, and other of the conspirators, informing her that they had been betrayed by Courtney, and exhorting her to retire from Ashridge, which, being near the metropolis and unfortified, left her at the mercy of the Queen and the council, to the strong castle of Donnington, which was near to the head-quarters of the rebels.

The day after the breaking-out of the Wyatt rebellion was known to the council, Mary sent a letter to Elizabeth, enjoining her to return immediately to court, and assuring her that she should be heartily welcomed; but as Elizabeth put no faith in these assurances, she took to her bed, sent word to the Queen that she was too ill to travel, and immediately afterwards fortified and garrisoned her house. This illness, whether real or feigned, in all probability saved her from a violent death. Mary allowed her a fortnight's respite, and during this eventful fortnight, Wyatt, at the head of a formidable army of insurgents, had unsuccessfully attacked the Queen in her palace at Westminster, and been conveyed, with the other leading rebels, to captivity in the Tower, when he and his fellow-rebels, to screen themselves, named Elizabeth and Courtney as the instigators of the uprising.

Mary, whose throne had been made to totter, signed the death-warrant of the unfortunate Lady Jane Grey and her husband, and as she now more than ever distrusted the loyalty of Elizabeth, she sent that Princess's maternal kinsman, Lord William Howard, together with Sir Edward Hastings and Sir Thomas Cornwallis, to bring her to the court at London. When they arrived, the Queen's physicians, Dr. Wendy and Dr. Owen—whom, it appears, by an original letter in Tytler's "Edward and Mary," which we have not space to insert, the Queen had kindly sent to tend her, and see that she was sufficiently recovered to bear the removal—decided that she might at once commence the journey without endangering her life. But, her object being to gain time, she refused to see the three commissioners; and when, after waiting half the day, they, at the late hour of ten at night, entered her chamber, she had retired to rest, and with affected amazement, exclaimed, "Is the haste such that it might not have pleased you to come to-morrow in the morning?"

They made answer that they were right sorry to see her in such a case.

"And I," quoth she, "am not glad to see you here at this time of night."

Her Grace was then informed that the Queen had sent her own litter for her accommodation, and that the next morning she would be removed. Her departure, which took place at about eleven in the morning, on Monday, the twelfth of February, excited the tears and lamentations of her afflicted household, who naturally gave way to the most painful forebodings. She reached Redburn, in a very feeble condition, the first night; on the second, she rested at Sir Ralph Rowlet's house, at St. Alban's; on the third, at Mr. Dod's, at Mimmes; on the fourth, at Highgate, where she stayed at Mr. Cholmeley's house for a night and a day, till her drooping spirits had revived, and her health somewhat recovered.

At Highgate, a number of gentlemen rode out to meet her, in testimony of their sympathy and attachment; and as she proceeded, the general feeling was further displayed, by crowds of people lining the pathways, who flocked anxiously around her litter, weeping and bewailing her unhappy fate. Her passage through Smithfield and Fleet Street, in a litter open at both sides, was followed by a hundred men, attired in coats of velvet, and a hundred others succeeded, in coats of fine red, trimmed with velvet; with this imposing train did Elizabeth pass through the Queen's garden to the court of the palace. This open support of the Princess by a formidable party in the capital, greatly disconcerted the plans of her enemies. They contented themselves, for the present, with detaining her in a kind of honourable custody at Whitehall. She demanded an interview with the Queen, but Mary refused to see her; and when the privy council examined her, she protested her innocence, and ignorance of the treasonable designs of Wyatt and his confederates. Lords Arundel and Paget, and the Emperor's ambassador, Renaud, urged that she should be immediately brought to the block as a traitress; but Mary abhorred the idea of shedding her blood; and at last, when all the lords of the council had individually refused to take charge of her, the Queen, for the security of her own person, resolved to send her to the Tower. This determination was announced to her by the Earl of Sussex, on the sixteenth of March.

Bishop Gardiner and two others came soon afterwards, and, dismissing her attendants, supplied their place with some of the Queen's servants, and set a guard round the palace for that night. In the morning, a barge was in readiness to convey her to the Tower: she entreated first to be permitted to write to the Queen, and the Earl of Sussex assenting, in spite of the opposition of another lord, and undertaking himself to be the bearer of her letter, she took the opportunity of repeating her protestations of innocence and loyalty, adding with much vehemence of manner:—"As for that traitor, Wyatt, he might peradventure write me a letter; but, on my faith, I never received any from him. And as for the copy of my letter to the French King, which is laid to my charge, I pray to God confound me eternally, if ever I sent him word, message, token, or letter, by any means."

Her letter failed to procure an interview with the Queen; and the next day, being Palm Sunday, strict orders were issued for all the people to attend the churches, and carry their palms, whilst, in the meantime, Elizabeth was privately removed to the Tower, attended by the Earl of Sussex, the Lord Treasurer, three of her own ladies, three of the Queen's attendants, and some of her officers. On reaching the place of her destination, she for a long time refused to land at Traitor's Gate; and when one of the lords declared "that she should not choose," and, at the same time, offered her his cloak to protect her from the rain, she retained enough of her high spirit to throw it from her with a good dash; and as she set her foot on the ill-omened stairs, she exclaimed: "Here landeth as true a subject, being a prisoner, as ever landed at these stairs; and before thee, O God! I speak it, having no other friend but thee alone."

On seeing a number of warders and other attendants drawn out in order, she asked, "What meaneth this?" Some one answered, that it was customary on receiving a state prisoner.

"If it be," said Elizabeth, "I beseech you that, for my cause, they may be dismissed."

Immediately the poor men kneeled down and prayed God to preserve her; for which action they all were severely reprimanded the next day. Going a little further, she sat down on a stone to rest herself; the lieutenant urged her to rise and come in out of the cold and wet, but she answered, "Better sitting here than in a worse place; for God knoweth whither you bring me."

On hearing these words, her gentleman-usher wept, for which she reproved him, saying, "You ought rather to be my comforter, especially since I know my own truth to be such, that no man shall have cause to weep for me." Then rising, she entered the prison, and its gloomy doors were locked and bolted on her. Shocked and dismayed, she collected her servants around her, called for her prayer-book, and devoutly prayed that she might "build her house upon the rock." Her conductors then retired; and her firm friend, the Earl of Sussex, took the opportunity of reminding all whom it might concern, that the Princess was to be treated in no other manner than they might be able to justify, whatever should happen hereafter; and that they were to take heed to do nothing but what their commission would bear out. To this the attendants cordially assented; and, having performed their office, the two lords took their departure.

A few days after her committal, Gardiner, and other privy councillors, came to examine her, respecting the conversation she had held with Sir James Croft on her removal to Donnington Castle. Elizabeth said, after some recollection, that she had in truth such a place, but that she had never occupied it in her life, and she did not remember that any one had moved her so to do. Then, to enforce the matter, they brought forth Sir James Croft; and Gardiner demanded what she had to say to that man. She answered, that she had little to say to him, or to the rest that were in the Tower. "But, my Lords," said the Princess, "you do examine every mean prisoner respecting me, wherein you do me great injury. If they have done evil and offended the Queen's Majesty, let them answer for it accordingly. I beseech you, my Lords, join not me in this sort with any of these offenders; and, concerning my going to Donnington Castle, I do remember that Master Hobby, and my officers, and you, Sir James Croft, had such talk. But what is that to the purpose, my Lords, but that I may go to mine own houses at all times?" Then the Earl of Arundel, kneeling down, said, "Your Grace sayeth true, and certainly we are very sorry that we have troubled you about so vain a matter. Elizabeth replied, "My Lords, you do sift me very narrowly; but I am well assured you will not do more to me than God hath appointed; and so God forgive you all."

Wyatt was at length, on the eleventh of April, condemned to death; when he confounded all the hopes and expectations of the enemies of Elizabeth, by strenuously and publicly declaring her entire innocence of any participation in the treasonable designs.

One only resource now remained to the Court, in their endeavours to ruin Elizabeth. They thought, that a long-continued absence, whilst it might gradually weaken the affections of the people, would afford them many opportunities for injuring or supplanting her, and it was therefore resolved to provide for her a kind of honourable banishment. Her confinement had been rendered as uncomfortable as it could well be. After a month's close imprisonment in the Tower, by which the health of the Princess had severely suffered, she obtained, with great difficulty, permission to walk in the state apartments, under the close superintendence of the constable of the Tower and the Lord Chamberlain, with the attendance of three of the Queen's servants; the windows being shut, and the Princess not allowed to look out. Afterwards she had the liberty of walking in a small garden, the gates and doors being carefully closed; and the prisoners, whose rooms looked into the garden, being at such times closely watched, to prevent the interchange of any word or sign. Even a little child of five years of age, who was wont to cheer her by his daily visits, and to bring her flowers, was suspected of being employed as a messenger between the Princess and the Earl of Devonshire,* and in spite of

* Courtney, Earl of Devonshire, was then a prisoner in the Tower; he had been apprehended on the twelfth of the preceding February, at the house of the Earl of Sussex.

the innocent simplicity of his answers, he was ordered to visit her no more! The next day, the poor child peeped in through a hole in the door, as she walked in the garden, and cried out—"Madam, I can bring you no more flowers!"—for which innocent remark, his father, one of the inferior officers of the Tower, was severely lectured, and ordered to keep his boy entirely away from the Princess.

From the commencement of her incarceration in the Tower, orders had been given by the Queen and her Court that mass should be regularly performed before the Princess and her attendants, in her apartment. Elizabeth did not feel any great repugnance to this rite—and thus deprived the council of all pretext for persecuting her on the score of religion; but some of her attendants were not so submissive, and she had the pain of seeing Mrs. Sands, one of her ladies, forcibly carried away, under a charge of heresy, and her place supplied by another, whose religious sentiments were more in unison with the court. All these severities, however, failed in their intended purpose; neither sufferings nor menaces could induce the Princess to acknowledge herself guilty of any offence against her sister. Queen Mary, about this time, was attacked with a severe indisposition, and Gardiner taking advantage, it is supposed, of the circumstance, sent a privy council warrant to Bridges, the Lieutenant of the Tower, for the instant decapitation of Elizabeth. Bridges, perceiving that the Queen's signature was not attached to the warrant, made a personal application on the subject to Mary, who, on hearing of the murderous plot, and providential escape of the Princess, again called her sister; and to preserve her from the future machinations of her enemies, ordered Sir Henry Bedingfield, a Norfolk knight, on whose courage and honour she could rely, to convey her to Woodstock, and there strictly guard her from the base designs of her foes, and from joining in the intrigues of her disaffected friends. Elizabeth, however, derived but little momentary benefit from this approaching change, as she still remained a closely guarded prisoner.

Sir Henry Bedingfield entered the Tower, at the head of a hundred of his men; and Elizabeth, struck with dismay at the unexpected sight, demanded whether the scaffold which had served for the execution of Lady Jane Grey, had been removed? On being informed that it was, she was somewhat comforted; but soon a frightful rumour reached her, that she was about to be carried away by Sir Henry and his soldiers, no one knew where. She immediately sent for Lord Chandos, constable of the Tower, whose humanity and courtesy had induced him to soften, as much as possible, the hardships of her lot, and closely questioning him, he at length plainly told her, that there was no help for it; orders had been given, and she must be consigned to the care of Bedingfield, to be conveyed to Woodstock. Anxious and alarmed at this intelligence, she inquired of her attendants, what kind of man this Bedingfield was; and whether, in the event of her murder being determined on, his conscience would allow him to see it perpetrated? None of her attendents could satisfy her on this point; all they could do was, to implore her to put her trust in God, as her only refuge in the hour of danger.

After suffering a close imprisonment of three months, in the Tower, she was at length, on the nineteenth of May, escorted out of that gloomy fortress; and, under the charge of Bedingfield and his troop of a hundred horsemen, conducted to Richmond palace, where the court was then held. She was still treated as a captive. The manners of Bedingfield she deemed severe; and such terror did she conceive from the appearances around her, that, sending for her gentleman usher, she desired him, and the rest of her officers, to pray for her: "For this night," added the unhappy Princess, "I think to die!" The gentleman, greatly affected, encouraged her as well as he was able; then going to Lord Williams, who was walking with Bedingfield, he called him aside, and implored him to tell him, sincerely, whether any michief were designed against his mistress that night or no; adding, "That I and my men might take such part as God shall please to appoint. For, certainly, we will rather die than she should secretly and innocently suffer." To which Lord Williams replied, "God forbid that any such wicked purpose should be wrought; and rather than it should be so, I also am ready to die at the feet of the Princess."

Amidst these gloomy apprehensions, Elizabeth was surprised by a message from the Queen, offering her immediate liberty, on condition of her accepting the hand of the reigning Duke of Savoy in marriage. But the firm mind of Elizabeth was not thus to be shaken, nor her penetration deceived. She believed that it was banishment which was intended in the guise of marriage; that she was required to exchange the succession to an independent English crown, for the matrimonial alliance of a foreign prince; and she had the magnanimity to firmly negative the offer, which was no sooner declared, than orders were issued for her immediate removal to Woodstock, in Oxfordshire. While crossing the river, at Richmond, on this melancholy journey, Elizabeth perceived, on the opposite side, "certain of her poor servants," who had been prevented giving their attendance during her imprisonment in the Tower, and who were now anxiously waiting to see her again. "Go to them," said she to one of her men, "and say these words from me: 'I am driven like a sheep to the slaughter.'"—Travelling leisurely on horseback, the journey occupied four days; and the slowness of her progress afforded an opportunity for some striking marks of popular feeling. Various little gifts were presented by the people on the way-side; for which Bedingfield was enraged, calling them traitors and rebels. As she passed through the villages, the bells of the churches were rung in token of joy for her supposed liberation; but the populace were soon undeceived, and informed she was still a prisoner and in disgrace; and Bedingfield ordered the unhappy ringers to be put in the stocks, as a reward for their labours! On the third evening, the Princess arrived at Ricot, the seat of Lord Williams, where its owner introduced her to a large circle of nobility and gentry, whom he had invited to welcome her. The suspicious mind of Bedingfield was aroused at the sight of such an assembly: the soldiers were ordered to keep strict watch; he insisted that none of the guests should be permitted to pass the night in the house, and demanded of Lord Williams, if he were aware of the consequences of thus entertaining the Queen's prisoner? To which the noble host replied, "I know well enough what I am about, and am resolved that her Grace may, and shall, be merry in my house this night." In the morning she departed for Woodstock, where, under the severe inspection of Bedingfield, she found herself once more a prisoner. No visitor was allowed to approach her dwelling: the doors were closed upon her; and a military guard kept watch, day and night, around the walls of her prison. Indeed, her residence at Woodstock, though less painful than her imprisonment in the Tower, was yet a state of rigorous confinement, in which she was haunted with cares and anxieties, which deprived her youth of all its bloom and vivacity, and seriously affected her constitution. On the eighth of June her health was so much impaired, that two physicians were sent from the Court to attend upon her. On returning to the Queen, they made a favourable report of her behaviour, and of the dutiful humility she evinced towards her Majesty. She was soon after advised to make all due submission to the Queen, but, with her wonted constancy, she declined; though this was the only condition in which she could hope for deliverance. Her situation, therefore, was painful in the extreme. Hearing, one day, out of her garden at Woodstock, the voice of a milk-maid, singing joyously, she exclaimed, with emotion: "O that I too were a milk-maid! for her situation is happier and far merrier than mine!"

Sir Henry Bedingfield continued his severe vigilance over the Princess : his task was a difficult and ungracious one. On one occasion, observing him lock the gate of the garden while she was walking in it, Elizabeth reproached him, and called him her gaoler; when he, on his knees, entreated her Grace not to give him that ugly name in future, for he was appointed to be one of her officers and protectors. Her correspondence was watchfully restricted. When, after urgent application to the council, she was at length permitted to write to the Queen, Bedingfield looked over her shoulder as she wrote, took the paper into his own keeping when she laid it down to rest herself, and again brought it back to her, when she resumed her pen. With his utmost precaution, however, he was unable entirely to cut off all communications with her friends. Through the agency of a visitor to one of her ladies, Elizabeth received the satisfactory assurance, that none of the prisoners in the rebellion of Wyatt had been induced to utter any thing against her. In allusion to this intelligence, she wrote with a diamond, on a window in her apartment, this homely, but expressive distich :—

"Much suspected, of me
Nothing proved can be,
Quoth Elizabeth prisoner."

"The plots," says Sir John Harrington, "laid to entrap the Lady Elizabeth by Gardiner, Bishop of Winchester, and his terrible hard usage of all her followers, I cannot scarce think of with charity, nor write of with patience. My father, for only carrying a letter to the Lady Elizabeth, and professing to wish her well, he sent to the Tower for twelve months, and caused him to expend a thousand pounds, ere he could be free of that trouble. My mother, who then served the Lady Elizabeth, he caused to be removed from her, as a heretic, insomuch that her own father durst not take her into his house. So I may in some sort say, this Bishop persecuted me before I was born."

The marriage of Mary to Philip of Spain, the arrival of Cardinal Pole, and the re-establishment of Popedom, so increased Elizabeth's fears, that her prudence prompted her to frequently hear mass and attend the confessional. It was at this trying period that, when asked by Gardiner what it was she conceived she received in the blessed sacrament, she made the celebrated response—

"Christ was the word that spake it;
He blessed the bread and brake it.
And what the word did make it,
That I revere and take it."

About the close of this year, Sir Nicholas Throgmorton, Dudley, and all the other prisoners, who participated in the usurpation of Lady Jane Grey, or the rebellion of Wyatt, were liberated from the Tower, at the intercession, it is said, of King Philip, who soon afterwards, and, according to the assertions of some historians, with a view to exclude Mary, Queen of Scots, from the throne of England, in the event of the Queen dying without issue, employed his good offices in the cause of the Princess and the Earl of Devonshire — two personages still more interesting to the feelings of the people.*

It is well known, however, that Elizabeth's enemies were still powerful. Lord Paget, notwithstanding his having waited on the Princess at table, was heard to declare, "that the Queen would never have peace in the country till her head was smitten off;" and the Bishop of Winchester never ceased regarding her with an evil eye. Lord Williams begged that he might be permitted to take her from Woodstock to his own house, offering large bail for her safe keeping, but this indulgence was refused. Philip was now more than ever bent on her deliverance. The moment was favourable for his purpose. Mary, happy in her hope of giving an heir to the crown, no longer opposed the wishes of her husband; and the privy council, believing the Queen pregnant, viewed the Princess with less bitterness. Accordingly, in December, 1554, Elizabeth took her final departure from Woodstock, and proceeded, under the escort of Bedingfield and his men, to Hampton Court. She was met at Colnebrook by her own

* See Memoir of Mary.

gentlemen and yeomen, to the number of sixty: "much to all their comforts," says Fox, in his Martyrology, "notwithstanding they were immediately commanded, in the Queen's name, to depart to town, and she was not even suffered once to speak to them."

On the following day she reached Hampton Court; but the doors were closed upon her, and she was guarded, as at Woodstock, for a whole fortnight, without any one having access to her, save her own immediate attendants. At the end of this period, she was visited by Lord William Howard, son of the Duke of Norfolk, "who very honourably used her," and through whom she requested to speak to some of the privy council. In consequence, several members, headed by the Bishop of Winchester, waited upon her, and "humbled themselves before her with all humility." Nevertheless, they seized the opportunity, to urge her once more to make submission to the Queen, as a necessary preliminary to obtaining the royal favour. But Elizabeth, with marked firmness, declared, that rather than do so, she would lie in prison all the days of her life; adding, that she begged no mercy at her Majesty's hand, but rather the law, if ever she had offended her in thought, word, or deed. "And besides this," added the Princess, "in yielding, I should speak against myself, and confess myself an offender, by occasion of which the King and Queen might ever after conceive of me an ill opinion; and it were better for me to lie in prison for the truth, than to be abroad and suspected."

The councillors then departed, promising to deliver her message to the Queen. The following day, the Bishop of Winchester again waited upon her, and told her, that "her Majesty marvelled she should so stoutly carry herself, denying to have offended; so that it should seem the Queen had wrongfully imprisoned her; and that she must tell another tale ere she recovered her liberty." To which Elizabeth replied, "I will stand to my former resolution; for I will never belie myself."

"Then," said the Bishop, "your Grace hath the 'vantage of me and the other councillors, for your long and wrong imprisonments."

"I take God to witness," rejoined Elizabeth, "that I seek no 'vantage against them for their so dealing with me."

Gardiner and the rest then kneeled, and took their departure—the Princess being again locked up.

A week after this interview, Elizabeth received an unexpected summons from the Queen, when she was conducted by torch-light to the royal apartments. Mary received her in her chamber, to which she now secluded herself, in expectation of that joyful event, which was destined never to take place. The Princess, on entering, knelt down, "as became a true and loyal subject;" adding, "I do not doubt your Majesty will one day find me to be such, whatever reports may have stated to the contrary." The Queen expressed at first some dissatisfaction at her still persisting so strongly in her assertions of innocence; but on Elizabeth's replying, in a submissive tone, that it was her business to endure what her Majesty was pleased to inflict, and that she should make no complaints; Mary, somewhat appeased, put a ring on her finger, of the value of seven hundred crowns, and dismissed her with kindness. Sir Thomas Pope was again appointed to reside with her, with the hope of adding to her comforts.

Philip still persisted in his intention of marrying Elizabeth to the Duke of Savoy; but as severity had already been resorted to in vain, to induce the Princess to comply with his wishes, he now resolved to try more lenient measures. The Duke, who had attended Philip to England, was still in town; and as he was a Prince of merit and talents, and in the prime of life, it was thought that a personal interview might incline Elizabeth to lend a more favourable ear to his proposal. She was accordingly invited to share at the ensuing Christmas festivities, celebrated by Philip and Mary, at Hampton Court. On the eve of that festival, the great hall of the palace being illuminated with a thousand lamps, the King and Queen supped therein, the Princess being seated at the same table, next to the cloth of state. After supper, Lord Paget served her with a perfumed napkin, and a plate of preserved fruits; but she retired to her ladies before the revels and masquerades began. On St. Stephen's day, she heard matins in the Queen's closet, adjoining the chapel, when she was attired in a robe of white satin, strung all over with large pearls; and, on the twenty-ninth of December, she accompanied their Majesties and the nobility to witness a grand tournament, at which two hundred spears were broken by the combatants.

That she was treated at this period with the greatest respect by the highest nobles in the realm, is fully corroborated by the following anecdote, related by Holinshed:—"A servant of the Princess had summoned a person before the magistrates for having ascribed to Elizabeth the opprobrious epithet of *jilt*, and for having made use of other disparaging language respecting his royal mistress. 'Was it to be endured,' asked the prosecutor, 'that a low fellow, like this, should speak of her Highness [Elizabeth] thus insolently, when the highest personages of the land treated her with every mark of respect? I saw yesterday,' added he, 'at court, that my Lord Cardinal Pole, meeting her in the presence-chamber, knelt before her, and kissed her hand; whilst King Philip made such obeisance to her, that his knee touched the ground.'"

After the reconciliation with her sister, Elizabeth removed to one of the royal residences in the vicinity of the metropolis, and subsequently established herself permanently at the palace of Hatfield, in Hertfordshire. In the beginning of September, 1555, King Philip, the husband of Mary, mortified by the Parliament refusing him the ceremonial of a coronation, disappointed in the hopes of an heir, and disgusted by the overfondness of a wife destitute of every personal attraction, quitted England for the continent, and did not revisit it for a year and a half. However Elizabeth might regret his absence, as depriving her of a powerful protector, she was now so firmly established as next heir to the crown, that she felt perfectly secure against any attempt to degrade her from her royal station; and her reconciliation with the Queen procured for her frequent admission to court.

In Strype's Memorials, it is stated, that "a few days after the King's departure, the Queen, the Lady Elizabeth, and all the court did fast from flesh, to qualify them to take the Pope's jubilee and pardon, granted to all, out of his abundant clemency." A few weeks subsequently, the death of Elizabeth's enemy, the Bishop of Winchester, restored her to a degree of happiness and comfort, of which she had long been estranged. Nevertheless, as she deemed it wise to retire from the public gaze, she again turned her attention to the peaceful pursuits of literature; and, under the able tutorship of the celebrated Roger Ascham, resumed the study of the Greek and Latin classics.

The disappointment of the Queen in her hope of giving an heir to the throne, her subsequent ill state of health, and the refusal of the Parliament to allow the coronation of her husband, conferred a growing importance on Elizabeth. In November, 1556, she came in state to Somerset Place, to take up her abode for the winter, when a court was immediately formed around her. She was invited to London, for the purpose of receiving a second, and more formal offer, of the hand of the Duke of Savoy, whose suit was enforced by the King with the whole weight of his influence. This alliance had been the subject of earnest correspondence between Philip and the council of Mary; the imperial ambassadors were waiting in England for her answer; and the disappointment of the hopes of the royal party, when Elizabeth reiterated a decided refusal of the proffered marriage, terminated by her quitting London in the month of December, somewhat in disgrace. Indignant at the resistance so repeatedly offered by the Princess to his views on this subject, Philip urged the Queen to interpose in such a manner as to compel obedience; but Mary took part with her sister, and having resolved to protect her from the violence of the King, wrote to him, that "unless the Parliament first gave its consent, the accomplishment of the marriage would fail to procure the advantages he anticipated from the union; but that, however this might be, *her conscience would not allow her to press the matter further.*" Philip, nevertheless, was so far from giving up his favourite topic, that he soon afterwards sent to England the Duchesses of Parma and Lorraine, for the purpose of conducting the Princess Elizabeth into Flanders: but again he was frustrated in his object, Mary would not permit these ladies to pay the Princess a single visit at Hatfield; and her reception of them was such, that they speedily returned to their own country.

A cordiality of feeling, and frequency of intercourse, now took place between Mary and Elizabeth, which even the insurrection attempted in the spring and summer of 1556, in the Princess's name, had in nowise interrupted. In February, 1557, the Princess arrived at Somerset Place, attended by a numerous retinue, whence she waited on the Queen at Whitehall; and in the ensuing spring, her Majesty honoured her by returning her visit at Hatfield. The royal guest was entertained with every species of courtly splendour. On the morning after her arrival, the Queen and the Princess, after attending mass, assisted at a grand exhibition of *bear-baiting*,* "with which their Highnesses were right well content." In those days, this barbarous species of combat was accounted genteel "sport for ladies!"

In the evening, the rooms were adorned with a splendid suit of tapestry, representing "the hangings at Antioch." After supper, a play was got up by the choristers of St. Paul's, then the most renowned actors in London; and after it was over, the Princess performed on the virginals, accompanied by the voice of one of the choristers.

Elizabeth was afterwards gratified by another entertainment, suited to the temper of the age. She was invited by Sir Thomas Pope to repair to Enfield Chase, to enjoy the favourite diversion of hunting the hart. Twelve ladies, attired in white satin, attended her on their "ambling palfreys," together with twenty yeomen, clad in green. At the entrance of the forest she was met by fifty archers, in scarlet boots and yellow caps, armed with gilded bows; one of whom presented to her a silver-headed arrow, winged with peacocks' feathers. At the conclusion of this fête, the Princess was presented by the principal sportsman, agreeably to the established laws of the chase, with a knife, and, as first lady on the field, she cut the buck's throat with her own fair and royal hand.

In the course of the following summer, the Queen invited her sister to a grand entertainment at Richmond. The Princess was brought from Somerset Place in the Queen's barge, which was richly hung with garlands of artificial flowers, and covered with a canopy of green sarcenet, wrought with branches of eglantine in embroidery, and sprinkled with blossoms of gold. In the royal barge she was accompanied by Sir Thomas Pope, and four ladies of her chamber. Six boats followed, filled with her retinue, habited in russet damask and blue embroidered satin, tasselled and spangled with silver; their bonnets of cloth of silver, adorned with green feathers. The Queen received her in a sumptuous pavilion in the labyrinths of the garden. This pavilion was of cloth of gold and purple velvet, made in the form of a castle; its sides were divided into compartments, bearing alternately the *fleur-de-lis* in silver and the pomegranate, the bearing of Granada, in gold. A sumptuous banquet was here served up to the royal ladies, in which there was introduced a pomegranate tree, in confectionery work, bearing the arms of Spain. There was no masking or dancing, but numerous minstrels performed. The same evening, the Princess returned to Somerset Place, and the following day to Hatfield.

A new suitor now entered the field, as a candidate for the hand of Elizabeth.

* The exhibition of bear-baiting always delighted Elizabeth. Mary, it is believed, never but on this occasion, witnessed this cruel sport.

This was Prince Eric, the eldest son of the King of Sweden. The affair was entrusted to the Swedish ambassador, who, by the direction of his sovereign, made his application to the Princess herself, without previously consulting the Queen and her council. Elizabeth made this circumstance a pretext for rejecting a proposal which she felt no inclination to encourage, and she declared that she could never listen to any overtures of this nature, without receiving the previous sanction of her Majesty. The ambassador pleaded in answer, that his master, in the character of a lover, had judged it becoming that his first application should be made to herself; but that, should he obtain her consent, he would then make his demand in form to the Queen. The Princess replied, "If it were to depend on myself, a single life would ever be my choice;" and then finally dismissed the ambassador.

Having learned from Sir Thomas Pope all the particulars of this affair, the Queen directed him to express to her sister her high approbation of her dutiful conduct on this occasion; and she also desired him to ascertain the sentiments of Elizabeth on the subject of matrimony. This he did, and communicated the same to his sovereign in the following letter:—

"Hatfield, April 26th, 1558.

"SIR THOMAS POPE TO QUEEN MARY.

"First after I had declared to her Grace, how well your Majesty liked her prudent and honourable answer to the King of Sweden's messenger, I then opened to her the purport of the said messenger's mission; which, after her Grace had heard, I said your Majesty had sent me, not only to declare the same, but also to understand how her Grace liked the said motion. Whereunto, after a little pause, she answered;—'Master Pope, I require you, after my most humble commendations to her Majesty, to render unto the same like thanks, that it pleased her Majesty of her own goodness, to conceive so well of my answer to the said messenger; and here withal, of her princely commendation, with such speed to command you to signify the same unto me: who before remained wonderfully perplexed, fearing that her Majesty might mistake the same: for which goodness I acknowledge myself bound to honour, serve, love, and obey her Highness during my life. Requiring you also to say unto her Majesty, that in the King my brother's time there was offered me a very honourable marriage, or two; and ambassadors sent to treat with me touching the same; whereupon I made my humble suit unto his Majesty, as some yet living can testify, that he would give me leave, with his grace's favour, to remain in that estate I was, which of all others best agreed with me, or pleased me most. And in good faith, I pray you say unto her Majesty, I am even at this present moment of the same mind, and so intend, to continue, with her Majesty's favour: assuring her Majesty I so well like this estate, as I persuade myself there is not any kind of life comparable to it. And as concerning my liking the said motion made by the said messenger, I beseech you say unto her Majesty, that in my remembrance I never heard of his master before this time; and that I so well like both the message and the messenger, as I shall most humbly pray God on my knees, that from henceforth I never hear of the one nor the other. I assure you, that if he should afterwards repair unto me, I would forbear to speak to him. And were there nothing else to move me to dislike the motion, other than that his master would attempt the same without making her Majesty privy thereto, it were cause sufficient.'

"And when her Grace had thus ended, I was so bold as of myself to say unto her Grace, her pardon first required, that I thought few or none would believe, but that her Grace could be right well content to marry; so that there were some honourable marriage offered her by your Majesty, or by your Majesty's consent. Whereunto her Grace answered:—'What I shall do hereafter I know not; but I assure you, upon my truth and fidelity, and as God is merciful unto me, I am not at this time otherwise minded than I have declared unto you; no, though I were offered the greatest prince in all Europe.'" Sir Thomas Pope then slyly remarks: "And yet perchance your Majesty may conceive this rather to proceed from a maidenly shamefacedness, than upon any such certain determination."

At the period when Mary lay on her death-bed, Elizabeth was on friendly terms both with her and with Philip. The Spanish King (then on the continent), on hearing of Mary's dangerous situation, sent Count Feria with a letter to her, urging her to name Elizabeth as her successor. This Mary had already done; but Feria waited on the Princess on the tenth of November, and proffered her the good-will of his master, with whom he artfully assured her that the declaration of the Queen in her favour had originated. She gave the ambassador a cordial reception, received Philip's proffer of friendship with courtesy, but firmly protested that it was neither to him, to her sister Mary, or to the council that she was indebted for her position in the succession, but to her own birth, and, above all, to the hearty good-will of the people generally. The Queen, a few days before her demise, which took place on the seventeenth of November, 1558, sent the Countess of Feria to deliver to Elizabeth the custody of the crown jewels. To these, Philip, to claim to himself the merit of sending them, caused to be added a present of his own, a valuable casket of gems which he had left at Whitehall, and which he knew Elizabeth greatly admired. In compliance with Mary's request, Elizabeth swore to continue the church of Rome. "She prayed God," says the Countess of Feria, "that the earth might open and swallow her alive if she were not a true Roman Catholic;" doubtless, a most awful perjury, Elizabeth, according to all evidences, being at the time a Protestant at heart. During the last week of Mary's life the time-serving courtiers flocked to Hatfield to pay their adulations to Elizabeth, who, when informed by a deputation of the council, that Mary had expired, although fully prepared for the announcement, affected great amazement, deeply sighed, and sinking on her knees, exclaimed with a solemn voice:—"It is the Lord's doings! it is marvellous in our eyes!"

CHAPTER IV

Accession of Elizabeth—Her Privy Council—Entry into London—Preparations for her coronation—Splendid costume—Procession from Westminster to the Tower—Her passage through the City—Pageants—Re-establishes the Protestant Church of England—Her reply to the Speaker's address exhorting her to marry—Proposals of marriage from Philip of Spain—The Arch-Duke Charles—The Kings of Sweden and Denmark—Popularity of Elizabeth—Her residence at Greenwich—Her band of gentlemen pensioners—Her royal progresses—The Duchess of Suffolk—Royal proclamation against luxury in dress—Act of Parliament against witchcraft.

HE death of Mary was announced to both houses of Parliament then sitting, by the Lord Chancellor Heath. After a short pause, the members gave vent to their feelings of royalty, by joyful shouts of "God save Queen Elizabeth! long and happily may she reign!" The new sovereign was immediately afterwards proclaimed before the palace in Westminster, and also at the Cross in Cheapside. The bells of the churches were set ringing; bonfires were kindled, tables were spread in the streets agreeably to the hospitality of the times, and there was "plentiful eating, drinking, and making merry." On the following Sunday, *Te Deum* was sung in the churches, and the general joy among all classes was unbounded.

Elizabeth held her first privy council at Hatfield. Sir Thomas Parry was declared Comptroller of her Household; Sir Edward Rogers, Captain of the Guard; and Sir William Cecil, Principal Secretary of State. The first of these personages had filled, for many years, the office of cofferer to the Princess, and was completely in the secret of her confidential intercourse with Lord Seymour, the Lord High Admiral, and whose fidelity in that delicate affair had withstood all the threats and artifices of the Protector. Cecil was already known to the public, and his nomination to such an important office was a happy omen for the Protestant cause, of which he was the adherent. He maintained a secret and intimate correspondence with Elizabeth during the whole period of her adversity, and assisted her on many trying occasions with his salutary advice. On appointing him a member of her privy council, Elizabeth addressed him in the following terms:—"I give you this charge, that you shall be of my secret council, and content yourself to take pains for me and my realm. This opinion I have of you, that you will not be corrupted with any gift; and that you will be faithful to the state; that without respect to my private will, you will give me that counsel that you think best, and that if you shall know any thing necessary to be declared to me of secrecy, you will show it to myself only; and be assured I will not fail to keep taciturnity therein."

On the twenty-third of November, the Queen repaired to her capital, attended by a train of a thousand nobles, knights, gentlemen and ladies; and took up her temporary residence at the monastery of Chartreux, or Charter House, then the abode of Lord North. It was a splendid building, and afforded ample accommodation for a royal retinue. Her next removal, agreeably to ancient custom, was to the Tower, and on this interesting occasion, all the streets from the Charter House were laid with fine gravel; musicians and singers were stationed by the way: and a vast assemblage of people freely tendered their joyful and admiring acclamations. The Queen passed along, splendidly attired in purple robes, and mounted on her palfrey, richly caparisoned. She was preceded by her heralds and great officers of state, and returned the salutations of her loving subjects with the most graceful affability.

Immediately on entering the royal apartments in the Tower, she, on her knees, returned humble and fervent thanks to that Providence which had hitherto protected her. How different must have been her sensations now from what they were when she had been led a prisoner under these walls! She had formerly entered that fortress by the traitors' gate, as a terrified and defenceless Princess, without hope of deliverance, and apprehensive of a violent death. She now returned to take legal possession of it, surrounded in all the pomp of royalty, by her ministers of state, and welcomed by the applause of the people. She was attended on her visit to the Tower by Lord Robert Dudley, one who, like herself, had been a prisoner there. He was now appointed Master of the Ordnance, and was regarded by his royal mistress with peculiar favour. His personal graces and elegant accomplishments were sufficiently striking to dazzle the eyes and charm the heart of a youthful Queen, possessed of a lively fancy, and now absolute mistress of her own actions. The circumstance of his being already married, blinded her, no doubt, as to the real nature of her sentiments towards him; or it was regarded by her as a sufficient sanction, in the eyes of the nation, for all those marks of favour and esteem with which she was pleased to honour him.

The illustrious family of the Howards came in for a large share of the Queen's bounty; the Duke of Norfolk, her second cousin, was invested with the order of the Garter. Her great uncle, Lord William Howard, created Baron of Effingham by Mary, was continued by Elizabeth in the high office of Lord Chamberlain. Lord Thomas Howard, who had treated her with distinguished respect on her arrival at Woodstock from Hampton Court, now received the title of Viscount Bindon, and continued much in favour to the end of his life. Sir Francis Knolles, whose wife was one of Elizabeth's nearest kinswomen, was sworn in a member of the privy council, together with Sir Richard Sackville. But of all her relations, Henry Carey, son of Mary Boleyn, the Queen's aunt, was the most deserving of her gratitude. He had expended thousands of his patrimony in her service, during the period of her imprisonment, and she liberally requited his friendship, by conferring on him the title of Baron Hunsdon; together with the royal residence of that name, its surrounding park, and several beneficial leases of crown lands. Lord Hunsdon, however, was as little skilled in that sentimental gallantry which Elizabeth required from her courtiers, as in the circumspect and tortuous policy which she approved in her statesmen. "As he lived in a ruffling time," says Naunton, "so he loved sword and buckler men; and such as our fathers were wont to call *men of their hands;* of which sort he had many brave gentlemen that followed him; yet he was not taken for a popular or dangerous person." It was said of him, that "his Latin and his dissimulation were both alike, and his custom in swearing and obscenity in speech, made him appear a worse Christian than he really was."

The following characteristic anecdote of this worthy is related by Fuller;—"On one occasion, his neighbour, Mr. Colt, chanced to meet him coming from Hunsdon to London, in the equipage of a nobleman of those days. The baron, on calling to mind some former grudge, gave him a sound box on the ear; Colt immediately returned the principal with interest; and thereupon his servants, drawing their swords, swarmed around him. 'You rogues!' said my lord, 'may not I and my neighbour exchange a blow but you must interfere?' His servants withdrew, and thus the quarrel was begun and ended in the same minute." The Queen's attachment to her relations was so remarkable, that even Leicester, in the height of his favour, felt that he must hold sacred their claims to her regard. Accordingly he used to remark, in allusion to Sackville and Hunsdon—"Those were of the tribe of Dan, and were *Noli me tangeres!*" (Touch me nots.)

After spending a few days in the Tower, Elizabeth passed by water to Somerset Place, whence she removed to the palace of Westminster, where she kept her Christmas. Great preparations were now making for her coronation at Westminster Abbey. The people were resolved, on that festive occasion, to lavish, in honour of their new sovereign, every demonstration of loyalty and affection. The costume of that age was magnificent. Gowns of velvet or satin, richly trimmed with silk, furs, or gold lace; costly gold chains; and caps or hoods of rich materials, adorned with feathers, decorated on all occasions of ceremony the persons, not only of nobles and courtiers, but of their retainers, and even of the substantial citizens. The attire of the ladies was proportionally splendid. Hangings of cloth, of silk, and of velvet, cloth of gold and cloth of silver, or "needlework sublime," adorned, on days of family festivity, the principal chamber of every house of respectable appearance; and these on public festivals were suspended from the balconies, and combined with the banners and pennons floating overhead, gave to the streets an appearance resembling a suite of long and gaily dressed saloons. Every circumstance tended to render the public entry of Queen Elizabeth the most gorgeous, and at the same time the most imposing, spectacle ever exhibited in the capital of Britain.

On the twelfth of January, 1559, her Majesty was conducted from her palace in Westminster to the royal apartments in the Tower; and a splendid water procession was appointed for the purpose. At this period, the streets of London were narrow and ill-paved, the roads bad, and the luxury of a carriage unknown. The Thames, therefore, was the great thoroughfare of the metropolis.

The old palace of Westminster, as well as the palaces of Richmond and Greenwich, the favourite summer residences of the royal family, stood on its banks: the court, therefore, passed from one palace to the other in their state barges. The nobility were beginning to occupy, with their mansions and gardens, the space between the Strand and the river; and it had become a prevailing fashion among them, to vie with each other in the splendour of their barges and the richness of the liveries of the rowers, who were all distinguished by the crests or badges of their noble owners. The corporation and trading companies of the City of London possessed, as at present, their state barges, enriched with carved and gilded figures, and decked and trimmed with targets and banners. These were all drawn out in grand array; and to enliven the pomp, "the bachelors' barge of the Lord Mayor's company, viz. the Mercers', was attended by a *foist* with artillery aboard, shooting off lustily as they went, with great and pleasant melody of instruments, which played in a most sweet and heavenly manner." In this state they rowed up to Westminster, and attended her Majesty with the royal barges back to the Tower.

The passage through the city took place two days afterwards. Her Majesty issued forth, drawn in a superb chariot, preceded by trumpeters and heralds in their coat-armour; and "most honourably accompanied by gentlemen, Barons, and the higher nobility of the realm; as also by a notable train of ladies. The ladies were on horseback, and both they and their lords were habited in crimson velvet, with which their horses were also caparisoned. This retinue of fair equestrians, constantly attendant on the person of the maiden queen in all her public appearances, produced a striking effect. As they approached, the air was rent by the acclamations of the citizens, who had erected across the principal streets a series of solemn pageants, in the manner of triumphant arches. On these were inscribed illustrative sentences in English and Latin: a child was stationed in each, who explained to the Queen, in English verse, the meaning of the whole. The first consisted of three stories, represented by living figures: Henry the Seventh and his royal spouse, Elizabeth of York, from whom her Majesty derived her name—Henry the Eighth and Anne Boleyn, and lastly, her Majesty in person, all attired in royal robes. The verses described the felicity of that union of the houses to which she owed her existence. The second pageant was styled "the seat of worthy governance;" on its summit sat another representative of the Queen; underneath were the cardinal virtues, trampling under their feet the opposite vices. The third exhibited the eight Beatitudes, all ascribed, with much ingenuity of application, to Her Majesty. The fourth represented, in lively contrast, the images of a decayed and flourishing commonwealth; and from a cave below, issued Time, leading forth his daughter Truth, who held in her hand an English Bible, which she offered for the Queen's acceptance. Elizabeth received the volume, and reverently pressing it with both hands to her heart and her lips, declared aloud, amidst the tears and grateful benedictions of her people, that she thanked the city more for that gift than for all the costly magnificence they had bestowed upon her; and that she would often read over that blessed book. The last pageant exhibited "a seemly and mete personage, richly apparelled in parliamentary robes, with a sceptre in her hand, over whose head was written:—'Deborah, the judge and restorer of the house of Israel!'" The Recorder of London then approached her Majesty's chariot, near the further end of Cheapside—where ended the long array of the city companies, which had lined the streets all the way from Fenchurch Street—and presented her with a splendid purse, containing one thousand marks in gold. To crown the whole, those two celebrated personages, Gog and Magog, deserted on this memorable day their accustomed stations in the Guildhall, and reared up their stately dimensions on each side of Temple Bar; with joined hands they supported above the gate a copy of Latin verses, in which they obligingly expounded to her Majesty the sense of all the pageants which had been presented to her view; concluding with compliments and felicitations suitable to the happy occasion. The Queen, in a few cordial words, thanked the citizens for all their cost and pains, assured them that she would "stand their good queen;" and passed the gate amidst thunders of applause.

The following traits of Elizabeth's behaviour on this auspicious day, are recorded, with affectionate delight, by Holinshed, our early English chronicler:—"'Yonder is an ancient citizen,' said one of the knights attending on her person, 'who weepeth, and turneth his face backward: How may it be interpreted? That he doth so for sorrow or for gladness?' With a just and pleasing confidence, the Queen replied, 'I warrant you it is for gladness.' How many nosegays," proceeds the same chronicler, "did her Grace receive at poor women's hands on that joyful day? How many times staid she her chariot when she saw any simple body offer to speak to her Grace? A branch of rosemary given her Grace with a supplication by a poor woman about Fleet Bridge, was seen in her chariot till her Grace came to Westminster."

"Her Majesty was twenty-five years of age at this auspicious period. She was a lady of passing beauty, of majestic deportment, and so rarely qualified by adversity, and so well accomplished by experience (which are most effectual tutors), that she had purchased prudence and judgment far above the capacity of her age. She was possessed of pregnant wit and wisdom, and virtues which gained for her the name and fame of a gracious and popular princess."

The ceremonies of the coronation took place on the following day; regulated in everything by ancient custom, they afforded little scope for that display of popular sentiments, which had given so intense an interest to the procession of the previous day. Great perplexity was occasioned by the refusal of the whole bench of bishops to perform the coronation service; but at length, Ogelthorp, Bishop of Carlisle, was gained over by the court, and the rite was duly celebrated. This refusal of the bishops was wisely overlooked by the government; but it no doubt proceeded partly from a conviction that the marriage of Henry the Eighth with Catherine of Arragon having been declared lawful and valid, Elizabeth, as the child of Anne Boleyn, must be regarded as illegitimate, and incapable of succeeding to the throne; and partly through a suspicious fear of the Roman religion, conceived because her Majesty had been brought up from the cradle in the Protestant faith. It appears also, that Elizabeth had a little before forbidden a bishop, at divine service, from lifting up and adoring the host; she likewise permitted the litany, epistles, and the gospels to be translated into English, which they held as execrable. "Yet Queen Elizabeth," says an early and accurate historian, "was truly godly, pious, and zealously devoted; for her Majesty was no sooner out of her bed, than she fell upon her knees in her private closet, and prayed to God devoutly. Certain hours were by her Majesty reserved, and devoted to the Lord. Moreover, her Majesty never failed every Lord's day and holy day to frequent the chapel; neither was any prince ever more conversant in divine service, or conducted himself with more devotion than her Majesty. She zealously heard all the sermons in Lent, being attired in black, and very diligently gave attention thereto, according to the ancient use and custom; although she said, and oft-times repeated, that which she had read of Henry the Third, her predecessor, that her Majesty had rather in her prayers speak to God devoutly, than hear others speak of Him eloquently. And concerning the cross, our Blessed Lady and the saints, she never conceived irreverently of them, neither spake herself, nor suffered any others to speak of them, without a certain kind of reverence."

In all probability, had she found herself free to follow entirely the dictates of her own inclinations, Elizabeth would have established in the church a kind of medium, like that devised by her father, for whose authority she had the highest veneration. To the end of her reign she never could be reconciled to married bishops; and with respect to the clergy generally, she preferred the single man before the married one. Lord Bacon relates the following anecdote: — "Queen Elizabeth, on the morrow of her coronation (it being the custom to release prisoners at the inauguration of a prince), went to the chapel; and in the great chamber, one of her courtiers, who was well known to her, either out of his own motion, or by the instigation of a wiser man, presented her with a petition; and before a great number of courtiers, besought her with a loud voice, that now this good time there might be four or five more principal prisoners released; these were the four evangelists, and the apostle St. Paul, who had long been shut, in an unknown tongue, as it were, in prison, so as they could not converse with the common people. The Queen answered very gravely, that it was best first to inquire of themselves whether they would be released or not."

Immediately on her accession, Elizabeth resolved to abolish the Catholic religion as speedily as prudence would permit. According to Stowe, the moment she had called together her first privy council, she began to put into practice that oath of supremacy which her father, Henry the Eighth, first ordained. Amongst the many who refused that oath, was the Lord Chancellor, Dr. Heath. Yet the Queen, having a good respect for him, would not deprive him of his title, but committed the custody of the great seal to Sir Nicholas Bacon, who from that time was called Lord Keeper, and by the authority of parliament exercised the power and prerogative of the Lord Chancellor, Dr. Heath only retaining the empty title. "At this same time," proceeds the faithful chronicler, "the English nation was wonderfully divided in opinion, as well in matters of ecclesiastical government, as in divers points of religion, by reason of three important theological changes within the brief period of twelve years. King Henry the Eighth retained the ecclesiastical supremacy, with the first fruits and tenths; maintained seven sacraments, with obits and mass for the quick and the dead. King Edward abolished the mass, authorised one book of common prayer in English, with hallowing the dead, and wine, &c., and established only two sacraments. Queen Mary restored all things according to the Church of Rome, re-established the papal supremacy, and, in fact, permitted nothing within her dominion that was was repugnant to the Roman Catholic Church; but the death of Mary was the ruin of all Abbots, Priors and Prioresses, Monks and Nuns. Elizabeth, on her accession, commanded that no one should preach without a special license, that such rites and ceremonies should be used in all churches as had been used in her Highness's chapel, and that the epistle and gospel should be read in the English tongue; and in her first parliament, held at Westminster, in January, 1559, she expelled the papal supremacy, resumed the first fruits and tenths, repressed the mass, re-introduced the Book of Common Prayer and the Sacraments in the English tongue, and finally and firmly re-established the Protestant Church of England." Whilst these matters were pending, Elizabeth, to prevent the Londoners from hearing political sermons, locked up the pulpit of St. Paul's Cross, and herself, as an act of expediency, attended mass in her own chapel, and outwardly conformed to the ceremonies of the Catholic Church.

In the same parliament that had re-established the Protestant Church of England, two questions were agitated, personally interesting to the Queen, her title to the crown, and her marriage. By the counsels of the keeper of the seals, Sir Nicholas Bacon, she refrained from requiring of parliament the repeal of those acts of her father's reign which had declared his marriage with Anne Boleyn, her mother, null and void, and herself illegitimate. Reposing in the well-known maxim of law, that the crown once worn takes away all defects in blood, she contented herself with an act declaratory in general terms of her right of succession to the throne, and thus she tacitly admitted Anne Boleyn's guilt.

In reply to the address of the Parliament, requesting her to enter the married state, she said:—"In a thing which is not very pleasing to me, the infallible testimony of your good will, and all the rest of my people, is most acceptable. As concerning your eager persuasion of me to marriage, I must tell you, I have been ever persuaded, that I was ordained by God to consider, and, above all, to do those things which appertain to his glory. And therefore it is, that I have made choice of this kind of life, which is most free, and agreeable for such human affairs as may tend to his service alone; from which, if either the marriages which have been offered to me by divers powerful princes, or the danger of attempts made against my life, could no wise divert me, *it is long since I had any joy in the honour of a husband;* and this is what I thought, when I was a private person; but when the public charge of governing the kingdom came upon me, it seemed to me an inconsiderate folly, to draw upon myself the cares of marriage. To conclude, I am already bound unto a husband, which is the kingdom of England, and let that suffice you:" *then, stretching out her hand, and shewing the ring with which she was given in marriage, and inaugurated to her kingdom,* she said, "*Reproach me no more* that I have no children; for every one of you, and as many as are English, are my children and kinsfolks, of whom, so long as I am not deprived (and God will preserve me), you cannot charge me, without offence, to be destitute. But in this I must commend you, that you have not appointed me a husband: for that were unworthy the majesty of an *absolute* princess, and the discretion of you who are born my subjects. Nevertheless, if God hath ordained me to another course of life, I promise to do nothing to the prejudice of the commonwealth; but, as far as possible, to marry a husband as shall be careful for the common good. And if I persist in remaining single, I feel assured that God will so direct my counsels and yours, that you shall have no cause to doubt of a successor, who may be more profitable for the commonwealth than he who may proceed from me, since the posterity of good princes doth oft-times degenerate. Lastly, this may be sufficient, both for my memory, and for the honour of my name, that when I have expired my last breath, these lines may be inscribed on my tomb:—

HERE LIES INTERR'D ELIZABETH,
A VIRGIN PURE UNTIL HER DEATH."

When Elizabeth conveyed to Philip of Spain the formal announcement of the death of his late wife, Queen Mary, she added her own anxiety to preserve his friendship. To this letter Philip, who had long felt an attachment to Elizabeth, and wished, by a union with England, to counterbalance the united powers of France and Scotland, replied by an offer of his hand! He undertook to procure from the Pope the necessary dispensation for the marriage, which he seemed confident would be granted with alacrity; and ere Elizabeth's answer could reach him, he dispatched envoys to Rome for this purpose. A princess of a character less firm and sagacious than the Queen, might have found in the splendour of Philip's rank and power temptations not to be resisted. But Elizabeth well knew how odious Philip's marriage with her sister had been to the nation. She believed, if she gave him her hand, the legality of the marriage would be questioned. She sympathized in the religious sentiments of her Protestant subjects; she felt, too, all the pride of being independent, and looking round with cheerful confidence on a people who almost adored her, she formed the patriotic resolution to wear her English diadem by the suffrage of the English nation alone, exempt from the participation of one who ranked among the first monarchs of Europe. The Spanish ambassador represented to the Queen, that a negative could not be given to the offer of Philip, without deeply wounding his pride and his feelings. However, the King of Spain soon consoled himself for this disappointment, by marrying the daughter of the King of France.

Proposals for the hand of Elizabeth

now poured in from almost every court in Europe. The Archduke Charles, son of the Emperor Ferdinand of Austria, was the next suitor; but his overtures were also declined without hesitation, although afterwards renewed with some prospect of success. Eric, who had now ascended the throne of Sweden, sent over his brother, the Duke of Finland, to plead once more with Elizabeth for the honour of her hand; and the King of Denmark, being determined that his neighbour should not bear off so glorious a prize without a contest, lost no time in dispatching his nephew, the Duke of Holstein, on the same distinguished errand. The Duke of Finland was received with high honours. Lord Robert Dudley and the Earl of Oxford set out for Colchester to meet him, and conduct him to London. He was received at the corner of Gracechurch Street by Lord Ambrose Dudley and the Marquis of Northampton, attended by many gentlemen and ladies; thence, followed by a great troop of yeomen of the guard and gentlemen, wearing gold chains, he proceeded to the palace of the Bishop of Winchester, in Southwark, which was hung with rich cloth of arras, wrought with gold and silver, and silk. The Duke of Holstein on his arrival was lodged at Somerset Place, the use of which the Queen had granted to Lord Hunsdon. This Duke had sanguine expectations of success in his suit; but the royal and fickle fair one deemed it enough to acknowledge his pains, by granting him an honourable reception, the order of the Garter, and a yearly pension!

Elizabeth now frequently appeared in public, and neglected no opportunity of increasing her popularity with the nation. On one occasion she visited the royal mint, to inspect a new coinage about to be issued, which she had the merit of restoring to its proper standard. She also went over the Priory of St. Mary Spittle, in Bishopsgate Street, noted for its famous pulpit cross; where, on particular days, the Lord Mayor and Aldermen attended to hear sermons. She was attended, as Stowe informs us, "by a thousand men in *harness*, with shirts of mail, corselets, and morice pikes; besides ten great pieces carried through the city unto the court, with drums and trumpets sounding, and two morice dancings; and in the cart two white bears."

Again, having honoured the Earl of Pembroke with her company to a splendid supper at Baynard's Castle, in Thames Street, she afterwards took boat and was rowed up and down the river; hundreds of barges rowing alongside of her, and thousands of people thronging at the water-side to gaze upon her Majesty, rejoicing to see her, and to partake of the music and sights upon the river.

The peer thus honoured was the brother-in-law of Catherine Parr; Elizabeth entertained great respect for his experience and capacity, admitted him to her privy council, and named him, with the Marquis of Northampton, the Earl of Bedford, and Lord John Grey—all leading men of the Protestant party—to assist at the meetings of divines and men of learning, by whom the religious establishment of the country was settled.

The arrival of ambassadors of high rank from the King of France, on the occasion of a peace recently concluded with that country, afforded the Queen another opportunity of displaying all the magnificence of her court. The Duke de Montmorenci, the chief of the embassy, was lodged at the Bishop of London's Palace; and the houses of the dean and canons of St. Paul were filled with his numerous retinue. The gorgeousness of the ambassadors' dress was the theme of admiration. The day after their arrival they were conducted in state to the court, where they supped with the Queen, and afterwards partook of a goodly banquet, with all manner of entertainment, until the hour of midnight. The next day her Majesty gave them a sumptuous dinner, followed by a baiting of bulls and bears! "The Queen herself stood with them in a gallery, enjoying the pastime, till six o'clock; when they returned by water, to sup with the Bishop of London. On the following day, they visited the Paris Garden, then a favourite place of amusement, on the Surrey side of the Thames, and were there entertained with another exhibition of bull and bear baiting." They departed in two days afterwards, "taking their barge towards Gravesend," highly delighted with their hospitable reception, and carrying with them a number of mastiffs, given them to hunt the wolves in the forests of France.

The Queen, at this period, took up her residence in her favourite summer palace at Greenwich, and the London companies were ordered to muster their men-at-arms in the adjoining park. Of the fourteen hundred men assembled on this occasion, eight hundred were armed in fine corselets, bearing the long Moorish pike; two hundred were halberdiers, wearing another species of armour, called Almain or German rivets; and the gunners or musketeers were equipped in coats of mail, with morions or steel caps. Her Majesty, surrounded by a splendid court, beheld their evolutions from a gallery over the park-gate. A few days afterwards, the Queen's pensioners were appointed to "run with the spear"—a chivalrous exhibition, which delighted the warlike imagination of Elizabeth. In the park of Greenwich, a banqueting-house was erected for her Majesty, "made with fir poles, decked with branches of birch, and all manner of field and garden flowers." Tents were also erected for her household, and a place prepared for the tilters. After the exercises were over, the Queen gave a supper in the banqueting-house, which was succeeded by a masque, and a splendid banquet. "And then followed great casting of fire-works and shooting of guns till midnight." The band of gentlemen pensioners, the boast and ornament of Elizabeth's court, was the most splendid establishment of the kind in Europe. It was composed of the flower of the English nobility; and to be admitted to serve in its ranks, was regarded as a distinction worthy the ambition of young men of the highest families. It was a saying of the Earl of Clare, that while he was a pensioner of Queen Elizabeth, he did not know a *worse man* [one of less wealth and distinguished birth] in the whole band than himself; yet he was then inheriting an estate of four thousand a year. "It was the constant custom of the Queen," says Collins, "to call out of all counties in the kingdom, the gentlemen of the greatest hopes and of the best fortunes and families, and with them to fill the more honourable places of the household servants; by which she honoured them, obliged their kindred and alliance, and fortified herself."

On the seventeenth of July, 1559, Elizabeth set out on the first of those royal *progresses*, which form so striking a feature in her domestic history. "In these journeys," says Bohun, "she was most easy to be approached; private persons and magistrates, men and women, country people and children, came joyfully and without fear to wait upon her. Her ears were then open to the complaints of the afflicted, and of those that had been in any way injured. She would not suffer the meanest of her people to be shut out from the place where she resided; but the greatest, as well as the least, were then in a manner levelled. She took with her own hand, and read with the greatest kindness, the petitions of the poorest rustics. And she would frequently assure them, that she would take particular care of their affairs; and she would ever be as good as her word. She was never seen angry with the most unseasonable of uncourtly approach; she was never offended with the most impudent or importunate petitioner. Nor was there any thing in the whole course of her reign that more won the hearts of the people, than this her wonderful facility and condescension, and the sweetness and pleasantness with which she entertained all who came to her."

The first stage of the Queen's progress was to Dartford, in Kent, whence she proceeded to Cobham Hall, where she was sumptuously entertained by Lord Cobham, a nobleman who enjoyed a large share of her royal favour. Eltham was her next stage; and she next visited the Earl of Arundel, at the magnificent palace of Nonsuch.

The Earl received her with the utmost magnificence. On Sunday night, a banquet, a mask, and a concert were the entertainments. The next day she witnessed a hunt, from a standing erected for her in the park, and the children of St. Paul's performed a play; after which, a costly banquet was served up in gilt dishes. On her departure, she was presented with a cupboard of plate by the noble host, who, on this occasion, looked to a high and splendid recompense—not less than the fair hand of the illustrious Queen herself; but, like other and more illustrious suitors, he was doomed to disappointment.

During the summer of this year, a pompous funeral ceremony took place in St. Paul's Cathedral, in memory of Henry the Second, of France. A hearse, magnificently adorned with the banners and escutcheons of the deceased, was placed in the church; a numerous train of lords and gentlemen attended as mourners; and all the ceremonies of a real funeral were duly performed. This was a customary tribute, at that period, among the Princes of Europe to the memory of each other. In the month of December following, the Duchess Dowager of Suffolk was interred, with much pomp, in Westminster Abbey. She was the grand-daughter of Henry the Seventh. After the tragical end of her misguided husband, and of Lady Jane Grey, her eldest daughter, the Duchess was permitted to remain in unmolested privacy; and she had subsequently rendered herself utterly insignificant, by an obscure marriage with one Stoke, a young man who was her master of the horse. When the news of this connection reached the ears of Elizabeth, she exclaimed, with surprise and indignation—"What! has the Duchess married her horse-keeper?" To which Cecil replied, with unpardonable freedom, "Yes, Madam, and she says your Majesty would like to do so too!" We need hardly remark, that her favourite, Lord Robert Dudley, at that time filled the office of Master of the Horse to the Queen. His long intimacy with the Queen was apparent to all observers, and occasioned fears and jealousies to her best friends and wisest counsellors.

A royal proclamation was this year issued, to check the prevailing luxury in dress, which at that period was inveighed against by Bishop Pilkington, who, in his sermons, cautions the people against wearing "fine-fingered rufflers, with sables about their necks, corked slippers, trimmed buskins, and warm mittens. These tender Parnels," says the homely bishop, "must have one gown for the day, another for the night; one long, another short, one for winter, another for summer. One furred through, another but faced; one for the work-day, another for the holy-day. One of this colour, another of that. One of cloth, another of silk or damask. Change of apparel; one afore dinner, another after; one of Spanish fashion, another of Turkey. And, to be brief, never content with enough, but always devising new and strange fashions. Yea, a ruffian will have more in his ruff and his hose, than he should spend in a year: he who ought to go in a russet coat, spends as much on apparel for himself and his wife, as his father would have kept a good house with." The affectation of wearing by turns the costume of all nations of Europe, with which the Queen herself was not a little accustomed, may be partly traced to the habit of importing articles of dress from abroad, and partly to the taste for travelling, which, since the revival of learning, had been laudably prevalent among the nobility and gentry.

An act of Parliament was also passed in this year, which is illustrative of the fanaticism of the early Protestant divines. The Catholics were accused of employing enchantment and witchcraft in their religious services, and it was feared "by many good and sober men" that these dealers in the black art might even bewitch the Queen herself. It was thought necessary, therefore, by the *enlightened* Parliament of Elizabeth, to forbid, under the penalty of death, the use of these mysterious practices. The *learned* Bishop Jewel led the way in inspiring these superstitious terrors. In a discourse delivered before the Queen and her court, he says, "Witches and sorcerers within the last few years have marvellously increased within your Majesty's dominions. *These eyes have seen most evident and manifest marks of their wickedness.* Your Majesty's subjects pine away even unto death; their colour fadeth; their flesh rolleth; their speech is benumbed; their senses are bereft. Wherefore your poor subjects most humble petition to your Majesty, that the laws touching such malefactors may be put in due execution. For the shoal of them is great, their doings horrible, their malice intolerable, the examples most miserable. And I pray God they may never practise further than upon your Majesty's subjects."—Verily, we are much indebted to the Parliament of Queen Elizabeth, for so effectually putting down the odious practices of these dealers in the black art!

CHAPTER V.

Sir Thomas Chaloner—Mysterious death of Lady Dudley—Curious particulars respecting Dudley and Elizabeth—Mary, Queen of Scots—The Queen and the Dean of Christchurch—Description of St. Paul's in the time of Elizabeth—Splendid present from Eric, King of Sweden, and preparations for his visit—Elizabeth's cruel treatment of the Earl and Countess of Hertford—False likenesses of the Queen—Royal visit to Cambridge.

AT the close of the year 1559, Sir Thomas Chaloner,—the first ambassador named by Elizabeth,—in a postscript to one of his official letters to Secretary Cecil, thus states his opinion on a point of great delicacy in the personal conduct of her Majesty:—

"I assure you, Sir, these folks are broad-mouthed, where I spoke of one too much in favour, as they esteem. I think ye guess whom they named; if ye do not, I will in my next letters write further. To tell you what I conceive—a young Princess cannot be too wary what countenance or familiar demonstration she maketh to one more than another. This delay of ripe time for marriage, ministreth matter to lewd tongues to descant upon, and breedeth contempt. I would I had but one hour's talk with you. If I trusted not your good nature, I would not write thus much; which, nevertheless, I humbly pray you to receive as written to yourself."

The sentiments of Cecil, respecting the Queen's extraordinary behaviour to Dudley, exactly coincided with those of his friend Chaloner; and fears for the reputation of Elizabeth gave additional urgency, at this period, to those pleadings in favour of matrimony, which her council felt compelled to press upon her attention so often and so much in vain. Alas! for the honour of the maiden Queen—her constant and invariable refusals of all matrimonial offers are easily accounted for—she loved, and was beloved in return, by a man already yoked to a helpmate—a pampered minion!—and a circumstance soon after occurred, which rendered her anticipated choice of a husband an object no longer of hope and joy, but one of general dissatisfaction and alarm.

At the moment when the whispered scandal of the court had apprised Lord Dudley how obvious to all observers the partiality of his Sovereign had become;—at the moment when her rejection of the proposals of so many foreign Princes had confirmed the suspicion, that her heart and affections were placed on one of her own subjects:—at such a moment, when, in short, every thing conspired to sanction hopes in the breast of Dudley, which, under any other circumstances, would have appeared visionary and presumptuous;—at the very juncture most favourable to his ambition, but most perilous to his reputation, Lord Robert Dudley lost his wife—by a sudden and mysterious fate. This unfortunate lady had been sent by her husband, under the protection of Sir Richard Verney, one of his retainers, to Cumnor House, in Berkshire; a solitary mansion, inhabited by Anthony Foster, also a dependant of Dudley, and bound to him by *particular* obligations. Here she soon after met with an untimely death; and Verney and Foster, who appear to have been *alone* in the house with her, gave out that it happened by an accidental fall down stairs. But this story gained so little credit in the neighbourhood, that reports of the most dreadful import were quickly propagated. These rumours soon reached the ears of the conscientious Thomas Lewer, Prebendary of Coventry, who immediately addressed to the Secretaries of State an earnest remonstrance, still extant, beseeching them to cause strict inquiry to be made into the affair; *as it was the universal belief that the lady had been murdered.* No steps were taken in consequence of this application; it was of too dreadful a nature, and involved consequences which might well make sycophants shudder. It is, however, a fact, that not only the popular voice, which was ever hostile to Dudley, continued to accuse him as the perpetrator or contriver of her fate, but Cecil himself, in a memorandum drawn up some years after, of "reasons against the Queen's making Dudley her husband;" mentions, among other objections, "that he was rendered infamous by the death of his wife." It is also certain that the Queen took no cognizance of this affair, beyond declaring "that Dudley was then in the court, and none of his at the attempt at his wife's house, and that it fell out as should neither touch his honesty nor honour." In the opinion of the whole country, however, this miserable favourite ever after passed for a dark and dangerous intriguer, capable of perpetrating any villany, and skilful enough to conceal his atrocity under a cloak of artifice and hypocrisy, impenetrable to the too partial eyes of the credulous Elizabeth, though obvious to all the world beside. This idea of his character caused him afterwards to be accused of attempting the lives of several other persons, who opportunely perished to facilitate his guilty purposes.

The statements in the Burleigh Papers, that Elizabeth, upon returning one dark night from an evening entertainment at Lord Dudley's, fell into conversation with his torch-bearers, and told them that she would make Dudley the best man that ever bare his name—meaning, that she would marry him—is too absurd to be accredited. When Elizabeth travelled on these occasions, she was always attended by courtiers, and surrounded by her guards: besides, she was not the Princess to make confidants of such mean-born persons as torch-bearers.

In 1560, Francis the Second died, when his beautiful widow, the unfortunate Mary, Queen of Scots, at the earnest entreaty of her Scottish subjects, resolved to return to the kingdom of her ancestors; and, with this view, she sent to request a safe conduct from the hands of Elizabeth, who replied, that Mary had only to ratify the treaty of Edinburgh (by one article of which Mary was never to resume the arms of England), and instructed Throgmorton, the English ambassador at the court of France, strongly to urge her immediate compliance with this demand. The Queen of Scots, however, as the nearest heir to the English crown, persisted in her resolution to maintain her lawful rights, and assured Throgmorton, that she was vexed at having exposed herself needlessly to such a refusal; and that doubtless she would be enabled to return to her own country without the permission of Elizabeth: she then abruptly put an end to the interview, and reached Scotland in safety. The enmity between these illustrious kinswomen henceforth became irreparable. A personal conference between the two Queens was proposed to be held at York, but Elizabeth ultimately declined the interview, being unwilling to afford her beautiful and captivating rival an opportunity of winning upon the affections of the English people.

The zeal against popery now shewed itself by many acts of the Queen and her government. All the altars in Westminster Abbey were ordered to be pulled down, and, about the same time, a remarkable scene occurred between Elizabeth and the dean of Christchurch, Dr. Sampson. On new year's day, 1561, her Majesty went in state to St. Paul's, when a sermon was preached by the dean. Thinking to gratify her, on that day, with an elegant and appropriate present, the worthy doctor had procured some illuminated prints, illustrative of the acts of the saints and martyrs, which he caused to be inserted in a richly-bound prayer-book, and laid on the Queen's cushion for her use. Her Majesty opened the volume, but on beholding the prints she changed colour, frowned, and called to the verger to bring her the book she was accustomed to have. The service ended, she went into the vestry, and inquired of the dean who had brought that book? and when he explained that he had intended it as a present for her Majesty, she lectured him severely; inquired if he was ignorant of her proclamation against images, pictures, and Romish reliques in the churches, and of her aversion to all idolatry; and strictly ordered that no similar mistake should occur in future. It is singular, that, at this very time, Elizabeth kept a crucifix in her own private chapel, and that the dean of Christchurch was so far from being popishly inclined, that he had, only the year before, refused the bishopric of Norwich on account of the habits and ceremonies attending the office. But Elizabeth was fond of showing her zeal on all public occasions against the Papists, on whose downfall her existence as a Queen depended.

This year the steeple of St. Paul's Cathedral, the loftiest in the kingdom, was struck by lightning, and utterly destroyed, together with the bells and the roof. The papists represented the accident as a judgment of heaven for the discontinuance of the matins and other services which were wont to be performed in the church, whilst the Protestants regarded it as a judgment for the abuses by which the church had formerly been polluted, under the sway of the papists. In a pamphlet published at the time, the Bishop of Durham says:—"No place had been more abused than St. Paul's—it was no wonder, therefore, that God had overthrown it now. From the top of the spire, at coronations or other solemn triumphs, some for vain glory had used to throw themselves down by a rope, and so killed themselves, vainly to please other men's eyes. At the battlements of the steeple, their popish anthems were sometimes used to call upon their gods, with torch and taper in the evenings. In the top of one of the pinnacles was Lollard's tower, where many an innocent soul had been by them cruelly tormented and murdered. In the middlemost alley was their long censer, reaching from the roof to the ground; as though the Holy Ghost came down in their censing, in the likeness of a dove. In the arches, men commonly complained of wrong and delayed judgments in ecclesiastical causes: and divers persons had been condemned there, by Annas and Caiaphas, for Christ's cause. Their images hung on every wall, pillar, and door, with their pilgrimages and worshipping; passing over their massing and many altars, and the rest of their popish service. The south alley was for usury and popery; the north for simony; and the horse-fair in the midst for all kind of bargains, meetings, brawlings, murders, conspiracies. The font for ordinary payments of money, was as well known to all men as the beggar knows his dish. So that without and within, above the ground and under, over the roof and beneath, from the top of the steeple and spire down to the low floor, not one spot was free from wickedness."

Eric, now King of Sweden, whose hopes of ultimate success in his matrimonial addresses to Elizabeth were continued, in spite of the repeated denials of the Queen, had sent to her Majesty a royal present, and declared his intention of following in person. The present, which consisted of eighteen large piebald horses, and two *ship loads* of the most precious articles, the produce of his country, was well received; but as Elizabeth was determined not to relent in favour of her royal lover, she wrote to him, expressing her anxious hope that he would spare himself the fatigue of a fruitless voyage. Fearing, however, that he might be already on his journey, she made preparations for receiving him with hospitality and splendour. Amongst the state papers of the time, we find a letter from the Lords of the Council to the Lord Mayor, setting forth: "That whereas certain bookbinders and stationers did utter certain papers, wherein were printed the face of her Majesty and the King of Sweden; although her Majesty was not displeased that either her own face, or that of this King, should be pourtrayed, yet to be *joined* in the same paper with him, or any other Prince who was known to have proposed marriage to her, was what she could not allow. Accordingly, it was her pleasure, that the Lord Mayor should seize all such papers, and pack them up, so that none of them should get abroad, otherwise she might seem to authorize this joining of herself in marriage to him, which might affect her honour." Next we have a letter to the Duke of Norfolk, directing the manner in which he should meet the King, if he landed in Norfolk or Suffolk, which thus concludes:—"Because the Queen's Majesty is a maid, in this case would many things be omitted in honour and courtesy, which otherwise were meet to be showed to him, as in like cases hath been of Kings of this land to others; and therefore it shall be necessary, that the gravest of her council do, as of their own judgment, excuse the lack thereof to the King; and yet, on their own parts, offer the King all the supplemental honours in their power, with all due reverence."

Notwithstanding these preparations, the King of Sweden never made his appearance, he having received the answer of Elizabeth at the moment of embarking for England. Elizabeth ought certainly not to have accepted the magnificent present of the disappointed Eric; but we suppose that would have been contrary to the royal etiquette, or, at least, that the maiden Queen whose acquisitiveness was remarkable, so represented it.

Whilst the Queen was at Ipswich, in the autumn of 1561, the court was startled by the discovery that the Lady Catherine Grey—the heiress of the house of Suffolk, who was formerly united to Lord Herbert, son of the Earl of Pembroke, (on the same day that her eldest sister, the unfortunate Lady Jane Grey, married Guildford Dudley), but whose union with that nobleman had been dissolved, at the instance of the Earl of Pembroke—had stolen a match with the Earl of Hertford, son of the Protector Somerset, and was on the point of becoming a mother. On being questioned, the lady admitted the fact, confessed her pregnancy, and declared herself to be the lawful wife of the Earl. Her degree of relationship to the Queen was not so near as to render her marriage without the royal consent illegal; yet, by an arbitrary and cruel stretch of authority, Lady Catherine was immediately sent prisoner to the Tower. The Earl of Hertford, her husband, was also committed to the same place, on the charge of having seduced a royal maiden.—The unfortunate lady, and those who had been in her confidence, were treated with harshness and indignity. From the Queen's warrant to Mr. Warner, Lieutenant of the Tower, we learn the cruel advantage taken of her situation:—"Our pleasure is, that ye shall, by our command, examine the Lady Catherine very strictly; how many hath been privy to the love between her and the Earl of Hertford from the beginning, and let her certainly understand, that she shall have no manner of favour, except she will show the truth, not only what ladies or gentlewomen of this court were privy thereto, but also what lords and gentlemen. We earnestly require you to use your diligence in this matter. Ye shall also send to Alderman Lodge, secretly, for St. Low, and shall put her in awe of divers matters, as if confessed by the Lady Catherine, and so also deal with her, that she may confess to you all her knowledge touching this affair. It is certain that there hath been great practices and purposes; and since the death of Lady Jane Grey she hath been most privy thereto. And as ye shall see occasion, so ye may keep St. Low two or three nights, more or less, and let her be returned to Lodge's, or kept still with you, as ye shall think meet."

The Countess of Hertford gave birth to a male child soon after her imprisonment, which was regarded as illegitimate, and the unfortunate parent was doomed to a further imprisonment, at the arbitrary pleasure of the maiden Queen! The birth of a second male child,* the fruit of stolen meetings between the captive pair, aggravated, in the jealous eyes of the match-marring sovereign, their common guilt! It was a glorious opportunity for Elizabeth to vomit forth her spleen, on account of her own intrigues, when Princess, with the late Lord Admiral Seymour having been detected and exposed. Warner, the Lieutenant of the Tower, was dismissed, for permitting or conniving at what the Queen was pleased to term "their illicit intercourse;" and the Earl of Hertford was sentenced, in the iniquitous Star Chamber, to a fine of fifteen thousand pounds (an immense sum in those days), for the double offence of corrupting a female of the royal blood, and of breaking his prison to repeat the offence!

It was some consolation to this persecuted pair, to learn, that, under all their accumulated sufferings, the public voice was unanimous in their favour. No one for a moment doubted but that they were lawfully married;—a fact afterwards fully established, and it was naturally asked "by what right, or on what principle, her Majesty presumed to keep asunder those whom God had joined together in wedlock?" But this sympathy of the people only stimulated the Monarch to greater cruelty. It was necessary to intimidate the people by strong measures! To the eternal disgrace of Elizabeth's character and government, she barbarously and illegally detained her ill-fated kinswoman, first in the Tower, and afterwards in private custody, till the day of her death in January, 1567;* and her husband having already added to the original offence of marrying a princess, the further crime of begetting legitimate children, was sentenced, in addition to his heavy fine, to a long imprisonment of nine years! So much for the jealous spleen of the maiden Queen! It is, however, some satisfaction to find, that by a process in the ecclesiastical court, with which the Queen could not interfere, the Earl of Hertford finally succeeded in establishing the legitimacy of his children.

The royal virgin being now in her THIRTIETH YEAR, was so annoyed on account of certain ill-favoured likenesses of her gracious countenance, which had obtained general circulation, that her minister Cecil drew up and published a proclamation, stating that none of her portraits hitherto published came up to the original; that she had resolved, by the advice of her council, to procure an exact likeness from the pencil of some "cunning painter," and therefore she strictly forbade any one to publish new portraits of her "person or visage" without license, or to sell or exhibit the old ones until they had been remodelled according to the correct likeness to be forthwith published by authority.

This was a strange topic for the deliberation of the wise Elizabeth and her enlightened ministers! But it appears, the perpetual subject of marriage was again agitated by her Parliament and by foreign Princes. According to Strype, "The Duke of Wirtemburg, a German Protestant Prince, had lately, in the

* Sir Egerton Brydges, in Collins's Peerage, says that she had three children; Edward, who died young; Edward, Lord Beauchamp, and Thomas, who married Isabella, daughter of Edward Onley, of Catesby, in Northampton.

* Perhaps Katherine Grey's real crime in the eyes of Elizabeth was her being the sister of Lady Jane Grey, and the heir of the house of Suffolk, upon which it was generally considered that the right to the crown had devolved.

most friendly manner, offered his services to the Queen, in case she were minded to marry. To which she gave him this courteous and Princely answer:—

"London, January 27th, 1563.

"That although I never yet was weary of single and maiden life, yet indeed I was the last issue of my father left, and the only one of his house; the care of my kingdom and the love of posterity did counsel me to alter this course of life. But, in consideration of the leave that my subjects have given me, in ampler manner to make my choice than they ever did to any Prince before, I am even in courtesy bound to make that choice which should be for the best for my subjects and the state. And for that you have therein offered your assistance, I do hereby graciously acknowledge the same, promising to deserve it hereafter."

It does not appear that the Duke tendered his own hand to Elizabeth for her acceptance after this gracious message!

In the summer of 1564, her Majesty's intention of honouring the University of Cambridge with her royal presence was announced to the Secretary of State, who was Chancellor of the royal foundation. The heads of the University, therefore, sent a respectful letter to Dudley, who was the high steward, entreating him to commend to her Majesty their royal services. Cecil arrived at Cambridge the day before the Queen, to get all in readiness for her reception. He received the customary offering of two pair of gloves, two sugar-loaves, and a march-pane. Lord Dudley and the Duke of Norfolk were complimented in a similar manner; and gloves of a finer fabric, and confectionary of a more sumptuous description were presented to Elizabeth in person. On her reaching the door of King's College Chapel, the chancellor knelt down and welcomed her; and the orator, kneeling on the church steps, harangued her for nearly half an hour. "First, he praised and commended many and singular virtues planted and set in her Majesty; which, not approving of, she shook her head, bit her lips and fingers, and anon broke forth into passion in these words:—'It is not true—it is not true.' " On his praising her virginity, however, she said to the orator; 'God's blessing on thy heart! there continue.' After that, he described the joy of the university at her presence.

"When he had finished, the Queen commended him, saying she would answer him again in Latin, but for fear she should speak false Latin; and then they would only laugh at her!" She then went in state to the chapel, where *Te Deum* was sung, and the evening service performed with all imaginable pomp. The next morning, being Sunday, she went thither again to hear a Latin sermon, and in the evening the body of this solemn edifice was converted into a temporary *theatre*, where she was gratified with the representation of a tragedy of Plautus. The performance of plays on Sundays was not at this period forbidden; but certainly the converting of a sacred edifice, in a royal university, into a theatre, was a breach of decorum in the enlightened age of Elizabeth. The third day of the royal visit was occupied by a public disputation in the morning, and a Latin play on the story of Dido, in the evening. On the fourth day, an English play, entitled Ezekias, was performed before her Majesty and suite. The next morning she visited the different colleges; at each of which a Latin oration was delivered before her, and she was presented with a parting present of gloves and confectionary, together with a volume, richly bound, containing the verses in English, Latin, Greek, Hebrew, and Chaldee, composed by the members of each college in honour of the occasion.

She afterwards repaired to the church of St. Mary, where a long and learned disputation, by doctors in divinity, was prepared for her edification. When it was ended, "the lords, and especially the Duke of Norfolk and Lord Robert Dudley, kneeling down, humbly desired her Majesty to speak something to the university in Latin. The Queen at first refused, saying, 'If I might speak my mind in English, I would not stick at the matter.' But understanding, by Mr.

Secretary Cecil, that nothing might be said openly to the university in English, she required him the rather to speak for her; because he was Chancellor, and the Chancellor is the Queen's mouth. Whereunto he answered, that he was Chancellor of the University, and not her Majesty's Chancellor. Then the Bishop of Ely, kneeling, said that three words from her royal mouth would suffice. By entreaties so urgent, the Queen suffered herself to be prevailed upon to deliver a royal speech, which had no doubt been prepared for the occasion, and in which she set forth her attachment to learning, promised to confer some substantial benefit on the University, and, in conclusion, said, 'should I be overtaken by death, before I have been able to perform this my promise, I will not fail to leave some great work to be executed after my decease, by which my memory may be rendered famous, others excited by my example, and all of you animated to greater ardour in your classical studies.'"

Alas! for royal promises! the pledge, thus solemnly and publicly given, was never carried into effect. An annuity of twenty pounds, with the title of "Queen Elizabeth's scholar," was bestowed on a youth, of the name of Preston, whose masculine beauty and graceful action in the play of Dido had particularly caught the royal fancy. This was the only solid benefit bestowed by her Majesty!

CHAPTER VI.

Honours showered on Dudley—His interviews with the Queen—One mistress and no master—Spirited conduct of Elizabeth—Enmity between Sussex and Leicester—Marriage of Lady Mary Grey—Autograph Letter of Elizabeth on the State of Ireland—Birth of James the Sixth—Elizabeth's affected joy on the occasion—Discord between the Queen and her Parliament—Royal visit to Oxford—The murder of Darnley and liberation of the Countess his mother.

LIZABETH, after her return from Cambridge, resolved to gratify her feelings, by conferring on her beloved Dudley some signal marks of her royal esteem. She, accordingly, created him Baron Denbigh and Earl of Leicester, accompanied by the munificent gift of Kenilworth Castle, park, and manor. Sir James Melville, the envoy of Mary, Queen of Scots, in his intertaining Memoirs, gives the following interesting description of the ceremonial of this creation:—"It was performed at Westminster, with great solemnity, the Queen herself helping to put on his mantle, he sitting upon his knees before her, with great gravity. But she could not refrain from putting her hand in his neck, smilingly tickling him; the French ambassador and I standing by. Then she turned round, and asked me how I liked him? I answered, that as he was a worthy servant, so he was happy in having a Princess who could discern and reward good service. 'Yet,' she replied, 'you like better yonder tall lad,' pointing towards my Lord Darnley, who, as nearest Prince of the blood, bore the sword of honour that day before her. She took me to her bed-chamber, and opened a little cabinet, wherein were divers little pictures, wrapped in paper, with their names written on them in her own hand. On the first that she took up was written, 'my lord's picture.' I held the candle; and when at length she permitted me to see it, I found it to be the Earl of Leicester's picture! I desired that I might have it to carry home to my Queen (Mary, of Scotland), which she refused, alleging that she had but that one picture of his. I said, 'Your Majesty hath here the original,' for '*I perceived him at the furthest part of the chamber*, speaking with Secretary Cecil. She showed me also a fair ruby, as great as a tennis-ball; I desired that she would send either it or my Lord of Leicester's picture, as a token to my Queen. She said, that if the Queen would follow her counsel, she would, in process of time, get all that she had; that, in the meantime, she was resolved to send with me, as a token, a fair diamond. I was conveyed by Leicester in his barge from Hampton Court to London. By the way, he inquired of me, what the Queen of Scots thought of him, and of the marriage proposed by Randolph, on the part of Elizabeth? Whereupon I answered very coldly, as I had been commanded by my mistress. Then he began to purge himself of so proud a pretence as to marry so great a Queen, *declaring that he did not esteem himself worthy to wipe her shoes;* and that the proposition of the marriage proceeded from Cecil, his secret enemy: 'For if,' added he, 'I should have appeared desirous of that marriage, I should have offended both the Queens, and thus lost their favour.'"

There can be no doubt that Elizabeth devised this matrimonial project of uniting Leicester with the beautiful Mary, Queen of Scots, purely as a romantic trial of his attachment to herself, and pleased her fancy with the idea of his rejecting for her own sweet self, a younger and a fairer queen! thinking it would give him consequence, in the event of making him her own husband. Certain it is, that when the Queen of Scots appeared to incline to a speedy conclusion of the business, and prayed Elizabeth to know on what conditions she would give her approbation to the union, the earnestness in the cause, which she had hitherto displayed, immediately ceased!

The Memoirs of Sir James Melville describe some highly entertaining scenes, of which he was an eye-witness, in the court of Elizabeth.

The son of the Elector Palatine, Duke Casimir, having made an offer of his hand to Queen Elizabeth, requested Melville, in passing through England, on his way to his own country, to convey his picture to her Majesty. The envoy was also furnished with portraits of the other branches of the electoral family. On his arrival in London, in 1564, he immediately repaired to Hampton Court, and, delivering his credentials, was forthwith admitted into the presence of her Majesty. After some discourse with the Queen, on some minor subjects, Sir James took the opportunity of breaking forth into earnest commendation of the elector, "whose service, nothing," said he, "but my duty to my own sovereign could have induced me to quit." Adding—"For the remembrance of so good a master, I desired to carry home with me the portraits of himself, his sons and daughters." "So soon as she heard me mention the pictures," continues Sir James, "she inquired if I had the picture of Duke Casimir, desiring to see it. And when I alleged that I had left them in London, and that I was ready to go forward on my journey, she said I should not depart till she had seen the pictures. So the next day I delivered them all to her Majesty, and she desired to keep them all night; she then called on my Lord Dudley to be judge of Duke Casimir's picture, and appointed me to meet her the next morning in her garden, where she caused them all to be delivered to me, giving me thanks for the sight of them. I then offered to her Majesty all the pictures, so she would permit me to retain the Elector's and his lady's, but she would have none of them. I had also sure information, that first and last she heartily despised the said Duke Casimir."

Elizabeth now told Sir James, that she intended soon to propose, as fit matches for his Queen, two noblemen, one or other of whom she hoped to see her accept for a husband. These two were Dudley, and Lord Darnley, eldest son of the Earl of Lennox, by the Lady Margaret Douglas.

A few weeks after Melville had returned to Scotland, Mary thought good to despatch him again to London, "to deal with the Queen of England, with the Spanish Ambassador, with my Lady Margaret Douglas, and with sundry friends she had in England."

"Having arrived in London," says Sir James, "I lodged near the court, at

Westminster. My host immediately gave notice of my coming; and that same night, her Majesty sent Mr. Hatton to welcome, and to inform me, that the next morning she would give me audience in her garden at eight o'clock. Accordingly, Mr. Hatton, and Mr. Randolph, late agent for the Queen of England in Scotland, came to my lodging, to convey me to her Majesty, who was, as they said, already in the garden. With them came a servant of my Lord Robert's, with a horse and foot mantle of velvet, laced with gold, for me to ride upon, which servant, with the said horse, waited upon me all the time that I remained there.

"At another interview, Elizabeth inquired if the Queen had sent any answer to the proposition of marriage made to her through Mr. Randolph. I answered, as I had been instructed, that my mistress thought little or nothing thereof. Adding, that the Queen, my mistress, is minded to send on her part, my Lord Murray, and the Secretary, Lidingtoun, and expects your Majesty will send my Lord of Bedford, and my Lord Robert Dudley. She answered,—That it appeared I made but small account of my Lord Robert, seeing that I named the Earl of Bedford before him; but that ere long she would make him a far greater earl, and that I should see it done before my return home, for she esteemed him as her brother and best friend, whom she would have herself married, had she ever minded to have taken a husband. But being determined to live single, she wished the Queen, her sister, might marry him, as meetest of all others with whom she could find in her heart to propose. For, being matched with him, it would remove out of her mind all fears and suspicions, of being offended by any usurpation before her death. Being assured that he was so loving and trusty, that he would never suffer any such thing to be attempted during her time; and that the Queen, my mistress, might have the higher esteem of him, I had been required to stay till I should see him made Earl of Leicester and Baron of Denbigh. She appeared to be so affectionate to the Queen, her good sister, that she expressed a great desire to see her. Then she took out of a little cabinet the Queen's picture, and kissed it, and I ventured to kiss her hand, for the great love evidenced therein to my mistress. She inquired of me many things relating to the kingdom of Scotland, and other countries wherein I had travelled. She caused me to dine with her dame of honour, my Lady Strafford, (an honourable and goodly lady, who had been banished to Geneva during the reign of her predecessor), that I might be always near her, so that she might confer with me.

"At divers meetings we had conversations on different subjects. The Queen, my mistress, had instructed me to leave matters of gravity sometimes, and cast in merry purposes, lest otherwise she should be wearied; she being well informed of her natural temper. Therefore, in declaring my observations of the customs of Holland, Poland, and Italy, the buskins of the women were not forget; and what country weed I thought best becoming gentlewomen. The Queen said she had clothes of every sort, which every day thereafter, so long as I was there, she changed. One day she had the English weed, another day the French, another the Italian, and so on. She asked me which of them became her best? I answered, in my judgment the Italian dress; which answer I found pleased her well, for she delighted to show her golden-coloured hair, wearing a caul and bonnet, as they do in Italy. Her hair was rather reddish than yellow, curled in appearance naturally. She desired to know what colour of hair was reputed best; and whether my Queen's hair or her's was best; and which of them was fairest? I answered, the fairest of them both was not their worst faults. But she was earnest with me to declare which of them I judged fairest. I said she was the fairest queen in England, and mine in Scotland; yet still she appeared earnest. I then told her, they were both the fairest ladies in their respective countries; that her Majesty was whiter, but my Queen was very lovely. She inquired, which of them was highest in stature? I said, my Queen. Then, said she, she is too high, for I myself am neither too high nor too low. Then she asked, what exercises she used? I replied, that when I received my despatch, the Queen was lately come from the Highland hunting. That when her more serious affairs permitted, she was taken up with reading of histories; that sometimes she recreated herself in playing upon the lute and virginals. She inquired if she played well? I said, reasonably for a queen.

"That same day, after dinner, my Lord of Hunsdon drew me up to a quiet gallery, that I might hear some music—but he said he durst not avow it—where I might hear the Queen play upon the virginals. After I had hearkened a while, I stood by the tapestry that hung before the door of the chamber, and seeing her back was towards the door, I ventured within the chamber, and stood at a pretty space, hearing her play excellently well; but she left off immediately, as soon as she turned about and saw me. She appeared surprised, and came forward, seeming to strike me with her hand; alleging that she used not to play before men, but when she was solitary, to shun melancholy. She asked how I came there? I answered, as I was walking with my Lord of Hunsdon, we passed by the chamber door—I heard such melody as ravished me, whereby I was drawn in ere I knew how; excusing my fault of homeliness, as being brought up in the court of France, where such freedom was allowed; declaring myself willing to endure whatever punishment her Majesty should be pleased to inflict upon me, for so great an offence. Then she sat down low upon a cushion, and I upon my knees by her, but with her own hand she gave me a cushion to place under my knee; which at first I refused, but she compelled me to take it. She then called for my Lady Strafford out of the next chamber, for the Queen was alone. She inquired whether my Queen or she played best? In that I found myself obliged to give her the praise. She said my French was very good; and asked if I could speak Italian, which she spoke reasonably well. I told her Majesty I had no time to learn that language, not having been above two months in Italy. Then she spoke to me in Dutch, which was not good; and would know what kind of books I most delighted in, whether theology, history, or *love matters!* I said I liked well of *all* the sorts.

"I now took occasion to press earnestly my despatch: she said I was sooner weary of her company than she was of mine. I told her Majesty, that though I had no reason to be weary, I knew my mistress's affairs called me home. Yet I was detained two days longer, that I might see her dance, as I was afterwards informed. Which being over, she inquired of me whether she or my Queen danced best? I answered the Queen danced not so *high*, nor so disposedly as she did. Then again she wished that she might see the Queen at some convenient place of meeting. I offered to convey her secretly to Scotland, by post horses, clothed like a page; that under this disguise she might see the Queen; as James the Fifth had gone in disguise with his own ambassador, to see the Duke of Vendome's sister, who should have been his wife. Telling her that her chamber might be kept in her absence as though she were sick, that none need be privy thereto, except Lady Strafford, and one of the grooms of her chamber. She appeared to like that kind of language, but only answered it with a sigh, saying, 'Alas! if I might do it thus!' I then withdrew."

"About this period," says Naunton, in his *Fragmenta Regalia*, "Bowyer, a gentleman of the black rod, being charged by the Queen's express command to look precisely into all admissions into the privy chamber, one day stopped a very gay captain, a follower of Leicester's, from entrance, for that he was neither well known, nor a sworn servant to the Queen: at which repulse, the gentleman, bearing high on my lord's favour, told him, he might perchance procure him his discharge. Leicester coming in at this moment, said publicly (which was none of his wont), that

Bowyer was a knave, and should not continue long in his office; and so turning about to go into the Queen's chamber; but Bowyer, boldly stepping before him, and falling at the Queen's feet, related the story, and humbly asked whether Leicester was King, or her Majesty Queen? Whereunto she said, with her wonted oath, 'God's death! my lord, I have wished you well, but my favour is not so locked up for you, that others shall not partake thereof; for I have many servants, to whom I shall, at my pleasure, bestow my favour, and likewise resume the same: *and if you think to rule here*, I will take a course to see you forthcoming; *I will have here but one mistress and no master!* and look that no ill happen to him, lest it be required at your hands!' which words so quelled my Lord of Leicester, that his feigned humility was long after one of his best virtues!"

That sincere, upright, courageous nobleman, the Earl of Sussex, and Lord Chamberlain, was endowed with sufficient penetration to detect, beneath the veil of artifice and hypocrisy under which they were concealed, the monstrous views of the Queen's favourite, Leicester; and he could not, without disgust and indignation, behold a Princess, whose blood he shared, and in whose service he had entered with devotion, the dupe of so despicable and pernicious a sycophant. That influence which he saw Leicester abuse, to the dishonour of the Queen and the detriment of the country, he undertook to overthrow, by fair and public means; and without motives of personal interest or ambition. There mingled also in the breast of the high-born Sussex, a thorough disdain of the origin of Dudley, with a just abhorrence of his character and conduct. He was wont to say of him, that two ancestors were all that he could remember—his father and grandfather—both traitors to their country. His sarcasms roused in Leicester the most deadly animosity. With the exception of Cecil and his friends, who remained neuter, the whole court divided into factions upon the quarrel of these two powerful peers: and to such extremity were matters carried, that for some time neither of them would stir abroad without a numerous armed train. The Queen herself had much difficulty in restraining these noblemen from breaking out into actual violence: at length, however, she summoned them both into her presence, and forced them to a temporary reconciliation.

The storm, under which the favourite had yielded for a time, quickly passed over, and he once more resumed his haughty demeanour. To revenge himself on Sussex was, however, beyond his power. The well-grounded confidence of Elizabeth in his abilities and his attachment to her person, he found to be immoveable; but he so far succeeded as to induce Elizabeth to send his adversary to an honourable exile, in the shape of an embassy to the Imperial court. When Sussex returned from this mission, the Queen named him Lord President of the North—an office which equally removed him from court intrigue. Not long after, the hand of death terminated his honourable career and the implacable enmity of Leicester. As he lay on his death-bed, Sussex thus addressed his surrounding friends:—"I am now passing into another world, and must leave you to your fortunes, and to the Queen's grace and goodness: but beware of the *gipsy* Leicester, for he will be too hard for you all; you know not the *beast* so well as I do!"

About this period [1566] the beautiful Lady Mary Grey, sister to the celebrated Lady Jane and Lady Catherine Grey, of royal lineage, married Martin Kays, of Kent, esquire, a judge at court. "Mary Grey," says Fuller, "frighted with the infelicity of her two eldest sisters, Jane and Catherine, forgot her honour to remember her safety; and married one whom she could love and none need fear, Martin Kays, of Kent, who was a judge at court—(but only of doubtful casts at dice, being sergeant porter)—and died without issue." Elizabeth, according to her usual practice in similar cases, when the blood royal was defiled, sent both husband and wife to prison. The unfortunate lady did not, it would appear, sufficiently "remember her safety" in forming this connection, obscure and humble as it was; for all matrimony had now become offensive to the match-marring Queen. After the death of her husband, Lady Mary Grey was consigned to the care of Sir Thomas Gresham, the eminent merchant, where she remained for three years, and was then liberated, through the kind intercession of Sir Thomas, who wrote to Lord Burleigh on her behalf.

Elizabeth was remarkably fond of proverbs and quaint aphorisms; and although throughout her epistolary correspondence this marked trait in her character is evident, it is nowhere so fully displayed as in the subjoined pedantic letter, in which she prescribes to Sir Henry Sidney, the Governor of Ireland, the part he is to take on the occasion of the fierce feud between the Irish Earls of Desmond and Ormond :—

"Harry,

"If our partial slender managing of the contentious quarrel between the two Irish Earls did not make the way to cause these lines to pass my hand, this gibberish should hardly have cumbered your eyes; but warned by my former fault, and dreading worser hap to come, I rede you take good heed that the good subjects lost state be so revenged, that I hear not the rest be won to a right byeway to breed more traitor's stocks, and so the goal is gone. Make some difference between tried, just, and false friends. Let the good service of well-deservers be never rewarded with loss. Let their thanks be such as may encourage more strivers for the like. Suffer not that Desmond's denying deeds far wide from promised works, make you trust to other pledge than either himself or John for gage: he hath so well performed his English vows, that I warn you to trust him no longer that you see one of them. Prometheus let me be; *Epimetheus* hath been mine too long. I pray God your old strange sheep, late (as you say) returned into the fold, wore not her woolly garment upon her wolvy back. You know a kingdom knows no kindred; *si violandum jus regnandi causa.* A strength to harm is perilous in the hand of an ambitious head. Where might is mixed with wit, there is too good an accord in a government. Essays be oft dangerous; especially when the cup-bearer hath received such a preservative as, what mightsoever betide the drinker's draught, the carrier takes no bane thereby.

"Believe not, though they swear, that they can be full sound whose parents sought the rule that they full fain would have. I warrant you they will never be accused of bastardy; you were to blame to lay it to their charge; they will trace the steps that others have passed before. If I had not espied, though very late, legerdemain used in these cases, I had never played my part. No, if I did not see the balances held awry, I had never myself come into the weigh-house. I hope I shall have so good a customer in you, that all other officers shall do their duty among you. If aught have been amiss at home, I will patch, though I cannot whole it. Let us not, nor no more do you, consult so long as till advice come too late to the givers; where then shall we wish the deeds while all was spent in words? A fool too late bewares when all the peril is passed. If we still advise, we shall never do; thus are we still knitting a knot never tied; yea, and if our loom be framed with rotten hurdles, when our web is well nigh done, our work is to begin anew. God send the weaver true 'prentices again, and let them be denizens, I pray you, if they be not citizens; and such, too, as your ancientest aldermen, that now dwell in your official place, have had best cause to commend their good behaviour.

"Let this memorial be only committed to Vulcan's base keeping, without any longer abode than the reading thereof; yea, and with no mention made thereof to any other wight. I charge you as I may command you. Seem not to have had but the secretary's letter from me.

"Your loving Mistress,

"Elizabeth, R."

In June, 1566, Mary, Queen of Scots, was safely delivered of a son. Sir James Melville was immediately dispatched with the news to Elizabeth; and, in his "Memoirs," we have the following graphic sketch of his mission :—" By twelve of the clock I took horse, and was that night at Berwick. The fourth day after, I was at London, and did first meet with my brother Robert (then ambassador to England), who that same night sent and informed Secretary Cecil of my arrival, and of the birth of the Prince, desiring him to keep it quiet till my coming to court to announce it myself unto her Majesty, who was residing for the time at Greenwich, where she was in great mirth, dancing after supper. But so soon as the Secretary Cecil whispered in her ear the news of the Prince's birth, all her mirth was laid aside for that night; all present marvelling whence proceeded such a change, for the Queen did sit down, putting her hand under her cheek, and bursting out to some of her ladies, that the Queen of Scots was mother of a fair son, *while she was but a barren stock!*

"The next morning was appointed for me to get audience; at which time my brother and I went by water to Greenwich, and were met by some friends, who told us how sorrowful her Majesty was at my news; but that she had been advised to show a glad and cheerful countenance: which she did in her best apparel, saying that the joyful news of the Queen, her sister's delivery of a fair son, which I had sent her by Secretary Cecil, had recovered her out of a heavy sickness, which she had lain under for fifteen days. Therefore, she welcomed me with a merry face, and thanked me for hastening to give her that welcome intelligence. The next day, she sent me her letter, with the present of a rich chain."

Elizabeth accepted, with a good grace, the office of sponsor to the young Prince of Scotland; sending thither, as her proxies, the Earl of Bedford, a son of Lord Hunsdon, and several knights and gentlemen. These met with a cordial reception from Mary, who was now at open variance with her husband. The present sent by Elizabeth, as the royal godmother, consisted of a rich font of pure gold, of the value of upwards of one thousand pounds; in return for which, rings, rich chains of diamond and pearl, and other precious jewels, were bountifully bestowed on the proxies of Elizabeth.

The delicate subject of a successor to the throne was again revived in the House of Commons, in defiance of the opposition of the court party, who reiterated "that the Queen was moved to marriage, and inclined to prosecute the same." A motion was carried, and a committee appointed to confer with the lords on the subject. The Queen then required a deputation from both houses to wait upon her, which having been agreed to, the lord keeper explained their sentiments, in a long speech, to which her Majesty was pleased, in her usual indirect way, to reply: "As to my marriage, a silent thought might serve. I thought it had been so desired that no other tree's blossom should have been minded, or ever any hope of fruit had been denied them. But if any doubted that I am by word or determination never bent to tread in that kind of life, I desire them to put aside that sort of heresy; for their belief is indeed mistaken. And although I might think it best for a private woman, yet I strive with myself to think it not meet for a Princess. As to the succession, I desire them not to think that they had needed this desire, if I had seen a time so fit, and it was so ripe as to be declared. That for their comfort, I had good record in that place that other means than they mentioned had been thought of for their good, as much as for my own surety; which, if they could have been conveniently executed, it had not been now deferred or over-slipped. That I hope to die in quiet, with *Nunc Dimittis*, which could not be without I see some glimpse of their following surety after my graved bones."

These vague and unmeaning sentences tended little to the satisfaction of the House of Commons; and a motion was made and carried, to persevere in the remonstrance against the Queen's delaying her marriage any longer. At this bold step her Majesty was so enraged, that she communicated, through Sir Francis Knolles, her positive command to the house, to proceed no further in this business, satisfying themselves with the promise of marriage which she had made on the solemn word of a queen. But Paul Wentworth, a sturdy, independent member of the Commons, would not tamely submit to this prohibition; and he again moved the house on the question, whether the late command of her Majesty was not a breach of its privileges? The Queen hereupon issued an injunction, that there should be no debates on this point; but the tone of resistance was so loud in the Commons against this her arbitrary interference, that she found it expedient, a few days after, to rescind both orders, insisting, however, on the condition, that the delicate subject should not at this time be further debated.

On proroguing Parliament, Elizabeth acquainted both houses with her extreme displeasure at their interference regarding a successor; a subject which she always chose to regard as belonging exclusively to her prerogative, and that though they might, perhaps, have after her one more learned or wiser, yet, she assured them, none could be more careful over them. And, therefore, she bade them henceforth beware how they proved the patience of their Prince, as they had now done that of their Queen. Notwithstanding, she did not mean to make a Lent at Christmas, the most part of them, therefore, might assure themselves, that they departed high in her grace and favour. The Commons had offered her an extraordinary subsidy, on condition of her naming her successor, which she refused. Even of the ordinary supplies she remitted one fourth, smilingly remarking, "It is as well for me to have money in the coffers of my subjects, as in my own!" It was in this way she trifled with the feelings of the nation!

In the Autumn of 1566, the Queen consented to honour with her presence the University of Oxford, of which her favourite, Dudley, now Earl of Leicester, was elected chancellor. She was received with the same ceremonies as at Cambridge. Learned addresses and exhibitions awaited her, and she harangued the heads of the University, not in Latin, but in Greek! In Warton's History of English Poetry, we find the following particulars of this celebrated visit.

"In the magnificent hall of Christchurch, the Queen was entertained with a Latin comedy, entitled Marcus Geminus, the Latin tragedy of Progne, and an English comedy on the story of Palamon and Arcite; all acted by students of the University. When the last play was over, the Queen summoned into her presence the poet (Richard Edwards), whom she loaded with thanks and compliments; and at the same time turning to her lords, she remarked, that Palamon was so justly drawn as a lover, that the author must have been in love himself; that Arcite was a right martial knight, having a swart and manly countenance, yet with the aspect of a Venus clad in armour; that the lovely Emilia was a virgin of uncorrupted purity and unblemished simplicity; and that though she sung so sweetly, and gathered flowers alone in the garden, her deportment was chaste and maidenly. The part of Emilia, the only female part in the play, was acted by a boy of fourteen, whose performance so captivated her Majesty, that she made him a present of a purse of gold. During the performance, a cry of hounds, belonging to Theseus, was counterfeited without, in the great square of the college. The young students not in the secret, thought it a real chase, and were seized with a sudden transport to join the hunters; at which the Queen cried out from her box, 'Oh, excellent! these boys, in very troth, are ready to leap out of the windows to follow the hounds!'"

The Vice-Chancellor was Dr. Lawrence Humphreys. He had lately been distinguished for his strenuous opposition to the Queen's injunctions, respecting the habits and ceremonies of the University. When he came forth in procession to meet her Majesty, on this auspicious visit, the Queen could not refrain saying, with a gracious smile, as she extended to him her hand to kiss—"That loose gown, doctor, becomes you mighty well; I wonder your notions of things should be so narrow!"

The husband of the unfortunate Mary, Queen of Scots, perished by a violent death, on the ninth of February, 1567. Elizabeth displayed on this tragical occasion the utmost moderation and kindness. She announced to the Countess of Lennox, the mother of Darnley, whom she had arbitrarily imprisoned in the Tower, the frightful catastrophe which had closed the history of her ill-fated son. The liberation of the Countess immediately followed; and the Earl, her husband, soon after gratified Elizabeth in her desire of interfering with her advice and assistance, by procuring her aid to obtain an extension of the time allowed him to bring forward his proofs against Bothwell, whom he had publicly accused of the assassination of her son. In the Burleigh Papers there is a curious letter from Secretary Cecil to Sir Henry Norris, ambassador in France, in which the following allusion is made to this subject:—

"I have stayed your son from going hence now these two days, upon the Queen's command, for that she would have him to know as much of the truth of the circumstances of the murder of the King of Scots as might be; and hitherto the same is hard to come by, otherwise than general rumours. The Queen's Majesty sent yesterday my Lady Howard and my wife to the Lady Lennox, in the Tower, to open this matter unto her; she could not, by any means, be kept from such passions of mind as the horribleness of the fact did inspire. And this last night were with the said lady, the Dean of Westminster and Dr. Huick; and I hope her Majesty will show some compassion for the said lady, whom any humane nature must needs pity."

CHAPTER VII.

Interesting letters from the Earl of Sussex to Elizabeth—Mary, Queen of Scots, escapes from Lochleven Castle into England—Elizabeth detains her in captivity, and frustrates her proposed marriage with Norfolk—Papal Bull against Elizabeth—The Queen's visit to the Royal Exchange—Death of Throgmorton—Trial and execution of Norfolk—Sonnet by Elizabeth—Leicester's connection with Lady Sheffield—Another royal favourite—Lord Burleigh—Elizabeth and Lady Shrewsbury—Death of the Marshal of Ireland—Remarkable letter of Elizabeth respecting Leicester—The Duke of Anjou's proposal of marriage—Leicester's marriage—Rage of Elizabeth—Quarrel between Leicester and the French Envoy—A shot fired at the Queen.

THE murder of Darnley had procured Elizabeth some respite from the importunities of Parliament, relative to the succession; but it was necessary to take some active steps to redeem her promise respecting her marriage. Accordingly, the Earl of Sussex was despatched to Vienna, to congratulate the Emperor Maximilian on his coronation, and at the same time to treat with his brother, the Archduke Charles, respecting his long-agitated marriage with the Queen. The following interesting letters were the result of his mission:—

"Vienna, October, 1567.

"His Highness is in person taller surely a good deal than my lord marquis; his hair and beard of a light auburn; his face well proportioned, amiable, and of a good complexion; without show of redness or over-paleness; his countenance and speech cheerful, very courteous, and not without some state; his body well shaped, without deformity of blemish; his hands very good and fair; his legs clean, well proportioned, and of sufficient bigness for his stature; his feet as good as may be.

"So, as upon my duty to your Majesty, I find not one deformity, misshape, nor any thing to be noted worthy disliking in his whole person; but contrariwise, I find his whole shape to be good, worthy commendation and liking in all respects, and such as is rarely to be found in such a Prince. His Highness, besides his natural language of Dutch, speaketh very well Spanish and Italian, and, as I hear, Latin. His dealings with me are very wise; his conversations such as much contenteth me; and none returneth discontented from his company. He is greatly beloved here of all men; the chiefest gallants of these parts are his men, and follow his court; the most of them have travelled other countries, speak many languages, and behave themselves properly; and truly we cannot be so glad to have him come to us, as they will be sad to have him go from them. He is reported to be wise, liberal, valiant, and of great courage; which, in the last wars, he well shewed in defending his country from the Turks with his own force alone, and giving them divers overthrows when they attempted any thing against his rules; and he is universally (which I most weigh) noted to be of such virtue as he was never spotted or touched with any noteable vice or crime, which is much in a Prince of his years, endowed with such qualities. He delighteth much in hunting, riding, hawking, exercise of feats of arms, and hearing of music, whereof he hath good practice. He hath some understanding in astronomy and cosmography, and taketh pleasure in clocks that set forth the course of the planets.

"He hath for his portion the countries of Styria, Carinthia, Friola, Trieste, and Istria: and hath the government of what is left in Crotia; wherein he may ride without entering into any other man's territories, near three hundred miles.

On the twenty-sixth of October, he again writes to her Majesty:—

"Since the despatch of my other letters, upon the resolution of the Emperor and the Archduke, I took occasion to go to the latter; meaning to sound him to the bottom in all causes," and to find whether such matter as he had uttered to me before, proceeded from him, *bonâ fide*, or were but words of form.

"His Highness answered:—'Count, I have heard by the Emperor of the order of your dealing with him, and I have had dealings with you myself; wherewith he and I rest very well contented: but truly, I never rested more contented of any thing than I do of this dealing, wherein, besides your duty to her that hath trusted you, you show what you are yourself, for the which I honour you as you are worthy.'—Pardon me, I beseech your Majesty, in writing the words he spake of himself, for they serve to indicate his natural disposition and inclination:—'And although I have always had a good hope of the Queen's honourable dealing in this manner, yet I have heard so much of her not meaning to marry, as might give me cause to suspect the worst; but understanding by the Emperor your manner of dealing with him—perceiving as I do presently by your words, I think myself bound (wherewith he doffed his cap) to honour, love, and serve her Majesty while I live; and will firmly credit what you on her Majesty's behalf have said; and, therefore, so I might hope her Majesty would bear with me for my conscience.* I know not that thing in the world that I would refuse to do at her command. And surely I have from the beginning of this matter settled my heart upon her, and never thought of any other wife, if she would think me worthy to be her husband; and therefore be bold to inform her Majesty truly herein, for I will not fail in my part of anything, as I trust sufficient appeareth to you by what I have heretofore said.'

"In such like talk, to this effect," proceeds Sussex, "his Highness spent almost two hours with me, which I have thought my duty to acquaint your Majesty; and hereupon I gather, that reputation ruleth him much for the present in this case of religion; and that if God couple you together in liking, you shall have of him a true husband,

* The Archduke Charles was a Catholic.

a loving companion, a wise counsellor, and a faithful servant; and we shall have as virtuous a prince as ever ruled: God grant (though you are worthy a great deal better than he, if he were to be found) that our wickedness be not such as we should be unworthy of him, or of such as he is."*

Every reader must regret, who peruses these interesting letters, that the negotiation should, like all others that had preceded it, have failed of the desired success. Religion, it would appear, furnished the only objection which could be urged against the marriage; and the Archduke merely stipulated for the performance of Catholic worship in a private room of the palace, at which none but himself and his attendants should be present. He consented to accompany the Queen regularly to the services of the Church of England; and for a time to suspend the exercise of his own religion, should any disputes arise. In short, he asked no greater indulgence on this point, than what was enjoyed by all the ambassadors of Catholic princes. But even this, it was affirmed, was more than the Queen could grant with safety. The majority of the people, however, believed that Leicester, the Queen's favourite, was at the bottom of all—that he it was who thwarted the negotiations, by means of one of his own creatures, *for whom he had procured the second rank in the embassy of the Earl of Sussex.* He also laboured night and day in prejudicing the mind of Elizabeth against the proposed union, which would have put a finishing stroke to his favouritism.

On the second of May, 1568, Mary, Queen of Scots, who had for some time been confined a prisoner in Lochleven castle, by her rebellious subjects, escaped from thence by means of a youth named George Douglas, to whose brother she had been committed in charge, and repaired to Hamilton castle, where, with the unanimous consent of all the nobles, who flocked thither in great numbers, a definite decree was issued, declaring that the act of resignation, extorted by fear from the prisoner Queen, was null and void; and the Queen herself, being present, took a solemn oath that it was extorted and forced from her. In two days such multitudes repaired to her from all parts, that she raised an army of six thousand men, and forthwith attacked the rebel army, headed by the Regent Murray. The result of the battle was disastrous to Mary, who betook herself to flight, and rode the same day a distance of sixty miles; when coming by night to Maxweltown, the seat of Lord Herries, she preferred exposing herself to the mercy of the sea, and relying upon Elizabeth's protection, than upon the fidelity of her faithless subjects. But before embarking, she sent to her a special messenger, with a valuable diamond that Elizabeth had formerly given her for a pledge of their mutual love and friendship, to acquaint her that she meant to come to England, and demand succour from her, if her own subjects any longer pursued her by civil war. Elizabeth promised her all the kindness and love of a royal sister; Mary, however, did not wait the return of the messenger, but committed herself to the master of a small vessel, against the advice and counsel of her friends, and on the seventeenth of May, with Lords Herries and Fleming, and some few others, arrived at Warrington, in Cumberland. The same day, she wrote to Elizabeth a letter in French, detailing the wrongs she had suffered, her present misfortunes, and imploring to be admitted to a personal conference with her.

Elizabeth pretended to be moved by this affecting epistle, and in letters, and by the mouth of Sir Francis Knowles and others, she promised her assistance, according to the equity of her cause; but, nevertheless, she refused her access to her person, and commanded that she should be conveyed to Carlisle, where she might remain in security; and if her adversaries attempted any thing against her, the governor of the place and the gentlemen of the county would protect her. Having received this answer and refusal, Mary again wrote to Elizabeth, by the hands of Lord Herries, beseeching more earnestly than heretofore to be permitted to enter Elizabeth's presence,

* Lodge's Illustrations.

or else to be allowed to depart to France.

These letters, and the communications of Lord Herries, seemed to move Elizabeth to compassion for a Princess, her near kinswoman, and one who, in deep distress, had thrown herself upon the protection of the English Queen, with the sure hope of finding aid and succour; but this compassion, if sincere, speedily gave way to feelings of revenge, and a cruel, selfish policy, which led Elizabeth to violate all principles of right or justice, by detaining the royal fugitive, whom, in the end, she basely brought to the scaffold.

No greater proof can be given of the innocence of the unfortunate Mary, Queen of Scots, than the offer of marriage made her by the Duke of Norfolk, the highest nobleman at the court of Elizabeth; and nothing can more fully prove the secret rancour, malignity, and jealousy of Elizabeth, than her successful endeavours to prevent the match taking place. The first rumours of this intended marriage reached the ears of Elizabeth by some of those crafty and curious courtezans, who are always ready to pry into and find out the secrets of lovers. On learning how matters stood, the Duke of Norfolk laboured with his utmost power to make a proposition for this marriage with Mary to the Queen of England. For this end he consulted the Earls of Leicester and Pembroke, and Sir Nicholas Throgmorton, but finally kept putting it off, and deferring it from day to day, expecting a fitter time and opportunity. Cecil, seeing the Duke perplexed in his mind, and knowing also the cause, advised him to declare the matter at once to the Queen, in order that all obstacles to the match might the sooner be taken away. But the Earl of Leicester was averse to that proceeding, and promised to propound the same to her Majesty, when she should walk abroad in the fields. But whilst he, by great courtesy, thus deferred the matter, Elizabeth, being at Farnham, caused the Duke of Norfolk to approach near unto her table, and with a most grave and serious smile, warned him, "*That he who reposed, and rested himself on a cushion, should take heed, and look to himself.*" At the same time, the Queen took the Duke aside into a gallery, where she rebuked him sharply for having sought the Queen of Scots in marriage without her leave and permission, commanding him at his peril to prosecute the matter. The Duke promised to comply, but discerning that her Majesty was irritated against him, and perceiving, also, that many noblemen withdrew themselves by degrees from his familiarity, departed for London, without leave, and, upon the way, took up his abode at the mansion of the Earl of Pembroke—a nobleman who solaced and consoled him in his affliction. That very day, Elizabeth, moved with anger, refused to set at liberty the prisoner Queen; and to the Scottish ambassador, who implored it of her Majesty, she commanded that she should behave herself peaceably, *or else she should see shortly, those upon whom she most relied, cut off aud beheaded! The Duke of Norfolk was afterwards sent to the Tower.*

"Finally," says the early historian from whom we extract these interesting particulars, "the Earl of Leicester, being at Tichfield, and dreading the anger of Elizabeth, from the part which he had acted in this affair, feigned himself suddenly ill, and being immediately visited and *graciously comforted* by the Queen, he was seized with such fear, that her Majesty could easily discern it, *beholding his blood and vital senses to shrink in himself*, that he declared unto her all the business from the beginning, imploring her pardon with such sighs and tears, that the Queen could not refrain from embracing her favourite."

On the fifth of March, 1569, Pope Pius the Fifth fulminated a papal bull against Elizabeth, pronouncing her, the pretended Queen of England, an usurper of the sovereignty of the Church in England, a heretic, and a favourer of heretics, and excommunicating her, and absolving her subjects from their oaths of duty, fidelity, and obedience to her.

This sentence greatly discomposed Elizabeth, who was not prepared for such a mark of the Pope's displeasure. As a proof of the annoyance it caused her court, one Felton, who had fixed the bull upon the gate of the Bishop of London's Palace, was immediately taken, tried, found guilty, and hanged, close by the palace where he had stuck up the obnoxious instrument. He died, glorying in that he had suffered as a martyr to the Church of Rome. For the rest, the bull fell harmless on the head of Elizabeth. The principles of the Reformation had already made too much progress to be affected by the Pope's angry efforts, and the Catholic powers took no notice of the circumstance, but renewed their intercourse with the court of Elizabeth.

In January, 1571, the Queen, attended by a splendid train, entered the city of London, and, after dining with Sir Thomas Gresham, the founder of the Royal Exchange, repaired to the Bourse, and minutely visited every part of it. The merchants of London had hitherto been unprovided with any building in the nature of a Bourse or Exchange, such as were established in the great commercial cities of Flanders. This desideratum Sir Thomas munificently offered to supply, if the City would give him a piece of ground for the purpose, and to build them one at his own expense. Accordingly, the edifice was begun in 1567, and finished within three years. It was a quadrangle of brick, with walks on the ground floor for the merchants (who now ceased transacting their business in the middle aisle of St. Paul's Cathedral), with vaults for warehouses beneath, and a range of shops above, from the rent of which the proprietor sought some remuneration for his heavy outlay. The shops, however, let but slowly, and it was partly with the view of bringing them into vogue, that the Queen promised her countenance to the undertaking.

The spacious mansion of Sir Thomas Gresham, which Queen Elizabeth honoured with her presence, is situated in Bishopsgate Street, and is still extant. On the occasion of this memorable visit, the Queen caused proclamation to be made by sound of trumpet, that henceforward Sir Thomas Gresham's Bourse should be called "the Royal Exchange." Gresham, as an encouragement to the citizens, offered to let the shops rent-free for one year, to all such as would furnish them with wares, and wax-lights in honour of the Queen's visit; accordingly, a most gorgeous display was made, to captivate her Majesty, of the richest commodities and the most exquisite manufactures, from all quarters of the globe. The result satisfied the sanguine expectations of Sir Thomas, and ever afterwards the shops of the Royal Exchange became the favourite resort of the fashionable and mercantile world. The building was destroyed by the great fire of London. It was speedily rebuilt on a much more magnificent scale, adorned in the centre of the square, in niches in the walls, with stone statues of all the Kings and Queens of England. This last became a prey to destruction on the tenth of January, 1838. The new Royal Exchange, commenced in 1840, under the direction of the skilful architect, Mr. Tite, was opened by the Queen in state, accompanied by her ministers and a grand civic procession, on the twenty-eighth of October, 1844.

About the year 1571, died Sir Nicholas Throgmorton, the esteemed ambassador of Elizabeth—a man of experience, judgment, and energy. Being at supper at the house of the Earl of Leicester, while in the act of eating a salad, he was suddenly taken ill, and soon after expired. There were not wanting those who asserted that he had been poisoned by Leicester, whom he had deeply offended by quitting his party, to reconcile himself with Cecil, who had recently been invested with the dignity of Baron of Burleigh, in reward for his long and faithful services. The hostility of Leicester extended to other branches of the family of Throgmorton. On some slight pretext, he procured from his royal mistress the dismissal of Sir John Throgmorton, the brother of Sir Nicholas, from his office of Chief Justice of Chester—an unmerited disgrace, which Sir John did not long survive. The proud and haughty Elizabeth, and her favourite, Leicester, never forgot the manly bearing of Sir Nicholas, when he boldly gave the lie, by the production of his own diplomatic instructions, to the crafty declarations of his own Queen, when he found that she was bent on the ruin of the innocent Mary of Scotland.

After suffering a long imprisonment, the unfortunate Duke of Norfolk, the last of the Howards, was brought to trial, for the alleged offence of sending proposals of marriage to the unfortunate Queen Mary, while she was in the hands of her bitter enemy, Queen Elizabeth. That the Queen of England had the smallest right to interdict this marriage, is denied by the highest legal authorities. It was an act of cruel perfidy, and adds another deed to the catalogue of her numerous crimes. Norfolk had, in his first alarm at having been questioned on the subject by Elizabeth, in an unguarded moment, been induced to promise his Sovereign to abstain from prosecuting his suit with the Scottish Queen; but on recovering from his surprise, and recollecting the previous interchange between himself and Mary of the most solemn promises of marriage, he felt he was under obligations of too sacred a nature to be dissolved by any verbal promise subsequently made to Elizabeth. As a chivalrous knight and a gentleman, the Duke was bound in honour, not only to endeavour to procure the release of the captive Princess, by every lawful means in his power, but also to claim, at all hazards, the fair hand which had been plighted to him, in full reliance upon his honour and fidelity. Impressed with these sentiments, the Duke, in return to a letter of eloquent remonstrance from Mary, which she found means to convey to him, sent her an answer, replete with the most solemn assurances of his inviolable constancy. This letter was intercepted by the emissaries of Elizabeth, and the Duke was forthwith put on his trial, on the ridiculous pretence of an attempt to dethrone Elizabeth, by uniting with Mary for that ostensible purpose. The Parliament, which was again assembled after an interval of five years, passed some new laws for the protection of the Queen's person from the imminent perils by which they saw her environed. The illustrious Duke was now brought before the tribunal of the House of Lords, and having confessed his *guilt*, of intending to marry the Scottish Queen, he being a subject of the Queen of England, he was found guilty, and the Earl of Shrewsbury, as Lord High Steward, with tears in his eyes, pronounced sentence against him. The Queen hesitated for some time in signing his death-warrant, but at length the fatal order was issued, and this high-minded nobleman was beheaded on Tower Hill, amid the lamentations of the multitude. His last words were, "I die innocent, but God will not let my death be unrevenged!" Then he whispered something to the Dean of St. Paul's, who, turning to the people, said: "The Duke entreateth you all to pray with him, that God would be merciful to him; and *that you would be silent, that his spirit be not disturbed!*" He forgave his executioner, and refused to put the handkerchief over his face, which he offered him, saying, "*I fear not death!*" Then, kneeling down, his heart lifted up to God on high, he prostrated himself on the scaffold, the Dean praying intently with him; then laying his neck over the block, at one stroke his head was cut off, which the executioner held up!—a lamentable sight to the people, who sobbed aloud.—"It is almost incredible," says an early historian, who was present at the spectacle, "how dearly the people loved him, and how, by his natural benignity and courteous actions, he had gained the hearts of the multitude. He was so nobly born, so gentle by nature, so comely of person, of so manly an aspect, so perfect in every respect! He was, in a word, the greatest honour and ornament of his country!"

In Puttenham's "Arte of English Poesie," we find the following sonnet written by the Queen, soon after the execution of Norfolk. Its authenticity is unquestioned, and its principal merit consists in its being a royal effusion! and, so far, it is a curiosity worthy our transcribing:—

"The doubt of future foes exiles my present joy,
And wit me warns to shun such snares as threaten mine annoy;

For falsehood now doth flow, and subjects' faith doth ebb,
Which would not be if Reason ruled, or Wisdom weaved the web.
But clouds of toys untried do cloak aspiring minds,
Which turn to rain of late repent by cause of changed winds.
The top of hope supposed the root of truth will be!
And fruitless all their grafted guiles, as shortly ye shall see.
Those dazzled eyes with pride, with great ambition blinds,
Shall be unveiled by worthy wights, whose foresight falsehood finds.
The daughter of Debate, that eke discord doth sow,
Shall reap no gain where former rule hath taught still peace to grow.
No foreign banish'd wight shall anchor in this port,
Our realm it brooks no strangers' force, let them elsewhere resort.
Our rusty sword with rest shall first his edge employ,
To pull their tops that seek such change, and gape for joy."

In Lodge's Illustrations are given several letters from Lord Talbot to his father, the Earl of Shrewsbury, which disclose some curious details of the Queen's favourite, Leicester, and serve to more fully depict the recklessness of his character. In May, 1573, Lord Talbot thus writes:—"The Earl of Leicester is much with her Majesty; he is more than ever solicitous to please her, and is as high in her favour as at any period of his intercourse with the Queen; but there are two sisters, Lady Sheffield and Lady Frances Howard, who are also deeply in love with him, and consequently at variance with each other. On this account the Queen is very angry with them, and, of course, not well pleased with Leicester; and has set spies to watch his motions. To such open demonstrations of feminine jealousy does this great Queen condescend to have recourse! It appears, that a criminal intimacy was known to subsist between Leicester and Lady Sheffield, even before the death of her husband; in consequence of which, this event was generally attributed to the *Italian arts* of Leicester, Lord Sheffield's death being sudden, and preceded by violent symptoms. In the commencement of this year, Lady Sheffield bore him a son, whose birth was carefully concealed, from fear of giving offence to the Queen, though many asserted that a private marriage had taken place. Afterwards, Leicester forsook the mother of his child to marry the Countess of Essex, and the deserted lady became the wife of another." Many years after the death of Leicester, this son, who was styled Sir Robert Dudley, and to whom his father had left a great part of his fortune, laid claim to the family honours; bringing several witnesses to prove his mother's marriage, and, among others, the lady herself. The latter declared, on oath, that Leicester, in order to compel her to form that subsequent marriage in his life-time, which had deprived her of the power of reclaiming him as her husband, had employed the most violent menaces; and had even attempted her life by a poisonous potion, which had thrown her into a fit of alarming illness, and caused the hair of her head and her nails to drop off! After this extraordinary evidence, the heirs of Leicester endeavoured to stay proceedings; but Sir Robert Dudley died before the matter was adjusted. In the following reign the evidence was again renewed, and the title of Duchess of Dudley was conferred on the widow of Sir Robert; the patent setting forth, that the marriage of the Earl of Leicester with Lady Sheffield had been satisfactorily proved! —Such were the villanies of this celebrated favourite, and what must be the character of the maiden Queen in the eyes of posterity, when facts like these are proved!

Christopher Hatton was a new competitor for the smiles of royalty; and bright was the dawn of fortune and favour which at this period awaited him. He was of a decayed family of Northamptonshire, and had recently commenced the study of the law at one of the inns of court, when hope or curiosity prompted him to gain admittance at some court festival, where he had an opportunity of dancing before Elizabeth in a mask. His personal figure and graceful attitudes so captivated the fancy of the amorous Queen, that she immediately bestowed upon him such flattering marks of attention as could not be misunderstood, which at once decided the happy student to quit the dry profession of the law, for the more congenial pursuits of court favouritism. The handsome appearance and gay accomplishments of Christopher Hatton were unexpectedly found to be combined with an amiable heart and a solid understanding. He possessed a prudent, cautious temperament, with the most enlightened views of human nature; and, after mature deliberation, Elizabeth, with that penetrating judgment of men and measures which always distinguished her conduct, and in defiance of ridicule, and the opinions of the court, gradually promoted her new favourite, till at length she elevated him to the dignity of Lord Chancellor. He discharged the arduous duties of his high office with prudence and ability, and speedily became a general favourite. He was the only one of Elizabeth's ministers who lived and died a bachelor; consequently he was exempt from all those jealousies and vexations which awaited those of the royal favourites who dared to enter the married state. Lord Talbot mentions, that at this period Hatton was ill and confined to his bed, and that the Queen went daily to visit him; but that a party with whom Leicester was leagued, were doing all in their power to bring forward another royal favourite to supplant him. This gentleman's name was Edward Dyer: he had been for two years in disgrace; and as he was during all that time suffering under a bad state of health, Elizabeth was made to believe, that the continuance of her displeasure was the sole cause of his malady, and that his recovery was considered hopeless, unless he received her royal pardon. The Queen immediately, on hearing this, despatched to the sick favourite *a comfortable message*, on receipt of which, the poor, silly, weak gentleman was restored to health! Lord Talbot adds, "to the honour of Lord Burleigh, he concerned himself, as usual, only in state affairs, and suffered all these love matters and petty court intrigues to pass over without notice."

Mary, Queen of Scots, in the year 1574, obtained, not without difficulty on the part of Elizabeth, permission to repair to the baths of Buckstone (Buxton Wells) for the recovery of her health; and a similar motive led thither the Lord Treasurer Burleigh. Elizabeth remarked the coincidence, and when, a year afterwards, it again occurred, her displeasure broke forth into sudden violence. She openly accused her minister of entering into intelligence with Mary, by means of the Earl of Shrewsbury and his lady, under whose charge she remained at Buxton. It was with much difficulty that he succeeded in appeasing the Queen. The following extract from a letter, written by Burleigh himself to the Earl of Shrewsbury, will illustrate this striking fact:—

"My lord, it is over true, and over much against reason, that upon my being at Buckstone last year, advantage was sought by some that loved me not, to confirm in her Majesty a formal conceit which some had laboured to put into her head; that I was of late time become friendly to the Queen of Scots, and that I had no disposition to thwart her practices; and now, at my being at Buckstone, her Majesty did directly conceive that my being there was, by means of your lordship and my lady, to enter into intelligence with the Queen of Scots; and hereof at my return to her Majesty's presence, I had very sharp reproofs for my going to Buckstone, with plain charging of me for favouring the Queen of Scots; and that in so earnest a sort as I never looked for, knowing my integrity to her Majesty; but, especially, knowing how contrariously the Queen of Scots conceived of me for many things past. And yet, true it is, I never indeed gave just cause, by any private affection of my own, or for myself, to offend the Queen of Scots, but whatever I did was for the service of mine own lady and queen, which, if it were yet again to be done, I would do. And though I know myself subject to contrary workings of displeasure, yet I will not, for remedy of any of them, decline from the duty I owe to God and my sovereign queen. For I know and do understand, that I am in this contrary sort maliciously aspersed, and yet in secret sort; on the one part, and that of long time, *that I am the most dangerous enemy and evil willer to the Queen of Scots;* on the other side, that I am also a secret well-willer to her and her title; and that I have made my party good with her. Now, my lord, no man can make both these true together, but it sufficeth for such as like not me in doing my duty, to deprive me; and yet such sort is done in darkness as I cannot get opportunity to convince them in the light. In all these crossings, my good lord, I appeal to God, who knoweth, yea, I thank Him infinitely who directeth, my thoughts, to intend principally the service and honour of God; and jointly with that, the surety and greatness of my sovereign lady, the Queen's Majesty: and for any other respect but what may tend to these two, I appeal to God to punish me, if I have any. As for the Queen of Scots, truly I have no spot of evil meaning to her; neither do I mean to deal with any titles to the crown. If she shall intend any evil to the Queen's Majesty, my sovereign, for her sake I must and will impeach; and therein I may be unfriendly to her or worse. . . .

"My lord, I pray you bear my scribbling, which I think your lordship will hardly be able to read; and yet I would not use any man's hand in such a matter as this is.

"Your lordship's most assured at command,

"W. Burleigh.

"From Hampton Court, 25th December, 1575."

The Countess of Shrewsbury, a woman remarkable for a violent, restless, and intriguing spirit, concluded, in 1574, a marriage between Elizabeth Cavendish, her daughter by a former husband, and Charles Stuart, brother of Lord Darnley, and next to the King of Scots in the order of succession to the crowns, both of England and Scotland. The rooted enmity between Mary, Queen of Scots, and the house of Lennox was well known, notwithstanding which, Elizabeth at once suspected, that this union was the result of some private intrigue between Lady Shrewsbury and the captive Queen. In consequence, Elizabeth, with her usual cruelty in all cases of this description, committed to prison, not only the mother of the bride, but also the unfortunate Countess of Lennox, who was destined to undergo such an accumulation of sufferings for having been the innocent cause of inducing her son Darnley to marry the Queen of Scots, thereby giving an heir to the British throne! It was by such cruel acts of oppression and illegal violence that the fame of Elizabeth was tarnished, and her name handed down with infamy to posterity.

In the autumn of 1576, the death of Walter Devereux, Earl of Essex and Marshal of Ireland, took place in Dublin. No domestic event had for a long time occasioned so strong a sensation at the court of Elizabeth. His untimely end was deeply deplored. He was learned, talented, and of illustrious descent, deriving part of his hereditary honours from the noble family of Bourchier, through a daughter of Thomas of Woodstock, youngest son of Edward the Third. In his nineteenth year he succeeded his grandfather, as Viscount Hereford, and, coming to court, attracted the merited commendations of Elizabeth, and the jealousy of Leicester. During a short period, he was joined in commission with the Earls of Huntingdon and Shrewsbury, for the safe keeping of Mary, the Scottish Queen. In the troubles of Scotland, he joined the royal army with all the forces he could muster, and in reward for his services, Elizabeth conferred on him the order of the garter, and subsequently invested him with the dignity of Earl of Essex. By these marks of royal favour, the jealousy of Leicester was strongly excited. In 1575, he was, through the agency of Leicester, for his own vile purposes, sent to Ireland, with the title of Marshal of that country. His efforts to restore order in that distracted portion of the Queen's dominions, were unsuccessful. His court enemies, among whom Leicester was conspicuous, contrived to divert most of the succours designed him by him by his sovereign; and the bodily fatigue endured in his arduous duties, joined to the anguish of a wounded spirit, impaired his constitution, and, after repeated attacks, he at last fell a victim to dysentery. The symptoms of his disease were also ascribed to poison; and one of his attendants, who had a knowledge of medicine, seeing him in great agony, suddenly exclaimed:—"By heavens, my lord, you are poisoned!" The report spread like wild-fire, and Leicester, known to be his bitterest enemy, was immediately pointed at as the contriver of his death. Leicester, who was universally believed to be capable of any enormity, had long carried on an intrigue with the Countess of Essex, and his subsequent marriage with that lady served as a strong corroboration of the charge. This union, however, was not publicly declared till two years afterwards, although a criminal connection between the parties was stated to have existed during the life-time of the Earl, and a private marriage was huddled up with indecent precipitation on his decease.

Notwithstanding the dark suspicion to which the death of Essex had given birth, nothing could injure Leicester in the favour of his royal mistress. He, above all others, was emphatically the man according to her own heart. This is strikingly exemplified in the following authentic epistle addressed by Elizabeth, with unblushing effrontery, to the Earl and Countess of Shrewsbury, in the month of June, 1577:

"Our very good Cousins:—

"Being given to understand, from our cousin of Leicester, how honourably he was not only lately received by you our cousin, the Countess, at Chatsworth; and his diet by you both discharged at Buxtone; but also presented with a very rare present; we should do him great wrong (*holding him in that place of favour we do*) in case we should not let you understand, in how thankful a sort we accept the same at both your hands, *not as done unto him, but to our own self, reputing him as another self*; and, therefore, ye may assure yourselves, that we taking up on us the debt, *not as his, but our own*, will take accordingly, to discharge the same in such honourable sort, as so well deserving creditors, that ye shall never have cause to think ye have met with ungrateful debtors, &c., &c.

"Elizabeth."

In August, 1578, the Earl of Sussex wrote an eloquent letter to the Queen, urging her marriage with the Duke of Anjou. But, what was of more avail, the French Prince sent over to England, to plead his cause, an agent named Simier, a person of sparkling wit, brilliant conversational powers, and who was an adept at the art of ingratiating himself with royalty, by a thousand amusing and pleasing attentions; and by that inordinate flattery—the characteristic feature of his nation—which is rarely thrown away, even upon the gravest of mankind. A suit thus so agreeably urged, Elizabeth had not fortitude to dismiss abruptly: "Her Majesty," says Lord Talbot, "continueth her very good usage of Monsieur Simier, and all his suite; and he hath conference with her three or four times a week; and the Queen is always best disposed and pleasantest when she talketh with him, (as by her gesture appeareth) that is possible. The opinion of the Duke's coming over still holdeth." The influence of Simier over the Queen became at length so powerful, that Leicester, and his infamous adherents, reported that he had employed philtres, and other unlawful means, to inspire the Queen with love for his master! On his part, Simier amply retaliated these hostilities, by carrying to her Majesty the first tidings of the secret marriage of her favourite with the Countess of Essex; a fact which Leicester had studiously concealed from his royal mistress, and which none of her courtiers, who were aware of the circumstance, had the courage to communicate. It was by this time, however, widely known, as the Countess's father, Sir Francis Knolles, had insisted, for the sake of his daughter's reputation, which had been sullied by a previous illicit connection with

Leicester, that the celebration of the nuptials should be as public as possible.

The rage, vexation, and disappointment of the Queen, on hearing the Frenchman's disclosure of the marriage of her favourite, Leicester, exceeded all bounds of decency and decorum. That Leicester, the dearest of her favourites, should form such a connection, such an indissoluble tie, and that too with her own near relation, without even consulting her, imploring her sanction, or supplicating her forgiveness—and that, after having formed it, he should have concealed the horrid fact from her, when known to her whole court;—appeared, to her jaundiced eyes, the very acme of ingratitude, perfidy, baseness, and insult! Like a weak, disappointed, and jealous woman, she felt the injury inflicted on her happiness, and like an arbitrary, tyrannical Queen, she resented the indignity offered to her person!

She instantly ordered Leicester to be imprisoned in a small fort, then standing in Greenwich park; and she threw out the menace, and actually entertained the design, of sending him to the Tower. But the honourable and lofty mind of the Earl of Sussex, her royal kinsman, revolted against proceedings so violent, so lawless, and so utterly disgraceful in every point of view. He plainly, but firmly, represented to her the danger of the course she was about to pursue—that it was contrary to all right and justice, that any man, no matter his station, or under whatever circumstances he might be placed by any previous connection, should be punished for *lawful matrimony;* a state which was held in honour by all; and his known hostility to the favourite, giving weight to his remonstrance, when advocating a mild treatment, Elizabeth prudently curbed her anger, and shortly afterwards restored the Earl, not to favour, but, what was then more prized by him, to liberty. After a time, he was again admitted to her presence, but he never afterwards regained her affections; and his unfortunate Countess remained ever after the object of her utter aversion, antipathy, and hatred.

The quarrel between Leicester and Simier, in consequence of the French envoy disclosing the marriage of Leicester to the Queen, proceeded to such an extremity, that Simier believed his life to be in imminent danger from the attempts of his adversary. One of the Queen's guard, it is said, had actually been hired by Leicester to assassinate the envoy, and the plan was only frustrated by accident. Her Majesty even found it necessary, by a royal proclamation, to take Simier under her special protection. It was during the turmoil occasioned by these disgraceful proceedings, that, as the Queen was taking her accustomed recreation on the Thames, attended by this Frenchman, and several of her courtiers, a shot was fired into the royal barge, which narrowly escaped taking effect on the person of her Majesty, but severely wounded one of the royal boatmen. The shot was, doubtless, aimed at Simier, and when one of the lords expressed an opinion that it was pointed at her Majesty, the Queen promptly silenced him, declaring "that she would believe nothing of her subjects that parents would not believe of their children."

CHAPTER VIII.

Arrival of the Duke of Anjou—The Queen at length anxious to marry—Stubbs' book against the match—His cruel punishment—Death of Bacon—Arrival of Drake—The Queen's marriage revived—Splendid reception of the French Embassy—The Duke of Anjou's second visit to Elizabeth—Personal anecdotes of the Queen.

FTER this attempted assassination, Leicester found himself so coldly treated by Elizabeth, that, in a letter to Lord Burleigh, he threatened to banish himself; well knowing, perhaps, that, for fear of the consequences of such a step to the fame of his royal mistress, the threat would not be tolerated; whilst the French Prince adroitly seized the moment of the Earl's disgrace, to try the effect of personal solicitations on the heart of Elizabeth. He arrived, unexpectedly, and almost without attendants, at the gate of her palace at Greenwich, was graciously received by her Majesty, and, after several long conferences in private, took his leave and returned home, leaving his cause to the skilful management of his own agent, and the ambassadors of his brother, the King of France. At this period, the privy-council, by command of her Majesty, held long and frequent meetings, for the discussion of her proposed marriage with the Duke of Anjou. From the Burleigh Papers, where the discussions are given in detail, we extract the subjoined interesting particulars.

"The Earl of Sussex was still strongly in favour of the match. Lord Hunsdon followed on the same side, as did also the Earl of Lincoln, the Lord Admiral. Burleigh laboured to support the measure, but evidently against his judgment, and in order to please the Queen. Leicester openly professed to have changed his opinion, 'for her majesty,' said he, 'was to be followed.' Sir Walter Mildmay, Sir Ralph Sadler, and Sir Henry Sidney, strongly opposed the measure. On the whole, those who pronounced in favour of the marriage, did so almost avowedly in compliance with the wishes of the Queen, whose inclination to the alliance had become very ardent, since the visit of her youthful suitor; whilst such as opposed it were moved by strong and earnest convictions of the gross impropriety and thorough unsuitableness of the match with respect to Elizabeth herself, and of the evils which, on account of the difference of religion, it was likely to entail on the nation.

"Instead of immediately obeying her Majesty's command, that they should come to a formal decision on the question, they hesitated, temporized, expressed their readiness to be entirely guided, in a matter so personal to herself, by her feelings and wishes; and inquired whether, under all the circumstances, she was desirous of their coming to a full determination. This message was reported to her Majesty in the forenoon (October seventh, 1579), and she allowed herself to be well pleased with the dutiful offer of their services. Nevertheless, she uttered many speeches, and regretted, not without shedding tears, that she should find in her councillors, by their long disputations, any disposition to make it doubtful, whether there could be any more surety for her and her realm, than to have her marry and have a child of her own body to inherit, and so continue the line of Henry the Eighth; and she condemned herself for simplicity, in committing this matter to be argued by them; for that she thought to have rather had an universal request made to her to proceed in this marriage, than to have made doubt of it; and being much troubled herewith, she requested the bearers of this message to forbear her till the afternoon.

"On their return, she repeated her displeasure; then endeavoured, at some length, to refute the objections brought against the match; and finally, her great misliking of all opposition, and her earnest desire for the marriage, being reported to her faithful council, they agreed, after long consultations, to offer their services in furtherance of the marriage, should such really be her pleasure."

Matters were in this state, when the unfortunate Stubbs, a gentleman of Lincoln's Inn, wrote and published a book, entitled, "The Discovery of a gaping Gull, wherein England is like to be swallowed by another French marriage, if the Lord forbid not the bans, by letting her see the sin and punishment thereof." The author was known as a zealous puritan, and had given his sister in marriage to the celebrated Edmund Cartwright, the leader of the sect. A furious proclamation was issued against the book, by order of Elizabeth; all the copies were ordered to be seized and burned; and the author and publisher being proceeded against, in virtue of a severe statute of Philip and Mary, they were found guilty, and condemned to the barbarous punishment of amputation of the right hand.

On being brought to the scaffold to undergo this sentence, Stubbs addressed the multitude to the following effect:—

"I am come hither to receive my punishment, according to the law. I am sorry for the loss of my hand, and more sorry to lose it by judgment; but most of all with her Majesty's indignation and evil opinion. For my hand, I esteem it not so much; for I think I could have saved it, and might do yet; *but I will not have a guilty heart and an infamous hand.* I pray you all to pray with me, that God will strengthen me to endure and abide the pain that I am to suffer, and grant me this grace, that the loss of my hand do not withdraw any part of my duty and affection toward her Majesty." When the hand was ready on the block to be struck off, he said repeatedly to the people; "Pray for me, now my calamity is near at hand." And with these words it was smitten off, whereof he fainted away!

Stubbs was further punished, by an imprisonment of several months in the Tower; but under all these inflictions, his courage and cheerfulness were supported by a firm persuasion of the goodness of the cause for which he suffered. While in prison, he wrote many letters to his friends with his left hand, signing them *Secrevola;* a name which he adopted in memory of his punishment. Such was the high opinion entertained by Burleigh of his theological learning, and the soundness of his principles, that he afterwards engaged him to answer a violent work of Cardinal Allen, entitled, 'The English Justice,' a task which he performed with distinguished ability.

The learned Sir Nicholas Bacon, who, under the title of Lord Keeper, had exercised, from the beginning of Elizabeth's reign, the office of Lord High Chancellor, died in 1579, generally regretted. He filled this important post with superior assiduity, uprightness, and ability; and several pleasing traits are related of his polite and amiable disposition. On the occasion of a visit from Elizabeth, she graciously remarked, that his house was too little for him; "No, madam," replied the Chancellor, "but you have made me too little for my house!" By his second wife, one of the learned daughters of Sir Anthony Cook, a woman of a keen and penetrating intellect, he became the father of two sons, Antony and the renowned Francis Bacon, the splendid dawn of whose unrivalled genius his father was fortunate to behold.

Elizabeth frequently visited Sir Nicholas Bacon, conversed with him familiarly; took pleasure in the flashes of wit, which often relieved the seriousness of his wisdom; and flattered with kind condescension his parental feelings, by the extraordinary notice which she bestowed on his son Francis, whose brightness and solidity of parts early manifested themselves to her discerning eye; and caused her to predict, that her "little Lord Keeper would one day prove an eminent man."

In November, 1580, Admiral Drake, after being absent about three years, during which time he sailed round the world, reached Plymouth harbour in safety. He was the first Englishman by whom this great and novel enterprise, of sailing round the globe, had been successfully achieved; and both himself and his ship became the objects of public curiosity and wonder. His courage, skill, and perseverance were extolled in the highest degree; the wealth which he had brought home from the plunder of the Spanish settlements aroused the daring spirit of adventure peculiar to Englishmen, and half the youth of the country were eager to embark on voyages of discovery. Elizabeth was lost in admiration at the conduct of the valiant Drake, and during the spring of 1581, she accepted the honour of a banquet, on board the Admiral's ship, off Deptford: and conferred on him the order of knighthood, with many substantial marks of royal favour.

Amongst the numerous verses affixed to the ship on this occasion, were the following, written by a Winchester scholar:—

> "Drake, on the Herculean columns these words write:
> Thou further went'st than any mortal wight:
> Though Hercules for travel did excel,
> From him and others thou didst bear the bell."

The French envoy, Simier, who still remained in London, continued to keep alive the tender impressions excited in the heart of Elizabeth, by the personal attentions of the Duke of Anjou; and the King of France, now finding more leisure to attend to the subject of his brother's marriage with the Queen of England, sent over, in 1581, a splendid embassy, headed by a Prince of the blood, to arrange the terms of this august alliance. A magnificent reception was prepared by Elizabeth for these distinguished visitors. "She caused," says Holinshed, "to be erected on the south side of her palace of Whitehall, a vast banquetting house, built with timber, and covered with painted canvas, and decorated inside in the most extravagant style. Branches of fruits of various kinds were hung from festoons of ivy, bay, rosemary, and different flowers; the whole profusely sprinkled with gold spangles: the ceiling was painted of a sky colour, with stars, sunbeams, and clouds, intermixed with scutcheons of the royal arms; and a profusion of glass lustres illuminated the place. In this gorgeous palace the French ambassadors were entertained by Elizabeth, at several splendid banquets, while her ministers were engaged, at her command, in drawing up the marriage articles! In the meanwhile, several of her youthful courtiers prepared for the occasion, what they termed a triumph. The young Earl of Arundel, Lord Windsor, Sir Philip Sydney, and Faulke Greville, the four challengers, styled themselves the foster-children of Desire; and to that end of the tilt-yard where her Majesty was seated, they gave the name of the Castle of Perfect Beauty. This castle the Queen was summoned to surrender, in a very courtly message, delivered by a boy dressed in red and white, the colours of Desire. On her refusal, a mount, placed on wheels, was rolled into the tilt-yard; and the four cavaliers rode in, superbly armed and accoutred, each at the head of a splendid troop; and when they had passed in military order before the Queen, the boy who had delivered the former message, again addressed her in the following terms:—

"'If the message lately delivered unto you had been believed and followed, O Queen! in whom the whole story of virtue is written, with the language of beauty; nothing should this violence have needed in your inviolate presence. Your eyes, which till now have been wont to discern only the bowed knees of kneeling hearts, and inwardly turned, found always the heavenly peace of a sweet mind, should not now have their fair beams reflected with the shining of armour, should not now be driven to see the fury of desire, nor the fiery force of fury! But since so it is (alas! that it is so!), that in the defence of obstinate refusal there never groweth victory but by compulsion, they are come:—what need I say more? You see them, ready in heart, as you know, and able with hands, as they hope, not only to assail, but to prevail. Perchance you despise the smallness of number. I say unto you, the force of desire goeth not by fulness of company. Nay, rather view with what irresistible determination they approach; and how, not only the heavens send their invisible instruments to aid them [music is heard within the mount], but also the very earth, the dullest of all the elements, which, with natural heavings, still strives to the sleepy centre; yet, for advancing this enterprise, is content actively (as you shall see) to move itself upon itself, to rise up in height, that it may the better command the high-minded fortresses [here the mount rose up in height]. Many words, when deeds are in the field, are tedious both unto speaker and hearer. You see their forces, but know not their fortunes; if you be resolved, it boots not; and threats dread not. I have discharged my duty; which was, even when all things were ready for the assault, thus to offer parley; a thing not so much used as gracious in besiegers. You shall now be summoned to yield; which if it be rejected, then look for the affectionate alarm to be followed with desirous assault. The time approacheth, but no time shall stay me from wishing, that however this succeed, the world may long enjoy its chiefest ornament, which decks it with herself—with the love of goodness!'

"The rolling mount was now moved close to her Majesty, the music began to play, and one of the boys, accompanied with cornets, sung a fresh summons to the fortress to surrender. Another boy then, turning to the challengers and their retinue, sounded an alarm, the two cannons were fired, the one with sweet powder, and the other with sweet water, very odoriferous and pleasant; and the noise of the shooting was excellent melody within the mount. After that, there were a great store of pretty scaling ladders, and the footmen threw flowers and such fancies against the walls, with all such devices as might seem fit shot for Desire, all which continued till the defenders came in. These knights were above twenty in number, each accompanied by his servants, pages, and trumpeters. Speeches were then delivered to the Queen: several of the knights appearing in some assumed character. Sir Thomas Perrott and Anthony Cook personated Adam and Eve; the latter having hair hung all down his helmet. The messenger sent on the part of Thomas Ratcliff, described his master as a forlorn knight, whose despair of achieving the favour of his peerless and sunlike mistress, had driven him out of the haunts of men into a cave of the desert, where moss was his couch, and moss moistened with tears his only food. Even here, however, the report of this assault upon the Castle of Perfect Beauty had reached his ears, and roused him from his slumber of despondency; and, in token of his devoted loyalty and inviolable fidelity to his divine mistress, he sent his shield, which he entreated her to accept, as the ensign of her fame, and the instrument of his glory: prostrating himself at her feet, as one ready to undertake any adventures in hope of her gracious favour.

"Mercury appeared on the part of the four sons of Sir Francis Knolles, and described them as legitimate sons of Despair, brethren to hard Mishap; suckled with sighs and swathed up in sorrow; weaned in woe and dry-nursed by Desire; long time fostered with favourable countenance, and wed with sweet fancies, but now, alas! of late, wholly given over to grief, and disgraced by disdain. The speeches being ended, the tilting commenced, and lasted till night. It was resumed the next day with fresh magnificence, and a few more speeches. At length the challengers presented to the Queen an olive bough, in token of their humble submission, and both parties were dismissed with thanks and commendations."

The articles of the marriage treaty were at length completed between Elizabeth and the Duke of Anjou; and it was stipulated, that the nuptials should take place six weeks after the ratification: but Elizabeth, whose vagaries were not yet at an end, had insisted on a separate article, purporting that she should not be obliged to complete the marriage until further matters, not specified, should have been settled between herself and the Duke of Anjou. She sent Walsingham to open new negotiations at Paris; but no sooner were these satisfactorily terminated, than fresh difficulties were started. Walsingham, puzzled and perplexed by such capricious conduct, remained uncertain how to act; and at length, all the politicians, English as well as French, were equally disconcerted, and came to the unanimous opinion, that this strange fickleness could only be put an end to by Elizabeth herself. Nothing, therefore, remained for them, but to await, in anxious silence, her Majesty's pleasure. Not so, however, the royal lover, who conjecturing that a *tête-à-tête* with the object of his ambition would be more effectual than a thousand negotiators, brought to a speedy conclusion his campaign in the Netherlands, which a liberal supply of money from Elizabeth had rendered uniformly successful; and putting his army into winter quarters, hastened to throw himself at the feet of his royal mistress. He was welcomed with all the demonstrations of satisfaction which could revive the hopes of a suitor: every mark of honour, every pledge of affection, were publicly bestowed upon the Duke; and Elizabeth, at the conclusion of a splendid festival on the anniversary of her coronation, even went so far as to take a ring from her own fair hand and place it on the finger of her intended husband. This passed in sight of the whole court, who naturally regarded the action as a complete betrothment; and the long suspense being apparently now satisfactorily terminated, the feelings of each party broke forth in a variety of ways. Some rejoiced; others grieved and wondered; Leicester, Hatton, and Walsingham loudly exclaimed that ruin impended over the church, the country, and the Queen. The ladies of the court alarmed and agitated their mistress by tears and lamentations. Her Majesty passed a sleepless night amid her disconsolate handmaids. The next morning she sent for Anjou, and held with him a very long private conversation; after which he returned to his chamber, and hastily throwing from him the ring which she had given him, uttered many reproaches against the levity and fickleness of Englishwomen.

The French Prince was soon after called away to the Netherlands; and Elizabeth, with evident reluctance to part from him, went with him as far as Canterbury. She then dismissed him with a large supply of money, and a splendid retinue of English lords and gentlemen. The parting was mournful in the extreme: Elizabeth loth to let him go, and the Prince as loth to depart. Nevertheless, this favourite son of Catherine de Medici was a sufficient adept in the dissimulation of courts to assume with ease all those marks of complacency that the case required. Nor was Elizabeth less accustomed to the arts of feigning; she was careful, by every manifestation of friendship and esteem, to smooth over the affront which she had put upon the brother of the reigning monarch of France. The Duke of Anjou soon afterwards lost his life in the Netherlands, and thus finally terminated all hopes of the marriage of Elizabeth.

The pernicious effects of the flattery daily and hourly administered to Elizabeth, was, about this time, remarked by one of her domestic chaplains, who, in a sermon preached before the Queen, in her chapel royal, had the boldness to tell her, that "she who had been once meek as a lamb, was now become an untamable heifer!" for which reproof he, on descending from the pulpit, was sharply reprimanded by her Majesty, as "an over-confident and presumptuous parson, who insulted and dishonoured his sovereign."

The decay of her beauty was also an unwelcome truth, which all the artifices of adulation and flattery were unable to conceal from her inward conviction. During the latter years of her life, she could never behold her face in a mirror, without rage and disappointment. This circumstance in no small degree contributed to sour her temper, while, at the same time, it rendered the young, the lively, and the lovely of her court, the objects of her hatred and malignity. Sir John Harrington relates a striking anecdote of Elizabeth on this point:—"The Queen would often ask the ladies around her chamber, if they loved to think of marriage? And the wise ones did conceal well their liking thereto, as knowing the Queen's judgment in this matter. The fair cousin of Sir Matthew Arundel, not knowing so deeply as her companions the sentiments of her Majesty, was one day asked the same question, when she said, with great simplicity, she had thought much about marriage, if her father would but consent to the man she loved! 'You seem honest, i'faith!' said the Queen; 'I will sue for you to your father!' The damsel was not displeased at this, and when Sir Robert, her father, came to court, the Queen asked him respecting his daughter's sweetheart, and pressed his consenting to the marriage, if the match was a discreet one. Sir Robert, much astonished at this news, said he never heard that his daughter had a liking for any man; and wished to know who was the object of her affection—adding, he would give free consent to what was most pleasing to her Majesty's will and advice. 'Then I will do the rest,' saith the Queen. The young lady was called in; and the Queen told her that her father had given his free consent. 'Then,' replied the young lady, delighted, 'I shall be most happy, and please your Majesty.' 'So thou shalt,' retorted Elizabeth, with a malignant sneer, 'but not to be a fool and marry;—I have your father's consent given to me, and I vow thou shalt never get it into thy possession. So go to thy business; I see thou art a bold one, to own thy foolish propensities so readily!'"

The dangers which surrounded the Queen, since her cruel and unauthorized detention of the unfortunate Mary of Scotland, aggravated the harshness of her natural disposition. Plans of insurrection were frequently agitated by conspirators, but as often baffled by the extraordinary vigilance and sagacity of her ministers, while the courage displayed by Elizabeth herself on these occasions was truly admirable. It is related by Lord Chancellor Bacon, that the council once represented to her the danger in which she stood by the continual conspiracies against her life; and acquainted her that a man was lately taken into custody, who stood ready, in a very determined and suspicious manner, to do the deed: and they shewed her the weapon by which he intended to destroy her. They, therefore, advised her Majesty, that she should go less abroad to take the air, thinly attended, as was her wont on private occasions. But the Queen answered firmly—"I had rather be dead than placed in custody!"

Sir Walter Raleigh was deservedly a great favourite with Elizabeth; his comely person, fine address, and great experience in the arts of a courtier, raised him to such a height of royal admiration, as to excite the jealousy even of him who had long occupied the first place in the affections of her Majesty. During the early days of Raleigh's attendance, when a few handsome suits of clothes formed almost the whole of his worldly wealth, he was on one occasion accompanying the Queen in one of her daily walks, which she was fond of taking, in the hope of improving her complexion, when, on reaching a miry spot which she could not conveniently pass over, he, with an adroitness characteristic of the finished courtier, pulled off his rich plush cloak and threw it on the mud, to serve her for a foot-cloth. The Queen graciously accepted his obliging assistance, and it was afterwards quaintly remarked, "the spoiling of Raleigh's cloak hath gained him many handsome suits."

CHAPTER IX.

Leicester sent to Holland—Elizabeth's letter to him—Babington's conspiracy—His associates—Infamous conduct of Walsingham to entrap the Queen of Scots—Defeat of the conspirators—Their trial and execution—Mary removed to Fotheringay Castle—Her address to the Commissioners—Her trial and condemnation—Confirmed by the Parliament—Elizabeth's answer to the Parliament—Mary's dying request to Elizabeth—Her treatment of Mary.

OWARD the close of the year 1585, the Earl of Leicester was sent to the Netherlands, invested by Elizabeth with the title of "General of her Majesty's Auxiliary Troops" in that country. He had also the command of the royal navy. He was accompanied by the young Earl of Essex, Lords Audley and North, Sir William Russell, and many other knights, and attended by a chosen company of five hundred gentlemen. The Queen, on his departure, forbade him to entertain a thought of anything which would be unworthy either of her or of the office which he held. Having landed at Flushing, he was first met by his nephew, Sir Philip Sidney, governor of that city, and afterwards by all the towns of Holland and Zealand, with all sorts of honours, acclamations, triumphs, devoted panegyrics, banquetings, and the like. And in the month of July following he proceeded to the Hague, where the court of Holland, by means of the States General, by letters patent, gave to him the sovereign command and absolute authority over the United Provinces, under the title of "Governor and Captain General of Zealand, and the United and Confederate Provinces;" which so excited his pride and vanity, that he assumed the state and dignity of majesty itself, and thereby so highly offended the Queen, that she addressed to him the following severe reprimand:—

"You shall understand by this messenger, whom we have expressly sent over to you, with what contempt you have behaved yourself against our pleasure. We had not thought, that you, a man we have raised from the dust, and favoured above all others, would have violated, in so great a matter, our command with so great contempt, even in a matter which so much and nearly concerneth us and our honour. But though against your duty, you have made so little respect of our honour, yet think not that we are so graciously negligent in the repairing thereof, that we can pass over so great an injury with silence and oblivion. Therefore, we command you, that you, setting apart all excuses, incontinently, according to the faith and duty wherein you are bound to us, perform all whatsoever Heneage, our under-chamberlain, shall in our name declare unto you, except you will draw upon your head a greater danger."

This letter effectually put a stop to Leicester's ambitious prospects in the Netherlands. With feigned remorse, which he so well knew how to assume, he supplicated the forgiveness of Elizabeth, and the affair was soon after amicably adjusted.

In July 1586, soon after the conclusion of the treaty of friendship between Elizabeth and James the Sixth of Scotland, the celebrated Babington conspiracy was discovered, which ended in the trial, sentence, and execution of the unfortunate Mary, Queen of Scots—a fatal drama, which has marked on the character of Elizabeth a deep spot of infamy, and which we detail from the most authentic sources. Three individuals—Giffard, doctor in divinity, Gilbert Giffard, his brother, and Hodgson, priests of the English seminary at Rheims—believing that the famous bull of Pius the Fifth, against Queen Elizabeth, was dictated to him by the Holy Ghost, so far persuaded one John Savage, that it was meritorious to murder such as were excommunicated—that it was martyrdom to die in such a cause—that he, after awhile, freely and voluntarily avowed his determination to accomplish the deed. During the Easter holydays of that year, John Ballard, priest of the same seminary, after visiting many Papists in England and Scotland, and sounding their minds, returned to France, accompanied by Maude, a spy of Walsingham—a most crafty dissembler, who had seduced his easy nature, and treated with Bernardino Mendoza, then in the service of the King of Spain in France, and Charles Paget, who was wholly devoted to the Queen of Scots, respecting the means of invading England. But Paget clearly demonstrated, that it would be in vain to invade England so long as the Queen was living. Ballard, nevertheless, was sent back, and at Whitsuntide arrived in London, attired in silks, under the disguise of a soldier, and calling himself Captain Foscue. He consulted with Anthony Babington of Dethick, in Derbyshire, a young man of good family, of a haughty spirit, surpassing learning, and zealous in the cause of his religion; he had before been in France, where he became familiar with Thomas Morgan, a servant of the Queen of Scots, and the Bishop of Glasgow, her ambassador, who continually sounded in the ears of this ambitious youth, the heroic virtues of the great Queen of Scots, in whose service he might obtain the means to rise to great honours. Whereupon the young man conceived a certain hope, and Morgan, without his knowledge, commended him in letters to the Queen. On consulting with Babington, Ballard gave him to understand that the Queen of England had not long to live, as Savage, who had vowed her death, was then in London. Babington was of a different opinion, and thought it not fit that affairs of such magnitude should be committed to him alone, lest he should fail in the attempt, but to six valiant men, of whom he would have Savage to be one, to the end that he might not infringe his vow. Babington, therefore, contrived a new plan for the invasion of England by the foreign powers at enmity with the Queen—at what port they should land—what assistance should be given them; how the Queen of Scots should be set at liberty; and, lastly, for committing the tragical murder, as he called it, of the Queen of England.

Whilst Babington was intent on these matters, he received letters, by a boy unknown, from the Queen of Scots (stated by Mary on her trial to be forgeries), written in a familiar character betwixt them: wherein she gently blamed him for his long silence, and commanded him with all speed to send the packet of letters sent from Morgan, and delivered to him by the secretary of the French ambassador, which he did, and by the same messenger sent her a letter, by which "He excused himself for his silence, because he was destitute of opportunity to send to her, since she had been given into the custody of Sir Amias Poulet, that puritan, wholly devoted to Leicester, and a cruel and bitter enemy to the Catholic faith. He mentioned the conference he had with Ballard. He informed her, that six gentlemen were chosen to commit a tragical murder, and that he, with a hundred others, was ready to deliver her. And he desired her to propound rewards to the heroic actor of this tragedy, or to their posterity, if they died in the attempt." On the twenty-seventh, Mary was alleged to have replied to these letters, in the following manner:—"She praised his singular affection to the Catholic religion, and to herself; but she admonished him to be considerate in this enterprise, and that he should form an association amongst the authors and actors in the same, for fear of the Puritans; not to attempt any thing before he was sure of the foreign succours, to stir up some commotions in Ireland, whilst the blow was to be given here; to secure the Earl of Arundel and his brothers in the enterprise, with the Earl of Northumberland, and secretly to recal into the kingdom the Earl of Westmoreland, Paget, and others." As to the means for her deliverance, she prescribeth as follows:—"Either by overturning a cart in the gate-way, or setting fire to the stables, or by intercepting her when she should be riding to take the air, or recreate herself between Chartley and Stafford. Finally, she requested Babington to promise rewards to the six gentlemen, and to all the rest!"

Babington now associated with him several persons of rank and fortune, who were anxious to reestablish the Catholic religion, amongst whom were Edward Windsor, brother of Lord Windsor; Thomas Salisbury, of Denbighshire; Tilney, of a noble family: with one of the gentlemen pensioners of the Queen, whom Ballard had reconciled to the Catholic faith; Chidiock Tichbourne, of Hampshire, and Edward Abingdon, whose father was under-treasurer to the Queen's household—two brave youths; Robert Gedge of Surrey; John Travers; John Charnock of Lancashire; J. Jones, whose father was keeper of the wardrobe to Queen Mary; Savage, of whom we have spoken; Barnwell, of a noble house in Ireland; and Henry Dunn, clerk of the office of first fruits and tithes. Into this company one Polley insinuated himself, a man well instructed in the affairs of the Queen of Scots, expert in dissembling, and who from day to day laid open all their counsels to Walsingham, and by the mischievous advice which he suggested to these conspirators, being of themselves inclined to evil, he precipitated them into far worse matters, notwithstanding Naw, the Queen of Scots' secretary, had warned them against trusting him.

To these Babington communicated his plans, but not to every one wholly. He showed to Ballard, Tichbourne, and Dunn, his own letters, and letters of the Queen of Scots. He then solicited Tiiney and Tichbourne to do the deed. At first they refused to stain their hands in their Princess's blood. But Ballard and Babington laboured hard to convince them how just and lawful it was to kill Kings or Princes who had been excommunicated, and that if right were to be violated, it must needs be for the Catholic religion; yet, notwithstanding, they were with great difficulty persuaded to consent. Abingdon, Barnwell, Charnock, and Savage, yielded their ready consent, swearing to perpetrate the murder. Salisbury they could not possibly induce to be a regicide, nor listen to any thing more than to use his best endeavours for the deliverance of the Queen of Scotland. Babington chose Tichnor to be the odd man, over and above the number of those who were to do the deed, of whose secrecy, trust, and resolution he had no doubt; but he was then abroad. Babington ordered, that before taking the oath, they should not impart the affair to any living being. They afterwards met in St. Giles' Fields, to confer further; also at St. Paul's, and in taverns, where they often feasted, puffed up with vain hopes of preferment to great honours and dignities, whereupon they would often commend the noble courage of those valiant Scots, who had lately seized on the King's royal person at Stirling; and Girard, the Bourgonian, who slew the Prince of Orange at Delft. Indeed, they arrived at such a height of vanity, that they must needs have the pictures of the conspirators drawn on a table, and Babington in the midst, with this inscription:—"Such be my companions, who dare to encounter dangers." This table was once privately shown to Elizabeth, who could not discern or recollect any other man by his portrait, with the exception of Barnwell, who had at various times received access to her Majesty through the Earl of Kildare, in whose service he was; but, being pressed on the matter, she recollected him to be the same man that had once before attempted her life. One day, while walking abroad, she perceived Barnwell, whom she regarded with a fixed and undaunted countenance; then, turning suddenly towards Sir Christopher Hatton, captain of her guard, and others, she exclaimed, "Am not I fairly guarded now, having not one man of all my followers who is provided with a sword?" This Barnwell reported to the rest of his companions, telling them how easily it might then have been done, had he had his confederates with him; and Savage said the same thing.

After this, Babington's sole care was, how he might bring in the foreign aid.

To make sure, he resolved to pass into France, and to send Ballard before him on the same errand, for whom he had procured a licence to travel. And the better to avoid suspicion, he insinuated himself with Sir Francis Walsingham, by means of Polley already spoken of, whom he earnestly entreated to procure him a passport from the Queen to go into France, promising him he would use his zealous efforts to discover all the hidden plots the English fugitives had in hand relative to the Queen of Scots. Walsingham commended his purpose, promising him not only his passport, but greater matters. Nevertheless, he put off from time to time both the one and the other, having, in the mean-time, served his turn by his own agents, who had acquainted him before-hand with all the designs and doings of the conspirators, who thought themselves as secure as the sun. The person who discovered most of these matters to Walsingham, was one Gilbert Giffard, descended from the noble family of the Chillingtons, in Staffordshire, near Chartley, where the Queen of Scots had resided. He was sent by the foreign conspirators into England, under the name of Luson, to remind Savage of the vow he had made to act as their agent, and to keep himself close, and the letters of the Queen of Scots safe, until they could be sent over.

The foreigners, in order to try whether they might safely receive letters from England, sent several blank sheets of paper folded up in packets like letters, when, perceiving by the answers returned, that they had been delivered, they wrote in earnest, but in characters. Giffard, being either troubled in conscience, or corrupted with money, went secretly to Walsingham, to whom he discovered himself, stated for what purpose he was employed in England, offered him his services for the *love* he bore his Princess and country, and promised to make him acquainted with whatever letters came into his hands from the foreign agents or the Queen of Scots. Walsingham, embracing his offer, entertained him kindly, and sent him into Staffordshire, to visit Sir Amias Poulet, the keeper of Mary Queen of Scots, entreating him to give this Giffard leave to entice some of his servants. But the governor, unwilling that any servant of his should, by dissimulation or otherwise, be brought to turn traitor, seemed displeased with the notion. Nevertheless, he suffered him to practise his infamous arts until he had corrupted a brewer and a dealer in oatmeal, his near neighbours. These he made sure of: with a few crowns he easily induced the brewer to bore artificially a hole in the wall, wherein a stone could be easily put in and out. Through this hole he both delivered and received letters, which, by carriers appointed for the purpose, came to the hands of Walsingham, who opened them, took copies of them, read the cyphers by the skill of Thomas Philips, and by the device of Arthur Gregory, so closed them up again, that it could not be perceived they had been unsealed, and then forwarded them to whom they were directed. In this way were the first two letters intercepted, which the Queen of Scots was alleged to have written to Babington, and his answers to her, wherein was added a postscript in the same characters, in which were the names of six noblemen, as also other letters, all written in one day to the Spanish Ambassador, to Lord Paget, Charles Paget, the Archbishop of Glasgow, and Sir Francis Inglefield, all which were first transcribed, and then resealed and sent off to their respective destinations.

As soon as Elizabeth understood, by these letters, what a storm was about to burst over her head, as well from abroad as at home, she immediately gave orders for the apprehension of Ballard, who, ere he could depart for France, was unexpectedly taken at Babington's house. This step alarmed Babington, and he immediately went to consult Tichbourne, whose counsel was, for every man to save himself by flight. But Babington had a great mind to send forth Savage and Charnock to assassinate the Queen without delay, and first, the better to ensure his access to the court, to have him richly clothed: to effect this, he held a conference with the rest of the conspirators that day in St. Paul's. But changing his mind, and being greatly perplexed how to act, he at length importuned Walsingham by letters and personal entreaties, being then at court, forthwith to let him have his passport for France, and as he had especial use for Ballard's services, he prayed that he might be set at liberty. Walsingham put him off with fair promises, and entrusted the capture of Ballard to Young, the cunning entrapper of the Papists, and his assistants, advising him, as it were in kindness, to keep him out of the claws of such men; this he easily persuaded him to (being a young man), and to take lodgings in London for a while, till the Queen had signed his passport, and till he returned to London himself, that they might confer the more privately together on such great matters: otherwise, by his going so often up and down, which he must needs do if he lodged anywhere else, the foreign agents could not fail to grow suspicious of him on his going to France.

In the meanwhile Scudamore, a servant of Sir Francis Walsingham, was directed to have an eye upon him, to accompany him everywhere, giving him to understand that this was done to save him from the officers of justice. This web Walsingham had closely woven without the knowledge of the Queen's council, and thought to lengthen it a little more. But Elizabeth was impatient, and could not listen to any further delay, lest in not seeking to save herself when she might, she would seem rather to be tempting God than trusting in him. Accordingly, a letter was sent from Walsingham at court to his agent in London, to look a little more narrowly to Babington than he had hitherto done. This letter was delivered to him unsealed, while sitting at table next to Babington, who having read it with him, suspected that all was discovered, and speedily absconded, under the cover of night, with Gage, Charnock, Barnwell, and Dunn, to a place of concealment in St. John's Wood. Immediately it became known that they had fled, they were proclaimed traitors. Hunger forced them to retire to the houses of the Bellamys, near Harrow-on-the-Hill, a family zealously affected to the Roman religion, who hid them in barns, clothed them in rustic apparel, and relieved them with meat. But being discovered ten days after, they were conveyed prisoners to London, and the citizens, to express their joy on the occasion, set the bells ringing, made bonfires, and sung psalms: all which the Queen greatly commended, and expressed her thanks to the City authorities. In a short time, Abington, Salisbury, and the rest of the conspirators, were taken; and, when examined, by their own confessions proved their guilty designs.

Meanwhile, the Queen of Scots and her servants were kept in close custody, that she might not hear of that conspiracy which was known throughout the land. But as soon as the conspirators were taken, Sir Thomas Gorge was sent to inform her briefly thereof. He found that the unhappy Queen, not dreaming of any such matter, had obtained permission for a day's hunting, and was now mounted on horseback; but, on learning the tidings, she expressed a wish to dismount and return to her chamber. This, however, was not permitted, and, under various pretexts, she was conducted up and down the country, from one nobleman's house to another, and not suffered to return home. In the meantime, Sir John Manners and three others, in compliance with a commission from Elizabeth, proceeded to the apartments of Queen Mary, separately confined Naw and Curll—kept the rest of the servants from communicating with their royal mistress, or she with them;—and, breaking open the doors of her cabinet, they seized all her writing-desks and boxes, wherein were any letters under her own hand and seal. Then Sir Amias Poulet, as he was commanded, seized upon all her money, that she might have no means of bribing any one, promising to restore it to her again. The desks being opened before Queen Elizabeth, divers letters were found written to her by strangers, copies of such as she had written to various individuals, notes, memorials, and secret characters, with several amorous letters, and letters of condolence on her infamous captivity from some great men of England. Elizabeth, notwithstanding, passed them all over in silence, using her old device, *Video Taceoq.*;—"I see, and say nothing."

The infamous Giffard, who had played so conspicuous a part in this tragedy, was sent to France, as if he had been banished; but, before leaving, he left with the Ambassador of France an indented paper, requesting him not to deliver the Queen of Scots her letters, nor those of the foreign agents, to any but him who should produce a paper corresponding with that which he had secretly left with Walsingham. A few months afterwards, he was committed to prison for some gross misconduct, and ended his days miserably, confessing that the most of what he said was true, as was apparent by that which was found in his desk.

On the thirteenth of September, seven of the conspirators were arraigned, and condemned as traitors, and, two days afterwards, the other seven were called to the bar, found guilty, and condemned; one only, Polley, though he was equally guilty with all, saying that he had something to speak to Sir Francis Walsingham, which was not brought forth. On the twentieth of the same month, the first seven were hanged on a gibbet—a scaffold having been erected for that purpose in St. Giles' Fields, where they were wont to meet. They were no sooner hanged, than, whilst yet alive and conscious, they were cut down, and, with barbarous cruelty, embowelled and quartered. The first who was thus horribly butchered was Ballard, the arch traitor, after he had asked forgiveness of God and the Queen, if ever he had offended her. Then Babington, who remained undismayed (whilst the others, turning aside, prayed on their knees), confessed his faults ingenuously; and, being cut down from the gallows, and laying upon the block to be quartered, cried loud, in Latin, *Parce mihi, Domine Jesu.* Savage, the rope having given way, fell from the gibbet; but, being promptly snatched up by the gentlemen, had his members cut off, and was embowelled alive. Barnwell excused his crime out of a pretext of conscience and religion. Tichbourne most penitently confessed his offence, and was much pitied by the beholders: so also was Tilney. Abingdon, being of a furious and turbulent spirit, threatened that in a short time there would be no little bloodshed in England. The next day, the other seven being drawn to the same place, suffered the same punishment, but with less severity, by order of the Queen, who was alarmed by the first day's cruelty after she heard of it: for they hung till they were dead, and then were cut down, embowelled, and quartered.

After this execution, Naw, a Frenchman, and Curll, both secretaries to the Queen of Scots, being questioned as to the letters, notes, and characters found in the Queen's closet, confessed and attested that they were their own handwriting, dictated by her to them in French, taken by Naw, and translated by Curll into English, and written out in secret characters. Neither denied they that they had received letters from Babington, and that they, at her bidding, had written back to him again. It, however, appears, almost beyond a doubt, especially as Walsingham reproved Curll, as unmindful of the gracious favours he had received, for saying that he had confessed nothing but what his companion Naw urged him to do, and which he could not deny, that this confession was false; and extorted by bribery.

Presently after, Sir Edward Wotton was sent into France, to inform the King of this conspiracy, and to show the copies of those letters of the Queen of Scots, and of others of the nobility of England, to testify the truth of the charges, that the King might perceive in what peril the Queen was by the proceedings of Morgan, Charles Paget, and others then resident in France. The council could not for some time determine what was best to be done regarding the Queen of Scots. Some advised that she should be closely imprisoned for life; others were of opinion that she should be put to death, in due course of law, for fear of endangering religion!

But the Earl of Leicester thought it better to despatch her with poison! and sent a divine (!) to Sir Francis Walsingham, to tell him that he thought it might lawfully be done! Walsingham, however, was so far from consenting to have any violence offered to her, that he had prevented Morton's purpose, which was to have had her sent to Scotland, and assassinated on the borders! It was ultimately determined to issue out a commission to forty noblemen and privy councillors, empowering them "to try and pass sentence upon Mary, daughter and heir to James the Fifth, late King of Scotland and Dowager of France, pretending a title to the English crown," for having participated in the late wicked conspiracy.

The majority of these commissioners met on the eleventh of October, at Fotheringham, in the county of Northampton, whither the Queen of Scots had been removed. The following day, they sent to her Mildmay, Sir Amias Poulet, and Barker, notary public, who delivered to her the Queen's letters patent, authorizing the commission; which, when she had perused, with a bold spirit and majestic countenance, she answered, "I am sorry to be charged, by my sister the Queen, with that of which I am innocent; but let it be remembered that I am also a Queen, and not amenable to any foreign jurisdiction."

The next morning, Sir Amias Poulet and Parker, two of the commissioners, repaired to her, and shewed her her answer in writing, demanding whether she would persist therein; when, after having it read distinctly, she said she would persist, with this addition, "that the Queen wrote to me that I was subject to the laws of England, and to be judged by them, because I lived under their protection. To which I answer, 'That I came into England for aid; but having ever since been detained a prisoner, I could never enjoy the benefit of the laws, nor had I till this moment any one to instruct me therein.'" Afterwards, she was several times waited upon by the commissioners, with their council, but to their entreaty she replied that "she was herself an innocent Queen, and as such, she would rather perish, than answer as a subject or a malefactor."

At last, however, Sir Christopher Hatton, vice-chamberlain, thus addressed her:—"You are accused of a conspiracy against our sovereign lady the Queen, but not condemned. You say you are a Queen; admitted: yet are you not exempt from answering in such a case. If you are innocent, you dishonour your reputation by refusing to come to judgment. You protest yourself to be so, but the Queen thinks otherwise; and hath appointed persons honourable, wise, and upright, to examine your innocency: they must hear you with equity and favour, and will be very joyful if you can clear yourself of these crimes. Believe me, the Queen herself will greatly rejoice: for she assured me at my departure,' that no greater grief had ever befallen her, than this of your accusation; wherefore, setting aside this vain conceit of sovereignty, which at this time standeth you in no stead, shew yourself blameless; attract no more suspicion to yourself by subterfuge, but rather wipe away the spot which else will stick perpetually to your reputation."

These remarks of Hatton's caused Mary to waver, and a harsh note, received the following morning from Elizabeth,—who, after the charge of plotting against her life, says, "I order, charge, and command you to answer to the nobles and peers of my kingdom, as you would to myself, if I were present;" and proceeds: "I have heard of your arrogance; but act candidly, and you may meet with more favour,"—turned the balance; and, on the subsequent morning, the fourteenth of October, the Queen of Scots sent for the commissioners, and declared to them that, being persuaded by Hatton's reasons, after maturely considering them, she desired to purge herself of the imputed crime; and, accordingly, on the same morning, her trial commenced. The upper half of the great hall of Fotheringay Castle was railed off, and at the higher end was placed a chair of state, under a canopy, for the Queen of England. Upon both sides of the room benches were arranged in order, where sat the Lord Chancellor Bromley, the Lord Treasurer Burleigh, fourteen earls, thirteen barons, and knights and members of the privy council. In the centre was a table, at which the Lord Chief Justice, several doctors of the civil law, Popham, the Queen's attorney, her solicitors, serjeants, and notaries, took their places. At the foot of this table, and immediately opposite Elizabeth's chair of state, a chair, without any canopy, was placed for the Queen of Scots. Behind was the rail which ran across the hall, the lower part of which was fitted up for the accommodation of persons who were not in the commission.

There was never, throughout the whole of Mary's eventful life, an occasion on which she appeared to greater advantage than this. In the presence of all the pomp, learning, and talent of England, she stood alone and undaunted, evincing, in the modest dignity of her bearing, a mind conscious of its own integrity, and superior to the malice of fortune. Elizabeth's ablest statesmen and lawyers were assembled to probe her to the quick; to press home every argument against her which ingenuity could devise and eloquence embellish; to dazzle her with a blaze of erudition, or involve her in a maze of technical perplexities. Mary had no counsellor, no adviser, no friend. Her very papers, to which she might have wished to refer, had been taken from her; and there was none to plead her cause, or to defend her innocence. Yet was she not dismayed. She knew that she had a higher judge than Elizabeth; and that, great as was the array of lords and barons who appeared against her, posterity was greater than they, and that to its decision all things would be finally referred. Her bodily infirmities imparted only a greater lustre to her mental pre-eminence; and not in all the fascinating splendour of her youth and beauty—not on the morning of her first bridal-day, when all Paris shouted with acclamations in her praise—was Mary Stuart so much to be admired, as when, weak and worn out, she stood calmly before the myrmidons of a rival queen, to hear and refute their unjust accusations, her eye radiant once more with the brilliancy of earlier years, and the placid benignity of a serene conscience lending to her countenance an undying grace.

Elizabeth's Attorney-General opened the pleadings. He began by referring to the act of parliament, in which it was made a capital offence to be the person by whom any design was undertaken against the life of the Queen of England. He then described the late conspiracy, and attempted to establish Mary's connection with it, by producing copies of letters which he alleged she had written to Babington himself, and several of his accomplices. To these, having added Babington's letters to her, and the declarations and confessions which had been extorted from her secretaries, he maintained that the case was made out, and wound up his speech with a laboured display of legal knowledge and forensic oratory.

She was now called upon for her defence; and she entered upon it with dignity and composure. She denied all connection with Babington's conspiracy, in so far as he entertained any designs injurious to Elizabeth's safety or the welfare of her kingdom. She allowed that the letters which he had addressed to her might be genuine, but there was no proof that she ever received them. She maintained that her own letters were all garbled or fabricated; that, as to the confessions of her secretaries, they had been extorted by fear, and were, therefore, not to be relied on; but that, if they were in any particulars true, they must have been disclosed at the expense of the oath of fidelity they had come under to her when they entered her service; and that men who would perjure themselves in one instance, were not to be trusted in any. She objected, besides, that they had not been confronted with her, according to an express law of the thirteenth of Elizabeth, "that no one should be arraigned for intending the destruction of the Prince's life, but by the testimony and oath of two lawful witnesses, to be produced face to face before him:" she maintained that, even supposing she were to allow the authenticity of many of the papers adduced against her, they would not prove her guilty of any crime; for she was surely doing no wrong if, after a calamitous captivity of nineteen years, in which she had lost for ever her youth, her health, and her happiness, she made one last effort to regain the liberty of which she had been so unfairly robbed; but that, as to scheming against the life of the Queen, her sister, it was an infamy she abhorred: "I would disdain," she said, "to purchase all that is most valuable on earth by the assassination of the meanest of the human race; and, worn out as I now am with cares and suffering, the prospect of a crown is not so inviting that I should ruin my soul in order to obtain it. Neither am I a stranger to the feelings of humanity, nor unacquainted with the duties of religion, and it is my nature to be more inclined to the devotion of Esther than to the sword of Judith. If ever I have given consent by my words, or even by my thoughts, to any attempt against the life of the Queen of England, far from declining the judgment of men, I shall not even pray for the mercy of God."

Elizabeth's advocates were not a little surprised at the eloquent and able manner in which Mary conducted her defence. They had expected to have every thing their own way, and to gain an easy victory over one unacquainted with the forms of legal procedure, and unable to cope with their own professional talents. But they were disappointed and baffled; and, in order to maintain their ground even plausibly, they were obliged to protract the proceedings for two whole days. Nor, after all, did the commissioners venture to pronounce judgment, but adjourned the court to the Star-Chamber at Westminster, where they knew that Mary would not be present, and where, consequently, they would have no opposition to fear. On the twenty-fifth of October, they assembled there, and having again examined the secretaries Nawe and Curll, and who confirmed their former declarations, a unanimous judgment was delivered, that "Mary, commonly called Queen of Scots, and Dowager of France, was accessory to Babington's conspiracy, and had compassed and imagined divers matters within the realm of England, tending to the hurt, death, and destruction of the royal person of Elizabeth, in opposition to the statute framed for her protection."

The same day, the lords commissioners, and judges of the realm, declared:—"That this sentence did derogate nothing from the right or honour of James, King of Scotland; but that he remained, and was in the same rank, estate, and right as if it had never been." A few days afterwards, the Parliament approved and confirmed the sentence pronounced against the Queen of Scotland: all with one accord (by the Lord Chancellor) presented a petition to the Queen, wherein they desired, that, for the preservation of the true religion of Christ, the tranquillity of the land, the security of her person, the good of them all and their posterity, the sentence against Mary, Queen of Scots, might be publicly pronounced, according to the tenor of the law; alleging reasons drawn from the dangers stirred and practised against religion, her own person, and the realm, by her who was a mother-nurse of the Roman religion, and had sworn an inviolable accord to extirpate the religion now established, and had long since laid claim to the crown, Queen Elizabeth yet living; esteeming that (seeing she was excommunicated) it was lawful to conspire against her, and meritorious to take away her life. She had ruined some noble houses of the land, and had kindled the fire of rebellion in England. That to pardon her were to destroy the people, who much repined at her impunity; and that she could not be freed from the oath of conspiracy, otherwise than by punishment. And, lastly, they recited the example of the awful vengeance of God against King Saul, for not putting Agag and Benadad to death."

In reply to this address, Elizabeth said—"Now my life hath been attempted to be taken away, it grieveth me most, that it was by such a person as was of mine own sex, estate, and rank; to whom I was so far from bearing ill-will, that, on the contrary, after she had plotted divers matters against me, I wrote to her in private, that if in any writing secretly she would acknowledge them, I would bury them all in oblivion. Neither would I have done this to entrap her; for I knew already all she could confess: and, although the matter was at that pass, yet if she had but shewed herself truly penitent, none would have taken her cause against me in hand. Nevertheless, if only it had concerned mine own life, and not the safe-guard of my people (without ostentation be it spoken), I would willingly have pardoned her. If England by my death might flourish the more, or gain a better prince, I could be well content to lay down my life; for I desire to live solely for your good and that of my people. As touching these late treasons, I will not so much prejudice either myself, or the ancient laws of my country, in such fashion, as not to think this arch treason to be subject thereto, although this new law had never been made; the which (although some favourers of her have suspected so) was not made against her, but was so far from entangling her, that it was rather a pre-admonition to her not to come within the danger of it; nevertheless, you have, by this new law, brought me into such a narrow strait, that I am to determine upon the punishment of a Princess, my next kinswoman; whose practices have afflicted me with so great a grief, that, not to augment my sorrows in hearing it spoken of, I did willingly absent myself from this Parliament, and not (as some think) for fear of treachery. Notwithstanding, I will not leave (although I use few words of it) to put this secret out of my heart, which I have seen with mine eyes, and read the oath, by which some have bound themselves to dispatch me within one month. From hence I foresee your danger in my person, and certainly I shall be careful and diligent to repel it. But forasmuch as the matter now in hand is an example as important as rare, I deem you expect not that I should resolve anything for the present: for my manner is, even in things of less consequence, to be long in deliberating about that I must once resolve upon. I will pray to God Almighty, that he will illuminate my heart, to foresee what is commodious for the church, the commonwealth, and your safeties. Notwithstanding, lest delay should bring danger, you shall (as the opportunity of time will serve) understand my purpose. In the meantime, I would you should expect all the goodness from me, which good subjects may look for from a good Princess."

Twelve days afterwards, she sent the Lord Chancellor to the House of Lords, and Pickering to the Commons, entreating them to more seriously consider the matter, and to devise some more wholesome remedy, that the Queen of Scotland's life might be preserved and secured. After they had deliberated a long time, and considered that the good or ill of Princes concerneth their subjects, they, with one according voice, all adopted the same resolution which they had done before, grounded upon these reasons:—"That so long as the Queen of Scotland lived, Queen Elizabeth could not be secure, unless she would become penitent, and acknowledge her crimes; and that she should be kept more straitly, and bound by oath and writing; or that she should deliver hostages; or that she should depart the kingdom. Of her repentance they had no hope, for she had been ungrateful to Queen Elizabeth, who had saved her life, and would not so much as acknowledge her faults; as for a straiter guard, her hand-writing, oath, or hostages, they would be all as nothing; for that when Queen Elizabeth died, all these would vanish away instantly. As for departing the land (if she were out of it), they feared she would raise arms against it."

The Lord Chancellor and the Speaker of the Commons declared this resolution of the parliament to Elizabeth; importuning her earnestly, that the sentence should be put into execution: shewing her, "That if it were injustice to deny the execution of the law to the meanest subject, much greater would it be to refuse to grant it to the whole body of the people, who with one voice and will demanded it." To which she replied:—

"O how wearisome is that way where we find nothing but irksomeness whilst we are going in it; and when 'tis past, inquietudes! I am troubled this day (if ever the like) whether to speak or to hold my tongue; if I should speak, and not complain, I dissemble; if I hold my tongue, the pains you have taken are in vain; if I complain, it will seem strange; notwithstanding, I confess that my first request was both for your security, and mine own. Some other means should have been found out than what you now propound; insomuch, that I cannot but complain to you, though not of you; for that I learn by your demands, that my safety dependeth upon another's ruin. If any think that I have purposely prolonged the time, to purchase a counterfeit praise of clemency, undoubtedly they wrong me unworthily; and greater wrong they do me if they think that the commissioners durst pronounce no other sentence for fear of displeasing me, or seeming to neglect my safety. However, because it now clearly appeareth, that I cannot be safe unless she die, I am touched with a deep dolour. As concerning your demand, I entreat and charge you, to be content with this my answer. I commend your judgment, and apprehend the reasons thereof. But excuse me, I pray, for that doubtful perplexity of thought, which troubleth me. If I say I will not comply with your demand, by my faith! I shall say unto you more, perhaps, than I mean. If I should say that I mean to grant it, I should tell you more than is fit for you to know; thus I must deliver to you an answer, answerless." After this, the parliament was prorogued.

On the twenty-second of November Lord Buckhurst and Beale were despatched to announce to Mary, that judgment was given against her; that it was confirmed by authority of parliament, and its execution demanded for the sake of justice, security, and necessity. They, therefore, exhorted her, that after she had acknowledged her offences to God and Queen Elizabeth, to satisfy herself by repentance before she died; for, if she lived, the reformed religion in England could not stand. She replied, that "the judgment was unjust;" refused the Protestant bishop and the dean whom they recommended to her, and desired a Catholic priest to direct her conscience, and to administer the sacraments; she also greatly blamed the English nation, saying often:—"The English have many times murdered their kings; and it is no strange thing if they do the like to me, who am derived of their royal blood." The sentence was proclaimed in the month of December, with the sound of a trumpet, through the City of London, in presence of the Lord Mayor, the Sheriffs, and the Aldermen. Elizabeth protested that she had been drawn into it by necessity, and the earnest request of parliament. On the awful tidings reaching the ears of Mary, she, by permission of her keeper, Sir Amias Poulet, wrote the following affecting epistle to Elizabeth:—

"I put off all malice of heart towards you; giving thanks to God for this condemnation, seeing it was his good pleasure to terminate the irksome pilgrimage which I have had in this life; and I desire, for I can expect no good from hot-headed innovators, who hold the chiefest rank in England, that I may be beholden to you alone, and no other, for the benefits following: — First, that when my adversaries are glutted with my innocent blood, my body may be carried from thence, by my own servants, to some sacred and hallowed ground, there to be buried; and above all, into France, where my mother lyeth in rest; seeing that, in Scotland, they had offered violence to the dead bodies of my ancestors, profaned or despoiled the churches; and in England, I can hope for no burial, according to the Catholic solemnities, amongst the ancient kings my ancestors; and so my body, that never had rest so long as it was joined to my soul, may have some at last, after it has parted from it.

"Secondly, fearing the close tyranny of some, I desire that I may not suffer my punishment unknown to the Queen of England, in some secret place, but in the sight of my servants, and other people, that they may truly bear witness of my faith in Christ, of my obedience to the church, and of the end of my life, against the false testimony which my adversaries may declare abroad. — Thirdly, I desire that my servants may be suffered peaceably to depart whither they will, and to enjoy the legacies I have bequeathed them by my will. I beseech you, in the name of Jesus Christ, to grant me these things, by virtue of our alliance in blood, by the sacred memory of Henry the Seventh, our common progenitor, and by the princely honour which sometimes you display. I have great cause of complaint, that all my princely robes were taken away, by command of the councillors. I fear their malice will extend to worse things. If they had but shewn me, without fraud or falsehood, the papers which they took from me, it would clearly have appeared by them, that nothing would have caused my untimely death, but the doubtful care which some had of your Majesty's safety. Finally, I entreat you to return me an answer under your own hand, touching these things."

But, alas! no answer was returned by her unfeeling kinswoman.

In calmly weighing the conduct of Elizabeth and her Parliament, the intelligent part of the community considered that the unfortunate Mary was being cruelly dealt with. They reasoned that she was an absolute and free Princess, over whom God alone had the command; that she was very nearly allied to Queen Elizabeth; and that, being driven out of Scotland by her rebellious subjects, she had no sooner arrived in England, than Queen Elizabeth promised her, upon her princely word, by Henry Mildmore, to show her all courtesy, and to welcome her with all hospitality. Yet, contrary to this promise, she imprisoned her, and violated those sacred rights. That she could only be considered as a prisoner of war; and to such it was lawful to practise any means to effect her liberty and freedom. That she could not commit treason, because she was no subject; and that none hath power over an equal. That this circumstance had caused to be disannulled the sentence of the Emperor of Austria against Robert, King of Sicily, because he was not subject to his empire. That if ambassadors, who are but the servants of princes, shall conspire against those to whom they are employed in embassy, they are not culpable of treason, much less the princes themselves; and that the will ought not to be punished, unless it take effect. That it was a thing unheard of, for a queen to pass under the hands of a common executioner. That she was condemned contrary to the law of God, the Roman civil law, and the English; yea, even against the statute of the thirteenth of Elizabeth, whereby it was ordained, "That no person should be called into judgment for having attempted the ruin of the prince, but upon the testimony and oath of two lawful witnesses, who should be brought face to face before the accused;" whilst no witness was produced against her on her trial, but she was condemned from the testimony of two absent secretaries. Others loudly complained, that spies had been suborned, who, by forgery, false letters, and deceitful practices, had deluded the Princess, and exposed her to machinations, of which she would not even have dreamt, had she been left to that quiet and repose which was requisite in her situation. That, in short, a cruel, base, and unmanly advantage was taken of an unfortunate captive Princess, utterly powerless, and unable to contend against the malignity of a jealous Queen, and an enslaved, fawning, and persecuting Parliament.

CHAPTER X.

James the Sixth intercedes with Elizabeth for his mother—The King of France endeavours to save her—Elizabeth's reply to the King of France—Conspiracy of the French Ambassador—Elizabeth terrified by false reports—She at length signs the warrant for Mary's execution—Mary prepares for death—Her heroic behaviour and execution.

IN the meantime, James the Sixth, the youthful King of Scotland, who bore his unfortunate mother but little affection, was prevailed upon to write to Elizabeth:—"That it was most unjust, that the nobles, the councillors, and subjects of England should give sentence against a Queen of Scotland, born of the English blood; and as unjust also, that the Parliament should exclude the true heirs from the right of succession, and their lawful inheritance." He also sent Patrick Gray and Robert Melvin to declare to Elizabeth—"That the great proximity betwixt them would not let him believe that she would violate that renowned reputation which she from all parts had purchased by her virtues; and especially by her merciful policy, unstained hitherto by any spot of cruelty;" and to entreat her to spare the life of his unfortunate mother, Mary. But as they themselves secretly desired the death of the Queen of Scots, their efforts were ineffectual.

In November, an extraordinary ambassador arrived from France, to intercede for the condemned Princess. Accompanied by M. de Chateauneuf, the ordinary ambassador, he had audience with Elizabeth, and strenuously urged her not to carry the sentence against Mary into execution. Elizabeth replied, in a tone of asperity: "That the Queen of England hoped, that the most Christian King of France made no less reckoning of her than of the Queen of Scotland, who had practised her destruction; that whilst Mary liveth, there will always be new plots of mischief breeding; especially, because it is now come to that issue, that there is no hope left for the one, if the other be not extinct! In verity, either I shall dispatch her, or she me! And the shorter time her life shall last, the more celerity will the conspirators use to execute their plots. For whatever cause she was put in prison, she is to be punished for the fault she hath committed since the time of her imprisonment! And as she hath been found guilty by a just judgment, she ought to undergo punishment; for that which is just is honest, and that which is honest is also profitable. That punishment of death, justly inflicted, cannot be accounted bloody, no more than a wholesome medicine can be deemed hurtful. Howsoever the Guises, the Queen of Scotland's cousins, relish it, Queen Elizabeth hath more nearer cause to respect herself, her own safety, her nobility, and the good of her people, on whose love she wholly dependeth, than the discontent of any other whatsoever; and that the matter was now at that point, that the old proverb of the two Princes, Conradine, King of Sicily, and Charles, Duke of Anjou, might be used, and truly said of these two Queens:—'The death of Mary—the life of Elizabeth; and the life of Mary—the death of Elizabeth.'"

D'Aubespine, the ambassador for France in England, who was of the faction of the Guises, thinking that, if he could not by argument or reasons deliver the Queen of Scotland, he might yet do so by some mischievous craft, treated privately, first with one William Stafford, a youth, whose mother was one of the ladies of honour, about the killing of Queen Elizabeth. At first, he dealt with him in an under-hand way, but afterwards more plainly, by his secretary, Trappe, who promised him, if he performed the deed, that he should have thereby, not only great glory and a large sum of money, but also exceeding favour from his holiness the Pope of Rome, the Guises, and all true Catholics. Stafford, loathing such a monstrous mischief, declined the proposal: but, notwithstanding, mentioned to him one Modey, as a fit fellow to be employed in such an atrocity, and one who would use dispatch, though the murder were ever so bloody, for money. This Modey was a prisoner in London, and to whom Stafford made it known, that the French ambassador desired to speak with him. He answered, that he desired the same, if he were out of prison; entreating him, in the meantime, to speak with Cordalion, the ambassador's under-secretary, who was his familiar friend. The morrow after, Trappe and Stafford were sent to him; when Trappe (Stafford stepping apart) entered into conversation with Modey—how, and by what means, they might kill Queen Elizabeth. Modey advised to have it done by poison, or by bringing privately into the Queen's chamber a barrel of gunpowder, to be secretly set on fire. But Trappe did not like either of these modes, he being desirous of finding a resolute fellow who feared nothing—such a one as Bourgoignon, who slew the Prince of Orange.

Stafford quickly revealed this matter to the council, and Trappe, now preparing to set out for France, was apprehended, and, being examined, confessed the whole affair. Hereupon, on the twelfth of January, 1587, the ambassador was sent for to Lord Burleigh's, whither he came in the evening, and found assembled, by command of the Queen, the Lord High Treasurer, the Earl of Leicester, Sir Christopher Hatton (Vice-Chamberlain), and Mr. Secretary Davison, who declared, that they had invited him thither to acquaint him with the cause why they had arrested his secretary, Trappe, being on his way to France; and then informed him of the whole matter, as Stafford, Modey, and Trappe had confessed; and they had caused them to be brought in, to testify the same before his face. The ambassador, with great impatience, and bending his brows, stood up and declared, that he, being the King's ambassador, would not abuse his master, the King of France, nor prejudice other ambassadors in such a way as to be a hearer of accusations, be they what they may. But Cecil having answered him, that these things were not produced as accusations against him, but to let him perceive that they were neither false nor feigned, and to the end that he might take occasion to convict Stafford the more easily of calumny, he became more quiet. But as soon as Stafford came in, and had begun to speak, he interrupted him in a contemptuous manner, and swore that this fellow, Stafford, had first mentioned the matter to him, and that he had threatened to send him, bound hand and foot, to the Queen of England, if he dared to mention that affair again: and that, at the time, he forgave him, for the love and affection he had to his mother, his brother and sister. Stafford, falling on his knees, protested many times, as he hoped to be saved, that the ambassador had first broken the matter to him. The ambassador was then more angry than before; Stafford was ordered out of the room, and Modey was not even permitted to come in! Hereupon Lord Burleigh, out of his own words, and from the confession of Trappe, reproved him, but somewhat gently, for this intended mischief. The ambassador answered—"If he had been guilty, or acquainted with the matter, yet, as being an ambassador, he was not bound to reveal it to any but to his own King."

Burleigh answering, said:—"Admit it be not the part of an ambassador (which yet is a questionable matter) to discover such affairs only to their own King, still, when the life of a Prince is at stake, it is the part of a Christian to prevent such enormities; not only when the life of a Princess is concerned, but even that of any private Christian." This he stoutly denied, and recited the example of a French ambassador not long ago in Spain, who, knowing of a treacherous design against the King of Spain, although it affected his life, yet he discovered it not to him, but to his own King; for which he received great commendation, both of his King and council." Nevertheless, Lord Burleigh very gravely admonished him, hereafter to have a care how he offended her Majesty, and not to forget his duty, and the merciful disposition of her Majesty, who was loth to offend the good ambassadors, by punishing the bad.

From this attempt, the sworn enemies of the Queen of Scotland sought to do her hurt, and took advantage thereby to hasten her death; knowing that, in cases of extreme danger, fear leaveth no place for mercy, they added to the terrors of Elizabeth; spread alarming rumours, to the effect that:—

The Spanish fleet was already landed at Milford-Haven.

The Scots had arrived upon the borders of England.

The Duke de Guise was in Essex with a mighty army.

The Queen of Scots had broken prison, raised a great troop of soldiers, and began a rebellion in the North.

There were new plots in hand for murdering the Queen, and to burn the City of London; and, finally, that the Queen of England was dead!

By these and other alarming reports, by her own malice and fears, and by the importunities of her flattering advisers; Elizabeth was brought into such trouble and perplexity of mind, that she forthwith signed Mary's death warrant; being most of all urged to it by Patrick Gray, an infamous Scotchman, whom the King of Scotland had expressly sent to dissuade the Queen of England from putting his royal parent to death; but who grossly betrayed his sacred mission, continually and insiduously pouring these venomous words into the ears of Elizabeth—we blush for human nature as we record them—*Mortua non mordet:* "Being dead, she will bite no more!"

The courtiers were not alone in their thirst for the blood of the unfortunate Mary; but divers fiery-tongued preachers, also, forgetful of the precepts of their Divine Master, took occasion to exercise, with all fiend-like asperity, the heat of their desire, in urging the Queen to haste the death of the captive and now condemned Princess.

Wavering and undecided, Elizabeth now passed several days in gloomy solitude, frequently sighing deeply, and muttering, *Aut petre aut percute;* "Prevent the stroke by striking." Amidst these sensations, she at length signed the fatal warrant under the great seal of England, for the execution of her kinswoman, and delivered it to her secretary, Davison, to keep it private, as she alleged afterwards, not acquainting any therewith, lest haply, in this turbulent time of fear, some sudden violent danger might happen; or, in other words, that some means might be found to assassinate the Queen of Scots in prison. But the morrow after, some sudden affright mixing itself with her pensive thoughts and meditations, she changed her former purpose, and commanded Davison to dispatch the warrant forthwith. The secretary told her it was ready, and sealed. Then she grew very angry, saying, "He was too hasty!" But for all this, he went directly and laid the warrant before the council; who willingly believing what they so earnestly desired, that the Queen had given her commands for the execution; and, unknown to her, sent Beale, who, from a fervour of zeal which he bore to religion (!), was more easily bent against the Queen of Scotland than any other, with two executioners, and letters patent, granting authority to the Earls of Shrewsbury, Kent, Derby, Cumberland, and others, to proceed in this execution. And the Queen had told Davison that she had a purpose of dealing otherwise with the Queen of Scotland; yet, for all that, he did not stay or detain Beale.

On reaching Fotheringham Castle, the Earls found the unhappy Queen of Scotland with Sir Amias Poulet and Sir Drue Drury, to whose custody she had been committed; and then reading the fatal mandate, they admonished her to prepare herself to die the next morning. Mary, with heroic courage, answered;—"I never thought that my sister, the Queen of England, would have consented to my death, seeing I am not subject to your laws; but, since her pleasure is such, death to me shall be most welcome! And surely that soul were not worthy the eternal joys of Heaven, whose body cannot endure one stroke of a headsman!"

She desired them to send to her her almoner, her confessor, and Melvin, her steward. They refused to send her her confessor, and appointed for her comforters the Bishop and Dean of Peterborough, whose services she declined. Thereupon the Earl of Kent, a zealous professor of religion, remarked :—"Your life will be the death, and your death the life of our religion." Then, having alluded to Babington, she solemnly affirmed she never knew of his practices. She left the due revenge of all to God; and, inquiring what had become of Naw and Curll, she asked, "If ever it was heard of, in former times, that the servants should be suborned to betray their lady mistress to death, and also be admitted as evidences against her?"

When the Earls were departed, she supped, as her manner ever was, very temperately, and seeing her servants, both men and women, weeping and mourning, she comforted them, and bade them wipe their eyes, and rather rejoice with her, for that she was now about to depart from this gulf of miseries. Supper being nearly over, she drank the health of all her servants; who, in order, one by one, upon their knees took her pledge, mingling their tears with the wine, and craving pardon of her for whatever they had been negligent of in their duties; so did she likewise of them. After supper she perused her will, looked over the inventory of her wardrobe and jewels, and inserted the names of those to whom she had bequeathed any thing. To some of them she distributed money with her own hands. She wrote also to her confessor, desiring him to pray for her; aud to the King of France and the Duke of Guise she recommended her servants. This duty over, she retired to rest, slept a few hours, and, awaking, passed the rest of the night in prayer.

At the dawn of that fatal day, the seventh of February, she attired herself in such garments as she usually wore upon festival days; and calling her servants around her, she caused her will to be read, desiring them to take in good part the legacies she had given them, seeing it was not in her power to make them better. Then, wholly fixing her mind upon God, she betook herself to her oratory, where, with sighs and fervent prayers, she called upon God; till such time as the sheriff of the county signified to her, that she must come forth! Then forth she came, in carriage and demeanour princely and majestic; cheerful in countenance, and in attire modest and matron-like; she wore a linen veil over her head and before her face, which was uncovered; at her girdle hung her rosary, or row of beads, and in her hand she held a crucifix of ivory.

In the porch, or passage of her apartments, met her the Earl of Kent, and the other noblemen, where Melvin, one of her servants, falling on his knees, and pouring forth tears, bewailed his unlucky fate, that he was doomed to carry into Scotland the sad tidings of the tragical death of his beloved mistress. "Oh! weep not!" said the afflicted Queen, "for you shall shortly see Mary Stuart at the end of all her sorrows. You will report, that I die true and constant in my religion, and firm in my love to Scotland and to France. God forgive them who have thirsted after my blood, as the hart doth for the water-brook."

Tears flowed in torrents from her eyes; she repeated again and again, "Adieu—Adieu! Melvin!" he weeping all the while no less lamentably than his royal mistress. Then, turning herself towards the Earls, she entreated them, that her servants might be gently treated, that they might enjoy the things she had given them by her will, that they might be permitted to be with her at her death, and, lastly, that they might be safely sent home to their respective countries. Her first two requests were granted, but the Earl of Kent scrupled to comply with the last; when she said:—"Fear you not, Sir; the poor creatures desire nothing but to take their last leave of me; and I know my sister, the Queen of England, would not that you should deny me so small a request." The Earl then acceded to her wishes, and she named Melvin, Bourgoine (her physician), her apothecary, her surgeon, two of her maids, and some others; Melvin carrying up her train.

Then the noblemen, the two earls, and the sheriff of the county, going before, she came to the scaffold, which was erected at the upper end of the hall, upon which was a chair, a cushion, and a block, all covered with black. As soon as she was seated, and silence commanded, Beale read the warrant of execution, and Dr. Fletcher, Dean of Peterborough, made a long discourse on the condition of her life, past and present, and of the life to come. Twice she interrupted him, entreating him not to importune her; protesting that she was settled and resolved in the ancient Roman Catholic religion, and ready even now to shed her blood for the same. He vehemently exhorted her to be repentant, and with an undoubted faith to put her whole trust and confidence in Christ: but she answered him: That she had been born and brought up in this religion, and was ready to die in the same. Then the Earls offered to pray for her, but she replied, she would thank them if they would pray together with her, but to communicate in prayer with those of a different religion, were scandal and sin. Then they desired the Dean to pray, with whom, whilst the assembly about him joined in prayer, she, falling upon her knees, and holding the crucifix betwixt her hands, prayed in Latin with her own people, out of "The Office of our Blessed Lady." After the Dean had ended his prayers, she prayed in English for the church, for her son, and for Elizabeth, Queen of England. She forgave all her enemies, and kissing the crucifix, said, "As thy arms, O Lord Jesus Christ! were spread forth upon the cross, so receive me into the same arms of thy mercy, and pardon me my trespasses."

Then the executioner asked and received her forgiveness, and her servants took off her upper garments, crying and lamenting aloud; yet she remained in cheerful countenance, and bade them forbear their womanish weeping, saying, "Weep not, for I am at the end of all my calamities." Likewise, turning towards her other servants, who were most piteously weeping, she touched them with the sign of the cross, and smilingly bade them all an eternal adieu! Then, having a linen cloth before her face, she laid her head upon the block, reciting the psalm, "In thee, O Lord, have I put my trust, let me not be confounded for ever." Then, stretching forth her body, and many times repeating with ardour and devotion these words, "Lord, into thy hands I commend my spirit;" her head, at the third blow, was cut off, the Dean crying aloud, "So perish all the enemies of Queen Elizabeth!" to which the Earl of Kent responded, "So perish all the enemies of the gospel!" and the people being all absorbed in admiration and pity, not a voice was heard to cry "Amen!"

Thus died the beautiful, the pious, the ill-fated Mary, Queen of Scots, in the forty-sixth year of her age, and the eighteenth of her imprisonment.

CHAPTER XI.

Elizabeth's letter to James the Sixth—Grief of James—Indignation of the Scots on learning the death of Mary—Trial and condemnation of Secretary Davison for causing Mary to be beheaded without the knowledge of Elizabeth—Opinions of the judges—Davison's extraordinary private apology—Barbarous cruelties perpetrated by Elizabeth's sanction—Threatened invasion of Spain—Preparations against the Spanish Armada—Elizabeth's visit to the camp at Tilbury—Her speech to the soldiers.

MMEDIATELY the news of the death of Mary was brought to Elizabeth, who, it is alleged by all her defenders, was all this time unconscious of what had happened, she took it most impatiently to heart; her speech and countenance at once failed her; through the extremity of her grievous discontent, she became quite comfortless and disconsolate; and, attired in mourning weeds, she bitterly lamented the cruel part she had acted, and shed an abundance of tears. She sent for her council, and sharply rebuked them for their precipitancy, chased them out of her sight, and commanded them to be questioned on the subject. As for her unfortunate secretary, Davison, who had imagined he was acting the part of a zealous and faithful servant, she ordered him instantly to be brought into the Star Chamber, to be dealt with according to law! And as soon as her affected anguish and sorrow suffered her to write, she addressed the following letter to James the Sixth in her own handwriting, and dispatched it by the hands of Sir Robert Carey:—

"My dear brother,

"I would you knew (though not felt) the extreme dolour that overwhelms my mind for that miserable accident which (far contrary to my meaning) hath befallen. I have now sent this kinsman of mine, whom ere now it hath you to favour, to instruct you truly of that which is too irksome for my pen to tell you. I beseech you, that as God and many more know how innocent I am in this case, so you will believe me, that if I had directed ought, I would abide by it. I am not so base-minded that fear of any living creature or prince should make me afraid to do that were just, or deign to deny the same. I am not of so base a lineage nor carry so vile a mind, but as not to disguise fits not a king, so will I never dissemble my actions, but cause them shewn even as I meant them, thus; assuring yourself of me that as I know this was deserved, yet if I had meant it I would lay it on others' shoulders; no more will I not damnifie myself that thought it not; the circumstance it may please you to have of this bearer, and for your part, think you have not in the world a more loving kinswoman nor a more dear friend than myself, nor any that will watch more carefully to preserve you and your estate, and who shall otherwise persuade you, judge them more partial to others than you, and thus in haste I leave to trouble you, beseeching God to send you a long reign.

"Your most assured loving sister and cousin, "Elizabeth R.

"The 14th of February, 1506."

The sorrow, whether real or affected, which Elizabeth felt for the death of the Queen of Scotland, was not to be compared with that experienced by the King of Scotland. His anguish and irritation was so great, that he refused to receive in Scotland Sir Robert Carey, the son of Lord Hunsdon, who was sent with letters from Elizabeth to excuse her Majesty, and to cast the fault upon Davison and her council. He heard him but partly, and that from the mouth of another, and hardly received the letters he brought. He revoked the authority of his ambassador in England, and thought only of revenge for so great and grievous an injury offered to majesty and to the royal name. The Estates of Scotland, which were then assembled, protested to his Majesty, that they were ready and willing to revenge Mary's death, which they pronounced to be an injury and insult to the whole nation of Scotland. However, Elizabeth appeased the vengeance of James with a present of four thousand pounds, and her emissaries induced him to consider the death of his mother as a personal benefit to himself, as it had relieved him from the fears of a rival for his throne.

Whilst Sir Robert Carey was on his way to Scotland, to appease the wrath of King James, Elizabeth, alarmed at the consequences likely to ensue from the violent death of Mary, vented her rage upon her unhappy secretary, Davison, and immediately ordered him to be brought into the Star Chamber, before certain commissioners, viz.—Sir Christopher Wray, Lord Chief Justice of the Queen's Bench, who, for that time, was likewise made Lord Keeper of the Privy Seal; the Archbishops of Canterbury and York; the Earls of Worcester, Cumberland, and Lincoln; the Lords Grey and Lumley; Sir James Crofts, Comptroller of the Queen's House; Sir Walter Mildmay, Chancellor of the Exchequer; Sir Gilbert Gerard, Master of the Rolls; Chief Justice Anderson, of the Common Pleas; and Sir Roger Manwood, Chief Baron of the Exchequer. In the presence of these, Sir Francis Popham, Attorney-General, accused William Davison of contempt against her Majesty, of the breach of his allegiance, the neglect and omission of his duty, in causing Mary to be put to death, without the consent or knowledge of Elizabeth. Davison answered, "That he was sorry that he should be thus called before commissioners, touching the Queen of Scotland, and the judgment given against her, to the impeachment of his credit, if not to the final loss thereof. It grieved him to be accused of contempt against her Majesty, to whom, for her princely favours, he was so indebted, that his offence must thereby be the more intolerable. He confessed himself guilty of the crimes alleged against him. If in making his apology he should contest with the Queen, he should do that which was most unbeseeming the obedience of a subject, the respect of a servant, and the fidelity and reputation of a secretary. He protested that he had done nothing therein wittingly and willingly, but what he was persuaded was the Queen's will and pleasure. The Queen blamed him for having been overhasty in setting the great seal to the mandate; he declared, That she had darkly signified, but not expressly commanded, that he should keep it by him. Neither, as he thought, had he trespassed in a matter of secrecy, for he had not imparted it to any but the council. As to not revoking the warrant, after the Queen had given him to understand that she had altered her mind, he affirmed that it was agreed upon by the general consent of the council, that forthwith the warrant should be put in force, and the Queen of Scotland executed, for fear the Queen or state might be endangered." After this confession, Sir Thomas Egerton, the Queen's Solicitor-General, having read some part of it, began to question him. But he desired him to read it all through, and not select particular passages, though he would rather it were not read at all, because in it were contained some secrets not fit to be revealed.

Sir Thomas Gandy and Sir William Pickering, the Queen's Serjeants-at-law, declared that he had deceived the council by a false assurance that the Queen had granted that they should proceed to the execution of the Queen of Scotland. Here Davison, shedding tears, desired the lawyers not to urge him any further, but to remember, that he was not there to contest against the Queen; wherefore he wholly submitted himself to her Majesty's conscience, and to the censure of the commissioners.

The sentiments of the commissioners on the subject are so singular, that we cannot refrain from giving them at length, with Davison's extraordinary private apology, which will throw great light on this remarkable question, as to the guilt or innocence of Elizabeth, in the murder of one of the most unfortunate women of her times. Sir Roger Manwood, beginning, made an historical relation of the acts of the Queen of Scotland; how, from her tender age, she had usurped the arms of England; [this was the secret of all Elizabeth's animosity] and, continuing his discourse to Babington's conspiracy, he commended the sentence pronounced against her, by virtue of the law, made known the clemency of the Queen, and gave judgment, that Davison, for his inconsiderate anticipation, should be fined ten thousand pounds, and imprisoned during the Queen's pleasure. Sir Walter Mildmay, after declaring with what mature deliberation and settled gravity they had proceeded in judgment against the Queen of Scots, produced against Davison this passage from scripture, "The heart of the King is in the hands of the Lord;" and therefore none, much less a servant, ought fraudulently or covertly to anticipate the determinate purpose of princes, without whose advice nothing ought to be done, especially in matters of so great moment as the death of a prince. But he cleared Davison of malice; yet reproved him, as having been inconsiderate in princes' affairs, and too forward in preventing the Queen's determination. And for a caveat hereafter, to men of his rank and station, not to commit the like error, accorded with Sir Roger Manwood concerning his fine and imprisonment.

Sir Jacob Croft checked and chid him for having unwisely uttered the things which he ought to have concealed, for that princes impart that to some of their council, which they conceal from the rest. Baron Lumley was of opinion, with the judges, that the sentence against the Queen of Scots was justly given; yet seriously averred, that in the memory of precedent times, it was never heard or read of, so high a contempt to have been committed against a prince, as that the lords of the council, in the Queen's house, at the council table, where her Majesty was, as it were, President of the Council, should have decreed such a matter; and that without her privity, they, and Davison too, having free access unto her when they pleased; protesting, that if he had but one only son who was faulty in such a fact, he should deem him deserving of a very severe punishment. But being persuaded of the honest disposition of the man, he would condemn him to no further punishment than the other judges proposed.

Lord Grey, inflamed with religious zeal, in a set speech, yet somewhat exasperate, proceeded to say:—"Davison is accused with having behaved himself contemptuously against the Queen; and this contempt is urged to the full; for that he employed his diligence in dispatching the Queen of Scots; that he betrayed secrets, and concealed from the Queen the sending away of the warrant. But who was this Queen he was so busy in making away with? Was it not she, I pray you, by whose life our religion, the Queen, the kingdom, and every one of us were in continual danger? Yet it is for her being so cut off, that we have this day's business in hand! Now my opinion is, that he who hath delivered our country from such great evils deserves to be royally recompensed. I do not think he has revealed any secrets, for he imparted the matter only to the council, and the magistrates appointed for state affairs, whom chiefly it concerned to understand that and such like, and which the Queen herself before had uttered to several persons. If Davison have offended in any thing, it is chiefly in this, that the Queen meaning to take another course, he told her not that the warrant was already sent away. But unquestionably he was driven into a double doubt; whether to lose the Queen's favour in sending away the warrant without her knowledge, or by recalling it, to bring new plots and perils to the Queen. Who remembereth not how turbulent the time was? What fearful rumours were everywhere dispersed? If any wrong or violence had then happened to the Queen or our religion, whilst the mandate was in his hands, had not the fault truly been in him? Should not we, our wives, and children, have fallen furiously upon him?

Should we not have imbrued our hands in his blood—have cursed his imprudence, and have erected to his eternal ignominy a trophy of indiscretion, engraven in letters of blood? What mulct or penalty soever you impose upon him shall not displease me; but surely I will always hold him for an honest man." "This orator-like speech," says our historian, "which we heard Lord Gray make, was delivered with a good grace, and manly countenance."

The three Earls agreed in opinion with the rest, concerning the proposed penalty to be inflicted upon Davison, and with Lord Gray touching his reputation. The Archbishop of York discoursed on matters of religion, and shewed that blindness of heart, and natural corruption, were the fountains from whence evil floweth! The Archbishop of Canterbury approved the act, and commended the author of it, but disapproved withal the manner of proceeding adopted by Davison. Lastly, the Lord Keeper of the Privy Seal, having briefly recapitulated all the opinions of the commissioners, confirmed the penalty imposed by them, and declared, "That although the Queen, being justly moved to displeasure, had submitted her councillors to examination, yet, notwithstanding, she did then pardon them; acknowledging that what they had done was from a desire and design tending to the defence of religion and the state, and the repelling of imminent dangers."

Davison then humbly petitioned the commissioners, that they would entreat for him—not to be restored to the honourable place of secretary, nor to have his liberty granted him—nor his fine or punishment mitigated, but that he might yet be a partaker of her Majesty's gracious favour! The which, for all this, he never regained; nevertheless, the Queen sometimes supplied and relieved his wants!

Thus the secretary of Queen Elizabeth, a man of honest disposition and much esteem, not cunning, nor acquainted with the tricks of court, was purposely brought upon the stage to be an actor in this tragedy; and being put out of his part, as being at a nonplus in the last act, was for a long time after shut up in prison, to the great grief of many. Hitherto we have related what was publicly done against him. Now observe how he excuseth himself in the "Apology" which he made to Sir Francis Walsingham:—"The Queen," said he, "after the ambassadors of France and Scotland were departed, wished me to shew her the warrant for the execution of the sentence pronounced against the Queen of Scotland. Having shewn it, she willingly set her hand thereto, and bade me likewise affix the great seal of England, and jestingly said, 'You will shew this now to Walsingham, who is sick already, but will die when he sees it.' She added by and by, 'that she had put it off so long, because she would not seem to be carried away by violence; yet, knowing well the necessity thereof.' Then blaming Sir Amias Poulet and Sir Drew Drury, for not having eased her of that care and trouble, she commanded Walsingham to know the cause of their cessation and delay. The day after I had sealed the warrant, she forbade me to do it; then on my telling her, that it was done already, she checked me for my diligence, saying; 'that by some wise men's advice, another course might have been taken.' I answered, that just courses are always good and sure. But fearing she would cast some blame upon me, as she had formerly done upon Lord Burleigh, about the Duke of Norfolk's death, I disclosed the whole matter to Sir Christopher Hatton; protesting, that I would never, hereafter, be so forward in so weighty a matter. Hatton presently discovered it to Burleigh, and he to the rest of the council, who all concluded upon the dispatch of the execution, and vowed to share the blame; and to effect it, they sent Beale instantly away with the warrant and letters. The third day after, perceiving the Queen to be troubled in mind at having the preceding night, as her Majesty said, dreamed of the Queen of Scotland's death, I asked her, if she had changed her purpose. She answered me, 'That some other means might have been used;' and then inquiring of me, whether I had received any answer from Sir Amias Poulet? I shewed her his letters, wherein he refused to undertake the execution, as unjust; to which, in great choler, she replied:—'He, and his confederates, are all faithless and perjured, in promising great matters and not performing them; but she should find some that for her sake would do it.' As for myself, I told her how ignominious it was, and into what perils she would bring Poulet and Drury. If she approved the deed being done, her renown would be blasted with injustice and disgrace, besides other dangers; and in disallowing it, she would ruin men of worthy merit, and their posterity for ever would be undone. To conclude, the very day that the Queen of Scotland suffered, her Majesty checked me jestingly, for that it was not yet dispatched!"

Although Elizabeth had sent her great rival, Mary, Queen of Scots to the grave, she was still harassed by continual rumours of plots against her life. Her cruel persecution of the Catholics was the immediate cause of these conspiracies. As an instance of the barbarity practised by her sanction, we mention the case of Margaret Middleton, who, for harbouring a Catholic priest, and refusing to either deny or admit the charge, was, with studied cruelty, crushed to death. "The place of execution," says an eye-witness, "was the Tolboth, six or seven yards from the prison. After she had prayed, Fawcet (one of the sheriffs) commanded them to put off her apparel; when she requested him, with the four women, on their knees, 'that for the honour of womanhood, this might be dispensed with;' but they would not grant it. Then she told them that 'the women might unapparel her, and that they would turn their faces from her during that time.' The women took off her clothes, and put upon her the long linen habit; then very quietly she laid her down upon the ground, her face covered with a handkerchief, and most part of her body with the habit; the dore was laied upon her; her hands she joined towards her face. Then the sheriff said 'Ye must have your hands bound.' Then two sergeants parted her hands, and bound them to two posts [in the print her feet are bound to two other]. After this, they laid weight upon her, which, when she first felt, she said, 'Jesu! Jesu! Jesu! have mercy upon me!' which were the last words she was heard to speak. She was dying about one quarter of an hour. A sharp stone, as much as a man's fist, had been put under her back; upon her was laid to the quantitie of seven or eight hundred weight, which, breaking her ribbs, caused them to burst forth of the skinne."—March 26, 1586.

In the mean time, while Queen Elizabeth, by these means, was endeavouring gently to calm the resentment of Scotland, she was furiously threatened by the King of Spain, who, though he as yet purposely avoided a declaration of war, was intently occupied upon the means of taking signal vengeance on the English, who had molested the Spaniards with continual piracies; surprized and pillaged divers towns, both in Spain and America; and lately, violating the majesty of all princes, had caused the Queen of Scots to be beheaded. It was represented to Philip, that the English navy was, neither in number, greatness, nor strength, comparable to the combined fleet of Spain and Portugal. That England was neither fortified nor furnished with commanders, soldiers, horses, or provisions for war, but destitute alike of friends and money. These representations were soon proved to have been wholly unwarranted. Elizabeth, with the view of protracting the designs of Spain, sent Sir Francis Drake with four sail of the line, well appointed, to the Spanish coast, and elsewhere, with orders to take, burn, and pillage all such ships as he could find, as well in the harbours and ports, as on the ocean! Drake, arriving in the straits of Gibraltar, entered the Haven, where, after having caused six large ships to fly under the forts for protection, he took and burnt about one hundred others; one of the vessels taken, being the valuable galleon of the Marquis of Santa-Cruz, called the Ragusa, richly laden with merchandise. Thence, returning to Cape St. Vincent, he there burnt all such ships and fishing-boats as lay at anchor in the roads. He then went to the Cascalet Haven, situated at the mouth of the Tagus, where he endeavoured to prevail on the Marquis of Santa-Cruz to fight; but the Marquis not daring to stir, allowed Drake to sail along the coast, and take their ships, without molestation. Then sailing towards the Azore Islands, Drake met and captured a large Spanish ship, richly laden, called the San Philip, returning from the East Indies.

By this short expedition of the valiant Drake, England was much enriched, and the Spaniards sustained so great a loss in munition and warlike preparations, that they were constrained to abandon their design of invading England for that year. From this time the English began with avidity courageously to assault those immense ships, resembling castles, which they had hitherto so much dreaded; but which, they now plainly discovered, conveyed the rich treasures of the Indies, and were not so impregnable as had been supposed.

In 1558, all Europe rang with the mighty preparations of King Philip, for the conquest of England. Queen Elizabeth, with singular diligence, had, during the past year, laboured hard, to prepare as many ships and warlike stores as possible. She selected Lord Howard of Effingham for the office of Lord High Admiral, a nobleman well skilled in navigation, prudent, valiant, industrious, and of great authority amongst seamen. The valiant Drake was appointed Vice-Admiral, and every effort was made to give the Spaniards a warm reception. Henry Seymour, the second son of the Duke of Somerset, was ordered to lie in wait upon the Belgic shores, with forty ships, English and Dutch, to prevent the Duke of Parma's approach. For the land service, twenty thousand soldiers were dispersed along the southern coast, and two armies of choice troops were levied and enrolled. An army of reserve, consisting of about thirty-six thousand men, was drawn together for the defence of the Queen's person, and appointed to march towards any quarter in which the most pressing danger should manifest itself. A smaller force of twenty-three thousand was stationed at a camp near Tilbury, to protect the capital, against which it was expected that the most formidable efforts of the enemy, on making good his landing, would be immediately directed. But it was on the spontaneous efforts of individuals that the safety of the country chiefly depended, and the first appeal made by the government to the patriotism of the people was answered with promptitude and spirit. A message was sent by the privy council to the corporation of London, to inquire what the City could raise for the public service? The City authorities requested to be informed what the council might think requisite in such an emergency? Fifteen ships and five thousand men was the answer. In two days afterwards, the corporation "humbly entreated the council, in sign of their perfect love and loyalty to Prince and country, to accept of thirty ships, amply furnished, and ten thousand men." And even as London gave precedent, the whole kingdom kept true rank and equipage. Lord Grey, distinguished by his rigour in suppressing the last Irish rebellion, was appointed president of the council of war. Lord Hunsdon, a brave soldier, distinguished in several regular campaigns in Scotland, was made general of the army of reserve; and the young Earl of Essex, a gallant nobleman, was selected to fill the post of general of cavalry in the main army. All these appointments gave general satisfaction; but the people were somewhat staggered by the nomination of Leicester,—the hated, disgraced, and incapable court favourite—to the high station of commander-in-chief of the army at Tilbury. Happily the naval service did its duty, without requiring the aid of such an imbecile; but the appointment of such a man must ever be regarded as one of the weakest acts into which Elizabeth was ever betrayed, by a blind and pernicious partiality.

All the preparations for defence being finally arranged, Elizabeth resolved to visit in person the camp at Tilbury, for the encouragement of her troops. Mounted on a noble charger, with a general's truncheon in her hand, a corselet of polished steel laced over her magnificent apparel; and a page in attendance, bearing her white plumed helmet; she rode bare-headed from rank to rank, with a courageous deportment and smiling countenance; and, amidst the loyal plaudits and shouts of military ardour, which burst from the animated and admiring troops, she harangued them in the following spirited speech:—

"My loving people: we have been persuaded by some that are careful of our safety, to take heed how we commit ourselves to armed multitudes, for fear of treachery; but I assure you, I do not desire to live to distrust my faithful and loving subjects. Let tyrants fear; I have always so behaved myself that, under God, I have placed my chiefest strength and safe-guard in the loyal hearts and good will of my people. And, therefore, I am come amongst you at this time; not as for my recreation or sport; but being resolved, in the midst and heat of the battle, to live or die amongst you all; to lay down for my God, my kingdom, and my people, my honour and my blood, even in the dust. I know I have but the body of a weak and feeble woman, but I have the heart of a King; and of a King of England too! and think it foul scorn that the King of Spain, the Duke of Parma, or any Prince of Europe, should dare invade the borders of my realm; to which, rather than any dishonour should grow by me, I myself will take up arms; I myself will be your general, judge, and rewarder of every one of your virtues in the field. I know already, by your forwardness, that you have deserved rewards and crowns; and we do assure you, on the word of a Prince, so they shall be duly paid you. In the meantime, my lieutenant-general shall be in my stead, than whom never Prince commanded a more noble and worthy subject! not doubting, by your obedience to my general, by your concord in the camp and your valour in the field, we shall shortly have a famous victory over those enemies of my God, of my kingdom, and of my people."

Elizabeth was delighted on this, as on all other occasions, to exalt the character of her favourite Leicester. Fortunately, his valour was not needed in the approaching contest with the Spaniards.

CHAPTER XII.

Defeat of the Spanish Armada—Details of the various actions—Joy of Elizabeth on the occasion—Death of the Earl of Leicester—Elizabeth's new favourite, the Earl of Essex—The rival favourites—Duel between Essex and Blount—Death of Walsingham—Essex intercedes with Elizabeth for Davison—Private marriage of Essex, and rage of Elizabeth—Rigid Parsimony of the Queen—Sir Christopher Hatton—The Queen and the Bishop of Ely—Sir John Perrot.

HE celebrated Spanish Armada, arrogantly named "The Invincible," now approached the coast of England; and the thunder of its ordnance was heard from the sea. It consisted of one hundred and thirty ships, filled with nineteen thousand two hundred and ninety soldiers, eight thousand three hundred and fifty marines, two thousand and eighty galley slaves, chained; and two thousand six hundred and thirty pieces of great ordnance. The general was Alphonso Guzman, Duke of Medina Sidonia, and under him was John Martinus Ricaldus, a most skilful navigator. On the twenty-eighth of May, they sailed from the Tagus, and bending their course towards Gallicia, they were dispersed by a strong tempest: so distressed and weather-beaten was the fleet, that Elizabeth was led not to expect it that year: and Secretary Walsingham wrote to the Lord High Admiral to send back four of the largest ships. But the Admiral entreated Walsingham not to believe the report, and expressed an earnest desire to retain the whole fleet, even at his own private expense—a proper rebuke of the parsimony of that period. Having a prosperous wind, the English Admiral sailed towards Spain, with the hope of surprising the weather-beaten ships in the harbour: when he was almost on the coast of Spain, the wind veered south; and he, who was commanded to defend the English shores, fearing that the same wind might waft the enemy's fleet towards England, quickly returned to Plymouth.

On the twelfth of July, the wind continuing favourable, the Duke of Medina, with his whole fleet, weighed anchor. He dispatched a vessel to announce to the Duke of Parma the approach of the Armada, and to inform him of other needful matters; for he had orders to join the forces and fleet of the Prince of Parma, and to waft them over to England, under the protection of his Armada, and to set on shore his land forces at the mouth of the Thames. On the sixteenth day, there was a great calm, and a thick fog covered the sea till noon, and then a strong north-wind blew, then a south-wind till midnight, and then an easterly; so that the Armada, being much scattered, could hardly be collected together, till it came within sight of England, which was on the nineteenth of the month: on which day the Admiral of England, being previously apprized by Captain Fleming that the Spanish fleet had arrived in the Channel, and was descried not far from the Lizard, the wind then keeping the English navy in port, he, with great difficulty, and no less industry and alacrity on the part of the sailors, himself not disdaining to pull at the hawser amongst the private seamen, at length brought his ships into the open sea. The next day, the English fleet came within sight of the Spanish Armada, which, in the form of a crescent, whose horns were at least some miles distant, was slowly approaching under full sail. The English purposely suffered them to pass by, that they might pursue them with a favourable gale of wind.

On the twenty-first of July, the Lord High Admiral sent before him a pinnace, called the Defiance, and, by discharging a piece of ordnance out of her, provoked the Spaniards to the fight: and presently out of his own ship, The Royal Ark, the Admiral thundered upon a huge vessel, which he took to be that of the Spanish Admiral, but which proved to be the ship of Alphonso Leva. At the same instant, Drake, Hawkins, and Furbisher, pealed terribly on the rear, commanded by Ricaldus, who performed all the duties of a valiant and discreet commander, in endeavouring to stay the ships under his command from flying, until his own ship, extremely battered with shot, became so unmanageable, that with much difficulty he kept his station. The Duke of Medina now reformed his dispersed ships, and with full sail held on his course. Nor could he do otherwise, as the wind was favourable for the English, and their ships attacked, retired, and re-attacked them upon every quarter, with incredible celerity. When they had continued the fight sharply for the space of two hours, the English Admiral thought it prudent to retire, as he hourly expected a reinforcement of forty sail.

The night following, a Spanish ship, the St. Katherine, being much shattered in the conflict, was received into the midst of the fleet to be repaired: and a large Catalonian ship, the Oquenda, in which was the treasurer of the fleet, was partly blown up with gunpowder, by the device of a Flemish gunner. But the fire was seasonably quenched by ships sent in for the purpose; one of these, a galleon of Peter Valdes, had the misfortune to fall foul of another ship, and the wind being stormy and the night dark, she was abandoned, and became a prey to Sir Francis Drake, who sent Valdes to Dartmouth, and gave his ship to be plundered by the marines. The

Spaniards were hotly pursued by the Admiral, with the ships Mary and Rose. The Duke of Medina was busied in putting his fleet in array of battle. He then sent Ensign Gliche to the Duke of Parma, to inform him of the state of the fleet, and committed the ship Oquenda, having first removed into other vessels her treasure and the marines, to the mercy of the seas. The same day, this splendid galleon, with fifty seamen, miserably maimed and half-burnt, fell into the hands of the English, and was sent into Weymouth.

On the twenty-third, at break of day, the Spaniards, having a prosperous north wind, turned sail towards the English, who, in order to get advantage of the wind, turned towards the west, and both fleets, after contending for the favour of the wind, prepared for action, and fought confusedly and with various success; while, in one place, the English valiantly brought out the ships dangerously hemmed in by the Spaniards; in another, Ricaldus, then in danger, with no less resolution disengaged his vessels. The lightning and thunder of the artillery was great on both sides, most of which, notwithstanding, came in vain from the Spanish ships—the shot flying clear over the English. Only one, Cock, an Englishman, in a small bark of his own, died gloriously in the midst of his enemies. The English ships being infinitely smaller than the Spanish, the British sailors dexterously evaded the enemy, discharged their shot with a sure and successful aim against the great sluggish ships of the foe, and then retired into the open sea. The Lord Admiral, however, was in no haste to grapple and fight hand-to-hand, for the enemy had a strong and well-appointed army on board; their ships were far more numerous, of greater burden, stronger, and higher in bulk: and they, fighting from above, threatened certain destruction to those that fought against them upon the lower ships: he also foresaw that the loss of his men would be much more prejudicial to him than the victory could be profitable. For, to be vanquished, was to bring the Queen into inevitable danger; and to be victor, was only to win a blaze of glory, at the great sacrifice of human life.

On the twenty-fourth, there was a mutual cessation of hostilities. The Lord Admiral dispatched several small barques to the adjoining ports of England for ammunition, and divided his whole fleet into four squadrons; the first he himself commanded, the second Drake, the third Hawkins, and the fourth Furbisher; and he appointed certain pinnaces, out of each squadron, to make impressions on the enemy in several quarters at the dead of night; but a calm following, that plan was abandoned. The twenty-fifth, which was St. James' day, a Portuguese galleon, the St. Anne, which could not keep company with the rest of the fleet, was attacked by several small English barques. Leva and Diego Enriquez, with three galleasses, now made their appearance, but the Lord Admiral, and Lord Howard in the Golden Lion (who, on account of the great calm, were fain to be towed by fishing-boats), so battered them with cannon, that not without great difficulty, and great loss of men, they sheered off, and afterwards the galleasses never offered to fight. The Spaniards report that, on that day, the English, at a nearer distance than ever, with their great ordnance, extremely distressed the Spanish admiral, slew many of his men, and shot down his mainmast; but that Mexia and Ricaldus came opportunely, and repelled the English. That then the Spanish Armada, accompanied by Ricaldus and others, attacked the English admiral, who escaped by the sudden changing of the wind; that thereupon the Spaniards left the pursuit, and holding on their course, sent a second messenger to the Duke of Parma, directing him, with all speed, to join his fleet with the King's Armada, and to send a supply of bullets. Of this the English were ignorant, who write that they shot off the lanthorn from one of the Spanish ships, the beak-head from another, and terribly raked a third; that the Nonsuch, Mary, and the Rose, having had only a short conflict with the Spaniards, left them, and, with other ships, went to the rescue of the Triumph, then in danger.

On the following day, the Lord Admiral, for their valour and fortitude, knighted Thomas Howard, the Lord Sheffield, Roger Townsend, John Hawkins, and Martin Furbisher. And it was determined thenceforth not to attack the enemy till they came to the straits of Calais, where Henry Seymour and William Winter awaited their arrival. So the Spanish fleet made sail, with a full south-west wind, the English fleet following them. But so far was the title of "Invincible," or the once terrible aspect of the Spanish Armada, able to frighten our wooden walls, that the youth of England, leaving their parents, wives, children, kindred, and friends, out of their dearer love of their country, with ships hired at their own expense, joined the fleet in great numbers, with that noble ardour, generous alacrity, and courage which distinguish Englishmen. Amongst others who thus rendered their able assistance, were the Earls of Oxford, Northumberland, and Cumberland; Sir Thomas and Sir Robert Cecil, Sir Henry Brooke, Sir Charles Blunt, Sir Walter Raleigh, Sir William Hatton, Sir Robert Carey, Sir Ambrose Willoughby, Sir Thomas Gerard, Sir Arthur Gorge, and other worthy knights of great credit and renown.

On the twenty-seventh, towards evening, the Armada cast anchor near Calais, and within cannon-shot of them lay the Admiral and the English fleet at anchor, whom Seymour and Winter soon joined. The number of the English ships amounted by this time to one hundred and forty, all able and ready for action, and yet there were not above fifteen of them which bore the weight and burden of the war, and repelled it. The Spaniards, by frequent messengers, urged the Duke of Parma to send forty fly-boats, without which they could not fitly fight with the English, on account of the magnitude and sluggishness of their ships, and the great dexterity and agility of the English; and they earnestly begged him to put instantly to sea with his fleet, whom the Armada would protect as it were with wings, till their arrival in England; but the Duke was prevented, by insurmountable obstacles, from acceding to their wishes..

By the command of Elizabeth, after the Spaniards had cast anchor, in the dead of night, the Admiral sent eight of his worst ships, daubed on the outsides with Greek pitch and rosin, and filled full of sulphur, and other materials quickly combustible, under the conduct of Young and Prouse, having a full gale of wind, directly upon the Spanish Armada; which, as the Spaniards saw approach nearer and nearer to them, (the flames shining and illuminating the ocean), thinking these terrific burning ships were filled with some deadly engines of destructien, set up such a howling and fearful outcry as rent the air, immediately weighed anchor, cut their cables, raised their sails, cried out to their rowers, and, struck with a horrible and panic fear, with impetuous haste betook themselves to a disastrous flight. In the confusion the Spanish Admiral's galliasse had her rudder broken, ran upon the sands on the following day, and, after a doubtful fight with Amias Preston, Thomas Gerard, and Harvey, was taken; Hugh Moncada, the captain, being slain, and the soldiers and marines either drowned or killed. In the meantime, a portion of the Spanish fleet rallied before Gravelin, and were fiercely attacked by Drake and Fenner, who shortly afterwards were joined by Fenton, Southwell, Beatson, Cross, Raymond, the Lord Admiral himself, Howard, and Sheffield. The Duke, Leva, Oquenda, Ricauld, and other Spaniards bravely sustained the charge; which was such that most of their ships were disabled, and the galleon, St. Matthew, commanded by Diego Pymental, and appointed to assist Toleda in the San Philip, was broken by the continual batteries of Seymour and Winter; and being driven towards Ostend, was taken by the Zealanders, off Flushing. Another galleon was sunk, and several ran aground on the sand-banks near the mouth of the Scheldt.

The last day of this month, at day-break, the wind veered to the north-west; and the Spaniards, striving to get into the straits again, were driven towards Zealand. The English, as the Spaniards believe, ceased their firing, perceiving some of their ships in great danger, and ready to run on the sands and shoals on the coast of Zealand. The next morning, however, with the aid of a favourable breeze, the Spaniards extricated themselves from danger, and the same evening, by common consent, they resolved to return to Spain by the Northern Ocean, as they wanted bullets and other necessaries; their ships were dismantled, and they had little hope of the Duke of Parma putting to sea.

In fact, the prowess and cool daring of the English had completely frustrated their designs, and filled them with terror: seeking only their own safety, they fairly fled before their daring pursuers; but the English, at the moment when they might have annihilated their invaders, were forced by the want of ammunition to return to port. The fugitives pursued their way unmolested by man, but they met with a more terrible enemy in the violent wind and waves of the Northern Sea. The shores of Scotland and Ireland were strewn with their wrecks, and when they terminated their unfortunate voyage, they had lost thirty of their largest ships, and upwards of ten thousand men.

In commemoration of this signal defeat, the Queen caused public prayers and thanksgiving to be made in all the churches of England, and went herself in triumph amongst the companies and corporations of London, who marched on each side of her Majesty, with their banners, and rode through the streets, which were richly hung with blue hangings. Thus attended, and in a chariot drawn by two horses, Elizabeth proceeded to St. Paul's, where she gave humble thanks to God, heard the sermon, which ascribed all the glory to God alone, and caused the ensigns taken to be there set up and shewn to the people. Then she assigned some revenues to the Admiral for the service he had performed with such happy success; praised highly her naval captains, as men born for the preservation of their country; and, as often as she saw any of those who had distinguished themselves in this memorable conflict, she would call them familiarly by their names, to acknowledge their services; she also rewarded the wounded and poorer sort with honourable pensions.

This public rejoicing was increased by the arrival of Sir Robert Sidney from Scotland, with letters for her Majesty, which assured her, that the King of Scots embraced most affectionately the Queen's friendship, made sincere profession of true religion, and would defend the same with all his might. Sir Robert had been sent to James the Sixth, when Great Britain was first threatened with the Spanish fleet, to acknowledge by his rejoicings and thanksgivings the good will which he before bore to the Queen, to praise his forwardness, to defend the common cause, to promise him reciprocal succour, if the Spaniards attempted any invasion in Scotland; and, to give him to understand with what ambition the Spaniards gaped after the whole monarchy of Great Britain, soliciting the Pope to excommunicate his royal person, and to exclude him out of the succession of the kingdom of England, to all which the King answered gaily and merrily:—

"I expect no other courtesy of the Spaniard, than such as Poliphemus promised to Ulysses; to wit, that he would devour him—the last of all his fellows."

In August, 1588, Leicester, whilst proceeding from Tilbury to his own castle of Kenilworth, was arrested in his progress by a severe illness, and after lingering for a few days, expired at Cornbury Park, in Oxfordshire; the cause of his death was a mystery, and such was the superstition of the age of Elizabeth, that it was judged necessary to take an examination before the privy council respecting certain magical practices, said to have been employed against his life. The son of Sir James Croft, Comptroller of the Household, made no scruple to confess, that he had consulted a magician, of the name of Smith, to learn who were his father's enemies in the council. The magician immediately mentioned the Earl of Leicester; and then, a little while after, he began flirting with his thumbs, exclaiming, in allusion to the device of this nobleman:—"The bear is bound to the stake!" and again, "nothing can now save the Earl of Leicester!" Notwithstanding the actual fulfilment of this denunciation, the magician was allowed to go unpunished!

Although Elizabeth was much grieved at the loss of her favourite, her joy, at the glorious news of the defeat of the Spanish Armada, greatly lessened the effect it would otherwise have produced. Leicester was the fifth son of John, Duke of Northumberland. Under King Edward, he was first gentleman of the King's Chamber; under Queen Mary, Master of the Artillery; and under Queen Elizabeth, (whose love for him was attributed, by the superstition of the times, to a kindred sympathy of spirits between them, occasioned, by some secret constellation, which the Greek astrologers called *Sinastria*, he having been born on the same day that Elizabeth was), he was Master of the Horse, Knight of the Garter, Privy Councillor, Steward of the Queen's House, Chancellor of the University of Oxford, Chief Justice in Eyre of all the forests beyond the Trent, the Queen's Lieutenant and Captain of the English forces against Spain, and Governor and Captain General of the united provinces of the Netherlands. Latterly he had indulged the vain hope of a new title of honour and authority, with sovereign power annexed thereto — a general lieutenancy under the Queen, throughout all England and Ireland, of which Elizabeth had granted him letters patent, for she could refuse nothing to her favourite lover; but Lord Burleigh and Sir Christopher Hatton boldly opposed such an act of folly, and succeeded in convincing Elizabeth of the extreme danger of giving too much power to one man alone. He was reputed a complete courtier; magnificent, liberal, a protector and benefactor of soldiers and scholars; very officious, cunning, and revengeful towards his enemies; skilful in temporizing, and an adept at serving his own turn by craft and duplicity. The Queen, who was hardly ever seen to remit anything due to her treasury, after his death caused his goods to be sold, to pay that which he owed to her bounty!

The death of Leicester, who had for thirty years been to Elizabeth an object of the most devoted tenderness, and upon whom she had lavished every honour, consistent with her own safety and independence, left a void in her existence, which she filled up by bestowing her tender regards on her engaging youthful kinsman, the Earl of Essex. The great disparity of years—the maiden Queen was fifty-six, and Essex but twenty-one years of age—gave to this new passion of Elizabeth an appearance of dotage, which afflicted all who admired her general good sense and dignity of conduct. Nor did she long enjoy that felicity in the society of her new favourite, which she fondly imagined would last for ever. Essex soon began to look with a kind of loathing upon the partiality of his royal mistress. His careless indifference soon admonished her, that her affection was not reciprocated, and that Essex had been actuated solely by interested motives, for the encouragement he had given to her advances. As this mortifying conviction came home to her bosom, Elizabeth grew restless, irritable, and capricious to excess. She watched all his motions with a self-tormenting jealousy, and gave a ready ear to the most malicious insinuations of his enemies; and her heart at length becoming callous by repeated insults, she began to visit his delinquencies with the most unrelenting severity. On discovering that he had absented himself from court, and from the duties of his office as Master of the Horse, to embark in the unfortunate expedition to Portugal, which was undertaken in the spring of 1589, with the design of placing Don Antonio on the throne of that kingdom, she instantly dispatched a peremptory order for his return, enforced by menaces of her utmost indignation in case of disobedience; but he had already put to sea. During the five months of his absence, the court was in commotion, from the eccentricities of Elizabeth, occasioned by his absence. But the laurels with which he had encircled his brow proved his protection. She had listened with a secret satisfaction to the traits of valour and generosity which he displayed, and which were communicated to her from various channels. Her tenderness revived at the recital of the perils and dangers to which he was daily exposing himself; and her joy at his safe return, too lively and too natural for concealment, deprived her wholly of the power to chide; and his pardon was granted even before he could utter a word of explanation. Essex had too much penetration, not to be deeply touched by this affectionate behaviour of Elizabeth; he renewed his efforts to please, and with so signal a success, that he was soon confirmed in the royal favour, and his attachment was rewarded by some munificent grants from the revenues of the state.

In the early days of his favour, Essex, conscious of his power over his royal mistress, assumed the right of treating as interlopers such as advanced too rapidly in the good graces of his Sovereign. Naunton, in his "Fragmenta Regalia," relates the following incident, as having occurred at this period: "My Lord Mountjoy being but newly come to court, and then but Sir Charles Blount, had the good fortune one day to run very well a-tilt; and the Queen therewith was so well pleased, that she sent him a token of her favour—a Queen at chess, of gold, richly enamelled; which his servants had the next day fastened on his arm, with a crimson ribbon; which my Lord of Essex, as he passed through the privy chamber, espying, with his cloak cast under his arm, the better to commend it to the view; inquired what it was, and for what cause it was there affixed. Sir Fulk Greville told him that it was the Queen's favour, which the day before, and after the tilting, she had sent him; whereat my Lord of Essex, in a kind of emulation, and as though he would have limited her favour, said:—'Now I perceive every fool must have a favour!' This bitter and public affront came to the ears of Sir Charles Blount, who sent him a challenge, which was accepted by my Lord; and they went near Marylebonne park, where my Lord was hurt in the thigh, and disarmed. The Queen missing the men, was very curious to learn the truth; and when at last it was whispered out, she swore by God's death, it was fit that some one or other should have taken him down, and teach him better manners, otherwise there would be no rule with him." Essex could not better have paid his court to Elizabeth, than by fighting a duel for her sake; for she had the weakness to imagine, that her personal charms were the sole cause. She compelled, however, the rivals to be reconciled, under the threat of her severest displeasure; and from that day all the outward marks of friendship were preserved between them. But Elizabeth was not the only cause of this duel. It appears that Sir Charles Blount had conceived an ardent passion for a sister of the Earl of Essex; the same lady who was at one time intended to be the bride of Sir Philip Sidney. She returned his attachment; but her friends, thinking the match inferior to her pretensions, broke off the affair, and compelled her to give her hand to Lord Rich, a man of a disagreeable character, and the object of her strongest aversion. So, after her marriage, the unhappy lady found it impossible to forget the lover who had been torn from her by parental authority, and she suffered herself to be seduced by him into a criminal connection, which was not detected until it had subsisted for several years. A divorce followed; and her lover regarding himself as bound in love and honour to make her his wife, they were married during the life-time of her husband; hence the ill blood engendered in the breast of Essex.

In April, 1590, died Sir Francis Walsingham, principal Secretary of State, whose name is recorded as being intimately connected with the domestic policy of Elizabeth, during many of the most eventful years of her reign.

Essex was anxious to appoint, as his successor to the office of Secretary of State, the discarded Davison, who became a sacrifice, to atone, in some measure, for the cruel murder of the unfortunate Mary, Queen of Scots. It would appear that he had privately, with the knowledge of Elizabeth, been for some time performing the office of Secretary of State, during the illness of Walsingham. No one was more susceptible than Essex of generous emotions, and the extraordinary zeal which he displayed, during three years, in the cause of this unfortunate and ill-used man, can only be ascribed to motives of pure and disinterested friendship. He knew him to be a victim to the artful policy of his royal mistress; and he tried every effort in his power to restore him to his family and to society. Several letters have been printed from Essex to Davison, which reflect great light on the behaviour and sentiments of Elizabeth in this extraordinary matter, from which we select the following.

"I had some conversation with her Majesty yester-night, after my departure from you; and I did find that the success of my endeavours to serve you much outrun my expectation. I made her Majesty see what you had suffered in your health, in your fortune, in your reputation in the world, since the time that it was her pleasure to commit you. I told her how many friends and well-wishers the world did afford you, and how, throughout the realm, her best subjects wished she would do herself the honour to repair and restore to you that state which she had overthrown; your humble sufferings of these harms, and reverend regard to her Majesty, must needs move a Princess so noble and so just; and more I had said, if my gift of speech had been any way comparable to my love. Her Majesty, seeing her judgment opened by the story of her own actions, shewed a very feeling compassion towards you; she gave you many praises; and amongst the rest, what she seemed to please herself in was, that you were a man of her own choice. In truth she was so well pleased with those things that she spake and heard of you, that I dare (if of things future there be any assurance) promise to myself that your peace will be made to your content and the desire of your friends; I mean in her favour and your own fortune; to a better estate than, or at least the same, you had; which, with all my power, I will employ myself to effect." These sanguine hopes, however, were soon checked.

In a subsequent letter he says:—"I have taken my opportunity, since I saw you, to perform as much as I promised; and although I have been able to effect nothing, yet even now I have had better leisure to solicit the Queen than in this stormy time I did hope for. My beginning was, that I was entreated amongst others, to move her in your behalf; my course was to lay open your sufferings and your patience; in them you had felt poverty, restraint, and disgrace; and yet you showed nothing but faith and humility—faith, as being never wearied nor discouraged to do her service; humbleness, as being content to forget all the burdens that had been laid upon you, and to serve her Majesty with as frank and willing a heart as they that have received the greatest grace from her. To all this I received no answer, but in general terms;—that her honour was much touched; that your presumption had been intolerable, and that she could not let it slip out of her mind. When I urged your access, she denied it; but in such a manner that I had no cause to be afraid to speak again on the subject. When I offered to reply, she fell into other discourse; and so we parted."

On the death of Walsingham, he writes:—"Upon this unhappy event, I tried to the bottom what the Queen will do for you. I urged, not the comparison between you and any other, but in my duty to her and zeal for her service I did assure her, that she had not any other in England who would, for these three or four years, know how to support so great a burden. She gave me leave to speak; heard me with patience; confessed with me that none was so sufficient; and would not deny but that which she lays to your charge was done without hope, fear, malice, envy, or any regards of your own, but merely for her safety, both of state and person. In the end, she absolutely denied to let you have that place, and willed me to rest satisfied, for she was resolved. Thus much I write to let you know, I am more honest to my friends than happy in their causes." Essex now hazarded the step of writing himself to James the Sixth, requesting, as a personal favour, the forgiveness and good offices of this amiable monarch, in behalf of the man who bore the blame of his mother's death; but all his efforts were unavailing; the more Elizabeth reflected on this matter, the less she felt herself able to forgive the rash presumption of the man who had anticipated her final resolution on the fate of Mary. No doubt the fear of giving offence to the King of Scots, was the cause of all this harsh treatment of the Queen towards her unfortunate secretary. He did not long survive her cruel conduct.

In the course of this year, 1590, the Earl of Essex was privately married to Lady Sidney, the widow of Sir Philip Sidney, and the daughter of Walsingham. When her Majesty heard of this marriage, she did not scruple to shew herself highly offended. The circumstance of the union having taken place without the previous consent of the Queen, was the ostensible cause of her displeasure. But that ungenerous feeling, which rendered her the universal foe of matrimony, heightened on this occasion by a secret jealousy, too humiliating to be owned, and too powerful to be repressed, formed the more genuine causes of her deep vexation and disappointment. The secret of her heart was soon discovered by the court; for what vice can long lurk unsuspected in a royal bosom? One of her attendants, Stanhope, thus addresses Lord Talbot on this delicate subject:—"This night, God willing, she will go to Richmond; and on Saturday night to Somerset House; and if she could overcome her passion against my Lord of Essex for his marriage, no doubt she would be much quieter; yet doth she use it more temperately than was thought for, and, God be thanked, she does not strike all whom she threats! The Earl doth display good temper on the occasion, concealing his marriage as much as so open a matter may be; not that he denies it to any; but for her Majesty's better satisfaction, he is pleased that my lady shall live very retired in the house of her brother."

Elizabeth, having coolly reflected on the folly and disgrace of openly maintaining an ineffectual resentment, soon after re-admitted the Earl, apparently to the same station of favour as before; but she never entirely dismissed her feelings of mortification, or again reposed in Essex the same unbounded confidence with which she had once honoured him. In the autumn of the next year, she still retained such displeasure against Sir Robert Sidney, then resident abroad on foreign service, for having been present at a banquet given by Essex on the occasion of his marriage, that she could not be induced to grant him leave of absence for a visit to England.

Elizabeth was parsimonious to a fault. On one occasion she accepted, with thanks, an offer, privately communicated to her by some person, holding an inferior station in the customs, of a full disclosure of the impositions practised upon her in that department. She admitted this informer several times to an audience, imposed silence, in the tone of a mistress, on the remonstrances of her ministers, who indignantly urged that the *employé* was not of a rank to be thus countenanced in accusation of his superiors, and reaped the reward of this judicious conduct by finding herself entitled to demand from her farmer of the customs a revenue of forty-two thousand pounds, instead of twelve thousand, which he had formerly been in the habit of paying! She afterwards exacted from him a further advance of eight thousand pounds per annum; and she stimulated her Chancellor of the Exchequer to such a rigid superintendence of all the details of the public expenditure, as produced the most important results. In the ensuing Parliament, a conference was held between the two Houses, respecting a bill for making the patrimonial estates of accountants liable for their arrears to the Queen; and the Commons desiring that it might not have a retrospective effect, the Lord Treasurer pithily remarked: "My Lords, if any of you had lost your purse by the way, would you look back or forwards to find it? The Queen, then, hath lost her purse!"

This rigid parsimony was at once the virtue and the foible of Elizabeth. It endeared her to the people, whom it protected from the imposition of new and oppressive taxes; but, being joined to an extraordinary taste for magnificence in all that related to her personal appearance, it betrayed her into a thousand meannesses, which, in spite of all the fascinating arts in which she was an adept, served to alienate the affections of her court. Her nobles found themselves heavily burdened by the long and frequent visits which she paid them at their country seats, attended uniformly with an enormous retinue; as well as by the contributions to her jewelry and wardrobe, which custom required of them, under the name of New Year's Gifts; and on all occasions when they had favours, or even justice, to ask. Many of her courtiers regretted the day when first her hollow smiles and flattering speeches seduced them to years of irksome, servile, and fawning servility. Bacon, in his "Apothegms," relates, on this subject, the following anecdote:—"Queen Elizabeth, seeing Sir Edward * * * * * in her garden, looked out at her window, and asked him, in Italian, 'What does a man think of, who thinks of nothing?' Sir Edward, who had not received some of the Queen's grants so soon as he had hoped and desired, paused a little, and then made answer: 'Madam, he thinks of a woman's promise.' The Queen shrunk in her head, but was heard to say, 'Well, Sir Edward, I must not confute you: anger makes dull men witty, but it keeps them poor!'"

She was dilatory enough in suits of her own nature; and the Lord Treasurer Burleigh, being a wise man, and willing therein to feed her humour, would say to her: "Madam, you do well to let suitors stay; for I shall tell you, if you grant them speedily, they will come again the sooner." "Madam," said a popular poet, whose bounty had been intercepted by this minister:—

"You bid your treasurer, on a time,
To give me reason for my rhyme;
But from that time and that season
I have had nor rhyme nor reason."

Spenser, the author of the "Fairy Queen," had similar injuries to endure, as is evident from those energetic lines, in which the poet, from the bitterness of his soul, describes the miseries of a profitless court attendance:—

"Full little knowest thou, that hast not tried,
What hell it is in suing long to bide;
To lose good days, that might be better spent;
To waste long nights in pensive discontent;
To speed to day, to be put back to-morrow;
To feed on hope, to pine with fear and sorrow;
To have thy Prince's grace, yet want her peers';
To have thy asking, yet wait many years;
To fret thy soul with crosses and with cares;
To eat thy heart through comfortless despairs;
To fawn, to crouch, to wait, to ride, to run,
To spend, to give, to want, to be undone."

About the latter end of 1591, died Sir Christopher Hatton, Lord Chancellor. His death was attributed to the grief which he felt in consequence of her Majesty's having demanded of him, with a rigour which he had not anticipated, the payment of certain monies received by him for tenths and first fruits. The Queen, it is said, on learning to what extremity her severity had reduced him, paid him several visits, and endeavoured, by her gracious and soothing speeches, to revive his drooping spirits; but her repentance came too late. It is, indeed, certain that the Queen manifested great interest in the fate of her chancellor; she paid him, during his illness, extraordinary personal attentions; and, on his death, she remitted to his nephew and heir, who was married to a granddaughter of Burleigh, all her claims on the property which he left behind. During his life, Hatton tasted largely of the solid fruits of the favour of his royal mistress. She persisted in the practice, originating in the reigns of her father and brother, of endowing her courtiers out of the spoils of the church. Sometimes, to the great scandal of the public, she would keep a bishopric many years vacant, for the sake of appropriating its whole revenues to secular purposes, and to her own favourites, and, still more frequently, the presentation to a see was given under the express condition that certain manors should be detached, or beneficial leases of lands and tenements granted to particular persons. Thus, the Bishop of Ely was required to make a cession to Sir Christopher Hatton, of the garden and orchard of Ely House, near Holborn; but on the decided refusal of the Bishop to surrender property which he regarded himself bound in honour and conscience to transmit unimpaired to his successors, Hatton instituted against him a chancery suit; and, having at length succeeded in wresting from him the land, he there built a splendid mansion, surrounded by gardens, which have been succeeded by a street still bearing his name—"Hatton Garden." He had even sufficient interest with her Majesty to cause her to address to the Bishop of Ely the following violent and unfeminine letter:—

"Proud Prelate—I understand you are backward in complying with your agreement; but I would have you to know, that I, who made you what you are, can also unmake you; and if you do not forthwith fulfil your engagement, by God I will immediately unfrock you!

"Yours, as you demean yourself,

"ELIZABETH."

Sir Christopher Hatton was early brought into the notice of Elizabeth by his great skill in dancing! and even after he had attained the dignity of Lord Chancellor, he used to lay aside his robes to dance, on occasions of festivity. This circumstance is thus pleasantly alluded to by Gray:—

"In Britain's isle, no matter where,
An ancient pile of building stands,
The Huntingdons and Hattons there
Employed the power of fairy hands,
To raise the ceilings' fretted height,
Each pannel in achievements clothing,
Rich windows that exclude the light,
And passages that lead to nothing.
Full oft within the spacious walls,
When he had fifty winters o'er him,
My grave Lord Keeper led the brawls,
The seal and maces danced before him!
His bushy beard, and shoe-strings green,
His high-crowned hat, and satin doublet,
Moved the stout heart of England's Queen,
Though Pope and Spaniard could not trouble it."

Towards Sir John Perrot, Hatton acted the part of an intriguing enemy, being provoked by the taunts which Sir John was continually throwing out against him, as one who had "entered the court as a galliard." Sir John Perrot derived his name and large estates from a wealthy family of that name, seated at Haroldstone, in Pembrokeshire. But his features, his figure, his air, and common fame, gave him for his father no less a personage than Henry the Eighth; nor was his resemblance merely external: his temper was haughty and violent, his demeanour blustering, his language coarse and abusive to excess; yet he was neither destitute of merit nor talent. As Lord Deputy of Ireland, from 1548 to 1588, he had made the most praiseworthy efforts towards the pacification of that unhappy and ill-governed country. His policy was liberal and benevolent; but his attempts at reformation armed against him a host of foes, among whom was the Archbishop of Dublin, whom he had exasperated by proposing to apply the revenues of St. Patrick's Cathedral to the foundation of an University in the capital of Ireland. He was often unguarded enough to give vent, in gross invective, against the person of her Majesty, to the great vexation which he, in common with all governors of Ireland under Elizabeth, was doomed to endure, from the scantiness of her supplies and the magnitude of her requisitions. His words were all carried to the Queen, mingled with such artful insinuations as tended to give to the mere unmeaning ebullitions of a hasty temper an air of deliberate contempt towards his sovereign. Just before the sailing of the Spanish Armada, Perrot was recalled, partly at his own request. A rigid inquiry was then instituted into all his actions, words, and behaviour in Ireland, and he was committed to the friendly custody of Burleigh. Afterwards, Lords Hunsdon and Buckhurst, with three other councillors, were ordered to search and seize his papers, in the house of the Lord Treasurer, without the sanction of this great minister, who was offended and alarmed at the step. Perrot was sent to the Tower, and, in April, 1592, put on his trial for high treason! The principal charges against him were —his contemptuous words of the Queen, his secret encouragement to rebellion and the Spanish invasion, and his harbouring of traitors. Of all these charges, with the exception of the first, he proved his entire innocence; and on that of contempt, he excused himself by the heat of his temper, and the absence of all evil intention. He was, nevertheless, found guilty; and, on leaving the bar, he exclaimed, "God's death! will the Queen suffer her brother to be offered up as a sacrifice to the envy of my frisking adversaries?"

The Queen felt the force of this appeal to the ties of blood. It was long before she could be induced to confirm the sentence; and she would never sign the warrant for its execution. Happy had it been for her peace of mind had she exhibited the same firmness with regard to the unfortunate Mary. Burleigh shed tears on hearing the verdict, saying, with a sigh, that hatred was always the more inveterate the less it was merited. When her first moments of anger had passed away, Elizabeth was now frequently heard to repeat the words of the Emperor Theodosius: — "Should any one have spoken evil of me, if through levity, it should be despised; if through insanity, pitied; if through malice, forgiven." She also said, in language more familiar to her, and swore a great oath, that they who accused Perrot were all knaves, and he an honest and faithful man. It was, accordingly, thought that she entertained the design of pardoning him, but her intentions were never carried into effect; and, in September, 1592, six months after his condemnation, this victim of inveterate malice perished in the Tower, of disease brought on by confinement, but more likely of a broken heart.

CHAPTER XIII.

Elizabeth and Sir Walter Raleigh—Sir Robert Carey—Shakspeare—Regulations of Elizabeth respecting the Drama—Tarleton, the jester—Meeting of Parliament—Haughty language of the Queen—Committal of Wentworth and other Members to the Fleet—Attempt to poison the Queen—Expedition to Cadiz—Elizabeth's care of Essex—His gallant conduct—Deaths of Lord Hunsdon and the Bishop of London—The Queen and Essex—Violent Quarrel between them—Death of Burleigh—Sir Roger Aston—Spenser.

IN 1592, Sir Walter Raleigh, anxious, by some splendid exploit, to revive the declining favour of Elizabeth, projected a formidable attack on the Spanish settlements in America, and engaged a large number of volunteers in the enterprise. But unavoidable obstacles arose, by which the fleet was detained till the proper season for its sailing was past. Raleigh was recalled to court, and the command of the expedition was entrusted to Furbisher. The only fortunate result of the enterprise was, the capture of one wealthy carrack, and the destruction of a second. In the meantime, Raleigh was amusing himself by an intrigue with one of her Majesty's maids of honour—a daughter of the celebrated Sir Nicholas Throgmorton. The Queen, in the heat of her indignation at the scandal brought upon her court by the consequences of this amour, resorted, as usual, to a rigour beyond the laws; and, though Sir Walter offered immediately to make the lady the best reparation in his power, by marrying her, which he afterwards did, Elizabeth unfeelingly published her shame, by sending both parties to the Tower! Sir Walter remained a prisoner during several months. Meanwhile, his ships returned from their cruise; and the profits from the sale of the captured carrack were to be divided among the Queen, the admiral, the sailors, and all who contributed to the outfit. Disputes arose: her Majesty was dissatisfied with the share allotted to her; and, taking advantage of the situation into which her own despotic violence had thrown Raleigh, she compelled him to buy his liberty, and the undisturbed enjoyment of all he held under her, by the sacrifice of no less than eighty thousand pounds, due to him as admiral! Such was the disinterested moral purity of the Virgin Queen!

Sir Robert Carey, the third son of Lord Hunsdon, was, at this period, a young man, and an assiduous attendant on the court of Elizabeth. Being a younger son, he had no patrimony; he received from the exchequer only one hundred pounds per annum during pleasure; and by the style of life which he was obliged to adopt, he had incurred a debt of a thousand pounds. In this situation he married a widow of five hundred pounds per annum, and some ready money. His father evinced no displeasure on the occasion; but his other friends, especially the Queen, were so much offended at the match, that he took his wife to Carlisle, and remained there, without going near the court, till the following year. Being then obliged to visit London on business, his father suggested the expediency of his paying the Queen the compliment of appearing on her birth day. Accordingly, he secretly prepared caparisons, and a present for her Majesty, at the cost of upwards of four hundred pounds; and presented himself in the tilt-yard, in the character of "a forsaken knight, who had vowed solitariness." The festival over, he made himself known to his friends in court; but the Queen, though she had received his gift, would not notice him. Soon after, the King of Scots sent to Carey's elder brother, then Marshal of Berwick, to beg that he would wait upon him, to receive a secret message, which he wished to be transmitted to the Queen. The Marshal wrote to his father, to inquire her Majesty's pleasure in the matter. She answered, "that she did not choose that he should stir out of Berwick;" but knowing, though she would not know it, that Sir Robert Carey was in court, she at length said to Lord Hunsdon, "I hear your fine son, who has married lately so worthily, is hereabouts. Send him, if you wish to know the King's pleasure." His lordship answered, "that he knew he would be happy to obey her commands." "No," said she, "do you bid him go, for I have nothing to do with him." Sir Robert Carey thought it hard, to be sent off without first seeing the Queen: "Sir," said he to his father, who urged his going, "if she be on such hard terms with me, I had need be wary what I do. If I go to the King without her license, it were in her power to hang me on my return; and that, for anything I see, it were ill trusting her." Lord Hunsdon "merrily" told the Queen what he said. "If the gentleman be so distrustful," she said, "let the Secretary make out a safe conduct to go and come, and I will sign it."

On his return, with letters from James the Sixth, Sir Robert hastened to court, and entered the presence chamber, splashed and dirty as he was; but, not finding the Queen there, Lord Hunsdon went to announce his son's arrival. She desired him to receive the letter or message, and bring it to her. But young Carey knew the court and the Queen too well, to consent to give up his dispatches, even to his father; he insisted on delivering them himself; and, at length, with much difficulty, gained an audience of the Queen. The first encounter was "stormy and terrible," which he passed over in silence; but, when the Queen had "said her pleasure" of himself and his wife, he made her a courtly excuse; with which she was so well appeased, that she at length assured him all was forgiven and forgotten, and received him into her wonted favour.

After this happy conclusion of an adventure so perilous to a courtier of Elizabeth, Carey returned to Carlisle, and his father's death soon occurring, he had orders to take upon himself the government of Berwick till further notice. In this situation he remained a year without salary; impairing much his small estate, and unable to procure from court, either an allowance, or leave of absence, to enable him to solicit one in person. At length, emboldened by necessity, he resolved to hazard the step of going up to court without permission. On his arrival, however, neither Secretary Cecil nor his own brother would venture to introduce him to the presence of the Queen, but advised him to hasten back before his absence should be known, for fear of her anger. At last, as he stood sorrowfully pondering on his case, a gentleman of the chamber, touched with pity, undertook to mention his arrival, in a way which should not displease the Queen: and he opened the matter by telling her, that she was more beholden to the love and service of one man than of many whom she favoured more. This excited her curiosity; and, on her asking who this person might be, he answered that it was Sir Robert Carey, who, unable longer to bear his absence from her sight, had posted up to town to kiss her hand, and instantly return. Elizabeth, much pleased, sent for him directly, received him with greater favour than ever, allowed him, after the interview, to lead her out by the hand; which seemed to his brother and the Secretary nothing less than a miracle; and what was more, granted him five hundred pounds immediately, a patent of Warden of the East Marshes, and a renewal of his grant of Norham Castle.

The immortal bard of Avon flourished in the reign of Elizabeth. As a dramatic author, the never-failing attraction of his pieces brought over-flowing audiences to the Globe Theatre, in Southwark, of which he became a joint proprietor. Lord Southampton bestowed on him a munificent donation of a thousand pounds, to enable him to complete a purchase, and introduced him to the notice of his beloved friend, the Earl of Essex. This led to the immediate patronage of Elizabeth, who was not slow in discovering his transcendent genius. She caused many of his plays to be represented before her, and the *Merry Wives of Windsor* owed its origin to the Queen's desire to see the character of Falstaff exhibited in the light of a lover.

During the early part of her reign, Sunday being still regarded principally in the light of a holiday, the Queen selected that day especially for the representation of plays at court; and by her licence, Burbage authorised dramatic performance at the public theatre, *on Sundays only*, out of the hours of prayer. Five years after, Gosson, in his *School of Abuse*, complains, that the players, "because they are allowed to play every Sunday, make four or five Sundays at least every week." To limit this abuse, an order was issued by the Privy Council, in 1591, prohibiting plays from being publicly acted on Thursdays; because on that day bear baiting and similar pastimes had usually been practised; and, in an injunction to the Lord Mayor, four days after, the representation of plays on Sundays was utterly condemned; and it was further complained, that on "all other days of the week, in divers places, the players do use to recite their plays, to the great hurt and destruction of the game of bear baiting, and like pastimes, which are maintained for her Majesty's pleasure." The Queen also thought proper to appoint commissioners, to inspect all performances of writers for the stage—a dramatic censorship—with full powers to reject and obliterate whatever they might esteem unmannerly, licentious, or irreverent—an excellent regulation, which has continued down to the present day. Nevertheless, no one enjoyed more than Elizabeth, the most licentious jests and merry conceits of the age. "At supper," says Bohun, "the Queen would divert herself with her friends and attendants, and if they made her no answers, would put them upon mirth and pleasant discourse, with great civility. She would then admit Tarleton, a famous comedian and pleasant jester, and other such men, to divert her with stories of the town, and the common jests and incidents of the day. Tarleton, who was then the best comedian in England, had composed a pleasant play, and when it was acting before the Queen, he pointed at Raleigh, and said, 'See the knave commands the Queen!' for which Elizabeth corrected him by a frown; yet he had the temerity to add, that he possessed too much and too intolerable a power: and, going on with the same liberty, he reflected on the too great influence of another royal favourite, which was so universally applauded by all present, that Elizabeth thought it prudent to hear these reflections with seeming unconcern. But yet she was so offended, that she forbad Tarleton, and all other jesters, from coming near her table in future."

The state of her finances compelled Elizabeth to summon a parliament in the spring of 1593, after a long respite of four years. She assumed a more haughty and menacing style than she had previously used. In answer to the three customary requests made by the Speaker, for the liberty of speech, freedom from arrests, and access to her person; she replied: that such liberty of speech as the Commons were justly entitled to—liberty, namely, of aye and no, she was willing to grant, but by no means a liberty for every one to speak what he listed! And if any idle heads should be found careless enough of their own safety to attempt innovations in the state, or reforms in the church, she laid her injunctions on the Speaker, to refuse all bills offered for such purposes, till they should have been examined by those who were better qualified to judge of these matters. She promised she would not impeach the liberty of their persons, provided they did not permit themselves to imagine that any neglect of duty would be allowed to pass unpunished, under shelter of this privilege; and she engaged not to deny them access to her person on weighty affairs, and in exercising their known rights, and fulfilling their duty to their country. Peter Wentworth, whose courageous and independent spirit had already drawn upon him repeated manifestations of royal displeasure, presented a petition to the Lord Keeper, praying the upper house to join with the lower, in a supplication to the Queen, to fix the succession to the crown. This subject was gall and wormwood to the Queen; her rage at the bare mention of a matter so offensive to her, was excited to such a pitch, that she instantly ordered Wentworth to be committed to the Fleet prison, together with Sir Thomas Bromley, who had seconded him, and two other members, to whom he had imparted the business; and, when the house was preparing a petition for their release, some privy councillors dissuaded the members against such a step, as one that could only give additional offence to her Majesty.

Soon afterwards, James Morrice, an eminent lawyer, Attorney of the Court of Wards, and Chancellor of the Duchy, made a motion for redress of the abuses in the Bishops' courts; and especially of the monstrous ones committed under the high commission. Several members supported the motion; but the Queen, in great wrath, sent for the Speaker, required him to deliver up to her the bill, reminded him of her strict injunctions at the opening of the session, and testified her extreme indignation and surprise at the boldness of the Commons, in intermeddling with subjects which she had expressly forbidden them to discuss. She informed him, that it lay in her power to summon parliament and to dismiss them at her pleasure; and to sanction or reject any determination of theirs: that she had at present called them together for the twofold purpose of enacting further laws for the maintenance of religion, and of providing for the national defence against Spain; and that these ought to be the subjects of their deliberations! As for Morrice, he was seized by a serjeant-at-arms in the house itself, stripped of his offices, rendered incapable of practising as a lawyer, and committed to prison, whence he soon after addressed to Burleigh a spirited remonstrance, in which he says:—

"Bills of assize of bread, shipping of fish, pleadings, and such like, may be offered and received into the house, and no offence to her Majesty's royal command; but the great causes of the law and public justice, may not be touched without offence. Well, my good lord, be it so, yet I hope her Majesty and you of her honourable privy council, will at length thoroughly consider these things, lest, as heretofore we prayed, 'From the tyranny of the Bishop of Rome, good Lord deliver us!' we be compelled to say, 'From the tyranny of the clergy of England, good Lord deliver us!'"

In October following, the Earl of Essex ventured to mention to her Majesty this persecuted patriot, as qualified for the office of Attorney-General; when "her Majesty acknowledged his talents, but said, his speaking against her, in such a manner as he had done, should be a bar against any preferment at her hand." He was kept for many years a prisoner in Tilbury Castle, and died in 1596. The House of Commons submitted, without further question, to the will of an imperious Queen, and passed, with little opposition, "An act to retain her Majesty's subjects in their due obedience," which is strongly illustrative of the tyrannical acts of the reformed church of the age of Elizabeth. By this cruel law, all persons above the age of sixteen, who should refuse during a month to attend the established form of worship, were to be imprisoned; when, should they further persist in their refusal during three months longer, they must abjure the realm; but, in case of their rejecting this alternative, on returning from banishment, their offences were declared felony, without benefit of clergy! The business of supplies was next taken into consideration, and the Commons voted several subsidies; but this not appearing to the ministry sufficient for the exigencies of the state, the peers were induced to request a conference with the House of Commons for an augmentation of the grant. The Commons at first rejected this interference with their acknowledged privilege of originating all money bills; but fear of the well-known consequences of offending their superiors, prevailed over their indignation; and both the conference and the additional supplies were acceded to. Some debate, however, arose on the time to be allowed for the payment of so heavy an imposition; and the illustrious Bacon, then member for Middlesex, enlarged upon the distress of the people, and the danger lest the House should, by this grant, be establishing a precedent against themselves and their posterity, in a speech, to which Sir Robert Cecil replied, with much warmth. Her Majesty showed a resentful remembrance of this speech of Bacon, on his appearing soon after as a candidate for the office of Attorney-General. His cousin, also, Sir Edward Hobby, took such an active part in some of the questions now at issue between the Crown and the Commons, as procured him an imprisonment till the end of the session, when he was liberated, "but not without a notable public disgrace, laid upon him by her Majesty's royal censure, delivered amongst other things, by herself, after my Lord Keeper's speech."

The Queen, in her speech to parliament, on proroguing the House on this occasion, animadverted in severe terms on the opposition displayed by many of the members; reiterated the lofty claims with which she had opened the session; and pronounced an eulogium on the justice and moderation of her government! She also entered into the grounds of her quarrel with the King of Spain; showed herself undismayed by the apprehensions of any thing which his once dreaded power could attempt against her; and added, in her characteristic style, adverting to the defeat of the great armada, this energetic warning:—"I am informed, that when he [Philip of Spain] attempted this last invasion, some upon the sea-coast forsook their towns, fled up higher into the country, and left all naked and exposed to his entrance. But I swear unto you, by God, if I knew those persons, I would teach them what it is to be fearful in so urgent a cause!"

In 1594, Philip the Second sought a base revenge upon Elizabeth, for the successive defeats he had experienced in his attempts to invade England. He proposed, through secret agents, vast rewards to any one who would attempt her destruction. It was no easy task to discover persons sufficiently rash to undertake, from mere mercenary motives, a villany so atrocious. But at length Fuentes and Ibarra, joint governors of the Netherlands, succeeded in bribing Dr. Lopez, domestic physician to the Queen, to mix poison in her medicine. Essex, whose watchfulness over the life of his sovereign was unceasing, was the first to give notice of this atrocious plot. At his instance, Lopez was apprehended, examined before Essex, the treasurer, the Lord Admiral, and Robert Cecil, and committed to custody in Essex's house. But nothing decisive appearing on his first examination, Cecil represented the charge as groundless, and the Queen, sending in anger for Essex, called him "a rash and daring youth," and reproached him for bringing, on slight grounds, so heinous a charge upon an innocent man. The Earl, indignant at finding his diligent services thus repaid, through the successful artifice of his enemy Cecil, quitted the royal presence in great rage; and, as was his practice on like occasions, shut himself up in his chamber; which he refused to quit, till the Queen herself sent the Lord Admiral a few days afterwards to mediate a reconciliation. Lopez was again subjected to fresh interrogatories, when, being threatened with the torture, he was induced to confess that he had received a bribe from the King of Spain; but he persisted in denying that it was ever his intention to perpetrate the odious crime. This subterfuge, however, did not save him from an ignominious death, which he suffered, with two others, whom the governors of the Netherlands had hired for a similar undertaking. The Spanish Court disdained to return any satisfactory answer to the complaints of Elizabeth, respecting these atrocious designs against her life; but either shame, or the fear of reprisals, deterred it from any repetition of such dangerous experiments against the life of the Queen of England.

About two years afterwards, however, an English jesuit, named Walpole, who was settled in Spain, and intimately connected with the noted Father Parsons, instigated an attempt, worthy of notice, from the singular circumstances attending it. In the last voyage of Drake to the West Indies, a small vessel of Walpole's was captured, and carried into a port of Spain, on board of which was one Squire, formerly a purveyor for the Queen's stables. This prisoner Walpole converted to Popery, and by insidious arguments, persuaded him to make an attempt against the life of Elizabeth; an enterprise, he assured him, which would be attended with little personal danger, and, in case of the worst, be rewarded by an immediate admission to the joys of heaven. He then presented to Squire a packet of poison, which he enjoined him to spread on the pommel of the Queen's saddle. The Queen, in mounting, would transfer the ointment to her hand; with that she was likely to touch her mouth or nostrils; and such was the virulence of the poison, that certain death would inevitably ensue. Squire returned to England, and enlisted for the Cadiz expedition; and, on the eve of its sailing, took the preparation and disposed of it as directed. Desirous of adding to his merits, he, during the voyage, anointed, in like manner, the arms of the Earl of Essex's chair. The failure of the application in both instances greatly surprised him. To Walpole it appeared so unaccountable, that he was persuaded Squire had deceived him; and, actuated at once by the desire of punishing his defection, and the fear of his betraying such secrets of the party as had been confided to him, he consummated his villany, by artfully conveying to the English government an intimation of the plot. Squire was apprehended, and at first denied all; "but, by good counsel, and the truth working within him," he was brought to confess what could not otherwise have been proved against him; and suffered penitently for his offence.

In June, 1596, a formidable armament was fitted out for Cadiz. The Lord High Admiral, Lord Howard of Effingham, commanded the fleet. The Earl of Essex was appointed general of all the land-forces, and spared neither trouble nor expense in his preparations for the enterprise. Lord Thomas Howard, Sir Walter Raleigh, Sir Francis Vere, Sir George Carew, and some others, held subordinate commands, and formed together a council of war. Elizabeth herself composed on this occasion a prayer for the use of the fleet; and she sent to her Lord High Admiral, and to the Earl of Essex, "jointly, a letter of licence to depart; besides comfortable encouragement. But our commander," adds a friend of Essex, "had a letter fraught with all kind of promises and loving offers, as the like, since he was a favourite, he never had." On the arrival of the expedition off Cadiz, Essex proposed that an attack should be made by the fleet on the ships in the harbour, but the Lord Admiral remonstrated against the rashness of such an attempt, and prevailed on several members of the council of war to concur with him. At length the arguments of the more daring party prevailed, and Essex, with that generous and noble ardour which distinguished him, threw his hat into the sea, in a wild transport of joy, on hearing that the Lord Admiral consented to make the attack. He was now made acquainted with a secret order of the Queen, dictated by her tender care for the safety of her young favourite—that he should by no means be permitted to lead the assault;—and he reluctantly promised an exact obedience to the mortifying commands of the Queen. But, no sooner was he in presence of the enemy, than his natural impetuosity would brook no control. He forgot his promise, and rushed into the heat of the action. The Spanish fleet was speedily driven up the harbour, where the Spanish admiral's ship, and another first-rate vessel, were set on fire by their own crews, and the rest run aground. Of these, two fine ships fell into the hands of the English; and the Lord Admiral, having refused to accept any ransom for the remainder, they were all, to the number of fifty, burned by order of the Spanish admiral.

In the meanwhile, Essex landed his men, and marched to the assault of Cadiz. The town was well fortified; and the English were on the point of being repulsed from the gate, which they had attacked, when Essex, at the critical moment, rushed forward, seized his own colours, and threw them over the wall; "giving a most hot assault unto the gate, where, to save the honour of their standard, happy was he that could first leap down from the wall, and with shot and sword make way through the thickest press of the enemy." The town being thus taken by storm, was given up to plunder; but Essex, whose humanity equalled his courage, put an immediate stop to the carnage, caused the women, children, and the religious orders, to retire to a place of safety, ordered the prisoners to be treated with the utmost lenity, and permitted all the citizens to withdraw, on payment of a ransom, before the place, with its fortifications, was committed to the flames. On his return to England, from an expedition so glorious to himself, Essex was welcomed by the Queen and by the people with every demonstration of joy and affection. But his adversaries, to lessen the glory of his exploits, ascribed to the naval commanders a principal share in the success at Cadiz, which he accounted all his own. It was suggested to the Queen that she might reimburse herself for the expenses she had incurred, out of the rich spoils taken at Cadiz; and no sooner had this project gained possession of her mind, than she began to quarrel with Essex, for his lavish distribution of prize-money. She insisted that the commanders should resign to her a large share of their gains; and even had the meanness to cause the private soldiers and sailors to be searched, before they quitted their ships, that the value of the money, or other booty, which they had taken possession of, might be deducted from their pay!

Lord Hunsdon, the nearest kinsman of the Queen, died in 1596. On hearing of his illness, Elizabeth resolved at length to confer upon him the title of Earl of Wiltshire, to which he had some claim, as nephew and heir-male to Sir Thomas Boleyn, her Majesty's grandfather, who had borne that dignity. She, accordingly, honoured her kinsman with a visit, and caused the patent and the robes of an earl to be brought and laid upon his bed; but the venerable old man, preserving to the last the blunt honesty of his character, declared, that if her Majesty had accounted him unworthy of that honour whilst living, he accounted himself unworthy of it now that he was dying; and, with this refusal, he expired.

Fletcher, Bishop of London, "a comely and courtly prelate," also died the same year. His talents and deportment pleased the Queen; and it is mentioned by Harrington, as an indication of her special favour, that she once quarrelled with the Bishop for wearing too short a beard. He afterwards gave her more serious displeasure, by marrying a gay and fair court lady, of good quality; and he had scarcely pacified her Majesty, by the offer of a grand entertainment at his house in Chelsea, when he was carried off by a sudden death, through an immoderate use of the new luxury of smoking tobacco. He was the father of Fletcher, the great dramatic poet, and was succeeded by Bishop Vaughan, who, on one occasion, preached before the Queen, on the vanity of decking the body too finely, which so offended her Majesty, that she told her ladies, if the Bishop held more discourse on such matters, she would fit him for heaven; but he should walk thither without a staff, and leave his mantle behind him. Perchance, the Bishop had never sought her Highness's wardrobe, or he would have chosen another text.

Elizabeth's captious favour towards Essex, and the arts used by him to gain his points on all occasions, are strikingly illustrated in the letters of Rowland White, in the Sidney Papers. "On February twenty-second, 1597, my Lord of Essex kept his bed the most part of yesterday; yet did one of his servants tell me, he could not pity him; for he knew his lord was not sick. There is not a day passes that the Queen sends not often to see him; and himself every day goeth privately to her. My Lord of Essex comes out of his chamber in his gown and nightcap." Again, "Full fourteen days his Lordship kept in doors; her Majesty resolved to break him of his will, and to pull down his great heart; but she found it a thing impossible, and says he holds it from the mother's side; but all is well again, and no doubt he will grow a mighty man in our state. The Queen had of late used the fair Mrs. Bridges, one of her maids of honour, harshly, with words and blows. It is spied out by envy, that the Earl of Essex is again fallen in love with her. It cannot fail to come to the Queen's ears; and then is he undone, and all that depend on his favour. I acquainted you with the care had to bring my Lady of Leicester to the Queen's presence. It was often granted, and she was brought to the private galleries, but the Queen as often found excuse not to come. Upon Shrove Monday, the Queen was persuaded to go to Mr. Comptroller's at the tilt end; and there was my Lady of Leicester, with a fair jewel of three hundred pounds value. A great dinner was prepared by my Lady Chandos; the Queen's coach got ready, and all the world expecting her Majesty's coming, when, upon a sudden, she resolved not to go; and so sent word. My Lord of Essex, who had kept his chamber all the day before in his night gown, went up to the Queen the private way; but all would not prevail; and as yet my Lady Leicester hath not seen the Queen. It had been better not moved, for my Lord of Essex, by importuning the Queen in these unpleasing matters, loses the opportunity he might take to do good unto his ancient friends." Again, he writes:—"My Lady Leicester was at court; kissed the Queen's hand and her breast, and did embrace her; and the Queen kissed her. My Lord of Essex is in exceeding favour here. Lady Leicester departed from court exceedingly contented; but, being desirous again to come to kiss the Queen's hand, it was denied; and, as I heard, some unkind words were given out against her."

Essex's decline in the favour of his royal mistress was now rapidly approaching. Confident in her affections, he suffered himself to forget that she was still his Queen. He often neglected those little attentions which would have gratified her: on any occasional cause of ill-humour, he would drop slighting expressions respecting her age and person, which, if they reached her ear, could never be forgiven. On one memorable instance, he treated her openly, and in her presence, with the greatest indignity. A dispute had arisen between them in presence of the Lord Admiral, the Secretary, and the Clerk of the Signet, respecting the choice of a Commander for Ireland, the Queen resolving to send Sir William Knolles, the uncle of Essex, while he vehemently supported Sir George Carew, because the latter had given him some offence, and he wanted to get rid of him. Unable, either by argument or persuasion, to prevail over the resolute will of her Majesty, the favourite at last so far forgot himself as to turn his back upon his royal mistress, with a laugh of contempt!—an outrage which she revenged after her own manner, by soundly boxing his ears, and bidding him "Go, and be hanged!" This unexpected attack so inflamed the blood of Essex, that, forgetting it proceeded from an enraged woman and a Queen, he clapped his hand on his sword, and while the Lord Admiral hastened to throw himself between them, he swore that not from Henry the Eighth himself, would he have endured such an indignity; and, foaming with rage, he rushed out of the palace. His sincere friend, the Lord Keeper, immediately addressed to him an admonitory letter, urging him to lose no time in seeking, with humble submission, the forgiveness of his offended mistress. Essex replied in the following eloquent and manly manner:—

"But, say you, I must yield and submit. I can neither yield myself to be guilty, nor allow this imputation laid upon me to be just. I owe so much to the Author of all truth, that I can never yield falsehood to be truth, nor truth to be falsehood. Have I given cause, ask you, and take scandal when I have done? No; I gave no cause to take so much as Fimbria's complaint against me. I patiently bear all, and sensibly feel all that I then received, when this scandal was given me. Nay, more, when the vilest of all indignities are done unto me, doth religion enforce me to sue? or doth God require it? Is it impiety not to do it? What! cannot princes err? cannot subjects receive wrong? Is an earthly power or authority infinite? Pardon me, pardon me, my good lord, I can never subscribe to these principles! Let Solomon's fool laugh when he is stricken; let those that mean to make their profit of princes show they have no sense of princes' injuries; let them acknowledge an infinite absoluteness on earth, who do not believe in an absolute infiniteness in heaven. As for me, I have received wrong, and feel it. My cause is good; I know it; and whatsoever come, all the powers on earth can never show more strength and constancy in oppressing, than I can show in suffering whatsoever can or shall be imposed upon me."

Several other friends of Essex—his mother, his sister, and the Earl of Northumberland, her husband—urged him, in like manner, to return to his attendance at court, and seek her Majesty's forgiveness; while the Queen, on her part, secretly uneasy at his absence, permitted certain persons to go to him, as from themselves, and suggest terms of accommodation. Sir George Carew was made Lord President of Munster, and Sir William Knolles assured his nephew of his earnest wish to serve him. At length, this extraordinary quarrel was made up, and Essex again appeared at court as powerful as ever: but, from this time, the sentiments of the Queen for her once-cherished favourite partook more of the nature of fear than of love, and confidence was never afterwards re-established between the parties.

The death of Lord Burleigh, the great minister of Elizabeth, took place in 1598. He was in the seventy-eighth year of his age, and had been identified with her government during the long period of forty years. His native quickness of apprehension was supported by an astonishing force and steadiness of application, and by an exemplary spirit of order. His morals were correct; his sense of religion uniform, profound, and practical. In his declining years, harassed by disease and care, and saddened by the loss of an affectionate wife, he became peevish and irascible: but his heart was good; in all the domestic relations he was fond and indulgent; faithful and tender in his friendships; nor could he be accused of pride, treachery, or vindictiveness. Rising by the strength of his own merits, unaided by birth or connections, he formed the resolution of attaching himself to no party. Towards the Queen, his demeanour was in the highest degree obsequious, and on no occasion did he hesitate in the execution of any of her commands. That he accepted bribes for church preferment, there is abundant evidence; but his royal mistress both expected and desired that emolument should be derived by him, and those under him, from such a source. Thus, we find it recorded in "Birch's Memoirs," that Bishop Fletcher had "bestowed in allowances and gratifications to divers attendants about her Majesty, since his preferment to the see of London, the sum of three thousand one hundred pounds; which money was given by him, for the most part, by her Majesty's direction and special appointment." Indeed, the corruption of the court of Elizabeth was so gross, that no public character disdained the influence of gifts and bribes; and we find Lord Burleigh inserting the following moral and prudential rules for the guidance of his son Robert:—"Be sure to keep some great man thy friend; but trouble him not for trifles. Compliment him often; present him with many, yet small gifts, and of little charge. And if thou hast cause to bestow any great gratuity, let it be some such thing as may be daily in his sight. Otherwise, in this ambitious age, thou shalt remain as a hop without a pole, live in obscurity, and be made a football for every insulting companion."

Elizabeth felt severely the loss of her favourite servant, counsellor, and friend. Contrary to her custom on such occasions, she wept much, retired for a time from all society; and, to the end of her life, she could never bear to pronounce his name without tears. Her uniform behaviour towards him evinced her deep sense of his fidelity and merits as a minister, and her affection for him as a man. In his latter years, she constantly made him sit in her presence, on account of his being troubled with the gout, and would pleasantly tell him, "My lord, we make much of you, not on account of your bad legs, but your good head." In his occasional fits of melancholy and retirement, she would woo him back to her presence by kind and playful letters; and she positively refused to accept of his resignation, when his bodily infirmities increased upon him. She constantly visited him when confined by sickness; and on one of these occasions, being humbly requested by his attendant to stoop as she entered at the door of his chamber, the Queen replied, with much feeling and dignity: "For your master's sake, I will, though not for the King of Spain!"

Elizabeth regularly maintained a correspondence with her kinsman and heir, James the Sixth of Scotland. Sir Roger Aston was frequently the bearer of these friendly epistles. "He was an Englishman born," says Welden, "but was brought up wholly in Scotland, and had served the King many years as his barber; he was honest, free-hearted, and of an ancient family in Cheshire, but of no breeding answerable to his birth. Yet was he the only man ever employed as a letter-carrier between the King and the Queen Elizabeth. He was in good esteem with her Majesty; and received many royal gifts, which enriched him, and gave him a better revenue than most gentlemen in Scotland. For the Queen found him as faithful to her, as to his master. In this, his employment, I must not pass over one pretty passage I have heard him himself relate. That whenever he came to deliver letters from his master, James the Sixth, to Elizabeth, he was placed in the lobby, where he might see the Queen dancing to a little fiddle; which was to no other end than that, on his return, he should pronounce it to be next to impossible for James to succeed to the throne of the gay, vigorous Elizabeth, who, to all appearances, would outlive the Scottish monarch."

Although in her letters to James the Sixth, Elizabeth did not hesitate treating him as the undisputed heir to the throne, she still pertinaciously refused to publicly declare her successor. Sir John Harrington relates the following lively anecdote on this subject:—"I no sooner remember this famous and worthy prelate (Hatton, Archbishop of York), but methinks I see him in the chapel at Whitehall, Queen Elizabeth at the window in the closet; all the lords of the parliament, spiritual and temporal, about them; and then, after his three obeisances, that I hear him out of the pulpit thundering this text: 'The kingdoms of the earth are mine, and I do give them to whom I will; I have given them to Nebuchadnezzar and his son, and his son's son:' which text being produced, taking the sense rather than the words of the prophet. He showed how oft our nation had been a prey to foreigners; and finally, conquered and reduced to subjection by the Normans, whose posterity continued in great prosperity to the days of her Majesty, who for peace, for plenty, for glory, for continuance, had exceeded them all; who had lived to change all her councillors but one; all officers twice or thrice; some bishops four times: only the uncertainty of succession gave hopes to foreigners to attempt fresh invasions, and breed fears of a new conquest. The only policy left to quail those hopes, to assuage those fears, was to establish the succession: and at last, insinuating, as far as he durst, the nearness of blood of our present sovereign, he said plainly, that the expectations and presages of all writers went northward, naming Scotland without any circumlocution, 'which,' said he, 'if it prove an error, yet it will be found a learned one.'

"All who knew Elizabeth's disposition, imagined that such a discourse was as welcome as salt to the eyes; or, to use her own words, 'to pin up her winding sheet before her face, so to point out her successor, and urge her to declare him;' wherefore, we all expected that she would have been highly offended: but when the sermon was finished, and she opened the window, we found ourselves deceived; for very kindly and calmly, without shew of offence (as if she had but waiked out of some sleep), she gave him thanks for his very learned discourse. Yet, when she had better considered the matter, in private, she sent councillors to him with a sharp message, to which he was glad to give a patient answer."

The death of her Majesty's poet-laureate, the immortal Spenser, under circumstances of severe distress, now excited the commiseration and regret of all the friends and patrons of English genius. After witnessing the destruction of his whole property by the Irish rebels, the unfortunate poet had fled to England for shelter;—the annuity of fifty pounds a year, which he enjoyed by virtue of his office, was apparently his only resource; and, having taken up his melancholy abode in an obscure lodging in London, he pined away under the pressure of penury and grief. Spenser was interred with great solemnity in Westminster Abbey, by the side of Chaucer; the generous Essex defraying the cost of the funeral, and walking himself as a mourner. Alas! would to God that the patrons of genius would only take the trouble to inquire into the circumstances of such men whilst they are yet living, their munificence would be more appreciated by posterity, than by paying funeral honours, or raising sculptured monuments to the memory of departed worth! That ostentatious, but munificent woman, Anne, Countess of Dorset, erected a handsome monument to his memory; and his brother poets who attended his funeral, threw elegies and sonnets into his grave.

CHAPTER XIV.

Essex appointed Lord Lieutenant of Ireland—His letter to Elizabeth—His departure for Ireland—Unexpected return—Sir John Harrington—Behaviour of Elizabeth—Disgrace of Essex—Elizabeth denies him a last favour—His revolt—Trial and execution—Grief and illness of the Queen—Story of the ring—Death of Elizabeth—Her burial—Tomb—Epitaphs—Character—Laudatory rhymes—Bishop Hall's Eulogium.

N 1598, the state of Ireland was in every respect deplorable:—the whole province of Ulster was in open rebellion, under Tyrone; and the rest of the country reduced to despair by innumerable oppressions, and by the rumour of further severities meditated by the Queen of England. In this state of things, Elizabeth, notwithstanding the unwillingness she felt at parting with her favourite Essex, resolved to appoint him to the high office of Lord Deputy of Ireland. The friends of the Earl eagerly forwarded his appointment, by eulogiums of his valour and genius, and imprudent anticipations of his certain and complete success. But Essex himself began to look upon the appointment as a kind of banishment. Secretary Cecil, in a letter dated December the fourth, 1598, states, that "the opinion of the Earl's going to Ireland had some stop; by reason of his lordship's indisposition to it, except with some such conditions as were disagreeable to her Majesty's mind; although," he added, "the cup will hardly pass from him in regard of his worth and fortune; but if it do, my Lord Montjoy is named." In the midst of the difficulties thus thrown in the way, Essex endeavoured to work upon the feelings of Elizabeth, by the following somewhat romantic epistle:—

"To the Queen.

"From a mind delighting in sorrow, from spirits wasted with passion, from a heart torn in pieces with care, grief and travel—from a man that hateth himself, and all things else that keep him alive, what service can your Majesty expect; since any service past deserves no more than banishment and proscription to the cursedest of all islands? It is your rebel's pride and succession must give me leave to ransom myself out of this hateful prison, out of my loathed body; which, if it happeneth so, your Majesty shall have no cause to dislike the fashion of my death, since the course of my life could never please you.

"Happy could he finish forth his fate
In some unhaunted desert more obscure,
From all society, from love and hate
Of worldly folk; then should he sleep secure;
Then wake again and yield God ever praise,
Content with hips and haws, and brambleberry;
In contemplation passing out his days,
And change of holy thoughts to make him merry.
Who when he dies, his tomb may be a bush
Where harmless robin dwells with gentle thrush.

"Your Majesty's exiled servant,
"Robert Essex."

The obstacles which had delayed the appointment of Essex, were gradually removed; the Queen consented to invest him with more ample powers than had ever before been conferred on a lord deputy. All his requisitions of men and supplies were complied with, and an army of twenty thousand foot and two thousand horse—a larger army than had ever been sent to Ireland—was placed at his disposal. At parting, the tenderness of the Queen revived in full force; and she dismissed him with expressions of regret and affection, which, as he afterwards professed to her, had "pierced his very soul." The people followed him with acclamations; and the flower of the nobility, as in the Cadiz expedition, attended him as volunteers. He embarked about the end of March, 1599; and, landing at Dublin, after a dangerous passage, his first act was, in direct opposition to the Queen's orders, to appoint his friend, the Earl of Southampton, to the office of general of the horse. He abandoned his original intention, of marching immediately against Tyrone, and devoted his early efforts to the suppression of a minor revolt in Munster; but in this he encountered a resistance so formidable, and found himself so ill supported by his troops, whom the nature of the service speedily disheartened, that after about four months, wasted in petty encounters, the army returned, sick, wearied, and greatly reduced in number. Essex, on learning that the Queen was much displeased at this expedition into Munster, and the appointment he had conferred on Southampton, addressed an eloquent letter to the Privy Council, in which, after declaring that he had done his duty to the best of his abilities and judgment, he says, "touching the displacing of the Earl of Southampton; your lordships say, that her Majesty thinketh it strange, and taketh it offensively, that I should appoint him general of the horse; seeing not only her Majesty denied it when I moved it, but gave an express prohibition to any such choice. I remember that her Majesty, in her privy-chamber at Richmond, I only being with her, showed a dislike of his having any office; but my answer was, that if her Majesty would revoke my commission, I would cast both it and myself at her Majesty's feet; but if it pleased her Majesty that I should execute it, I must work with my own instruments. O! miserable employment, and more miserable destiny of mine, that makes it impossible for me to please and serve her Majesty at once! Was it treason in my Lord of Southampton to marry my poor kinswoman, that neither long imprisonment, nor any punishment besides that hath been usual in like cases, can satisfy and appease? Or, will no kind of punishment be fit for him but that which punisheth, not him, but me, this army, and this poor country of Ireland? Shall I keep the country when the army breaks? Or, shall the army stand when all the volunteers leave it? Or, will any voluntaries stay, when those that have will and cause to follow are thus handled? No, my lords, they already ask passports, and that daily."

Notwithstanding this eloquent appeal, the Queen still persisted in requiring Essex to displace his friend; and even chid him severely for delay, after once learning her displeasure on this point. Success in the main object of his expedition might still, however, have enabled him to triumph over his court enemies, and effect a reconciliation with his offended mistress; but fortune had now turned its back upon him. The necessity of quelling some rebels in Leinster again prevented his march to Ulster. But by this time the season had so far advanced, and the army had become so sickly, that both the Earl and his council were of opinion, that nothing effectual could be done; and, at the first notice of his intended march, great part of his forces deserted. He, nevertheless, proceeded, and, in a few days, came in sight of the main army of the rebels, much more numerous than his own. Tyrone, however, would not venture to give him battle, but demanded a parley. This was granted, a conference was held, and a truce concluded, to be renewed every six weeks, till terms of peace should be finally agreed upon. During the whole of this time, sharp letters were passing between Elizabeth, her privy council, and the Earl.

The Queen remonstrated with Essex against his contemptuous disobedience of her orders, and his wasting, in frivolous enterprizes, vast supplies of men and money which she had entrusted to him for a great and specific purpose. Apprehensive, lest by his remaining longer in Ireland, he should be irrecoverably lost in the affections of her Majesty, he resolved to risk another act of disobedience—that of leaving for a while his important charge, and hastening to throw himself at the feet of an exasperated, but, he flattered himself, not a relentless mistress. Accordingly he embarked with his household, and a number of his favourite officers, and arrived at the court, which was then held at Nonsuch, on the morning before Michaelmas-day. On alighting at the gate, covered with mud and dirt, he hastened up stairs; passed through the presence and privy chambers, and never stopped till he reached the Queen's bed-chamber, where he found her Majesty newly risen, with her hair all hanging about her face. He kneeled and kissed her hands; and she, in the agreeable surprise of beholding at her feet one whom she still loved, received him so kindly, and listened with such favour to his excuses, that on leaving her, after a private conference of some duration, he appeared in high spirits, and thanked God, that though he had suffered many storms abroad, he found a sweet calm at home. He waited on her again, as soon as he had changed his dress, and after a second long and gracious conference, was freely visited by all the lords, ladies, and gentlemen at court, excepting the Secretary and his party, who appeared somewhat shy of him. But all these fair appearances quickly vanished. On again visiting the Queen in the evening, he found her much changed towards him; she began to call him to account for his unauthorized return, and the hazard to which he had exposed Ireland. Four privy councillors were appointed by her to examine him that night, and hear his answers; but nothing was concluded, the matter being referred to a full council, summoned for the following day, Essex, in the mean time, being commanded to keep his chamber. The council having met, the Earl answered with great gravity and discretion the following charges brought against him: "His contemptuous disobedience of her Majesty's orders and will in returning; his presumptuous letters written from time to time; his proceedings in Ireland contrary to his instructions; his rash manner of coming away from Ireland; his over-boldness in going the day before to her Majesty's presence to her bed-chamber; and his making of so many idle knights." After the council had heard his defence, they remained awhile in consultation, and then made their report to the Queen, who said, "she would take time to consider his answers." In the meanwhile, the proceedings were kept very private, and the Earl continued a prisoner in his own apartment.

An open division now took place between the two great factions which had long secretly divided the court. The Earls of Shrewsbury and Nottingham, Lords Thomas Howard, Cobham, and Grey, Sir Walter Raleigh, and Sir George Carew, espoused the cause of the Secretary; while Essex was followed by the Earls of Worcester and Rutland, Lords Montjoy, Rich, Lumley, and Henry Howard, the last of whom was already suspected of treachery towards his friend and patron. Sir William Knolles also joined the party of his nephew, with many other knights and gentlemen. Lord Effingham, though son of the Earl of Nottingham, who espoused the opposite party, was often with Essex, and protested all service to him. "It is a world to be here!" continues Whyte, in the "Sidney Papers," from which these interesting particulars are gleaned; "and see the humours of the place." On the second of October, Essex was commanded to retire from court, and committed to the custody of the Lord Keeper, with whom he remained at York-House.

Harrington, the wit and poet, had the misfortune to be one of the three-score "idle knights" dubbed by the Lord Deputy, during his short and inglorious career in Ireland; and also one of the officers selected to accompany him in his return; and we learn from his own letters in what manner his royal godmother welcomed him on his arrival:—

"My worthy Lord,

"I have lived to see that d—— rebel Tyrone brought to England, courteously honoured, favoured, and well-liked. Oh! my lord, what is there which doth not prove the inconstancy of worldly matters! How did I labour after that knave's destruction! I was called from my home by her Majesty's command, adventured perils by sea and land, endured toil, was near starving, ate horse-flesh at Munster, and all to quell that man, who now smileth in peace at those who did hazard their lives to destroy him. I obeyed in going with Essex to Ireland, and obeyed in coming with him to England. But what did I gain? why, truly, a knighthood, which had been better bestowed by her that sent me, and better spared by him that gave it. I shall never put out of my memory her Majesty's displeasure: I entered her chamber, but she frowned, and said, 'What! did the fool bring you too? Go back to your business!'"

In a letter to Mr. Robert Markham, Harrington says:—

"My good Cousin,

"Herewith you will have my journal, with our history during our march against the Irish rebels. I did not intend any eyes should have seen this matter, but my own children's; yet, alas! it happened otherwise; for the Queen did so ask, and I may say, demand my account, that I could not withhold showing it; and I, even now, almost tremble to rehearse her Majesty's displeasure hereat. She swore, by God's son, we were all idle knaves, and the Lord Deputy worse, for wasting our time and her commands, in suchwise as my journal doth write of. She chafed much, walked fastly to and fro, looked with discomposure in her visage; and, I remember, she caught my girdle when I knelt to her, and swore, 'By God's son, I am no Queen: that man (meaning Essex) is above me! Who gave him command to come here so soon? I did send him on other business!' It was long before more gracious discourse fell to my hearing; but I was then put out of my trouble, and bid go home. I did not stay to be bidden twice; if all the Irish rebels had been at my heels, I should not have made better speed, for I now fled from one whom I both loved and feared too."

Our readers will, no doubt, be gratified to learn some further particulars of Sir John Harrington, the author of these amusing letters. He was the godson of Elizabeth, being the child of her faithful servants, James Harrington and Isabella Markham. He was born in 1566, and, after the usual course of school and college education, young Harrington presented himself at court, where his wit and learning soon procured him a rather dangerous distinction. A satirical poem was traced to him as its author, containing certain allusions to living characters, which gave so much offence at court, that he was threatened with the tender mercies of the star-chamber; but the secret favour of Elizabeth towards a godson whom she loved, and who amused her, saved him from this very serious kind of retaliation. Soon afterwards, he translated a tale out of Ariosto, which proved highly entertaining to the court ladies, and so pleased the Queen, that, in affected displeasure at certain over-free passages, which she secretly glozed over, she ordered him to appear no more at court—till he had translated the whole poem! The royal command was obeyed with alacrity; and he speedily committed his Orlando to the press, with a dedication to her Majesty! Before this time, our sprightly poet had found means to dissipate a considerable part of the large estate to which he was heir; and being inclined to follow the friendly counsels of Essex, who bade him "lay good hold on her Majesty's bounty, and ask freely," he dexterously opened his case, by the following lines, slipped behind her cushion:—

"For ever dear, for ever dreaded Prince,
You read a verse of mine a little since;
And so pronounced each word and every letter,
Your gracious reading graced my verse the better;
Since then your Highness doth by gift exceeding,
Make what you read the better for your reading;
Let my poor Muse your pains thus far importune,
Like as you read my verse, so—read my fortune.
"*From your Highness's saucy Godson.*"

Of the various little arts of pleasing to which Harrington applied himself, some amusing instances are given in his own note-book, kept by himself:—"I am to send good store of news from the country, for her Highness' entertainment. Her Highness loveth merry tales." "The Queen stood up and bade me reach forth my right hand to rest her thereon. O! what sweet burden to my next song. Petrarch shall eke out good matter for this business." "The Queen loveth to see me in my new frize jerkin; and saith 'tis well cut. I will have another made like to it. I do remember she spat on Sir Matthew's fringed cloth, and said the fool's wit was gone to rags. Heaven spare me from such a jibing!" "I must turn my poor wits towards my suit for the lands in the north—I must go in an early hour, before her Highness hath special matters brought up to counsel on. I must go before the breakfast covers are placed, and stand uncovered as her highness cometh forth from her chamber; then kneel, and say, 'God save your Majesty! I crave your ear at what hour may suit for your servant to meet your blessed countenance.' Thus will I gain her favour to follow me to the auditory.

'Trust not a friend to do or say,
In that yourself can sue or pray.'"

The lands alluded to, formed a large estate in the north of England, which an ancestor had forfeited by his adherence to the House of York, during the civil wars, and which Harrington was now endeavouring to recover. "Yet will I venture," writes he to a friend, "to give her Majesty five hundred pounds in money, and some pretty jewel or garment, as you shall advise; only praying her Majesty to further my suit with some of her learned counsel, which I pray you to find some proper time to move in. This some hold as a dangerous adventure, but five-and-twenty manors do well justify my trying it."

This singular paragraph proves, to demonstration, the avarice and corruption of the age of Elizabeth. When sovereigns lead the way to such venality, there is no knowing where it may end.

The fate of Essex remained long in suspense, while several little circumstances indicated the strength of the Queen's resentment against him. To the personal request of Lady Walsingham, she peremptorily denied the Earl permission, even to write to his Countess, her daughter, who was in childbed, and exceedingly troubled at neither seeing nor hearing from her husband. She also refused to allow his family physician access to him, though he was now so ill as to be attended by several other physicians; with whom, however, Dr. Brown was permitted to consult; at the same time it was given out, that if he would beg his liberty for the purpose of going back to Ireland, it would be granted him. But he was resolute never to return thither, and professed a determination of leading henceforth a retired life in the country, free from all participation in public affairs. His sisters, Lady Rich and Lady Southampton, quitted Essex House and went into the country, because the resort of company to them had given great offence. He himself neither saw, nor desired to see, any one. His very servants were afraid to meet in any place to make merry, lest it might be taken ill..

"At the court," says Whyte, "Lady Scrope is only noted to stand firm to him; for she endures much at her Majesty's hands, because she daily does all kind of offices of love to the Queen in his behalf. She wears all black; she mourns and is pensive, and joys in nothing but in being solitary and alone. And 'tis thought she says much that few would venture to say but herself." This noble and generous woman was daughter of the first Lord Hunsdon, and nearly related both to Essex and the Queen.

Towards the middle of October, strong hopes were entertained of the Earl's enlargement. The Secretary expressed to him the satisfaction he felt in seeing her Majesty so well appeased by his demeanour, and his own wish to promote her good. The reasons which he had assigned for his conduct in Ireland appeared to have satisfied the privy council and mollified the Queen. But her Majesty characteristically declared, that she would not bear the blame of his imprisonment; and before she and her council could settle among them on whom it should be made to rest, a new cause of exasperation arose. Tyrone, in a letter to Essex, which was intercepted, declared that he found it impossible to prevail on his confederates to observe the conditions of truce agreed upon between them; and the Queen, relapsing into anger, triumphantly asked if there did not now appear good cause for the Earl's committal? She immediately made known to Lord Montjoy her wish that he should undertake the government of Ireland; but the friendship of this nobleman to Essex induced Montjoy to excuse himself. The council unanimously recommended to her Majesty the enlargement of Essex, but she angrily replied, that such contempts as he had been guilty of ought to be openly punished, and caused heads of accusation to be drawn up against him. All this time Essex continued ill, and his once high spirit now condescended to such supplications as the following:—

"To the Queen.

"When the creature entereth into account with the Creator, it can never number in how many things it needs mercy, nor in how many it receives it. But he that is best stored must still say, *da nobis hodie;* and he that hath showed most thankfulness, must ask again, *quid retribuamus?* And I can no sooner finish this my first audit, most dear and most admired Sovereign, but I come to consider how large a measure of this grace, and how great a resemblance of his power, God hath given you upon earth; and how many ways he giveth occasion to you to exercise the divine offices upon us, that are your vassals. This confession best fitteth me, of all men, and it is now most joyfully and most humbly made by me. I acknowledge, upon the knees of my heart, your Majesty's infinite goodness in granting my humble petition. God, who seeth all, is witness how faithfully I do vow to dedicate the rest of my life next after my highest duty, in obedience, faith, and zeal to your Majesty, without admitting any other worldly care; and whatsoever your Majesty resolveth to do with me, I shall live and die,

"Your Majesty's humblest vassal,

"Essex."

Two months afterwards, perceiving no immediate prospect of his restoration to liberty, he again addressed her Majesty in the following style:—

"Before all letters written with this hand be banished, or he who sends this enjoin himself eternal silence, be pleased, I humbly beseech your Majesty, to read over these few lines. At sundry times, and by several messengers, I received these words as your Majesty's own—that you meant to correct, but not to ruin. Since which time, I do not only feel the intolerable weight of your Majesty's indignation, but, as if I were thrown into a corner like a dead carcase, I am gnawed on, and torn by the vilest and basest creatures. The tavern-hunter speaks of me as he lists; already they print me, and make me speak to the world; and shortly they will play me upon the stage. The least of these is a thousand times worse than death. But this is not the worst of my destiny; for your Majesty, who hath mercy for all the world but me—who hath protected from scorn and infamy all to whom you once vowed favour, but Essex—and never repented you of any gracious assurance you had given, till now—your Majesty, I say, hath now, in this eighth month of my close imprisonment—as if you thought my infirmities, beggary, and infamy too little punishment for me—rejected my letters, refused to hear of me; which to traitors you never did. What, therefore, remaineth for me? Only this, to beseech your Majesty, on the knees of my heart, to conclude my punishment, my misery, and my life together, that I may go to my Saviour, who hath paid himself a ransom for me; and to whom, methinks, I still hear calling me out of this unkind world, in which I have lived too long, and once thought myself too happy!

"From your Majesty's humblest servant,

"Essex."

At length the Queen commanded that eighteen commissioners be selected out of the Privy Council, to discuss his conduct, hear his accusation and defence, and finally pronounce upon him such a censure—for it was not to be called a sentence—as they should deem meet. The pathetic eloquence of the noble prisoner moved many of the council to tears; and even his enemies were affected. Finally, it was the unanimous sentiment of the council, that the Earl should abstain from exercising the functions of Privy Councillor, Earl Marshal, or Master of the Ordnance; that he should return to his own house, and there remain a prisoner as before, till it should please her Majesty to remit the sentence.

This censure tranquillized, but did not destroy the Queen's wrath against Essex. A few days afterwards, her Majesty repaired to Lady Russel's house, in Blackfriars, to grace the nuptials of her daughter, a maid of honour, with Lord Herbert, son of the Earl of Leicester; on which occasion she was conveyed from the water side in a half-litter, borne by six knights. After dining with the wedding company, she passed to the neighbouring house of Lord Cobham to sup. Here she was entertained with a mask by eight ladies, who, after performing their appointed parts, chose out eight ladies more to dance the measure; when Mrs. Fitton, the principal masker, came, and "wooed" the Queen also to dance. Her Majesty inquired who she was? "Affection," she replied. "Affection!" exclaimed the Queen, "is false." Yet she rose and danced!

In August, 1600, the Earl was acquainted in due form, by the Privy Council, that his liberty was restored, but that he was still prohibited from appearing at court. He answered, that it was his design to lead a retired life at his uncle's, in Oxfordshire; yet he begged their intercession, that he might be admitted to kiss the Queen's hand before his departure. But this was too great a favour to be granted; and he was informed, that though free from restraint, he was still to consider himself as in disgrace; a circumstance which deterred all but his nearest relations from resorting to him.

The following interesting letter from Sir Robert Sidney to Sir John Harrington, affords an insight into the character and conduct of Elizabeth at this period:—

"Worthy Knight;

"Your present to the Queen was well accepted of; she did much commend your verse, nor did she less praise your prose. The Queen has tasted your dainties, and saith you have marvellous skill in cooking of good fruits. If I can serve you in your northern suit, you may command me. Visit your friends often, and please the Queen by all you can; for all the great lawyers do much fear her displeasure. I do see the Queen often; she doth wax weak since the late troubles, and Burleigh's death doth often draw tears from her goodly cheeks; she walketh out but little; meditates much alone; and sometimes writes in private to her best friends. Her Highness hath done honour to my poor house by visiting me; and seemed much pleased at our efforts to amuse her. My son made her a fair speech, to which she made a gracious reply. The women danced before her, whilst the cornets saluted from the gallery; and she vouchsafed to eat two morsels of rich comfit cake, and drank a small cordial out of a golden cup. She had a marvellous suit of velvet, borne by four of her first female attendants, in rich apparel; two ushers went before; and at going up stairs she called for a staff; and was much wearied in walking about the house, and said she wished to come another day. Six drums and six trumpets remained in the court, and were sounded at her approach and departure. My wife bore herself in wondrous good liking, and was attired in a purple kirtle fringed with gold; and myself in a rich band and collar of needlework; and wore a goodly stuff of the bravest cut and fashion, with an under body of silver and loops. The Queen commended much our appearance, and smiled at the ladies, who, in their dances, often came up to the step on which the seat was fixed, to make their obeisance, and so fell back into their order again. The younger Markham did several gallant feats on a horse before the gate, leaping down and kissing his sword, then mounting swiftly on the saddle, and passing a lance with much skill. When the day was well nigh spent, the Queen went and tasted a small beverage, that was set out in divers rooms where she might pass; and then, in much order, was attended to her palace, the cornets and trumpets sounding through the streets."

The fate of the royal favourite, Essex, was now approaching a crisis. The perseverance of the Queen in refusing to re-admit him to her presence, caused him the most tormenting anxiety; and he at length resolved to bring her disposition towards him finally to the test. The period for which he held the lucrative farm of sweet wines would expire at Michaelmas; he was soliciting its renewal; and on the doubtful balance of success or failure his future conduct would hinge. On this occasion he spared no expressions of humility and contrition which might soften the obdurate heart of his royal mistress. He professed to kiss the hand and the rod with which he had been corrected—to look forward to the time when he could again behold those blessed eyes, so long his cynosure, as the only real happiness which he could ever enjoy; and he declared his intention, like Nebuchadnezzar, to make his habitation with the beasts of the field—to eat hay like an ox, and to be wet with the dews of heaven, until it should please the Queen to restore him. To Lord Henry Howard, who was the bearer of these humiliating expressions, the Queen declared her unfeigned satisfaction to find him in so proper a frame of mind; she only wished, she said, "that his future actions might harmonize with his words; and, as he had long tried her patience, it was proper that she should make some experiment of his sincerity. Her father never would have endured such perverse conduct; but she would not now look back; 'all that glittered was not gold;' but if such results came forth from her furnace, she should ever after think the better of her crucible." But having soon after detected the secret motive for all these moving expressions of penitence and devotion, her disgust against Essex was revived; and she not only finally rejected his suit, for the renewed contract of wines, but added these coarse and insulting words; that "an ungovernable beast must be stinted of his provender, in order to bring him under proper management!"

The spirit of Essex could endure no more; rage took possession of his soul! and, equally desperate in fortune and in mind, he was ready to engage in any enterprise which his bitterest enemies could desire. In return for the vulgarity of the Queen, he used the equally coarse expression, which was eagerly and maliciously reported to her by certain ladies of the court, "that through old age, the mind of the Queen had become as crooked as her carcase:" words alone sufficient to cool the ardour of the most indulgent mistress.

In his extremity, Essex applied to the King of Scotland, urging him to lose no time in claiming, by his ambassadors, a solemn acknowledgment of his title to succeed to the throne of England. In the mean time he formed a council of five of his most devoted friends:—the Earl of Southampton, Sir Charles Danvers, Sir Ferdinand Gorges, Sir John Davis, Surveyor of the Ordnance, and John Littleton, Esq., of Frankley. By this junto, which met privately at Drury House, a plot against the crown was matured. The Earl delivered in a list of a hundred and twenty nobles, knights, and gentlemen, on whose attachment he thought he could rely; it was then agreed that an attempt should be made to seize the palace, and to compel the Queen to remove from her councils the enemies of the Earl, and to summon a new Parliament; and their respective parts were allotted to the destined actors in the scene of rebellion. In the mean while, the extraordinary bustle at Essex House could not escape the vigilance of government; and measures were immediately taken for obtaining intelligence of all that passed within its walls. Lord Henry Howard was the first to betray his friend; and a domestic of Essex, who had been brought up with him from infancy, and who was in his entire confidence, had also the baseness to reveal his counsels. On the seventh of February, 1601, the Privy Council, being fully informed of his proceedings, dispatched Secretary Herbert to summon Essex to appear before them. But, apprehensive that he was betrayed, and conscious that the steps he had taken were not to be justified, the Earl excused himself from attending the council; and, summoning around him the most confidential of his friends, he represented to them that they were on the eve of being sent to prison; and bade them decide whether they would quietly submit to their enemies, or attempt thus to carry their plans into effect. In the course of the discussion which followed, a person entered, who pretended to be deputed by the City of London to assure the Earl of their cordial co-operation in his cause. This decided the matter; Essex, with a more cheerful countenance, began to expatiate on the affection borne him by the City, and his expectation of being joined by Sheriff Smith with a thousand of the trained bands which he commanded. The next morning was fixed upon for the insurrection; and, in the mean time, emissaries were dispatched about town in all directions, to spread among the friends of the Earl the alarm of a design upon his life, by the agents of Lord Cobham and Sir Walter Raleigh.

Early in the morning, the Lord Keeper, the Lord Chief Justice, and Sir William Knowles, Comptroller of the Household, arrived at Essex House, and demanded entrance in the name of the Queen. They, themselves, were with difficulty admitted through the wicket of the gate, which was now kept shut and guarded; and all their servants were excluded except the purse-bearer. They beheld the court-yard filled with a confused multitude, in the midst of which stood Essex, accompanied by the Earls of Southampton and Rutland, and many others. The Lord Keeper demanded, in the name of her Majesty, the cause of this unusual concourse; adding an assurance, that if any one had injured his Lordship he should find redress. Essex, in a vehement manner, complained of letters counterfeited in his name; of designs against his life; of perfidious dealings towards him; but the conference was interrupted by the clamours of the multitude, some of whom threatened violence to the emissaries of the court. Without further parley Essex conducted them into the house, where he ordered them to be safely kept, as hostages, till his return from the City, whither he was hastening to take measures with the Lord Mayor and Sheriffs to accomplish his purpose. He then entered the City, attended by the Earls of Southampton and Rutland, Lords Sandys and Monteagle, Sir Charles Danvers, Sir Christopher Blount, and many others. On passing through Fleet Street, they cried out, "For the Queen! for the Queen!" They also gave out that Cobham and Raleigh intended to have murdered Essex in his bed.

The people, being partial to Essex, eagerly believed that he and the Queen were reconciled, and that she had appointed him to ride in that triumphant manner through the City to his house in Seething Lane. However, the Lord Mayor received timely information from the privy council of the real state of affairs, and, by eleven, the gates were closed and strongly guarded. Though greatly disconcerted at seeing no preparations for joining him, Essex repaired to the house of Sheriff Smith, but this officer slipped out at the back door, and hastened to the Lord Mayor for instructions. The Earl next proceeded to an armourer's, and demanded ammunition, which was refused; and while hastening to and fro, without aim or object, Lord Burleigh boldly entered the City, with a garter king-at-arms, and half a score horsemen, and proclaimed the Earl and his adherents to be traitors to their country. One of the attendants of Essex discharged a pistol-shot at Burleigh, without effect; but the multitude showed no dispositon to molest him, and he hastened back to assure the Queen that there was no danger of a commotion in the City. The palace was now fortified and strongly guarded, the streets blocked up with carts and coaches; and the Earl, after wandering about the City till two o'clock, and finding that none of the citizens would join him, and that many of his original followers had deserted him, determined to make his way back to Essex House. At Ludgate, he was opposed by a body of troops, posted there by order of the Bishop of London; when, drawing his sword, he directed Sir Christopher Blount to attack them; "which," says Birch, "he did with great bravery, and killed Waite, a stout officer, who had been formerly hired by the Earl of Leicester to assassinate Sir Christopher, and was now abandoned by his company." But Essex was speedily repulsed with the loss of one young gentleman killed, and Sir Christopher Blount wounded and taken prisoner. Then retreating with his diminished band to the river-side, the Earl returned by water to his own house. Here he was much disappointed to find that his three prisoners had been liberated in his absence by Sir Ferdinand Gorges; but still clinging to his hopes of an insurrection in his favour, he proceeded to fortify his house. It was soon, however, invested by a considerable force, under the orders of the Lord Admiral, the Earls of Cumberland and Lincoln. Sir Robert Sidney summoned the little garrison to surrender, when the Earl of Southampton demanded terms and hostages, but being answered that none would be granted to rebels, except that the ladies and their female domestics would, if they desired, be permitted to depart, the besieged declared their resolution to hold out, and the assault commenced. Lord Sandys advised Essex to cut his way through the assailants, it being more honourable for men of quality to die sword in hand than by the axe of the executioner; but the Earl, who had resigned all hopes of life, was easily moved by the tears and entreaties of the surrounding females, to adopt less courageous counsels. Captain Owen Salisbury, a brave veteran, seeing that all was lost, planted himself at a window, bare-headed, and received a bullet on the side of his head from one of the assailants. "Oh!" cried he, "that thou hadst been so much my friend to have shot but a little lower!" He died, notwithstanding, the following day. About six in the morning, the Earl announced his willingness to surrender, on receiving assurance, for himself and friends, of civil treatment and a legal trial; and permission for a clergyman, named Aston, to attend him in prison: the Lord Admiral replied, that of the first two articles there could be no doubt, and he would intercede for the last. The house then capitulated, with all its inmates. During the night, the principal offenders were sent to Lambeth Palace, and the following day they were conveyed to the Tower, while those of an inferior rank were committed to gaol.

On the ninth of February, Essex and Southampton were brought to trial before the House of Peers—Lord Buckhurst sitting as Lord High Steward. Essex pleaded not guilty, professed his loyalty to his Queen and country, and assigned, as his motive for the late attempt, that it was an act of self-defence against the machinations of his enemies, who plotted his life. Whatever construction lawyers might put upon it, the necessity of self-defence against Cobham, Raleigh, and Cecil, had impelled him to raise the City, and he was consoled by the testimony of an approving conscience. Lord Cobham here rose and protested that he had never acted with malice against the Earl, although he had disapproved of his ambition. "On my faith," replied Essex, "I would have given this right hand to have removed from the Queen such an informer and calumniator!" The Earl of Southampton also pleaded not guilty, and professed his inviolate fidelity towards her Majesty, and conducted himself with an ingenuous modesty of behaviour which won all hearts. After a trial, which lasted eleven hours, a verdict of guilty was unanimously pronounced on both earls. In an affecting manner, Southampton implored all present to intercede for him with her Majesty; and Essex, with great earnestness, joined in this prayer of his unfortunate friend: as to himself, he said, he was not anxious for life; wishing for nothing more than to lay it down with entire fidelity towards God and his Queen. Yet he would have no one insinuate to the Queen that he despised her mercy, though he should not too submissively implore it; and he hoped all men would in their consciences acquit him, though the law had pronounced him guilty. Such was the lofty tone assumed by Essex.

Elizabeth behaved on the occasion of this insurrection with her wonted fortitude. Even when Essex was actually in the City, and a false report was brought to her of its revolt, "She was never more amazed," says Cecil, "than she would have been to have heard of a fray in Fleet Street." But when, in the further progress of this affair, she beheld her once loved Essex brought to the bar for high treason, and condemned by the unanimous verdict of his peers—when it rested solely with herself to take the forfeit of his life, or interfere by an act of special grace for his preservation—her grief, agitation, and perplexity became extreme. She still loved him, and remembered with fondness the affectionate zeal with which he had served her; but whilst her heart was pleading for his forgiveness, one of his followers was seized in an attempt to enter the palace for the purpose of compelling her to sign a warrant for the release of the two Earls. This alarmed the fears of Elizabeth. Irresolute for several days, she at one time ordered, then countermanded, the order for his execution; then, repenting her weakness, she signed a second warrant, in obedience to which he was finally brought to the scaffold, on the twenty-sixth of February, 1601. He had requested of the Queen that he might be put to death in as private a manner as possible, within the walls of the Tower. His wish was willingly complied with; but about a hundred nobles, knights, and gentlemen witnessed the awful scene, from seats placed near the scaffold. Sir Walter Raleigh stationed himself at the window of an armoury, whence he could see all that passed, without being perceived by the Earl: the sorrowful spectacle melted even him to tears.

The life of Southampton was spared, at the intercession of Cecil; but he was confined in the Tower until the death of the Queen. Four only of the principal conspirators suffered capitally—these were Sir Christopher Blount, Sir Charles Danvers, Sir Gilly Melrick, and Henry Cuff.

The peace of mind of Elizabeth received an incurable wound by the loss of her unhappy favourite. In the following letter from Sir John Harrington to Sir Hugh Portman, dated October 9th, 1601, nearly eight months after the fatal event, we have a vivid description of her feelings:—

"For six weeks I left my oxen and sheep, and ventured to court. Much was my comfort in being well received, notwithstanding it is an ill hour for seeing the Queen. The mad-caps are all in riot, and much evil threatened. In good sooth, I feared her Majesty more than the rebel Tyrone, and wished I had never received my Lord of Essex's honour of knighthood. She is quite changed in countenance, and unattired; and these troubles waste her much. She disregardeth every costly cover that cometh to the table, and taketh little but manchet and succory pottage. Every new message from the City doth disturb her, and she frowns on all the ladies. I had a sharp message from her, brought by my Lord Buckhurst, namely this:—'Go tell that witty fellow, my godson, to get home; it is no season now to fool it here!' I liked this as little as she doth my knighthood; so took to my boots, and returned in bad weather to the plough. I must not say much, even by this trusty and sure messenger; but the many evil plots and designs hath overcome all her Highness' sweet temper. She walks much in her privy-chamber, and stamps with her feet at ill news, and thrusts her rusty sword at times into the arras in great rage. My Lord Buckhurst is much with her, and few else, since the City business; but the dangers are over, and yet she always keeps a sword by her table. I obtained a short audience at my first coming to court, when her Highness told me, if ill-counsel had brought me so far from home, she wished heaven might mar that fortune which she had mended. I made my peace in this point, and will not leave my poor castle of Kelsten, for fear of finding a worse elsewhere, as others have done. I could not move in any suit to serve your neighbour B., such was the face of things; and so disordered is all order, that her Highness has worn but one change of raiment for many days; and swears much at those that cause her griefs in such wise, to the no small discomfiture of all about her, more especially our sweet Lady Arundel."

In the month of October, the Queen summoned her last Parliament! Her procession to the House had something gloomy and ominous; the people still resenting the death of their favourite, Essex, whom they never could be taught to regard as a traitor to his Sovereign, refused to gratify her ears, as they had been wont to do, with those affectionate exclamations, on which Elizabeth had ever set so high a value.—The following year was barren of domestic incident. The Queen continued to pursue, from habit, amusements for which she had lost all relish. She went a-Maying to Mr. Buckley's, at Lewisham, and paid several other visits in the course of the year; but all her efforts to chase away melancholy were unavailing—the image of Essex still haunted her imagination. About the beginning of June, during a conversation with M. de Beaumont, the French Ambassador, she owned herself weary of life; then, sighing heavily, whilst her eyes filled with tears, she again adverted to the death of Essex, and mentioned, that being apprehensive, from his ambition and the impetuosity of his temper, of his throwing himself into some rash design which would prove his ruin, she had repeatedly counselled him, during the last two years, to content himself with pleasing her, and to forbear treating her with the insolent contempt which he had lately assumed; above all, not to touch her sceptre, lest she should be compelled to punish him by the laws of England, and not according to her own laws, which he had found too mild and favourable to give him any cause of fear; but that her advice, however salutary and affectionate, had proved ineffectual to prevent his ruin.

On the twenty-seventh of December, 1602, Sir John Harrington, in a letter to his wife, gives the following melancholy picture of the state of the Queen:—

"Sweet Mall,

"I herewith send thee, what I would to God none did know, some ill-bodings of the realm and its welfare. Our dear Queen, my royal godmother, and this state's natural mother, doth now bear some show of human infirmity; too fast, for that evil which we shall get by her death, and too slow for that good which she shall get by her release from pains and misery. It was not many days since I was bidden into her presence; I blessed the happy moment, and found her in a most pitiable state. She bade the Archbishop ask me if I had seen Tyrone? I replied, with reverence, that I had seen him with the Lord Deputy. She looked up with much choler and grief in her countenance, and said: 'Oh! now it mindeth me that you were one who saw this man elsewhere;' alluding to a conference held with Essex; and hereat she dropped a tear, and smote her bosom. She held in her hand a golden cup, which she often put to her lips; but, in truth, her heart seemeth too full to need more filling. This sight moved me to think of what passed in Ireland; and, I trust, she did not less think on some who were busier there than myself. She gave me a message to the Lord Deputy, and bade me come to the chamber at seven o'clock. Hereat some who were about her did marvel, as I do not hold so high place as those she did not choose to do her commands. Her Majesty inquired of some matters I had written; and as she was pleased to note my fanciful brain, I was not unheedful to feed her, and read some verses, whereat she smiled once, and was pleased to say: 'When thou dost feel creeping time at thy gate, these fooleries will please thee less; I am past relish for such matters; thou seest my bodily meat doth not suit me well; I have eaten but one ill-tasted cake since yester-night.'"

Notwithstanding the state of bodily and mental indisposition in which Harrington thus graphically described the Queen, she continued to take her accustomed exercises of riding and hunting, regardless of the inclemencies of the season. One day, in January, 1603, she visited the Lord Admiral at Chelsea, and, about the same time, removed to her palace at Richmond, for the benefit of her declining health. In the beginning of March, her illness suddenly increased; and at this period her kinsman, Sir Robert Carey, arrived from Berwick to visit her. In his Memoirs, we have the following relation of his last interview with Elizabeth:—"When I came to court, I found the Queen ill disposed, and she kept her inner lodging; yet she, hearing of my arrival, sent for me. I found her in one of her withdrawing-chambers, sitting low upon her cushions. She called me to her; I kissed her hand, and told her it was my chiefest happiness to see her in safety and in health, which I wished might long continue. She took me by the hand, and wrung it hard, and said, 'No, Robin, I am not well;' and then discoursed with me of her indisposition; and that her heart had been sad and heavy for ten or twelve days: and in her discourse, she fetched not fewer than forty or fifty great sighs. I was grieved at the first to see her in this plight, for in all my lifetime I never knew her fetch a sigh, but when the Queen of Scots was beheaded. Then, upon my knowledge, she shed many tears and sighs, manifesting her innocence that she never gave consent to the death of that Queen. I used the best words I could to persuade her from this melancholy humour, but I found it was too deep rooted in her heart, and hardly to be removed. This was upon a Saturday night, and she gave command that the great closet should be prepared for her to go to chapel the next morning. The next day, all things being in readiness, we long expected her coming. After eleven o'clock, one of the grooms came out, and bade us make ready for the private closet—she would not go to the great. There we stayed long for her coming, but at last she had cushions laid for her in her privy chamber, hard by the closet door, and there she heard service.

"From that day forward she grew worse and worse. She remained upon her cushions four days and nights at least. All about her could not persuade her either to take any sustenance or go to bed. The Queen grew worse and worse, because she would be so; none about her being able to go to bed. My Lord Admiral was sent for (who by reason of my sister's death, who was his wife, had absented himself some fortnight from court);—what by fair means, what by force, he got her to bed. There was no hope of her recovery, because she refused all remedies. On Wednesday, the twenty-third of March, she grew speechless. That afternoon, by signs, she called for her council; and, by putting her hand to her head when the King of Scots was named to succeed her, they all knew he was the man she desired should reign after her. About six at night, she made signs for the Archbishop and her chaplains to come to her; at which time I went in with them, and sat upon my knees, full of tears, to see that heavy sight. Her Majesty lay upon her back, with one hand in the bed and the other without. The Archbishop kneeled down by her, and examined her first of her faith; and she so punctually answered all his several questions, by lifting up her eyes and holding up her hand, that it was a comfort to all beholders. After he had continued long in prayer, till the old man's knees were weary, he blessed her, and meant to rise and leave her. The Queen made a sign with her hand. My sister Scrope knowing her meaning, told the Archbishop that the Queen desired he would still pray. He did so for a long half hour after, and then thought to leave her. The second time she made sign to have him continue in prayer. He did so for half an hour more, with earnest cries to God for her soul's health, which he uttered with that fervency of spirit as the Queen, to all our sight, much rejoiced thereat; and gave testimony to us all of her Christian and comfortable end. By this time it grew late, and every one departed, all but her women that attended her. Between one and two o'clock of the Thursday morning, he whom I left in the cofferer's chamber, brought me word that the Queen was dead."

Grief for the untimely death of the

Earl of Essex, with which she had long maintained a secret struggle, burst forth at the last with a violence she could not control, and rapidly completed the decay of her constitution, already undermined by the cares and anxieties incident to her exalted station.

In "Osborne's Memoirs of Queen Elizabeth," is related a remarkable anecdote, on the authority of Sir Dudley Carleton, the English Ambassador in Holland, with which we shall conclude the eventful life of one of the most extraordinary women in ancient or modern times:—"The Countess of Nottingham, who was a relation, but no friend, of the Earl of Essex, being on her death-bed, entreated to see the Queen, declaring that she had something on her mind of which she was anxious to disburthen herself before she could leave this world. On this being communicated to the Queen, she immediately resolved to comply with the wish of the dying Countess. On her Majesty's arrival, and being conducted into her apartment, the Countess produced a ring, which she said 'the Earl of Essex had sent to her after his condemnation, with an earnest request that she would deliver it to the Queen in person, as the token by which he implored her mercy; but which, in obedience to her husband, to whom she had communicated the circumstance, she had hitherto withheld; for which cruel act of treachery she now humbly entreated the forgiveness of her Majesty.' On sight of the precious ring, Elizabeth instantly recognized it as one which she had herself presented to her unhappy favourite, on his departure for Cadiz, with the tender promise, that of whatsoever crimes his enemies might have accused him, or whatsoever offences he might actually have committed against her, on his returning to her that pledge of her affections, she would either pardon him, or, at least, admit him to justify himself in her presence! Transported with grief and rage, on learning the barbarous infidelity of which her beloved Essex had been the victim, and herself the dupe, the Queen shook in her bed the dying Countess, and exclaimed with vehemence, that 'God might forgive her, but she never could.'*

"Returning to her palace in a state of mind terrible to behold, Elizabeth surrendered herself, without a ray of comfort, to the despair which seized her heart on this fatal disclosure. Hence the intensity of her mental sufferings—her obstinate silence, interrupted only by sighs, groans, and broken indications of a deep-felt sorrow which she could not reveal; hence the days and nights passed by her on the floor, reclining on cushions, afraid to go to bed, from an inward consciousness that if she did so she would never rise again—sleepless—her eyes fixed, and her finger pressed upon her mouth; hence all those heart-rending symptoms of incurable and mortal anguish, which gradually led, in the space of twenty days, to the lamentable termination of a long life of power, prosperity, and national glory. She expired on the twenty-fourth of March, 1603, in the seventieth year of her age, and the forty-fifth of her reign."

By order of Cecil, and contrary to Elizabeth's express commands, her body was embalmed. It was then conveyed by water to Whitehall, where it was nightly watched by six ladies, till the preparations were completed for the funeral, which was solemnized with royal splendour on Thursday, the twenty-eighth of April. "The royal corpse," says Stowe, "embalmed, lapped in lead, and covered with purple velvet, was laid on a chariot, drawn by four great horses, trapped in black velvet; on the body was placed a wax effigy of Elizabeth in her parliament robes, with a crown on her head, and a sceptre in her hand. The mourners, in black, were about one thousand, and consisting of the nobility, the honourable of estate, the officers and servants of the royal household, the gentlemen of the Royal Chapel, the choir of the college, and many others, conveyed the body, in so-

* Lingard rejects the story of the ring, because it has not been mentioned by any of those who have related the occurrences of the Queen's malady; and, indeed, as it rests only on historical tradition, its authenticity must be deemed doubtful.

lemn state, from Whitehall to Westminster Abbey, where, after Anthony Wood, Bishop of Chichester, had preached a learned funeral sermon, it was interred with the usual ceremonies in the vault of her grandfather, Henry the Seventh, in his most beautiful chapel; and in the same grave with her sister, Mary, Queen of England. "As the funeral procession passed through Westminster," proceeds the quaint chronicler, "the City was surcharged with multitudes of all sorts of people in the streets, houses, windows, leads, and gutters, that came to see the obsequie. And when they beheld her statue, or picture, lying upon the coffin, set forth in royal robes, having a crown upon the head thereof, and a ball and sceptre in either hand; there was such a general sighing, groaning and weeping, as the like hath not been seen or known in the memory of man; neither doth any historian mention any people, time, or state, to make like lamentation, for the death of their sovereign." Her successor, James the First, erected a noble monument to her memory, in Westminster Abbey. Amongst the complimentary epitaphs hung up in her honour, in numerous churches, throughout the realm, occur the following:—

'If royal virtues ever adorned our crown:
If ever mildness shined in majesty:
If ever honour, honoured true renown:
If ever courage dwelt in clemency:
If ever Princess put all Princes down:
For temperance, prowess, prudence, equity:
This, this was she, that in dispite of death,
Lives still admired, adored Elizabeth."

"In Bohun's Character of Queen Elizabeth," we have the following description of her habits of life, amusements, and magnificence:—"First, in the morning, she spent some time at her devotions; then she betook herself to the dispatch of her civil affairs; reading letters; dictating answers; considering what should be brought before the council, and consulting with her ministers. When she had been thus occupied, she would walk in a shady garden, or pleasant gallery, without any other attendance than that of a few learned men. Then she took her coach, and passed, in the sight of her people, to the neighbouring groves and fields, and sometimes would hunt or hawk. There was scarce a day but she employed some part of it in reading and study; sometimes before she entered upon her state affairs, sometimes after them. She slept little, seldom drank wine, was sparing in her diet, and a religious observer of the fasts and festivals of the Church. She sometimes dined alone, but generally had some of her friends with her. At supper she would divert herself with her attendants and friends; and if they made her no answer, would put them upon mirth and pleasant discourse with great civility. She would then also admit Tarleton, a famous comedian and pleasant talker, and other such men, to divert her with stories of the town, and the common jests and accidents. She would recreate herself with a game of chess, dancing or singing. She would often play at cards, and if at any time she happened to win, she would be sure to demand the money. She was waited on in her bed-chamber by married ladies of the nobility; the Marchioness of Winchester, Lady Warwick, and Lady Scrope; and here she would seldom suffer any to visit her but Leicester, Hatton, Essex, Nottingham, and Raleigh. Some lady always slept in her chamber; and besides her guards, there was always a gentleman of good quality, and some others, up in the next chamber to wake her if anything extraordinary happened. She loved a prudent and moderate habit in her private apartment, and conversation with her own servants; but when she appeared in public, she was ever richly adorned with the most valuable clothes; set off again with much gold, and jewels of inestimable value; and on such occasions she ever wore high shoes, that she might seem taller than indeed she was. The first day of the Parliament, she would appear in a robe embroidered with pearls; the royal crown on her head, the golden ball in her left hand, and the sceptre in her right; and, as she never failed then of the loud acclamations of her people, so she was ever pleased with them, and went along in a kind of triumph, with all the ensigns of majesty. The royal name was ever venerable to the English people; but this Queen's name was more sacred than any of her ancestors. In the furniture of her palaces she ever affected magnificence and an extraordinary splendour. She adorned the galleries with pictures by the best artists; the walls she covered with rich tapestries. She was a true lover of jewels, pearls, all sorts of precious stones, gold and silver plate, rich beds, fine couches and chariots, Persian and Indian carpets, statues, medals, &c., which she would purchase at great prices.* Hampton Court was the most richly furnished of all her palaces; and here she had caused her naval victories against the Spaniards to be worked in fine tapestries, and laid up among the richest pieces of her wardrobe. When she made any public feasts, her tables were magnificently served, and many side-tables adorned with rich plate. At these times, many of the nobility waited on her at table. She made the greatest displays of her regal magnificence when foreign ambassadors were present. At these times she would also have vocal and instrumental music during dinner; and after dinner, dancing."

Rapin says, she is accused of not being so chaste as she affected to appear; and that some assert that there are now in England the descendants of a daughter she had by Leicester. Lingard gives credit to a report that she had a son by Leicester, who, under the name of Arthur Dudley, lived for some time at Madrid, and was honoured by the King of Spain with the distinctions due to royalty. Dr. Walker says, it is amazing that Hume should record of Queen Elizabeth such consummate vice and abandonment as he does, and yet struggle to ally all her actions with moral or political virtue. He tells us, she was so passionate and vulgar as to beat her maids of honour. Her avarice, in some measure, he allows, induced her to take one hundred thousand pounds from the booty of Raleigh, and to countenance Drake's pillaging the Spaniards, even during peace; and the same passion prevented her love for Leicester going further than the grave—for she ordered his goods to be disposed of at a public sale, to reimburse herself of some money which he owed her. But violent as this passion was, it was still weaker, as Hume observes, than her lustful appetite; for it is computed by Lord Burleigh, that, not to mention Leicester, Hatton, Mountjoy, and other paramours, the value of her gifts to Essex alone amounted to three hundred thousand pounds. Hume also informs us, that her politics were usually full of duplicity and artifice, and that they never triumphed so much in any contrivances as in those which were conjoined with coquetry. He further shows us that she had an utter disregard for truth, by stating that, after promising to support the Scottish malcontents, she secretly seduced the leaders of them to declare before the ambassadors of France and Spain that she had not incited them, and the instant she had extorted this confession, she chased them from her presence, called them unworthy traitors, and so forth. Hume also tells us that

* No Sovereign was more fond of display than Elizabeth. We are assured, that at her death, three thousand complete habits were found in her wardrobe, with a numerous collection of jewellery, for the most part presents, which she received from petitioners, from her courtiers, and from those whom she had honoured by visits at their mansions. The following extracts from a MS. in the British Museum, entitled "A Book of Queen Elizabeth's Jewels," taken in July, 1587, may, perhaps, amuse the reader.

"*Item*, One little flower of gold, with a frog thereon, and therein, Monsuier, *his phisnamye*, and a little pearl pendant. This was probably a brooch.

"*Item*, A little bottle of amber, with a foot of gold; and, on the top thereof, a bear with a ragged staff; the bear and staff was Leicester's device.

"*Item*, A tooth-pick of gold, like a bittern's claw, garnished with four diamonds, four rubies, and four emeralds; being all but sparks.

"*Item*, A nutcracker of gold, garnished with sparks of diamonds."

When Hentzner saw Elizabeth, in her sixty-seventh year, she wore false hair, and that red. In the jewel books here mentioned, we have a long list of her Majesty's wigs, or rather head-dresses; they are called at the head of the page "*attiers*."

"*Item*, One caul of hair, set with pearls, in number forty-three.

"*Item*, One caul of hair, set with pearls of sundry sort and bigness, with seed pearl between them, cheveron-wise, one hundred and ninety-one.

"*Item*, One caul, with nine true-loves of pearl, seven buttons of gold; in each button a ruby."

malignity made an ingredient in her character. Her conduct to Mary, Queen of Scots, proves her capable of the basest treachery, and of deliberate murder. Now, with such an avowed accumulation of vice, with vulgarity, avarice, lust, duplicity, lying, malignity, treachery, and murder, no excellence is compatible. Mr. Hume and others may, if they please, applaud in her that force of character which is, indeed, necessary to virtue as well as to vice, but which, in her, as it led only to the perpetration of crimes, is infinitely more deserving of blame than of applause.

Perhaps the death of no sovereign occasioned the production of such a mass of doggrel rhyme as that of Elizabeth. The following, on the removal of her body from Richmond to Whitehall, was greatly admired:—

"The Queen was brought by water to Whitehall,
The oars at every stroke did tears let fall;
More clung about the barge: fish under water
Wept out their eyes of pearl, and swam blind after.
I think the bargemen might, with easier thighs,
Have rowed her thither in her people's eyes:
For howsoever thus much my thoughts have scann'd,
She would have come by water, had she come by land."

The following lines occur in one of the Cottonian MSS., in the hand-writing of Camden, the historian.

"Whom princes serve, and realms obey,
The greatest of Briton kings begot;
She came abroad e'en yesterday,
When such as saw her knew her not:
For one would ween, that stood afar,
She were as other women are.

In truth, it fares much otherwise;
For whilst they think they see a queen,
It comes to pass, ye can devise
No stranger sight for to be seen;
Such error falls in feeble eye,
That cannot view her stedfastly.

How so, alas! forsooth it is,
Nature, that seldom works amiss,
In woman's breast, by passing art,
Hath harbour'd safe the lion's heart,
And featly fixed, with all good grace,
To SERPENT'S *head* an ANGEL *face*."

We conclude the memoirs of one of the most revered of England's sovereigns, with the eulogium pronounced to her memory by the eloquent Bishop Hall, in his sermon at Paul's Cross, on the anniversary of the accession of King James:—

"O blessed Queen! the mother of this nation, the nurse of this church; the glory of womanhood, the envy and example of foreign nations; the wonder of time—how sweet and sacred shall thy memory be to all posterity! How excellent were her masculine graces, of learning, valour, and wisdom, by which she might justly challenge to be the queen of men! So learned was she, that she could give present answer to ambassadors in their own tongues; so valiant, that, like Zisca's drum, she made the proudest Romanist to quake; so wise, that whatsoever fell out happily against the common adversary in France, Netherland, Ireland, it was by themselves ascribed to her policy. Why should I speak of her long and successful government, of her miraculous preservations, of her famous victories; wherein the waters, wind, fire, and earth fought for us, as if they had been in pay under her; of her excellent laws and careful execution? Many daughters have done worthily, but thou excellest them all. Such was the sweetness of her government, and such the fear of misery in her loss, that many worthy Christians desired that their eyes might be closed before hers. Every one pointed to her white hairs, and said, with that peaceable Leontius, 'when this snow melteth, there will be a flood.'"

ANNE OF DENMARK,

Queen of James the First.

CHAPTER I.

Anne's parentage—Birth—Education—Orkney and Shetland Isles—James the Sixth of Scotland resolves to marry a Princess of Denmark—Obstacles—He at length fixes on Anne—The betrothment—Anne embarks for Scotland—Is driven by storms to Norway—James goes in person to fetch her home—Marries her at Upslo—Takes her to Copenhagen, where they pass the winter with her relatives—He conducts her to Scotland—Her coronation—Bothwell and the witches—Prince Henry born, and consigned, according to custom, to the keeping of Earl Marr—Anne desires to bring him up herself—The King objects—Conjugal strife—Elizabeth born—The Gowrie plot—Anne's base suspicions of the King—Ruin of the Ruthvens—Prince Charles born—Anne's kindness to Beatrice Ruthven.

NNE of Denmark, a Princess of inferior intellect, and the first Queen Consort of Great Britain, was the second-born child of Frederick the Second, King of Denmark, and his wife, Sophia, daughter of the Duke of Mecklenburg. She first saw the light at Scanderburg, in December, 1575. She received but a superficial education, and such was the etiquette of the Danish Court, or the neglect of her nurses, that she could not walk till after she had entered her tenth year. As Denmark had, in the preceding century, pawned the sovereignty of the Orkney and Shetland isles to Scotland, it was resolved, about the year 1584, to entirely relinquish the sovereignty to the Scottish crown, on condition that the young Monarch, James the Sixth of Scotland, him who on the death of Queen Elizabeth ascended the throne of England, and afterwards assumed the title of James the First, King of Great Britain and Ireland, should marry one of the Danish King's daughters. Accordingly, in 1585, King Frederick the Second of Denmark sent ambassadors to King James, in Scotland, with an offer of the choice in marriage of his two daughters, Elizabeth or Anne, both of whom had been educated as staunch Lutherans, and with instructions, that in case James felt no inclination to accept the offer, to demand the immediate restitution of the Orkneys and the Shetlands; which, although but small barren islands, are of great value to the British crown, as needful links of the insular sovereignty of the ocean. At this period James's marriage was a subject of contention between his captive mother, Mary, Queen of Scots, and his match-marring godmother, Elizabeth, Queen of England. Mary being Catholic, and, moreover, anxious to strengthen the power of Scotland against England, wished him to wed one of the daughters of King Philip the Second of Spain; whilst Elizabeth declared she would pay the whole expense of the wedding, if he would take to wife Gustavus Vasa's grand-daughter, the Protestant Princess

Anne of Denmark.

of Sweden. The government of Scotland, however, being anxious to retain possession of the Orkneys, and desirous to avoid a naval war with their powerful neighbour, Frederick the Second, gave the Danish ambassadors a cordial reception, and dispatched James's old schoolmaster, Peter Young, to the court of Denmark, to forward the arrangements for the match. Meanwhile, Elizabeth, who, by bribery and other means, had secured the majority in the Scottish Government, brought Mary, Queen of Scots, to the block, and succeeded in delaying the Danish match for about three years.

At the close of 1587, the exasperated King of Denmark threatened Scotland with war, if the Orkneys were not promptly restored. King James took the hint, and again dispatched Peter Young, and with him, Crownel Stuart, to the Danish Court. In the summer of 1588, these commissioners returned, "well rewardit and well contentit," and reported so favourably of the Princesses; pronouncing them to be "braw lassies," with a "routhie tocher" [plentiful marriage portion], that James instantly dispatched Crownel Stuart and the Bishop of St. Andrew's, to conclude the match with the Danish King's eldest daughter. Just as this embassy had embarked, and through the intrigues of Queen Elizabeth, who took infinite pleasure in traversing the matrimonial desires of all within her reach, commissioners from the King of Navarre landed in Scotland, and offered to James the hand of Katherine of Navarre, a Princess old enough to be his mother. With the object of this commission, Elizabeth, with all speed, acquainted the Danish sovereign; who, on discovering that the information was correct, flew in a rage, told the Scotch ambassadors to their faces, they were a set of cheats; betrothed his eldest daughter to the Duke of Brunswick, and vowed to regain the sovereignty of his islands, cost him what it might. The Scotch ambassadors endeavoured to soothe him, and after much bickering, it was arranged that James should wed his younger daughter, Anne, if the espousals took place before the first of May, 1589; but, if not, the engagement should then be null and void, and the islands should be restored. When the Scotch commissioners returned, they brought to James an exquisite miniature of the beautiful Anne of Denmark, which so excited his love, that shortly afterwards he told his council, that "having prayed and avised with God aboon twa weeks, he had resolvit to wed bonnie Anne of Denmark." The majority of the council being the paid creatures of Queen Elizabeth, strongly opposed the match; but James, impressed with a belief that, to secure the royal lassie, "she must be wooed and married, and a'" before the first of May, 1589, effectually terminated their artful procrastination, by paying the artisans of Edinburgh, to rise in insurrection in favour of the Danish match; an uprising, which so alarmed the council, that they instantly dispatched the Earl Marshal of Scotland, the Constable of Dundee, and the Lord Andrew Keith, to Denmark, to espouse the Princess Anne, in the King's name. Meanwhile, the death of the Danish Monarch, which took place at the close of 1588, deprived Anne of the rank of a reigning King's daughter, and, indeed, so altered the position of affairs, that, although James's proxies did not reach Denmark before the middle of June, more than six weeks after the extreme time specified for the betrothment, by the late Frederick the Second, they met with a cordial reception, and on the twentieth of August, 1589, Anne was married by proxy to the King of Scots, at the strongly fortified castle of Cronenburg, in the island of Zealand.

In September, the Scotch proxies and the royal bride embarked with their retinue for Scotland, with a fleet of eleven ships, under the command of Peter Munch, the Danish Admiral. But they had scarcely put to sea, when a violent tempest arose, and although by strenuous exertions they twice obtained a glimpse of the Scottish coast, they were, at last, driven by the adverse winds to take refuge in a sound in Norway. Here the young Queen landed, and at the inhospitable village of Upslo, sought shelter from the severe frost which then set in, and bound the country around in fetters of ice. Meanwhile a young Dane, named Stephen Beal, braved the winds and the waves, and succeeded in carrying the news of her disasters to her spouse, who, resolving, like a true lover, to go in person and fetch her home, sailed for Norway, with a small squadron of five little vessels, on the twenty-second of October. After encountering a violent gale, which well nigh wrecked the tiny squadron, the adventurous James landed at Slaikray, in Norway, on the twenty-eighth; and travelling from thence through a barren country, where only ice and snow predominated; at last, after a diligent search, reached the wretched village of Upslo, on the nineteenth of November; and immediately at his coming, and without previous notice of his arrival, "passed in quitly," says the chronicler, "with bruites [boots] and all, to her highness, Anne, and saluted her with a kiss; quhilk she refusit, as not being the form of her country. But after a few words privately spoken between his Majesty and her, familiarite eusued." On the following Sunday, James married Anne, with all the pomp and ceremony the time and place permitted; and the next morning, in compliance with an old Scottish custom, he made her a grant of the valuable lordship of Dunfermline, in "morrowing gift." At this period the winter storms raged with such fury at Upslo, that James relinquished the idea of returning to Scotland till the ensuing spring. And whilst the royal pair were passing their honeymoon, with all the joy the fierce freezing season and rugged country would permit, ambassadors from Anne's mother, Sophia, arrived, with an invitation for them, if possible, to cross the mountains and pass the winter with her at Copenhagen. The invitation was accepted; and James and his bride, after encountering appalling dangers, succeeded in crossing the icy snow-shrouded Norwegian Alps, and on the twenty-first of January, voyaged over the stormy Sound from Sweden to Zealand, and were welcomed to Cronenburg Castle by Anne's mother, the Queen Regent, Sophia; her brother, the young King, Christian the Fourth; the Duke of Brunswick, who was about to wed her sister Elizabeth, and the leading nobles and ladies of the Danish Court. Here the royal pair were again married according to the rites of the Lutheran Church; and as Anne's dower, the Danish government surrendered to James the long disputed sovereignty of the Orkney and Shetland isles, and also agreed to pay him by instalments the sum of forty thousand crowns. The royal wedding was celebrated by wild uproarious carouses and disgraceful drinking bouts, which only more firmly rooted in James that debasing vice of inebriation, in which, from his earliest youth, he was wont to indulge. In one of his letters to his council, he says, "We are at Cronenburg, drinking and driving in the auld style." After waiting to witness the marriage of the Duke of Brunswick and Elizabeth of Denmark, James and his bride, at the earnest entreaty of the Scottish council, sailed from Cronenburg on the twenty-second of April, 1590; and after a pleasant voyage, landed at Leith, on the first of the succeeding month. Here they tarried till the sixth, when they proceeded to Edinburgh, where both Anne and the King were welcomed by the nobles and the populace with a frenzy of delight.

James's first care, on reaching Edinburgh, was to provide for his Queen a splendid coronation; and as he was not worth a pound of "ready siller," he begged loans and benevolences from his lairds, telling them, in his own quaint manner, "Ye would na that your King suld seem an unco scrub at sic a time." And from those he could not borrow he begged, saying, "Ye will rather hurt yoursel vera far, than gloam out the poverty of your Prince." On Sunday, the seventeenth of May, the coronation was solemnized according to the ancient ritual, and with all attainable pomp and magnificence, by Mr. Robert Bruce, a minister, assisted by the Duke of Lenox, the Lord Hamilton, and Mr. David Lindsay. The coronation festivities lasted till the middle of June, when the

King and Queen paid a short visit to the royal palace of Falkland, whither the Queen removed to her dower palace of Dunfermline, where she had scarcely arrived, when her dower and revenue were finally arranged, and her household appointed.

At this period, Francis Stuart, that nephew of the late turbulent Hepburn, Earl of Bothwell, to whom King James had granted the title of Bothwell, and who for some time had cherished hopes of succeeding to the crown of Scotland, was accused of having induced certain witches to raise the tempests that had well nigh shipwrecked the Queen on her late voyage. Bothwell boldly declared the charge groundless, but as everybody, from the King down to the meanest peasant, believed in wizards, witches, and witchcraft, his reasonable defence was not listened to; and to make the matter worse, several crazy old women sought their own destruction, by voluntarily giving themselves up as witches, and confessing that they had leagued with the sisters of their diabolical craft, in Scotland and Norway, against the Queen; and that by baptizing a cat, and then tying four joints of a dead man to poor pussy's feet, and flinging her into the sea; at the same time loudly crying out, "Behold there is no deceit amongst us," they had raised the storm which drove her Majesty to Norway for refuge, with the intention of drowning her. Annis Simpson, one of these mono-maniacs, of her own free will confessed that she had thus written to Marian Lenchop, a witch at Leith.

"Marion Lenchop, ye sal warn the rest of the sisters to raise the wind this day, at eleven hours, to stop the Queen's coming to Scotland."

The next day, she declared before the council, that, in compliance with this warning, the whole sisterhood of Scotch sorceresses, to the number of two hundred, met together at the midnight hour, at some ruins in the neighbourhood of Leith, and after performing a lot of absurd mummeries, which want of space prevents us from more than mentioning, they, with bare arms and dishevelled hair, all put to sea: each one carried a flagon of wine, and embarked, not in a boat, but in a separate sieve, and they all floated merrily on, chatting and quaffing their wine, till they reached North Berwick church, where they landed, and forming a circle, danced round and round, singing in chorus—

"Cummer, go ye before,
Cummer, go ye;
Gif ye will not go before,
Cummer, let me."

Every one believed this absurd fiction but James; and Annis, to convince him that she was a real witch, and had dealings with the evil one, called him aside and dispelled his doubts, by whispering in his astonished ear an exact detail of all that had passed between him and the Queen when they first met in Norway.* Accordingly, Annis Simpson, after a lengthy trial, which served but to increase the absurd belief in witchcraft and necromancy, was sentenced to be "*werriet*, and afterwards *brunt*."

Bothwell, on finding himself implicated in the confessions of Annis Simpson, escaped from prison; and from that day till the winter of 1593, continued to alarm the Queen and her attendants, by making desultory attacks on whatever palace her Majesty happened to sojourn in. His object, he gave out, was not to do personal injury to any one, but to obtain an audience with the King, to apologize to him, and to endeavour to convince him that he had had no dealings with the witches, and that the charge was vamped up against him by the cunning and malice of Chancellor Maitland. The aim, however, of Black Bothwell, as he was called after his escape from prison, was higher than this; for when, at the close of 1593, he, with a chosen band of rebels, found an entrance into Holyrood, where the King and Queen were then abiding, although he affected great humility, he virtually

* James was a sincere believer in demonology. From an elaborately-penned work on witchcraft, published first in Scotland, and afterwards in England, he demonstrated the existence of witches, and, as was believed, satisfactorily solved the interesting question, "Why the devil did work more with ancient women than others?"

made James and Anne his prisoners, and so detained them till the great enemy of his faction, Chancellor Maitland, was displaced and banished from court.

In February, 1594, Anne's first-born—a son—entered the world, at Stirling Castle—an event which destroyed the hopes of Bothwell, deprived him of his partizans, and forced him to seek refuge in France, where he died, a few years afterwards. The royal babe was christened Henry Frederick, with the baptismal rites of the Episcopal Church of Scotland; and Queen Elizabeth, who took upon herself the office of godmother, sent by her proxy, as a "god-bairn gift" to the infant Henry, a rich cupboard of gold and silver plate, which being of great value, and James being much in want of money, "was soon meltet and spendit."

The christening, which was solemnized with regal pomp and great rejoicing, gave infinite satisfaction to all concerned; but immediately afterwards commenced a time of domestic trouble for the royal pair. The Queen, who, with all her faults and weaknesses, was a truly fond mother, on learning that, in compliance with the laws of Scotland, her infant was to be taken from her, and brought up in Stirling Castle, under the immediate guardianship of the Earl and Countess of Marr, was overwhelmed with maternal anguish, and, at the moment of separation, she fell to the ground in a swoon. Month after month she begged of the King to let her have the bringing up of her own child. It availed not that James assured her that the insane act would doubtless be death to himself, as some faction, to obtain the ascendancy, would depose, perhaps murder, the King, tear the child from his mother, and exercise uncontrolled regal power during his minority. To this and other reasonable arguments, Anne only replied by tears, foolish entreaties, and still more foolish threats; and at length her perversity so increased, that, to obtain possession of her darling one, she intrigued with the council, obtained a majority of them in her favour, and, to procure funds for a rebellious journey which she contemplated making to Stirling, wrote to her jeweller the following terse, pithy epistle:—

"George Heriot,

"I earnestly desire you present to sent me £200, with all expedition, because I maun hest me away presently.

"Anna, R."

About this time, the King gave her permission to visit her son at Stirling; but as there was going to be a wedding there, she declared she would defer her visit, lest Marr should construe her presence at such a time into a personal compliment. The King, however, forced her to set forth, which she did with a most unwilling heart, and on reaching Linlithgow, she feigned sickness, took to her bed, and declared herself to be too ill to proceed farther. Shortly afterwards, when the King was absent on a progress, she planned an attempt to surprize Stirling Castle with an armed force, and tear the infant Prince from the hereditary guardianship of the Earl of Marr. The King heard of her design, hastened home in time to prevent it, forced her to accompany him to Stirling, permitted her to see and caress their child, and, on quitting the castle, left the following written command with Marr:—

"My Lord Marr,

"Because my own surety consisteth in the surety of my son, whom I have entrusted to your keeping, on the faith I have in your honesty, this I command you, out of my own mouth, being in company of those I like, otherwise for any charge or necessity which can come from me, you shall not, on any account, deliver him. And, in case of my death, see that neither *for the Queen* nor the estates, their pleasure, you deliver him till he be eighteen, and then not without he himself command you to do so. This from your assured friend,

"James, R."

"Streveling Castle, June 24th, 1595."

This injunction the King read aloud, and delivered to Marr, in the presence of the Queen, who, withal, continued to torment herself, annoy the King, and embroil the council, with the vain hope of obtaining possession of her young son, till her thoughts were, for a period, directed into another channel, by the birth of her second child, which took place at Falkland, on the fifteenth of August, 1596. The Princess was christened Elizabeth, the city of Edinburgh stood godmother to her, and she lived to be the heroic Protestant Queen of Bohemia—the ancestress of our present Sovereign, the Lady Victoria, whom God preserve!

On the twenty-fourth of December, 1598, Anne brought into the world her daughter Margaret, at Dalkeith Palace; and, at the close of the subsequent year, her son Robert, who died in early infancy, first saw the light. In August, 1600, the mysterious Gowrie plot occurred. On the day when John Ruthven, Earl of Gowrie, and his brother, Alexander, hoped to assassinate the King, James, who, with the Queen, was residing at Falkland, rose with the sun, and when Anne asked him why he was astir so early? he replied, "I am going a hunting, and hope to kill a fine buck before noon." But he had another object in view, on that eventful day, besides chasing the deer. Alexander Ruthven had informed him that a Jesuit, with a large pot-full of foreign gold coin, had been taken, and was then detained at his brother Gowrie's house at Perth; and as it was desirable that the King should examine him in private, James, on returning from the hunt, could call there and do so, whilst the hunting party were taking refreshment. Accordingly, James started out in the hope of enjoying the chase, and afterwards seizing the foreign gold, and detecting a Popish plot against the government. At noon, he and two of his attendants slipped from the hunting-party, and went to Gowrie House and partook of refreshments, after which, Alexander Ruthven conducted the King only, up a staircase, and through several apartments, the doors of which he locked behind him, into a small study, where stood a man clad in armour, with a sword and dagger by his side. The King, who expected to have found one disarmed and bound, started at the sight, and at that moment Ruthven, snatching the dagger from the girdle of the man in armour, made a murderous assault on the King, exclaiming furiously, "My father suffered unjustly by your command; his innocent blood calls for vengeance, and by this dagger shall that vengeance be executed!" James expostulated, entreated, flattered, but to no purpose. "You shall die!" shouted Ruthven, as he again sprung at the disarmed monarch with the fury of a hungry tiger; a fierce struggle ensued, in which the man in armour took no part. The King defended himself bravely, and whilst skilfully parrying the well-aimed blows of the death-doing dagger, dragged Ruthven, who held him by the throat, to an open window, out of which he, as he best could, shouted, with all his might, "Treason! treason! I am murtherit! Help, help, Lord Marr!"

His attendants heard and knew his voice, and, looking up to the window, saw that his face was red, and that a hand "sharply gripet his cheek and mouth." They sped to his assistance, and the brave Sir John Ramsay first entering the apartment, rushed upon Ruthven, and thrust him towards the stairs, where Sir Thomas Erskine and Sir Hugh Herries met and killed him. Gowrie now, with seven of his followers, fully armed, flew into the room, and loudly threatened to slay them all; but, notwithstanding the inequality of numbers, the King's attendants bravely encountered them, when Ramsay slew Gowrie on the spot, and immediately afterwards his seven followers, all maimed and bleeding, fled for their lives.

The report that James had slain John and Alexander Ruthven, but without any statement of the other particulars, speedily reached the ears of the Queen, and her maid, Beatrice Ruthven, sister to the departed Gowrie and his brother. Beatrice very naturally shed abundance of tears for the loss of her brothers; the Queen sympathizing with her; and, when the King returned, instead of flying into his arms and joyfully congratulating him on his fortunate escape from the assassin's dagger, she continued to weep, reminded him of his words when he left her in the morning, and told him she believed in her heart that the Ruthvens had not been conspirators, but his victims; nor could James, at that time, or ever afterwards, convince her to the contrary. A most base, most unwifelike accusation and suspicion; and which, had Henry the Eighth been her husband, would have cost her her head, but which, as it was, was, after a while, forgiven by her tender, indulgent lord.

The failure of the Gowrie plot was followed by the disgrace and utter ruin of the surviving Ruthvens. The dead bodies of John and Alexander were condemned and quartered, and the unfortunate Beatrice, although in no way implicated in the conspiracy, was deprived of all she possessed, torn from the Queen, and driven from Court to scorn, want, and misery.

On the nineteenth of November, 1600, Anne gave birth, at Dunfermline, to her second son, who was christened Charles, and afterwards ascended the throne of England as Charles the First. Her accouchement was protracted, the child was sickly, and for several weeks afterwards she was so feeble, that her life was despaired of. The King, who, as yet, had scarcely forgiven the misplaced sympathy she had, without caution or restraint, expressed for the Ruthvens, visited her, caressed her with conjugal tenderness, and gave to her midwife twenty-six pounds thirteen shillings and four-pence Scots; and to John Murray, for bringing him the news of her confinement, sixteen pounds Scots.

In 1602, the peace of the royal pair was again disturbed. The Queen, out of pure, disinterested compassion, privately sent for poor Beatrice Ruthven, secreted her in the royal palace of Holyrood the whole of one day and night; had much conference with her, pitied and consoled her, and sent her away loaded with gifts. The vigilant Sir Thomas Erskine detected this interview, and believing it to be the embryo of another dangerous plot, instantly imparted his discovery to the King. The intelligence aroused the anger and jealousy of James; he cross-questioned the Queen, had the domestics examined, and the whole case thoroughly investigated; but, at last, came to the conclusion that the Queen had neither done nor meant any harm in the matter, and therefore immediately resumed his affectionate manner towards her. It was these incidents that enabled the spies and ambassadors at the Scottish court, in 1602, to darkly hint that Anne had been detected in favouring a conspiracy against the King's life.

CHAPTER II.

James succeeds to the English throne—Journeys to England—Letter to Prince Henry—Basilicon Doron—Sonnet written by the King—Anne's rebellious visit to Stirling—Prince Henry is restored to her—Her Progress to England—James holds a Chapter of the Garter at Windsor—Coronation—The Plague—Ambassadors—Raleigh and Cobham—Conspirators tried—The Queen's winter evening amusements—Lion bait—Her progress through the City.

WE now come to the career of Anne as Queen of Great Britain and Ireland. On the day that Queen Elizabeth died, the twenty-fourth of March, 1603, James was proclaimed her successor. The whole inhabitants of Britain, as well as himself, had for some time anticipated the event which was now hailed with joy both by the English and the Scots, who testified their satisfaction at the union of the British islands under one sovereignty by their unanimous acclamations, bonfires, the booming of ordnance, and the ringing of bells. The moment Queen Elizabeth breathed her last, Lady Scrope, who was attending her, secretly dropped out of the window of the death-chamber a sapphire ring, which the King of Scots, who trusted not too implicitly in the faith of the Cecils, had placed in her hands to serve as a token of the important event. This ring her brother, Sir Robert Carey, who had been long waiting beneath the window in anxious expectation, no sooner caught up, than he hastened to Scotland swift as horse could carry him. He reached Holyrood Palace about two the next morning, boldly knocked up the King, and, as he anticipated, was the first to convey to him the welcome intelligence; and for his zeal was created Earl of Monmouth. Shortly afterwards an express from the privy council of England reached Holyrood, with a formal invitation for James to come to London, and ascend the throne of England as James the First; an invitation he was nothing loth to accept; but as England had proved fatal to so many of his predecessors, he wisely resolved to leave the Queen and his children behind him, and in the first instance cross the border without his family, and with but a small armed force. He commenced his journey on the third of April, bade a fond farewell to Anne in High Street, Edinburgh, in the presence of the populace, who joined their tears and lamentations with those of their deeply affected Queen; and as time did not permit him to pay a visit to his heir, Prince Henry, whom he left in the strongly garrisoned castle of Stirling, under the protection of the Earl of Marr; he, at his departure, addressed to him the following sensible fatherly epistle:—

"My Son,

"That I see you not before my parting, impute it to this great occasion, wherein time is so precious; but that it shall, by God's grace, shortly be recompenced by your comming to me shortly, and continual residence with me ever after. Let not these news make you proud or insolent, for a King's son and heir you were before, and no more are ye yet; the augmentation that is hereby like to fall unto you is but in cares and heavy burthens, be therefore merry but not insolent; keep a greatness, but *sine fastu*, be resolute but not wilful; keep your kindness, but in honourable sort choose none to be your play-fellows but them that are well born; and above all things, give never good countenance to any but according as ye shall be informed that they are in estimation with me. Look upon all Englishmen that shall come to visit you as upon your loving subject, not with that ceremony as towards strangers, and yet with such heartlyness as at this time they deserve. This gentleman whom this bearer accompanys is worthy and of good rank, and now my familiar servitor; use him therefore in a more homely loveing sort than others. I send you herewith my book, lately printed; studdy and profit in it as ye would deserve my blessing; and as there can no thing happen unto you whereof ye will not find the generall ground, therein if not the very particular point touched, so must ye level every man's opinion or advices unto you as ye find them agree or discord with the rules there set down, allowing and following their advices that agrees with the same, mistrusting and frowning upon them that advise you to the contrary. Be diligent and earnest in your studies, that at your meeting with me I may praise you for your progress in learning; be obedient to your master for your own weal and to procure my thanks, for in reverencing him ye obey me and honour yoursell. Farewell.

"Your loving father,
"James, R."

The book which the author-King sent with this letter, was entitled "The Basilicon Doron; or, his Majesty's Instructions to his dearest son, the Prince." Although it inculcated the Divine right of Kings with a vehemence scarcely suited to the present age, it met with the commendations of Bacon, Locke, Hume, and others.

The following sonnet addressed to Prince Henry, which would not dishonour any writer of that time, we extract from it, as a specimen of King James's powers as a versifier :—

"God gives not Kings the stile of Gods in vaine,
For on the throne his scepter do they sway;
And as their subjects ought them to obey,
So Kings should fear and serve their God again.
If then ye would enjoy a happy reign,
Observe the statutes of our Heavenly King,
And from His laws make all your laws to spring.
Since His lieutenant here ye should remain,
Reward the just, be stedfast, true, and plain,
Repress the proud, maintaining aye the right;
Walk always so, as ever in His sight,
Who guardes the godly plaguing the prophane;
And so ye shall in princely vertues shine,
Resembling right your mighty King divine."

The subjoined sonnet, also addressed to Prince Henry, although not appearing in the "Basilicon Doron," as printed, is prefixed to the autograph of this work, in King James's own hand, and which is still extant in the British Museum—

"Loe! heir my son a mirror viue and fair,
Quhilk schawis the schadow of a vorthie King;
Loe! heir a booke, a paterne, dois zow bring,
Quhilk ze sould preas to follow mair and mair.
This trustie freind the treuthe will never spair,
But give a guid advyse unto zow heir;
How it sould be zour chief and princelie cair,
To follow vertew,—vyce for to forbeare.
And in this booke zour lesson will ze leire,
For gyding of zour people, great and small;
Than as ze aucht gif ane attentive eare,
And paus how ze thir preceptis practise sall,
Zour father biddis zow studie, heir, and reid
How to become a perfyte King indeid."

When James bade farewell to the Queen, who at the time was several months advanced in pregnancy, he made arrangements for her to follow him in twenty days, if his reception in England was favourable, which, as every reader of general history knows, was so much so, that one of the Scotch nobles travelling in his train was heard to exclaim: "Thae Southerons wul spoil a gude King." In fact, at this period, the King enjoyed an enviable felicity; but as extremes meet, the folly and perversity of Anne was, at the same time, preparing both for him and herself another round of domestic troubles. Their son, Prince Henry, newly excited her scarcely controllable feelings of maternity by an affectionate letter, congratulating her on the accession of his father to the English throne, lamenting the absence of both his parents; and expressing a hope, that as the King was too far off, the Queen, his mother, would pay him a visit. When Anne received this letter, James had ordered the man she hated above all others, the upright Earl of Marr, to England; and the moment he had departed she mustered a strong party of the nobles of her faction, hastened to Stirling Castle, and endeavoured to intimidate the old Countess of Marr into the surrender of the Prince. The Countess admitted the Queen into the castle, but courageously refused entrance to her armed attendants; and when Anne made preparations to take her son away with her, the Countess declared, that she had the King's warrant for his detention, and that nothing short of an equal authority should induce her to surrender him. A stormy scene ensued, force was threatened; and in the end the Queen was carried to bed in hysterics, and shortly afterwards gave premature birth to a dead son. When King James received intelligence of this unpleasant event, the conjugal tenderness he bore to his spoilt wife overcame his anger. Resolving to restore her to health at any sacrifice, he instantly dispatched Lord Lennox to meet the Earl of Marr, who was on his road to London, and to deliver to him two royal orders; one being a command for him to hasten in the company of Lennox to Stirling, and endeavour to appease the Queen; and the other, a letter for Marr to give to the Queen, authorizing her to receive charge of Prince Henry, and conduct him to Holyrood. Marr and Lennox met at York, and instantly hurried on to Stirling. Their arrival threw the Queen into a fresh paroxysm of rage, and increased her illness, whilst such was her malice, or perversity, that she would neither see the Earl nor accept the Prince from his hands. In this dilemma the King was again applied to, and after he had addressed several soothing letters to his rebellious consort, without being able to induce her to comply with his wish, he directed Marr to consign Prince Henry to Lennox, who would hand him over to the Queen in due form. This arrangement appeased the wrath of the narrow-minded, self-willed Anne, who repaired with her first-born to Holyrood, where she took immediate measures for her departure for England.

The King, when at Berwick, on his progress to London, had written to the English Privy Council, as follows: "Forasmuch as we do intend to bring into this realm, as soon as possibly we can, both the Queen, our *wyfe*, and our two elder children, which be able to abide the travil, we must recommend to your consideration, the sending hither of such jewels and other furniture which doth appertain to the late Queen, as you shall think to be meet for her [Queen Anne's] estate. And also coaches, horses, litters, and whatsoever else you shall think meet." But the Privy Council having come to the conclusion that it was illegal to send the crown jewels out of England, refused to comply with this request; and James, in a second letter, written nine days afterwards, at Topeliff, says, "Touching the jewels to be sent for our wife, our meaning is, not to have any of the principal jewels of state sent, but only such as by the opinion of the ladies attendant about the late Queen, our sister, you shall find to be meet for the ordinary apparrelling and ornament of her; the rest may come after, when she shall be nearer hand. But we have thought good to put you in mind, that it shall be convenient, besides jewels, you send some of the ladies of all degrees, who were about the late Queen, as soon as the funeral* be passed, to meet her as far as they can, at her entry into the realm, as soon after, for that we hold needful for her honour. And that they do speedily enter into their journey, for that we would have her here with the soonest; and as for horses, litters, coaches, and other things of that nature, whereof we have heretofore written, for her use, we have thought good to let you know, that the proportion mentioned in your particular letter to us, shall suffice, in our opinion, for her. And so you may take order for the sending of them away with the ladies that are to come as before, as you shall think meetest." With this request the Privy Council willingly complied, and on the second of June, Anne, being sufficiently recovered in body and mind, set forth in her progress to London. Prince Henry and the Princess Elizabeth accompanied her, but the "babie Prince Charles" being young and delicate, was left at Dunfermline under the guardianship of Lord Fife. At Berwick, where her household was to be settled, that she might enter England with a retinue becoming her dignity, she found waiting her arrival, the Earls of Sussex and Lincoln, the Lords Compton and Norris, Sir George Carew, who James had appointed to be her Chamberlain, the Countesses of Worcester and Kildare, and the Ladies Anne Herbert, Scrope, and Richard Walsingham; but such was the Queen's love of old faces, or rather perversity, that she would not appoint one of these to her service; and knowing the power she had over the mind of her too fond husband, she tormented him by sending applicant after applicant to be confirmed in places which he very wisely had reserved for other, and, under the circumstances, far more suitable persons. Nor was the difficulty arranged till after the King had thrown himself into a rage, sworn dreadful oaths at some dozen of his disobedient consort's candidates, and at last vowed by all that was sacred, that he would cut off the head of the next applicant; a threat which none of the Queen's nominees had the courage to brave.

From Berwick the Queen and her children went in procession to York, where, on the eleventh of June, the Mayor, Aldermen, and citizens conducted them into the city with all considerable magnificence, presented them with valuable gifts of money, plate, and jewels, and entertained them with regal splendour till the fifteenth of June. On that day they went to Grimstone, where the Queen addressed the following pleasing

* The funeral of Queen Elizabeth, which was solemnized before either James or Anne arrived in London.

little note, letter it can scarcely be called, to the King.

"MY HEART,

"I am glad that Haddington hath told me of your Majesty's good health, which I wish to continue. As for the blame you charge me with, of lazy writing, I think it rather rests on yourself, because you be so slow in writing as myself. I can write of no mirth but of practising of tilting, of riding, of drumming, and of music, which is all, wherewith I am not a little pleased. So wishing your Majesty perpetual happiness, I kiss your Majesty's hand, and rest your

"ANNA, R."

At Dingley, near Leicester, the Queen parted with her daughter Elizabeth, who was conducted to Lord Harrington's seat of Combe Abbey, in the neighbourhood of Coventry, where she resided for several years, and completed her education under the tutorship of her governesses, the Ladies Harrington and Kildare. From Dingley, the royal travellers proceeded to Althorp, near Northampton; where, as they passed through the park on the evening of the twenty-fifth of June, they were entertained by a masque of fairies, produced by the transcendant genius of Ben Jonson, and performed in the open air, with the woods and verdure of an English park for the scenery, and with no other lights than the glorious lamps of heaven, which on that bright Midsummer night beamed down from the dark firmament with silvery softness, and rendered the magical scene doubly enchanting.

The next station of the royal progress was East Nestor, the seat of Sir George Farmer, where they were met by the King and his retinue, who, after accompanying them to Grafton, the seat of the Earl of Cumberland, and to Solden House, the mansion of the Fortescues, conducted them to Windsor Castle. The King and Queen tarried for several weeks at Windsor, and held court there with great splendour. On the second of July, James held a chapter of the garter, and created his son Henry, and several English and Scotch nobles, knights of the order; to which the King of Denmark and the Duke of Wertenburgh were at the same time elected. "The day of the garter festival," says the chronicler, "the great ladies of England, in honour of the Queen, and in discharge of their duties, came to the court at Windsor, to perform their homage to her highness. They, with great reverence, kneeling one by one, kissed her Majesty's hand, and it was hard to discern, whether the mildness of the sovereign, or the humility of the subject was greatest."

The King had long appointed his saint day, the festival of St. James, for the performance of his coronation; and, although the Cobham and Raleigh conspiracy had just been discovered, and a dangerous mortality raged in the city, he would admit of no postponement. This haste was necessary, as an opinion prevailed, that since parliament had not settled the succession, James could not be viewed as the actual possessor of the sovereignty of England till after he had been crowned. About the twentieth of July the royal pair removed to Hampton Court, where the King created several earls and barons. On the twenty-second their Majesties proceeded by water to St. James's Palace; and the King, to avoid the plague, there made Knights of the Bath preparatory to his coronation, instead of holding court for that purpose, as was customary, at the Tower. "Also," says the chronicler, "by reason of the dreadful pestilence then raging in the City of London, as God's visitation for our sins, and the plots which it was said were hatching against his Majesty's life, the King rode not from the Tower, through the city, in royal manner, as was customary at coronations, and to prevent the spread of the contagion—eight hundred and fifty-seven persons having died that week of the plague only, in the city and suburbs of London—all the citizens, excepting the Lord Mayor and Aldermen, were forbidden by proclamation to come to Westminster. On the twenty-fifth of July, being Monday, and the feast of St. James, the King, with his consort, the noble lady, Queen Anne, were together crowned and anointed at Westminster, by John Whitgift, Archbishop of Canterbury, in the presence of the nobility, in their robes and coronets; and the Lord Mayor and Aldermen of London, in gowns of crimson and scarlet; and twelve wealthy citizens, who were permitted to attend them. Although the august ceremony was solemnized in haste, and stripped of the "pomp and circumstances" of a city pageant, it was stated by royal proclamation, that the King and the Queen, with their son, Prince Henry, would pay the citizens a ceremonious visit, and partake of their hospitality, as soon as the pestilence had abated. The Queen, at her coronation, offended the religious sentiments of her English subjects, by refusing to take the sacrament according to the rites of the church of England; a refusal which doubtless proceeded from scruples of conscience, and for which she in justice cannot be blamed, especially as she had already, to please the Scots, forsaken the church of Luther, in which she had been educated, for the Calvinistic faith of Scotland.

Immediately after the coronation, the court hurried to Woodstock, where James and Anne sojourned till the middle of September. The pestilence followed their track, and cut off several of their servants; and it raged in the city with such awful severity, that the courts of law were removed, Bartholomew Fair and all fairs within fifty miles of the metropolis were suspended, and at last James issued several proclamations for preventing any further increase of buildings. But, despite the pestilence, the court was brilliant with foreign ambassadors extraordinary, who had arrived from France, Spain, and Flanders, to congratulate the King and Queen on their accession to the English throne, and to intrigue for the favour of the Scottish Prince, now that he was monarch of all the British isles. The Queen's brother, Ulric, Duke of Holstein, had also arrived, and charmed by the grace and beauty of Arabella Stuart, then the star of the English court, vainly endeavoured to win her heart. The Lady Arabella was the next heir to the crown of England after James and his family; and although the plot for which Raleigh, Cobham, and their associates were imprisoned, had, for its object, to "kill the King and his cubs," and place Arabella on the throne, James was so convinced of the entire innocence of that lady, that he allowed her to take precedence of all other ladies at court, next to the Queen, during the period that the Princess Royal was receiving her education. On the seventeenth of September the court removed to Winchester, where it remained whilst Raleigh, Cobham, and the other conspirators were tried. The trials were long and tedious, and although the evidence adduced was neither clear nor conclusive, the conspirators were found guilty, and condemned as traitors; but, with the exception of two priests and George Brook, not executed. They were brought to the scaffold one by one, and after making their confession and preparing themselves for the block, informed that the King had commuted their sentence to banishment or imprisonment. Raleigh, whose execution had been fixed for the subsequent Monday, was informed that it was for the present deferred. He remained a prisoner in the Tower, where he wrote his History of the World. The Queen pitied him, believed him innocent, and obtained for him many indulgences.

The Queen and her ladies had a dull time of it during this autumn: a dread of plots and the plague confined them within the walls of Winchester Palace; where, to dispel the gloom of the dreary November evenings, they played at "Titter my tat," "Merry trotter," "Rise, pig, and go," "Run, bull, and fetch it," and other juvenile sports, which they had learned in their infancy. To atone for the dreary life the Queen and her ladies had led during the autumn, the King caused the Christmas festivals to be graced by masques, ballets, and other magnificent entertainments, in which their Majesties and the leading nobles and ladies of the court acted the part of gods, goddesses, fays, furies, and river nymphs. The King, to redeem his promise of paying a state visit to the city immediately the pestilence had abated, brought the Queen and Prince Henry in private to the Tower, on the thirteenth of March, 1604. On their way, the royal party paid a private visit to Gresham's Exchange; and on taking up their lodgings at the Tower, says the continuator of Stowe, visited all the offices and store houses in that venerable fortress, including the Mint, where both the King and Queen coined some money with their own hands. They then went to see the lions, when the King, on being told that the English mastiff dog was as courageous as the lion, requested Edward Allen, late servant to the Lord Admiral, but now sworn Prince Henry's man, and the master of the bear gardens, to fetch secretly three of the savagest mastiffs in the garden, which being done, the King, Queen, and Prince, with four or five lords, went to the lions' tower, and caused the finest lion to be put into a separate den with one of the dogs. The dog instantly flew at the head of the lion, but the fierce carnivora immediately shook him off, seized him by the throat, and dashed him about the den. The King perceiving that although the dog was courageous, the lion, on account of his superior strength, had the best of it, ordered another dog to be put in the den. The mastiff in a moment sprang at the lion's face, but was as speedily shook off again by the angry king of the forests; when the last and the fiercest of the dogs was set on, he seized the lion by the lip, and in return was so pawed and clawed, that at length he let go his hold, when the lion, although so exhausted that he could not bite with any degree of force, seized him by the throat, and dragged him, as he had done the former dogs, about the den. Whilst this encounter was taking place, the other two dogs were fighting together in the lower room of the den; now, therefore, to enliven the sport, the lion was driven down to them, in the hope that he would attack them, but instead of doing so, he, on coming down, leaped over them, and rushed into an inner den, where he roared till the earth shook again, and out of which he could not be made to come. Thus ended the cruel sport, which so excited the attention of the august beholders, that Prince Henry charged Edward Allen to keep the only one of the three dogs who recovered from the wounds received in the terrific encounter, and make much of him, saying, "he that hath fought with the king of beasts should never afterwards fight with any inferior creature."

On the fifteenth of March, the King and Queen, with their son, Prince Henry, passed triumphantly from the Tower through the city of London to Westminster. The City Companies, marshalled according to their degrees, were placed in due order, the first beginning at the upper end of Mark Lane, and the last reaching to the conduit in Fleet Street, their seats being double, railed upon the upper part, whereon they leaned. Their streamers, ensigns, and banners, were set up in their respective places; and directly against them, and right through the City to Temple Bar, a single rail was erected, at a fair distance from the other, to keep back the multitude. The King, richly mounted on a white jennet, and under a rich canopy, sustained by eight gentlemen of the privy chamber, for the barons of the Cinque Ports, entered his royal city of London, and with the Queen and Prince Henry, also clad in rich array, passed on, with a numerous and gorgeous train, towards Westminster, through seven triumphal gates. The first gate was erected at the east end of Fenchurch Street, and on its top was a perfect model of Old London, extending the full width of the street, and showing the whole Thames front of the City, with all its churches and buildings minutely and elaborately detailed. The second gate, a most sumptuous piece of workmanship, was loftily raised in Gracechurch Street, by the Italians. The third was raised, by the Dutch, upon Cornhill, by the Exchange, and represented the seventeen provinces of Holland. Close to Mildred church, in the Poultry, a stage was erected, where, at the cost of the City, to delight the Queen with the music of her native land, the Danish March was performed, with great accuracy, by a band of nine trumpets and a kettle-drum. The fourth gate, through which their

Majesties passed, was erected by the citizens, at the Soper Lane end of West Cheap. Adjoining the east end of the great cross in Cheapside was erected a square, low gallery, four feet high, and set round with pilasters, where stood the aldermen, the chamberlain, the town-clerk, and the council of the City, and Sir John Montague, the city recorder, who delivered the following flattering address to the King:—

"High, imperial Majesty,—It is not yet a year in days since, with the acclamation of the people, the citizens, and the nobles auspiciously here, at this cross, was proclaimed your true succession to the crown. If then it was joyous, with hats, hands, and hearts lifted upwards to heaven, to cry 'King James,' what is it now to see King James! Come, therefore, O worthiest of Kings, as a glorious bridegroom through your royal chamber; but to come nearer—*adest quem querimus.* Twenty and more are the sovereigns we have served since our Conquest; but, conqueror of hearts! it is you and your posterity that we have vowed to love, and wish to serve, whilst London is a city. In pledge, thereof, my Lord Mayor, and the aldermen, and the commons of this city, wishing you a glorious reign, present your greatness with a little cup of gold."

On the conclusion of this fulsome address, the Recorder, in the name of the Lord Mayor and the whole City, presented a cup of gold to the King, another to the Queen, and a third to the young Prince Henry. After which, their Majesties proceeded forward to the little conduit at Paul's Gate, where was placed the fifth gate, arbour-like, and therefore called the Arbour of Music. Through this they passed to St. Paul's Churchyard, where the choristers of St. Paul's chaunted an anthem, as they slowly proceeded forward; and, at St. Paul's School, an address in Latin was read to them by one of the scholars. The sixth gate was a large triumphal arch, erected near the conduit in Fleet Street, and on which a large globe of the world moved, greatly to the delight of the Queen and Prince, who halted outside of the arch for several minutes to gratify their marvel-loving eyes. At Temple Bar, where the King bade a princely farewell to the Lord Mayor and the City, the seventh and last gate was erected, in imitation of the Temple of Janus. In the Strand was erected, by the city of Westminster and the duchy of Lancaster, a splendid pageant of a rainbow, with the sun, moon, and stars advancing between two pyramids. Their Majesties stopped awhile to gaze on this crude, childish orrery, and then proceeded on to St. James's, where the procession ended, and the King, Queen, and Prince passed the night.

CHAPTER III.

Anne senas for Prince Charles—Royal masques—Birth of Princess Mary—First royal Protestant baptism in England—Gunpowder plot—Visit of Christian the Fourth—Anne purchases Theobalds—Her extravagance—Love of cruel sports—Installation of the Prince of Wales—Overbury and Carr—Death of Prince Henry—Anne moans his loss—Marriage of her daughter Elizabeth—Commends Villiers to the King—Her letters to Villiers—Visit to Ladies' Hall—Falls sick—Intercedes for Sir Walter Raleigh—Grows worse—Takes to her bed—Professes herself a Protestant—Interview with Prince Charles—Her Death—Funeral—Missing jewels—Epitaph.

N the summer of 1604, the young Prince Charles, being sickly and rickety, was brought to England, and, by the Queen's desire, placed under the care of Lady Carey, the wife of Sir Robert Carey, him who rushed to Scotland with the first news of Queen Elizabeth's death. The Prince, when he arrived in England, was between three and four years old, and in a miserably crippled state, but, under the judicious management of Lady Carey, he daily gained health and strength; and, at last, to the infinite joy of his parents, walked, prattled, and played with ease and sprightliness. On Twelfth Day, 1605, he was formally created Duke of York. The royal boy and several nobles were, at the same time, installed Knights of the Bath, and the Queen celebrated the occasion by taking part in Ben Jonson's celebrated "Mask of Blackness." The facile poet, in compliance with the vulgar taste of her Majesty, introduced into this entertainment twelve African nymphs, daughters of the Niger, who made a voyage to England in search of a wash to whiten their complexions. The parts of these negresses, who did nothing but dance, were sustained by the Queen and the other ladies, with blackened faces, and the first scene displayed them seated on an enormous shell of mother-of-pearl. In regard to the Queen, who, observes Osborn, was gifted with "a skin far more fair and amiable than the features it covered," the choice of this repulsive disguise was peculiarly injudicious, and cast a grotesque air over the whole performance, which Sir Dudley Carleton, an eye-witness of the scene, thus describes:—

"At night, we had the Queen's mask, or rather pageant, in the banqueting-house. There was a great engine at the lower end of the room, which had motion, and in it were the images of sea-horses, and other terrible fishes, which were ridden by Moors. The indecorum was, that there was all fish and no water; at the further end was a great shell, in form of a scallop, wherein were four seated; on the lowest sat the Queen, with my Lady Bedford; on the rest were placed the Ladies Suffolk, Derby, Rich, Effingham, Ann Herbert, Susan Herbert, Elizabeth Howard, Walsingham, and Bevil. Their appearance was rich, but too light and courtesan-like for such great ones. Instead of visors, their faces and arms, up to the elbows, were painted black, which was disguise sufficient, for they were hard to be known; but it became them nothing so well as their own red and white; and you cannot imagine a more ugly sight than a troop of lean-cheeked Moors. The Spanish and Venetian ambassadors were both present, and sat by the King, in state, at which Monsieur Beaumont quarrels so extremely, that he saith the whole court is Spanish. But, by his favour, he should fall out with none but himself, for they were all indifferently invited to come as private men to a private sport, which, he refusing, the Spanish ambassador willingly accepted; and being there, seeing no cause to the contrary, he put off Don Paxis and took upon him El Senor Embassadour, wherein he outstripped our little Monsieur. He took out the Queen, and forgot not to kiss her hand, though there was danger it would have left a mark on his lips. The night's work was concluded with a banquet in the great chamber, which was so furiously assaulted, that down went tables and tressels before one bit was touched."

It was certainly unwise of the Queen to blacken her features, and, on that night of festivity, display her lean cheeks in the unbecoming disguise of an old negress, especially as she was by no means deficient in personal beauty. Cardinal Bentivoglio, who was her contemporary, says, "The Queen of England is one of the handsomest princesses of her time. She speaks the Italian language with fluency, shows a noble spirit, and is singularly graceful, courteous, and affable. She delights, beyond measure, in praises and admiration of her beauty, in which she has the vanity to think that she has no equal. Hence she makes public exhibition of herself in a thousand ways, and with a thousand different inventions, and sometimes to so great an excess, that it has been doubted which went furthest —the King, in the ostentation of his learning, or the Queen, in the display of her beauty. The Queen is much attached to the free mode of life customary in England; and as she is very affable, she often puts it in practice with the ladies, whom she admits to the greatest intimacy, visiting them by turns in their own houses, where she diverts herself with private amusements, laying aside all the dignity and majesty of a princess." Other contemporaries draw a less favourable portrait of Anne of Denmark. One writer, Molino, states, that "she is ordinary in countenance and port, and insupportably proud and disdainful to every one but those she likes."

James is described in equally various colours by different authorities. Cardinal Bentivoglio says, "he is rather above the middle size, of a fair and florid complexion, and of lineaments very noble to behold. But, in his carriage and demeanour, he discovers neither grace nor dignity; and he eats and drinks to excess, and disregards all regimen." Perhaps, however, the most curious picture of King James the First is that by Balfour, who says, "He was of middle stature, more corpulent, throghe his clothes, then in his bodey, zet fatt enouch; his clothes ever being made large and easie, the doubletts quilted for stelleto proofe, his breeches in grate pleits, and fully stuffed. He was naturally of a timorous dispositione, which was the greatest reasone of his quilted doubletts. His eyes large, ever roulling after any stranger cam in his presence, in so much as being out of countenance. His beard was werey thin, his toung too large for his mouthe, and made him drinke werey oncomlie, as if eatting his drinke, wich cam out into the cupe on each syde of his mouthe. His skin vas als softe as tafata sarsnet, wich felt so because he never washt his hands, onlie rubb'd his fingers ends slightly vith the vet end of a napkin; his legs wer verey weake, having had (as was thought) some foule playe in his youthe, or rather before he was borne, that he was not able to stand at seven zeires of age; that weaknis made him ever leaning on other men's shoulders." Wilson, who describes him as being "fond of such representations and disguises in their maskaradoes as were ridiculously witty and sudden," declares that, on one occasion, "a sucking pig—an animal which the King held in the utmost abhorrence—was swathed as an infant about to be christened. The Countess of Buckingham, disguised as a midwife, brought it, wrapped up in a rich mantle; the Duke attended as godfather; Turpin, in lawn sleeves, as minister; another brought a silver ewer with water; but, just as the service commenced, the pretended child betrayed itself by its cry, and the King turned aside, exclaiming, 'Away, for shame, away!'"

On the seventh of April, 1605, Anne gave birth to a daughter at Greenwich. As the King resolved to give the Princess the name of his own unfortunate mother, she was christened Mary, with the first Protestant baptismal rites that had ever been administered to a royal infant in England. The christening was solemnized, with regal pomp, in the chapel of Greenwich Palace; and the sponsors, Lady Arabella Stuart, and Duke Ulrick, the Queen's brother, who shortly afterwards returned to Denmark, presented the babe with valuable gifts. On the Whitsunday following, the Queen was churched; the ceremony performed, being, with a trifling exception, that prescribed in the present Book of Common Prayer by the Church of England; and at the conclusion, the King came forth, saluted her at the altar, and conducted her to his presence chamber. The Princess Mary was a delicate infant; she was never well; when scarcely three years old, a slow fever, which baffled the skill of the royal physicians, put a period to her unhappy existence.

The Gunpowder Plot, to blow up the King, Prince Henry, and the Parliament, at one fell swoop, on the fifth of November, 1605, but which fortunately was discovered and prevented before the hardened Guy Fawkes, to use his own words, when taken and examined, could "blow the Scottish beggars back to their native mountains," was not directed against the Queen, whose power the conspirators evidently deemed too weak to be feared; therefore the details of this horrible conspiracy, which are to be met with in the pages of every History of England, would be out of place here.

The Queen brought into the world her daughter Sophia, at Greenwich, on the twenty-second of June, 1606. The infant survived her baptism but a few days, and was privately interred in Westminster Abbey, and the mother was dangerously ill for some time afterwards.

On the sixteenth of July, Anne's brother, Christian the Fourth, of Denmark, arrived in England, on a visit to the King and Queen. James met him at Gravesend, and conducted him up the Thames to Greenwich Palace, where he entered the sick Queen's chamber, and had a tender interview with his affectionate sister. Shortly afterwards, Cecil gave a grand entertainment and masque at Theobalds, in honour of the royal stranger. Many of the noble performers in this masque presented themselves before the spectators in a state of disgusting intoxication, then the prevalent vice of the court, as will be seen by the following extract from a letter written by one of the guests: "Those whom I never could get to taste good liquor, now follow the fashion, and wallow in beastly delights. The ladies abandon sobriety, and are seen to roll about in intoxication. After dinner, the representation of Solomon, his temple, and the coming of the Queen of Sheba, was made, or (as I may better say) was meant to have been made. The lady who did play the Queen's part, did carry most precious gifts to both their majesties [James and Christian]; but forgetting the steppes arising to the canopy, overset her casket into his Danish Majesty's lap, and fell at his feet, though I rather think it was in his face. Much was the hurry and confusion, cloths and napkins were at hand to make all clean. His Majesty then got up and would dance with the Queen of Sheba, but he fell down and tumbled himself before her, and was carried to an inner chamber and laid upon a bed of state, which was defiled by the presence of the Queen. The entertainment and show went forward, and most of the presenters went backward or fell down, wine did so occupy their inner chambers. Now did appear in rich dress, Faith, Hope, and Charity; Hope did assay to speak, but wine did render her endeavours so feeble, that she withdrew. Faith was then all alone, for I am certain she was not joined with good works, and left the court in a staggering condition. Charity came to the King's feet, and seemed to cover the multitude of sins her sisters had committed in some sorte. She made obeysance and brought gifts; she then returned to Hope and Faith, who were both in a dreadful sick condition in the lower hall." Such is a sketch of this disgusting scene from the pen of the poet Harrington; a scene we should have passed over in silence, but that some writers have endeavoured to blacken the fame of Anne of Denmark, by stating that she sanctioned the drunken revel, and herself played the part of the Queen of Sheba, when, in fact, poor lady, she at the time was confined to her lying-in chamber at Greenwich, by sheer debility; and even had she have been recovered, her etiquette of mourning for the death of her infant, would have precluded her from attending masques and festivities. She was churched on the third of August, and she took no part in any festivity till Sunday, the tenth of August; "when," says the chronicler, "the King and Queen went from Greenwich by water to Chatham, with Prince Henry, King Christian, and a numerous retinue, where they partook of a sumptuous banquet on board the Elizabeth Jonas; which splendid ship was wonderously adorned with cloth of gold. The august visitors dined in the orlop deck, which was fitted up with a rich chair of estate and other costly furniture. After dinner, the royal party went from that ship to the White Bear, upon a bridge, about twelve score yards long, made of fir masts, railed on either side, which floated upon the water, and was broad enough for four men, abreast, to walk along it. When the Queen, the Kings, and the others had landed, and gone past the Windmill Hills, the vessels off Chatham and the Castle discharged their ordnance to the number of about one thousand two hundred shots. The Danish King then left them, and went on board his own ship for the night, and next day the King, the Queen, Prince Henry, and a retinue of nobles, partook of a farewell banquet, which he had provided for them, on board the largest of the Danish vessels. This gallant ship, called the Admiral, was of very high and narrow building; the bulkhead, the stern, and her three galleries, were finely gilded; and the waist and half-deck adorned with arras and other rich ornaments. Here the august visitors were very royally feasted, and as they sat at banquet they pledged each other to their lasting health and continuing amity; and every pledge drank was straightway known by sound of drum and trumpet, and the cannons' loudest voice, beginning ever in the Danish Admiral, seconded by the English block houses, and followed by the Vice-Admiral, and the other six Danish ships, ending always with the smallest." The entertainment was terminated by a grand pageant of fire-works, contrived by his Danish Majesty, but which, on account of the necessity of taking the tides, which served at four o'clock, was shorn of its brilliancy by being ignited in a bright sunny August afternoon. At a quarter to four the Queen and her spouse bade an affectionate adieu to their loving brother, King Christian, who, after a prosperous voyage of eight days, reached his own dominions in safety.

Immediately after the departure of Christian the Fourth* of Denmark, the King and Queen, both of whom were passionately fond of the pleasures of the chase, went to Windsor, where they daily hunted with falcons and hounds, till the autumn rains set in. In May, 1607, her Majesty had the felicity to receive possession of the seat of Theobalds, at Cheshunt, a magnificent building, which was levelled to the dust in 1650, and which she obtained from Cecil, Earl of Salisbury, in exchange for her dower palace of Hatfield. The event was marked by a royal entertainment given by her Majesty at Theobalds, on the twenty-second of May, when Anne took part in a masque produced for the occasion by the gifted Ben Jonson, who, to compliment the Queen's passion for hunting, introduced into the enchanting scene that beatiful lyric

"Queen and huntress chaste as fair."

In September, 1608, the Queen and Prince Henry stood sponsors to Frederick Henry Howard, second son of the Earl of Arundel; and, in the winter of 1609, it was found that the Queen, who was never remarkable for economy, was so deeply in debt, that the King, to satisfy the clamours of her creditors, and, if possible, prevent the recurrence of such a calamity, made her a present of twenty thousand pounds, and added to her jointure three thousand pounds per year out of the customs. Such was the delight taken by Anne of Denmark and her royal spouse in cruel sports, that, on the twenty-third of June, 1609, they proceeded to the Tower with the Princes Henry and Charles, and the Princess Elizabeth, to witness a combat between a lion, a bear, a horse, and dogs. The encounter was furious, the scene fearful and revolting, but the sight of blood and the roaring and howling of the savage beasts, as they fought for their lives, excited in the minds of the royal party only pleasurable feelings; nor is this a matter of surprise, for, in that age of barbarity, bear-baiting, cock-fighting, and other similar cruelties, were alike patronized by all classes, from the peer to the peasant.

Anne of Denmark, who we have seen was one of the tenderest of mothers, was at length afforded a fondly anticipated pleasure; her eldest son was created Prince of Wales, with all conceivable pomp and magnificence; and at the same time the Prince and twenty-five nobles were installed Knights of the Bath. "Wednesday, the thirtieth of May, 1610," says a contemporary, "the Prince being accompanied by divers young nobles and his own servants, rode about twelve at noon from St. James's to Richmond, where he supped, and reposed for that night. The next morning, the Lord Mayor, the Aldermen, and fifty-four of the companies of London, in their barges, with divers fair banners and streamers, proceeded along the Thames to Chelsea, where they attended the coming of the Prince, whose dinner was prepared at the court of Whitehall, and that of the Lord Mayor and the

* In July, 1614, the Danish Monarch paid another visit to England. He was not expected; travelled incognito, and took the Court by surprise. But he stayed only a fortnight, and during that time the Court was occupied in nothing but the ordinary round of royal pleasures. We have deemed it well not to detail the visit. The Queen received her brother with sisterly affection, parted from him in tears, and never saw him more.

several City companies, at their respective halls. But by reason of the low ebb, his Highness could not proceed forward till four in the afternoon. He was entertained by the way about Barnelms, with a banquet; and, coming to Chelsea, where the Lord Mayor and his train attended, there was a dolphin, upon whom sat Neptune; and upon a whale sat a water goddess, who delivered a complimentary address to the Prince, which being done, they proceeded toward the court; the inferior companies first, and the Lord Mayor's barge between, the two sea monsters next, before the Prince's barge, after which followed his own servants in several barges, and the barges of divers noblemen that attended his Highness on the way. When they came to Whitehall, his Highness took leave of the Lord Mayor and Aldermen, and landed at Whitehall Bridge. When he landed, a peal of chambers, placed directly opposite the court, on the Lambeth side of the river, were discharged, and he was received with due form by the officers of the King's household, and welcomed by the Queen, his mother, in the privy chamber." The ceremony, which it would be as tedious a task to narrate as to pursue, was forthwith performed with all possible solemnity. The youthful Henry was solemnly invested Prince of Wales, on the fourth of June, and the delighted Queen celebrated the event by taking part in two masques, written for the occasion by Ben Jonson, and by the respectable poet, Daniels. "In honour of the Prince's investure," proceeds our author, "there met in the tilt-yard, divers earls, barons, and others, being in rich and glorious armour; and having costly caparisons, wondrous, curiously, embroidered with pearls, gold and silver; the like rich habiliments for horses having never been seen before. These nobles presented their several ingenious devices and trophies before the King, Queen, and Prince, and then ran at tilt, where there was a world of people to behold them. And that night there were naval triumphs and pastimes upon the Thames, over against the court, with ships of war and gallies, fighting one against another, and against a great castle builded upon the water. After these mock battles, then, for an hour's space, there were many strange and variable fire-works in the castle, and in all the ships and gallies, without hurt to any person, which was singularly fortunate, the Thames being, in a manner, closely covered with boats and barges full of people, whilst the adjacent shore, on both sides, was surcharged with people, who were highly delighted with the magnificence of the spectacle."

Prince Charles, Duke of York, having now attained health and strength, he was taken from the care of the judicious Lady Carey, and placed under the tuition and training of tutors and companions selected by his brother, the Prince of Wales; to whom he shortly afterwards addressed the subjoined little letter, informing him that he hunts.

"SIR,

"Pleas your H. [Highness] I doe keepe your haires in breath, (and I have very good sport) I doe wish the King and you might see it. So, longing to see you, I kissse your hand, and rest

"Yours to be commanded,

"YORK.

"My maydes service to you.

"To his Hienesse."

About this time, Sir Thomas Overbury, the assistant of Robert Carr, the royal favourite, whose duty it was, as confidential secretary, to decipher the many letters which, in that intriguing era, were addressed both to the King and to the Queen in cypher, deeply offended Queen Anne, by making public the contents of several of her private letters, which had passed through his hands. Overbury treated the Queen's malice with derisive scorn, and for his temerity, suffered a short imprisonment; but Carr, who was created Viscount Rochester and Earl of Somerset, and on the death of Salisbury, in May, 1612, filled the post of Prime Minister and Secretary, endeavoured by every means in his power to conciliate her; but she very justly abhorred the selfish rapacity of his whole clique, and heartily despised both him and them.

Although James had been for years on the throne, he had failed to acquire a place in the affections of his English subjects. His love of pleasure, his extravagance, his partiality to favourites; and above all, his extraordinary notions of the Divine right of Kings, alarmed the patriots, and scandalized the religious portion of the community, and prevented him from obtaining the esteem of the people generally. But those who were discontented with their King, beheld in his heir a prince of the most promising virtues and abilities. "The following rhyme," says Harrington, "was common in the mouths of the people—

'Henry the Eighth pulled down the abbeys and cells,
But Henry the Ninth shall pull down bishops and bells.'"

A prediction, which, like many of the ultra-democratic absurdities of the present era, however popular, was too absurd to be fulfilled. Prince Henry, nevertheless, was looked upon by the more sober-minded as a most fit successor to the throne; the young Prince himself, faithful to the lessons formerly instilled into his mind by his mother, openly ridiculed the weakness of his father, and boasted that on his accession his conquering sword should add France to the possessions of the crown of England: hopes, which, to the sorrow of the nation and the deep dejection of his fond mother, were anticipated by an untimely death. In person he was tall, being more than six feet high when he reached his seventeenth year; he was large-boned, thin skinned, fair in complexion, and with a Grecian cast of features. He injured his health by long bathing after supper, by taking violent exercise during the greatest heats of summer, by recklessly exposing himself to the storms and rains of winter, and by indulging too freely in the luxuries of the table. In the spring of 1612, his health and spirits began to decline; during the summer he grew worse; as September drew to a close, he, on returning from his sports in the country, became alarmingly ill, and on reaching St. James's was attacked with an intermittent fever —a malady for which a specific was then unknown; and which, despite the efforts of the royal physicians, speedily assumed the form of a virulently infectious, putrid fever. The Queen, hitherto, had watched at the bedside of her unfortunate son; but immediately the malignant symptoms became evident, a dread of infection forced her to retire to her own palace of Somerset-house—called, in honour to her, whilst she held possession of it, Denmark House—where she remained in a miserable state of mind. Her whole thoughts were bent on the recovery of the death-sick Prince. She remembered that Sir Walter Raleigh had a quack medicine, which she had herself taken with success for an ague. For this nostrum she accordingly sent, in the hope of restoring her son to health. Sir Walter, who deeply lamented the Prince's danger, had full faith in the medicine, and with a large packet of it which had been carefully prepared for the purpose by his own hands, sent word, that, "with the exception of poison, it would cure all mortal diseases." The Prince swallowed a dose, revived for a short while, and then, about half-past seven in the evening of the sixth of November, 1612, breathed his last.

When the mournful tidings were conveyed to the impatient Queen, she fell into fearful paroxysms of rage, grief, and despair. She remembered the words of Sir Walter Raleigh's message, that the nostrum would cure all maladies but poison; and in the delirium of her grief, declared that poison, and not fever, had deprived her of her beloved son Henry. Her suspicions attributed the murderous deed to Sir Thomas Overbury, and a few days afterwards common report implicated the King in the transaction; a shameful libel, as James, although a weak monarch, was a worthy father, and with the Queen, equally bewailed the loss of their dear son. The body of the Prince was opened, and the still existing report of the surgeons, who made the *post-mortem* examination, render it evident that he died of a malignant fever.

The Princess Elizabeth was now, after her brother Charles, the next heir to the throne. She had had many wooers, and the Queen had deeply offended the religious prejudices of the English Protestants by desiring to marry her to the young King of Spain. The King, although allured by the splendour of the alliance, was after a time convinced of the folly of expecting a royal household divided in religion to prosper; and the union was declined. The pretensions of the other two suitors—the Prince of Piedmont, and Frederick Count Palatine of the Rhine—were about equal; but as the latter professed the reformed faith, he obtained the preference; the marriage articles were signed, and on the sixteenth of October, 1612, he landed in England to receive the hand of Anne's young and beautiful daughter, Elizabeth. Grand preparations were made for the occasion, but the unexpected death of Prince Henry caused the marriage ceremony to be delayed till the fourteenth of February, 1613, when it was solemnized at Whitehall with extraordinary splendour, in the presence of the royal family and the leading nobles and their ladies, who, although the court were still in mourning for Prince Henry, vied with each other in magnificence of dress. "At the betrothment, the King," says the MS. letter of Mr. Lewkner, "was present, brought in a chaire, for he was then so gowtie he could not goe, and the Queene no way affecting the match, kept her chamber." This was the first royal marriage celebrated according to the form in the Book of Common Prayer of the Church of England. Both their Majesties and Prince Charles were present; James wore a suit of black, and Anne was attired in white satin, and covered with the richest of the crown jewels. The dress of the Princess, and the extravagant cost of the ceremony and rejoicings, are thus detailed by Wilson:—

"In February, 1613, the Prince-Palatine, and that lovely Princess, the Lady Elizabeth, were married on Bishop Valentine's day, with all possible pomp and grandeur. Her vestments were white, the emblem of innocency; her hair dishevelled, hanging down her back at length, an ornament of virginity; a crown of pure gold upon her head, the cognizance of majesty, being all over beset with precious gems, shining like a constellation; her train supported by twelve young ladies in white garments, so adorned with jewels, that her passage looked like the milky way. She was led to church by her brother, Prince Charles, and the Earl of Northampton, the young batchelor on her right hand, and the old one on her left. And while the Archbishop of Canterbury was solemnizing the marriage, some coruscations and lightenings of joy appeared in her countenance, that expressed more than an ordinary smile, being almost elated to a laughter.

"She returned from chapel between the Duke of Lennox and the Earl of Nottingham, Lord High Admiral, two married men.

"To support the magnificence with which this ceremony was attended, the King was obliged to demand aids of his subjects, a custom usual on these occasions, and although intermitted for more than a century, he received twenty thousand five hundred pounds; yet how enormous soever the sum may seem, it was insufficient to defray the expence, which amounted to almost four times that sum.

"The city of London, that with magnificence had feasted the Prince-Palatine and his noble retinue, presented to the fair bride a chain of oriental pearl, by the hands of the Lord Mayor and aldermen, in their scarlet and gold chain accoutrement, of such a value, as was fit for them to give and her to receive, as it cost no less than two thousand pounds."

One round of masques, balls, displays of fire-works, sham naval and military battles, and other entertainments, continued till the twenty-fifth of April, when the Princess Elizabeth and her husband bade a final farewell to England. Immediately after their departure the Queen's health and spirits gave way, but she restored her constitution by a visit to the springs at Bath. The bath she used was ornamented with a cross, the crown of England, and the inscription *Anna Regina Sacrum*, and has ever since been known as "the Queen's Bath." In the disgraceful proceedings of the divorce of the Lady Frances Howard from her husband, the Earl of Essex, which took place in April, 1613, the Queen took no part; neither does it appear that Anne in any manner influenced James when he inhumanly incarcerated Arabella Stuart in the Tower for privately marrying the Earl of Hertford, although it would have redounded to her honour had she pleaded for the cruelly persecuted Arabella, who, after ineffectual efforts to escape, went mad, and died in a most deplorable condition on the twenty-seventh of September, 1615.

At this period the young, handsome, and accomplished George Villiers was first introduced to the notice of the King, who had grown weary of his favourite, Somerset. Just previously, Sir Thomas Overbury, whilst a prisoner in the Tower, was poisoned by the vengeance of Somerset's countess; rumour attributed the murder to Somerset, and he and his wife were now arrested, and with their accomplices tried and found guilty of the poisoning. Although the King, at his visit to Cambridge in 1615, took especial notice of Villiers, he refused to accept of his services, without the Queen would first recommend him, to fill the office of his confidential secretary. To Archbishop Abbot, who undertook to procure this formal recommendation from the Queen, Anne replied—

"My Lord, you know not what you desire. I know your master better than you all. If Villiers gains the royal favour, we shall all be sufferers; I shall no more be spared than others, for the King will teach him to treat us all with pride and contempt."

Abbott, who himself relates the anecdote, says, "The King would never admit any to nearness about himself, but such as the Queen should commend to him; that if she should complain afterwards of *the dear one*, he might make answer, 'It is long of yourself, for you commended him unto me.'"

However, whatever the Queen's misgivings might be, she shortly afterwards, in compliance with Abbott's repeated entreaties, earnestly besought her spouse to receive Villiers as a favourite, and on St. George's feast, 1615, the King sent for Villiers, knighted him with Prince Charles's sword, whilst the Queen stood by, and caused him to be sworn a gentleman of the privy chamber, with a yearly salary of one thousand pounds. The new favourite proved more grateful to Anne than she expected. He never gave her cause to quarrel with him, and as she found she could place unlimited confidence in him, she employed him as a monitor to correct the King's personal indiscretion and ill-behaviour, as will be seen by the subjoined letter from Queen Anne to Sir George Villiers.

"My kind Dog,

"I have received your letter, which is very welcome to me; you do very well in lugging the sow's ears [meaning in reprimanding the King], and I thank you for it, and would have you do so still, upon condition that you continue a watchful dog to him, and be always true to him. So wishing you all happiness.

"Anna, R."

The Queen, in reply to a letter of Villiers, informing her that, "in compliance with her command, he had pulled the King's ear till it hung like a sow's lug," wrote—

"My kind Dog,

"Your letter hath been acceptable to me; I rest already assured of your carefulness. You may tell your master that the King of Denmark hath sent me twelve fair mares, and, as the bringer of them assures me, all great with foals, which I intend to put into Byfield Park, where being the other day a hunting, I could find but very few deer, but great store of other cattle, as I shall tell your master myself when I see him. I hope to meet you all at Woodstock, at the time appointed, till when I wish you all happiness and contentment.

"Anna, R.

"I thank you for your pains taken in remembering the King for the paling of my park. I will do you any service I can."

To Sir George Villiers.

In March, 1617, James set out from Theobalds on his long-delayed progress to Scotland; the Queen accompanied him as far as Ware, and then bade him adieu, and proceeded to Greenwich Palace, where she resided during his absence. There was a boarding-school for young ladies at Deptford, known as Ladies' Hall; and whilst the King was away in Scotland, her Majesty honoured the establishment with a visit, and the pupils performed a masque for her entertainment. It being against all propriety to admit so audacious a god as Cupid into a ladies' boarding-school, the piece was entitled "Cupid's Banishment," and throughout the performance the God of Love was very properly shown neither favour nor mercy. Indeed towards the close of the masque he was rudely bundled out, and then the nymphs sang,

> "Hark, hark, to Philomel,
> Whose notes no song can parallel;
> Mark, mark, her melody,
> Still she descants on chastity.
> The diapason of her tone is—Cupid's gone,
> He's gone, he's gone, he's quite exiled,
> Venus' brat, peevish imp, fancy's child,
> Let him go, let him go, with his quiver and his bow."

All Anne of Denmark's letters are without date; the following seems written whilst James was in Scotland.

Queen Anne to King James.

"Sir,

"As nothing is more welcome to me than your letters (for which I thank you), so can they bring me no better tidings than of your good health, of me much desired; for I cease not to pray for the increase and continuance of your good, both of mind and body, and thereof rest assured, so kissing your hands, I remain she that will ever love you best.

"Anna, R."

About the period when the King returned from Scotland, the Queen was attacked with bodily infirmities, "which," says Chamberlayne, in a letter to Sir Dudley Carlton, dated October, 1617, "she would fain lay to the gout, although her physicians fear an ill habit, through her whole constitution." At the commencement of 1618, symptoms of confirmed dropsy became evident, and her spirits, as well as her bodily health, began to decline. To avoid the riotous revels in which James was wont to indulge at Shrovetide, she removed to her quiet chamber in Somerset House. But she had scarcely settled down, when the King, in the midst of his carouses, was attacked with the gout, and the Queen, sick as she was, visited him at Whitehall, and afterwards took him with her to Theobalds, and nursed him till he recovered. During the summer and autumn, Anne's health continued to decline. She removed to Oatlands, and thence to Hampton Court, where she grew worse, and suffered from a racking cough, and several times vomited blood. The King, when not confined to his chamber by sickness, paid her frequent visits, and on Sir Walter Raleigh, in an earnest appeal, imploring her to

> "Save him who would have died for her defence,
> Save him whose thoughts no treason ever tainted;"—

she made a passionate appeal to his Majesty on behalf of the brilliant but unfortunate Sir Walter; who, notwithstanding, had his head struck off by the executioner on the twenty-ninth of October, 1618. What effect his death produced upon Anne, now that her own life was drawing to a close, is not known. She continued to grow worse throughout the winter, and to add to the depression of her drooping spirits, the King, who had hitherto made a point of travelling three times a week from London to Hampton Court to see her, was laid up at Royston with an alarming fit of illness. James, urged by a suspicion that two of his wife's attendants, Danish Anna, and a Frenchman named Pierrot, would endeavour by some foul play to possess themselves of her valuable jewels, was anxious that the Queen should make her will; but her physicians, Drs. Mayerne, Atkins, and Turner, objected to her receiving more than a very gentle hint upon the subject. With this view, the Archbishop of Canterbury and the Bishop of London waited upon her, on the second of February, 1619, and in reply, she assured the prelates of her sure, although slow, recovery; adding, "you speak thus dismally, because your visit has fallen out on Candlemas, which ye know is always a day of gloom with the English;" in fact, she did not choose to take the hint.

A few days afterwards, and whilst she was making preparations for a visit she vainly hoped to receive from the King of Denmark, her cough assumed the form of a consumptive one. She took to her bed, first having the one "she loved best set up," and then rapidly sunk into the arms of death. On the last day of her existence, the Archbishop of Canterbury and the Bishop of London again visited her, and earnestly prayed with her; after which, she assured them "that she had set her heart on God, that she had no faith in saints nor in her own merits, and that she only looked to Christ, her Saviour, for the redemption of her soul." They then urged her to make her will; but as Pierrot and Danish Anne, to whom she now utterly consigned herself, feared they should have to account for the valuables they had grasped, if she consented, they prevailed on her to give the prelates an evasive answer, and urge them to retire. Canterbury went, however, promising to return in two days, but the Bishop of London remained at Hampton Court. Meanwhile, Prince Charles, whom she had sent for, was conducted to her presence, and after an affectionate conference, he, at her earnest request, retired to her chamber. Indeed, the Queen longed for the luxury of privacy, a luxury which, in those days, royal personages sighed for in vain. They were born in public, lived in public, even to dressing, eating, drinking, and undressing; and what must have been more trying, could not even die without being surrounded and watched in their last agonies by a host of attendants, princes, nobles, prelates, privy councillors, ambassadors, and others.

In the evening the Countesses of Arundel, of Bedford, of Derby, and Lady Carey, besides several lords and others, visited the dying Queen, and urged her to make her will; and after supper, Prince Charles again entered his chamber, but by her earnest desire soon afterwards retired; when she gave a peremptory order for no one but her two favourite domestics to enter her presence, and forbad any watch to be held. Her physicians visited her at the midnight hour, and the moment they were gone, she ordered Danish Anne to close the door, and lock out all that were out; and now she said, "Lay down by my side and repose, for you want rest." Half-an-hour afterwards she called for water to wash her eyes, but when the candle was brought she could not see the light—death had sealed her vision; which Danish Anne no sooner discovered, than she unlocked the doors, and called in the physicians, the bishops, the Prince, and all the lords and ladies of the household. It was one o'clock: the sinking Queen swallowed a cordial administered by her physicians, scribbled her signature to her will, and whilst the Bishop fervently prayed by her bed-side, gave several slight moans, and with a smiling countenance ceased to breathe, at a few minutes past one in the morning of the second of March, 1619.

Her loss was deeply mourned by the King, who at the time was confined to his chamber by a dangerous illness, but from which he had the good fortune to recover a few weeks afterwards. Her body was conveyed by water to Somerset House, and after laying in state there till the thirteenth of May, interred with royal obsequies in Westminster Abbey, Prince Charles and all the leading nobility attended the funeral. The Countess of Arundel was the chief lady mourner, and the funeral sermon was preached by the Archbishop of Canterbury. Shortly after the funeral, the King examined his departed consort's coffers and cabinets, and found that thirty-six thousand pounds' worth of her jewels, besides much money which he believed she had hoarded up, were missing; suspicion fell on Pierrot and Danish Anne; they were arrested and examined, but without any trace being obtained of the missing treasure, which, indeed, it appears never was found.

Anne of Denmark died in the forty-sixth year of her age; no monument was erected to her memory, but her hearse stood over her grave till the Civil Wars, when it was destroyed. Her consort, James the First, who did not again enter the married state, died on the twenty-seventh of March, 1625, and her only two surviving children, Charles, created Prince of Wales, in November, 1616, and afterwards Charles the First, and Elizabeth, Queen of Bohemia, were both singularly unfortunate.

Many epitaphs and poetical tributes were written to the memory of the fondly-beloved Queen of James the First. Of these, we select from Camden's Remains the following.

Epitaph on Queen Anne of Denmark.

"March, with her winds, hath struck a cedar tall,
And weeping April mourns that cedar's fall,
And May intends no flower that month shall bring,
Since she must lose the flower of all the spring.
Thus March's wind hath caused April's showers,
And yet sad May must lose her flower or flowers;
But though the beauteous queen so fondly loved,
Has left this earth to be enthroned above,
She's only changed, not dead; no good prince dies,
But, like the sun, doth only set to rise."

Henrietta Maria.

HENRIETTA MARIA,

Queen of Charles the First.

CHAPTER I.

Henrietta Maria, daughter of Henry the Fourth of France—Birth—Infancy—Education—Wooed by the Count of Soissons—Charles the First's adventures in search of a bride—His marriage with Henrietta negotiated—The marriage treaty—Nuptials solemnized in France—Henrietta conducted to England—Charles meets her at Dover—Conducts her to Canterbury—Marries her there—Aquatic procession up the Thames.

HENRIETTA MARIA, consort of Charles the First, and partaker of that weak, insincere monarch's calamities, was the youngest daughter, and the fifth and last child of the more famed than really illustrious Henry the Fourth of France, and of his wife, Mary of Medicis. She first saw the light at the Louvre, on the fourteenth of November, 1609; and, on the fourth of May, 1610, her father was stabbed to the heart by one Ravaillac, who, it is said, was instigated to the crime by the Jesuits. She took part at that monarch's funeral, which was solemnized with sad magnificence, on the thirteenth of the subsequent June; and at the inauguration of her brother, the young Louis the Thirteenth, she was carried in the procession by the Princess of Condé. During her infancy, she chiefly resided at the palaces of Blois and Fontainbleau. Before she had completed her third year, she was made one of the partakers in the marriage festivity of her sister, Elizabeth, with the King of Spain, which was celebrated, with all conceivable pomp and rejoicings, at the palace of the Place Royale; and, when six years old, she was present at the solemn delivering of her sister, Elizabeth, to the King of Spain, as his spouse, and the receiving of Anne, the Infanta of Spain, as the consort of Louis the Thirteenth. She was educated under the immediate supervisal of her mother, who instilled into her young mind extravagant ideas of the infallibility of royalty; and taught her to believe that "Kings are the visible gods of men, as God is the invisible King of men"—a false and dangerous doctrine, and a belief in which, doubtless, materially aggravated the sorrows of the unfortunate Queen Henrietta Maria.

The principal tutor of the Princess Henrietta was M. de Brevis—a man of energy, wisdom, and erudition; but the good that, in all probability, would have resulted from his sound teachings, was destroyed in the embryo by the egotistical weakness, pride, and vanity of Mary de Medicis, and by the bigoted religious counsels of the enthusiastic Mère Magdelaine — a sincere but narrow-minded ultra-popish Carmelite nun, who, in the doctrines of religion, completely controlled the mind of the Princess during her childhood. After the deservedly-unpopular Mary de Medicis was deprived of the regency, and sent captive to the castle of Blois, Henrietta shared her seclusion for about three years, when her presence was required at the marriage of her sister, Christine, with the Duke of Savoy; and, after the ceremony, she was not again permitted to return to her mother, who, however, in 1620, effected a reconciliation with her son, Louis the Thirteenth, and, from that time, obtained a greater influence in the government of France than she had ever before possessed.

Henrietta's first lover was the Count of Soissons. He claimed her hand as the reward for his valuable services at the siege of Rochelle; nor was his suit discouraged, till it was next to certain that the Princess would become the bride of Charles, the only surviving son of James the First. Impressed with a conviction that domestic happiness could not exist where love was wanting, Charles resolved, in person, to woo and win his destined bride. The first object of his love was Maria Althea, daughter of Philip the Third of Spain, and sister of the then reigning monarch, Philip the Fourth. To woo this Princess, Charles and the Duke of Buckingham, who accompanied him, set out in the disguise of English merchants. Travelling under the fictitious names of Tom Smith and John Brown, they, in their route, passed through Paris, where, without their disguise being detected, they obtained a view of the ladies of the French court, and witnessed the rehearsal of a court ballet, in which the Queen of France danced with the beautiful Henrietta, who, although scarcely fifteen, and girlish withal, on being informed of the Prince's adventures, exclaimed, with a sigh, " He need not have travelled so far as Madrid to search for a bride."

That Charles did not fall in love with Henrietta at this his first view of her, is evident by the subjoined letter, which he addressed to his father, James the First:—

" Sir,

" Since the closing of our last, we have been at court again (and that we might not hold you in pain, we assure you that we have not been known), where we saw the young Queen [of France], little Monsieur, and Madame, at the practising of a mask that is to be presented to the King, and in it there danced the Queen and Madame [Henrietta Maria], with as many as made up nineteen fair dancing ladies, amongst which the Queen is the handsomest, which hath wrought in me a greater desire to see her sister. So, in haste, going to bed, we humbly take our leave, and rest your Majesty's most humble and obedient son and servant,

" Charles."

" Paris, the 22nd of Feb."

" And your humble slave and dog,

" Steenie."

After a series of adventures, which we have no space to detail, Charles reached Madrid in safety, was honourably received there, saw the Princess, loved her, and, in the ecstacy of passion, wrote, or rather translated, from a Spanish verse, composed on the wooing—

"Charles Stuart am I,
Love guides me afar,
To the heavens of Spain,
For Maria, my star."

After much negotiation, the marriage-treaty was arranged, and the Infanta assumed the title of Princess of England; but, before the betrothal could take place, Charles was suddenly recalled to England; and as the people of both countries strenuously opposed the alliance, the match was broken off. However, previous to the formal nullification of the treaty, King James, by the desire of Charles, who, when at Madrid, had been requested by Elizabeth, the young Queen of Spain, to marry her sister, Henrietta-Maria, dispatched Henry Rich, Lord Kensington, to Paris, in the summer of 1624, to make private inquiry of the Queen-Mother, Mary of Medicis, who at that period completely ruled the reins of the state, whether a match between Charles and Henrietta was feasible, before any public treaty was entered upon. The Spanish ambassador at Paris guessed or learned the errand of this nobleman, and resolved, if possible, to thwart his purpose. However, after both parties had intrigued, quarrelled, and manœuvred, the Queen-Mother lent ear to the suit, and accepted the wooing ambassador's explanation of the breaking-off of the Spanish engagement. Kensington was a genuine specimen of politeness and discretion; he inflamed the fancy of the Prince and the Princess by artfully exaggerating their charms and virtues to each other; he wore at his bosom an elegant miniature of Charles, enclosed in a gold case, which, immediately the purport of his visit could no longer be kept secret, he took pleasure in displaying to the ladies at court, and, on one occasion, lent it for an hour, that Henrietta might contemplate it in private; whilst to Prince Charles he wrote as follows:—

"May it please your Highness,

"I find here so infinite a value of your person and virtue, as what instrument soever (myself the very weakest) having some commands, as they imagine, from you, shall receive excess of honours from them; they will not conceive me, nor yet scarce receive me, but as a public instrument for the service of an alliance that, above all the things in this world, they do so earnestly desire. The Queen-Mother hath expressed, as far as she thinks is fit, for the honour of her daughter, great favour and goodwill in it. I take the boldness to tell her (the which she took extremely well) that if such a proposition should be made, your Highness could not believe that she had lost her former inclination and desire in it. She said, your trust of her should find great respect. There is no preparation, I find, towards this business but by her; and all persuasions of amity made light that look not towards this errand; and, Sir, if your intentions proceed this way, as by many reasons of state and wisdom there is cause now rather to press it than slacken it, you will find a lady of as much loveliness and sweetness to deserve your affection as any creature under heaven can do; and, Sir, by all her fashions since my being here, and by what, from the ladies, I hear, it is most visible to me her infinite value and respect unto you. Sir, I say not this to betray your belief, but from a true observation and knowledge of this to be so. I tell you this, and must somewhat more, in way of admiration of the person of Madam, for the impressions I had of her were but ordinary, but the amazement extraordinary, to find her as, I protest to God, I did, the sweetest creature in France. Her growth is very little short of her age, and her wisdom infinitely beyond it. I heard her discourse with her mother, and the ladies about her, with extraordinary discretion and quickness. She dances, of which I am a witness of, as well as ever I saw any creature. They say she sings most sweetly: I am sure she looks so. Sir, you have thousands of servants here that desire to be commanded by you, but most particularly the Duc de Chevereau and Monsieur le Grand, who seek all opportunities to do you service, and hath credit and power to do so. Sir, if these that are strangers unto you are thus ambitious of your commands, with what infinite passion have I cause to beg them, that am your vassal, and have no other glory than to have you as

"Your Highness' most humble

"And obedient creature,

"Kensington."

When Kensington had sufficiently smoothed the way for the marriage, James sent, as his coadjutor, the Earl of Carlisle, the regular ambassador, to France. Carlisle was an empty-headed fop, and being a mere state puppet, the treaty for the alliance was negociated by Kensington. On obtaining a formal audience, the English ambassadors presented, by the Queen-Mother's permission, letters, and a portrait of Charles to the Princess. Henrietta received them with thanks repeatedly perused the Prince's *billet-doux* with tears of joy, and placed it with his portrait in her bosom, where she afterwards continued to wear them. In return, Charles received a beautiful miniature of the Princess. He gazed upon it with raptures; Henrietta was then but fifteen, yet in her was visible the budding charms of one of the sweetest, fairest queens in history. Nothing for an instant excited feelings of dissatisfaction, saving the diminutiveness of her stature; and the elegant Lord Kensington, in a letter to Charles, after alluding to the smallness of her person, artfully remarks, that her sister, Christine, now grown a tall, portly lady, was equally diminutive at her age.

Matters were in this state, when Lord Kensington requested an interview with Henrietta, to convey to her a private message from the Prince. "The Queen-Mother, after some hesitation, assented," writes Kensington; "but withal she would needs know what I would say unto her daughter.

"'Nay, then,' smilingly quoth I, 'your Majesty would impose upon me the like law that they in Spain did upon his Highness when he courted the Infanta.'

"'But the case is now different,' said she, 'for there the Prince was in person, here is but his deputy.'

"'But a deputy,' answered I, 'that represents his person.'

"'True,' rejoined the Queen, 'and yet I desire to know what you would say to my daughter.'

"'Nothing that is not fitting the ears of so virtuous a Princess.'

"'What is it then?'

"'Well, Madam,' quoth I, 'if you will needs know, it shall be much to this effect: that your Majesty having given me the liberty of some freer language than heretofore, I obey the Prince his commandments in presenting to her, your beautiful daughter, his service, not by way of compliment any longer, but out of passion and affection, which the beauty of her person and the virtues of her mind so kindled in him, that he was resolved to contribute the utmost he could to the alliance in question, and would deem the success thereof the greatest happiness that could befall him. Such, with some little other like amorous language, was to be my communication to your fair and royal daughter.'

"'*Allez, Allez,* I perceive no great danger in that,' smilingly answered the Queen-Mother; '*je me fie en vous, je me fie en vous.*'

"Neither did I abuse the trust," proceeds Lord Kensington, "for I varied not much in delivering my message to Henrietta, save that I amplified it a little more. She drank it in with joy, and with a low curtsey made her acknowledgments to the Prince, adding, that she was sincerely obliged to his Highness, and would think herself happy in the occasion that should be presented, by meriting the place she had in his good graces. I then," concludes the polite Ambassador, "turned my speech to the ladies that attended, and told them that since the Queen of France was pleased to give me this liberty, it would be henceforth well for them to act accordingly. I told them that his Highness, Charles, had her Grace Henrietta's picture, which he kept in his cabinet, and on which, since he could not have the happiness to behold her person, he continually fed his longing eyes and ardent passion. All which, and other such-like speeches, the royal maiden standing by, quickly took up, without letting any one of them fall to the ground."

Nothing now remained but to arrange the marriage-treaty; a task which proved so tedious and difficult, that Charles more than once despaired of success. Henrietta was a Catholic, the Prince a Protestant; the Pope, on this account, objected to the match, and declared that if it took place, religious discord would destroy the domestic happiness of the royal couple. However, after much discussion and intrigue, it was arranged that the Princess should have separate religious establishments of her own, and she and her servants should be permitted the full exercise of their religion; that Henrietta's children should remain under her care till they were thirteen years of age, (a clause injurious to the interests of both countries, and which gave to the future Queen of England power to bring up her offspring in the Catholic faith,) that her portion should be eight hundred thousand crowns, and that she should, for herself and for her descendants, renounce all right of succession to the crown of France. By a secret article, it was stipulated that James should cease to persecute the Catholics, and permit them the private and peaceable exercise of their worship. Such was the substance of the marriage-treaty, which was signed in December, 1624. Both parties expected to solemnize the nuptials immediately afterwards; but, to their surprise and vexation, after Charles had appointed the Duke of Chevereuse as his proxy, the nuncio Spada, by order of Pope Urban, refused to deliver the papal dispensation for the marriage until the promises in favour of the English Catholics were acknowledged publicly. Shortly afterwards, King James died, the Prince ascended the throne of Great Britain, under the title of Charles the First, and in the end, to avoid the scandal of the marriage being solemnized without the papal license, which the Queen-mother threatened should be done, Spada, by Urban's order, delivered the dispensation, and on Sunday, the twenty-fifth of April, 1625, Charles was solemnly married, by proxy, to Henrietta-Maria, at Notre-Dame cathedral. Scarcely was the ceremony concluded, when the Duke of Buckingham, with a large retinue of English nobles, unexpectedly arrived to escort the royal bride to England. The King, the Queen-mother, and the whole court of France prepared to accompany the young Queen of England in royal progress to the port of embarcation. The royal travellers set out in magnificent array, but illness forced the King of France to remain behind; and the sudden and alarming indisposition of Mary of Medicis detained Henrietta for a fortnight at Amiens, and threw a cloud of gloom over the august party, which was only dispelled by the Queen-mother's recovery; when they proceeded forward to Boulogne, where Henrietta, after receiving from her mother a letter, in which many sublime truths were combined with counsel that, under the circumstances, was highly pernicious and dangerous; and after taking leave, as she believed, for ever of those relations and friends who proceeded no farther with her—embarked on the eleventh of June, and, after a stormy passage, landed at Dover on Sunday, the twelfth, about eight in the evening, and "lay there in the castle that night." Tidings of her landing were swiftly carried to the King, who was then at Canterbury, impatiently waiting her arrival. "His Majesty," says a contemporary, "came to Dover castle at ten the following morning to visit her; and although she was unready and at breakfast, and he desired to wait till the repast was concluded, she hastened down a pair of stairs to meet him, and offered to kneel down and kiss his hand; but he wrapt her up in his arms with many earnest kisses. After this, as they stood conversing together, the King, surprised at finding her taller than he had expected—she reached to his shoulders—glanced downwards towards her feet, to discover if her height had been increased artificially; which she perceiving, and guessing his purport, showed him her shoes, saying, 'Sir, I stand upon mine own feet, I have no helps by art; thus high am I, and neither higher nor lower.' Having conversed together for an hour, the royal pair went forth into the presence, where the nimble, quiet, black-eyed, brown-haired, royal brunette recommended to her captivated spouse all her servants of quality by name." At dinner the King sat by her side and carved for her, and she ate heartily of the venison and pheasant which his Grace piled on her plate, notwithstanding her confessor (who all this while stood by her) had forewarned her; "that it was the eve of St. John the Baptist, a fast day, and that she should take heed not to set a bad example, or cause a scandle on her first arrival." The same day the royal party proceeded from Doncaster to Canterbury, and in the great hall there, Charles and Henrietta were that evening married in person. A sumptuous wedding supper was provided, "which being over," says one of the news letters, which, in the absence of regular newspapers, were then written, for the information and amusement of the wealthy, by professed intelligencers, "her Majesty retired for the night, and some space of time after, his Majesty followed her; and on entering his bed-chamber, the first thing he did was to bolt all the doors around (being seven) with his own hands, letting in but two of the bed-chamber to undress him, which being done, he bolted them out also. The next morning he lay till seven o'clock, and was pleasant with the lords that he had beguiled them, and hath ever since been very jocund."

On the fourteenth of June, the royal pair proceeded in state to Gravesend, and thence by water to Whitehall. "Yesterday," says a contemporary intelligencer, "I saw their Majesties coming up from Gravesend; the King looked exceedingly merry, the Queen is diminutive in stature, her head reaching only to his shoulder, but she is young enough to grow taller. A hope is entertained that she will, by God's blessing, embrace our religion. It is said that one of the English attendants asked her if she could endure a Huguenot; when she answered, 'Why not? was not my father one?' As she passed in royal procession up the Thames, she had a splendid view of our magnificent navy, which is about to put to sea, and which saluted her with a volley of fifteen hundred great shot; and the Tower gave her a deafening peal of ordnance. Throughout the voyage, the people cheered her, and she responded, by standing at her large window, which, although it rained hard, was wide open, and joyfully waving her hand to them. So they arrived at Whitehall, where they continue till Monday, when they go to Hampton Court. On Sunday, June the nineteenth, there is to be a great feast at Whitehall. The day they arrived in London, the bells rang all midnight, and all the streets were full of bonfires." Their solemn entry into the metropolis was prevented by the fearful ravages of a plague, which was pronounced, at the time, the most destructive in the memory of man. The King, Queen, and Court, after a short stay at Whitehall, removed to Hampton Court, and remained principally there and at Windsor, till the winter; whilst the public rejoicings in commemoration of the accession and marriage of Charles, were deferred till after the summer heats had subsided, and the alarming mortality somewhat abated.

CHAPTER II.

The Queen's French priests and attendants give offence to the King—The royal pair quarrel—Charles resolves to send home the French household—They take the oath of allegiance, and urge Henrietta to refuse being crowned—The King crowned without her—The Queen's French household turned out of Whitehall—Forced to depart the country—The French Ambassador effects a reconciliation between the King, Queen, and Buckingham—Henrietta consults a fortune-teller—Birth and death of Prince Charles James—Death of Buckingham—Birth of Charles the Second; and of the Princess Mary—The Queen's Catholic Chapels—Birth of James, Duke of York—Prynne and his Histriomastrix.

HE Queen had brought with her a large retinue of foreign attendants, catholic priests, and servants; these, before a month had elapsed, deeply offended the King, who, but for his agreement not to remove them without the consent of the Queen, would have packed them back to France without ceremony. The people, also, heartily hated them, on account of their religion; whilst they, it appears, equally detested the King and the people. According to the marriage articles, the Queen and her attendants were to be permitted the free exercise of their religion, and her Majesty was to have her chapel for that purpose. This was but partially granted, and at Whitehall the mass was scarcely tolerated. We give the particulars in the words of a contemporary intelligencer. "On Friday last the Queen was at her first mass in Whitehall, which was mumbled over at eleven o'clock, at which time she came out of her bedchamber, in her petticoat, with a veil upon her head, supported by the Count de Tilliers, her Lord Chamberlain, and followed by six women. Whilst they were at mass, the King gave order that no Englishman or woman should come near the place. These priests have been very importunate to have the chapel finished at St. James, but they find the King very slow in doing that. 'His answer,' one told me, was, 'that if the Queen's closet, where they now say mass, was not large enough, let them have it in the great chamber; and if the great chamber was not wide enough, they might use the garden; and if the garden would not suit their turn, then was the park the fittest place.' So, seeing themselves slighted, they grow weary of England, and wish themselves home again; besides, with all their stratagems, they cannot bring the King to be the least in love with their fopperies. They say there came some English papists to the Queen's mass on Sunday, whom she rebuked, and caused to be sent out." The same authority proceeds, "the friars so frequent the Queen's private chamber, that the King is much offended, and he so told them; 'having,' as he said, 'granted them more than sufficient liberty in public.' Mr. Mordant informs me, that 'the Queen, although little of stature, is of a pleasing countenance if she be pleased, but full of spirit and vigour, and seems of a more than ordinary resolution.' 'With one frown,' sayeth he, 'divers of us being at Whitehall to see her (being at dinner, and the room somewhat overheated with the fire and the company), she drove us all out of the chamber. I suppose none but a Queen could have cast such a scowl.'"

Unable to longer brook the overbearing influence of the French household over the mind of his fondly-beloved consort, Charles, burning with jealousy, resolved to send the whole retinue back again to France. To further this object, he dispatched the subjoined private communication to the Duke of Buckingham, who was then at Paris, as ambassador extraordinary:

"STEENIE,

"I writ to you by Ned Clark, that I thought I would have cause enough in a short time to put away the *Monsers* [her Majesty's French household], either on account of their attempting to steal away my wife, or of their making plots with my own subjects. For the first, I cannot say, certainly, whether it was intended, but I am sure it was hindered for the other, though I have good grounds to believe it, and am still hunting after it; yet, seeing daily the maliciousness of the *Monsers*, by making and fomenting discontentments in my wife, I could tarry no longer, after advertising of you that I mean to seek for no other grounds to cashier my *Monsers*, having, for this purpose, sent you this letter, that you may, if you think good, advertise the Queen-mother with my intentions; for this being an action that may have a show of harshness, I thought it was fit to take this way, that she to whom I have had many obligations may not take it unkindly, and likewise I think I have done you no wrong in my letter, though in some place of it I may seem to chide you. I pray you send me word with what speed you may, whither ye like this course or not; for, I shall put nothing of this in execution *while* [until] I hear from you; in the meantime I shall think of convenient means to do this business with the best mind, but I am resolved it must be done, and that shortly. So longing to see thee, I rest

"Your loving, faithful,

"Constant friend,

"CHARLES R.

"Hampton Court, the 20th of Nov., 1625."

With this, was sent to Buckingham another and a more sensible letter, meant to be shown to the Queen-mother, Mary of Medicis. This second letter Buckingham placed in the Queen-mother's hands, but withal, such was the force of circumstances, that Charles found it impossible to cashier the Queen's French retinue for upwards of six months afterwards.

The uncomplying bigotry and opposition of the French train continued. "The Queen's servants," says a news-letter, dated January twelve, 1626, "perceiving they would be discarded if they took not the 'Oath of Allegiance,' have now, I hear, all taken it. But they did so with great unwillingness, and a highly offensive display of importance and contrariety." Much, however, as Charles was incensed at this conduct, at the religious bigotry, and at the petty interference on every occasion, private and public, of his bride's household, he was further astonished and irritated to find that the Queen refused, and they encouraged her refusal, to attend his coronation. The second of February was chosen for the solemnization of the august ceremony; and, although Charles resorted to entreaties, persuasions, and threats, Henrietta could not, or would not, subdue her religious scruples. "I am a Catholic," said she, "and as the ceremony of crowning is Protestant, I abhor it, and will have nothing to do with it." A foolish piece of bigotry, which was never forgiven by the people, and which, in its consequences, proved highly injurious both to herself and to her husband.

King Charles was solemnly crowned and anointed at Westminster, and "the Queen," says a contemporary, "would neither be crowned, nor by any means be present in the church to see the solemnities and ceremonies. Though she was offered to have a place made fit for her, she would not go, but took a chamber at the palace gate, where she and her attendants might behold the procession going and returning. It was one of the most punctual coronations since the Conquest; the King took an oath, as his predecessors had taken it, to preserve the church the same as it was in the days of Edward the Confessor: as I found an entry into the church, I will mention what I saw. Just as I had taken my seat at the stage, on which stood the royal seat, his Majesty approached. He presented himself bare-headed to the people (all the doors being then opened for their entrance), the Archbishop on his right hand, and the Earl Marshal on his left; when the Bishop in a loud voice said to this purpose:—'My masters and friends, I am here come to present unto you your Sovereign, King Charles, to whom the crown of his ancestors and predecessors is now devolved by lineal right, and he himself has come hither to be settled on that throne, which God and his birth hath appointed for him, and, therefore, I desire you, by your general acclamation, to testify your consent and willingness thereunto.' Upon which, from some strange and unaccountable reason, every one remained silent, till my Lord of Arundel told them to shout; when, as if ashamed of their first oversight, some of them cried out, 'God save King Charles!' The other most remarkable incident at this coronation was, that the unction, to prevent its being seen, was performed behind a traverse, whence doubts were raised as to the validity of the coronation.

The refusal of the Queen to be crowned, caused the French ambassador, the Marquis de Blainville, to absent himself from the coronation, on the plea, that, under the circumstances, his presence would be viewed as an insult to the Queen, his master's sister. This irritated Charles, and cross words passed between him and his perverse spouse on the subject.

"There hath been some disagreement at court between their Majesties," says Mr. Mead, in a letter to Sir Martin Stuteville, dated February the twenty-fifth, "by reason of the French ambassador; but after three days' sullen silence, the King again spoke graciously to the Queen. Nevertheless, he forbad the ambassador the court, stopped all outward passage at the ports, and sent a messenger with letters to France." As weeks rolled on, the annoyances on both sides increased. The Queen and the French complained of the King and the English, whilst the King and the English equally censured the Queen and the French. At length, Charles resolved no longer to bear with the annoyance. "On Monday last," states a news-letter, dated July the fifth, 1626—"about three in the afternoon, the King, pressing into the *Queen's side* [her suite of chambers at Whitehall], and finding some Frenchmen, her servants, unreverently dancing and curvetting in her presence, took her by the hand, and led her into his apartments, locking the door after him, and shutting out all save the Queen. Presently, upon this, my Lord Conway called the French Bishop and others of that clergy into St. James's Park, where he told them the King's pleasure was, that all her Majesty's servants of that nation, men and women, young and old, should, without delay, depart the kingdom. The Bishop answered, that being an ambassador, he could not go unless commanded by the King, his master; but he was told, that the King, his master, had no power in England, and that if he were unwilling to go, he would be conveyed hence by force. Lord Conway, accompanied with Mr. Treasurer and Mr. Comptroller, then went to the Queen's apartments, and signified to all the other of the Queen's French servants that they must all depart thence to Somerset House, and remain there till they knew further of his Majesty's pleasure. The women howled and lamented as if they had been going to execution, but all in vain; for the yeomen of the guard, by Lord Conway's orders, thrust them, and all their country folk, out of the Queen's apartments, and locked the doors after them." Whilst this stormy scene was transacting, the Queen, who the determined Monarch detained in his own withdrawing rooms, flew in a violent rage, and vowing to bid farewell to her ill-used household, rushed to the window for that purpose. Charles seized both her hands, and implored her to quietly submit to what she could not prevent; but, although he exerted all his masculine strength, she succeeded in smashing several of the windows with her fists. "Howsoever," continues the news-letter, "I now hear her rage is appeased, and that the King and she went to Nonsuch, and have been very jocund together."

A few days afterwards, the King, leaving his consort at Nonsuch, went to Somerset House, "and in a set speech," remarks Mr. John Pory, in a letter, dated July, 1626, "told the French household that he hoped the good King, his brother of France, would not take amiss what he had done, for the French, he said (particular persons he would not tax), had occasioned many jars and discontents between the Queen and himself, such, indeed, as longer were insufferable. He prayed, them, therefore, to pardon him if he sought his own ease and safety, by dismissing them to their own country; and said, moreover, that he had given orders to his treasurer to reward every one of them for his year's service. So the next morning being Tuesday, there was distributed amongst them twenty-two thousand six hundred and seventy-two pounds in money and jewels. The King's magnanimity on this occasion, I think, proceeded from a desire to satisfy the rapacity of the Queen's clergy, who were the most superstitious, turbulent, and jesuited priests that could be found in France, very fit to make firebrands of sedition in a foreign state, so that his Majesty, whilst he retained them, did but nourish so many vipers in his bosom; nay, their insolence towards the Queen was not to be endured. No longer ago than on St. James's day last, they made her poor Majesty to walk on foot, some say barefooted, from her house at St. James's to the gallows at Tybern, thereby to honour the saint of the day by visiting that holy place, where so many martyrs, forsooth, had shed their blood in defence of the Catholic cause. Had they not also made her to dabble in the dirt on a foul morning, from Somerset House to St. James's, her Luciferian confessor riding along by her in his coach. Yea, they have made her to go barefooted to spin, to eat her meat out of wooden dishes, and to wait at table and serve her own servants, with many other ridiculous and absurd penances. And if these rogues dare thus, insultingly, laud it over the daughter, sister, and wife of such great

Kings, what slavery would they not make us, the people, to undergo? Besides all this, these French about her Majesty, are said to have corresponded with the Pope, the English papists, and the Spaniards, for the re-establishment of the Catholic religion. It was intended they should have immediately departed, but they are not gone yet. They have taken possession of all the Queen's apparel, linen, and jewels, which they found at Somerset House, and left her but one gown and two smocks to her back; and when intreated by the lords of the council to send her Majesty some apparel, they forwarded her only one satin gown, keeping all the residue to themselves. They brought her deeply in debt for purchases which they had made solely on their own account; and her Master of the Horse, the Count of Seipieres, laid claim to all the horses and furniture under his charge, but his claim was refused." Their struggles to delay their departure, at length so exasperated Charles, that he, in a rage, dispatched the subjoined order to the Duke of Buckingham.

"Steenie,

"I have received your letter by Dick Græme. This is my answer; I command you to send all the French away to-morrow out of the town, if you can by fair means, but (stick not long in disputing,) otherwise force them away; driving them away like so many wild beast, until you have shipped them, and so the devil go with them. Let me hear no answer, but of the performance of my command. So I rest,

"Your faithful, constant,

"Loving friend,

"Charles R.

"Oaking, the 7th of August, 1626."

Even this order, written as it was, too, entirely in the King's hand, was for several days disregarded by the detested French retinue. A contemporary, writing on the seventeenth of August, says: "Monday last, being the peremptory day for the dispatch of the French, the King's officers then attended them with coaches, carts, and barges, but they contumaciously refused to go, saying, 'they would wait till they had orders from their King;' and above all, the Bishop stood on his punctilios. This news being sent in post to the King on Tuesday morning, his Majesty dispatched to London the captain of the guard, attended with a competent number of his yeomen, together with heralds, messengers, and trumpeters. The heralds and trumpeters proclaimed the King's pleasure at the gate of Somerset House, and the yeomen proceeded to put in execution their order, which was, neither more nor less than to turn [the French out head and shoulders, and shut the gate after them; an extremity which, fortunately for all concerned, was not resorted to, as the French consented to depart the next tide. At that time my Lord Conway, Mr. Treasurer, and Mr. Comptroller, went to see them perform their promise, and brought the Bishop out of the gate to the boot of his coach, where, he making stand, requested and obtained permission to stay till the midnight tide, that he might depart private and cool. So, on Tuesday night, they lay at Gravesend, on Wednesday night at Rochester, on Thursday at Canterbury, and on Friday at Dover; from whence, God send them a fair wind. At their first setting out from London, they were very sullen and dogged, and the jeers and taunts of the riotous mob which had collected to see them driven forth, exasperated them almost to madness; but their kind entertainment by the way, quite dispelled their angry feelings by the time they arrived at Dover." The same intelligencer, in a letter, dated August the seventeenth, says, "The Queen's household is now settled, and consists chiefly of the old servants of Queen Anne of Denmark, who had been pensioned off; Lord Rutland refuses to be her Lord Chamberlain, but Sir Thomas Goring is her Vice-Chamberlain, Lord Percy, Master of her Horse, Lord Holland her steward, Lord Carew her receiver, Sir Thomas Savage her Chancellor, and so forth. Of her late French retinue, the following were permitted to remain in her service. Her nurse, her dresser, the Duchess of Tremouile, three of the most inoffensive of the chaplains, twelve musicians, a cook, a baker, a pantler, and a tailor."

This forcible dismissal of the Queen's French household was taken as a personal insult by her brother, Louis the Thirteenth. He refused to admit to his presence Secretary Carlton, who had been sent to Paris by Charles, to account for his conduct, and even threatened England with war, a calamity which was only averted for a while by the discretion and wise policy of the Duke de Bassompierre, who was sent to England to play the part of a peace-maker between the Queen and her husband. He found the royal pair greatly exasperated against each other. Henrietta was but sixteen, and quite too young and girlish to comprehend the causes that induced Charles to prevent her from exercising her private worship so publicly as she desired. She knew that the indulgence had been stipulated for in the marriage contract, and believing in the infallibility of royalty, attributed the deprivation not to the powerful Protestant voice of the people, but to the conjugal tyranny of her really indulgent lord, and to the interested suggestions of Buckingham, with whom she had quarrelled violently. To effect a reconciliation, Bassompierre held several private and separate interviews with the King, the Queen, and with Buckingham. Charles accused the French domestics with discovering all that passed between himself and his consort, and plotting to embroil them, and charged the clergy with forcing the Queen to do penances beneath the dignity of her Majesty, and to the injury of her health and the discredit of her reputation in England. The Queen passed over in silence all of these charges but one. It had been asserted that her clergy had compelled her, by way of penance, to make a pilgrimage to the gallows at Tyburn, to pray on the spot where the gunpowder conspirators had been executed; a charge she earnestly denied, and which Bassompierre, when pleading her cause before the Privy Council, thus accounted for. "The truth is," said he, "on the evening of one sultry day, the Queen, with her attendants, had taken the same walk through St. James's and Hyde Parks, which she had frequently taken with the King. But that she went in procession, approached the gallows nearer than fifty paces, or said prayers there, is what her enemies know to be base fictions of their own invention." After much exertion, repeated interviews, and telling the petulant Queen to her face that she behaved most unwife-like, and blamed the King unjustly, Bassompierre effected something like a reconciliation between the royal couple, and expressed himself satisfied. But on his return to France he was ungraciously received by the Monarch, and loudly censured by the Queen-mother and the courtiers. He had acted too honest, too candid a part to please them. They insisted that, by not enforcing the full performance of the articles of the marriage, he had compromised the dignity of his sovereign, and a war between England and France followed.

In 1627, Henrietta experienced hopes of maternity, and a belief in fortune-telling induced her to apply to the aristocratic prophetess, Lady Eleanor, the daughter of the Earl of Castlehaven and wife of Sir John Davys, the King's Attorney-General, who, in reply to her questions, told her that she would shortly have a son, who would be born, christened, and buried all in one day; that she would be happy for sixteen years, and that Buckingham, who had sailed to relieve Rochelle, would soon and safely return, but with little honour either to himself or to his country. The child was born rather before his time, in May, 1628. It entered the world in a languid state, proved a boy, was christened with protestant rites, Charles James, died on the day of its birth, und was buried before midnight. Charles laid the premature birth, and its consequences, to the door of Lady Eleanor, and forbad the Queen to again consult her. But the sybil so prided herself on the fulfilment of her predicated fate of the King's first-born, that she raised quite a commotion by prophesying on political, theologic, and other subjects, which did not concern her. The King, annoyed at her impertinece, sent Mr.

Kirk to request her husband to command her to bridle her tongue. This Mr. Kirk proved a faithless servant; for, after delivering the King's message, he, to please Henrietta, obtained from the Lady Eleanor a prediction that the Queen's next born would be a Prince, and a fine healthy child; and, afterwards, he provoked the King by publishing the prophecy, which was generally believed, and hailed with rejoicings and bonfires. Buckingham, the man to whose influence the Queen attributed most of the differences between herself and her husband, was assassinated on the twenty-third of August, 1628; and, after his murder, the conjugal happiness of the royal couple greatly increased. As predicted, the Queen's next born proved a fine healthy Prince, but he was so ugly, that the Queen was ashamed of him. He first saw the light at St. James's Palace, on the morning of the twenty-ninth of May, 1630. The same morning the King went in state to St. Paul's, and returned thanks to God for the happy event. At the noon-day hour a bright star appeared in the heavens, and the astonished populace viewed the phenomenon as a presage that—

"Now, there is born a valiant prince in the west,
That shall eclipse the kingdoms of the east."

The Prince was baptized Charles, with the ceremony prescribed in the Book of Common Prayer of the Church of England, on the last Sunday in June, in the chapel at St. James's, but not the Queen's Catholic Chapel; and he afterwards ascended the throne of England, by the title of Charles the Second. The sponsors were the zealous papists, Louis the Thirteenth and Mary of Medicis, and the Protestant Palgrave. Neither of them professed the tenets of the Church of England; and, whether for this or for any other reason, the Duke of Lenox, the Marquis of Hamilton, and the Duchess of Richmond stood proxies for them. These noble personages were attired in white satin, with rich crimson trimmings, and their stockings were of crimson silk. The profuse Duchess presented to the Prince a jewel worth seven thousand pounds; to Mr. Wyndham, to whose care he was confided, a gold chain, worth two hundred pounds; to his wet nurse, a native of Wales, three massive silver dishes, and a bowl and a ewer of solid silver; and to the midwife, the dry nurse, the rocker, and others, various pieces of plate.

On the fourth of November, 1631, Henrietta brought into the world her eldest daughter at St. James's palace; the baby was solemnly baptized Mary, and committed to the charge of Katherine, Lady Stanhope, who through life served her with fidelity, and had great influence over her.

In September, 1632, was commenced the building of a Roman Catholic Chapel, for her Majesty's use, at Whitehall; and the Queen, by laying the foundation stone with her own hands, greatly increased her unpopularity. Shortly afterwards, another Roman Catholic Chapel, for her use, was commenced at St. James's; they were both finished in about three years, when the Popish service was celebrated in them, with a splendour and publicity that greatly annoyed the Protestant public, and seriously injured the King's credit with his subjects. At Christmas, 1632, the Queen was confined to her chamber, at Whitehall, by indisposition; but about New-year's day she recovered, and to dispel the gloom occasioned at Court by her illness, invited the King, his nobles, and their ladies, to a twelfth-night entertainment at Somerset House, where his Majesty's players entertained the august company, by acting Fletcher's pleasing dramatic poem of the "Faithful Shepherdess."

When Charles could no longer delay his Scottish coronation, he invited the Queen to accompany him and share his inauguration. She, however, declared the ceremony would shock her religious feelings, and permitted him to depart to the North without her. By this northern progress and coronation the King added nothing to his popularity, and the Queen being in a situation which promised an increase of family, caused him to hurry homewards with marked precipitancy. Shortly after his return,

Henrietta presented him with their second son at St. James's Palace, on the thirteenth, or, according to other authorities, the fourteenth of October, 1633. The Prince was christened James, after his grandfather, James the First, by the new Archbishop, Laud, and then, according to custom, created Duke of York. He was placed under the charge of Lady Dorset, received a naval education, became one of England's most renowned admirals, and, on the sixth of February, 1685, succeeded to the throne by the title of James the Second. To commemorate the birth of Prince James, the gentlemen of Lincoln's Inn and of the Temple, entertained the Queen at their own cost, with a splendid masque and ballet. These magnificent entertainments lasted three days, cost twenty-two thousand pounds, and, although denounced by the Puritans as wasteful and extravagant, greatly benefitted the people, by distributing amongst them some of the hoarded wealth of these rich societies, to say nothing of the pleasure afforded by the spectacle.

In the first years of her marriage, the Queen had made such slow progress in the English tongue, that, to render the task at once easy and agreeable, Mr. Wingate, Barrister of Gray's Inn, who was appointed her tutor in 1632, caused Walter Montague's masque of the "Queen's Pastoral," to be performed by the Queen and her ladies at Whitehall. It was for the part the Queen enacted in this pastoral, which was a long, heavy piece, and took eight hours in the performance, that William Prynne inveighed so bitterly against her in his "Histromastrix." Charles, to be revenged on Prynne, caused him to be sentenced by the Star Chamber, to stand in the pillory, and lose his ears. This barbarous punishment, although the Queen interceded in favour of the victim, was inflicted in all its rigour.

CHAPTER III.

The Queen's short-lived felicity—Princess Elizabeth born—Shrovetide masques—Prince Charles and physic—Mary of Medicis comes to England—Execution of Strafford—Princess Elizabeth betrothed to the Prince of Orange—The Queen's plot to gain over the army detected—Mary of Medicis forced to leave England—Whilst Charles is in Scotland, the Parliament endeavours to deprive the Queen of her children—Insurrection of Irish Catholics—The King returns from Scotland—He and the Queen entertained by the London citizens—Arrest of the factious members of the Commons thwarted through the Queen's indiscretion—She goes abroad to raise arms for the King—Returns with a fleet of military stores—Her conduct in the north—Meets the King at Edge Hill—Her residence at Oxford—Adversity—Illness—Birth of Princess Henrietta Maria—Flight to France—Residence at the French court—Correspondence with her husband—Utter defeat of the Royalists at Naseby—The King refuses to forsake the Church of England.

AT this period, when the nation reposed in a deceptive calm, which shortly afterwards was succeeded by a rebellion so fierce and stormy, that the throne was overturned, and monarchy for awhile driven away from the kingdom, Henrietta vainly believed herself one of the most blessed and happiest of queens. Her husband sincerely loved her; in beauty she was peerless; all conjugal strife between herself and the King had ceased, and her children were healthy, thriving, and promising. Masques, ballets, and dramatic poems were written for her diversion and her improvement in the English language by Ben Jonson, and by Beaumont and Fletcher, and their effects were heightened by scenery, devised by the great architect, Inigo Jones. Her personal graces were pourtrayed by the matchless pencil of Vandyke, and, if possible, to render her immortal, the poet Waller hymned her praises in sweet and polished stanzas; but, alas for humanity, this state of felicity was too exalted to continue; the people, goaded by an unwise stretch of the royal prerogative, and a wild fanatic republican impulse, rushed to arms in defence of their liberty and rights. Bloodshed, treachery, anarchy, ensued, and a strong faction obtained the helm of government, beheaded the King, and convinced Henrietta that she was indeed the partaker of a destiny truly sad and calamitous.

On the twentieth of January, 1635, the Queen gave birth to the Princess Elizabeth at St. James's Palace. The succeeding Shrovetide was kept at the court and in London with maskings and disguises, in which Henrietta took a conspicuous part. She was present at the masked ball given by Lady Hatton at Ely Place, Holborn; and on Shrove Tuesday, she, and three of her ladies, visited the Temple masquerade, disguised as citizens' wives. In December, 1636, the Princess Anne was born. She was a delicate babe, and only lingered till December, 1640, when she expired. Her last words were, "Lighten mine eyes, O Lord, that I sleep not the sleep of death," a short prayer that she had been taught to repeat night and morning. It has been asserted, that her Majesty brought up her children in the Catholic faith; but as their governors and tutors were staunch supporters of the Church of England, this statement can be at least but partially true. The first letter extant that Henrietta wrote to Prince Charles, was an exhortation that he would take his physic. This motherly epistle, of which the subjoined is a copy, was written, it is supposed, in 1638, when the Prince was eight years old.

"CHARLES,

"I am sore that I must begin my first letter with chiding you, because I hear that you will not take *phisike.* I hope it was *onlie* for this day, and that to-morrow you will do it, for *yf* you will not, I must come to you and make you take it, for it is for your health. I have given orders to my Lord Newcastle to send *mi* word to-night, whether you will or not, therefore I hope you will not give *mi* the paines to go, and so I rest,

"Your affectionate mother,

"HENRIETTE MARIE, R.

"To my dear son, the Prince."

The Earl of Newcastle, who, in 1634, had been appointed Governor to the Prince, made remonstrances in compliance with the Queen's direction, and received in answer the subjoined terse, witty note. The original, which still exists, is entirely in the Prince's hand, in characters about the size of round text, and in lines ruled with a pencil above and below.

"MY LORD,

"I would not have you take too much phisick, for it doth *allwaies* make me worse, and I think it will do the like with you. I ride every day, and am ready to follow any other directions from you. Make haste to return to him that loves you.

"CHARLES, P.

"To my Lord of Newcastle."

When Mary of Medicis was banished from the court of France by the persecution of Cardinal Richelieu, Charles, whose subjects were about to burst out into open and overpowering rebellion, had the indiscretion to incur that iron-willed minister's hate, by welcoming her to England with all conceivable pomp and magnificence. The King met her at Harwich, and conducted her with royal dignity to London, where, attended by Charles and his court, she passed through the city on the sixteenth of November, 1639. The meeting of Henrietta and her mother on this occasion, affected to tears all who were present. When the carriage in which Mary of Medicis was seated arrived at St. James's, the Queen, although then near her time, and in utter disregard of all etiquette, rushed down stairs, hurried to the carriage door, and the instant her mother alighted, fell on her knees before her to receive her blessing, and the royal children who were at St. James's at the time followed out after their mother, and knelt around her. Henrietta took especial care that her mother was honoured at court with all the distinction and homage due to her exalted birth. To slight the mother was to offend the daughter; and yet, in return for this disinterested and affectionate kindness, Mary of Medicis, and her numerous train, embarrassed the King by their extravagance and rapacity, and then committed the folly of petitioning parliament for increased allowances. As the troubles of state, which we have no space to detail, thickened around Charles, Henrietta injured the cause she so earnestly desired to serve, that of her husband, by secretly intriguing with the parliamentary faction. Night after night she met the leaders of this party at the foot of the back stairs at St. James's, and although she promised them most extravagant rewards, she only succeeded in winning over Lord Digby; in fact, they visited her solely to elicit from her indiscreet tongue, intelligence valuable to them, but dreadfully injurious to the royalists. When the Parliament was about to wreak its vengeance on her faithful friend, Strafford, she exerted all her energies to save him, but her diplomacy rather injured than benefited his cause. He had endeavoured to crush the liberties of the people, and for his temerity he suffered on the scaffold. On the second of May, 1641, just ten days previous to the execution of Strafford, the Princess Royal, who was ten years of age, was betrothed to the Protestant Prince of Orange, a royal youth, in his eleventh year. The day following, the plot devised by the Queen to gain over the army, which was then alike at variance with the Crown and with the Parliament, having been disclosed by the treachery of her Majesty's Chamberlain, Sir George Goring, a mob of about six thousand of the citizens broke into Westminster Abbey, surrounded the Parliament, and whilst doing all the mischief usually done by revolutionary rioters, cried out for justice upon Strafford, and other incendaries, and to be secured from plots against the Parliament, and for the Earl's rescue. These riots alarmed the Queen-mother, Mary of Medicis, and not without reason. "When she came to England," says Whitelocke, "the people were generally discontent at her coming, and at her followers, which some observed to be the sword and pestilence, and that her restless spirit embroiled all where she came." The fatal influence which the Queen began to acquire was generally known, and had been remarkably evinced in the active part she had taken in the late plot. But the Queen-mother was again suspected of intriguing in affairs of state, and encouraging her daughter to do the same, and the populace of England began to treat her with the same insult which she had experienced elsewhere. The King, therefore, sent a complaining message on the subject to the Commons, who, whilst expressing their willingness to afford her all lawful protection, advised that she should seek safety by leaving the kingdom. She accordingly went to Holland, where she died. About the time of her departure, Henrietta was separated from the King, who, leaving her in England, proceeded to Scotland, on the ninth of August, 1641, where he made important concessions to the Scottish Covenanters. In his absence the Queen was dreadfully harassed. The first annoyance was occasioned by her happening to have all her children, except the Prince of Wales, to reside with her at Oatlands for a short while. The Parliament declared that she meant to make Roman Catholics of them, and under that pretence, examined and imprisoned her confessor, Father Philipps. This incident, Sir Edward Nicholas, the Royal Secretary, imparted by letter to the King, assuring his Majesty, that if he did not speedily dismiss the Queen's Catholic priests, the malignant jealousy of the Roundhead orators in the House of Commons would force him so to do. The King, however, rejected this advice, consulted the Queen on the subject, and as her conscience or obstinacy was unyielding, she retained her priests and confessors till the mob in the ensuing year destroyed every vestige of the Catholic chapel at Somerset House. That the Queen tampered with the religion of her children is probable; indeed, Father Cyprian, one of her Capucins at Somerset House, distinctly states, that she secretly gave a crucifix and a rosary to her eldest daughter Mary, and taught her the use of them—conduct which was probably conveyed by the first lady of the bedchamber, and her false, base friend, Lady Carlisle, to Lord Kimbolton, and Mr. Pym, two leaders of the Roundheads, with both of whom she was on terms of intimacy, and whom she, to the misfortune of the King and Queen, betrayed every incident that occurred in the royal household. At this juncture, the Parliament sent the Queen word, that she must surrender her children, lest she should make Papists of them. To obviate this necessity, she withdrew to Hampton Court, and contented herself with visiting her little ones. But this only increased the boldness of the patriots; reports were spread that she meant to flee the kingdom, and carry her children with her, and the Parliament issued orders for the military at Oatlands to watch and guard the royal palace there. Henrietta resolved to battle bravely in defence of her offspring; she believed the real purpose of her enemies was to abduct them from her, and to frustrate that purpose, she requested Lord Digby to surround with her friends all the mansions where she and her children were abiding, obtained the use of a number of fine horses, from one on whose loyalty she could rely, and regained the co-operations of Goring, and prevailed upon him to hold himself in readiness at Portsmouth, so that if hard pressed, she, as a last resource, could do what the patriots declared she had long decided upon, embark with her offspring for the continent. Her courage, energy, and promptitude astonished her enemies, and defeated their projects. Now that she was prepared for the attack, neither she nor her children were molested. The Parliament resorted to ingenious subterfuges for calling out the military of Oatlands, without royal authority, and every member of the Lower House took the pains to repeatedly declare that he had taken no part in it.

In the autumn of this year the Irish Catholics rose in insurrection, and attempted in one day to massacre all the Protestants in Ireland. A similarity of religion induced the Roundheads to accuse the Queen of having encouraged the massacre; but the accusation, like many others brought against Henrietta at this troublous period, was without foundation; indeed, the uprising was purely a Celtic one, and to break the fetters that bound Ireland to England, was the sole object of the rebels.

When the King commenced his homeward journey from Scotland, he dispatched to the Queen information of his intentions, and her Majesty, through Sir Edmund Nicholas, in the subjoined epistle, ordered the Earl of Essex, then Lord Chamberlain, and with whom she was not on the best of terms, to make the necessary preparations for the reception of his royal master.

"Master Nicholas,

"I desired you not to acquaint my Lord of Essex, of what the King commanded you, touching his coming. Now you may do it, and tell him that the King will be at Theobalds on Wednesday, and shall stop there; and upon Thursday he will dine with the Lord Mayor, and be at Whitehall, only for one night; and upon Friday, will go to Hampton Court, where he means to stay this winter. The King commanded me to tell this to my Lord of Essex, but you may do it, for their Lordships are too great princes now to receive any directions from me. Being all that I have to say, I shall rest your assured friend,

"Henriette Marie, R.

"For Master Nicholas.

"November 24th, 1641."

Charles returned on the twenty-fifth of November. On his entry to London, he was met by the Lord Mayor, the Sheriffs, and other opulent citizens. The Queen and all her children accompanied him; they dined in public, in the Guildhall, and as they retired to

Whitehall, were greeted with the loud and loyal congratulations of the numerous spectators. This burst of extreme loyalty highly gratified their Majesties, and taught Charles to meet his opponents in Parliament with more firmness; but the ill-starred monarch forgot that at this period the people were as much the slaves of the dominant faction as he himself. However, as the Commons had impeached the bishops at the close of December, and hinted at an impeachment of the Queen, Charles resolved to arrest five of the most factious of its members. This bold, but unfortunate design, he imparted to no one but the Queen. When he set out on the morning of the fatal fourth of January, 1642, he assured his consort if an hour elapsed without her hearing ill news from him, she would see him return the master of his kingdom. She anxiously waited till that tedious hour had flown, when as no news arrived, she believed the King victorious, and turning to the treacherous Lady Carlisle, exclaimed exultingly:—"Thank God, the greatest troubles are passed, for I have reason to believe that, by this time, Pym and his confederates are arrested, and the King is again master of his kingdom." Lady Carlisle, however, thought otherwise, for the moment she learnt the King's design from the too-confiding Queen, she betrayed it through one of her agents to Pym, and as she expected, so it happened. Before the King could reach the house, the marked members had fled, their party had rallied, and Charles was heard in silence, and retired amidst low but distinct murmurs of "privilege, privilege." When the Queen found the mischief her heedless prattling had done, she bitterly upbraided herself, owned her fault, and throwing herself into the arms of her tender husband, implored his forgiveness. Greatly to the credit of Charles, although the indiscretion had ruined him, he neither upbraided her nor treated her with less kindness than previously. A few days after this occurrence, the whole populace of London rose in insurrection, in defence, it was said, of the privilege of the House of Commons; and Charles, aware of the power, and distrusting the object of the patriots, fled, with the Queen and their family, to Hampton Court, on the evening of the tenth of January.

In this extremity the Queen resolved to proceed to Holland, under pretence of conducting her daughter Mary to her husband, the Prince of Orange; but, in reality, to solicit the aid of foreign powers, and to raise money on her jewels, and purchase arms and ammunition for her consort. As the Parliament had ordered the nobility to arm and prevent the King from going abroad, she, that the Commons might not interfere with her departure, prevailed upon Charles to give the royal assent to the act, excluding the Bishops from sitting as peers in the House of Lords. She was conducted by the King to Dover, where she embarked with her daughter, the Princess Mary, on the twenty-third of February. The parting was painful; "Perhaps," ejaculated the King, as he pressed his consort in his arms, "we may never meet again." "As the Lord wills it, so must it be," rejoined the weeping Queen. "But," interrupted the Princess, alarmed at the sorrow of her parents, and looking earnestly in the face of the unfortunate monarch, "but your Grace will come and see me when that naughty, naughty, Pym, has gone to prison; that you will, won't you?" The King took her in his arms, blessed her, smothered her in kisses, and then she and her mother embarked; whilst Charles, lingering on the shore, watched the vessel that bore them away till it was quite out of sight. On returning, he took up his residence at Theobalds; but, as the Parliament daily grew stronger and bolder, and at length, to get him in their power, invited him to fix his residence in London, he hastened with his sons to Newmarket, and thence to York, where, no longer controlled by the two Houses, he made preparations to defend his prerogatives by force of arms. The surrounding inhabitants welcomed him with acclamations and loyal addresses, and most of the leading nobles and gentry volunteered to serve in his cause. At Hull, however, he met with a signal defeat; Sir John Hotham, the Governor, when informed of his approach, ordered the drawbridge to be raised, the gates closed, and the walls manned, and on his arrival, peremptorily refused him admittance, either to the town or to the fortress.

The Queen's efforts in Holland were crowned with success. She won the good-will of the proverbially uncouth burgomasters, and by loans and what she borrowed on her jewels, raised about two million pounds sterling. On the second of February, 1643, she sailed from Scheveling, with a fleet of eleven vessels, commanded by Von Tromp, and freighted with military stores and ammunition; but she had scarcely put to sea, when a violent storm arose, and after a fortnight's tossing and tumbling on the troubled deep, the whole squadron, saving ten ships, which were lost, was driven back to the port from whence they set out. Nothing daunted, Henrietta, a few days afterwards, again set sail; the voyage was prosperous, and on the twentieth of February, she reached in safety Burlington Bay, where she landed on the twenty-second, greatly to the rage of Batten, the Parliamentary Admiral, who having cruised in the neighbourhood and failed to intercept her, vented his spleen, by, on the second night, the twenty-fourth of February, anchoring in the road, and at five in the morning, opening a sharp cannonade upon the house in which her Majesty slept. The danger so terrified the Queen, that she quitted her bed, and, "barefoot and barelegged," sought shelter in a neighbouring ditch, behind a hill, where she remained till the ebbing of the tide, when the firing ceased, and Batten sheered off.

Henrietta waited in the neighbourhood of Burlington till her stores and cannon were placed in order, and other preparations were made for marching. During this period she executed much business. Her affability, uprightness, and firmly-rooted conviction of success, animated all around her, and won over the people of Yorkshire to the royal cause. She distributed arms amongst those who volunteered in her service; and the following circumstance, mentioned by Bossuet, greatly increased her popularity. Her soldiers took prisoner one of the captains of the Parliamentary vessels, tried him, found him guilty of directing the cannon which bombarded her house at Burlington, and condemned him to be hanged—she went and stopped the procession which conducted him to execution—whether intentionally or if by accident is not stated—and after declaring that she had forgiven him, and as he had not killed her, he should not be put to death on her account; ordered him to be released on the spot, which so affected him, that he joined her standard, and prevailed upon several of his shipmates to follow his example. From Burlington the Queen marched across the wolds of Malton to York, with two hundred and fifty waggons loaded with stores and ammunition, escorted by two thousand cavaliers. She wrote to the King from York, on the twentieth of March, 1643, stating, "Sir Hugh Cholmondely [Governor of Scarborough] is come in with a troop of horse to kiss my hand, the rest of his people he has left at Scarborough, with a Parliament ship laden with arms. So this ship is ours as well as Scarborough." About this time negotiations were pending for a treaty of peace between the King and the Parliament. The Queen opposed the treaty; her reason for so doing she thus states,—"I hear from London that the Parliament will have no cessation of arms, and that in their treaty, they demand the surrender of forts, ships, and ammunition, and the disbanding of your [the King's] army. Certainly I heartily wish a peace, but as a first step to that peace, I would desire the disbanding of the perpetual Parliament;* a measure which those who are against you, as well as for you, earnestly desire, and which you must demand at first, or it will not be granted. Obtain this, and the rest will easily fol-

* The Long Parliament. This Parliament had, in fact, invested itself with paramount authority; since, on the tenth of May, 1641, it passed an act which prohibited the dissolution, prorogation, or adjournment of the present parliament, without the previous consent of the two houses.

low. Remember Hull and all Yorkshire is ours, which is a great advantage; and for myself, if you make peace and disband your army, before this perpetual Parliament is dissolved, I shall certainly go to France, for I have no desire to be grasped within the power of those who would use me ill, perhaps cruelly so." On the third of April she wrote to the King, "our army marches to-morrow, to put an end to Fairfax's excellency;" a measure highly needful, but not so easily accomplished as she had supposed. The King and Prince Rupert were bravely battling in the neighbourhood of Oxford, and in the midland counties; between them and Henrietta, Fairfax and Essex, at the head of the patriot army, had planted themselves; nor were they beaten out of the field till after some months had elapsed, and the Royalists had obtained several minor victories. The success of the Royalists enabled Henrietta to send a plentiful convoy to her husband in May, and shortly afterwards, she and her army advanced to Newark, whence, flushed with the late successes, she, on the twenty-seventh of June, wrote to the King, "I shall go hence on Friday; on Saturday I shall sleep at Werton, and from thence go to Ashley, where we will resolve what way to take . . . . As soon as we have resolved I will send you word . . . . For the safety of Nottinghamshire and Lincolnshire I leave two thousand foot (means to arm five hundred more), and twenty companies of horse under Charles Cavendish . . . The enemy have left in Nottingham (in garrison) one thousand. I carry with me three thousand foot, thirty companies of horse and dragoons, six pieces of cannon, and two mortars. Harry Jermyn commands the forces which go with me, as Colonel of my guard; Sir Alexander Lesley, the foot under him; Sir John Gerard, the horse; Robin Legge, the artillery, and I am *she-majesty generallissima* over all, and extremely diligent am I, too, with one hundred and fifty waggons of baggage to govern in case of battle." But, brave as her "she-majesty generallissima" might be, she felt no disposition to do battle with Essex, for in the same epistle she says, "Have a care that no troop of Essex's army incommode us;" a needless caution, for, at the time, the King and his loyal Cavaliers, with God save Queen Mary—the name by which Henrietta Maria was then designated in England—for their war-cry, were doing their best to keep the Earl in check, and so successful were their efforts, that the Queen and her army marched the whole distance from Yorkshire to Oxford without opposition. To their infinite joy, Charles and Henrietta met in the vale of Keynton, close to Edge Hill, on the thirteenth of July, and their previous career of triumph they and their partizans erroneously pronounced to be a sure omen of a speedy victory and peace. According to Clarendon, the King, at this period, could and would have made honourable and advantageous terms with the patriots, had not Henrietta, flushed with her recent successes, prevented him. She declared that the only effectual way of terminating the war was by conquest; a mistake, to use a mild expression, for which she ever afterwards greatly blamed herself. It, however, appears to us, that Charles, in this case, was the most culpable person; he should have calmly weighed the matter, and followed the dictates of his own judgment, instead of submitting to the will of his too sanguine consort; and, moreover, he must have been blind indeed, not to have perceived at a glance, that how anxious soever he might be to crush the unjust power—the unyielding opposition—of his bitterest opponents, some of whom, it must be admitted, were eager only in the pursuit of gold, place, power; whilst others, actuated by a wild revolutionary fanaticism, known at the time as levellers, were seeking to overthrow the King and the church, and establish the absurd social doctrine of equality; that to subdue the discontents of the people by force of arms, was but to supersede a lesser evil by a greater one, for neither the English nor the Scotch would tamely bow to the yoke of an absolute despotism.

The Queen remained at Oxford whilst a severe reverse came over the fortunes of the Royalists. When the powerful parliamentary forces approached that city in hostile array, Charles escorted "his wife," as he emphatically called his beloved Henrietta, to Abingdon, for safety. They parted in tears on the third of April, 1644, and never again met on earth. The prospect before the Queen was gloomy and forbidding; and, to add to her bodily sufferings, she was far advanced in pregnancy, and suffering from the torments of a rheumatic fever. To cure this malady she went to Bath; but in a brief time, circumstances forced her, ill as she was, to seek refuge at Bedford House, in the loyal city of Exeter. Here, in poverty, and in daily expectation that the city would be besieged, she wrote to the King's physician, Dr. Mayerne, earnestly requesting his professional aid; and about the same time, Charles wrote, "Mayerne, For the love of me, go to my wife." The faithful physician, although he deemed her Majesty's religion the chief cause of the troubles in England, hastened to her presence; and about a fortnight afterwards she brought a healthy daughter into the world, at Bedford House, Exeter, on the sixteenth of June. This event had taken place but a few days, when Essex, at the head of hostile forces, advanced to besiege the city; Henrietta, in alarm, sent to him for a passport to go to Bath or Bristol for the recovery of her health; but he insultingly answered, he intended himself to conduct her to London, where she had been impeached of high treason, for levelling war upon England. Delicate as she yet was from the effects of her confinement, she summoned all her energy and resolution, and in the dead of that same night rose from her sick bed, disguised herself, and with her confessor, and a lady and a gentleman, escaped to a hut, three miles out of Exeter, where she lay without food, under a heap of rubbish, for two days, whilst the revolutionary soldiers vainly searched around for her; fifty thousand crowns having been offered by the Parliament for her head. This peril passed, she and her three companions in adversity travelled to a poor cottage, in a wood, between Exeter and Plymouth, where she met her other attendants, who had escaped by stratagem out of Exeter; the whole party then proceeded to Pendennis castle, and the next day embarked for France. Meanwhile, Charles, aware of the danger of his "beloved wife," courageously fought his way to Exeter. He entered that city only a few days after Henrietta had sailed, took the little Princess, which the ill-starred Queen had, on her flight, left to the care of Lady Mortimer, and fondly kissing her, blessed her, and had her baptized Henrietta-Maria.

The Queen encountered many perils before she reached France. A parliamentary cruiser, commanded by Captain Batte, chased the vessel in which she embarked, fired at it, and disabled it, when Henrietta hastened on deck, took the command into her own hands, and with the false courage of an heroine of ancient Rome, charged the captain not to strike, but in the event of it being impossible to hold out any longer, to fire the powder magazine and blow them all up in the face of the foe. However, at the moment when all on board, save the Queen, gave themselves over for lost, six vessels hastened to their protection, out of the harbour of Dieppe, and forced the foe to make a hasty retreat. They then made for Dieppe, and were about entering the haven, when a storm arose and drove them to Chastel, near Brest, in Brittany, where having with difficulty effected a landing, they traversed the rocky coast on foot, till they discovered a rude village, when the fatigued Queen entered a poor fisherman's cabin, and thankfully reposed on a bed of straw. The poor Bretons took her and the people for pirates, but when she made known to them who she really was, the neighbouring gentry thronged to her, offered her their hearty congratulations, and, what was then infinitely more valuable to her, all the assistance in their power, and through their kindness she proceeded to the springs of Bourbon, in search of health and repose. The air and waters of her native land proved only slightly efficacious; indeed, severe mental and bodily trials had destroyed the vigour of her constitution; she was wasted to a skeleton, her beauty was for ever gone, and she bewailed her husband's misfortunes and the bereavement of her children with such severe and heart-piercing lamentations and tears, that a return of the buoyancy and vigour of youth was quite impossible. Her sister-in-law, Anne of Austria, liberally supplied her with money for her expenditure; and like a true wife, the affectionate Henrietta exercised a liberal parsimony, and sent every penny she could obtain or save to her distressed husband. Some authors affirm that Lord Jermyn, who retained his post in the Queen's household through all the reverse of her fortune, maintained her when in exile. "This," says Madam de Motteville, "is an error, for she had a large income settled upon her by her generous relations, which she regularly received till the civil war of the Fronde reduced those relatives to the same distressed condition with herself."

When Henrietta was sufficiently recovered to leave the baths of Bourbon, she was formally invited to court, and conducted thither in state by the Duke of Orleans and Mademoiselle de Montpensier, in August, 1644. The Queen-mother and her son welcomed her to the Louvre in person, and appointed St. Germains for her country seat. To this ancient château she retired in the autumn; and she was honoured with all the respect and deference due to a Princess of France. In gratitude to Heaven for her preservation from shipwreck, she, in September, presented to the chapel of our lady at Liesse one thousand five hundred livres, for a low mass to be said for her on every Saturday in perpetuity. She now made it at once her business and her pleasure to correspond with the King, and form around her a little court of his exiled partizans. Amongst these, were the literary stars, Denham, Cowley, and Waller. The latter was appointed to translate the letters which the royal pair addressed to each other in cypher; and so numerous and lengthy were these affectionate epistles, that for years it fully occupied his time by day, and not unfrequently encroached upon his nights.

In the spring of 1645, Henrietta became so alarmingly ill, that her life was despaired of. Charles therefore addressed his letters to her confidential secretary, Lord Jermyn, and requested him, whilst the Queen remained too unwell to read the correspondence herself, to impart to her only such portions of it as would be likely to cheer, and not trouble her: "Indeed," says the true and tender King, "act with such discretion in the matter, that her health, in the first case, be cared for, and my affairs afterwards." During the summer, the Queen was restored to convalescence. The subjoined letter shows the interest she continued to take in her husband's affairs.

Queen Henrietta to King Charles.

"Dear heart,

"I understand that the commissioners are arrived in London. I have nothing to say, but that you have a care of your honour, and that if you have a peace, it may be such as may hold, and if it fall out otherwise, that you do not abandon those who have served you, for fear they do forsake you in their need; also, I do not see how you can be in safety without a regiment of guards. For myself, I think I cannot be, seeing the malice which they have against me and my religion, of which I hope you will have a care of both; but, in my opinion, religion should be the last thing upon which you should treat for: if you do agree upon strictness against the Catholics, it would discourage them to save you; and if, afterwards, there should be no peace, you could never expect succour, either from Ireland or any Catholic Prince, for they would believe you would abandon them after you had served yourself."

On the seventeenth of January, 1645, the anxious Henrietta wrote to her struggling husband as follows:—

"My dear heart,

"Tom Elliot, two days since, hath brought me much joy and sorrow; the first to know the good estate in which you are, the other, the fear I have that you go to London. I cannot conceive where the wit was of those who gave you this counsel, unless it be to hazard your person to save theirs; but, thanks be to God, to-day I received one of yours by the ambassador of Portugal, dated in January, which comforteth me much to see that the treaty shall be at Uxbridge. For the honour of God, trust not yourself in the hands of these people, and, if you ever go to London before the Parliament be ended, or without a good army, you are lost. I understand that the proposition for the peace must begin by the disbanding of your army; if you consent to this, you shall be lost; they having the whole power of the militia, they have done, and will do, whatsoever they please. I received, yesterday, letters from the Duke of Lorrain, who sends me word, if his service be agreeable to you, he will bring you ten thousand men. Dr. Gaffe, whom I have sent into Holland, shall treat with him on his passage upon this business, and I hope very speedily to send good news of this, as, also, of the money. Assure yourself I will be wanting in nothing you shall desire, and that I will hazard my life, that is to die of famine, rather than not send it to you. Send me word, always, by whom you receive your letters, for I write both by the ambassador of Portugal and the resident of France. Above all, have a care not to abandon those who have served you, as well the bishops as the poor Catholics. Adieu."

The above letters are quoted from the King's cabinet, captured by the rebels at the battle of Naseby, a battle which destroyed Charles's last hopes of prevailing over the parliament by arms, and in which he lost more than three thousand men, nine thousand stand of arms, his park of artillery, the baggage of the army, and his private cabinet, containing his late correspondence with the Queen and the royalists. Out of these important private papers the Parliament published a selection, with remarks, in justification of their conduct; and, although Charles very naturally denounced the publication, he acknowledged that, as far as it went, it was genuine.

Desperate as was the position of Charles at this period, his confidence did not forsake him. What he could not procure by arms, he endeavoured to obtain by negotiation; and he might have succeeded, had it not been discovered that he was, at the same time, treating with the Independents, and with the Presbyterians of Scotland. In May, 1646, being unable to longer maintain the field, he escaped from Oxford in disguise, and trusting to the words of the Scots, threw himself on their generosity, and they basely sold him to the Parliament. The Queen strenuously urged him to save himself, by abandoning the Episcopal Church of England; but he firmly refused, declaring it was part of his kingly duty to foster that church of which he was the sworn defender. It was when the Scots had lost all hope of prevailing upon him to establish the Presbyterian creed throughout the kingdom, that one day, when he was at church at Newcastle, the minister, after uttering bold truths, ordered the factious psalm to be sung, beginning,—

"Why dost thou, tyrant, boast thyself,
Thy wicked deeds to praise?"

When he stood up in his place, forbad it, and called for the psalm, commencing,—

"Have mercy, Lord, on me I pray,
For men would me devour."

And the whole congregation good-naturedly indulged him.

CHAPTER IV.

Henrietta moans the surrender of Charles to the Scots—Escape of her eldest son, of her daughter, Henrietta Maria, and of James, Duke of York—War of the Fronde—The Queen in abject poverty—News of the execution of Charles the First horrifies her—Louis the Fourteenth pays her a visit of condolence—Unsuccessful adventures of Charles the Second in Britain—Cromwell's harshness towards her children—She founds the Convent of Shallot—Endeavours to convert her youngest son to the Catholic Faith—Drives him from her home—Death of Cromwell—Accession of Charles the Second—Henrietta negotiates the marriage of her daughter—Comes to England—Opposes the marriage of the Duke of York to Anne Hyde—Conducts her daughter, Henrietta, to France, and marries her to the Duke of Orleans—Returns to England—Succours the English Catholics—Illness—Goes to France in search of health—The great Plague of London—Her health still declines—Death—Burial—Surviving children.

THE surrender of Charles to the treacherous Scots sadly depressed the spirits of the Queen, and the first pleasure she experienced afterwards, was the arrival of her eldest son, Charles, Prince of Wales, in September, 1646; the Prince, when his father's fortunes became desperate, withdrew to Scilly, then to Jersey, and at last landed in France, and joined his disconsolate mother. About the same time Lady Morton succeeded in escaping, with the little Princess, Henrietta Maria, from the grasp of the Parliament, and conducted her, in safety, to the arms of her fond mother. To effect this escape, Lady Morton assumed the disguise of a poor French woman, fitted herself up a hump, with a bundle of dirty clothing; dressed the royal babe in rags, called her Pierre, a name closely resembling the sound uttered by the prattling infant, when she endeavoured to call herself Princess, and naming her her little boy, walked with her, on her back, from the nursery at Oatlands, to Dover; then crossed the channel to Calais, in the common packet-boat, without exciting suspicion, and hastening to Paris, presented the Princess to the enraptured Queen, who, fondly folding her little one in her arms, kissed her again and again; called her, her "child of benediction," and resolved to bring her up a Roman Catholic.

In May, 1648, Henrietta received the pleasing intelligence that her son James, Duke of York, had escaped from his confinement at St. James's, and reached the Downs in safety. He was about to proceed to his mother in France, but, on hearing of the revolt of the fleet from the patriot party, he changed his mind, and hastening to the Hague, encouraged the sailors, by taking upon himself the command; conduct which Henrietta highly commended.

When the war of the Fronde broke out in Paris, at the commencement of 1648, Henrietta urged her sister-in-law to avert the impending storm, by making reasonable concessions to the popular party. But the Queen-Regent not being one of those who took warning by the calamity of others, the war, which raged for about eighteen months, speedily assumed a most alarming aspect; and, ere it reached the crisis, Henrietta, Anne of Austria, and, indeed, all the royal family of France then in France, were reduced to such extreme destitution, that they had not wherewith to procure a dinner. The Queen strenuously exerted herself to put a period to the war of the Fronde; she gained the confidence of the house of Condé, the leaders of the popular party; and, at last, after both parties had suffered greatly, her representations were listened to, and peace effected.

To Henrietta, the Christmas of 1648 was a truly doleful one; she had vainly urged France, Holland, and Poland to aid her husband; and now shut up in the spacious Louvre, whilst all around her was one wild scene of insurrection and horror, and, with thoughts centred on the more distant, but, to her, more absorbing affairs of her unfortunate consort in England, whose letters could not reach her, on account of the besieged state of Paris; she and her daughter, the Princess Henrietta Maria, were actually famishing for want of bread, clothing, and fuel.

On the sixth of January, Cardinal de Retz, one of the most active of the insurrectionists, visited her; and, appalled by the destitution and misery which she endured, without a murmur, hastened to the Parliament of Paris, and, on the same day, prevailed on that assembly to vote her the very acceptable sum of twenty thousand livres. On this eventful day, when De Retz saved her and her daughter from perishing of cold and hunger, Henrietta, having received the affecting tidings that the dominant faction in England was about to sentence her husband to the scaffold, wrote an earnest dispatch to the French ambassador in England, imploring to be permitted to come to London, and see the unfortunate Charles the First. Enclosed in this dispatch, were letters to the Speakers of the Upper and Lower Houses of Parliament, and to Fairfax, the general of the army, beseeching from them the same indulgence. She also wrote to her husband, deeply sympathizing with his afflictions, and assuring him of her anxiety to help him, and her earnest desire, if she could not die for him, to die with him. These efforts of the sorrowing Henrietta were disregarded by the enemies of her husband, and the unfortunate Charles the First was tried, executed, and buried, before his consort, besieged as she was in Paris, received the appalling intelligence.

The misery and insults endured by the faulty, but greatly ill-used Charles the First, during his captivity; his unjust, partial, and unconstitutional trial; and his still more unjust execution, have been so fully detailed by modern writers, that we pass them by; simply remarking, that the murdered monarch was hurried to the scaffold by a small faction of bold and ambitious spirits, who had the address to usurp the government, and that the great majority of the people deeply deplored, and would fain have prevented his execution. As a proof of this, we extract the following passage from the life of Philip Henry, an eminent divine, written by his son Mathew, the author of the celebrated "Commentary on the Bible."

"At the latter end of 1648, he [Philip Henry] had leave given him [from college] to make a visit to his father at Whitehall, with whom he stayed for some time; there he was January the thirtyeth, 1649, when the King was beheaded; and with a very sad heart saw that tragical blow given. Two things he used to speak of, that he took notice of himself that day, which I know not if any of the historians mention. One was, that at the instant when the blow was given, there was *such a dismal, universal, groan among the thousands of the people that were within sight of it (as it were with one consent) as he never heard before*, and desired that he might never hear the like again, nor see such a cause of it. The other was, that immediately after the stroke was struck, there was, according to order, one troop marching from Charing-Cross towards King Street, and another from King Street towards Charing-Cross, purposely to disperse and scatter the people, and to divert the dismal thoughts which they could not but be filled with, by driving them to a shift, every one for his own safety."

King Charles had been beheaded ten days before the dreadful news reached the ears of Henrietta; the besieged state of Paris had stopped the couriers with dispatches to her from England, and she learned the sad tale of his trial and his death all in one day. Her secretary, Lord Jermyn, imparted the calamitous tidings to her, and it plunged her into grief too intense for utterance; for hours she neither moved, wept, nor spoke, but stood motionless in a stupor of sorrow, from which she was only aroused by the sympathy of the Duchess of Vendome; when, after indulging in a flood of tears, she exclaimed, "The loss of my crown I regret not; but, oh! to lose so kind, so virtuous, so wise, so indulgent a husband is a calamity indeed!" She then resolved to retire to a convent, and there weep out her sorrow unseen, and unknown, to all save her own faithful attendants. A few days afterwards, she took up her abode in the convent of Carmelites, in Paris, wherein she gave herself up to prayers, and the rigid forms, ceremonies, fasts, and mortifications usually indulged in by Roman Catholics on such occasions. But, in a brief time, she was forced to return to the Louvre, to advise and direct the conduct of her elder children. Her son, Charles the Second, by her desire, paid her a visit in the summer of 1649; and shortly afterwards, such were the commotions in Paris, pacific and conciliating as was her conduct, both to the popular and to the court party, that she was forced to retire from the Louvre to St. Germains. Her journey, especially through the streets of Paris, was fraught with danger. She was in deep mourning for her murdered husband; and Charles the Second, who was also in deep black, rode by the side of her coach, to protect her from the insults of the rabble, who, from a vague notion of bettering their own miserable state, denounced princes, and all that was princely.

When the civil war in Paris had abated, the widowed Queen returned with her son to the Louvre. Here, in August, 1649, Anne of Austria, and the youthful Louis the Fourteenth, paid her a state visit of condolence on the death of her husband; and, on this occasion, King Charles the Second was, for the first time, formally acknowledged at the court of France, where the charms and coquetry of Mademoiselle de Montpensier detained him for some time. Impelled by the desire of ascending his father's throne, Charles, despite the alarms and entreaties of his mother, who believed the time not yet ripe for striking the blow, ventured into his lost kingdom, to seek his fortune. Accompanied by his brother, James, Duke of York, he landed at Jersey, in September, 1649, where he was acknowledged King of Great Britain; he then proceeded to Scotland, and commenced a series of adventures, till his escape after the disastrous defeat at Worcester, when, to the joy of Henrietta, who had given him over for lost, he found his way back to her at Paris, in October, 1651. "His daring adventures and hair-breadth escapes," says an esteemed historian, "were listened to with interest; and his conduct was made the theme of general praise. That he should be the heir to the British crowns, was the mere accident of birth; that he was worthy to wear them, he owed to the resources and energies of his own mind." In a few months, however, the delusion vanished; Charles had borne the blossoms of promise—they were blasted under the withering influence of pleasure and dissipation.

Two of Henrietta's children, the young Duke of Gloucester, to whom she had given birth in November, 1640, and his sister, the Princess Elizabeth, still remained prisoners in England; the former was too young to feel the degradation of his situation, but the Princess, conscious of her position, was sent from St. James's to Carisbroke Castle—the prison from whence her father was taken to be tried and executed—where she gave way to such anguish, that she fell into a nervous fever, of which she expired on the eighth of September, 1650. The Queen, on hearing of her death, wept bitterly, as also did her affectionate brothers and sisters. She was interred with but little ceremony at Newport, sixteen days after her demise.

It was whilst the protracted negotiations for peace between France and the iron-willed Cromwell were pending, that Henrietta Maria took occasion to demand, by the voice of Cardinal Mazarin, the payment of her dower as Queen-dowager of England. "She has no right to this dower," was the Protector's stern reply; "for the people of England have never recognized her as Queen." As previously shewn, she, in her girlhood, had refused to share the coronation ceremonies with her husband;

and it was upon this truly unwise refusal, that her dower was now denied her; an insult so irritating, that Henrietta exclaimed, "If the English did not consider me the wife and consort of their late sovereign, what then have I been? surely, they would not question the legality of my marriage? However," she proceeded, with dignity, "as King Louis the Fourteenth chooses to submit to such a false stigma on the royal house of France, I must rest contented; especially, as my husband's loyal subjects always respected me as their Queen." Although Henrietta failed to obtain her dower revenues, she procured the release of her young son, the Duke of Gloucester. Cromwell permitted him "to transport himself beyond seas," and he immediately flew to the arms of his mother. By the treaty of peace, signed in October, 1656, it was provided, that Charles Stuart (Charles the Second), his brother, the Duke of York, Ormond Hyde, and fifteen other adherents of the exiled Prince, should be excluded from the kingdom of France.

As Henrietta admitted Charles's authority as King over her children, she entreated him, when he was about to depart, to permit her son Henry to remain with her. He at first objected, fearing that the Prince's religious sentiments would be tampered with; but when the Queen, who was already educating her last-born in the Catholic faith, solemnly promised to do nothing of the kind, he consented, and immediately afterwards wandered out of France, and settled at Cologne. The Queen-regent of France, on account of her discourtesy in driving Charles out of her territory, added two thousand francs per month to Henrietta's pension.

In December, 1652, Henrietta's gentle, discreet confessor, Father Philips, died, and his post was filled by the Abbé Montague, a restless, intriguing Jesuit, who speedily destroyed the peace of Charles the First's family. He first, under a representation that it was sinful to permit the celebration of the Church of England service at the Louvre, caused Henrietta's establishment there to be broken up, and her residence to be changed to the Palais Royal, where the Queen-mother of France resided; a measure which greatly disconcerted the English exiles—most of whom professed the Church of England faith. The change also severely affected the Queen; she was forced to live in public with the French court, whilst her delicate health required retirement; she therefore founded the convent of Challot, into which she retired, and where she placed her daughter, Henrietta Maria, to be educated. The wily Jesuit next prevailed on Queen Henrietta to convert her Protestant children to the Catholic Church. This task of love she commenced by urging her youngest son, Henry, Duke of Gloucester, to abandon the Church of England. Finding entreaties, persuasions, and threats, to be alike vain, she resolved to send him to the Jesuits' College; but he promptly refused to comply. Stormy altercations ensued, in which Montague and the young Prince's faithful tutor, Mr. Lovet, took an active part. Meanwhile, Prince Henry applied to his brother Charles, who, in an affectionate letter, replied, "I understand Mr. Montague and your mother are endeavouring to pervert you from your religion; if you hearken to them or any one else in this matter, you must never think to see England or me again. Do not let them persuade you, either by force or fair promises. I hear there is a purport to put you into the Jesuits' College, which I command you, on the same grounds, never to consent unto. Remember the last words of your dead father, which were to be constant to your religion; which, if you do not observe, this shall be the last time you will hear from me." Notwithstanding this royal mandate, Henrietta one day took Prince Henry aside, kissed and caressed him, and prevailed on him to once more listen to the persuasions of Montague. He gave the crafty Jesuit audience in his private chamber in the Palais Royal, listened to his arguments for more than an hour, and dismissing him, said, "Inform my mother that I adhere more firmly than ever to the religion of the Church of England."

"Then it is her Majesty's command,

that you never more enter her presence," replied Montague, as he abruptly quitted the apartment.

This message smote Gloucester with despair; he instantly employed the intercession of his brother, the Duke of York, but to no purpose. "I will discuss the subject with neither of you," replied the enraged Queen, "but through the medium of my confessor. Gloucester must comply, or I renounce him for ever."

The subsequent Sunday morning the Jesuit called on the Prince, entreated him for his mother's sake to succumb to her wish, and advised him to speak with her as she went to mass; at that moment the Queen passed to enter her coach, the Prince rushed out, kneeled before her, and implored her blessing; but, to her disgrace, she repulsed him with an angry glance, and passed on. He returned in despair, and when the diplomatic Jesuit, who had watched the meeting from the window, asked why he was weeping, retorted with disdain, "Because, sir, my mother, in compliance with your unchristian advice, has commanded me never again to enter her presence." He then turned from the base Jesuit, and it being service-time, went with his brother, the Duke of York, to Sir Richard Brown's private little chapel, and there took part in the holy devotions of the Church of England. The Prince—he was but fourteen—was now forced to endure a severe trial; when the dinner hour arrived, he learned with astonishment, that his mother refused his common sustenance; by her strict injunctions no dinner had been provided for him, and he was forced to accept the hospitality of Lord Hatton, who generously offered to serve him to the utmost of his power; before night his apartments were dismantled, the sheets stripped from his bed, his servants told to depart, and his horses turned adrift out of their stables. When he received this very unnatural harshness from his mother, he was penniless; but Hyde, Ormond, and other Church of England Royalists, generously provided for his maintenance. The Duke of York, by his constancy to the Church of England, and the assistance he afforded his younger brother, also deeply offended the priest-ridden Henrietta; but at the moment when, in all probability, he would have been dismissed with his mother's malediction, Charles the Second, at the instigation of the Princess of Orange and of the Queen of Bohemia—both staunch Protestants—wrote a formal letter to his mother, demanding the Duke of Gloucester as his subject; a demand which Henrietta was forced to comply with. The young Duke, to his infinite joy, set out on his journey to his brother in December, 1654, and before his departure, his reluctant mother summoned him to her arms, kissed him, blessed him, and promised to cease persecuting him. This unwarrantable cruelty to her youngest son is the worst, the most reprehensible deed committed by Henrietta; and certainly her confessor, by urging her to it for her soul's sake, proved himself, although a priest, a base, heartless wretch.

Two years after these unpleasant occurrences, the Princess of Orange visited Henrietta, and effected a reconciliation between her and her sons. The Duke of York escorted his sister, the Princess, to Paris, and about this time it was, that he fell in love with the more fascinating than beautiful, Anne Hyde, of whom he says, "she had all the qualities proper to inflame a heart, and she brought my passion to such a height, that the winter before the King's restoration, I resolved and promised to marry her." The gossip story mentioned by Pepys and by Reresby, that about this time Queen Henrietta married Lord Jermyn, and shortly afterwards brought him a daughter, must be deemed an unfounded slander. It has all the appearance of an improbability, and after a diligent research, not a jot of evidence can we find in support of it.

The death of Cromwell, on the third of September, 1658, although not followed by the immediate restoration of Charles the Second, raised hopes in the minds of Henrietta, that a brighter era was at hand for her and her family; and, when intelligence reached her, that on the eighth of May, 1660, Charles the Second was proclaimed in London, she became frantic with joy; gave a magnificent ball, to which was invited all the French courtiers, and every English gentleman in France, be his politics or religion what it might; and hastened with the glad tidings to the Nuns at Chaillot, where she took up her abode for a time, and where Charles the Second, on his road to England, paid her a visit incognito, to consult her in the matter. Although she strained every nerve on his behalf, made alliances in his favour, and obtained for him fifty thousand crowns from the Duchess of Savoy, she was not a witness to the exuberant joy of the restoration on the memorable twenty-ninth of May, 1660; her absence is thus noted by Cowley.

"Where's now the royal mother, where?
To take her mighty share
In this inspiring sight;
And with the part she takes to add to the delight.
Ah! why art thou not here?
Thou, always best, and now the happiest Queen,
To see our joy, and with new joy be seen."

Her absence was occasioned by the arrangements she was making for the betrothment of her daughter Henrietta Maria, to her nephew, Philippe, Duke of Orleans; and, immediately these arrangements were settled, as far as they could be in France, (the English Parliament had to fix the Princess's dower,) she resolved to go to England, where she hoped to take possession of her long-withheld dower; to prevent the marriage of the Duke of York to Anne Hyde, and to again behold her son, the Duke of Gloucester: but she only obtained one of these objects. Before she sailed, York was married, and the small-pox had carried the lamented Gloucester to an early grave. She embarked with her daughter Henrietta Maria, from Calais, on the eighteenth of October, 1660, on board the English fleet, under the command of the Duke of York, who had just previously married the charming Anne Hyde; an act for which she severely reprimanded him, the moment he entered her presence. The voyage was protracted, by an unusual calm; for a whole day and night the ships lazily rolled on the glossy, rippleless sea; at last, in the afternoon of the second day, a gentle breeze sprung up, and wafted the fleet in safety to Dover, where Charles the Second received his mother and his sister with royal magnificence. In the evening he entertained them with a sumptuous banquet at Dover Castle, where every member of the Stuart family assembled to welcome them; and where Prince Rupert and the Princess of Orange honoured them with particular attention. From Dover, the royal party proceeded to Gravesend, whence the King conducted his mother to Whitehall, on the second of November. Pepys thus alludes to her arrival. "To Whitehall, where I saw the boats coming, very thick, to Lambeth, and all the stairs to be full of people. I was told the Queen was coming, so I got a sculler for sixpence, to carry me to the royal barge and back; but I could not get to see the Queen. * * * I observe, this night, very few bonfires in the City, not above three in all London, for the Queen' s coming; whereby, I guess that her coming do please but very few." The next day, Henrietta held a grand levée at Whitehall; and "on the twenty-second," says Pepys, "Mr. Fox did take my wife and I to the Queen's presence chamber, where he got my wife placed behind the chair; and the two Princesses came to dinner. The Queen is a very little plain old woman, with nothing in aspect or garb more than an ordinary woman. The Princess of Orange I have often seen before. The Princess Henrietta is very pretty, but much below my expectation; and her dressing of herself, with her hair frized short up to her ears, did make her seem so much the less to me. But my wife standing near her, with two or three black patches* on, and well dressed, did seem to me much handsomer than she."

The marriage of James, Duke of York, to Anne Hyde, was a source of great trouble to the royal family. Anne was of quite inferior rank to the Duke,

* Court plaster. It was then fashionable, and deemed ornamental, for ladies to bedeck their face with small patches of court plaster.

and, on this account, Queen Henrietta and her daughters despised her. The Princess of Orange declared she would never yield precedence to her; and, at the same time, Charles Berkley came forward, swore that Anne had long been his mistress, and brought as witnesses of her licentious conduct, the Earl of Arran, Jermyn, Talbot, and Killigrew. These, and other false witnesses, and unfaithful councillors — some divines and some lawyers—whom the Princess of Orange had suborned, at last, so shook the resolution of the Duke, that he assured his mother and sister he could no longer own Anne for his wife. Meanwhile she was delivered of a son; and whilst in the throes of labour, she solemnly vowed, in the name of the living God, that the Duke was the father of her son, and that she had always been faithful to him. For several weeks James had not visited his wife; his mind was racked with doubts, and the birth of the child so increased his distress, that he was laid on a bed of sickness. His brother, the King, subdued by his passionate importunity, had sanctioned the match, and he now generously took the part of the distressed Anne. Matters were in this state, when the Princess of Orange was attacked with the small-pox, of which she died, on the twenty-fourth of December, 1560. A few hours before she expired, she confessed that Anne had been foully slandered, and was innocent of the crimes imputed to her. Berkley, to save himself, it is supposed, by confessing his guilt, hastened on the following day to the sick Duke, and, on his knees, pronounced all that he had said against Anne to be false; "she had never been his mistress, and, to the best of his knowledge and belief, she was one of the best, most virtuous wives in Christendom. Under a belief that the marriage would prove the ruin of his royal highness, he had invented and propagated the calumny, but he now repented of the crime, and implored the Duke's pardon." James, no less pleased than surprised by the confession, forgave Berkley; and then, hastening to his wife, kissed and blessed her and his little one, and publicly recognised her as his Duchess. The reconciliation greatly irritated Queen Henrietta; and when the King urged her to forgive them, she passionately replied, "Never; and if you attempt to bring that woman here, out I go." Her malicious opposition, however, was short-lived. Deeply impressed by the death-bed remorse of the Princess of Orange, and urged by the earnest entreaty of the French Minister, Mazarin, who was anxious to conciliate Anne's father, the Chancellor Clarendon, Henrietta—she was about to proceed to France—sent for the Duke and Duchess of York, and gave them her blessing. On the festival of the New Year, January the first, 1661, but two days after the burial of the Princess of Orange, in the Stuart vault, in Westminster Abbey, she publicly recognised them at Whitehall. Pepys says, "To-day, January the first, Mr. Moore and I went to Mr. Pierce's in our way, seeing the Duke of York bring his lady to-day, to wait upon the Queen-mother, the first time that ever she did since that business; and the Queen-mother is said to receive her now with much respect and love." On the same day, Henrietta gave audience to Lord Clarendon, the father of the Duchess of York, when mutual apologies were exchanged, and a reconciliation effected between the long-estranged Queen and Chancellor. The next day, the Queen, dreading lest her best-beloved child, the Princess Henrietta Maria, should fall a prey to the small-pox, removed with her to Hampton Court; and so soon as the Parliament had settled upon the princess forty thousand jacobuses,* by way of portion, and twenty thousand as a present, proceeded with her, under the escort of the King in person, to Portsmouth, and there embarked with her for France, on board the London, one of the finest ships in the royal navy, on the ninth of January, 1661. The vessel sailed with a fair wind; but, as usual with the Queen when at sea, a series of misfortunes followed. "This day, January the eleventh," says Pepys, "comes news

* Gold coins of the value of twenty-five shillings each, sterling, struck in the reign of James the First.

to the City, by letter, from Portsmouth, that the Princess Henrietta Maria fell sick of the measles (at first thought to be the small-pox) on board the London, after she and the Queen were under sail. Therefore, the royal voyagers returned to Portsmouth harbour. In their way, by neglect of the pilot, the vessel ran upon the Havre sand, grounded, and narrowly escaped being wrecked. The Queen and the Princess continue on board, and her Majesty does not intend to sail again till her daughter has recovered." A fortnight afterwards, the Princess being pronounced sufficiently convalescent, Henrietta sailed with her to Havre. The voyage was short and pleasant, and on landing, the royal mother and daughter were escorted by the governor of Normandy, at the head of the leading Norman nobles, to his chateau, in the vicinity of Rouen, and there magnificently entertained. Afterwards they were conducted to Pontoise, where Louis the Fourteenth, his Queen, Maria Theresa, and the Duke of Orleans met them, and accompanied them in state to Paris. At the end of Lent, a dispensation for the marriage of the Princess Henrietta Maria and the Duke of Orleans was obtained; and on the thirty-first of March, 1661, the marriage was solemnized in the private chapel, at the Palais Royal, in the presence of the most illustrious personages in France. Immediately afterwards, the Duke insisted on withdrawing his bride from her mother to his own palace. To Queen Henrietta the separation was painful in the extreme: her beloved daughter was but sixteen; she feared the temptations of the dissipated court would be too great for the young sprightly Princess; and so it turned out. The young Duchess speedily injured her health and her reputation, by being the foremost at all the court balls, masques, and other nocturnal and not too reputable entertainments.

When the Queen parted from her daughter, she retired to her rural château of Colombe, situate about five miles from Paris, near the Seine, where she resided in peaceful retirement. From Colombe, she addressed several epistles to the Duchess of Orleans, urging her, for her soul's sake, to improve her conduct; but her residence at this delightful retreat was of no long continuance. She last quitted the shores of England, under a promise of returning again after effecting her daughter's marriage, and settling in the country whence she obtained her dower. To redeem this promise, she, after inviting and sumptuously entertaining the Duke and Duchess of Orleans, and with scalding tears parting with the Duchess, as she dolefully believed for ever, on earth, proceeded to Calais, embarked there, braved a storm in crossing the Channel, and reached England in safety. On the twenty-eighth of July, Charles the Second and Katherine of Braganza, whom he had lately wedded, welcomed her with royal magnificence to Greenwich, where she then took up her abode; Somerset House being at the time under repair. Shortly afterwards, she joined in the aquatic procession, when Queen Katherine came in state down the Thames, from Hampton Court, to take possession of Whitehall. In the course of the summer, Henrietta changed her residence, from the old dilapidated palace at Greenwich, to her own palace of Somerset House, which, by her desire, had been enlarged and beautified. She lived on terms of amity with her daughters-in-law, Katherine of Braganza, and the Duchess of York. In compensation for her dower lands, which had been shared by the revolutionists, the Parliament, in 1661, granted her thirty thousand pounds per year, and to this pension Charles added an annuity of another thirty thousand pounds, from the Exchequer. She lived considerably within this income, and every quarter distributed the overplus amongst the deserving poor and unfortunate. Somerset House was her principal residence, and it was in her Catholic Chapel there, that the persecuted Papists of London congregated. She devoted great attention to the care of this little flock, and talked of establishing Catholic Chapels in several of the leading cities in England; but this last object, which would have rendered her highly unpopular, was thwarted by the decay of her health. In 1664, the fogs of London greatly affected her chest, and she suffered much from general debility. Charles the Second urged her to seek health at the baths of Bourbon; and at length, after, in compliance with her earnest entreaty, he had promised not to close her Catholic Chapel at Somerset House, nor molest her religious establishments there, during her absence, she resolved to pay a visit to France. When ready to depart, she called her priests and confessors around her, bade them an affectionate farewell, told them "she hoped soon to return, and charged them, as they would answer before God, to, in the mean time, faithfully and diligently perform their duty to the English as well as the French Catholics."

She embarked at the close of June, 1665, in a vessel commanded by the Duke of York, who had just gained a great naval victory over the Dutch, off Harwich; landed at Calais in safety, proceeded direct to Paris, and took up her residence at her favourite château of Colombe. In this peaceful abode we will leave her, and glance at that terrible visitation, the Great Plague of London, which had broken out previous to her departure from the Metropolis.

The pestilence began in Long Acre, * at the close of 1664, when two or three persons suddenly dying in one family, the timid neighbours took the alarm and removed into the City, whither it is supposed they carried the infection. Here it gathered strength from the denseness of the population, and soon its ravages became extensive. The lower classes were seized with a panic, and entertaining an absurd, but popular notion, that the plague visited London every twenty years, they took no means to counteract it. A three months' frost, which set in in December, suspended the ravages of the pestilence; but no sooner had a thaw succeeded, than it burst forth with increased force. As the spring passed on, it extended to several parishes; and, at last, its ravages became so alarming, that the magistrates issued an order, dated July the first, 1665, to shut up all the infected houses, which were marked with a red cross, one foot in length, painted on the door, with the words, "Lord, have mercy upon us!" placed above it. From that moment the house was closed, and guards were constantly in attendance to supply the sick with necessaries, and to prevent the inmates from quitting the house, for at least a month. This precaution is thought to have done much injury. If the destroyer, when only stalking forth amongst men free to fly from his approach, and to shrink from contact with him, committed such havoc, it may be imagined how fell his ravages must have been amongst persons thus pent up together. Even those who retained full possession of health, might calculate the hours they had still to live; those who to-day turned out the bodies of their lifeless companions, might lay their certain account with following them on the morrow; no hope of escape being left to any, all must have prepared to die; and this consolation, at least, they must have had, that neither fear nor apprehension could any longer interfere with the tender offices of friendship and affection. The surviving son needed not to shrink from closing the eyes of his dying parent, nor the widowed wife to pillow her head on the cold breast of her departed spouse. An eye-witness says, "Many who were lost, might have been alive, had not the tragical mark upon their door drove proper assistance from them." The same author adds, that "the mortality amongst the people thus shut up, was greatly increased by the wicked practices of the nurses. Those wretches," he remarks, "out of greediness to plunder the dead, would strangle their patients, and charge it to the distemper in their throats, whilst others would directly convey the pestilential taint from sores of the infected to those who were well."

The alarm of the citizens was aggravated by several publications which were issued in the early stages of the plague, bearing most portentous titles, and all foretelling the destruction of the City. One of these pamphlets was entitled "Fair Warnings," a second, "Britain's Remembrancer," and a third, had for its title an epigram, "Come out of her, my people, lest ye be partakers of her

* This account is a slightly altered extract from Percy's History of London.

plagues." Fanatics or missionaries ran through the streets, agitated and agitating by their oral denunciations and predictions. One man ran about in a state of wild disorder, crying day and night, like the man mentioned by Josephus, whose "Woe to Jerusalem!" proceeded and foretold its fall; he walked quickly, and with sepulchral voice, and countenance beaming with horror, continually ejaculated, "Oh, the great and dreadful God!" Another man, pretending a more than human authority for preaching to the City, went about like Jonah in the city of Nineveh, crying out "Yet a few days, and London shall be destroyed."

In the months of May, June, and July, the plague had continued with more or less severity; but in August and September it quickened into dreadful activity; sweeping away three, four, five, and sometimes eight thousand persons in a week. Then it was that the whole British nation wept for the miseries of the Metropolis. In some houses carcases lay waiting for burial, and in others, persons in their last agonies. In one room were heard dying groans, in another the ravings of delirium, mingled with the wailings of relations and friends, and the apprehensive shrieks of children. Infants were smitten with death at the moment of their birth. Some of the infected ran about staggering like drunken men, and fell, and expired in the streets; whilst others lay half dead, never to be waked, but by the last trumpet. At length the physician and the divine received the stroke of death, in the exercise of their humane and holy offices; business was suspended, the bells seemed hoarse with tolling, and the sextons were not sufficient to bury the dead, with which the church-yards were so glutted, that they were thrown into pits in heaps of thirty or forty together, without coffins, mourners, or funeral service. When the disease was at its height, and more than twelve thousand perished in one week; fires of sea-coal were, by order of the Privy-Council, kindled in the streets, in the proportion of one fire to every twelve houses, with the fallacious hope of dissipating the pestilential miasma; but "before three days had expired, the heavens so wept for the fatal mistake, as to extinguish even the fires with their showers." A fatal night succeeded, in which more than four thousand persons expired. Those moving sepulchres, the dead carts, continually traversed the streets, whilst the appalling cry, "Bring out your dead!" thrilled through every soul not yet dead to feeling. At last the dead carts were insufficient for the office, and the houses and streets were rendered tenfold more pestilential by their unburied dead. The change that now took place in the feelings of the people, is thus vividly described by Defoe. "As I have mentioned how the people were brought into a condition to despair of life, and abandon themselves, so this very thing had a strange effect among us for three or four weeks; that is, it made men bold and venturous; they were no more shy of one another, or restrained within doors, but went any where and every where, and began to converse. One would say to another, 'I do not ask you how you are, or say how I am. It is certain we shall all go, so 'tis no matter who is sick or who is sound;' so they ran deliberately into any place or company."

The dead now were no longer numbered, for the parish clerks and sextons perished in the execution of their office. In the parish of Stepney alone, one hundred and sixteen sextons, grave-diggers, and carters employed in removing the dead bodies, died in one year. Ten thousand houses were at one time deserted, and it is said that during the plague, not fewer than two hundred thousand persons quitted the metropolis:—

> "Empty, the streets, with uncouth verdure clad,
> Into the worst of deserts sudden turned
> The cheerful haunts of man."

In the last week of September the plague began to abate, and the bills of mortality fell from upwards of eight thousand to little more than six thousand, weekly. Every succeeding week the number of victims diminished, so that by the subsequent February, the pestilence had wholly ceased. The number that perished during this plague, according to the returns, was sixty-eight thousand five hundred and ninety;

but Defoe asserts, "that the number was, at least, one hundred thousand." The lives of numbers were preserved by means of shipping on the Thames, into which the infection did not reach, except in very few instances.

The survivors of the dreadful calamity would have perished of famine, but for the bounty of the affluent. The money subscribed is said to have amounted to one hundred thousand pounds a week, to which Charles the Second humanely gave one thousand pounds weekly. In the parish of Cripplegate alone, the disbursements to the poor amounted to seventeen thousand pounds a week. But even when the poor had obtained the money, they feared to lay it out in provisions, lest they should, by some means, catch the infection. If they bought a joint of meat in the market, they would not receive it from the hand of the butcher, but take it off the hooks themselves; the butcher, equally cautious, would not touch the money, but had it dropped into a pot of vinegar, kept for the purpose. Workmen were equally cautious with their masters, and even members of the same family with each other.

To return to the subject of this memoir: Henrietta was relieved, but not cured, by the waters of Bourbon; consumption, and a complication of other maladies, slowly, but fatally undermined her constitution. In August, her situation became such, that the four leading physicians in France attended her. In truth, she was in the last stage of consumption, and a too-powerful dose of opium, administered by order of M. D'Aquin, her physician, sent her into a sleep from which she never again woke. The day before her death, she was more cheerful than usual; after partaking of supper she swallowed the opium draught, went to bed, and fell into a calm sleep. At day-break her attendants approached her bed-side, to administer another draught; she made no reply to their reiterated questions; they touched her, and finding that she moved not, became alarmed, and sent for priests and physicians; when they arrived, she slightly breathed but was quite unconscious, The priests prepared the sacrament of extreme unction, and soon afterwards her gentle respirations ceased, and her soul passed to eternity. She died in her sixty-first year, on the morning of the twenty-first of August, 1669, at her favourite residence of Colombe. Couriers were immediately dispatched, with the fatal tidings, to the relations and friends, and the subsequent night her heart was taken out and presented to her convent at Chaillot; whither her body, after being embalmed, was conveyed, previous to the funeral. The royal corpse lay in state at Chaillot, till the second of September. On the evening of that day, immediately darkness had set in, it was carried in grand funeral procession, by torch-light, to the royal tombs, in the Abbey of St. Denis, and there interred with imposing funeral rites. Twenty-eight days afterwards, another magnificent service was performed to the memory of the Queen of Charles the First, by the nuns of Chaillot, at which her bereaved daughter, Henrietta Maria, Duchess of Orleans, took a conspicuous part, and Bossuet delivered the renowned funeral oration, which at once stamped his reputation as one of the greatest orators of his times. The courts of France and of England went into deep mourning for the departed Queen. Charles the Second deeply deplored the loss of his mother, and gave the sisterhood of Chaillot two thousand jacobuses, to erect a chapel for the reception of her heart.

Henrietta died intestate, but not in debt. According to the then law of France, Louis the Fourteenth was heir to her effects; but he waived his claim in favour of Charles the Second, and Charles presented all her furniture to the nuns of Chaillot, who, on the tenth of every month, said mass for the repose of her soul. Henrietta left but three surviving children, Charles the Second, James, Duke of York, who, on the death of his brother, ascended the throne of Great Britain, and the beautiful Duchess of Orleans. The Duchess survived her but a few months. She died, suddenly, in June, 1670; some say of poison, and others of cholera.

KATHERINE OF BRAGANZA,

Queen of Charles the Second.

CHAPTER I.

Katherine's Birth—Parentage—Education—Income—Suitors—Match proposed between her and Charles the Second—Dower—Charles agrees to the match—Futile opposition of Spain—Charles crowned—Marriage treaty signed—Opposition of Lady Castlemaine—Katherine sails to England—Is married to Charles, who is delighted with her person and manners, but continues his amours with Castlemaine—Endeavours to make Castlemaine one of the Queen's ladies—Katherine refuses to accept her—Quarrels with him—Clarendon urges her to comply—Temporary reconciliation—The Queen-mother approves her conduct—Her first state visit to London—Lady Castlemaine thrust upon her—The King and courtiers insult her—She accepts the services of Castlemaine—Royal ball—State of public matters.

KATHERINE OF BRAGANZA, the well - intentioned, but ill-used Queen of Charles the Second, first saw the light at the delightful palace of Villa Viçosa, in Portugal, on the twenty-fifth of November, 1638, the very day of the year—an auspicious day for Portugal—on which her father, John, Duke of Braganza, instigated by the ambition of her mother, Donna Luiza, the daughter of the Duke of Medina Sidonia, undertook to emancipate his bleeding country from the yoke of tyrannic Spain, or die in the attempt. This important revolution was effected with ease and celerity. The people were disgusted with the rigorous and impolitic administration of Olivarez. Duke John was a descendant of the ancient Kings of Portugal; he, at this time, had the command of the army; and, being seconded in his views by the patriotic spirit of the nation, he hastened to Lisbon, where he caused himself to be proclaimed King, by the title of John the Fourth. The Spanish guards were attacked and routed, and the chief partisans of the government put to death by the populace. All the principal towns followed the example of the capital, and shortly afterwards, all the foreign settlements. From that era, the twenty-fifth of November, 1640, Portugal became an independent sovereignty, after having been for sixty years an appanage of Spain.

Immediately after John the Fourth had defeated the Spanish forces in 1640, Charles the First recognized him as sovereign of Portugal, a service refused to him by the Pope, and by all the Catholic courts of Europe, excepting France, and which emboldened him to

Catherine of Braganza.

propose, through his Ambassador, the marriage of his daughter, Katherine of Braganza, with the Prince of Wales, afterwards Charles the Second; a proposal to which the needy English monarch listened with stoical indifference. Katherine was educated in a convent, under the immediate superintendence of her wise, energetic mother, the Queen of Portugal; and in November, 1654, her father, out of the unbounded affection he bore her, gave her, besides other sources of income, the island of Madeira, the city of Lanega, and the town of Mour; but with a proviso, that if she married out of the kingdom, she should exchange them for a suitable equivalent from the nation. Shortly afterwards her father died, and her eldest brother, Don Alphonso, being too young to reign, her mother assumed the regal authority, which she exercised for ten years, with such success, that the independence of Portugal was firmly established, the commerce and trade of the nation enlarged, and the social condition of the people greatly meliorated.

Many were the offers made for the hand of the Infanta Katherine; but her mother, foreseeing the restoration of Charles the Second, refused them all, with the secret intention of marrying her to that sovereign. Donna Luiza's first proposals for this match were made to General Monk, by a clever Jew, who at the time almost ruled her cabinet. But Monk felt no desire to wed his sovereign to a Catholic. Meanwhile, Charles himself fell in love with Henrietta, the young Princess of Orange, and had the mortification to learn that her mother, the Princess-dowager of Orange, peremptorily refused his offer for her hand, with the cutting remark, that "although the son of a King, he was but a poor exile, and therefore she could not think of throwing her daughter away upon him." Charles also made the offer of his hand to the niece of the Cardinal Mazarin, but with no better success. In a few weeks, however, the tide of popular feeling in England turned in favour of royalty, and when a deputation from the Parliament arrived at Breda, presented the royal Stuart with fifty thousand pounds, and invited him to return and take possession of his throne, both the Princesses of Orange and Mazarin sought to renew the negotiation, but to each of them Charles answered, "I was too poor for the lady in my adversity, now she is not exalted enough for me."

Shortly after Charles the Second had been restored to the throne, his more sober friends, perceiving what scandal his immoralities gave rise to, urgently entreated him to marry, and at last he seriously resolved to choose a consort. Whilst pondering on the subject, and yet undecided as to which of the marriageable Princesses of Europe he should offer his hand, his mother, at the secret instigation of the French court, directed his attention to Katherine of Braganza. France, be it observed, had aided Portugal to preserve its independence against Spain, but, by the recently concluded treaty of the Pyrenees, Louis had bound himself to afford no further assistance to the Portuguese patriots; he, however, to prevent that country from being again incorporated with Spain, determined to procure the marriage of the Donna Katherine to Charles the Second; and afterwards, through England, to afford that assistance to Charles's wife's family, which he otherwise could not do without violating the treaty. He wrote to the court at Lisbon, proposing the match; Donna Luiza thanked him, and as his advice accorded with her own politic views on the subject, immediately adopted it. The business was opened by Don Francisco de Mello, the Portuguese Ambassador in England. He proposed the match to the King's Lord Chamberlain, the Earl of Manchester, and on the following day paid Charles a visit in person, and offered with the Princess a dower of five hundred thousand pounds in ready money, and to annex Tangiers, on the coast of Africa, and Bombay, in the East Indies, to the crown of England for ever; and to grant to the English a free trade to Portugal and to the Portuguese colonies. Charles, who greatly needed money, lent a willing ear to the proposal, consulted a secret council composed of

Clarendon, Ormond, Southampton, Manchester, and Nicholas, and, in compliance with their advice and his own inclination, caused De Mello to be given to understand that the proposal would be accepted. To facilitate the negotiation, De Mello returned to Portugal, with letters from Charles to Katherine, to her mother, the Queen-regent, and to her brother, the young King, in favour of the marriage. The court at Lisbon, overjoyed at the prospects of the alliance, conferred the title of Count Da Ponte upon De Mello, and dispatched him to England, with full powers to conclude the marriage. At the commencement of 1661, he arrived at London, when, to his surprise, he was received with great coolness at court; in fact, in his absence, Vatteville, the Spanish Ambassador, had informed Charles, that Katherine was known to be incapable of becoming a mother; she was ugly and deformed, and his marriage with her would lead to a war with Spain and other evils; but if he would take one of the Princesses of Parma, the King of Spain would give with either of those ladies as large a dower as would be given with a daughter of Spain. These suggestions, seconded by the efforts of the Earl of Bristol, the enemy of the Portuguese match, induced Charles to dispatch that nobleman to Parma, to obtain information regarding the two Princesses. He saw them on their way to church; the one sight convinced him that the one was too ugly, the other too corpulent, to be recommended to the royal choice. The ill success of Bristol's mission urged Vatteville to make further efforts against the Portuguese match; he, in the name of his royal master, offered to dower a Princess of Denmark or of Saxony, or the Princess Henrietta of Orange; or, indeed, any lady Charles chose to accept as a bride, whether Catholic or Protestant, saving Katherine of Braganza. But the English monarch turned a deaf ear to his proposals. The amount of the dower, the urgent entreaties of Louis the Fourteenth, who, to secure the Portuguese match, offered him a dower of fifty thousand pounds and other valuable services; and what, perhaps, outweighed all other considerations, the confirmation of De Mello's account of the Infanta's personal charms and agreeable manners, by several trustworthy persons who had lately returned from Portugal, completely turned the balance in favour of Katherine. Her portrait was shewn to Charles—he pronounced it beautiful; and after a full council of eight-and-twenty members had, without a dissentient voice, decided in favour of the match; he sent for the Portuguese Ambassador, received him with marked distinction, and acquainted him with his earnest desire to marry the Infanta without further delay. De Mello received the communication with infinite satisfaction, and assured Charles, that the Queen-mother, to show the confidence she reposed in his honour, had resolved to send her daughter to him unmarried. The motive which really induced the politic Donna Luiza to dispense with the betrothment of her daughter by proxy, was, that the marriage being between a Protestant and a Catholic, a dispensation was necessary; and as the see of Rome had never acknowledged the independence of Portugal, the Pope, in the dispensation, would mention Katherine, not as the Infanta of King John the Fourth of Portugal, but simply as the daughter of the late Duke of Braganza—a slight which the jealous Queen-mother and her court would on no account submit to.

To prevent the occurrence of unpleasantnesses similar to those which dimmed the lustre of his father's coronation, Charles resolved to be crowned before his marriage with the Catholic Katherine was solemnized. His inauguration was performed with the usual ceremonies, pomp, and rejoicing, on the twenty-third of April, 1661. The Parliament met on the eighth of May; the King opened the session in person, and in his speech to both houses, informed them of his intended marriage. Both the Lords and the Commons voted him congratulatory addresses, and in June the treaty was signed, and the Earl of Sandwich dispatched with a fleet to cruise in the Mediterranean, and after teaching piratical Algiers and Tunis to pay due respect to the British flag, and taking possession of Tangiers, to bring the Portuguese Princess to England. Meanwhile, Vatteville, the disappointed Spanish ambassador, endeavoured to excite the rabble of London to rise in riot, in opposition to the introduction of a Popish Queen into Protestant England; but his efforts were vain. All classes, disgusted with the King's amours with Mrs. Palmer, afterwards Lady Castlemaine, thought it better that he should have a Catholic Queen, than no Queen at all. To Mrs. Palmer, with whom the King, although professing himself to be a married man, continued to live on terms of the most disgraceful familiarity, the approaching marriage was a subject of great annoyance and anxiety. To pacify the temper of this bad, bold woman, Charles usually dined and supped at her house; created her reluctant husband Earl of Castlemaine, and solemnly promised to appoint her one of the ladies of the bedchamber to his Queen.

Meanwhile, the Earl of Sandwich reached Lisbon, and after many ceremonies, and much tedious delay, was forced by the artful Queen Regent to receive but half of the sum promised with Katherine—and that not in money, but in merchandize; and to accept a bond from the crown of Portugal for the payment of the residue, within a year. He sailed from Lisbon, with the royal bride, on the fifteenth of April, 1662. The parting of Katherine from her mother, is thus recorded by a contemporary poet:—

"Here the two Queens took leave, but in such sort,
As with amazement filled the thronged Court.
Their carriage more than masculine, no tear
From either of their Majesties appear.
Art conquered nature, state and reason stood
Like two great consuls, to restrain the flood
Of passion and affection, which, nevertheless,
Appeared in sad, but prudent comeliness.
A scene so solemn, that the standers by,
Both lords and ladies, did that want supply.
In this great concourse, every one appears
Paying a tribute to them, in their tears."

The voyage was tedious and stormy; in the channel it blew such a gale, that the fleet sought shelter in Mount Bay, till the storm subsided, and a favourable breeze sprung up. Off the Isle of Wight, they met the Duke of York, who, at the head of five frigates, had put to sea, to meet his future sister-in-law. The Duke paid a visit to the royal bride, on board the Royal Charles, the vessel in which she sailed; and although, being the King's brother, he might have saluted her, he, out of a delicate regard to her feelings, and that he might not be the first man to offer that compliment to his Queen, simply kissed her hand. He then introduced to her several noblemen, amongst whom were the Earl of Chesterfield and the Duke of Ormond, who brought her a letter from the King; and after they had kissed her hand, he seated himself by her side, and familiarly conversed with her in Spanish. Henceforth, he daily visited the Queen to the end of the voyage; and her Majesty, emerging from the almost oriental state of seclusion in which she had hitherto kept herself, welcomed him with winning sweetness. Pepys says, that Mr. Creed, secretary to Lord Sandwich, informed him "how recluse the Queen had ever been, and all the voyage never came upon the deck, nor put her head out of her cabin, but did love my lord's music, and would send for it down to the state room, and she set in her cabin within hearing of it." He also states, that the Queen gave no rewards to any of the captains or officers, but only to my Lord Sandwich, and that was a bag of gold, which was no honourable present, of about one thousand four hundred pounds sterling. The Portuguese writers, however, assure us, "that she liberally rewarded the commanders and the officers of the ships, and gave money to be distributed amongst the common sailors."

The fleet anchored at Spithead on the thirteenth of May; and on the same day Katherine landed, and was conducted to the King's house, at Portsmouth; "where," says the Earl of Sandwich, "she took up her lodgings, received my Lady Suffolk, and the other ladies of her household, very kindly, and appointed them this morning to come and put her in that habit they thought would be most pleasing to the King; and I doubt not, but when they shall have done their part, she will appear with much more advantage, and very well to the King's contentment. She is a Princess of extraordinary goodness of disposition, very discreet and pious, and there is every hope that she will make the King and all of us happy." The news of her Majesty's landing was swiftly carried to Charles by her Lord Chamberlain; but the real or pretended necessity of bringing the session to a close, detained the King in London for five days afterwards; and during this time, he disgraced himself, by daily dining and supping with the detestable Lady Castlemaine.

"On the twenty-first of May, 1662," Pepys remarks, "Lord Sandwiche's housekeeper, Sarah, told me how the King dined at my Lady Castlemaine's, and supped every day and night the last week; and that the night that the bonfires were made for the joy of the Queen's arrival, the King was there, but there was no fire at her door, though at all the rest of the doors almost, in the street, which was much observed; and that the King and she did send for a pair of scales and weighed one another, and she, being near going to bed, was said to be the heaviest." Charles left London on the nineteenth of May, and reached Portsmouth on the next day. Katherine was confined to her bed with a cold, and slight sore throat; but he hastened into her chamber, affectionately embraced her, earnestly conversed with her in Spanish, and on returning to his own apartments, highly commended her person and manners. Some writers affirm that, on first seeing her, he declared she was "as ugly as a bat;" but the subjoined letter, written by himself to Clarendon, on the morning of his marriage, fully disproves the assertion:—"Her face, my Lord, is not so exact as to be called a beauty, though her eyes are excellent good, and not anything in her face that, in the least degree, can *shoque* one. On the contrary, she has as much agreeableness in her looks, altogether, as ever I saw; and, if I have any skill in physiognomy, which I think I have, she must be as good a woman as ever was born. Her conversation, as much as I can perceive, is very good; for she has wit enough, and a most agreeable voice. You would much wonder to see how well we are acquainted already. In a word, I think myself very happy, for I am confident our two humours will agree exceedingly well together."

On the twentieth of May, the health of the Queen having greatly improved, it was resolved that the nuptials should take place the next day. Since her arrival, Katherine had been earnestly importuned to waive her claim of having the marriage celebrated after the Catholic rites; but, as she remained inflexible, it was performed with all possible privacy, on the morning of the twenty-first of May, in her bed-room, by her almoner, the Lord Aubigny. Phillip, afterwards Cardinal Howard, and five others, attended as witnesses, and every person present was sworn to profound secrecy. After dinner, the ceremony was publicly solemnized, after the form established by the Church of England, in the great hall or presence chamber, by the Bishop of London. A rail across the hall divided the royal party from the concourse of nobles and gentry who witnessed the ceremony. When the King and Queen had taken their places under a rich canopy, the Bishop performed the nuptial rites prescribed in the Book of Common Prayer, and pronounced them married, "in the name of the Father, the Son, and the Holy Ghost." "Long may they live!" responded the spectators, with hearty shouts; and, in conclusion, the ribbons, which the bride wore in profusion, were cut from her dress, and distributed in small portions, as wedding favours, amongst the assembly. Whilst the scramble for these eagerly-sought fragments was going on, Charles conducted his consort to her apartments, where the principal ladies and nobles at court kissed her hand. The marriage was entered in the parish register of St. Thomas à Becket, Portsmouth, in the following words: "Our most gracious sovereign lord, Charles the Second, by the grace of God, King of Great Britain, &c.; and the most illustrious Donna Katherine, Infanta of Portugal, daughter of the deceased Don Juan, King of Portugal, and sister to the present Don Alphonso, King of Portugal, was married at Portsmouth, upon Thursday, the twenty-first of May, 1662, being the fourteenth year of his Majesty's reign; by the Right Reverend Father in God, Gilbert, Lord Bishop of London, Dean of his Majesty's Chapel Royal; in the presence of several of the nobility of his Majesty's dominions and Portugal."

After the fatigues of the ceremony, the Queen, who was yet weak, from the effects of her late indisposition, retired to repose in her chamber. The King took his supper with her on her bed; and so little did he know his own heart, that four days afterwards he wrote to Clarendon—"I cannot easily tell you how happy I think myself; and I must be the worst man living—which I hope I am not—if I be not a good husband."

Katherine and her royal spouse left Portsmouth on the twenty-seventh, tarried on the night of the twenty-eighth, at Windsor; and on the twenty-ninth, the anniversary of Charles's birth and restoration, reached Hampton Court, where the state officers, the nobility, gentry, and ladies of the Court were waiting to greet their Queen on her arrival. She cheerfully received their congratulations, permitted them to kiss her hand, and on the Duchess of York being presented, took her in her arms, called her sister, and affectionately saluted her. The personal charms of Katherine, if not transcendant, were evidently above mediocrity. On this subject, Pepys remarks—"The Queen was brought a few days since to Hampton Court, and all people pronounce her to be a very fine and handsome lady, and very discreet; and that the King is pleased enough with her, which I fear will put Madam Castlemaine's nose out of joint. The Court is wholly now at Hampton. On the third of June," he proceeds, "I found the Countess of Sandwich come from Court, where the Queen had used her very civilly; and the Countess tells me she is a very pretty woman. Yesterday, Sir R. Ford told me the Aldermen of the City did attend her [Majesty] in their habits, and did present her with a gold cup, and one thousand pounds in gold therein. But he told me that they were so poor in their chamber, that they were fain to call two or three Aldermen to raise fines to make up this sum."

For a few weeks after their marriage, the royal pair lived in perfect harmony. Foregoing the strict exercise of her religious devotions, Katherine, by the advice of the Portuguese Ambassador, overlooked the dissipation of the gay Court, and, to please her witty, licentious husband, frequently appeared in public, and took part with him in sylvan and aquatic sports, balls, concerts, and other entertainments; whilst Charles, charmed with the grace, winning manners, and freshness of his bride, made her his first and earnest care. The first interruption to Katherine's dream of wedded felicity, was occasioned in July, by the King's resolution not to estrange himself from Lady Castlemaine. She had borne him a son since the Queen's arrival; he had stood godfather to that son; and her husband had withdrawn in disgust to France, with a view of separating from her for ever. Charles, therefore, began to consider that she had more than ordinary claims upon him for protection; and, erroneously believing Katherine to be in profound ignorance of his amours with her, placed her name at the head of the list of ladies whom he recommended to the Queen for appointments in her household. Katherine instantly drew her pen through the abhorred name. "I hear," says Pepys, "that the Queen did prick her out of the list presented her by the King, desiring that she might have that favour done, or that he would send her back again to Portugal; and that the King was angry, and the Queen discontented a whole day and night upon it; but, at last, the King hath promised to have nothing more to do with Lady Castlemaine." A promise he directly afterwards violated, by leading "the lady," as Castlemaine was usually designated, into the Queen's chamber, and presenting her to her Majesty, in the midst of a brilliant Court. Katherine subdued her feelings for the moment, received her rival graciously, and permitted her to kiss her hand. But the effort nearly cost her her life; in a few minutes her eyes were suffused with tears, the blood gushed from her nose, she changed colour, shrieked, and was carried to her apartment in a fit. Charles pronounced this incident an insult to himself and to Lady Castlemaine; he vowed that he would never submit to the jealous whims of his wife; and told Katherine, as she had put a public insult upon Lady Castlemaine, she must, to make her a becoming reparation, receive her as a lady of her bed-chamber. This, the Queen very properly refused; when Charles resolved, as her husband and King, to enforce compliance. The profligate at Court, applauded his resolution; and on Clarendon and Ormond venturing to remonstrate against it, he silenced them by addressing the subjoined letter to Clarendon:—

"Hampton Court.

"I forgot, when you were here last, to desire you to give Brodericke counsel not to meddle any more with what concerns my Lady Castlemaine, and to let him have a care how he is the author of any scandalous reports: for, if I find him guilty, I will make him repent of it to the last moment of his life; and now I am on this matter, I think it necessary to give you a little good counsel in it, least you may think that by making a further stir in the business, you may divert me from my resolution, which all the world shall never do; and I wish I may be unhappy in this world, and in the world to come, if I fail in the least degree of what I have resolved: which is of making my Lady Castlemaine of my wife's bed-chamber; and whosoever I find may endeavour to hinder this resolution of mine (except it be only to myself), I will be his enemy to the last moment of my life. You know how true a friend I have been to you; if you will oblige me eternally, make this business as easy to me as you can, of what opinion soever you are of, for I am resolved to go through with this matter, let what will come of it; which, again, I solemnly swear, before Almighty God. Therefore, if you desire to have the countenance of my friendship, meddle no more with the business, except it be to beat down all false and scandalous reports, and to facilitate what, I am sure, my honour is so much concerned in. And whosoever I find to be my Lady Castlemaine's enemy in this matter, I do promise, upon my word, to be his enemy as long as I live. You may show this letter to my Lord Lieutenant [Ormond]; and, if you have both a mind to oblige me, carry yourselves like friends to me in this matter. CHARLES R."

This letter alarmed Clarendon into undertaking an office he detested. He endeavoured, by all the art and sophistry of which he was master, to prevail on the persecuted Queen to succumb to the base wishes of her husband; but she refused to listen to his advice; and Charles, in revenge, subjected her to painful indignities, seldom entered her presence, sent her country-women back to Portugal, and grossly insulted the Portuguese Ambassador. The arrival of the Queen-mother, Henrietta Maria, to congratulate the King and Queen on their marriage, led to a temporary reconciliation between the royal pair. They visited her at Greenwich, on the twenty-eighth of July; she, as loudly as prudence permitted, expressed her abhorrence of the painful mortifications to which Katherine was subjected; and when Charles and his consort returned to Hampton Court, they, to the delight of all right-minded persons, supped together in public. On the twenty-third of August, the King, Queen, and Court, proceeded down the Thames, from Hampton Court to London. It was the Queen's first public entry into the Metropolis; and Evelyn, who was a spectator, pronounces the spectacle magnificent; the decorations of the barges and boats, rich and costly; the music of the bands on the water, sweetly enchanting, and the thunder of the ordnance startling and awful. Pepys, who witnessed the scene off the roof of the banqueting-house at Whitehall, says, "All the show consisted, chiefly, in the number of boats and barges, and two pageants, one of a king, and another of a queen, with her maids of honour sitting at her feet, very prettily. Anon came the King and Queen, in a barge, under a canopy, with a thousand barges and boats, I know, for we could see no water for them, nor discern the King nor Queen. And so they landed at Whitehall Bridge, and the great guns on the other side went off." Lady Castlemaine was not permitted to take part in this procession; but, shortly afterwards, the King again introduced her to Court, and she, with shameless effrontery, mingled with the most exalted personages, in the presence-chamber of the Queen, and of the Queen-mother. "On the seventh of September," remarks Pepys, "meeting Mr. Pierce, the surgeon, he took me into Somerset House, and there carried me into the Queen-mother's presence-chamber, where she was, with our Queen sitting on her left hand, whom I never did see before; and, though she be not very charming, yet she hath a good modest and innocent look, which is pleasing. Here, I also saw Madam Castlemaine; and, which pleased me most, Mr. Crofts,* the King's bastard; a most pretty spark, of about fifteen years old, who I perceive do hang much upon my Lady Castlemaine, and is always with her; and I hear that both the Queens are mighty kind to him. By and by, in comes the King, and, anon, the Duke of York and his Duchess; so that they being well together, was such a sight as I never could, almost, have happened to see with so much ease and leisure. They staid till it was dark, and then went away; the King and his Queen, and my Lady Castlemaine, and young Crofts, in one coach, and the rest in other coaches. Here were great store of great ladies, but very few handsome ones. The King and Queen were very merry, and he would have made the Queen-mother believe that the Queen would shortly present him with an heir, and, indeed, declared that she said so." The assertion, it appears, wounded the feelings, and shocked the modesty of the young Queen, who, knowing but little English, and unaware of the strength of the expression she used, answered, 'You lie!' which was the first English word that I ever heard her say; and it made the King good sport, for he would have made her say in English, 'Confess and be hanged.'"

The contention between the royal pair still continued. Lady Castlemaine, with unparalleled effrontery, entered the Queen's presence where and when she pleased; she daily received the attention of the King and his courtiers, whilst her Majesty sat by alone, silent and unnoticed. The Queen was never free from her company; she thrust herself into the royal coach whenever Katherine went out, whether to visit a friend, or to a public entertainment; and, at last, to the scandal of all good Protestants, she even attended her to mass, an incident thus noted by Pepys, in his Diary:—"On the twenty-first of September (Lord's Day), to the park. The Queen coming by in her coach, going to her Chapel, at St. James's; the first time I had been ready for her. I crowded after her, and I got up to the room where her closet is, and there stood, and saw the fine altar ornaments, and the friars in their habits, and the priests come in with their fine crosses and many other fine things. * * * The Queen very devout. *But what pleased me best, was to see my dear Lady Castlemaine, who, though a Protestant, did wait upon the Queen to chapel.* Not understanding the sermon, which was in Portuguese, I went up to the Queen's presence-chamber, where she and the King were expected to dine; but her Majesty staid at St. James's, and the King dined alone in his own chamber." Matters remained in this state for several weeks longer; when Katherine, wanting resolution to maintain the unequal contest, accepted the services of Lady Castlemaine, and even treated her with all outward show of kindness, in private, as well as in public. By this sudden change of conduct towards her rival, Katherine hoped to conciliate the King

* Son of Charles the Second, by Lucy Waters. He was created Duke of Monmouth.

and her enemies. But in this she was mistaken. Charles prided himself in the victory he had obtained over what he was pleased to designate her crafty, perverse temper; and those who had previously admired her constancy, her greatness of soul in suffering the trials of conjugal persecution, rather than countenancing her base rival, pronounced her a "mutable woman, hard to know, and difficult to serve." She, however, was neither so malicious nor energetic as some Princesses; otherwise, instead of tamely submitting to her husband's tyrannic will, she would have placed herself at the head of the disaffected, a formidable and daily increasing party, who denounced the sale of Dunkirk to the French; disgusted at the profligacy and extravagance of the King and the Court, sympathised with the virtuous ill-treated Queen, and loudly complained of the influence and insolence of Lady Castlemaine. "Strange," remarks Pepys, "how the King is bewitched to this pretty Castlemaine; her interest at Court is now greater than the Queen's; and she, with Sir Charles Barkeley and Sir H. .Bennett, both of whom she hath brought in, hath more influence with the King than any one else at Court."

King Charles and his gay Court danced out the year 1662 at a grand ball, held at Whitehall; which Pepys, who was present, thus mentions in his amusing Diary:—"Mr. Povy and I to Whitehall, he taking me thither, to carry me to the ball given this night by the King. He brought me first to the Duke's Chamber, where I saw the Duke and his Duchess at supper; and thence into the room where the hall was to be crammed with fine ladies, the greatest of the Court. By and by comes the King and Queen, the Duke and Duchess, and all the great ones; and after seating themselves, the King takes out the Duchess of York, and the Duke the Duchess of Buckingham, the Duke of Monmouth my Lady Castlemaine, and so other lords and other ladies, and they danced the 'Brantle.' * After that, the King led a lady a single 'Coranto;'† and then the rest of the lords, one after another, other ladies; very noble it was, and great pleasure to see. Then to country dances, the King leading the first, which he called for, which was, says he, 'Cuckolds, all away,' the old dance of England. Of the ladies that danced, the Duke of Monmouth's mistress, and my Lady Castlemaine, and a daughter of Sir Henry de Vic's, were the best. The manner was, when the King danced, all the ladies in the room, and the Queen herself stood up, and, indeed, his Majesty dances easily and much better than the Duke of York. Thus ends this year," proceeds Pepys. "Public matters stand thus. The King is bringing, as is said, his family and navy, and all other his charges, to a less expense. In the mean time, himself following his pleasures more than with good advice he would do, at least, to be seen to all the world to do so. His dalliance with my Lady Castlemaine being public ever day, to his great reproach, and his favouring of none at court so much as those that are the confidants of his pleasure, as Sir H. Bennett and Sir Charles Barkeley, which good God put it into his heart to mend, before he makes himself too much contemned by his people for it. * * * He sups, at least, four times every week with my Lady Castlemaine, and most often stays till the morning with her, and goes home through the garden all alone, privately, and that so as the very sentries take notice of it and speak of it." The public loudly condemned these shameful doings of the King and his paramour. But Charles disregarded the clamours of the people, and carried her with him to Windsor, where, with his profligate Court, he celebrated the festival of St. George with unusual magnificence, in honour of the Duke of Monmouth's marriage with Lady Anne Scott, heiress of Buccleugh. "I did hear," says Pepys, "that the Queen is much grieved of late at the King's neglecting her, he not having supped with her this quarter of a year. She was at Windsor, at the St. George's feast there [April the twenty-third, 1663], and the Duke of Monmouth, dancing with her, with his hat in his hand, the King came in and kissed him, and made him put on his

* A cheerful dance resembling a cotillion.

† A slow dance, in three-quarter time.

hat, which everybody took notice of; indeed, Monmouth is in so great splendour at Court, and so dandled by the King, that some doubt that if the King should have no child by the Queen, which there is yet no appearance of, whether he would not be acknowledged for a lawful son."

CHAPTER II.

Katherine bears her wrongs with meekness—The legality of her marriage challenged—Her monies withheld from her—Her correspondence with the Pope—Charles neglects Castlemaine for Frances Stuart—Katherine seeks health at Tunbridge Wells—The King's amours with Castlemaine and others, continue—Her Majesty grows worse—Becomes dangerously ill—Afflicting interview between her and Charles—She recovers—The King again neglects her for his lemans—Castlemaine turns Catholic—Katherine's Master of her Horse dismissed against her will—Her economy—She visits the fleet at Chatham—Retires from London, on account of the Plague—Miscarries—Goes in mourning for the death of her Mother—Again visits Tunbridge Wells—Charles's amours with Nell Gwynn and Mrs. Davis commence—The Fire of London—Fashions at Court—Queen's birthday.

ATHERINE continued to bear her wrongs with meekness; she abstained from all political intrigue, continually studied to please her husband, and performed the duties of her exalted station with becoming grace and dignity. The creatures of Castlemaine, in the impeachment against Clarendon, ventured to challenge the legality of her marriage; but the King viewed the act as a personal insult to himself, and silenced them with oaths and frowns. Another annoyance endured by the patient Queen was, that a large portion of her income was withheld from her; a deprivation she bore with, till informed that forty thousand pounds per annum was charged to her account, in the expenses of the crown, laid before Parliament; "when," remarks Pepys, "she took order to let them know, that as yet, she had received for the maintenance of her whole household but four thousand pounds, which is, certainly, a notable act of spirit." The moral courage displayed by Katherine on this occasion, increased the King's respect for her. She accompanied him on his state visit to the City, on the twentieth of May, and he rejoiced with her at the news of the battle of Amexial, a battle which, to her joy, completely established the independence of Portugal, and secured the crown to her family. It was her anxiety for the recognition of the regal rights of her brother and his heirs, that induced her to dispatch Bellings with letters to the Pope, and to several of the Cardinals, urging the Holy See to recognize the independence of Portugal, and expressing an earnest desire for the reestablishment of the papal supremacy in England; an unlawful and unwarrantable proceeding, on which Titus Oates and his confederates probably built their pretended diabolical plots, and which did not escape the notice of her enemies.

"On the tenth of July," writes Samuel Pepys, "Mr. Pierce, the surgeon, tells me that, for certain, the King is grown colder to my Lady Castlemaine than ordinary, and that he believes he begins to love the Queen, and make much more of her than he used to do." Two days afterwards, the same authority states, "On hearing that the King and Queen rode abroad with the ladies of honour to the park, and, seeing a great crowd of gallants staying here to see them return, I also staid walking up and down.

By and by, came the King and Queen, her Majesty attired in a white laced waistcoat and a crimson short pettycoat, with her hair dressed *à la négligence*, looked mighty pretty; and the King rode hand in hand with her. Here was also my Lady Castlemaine, riding among the rest of the ladies, but the King took, methought, no notice of her; and when she alighted, no one pressed as she seemed to expect, and staid for to take her down; so she was taken down by her own gentlemen. She looked mighty out of humour, and had a yellow plume in her hat, which all took notice of, and yet it is very handsome; but, very melancholy, nobody spoke to her, nor did she so much as smile or speak to any body. I followed them up into Whitehall, and into the Queen's presence, where all the ladies walked, talking, and fiddling with their hats and feathers, and changing and trying one another's, by one another's heads, and laughing. But it was the finest sight to me. considering their great beautys and dress, that ever I did see in all my life. But, above all, Frances Stuart in this dress, with her hat cocked, and a red plume, with her sweet eye, little Roman nose, and excellent *taille*, is now the greatest beauty I ever saw, I think, in my life. And if ever woman can, does exceed my Lady Castlemaine, at least in this dress; nor do I wonder if the King changes, which I verily believe is the reason of his coldness to my Lady Castlemaine." Charles, however, could not, or would not, immediately, cast off his imperious mistress. On the twenty-second of July, writes our author, "Captain Ferrers tells me that my Lady Castlemaine is now as great again as ever she was, and that her going away was only a fit of her own, upon some slighting words of the King; so, that she called for her coach at a quarter of an hour's warning, and went to Richmond; and the King, the next morning, under pretence of going a hunting, went to see her and make friends, and never went a hunting at all. After which she came back to Court, and commands the King as much as ever, and hath and doth what she will. No longer ago than last night, there was a private entertainment made for the King and Queen, at the Duke of Buckingham's, and she was not invited; but, being at my Lady Suffolk's, her aunt's, she was heard to say, 'Well, much good may it do them, and for all that, I will be as merry as they;' and so she went home, and caused a great supper to be prepared. And, after the King had been with the Queen at Wallingford House, he came to my Lady Castlemaine's, and was there all night, and my Lord Sandwich with him. Ferrers tells me, 'he believes, that as soon as the King can get a husband for Frances Stuart, my Lady Castlemaine's nose will be out of joint, for that she comes to be in great esteem, and is more handsome than she.'"

The degradations and annoyances to which the Queen was subjected by her selfish and inconstant lord, impaired her health. For recovery, she resolved, by the advice of her physicians, to visit the Wells of Tunbridge. Poverty however prevented herfrom so doing till the close of July, when the King accompanied her thither; not, it is said, out of conjugal affection, but because he was enamoured of the beautiful Frances Stuart, who was in attendance on her Majesty as maid of honour. After a month's sojourn at Tunbridge, their Majesties went on a progress to Bath, Oxford, and other places in the Western and Midland counties, and returned, with the Court to Whitehall, in the first week of October. The Tunbridge waters and country air effected no improvement on the health of Katherine; her malady was not bodily, but mental. It sprung from the conjugal inconstancy of the King, who declared he could not, but who, in truth, would not, remain true to his spouse. "My Lady Castlemaine, I hear," writes Pepys, "is in as great favour as ever; the King supped with her the very first night he came from Bath; when there being a chine of beef to roast, and the tide of the Thames rising into their kitchen, so that it could not be roasted there, and the cook telling her of it, she answered; 'Zounds! she must set the house on a fire, but it shall be roasted.' So it was carried to the house of Mrs. Sarah's husband, and there rested." A few days after her return to Whitehall, Katherine's illness assumed the form of a dangerous fever. Her death was hourly expected, which so affected Charles, that, hastening to her bedside, he threw himself on his knees, bitterly wept, confessed he had wronged her, and implored her to live for his sake. Katherine mingled her tears with his, expressed herself ready and willing to die, and leave all the world but him; and assured him that, from her heart, she forgave him. The scene was heart-rending,—doleful cries and lamentations burst from all present; and at last, when the King was on the point of fainting, his attendants removed him by force to an adjoining chamber.

The progress of Katherine's illness is thus chronicled by Pepys:—"October the seventeenth. Some discourse of the Queen's being very sick, if not dead, the Duke and Duchess of York being sent for betimes, this morning, to come to Whitehall to her.—Nineteenth. I hear that the Queen did sleep five hours pretty well to night, and that she waked and gargled her mouth, and to sleep again; but that her pulse beats fast, beating twenty to the King's, or my Lady Suffolk's eleven; but not so strong as it was. It seems she was so ill as to be shaved, to have pidgeons put to her feet, and to have the extreme unction given her by the priests, who were so long about it, that the doctors were angry. The King, they all say, is fondly disconsolate for her, and weeps by her, which makes her weep, which one this day told me he reckoned a good sign, for that it carries away some rheume from the head.—Twentieth. Mrs. Sarah tells me that the Queen's sickness is the spotted fever; that she is as full of spots as a leopard; and that the King doth seem to take it much to heart, for that he hath wept before her; but, for all that, he hath not missed one night since she was sick, of supping with my Lady Castlemaine, which I believe is true; for she says that her husband hath dressed the suppers every night; and I confess I saw him, myself, coming through the street, dressing up a great supper to-night, which Sarah says is also for the King; which is a very strange thing.—Twenty-second. This morning, hearing that the Queen grows worse again, I sent to stop the making of my velvet cloak, till I see whether she lives or dies.—Twenty-third. The Queen slept pretty well last night, but the fever continues upon her still. It seems she hath never a Portuguese doctor here.—Twenty-fourth. The Queen is in a good way of recovery, and Sir Francis Prujean hath got great honour by it, it being all imputed to his cordial, which, in her despair, did give her rest, and brought her to some hopes of recovery.—Twenty-sixth. Dr. Pierce tells me that the Queen is in a way to be pretty well again, but that her delirium in her head continues still, that she talks idle, not by fits, but always, which in some lasts a week after so high a fever, in some more, and in some for ever; that this morning she talked mightily that she was brought to bed, and that she was troubled that her boy was but an ugly boy. But the King being by, to please her, said, 'No, it is a very pretty boy;' 'Nay,' said she, 'if it be like you, it is a fine boy indeed, and I would be very well pleased with it.'—Twenty-seventh. Mr. Coventry, to-day, tells me that the Queen had a very good night last night, but yet it is strange that she still raves, and talks of little more than her children, and fancies that she hath three children, and that the girls are very like the King. And this morning, about five o'clock, the physician feeling her pulse, thinking to be better able to judge, she being still and asleep, waked her, and the first words she said were, 'How do the children?'—Thirty-first. The Queen continues light-headed, but hopes are entertained of her recovery.—November four. She is mending apace. —Tenth. I hear she is now well again, and that she hath bespoken a new gown."

The King's affection for Katherine during her illness appears to have ceased the moment he learned she was out of danger; and no sooner had she recovered, than he openly devoted himself to the fair Frances Stuart. "On the ninth of November," Pepys observes, that "the King is now become enamoured with Mistress Stuart; he gets into corners, and will be with her half an hour together, kissing her, to the observation of all the world; and she now stays by herself, and expects it as my Lady Castlemaine did use to do, to whom the King is still kind, so as to now and then go to her, but with no such fondness as he used to shew." Castlemaine, perceiving that the King's affection for her was on the decline, artfully paved the way for a reconciliation with her ill-used husband, by embracing the Catholic faith. "I hear for certain," says the gossiping Pepys, "that my Lady Castlemaine is turned papist, which the Queen for all does not much like, thinking that she does it not for conscience' sake." She was madly jealous of Francis Stuart, her young rival in the King's affections—a bitter sentiment she took every opportunity, public as well as private, of displaying to the full. Very different was the conduct of the meek, but shamefully slighted Queen, at this period. "Mr. Pierce told me," remarks the previously quoted contemporary, "how the King still doats upon his women, even beyond all shame; and that the good Queen will of herself stop before she goes into her dressing-room, till she knows whether the King be there, for fear he should be, as she hath sometimes surprised him, with Frances Stuart; and that some of the best part of the Queen's jointure are contrary to faith, and, against the opinion of my Lord Treasurer and his council, bestowed or rented, I know not how, to my Lord Fitz-Harding, Frances Stuart, and other members of that crew." Another indignaity put upon Katherine, was the dismissal by the King of Mr. Montague, the master of her horse, in May. "His fault, I perceive," remarks our quaint author, "was his pride, and most of all, his affecting to be great with the Queen; and it seems, indeed, he had more of her care than anybody else, and would be with her talking alone two or three hours together, insomuch that the lords about the King, when he would be jesting with them about their wives, would tell the King that he must have a care of his wife too, for she hath now a gallant; and they say the King himself did once ask Montague how his mistress, meaning the Queen, did. He grew so proud, and despised everybody, besides suffering nobody, he or she, to get or do anything about the Queen,—that they all laboured to do him a good turn. They all say that he did give some affront to the Duke of Monmouth, which the King himself did speak to him of. But strange it is, that this man should, from the greatest negligence in the world, come to be the miracle of attendance, so as to take all offices from everybody, either men or women, about the Queen." Her Majesty was so grieved at his discharge, that she would admit no one else to his office till after his death, which took place in 1665.

Unlike the pomp-loving King and his mistresses, who in splendour rivalled the fabled princes of the east, and decorated their apartments with all that luxury could devise, or wealth procure, Katherine observed a rigid economy, and, in private as well as public, avoided extravagant magnificence and ostentatious display. To her simplicity of taste in the furniture and fittings of her private apartments, Pepys bears evidence in the following words:—

"June twenty-fourth, 1664. To Whitehall; and Mr. Pierce showed me the Queen's bed-chamber, and her closet, where she had nothing but some pretty pious pictures and books of devotion; and her holy water at the head, as she sleeps with a clock by her bedside, wherein a lamp burns that tells her the night. Thence he carried me to the King's closet, which was decorated with such a variety of pictures, and other things of value and rarity, that I was properly confounded, and enjoyed no pleasure in the sight of them, which is the only time in my life that ever I was at a loss for pleasure in the greatest plenty of objects to give it me."

On the fourth of July, 1664, the King took Katherine and his mother, Henrietta Maria, to view the fleet at Chatham, before it sailed on its voyage of hostility against Holland. The sight so pleased the Queen, that in the subsequent October she went to Woolwich to see a ship launch, which is thus mentioned by the observant Pepys: "At Woolwich. There up to the King and Duke [of York]. Here I staid about with them while the ship was launched, which was done with very good success, and the King did very much like the ship, saying she had the best bow that ever he saw. But Lord, the sorry talk and discourse among the great courtiers round about him, without any reverence in the world, but with so much disorder. By and by, the Queen comes, with her maids of honour, one thereof, Mistress Baynton, and the Duchess of Buckingham, had been very sick, coming by water, in the royal barge, the water being very rough; but what silly sport he made with them in very common terms, methought was very poor, and below what people think these people say and do."

The rejoicings for the victory obtained over the Dutch by the Duke of York, on the third of June, 1665—the most glorious action hitherto fought by the navy of England—were deeply depressed by the terrible visitation of the great plague,* which filled all hearts with awe, and which increased so rapidly in Westminster, that on the twenty-ninth of June, the King, Queen, and court removed to Hampton Court; but as the plague followed them thither, they, on the twenty-seventh of July, departed for Salisbury. On this occasion the Queen and her ladies affected a new travelling costume. Pepys, who saw them set out, remarks: "It was pretty to see the young pretty ladies dressed like men, in velvet coats, caps with ribbons, and with laced bands, just like men. Only the Duchess of York, who has lately grown too fat to be graceful, it did not become." As the air of Salisbury disagreed with the King, and as one of the grooms died there of the plague, the court removed to Oxford, where, on the tenth of October, the King opened parliament, who voted him a supply of one hundred thousand pounds, for carrying on the war against the Dutch. The King removed to Hampton Court in January, 1666; the Queen, being enceinte, remained at Oxford, as it was fondly hoped, till she had presented her husband with an heir; but, unfortunately, she miscarried, and when she joined the King in February, it was only to be frowned upon by him, and to be derided by Lady Castlemaine, who had just presented him with a fine boy, and who maliciously insinuated that Katherine was incapable of bringing him an heir. In March, the Queen received the mournful tidings of the death of her beloved mother, Donna Luiza, widow of John the Fourth, of Portugal. The court went in deep mourning on this occasion; all the ladies were ordered to wear black, with their hair plain, and without patches on their face; "a mode of dress," says a contemporary, "in which Lady Castlemaine appears quite an ordinary woman, and nothing like so pretty as Frances Stuart." "In June," remarks Pepys, "the Queen, in ordinary talk before the ladies in her drawing-room, did say to my Lady Castlemaine that she feared the King did take cold by staying so late abroad at her house. She answered before them all, that he did not stay so late abroad with her, for he went betimes thence, though he did not before one, two, or three in the morning, but must stay somewhere else. The King then coming in, and hearing her, did whisper in her ear aside, and told her she was a bold, impertinent woman, and bid her to be gone out of the court, and not come again till he sent for her: which she did presently, and took a lodging in Pell Mell, and kept there two or three days, and then sent to the King to know whether she might fetch her things away out of her house. The King sent to her she must come and view them, and so she came; and the King went to her, and now they are as great friends as ever. I am told she did in her anger say she would be even with the King, and print his letters to her, a threat which greatly terrified the King." In July, the Queen and her train paid another visit to Tunbridge Wells. Her Majesty, to heighten the pleasure of her sojourn at this fashionable place of resort, sent for the players —an unwise act, followed by a dis-

* See p. 707.

graceful intimacy between Charles and the two actresses, Mrs. Davis and Nell Gwynn, and by the latter being appointed one of the ladies of the chamber to Queen Katherine.

In September, 1666, burst forth that terrible conflagration known in history as the Great Fire of London, and to which many writers believe we owe the complete extinction of the plague. It originated about two on the morning of Sunday, the second of September, at a bakehouse in Pudding Lane, near Fish Street Hill, a confined part of the metropolis, which then consisted only of narrow lanes and passages, and houses principally of wood or lath and plaster, and filled with tar, oil, ropes, and other combustible ship stores. To these buildings it spread with a force and rapidity which defied the power of buckets, and to add to the misfortune, the pipes from the New River were found empty, and the engine which raised water from the Thames was reduced to ashes. The Lord Mayor, who arrived at the spot about an hour after the outburst, was advised to intercept the progress of the flames, by pulling down some of the houses; but he answered, "Lord! what can I do? I am spent, people will not obey me. I have been pulling down houses, but the fire overtakes us faster than we can do it." By eight in the morning it had reached London Bridge, "and there dividing, left enough to burn down all that had been erected on it since the last great fire in 1633, and with the main body pressed forward into Thames Street," which was charged with combustible material, that augmented it very considerably, raging the whole day, and striking the inhabitants with such terror, "that," says Lord Clarendon, "all men stood amazed as spectators, only no man knew what remedy to apply, nor the magistrates what orders to give." Evelyn remarks: "The conflagration was so universal, and the people so astonished, that from the beginning, I know not by what despondency or fate, they hardly stirred to quench it, so that there was nothing heard or seen but crying out and lamentation—running about like distracted creatures, without at all attempting to save even their goods—such a strange consternation there was upon them." The conflagration, which at first took an easterly direction, proceeded so rapidly, that to prevent it reaching the Tower, several houses were pulled down. But the "bright flame," which had raged in that direction all Monday, in the night took other courses. The wind changed, and blew with so great and irresistible violence, that it scattered the fire from pursuing the line that it was in, with all its force, and spread it over the city, so that they who went late to bed at a great distance from any place where the fire prevailed, were awakened before morning with their own house being in a flame. On Monday, Gracechurch Street, and part of Lombard Street, and Fenchurch Street, were in flames; the fire then was burning in the form of a bow—"a dreadful bow," says the Rev. T. Vincent, "such as mine eyes never had before seen." The night of Monday was more dreadful than the preceding one. The destroying element, after spreading westward along the bank of the Thames, as far as Queenhithe, and in a parallel direction to Cornhill and the Royal Exchange, and northward to Dowgate and Watling Street, divided itself into four branches, which united in one great flame at the eastern end of Cheapside. On Tuesday the whole of that street was in flames, and the fire was seen leaping from house to house and street to street, a great distance one from the other. The impetuous flames now reached St. Paul's Cathedral, "the stones of which," says Evelyn, "flew like granados, melting lead, running down the streets in a stream, and the very pavements glowing with a fiery redness so as no horse nor man was able to tread on them, and the demolition had stopped all the passages, so that no help could be applied." The neighbouring streets shared the same fate, and the scene was appalling. "All the sky," proceeds the author just quoted, "was of a fiery aspect, like the top of a burning oven, and the light seen for about forty miles round for many nights. God grant may eyes may never behold the like, now seeing about ten thousand houses all in one flame, the noise and cracking, and thunder of the impetuous flames, the shrieking of women and children, the hurry of people, the fall of towers, houses, and churches, was like an hideous storm; and the air all about so hot and inflamed, that at last one was not able to approach it, so that they were forced to stand still and let the flames burn on, which they did, for near two miles in length and one in breadth. The clouds of smoke were dismal, and reached upon computation near eighty miles in length. Thus I left it this afternoon, bearing a resemblance of Sodom on the last day: London was, but is no more."

But the devouring element still continued to leap from house to house, and street to street, with lawless power; on the day and night of Tuesday, sweeping away Ludgate Hill, the Old Bailey, and the Inner Temple; when the Court at Whitehall, in alarm, caused several houses to be blown up with gunpowder, a plan which saved the palace and Westminster Abbey, and which, if adopted at the commencement of the conflagration, as suggested by some seamen, might have saved half the City; but this, "some tenacious and avaricious men, aldermen and others, would not permit, because their houses must have been the first." On Wednesday morning, the wind, which before blew a hurricane, was hushed to a dead calm, the fire was stayed, and a remnant of London was saved. The first effectual check that the fire encountered, was the brick buildings of the Temple, which were only partly consumed; and although the fire broke out again there on Thursday evening, the Duke of York effectually stopped its progress, by blowing up the neighbouring houses. According to the official gazette of the fire, it laid waste four hundred and thirty-six acres, and was finally stopped "at the Temple Church, near Holborn Bridge, [Giltspur Street, Smithfield], Cripplegate, near the lower end of Coleman Street, at the end of Basinghall Street, at the upper end of Bishopsgate Street and Leadenhall Street, at the Standard, in Cornhill, at the Church in Fenchurch Street, near Clothworkers' Hall, in Union Lane, at the middle of Mark Lane, and at the Tower Dock." Of the six-and-twenty wards, it utterly destroyed fifteen, and left eight others shattered and half burnt. It consumed four hundred streets, thirteen thousand two hundred dwelling-houses, eighty-nine churches, numerous chapels, four of the City gates, the greater part of Guildhall, and numerous public buildings, hospitals, schools, libraries, and other stately edifices. It is calculated that the property destroyed could not be less than ten millions sterling.

Meanwhile, to aggravate the distress of the ruined citizens, the most alarming reports were spread. "It was said, and believed, that men had been seen throwing fire-balls into houses as they passed through the streets, and that the French and the Dutch had combined with the republicans and the papists to destroy the city. These absurd stories increased the general confusion and terror, and those who were laudably labouring to extinguish the flames, or hurrying away with their families and goods to places of safety, were obstructed by the flight of cowards from the imaginary massacre, and the march of the brave, who took up arms to oppose the murderers, and maltreat every foreigner and papist they met with. The most mischievous of these reports was circulated on the Wednesday night; word was conveyed to the distressed inhabitants lying in tents in the neighbouring fields, that "the French were coming armed against them, to cut their throats, and spoil them of what they had saved out of the fire.' Despair roused the citizens, and, fired with indignation, they prepared to defend themselves; but the coming morning dispelled their fears, and brought with it the joyous prospect that the fire was effectually quenched, and that no more calamity threatened them. The King and the Duke of York took an active part in arresting the progress of the flames. "It is not, indeed, imaginable," says Evelyn, "how extraordinary the vigilance and activity of the King and the Duke was, even labouring in person, and being present to command order, reward, or encourage workmen." To this energy, and to a corresponding vigilance on the part of the magistracy and the train bands, must be attributed the circumstance, that so few lives were lost, and so few robberies were committed.

The conduct of the Queen on this distressing occasion is no wherechronicled; but, just after the calamity, it is recorded, she adopted the fashion introduced by two of her maids of honour, which is thus described by Pepys:—"Walking in the galleries at Whitehall, I find the ladies of honour dressed in their riding garbs, with coats and doublets with deep skirts, just for all the world like mine, and buttoned their doublets up the breast, with perriwigs and with hats; so that only for the long petticoat dragging under their men's coats, nobody could take them for women in any point whatever. It was an odd sight, and a sight that did not please me." In October, the writer we have just quoted says, "Pierce tells me that Lady Castlemaine is again about to become a mother, and that the King still intrigues with Frances Stuart, who, he says, is a most good-natured lady. This day the King begins to put on his vest, and I did see several persons of the House of Lords and Commons too, great courtiers, who are in it, being a long cassock close to the body of black cloth, pinked with white silk under it, and a coat over it, and the legs ruffled with black riband, like a pigeon's leg; and, upon the whole, I wish the King may keep it, for it is a very fine and handsome garment." "It, however," remarks Evelyn, "was too good to hold; we could not leave the monsieur's vanities long, so again returned to the fashions of France." About this time, Katherine, having a small well-turned foot, endeavoured to introduce dresses with short skirts; but her effort to set the fashion, like that of the King's, completely failed. The Court beauties being tall and graceful in figure, they preferred wearing flowing draperies, and all other ladies imitated their example.

This year the Queen's birth-day was celebrated by a grand ball at Whitehall; and the court being still in mourning for her Majesty's mother, leave was given to wear silver and white lace on that day. Pepys, who clambered up to a loft, where with much trouble he could view the imposing spectacle, says, "Anon, the house grew full, the candles were lighted, and the King and Queen and all the ladies sat. It was indeed a glorious sight to see Frances Stuart in black and white lace, and her head and shoulders dressed in diamonds and the like, many great ladies more, only the Queen none; and the King in his rich vest of rich silk and silver trimming, as the Duke of York and all the dancers wore some of cloth of silver, and others of other sorts, exceeding rich. Presently, after the King was come in, he took the Queen, and about fourteen more couple there were, and began the *bransles*. * * * After the *bransles*, then to a *corant*, and now and then a French dance; only Mrs. Stuart danced mighty finely, and many French dances, especially one the King called the 'new dance,' which was very pretty; but, upon the whole, the dancing of itself was not extraordinary pleasing, although the clothes and sight of the persons were, indeed, worth my coming, being never likely to see more gallantry while I live, if I should come twenty times. About twelve at night it broke up."

CHAPTER III.

Fall of Clarendon—Killigrew reproves the King—Castlemaine created Duchess of Cleveland—Buckingham offers to kidnap the Queen—Her divorce projected—A precedent established—Charles refuses to dissolve his marriage—Her interview with the Duchess of Orleans—The Duchess of Portsmouth—Frolic at Saffron Walden Fair—Tea—Shaftesbury's futile efforts to divorce Katherine—Arrival of the

Duchess of Mazarin—Scheme to nullify the Queen's marriage—Popish plot scheme, levelled against the Queen and others, creates a general panic—At length checked by the King suddenly dissolving Parliament.

FOR some time it had been rumoured that the King projected a divorce from the Queen, with a view to marry Frances Stuart. Clarendon put faith in the rumour, and deeply offended the enamoured sovereign, by prevailing upon the Duke of Richmond to marry the fair lady. The enemies of the luckless minister took advantage of the circumstance to raise a popular cry against him. They painted on the gate of his mansion a large gibbet, with the following epigram beneath it :—

"Three sights to be seen ;
Dunkirk, Tangiers, and a barren Queen."

And on account of the childless marriage of the King, wrote—

"God bless Queen Kate,
Our Sovereign's mate,
Of the royal house of Lisbon;
But the devil take Hyde,
And the bishop beside,
Who made her bone of his bone."

Katherine, believing that the chancellor suffered persecution chiefly on her account, exerted all her power in his behalf, but without effect, and in the end he was banished the country. For a period after the fall of Clarendon, we hear no more of the Queen's divorce. The King, who condescended to dance with her at a masked ball at Whitehall, in April, 1667, continued to lead a worthless, profligate life. "Mr. Pierce," says Pepys, "did tell me as a great truth, as being told to him by Mr. Abraham Cowley, the poet, who was by and heard it, that Tom Killigrew should publicly tell the King, that his matters were coming into a very ill state, but that yet there was a way to help all. Says he :—'There is a good, honest, able man, that I could name, that if your Majesty would employ, and command to see all things well executed, all things would soon be mended; and this is one Charles Stuart, who now spends his time in employing his lips about the Court; but if you would give him this employment, he were the fittest man in the world to perform it.' This, he says, is most true; but the King, instead of profiting by it, lays all business aside, and attends to nothing but his pleasures, which is a sorrowful consideration."

Another time Mr. Killigrew paid his Majesty a visit in his private apartments, habited like a pilgrim who was bent on a long journey. The King, surprised at the oddity of his appearance, immediately asked him what was the meaning of it, and whither he was going. "To hell," bluntly answered the wag. "Prythee, what can your errand be to that place?" demanded the King. "To fetch back Oliver Cromwell," rejoined he, "that he may take some care of the affairs of England, for his successor takes none at all." It was about this period that a court wit wrote on the chamber door of Charles II.—

"Here lies the mutton-eating King,
Whose word no man relies on ;
Who never said a foolish thing,
Nor ever did a wise one."

Lady Castlemaine's influence still continued. At a court masquerade, she, to outshine the Queen, appeared in jewels, valued at forty thousand pounds. The King, about this time, "paid thirty thousand pounds to clear her debts," and, to gratify her vanity, created her Duchess of Cleveland, with reversion to Charles and George Fitzroy, her children by him. At her earnest entreaty, he released from the Tower, and took again into favour the unprincipled Buckingham, who now strenuously advised him to put away his Queen, whose repeated miscarriages proved that she was incapable of bearing him an heir. Buckingham had offered to steal her Majesty away, and convey her to a distant region, where she would be well cared for, and never more heard of. Charles rejected the project with horror, but he listened with more attention to the suggestion that he should take another wife. He even consulted lawyers and divines; and Dr. Gilbert Burnet, author of the "History of the Reformation," and other works, in two treatises, entitled "Solution of the Two Cases of Conscience, one touching Polygamy, the other Divorce;" decided that, according to Scripture, barrenness in the woman furnished, in certain cases, a lawful cause for polygamy or divorce. The promising state of the Queen, however, prevented further proceedings, till the hopes of her giving an heir to England again proved delusive, when Charles seriously contemplated being divorced from her; and, as no case could be found in which a divorce had been pronounced, pending the lives of the parties, where such parties had been previously legally married, Buckingham undertook to create a precedent. "Lady Ross," says the learned Dr. Lingard, "had long lived in adultery; she had been separated from her husband by a sentence of the ecclesiastical judge, and her children, by her paramour, had been declared illegitimate by act of parliament. A more favourable case could hardly be wished for, and a bill was introduced into the upper house to enable Lord Ross to marry again. Its object instantly transpired, and the royal brothers exerted all their influence, the King to support the Duke of York to oppose the bill. The latter not only obtained the votes of his friends and dependents; but, as the question involved a point of doctrine respecting the indissolubility of marriage, he was joined by all the bishops, with the exception of those of Durham and Chester, by the Catholic peers, and by such of the Protestant peers as deemed it proper to follow, on theological grounds, the opinion of the prelates. The second reading was carried by only a small majority; before the third reading, Charles adopted a measure to animate his friends, which surprised both the house and the nation. One morning he suddenly entered, took his seat on the throne, and desired the lords to proceed as if he were not present, for he came only to renew a custom which his immediate predecessors had allowed to fall into desuetude, that of attending their debates. James, who saw the motive of his brother, was stimulated to more active exertions; and when, on the twenty-eighth of March, 1670, the third reading was carried against him by a majority of two; entered his protest on the journals, in which he was followed by thirteen spiritual and fifteen temporal peers. Buckingham triumphed, and yet he gained nothing by the victory. He served a fickle and uncertain master, who changed his resolution according to the impulse of the moment. Charles had entertained with pleasure the project of divorce, so long as its accomplishment appeared distant; but when the effort was to be made, his sense of justice, perhaps his good nature, assumed the ascendancy, and he refused to avail himself of the benefit, to the prejudice of an unprotected and unoffending female. The precedent, however, has not been lost to posterity; and the permission to marry again, which was, in this instance, granted to Lord Ross, forms the authority for the similar permission, which has since been regularly inserted in bills of divorce."

Whilst these plots were in agitation, Katherine surprised the world by an imitation of the King and his gay crew, plunging into all the mad revels of the Court, attending theatres and masquerades, and going about in masks and other disguises in quest of gay scenes and mirthful adventures. In May 1670, she had the pleasure of making the acquaintance of Charles's sister, Henrietta Maria, Duchess of Orleans; the interview took place at Dover, whither the Duchess had come to conclude the long-pending secret treaty between Louis the Fourteenth and King Charles. By one of the articles of this degrading treaty, Charles undertook to publicly profess himself a Catholic, and by another, he was rendered a pensioner of France. He knew that Louis had bribed the leading personages of the English Court, and had handsomely paid the more potent of the republican party to incite their countrymen to rebellion, and being extravagant and indolent, he preferred receiving from a foreign power supplies which his own subjects would have grudgingly granted, or perhaps boldly refused. A few weeks after her return to France, the Duchess of Orleans died, and, in the subsequent November, the King sent for her favourite, Mademoiselle Querouaille; forced the Queen to accept her as one of her maids of honour, and soon after made her one of his mistresses. "I saw that famous beauty, Mademoiselle Querouaille," remarks Evelyn, "and, in my opinion, she is of a childish, simple, and baby face." She became one of Charles's most rapacious, extravagant ladies, and after bearing him a son, was created Duchess of Portsmouth. Her splendid apartments at Whitehall, were furnished with "ten times the glory and richness of the Queen's, with massive services of plate, and whole tables and stands of incredible value."

On the thirty-first of March, 1671, the Duchess of York died at St James's, having been the mother of eight children, of whom only two daughters reached maturity, Mary and Anne, both afterwards Queens of England. The Queen was present at her death, "but she did not," as Burnet asserts, "prevent Blandford, her Protestant confessor, from administering the sacrament to her;" for the Duke, who was in an adjoining apartment, informed him, that "she had embraced the Catholic faith, and, on that account, he contented himself with making her a short Christian exhortation." Sir Walter Scott, in his notes to Dryden's works, remarks, that "Katherine's greatest fault was, her being educated a Catholic; her greatest misfortune, bearing the King no children; her greatest foible, an excessive love of dancing;" another of her weaknesses, one may add was a love of frolic, which occasionally led her to forget her dignity, and get into rather awkward scrapes. When her Majesty, with the King and the Court, was being magnificently entertained at Audley End, in September, 1671, she and the Duchesses of Richmond and Buckingham went disguised as rustics to Saffron Walden fair, in the neighbourhood; but they so overdid their disguises, that the real rustics, believing them to be a company of strolling players, followed them in a crowd. The Queen went into a booth to purchase a pair of yellow stockings for her sweetheart; one of the customers there recognised her, and immediately the whole fair crowded to gaze on her, and forced her and her party to ride back in dismay to Audley End, as fast as their horses would carry them, with a host of rude horsemen behind them, all eager "to get as much gape as they could." Some writers assert that, that sober beverage tea, was first brought to England by Katherine of Braganza; and, although this must be an error, as, twenty months before her arrival in England, Pepys entered in his Diary, "I did send for a cup of tea, a China drink, of which I never had drunk before;" she was certainly the first tea-drinking Queen of England. She commended its use, and Waller, in his complimentary poem on her marriage, says:—

"The best of Queens, and best of herbs, we owe
To that bold nation who the way did show,
To the far region, where the sun doth rise,
Whose rich productions we so justly prize."

In 1671, the Queen accompanied her husband to Newmarket races; but took no part in the rude, riotous proceedings, in which he and his profligate associates, men and women, then indulged. She, it appears, had but little taste for the polite arts: painting, sculpture, and architecture, owe nothing to her Queenly patronage; and, although entranced by the operatic music of Italy, she found no charm in the matchless compositions of the transcendent Purcell, or in the soul-stirring music in Macbeth.

In 1673, the new Lord Chancellor, Shaftesbury, without even consulting the King, appointed a day for it to be moved in the Commons,—"that for the security of the established religion, the Parliament should request his Majesty to divorce Queen Katherine, and wed a Protestant consort;" but, before the day arrived, it was named to Charles, and he so promptly and forcibly negatived it, that his profligate ministers did not molest the Queen again for about five years. In 1675, the Queen was alarmed by the arrival of the celebrated Hortensia Mancini, Duchess of Mazarin. She came to England in consequence of the intrigues of the Duchess of Portsmouth's enemies, who hoped that the revival of the King's passion for his "old love," might destroy the ascendancy of the reigning favourite. Charles gave her a pension of four thousand pounds a year, and a residence at Chelsea; but she neglected her game, and by engaging in another amour, defeated the object for which she came to England.

Katherine was present at the marriage of William, Prince of Orange, to the Duke of York's eldest daughter, Mary, at Whitehall, on the fourth of November, 1677; she danced at the bridal ball, and took part in the gorgeous festivity that marked the occasion, but she did so with a heavy heart. For more than five years the King had so completely withdrawn himself from her company, that he ceased to live with her, and now he rarely, if ever, spoke to her, except in public. About this time, Shaftesbury, perceiving the paternal fondness of Charles for his natural son, the Duke of Monmouth, resolved to, at one stroke, set him up as a competitor for the crown, in opposition to the Duke of York, and nullify the Queen's marriage. He hinted to his Majesty, that if he would acknowledge he had privately married Lucy Walters, the mother of Monmouth, witnesses could be procured to confirm it with their testimony. But Charles, heavy as his failings were, being too proud and honourable to disown his lawful wife, and unjustly deprive his brother of his right of succession, by bribery and perjury, answered with indignation:—"Much as I love the Duke, I would rather see him hanged at Tyburn, than own him for my legitimate son;" and, shortly afterwards, he, to punish Shaftesbury for his duplicity and treachery, caused him to be ejected from the Privy Council—an act which so annoyed the haughty minister, that he joined the opposition; and in the hope, it is said, of bringing the Queen and the Duke of York to the block, set afloat, or, what seems more probable, supported, and, after a period, urged forward, the horrible imposture known as the Popish or Jesuits' plot.* This plot, forged by Titus Oates, Dr. Tonge, and a chemist named Kirby, was opened by Kirby accosting the King as he was walking in St. James's Park, and, in an under tone, begging his Majesty not to separate from the company, because his life was in danger. The alarming intelligence led to an interview in the evening, when Tonge attended with a written statement, known in history as "The Narrative;" setting forth that the Jesuits in London had organized a conspiracy to murder the King, destroy London by fire, and subvert by force the Protestant religion; and was referred by Charles, who put no faith in his improbable tale, to the Lord Treasurer. Danby, at this period, suspected that the Parliament, which was about to meet, would impeach him of high treason for his ministerial misdoings. Nothing would be more likely to avert the blow, than the agitation which, with management, might be produced by this sham popish plot; besides, he secretly hated the Duke of York. The Duke had lately embraced the Catholic faith, and the measure would, doubtless, add to his unpopularity; these, and other considerations, induced the crafty minister to countenance the conspirators, and magnify their improbable statements. But when he requested to lay "the Narrative" before the Privy Council, Charles hastily exclaimed:—"No, not even before my brother; it would only create alarm, and may, perhaps, put the design of murdering me into the head of some individual, who, otherwise, would never have entertained such a thought." Finding his pretended discovery slighted by the King, and distrusting the intentions of the council, Oates, to compel public attention to the subject, went before Sir Edmondbury Godfrey, and made affidavit to the truth of

* Want of space compels us to confine our details of this pretended plot to the attempts of Oates and his patrons, and accomplices in crime, to fix the charge of treason and murder on the Queen and her servants.

"the Narrative," and denounced certain persons as conspirators. One of the denounced was Godfrey's friend, Coleman. Godfrey, in alarm, instantly wrote, warning him of his danger; and he, without a moment's delay, revealed the secret to the Duke of York, who, believing the plot to be devised against himself, prevailed on the King to institute a strict inquiry as to the truth or falsehood of the informer's statements. Oates was now called before the council, and the assurance with which he delivered his long, thrilling narrative, imposed on many of his hearers; but the King and the Duke of York were more than ever convinced of the imposition. Charles desired Oates to describe Don John, to whom he pretended he had been introduced at Madrid; and, without hesitation, he replied that, "he was a tall, spare, and swarthy man." The King turned to his brother, and smiled, for both knew, from personal acquaintance, that Don John was low of stature, corpulent, and fair of complexion. "And where," said Charles, "did you see La Chaise, the French King's confessor, pay down the ten thousand pounds which you have just stated he subscribed, in furtherance of the plot?" "In the house of the Jesuits, close to the Louvre," boldly answered Oates. "Man alive!" exclaimed the King, provoked at his effrontery, "the Jesuits have no house within a mile of the Louvre." Oates had now completely committed himself; but a lucky incident again restored him to something like credit. Coleman's papers were seized, and amongst them was found a copy of a letter which he had sent to Father La Chaise, proposing that Louis should furnish him with twenty thousand pounds, to be employed in England, to equally further the interests of France and of the Catholic Church. This letter, be it observed, was no proof of his connection with the proclaimed popish plot, but simply an evidence that he was one of the many mercenary agitators of that period. Nevertheless, false evidence was adduced against him; he was tried, convicted, and on the third of December, suffered on the scaffold. In October, whilst the King and Court were absent on pleasure, the public excitement was increased, by a report that Godfrey, before whom Oates had made his affidavit, had been murdered by the Jesuits. He had been missing for five days; his body was found in a dry ditch, on Primrose Hill, resting on the knees, breast, and left side of the face, with a sword, said to be his own, thrust right through it, in the region of the heart, and with a deep purple crease round the neck. Godfrey's death is to the present hour involved in mystery; he was of a melancholic disposition, and, as his father committed suicide, some writers believe that he perished by his own hands; others as confidently assert that he was the victim of the fabricators of the plot; and the people, at the time, insisted upon it, that the Jesuits had assassinated him; and to strengthen this impression, his funeral was conducted with extraordinary pomp and magnificence. The minds of all classes became so inflamed, that the general business of life was interrupted, horrible, but grossly absurd rumours were circulated and believed; and when the public frenzy had reached its height, all was confusion, panic, and clamour.

When the Parliament met, the houses neglected all other business, to listen to the narratives of Oates and Tonge. The hirelings of the King of France were stirring up all conceivable emotion; as, also, were the emissaries of the Prince of Orange, who, with the cry of "No Popery!" earnestly endeavoured to procure the exclusion of the Duke of York from the succession. Danby, to avert his impeachment, joined lustily in the "No Popery" cry. "He fancied," says James the Second, in his Memoirs, "that by crying out against popery, he should pass for a pillar of the Church, and ward the blow which he foresaw was falling on his shoulders; but my Lord Shaftesbury, who soon found out his drift, said, 'Let the Treasurer cry as loud as he pleases against popery, and think to put himself at the head of the plot; I will cry a note louder, and soon take his place.'" Shaftesbury kept his word, through his influence a parliamentary committee was appointed to investigate the matter to the bottom; when, the popular party being greatly in the majority, Oates was pronounced the saviour of his country, rewarded for his infamy with a pension of one thousand two hundred pounds per year, and encouraged to denounce all the Catholic peers who would be likely to oppose the condemnation of the Queen and the Duke of York.

Although, since the pretended popish plot was brought before the public, several persons had, on the unsupported evidence of Oates, been sent to prison and interrogated, no prosecution was instituted; because, to establish the guilt of the accused, the law required the concurrent testimony of two witnesses. The first week in November, this difficulty was overcome; William Bedloe, a felon who had just been discharged from Newgate, in the hope of obtaining the reward, protection, and free pardon offered by royal proclamation to the discoverer of the assassins of Sir Edmondbury Godfrey, came forward, and declared upon oath, that the assassination had been committed at Somerset House, where the Queen lived, by Le Fevre and Walsh, two Jesuits, by Belasyse, a gentleman, and by a waiter in the Queen's chapel, who stifled their victim between two pillows; that the body lay for two days on the Queen's back stairs; that he had been offered two thousand guineas to assist in removing it, and that at last it was carried away on Monday night by three of the Queen's people. Five days afterwards, he deposed, "that in the beginning of October, he had been offered four thousand pounds to commit a murder; that Godfrey was inveigled into the court of Somerset House about five o'clock, and murdered on the spot;" but he now recollected that the magistrate was not, as he had previously deposed, stifled between pillows—that story was contradicted by the appearance of the corpse—but strangled with a linen cravat. He pointed out to the Duke of Monmouth the room where he asserted the body was deposited, and stated that he saw standing round it the four assassins, and Atkins, clerk to Mr. Pepys of the Admiralty. But, unfortunately for the plausibility of this tale, he had fixed the time of the murder at the very hour when the King was on a visit to her Majesty at Somerset House; an hour when such an atrocious act would have been discovered on the instant by the guards, the sentinels, or the numerous court attendants; and the place where he stated the body had been concealed, was the room appropriated to the use of the Queen's footmen, who were there in waiting from morning till night Bedloe's incredible deposition was disbelieved by Charles, who pronounced him a great rogue; but the excited public hailed it as a confirmation of that of Oates; and at last, such was the effrontery of this new impostor, such the treachery of the popular leaders, that although on his first examination he had sworn that he knew nothing whatever of Oates or his trumped-up plot, he now found it convenient to forget that he had ever so stated, and to make all his depositions harmonize with his brother informer. The excitement still continued, and was fomented by the baseness or credulity of the popular leaders; the Parliament deprived the Catholic peers of their seats; it was rumoured, and generally believed, that Godfrey was murdered by the Queen's desire; and Oates at last resolved to accuse the Queen of a design to poison the King. To accomplish this daring purpose, Mrs. Elliot, the wife of one of the gentlemen of the King's bed-chamber, waited on his Majesty, and solicited a private audience for Oates, who desired to impart some important information, tending to criminate the Queen. Charles heard her with impatience and incredulity; and when she hinted at a divorce, told her he would never abandon an innocent woman. A dread of being denounced as a Catholic, and perhaps deposed by his excited subjects, prevented Charles from strenuously opposing the popular delusion. Oates, therefore, obtained the desired audience, and was afterwards examined by Secretary Coventry, and by the Privy Council. He stated, that in the preceding July, he saw a letter, in which it was affirmed by Wakeman, her Majesty's Catholic physician, that the Queen had been prevailed upon to sanction the murder of the King; and that, a few weeks afterwards, he went with several Jesuits to Somerset House, and there waited in the anti-chamber, whilst the Queen gave them audience. They left the door ajar; he listened, and heard a female voice exclaim, "I will no longer suffer such indignities to my bed! I am content to join in procuring his death, and the propagation of the Catholic faith." When the Jesuits came out, he peered into the room, and saw no one there but a woman, whom he took to be the Queen. The King, convinced that this story was a fabrication, insisted on Oates pointing out the room and anti-chamber which he had described. The impostor traversed Somerset House "through and through;" and at last, being unable to fix upon a place, excused himself, on the plea that "his memory was fickle." Bedloe, undismayed by this blunder of his coadjutor in crime, came forward as a witness to support his testimony. He swore that he had witnessed a conference at Somerset House, between the Queen and two French clergymen, in the presence of Lord Belasyse, Coleman, and some Jesuits; and was afterwards informed by Coleman, that at the first proposal of the King's murder, Katherine burst into tears; but that the reasonings of the French Jesuits had prevailed over her objections, and that she had reluctantly signified her consent. In reply to the question, why he had not imparted this startling evidence before? he answered, that "it had escaped his memory;" and the majority in Parliament believed, or affected to believe him.

As the plot thickened, the memory of Oates also continued to improve. He affirmed that Wakeman had agreed with Father Harcourt, for a reward of fifteen thousand pounds, five thousand of which he had received in advance, to prepare a certain poison, which the Queen was to administer to the King. And on the twenty-eighth of November, immediately after Bedloe had delivered his deposition to the House of Commons, he advanced to the bar, raised his voice, and exclaimed, "I, Titus Oates, accuse Katherine, Queen of England, of high treason!" The members not in the secret were amazed and dumbfounded; and before they could recover from their consternation, the House voted an address to the King for the removal of the Queen and her household from Whitehall, and sent a message to the Lords, soliciting their concurrence; but the Lords, instead of immediately seconding this hasty vote of the Commons, examined Oates and Bedloe, and, dissatisfied with their evidence, refused to brand their Queen as a traitress, and appointed a committee to state the reasons of their refusal. Shaftesbury and two others protested against this vote; but the majority had the prudence and the decency to acquiesce, and instead of proceeding with the charge against the Queen, prepared an address to the King, for the apprehension of all Catholics within the kingdom, and, upon the unsupported testimony of the base Oates and Bedloe, impeached five of the principal Catholic lords. By this time so powerful had become the agitating faction, that Charles, resolved as he was to shield Katherine from their merciless grasp, found it impossible to extend the royal protection to their numerous other victims. Thirty thousand Catholics were mercilessly driven out of London; every day some innocent but unfortunate creature was arrested, and afterwards executed in opposition to all law and justice. The Queen fully expected to be brought to the block, but the King swore that she should not be sacrificed; and, to convince her enemies that he was in earnest, sent for her to live with him at Whitehall, and treated her with the most marked attention and respect. "He said to me," remarks Burnet, "that considering his faultiness towards her in other things, he thought it a horrible thing to abandon her."

The venal agitators had driven the Duke of York from the board of the Privy Council, and although foiled in their efforts to impeach the Queen of treason, they paved the way for another attempt, by inducing Bedloe to denounce Miles Prance, silversmith to her Majesty, as one of the murderers of Sir Edmondbury Godfrey. Prance was hurried to Newgate, and there accused, threatened, and at last, under a promise of pardon, induced to confess himself guilty, and name as his accomplices, Hill, Green, and Berry, three of the Queen's inferior domestics at Somerset House, who were arrested, tried, and, despite their earnest protestations of innocence, condemned and executed, in February, 1678. Prance, stung with remorse at having accused three innocent men of murder, desired to be brought before the King and council, and on his knees protested that his accusation was false, for he knew nothing of the murder or the murderers. He was remanded to Newgate, chained to the floor in the condemned cell, and driven almost to madness by the harshness of his keeper, Boyce, who assured him that he would be hanged if his statements did not agree with Bedloe's evidence, and at last cajoled him into confessing the "manner and circumstances of the murder, the pretended conspiracy to assassinate the Earl of Shaftesbury, and the vile practices of several popish priests." He in the end became one of Oates' suborned witnesses.

In 1679, the King, to gratify and appease the people and the Parliament, ordered the Duke of York to withdraw to the continent. The Duke complied; but as Shaftesbury had flattered Monmouth—the King's natural son—with the hope of succeeding to the crown, and as the story of a contract of marriage passed between Charles and Monmouth's mother, had been spread abroad and believed by the people generally, the King, at the request of the Duke and the Queen, issued a proclamation, in which he solemnly declared that "he had never been married, nor contracted to any woman whatsoever, but to his wife, Queen Katherine." At this period the Queen fully expected that her enemies would succeed in their efforts to bring her to the block; but, whilst glorying in their success, they experienced a severe and unexpected reverse. Sir George Wakeman, the Queen's physician, and Marshall, Rumby, and Corker, three Jesuits who together were indicted on the charge of conspiring with the Queen to take the King's life, were acquitted, and Oates and Bedloe, their accusers, reduced to the necessity of defending themselves from the imputation of perjury. On this trial, the judge, the Lord Chief Justice Scroggs, who had hitherto exaggerated the plot, and browbeat the prisoners, delivered a favourable charge to the jury, which so irritated Oates and Bedloe, that they accused him to his face of partiality, declared that they would never more give evidence in any court in which he presided, and exhibited articles against him before the council. In August, an alarming fever confined the King to his bed; and the popish plot agitators affirmed, and the people believed, that he had been poisoned. Immediately the symptoms of his malady became alarming, he sent for the Duke of York from Brussels. The Duke lost not a moment; but before he reached Windsor, the King was convalescent. In September, the King, Queen, and the whole court, made a progress to Newmarket, and in the subsequent August, Katherine's false accuser, Bedloe, was stopped in his iniquitous career by the hand of death. He expired at Bristol; and just previously sent for the Chief Justice North, and before him and several others, declared that all the evidence which he had given regarding the popish plot was true; but when North was about to retire, he called him aside, and immediately all had left the room but his wife and North's clerk, swore that the Queen had given money for the propagation of the Catholic faith, but was, as far as he knew, ignorant of any plot against the King's life. Katherine was still persecuted by her enemies, but all their efforts failed to implicate her in the crimes of murder and high treason. When Francisco de Feria accused the Portuguese ambassador of having offered him a reward to murder Shaftesbury, Oates, and Bedloe, the attempt to make a case against her Majesty signally failed; which so annoyed Shaftesbury, that in November, on the bill for the exclusion of the Duke of York, being thrown out by the Lords, he proposed what he described as "the sole remaining chance for the security of liberty and religion;" a bill of divorce, which, by separating the King from

Katherine, might enable him to marry a Protestant princess, and leave the crown to his legitimate issue. The Earls of Essex and Salisbury, and the Lord Howard of Escrick, warmly supported the motion. But the King refused to relinquish his innocent consort, as a prey to a murderous faction; and by openly soliciting the votes of the peers against the measure so intimidated its originators, that it was abandoned, and never again brought forward.

The Queen witnessed, from a private box in Westminster Hall, the trial of Lord Stafford. The unfortunate lord was pelted and hooted at by the rabble, treated with gross injustice and indignity by the Court, accused by Oates and others of being one of the popish plot conspirators; and, although the evidence of his accusers was gross and groundless, found guilty, condemned, and on the twenty-ninth of December, 1680, beheaded on Tower Hill. Early in 1687, the reputation of Katherine was attacked by the false accusation of a new informer in the popish plot scheme. Fitzharris, a pensioner of the Duchess of Portsmouth, and a tool of the Shaftesbury faction, came forward, and after accusing the Duke of York and the Catholics of high crimes and misdemeanours, charged the Queen with an intent to poison the King. Charles, annoyed at the daring of the patrons of the plot, resolved to thwart their purpose. Having summoned Parliament to meet at Oxford, on the twenty-first of March, he and his consort left Windsor on the fourteenth, and were escorted to the city of learning by a troop of horse-guards, and with all conceivable pomp. Throughout the journey they were greeted with joyful acclamations, and on their arrival the bells rang, bonfires blazed, the people hailed them with loyal enthusiasm, and the University and the Corporation welcomed them with addresses, banquets, balls, and rejoicings. The King had entered Oxford but three days, when Shaftesbury, at the head of the popular party, arrived, in rival magnificence, themselves, armed and attended by a powerful force of armed men, wearing round their hats a ribbon, with the inscription—"No popery, no slavery." Charles opened the Parliament in person; but as the Whigs,* the name by which the popular party was now known, were bent upon using Fitzharris and his falsehoods, to keep alive the popular excitement, and, if possible, to effect the destruction of the Queen and the Duke of York, the King resolved upon the bold step of dissolving the Parliament, after it had set but six days. The majority in the Commons believing that the sessions would be long, and victory certain, resolved, in opposition to the known desire of his Majesty, that Fitzharris, instead of being tried for high treason in the Court of King's Bench, should be impeached, that they might draw from him certain statements which they could use against the Queen, the Duke, or those immediately connected with them. They sent a message, to this effect, to the Lords, and were answered, "that their Lordships had resolved that Fitzharris should be proceeded with according to the course of common law, and not by way of impeachment in Parliament." The Commons, in retaliation, voted this resolution of the Lords "an obstruction to the further discovery of the popish plot," and ordered that bills should be immediately brought in for the further exclusion of papists. This order was voted on the Saturday; and on the subsequent Monday, Charles hastened in a sedan chair, followed by a second chair, carrying the royal robes to the House of Lords. He entered, unattended, took his seat upon the throne, and having caused the Commons to be summoned into his presence, told them that "proceedings which had began with violent dissensions between the two houses, could not end in good;" and immediately, the Chancellor, by his command, declared the Parliament dissolved. As the King had kept his intentions a profound secret, they were struck dumb with surprise; and before they had time to rally, Charles and Katherine entered

* It was about this period that the appellation of Whig and Tory became permanently affixed to the two great political parties, which for a century and a-half had divided the nation.

their carriages, and, escorted by the royal guard, drove off to Windsor, with a precipitation which gave birth to a belief that this hasty dissolution had been provoked by the discovery that the enemies of the Court had conspired against his person. The next day, their Majesties proceeded to Whitehall.

"This vigorous measure," remarks an esteemed historian, "though it might have been foreseen, astonished the patrons of the plot, deprived them of all spirit, and reduced them to absolute despair. They were sensible, though too late, that the King had taken his final resolution, and was determined to endure any extremity, rather than submit to those terms which they had resolved to impose upon him. They found that he had patiently waited till affairs should come to full maturity, and having now engaged a national party on his side, had boldly set his opponents at defiance. No Parliament, they knew, would be summoned for some years, and during that long interval the Court, though, perhaps, at the head of an inferior party, yet being possessed of all authority, would have every advantage over a body dispersed and disunited. These reflections crowded on every one, and all the exclusionists were terrified, lest Charles should immediately take revenge on them for their long and obstinate opposition to his measures. The King, on his part, was no less apprehensive, lest despair might prompt them to have recourse to force, and make some sudden attempt on his person; both parties, therefore, hurried from Oxford, and, in an instant, that city, so crowded and busy, was left in its usual emptiness and tranquillity."

By the order of Charles, Fitzharris was brought to trial in the Court of King's Bench, for high treason. The Court pronounced him guilty; and to save himself, he confessed, upon oath, to the council that Treby, the Recorder, and Bethel and Cornish, the Sheriffs, had induced him to accuse the Queen and the Duke of York, and that Lord Howard was the real author of the libel for which he stood condemned. But these efforts availed him not. Charles resolved that he should die, and he was executed on the first of July. With him suffered the innocent Oliver Plunket, the titular Archbishop of Armagh, and the last of the victims sacrificed to the imposture of the Popish Plot. The Earl of Essex, who had been Lord Lieutenant of Ireland, earnestly solicited the King to pardon the aged Plunket, declaring that, "from his own knowledge, the charge against him could not be true;" but Charles indignantly replied: "Then, my lord, be his blood on your own conscience; you might have saved him, if you would. I cannot pardon him, because I dare not." This too was the true state of the case; indeed, had the Merry Monarch been endowed with an ordinary amount of moral courage and energy, the Popish Plot agitation scheme would have been destroyed in the embryo, instead of being allowed to grow up to a giant bogie, for cunning, unprincipled statesmen and impostors to frighten the nation with.

CHAPTER IV.

Imprisonment and fall of Shaftesbury, the leader of the Popish Plot Patrons—The Queen sues her Treasurer for the arrears of her income—Waller's complimentary stanzas to her—Meal-Tub and Rye-House Plots—Russell and Sidney executed—Remarkable Frost—Katherine's birth-day—Death of King Charles the Second—Advancement of the nation during his reign—His children—His loss bewailed by Katherine—Her kindness to Monmouth—She requests, and obtains, Don Pedro's permission to return to Portugal—Verifies the birth of the Prince of Wales—Is insulted by Mary the Second—Returns to Portugal—Is honoured and respected by the Portuguese—Nominated Queen Regent—Her last illness—Death—Pompous funeral—Prayed for in England as Queen Dowager—Will.

THE decay of the popish plot scheme encouraged the Court party to institute proceedings against Shaftesbury. Six Irish witnesses accused him of having suborned them to give false testimony against the Queen, the Duke of York, the Lord Lieutenant, and the Lord Chancellor of Ireland. He was committed, and, on his road to the Tower, hooted by the same rabble that had before assailed his victims on their way to trial and execution, with hisses and yells. However, the grand jury ignored the bill against him ; but the publication of his papers shortly afterwards, exposed his base intentions, and deprived him for ever of all influence and popularity.

In 1682, the Queen, whose income since the death of Charles's mother, Henrietta Maria, amounted to about fifty thousand pounds per year, was greatly straitened in purse, on account of her monies not having been duly paid to her, as they fell due, by the government. She considered her treasurer greatly at fault in the matter, and even had the weakness to institute law proceedings against him for the arrears ; but, of course, he was neither in law nor reason accountable for the deficiencies of her receipts.

On New Year's Day, 1683, Waller dedicated to the Queen the subjoined complimentary stanzas :—

" What revolutions in the world hath been,
How are we changed since first we saw the Queen :
She, like the sun, does still the same appear,
Bright as she was at her arrival here ;
Time has commission mortals to impair,
But things celestial is obliged to spare.
May every new year find her still the same,
In health and beauty, as she hither came ;
When Lords and Commons, with united voice,
The infanta named, approved the choice ;
First of our Queens, whom not the King alone,
But the whole nation lifted to the throne."

After alluding to the victories obtained by the Polish King, John Sobieski, over the Turks, the poet thus concludes :—

" His conduct wins the day,
And her example chases vice away ;
Though louder fame attend the martial rage,
'Tis greater glory to reform the age."

Unfortunately, excellent as was the example set by Katherine, it was devoid of the power to " chase vice away" from the licentious Court, or to reform the age, a glory erroneously attributed to it by the high-minded poet. Charles, it is true, had paid great attention to his consort since the shafts of the Popish Plot impostor had been levelled against her ; but, alas ! for humanity ! he still continued to gratify his partiality for his mistresses, with whom he openly toyed and flirted, in public as well as in private. The King's conduct was imitated by his obsequious courtiers, and in the end, despite the worthy example of the despised Queen, virtue was openly reproached at Court as a thing to be despised.

With the Meal-Tub plot, the Rye-House plot, and the various other conspiracies, sham and real, set afloat at this era of popular excitement and delusion, we have nothing to do, not one of them being directed against, nor in any way supported by Katherine. The Rye-House conspirators intended to murder the King and the Duke of York as they returned from Newmarket; but an accidental fire at the King's mansion there, forced the royal brothers to come to London two days before the appointed time, and thus they escaped the threatened danger. It was for this conspiracy that Lord William Russell and Algernon Sidney were beheaded; the former on the twenty-first of July, the latter on the seventh of December, 1683.

This winter a terrible frost occurred. It began in December, 1683, and continued till February, 1684, with such remarkable severity, that the forest trees, and even the oaks, in England, were split by it ; most of the hollies were killed, and nearly all the birds perished. On the twenty-fourth of January, Evelyn writes :—" The frost continuing more and more severe, the Thames, before London, was planted with booths, in formal streets ; all sorts of trades and shops furnished and full of commodities, even to a printing press. * * * Coaches plied from Westminster to the Temple, and from several other stairs to and fro, as in the streets; slides, sliding with skates, a bull-bating, horse and coach races, puppet plays and interludes, cooks tipling, and other lewd places, that it seems to be a Bacchanalian triumph or carnival on the water. [This carnival, or fair, was visited by the King and Queen, when a whole bullock was roasted on the ice.] London, by reason of the excessive coldness of the air hindering the ascent of the smoke, was so filled with fuliginous steam of the sea-coal, that hardly could one see across the streets, and this filling the lungs with its gross particles, exceedingly obstructed the breast."

In the subsequent November, Katherine's birth-day was commemorated with unusual magnificence. Bonfires blazed, the bells rung, the tower-guns boomed, and brilliant fireworks, and sham acquatic fights and skirmishes, enlivened the bosom and banks of the Thames. It was a holiday for all London, and the rejoicings at Court closed with a grand ball at Whitehall. The display of fireworks cost one thousand five hundred pounds; they far surpassed any previous attempt of the kind. "The Court," remarks Evelyn, "had not been so brave and richly apparelled since his Majesty's restoration." But the reign and life of Charles were now fast hastening to a close. With the coming of the new year, his health visibly declined; still he could not find resolution to relinquish his evil ways, or his licentious companions. The evening of February the first, the last Sabbath he lived to look upon, he spent with his dissolute associates, in a manner most unrighteous and unworthy of a Christian King. The courtiers were gambling, with a bank of two thousand pounds before them. Charles was sitting, at the same table, in open dalliance with his lemans, the Duchesses of Portsmouth, Mazarine, and Cleveland; whilst a French youth amused them by singing love songs. From this scene of profanity and dissoluteness, the King proceeded to the apartments of the Duchess of Portsmouth, where, being too unwell to partake of a substantial supper, he ate two or three spoonfuls of soup. After passing a feverish and restless night, he rose at an early hour. To his attendants he appeared to be labouring under an affection of the brain; he was drowsy and absent, his gait was unsteady, and his speech embarrassed. About eight, as he walked across his chamber, he was seized with a strong fit of apoplexy; Lord Aylesbury caught him as he fell, and Dr. King, a physician, who had practised as a surgeon, being in an adjoining room, hastened to his assistance, and instantly opened a vein. The blood flowed freely, and stimulating remedies being applied, the royal patient in about two hours recovered his faculties. He suffered a relapse in the evening, passed a bad night, but so improved in the course of the next day, that hopes were cherished of his recovery. But in twenty-four hours the King's strength was exhausted. Medicine was administered without effect, and on the fourth evening it became evident that his dissolution was at hand. With all his faults, Charles was deeply beloved by his subjects. "The announcement of his malady spread a gloom over the metropolis; the report of his convalescence, the next day, was received by the citizens with expressions of joy, by the ringing of bells and numerous bonfires. When, at last, the danger became manifest, crowds hastened to the churches to solicit from heaven the health of their sovereign, and we are told, that repeatedly the service was interrupted by the sighs and sobs of the congregation. In the two royal chapels the ministers succeeded each other in rotation, and the prayers were continued every two hours till his death."

The King, on recovering his speech, after the first attack, asked for the Queen, and found she was by his side. Instantly, on hearing of his illness, she had rushed to his presence, and the Duke of York had preceded, and the Duchess of York soon followed her Majesty. Katherine remained speechless for some time, but, after awhile, she called the Duchess of York aside, and said to her:— "Sister, I beseech you to tell the Duke, who knows the King's sentiments with regard to the Catholic religion as well as

I do, to endeavour to take advantage of some good moments." Shortly afterwards, the sight of her husband's sufferings threw her into fits, and she was carried out of the room. The Duchess of York took the earliest opportunity to impart the Queen's desires to the Duke, her husband, who answered, "I know it, and think of nothing else." Interest as well as affection, caused the Duke to remain a constant attendant on his death-stricken brother. The Archbishop of Canterbury, and the Bishops of London, Durham, Ely, Bath and Wells, were also present, and in turn watched during the night in the King's chamber. On Thursday morning the holy Kenn, Bishop of Bath and Wells, seized a favourable moment to warn the royal sufferer of his danger, and implore him to prepare for death. Charles received the announcement with resignation, and the Bishop proceeded to read the office appointed for the sick and dying. On coming to the rubric, respecting confession, he paused, and asked his Majesty "if he repented of his sins?" The King answered in the affirmative; and the prelate having pronounced the absolution, from the service for the sick, inquired if he might proceed to the administration of the sacrament? Charles made no reply. Kenn repeated the question in a louder voice, and the reluctant Monarch rejoined in a faint tone, "There will be time enough for that yet." The elements were, however, brought and placed on a table; but when the question was again put to the dying man, he replied:—"I will think of it."

Meanwhile, Barillion, the French ambassador, at the instance of the Duchess of Portsmouth, took the Duke of York aside, and reminded him of his brother's secret perference of the Catholic worship. The Duke, however, scarcely knew how to act. By law, it was treason to reconcile any one to the church of Rome, and he indulged a hope, that Charles would free him from responsibility, by openly declaring the state of his mind. But being disappointed, he in the evening requested the company to withdraw from the bedside, and kneeling down, whispered in the King's ear, "Shall I send for a Catholic priest?" "For God's sake do!" replied Charles; "but," added he, "will it not expose you to danger?" "I care not for danger," replied the afflicted brother, who, after sending in search of a priest, turned to the company in the sick chamber, and said aloud, "The King requires all present to quit the apartment, except the Earls of Bath and Feversham." Shortly afterwards, Father Hudleston—him who, in 1651, had saved the King by concealing him—disguised in the costume of a Church of England clergyman, was led in secret through the Queen's apartments, and introduced through a private door into his Majesty's bed-chamber. The Duke of York introduced him to the King with these words: "Sir, this worthy man once saved your life; he now comes to save your soul." The priest went on his knees by the bed-side, and Charles having welcomed him, told him that "he desired to die in the faith and communion of the holy Roman Catholic church:" made his confession, and declared that he was in charity with all the world; that with all his heart he pardoned his enemies, and desired pardon of all those whom he had in any wise offended; and that if it pleased God to spare him longer life, he would amend it, detesting all sin. "I then," says Hudleston, "desired him to say with me this little act of contrition:—

"'Oh! my Lord God, with my whole heart and soul I detest all the sins of my life past, for the love of Thee, whom I love above all things; and I firmly purpose by thy Holy Grace never to offend Thee more. Amen! sweet Jesus, amen! Into Thy hands, sweet Jesus, I commend my soul. Mercy, sweet Jesus, mercy!'"

Hudleston then anointed him, administered the eucharist, and withdrew. The excitement caused the King to rally; but, an hour afterwards, he became worse, and the physicians declared that he could not live another twenty-four hours. During the night his sufferings were severe, but he bore them with fortitude and resignation. "He often," remarks a contemporary, "in extremity of pain, would say he suffered, but he thanked God that he did so, and that he suffered patiently. He every now and then would seem to wish for death, and beg the pardon of the standers-by and those that were employed about him, that he gave them so much trouble, saying he was weary of this world, that he had had enough of it, and he was going to a better." The sorely sick Queen, being strictly forbidden by her physicians and her friends, from being carried into her husband's chamber till the violence of her grief had subsided, by a messenger excused her absence, and implored the dying Monarch to pardon her offences. "Alas! poor woman," he said, with a faint voice, "she beg my pardon! —I beg hers, with all my heart;—take back to her that answer." About two in the morning, he cast his eyes upon the Duke, who was kneeling by his bedside, kissing his hand, and thanked him for having always been the best of brothers and friends; begged his pardon for the trouble which he had given him from time to time, and told him now he freely left him all, and begged of God to bless him with a prosperous reign. He never mentioned the name of the Duke of Monmouth; but sending for his other illegitimate sons, he recommended them to the care of James, and drawing each to him, one by one, on the bed, gave them a father's blessing. The bishops, moved by this sight, urged him as the Lord's anointed, and the father of his country, to bless all present in the name of the whole body of his subjects; every one in the chamber instantly went down on his knees, and Charles, being raised up, pronounced a solemn blessing over them. He then entreated the Duke of York not to let "poor Nelly Gwyn starve," and for his sake to protect the Duchesses of Portsmouth and Cleveland. Afterwards he endeavoured to repose, but his next slumber was to be the sleep of death. Shortly after six in the morning, he complained of an acute pain in the right side, accompanied with a difficulty of breathing; as a remedy, eight ounces of blood were taken from his arm; the relief was but temporary: he continued to sink, his speech failed at eight o'clock, his consciousness at a quarter past ten, and he calmly expired about noon, on the sixth of February, 1685, in the fifty-fourth year of his age. On the fourteenth of February he was interred, at midnight, in Westminster Abbey; and as he had embraced the proscribed Catholic faith, his funeral was performed with but little pomp or parade.*

Charles, great as were his failings or vices as a sovereign and a man, was sincerely beloved by his subjects. During his reign, Chelsea College, the Observatory at Greenwich, and the Royal Society were founded, trade and commerce flourished, the arts improved, and the wealth and the comforts of the people greatly increased. He left no issue by his Queen; and of his numerous illegitimate children, he acknowledged James, Duke of Monmouth, by Lucy Walters; Charlotte, Countess of Yarmouth, by Lady Shannon; Charles, Duke of Southampton; Henry, Duke of Grafton; George, Duke of Northumberland; Charlotte, Countess of Litchfield, by the Duchess of Cleveland; Charles, Duke of St. Alban's, by Nell Gwyn; Charles, Duke of Richmond, by the Duchess of Portsmouth; and Mary, Countess of Derwentwater, by Mary Davies.

Katherine of Braganza deeply mourned the loss of her beloved husband. For several weeks after his death, she confined herself to a chamber of mourning, where the daylight was shut out and tapers kept burning, and where the floor, the walls, the ceiling, the bed she reclined on, and, in fact, every thing the eye could rest upon, was black. James the Second treated her with kindness, and permitted her to remain at Whitehall till the second week in April, when she removed to her own palace, Somerset House, where she resided with the splendour and dignity becoming a Queen Dowager of England.

To the equally unworthy and unfortunate Duke of Monmouth, Katherine behaved with a kindness which he little deserved, but which did credit to her

* It may be observed, that Burnet's account of the death of Charles contains so many misstatements, that it cannot be relied on. In the above narrative, his errors and falsehoods are carefully avoided.

heart. At the time of the Popish Plot, he had united with those who thirsted for her life; he had repeatedly endeavoured to invalidate her marriage with Charles the Second; yet when he was apprehended for the part he had taken in the Rye-House plot, she successfully solicited his father to forgive him; in fact, he never got into trouble but she stood his friend. Her last efforts on his behalf were, however, unsuccessful: after he was condemned to death in 1685, he wrote and implored her to intercede for him with his uncle, James the Second. She did so with great earnestness, and the King granted him an interview, but not a reprieve. Subjoined is a copy of Monmouth's letter to her on this occasion:

"From Ringwood, the 9th of July, 1685.

"MADAM,—Being in this unfortunate condition, and having none left but your Majesty that I think may have some compassion of me, and that for the last King's sake, makes me take this boldness to beg of you to intercede for me. I would not desire your Majesty to do it, if I were not from the bottom of my heart convinced how I have been deceived in it, and how angry God Almighty is with me for it; but I hope, Madam, your intercession will give me life to repent of it, and to show the King how really and truly I will serve him hereafter; and I hope, Madam, your Majesty will be convinced that the life you save shall ever be devoted to your service, for I have been, and ever shall be, your Majesty's most dutiful and obedient servant, MONMOUTH."

Shortly after the death of her beloved husband, Katherine requested of her brother, Don Pedro, permission to return to Portugal, and end her days there. The request was cheerfully granted, but she delayed her departure, in the hope of obtaining the thirty-six thousand pounds which she claimed from the crown for arrears of income. She was present when the Queen of James the Second gave birth to an heir to the throne, stood godmother to the royal babe, and afterwards, by the King's desire, attended, with other noble personages, before the Privy Council, at Whitehall, to verify his birth; when called, she said, "The King sent for me to the Queen's labour; I came as soon as I could, and never left her till she was delivered of the Prince of Wales." The King deemed her evidence of great weight; and by all reasonable persons, who were not swayed by party considerations, it was viewed as a refutation of the widely-spread calumnies cast on the royal infant's birth.

Katherine took no part in the excitement occasioned by the landing of the Prince of Orange; but when King James, after his first flight, returned to London, he, before proceeding to Whitehall, called at Somerset House, had an interview with her, and learned from her lips the fate of her Lord Chamberlain, Feversham, who had been unjustly arrested and sent to the Tower by the Prince of Orange. The same evening that James retired to Rochester, December thirtieth, the Prince of Orange called upon Katherine, and finding her overcome with sadness and *ennui*, demanded, "Why she was not playing at basset?" The Queen Dowager, being desirous to intercede for Feversham, replied, "Because my Lord Chamberlain, who always keeps the bank, is absent." "Then he shall not be absent longer," rejoined the Prince; and that same night Feversham was set at liberty. After the expatriation of James the Second and his consort, Katherine suffered from repeated annoyances and insults. In July, 1689, the Commons voted that her popish servants should be limited to eighteen in number; and William the Third, when about to proceed to Ireland, sent Lord Nottingham to inform her, that as intelligence had reached him of great meetings against the government being held at her residence of Somerset House, he wished her to remove to Windsor or Audley End. This and many other indignities endured by Katherine at this period, emanated from Queen Mary, who bitterly hated the Queen Dowager, and subjected her to such restraints and espionage, that in 1691, she gave formal notice to the government of her intention to quit England for ever. But at that instant not a ship could be spared to convey her over seas: every vessel was required to oppose the French fleet, then hovering off Plymouth; and it was not till the thirtieth of March, 1692, that she was enabled to commence her long-desired journey. Having granted pensions to the members of her household, which she punctually paid to the hour of her death, she, with a small retinue of English ladies of rank, crossed the channel, travelled through France and Spain, and on the twentieth of January, 1693, entered Lisbon, amidst the acclamations of the people and the rejoicings of the court. Don Pedro met her in the street of Lumar, greeted her affectionately, and conducted her to the Quinta de Alcantara, a royal suburban mansion assigned to her use, where she made the acquaintance and won the undying friendship and affection of his Queen, Donna Maria Sophia. After a time, she, to improve her declining health, removed first to the palace of the Conde de Redonda, and then to that of the Conde de Aveiras, at Belem. For the same reason she made a progress to the place of her birth in the spring of 1699; throughout this journey the nobles and the people, mindful that her alliance with Charles the Second had secured to them their independence as a nation, treated her with all conceivable respect and honour, and, indeed, even the loyal in England still revered her memory. In 1700, Pepys, writing to his nephew, who was then travelling in Portugal, says, "If this reaches you at Lisbon, I give you in charge to wait upon my Lady Tuke, one of the ladies attending my once royal mistress, our Queen Dowager; nor if she offer you the honour of kissing the Queen's hand, would I have you to omit the presenting her Majesty in most humble manner with my profoundest duty, as becomes a most faithful subject."

When the unfortunate James the Second died, Katherine, as a tribute to his memory, ordered Somerset House, which she still retained, to be hung in black, and her servants there to wear mourning for a twelvemonth. While on her journey to Portugal, the Queen Dowager had been laid up for some time with the erysipelas, and in the spring of 1704 she suffered from an alarming attack of the same disease. She, however, recovered; and, weak and deficient of regnal talents as most of her English subjects had considered her, the men of her own country so highly esteemed her wisdom and powers to govern, that when ill-health forced Don Pedro to retire to Beira for change of air, he placed the reins of government in her hands; and such was the success and popularity of her rule, that in 1705, when Don Pedro's illness became alarming, she was solemnly constituted Queen Regnant. She, however, did not live long to enjoy her successes as a reigning sovereign. A violent and unexpected attack of cholic put a period to her existence on the thirty-first of December, 1705, and in the sixty-eighth year of her age. The King, her brother, on hearing of her illness, hastened to her presence, and summoned a council of state in the palace of Bemposta, where she then lay; but before the necessary measures for his resumption of the regal prerogatives were completed, she had breathed her last. She was interred in the monastery of Belem with the most imposing funeral rites: Don Pedro was too unwell to attend, but the whole of his court and all his retinue followed; for eight days public business and amusements were suspended, and the ministers and their families, and the court and their attendants, wore deep mourning for a year; in fact, all Portugal mourned her death as a national calamity. She was prayed for as Queen Dowager in the churches in England in the reigns of James the Second, William and Mary, and Anne. By her will, dated the fourteenth of February, 1699, she appointed her tried and faithful old Lord Chamberlain, the Earl of Chesterfield, her principal executor, but ill health caused him to decline the office; she instituted Don Pedro her heir, and as she died extremely rich, left bountiful legacies to all her relations and friends, munificent bequests to several Portuguese monasteries and convents, founded a Jesuit college for the education of missionaries for India, and ordered large sums to be distributed in alms to the poor.

MARIA BEATRIX,

Queen of James the Second.

CHAPTER I.

Maria Beatrix—Birth—Parentage—Education—Demanded in Marriage by James Duke of York—Yields with reluctance—Espoused by proxy—The Marriage opposed by the Parliament and the People—Journey to England—Received by the Duke of York at Dover—Married to him in person—Proceeds to London—Kindly received by King Charles the Second—Residence at St. James's—Persecuted by the popular party—James takes her on a progress—Witnesses the mock siege of Maestricht—Birth, christening, and death of her first child—Maligned by Lugancy the informer—Inconstancy of her husband—Injures her reputation and offends the Queen by visiting the Duchesses of Mazarin and of Portsmouth—Birth and death of her children Isabella and Charles.

HAT queen of misfortune and sorrow, Maria Beatrix, consort of the ill-starred James the Second, the last of the Stuart kings, was born at the ducal palace in the city of Modena, on the fifth of October, 1658. Her father, Alphonso d'Esté, Duke of Modena, was a martyr to the gout, of which he died after a short but promising reign of four years. On his demise he left to his duchess, Laura Martinozzi, the regency of Modena and the guardianship of their offsprings, Francis the Second, his successor, and Maria Beatrix, known also as Mary Beatrice, the subject of the present memoir. The Duchess of Modena herself superintended the education of the orphan son and daughter, and although a fond parent, treated them with censurable severity. To Maria she strictly forbad cakes and sweetmeats, forced her greatly against her will to eat *soupe maigre* at her meals; one day smartly boxed her ears, because in repeating the Benedicite she had forgotten one of the verses; and another time, when she was frightened at the sweeps who had come to cleanse the chimney of her nursery, seized her by the hand, and to convince her that her fears were groundless, caused the men of soot to draw near and speak to her, which, as she stated in after-life, nearly terrified her into fits. To finish her education, she was sent to a convent of Carmelite nuns; and the life she led there, so imbued her mind with spiritual romance, that she was preparing to take the veil, when, to her discomfiture, James, Duke of York, afterwards James the Second, sued and obtained her reluctant hand in marriage.

Thus wrapped in the mysticisms of the Catholic faith, and dreaming of nought but veils and rosaries, we leave the fair young recluse, to glance at the romantic circumstances which led to her marriage. In 1660, James, then Duke of York, married Anne Hyde: the match brought him little happiness and much trouble; it involved him in the unpopularity of her father, the Chancellor Clarendon, and entailed upon him the hatred and opposition of Buckingham, Shaftesbury, and their party, who, to prevent the possibility of his avenging on them the injuries they had inflicted on his father-in-law, were unceasing in their efforts to deprive him of his right of succession. All his children by Anne Hyde died in their youth, saving the two daughters, whose unnatural conduct so embittered his declining years; and in 1671 Anne herself breathed her last. To fill her place, he set his heart upon Susanna Armine, widow of Sir Henry Bellasis. But as this lady was a Catholic, and far beneath him in rank, and moreover as he himself had just previously damaged his reputation in England by embracing the Catholic faith, his brother, King Charles the Second forbade the match, and induced him to solicit the hand of the Archduchess of Inspruck, a princess who, singular to relate, was also a Catholic. This suit was accepted, the marriage treaty concluded, and in 1673, his warm friend, the Earl of Peterborough, set out for Vienna to marry the Archduchess by proxy. Peterborough, however, was arrested on his journey by the provoking news that the Archduchess had changed her mind, and was about to become the bride of the Emperor Leopold the First. He wrote to James, who in reply commissioned him to choose a wife for him elsewhere, and directed his especial attention to Maria Beatrix, of Modena; Mary Anne of Wirtemburg; the Duchess of Guise, a widow; and Mademoiselle de Rais. The two latter ladies he saw at Paris, and dismissed at once; the one being delicate in constitution, the other ordinary in person and features. He obtained the sight of a portrait of Maria Beatrix, and was enraptured with it; but, to his chagrin, learned that she was fully bent on taking the veil. Next, by direction of James, he hastened to the presence of Mary Anne of Wirtemburg; and charmed by her beauty, grace, and manners, reported favourably of her, and led her friends to hope that he would shortly be commissioned to make a formal demand of her hand. Matters were in this state, when the Duke of York, in compliance with the policy of the King and Privy Council, commanded him to privately leave Paris, proceed incognito to Dusseldorf, and at the court there endeavour to obtain a sight of the Princess of Newburgh. He instantly complied. After some trouble, and being taken for the Duke of York in disguise, he effected the object of his mission, reported unfavourably of the lady, and was ordered back to Paris to complete the arrangements for the marriage with Mary Anne of Wirtemburg. Without delay he hastened to the convent at Paris, where the Princess resided, and assured her that she might shortly expect a formal demand for her hand from the Duke of York; he then returned to his own home, where, to his surprise and annoyance, he found dispatches ordering him to break off all negotiation for the intended marriage with her, and to learn, with all speed, if the daughter of the Duc D'Elbœuf would be a suitable lady for James to marry. Mortified as he was, he got a sight of Elbœuf's daughter, found her to be a girl of thirteen, very childish for her years, and one he could not think of bringing home as a bride for the heir-apparent to the throne of England. No other course was now open but to make a formal demand of the hand of the Princess of Modena. Peterborough received dispatches for this purpose from the King and the Duke of York, and at once set out on his mission, travelling as before, incognito. His secret was known at the court of Modena before he arrived there. The Duchess of Modena opposed, or rather affected to oppose, the match, till the King of France interceded in its favour, when she received Peterborough with courtesy, overcame her daughter's opposition to enter the married state, and dispatched the Abbe Dangeau to Rome for a dispensation, which was necessary for the marriage, on account of the Duke of York not having made a formal public confession of his conversion to the Roman Catholic Church. The Pope, however, declined to immediately grant the dispensation; when, as it was important that the ceremony of the espousals should be performed before the meeting of the British parliament, which now drew nigh, and as the Bishop of Modena peremptorily refused to officiate, Maria was married without a dispensation, and in defiance of the Pope's interdict, by a poor priest, an Englishman, named White, to the Duke of York, by proxy, on the thirtieth of September; and what heightens the singularity of these espousals, the Duke of York was a Catholic, whilst his proxy, the Earl of Peterborough, was a member of the Protestant Church of England. At the period of her marriage Maria was scarcely turned fifteen; she was womanly of her age, a captivating brunette, but unconscious of her charms. Her portion was one hundred thousand francs, and Louis the Fourteenth, who always considered her as his adopted daughter, paid part of it.

The marriage was commemorated by balls, pageants, feats of arms, banquets, and other demonstrations of public rejoicings, which lasted for several days; meantime the fair young bride, although forced to take part in the festivity, was miserable, sullen, and melancholy: she had violently but vainly struggled to preserve her maiden independence, the irrevocable vow her reluctant lips had been forced to pronounce; and when the time for her departure for England was named, she cried bitterly for two whole days and nights, and would not be pacified till her mother consented to accompany her; an arrangement opposed to the express orders of the Duke of York, who, for obvious reasons, desired that his Duchess should come to England without foreign attendants, but to which Peterborough was compelled to consent. Maria left Modena about a fortnight after the solemnization of her marriage, accompanied by her mother, her brother, the young Duke of Modena, her uncle, Prince Rinaldo D'Esté, and a princely train of nobles. The Earl of Peterborough and his suite escorted her to Paris; but on reaching the border of France, her brother and most of the nobles who had attended her out of respect to the house of Esté, returned. At Paris, Louis the Fourteenth and the most exalted and illustrious personages in France entertained her with regal magnificence, and treated her with all conceivable honour and distinction. These princely favours she returned with becoming grace and dignity, and was about to set out for England, when a violent attack of fever laid her up and forced her to keep her bed for a fortnight. Before she was convalescent the Parliament in England met, and the Commons voted an address to the King, praying that he would not permit the projected marriage between James and the Princess of Modena to take place. Charles answered, "Your request has come too late, the marriage has already been solemnised, and the Duchess of York is already on her road to England." The Commons, nothing daunted, voted a second address, beseeching his Majesty to stop Maria at Paris, and prevent the consummation of the marriage; and being answered that the King could not in honour break a contract of marriage that had been solemnly executed, they became enraged, threatened to stop the supplies, voted the standing army a grievance, and petitioned the King to appoint a day of general fasting, that God might avert the dangers with which the nation was threatened. The next day being the fifth of November, the London apprentices burnt Guy Fawkes and the Pope, with ceremonies and allusions that fully marked their abhorrence of the Duke's change of creed, and marriage to a Catholic princess. "This opposition of the Commons and the people struck the courtiers with consternation, and the Earl of Arlington implored his Majesty either to prevent the departure of Maria from Paris or to insist that James, after his marriage, should withdraw from public notice and lead the life of a country gentleman. Charles answered, that the first was incompatible with his honour, and the second would be an indignity to his brother."

Meanwhile, the unwilling Duchess left Paris, journeyed to Calais, and there embarked with her mother, her uncle, and a numerous retinue, partly English, but mostly foreign, on the twenty-first of November, 1673. A favourable wind wafted the royal party to Dover with speed and safety. The Duke of York awaited their arrival on the sands, received his young bride in his arms as she landed, and although she manifested unmistakeable evidence of aversion to him, tenderly saluted her, and courteously conducted her to her lodgings, where he left her for a short while to repose with her mother. "The same evening," remarks Clark, in his Life of James the Second, "the Duke and Duchess of York, and the Duchess of Modena, with their attendants, the Earl of Peterborough being also present, being assembled together in the state drawing-room, Dr. Crew, Bishop of Oxford, asked the Duchess of Modena and the Earl of Peterborough whether the said Earl had married the Duchess of York as proxy of the Duke, which they both affirming, the bishop then declared it was a lawful marriage." But, according to another equally reliable authority, Crew, after receiving the affirmation of the Earl and the Duchess, married the royal pair after the forms of the Church of England, and on the same night the marriage was lawfully consummated. Maria's proxy wedding-ring was set with a diamond; that which her spouse himself placed on her finger was ornamented with a small ruby; the former she called the diamond of her marriage, the latter she prized as her true marriage-ring, would on no account remove it from her finger, and as her spouse had placed it, so wore it to the day of her death.

Their highnesses remained at Dover but two days; during this time, the Earl of Berkshire, probably at the request of the King, urged the Duke to solicit permission to withdraw from public life, and retire with his duchess to Audley End. James answered, "My interest requires that I should be on the spot to oppose the intrigues of my foes, and my duty forbids me to desert my brother without the royal command." From Dover James and Maria, with their suite, journeyed overland by short stages to Gravesend, where, on the morning of the twenty-sixth of November, they embarked for London. Off Greenwich, they were met by the King and his courtiers, and entering the royal barge, proceeded to Whitehall, where Maria and her distinguished retinue were cordially welcomed by Queen Katherine of Braganza and her ladies. As the marriage was exceedingly unpopular, the bridal progress was neither attended by admiring crowds, nor enlivened by blazing bonfires, and other demonstrations national enthusiasm; but withal, the purity of morals and manners, the youth, innocence, and captivating charms of Maria Beatrix, disarmed the malignity of her assailants, the enemies of the court, and won for her the homage of the disinterested. The aged Waller hymned her praises in soft-flowing numbers; and Granville, Earl of Lansdown, struck by her gentleness and surpassing loveliness, wrote—

Our future hopes from this blest union rise,
Our present joy and safety from her eyes;
Those charming eyes, that strive to reconcile
To harmony and peace this stubborn isle.

The Duke and Duchess of York removed to St. James's Palace, the Duke's usual residence; and on the sixth of December the resident ambassadors and envoys from the various courts waited on them, and formally congratulated them on their marriage. They, however, were allowed but little peace by the popular party, who assumed such a powerful and menacing attitude, that the King, to stifle their clamours, permitted the penal laws against Catholics to be enforced with rigour, forbade by an order in council any popish recusant to walk in St. James's Park, or visit St.

James's Palace, and refused to Maria the use of the public Catholic chapel at St. James's, which had previously been stipulated in her marriage articles, under pretence that it was required for the use of the Queen-mother, Henrietta, and her household.

On the thirtieth of December, the Duchess of Modena bade adieu to her daughter and to England, and shortly afterwards James took his young bride on a progress to see some of the most important and interesting places in England. On her return, Maria was entertained by a brilliant succession of fêtes, balls, and theatrical performances; and in the summer, when the court was at Windsor, she was one of the noble personages who witnessed the representation of the siege of Maestricht; a chivalric pageant, got up for the amusement of their Majesties and the court, and the last of the kind performed in England in the presence of royalty. A huge model of the city and fortifications of Maestricht was erected in a field close to Windsor Castle. The Duke of York, and his rival, Monmouth, at the head of a little army of courtiers, played the part of the besiegers; the city held out, trenches were opened, mines sprung, batteries erected, a fierce cannonade was kept up on both sides, prisoners were taken, grenades thrown, breaches made; and at last, after the whole business of a siege had been displayed with skill and success, the city was taken, amidst the huzzas of the delighted spectators.

On the tenth of January, 1675, exactly twenty-five minutes after four in the afternoon, Maria gave birth to her first child, a daughter, at St. James's Palace. She earnestly wished to bring up the babe in her own religion; but her husband told her that it would be impossible, as it had been moved in Parliament by the bishops that their offspring should be educated in the religion of the realm, and the King had expressed his pleasure that it should be so. She, however, in defiance of husband, King, and Parliament, sent for her confessor, Father Gallis, a few hours after the birth of the infant, and prevailed on him to at once privately christen it in her bedroom, with the rites of the Roman Catholic church. She then told the King what she had done, and implored him to prevent the reiteration of the baptism; but he disregarded her entreaty, and the child was christened Katherine Laura, with the rites of the Church of England, in the chapel-royal. The sponsors were the Duke of Monmouth and the Princesses Mary and Anne, and the previous baptism was kept a profound secret. She was a delicate child, and, to the great grief of her parents, died of a convulsion fit, in the tenth month of her age, and was buried on the fifth of October, 1675, in the vault of Mary, Queen of Scots, in Westminster Abbey.

In October, 1675, Maria was annoyed and alarmed by the attempt of the impostor, Lugancy, to cast obliquity on her name. This adventurer, a French felon, and the prototype of the renowned Titus Oates, pretended to be a converted Jesuit, and gave information that "Father St. Germain," who for greater effect was described as confessor to the Duchess of York, "had surprised him at his lodgings, and holding a poniard to his breast, had compelled him, with the threat of instant death, to sign a recantation, and a promise to return to his native country." This improbable tale was introduced to the notice of the Commons by Lord Russell. The Parliament, the court, the city, the country, instantly took the alarm; the papists were treated with additional severity; and Lugancy was examined by the Commons, and deposed, "that in a short time Protestant blood would flow through the streets of London; that the King was at heart a Catholic; and that there was an infinite number of priests and Jesuits in London, all plotting to murder the Protestants." Shortly afterwards, Du Maresque, an upright French clergyman of the Reformed Church, published a history of the impostor's adventures in France. The work destroyed Lugancy's credit with the Parliament; but such was the blindness of sectarian prejudice, that Compton, Bishop of London, and the great patron of converts from Popery sent him to Oxford, and caused him to be ordained a minister of the Church of England, and made vicar of Dover Court, in Essex.

Shortly after the departure of her mother, Maria became deeply attached to her husband; to use the words of a contemporary, "she loved him too well, and to her sorrow discovered that she was not the sole object of his affection. He maintained a disgraceful intimacy with the titled courtezans at court, and even with several of the ladies in her household; and when the unpleasant truth reached her ears, she assailed him with tears and reproaches. But she being a girl, and he of mature years, he disregarded her upbraiding, felt flattered by her jealousy, and continued to indulge his inconstant passion till time developed her character, endowed her with matronal port and dignity, and taught him to esteem and admire her."

In 1675, James permitted his young, inexperienced wife to visit her disreputable relation, the Duchess of Mazarine, who had just arrived in England, and already played the part of an intriguing courtezan at court. That most imperious of the King's mistresses, the Duchess of Portsmouth, annoyed that the like honour had not been paid to her, told James that she considered herself entitled to as much attention from his consort as Madam Mazarine: and, whether from fear of her malice, or any other cause, the Duke of York, a few days afterwards, had the folly to introduce his Duchess to her. The meeting took place at Portsmouth's apartments at Whitehall; the King was present, and thanked Maria for consenting to make the acquaintance of his most esteemed favourite; but her indiscretion cost her the marked displeasure of the Queen, who, at a dress ball given by her Majesty that very night, turned from her with scorn, in the presence of the whole court. This emphatic censure from her virtuous sister-in-law deeply wounded the feelings of the impolitic, but well-intentioned Duchess of York; Mazarine she viewed as a relation and friend, and of her immoral doings she knew but little; Portsmouth she had visited against her will, and by the express command of her husband, therefore, however unpardonable her folly, that of her spouse, the Duke of York, was infinitely more so; for, by not preventing her visit to Mazarine, he had incurred the ill-will both of the Queen and Portsmouth, the latter of whom was intriguing with Shaftesbury and Russell to effect his exclusion from the succession, at the very time that he forced his wife to make her acquaintance.

On the eighteenth of August, 1676, at five minutes past eight in the morning, Maria's second child—a daughter—entered the world. The infant was christened Isabella, by Dr. North, Prebendary of Westminster, and died when five years old. Maria was present when the Prince of Orange was married to her step-daughter, the Princess Mary, on the fourth of November, 1677; and three days afterwards, remarks Dr. Lake, "the Duchess was safely delivered of a prince, to the great joy of the whole court, except the Clarendon party. The child is but little, but sprightly, and likely to live."

The evening after his birth, he was christened with great pomp, by Dr. Crew, by the name of Charles, after the King, who stood godfather, and created him Duke of Cambridge. The other godfather was the Prince of Orange. His sister, the Princess Isabella, was godmother, and being only fifteen months old, her governess, Frances Villiers, stood as her proxy. The infant Charles, although a healthy babe, was short-lived; four days after his birth the small-pox broke out at St. James's, he caught the infection, his ignorant nurses drove the eruption inward, and on the eleventh of December he died in a convulsion fit. The next day his remains were interred in the vault of Mary, Queen of Scots, in Westminster Abbey. His death overwhelmed the Duke and Duchess of York with grief; the whole court expressed their sorrow by going into mourning, and the lamented event was announced to all the sovereigns of Europe, who in return sent letters of condolence to the bereaved Duke and Duchess.

CHAPTER II.

Maria visits her step-daughter, Mary, at the Hague—Her husband plotted against by Oates and his abettors—He is driven from the council-board—Maria embarks with him for Holland—He is falsely accused of an intent to invade England—Unpopularity in England increases—Attempt to pass the Exclusion Bill—The Duke and Duchess joined by their daughters Anne and Isabella—Visited by Maria's mother—Return, with their family, to England—Leave the Princesses at St. James's, and travel to Scotland—Received there with hearty congratulations—Recalled to England—Welcomed by the King, and feasted by the civic authorities of London—Their enemies again intrigue against them with success—They return to Scotland—Their popularity there—Their prospects in England gloomy and forbidding—The Fitz-Harris Plot—Their daughter Isabella dies, and the Princess Anne joins them—James is shipwrecked—They again return to England——Birth and death of their daughter, Charlotte Maria.

ARIA'S step-daughter, Mary of York, had been married to the Prince of Orange but a few months, when news arrived that she was ill in body, and dejected in mind. The Duke of York, anxious for the welfare of his daughter, prevailed on Maria to pay her a visit in private; and when the matter was arranged, he wrote to the Prince of Orange, informing him that " the Duchess of York and the Princess Anne intend coming to the Hague, very incognito, and that they would take Lord Ossory for their governor." He also addressed the same information to Sir William Temple, the British resident at the Hague, who, in answer, stated, " It will be difficult to help her Highness to be incognito in this place. The Prince being yet absent, I spoke of it to Monsieur Van Lewen, who was hard to be persuaded that the honours due to her Highness by the States upon such occasions should not be performed solemnly, at her landing. But having acquainted him with the absoluteness of your Highness's commands * * * I prevailed on him to make no mention of it to the States till the Prince's return. For a house to receive her Highness and Lady Anne, with their attendants, there is no choice at all in it: and so the Princess Dowager's house is making ready for this purpose, and will, I doubt not, be in order by to-morrow." This letter was written on the first of October, and about the same day Maria Beatrix and the Princess Anne reached the Hague. They preserved their incognito, and after a stay of eight days, returned to England in safety. That they had met with a gratifying reception, is evident by the subjoined extract from a letter addressed by James to William of Orange:

"London, Oct. 18th.

" We came thither on Wednesday, from Newmarket, and the same night, presently after eleven, the Duchess, my wife, arrived here, so satisfied with her journey and you, as I never saw anybody; and I must give you a thousand thanks from her and from myself for her kind usage by you."

On reaching England, Maria found her husband vainly striving to quell the storm which his enemies had raised against him, the Queen, and the Catholics. The infamous Titus Oates and his confederates, by their gigantic popish plot scheme, which we have detailed in the memoirs of Queen Katherine of Braganza, had thrown the nation into a ferment. The majority of the Commons breathed vengeance against the Catholics; the public mind was kept in a state of intense terror and excitement by the promulgation of absurd, but alarming reports, of the bloody designs of the papists; and at length, when the frenzy of the people was at its height, the triumphant faction forced James to relinquish his seat in the council, and then demanded that he should be excluded from the royal presence. The good nature of Charles revolted from proceedings so harsh and ungracious, and, to induce his brother to defeat the machinations of his foes, by retiring to the fold of the Established Church, he commissioned the Archbishop of Canterbury, and other prelates, to wait on him, and endeavour to overcome his objections; but, unlike the easy-minded, merry monarch, James refused to serve his interest at the expense of his conscience. Charles then urged him to go abroad for a short time. James replied, "I am willing to submit to your Majesty's wish, but must request from your hand a written order to quit the kingdom, that I may not appear to flee like a coward or a culprit." Charles immediately gave the order, in the form of an affectionate letter, of which the subjoined is a copy:—

"I have already given you my resolutions at large, why I should think it fit that you should absent yourself for some time beyond the seas. As I am truly sorry for the occasion, so may you be sure I shall never desire it longer than it will be absolutely necessary for your good and my service. In the meantime, I think it proper to give it you under my hand, that I expect this compliance from you, and desire it may be as soon as conveniently you can. You may easily believe with what trouble I write — there being nothing I am more sensible of than the constant kindness you have ever had for me. I hope you are as just to me, to be assured, that no absence, nor anything else, can ever change me from being truly and kindly yours. C.R.

"Feb. 28th, 1679."

On the fourth of March, the Duke and Duchess of York, after having made hasty preparations, embarked for Holland. The King accompanied them to the port of embarcation, and separated from them with tears. After a stormy passage, they landed in safety, and the Prince of Orange, with a retinue of his nobles, received them, and conducted them with pomp to the Hague. Here they were treated with all the honour and respect due to their exalted rank; but after a short stay, they proceeded to Brussels, and took up their abode in the house where Charles the Second had resided when in exile. In England the Duke's unpopularity continued to increase. It was stated before the committee of secrecy, that he intended to come back in June with a powerful body of French troops, to massacre the Protestants. Yet at this very time he was strenuously urging those at the head of the navy department to more effectually guard the coast of England against the threatened French invasion. He wrote to Pepys, the Secretary to the Admiralty, on the subject, who, in reply, says:—

"I acknowledge, with all humility and thankfulness, the honour of your Highness's letter, and do with equal shame and grief, observe how much your Highness's solicitude, even at this distance, for the security of this kingdom against the power of France, does exceed all that we ourselves expressed upon that subject, otherwise than by a general but inactive restlessness under our apprehensions of the danger, but without any alteration made since your Royal Highness's departure, in the state of our ships or coasts, other than what is consequential to their having laid so long neglected."

But, despite James's patriotic intentions, the House of Commons, on the twenty-seventh of April, voted that "the Duke of York's being a papist, the hope of his coming to the crown had given the greatest countenance and encouragement to the conspiracies and designs of the papists." The bill of exclusion was next read for a second time, and the House would have passed it, had not Charles unexpectedly prorogued Parliament. When the Duke and Duchess had reluctantly gone out of England, they, by the King's desire, left their daughters, Anne and Isabella, behind, that it might not be said that they went to seduce them from the Protestant church; but they found the separation so painful, that early in August, the Duke requested, and the King permitted, their children to join them. On the nineteenth of the same month, Anne and her infant half-sister, Isabella, commenced their journey, and, after a prosperous voyage, reached Brussels in safety, greatly to the delight of their fond parents. Just previously, Maria enjoyed the happiness of a visit from her mother, the Duchess of Modena, from whom she had been separated ever since her marriage. Meanwhile, the Duke of York bore his exile with impatience. He feared that in his absence his enemies would deprive him of his dearest rights; he frequently requested to be permitted to return, but was invariably answered that he must wait till the excitement raised by the Popish Plot imposture had subsided. "Indeed," said Charles, in one of his letters, "I should be very unwilling to have a question brought upon the stage, whether or not you should be secure, and you at the same time present, considering how easy it is to have false witnesses, till Oates and Bedloe have their due." This reply almost paralyzed James; but shortly after its arrival, he received a message, apprising him that the King was seriously ill, and desired him to instantly hasten to his presence, with all possible secrecy; but on condition that he took the whole responsibility of his return on himself, and went back to Brussels immediately after the King had recovered. James lost not a moment. Leaving his Duchess and daughters behind, he set out in disguise, on the eighth of September, with only four attendants, travelled under a feigned name, reached Windsor at seven o'clock on the morning of the twelfth, and was the first to announce his arrival to the King. Charles, who was now convalescent, was up, and at his toilet. On entering his presence, James knelt at his feet, and apologized for returning without being recalled; the King bade him rise, tenderly embraced him, and assured him he was welcome,—the courtiers then flocked round him, and, whether his enemies or his friends, equally offered him their congratulations. During this visit, James obtained the royal permission to transfer his residence from Brussels to Edinburgh. He left London on the twenty-fifth of September, and rejoined his wife and daughters on the first of October. His intended change of residence was officially announced in the Gazette.

On the third of October, the Duke and Duchess of York, with their two daughters, Anne and Isabella, and the Duchess of Modena, left Brussels, and, after a long and stormy voyage, reached the Hague on the sixth, took up their residence at the Old Court Palace, and were welcomed and entertained there by the Prince and Princess of Orange. On the seventh, the Duke of York received an express from King Charles, commanding him to sail to the Downs, and to wait there for further orders. He lost no time in complying with this mandate. On the ninth, he and his consort, with their two daughters, bade an affectionate farewell to the Duchess of Modena, and, with their suite, commenced their voyage. At the Maesland Sluys, the Prince and Princess of Orange, who had accompanied them thus far, parted from them with all the outward show of sincere affection. After a stormy passage, from which Maria suffered severely from sea-sickness, they reached the Downs, where orders to immediately proceed to Scotland by sea awaited them. To comply would have been to hazard the life of the sorely sick Duchess; James, therefore, wrote to Charles, and obtained from him permission to travel to Edinburgh overland. The royal party landed at Deal, and, to the surprise of the Court, and annoyance of the popular faction, reached St. James's

Palace on the night of the twelfth of October. The King cordially welcomed them, and assured the Duke that it was out of his power to shield him from the malignity of his foes, if he remained in England. A week afterwards, the reluctant King was formally compelled to request his persecuted brother to hasten his departure to Scotland. It was resolved that the Princesses Anne and Isabella should remain at St. James's Palace; and Charles earnestly pressed Maria, who had vomited blood at sea, and was still in a dangerous state of health, also to remain at Court, as it was arranged that the Duke should return about the middle of the subsequent January. She, however, turned a deaf ear to his entreaties, and "chose rather even, with the hazard of her life, to be the constant companion of the misfortunes and hardships of the husband she so sincerely beloved." Their Highnesses set out for Scotland on the twenty-seventh of October. They found the journey slow and wearisome; rains, fogs, and almost impassable roads, rendered the progress harassing and comfortless. At Hatfield, and at York, they were received with marked neglect and ill-will; but in Scotland their reception was enthusiastic; two thousand of the Scottish gentry conducted them in procession from the border to Lenthington, where they were splendidly entertained till the fourth of December, when, attended by the Lords of the council, and the leading nobles of Scotland, they entered Edinburgh in grand procession, and were feasted and entertained with regal magnificence at the cost of the loyal Corporation. The Duke and his English retinue were complimented with the freedom of the city; a special entertainment was provided for his Duchess and her ladies; and although his right was contested, he took his place in the privy council, but wisely abstained from all connection with either of the parties which then divided that kingdom. Meantime, the current of popular opinion in England began to turn in his favour; numerous loyal addresses were presented to the King; all moderate men openly denounced the doings of the dominant faction, and the men of Norfolk even ventured to offer thanks to his Majesty for the recall of the heir-apparent from Flanders. Encouraged by these and other equally evident demonstrations of the loyalty of his subjects, Charles resolved to redeem the promise he had made to recall the Duke and Duchess of York, early in the ensuing year. Entering the council chamber, on the twenty-eighth of January, 1680, he stated to his council assembled there, that he had derived little benefit from the absence of his brother; that he deemed it unjust to take from a Prince, whose rights were assailed, the opportunity of defending them in his place in Parliament, and, therefore, had commanded his Highness to quit Edinburgh, and return to his former residence at St. James's. This unexpected announcement so startled and annoyed the leaders of the factious demagogues, that, three days afterwards, Shaftesbury, Russell, Cavendish, Capel, and Powell, tendered their resignation; and Charles replied, that "he accepted it with all his heart."

James and Maria, on receiving the welcomed summons to England, warmly thanked the Scots for the kindness and the honour they had done them, and with all haste put to sea. After a rather boisterous voyage, they reached Deptford on the twenty-fourth of February, and immediately proceeded in a barge to Whitehall, where the King received them with brotherly affection. The next day they took up their abode at St. James's, where the Duchess, overcome by the strong impulses of maternal affection, embraced her own young Isabella with tears of joy, and then warmly saluted her step-daughter, Anne. By the Court party their return was hailed with enthusiasm, and in London the popular current had turned so completely in their favour, that the civic powers presented to each of them congratulatory addresses; and the next day the King and the Duke were feasted with a sumptuous supper by the Lord

Mayor, and the public joy at their presence was testified by the ringing of bells, the blazing of bonfires, and a general and profuse illumination.

The conduct of their Highnesses at this period was wise and conciliatory. Maria's purity of life, and her affectionate conduct as a wife and a stepmother, won for her the unsought goodwill of the public. At the close of September she visited Cambridge, and after giving a grand ball there, proceeded to Newmarket, where, with the Duke her husband, and the King and Queen, she remained during the races in October. Since the Duke of York's return, his enemies had closely watched his conduct; they viewed his increasing popularity with alarm, and resolved to again force him from the land of his birth. With this view, Shaftesbury, Russell, Huntingdon, and others of their party, went to Westminster Hall, and offered, before the grand jury there, six reasons why they should present him for recusancy, and indict the Duchess of Portsmouth as a national nuisance. The Duchess certainly was a national nuisance; but their purport was not to reform the morals of the Court, but to terrify her into using her almost absolute influence over the King to effect the downfall of the Duke; and it was principally her earnest entreaties which prevailed on his Majesty to notify to his brother, on the eighteenth of October, that he must return to Scotland. Overcome with despair at these words, the unfortunate James requested and obtained from Charles a promise that he would never surrender the rightful descent of the crown, the regal authority over the Parliament, and the command of the naval and military forces. He also requested a general pardon, as a protection against the malice of his enemies in his absence. This the King refused, on the plea that it would be derogatory to the honour of both of them. James viewed the refusal as a proof that he was abandoned by his brother; and, overcome by despair and indignation, declared, if his enemies dared to persecute him further, he would seek the aid of the French King, rather than their audacity should pass unavenged. Barillon, the French ambassador, caught up the angry remark, and by profuse offers of money and arms, urged him to raise the sword of insurrection. James, however, spurned the proposal; and on the twentieth of October, the day before the meeting of Parliament, set out with a heavy heart, and accompanied by his faithful consort, on his voyage to the north. After a protracted stormy passage, they neared the Scotch coast, reached Leith in safety, and thence proceeded to Holyrood House, where they took up their abode. The Scots, as before, greeted them on their arrival with every conceivable expression of joy. "When they landed," says a contemporary, "the shore was thronged with people of all ranks, who, flinging their bonnets in the air, so loudly and continuously shouted, 'Lord preserve your Highness!' 'God save the King!' and the like, that they almost drowned the booming of the cannons, the ringing of the bells, and the noise of the trumpets and the drums. All the high and noble personages in Scotland met their Highnesses in Leith, and conducted them with all conceivable pomp and ceremony to Holyrood House. The Archbishops of St. Andrew's and Glasgow complimented them in the name of the kirk, the governor of Edinburgh Castle delivered to James the keys of the castle; and the night through, the city was enlivened by the ringing of bells and the blaze of many and great bonfires, around which the joy-intoxicated citizens assembled, and with smiling faces drank the health of their Majesties and their Highnesses."

James and Maria succeeded in retaining their ascendancy over the hearts of the aristocracy and the people of Scotland. They kept a brilliant court at Holyrood, to which all persons of rank or distinction resorted. As they professed an unpopular creed, they performed their religious rites with all possible privacy; and they frequently rode out in public, and made it a point to maintain an affable deportment towards all persons.

The Duke frequently played at the then popular game of golf, and increased his popularity by choosing citizens and mechanics for his partners on these occasions; whilst the Duchess, by her gracious deportment, purity of mind, and engaging manners, won the hearts of the Scotch ladies, whom she frequently entertained at levees and social evening parties. To avoid all appearance of disgrace, the Duke had entered Scotland as the immediate representative of his royal brother. He arrived in troublous times, but by a judicious employment of the influence of his exalted rank, he put a check to the evils which arose from the family feuds amongst the nobility; and by discountenancing the horrible execution of the Cameronians, religious fanatics who had risen in insurrection, denied the authority of the King, and murdered Archbishop Sharpe, and to whom he offered a pardon on the easy terms that they would cry, "God save the King!"—restored the nation to comparative tranquillity.

Meanwhile, their Highnesses' prospects in England were anything but cheering. The bill for the exclusion of the Duke from the succession, was passed by the Commons, and only thrown out of the Lords by the opposition of the bishops. The project for banishing James, with the empty title of King, to the distance of five hundred miles from England, and investing the regal power in the Prince and Princess of Orange, as regents for him, was started, and Charles was urged to permit Monmouth to be named as his successor. As none of these measures succeeded, a plot, in which it was pretended that the Duke and Duchess were deeply implicated, was devised. Fitzharris,* an obscure Irishman, came forward, and deposed that Montecuculli, the late agent of the Duchess of Modena, had offered him ten thousand pounds to murder the King; that the Duke was privy to the plot; that powerful forces were to come from France and Flanders to place him on the throne; and that it was proposed, in the event of success, to boil down the bones of the Protestant leaders, and make of them a *sainte ampoule* for the coronation of the future Catholic Kings of England. The Whig leaders carried this absurd fiction to Parliament, "declared, on their souls, that they believed every word of it, and with great pathos and eloquence descanted on the horrible practices of the Duke and Duchess of York, and the Catholics generally." Charles, however, defeated their murderous designs, by suddenly dissolving parliament, and causing Fitzharris to be proceeded against for high treason in the Court of King's Bench. The intelligence of these doings seriously alarmed James and Maria; and, to add to their afflictions, their daughter Isabella died at St. James's Palace, on the fourth of March, 1681, in the fifth year of her age. The bereavement threw the Duchess into a state of deep despondency, which affected her health. James, who was also overcome with melancholy, wrote to his brother, and requested that they both might return, if it was only to restore themselves to convalescence. In reply, Charles, by the advice of Halifax, assured the Duke that he must not expect to again visit England till he had conformed to the Established Church. James, however, unhesitatingly refused to act the hypocrite. In his letter on the subject, he says, "I cannot in conscience do what you so press me to; besides, it would be of little use or advantage, for the Shaftesburian and republican party would say it was only a trick, that I had a dispensation, and that I was still a Catholic in my heart, and say there was more reason to be affeared of popery than ever." Although James's request was denied, the Princess Anne, by the King's permission, sailed to Leith, and, to her infinite delight, joined the company of her persecuted father and stepmother on the seventeenth of July. Twelve days afterwards, the Duke, in quality of Royal Commissioner, opened the Scottish parliament with a speech. To conciliate the members, he invited them all to a sumptuous banquet; and, in return, the city of Edinburgh feasted

* See Memoir of Katherine of Braganza, page 735.

and entertained the Duke and Duchess, the Princess Anne, and the whole Court of Scotland. These festivities terminated, James made a progress to several of the leading towns, and throughout the journey his reception was enthusiastic. About this time, the Duchess of Portsmouth entreated his Majesty to grant her five thousand pounds a year out of James's income from the post office. Charles promised compliance, and, to redeem his promise, sent for his brother to come and arrange the matter with him. The Duke was displeased with the purpose for which he was recalled, especially as he was not permitted to bring his Duchess and his daughter with him. He, however, embarked with all speed at Leith, landed at Yarmouth in March, and immediately proceeded to the presence of Charles, who received him with brotherly affection, granted him permission to reside in England, and, after detaining him for about two months, sent him back to fetch his Duchess and his daughter Anne. At this time Maria was enceinte, and a desire that the babe should be born in London, was the principal, perhaps the only cause of the King's recalling her to Court.

At nine in the morning, on the fourth of May, the Duke embarked for Edinburgh: the weather was foul, dirty, and foggy; the careless pilot took a dangerous course; and on the morning of Sunday, the sixth, the vessel was wrecked. Sir James Dick, Provost of Edinburgh, and one of the passengers, in his details of this catastrophe, remarks, "At eleven o'clock in the morning, the man-of-war called 'the Gloucester,' Sir John Barrie, Captain, wherein his Highness was, and a great retinue of noblemen and gentlemen, whereof I was one, did strike in pieces, and did wholly sink in a bank of sand called the Lemon and Ore, about twelve leagues from Yarmouth. This was occasioned by the wrong calculation and ignorance of a pilot, and put us all in such consternation that we knew not what to do, the Duke and all that were with him being in bed when she first struck. The helm having broken, the man working it was killed by the force thereof at the first stroke. When the Duke got his clothes on, and inquired how things stood, the vessel had nine feet of water in her hold, the sea was fast coming in at the gun-ports, and the seamen and passengers were not at command, as every man was studying his own safety. This forced the Duke to go out at the large window of the cabin, where his little boat was ordered quietly to attend him, lest the passengers and seamen should throng so in upon him, as to overset his boat. This was accordingly so conducted that none but the Earls of Wilton and Aberdeen, Churchill and two of the bed-chamber men, went with him. They were forced to draw their swords, to hold people off." Sir James Dick, with the Earl of Middleton, the Laird of Touch, and numerous others, then entered the long boat, into which so many leaped, that, remarks our author, "Laird Hopton, Mr. Littledel, and others, all being at the place when I jumped, would not follow, because they considered it safer to stay in the vessel than to expose themselves to our hazard. We were so thronged one had no room to stand; and if the rest had not thought us all dead men, I am sure many more would have jumped in upon us." Both boats safely reached the "Mary yacht," from which a rope was cast, so as to bring them to the lee side of the vessel, "when," says Sir James Dick, "every man climbed for his life, and so did I; taking hold of a rope, I made shift upon the side till I came within men's reach, and was hauled in. I then looked back, but could not see one bit of our great ship above water, but only about a Scots ell long of the staff upon which the royal standard stood; for with her striking she had come off the sand-bank, which was but three fathoms, and her draught was eighteen feet. There was eighteen fathom water on each side when she struck, and she sunk in the deepest place. Now if she had continued upon the three fathoms, and broke in pieces there, all would have had time to save themselves; but such was the misfortune, that she was wholly overwhelmed, and all were washed into the sea that were upon her decks: there would have been a relief by boats, if she had stood half-an-hour longer." Hume, following the false assertions of Burnet, in his mention of this catastrophe, makes the following mis-statement: "*The Duke escaped in the barge*, and it is pretended that whilst many persons of rank and quality were drowned, and among the rest Hyde, his brother-in-law, *he was very careful to save several of his dogs and priests*, for these two species of favourites are coupled together by some writers. It has likewise been asserted, *that the barge might safely have held more persons*, and that some who swam to it were thrust off, and even their hands cut, in order to disengage them." Now, according to Sir James Dick's account, the Duke did not go in the barge or long-boat at all, but in his own *little boat;* and according to other contemporaries, the boat was crowded, and withal the Marquis of Montrose, who was struggling with the waves, and a poor fiddler who clung to the side, were taken in, the former by James's own hands, and the latter by his expressed command. As to priests or dogs, according to the best-authenticated evidence, not one of either was in the boat.

James completed his voyage in the "Happy Return," landed at Leith at eight in the morning, on the seventh of May, and proceeding at once to his Duchess, was the first to announce to her the peril in which he had been involved. His arrival was marked by all conceivable demonstrations of public joy; all Edinburgh was illuminated, congratulatory addresses were presented to him, and songs were sung in commemoration of the event. Although James had so narrowly escaped when the ill-fated "Gloucester" went down with nearly two hundred persons on board, he resolved, like a true blue-jacket, to bring his wife and daughter to London by sea, and not, as many of his Scottish friends advised him, overland; Maria willingly consented to with him brave the perils of the deep, and a popular song of the time contains the subjoined pleasing allusion to her departure:

"The wandering dove that was sent forth
To find some landing near,
When England's arch was tosst on floods
Of jealousy and fear:
Returns with olive branch of joy,
To set the nation free
From Whiggish rage, that would destroy
Great York and Albany."

After James had formally bade farewell to the Scotch council, the nobles, the authorities of Edinburgh, and others, he proceeded with his Duchess and his daughter to Leith, and there embarked with them in the "Happy Return." This time the voyage was safe and prosperous. They entered the Thames on the twenty-fifth of May, were met by the King, and received on the royal barge at Erith; and amidst the booming of guns, and the acclamations of thousands of spectators, proceeded up the river in grand procession to Whitehall. The same day, the Lord Mayor and aldermen congratulated them on their return, all the bells in London were set ringing, and at night the city was brilliantly illuminated. Maria, who with James, her husband, now took up her abode at St. James's Palace, requested and obtained the royal permission to have her mother present at the approaching accouchement. The Duchess of Modena received the invitation with pleasure, and hastened to England without ceremony or delay. Her arrival in London was no sooner known, than the exclusionists, who, although outnumbered were not beaten, resolved, should the infant prove a boy, to circulate a report that it was a spurious child, brought over by the Duchess to deprive the Protestant heiress of the crown, and that the real babe was a daughter. They even set rumours afloat in furtherance of their base designs. But their factious proceedings were cut short by Maria giving birth to a Princess several weeks sooner than was expected. The infant entered the world on the fifteenth of August, 1682, was christened Charlotte Maria by the Bishop of London, and eight weeks afterwards died in a convulsion fit.

CHAPTER III.

Maria Queen of England—Mourns the death of Charles II.—Her husband's conduct on their accession—She urges her brother to marry against his will—Her regalia—Coronation—Conduct to the King's mistress, Katherine Sedley—Goes in state to mass—Attends the opening of Parliament—Monmouth rebellion—He implores her intercession—Is executed—The King's clemency to Story, and kindness to the French Protestant refugees—Maria's abhorrence of Father Petre—Mourns the death of her mother—Visits Bath—Is enceinte—Scandalous reports—Apprizes the Princess of Orange of her situation—Sudden illness—Removes to Whitehall—Gives birth to a Prince—Extraordinary circumstances attending her confinement—Illness of the infant—Reports of his death circulated—Public thanksgiving and rejoicing—Maria surprised at the coolness of the Princess of Orange—The Prince fed upon currant gruel—He becomes dangerously ill—His death again reported—Maria visits him—He recovers.

ROM this period we have nothing of importance to relate of Maria Beatrix, previous to the accession of her husband as James II., on the sixth of February, 1685. She was present at the death of Charles II., "was a most passionate mourner, and so tender-hearted as to think a crown dearly bought with the loss of suc a brother." Immediately Charles had breathed his last, James, overcome with grief and fatigue, withdrew to his closet to repose. After the lapse of about an hour, he met the council, and was immediately hailed as King. He then addressed the assembly, told them how deeply he deplored the loss of his beloved brother, and proceeded, "I have been reported a man of arbitrary power, but that is not the only story which has been made of me. I shall make it my endeavour to preserve this government as it is now by law established. I know the principles of the Church of England are for monarchy, and the members of it have shown themselves good and loyal subjects; therefore I shall always take care to defend and support it. I know, too, that the laws of England are sufficient to make the King as great a monarch as I can wish; and as I shall never depart from the just rights and prerogatives of the crown, so I shall never invade any man's property. I have often heretofore ventured my life in defence of the nation, and I shall still go as far as any man in preserving it in all its just rights and liberties." This declaration was joyfully received, and James was immediately proclaimed at the gates of Whitehall, at Temple Bar, and at the Royal Exchange. The first few days of her accession as Queen-consort, Maria was occupied with her royal husband in receiving condolences and compliments from the prelates, lords, ambassadors, and other functionaries. She wore deep mourning for her departed brother-in-law; and, what is remarkable, her first act as Queen was a tyrannical endeavour to force her bachelor brother, the Duke of Modena, to enter the married state with the rich heiress, Mademoiselle de Bouillon, a lady of her own choosing. The twenty-third of April—St. George's day—was appointed for the coronation of her and her lord. Since Anne Boleyn, but one Queen-consort, Anne of Denmark, had been crowned in England; and on this account the claims for the performance of various ancient services were so numerous, that to decide them an especial court was opened at Westminster, on the thirtieth of March. As the crown jewels had been plundered by the Roundheads during the Civil War, the Queen's crown and other regal ornaments were made expressly for her, and that at a most extravagant cost; her imperial diadem, set with diamonds, rubies, and other precious stones, was of itself valued by the goldsmith who made it, at £111,900. However, to retrench in other particulars, the King dispensed with the procession through the city, and other expensive but not really important details. King James observed the ancient custom of washing the feet of poor men, and touching for the King's evil. On the morning of the coronation, the Queen, in her state robes and jewels, and with a richly jewelled gold circlet on her head, went privately in her chair from St. James's Palace to Whitehall, and thence to Westminster Hall, where she reposed in the court of wards till the King had arrived; when she entered the hall in procession, and took her seat under a canopy close to that of the King. The regalia were then delivered with much ceremony to the nobles appointed to carry them, after which the royal pair walked in procession from Westminster Hall to the Abbey; the way was strewn with flowers, drums beat, trumpets sounded, and a choir of vocalists marched in the procession, singing the admired anthem, "O Lord, grant the King a long life." They entered the Abbey by the west door, and immediately proceeded to their chairs of state. The Bishop of Ely preached the sermon, the hymn "Veni Creator" was sung, and first the King and then the Queen were crowned and anointed. "The King and Queen," says Burnet, "resolved to have all things done in the Protestant form, and to assist in all the prayers, only they would not receive the sacrament. In this certainly his Majesty's priests dispensed with him, and he had such senses given of the oath, that he either took it as a sin, with a resolution not to keep it, or he had a reserved meaning in his own mind." One remarkable incident occurred at their coronation; the King's crown—it had been made for Charles II.—was so large, that when placed on his head by Archbishop Sancroft, it tottered, and Mr. Henry Sidney, putting forth his hand to save it from falling, remarked, with more wit than truth, "This, your Majesty, is not the first time the crown has been supported by my family." Trifling as this incident was, it was regarded by Maria Beatrix, and nearly all present, as a foretoken of evil. Of the devout behaviour of the Queen during the service, Dr. Patrick speaks with pleasure: "I observed," he remarks, "a vast difference between the King's behaviour and the Queen's. At the reading of the Litany they both came to kneel before the altar, and she answered to all the responses, but he never moved his lips. She expressed great devotion, but he little or none, often looking about as unconcerned. When she was anointed and crowned, I never saw greater devotion in any countenance; the motion of her body and hands was very becoming, and she answered 'Amen' to every prayer with humility, seriousness, and composure of spirit."

The solemnities concluded, their Majesties returned in procession to Westminster Hall, and reposed in separate apartments till the company had taken their seats at the seven principal tables in the banqueting-hall; they then entered, wearing their crowns, and bearing in either hands their sceptres and rods, and took their seats in the chairs of state at the head of the royal tables. The ceremonies at the banquet resembled those observed at previous coronations, the dishes, more than a thousand in number, were various, rich, and rare, the wines choice and abundant. When their Majesties had washed their hands, and grace had been said by the dean of the Chapel Royal, they sat down to dine. After the first course, the royal champion, Sir Charles Dymock, rode into the hall on a richly trapped steed, and three successive times pronounced the accustomed challenge, and flung down his gauntlet without any objection being offered. Then Garter, with the other kings-at-arms, and the heralds, cried largess in the usual manner, and proclaimed the King's style and titles. During the second course, the Mayor of

Oxford, and the Lord Mayor of London, with twelve of the citizens, as assistants in the buttery, presented the King with wine, and received the bowls and the cup as their fees. When the banquet was ended, and grace said, their Majesties washed their hands, proceeded in procession to the court of wards, ceremoniously delivered their regalia there, and at half-past seven in the evening returned as they came to Whitehall. The fatigue and the excitement of the day so affected the Queen, that she was unwell for a week afterwards.

Although James had sacrificed place and power to the profession of his religion, he, in open disregard to its precepts, still cohabited with his audacious mistress, Katherine Sedley. This infamous woman was stately in person, but so far from beautiful in face, that Charles II. used to say that his brother had her by way of penance. James, who was captivated by her wit and brilliant conversation, and believed himself the father of her two children, made her one of the Queen's maids of honour, created her Countess of Dorchester for life, settled on her an income of £2000 a year, and made her a present of a splendid mansion in St. James's Square. Sedley professed the Church of England faith, and Rochester, in the hope of being able to govern the King through the mistress, urged James, whose blind zeal for Romanism he improperly attributed to the influence of Maria Beatrix, to bestow on her that favour and confidence which the Duchess of Portsmouth had enjoyed in the late reign. The Queen, however, was not of a temper to submit to these indignities without a struggle. Sick with mortification, she took to her chamber, where, by the advice of Sunderland and Father Petre, she summoned these two intriguers, together with the most distinguished Catholic clergy and noblemen at court, to her presence, and then sent for the King. When James arrived, she, with sobs and tears, upbraided him with his infidelity, and declared if he did not give up his mistress, she would retire to a convent. The whole assembly, including Father Petre, the King's priest and confessor, united their remonstrances with hers; and James, surprised and abashed, promised to separate from Sedley for ever, and instantly dispatched an order commanding her to withdraw from Whitehall, and retire to the continent. But Sedley scorned the order, declared she was a free-born Englishwoman, and would reside where she pleased; and if the King wished to remove her he must do so by force, and then she would apply for a writ of habeas corpus, and recover her liberty. James overlooked her insolence, and, to induce her to withdraw from court, made her a present of a valuable estate in Ireland, to which she retired. After an exile of six months, she returned, and the King continued to visit her as well as his other mistresses; but as he did so with all possible privacy, the Queen had the good sense to generally act as if ignorant of his improprieties.

James, although well-intentioned, knew not how to retain the affection of his subjects. Almost his first acts as a sovereign offended the prejudices of the Church of England Protestants. He opened his own Catholic chapel at Whitehall, and there ostentatiously practised the ceremonials of his religion; and with a view to establish liberty of conscience and freedom of worship—measures far in advance of the age—he charged the judges to discourage religious persecutions, and ordered, by proclamation, the discharge of all persons confined for non-conformity; when, to the alarm and annoyance of the Established Church, several thousand Catholics, and twelve hundred Quakers, were released from prison. On the twenty-second of May, 1685, the King opened the parliament in person; the Queen and Anne of Denmark attended in private, and witnessed the ceremony, and, remarks Evelyn, "as her Majesty was there when prayers were said, and several of the lords took the oath, she heard the Pope and the worship of the Virgin renounced very decently." The Commons, by shouts of "*Vive le Roi!*" and afterwards by settling the revenue, in compliance with the royal wish, demonstrated their loyalty; but the rebellion of Argyle in Scotland, and of Monmouth in England, caused James some anxiety. Monmouth landed at Lyme, in Dorsetshire, on the eleventh of June, 1685, and, in a flaming proclamation, denounced the King, by his former title of Duke of York, as a murderer, a traitor, and a tyrant, who had burnt the city of London, supported the Popish Plot, caused Godfrey and the Earl of Essex to be massacred, and his brother, the late King, to be poisoned. In a week he found himself at the head of ten thousand men; and being received with enthusiasm at Taunton, he had the folly to take upon himself, by solemn proclamation, the title of King James the Second, and to set a price on the head of James, Duke of York. But he reaped little benefit from the assumption of royalty. Scarcely a nobleman or gentleman of opulence joined his standard, his forces were undisciplined, and the news of the defeat and capture of Argyle in Scotland, on the seventeenth of June, threw him into an agony of despair. On July the sixth, not three weeks afterwards, his army was routed at Sedgmoor, and on the eighth he himself was taken concealed in a ditch covered with fern. The love of life induced him to write to James a supplicatory letter, imploring mercy, and soliciting a personal interview, as he had an important secret to reveal, which he dared not commit to paper. He also wrote to the Queen and the Queen-dowager, begging them to intercede in his behalf. The interview was granted; he threw himself at the King's feet, and earnestly entreated and fondly anticipated the royal clemency; but James told him that he had rendered himself incapable of pardon, by usurping the title of King. He was beheaded on Tower Hill, on the fifteenth of July, 1685. On the scaffold he exhibited such symptoms of spiritual blindness, that whilst he was preparing for the block, the prelates in attendance prayed "that God would accept his repentance, his imperfect repentance, his general repentance." The headsman was so nervous or unskilful, that unable to effectively execute his horrible task at the third stroke, he flung down the axe, and swore that his heart failed him, and he would do no more; but the sheriffs forced him to proceed, and at the fifth blow the head was severed from the mangled body. The cruelties inflicted on the rebels by the inhuman Kirk and the drunken Judge Jeffreys, are attributed by general history to the orders of James; but the King, so far from sanctioning such barbarous severity, "compassioned his enemies so much," says the Duke of Buckingham, "as never to forgive Jeffreys in executing such multitudes of them in the west, contrary to his express orders." The King's conduct to the rebel Story, may be related as a proof that his Majesty was not the revengeful butcher his enemies would have us suppose. Story, when taken for assisting Monmouth, was ordered before the King and the council; the order being unexpected and prompt, his keeper, without giving him time to prepare himself, cautioned him to answer the questions in a plain, correct manner, and immediately brought him in a coach. On entering the council-chamber, his haggard and squalid appearance surprised and frightened all present. When the King cast his eyes upon him, he exclaimed, "Is that a man, or what is it?" "It is Story, your majesty," said one of the council. "Oh! Story," remarked the King, "I remember him, he is a rare fellow, indeed;" then turning to him, "Pray, Story," said he, "you were in Monmouth's army in the west, were you not?" "Yes, an't please your majesty," replied Story, with ready frankness. "You were a commissioner there, were you not?" said the King. "Yes, an't please your majesty," again answered Story. "And you made a speech before crowds of people?" "Yes, an't please your ma jesty." "Pray," proceeded the King, "if you have not forgotten what you said, let us have a specimen of your rhetoric on that occasion." "I told them, an't please your majesty, that you fired the city of London." "A rare rogue, upon my word!" said the king; "and, pray what else did you tell them?" "That you poisoned your brother, an't please your majesty." "Impudence in the utmost height," remarked James; "pray let us know something further." "I also told them," answered Story, with great sangfroid, "that you had determined to make the nation both papists and slaves." "A rogue with a witness!" exclaimed the King; "and to all this, I doubt not but a thousand other villanous things were added. But what would you say, Story, if, after all this, I were to grant you your life?" "That I would pray for your majesty as long as you lived," rejoined Story, with a submissive bow. "Well then," said James, "in conclusion I freely pardon all that is past, and hope that you will not, for the future, represent your king as inexorable." This is not the only well-authenticated instance of James's clemency. He pardoned Ferguson and Hook—the former had drawn up Monmouth's proclamation, the latter had conspired to shoot him—and he mitigated the severity of the sentence of several others who had personally injured him. He also, although a Catholic, condemned the revocation of the Edict of Nantes, as unchristian and impolitic; and afforded such encouragement to the French Protestants, that at last, nearly fifty thousand of them settled in England. But in this the nation believed him insincere. How, it was asked, could a monarch be favourable to Protestantism, who had, in violation of the laws of the realm, sent an embassy to Rome, and established a secret board to watch over the interests of the Catholics? Impressed with these sentiments, the parliament which met in November so strenuously opposed his proposition for a standing army, the officers in which were to be exempted from the test act, that he suddenly prorogued the houses, with a secret resolution of acting in future without their advice.

Their Majesties spent the summer of 1686 at Windsor and the King, in the presence of the Queen, several times reviewed his army of 16,000 men, who were encamped on Hounslow Heath, and pronounced to be the finest, the best appointed, and the best disciplined soldiers in Europe. From Windsor, the royal pair went on a short progress, and returning to Whitehall in October, kept the anniversaries of their birth-days—they both happened in this month—with great splendour. The Catholic chapel built for their express use, was opened on Christmas eve, and they kept the Christmas festival with regal pomp and liberality. The disgrace of Rochester has by some writers been erroneously attributed to the malice of the Queen; it was really occasioned by the intrigues of Sunderland and Father Petre. The latter had been named in the subsequent summer one of the privy council, an appointment which James knew to be impolitic, and for which he could only account by stating, "that he was so bewitched by my Lord Sunderland and Father Petre, as to let himself be prevailed upon to do so indiscreet a thing." The Queen disliked Petre; she called him a wicked man, and told the King that his elevation to the council would "give great scandal, not only to Protestants, but also to Catholics, as contrary to their rules." This summer their Majesties added to their unpopularity, by giving a pompous public reception to the nuncio D'Adda; and on account of the death of the Queen's mother, the Duchess of Modena, on the nineteenth of July, the court went into deep mourning. Maria deeply deplored the loss of her beloved mother. The affliction injured her health, and on the sixteenth of August, she, by the advice of her physicians, set out for Bath, to take a course of the waters there. The King paid her a short visit in September; and as the hot bath and the mineral waters greatly improved her health, she, on the sixth of October, rejoined his Majesty at Windsor, and from thence went with him to Whitehall on the eleventh, where his birth-day was kept with unusual magnificence.

Towards the close of November, it became evident that the Queen was pregnant. James hailed the circumstance with undisguised joy, announced it by proclamation in the Gazette of December twenty-third, and at the same time ordered a day of thanksgiving to be observed, and a prayer to be said in all the churches for the fruition of his hopes. He promised himself that the child would prove a boy; the Catholic party shared his exultation; but his married daughters and their consorts regarded the crown as their natural inheritance; and that their claim might not be superseded by those of an infant half-brother, they secretly favoured the King's enemies, and caused rumours to be industriously circulated, "that the Queen's pregnancy was a mere pretence, the first act of a farce, which would end in the production of a suppositious child, a false Prince of Wales, to the exclusion of the true Protestant heirs." In ordinary circumstances so improbable a tale would not have found credit; but it was eagerly received by the prejudice of party, and to give a greater air of probability, the story of Queen Mary's "mock conception," by Fox, the martyrologist, was reprinted and distributed among the people.

In December, the Queen, in an affectionate letter, informed her step-daughter, the Princess of Orange, of her situation. On the twenty-first of February, 1688, she again wrote, stating that she reckoned herself gone about twenty weeks, and that she was doing well. She continued to do well till the seventh month, when she became so alarmingly ill that a miscarriage was anticipated, and for several days her life was despaired of. Immediately the danger was over, James wrote as follows to the Prince of Orange.

"Whitehall, May 11th, 1688.

"My going to Chatham on Tuesday last, prevented me from writing to you by that day's post, to let you know I had received yours of the eleventh. I found my ships and stores in very good condition, and chose one of my new third-rates to be fitted out to carry the Queen-dowager, when she goes to Portugal. I came back thither yesterday morning, and found that my Queen had not been well, and was in some fears of her coming before her time; but, God be thanked, she was very well all day yesterday, and continues so now, so that I hope she will go out her full time * * * *I have no more to say, but that you shall find me as kind to you as you can expect.*

"To my son, the Prince of Orange.

"JAMES R."

The concluding paragraph in this letter is an evident allusion to the Prince of Orange's project to deprive James of the crown. At the close of the preceding summer, Louis XIV. had warned the King of his son-in-law's base intentions, and offered him assistance; which he then refused, but which he afterwards solicited, when it was too late.

Maria, who continued in a delicate state of health till after her accouchement, resolved to lie-in at Windsor; but as her time drew near, she, to silence the slanders of her enemies, determined that the event should take place at St. James's Palace with all possible publicity. "The Queen and I intend to lie at James's to-morrow [Saturday] night, she intending to lie in there," remarks the King in a letter addressed to his daughter Mary, dated June eighth, 1688. Throughout that day (June ninth,) the Queen was restless and anxious, and when told that the workmen at St. James's could not possibly finish in time to put up her bed that night, she angrily answered—"I mean to lie there to-night, even though it be upon the boards." At a late hour at night, the arrangements having been hastily concluded, her Majesty was carried in a sedan from Whitehall to St. James's Palace. About eight the next morning, it being June the tenth, Trinity Sunday, she requested the King to summon immediately every one he intended to witness the birth of their offspring. Margaret Dawson was the first to obey the summons; she found the Queen alone, depressed in spirits, chilly and trembling; by her orders the bed was made and warmed with a warming-pan full of hot cinders, before the Queen entered it. Upon this incident, which happened at eight in the morning, whilst the Prince was not born till ten, was founded the slanderous report that a spurious child had been introduced beneath the bed-clothes, in a warming-pan. When the Queen had got into bed, she asked the King if he had sent for the Queen Dowager. "I have sent for everybody," he answered. And so it appeared, for in an hour, the lying-in chamber was crowded with sixty-seven persons. Amongst those who attended as witnesses, were the Queen-dowager, the Countess of Sunderland, and many ladies of rank, besides eighteen members of the privy council. Burnet remarks that the Protestant ladies that belonged to the court, were all gone to church, before the news was let go abroad; but he neglects to add, that they were all sent for, by the Queen's desire. At ten o'clock the child was born, and instantly shown to three of the Protestant ladies present. By a preconcerted sign, the midwife telegraphed to the King that it was a boy; but James, not satisfied with this secret signal, exclaimed aloud—"What is it?" "What your Majesty desires," answered the nurse, who, taking the babe in her arms, carried it into an adjoining apartment, where it was shown to all who had witnessed the birth, and by them pronounced to be a fine, healthy Prince. James, to testify his joy at the event, knighted the Queen's physician on the instant by her bed-side; made rich presents to his ministers and others; caused the guns to be fired, and the bells to be rung; ordered a day of general thanksgiving and festivity, and gave a considerable sum in charity to the poor. Better would it have been for the interests of the misguided monarch, had he have celebrated this event by a general pardon, and the release of the bishops who just previously had been sent to the Tower for refusing to cause his declaration of liberty of conscience to be read in their churches. But James was too obstinate to yield, too upright to attempt to pervert the course of justice; and the trial and acquittal of the prelates greatly accelerated the destruction of his regal power.

A few hours after his birth, the careless nurse gave the Prince too strong a dose of medicine; it rendered him fractious, and the dose was repeated, till at last he became so ill that at three in the morning, he was thought to be dying; the King was called out of his bed, and the whole palace was thrown into a state of consternation. The physicians were sent for, and after they had given him more physic, and made an issue in his little shoulder, he recovered. But the King's enemies turned the event to their own account, by circulating a report that the Prince had died; and to personate him, another and a spurious child had been substituted.

Although their Majesties were annoyed at the libels issued against them from the Dutch press, and informed of the designs of the Prince of Orange, they continued their friendly correspondence with him and his consort. In a letter, dated the twelfth of June, James informed him of the birth of the Prince in the following words:—"The Queen was, God be thanked, safely delivered of a son, on Sunday morning, a little before ten. She has been very ill ever since; and the child was somewhat ill this last night, of the wind; but is now, blessed be God, very well again, and like to have no return of it, and is a very strong boy." The public thanksgiving for the birth of the Prince of Wales took place on the seventeenth of June, and shortly afterwards, the Lord Mayor and Aldermen of London kissed the Prince's hand, and presented him with a purse of gold. The cities of Edinburgh and York presented their Majesties with congratulatory addresses, and the University of Oxford and the laureate Dryden commemorated the event in complimentary poems; but to counteract the impressions which these royal odes might make on the public mind, the Orange faction, in sarcastic rhymes, attacked the character of the Queen, and insinuated that the Prince was a spurious child. At the court of France, the news of the Prince's birth was received with infinite satisfaction. All the ladies at St. Cloud drank his health, and the Duke of Burgundy caused threescore of fusees to be fired. A contemporary remarks, "The mobile at Amsterdam did, at the English consul's, celebrating the birth of the Prince of Wales, commit such rudeness as requires severe resentment. At the same time, they tell us of the extraordinary joy at Rome upon the Prince's birth, and that it was expected his Holiness would suddenly nominate M. Barberino, or some other prelate, to carry his Royal Highness the blessed clouts."* The joyful Queen rapidly recovered; at the lapse of a fortnight she received visits from ladies, and on the twenty-eighth she gave audience to the Dutch ambassador extraordinary, who conveyed to her the deceitful compliments of William and Mary of Orange. Eight days afterwards, she addressed to her step-daughter, Mary, a letter, commencing—"The first time that I have taken pen in hand since I was brought to bed is this, to write to my dear *Lemon.*" This one sentence, unfortunately all that has been preserved, of an epistle in which the Queen, discarding the stiffness and formality of royalty, playfully addresses the Princess of Orange by the pet name of Lemon, fully indicates the familiarity, if not affection, subsisting between the royal ladies at this period.

"Their Majesties and the Prince," observes a news letter, dated the seventh of July, 1682, "continue in very good health. The King hath declared the Prince Prince of Wales, though he is not yet created, and hath ordered him to be prayed for in all churches under that title. About fifteen days hence, the court will be removing to Windsor, and the Prince to Richmond. About the tenth of this month, the Queen's majesty intends to come abroad, her month being then out; and to welcome her Majesty, there are eight or nine vast engines made upon the Thames, of different forms and figures, which are to play several sorts of fire-works within a few nights after. At the lapse of a month, Maria left her chamber and returned from St. James's to Whitehall; but on the following day the Prince became so alarmingly ill, that the display of fire works was postponed; and the Princess Anne exaltingly wrote to her sister Mary, that, "to all appearances, he would soon become an angel in heaven." The Queen deplored his illness; and the sarcasms and vulgar low poems with which his birth and his state audiences—he had actually been paraded through the ceremonies of giving audience to the foreign ministers and others—had been assailed, so annoyed her, that, leaping from one extreme to the other, she, under a pretended dread of his catching the small-pox, shut him up, and would not permit any one to visit him but the nuncio. However, in a few days his health improved; and "this evening, the seventeenth of July," writes the Ellis correspondent, "the fire-works upon the Thames will be played in honour of his birth. The designs of them are very ingenious, and too long to be here inserted. There are several thousands of baloons that are to be shot into the air, and then to fall into the river, and represent several figures. There are twelve mortars that are to cast granado shells into the air, which, when they break, will discover odd mixtures and shapes; the figure of Bacchus representing Plenty, out of whose great tun and belly are to be discharged about eight or nine barrels of combustibles. There are also two large female figures, which represent Fecundity and Loyalty; the emblems of the first are a hare and a hen and chickens, each of which are in their proper time to act their part in the magnificent show of this evening. Two days afterwards," our author proceeds, "the Lady Marquis of Powis, governante to the Prince, hath taught his royal highness a way to ask already; for a few days ago, his royal highness was brought to the King with a petition in his hand, desiring that two hundred hackney coaches may be added to the four hundred now licensed, but that the revenue for the said two hundred might be applied towards the feeding and breeding (bringing up) of foundling children. The idea of founding a Foundling Hospital emanated from the Queen; and she hoped, by connecting the name of her infant son with the benevolent purpose, to obtain for him the good-will of the nation. At the same time, the report that he had died was so generally believed, that she found it necessary to send him daily into the park, under pretence of taking the air, but really that he might be seen by the deluded public.

* MS. Donat. Vol. Brit. Mus. 4194, p. 239.

James, although credibly informed that the Emperor and the Pope were encouraging the Prince of Orange to expel him from the throne, still carried on a correspondence with his treacherous son-in-law. On the twenty-second of July, he replied to William's insincere congratulations on the birth of the Prince of Wales, in the subjoined rather cold, distrustful lines :—

"July 22nd, 1688.

"I have had yours by Mr. Tulestein, who has, as well as your letter, assured me of the part you take on the birth of my son. I would not have him return without writing to you by him, to assure you *I shall always be as kind to you as you can with reason expect.*"

At the same time, the Queen, who evidently believed that the Prince of Orange sincerely sympathised in the maternal joy, dispatched to him the subjoined friendly letter :—

"July 24th, 1688.

"The compliments Mr. Tulestein made me from you, and the letter he brought over, are so obliging, that I know not which way to begin to give you thanks for it. I hope he will help me to assure you that I am very sensible of it, and that I desire nothing more than the continuance of your friendship, which, I am sure, mine shall always one way deserve, by being, with all the sincerity imaginable, truly yours, M. R."

Maria d'Este was surprised that she had not received the fondly-anticipated congratulation on the birth of her son, from her step-daughter Mary. She had written to her an affectionate letter on the sixth of July. Seven days afterwards, she, in a friendly epistle, informed her that "she had come a month sooner than she had expected, and if the child had not been bigger and stronger than any she had ever had, she should have thought he had come before his time." Yet, withal, the Princess of Orange had neglected to express tenderness towards her infant half-brother, the young Prince of Wales. The Queen, who had the weakness to attribute Mary's unkindness to a diminution of affection towards herself, in an expostulatory letter, dated Windsor, the thirty-first of July, remarks: "I suspect you have not been so kind to me as you used to be, and the reason I have to think so is (for since I have begun, I must tell you all the truth), that since I have been brought to bed you have never once, in your letters to me, taken the least notice of my son, no more than if he had never been born, only in that which M. Tulestein brought, that I looked upon as a compliment that you could not avoid, though I should not have taken it so, if ever you had named him afterwards."

As the Queen's former children had all died of convulsions, the physicians advised that the Prince of Wales should be fed by the spoon; but "instead of milk," writes the nuncio, "they gave him an aliment called watter gruell, composed of barley flour and water boiled together and sweetened with sugar, and to which, at times, was added a few currants." This very improper diet injured the health of the royal babe. On the seventeenth of July he was sent to Richmond for change of air; but as his diet was not changed, he continued to grow worse. "Their Majesties have passed three or four days at Richmond, with the Prince of Wales," writes the Ellis correspondent on the seventh of August, "his Royal Highness having continued dangerously indisposed by indigestion, inflammation, and other alarming maladies. Several consultations of doctors and midwives, and nurses, have been had, and at last it was resolved his Highness should have the breast, and a fresh countrywoman hard by was had on Saturday, and he hath been suckled, and been much better. The Queen resolved to continue with the Prince at Richmond till he be well, and in a condition to be removed to Windsor."

The day that their Majesties arrived at Richmond, Colonel Sands, gentleman waiter to the Princess Anne, was sent by her from Tunbridge (where she then was) to the royal nursery, to inquire after the Prince's health. Going up immediately to the King, he entered the nursery, and there saw, lying in the cradle, a pale, long-visaged child, with red spots on his face, and, to all appearances, dying of convulsions. Presently afterwards, the nurses in the room came and turned him out, saying, the Prince was asleep. As he was retiring, he met the King, who, with a troubled countenance, asked him if he had seen the Prince. Sands answered that he had not, when the King's countenance brightened up. After dinner, being called, by the King's orders, to look at the Prince, he entered the nursery, but was shown a fine healthy babe, which he really believed was not the child he had seen in the morning, but one that had been substituted in that infant's place. This tale Sands, who, by his own account, told his Sovereign a falsehood, related to the Princess Anne. She believed, or affected to believe it, caused it to be circulated, and the unfaithful chronicler, Burnet, incorporated it, along with other absurdities and untruths, in his History of his Own Times.

"At Richmond," remarks the writer of the Ellis letters, "the Prince of Wales continues to suck the nurse allowed him, and it hath that good effect which is natural and usual to children. * * * * The nurse is the wife of a tile-maker, and seems a healthy woman. She came in her cloth petticoat and waistcoat, and old shoes, and no stockings; but she is being rigged out by degrees, that the surprise may not alter her in her duty and care. A £100 per annum is already settled upon her, and two or three hundred guineas already given, which she saith that she knows not what to do with." On the ninth of August, the Queen considered the Prince sufficiently recovered to accompany her to Windsor. "On Saturday last," proceeds our author, "his Royal Highness the Prince of Wales was removed from Richmond to Windsor, where he is lodged in the Princess of Denmark's house, which was Mrs. Ellen Gwyn's, and is well recovered of his late indisposition, to the joy of the whole court and kingdom. His Highness's nurse is also in health and good plight, being kept to her old diet and exercise. She hath also a governess allowed her, an ancient gentlewoman, who is with her night and day, at home and abroad." It was the wish of the King's enemies that the royal babe should die; twice he had been in a dangerous state, and his present thriving condition so completely disappointed their expectations, that they vented their spleen by circulating reports that the present Prince of Wales was a suppositious child, whose real mother was his nurse, the tile-maker's wife. This month, Mary of Orange, in a letter to the Queen, at last condescended to mention the Prince of Wales, but with such indifference and cold formality, that, on the seventeenth of August, Maria wrote in answer: "Even in this last letter, by the way you speak of my son, and the formal name you call him by, I am confirmed in the thoughts I had before, that you have for him the last indifference. The King has often told me, with a great deal of trouble, that as often as he has mentioned his son in his letters to you, you never once answered anything concerning him." This epistle the cold-hearted Princess of Orange endorsed, "Answered, that all the King's children shall ever find as much affection and kindness from me as can be expected from children of the same father."

CHAPTER IV.

The King and Queen at last convinced of the designs of William of Orange—Maria's last letter to the Princess of Orange—Impolicy of James—The Prince christened—His birth publicly verified—William of Orange lands—The King hastens with the Prince from London—Maria remains at Whitehall—The King's dangerous illness—General state of excitement and alarm—Prince George of Denmark and others desert to the Prince of Orange—Princess Anne absconds from Whitehall—

James gives up all for lost—Maria escapes with her son to France—Her anxiety for her husband's safety—Proceeds to Boulogne—Hears of James's arrest—Sets out for St. Germains—Receives intelligence of her consort's landing at Boulogne—Welcomed to St. Germains by Louis XIV.—Arrival of her husband—Marked kindness of Louis to the royal fugitives—Absurd etiquettes practised at the Court of France—James proceeds to Ireland—During his absence Maria resides in the convent at Chaillot—Her efforts to assist his cause—He is defeated at the Battle of the Boyne—Returns to the Queen, disappointed and dejected—Maria again pregnant—Her husband makes another futile effort to recover his lost crown—She gives birth to the Princess Louisa Maria—Her kindness to the exiles at St. Germains—James and his gentlemen-pensioners—Jacobite song.

BY this time every one but the King and Queen felt convinced that the Dutch armament was fitted out for the invasion of England. Louis XVI. again warned James of his danger, and offered him ships and troops for his defence. But he scornfully refused the proffered aid, declaring that he could not believe his own children to be capable of compassing his ruin; nor was he convinced of the agonizing truth till the eighteenth of September, when the admiral in the Downs informed him, by express, that the Dutch fleet was in sight. He hurried to London, to take steps for assuming the defensive; and the next day the Queen and the Prince of Wales left Windsor, and met him at Whitehall. "On the twenty-fourth of September," remarks the Ellis correspondent, "the Lord Mayor and Aldermen waited on the King and Queen, to pay their duty upon their Majesties' return from Windsor. His Majesty, in gracious return to the compliment, took notice of the report as if the Dutch intended to attempt upon England, and bid them not be concerned, that he would stand for them as his Majesty hoped they would stand for him; as he had often ventured his person heretofore in defence of the monarchy, so would he go as far as anybody to do it still, against anybody that should offer to disturb our quiet, or to that effect." The report that the Dutch fleet was hovering on the coast, excited alarm, suspense, and distrust; yet the too-confiding Queen continued to correspond with the Princess of Orange. On the twenty-first of September, she excused herself from not writing before, as the Princess Anne came to see her last post, after an absence of two months. On the twentieth of the same month she wrote to her once-loving step-daughter, Mary of Orange: "I am much put to it what to say, at a time when nothing is talked of here but the Prince of Orange's coming over with an army. This has been said a long time, and believed by a great many; but I do protest to you, I never did believe it till now very lately, that I have no possibility left of doubting it. The second part of this news I will never believe, that is, that you are to come over with him, for I know you to be too good, that I don't believe you could have such a thought against the worst of fathers, much less perform it against the best that has always been kind to you, and, I believe, has loved you better than all the rest of his children." As might be expected, this appeal to filial duty was disregarded; and on the fifth of October (her Majesty's birth-day, and the last she was destined to commemorate in England) Maria again wrote to her unfeeling step-daughter as follows:—"I don't well know what to say; dissemble I cannot; and if I enter upon the subject that fills everybody's mind, I am afraid of saying too much, and, therefore, I think the best way is to say nothing." Research has failed to discover an answer to either this, the last letter written by the Queen to the Princess of Orange, or the two preceding epistles; and as Mary knew that she could not justify the conduct of herselt or of her ambitious husband, she, in all probability, passed them over in silence.

Meanwhile James perceived the impolicy of his past misrule; and now that he had let the birth of his son slip by, the golden moment when he might have made concessions without impairing his dignity, he hastened, with an ill grace, to repair his former errors. He courted and conciliated the bishops, proclaimed the free and unbiassed election of a parliament to meet in November, restored the old charter to the city of London, gave up the contest he had so unwisely entered upon with Oxford, and made other important concessions, in the hope of averting the storm which threatened to sweep him from off his throne. But he was blind to the fact known to most of his subjects, that his daughter, many of his ministers and courtiers, and three of the bishops, had pledged themselves to the service of William, and, by their emissaries, were secretly sowing the seeds of disaffection in the army and the navy, and inciting the people to rebellion. James was, certainly, a bigoted, despotic prince, and such was his want of tact, that he chose the present inauspicious period for the baptism of the Prince of Wales; and much to the annoyance of his Protestant subjects, the pope, represented by D'Adda, stood godfather, and Katherine of Braganza godmother. The ceremony was performed with great solemnity in the Catholic chapel at St. James's. Father Saban officiated, and named the Prince James Francis Edward.

On the nineteenth of October, William sailed for England with his invading host; but at night a tempest arose, shattered the fleet, and caused a new respite for James. Meanwhile the Prince of Orange, in two printed declarations, endeavoured to persuade the people of England and Scotland of the rectitude of his intentions, and to convince them that their welfare and his interests imposed on him the duty of inquiring into the birth of the pretended Prince of Wales. At the same time was published a pamphlet, said to have been written by Dr. Burnet, but purporting to be a memorial from the Protestants of England to the states, setting forth the despotism of James, and declaring that the Queen's pregnancy was a pretence, and the birth of the Prince of Wales an imposture. Other similar slanders were also published, in all of which the King was charged with imposing a spurious heir upon the nation. James had hitherto disregarded these fabrications; it was evident they could no longer be passed over in silence; and after overcoming the struggles of pride in his own breast, and the more delicate scruples of his consort, he, on the twenty-second of October, summoned an extraordinary council at Whitehall, where, in the presence of Prince George of Denmark, the privy council, the peers spiritual and temporal residing in the vicinity of the capital, the law officers of the crown, and the Lord Mayor and Aldermen of London, he stated "that he called them together upon a very extraordinary occasion, but that extraordinary diseases have extraordinary remedies. That the malicious endeavours of his enemies had so poisoned the minds of some of his subjects that, by the report he had had from all hands, he had reason to believe that very many men did not think this son, with which God had blessed him, to be his, but a supposed child. But he might say that, by a particular Providence, scarcely any Prince was ever born where there were so many persons present; that he had taken this time to have the matter heard and examined there, expecting that the Prince of Orange, with the first easterly wind, would invade this kingdom. As he had often ventured his life for the nation before he came to the crown, so he thought himself more obliged to do so now as King, and did intend to go in person against him, whereby he might be exposed to accidents; and, therefore, he thought it necessary to have this now done, in order to satisfy the minds of his subjects, and to prevent the kingdoms being engaged in blood and confusion after his death. That he had desired the Queen Dowager to give herself the trouble to come hither to declare what she knew of the birth of his son, and that most of the ladies, lords, and other persons who were present, were ready to depose upon oath their knowledge of the matter."

The birth of the Prince was then verified by the Queen Dowager and seventeen Catholic and twenty-three Protestant nobles and ladies, besides the Queen's midwife, nurses, and physicians. The depositions of all, with the exception of the Queen Dowager, were taken upon oath. They still exist, and, together, form most minute and conclusive evidence of the birth and legitimacy of the son of James II. and Maria Beatrix. After the witnesses had been examined, the King informed the assembly that he had requested the Princess Anne to attend, but that she had absented herself on the plea that she was *enceinte*. He then added, that, "though he did not question but that every person there was satisfied in this matter, yet, by what they had heard, they would be better able to satisfy others, that, besides, if he and the Queen could be thought so wicked as to endeavour to impose a child upon the nation, they saw how impossible it would have been; neither could he himself be imposed upon, having constantly been with the Queen during her pregnancy and the whole time of her labour; that there was none of them but would easily believe him, who had suffered so much for conscience' sake, incapable of so great a villany, to the prejudice of his own children; and that he thanked God that those who knew him knew well that it was his principle to do as he would be done by, for that was the law and the prophets, and he would rather die a thousand deaths than do the least wrong to any of his children."

These proceedings satisfied the King's friends, but failed to silence the malicious slanders of his enemies. Their Majesties and their innocent infant were made the subjects of obscene jests, and it was objected that the Princess Anne had not been present either at the birth or at the investigation; but the truth was, she had purposely gone to Bath, that she might not be present at the lying-in; and as to her excuse of pregnancy, when requested to attend the investigation, her husband, the Prince George, assured Clarendon it was a falsehood, which, he says, so startled him, that he exclaimed, "Good God bless me! nothing but lying and dissimulation in the world."

On the first of November, William again sailed from Helvoetsluys. It was expected that he would make his descent on the coast of Yorkshire; but after steering northward for twelve hours, he changed his course, passed the royal fleet in the Downs, and, on the fifth, entered Torbay, where he landed without opposition. The news surprised and confounded James, and, to add to his embarrassment, many of the peers, spiritual and temporal, showed evident signs of disaffection. His advisers were too timid and too treacherous to afford him wise counsel; and after having frittered away ten precious days in the metropolis, he resolved to proceed to Salisbury plain, the rendezvous of the royal forces, and head his army in person. "This day, the seventeenth of November, at two," writes one of the courtiers, "his Majesty marched for Windsor with the Prince of Wales. They will be to-morrow at Basingstoke or Andover. The Queen is still here. This is a lamentable time with us all." The next day the King sent the Prince on to Portsmouth, that, if necessary, he might be conveyed in secret to France. The Queen parted from her husband and infant with unfeigned sorrow, and during their absence remained in a state of agonizing suspense. She continued to hold the court at Whitehall. Clarendon says, he called upon her on the twenty-second of November, when she told him that the King intended nothing but a general liberty of conscience, which she wondered could be opposed; that he always intended to support the religion established, being well satisfied of the loyalty of the Church of England. This statement, however, is contradicted by the King's own writing. In the Latin letter, which he addressed to the Holy See, and which Lord Milford presented to the Pope, James expressly says, "The only source of the rebellion against us is, that we embrace the Catholic faith; and we do not disown that to spread the same, not only in our three kingdoms, but over all the dispersed colonies of our subjects in America, was our determination."

His Majesty reached Salisbury on the nineteenth, reviewed that portion of his troops that lay there, and appointed the next day for the inspection of the division at Warminster. But in this he was prevented by a profuse bleeding at the nose, which recurred at intervals during that and the three following days. The alarming attack was induced by anguish of mind and bodily fatigue, and the excessive loss of blood prostrated his animal system, and completely incapacitated him from mental or bodily exertion. At this distressing moment the mercenary Churchill, afterwards Duke of Marlborough, went over, with Grafton and others, to the Prince of Orange. James, in bewilderment, withdrew, with his infantry, to Andover, and there he had scarcely arrived, when his son-in-law, Prince George of Denmark, and the Duke of Ormond, with Lord Drumlanrig and Mr. Boyle, also deserted to the enemy. Meanwhile the whole nation was in a state of excitement. To bespatter the Queen, who, with anxious heart, still resided at Whitehall, the Orange faction dipped their pens in the foulest slime of infamy; and on the night of the twenty-fifth, the Princess Anne decamped from Whitehall, and succeeded in joining her husband in Northampton. The domestics affected to be ignorant of her disappearance till the next morning, when they rushed to the Queen's apartments and imperiously demanded their mistress, whilst a mob in the street raised a cry that she had been murdered by the Papists. Shortly afterwards, the King returned dispirited to his capital. The receipt of the intelligence overwhelmed him. Bursting into tears, he exclaimed, "God help me! my very children have forsaken me. Oh, if mine enemies only had cursed me, I could have borne it." The Queen endeavoured to soothe him; but he was so unnerved by the shock, that for several days afterwards he exhibited occasional aberrations of intellect.

The hopelessness of the royal cause became daily more apparent. Newcastle, York, Hull, Bristol, and Plymouth, were in the hands of the Orange partizans, and the people of Nottingham passed a resolution, the language of which dreadfully alarmed the King. "We own," said they, "that it is rebellion to resist our King that governs by law, but *he* was always accounted a tyrant that made *his* will a law. To resist such an one we justly esteem it no rebellion, but a necessary defence." James himself gave up all for lost, and, instead of summoning his energies to oppose the stealthy but successful progress of the Prince of Orange, thought only of providing for the safety of the Queen and their son. He had persuaded himself that his opponents wished to murder the young Prince. To Lord Dartmouth he wrote, "'Tis my son they aim at, and it is my son I must endeavour to preserve; therefore, I conjure you to get him sent in a yacht to France with all possible secrecy, and I shall look upon this as one of the greatest pieces of service you can do me. Four times did he repeat this command. But Dartmouth disapproved of sending the heir-apparent out of the kingdom, and, in reply, wrote, "Pardon, sir, if, on my bended knees, I beg of you to apply yourself to other counsels, for the doing this looks like nothing less than despair, to the degree of not only giving your enemies encouragement, but distrust of your friends and people, who, I do not despair, will yet stand by you in the defence and right of your lawful successor." This letter induced James to alter his arrangements, but not his purpose. The Prince was brought from Portsmouth to Whitehall, and it was resolved that the royal mother and son should escape together to France. Maria at first objected to this arrangement. She could separate from her child, she said, but her husband she could not, would not, leave in his present distress. Nor was she prevailed upon to accompany the Prince, till the King had solemnly promised to follow her in twenty-four hours.

The time appointed for the escape of the Queen and her son was the night of Sunday, the ninth of December. On that night, their Majesties retired to bed as usual; but, about twelve o'clock, they rose, and the Queen attired herself in the disguise of an Italian washerwoman, with the little Prince done up in the form of a bundle of linen, which, when necessary, she should carry under her arm. Thus prepared, she made the King repeat his promise to follow her in twenty-four hours, parted from him in tears, and, attended by two nurses, and conducted by Count de Lauzun and St. Victor—two brave Frenchmen, who generously came to England, and volunteered their services to the distressed King and Queen—stole out of Whitehall, proceeded in a coach, prepared for the purpose, to the Horseferry, at Westminster, and, although the night was dark, stormy, and freezing, stepped intrepidly into a small open boat, crossed the Thames in safety, and landed at Lambeth. Here the coach that had been ordered was not in attendance; the rain fell in showers, and the royal fugitives were forced to wait for half an hour or so under the open shelter of the walls of Old Lambeth Church. Fortunately the child slept the whole time; and when an inquisitive stableman from a neighbouring inn made towards the Queen, with a lighted lanthorn in his hand, St. Victor effectually checked his curiosity by running against him as if by accident, and sending him and his lanthorn rolling in the mire. At length they entered the coach and drove to Gravesend, where they took their places in a common yacht, bound for Calais, on board of which they found several of the Queen's household, who, like herself, were disguised in humble dress, and, to avoid exciting suspicion, made an appearance of being strangers to each other. The wind being fair, the yacht put to sea the moment the Queen and her party came on board. They sailed past the Dutch men-of-war in the channel unquestioned; but they encountered a violent gale. Maria and all the passengers were attacked with violent sea sickness, and, to aggravate her Majesty's sufferings, those of the crew who waited on the distressed ladies believed her to be what she professed, a poor foreign washerwoman, and therefore paid no attention to her personal comforts. The yacht reached Calais on the eleventh of December, and at nine in the morning the distressed Queen landed with her infant son. She took up her residence in a private house, insisted on preserving a strict *incognito*, and wrote to Louis XIV., that "she had crossed the sea in her distress, to seek consolation and protection from the greatest monarch in the world." Having heard nothing but alarming rumours of the King for two days, Maria, in a state of agonizing doubt and suspense, proceeded, on the thirteenth, to Boulogne, where she hoped to receive more certain intelligence. On the nineteenth, she learned that her consort had been arrested. The news struck her dumb. Her first impulse was to return to him and share his misfortunes, whatever they might be; but as every one persuaded her from so impolitic a step, and as the French King had sent her condoling letters and a princely escort to conduct her to Paris, she at length yielded, and on the twentieth of December, proceeded on her journey. When within a few miles of Montrieul, she received intelligence that James was still at Whitehall, but that nearly all the courtiers and peers had deserted him, and that he was too dejected, unnerved, careworn, and imbecile, to think of anything but saving his own life, which he believed the Prince of Orange was anxious to take, by flying to France. From Montrieul the exiled Queen passed through Abbéville and Poix to Beauvais, where she remained till the twenty-fifth, and learned with joy that her husband had left London for Rochester. On reaching Beaumont, a message from the court of France apprised her of the landing of James near Boulogne. The news threw her into raptures. She instantly wrote and dispatched an affectionate letter to him, and then gave way to transports, which were followed by hysterics and a severe attack of spasms. On the twenty-eighth of December she was met at the pretty little village of Chatou by Louis XIV., who cordially welcomed her, tenderly kissed the little Prince of Wales, placed her at his right hand in his own coach, and in this manner conducted her to the splendid palace of St. Germains. When they alighted he gracefully led her into the inner court, told her the whole palace, with its superb furniture and appointments, was at her service, then showed her the sumptuous nursery apartments that had been fitted up expressly for the Prince of Wales, and shortly afterwards departed. To relieve her pecuniary embarrassments without wounding her pride, he had placed 6000 louis-dors in an elegant and attractive casket, stood the casket on her toilet, and ordered the royal upholsterer to present her with the key of it; but this she had scarcely received, when a messenger from James brought the joyful intelligence that he would sleep at Breteuil, and in the afternoon of the morrow arrive at St. Germains. True to his word, the expatriated monarch reached St. Germains at the appointed time. Louis met him in the hall of guards, greeted him with sincere tokens of friendship, and, introducing him to the Queen, said, "Madam, I present to you one whom you will be delighted to behold." Maria shrieked, fell into his arms, and burst into tears. The next day Louis sent him a gracious compliment, and with it the very acceptable present of £10,000. Indeed, the French Sovereign received the royal fugitives with expressions of sympathy and tokens of kindness and munificence that did honour to his heart. He paid them the same honours as if they had been in possession of the British throne, and allowed them 50,000 francs per month for the support of their household. But whilst mourning over their fall in royal but borrowed splendour, Maria and her husband, to their annoyance, were compelled to observe the nonsensical ceremonials and etiquettes then the vogue at the court of France. They were bewildered by the importance attached, by the French nobles and ladies, to the seats they occupied. Some claimed the right to sit in their presence in a superb easy chair, called a *fauteuil*, whilst to others, according to their rank, precedence assigned less costly *fauteuils*, then arm chairs, of various prescribed dimensions, and, lastly, stools. Maria, however, conducted herself with surpassing grace, dignity, and discretion. Louis pronounced her a model of queenly perfection, and, in an instant, all the Duchesses of France hastened to St. Germains to court her good-will. She won the esteem of the dauphin, and policy taught her to propitiate that influential mistress of Louis XIV., Madam de Maintenon.

On the twenty-eighth of February, 1690, the self-banished James proceeded on his expedition to Ireland; during his absence, Maria retired, with her beloved son, from St. Germains to the seclusion of the convent at Chaillot, where she passed much time in prayers for his safety and success; but, at the solicitation of the King of France, she occasionally emerged from her retirement, to take part in the court balls and fêtes, a sacrifice willingly made by the anxious Queen, in the hope of obtaining supplies of money and arms for her distressed husband. Louis, however, could not afford to lavish wholesale sums on the Irish war, and when at last he succumbed to her earnest entreaties, the aid afforded was insufficient. To assist James's cause in Scotland, Maria pawned some of her jewels, and "sent," writes the brave Dundee, "£2000 sterling to London, to be paid to me for the King's service, and two more are coming. I did not think the Queen had known anything of our affairs. I received a very obliging letter from her by Mr. Crain." She also wrote to many other of her husband's old friends in Scotland, and, to leave no stone unturned, she dispatched Lord Melfort to Rome, to solicit assistance from the Pope; but all that could be obtained from his holiness, was a profession of sympathy for the Stuart cause, and a promise of his prayers. A rumour that success had attended the arms of her absent lord, and her all-absorbing love for him, prompted her to address to the Earl of Tyrconnel, who at the time was earnestly assisting James to maintain his regal dignity in Ireland, an importunate epistle, dated from St. Germains, April 5th, 1699, in which, after observing, "I beg of you to take care of the King, and not to let him be so encouraged by the good news he will hear, as to endanger himself or his cause by going too hastily into England;" proceeds: "Pray put his Majesty often in mind of being careful of his person, if not for his own sake, for mine, my son's, and all our friends, that are undone if anything amiss happens to him. I dare not let myself go upon this subject, I am so full of it; I know you love the King, I am sure you are my friend, and therefore I need say the less to you; but cannot end my letter without telling you that I never in my life had a truer or a more sincere friendship for anybody than I have for you.

"M. R."

Just after penning this letter, Maria had the happiness to prevail on Louis to dispatch to Ireland that fleet which drove William's squadron out of Bantry Bay, and land a much-needed supply of arms, ammunition, and money for her husband. The news of the success of this expedition delighted her; and on learning that the French admiral had defeated the English fleet off Beachy Head, in the beginning of July, she wrote him a complimentary letter, congratulating him on his success, and thanking him for opening the way for the return of herself and her royal lord to their usurped throne. But her rejoicings were premature; three weeks before this hopeful letter was penned, James's army had been completely defeated and routed in the sanguinary battle of the Boyne, and the unfortunate monarch had precipitately fled to Dublin, and thence to Waterford, where, with Tyrconnel and a few faithful adherents, he put to sea, and, after a prosperous voyage, landed at Brest on the tenth of July. There he remained, for the necessary purpose of sending all possible relief and encouragement to his adherents in Ireland and Scotland, till the twentieth, when he hastened to the presence of the Queen. The royal pair, as may be supposed, marked their meeting with the fondest expressions of affection: and James, in allusion to his defeat at the Boyne, told Maria, "that he knew he should be censured for having risked so unequal an encounter, but that he had no other post so advantageous, and was loth to relinquish the enterprise without an effort." Maria, with her husband—they now were king and queen only in name—paid a state visit to Louis the Fourteenth in October. Towards the close of the subsequent month, she, to her joy, proved enceinte; her situation was made known in January, 1692, and shortly afterwards James sent the subjoined letter to the peers and peeresses, the wife of the Speaker of the Commons, the lady mayoress of London, the wives of the sheriffs, and to the eminent accoucheur, Dr. Chamberlain:

"James R.

"Right trusty and well-beloved cousin and counsellor, we greet you well. Whereas, our royal predecessors used to call such of their privy council as could conveniently be had, to be present at the labour of our queens, and witness of the births of their children, and that we have followed their example at the birth of our dearest son, James, Prince of Wales, however that precaution was not enough to hinder us from the malicious aspersion of such as were resolved to deprive us of our royal right, that we may not be wanting to ourself, now it hath pleased Almighty God, the supporter of truth, to give us hopes of further issue, our dear consort, the Queen, being big and drawing near her time, we have thought fit to require such of our privy council as can come, to attend us here in St. Germains, to be witness to our said consort the Queen's labour. We do hereby signify this our royal pleasure to you, that you may use all possible means to come with what convenient haste you can, the Queen looking about the middle of May next. And that you may have no scruple on our side, our dear brother, the most christian king, has given his royal word and promise to you, as we hereby do, that you shall have leave to come, and the Queen's labour being over, to return with all safety. The iniquity of the times, the tyranny of strangers, and misled party of our own subjects, brought us under the necessity of using this unusual way; yet we hope it will convince the world of the truth and candour of our proceedings, to the mortification of our enemies. We, not doubting of your compliance herewith, bid you heartily farewell. Given at our court at the castle of St. Germains, the second day of April, N.S. 1692, and in the eighth of our reign."

At this period, James was led to hope that he would yet regain his lost crown. The King of France was making great preparations to assist him. One-third of the clergy of the Church of England remained true to their allegiance, and were anxious for his restoration. His daughter, Anne, had sought to be reconciled to him, and he had received assurances, that the army, commanded by Marlborough, and the fleet by Russell, would declare in his favour, and that the people, generally, were disgusted with the extravagance and misrule of William and his courtiers. Immediately the French fleet was ready, he resolved to sail for England, and recover his sceptre from the grasp of his too-ambitious Dutch son-in-law. Having invested his son, the Prince of Wales, who was now a fine boy, in his fourth year, with the order of the garter, and departed from his Queen, in sorrow, on the twenty-first of April, he hastened to La Hogue, where, to crown his misfortunes, he witnessed the disastrous defeat of the French fleet, by the combined English and Dutch navy. Although this action completely annihilated his hopes, when he saw the English sailors courageously boarding the French vessels, he, with an irrepressible burst of national enthusiasm, exclaimed, "My brave English! my brave English!" He lingered at La Hogue for upwards of three weeks, bemoaning his misfortunes, with a dejection bordering on insanity. Maria, in compliance with his commands, deferred her visits to her favourite convent at Chaillot, till his return. This took place on the twenty-first of June, and, just a week afterwards, she gave birth to a daughter, at St. Germains, in the presence of the great ladies of the French court, the Archbishop of Paris, Madam Meereroon, the wife to the Danish Ambassador; all the English nobles and their ladies, who had followed their sovereigns into exile, and other exalted personages. The royal babe was christened Louisa Maria, with great pomp, in the chapel-royal of St. Germains. She was held at the font by the Duchess of Orleans, Louis XIV stood godfather, and James fondly called her *La Concolatrice*, his comforter.

At this period, the palace of St. Germains was crowded with noble Jacobite emigrants, and the town was filled with numerous Scotch, English, and Irish families, who had sacrificed their all, in futile efforts, for the restoration of James II. To relieve their destitution, Maria religiously denied herself luxuries, and, at times, almost necessaries. James would frequently call the more modest and indigent of them into his cabinet, and distribute to them, folded up in paper, various sums of money, according to the merit, the quality, or the exigency of each. The gentlemen he had saved from starvation, by embodying them as his household troops; but Louis XIV., whose pensioner he himself was, desired him to disband them. He complied with regret, and when he reviewed them for the last time, he "passed along their ranks, and wrote in his pocket-book, with his own hand, every gentleman's name, and gave him his thanks, in particular; then, removing to the front, bowed to the body, with his hat off. After he had gone away, he returned, bowed to them again, and burst into a passion of tears. The regiment kneeled, bent their heads and eyes steadfast on the ground, and then rose and passed him with the usual honours of war." Meanwhile, the deposed King and his consort were fondly remembered by the Jacobites in England, who, that their cause might not be forgotten, sung at their convivial meetings the subjoined and other enigmatical songs.

"To one King, and no King, one uncle, and father;
To him that's all these, yet allowed to be neither.
Come, rank round about, and hurrah to our standard,
If you'll know what I mean, here is a health to our landlord.

To one Queen, and no Queen, one aunt, and no mother;
Come, boys, let us cheerfully drink off another.
And now to be honest, we'll stick by our faith,
And stand by our landlord, as long as we've breath.

To one Prince, and no Prince, one son, and no bastard;
Beshrew them that say it, a lie that is fostered.
God bless them all three, we'll conclude with this one—
It's a health to our landlord, his wife, and his son.
To our monarch's return, one more we'll advance.
We've a King that's in Flanders, another in France.
Then about with the health, let him come, let him come then;
Send the one into England, and both are at home then."

CHAPTER V.

Death of Mary II. revives the hopes of the Jacobite partizans—Louis XIV. prepares an armament to assist James in the recovery of his realms, but prevents it from sailing—Peace of Ryswick—William acknowledged by France King of Great Britain—Louis demands the payment of Maria's dower—Parliament grants it, but William applies it to his own use—William endeavours to drive Maria and her consort from St. Germains—Prior, the poet's, letter—Maria attacked with influenza—Growing importance of her son—Illness, sufferings, and death of James II.—His obsequies—Anguish of the Queen—Louis XIV. pays her a visit of condolence, and acknowledges her son King of England—James's religious practices whilst in France—Maria's letter of James's forgiveness, to Anne of Denmark—The first acts as guardian to her son—Fuller's libel—Her son attainted and abjured by the British Parliament—The Lords endeavour, but the Commons refuse to attaint Maria—She is seized with dangerous illness—William III. dies, and Anne of Denmark succeeds him—Maria slowly recovers.

HILST James and Maria were leading the life of rigid ascetics in France, and occupying their time in visits to convents and monasteries, and inflicting on themselves austere penances, their friends in Britain were anxiously plotting to restore them to their regal dominions; and the death of Queen Mary II., in 1694, induced the Jacobite partizans to again count on success. They anticipated that the Princess Anne, who stood nearer in relationship to the crown than William, would attempt to invalidate his title. But in this they were mistaken. Anne knew that her claim rested on the same authority as William's title—the will of the people; and she had the duplicity to court his friendship, and, at the same time, to carry on a secret correspondence with her unfortunate father. "The Princess Anne," remarks James II., in the journal of his life, "notwithstanding the professions and late repentance, appeared now to be more satisfied that William should remain, though he had used her ill, and usurped on her rights, than that her father, who had always cherished her beyond expression, should be restored. But his own children had lost all bowels of compassion and duty for him." Although greatly afflicted at his eldest daughter's death, James did not attempt to make a descent in England at the time. But in February, 1695, he, at the urgent entreaty of his adherents in London, resolved upon making another effort to recover his lost realms. With this view, troops were got ready, French vessels were prepared to carry them across the channel, and James proceeded to Calais; but, ere he could embark, Louis XIV., who was willing to aid an insurrection in England, but unwilling to risk the chance of exciting one, sent orders, that the transports were not to weigh anchor till the certain news of a rising in England or Scotland had been received. At this juncture, the discovery of Barkley's base plot against William's life frustrated the scheme devised by the more moderate Jacobites for the intended revolt, in conjunction with the proposed landing of "the King over the water," as they enigmatically designated James; and, to crown the misfortune, a terrific storm arose and wrecked the French fleet, which should have conveyed the deposed King and his little armament across the channel. On the twenty-third of March, James retired to Boulogne, and there waited, whilst Maria Beatrix earnestly besought Louis to permit Mary to proceed to England, with the proposed French forces. Louis, however, was inexorable, and the reluctant James returned to his condoling consort at St. Germains, only to weep over the bitter disappointment of his hopes. Meanwhile, he was offered the crown of Poland; but, by the advice of Maria, he refused to accept it. He had resolved, he said, to hold himself, till death, free to return to his own realm; England was, alone, dear to him as a nation, and he hoped his people would yet unite in recalling him.

After the death of Colbert, the finances of France fell into such disorder, that Louis XIV., unable longer to maintain his stand against England and her allies, became anxious for a general peace. For this purpose a congress was held at Ryswick, in 1697, and, after much diplomatic manœuvring, the terms were arranged. To the painful annoyance of James and his consort, one of the leading articles stipulated the recognition of William as King of Great Britain and Ireland. But, although James was forced to cede this point, he insisted on the payment to Maria of the dower settled on her by the British parliament as Queen of James II. The demand was just and reasonable; Maria had done nothing to forfeit her claim on the revenue of England as a Queen-consort, and to the British plenipotentiaries' absurd objections thereto, Louis replied that the appanage of the consort of James II. had been settled upon her by act of parliament, that act had never been repealed, and therefore that she had an incontestable right to all the arrears of the revenue due to her as Queen consort since she left England, as well as to all these which shall become due to her hereafter.

The spirit in which William's privy council met the claims of Maria d'Este, may be gleaned from the subjoined extract from an official dispatch of Sir Joseph Williamson:—

"As to the late King James's Queen's jointure, which the French stick hard upon to be made good, it is a point of that delicacy that we are not willing hitherto to entertain it as any matter of our present business. If she have by law a right, she be to enjoy it, if not, we are not here empowered to stipulate anything for her; and so we endeavour to stave it off from being received as any part of what we are here to negotiate. However, it seems to be of use, if Mr. Secretary Vernon can do it without noise or observation, to get an account of all that matter, how it now stands, and what settlements were made by the marriage articles, if any. What, if any kind have been made on her, and how far, according as the law now stands, those that have been made will take. A private knowledge of this, if we could get it in time, might be of good help to us to stave off the point which, as we think, cannot so much as be openly treated on by any of us without inconveniences that will follow."

Meantime Maria arranged that her dower should be transmitted to her through the medium of Louis XIV. But she might have spared herself these pains: William signed the treaty, stipulating it to her, and then defrauded her, and deceived the British parliament by charging, on that account, the annual sum of £50,000, which he applied wholly to his own uses. By a secret article in the treaty of Ryswick, William agreed to adopt James's son, the Prince of Wales, as his successor, provided that James would relinquish his own claim to the crown of Great Britain, and not attempt to drive him (William) from the disputed throne. This the Orange partizan, Dalrymple, pronounces to be an intended piece of generosity towards the exiled family; but the Jacobites denounced it as a scheme of William's to get the young Prince of Wales into his power, and then retain him as an hostage against

James, and as a check upon the probable intrigues of Anne and her partizans. But, however this may be, when Maria was informed of the project, she declared, with great vehemence, that, much as she loved her son, she would rather see him dead at her feet, than permit him to be instrumental to his father's wrongs. James acquiesced in this sentiment, added that he would never trust his son to the keeping of the treacherous Prince of Orange, and instantly spurned the proposal with indignity. William III., now that he was formerly recognized as King of England by Louis XIV., laboured to drive his unfortunate step-parents from St. Germains; but, although he thrice repeated the unjust demand, the French King—to his honour be it recorded—thrice firmly negatived it.

Prior, the poet, who was secretary to the splendid embassy sent by William to the court of France after the Peace of Ryswick, remarks,in a letter addressed to Halifax, "I found old James and all his court the other day at St. Cloud. *Vive Guillaume!* You never saw such a strange figure as the old bully, James II., is; lean, worn, and shrivelled, not unlike Neale, the projector. The Queen, Maria Beatrix, looks very melancholy, but otherwise well enough. Their equipages are all very ragged and contemptible. I have written to my Lord Portland the sum of several discourses I have had with M. de Lauzun, or rather he with me, about the pension which we were to allow the Queen. If we do not, I, or rather my Lord Jersey, should now be furnished with some chicaning answers when we are pressed on that point, for it was fairly promised, that is certain." Prior's remark in this coarse letter, as to the fact of the promise, was correct, at least the parliament thought so, granted the dower, and believed it was paid, although, in fact, it never found its way further than the pockets of William III.

In the winter of 1699, James, Maria, and their son, the Prince of Wales, all suffered from attacks of influenza, so severe and protracted, that they did not recover their health and vigour till the subsequent spring. Of the growing importance of the Prince of Wales, Manchester, the British ambassador in France, bears witness. "Last Thursday, the twenty-second of May, 1700," he writes the Earl of Jersey, "was a great day here. The Prince of Wales, as they call him, went in state to Notre Dame, and was received by the Archbishop of Paris with the same honours as if the French King had been himself there. After mass he was entertained by him, and your Lordship may easily imagine that all the English that are here ran to see him." The death of Anne of Denmark's only surviving child, the young Duke of Gloucester, in August 1700, augmented the respect paid by the court of France to the heir of James II. "The melancholy news produced a great effect here," reports William's ambassador. "The Prince of Wales is shortly to be at Fontainebleau for the first time: an apartment is now preparing for him." On the eighth of September the ambassador again writes—"The whole court of St. Germains, saving the king and queen, is actually in mourning One of the cabinet there declared that they, so far from expecting an official notification of the Duke of Gloucester's death, considered that King James himself ought rather to notify it to other Princes. I must also tell you," proceeds Manchester, "that the court of France goes to Fontainebleau on the twenty-third instant, and the late King [and Queen] of England and the Prince of Wales, on the twenty-seventh. There are great numbers of English; and at St. Germains, every day fresh arrivals come to make their court there." A few weeks later, some of the Stuart partizans, it would appear, became anxious that Maria's son should, unknown to his parents, unite with them in the hazardous project of crossing the channel, landing in England, and rising the people in their favour. On the eleventh of December, Manchester writes—"They have, at St. Germains, an apprehension that the Prince of Wales will be carried away into England with his own consent, and upon this they have increased his guards from six to fourteen. They think their game so very sure, that ther is no occasion he should take such a step." It was certainly wise of the royal exiles to prevent the premature appearance of their beloved son in England, although had James himself landed at this time in the realms he had so foolishly deserted, his efforts, if prudently directed, would, doubtless, have been successful. Nearly all the Irish, and a good half of the English, weary of heavy taxation and ruinous wars, openly and loudly clamoured against the Dutch Sovereign, whilst the Scots moaned the absence of the deposed monarch and his consort, as a national calamity.

But the unfortunate James II. was never again to set foot in England. The flame of his life was about to flicker, brighten up for a moment, and then expire for ever. He was attacked with the first serious symptoms of his approaching end suddenly and unexpectedly. Whilst their Majesties were at chapel on the fourth of March, 1701, the choir sung the anthem, "Remember, O Lord, what is come upon us; consider and behold our reproach; our inheritance is turned to strangers, our houses to aliens." Those words the King applied to himself. They recalled to his mind the base conduct of his daughters, and his own fallen condition, in vivid, agonizing colours. His enfeebled frame was unable to withstand the shock, and before the anthem was ended, a torrent of blood gushed from his mouth and nostrils, and he sunk to the ground in a fit of sanguineous apoplexy. He was immediately carried to his chamber, and put to bed. The afflicted Queen struggled to conceal her own distress of mind, anxiously watched by his bed-side, and exerted her utmost energies to alleviate his sufferings. But neither the tender care of his consort nor the skill of his physicians could save him from an attack of paralysis, and at last it was resolved that he should try the waters of Bourbon. "They intend," writes a contemporary, "to pump his right arm, which he has lost the use of, and he is to bathe, and drink the waters." He set out on his journey on the fifth of April, accompanied by his affectionate Queen. Louis provided the funds for the occasion. "They (James and Maria)," remarks the English ambassador, "desired but 30,000 livres of the French court for this journey, which was immediately sent them in gold. I don't know but they may advise him (James) after that to a hotter climate, which may be convenient enough on several accounts. In short, his senses and memory are very much decayed, and, I believe, a few months will carry him off." On the first day, James and Maria reached Paris, and thence, passing onward, by short stages, from convent to convent, arrived at Bourbon on the nineteenth. During their sojourn at Bourbon, they paid ceremonious visits to the monasteries and other religious houses in the neighbourhood, and charmed and edified all present by their humility and pious conversation. The baths of Bourbon effected so rapid a change in James, for the better, that at the commencement of the second week in June the royal pair returned to St. Germains. Maria, however, had the sorrow to find that the improvement in her beloved consort's health was but transitory. "June the fifteenth," writes the Earl of Manchester, "King James is so decayed in his senses, that he takes care of nothing, all things going direct to the Queen." In another dispatch, dated the thirteenth of July, our authority proceeds: "The late King was taken with another fit of apoplexy, and it was thought he would not have lived half an hour. His eyes were fixed, and I heard yesterday he was ill again. He is so ill decayed, that by every post you may expect to hear of his death." From this second attack James sufficiently recovered to linger through the summer. The Queen was constantly by his side, and, supported by her willing arms, he, on fine days, would frequently walk in the parterre, or on the terrace at St. Germains. His end was hastened by the recurrence of the incident which caused his attack of apoplexy in the preceding March. Whilst he was at mass, on Friday, the second of September, the choir, with blamable indiscretion, again sung the anthem, "Lord, remember, what is come upon us," &c. James, as on the former occasion, applied the words to himself, and, overcome with agonizing emotion, fell into the Queen's arms, and was carried to his chamber in a strong fit. Maria, as before, watched with tender care by his bed-side. On Saturday he rallied, but on Sunday he was attacked with a more severe fit than before, and when his clenched teeth were forced open, an alarming torrent of blood gushed from his mouth. The affrighted Queen, although unable to conceal her emotion, insisted on remaining by his bed-side, and when the hœmorrhage subsided and his consciousness returned, she became frantic with joy. In fact, James was more collected than his consort. He felt that his end was drawing nigh, and sending for the Prince of Wales, he embraced him, and exhorted him to serve God with all his power; never to put the crown of England in competition with his eternal salvation: if Providence placed him on the throne of his ancestors, to govern his people with justice and clemency, to honour his mother, and to be a kind brother to his sister Louisa. The dying father also blessed and admonished the Princess Louisa, and, at parting, implored her to serve her Creator in the days of her youth, to consider virtue as the greatest ornament of her sex, and to closely follow the steps of that great pattern of it, her calumniated mother, whose virtues, he felt assured, would be made, by Time, the mother of truth, to shine with the brilliancy of the sun itself. The Earl of Manchester, William the Third's ambassador at the Court of France, kept a keen watch on the proceeding of Maria and her dying lord. From his dispatches we extract the subjoined:—

"Paris, Sept. 7th.—On Sunday last, King James had several fainting fits, which lasted so long, that they thought him dead; but they brought him at last to himself. He received the extreme unction, and seems much resigned. He exhorted the Prince of Wales to keep his faith, shewing him of how little value a crown was in comparison to his salvation. He continued long on this subject, and told the curate of St. Germains that he would be buried in their church without pomp, and with only an inscription, 'J. R. of England.' The physicians cannot tell what his distemper is. They think that an imposthume is broke; for a great deal of corruption and blood comes continually from him. Yesterday he had another fit, which lasted an hour. The French King and the whole court have been to take their leave of him; but he was not dead last night, though none expect he can recover.

"Paris, Sept. 9th.—King James is still alive, but without hopes of recovery. He seems much resigned, and has exhorted the Lords Middleton and Griffin, and the rest of his Protestant servants, to embrace the Roman religion. They talk much of what King James said to the P. [prince] to keep stedfast to his religion, and not depart from it on any account whatsoever. I can tell you that the moment King James dies, the other will take the title of King of England, and will be owned as such by those of St. Germains. The French King is now at Marly, and at his return he goes to Fontainebleau, so it may be easily contrived not to see the P [prince] till his return. The Queen will be in a convent at Chaillot till the King is buried, and the P. [prince] at the Duke of Lauzun's, at Paris, and after that they will return to St. Germains. I doubt not but the French will call him *Roi d'Angleterre*.

"Sept. 14th.—It was expected that King James would have died last night, but he was alive this morning, though they expect he will expire every moment, being dead almost up to the stomach, and he is sensible of no pain.

"Sept. 16th.—We have been ever since Tuesday expecting to hear of the death of the late King. His grand distemper now is a lethargy, and he is often thought dead, though with cordials *et cetera* they keep him up without any hopes of recovery. The King of France was that day to see him, and then he declared publicly that he would own the P. [prince] for King of England, and ordered the captains of the guards to pay him the same honours they did to the late King James. This is what his Majesty may rely upon."

When the pangs of death came visibly upon James, his confessor requested Maria to withdraw, as he was about to offer up prayers for a departing soul, and her tears and sobs might disturb her husband and distract his attention from the holy service. She reluctantly consented; but the fervour with which she kissed the dying King's hands aroused him from his lethargy, and a painful scene ensued. Maria wept, wrung her hands, and, unable to restrain her feelings, implored him either to live for her or to let her die with him. James, who retained his consciousness to the last, told her, with remarkable calmness and resignation, that it was wicked not to submit with pleasure to the will of God. "Besides," he remarked, "I am going to be happy, and for ever I will pray for you; and you, therefore, instead of weeping, should rejoice at my departure." Maria was carried out in hysterics, and when, a few hours afterwards, she learned the terrible truth that her consort was no more, she shrieked out, "O God, is it, then, over?" and in agony of bitter sorrow, rolled herself on the floor, tore her hair, wept a flood of tears, and, at last, sunk into a swoon; "but," remarks a contemporary, "when this sudden paroxysm of grief had subsided, she expressed sorrow for not having freely resigned herself to the will of God, prayed fervently for fortitude to withstand the shock, and never again gave way to uncontrolled despair."

King James II. expired between three and four o'clock, in the afternoon of Friday, the sixteenth of September, N.S., 1701, with great marks of devotion; and, immediately afterwards, the Prince of Wales was proclaimed King of Great Britain, Ireland and France, by the title of James III. "There was no other ceremony," writes the Earl of Manchester, "than that the Queen waited on him, and treated him as King; whilst those at St. Germains kissed his hands, and the French complimented him. What was done in the town, was done in a tumultuous manner. Some say there was a herald, an Irishman. Lord Middleton did not appear, because he could not tell how the title of France would be taken here, had they done it in form. Lord Middleton brought the seals to him, which he gave to him again. Others did the like. I am told, that before the French King made this declaration, he held a council at Marly, where it took up some time to debate, whether he should own him or no; or if he did, whether it ought not to be deferred for some time. The secret of all this matter is this, that, in short, there was a person that governs here, who had some time since promised the Queen that it should be done; so that whatever passed in council, was only for form's sake."

A few hours after the death of her beloved husband, the sorrowing Maria d'Este retired to her favourite convent at Chaillot, and there solaced her grief by prayer, and by rigid observances of the ceremonious and the superstitious rites prescribed by the Church of Rome for those who have been bereaved of a dear relation. On the seventeenth, the body of James II. was embalmed; his heart was placed in a golden urn, and presented to the convent at Chaillot; his bowels were privately interred in the church of the Benedictines, Fauxbourg de St. Jacques, Paris, whither his body was conveyed with but little pomp; and after the obsequies were solemnized, left uninterred in one of the chapels, a circumstance occasioned by his having desired in his will to be buried in Westminster Abbey. On the nineteenth, Maria returned to St. Germains; and on the twentieth, Louis XIV. came thither to pay her a visit of condolence, and to compliment her young son as King of England. "When the French monarch arrived at St. Germains," writes Charles Lyttelton to his father, "the youthful King of England met him at the top of the stairs, and after they had embraced one another, conducted him into the mourning chamber, where the Queen, Maria Beatrix, laid upon the bed to receive him [according to the custom of France]. After the ceremonies were finished, the King conducted him back to the top of the stairs, always giving him the right hand."

The Earl of Manchester, in his despatches to England, alludes to the events of this period in the following words:—"September twenty-one.—I did not go to Versailles yesterday, for I thought it not proper till I had his Majesty's orders. I was satisfied that the whole discourse would be of their new *Roi d'Angleterre*, and of the King going to make him the first visit to St. Germains, which he did that day. He stayed but little with him, giving him the title of Majesty. He was with the Queen a considerable time. The rest of the Court made their compliments the same day.

"September twenty-three. The French King made the P. (Prince) the first visit. The next day, the P. (Prince) returned the visit at Versailles; when the French King treated him with the same respect that he was used to treat his father. All the ceremonies passed to the perfect satisfaction of those at St. Germains.

"September twenty-four.—I have seen M. de Torcy, and can perceive from him that the French King was brought to do this at the solicitation of the Queen, at St. Germains. It is certain that M. de Torcy, as well as the rest of the ministers, was against it, and only the Dauphin, and Madame de Maintenon, whom the Queen had prevailed with, carried this point. The will of the late King James is opened, but not yet published; but I hear it is to be printed. What I have learned of it is, that the Queen is made Regent; the French King is desired to take care of the education of the P. (Prince); that, in case he be restored, the Queen is to be repaid all that she has laid out of her own; that all other debts which they have contracted since they left England, and what can be made out, shall be paid. That the new King shall not take any revenge against his father's enemies, nor his own. That he shall not use any force in matters of religion, nor in relation to the estates of any person whatsoever. He recommends to him all those that have followed him. I am told that Lord Perth is declared a Duke, and Caryl a Lord. I do not doubt but we shall hear of several new titles and garters. Certainly there ought to be some stop put to all this, else we shall not know where we are."

James's will is dated November the seventeenth, 1688; it was made by him when he was about to join his army at Salisbury, just after the Prince of Orange had landed. By that testament he desired that his body be privately interred in Henry the Seventh's chapel; named his son Prince James his sole heir, constituted Maria as his executrix, and the guardian of their son, and appointed a council, consisting of Prince George of Denmark, the Dukes of Newcastle and of Queensbury, the Earls of Lindsay, of Nottingham, and of Perth, and other nobles; some of whom proved friends, some foes, to assist her in her important duties. By virtue of this will, Maria took upon herself the title of Regent of England; and the King and the Court of France treated her as such.

During his sojourn in France, James led a devout, harmless life; hunting was his chief diversion. Father Brettonneau says, "King James never missed going to La Trappe once a year. He would stay there three or four days, which he passed in long meditations and spiritual conferences with the abbot and his confessor, whom he took with him. He assisted at the choir hours, except at night. He ate nothing but eggs, raisins, and pulse, unless he was indisposed. His self-abhorrence, and holy confession for his sins, inspired him with such a spirit of mortification, as would have carried him too far, if his confessor had not opposed it, and moderated his austerities. He kept very severe fasts, and would upon certain days bind his body with a very sharp-pointed iron chain. His-self discipline was very rigorous, and, withall, he took such care to conceal those exercises of penance, that having once, by chance, left his instrument of discipline in a place where the Queen found it; he so blushed, that her Majesty had never in her life before seen him in such confusion." James himself asserts: "Forasmuch as it has pleased the divine goodness graciously to touch my heart, when I was at La Trappe, more sensibly than ever; I have since, by the aid of the same grace, done my utmost to reform and amend my life. After I had been there two or three days, which,

I thank God, I continue to do every year since my return from Ireland, I perceive I have made a considerable improvement, for I begin to have a more perfect knowledge of the vanity of human grandeur. I was very well convinced that nothing ought to be more passionately desired than the love of God; and that it is the duty of every good Christian to mortify himself, especially such a wretch as I am, who have lived so many years in an almost continued state of sin; till, at last, it has pleased thee, Oh, my God! out of thine infinite mercy, to call me back to myself, by thy fatherly corrections."

James, on his death-bed, had charged Maria to inform his daughter, Anne of Denmark, that, with his expiring breath, he had forgiven her and blessed her. This painful duty Maria performed, by addressing the subjoined cold, but sincere and truthful epistle to the criminal Princess, Anne.

"September 27, 1701.

"I think myself indispensably obliged to defer no longer the acquainting you with a message which the best of men, as well as the best of fathers, has left with me for you. Some few days before his death, he bid me find means to let you know that he forgave you from the bottom of his heart, and prayed God to do so too; that he gave you his last blessing, and prayed to God to convert your heart, and confirm you in the resolution of repairing to his son the wrongs done to himself; to which I shall only add, that I join my prayers to his, herein, with all my heart; and that I shall make it my business to inspire into the young man, who is left to my care, the sentiments of his father, for better no man could have."

Maria's first act, as guardian of the Prince, her son, was to publish a manifesto in his name, setting forth his claims to the crown of England. As Mary had died without children, and Anne was childless, he had become heir presumptive to those in whom the parliament had settled the succession in 1689. His friends anticipated, and his enemies feared, that his peaceful restoration was at hand. A month had not elapsed from the time of James II.'s death, before Fuller, at the instigation, it is supposed, of some of the Dutch cabinet, reprinted and circulated his libellous tract entitled "A full demonstration that the pretended Prince of Wales was the son of Mrs. Mary Gray, undeniably proved, by original letters of the late Queen [Maria Beatrix] and others, and by depositions of several persons of worth and honour never before published, and a particular account of the murder of Mrs. Mary Gray, at Paris; humbly recommended to the consideration of both houses of parliament." Of the character of this Fuller, some idea may be formed from the fact that the House of Commons, on the twenty-fourth of February, in the fourth year of William and Mary, declared "that the said Fuller was a notorious impostor and cheat, and a false accuser, having scandalized their Majesties and the government, abused the house, and falsely accused several persons of honour and quality, for all which offences they voted an address to his Majesty, to command his attorney-general to prosecute him." On the present occasion, the house voted "that Fuller, having taken no warning by the censure received from the House of Commons on the twenty-fourth of February, 1691, and the punishment inflicted on him by the just sentence of the law [he was tried and condemned to the pillory as an impostor], has repeated his evil practices by several false accusations in divers scandalous pamphlets; this house doth declare the said William Fuller to be a cheat, a false accuser, and an incorrigible rogue, and hath ordered that Mr. Attorney do prosecute him for his said offences."

The libel nevertheless well answered the purpose for which it was intended, that of strengthening the feeling in England against Maria Beatrix and her son. The city of London, and the several counties and corporations of England, drew up addresses to William, expressive of the deepest indignation at the French King's presumption, and of their determination to defend, with all their power, his Majesty's person and government against any attempted invasion of his crown or dignity. The whole nation clamoured aloud for war with France. The parliament voted that they would vigorously assist the King and his successors against the pretended Prince of Wales and all other pretenders whatsoever. The Commons brought in a bill for attainting the pretended Prince of Wales, which, being sent up to the Lords, passed with an additional clause of attainder against "Maria, his pretended mother;" but the Commons stoutly declared against this additional clause, and the bill was passed without it. Immediately afterwards, the Lords, a majority of whom were the willing tools of William III. and his cabinet, passed another bill for the attainder of "Maria, late wife of the late King James," but with no better success than before. The Commons, disgusted at the idea of attainting the innocent widow of their late sovereign, threw the bill under the table, without even putting it to the question. Next, both houses passed an act for abjuring Maria's beloved son, entitled, "An act for the further security of her Majesty's person, and the succession of the crown in the Protestant line, and extinguishing the hopes of the pretended Prince of Wales and all other pretenders, and their open and secret abettors." This bill had been strongly opposed by the Jacobites; they had hoped that the King, who was dangerously ill, would die without giving the royal assent to it—but in this they were mistaken; immediately it had passed the houses, the royal fac-simile was stamped on it by a special commission, and the next day, being the eighth of March, 1702, William III. breathed his last.

Meanwhile Maria, who still deeply mourned the death of her beloved husband, was too weak in body, too feeble in mind, to successfully grapple with the difficulties that surrounded her. The passing of the bills for the attainder, and the abjuration of her son, overwhelmed her with sorrow; she was attacked with an alarming illness, and when the news of the death of William reached St. Germains, she was suffering from palpitation of the heart, and from the first symptoms of a cancer in the breast, and other dangerous maladies. She was far too ill to attend the deliberations of her council; and her cabinet, although it was distracted with jealousies, and could do nothing of importance without her, yet dared not endanger her life, by consulting her. The Prince, her son, could not embark for Britain without her consent, and the Jacobites in England, Scotland, and Ireland, although numerous and wealthy would not attempt a rising, unless him, for whom they were willing to draw their swords, was present to cheer them on. Besides, neither France nor Spain then felt inclined to lend effectual aid to the cause of the royal Stuart, and many thought that the reign of the new Queen Regnant of England would be short, and that the whole realm would cheerfully hail the pretended Prince of Wales, as the son of James II. and Maria was now generally called, as her successor. Thus it was that Anne of Denmark ascended the throne of Great Britain, without a shadow of opposition.

Maria's progress to convalescence was slow. In September, 1703, she wrote to the abbess of Chaillot, that her breast had been lanced, and the operation, although painful, had eased the pangs of the cancer, and effected a marked improvement in her general health. Her dreadful malady, however, afterwards increased in severity to that degree, that, in a letter to the abbess of Chaillot, dated August, 1705, she says, "I suffer from pangs in my breast almost constantly, and I seldom have any rest at night." But again it would appear the progress of her deadly disease was arrested by the skill of her surgeon, DeBeaulieu, who in the subsequent September performed another operation on her breast, when, to the surprise of herself and her friends, she again became convalescent. The health of the Prince, her son, also was now fully established.

CHAPTER VI.

Maria's son attempts to invade Scotland unsuccessfully—A price set on his head—Queen Anne names him "the Pretender"—Marlborough intrigues in his favour—Maria writes to Marlborough—Pecuniary distress forces her to reside at Chaillot—She pays Louis a visit of condolence on the death of the Dauphin—Renewed correspondence with Marlborough—Death and burial of her daughter, the Princess Louisa—Her son ordered to quit France—Her conciliatory letter to Lord Middleton—Treaty of Utrecht signed—Pretender banished from France—Distress and starvation at St. Germains—Maria's income in arrears—Madame de Maintenon procures her a payment—She receives a portion of her dower from England—Jacobite song—Death of Queen Anne—Accession of George I.—Vehement demonstrations in favour of the Pretender—Maria visits him at Lorraine—His misfortunes enhanced by the death of Louis XIV.—When too late, he sails for Scotland—Maria receives cheering, but false, accounts of his progress there—The expedition fails—He visits his mother incognito—Discharges Bolingbroke from his service—Terrible execution of his partizans in England—He retires to Avignon—Sweden, Spain, and Russia make secret preparations to assist him—The scheme detected and prevented—Maria's last illness—Death—Virtues—Slandered—Poverty—Obsequies—Closing career of the Pretender.

EVER since the death of William III., the Jacobite agents in England and Scotland had maintained a secret correspondence with the exiled court at St. Germains, and frequently, but vainly, importuned Maria to procure money, arms, and other assistance from the King of France, in support of the cause of her son. The Scotch, at the crisis of the union, were most earnest in their entreaties for the means to rise and proclaim the son of James II. and Maria Beatrix, by the title of James VIII., King of Scotland; but every time Maria broached the subject, Louis XIV. put her off till the spring of 1708, at which period he resolved to send an expedition, headed by the prince, her son, in person, to make a descent on the coast of Scotland. The fleet was prepared at Dunkirk, but the Chevalier de St. George (the name which the prince assumed in this adventure), when about to embark, was seized with measles: this caused a delay of several days; and when, at last, Fourbin, the French admiral, put to sea, the weather proved foul and stormy, and on his entering the Frith of Forth, near Edinburgh, the English fleet chased him and took one of his men-of-war, which so alarmed him that he would not permit the prince to land, and returned to France without attempting, much less accomplishing, the presumed object of his mission. In the absence of her beloved son, Maria had retired with her daughter, Louisa, to her favourite convent at Chaillot, and there, assisted by the nuns, offered up prayers for his safety and success. His return and disappointment troubled, but did not astonish her; for a few nights previously an old woman had appeared to her in a dream, and told her that this time he would not land; a vision which both herself and the superstitious nuns interpreted as a sure omen of the failure of the expedition. This attempted invasion of Scotland caused an alarming run upon the Bank of England for gold, and so terrified Queen Anne, that her cabinet set a price on the head of her unfortunate half-brother, and she herself did much to exclude him from the throne, by now, in her address to parliament, styling him "the Pretender," a name by which he was ever afterwards known in England. After this failure, the Pretender served in the French army in the Low Countries, where he proved himself a courageous and energetic soldier, and at the battle of Oudenarde witnessed the superior military genius of the Duke of Marlborough, with whom he was carrying on a secret correspondence. That Marlborough was at heart favourably disposed towards the son of James II. cannot be doubted. When Louis XIV. made ineffectual negociations for peace in the summer of 1708, Marlborough mentioned the exiled Prince to the French minister, Torcy, in terms of affection, and even advised Torcy to renew the demand of Maria's dower. "Insist on that article to the Viscount Townshend," said he; "that lord is a sort of inspector over my conduct. He is an honest man but a whig; I must speak like an obstinate Englishman in his presence." Again, in his conference with the Pretender's natural brother, Berwick, Marlborough remarked, "As the English will never permit France to impose a sovereign on them, I hope to extricate the Prince from the influence of France, and then by prudent arrangements to unite all persons in acknowledging him as the successor to his sister Anne's throne." Marlborough, likewise, whilst the hostile armies were encamped in the neighbourhood of Fort Scarfe, sent a party of his officers to the Pretender, who was then serving in the French army under Villars, with a polite request that he would favour them with an audience, they being anxious to behold the son of their late beloved King James II. The audience was willingly granted, and the jacobite officers were each presented with a medal bearing the likeness of the Chevalier St. George, and wrapped in paper, on which was written the subjoined enigmatical, but significant allusion to the bravery of the exiled prince at the murderous battle of Malplaquet: "The medal is good, for it bore six hours' fire; you know it was hot, for yourselves blew the coals, on the memorable 11th of September, 1709. You know it was then well tried." Besides encouraging those petty treasons, Marlborough carried on at this time, through his nephew Berwick, a secret correspondence with Maria Beatrix, who, in reply to one of his letters, in which he informed her of his intention to resign his appointments under Queen Anne, makes mention of her son by the fictitious name of Mr. Matthews. "I was glad," she writes, "to find you still continued in your good resolution towards *Mr. Matthews* [the Prince]. I was surprised, on the other hand, to see you had a design of quitting everything immediately after the peace was concluded, for I find that to be the only means of rendering you useless to your friends, and your retreat may prove dangerous to yourself. You are too large a mark and too much exposed for malice to miss, and your enemies will never believe themselves in safety till they have ruined you. But as you are lost if you quit your employments, I see likewise, on the other hand, that it will be difficult for you to keep yourself in office as things are now situated, so that your interest itself now declares for your honour. * * * The advice you gave us in sending us to the new favourite,* is very obliging; but what can we hope from a stranger who has no obligations to us? Whereas, we have all the reason in the world to depend upon you, since we have now but the same interest to manage, and you have the power to put *Mr. Matthews* in a condition to protect you. Lay aside then, I beseech you, your resolution of retiring, take courage, and without losing more time, send us a person in whom we can have entire confidence; or if you have not such a man with you, allow us to send you one whom we may trust, in order to concert matters for our common interest, which can never be properly done by letters. * * * I must not conclude without thanking you for promising to assist me in my suit [her endeavour to procure the payment of her dower], at the treaty of peace. My cause is so just that I have every reason to hope I shall gain it, at least I conceive that Mr. Matthews's sister [Queen Anne] is of too good a disposition to oppose it." The poor Queen at this time was suffering from pecuniary distress, and stood greatly in

* Mrs. Masham, who had secured the esteem of Queen Anne.

need of the income so justly her due as Queen-dowager of England. Louis XIV. was so impoverished by the expenses of the protracted war, that he could afford to allow her but little, and that little was greatly reduced by the peculations of the French exchequer, who, when she expostulated with them on their mal-practices, boldly told her if she did so again, they would stop her income altogether. Under these circumstances she, still to meet the demands on her impoverished purse for the relief of the distressed emigrants at St. Germains, retired with her daughter to her favourite convent at Chaillot, where she afterwards chiefly resided. For her apartments at this convent she paid, or rather agreed to pay, a yearly rent of 4,000 francs, and as she could live there at a very trifling cost, and indulge to the full those ascetic superstitious habits which she erroneously but sincerely believed to be pleasing to the Almighty and necessary to salvation, she ceased to consider St. Germains as her residence, and only occasionally visited there, to serve the interests of her son. On the death of the Dauphin, in the spring of 1711, Maria paid Louis a visit of condolence at Marly, and afterwards, accompanied by her son and daughter, who were in deep mourning for the occasion, (she herself was already in black, a costume she wore in memory of her departed husband to the day of her death), paid state visits of sympathy to all the members of the royal family.

The preliminary treaties for the peace of Utrecht greatly excited the Queen and the exiles at St. Germains. The hope that she would at length receive her dower, and the fear that Louis the Fourteenth would be compelled to repudiate her son's title and cause, at once raised and depressed the spirits of the sorrowing Maria. The disgraced and double-dealing Marlborough renewed his secret correspondence with the widow and son of James the Second, and he even had a personal interview with the Jacobite agent, Tunstal, who with studied mystification wrote to Middleton—"I had two long conferences with him about *Mrs. Bernard's* [Maria's] *lawsuit* [dower] and *Mr. Kelly's* [the Pretender's] affairs, as to both which he shows a good will, and gives, in appearance, sincere wishes; but how far he will be able to work effectually in the matter, I leave you to judge. First, as to *Mrs. Bernard's deed*, [clause for the payment of Maria's dower], he says it must be insisted upon in time, for he looks upon it as certain that an *accommodation* [peace] will be made; and if he should be found capable of helping or signing this deed, he assures *Mrs. Bernard* of his best service." The court of St. Germains, however, it appears, placed little reliance in the professions of one who had played a grossly treacherous part to his old master, James the Second, as may be gathered from an answer to this dispatch written by Middleton, in which he says: "He [Marlborough] might have been great and good, but God hardened Pharaoh's heart, and he can now only pretend to the humble merit of a post-boy, who brings good news to which he has not contributed." Whilst rejoicing over the prospect of obtaining her unjustly-withheld dower, Maria was called upon to moan the death of the Dauphin, the Dauphiness, and their eldest son, a domestic calamity which overwhelmed Louis the Fourteenth with sorrow, darkened the political horizon of the widow and son of James the Second, and was followed in a few weeks by a bereavement little anticipated by the court at St. Germains. On the thirtieth of March, 1712, the King of England, as the Pretender was usually styled in France, proceeded to Chaillot, and the same evening conducted his mother and sister from the convent to St. Germains. A few days afterwards, he was attacked with the small-pox, and although he recovered, his sister, the Princess Louisa, caught the infection, of which she expired at seven minutes to nine on the morning of Monday, the eighteenth of April. The affliction distracted the poor Queen, and threw her into a violent fever; the prince was not yet out of danger, and for several days the life of the mother and of the son was equally despaired of; indeed, it was reported that the prince was dead. "I and mine," writes a London Jacobite to one of Maria's ladies, "have so shared in your bereavement, that we thought our sorrows could have no addition when we heard your chevalier was recovered; but now we find our mistake; for since we had yours to my daughter Jenny, 'tis said at court he is despaired of, and on the Exchange that he is dead, that he ate too much meat, and got a cold with going out too soon. * * * I cannot help being anxious for his health, notwithstanding your assurances of his recovery; for we have so many cruel reports about him, that it is enough to make us distracted. Pray assure his afflicted mother of my most humble duty. God in heaven send her comfort, for she wants it; nothing but her goodness could resist such a stroke."

The heart of the promising young flower of St. Germains, Princess Louisa, was deposited beside that of her father's, in the convent of Chaillot, and her body was placed by the side of his, in the church of the English Benedictines, Paris. Immediately Maria had sufficiently recovered, Louis the Fourteenth and Madame de Maintenon paid her visits of condolence, and kindly assured her that the whole court of France deeply deplored her loss. Maria did not return to her friends at Chaillot till the end of July, and when she arrived she burst into tears, and exclaimed :— "Alas! alas! the house is desolate; this is not as it used to be; but, oh God, thou art just and holy: it has pleased thee in thy infinite wisdom to take the child and leave the mother; and hard though it be to part, yet will I ever pray. God, thou art the master, thy holy will be done, and thy hallowed name be praised and blessed to all eternity." She then visited the chapel, where the hearts of her beloved husband and child were enshrined, prayed for the eternal repose of their souls, and returned to her apartments choked with sorrow, and blinded with tears. Before the fallen Queen had recovered from this shock, she was forced to submit to the estrangement of her beloved son. By order of the French ministers, the Chevalier de St. George quitted St. Germains on the eighteenth of August, and proceeded to Livry, where he was permitted to take up his residence, previous to his final departure from France. From Livry he paid several visits to his mother at Chaillot, and he visited the opera at Paris on the same night that Lord Bolingbroke, the English ambassador extraordinary for the peace, went there in state. On the first of September, Maria, and the nobles and ladies who shared her exile, paid a formal visit to her son at Livry. The next day, the mother and son parted in sorrow, and after three days' journey, the Pretender reached Chalons-sur-Marne, where he was to await the events of the negotiations at Utrecht. Throughout the autumn the Queen suffered from ill health, and from a melancholy depression of spirits, occasioned by her domestic misfortunes. In December, her sorrows were increased by the news of her son's coolness to the Earl of Middleton, his chief counsellor. Middleton had been charged with betraying the Pretender's state secrets to Queen Anne's cabinet, a charge which he disproved with indignation, and then offered to resign his thankless, profitless post; which so alarmed Maria, who had every confidence in the integrity and ability of the Earl, that she addressed to him the subjoined conciliatory epistle :—

"St. Germains, January 28th, 1713.

"I have not had the heart all this while to write to you upon the dismal subject of your leaving the King, but I am sure you are just enough to believe that it has and does give to me a great deal of trouble, and that which I see it gives the King increases mine. You tell me in your last letter, upon Mr. Hamilton's coming away, that if your opinion had been followed, you had gone first, but if mine were, you should never go first nor last. But, alas! I am grown so insignificant and useless to my friends, that all I can do is to pray for them, and God knows my poor prayers are worth but little. I own to you that, as weary as I am of the world, I am not yet so dead to it as not to feel the usage the King and I meet with. His troubles are more sensible to me than my own, and if all fell only on me, and his affairs went well, and he more easy, I think I could be so too; but we must take what God sends, and as he sends it, and submit ourselves entirely to his will, which I hope in his mercy he will give us grace to do, and then, in spite of the world, all will turn to our good.

"You told me in one of your former letters that you were charmed with the King being a good son. What do you think, then, that I must be, that am the poor old doting mother of him? I do assure you his kindness to me is all my support under God, and I am confirmed of late more than ever in my observation that the better you are with him, the kinder he is to me; but I am also charmed with him for being a good master, and a true friend to those who deserve it of him, though I am sorry from my heart that you have not had so much cause of late to make experience of it.

"M. R.

"I say nothing to you of business, nor of Mr. Hamilton, for I write all I know to the King, and it is to no purpose to make repetitions. I expect, with some impatience and a great deal of fear, *Humphrey's* [Queen Anne's] decision as to *France* [the Pretender's being permitted to reside within the dominions of the Duke of Lorraine]."

A measure which ultimately was privately consented to by Anne, and publicly opposed by her ministers.

Maria prevailed upon Middleton to retain his post, but she had scarcely ceased to rejoice over the success of her mediation, when the treaty of Utrecht was signed (March the thirtieth, 1713); and to fill her cup of sorrow to overflowing, it was therein stipulated that the King of France recognized the limitation of the succession to the kingdom of Great Britain in the Protestant line of Hanover, and that he and his heirs engaged that the person who, since the decease of King James the Second, has taken upon himself the title of King of Great Britain, shall not be permitted to reside in France; and that the King of France agreed for himself and his heirs not to disturb the Queen of Great Britain, her heirs and successors of the Protestant line, nor to give aid, favour, nor counsel, directly or indirectly, by land or by sea, to any person who shall oppose the Protestant succession. Again and again did the fallen Queen read these articles, with tearful eyes and aching heart. "The King of France," she remarked to the nuns of Chaillot, "was forced to consent to the terms of this harsh treaty, for it was only on these conditions that the English would have made peace. However," she concluded, "my son has sent a protest to the plenipotentiaries at Utrecht, asserting his title to the crown of Great Britain; but I fear it will avail him not; for although I have lately received assurances that the Scots and the Irish are sincerely attached to the house of Stuart, they are without money, arms, or wise, energetic leaders."*

As the autumn advanced, the distress of her followers at St. Germains induced Maria to borrow money at a high interest, to relieve their pressing necessities, and then to intreat Madame de Maintenon to lay her own pecuniary difficulties before Louis the Fourteenth. Her pride was wounded at having to make this appeal; but all the Jacobites at St. Germains were dying of hunger, and the French officials had allowed her income to run considerably in arrears. Madame de Maintenon wrote her a sympathizing letter in reply, and a few days afterwards she received the acceptable sum of fifty thousand livres, nearly the whole of which she immediately distributed amongst her famishing followers.

At this period the expenses of the late war had so completely exhausted the finances of France, that Maria again found it impossible to procure the regular payment of her income; and at the commencement of 1714, the Jacobites at St. Germains, most of whom depended on her munificence for subsistence, were once more threatened with the horrors of starvation. But at this distressing moment, when another appeal to the kind intercession of the all-potent Madame de Maintenon appeared inevitable, Maria, to her joy, received the first and only payment of a portion of the jointure settled on her by the government

* From MS. in the possession of J. Chidley, Esq.

of England. She claimed £50,000 per annum; but the lord treasurer, Harley, reduced this amount by £3000, and sent her £11,750, as the first quarter's payment, a sum she thankfully received, in the hope of reconciling Queen Anne to her son, and also that she herself might alleviate the misery of the famishing emigrants at St. Germains. Meanwhile the Pretender continued to reside within the dominions of the Duke of Lorraine, and reports were circulated that he had abjured the faith of Rome for that of the Protestant Church of England, in the hope of securing the crown of Great Britain. These reports caused the bigoted Maria, for such it must be allowed she really was, great uneasiness, till they were firmly contradicted by the Pretender himself, who, in a letter addressed to her on the thirtieth of December, 1713, assured her that they were quite without foundation, and that he would sooner lay dead at her feet than abandon his faith; a communication which in itself afforded a sufficient reason for excluding him from the throne of a Protestant kingdom, but to which the English and Scotch Jacobites were blinded by their hot partizan zeal. They hoped at Queen Anne's death, which was generally believed to be at hand, to hail him as her lawful successor; and when she and her cabinet made ineffectual efforts to remove him from the court of Lorraine, they composed and sung at their private convivial meetings the following spirited song:—

Tune—Over the hills and far awa'.

"Bring in the bowl, I'll toast a health
To one that has neither land nor wealth;
The bonniest lad you ever saw,
Is over the hills and far awa'.
Over the hills, and over the dales,
No lasting peace till he prevails;
Pull up, my lads, with a loud huzza,
A health to him that's far awa'.

By France, by Rome, likewise by Spain,
By all forsook, but Duke Lorraine;
The next remove appears most plain,
Will be to bring him back again.
Over the hills and far awa',
Over the hills and far awa',
The bonniest lad you ever saw,
Is over the hills and far awa'.

He knew no harm, he knew no guilt,
No laws had broke, no blood had spilt;
If rogues his father did betray,
What's that to him that's far away?
Over the hills and far awa',
Beyond the hills and far awa';
The wind may change and fairly blaw,
And blaw him back that's blown awa'."*

Queen Anne died the first of August, 1714: the news of the event was carried to Maria with eagle's wings, and she in all haste imparted it by express to her son at Lorraine, who, without delay, proceeded incognito to Paris, to consult his mother and his leading partizans, on the propriety of hastening to England to assert his rights. The secret of his arrival in the neighbourhood of Paris was quickly carried to the court of France, and as Louis XIV. felt no inclination to wage another war with England, he sent De Torcy to request, and if needful, to order him immediately and privately to quit France. The request sufficed; indeed, by not being present at the death of Anne, he had lost his best chance of success; besides, he had not been invited to England, he had neither money, men, nor ships to cross the channel with, and George I. had been proclaimed without opposition: he therefore had but one reasonable alternative, that of returning to Lorraine, and there awaiting the course of events. On reaching Plombiere, in Lorraine, he issued a proclamation, setting forth his claim to the crown of Great Britain, and the late Queen Anne's intentions in his favour; which was followed by the disgrace of Harley, Bolingbroke, Ormond, and several other noblemen, who in Anne's reign had for venal purposes, rather than from principle, corresponded with the court at St. Germains. Meanwhile Maria suffered from an alarming illness; and although, contrary to all expectations, she recovered, the shock had irreparably injured her physical powers. In the spring of 1715, the populace of England and Scotland rose in riot in favour of the Pretender. The cries of "No Hanover!" "St. George for England!" and "Down with the Roundheads!" were echoed throughout London, Oxford, and most of the

* Ellis's Royal Letters, second series, vol. iv., p. 281.

principal cities; the effigy of William III. was burnt; and at Edinburgh and other towns in Scotland, the health of the disinherited representative of the Stuart dynasty was publicly drank, amidst the maddening huzzas of the people. These enthusiastic demonstrations afforded him whose interests they were meant to serve, another opportunity to make a perhaps successful clutch at the crown that he hoped, but was destined never, to wear. Again, however, the auspicious moment was allowed to slip by. Maria was alarmed for the safety of that son which her enemies had represented as a supposititious child, and her maternal fears paralyzed the efforts of the leaders of the Stuart partizans. Although in a state of painful debility, she in June proceeded by easy stages to Plombières, met her son there, accompanied him to the court at Bar, and entreated him, for her sake, not to endanger the lives of himself and his dearest friends by attempting a descent either on England or Scotland, without an ample supply of money, ships, arms, and men. The proceedings of the fallen Queen and her cabinet were closely watched by the Earl of Stair, the English ambassador in France; who, in one of his dispatches, dated July twenty-fourth, remarks, "I sent Barton to Lorraine, to be informed of the Pretender's motions. I met the Abbe du Bois in a wood, and gave him an account of the intelligence I had concerning the Pretender. I desired he would be particularly careful in informing himself concerning the Pretender's designs, and how far the court meddled with them." Five days afterwards, Stair again reported to his cabinet, "Barton has this day returned from Bar; he informs me that the Pretender is still there with his mother, Queen Maria, everything is quiet, and but few people are there. They talk of the Pretender going to Britain as soon as his mother has returned to Chaillot."

Maria set out on her homeward journey early in August, and on reaching St. Germains she prevailed upon Louis XIV. to order an army and a fleet to be prepared for the invasion of Scotland by her son. This kind act of the old French King again cheered the heart of the sorrowing Queen, but her joy was of brief duration. Louis XIV. expired on the first of September, and Orleans, the new regent, being at that time indifferent to the interests of Maria and her son, and unwilling to give serious offence to George I., he, at the request of the English ambassador, prevented the armament which was already prepared for the Pretender from sailing, and had the ships unloaded, and the arms, ammunition, and stores, shut up in the royal arsenal of France. Nevertheless, the royal Stuart left Bar in the last week of October, with the determination of proceeding to Scotland, where his standard had already been raised. He entered France in disguise, and was so dodged and sharply watched by the spies of the English ambassador, that finding it impossible to reach the coast without danger, he proceeded to Paris, took Chaillot in his route, and bade a tearful farewell to his mother; and, after narrowly escaping the murderous knife of the assassin at the little village of Nonancourt—the tempting bribe of £200,000 had been set on his head by the British government—at length embarked, with but few attendants, on board a small vessel at Dunkirk. His arrival in Scotland he announced to his secretary of state, Lord Bolingbroke, in the following words:—

Peterhead, Scotland, Dec. 22, 1715.

"I am at last, thank God, in my own ancient kingdom, as the bearer will tell you, with all the particulars of my passage and his own proposals of future service. Send the Queen the news I have got, and give a line to the Regent *en attendant*, that I send you from the army a letter from our friend, to whom I am going to-morrow. I find things in a prosperous way. I hope all will go well, if friends on your side do their part as I shall have done mine. My compliments to Magni; tell him the good news; I don't write to him, for I am wearied, and won't delay a moment the bearer. "J. R."

In another letter to Bolingbroke, dated January second, 1716, he remarks, "All was in confusion before my arrival.

I have been obliged to send back to France one of my experienced officers, on account of the disgust the Highlanders have got of him, which is altogether inexplicable. The Highlanders returned home, and but four thousand men left in Perth. Had I retarded some days longer, I might have had a message not to come at all. My presence, indeed, has had, and will have, I hope, good effect. The affection of the people is beyond all expression. I send to the Queen, my mother, all the letters I mention here, that she may peruse them, and then agree with you the best ways of forwarding them. You will shew her this for mine to refer to it."

From the period of her separation from the Pretender at Chaillot, till the tenth of January, 1716, when the above and other letters were placed in her hands, Maria had remained in painful uncertainty of what had become of him. The distressing intelligence of the surrender of the rebels in the north of England, and the defeat of the Stuart partizans at the battle of Dumblane, had reached her just previous to Christmas, and blighted her fondly-cherished hopes of the success of the Stuart cause. These severe trials she bore with christian fortitude and resignation; but the news that the Chevalier de St. George had reached Scotland in safety, threw her into a transport of joy, which overpowered her enfeebled constitution, and brought on a severe attack of nervous fever, from which she only recovered with slowness and difficulty. Whilst yet too unwell to leave her sick chamber, Maria received several cheering but false accounts from Scotland, and when at last she was made acquainted with the unsuccessful issue of the efforts of her son and his Scotch partizans, her troubles were aggravated by the conduct of Lord Bolingbroke, who treated her with marked disrespect, refused to ask her opinion on what measures should be adopted for the furtherance of the Stuart cause, and squandered on his own wicked mistresses the money that had been confidentially entrusted to him by the Pretender to buy powder and arms with. At the close of February, the fallen Queen again embraced her beloved son, who, when his cause had become desperate in Scotland, had sailed to Gravelines, and thence proceeded incognito to St. Germains, where, as his presence in France was interdicted, he, after staying three or four days, bade his mother an affectionate adieu, and set forth under pretence of proceeding to Chalons-sur-Marne, and there tarrying till the Duke of Lorraine had, as a matter of etiquette, granted him permission to take up his residence at Bar. However, on reaching Malmaison, he, to the annoyance of his mother, and to the injury of his best interests, altered his course and hastened to the chateau of the intriguing politician, Mademoiselle de Chausserage, at Neuilly, where he had private conferences with the Spanish and Swedish ambassadors, and received from them assurances of good-will and support. The Chevalier being quite dissatisfied with the conduct of the accomplished but unprincipled Bolingbroke, he at once dismissed him without so much as granting him a personal interview. "The friends of Bolingbroke," writes a contemporary, "reported that he was dismissed by the advice of the unfortuuate Maria Beatrix, and from thence drew malicious inferences; but you may be assured that it was the concurrent opinion of the Duke of Ormond, and all the Pretender's friends here, to displace him, and that her Majesty had no hand in his removal." Lord Stair, who well knew that Bolingbroke was carrying on a series of treacherous intrigues with the Walpole ministry, describes this rupture to Horace Walpole in the following sarcastic sentences:—

"Poor Harry [Bolingbroke] is turned out from being Secretary of State, and the seals are given to Lord Mar; they call him knave, and traitor, and God knows what. I believe all poor Harry's fault was that he could not play his part with a grave face enough; he could not help laughing now and then at such kings and queens. He had a mistress here at Paris, and got drunk now and then; and he spent the money upon his mistresses that he should have bought powder with for the insurgents in the north, and never went near the Queen. For the rest, they [the Stuart partizans] begin to believe that the King is unlucky, and that the westerly winds and Bolingbroke's treasons have defeated the finest project that ever was laid."

The failure of the late Jacobite rising in Scotland severely distressed the disappointed Queen, and did irreparable injury to the cause of her son. As the spring of 1716 advanced, every post from England brought tidings to the dejected widow of James II. of the tragic end of the unfortunate Stuart partizans who fell into the hands of the British government. More than a thousand of the common rebels were transported to the colonies, and the Earls of Derwentwater and of Kenmure, and many other nobles and gentlemen, some of whom had departed from St. Germains a few months previously, full of hope, to join the Jacobite rising in the north, were executed, for the most part, with all the barbarous accompaniments of drawing and quartering. The position of the Pretender himself was by no means a pleasing one. The menaces of England compelled the reluctant Duke of Lorraine to deny him an asylum at Bar; the vassal princes of France and Germany were forced to exclude him from their dominions; and in the end he took up his residence at Avignon. Disastrous, however, as was the result of the Jacobite insurrections in 1715 and 1716, the widow and the son of James II. still cherished hopes of renewing the contest. The Pretender appealed to Sweden, Spain, and Russia, and after some intriguing, prevailed upon the three powers to make secret but formidable preparations for invading Scotland, and placing him upon the throne of Great Britain. With this object vessels and arms were prepared, and a merchant engaged to "forthwith remit £20,000 into France to the Queen Dowager of England [Maria Beatrix], who was to pay it to the person appointed to superintend the financial department." But on the twenty-ninth of January, 1717, at the moment when every one in the scheme entertained the most sanguine expectations of success, General Wade, by the authority of the British cabinet, to whom secret information of the intrigue had been conveyed, arrested Count Gyllenborg, the Swedish ambassador at London, and seized his papers; a blow which at once exploded the plot, and annihilated the hopes of the Jacobites.

To afford encouragement to the blighted cause of her son, Maria at this period made St. Germains her chief residence. She paid a short visit to Chaillot in the summer, and although suffering severely from physical debility—the cancer in her breast had again broke out with a violence that defied the skill of her physicians—she occupied herself at the close of this year and the commencement of 1718, in corresponding with the leading Jacobites in England and Scotland. In April she was attacked with her last illness. At first, the symptoms were not alarming; but on the second of May she wrote to the Abbess of Chaillot, that she had "resigned all hope of recovery." On the evening of the sixth she received the last sacraments of the Catholic church; she then bade an affectionate farewell to her friends and attendants, whom she requested to pray for herself and her son; and after sending a messenger to beseech the Regent, Orleans, and the young King, Louis XV., to show kindness to her son, her servants, and her destitute dependants at St. Germains, listened with composure to the prayers for a departing soul, and expired without a struggle at a quarter to eight on the morning of May the seventh, 1718, in the sixtieth year of her age, the seventeenth of her widowhood, and the thirtieth of her exile.

More shrewd, more worldly-wise princesses than Maria Beatrix, of Modena, are to be met with in the pages of regal biography, but certainly the names of none are recorded, either in the annals of ancient or of modern times, who were more well-intentioned, more pure-purposed, more anxious to do all possible good, to shun all seeming evil, than the unfortunate, the grossly calumniated consort of James II., a Queen who, although she never employed pen or tongue to slander her personal or political enemies, and with her last breath had forgiven her numerous persecutors and slanderers, had expired but a few days, when one of those false witnesses had the hardihood to assert, in the Dutch Gazette, the crude fabrication that, in her dying moments, she had solemnly asserted that she was not the mother of her beloved son, the Chevalier St. George.

Maria Beatrix died in poverty. The government of France defrayed the expences of her obsequies which were performed with a solemnity befitting her rank, but without pomp, in the convent of Chaillot, on the twenty-seventh of June. In compliance with the instructions in her will, her heart was placed beside that of her husband and daughter at Chaillot, and her body was also conveyed to that convent, there to remain unburied till the time arrived when, as it was hoped, it could find a final resting place, together with the remains of her consort and her daughter Louisa in the royal sepulchre at Westminster. The Regent, Orleans, who, profligate as he himself was, had always sincerely reverenced and compassioned the virtuous, holy-minded Queen of many afflictions, ordered a court mourning for her, and generously provided for her Jacobite servants and dependants, who with their descendants were permitted to remain at St. Germains till the period of the French revolution, when all that was royal or holy was plundered, destroyed, or banished from bleeding France.

The Chevalier de St. George, or, as he is more usually styled in our histories, the Pretender, survived his mother many years. In August, 1718, he was married to the Princess Clementina, the third daughter of Prince James, the eldest son of the illustrious John Sobieski, King of Poland. This lady bore him two sons; but domestic disagreement, and jealousy of the wife of a Colonel Hay, induced her to separate from him, and retire to the convent of St. Cecilia. She died on the eighteenth of January, 1735, in her thirty-fourth year, at Rome, where the Pretender also breathed his last, on the thirtieth of December, 1765, at the advanced age of seventy-eight.

MARY THE SECOND,

Third Queen Regnant, and Queen of William the Third.

CHAPTER I.

Mary II.—Parentage—Birth—Early life—Education—William of Orange refuses her hand in marriage—Regrets so doing—Comes to England to obtain her hand—He succeeds—Mary is married to him—His ruse to win popularity—Mary embarks with him for Holland—Rejoicings on their reaching the Hague—William's amours with Elizabeth and Mary Villiers—Dr. Hooper appointed almoner to Mary—Her unhappy life—Illness—Visited by Maria Beatrix and the Princess Anne; and by her exiled father, the Duke of York—Evil conduct of her maids of honour—Dr. Hooper returns to England—Is succeeded at the Hague by Dr. Ken—Ken's worthy conduct—He is disgusted with William's boorishness and brutality—Mary's observance of the Sabbath.

MARY THE SECOND, known in early life as Mary of York, was the daughter of James, Duke of York, (afterwards James II.), and his first wife, Anne Hyde, the more captivating than beautiful daughter of Sir Edward Hyde, Chancellor of the Exchequer and Earl of Clarendon. She was ushered into the world at St. James's Palace, about three minutes past six in the evening of April the thirtieth, 1662, and a few days afterwards was christened Mary, after the unfortunate Mary, Queen of Scots, with the ceremony prescribed in the Book of Common Prayer of the Church of England, in the chapel at St. James's. Her sponsors were Prince Rupert and the Duchesses of Buckingham and Ormond. In June, she was taken to a nursery established for her at Twickenham Palace, the residence of her grandfather, Clarendon, where she remained till the incursions of the plague caused that establishment to be broken up, and her residence to be fixed at the palace of Richmond, a lease of which was granted to her appointed governess, Lady Villiers, with whose daughters she and her sister, Anne, were brought up in their early youth. She was a fine, healthy babe, and her fond father frequently nursed and dandled her, whilst transacting the naval business of the country as Lord High Admiral. When she was little more than two years old, the minute observer, Pepys, remarks in his journal, "I was with the Duke of York, and saw him with great pleasure play with his little girl, just like an ordinary private father of a child." Her brother James was born on the twelfth of July, 1663. Anne, her sister, afterwards Queen of England, entered the world in February, 1664, and her brother Edgar, who like James died in his childhood, was born on the fourteenth of September, 1667. When only nine years old, the Lady Mary had the misfortune to lose her mother. In August, 1670, the Duchess of York, who had long been ailing, abjured the Church of England for the Roman Catholic faith, and on the thirty-first of the subsequent March, breathed her last, at St. James's Palace. The Duchess had brought her husband a family of eight children; of these, four survived her—Lady Katherine and Duke Edgar, both of whom died in less than a year after, and the Ladies Mary and Anne, who both lived to embitter the last days of their unfortunate father, and to wear the greatly-prized crown of their ancestors.

The Duke of York was at this time suspected of being a convert to the Church of Rome, and his marriage with an Italian Princess of the Catholic House of Este, in November, 1673, rendered him so completely unpopular, that the King endeavoured to appease the wrath of his popery-hating English subjects, by taking the Ladies Mary and Anne from the superintendnece of their father, and appointing as their tutor Henry Compton, Bishop of London, a prelate who, at the age of thirty, had exchanged the sword and helmet for the crosier, and who, possessing little learning himself, paid no regard to the education of his fair young pupils, but left them either to attend to their studies or not just as they pleased. As to Anne, she did little else but play or make mischief; she grew up in a state of blissful ignorance, and even in her old age was unable to construct or even spell her letters with ordinary accuracy or elegance. Not so, however, with Mary; blessed with a faithful memory, a love of study, and an aptitude for literature and art, she grew up a worthy English and French scholar, and took lessons in drawing, with encouraging success, from Master and Mistress Gibson, the two dwarf protegées of the Queen-mother, Henrietta Maria. Dr. Lake and Dr. Doughty filled the offices of assistant tutor and chaplain to the Princesses; and, what is also worthy of remark, Anne Trelawney was the Lady Mary's playfellow, and Sarah Jennings, afterwards Sarah Churchill, Duchess of Marlborough, was the most esteemed playmate of the Princess Anne of York.

The royal sisters, Mary and Anne, who in their early youth were never apart, were first introduced to court on the second of December, 1674, when they took part in a ballet written for the occasion by the poet Crowne, entitled "Calista, or the Chaste Nymph." Dryden wrote the epilogue to this ballet, which was addressed to the king, and in the course of which he highly complimented the daughters of the Duke of York and Anne Hyde.

The Ladies Mary and Anne afterwards performed in Lee's "Mithridate" and other plays, the accomplished actress, Mrs. Betterton, training and instructing them in their parts; and from her lessons they both derived the accomplishments so useful to them as Queens, of delivering addresses and speeches with grace, ease, just expression, and a clear, sweet, and distinct voice.

When Mary was fourteen, Compton, between whom and the Duke of York a feud had long existed, requested the Duke to allow him to confirm her. York replied with warmth—"I have not instructed my daughters in my own religion, because in that case they would have been taken from me. Therefore, as I cannot communicate with them myself, I am decidedly against their receiving; but you can tell the King what has passed between us, and obey his orders." The next day, Compton waited upon Charles, and about a week afterwards, he, in compliance with the royal will, and to the satisfaction of the nation, confirmed the Lady Mary of York with due solemnity in the chapel belonging to Whitehall Palace.

In 1674, Lord Arlington, in the hope of supporting his declining credit with the King, advised His Majesty to negotiate a marriage between William, Prince of Orange, and the Lady Mary of York. Great results were anticipated from the match: indeed, as the Prince was a Protestant, Charles and his council believed that it would greatly allay the religious apprehensions of the people, whilst, as it opened to him (the Prince of Orange) a prospect of succeeding to the throne of Great Britain, they considered that in return he would sever his connections with the popular leaders in England, and second Charles in his efforts to negotiate a general peace. Accordingly, the Earl of Ossory, by command of the King, proceeded to the Hague, under pretence of visiting some relations there, but for the real purpose of hinting to William that if he would assist Charles in pacifying Europe, he should receive as a reward the hand of his fair young cousin, the Princess Mary. William, who knew that the Duchess of York was then in an advanced state of pregnancy, received Ossory with courtesy; but the instant he broached the subject, interrupted him by remarking, with an air of rudeness, that in the existing circumstances he was not in a condition to think of a wife. This unceremonious refusal of the hand of a Princess, in rank far above himself, succeeding events taught him to deeply regret. He had insulted the Duke of York, and deeply offended Charles II., the only monarch who could assist him to conclude a honourable peace, or to carry on the war with advantage. He perceived the necessity of seeking a reconciliation, and with that view, remarks Sir William Temple, "he met me one morning by appointment in the garden of his Hounslardyke palace, and there, after telling me that his friends often pressed him to marry, and descanting on the offers he had received from high-born damsels in France and Germany, and discoursing on love and marriage matters, remarked that he wished to know somewhat of the person and disposition of the young Lady Mary; for though it would not pass in the world for a Prince to seem concerned in those particulars, yet for himself he was so, and to such a degree, that no circumstances of fortune and interest would engage him without those of person, especially those of humour and disposition. As for himself, probably he would not be very easy for a wife to live with; he was sure he should not, to such wives who were generally in the courts of this age; that if he should meet with one to give him trouble at home, it was what he should not be able to bear, who was like to have enough abroad in the course of his life. Besides, after the manner in which he was resolved to live with a wife, which should be the very best he could, he would have one that he thought likely to live well with him, which he thought chiefly depended on her disposition and education; and that if I knew anything particular in these points of the Lady Mary, he desired I would tell him freely." Temple replied, "that of his own observation he knew nothing of the temper and disposition of the Princess, but that he had heard her highly spoken of by his wife, his sister, and also by her governess, Lady Villiers." The Prince, in conclusion, told Temple that he meant to write to the King and the Duke of York on the subject, and requested that Lady Temple, who was about to return to England, should be the bearer of the letters. A few days afterwards, the Prince brought his letters to Lady Temple, and she immediately proceeded to England with them, and presented them to King Charles and his brother James.

At the close of the campaign in 1677, William went in person to seek the hand of the presumptive heiress to the crown of England. After a protracted, stormy voyage, he landed at Harwich, on the ninth of October, and at once hastened to Newmarket, where his uncles, Charles II. and the Duke of York, were enjoying the Newmarket races. The Lord Treasurer Danby, and Sir William Temple, who had returned from the embassy, were devoted to the Prince's interests, and were the only persons, saving the King and the Duke, to whom the object of his journey was known. He was received by Charles and his brother with marked attention; but, to their astonishment, he informed them through Temple that he was resolved to see the Princess Mary, before entering into discussions of business, as until he had made himself acquainted with her, it was impossible for him to be in love with her. Charles, with a laugh, answered, "I suppose his whims must be humoured;" and leaving Newmarket sooner than he had intended, conducted him to Whitehall, and introduced him to his prospective bride, with whose person and deportment he pretended to be so well satisfied, that he immediately made his suit to the King, who acquiesced in it on condition that he agreed to Charles's views in regard to the peace on the continent. But to this he demurred: "he must end his marriage before he entered upon the peace treaty," he said, "otherwise his allies would be apt to believe that he had made his match at their cost; and for his part, he would never sell his honour for a wife." Nevertheless, the King remained firm to his resolution for several days; when, just as the negociation appeared to be on the point of terminating unsuccessfully, Temple one night, after supper, paid a visit to the Prince of Orange, who with an angry scowl, and in tones of strongly-marked discontent, told him "that he repented coming into England, and resolved to be gone in two days, if the King continued in his resolution of treating upon the peace before he was married; but before he went, the King must choose how they should live hereafter, for he was sure it must be either like the greatest friends or the greatest enemies, and desired Temple to let his Majesty know so next morning, and give him an account of what he should say upon it." To this insulting message from his ungrateful nephew of Orange, the facile, thoughtless Charles answered, after a short pause—"Well, I never yet was deceived in judging a man's honesty by his looks, and if I am not deceived in the Prince's face, he is the honestest man in the world. I will trust him, and he shall have his wife, and you, Sir William Temple, shall go immediately and tell my brother so, and that it is a thing I am resolved on." This Temple did, and the Duke of York, after overcoming the momentary surprise, answered, "The King shall be obeyed, and I hope all his subjects will learn of me their duty to their sovereign;" adding, "I tell him my opinion very freely upon all things, but when that's done, and I know his pleasure upon it, I obey him."

The same day, the marriage articles were drawn up, and on that following, Charles, accompanied by the Duke, his brother, entered the council-chamber, and announced to the assembled lords, "that he had concluded a marriage between his nephew, the Prince of Orange, and his niece, the Princess Mary, for the purpose of uniting the different branches of his family, and of proving to his people the interest which he took in the security of their religion." "And I," added the Duke, "as father of the bride, have given my consent, a consent which will prove the falsehood of the charges so often made against me, that I meditate changes in the Church and State. The only change which I seek is to secure men from molestation in civil concerns, on account of their opinion on religious matters." A short while previously, the Duke had endeavoured to negotiate the marriage of his daughter Mary to the Dauphin of France; but, after some secret intriguing, the French proposed to marry her to the Prince de Conti, an offer which the Duke rejected with marked displeasure. As to the poor bride, she was not so much as asked if she had any objection to enter the married state; and when the Duke of York took her into her closet, on the twenty-first of October, and informed her of the proposed marriage between her and the Prince of Orange, she wept bitterly all that afternoon, and all the following day. Indeed, for her the suit had no charms, she had already fixed her affections on a handsome young Scotch noble; but alas! for the fate of princesses, in these matters the will of the reigning sovereign was law: she was compelled to dry up her tears, stifle her sorrow, and with an outward semblance of gladness receive, during the subsequent week, the congratulations of the Privy Council, the Judges, the Lord Mayor and Aldermen of London, and others, and to attend a grand entertainment given bv the citizens of London, in honour of the occasion.

On Sunday, the fourth of November, 1677, the Lady Mary of York was solemnly married to William, Prince of Orange. The nuptials were performed in the bride's bed-chamber, by Compton,

Bishop of London, and in the presence of Charles II., his consort, Katherine of Braganza, and the Duke and the Duchess of York. Charles gave his dejected niece away, and was unusually merry on the occasion. In reply to the question, "Who gives this woman?" he loudly exclaimed, "I do;" and when the bridegroom, at the moment of endowing his bride with all his worldly goods, placed a handful of gold and silver coin on the prayer-book, Charles, with an arch look, told his niece to take it up and put it in her pocket, for it was all clear gain. The ceremony concluded, the newly-wedded pair were formally congratulated by the court and the foreign ambassadors; and at night, after partaking of a right royal supper, they received the accustomed honours from the King, Queen, and court in bed.

On the following morning, the Prince presented his bride with jewels worth £40,000; and as the alliance, on account of its being a Protestant one, was highly popular both in England and Scotland, the royal coupie received the congratulations of the court, the judges, the foreign ambassadors, the Lord Mayor of London, and others; whilst throughout the chief cities in Great Britain the bells rang, the cannon boomed, the conduits ran with wine, and the people drank the health of their Highnesses with long and loud acclamations.

The Princess Mary had been married but two days, when the birth of a fine healthy brother destroyed the probability of her succeeding to the throne of Great Britain. William of Orange viewed the event as a misfortune; and, although he stood sponsor to the unwelcome babe, he exhibited marked symptoms of disappointment and vexation. At this period the small-pox was raging at St. James's, the Lady Anne of York was confined to her bed with it, and although Mary was urged by the Duke of York, and by the Prince her husband, to quit the infected palace, neither threats, persuasions, nor the danger of infection could prevail. She wished to be near her sorely sick sister, she said, till the hour of her departure from England; a concession which she succeeded in wringing from her husband and her indulgent father.

On the thirteenth of November, a grand banquet and ball was given at court in honour of her nuptials; it was the Queen's birthday, and on that account the entertainment was unusually splendid. The bride was dressed in rich apparel and costly jewels, joy and mirth reigned around, but she in whose honour all this pomp and rejoicing took place, was sad at heart and ready to burst with grief; the whole evening her unkind husband neither spoke to her nor paid her the least attention. She expected she should have to leave all that was most dear to her on the morrow, and embark with him for Holland; whilst, to complete her misery, she was not permitted to see her dangerously-ill sister Anne, whom fear taught her to believe she was doomed never again to behold on this side of the grave. However, on the next day an easterly wind set in, and detained the royal travellers till the morning of the nineteenth of November, when a favourable westerly breeze sprang up, and as the tide served, the weeping Princess entered the royal barge at Whitehall stairs, and, accompanied by her husband, her father, and her uncle, and many of the nobility, proceeded down the Thames to Erith, where she bade them a most affecting farewell, and shortly afterwards embarked with her husband and retinue, and sailed down the river as far as Sheerness; when a contrary wind detained the fleet for nearly forty hours, a circumstance of which the crafty Prince of Orange took advantage by a dexterous manœuvre to damage the reputation of the Duke his uncle, and increase his own popularity with the English people. He landed with his bride and four attendants, crossed over to Canterbury, and repairing to an inn there, gave out that the King and the Duke of York had, from sheer jealousy, lest they should have been invited by the Lord Mayor to a civic feast, unkindly hurried them out of London in a destitute condition. He sent his favourite, Bentinck, to apply to the corporation of Canterbury for a loan of money; but, as the case was an ugly one, the mayor and his brethren, upon mature consideration, refused the request. However, Dr. Tillotson, who happened to be present, hastened home immediately, collected together what plate and money he had at command, and carried them to the inn, and presented them to Bentinck for the service of their Highnesses. The present was accepted with grateful acknowledgments, the doctor was permitted to kiss the hand of the Princess, and thus many of the nobility and gentry of Canterbury were induced to believe that the King and the Duke of York had, in a fit of jealousy, packed off the Prince and Princess of Orange in a state of deplorable destitution, whereas the very reverse was the fact. Mary and her husband, as previously stated, had already attended the civic feast in London, and William, so far from being in a state of abject poverty, had, on quitting Whitehall, received the first instalment of the £40,000, the marriage portion of his bride. "In this his object to obtain partizans, the wily Prince," remarks a contemporary, "at least partially succeeded. By this accident, the kind-hearted Tillotson began that acquaintance and correspondence with the Prince and Princess of Orange as afterwards advanced him to the archbishopric."

The Princess Mary proceeded with her royal lord from Canterbury on the twenty-seventh of November, embarked the next day at Margate, and after a stormy passage, landed at the Dutch town of Tethude, and at once proceeded to Hounslardyke palace. On the fourteenth of December, she and her husband made their public entry into the Hague with all conceivable pomp and splendour. The bridge of the Hague was tastefully decorated with flowers and evergreens, beneath which was a laudatory inscription in Latin.

The road through which they passed was lined by several companies of the burghers in arms. Four-and-twenty virgins walked in procession on each side of their Highnesses' carriages, chaunting joyous songs, and strewing the way with herbs and flowers; and at the town-house, and in the Hoogstraet, they passed under triumphal arches adorned with the arms of their Highnesses, and other appropriate and elegant devices. In the evening a grand exhibition of fireworks took place, and the next day William and his bride received the compliments and congratulations of the leading Dutch nobility.

The Princess was attended to Holland by Lady Inchiquin—Mary Villiers—and by Elizabeth and Anne Villiers. The two latter sisters won the heart of William of Orange, and to the disgrace of him and themselves, and to the sorrow of Mary of Orange, prostituted their charms to his passion shortly after their arrival at the Hague. Louis XIV. took umbrage at this marriage. The Duke of York, he said, had given his daughter to the mortal enemy of France. The fault, however, did not lay with the Duke, but with his brother, King Charles, who, when reminded by one of York's friends that he had promised never to give the Princess Mary in marriage without the approbation and consent of her father, exclaimed, "So I did, man; but, odds fish! James *must* consent to this."

At the commencement of 1678, Dr. Hooper was appointed almoner to the Princess of Orange. On reaching Holland, he had a chapel fitted up for her use, and he paid great attention to her spiritual wants, and prevailed upon her to attend divine worship twice a day; but he could not induce her to suppress that passion for gambling which she indulged to the last years of her existence.

It was long before Mary became reconciled to her changed destiny; and she had been in Holland but a short while, when distress of mind, occasioned by the conjugal infidelity and harshness of her husband, combined with change of climate, brought on a severe attack of bilious fever, which, after its more dangerous symptoms had passed away, changed into a slow intermittent, which hung long upon her, and, in conjunction with a miscarriage that she had in April, brought her to the verge of the grave. To cheer her drooping spirits (she had again proved enceinte), her father, the Duke of York, resolved to send his duchess, Maria Beatrix, and the Princess Anne, who had quite recovered from the small-pox, on an incognito visit to her. This he announced to the Prince of Orange in a letter dated September the twenty-seventh, 1678, in which he says, "The duchess and my daughter Anne intend to make your wife a visit very incognito, and have yet said nothing of it to anybody here but His Majesty, whose leave they asked, and will not mention it till the post be gone * * * They intend to set out from hence on Tuesday next, if the wind be fair; they bid me tell you they desire to be very incognito, and they have Lord Ossory for their escort. I was very glad to see by the last letters that my daughter continued so well, and I hope now she will go out her full time. I have written to her to be very careful of herself, and that she would do well not to stand too long, for that is very ill for a young woman in her state."

On the first of October, Maria Beatrix and the Princess Anne set out for the Hague, where they arrived in safety a few days afterwards, and were received with marked distinction and good will by the Prince of Orange, and with rapturous joy by Mary, whose transports on again beholding that sister whose life she had despaired of when she quitted England, amounted, it is said, almost to madness.

The Princess of Orange had enjoyed the company of her step-mother and her sister but a few days, when they bade her adieu and returned to England. In the spring of the next year, 1679, her father, who was banished for a time on account of his religion, visited the Hague; an event which afforded her infinite pleasure, as she had not yet learned to dishonour and persecute one of the best of parents. The Duke of York reached the Hague in March. Mary was still suffering from the intermittent fever. In April he wrote to Lawrence Hyde, "My daughter's ague fit continues still; her eleventh fit is now upon her; but as the cold fit is not so long as usual, I have hopes it is going off." To the Prince of Orange he wrote, "Thank God, my daughter has missed her ague; I trust she will have no more attacks, now that the warm weather is set in. * * * I hope that her journey to Dieren will completely cure her." This Dieren was one of the Prince of Orange's rural palaces, and thither the Prince, the Princess, and their court removed. The change effected a marked improvement in Mary's health, and a short visit to the baths at Aix-la-Chapelle completely restored her to convalescence.

The Duke of York, during his exile in Brussels, had prevailed upon Charles II. to send to him his daughters Anne and Isabella; and when he again visited the Hague, in September 1679, he was accompanied by his Duchess and these Princesses. The greatest harmony existed amongst the family of the Duke of York at this period; and on the Duke and his family returning to Brussels, Mary parted from them in tears. This was the last time she saw her father. But as yet she loved him; and although her husband was secretly plotting with Russell, Sunderland, Sidney, Oates, and their faction, to deprive him of his succession to the crown, there is every reason to believe that she was not made acquainted with their intrigues till some time afterwards.

At this period, the evil conduct and overwhelming influence of Mary's maids of honour were a ceaseless cause of trouble and annoyance to her, but of great gratification to her husband. They gave dinner parties and other entertainments to the foreign ministers, who, be it observed, were sent, not to William of Orange, but to the States of Holland; and artfully drew from them intelligence of their intended proceedings with the States, and imparted the same to the Prince of Orange. At the head of this clique was Elizabeth Villiers, the acknowledged leman of Prince William, and next to her in authority stood Anne Villiers, who about this time became the wife of the Prince's favourite minister, Bentinck, but who withal, if reports are to be accredited, still continued to walk in the same infamous path as her sister Elizabeth; circumstances which rendered Mary's position truly commiserable, especially as both these bad, bold ladies were the daughters of her governess, and some years older than herself.

The Prince of Orange, although professing to be a Protestant, was at heart an enemy to the Church of England; and Mary's almoner, Dr. Hooper, unable to longer bear his boorish insults, at length resigned his appointment in disgust, and was succeeded, in 1679, by the high-minded and conscientious Dr. Ken. On reaching the Hague, Ken prevailed upon the Princess of Orange, who had been induced by her husband to attend the worship of the Brownists, to remain firm to the faith of the Church of England; and shortly afterwards, he gave mortal offence to Prince William, by the part he took in the marriage of Mary Worth, one of the Princess's maids of honour, to William's near kinsman and favourite, Count Zulestein. The Count had ruined the reputation of Miss Worth, promised to marry her, and then, at the instigation of the Prince of Orange, refused to fulfil his promise. The Princess laid the case before Dr. Ken, and he, worthy man, sought a personal interview with Zulestein, and prevailed on him to make the unfortunate girl his wife. Accordingly, one morning, whilst the Prince of Orange was gone on business to Amsterdam, the Princess called the parties together, and Ken united the frail lovers in the holy bonds of matrimony in her chapel. When the Prince returned, and found that the marriage had been consummated, he raged and stormed at the Princess Mary, and vehemently reproached Ken, who answered by begging permission to return to England. But Mary entertained profound respect for her pastor, and with tears of sincerity implored him not to forsake her; and at last, William, fearing that his interests in England would be injured by his conduct, begged Ken to remain with the Princess for another twelve months. The prelate complied with reluctance, for he was disgusted at the brutality of the Prince of Orange as a husband. On the twenty-first of March, 1680, Sidney entered in his journal, "Dr. Ken is very much dissatisfied with the Prince of Orange; he thinks he is not kind to his wife, and he is determined to speak to him about it, even if he turns him out of doors." A few weeks afterwards, Sidney wrote, "Sir Gabriel Sylvius and Dr. Ken are both here, and both complain much of the Prince, especially of his usage to his wife; they think she is aware of it, and that it doth greatly contribute to her illness; they urge strongly her going to England, but they think he will never consent."

It was at this period that the Princess Mary, fond as she was of Sunday card-playing, denied herself the gratification of a terrible but exciting sight, rather than break the Sabbath-day. One Saturday evening, a vessel was stranded near the Hague, which multitudes went to see, and which she also wished to have seen. But to some who solicited her to go, she said she thought it too late that night, and she supposed it would be shivered to pieces by Monday morning. "Yet I am resolved," she added, "not to give so ill an example as to see it on the Lord's day."

CHAPTER II.

Mary rendered subservient to her husband's will—Her feelings outraged by William—Dr. Ken is succeeded by Dr. Covell as her almoner—Her coquetry with Monmouth—Her father's accession produces a marked change at the Orange court—She neglects the Church of England worship at the instigation of her husband—

Dr. Covell's letter detailing her husband's brutality, intercepted by William; who dismisses the Doctor, Miss Trelawney, and others of Mary's true friends—Burnet at the Hague—Mary obtains a body-guard for her husband—Unites in his efforts to usurp the throne of her father, James II.—Intrigues with the Orange faction in England; and with her sister Anne—Hypocritical correspondence with her father and step-mother—Promises to William her regnal authority—William embarks for England—Mary at the Hague prays for his safety and success—William's expedition—Mary lands in England—Her unfilial glee at Whitehall—Proclaimed joint Sovereign with her husband—Expels the fiddlers from the Chapel-Royal—Irreverence of William—Burnet elevated to the see of Salisbury—Nonjurors.

FROM the year 1680 to 1684, Mary lived in a state of restraint and seclusion bordering on captivity. It was during this period that William succeeded in breaking down her spirit, and making her subservient to his own ambitious will. He surrounded her with spies and malicious rivals, terrified her by menaces and authoritative commands, persecuted her for her filial regard to her father, who, he assured her, was guilty of the crimes laid to his charge by the concoctors and abettors of that monstrous bugbear, the Popish Plot, and humbled her to the dust by shewing preference for her maids of honour. Dr. Ken, who found he could no longer be of service to the persecuted Princess, returned to England, and the eccentric Dr. Covell accepted the appointment of head of the Church of England chapel at the Hague.

The last time that Mary expressed repugnance at any outrage or insult offered by the Prince of Orange to her family, was on the thirtieth of January, 1685. On that day, which being the anniversary of the death of her grandfather, Charles I., was usually kept by her family with great solemnity; she had assumed the garb of mourning, and was sitting alone in her chamber, with the view of passing the whole day in prayer and fasting, when William entered and sternly bade her doff her weeds and robe herself in her gayest apparel, as he meant her to dine with him in public. She was obliged to obey; but at the dinner-table she refused to partake of a single dish. In the evening he further outraged her feelings, by compelling her to accompany him to the play. From this time we hear no more of the filial affection of Mary. Henceforth she first secretly, and then openly, supported her husband's purpose of grasping at the crown of Great Britain, to the prejudice of her own father, the Duke of York.

When the Duke was restored to his place in the succession, and recalled in the autumn of 1679, Monmouth, who at the same time was sent into exile, was received at the Hague with the most marked favour and attention by the Prince of Orange. The Prince invited him to hunt at Dieren, and permitted, nay, encouraged Mary to dance, dine, promenade, and even coquet with him, and receive and countenance his mistress, Lady Harriet Wentworth, only daughter and heiresss of the Earl of Cleveland. These proceedings produced a letter of remonstrance from the Duke of York to the Princess, who on reading it burst into tears, and exclaimed, "Alas! what can I do? the Prince is my master, and will be obeyed." However, there is room for suspecting that Mary really entertained a tender penchant for Monmouth, and granted him improper liberties. She still continued to toy and coquet with him; and at the close of 1684, she, in reply to another letter of reproof from her father, wrote, "I am happy and contented, and *not kept in awe by my husband.*"

The news of the death of Charles II., and the peaceful accession of James II., produced a marked change at the Orange court. Monmouth, after holding a private conference with Prince William till midnight, secretly departed from the Hague before the dawn of the following morning. A few days afterwards, the Prince took an affectionate letter which King James had sent to Mary, announcing his accession, and read it to the assembled States, as if it had been sent to himself. At the same time he wrote to James an humble apology for his past conduct, and promised to break off all communication with Monmouth, and be to him (James) a true, faithful, and zealous son-in-law, to the last breath of his life; apologies and protestations which James had the weakness to accept and rely on.

Since the arrival of Dr. Covell, Mary had again neglected the worship of the Church of England for that of the Brownists; and Covell, by urging her to remain steady to the faith in which she had been baptized, had given great offence to the Prince of Orange, who, at this period, succeeded in intercepting the subjoined letter, which Covell had addressed to Mr. Skelton, the ambassador; and after copying it, had the weak audacity to send it to Mary's uncle, Lawrence Hyde, enclosed in an epistle detailing the particulars of the discovery, and denouncing Covell as a great knave, and an unfaithful servant to the Princess of Orange.

"Dieren, October 5, 1685.

"Your honour may be astonished at the news, but it is too true that the Princess's heart is like to break, and yet she every day, with Mistress Jesson and Madam Zulestein, counterfeits the greatest joy, and looks upon us as dogged as may be. We dare no more speak to her. The Prince hath infallibly made her his absolute slave, and there is an end of it. I wish to God I could see the King give you some good thing for your life, beyond the power of revocation, as I fear the Prince will for ever rule the roast.† * * * But I wonder what makes the Prince so cold to you. None but infamous people must expect any tolerable usage here. * * * I do not wonder at the behaviour of the new marchioness, Katherine Villiers,† it is so like the breed. * * * What would you say if the Princess should take her into the chapel, or in time into the bed-chamber? I cannot fancy the Villiers' sisters will long agree. * * * The Princess is just now junketing with Madam Bentinck and Mrs. Jesson, in Madam Zulestein's chamber."

The Prince of Orange on obtaining possession of this letter, which truly depicts the slavery to which Mary was reduced by her stern husband and his favourite, Elizabeth Villiers, dismissed Dr. Covell without ceremony; and under pretence that Miss Trelawney, Mary's old and attached play-fellow, Mrs. Langford, her nurse, and Mr. Langford, one of her chaplains, had been leagued with him, discharged them from the service of the Princess without warning or common civility. Mary was greatly distressed at their departure, but the cold, calculating Prince, unmoved by her tears and entreaties, sternly bade her retire to her chamber if she must weep her eyes out, and not show to the world what a weak, foolish creature she was.

As Covell's letter was addressed to the envoy, Skelton, the Prince of Orange demanded his removal; but James refused to comply, and Skelton remained, and from time to time faithfully informed his master of the intrigues of the Prince; information to which James, unfortunately for himself, turned "a deaf ear." "I cannot," said the too confiding King, "suspect the faith of a son and daughter who are writing me affectionate and confidential letters by every post."

The Prince of Orange had hitherto been without a body-guard; in the spring of 1686, the conjugal care of the Princess obtained for him this important adjunct of royalty, an event said to have been brought about by the sagacity of Dr. Burnet, who having just arrived in Holland, hastened to the presence of Mary, and informed her that he had discovered a horrible plot against the liberty, or perhaps the life of her husband; which so alarmed her, that she

† For the sake of brevity, the passages foreign to our immediate purpose are left out.

† Katherine Villiers had lately arrived at the Orange court, and married there the Marquis de Puissars.

applied to the States, and obtained from them the appointment of a body-guard for the Prince, which he ever afterwards retained. From this time Burnet's influence at the court of Orange became considerable; an influence so displeasing to King James, that he wrote to Mary, "Burnet is a flatterer, a dangerous man, an ill man, a man not to be trusted. His conversation is pleasant, his genius great, but he wants honesty, moral worth, and a high principle." Mary, however, thought otherwise, and she listened with pleasure to the conversation of the great polemic and political controvertist, who had been especially commissioned to expound to her the intrigues by which the Orange faction in England were working the deposition of her father, James II., in the hope of placing her and her husband on the throne of that unfortunate monarch. "She knew but little of our affairs," remarks Burnet, in his History of His Own Times, "till I was admitted to wait upon her, and I began to lay before her the state of our court, and the intrigues in it ever since the Restoration, which she received with great satisfaction and true judgment and good sense in all the reflections she made."

In 1687, James's cabinet minister, Sunderland, whilst pretending to be a convert to the faith of Rome, and a true and loyal servant to his master, was secretly promoting the cause of the Prince and Princess of Orange. In a letter, the joint composition of himself and his wife, and addressed to Mary and her aspiring husband, the Prince, occur the subjoined passages, illustrative of the intriguing correspondence which Mary at this time commenced, and afterwards so largely carried on with almost all her father's personal or political enemies.

"Some papists the other day said that my Lord Sunderland did not dance in a net, for they very well knew that, however, he made King James believe there were dispensations from Holland as well as from Rome; and that they were sure I held a correspondence with the Princess of Orange. This happened the day I first heard of the propositions respecting the Test Act, which made me defer sending till the King had spoken to me of it, which he has done. And as I could very truly, so did I assure his Majesty that I never had the honour to have any commerce with the Princess of Orange, but about treacle-water or work, or some such slight thing. I did also assure his Majesty that if there had been any commerce, I should never be ashamed, but, on the contrary, proud to own it, seeing he must be sure that the Princess could never be capable of anything with anybody to his disservice. * * * If by the bearer your Highness will be pleased to let me know my letter came safe to you, I shall be very happy. A. SUNDERLAND."

About this time, Mary carried on a more than merely complimentary correspondence with Lady Russell; and she also addressed a kindly worded letter to Archbishop Sancroft, in the hope of winning him over to the Orange interest. The worthy primate prepared an answer breathing regret at the cession of James II. from the Church of England, but this on consideration he withheld, and merely acknowledged the compliment in a short polite note. In December, Mary received from her father a long letter, written with his own hand, containing the motives of his conversion to Popery. She answered it in an equally long epistle, which Dr. Stanley, who was then her almoner, highly commended, and, to flatter her vanity, sent to the primate Sancroft, with a request that he (Sancroft) would favourably notice it, adding, "If you do this, and send it secretly through Dr. Tennison, to her Royal Highness, I believe it will be very acceptable to her." But as Sancroft was not disposed to encourage a daughter to make a public parade of the errors of her father, even though she might have truth on her side, he resolved not to gratify Mary's unfilial ambition, and passed the matter over in silence.

At the close of 1687, it became known that James's consort, Maria Beatrix, was enceinte. This gave fresh impetus to the Orange faction in England, whose secret correspondence with William and Mary became every day more spirited, and more decidedly revolutionary. Almost every one of King James's courtiers and attendants were enleagued with Mary and her husband, and treacherously plotting the ruin of their royal master. The Princess Anne had become the wife of Prince George of Denmark in July, 1683, and she and the premier, Sunderland, were at once the most active and the most powerful of the Orange faction. In allusion to the expected birth of an heir presumptive to the throne, Anne, in a letter to Mary, remarked, "It is to be feared that Mansell [King James II.] will have a son. * * * As to Mansell's wife, she looks as if she were afraid one should touch her, and whenever I have happened to be in the room as she has been undressing, she has always gone in the next room to put on her smock. These things give me so much cause of suspicion, that I believe when she is brought to bed nobody will be convinced 'tis her child, except it prove a daughter." A few days afterwards, Anne, in another letter, assured Mary that she for one should not believe the expected royal infant to be the Queen's child, if it proved a son. She happened to be out of town when the Queen gave birth to a son, which took place June the tenth, 1688, and wrote to her sister Mary as follows: —"My dear sister can't imagine the concern and vexation I have been in, that I should be so unfortunate to be out of town when the Queen was brought to bed, for I shall never now be satisfied whether the child be true or false. It may be it is our brother, but God only knows, for she never took care to satisfy the world, or give people any demonstration of it. It is wonderful, if she had really been with child, that nobody was suffered to feel it stir but Madame Mazarine and Lady Sunderland, who are people that nobody will give credit to."

Mary's answers to these venomous epistles have not been found, but with all possible caution and secresy she united with her sister Anne in spreading the reports that he was a supposititious child, although there is too much reason for believing that she in her heart accredited his identity.

Meanwhile Mary was greatly embarrassed and annoyed by the receipt of friendly epistles from her father, James II. and his consort, Maria Beatrix.* Her answers are not forthcoming; but when her father, on learning that the Prince of Wales was not regularly prayed for in her Protestant chapel at the Hague, wrote and asked her to explain if cause of offence had been given, she answered—

"Hague, August 17, 1688.

"Sir,—Being to go to Loo next Thursday, if it please God, I am come to this place (Hague) to go *bake* at night. Last Thursday I received your Majesty's of the thirty-first of July, by which I see you had heard that the Prince of Wales was no more prayed for in my chapel; but long before this you will know that it had *onely bin sumetimes* forgot. M. d'Albeville can assure you I never told him it was forbid, so that they were only conjectures made upon its *bein sumetimes* neglected; but he can tell, as I find your Majesty already knows, that the Prince of Wales was prayed for here long before it was done in England. This excessive hot weather continues longer than I ever knew it, which I shall find sufficiently in my journey. I have nothing more to add at present, than only to beg your Majesty to believe, wherever I am, I shall still be your Majesty's most obedient daughter and servant,

"Marie."

The correspondence between James and Mary was constant till within a few days of William's landing in England. Research has failed to bring to light the letters addressed by Mary to her father at this period, but portions of the gentle, reasonable, affectionate replies of James II. are still extant.

These epistles, which indeed do honour to the heart of their royal author, if they touched the conscience, produced no perceptible change in the conduct of Mary, who, at the close of September, and to deceive her father, and prevent him from discovering the design of her

* See Memoirs of Maria Beatrix.

husband, assured him that the sole object of William's visit to Minden, was to hasten the advance of his German allies to the Rhine, that they might be ready to oppose the French army; a deception which worked so admirably, that James put no faith in the warning of Skelton, his ambassador, who had just returned from the Hague, refused to accept the offer of Louis XIV. to intercept the Dutch armament preparing to invade England, under an impression that Mary's solemn assurance that that armament was preparing to repel the anticipated attack of France was to be relied on; and even so late as the commencement of October, actually offered the Prince of Orange the assistance of naval and military forces.

At this period Burnet did his patron a valuable service, by persuading Mary that the law of England, which in the event of her succeeding to the throne of her father would place the whole royal power in her hands, to the prejudice of her husband, was contrary to the law of God, and therefore she was bound in conscience to delegate to William the sovereign authority the moment she herself became possessed of it. Impressed with this sentiment, she sent for William, who that day was hunting, and in the presence of the expectant divine, made to him a solemn promise that whatever authority might subsequently devolve on her, he should always bear the rule; "she did not think," she said, "that husbands should ever be ruled by their wives, but whilst she practised one command, 'Wives, be obedient to your husbands in all things,' she deemed it but just that he should practise the other, 'Husbands, love your wives.'" By these words, she alluded to his disgusting intimacy with Elizabeth Villiers; an intimacy which deeply mortified her, and laid her open to daily insults and wrongs from the base Elizabeth, and to the jeers and the pity of the world at large.

When William had made all needful preparations for sailing from Helvoetsluys, in pursuit of the English crown, he, in solemn tones, delivered to the States the subjoined oration:—

"My Lords,—I am going to the navy to embark. I hope you do not take it ill that I do not make it known to you all where I am going. I will assure your lordships, that what I am designing is for the good of the Protestant religion in general, and of your States in particular, as is not unknown to some of you. I will either succeed in it, or spend my blood to the last drop. My Lords, your trust in me and kindness to me at this time is unbounded; if I live and make it not the business of my life to make your lordships suitable return for it, may God blast all my designs, and let me pass for the most ungrateful wretch that ever lived."

His trusty adherent, the aged pensionary, Herr Fagell, to whom was committed the task of answering, said in reply—

"Sir,—My Lords the States are not at all displeased that you conceal from them your design; they do repose an entire confidence in your Highness's conduct, zeal to the Protestant religion, and affection to their State, otherwise they would never have given you the absolute disposal of their navy, their armies, and their money. My Lord, the States wish you all the success in your designs, and have ordered a public fast and prayers to God for your success through all your dominions; and beg of your Highness not to venture your life and person unnecessarily; for though their navy and their army be the very sinews of their State, your person is more considerable to them than both."

At these words the old man burst into tears, and every one present was deeply affected, saving the Prince, who remained unmoved; a selfish apathy, which his admiring friends mistook for firmness and magnanimity.

"The fast day," observes the learned Dr. Lingard, "was celebrated at the Hague with extraordinary solemnity, and the service of three long sermons; separated by prayers of equal duration, was protracted from ten and a-half in the morning, till half-past seven in the evening. During the whole time the Princess Mary attended at the great church, and bore without shrinking the gaze of an immense multitude. Hers, indeed, was a most singular situation. She could not pray for the success of her husband, without praying for the dethronement of her father. But whatever passed within her breast, whether she looked with sorrow on the calamities which threatened her parent, or flattered her own vanity with the near prospect of a crown, she was able to disguise her feelings. Mary listened to the preachers, and joined in the prayers with as much apparent tranquillity as if she had nothing to hope or fear from the result."

This apathy, however, it appears was but affected. Burnet, who accompanied the Prince as spiritual director of the invading armament, and other high witnesses, assure us that as the time approached for her husband's departure, she grew hourly more thoughtful and dejected.

"She was very solemn and serious," remarks this celebrated divine, "and prayed very earnestly to God to bless and direct us. At last, the Prince of Orange went on board, and we all sailed the night of the nineteenth of October, 1688, when directly a great storm arose, and many ships were, at the first alarm, believed to be lost. The Princess of Orange behaved herself as her friends had expected. She ordered prayers four times a day, at which she herself assisted with great devotion."

We extract the following as the reasons which led to the revolution, from a tract published in 1698:—"The King (James) committed two fatal errors in his politics. The first was his falling out with his old chronies the priests, who brought him to the crown in spite of his religion, and would have supported him in arbitrary government to the utmost; nay, popery (especially the worst part of it, viz. the domination of the church) was not so formidable a thing to them, but with a little cookery it might have been rendered palatable. But he had priests of another sort who were to rise upon their ruins; and he thought to play an easier game by caressing the Dissenters, imploying them, and giving them liberty of conscience: which kindness looked so preposterous, that the wise and sober men among them could never heartily believe it, and when the Prince of Orange landed, turned against him.

"His second error was the disobliging his own army, by bringing over regiments from Ireland, and ordering every company to take in so many Irish papists; by which they plainly saw that he was reforming his army, and would cashire them all as fast as he could get papists to supply their room. So that he violated the rights of the people, fell out with the Church of England, made uncertain friends of the Dissenters, and disobliged his own army; by which means they all united against him, and invited the Prince of Orange to assist them: which invitation he accepted, and landed at Torbay the fifth of November, 1688, publishing a declaration which set forth all the oppressions of the last reign (but the keeping up a standing army), declared for a free parliament, in which things were to be so settled that there should be no danger of falling again into slavery, and promised to send back all his foreign forces as soon as this was done.

"When the news of his landing was spread through England, he was welcomed by the universal acclamations of the people. He had the hands, the hearts, and the prayers of all honest men in the nation: every one thought the long-wished-for time of their deliverance was come. King James was deserted by his own family, his court, and his army. The ground he stood upon mouldred under him; so that he sent his Queen and foundling to France before him, and himself followed soon after. When the Prince came to London, he disbanded most of those regiments that were raised from the time he landed; and King James's army that were disbanded by Feversham, were ordered to repair all again to their colours."

The following is from the declaration of the Prince of Orange alluded to above. "We are confident that no persons can have such hard thoughts of us, as to imagine that we have any other design in this undertaking, than to procure a settlement of the religion, and of the liberties and properties of the subjects upon so sure a foundation, that there may be no danger of the nations relapsing into the like miseries at any time hereafter. And as the forces we have brought along with us, are utterly disproportioned to that wicked design of conquering the nation, if we were capable of intending it; so the great numbers of the principal nobility and gentry, that are men of eminent quality and estates, and persons of known integrity and zeal, both for the religion and government of England; many of them being also distinguished by their constant fidelity to the crown, who do both accompany us in this expedition, and have earnestly solicited us to it, will cover us from all such malicious insinuations. For it is not to be imagined, that either those that have invited us, or those that are already come to assist us, can join in a wicked attempt of conquest, to make void their own lawful titles to their honours, estates, and interests. We do, therefore, invite and require all persons whatsoever, all the Peers of the realm, spiritual and temporal, all Lords Lieutenants, Deputy-Lieutenants, and all gentlemen, citizens, and other commons of all ranks, to come and assist us in order to the executing of this our design, against all such as shall endeavour to oppose us, that so we may prevent all those miseries which must needs fall upon the nation's being kept under arbitrary government and slavery; and that all the violences and disorders which have overturned the whole constitution of the English government, may be fully redressed in a free and legal parliament."

As the period of which we are now writing is one of the most interesting in our national history, we subjoin a detail of the events which followed the arrival of the Prince William, taken from a curious Tract entitled "King William and Queen Mary Conquerors," and which was ordered by the Parliament to be burnt by the common hangman.

"November the twentieth, there happened a skirmish at Wincanton, between a detachment of seventy horse, and fifty dragoons and grenadiers, commanded by Sarsfield; and about thirty of the Prince of Orange's men, commanded by one Campbel: where, (saith my author,) notwithstanding the great inequality of the numbers, the latter fought with that desperate bravery, that it struck a terror into the minds of the army.

"At Salisbury the King was deserted by part of his army, (as he had been, before his leaving the Whitehall, by the Lord Cornbury, and such as would follow him), particularly by the Duke of Grafton, and the Lord Churchill, and, either there or at Andover, by Prince George of Denmark himself: upon which the King and his army were so disheartened, that upon a false alarm made, either with design or by accident, on the twenty-fifth of November they left Salisbury, the army retreating to Reading, and the King to Andover; and on the twenty-sixth, in the evening, he returned to London.

"The army at Reading, upon another false alarm, on the eighth of December retired in great haste to Twiford Bridge; and endeavouring to regain their post, a party of the Prince's men, who were sent for by the inhabitants of Reading, upon their threatening to plunder and fire the town, attacked the Irish Dragoons and slew fifty of them.

"The King being returned to London, and having now no longer any confidence in that way of deciding the dispute that he himself had chosen, on the twenty-eighth of November, in a privy council, ordered the Lord Chancellor to issue out writs for the sitting of a Parliament on the fifteenth day of January following.

"But the reader must observe, that this was not done until he was forced to it; and therefore, the Prince was now no longer under any obligation to the King, of standing to the decision of a Parliament. He might, had he pleased, without any injustice with respect to him, have made use of his good fortune, and pursued the advantage he had gained; which must, in all likelihood, have ended in victory; the Earl of Feversham, the King's General, not having with him, at that time, above four thousand men.

"But yet such was his moderation,

that upon the King's sending the Lords Hallifax, Nottingham, and Godolphin, to treat with him, and to adjust preliminaries to the holding of a Parliament, he, with the advice of the lords and gentlemen of his party, accepted the motion, and, as things then stood, returned a most reasonable answer. The which was sent to the King before his first attempt to withdraw himself out of the nation; and yet he did not alter his resolution to do it: it was sent to his Majesty by an express, and yet he resolved to leave the town; and ordered all those writs for the sitting of the Parliament, that were not sent out, to be burnt; and a caveat to be entered against the making use of those that were.

"And at the same time, he sent orders to the Earl of Feversham to disband the army, and dismiss the soldiers, (which was accordingly done) telling him in his letter, that things being come to that extremity, that he had been forced to send away the Queen and his son, that they might not fall into the hands of the enemy, he himself was obliged to do the same thing. And presently after, his Majesty was taken by the inhabitants of Feversham in a small vessel, endeavouring to go out of the nation.

"And after this it is manifest the Prince never considered him as King of England, but as his prisoner, or as a person conquered. It is true, the Lords invited him back to London, but it was without the Prince's consent, and in all likelihood without his knowledge. For although he treated him with all imaginable respect, as a person so nearly related to himself and the Princess, and with a due regard to Majesty, with which he had been so lately vested; yet still it was but like a person conquered. For, understanding he was at Rochester, he sent to him to continue there, by Monsieur Zulestein; but he missing of him, he sent another order after him, to remove from Whitehall, whither he was gone, to Ham. The message was to be delivered by the Marquess of Hallifax, the Earl of Shrewsbury, and the Lord Delamere, after the Prince's Guards were in possession of the posts about Whitehall, and a note drawn up to that purpose.

"Likewise the Prince committed the Earl of Feversham to the castle of Windsor, who had been sent by the King to invite him to St. James's. And if he committed the servant to prison, it is not hard to determine in what condition he judged the master to be. Princes do not use to imprison each other's servants sent on kind messages, while their masters are free; that is, as King James in his reasons for withdrawing himself from Rochester, words it, against the practice and law of nations.

"But the truth is, he considered him as a Prince conquered by him, and treated him accordingly, although with imaginable respect, and with great tenderness."

"The act 1 William and Mary," remarks another contemporary, "declaring the rights and liberties of the subject, and settling the succession of the crown, recites the very instrument of conveyance of the crown to the Prince and Princess; which begins in these words: 'Whereas the late King James II., by the assistance of divers evil counsellors, judges, and ministers employed by him, did endeavour to subvert and extirpate the Protestant religion, and the laws and liberties of this kingdom:' which is there made out, by an enumeration of sundry particulars. And not long after, there are these words: 'And whereas the late King James II. having abdicated the government, and the throne being thereby vacant,' the two House of Parliament do thereupon invest the Prince and Princess of Orange with the crown.

"King James endeavoured to subvert the government, as they favourably word it; or rather, he had long before wholly subverted and overthrown the government, as the Prince of Orange's declaration speaks, (which this very act has annexed and made parcel of the crown, and expresses to be the only means of redressing that mischief)."

While these important events were taking place, Mary remained unnoticed in Holland; the Prince, who resolved to owe nothing to the presence or pretension of his consort, made sure of obtaining the crown as his own, for life, before he commanded her to come to England. She embarked at the

Brill, on the tenth of February, 1689; after a swift, pleasant voyage, landed at Gravesend, and thence hastened to Greenwich Palace, where the Princess Anne, and Prince George of Denmark, after cordially welcoming her, entered the royal barge and proceeded with her up the Thames to Whitehall Stairs, where they all three landed, amidst the acclamations of thousands of spectators. The moment Mary's arrival became known, the metropolis was lit up with bonfires, the bells were rung, the guns fired, and the pope, together with father Petre, and the yet unconscious rival brother of the Princess Mary and Anne, known in after-years as the Pretender, were duly burnt in effigy. The conduct of Mary when she met the numerous and brilliant court assembled to greet her, was highly reprehensible. There was a levity and gaiety in her manners, which by no means suited a daughter taking possession of the spoils of an exiled, a deeply-injured, and an affectionate father. "She seemed quite transported with joy," remarks Evelyn, "and came into Whitehall laughing and jolly as to a wedding." "She gave proof," wrote Lady Churchill, "that she wanted bowels the day she came to Whitehall. She ran about it, looking into every closet and conveniency, and turning up the quilts upon the beds, as people do when they come into an inn, with no other sort of concern in her appearance but such as they express; conduct I thought mighty strange; for King James, although deposed, was still her father, who had been so lately driven from that chamber, and from that bed; and if she felt no tenderness, I thought she should at least have looked grave at so melancholy a reverse of his fortune."

Mary's panegyrist, Burnet, after admitting that, on her arrival at Whitehall, she put on an air of indecent and censurable gaiety, remarks, "I took the liberty to ask her how it came that what she saw in so sad a revolution in her father's person, had not made a greater impression on her. She took this freedom with her usual good nature, and answered with becoming gravity, that 'she felt the sense of it very lively in her thoughts, but that the letters which had been writ to her, had obliged her to put on a cheerfulness, in which she might possibly go too far, as she was obeying this instruction in those letters, and not acting in accordance with her own will." A lame excuse evidently, for her husband's directions doubtless had reference only to her public conduct as Queen, and not to her deportment in private. William surely did not command her to hurry from chamber to chamber, the moment she arrived, and, with a joyous heart and merry smiles, gaze on the princely possessions that had fallen within the grasp of herself and her husband. He certainly was too discreet, too worldly-wise to dictate such a needless exhibition of heartless glee; therefore, the only conclusion to be arrived at is, that she overlooked her father's miserable reverses, to exult over her own fortune, in becoming the mistress of his palace, and all the personal property which he and his Queen had left there.

The next day, February thirteen, was ordered for the proclamation of the new sovereigns. The day was cold, dark, and rainy, nevertheless all London was astir. Shortly before noon the two Houses went in procession to Whitehall, where they took up their places at the lower end of the banquetting hall. William and Mary, in robes of state, but without crowns or circlets, entered from the other end, and took their seats under the royal canopy, when the usher of the black rod conducted the speaker and members of the Lords and Commons as far as the steps. The clerk then read the declaration of rights, and the Marquess of Halifax tendered to the Prince and Princess the crowns of England, France, and Ireland; in the name of the assembled Lords and Commons, William answered for himself and his wife, that they accepted the offer with thanks, the more so, as it was a proof of the confidence reposed in them by the whole nation. And he added, "As I have no other intention in coming hither than to preserve your religion, laws, and liberties, you may be sure that I shall endeavour to support them, and be willing to concur in anything that shall be for the good of the kingdom, and to do all that is in my power to advance the welfare and the glory of the nation." The Princess made several curtsies, and "when her father's faults were named, she looked down as if she were troubled." Immediately the signatures of William and Mary were affixed to the declaration of rights, they were proclaimed by the style and title of William III. and Mary II.

This same afternoon, the Queen, to sustain her assumed character for piety, and to learn if James II. and his son were still prayed for in Sancroft's chapel, sent two of her chaplains to request for her the Archbishop's blessing. "Tell her," answered the unswerving primate, "to first ask her father's blessing, for without that mine would avail her nought." On the day following, she took up her abode at St. James's, and in reply to Dr. Bates, who, in the name of the Dissenters of England, expressed to her a desire that a general union should take place between them and the Church of England; remarked, with the skill of an experienced diplomatist, "I will use all endeavours for promoting any union necessary for edifying the church; I desire your prayers." Shortly afterwards, Mary obtained the approbation of her Protestant subjects, by expelling "the fiddlers" from her chapel at St. James's; but as her Dutch spouse pertinaciously insisted upon wearing his hat in church, the people openly murmured at his irreverence.

William had been on the throne but a few days, when he withdrew with his consort to Hampton Court, where, under a pretence of ill health, but really to conceal his petulancy, he secluded himself in his closet, and only came to town on council days; "so that," says Burnet, "the gaiety and diversions of a court, to which the nation had been so much used in the two former reigns, quite disappeared, which gave great disgust. The Queen, however, set herself to make up what was wanting in the King, by a great vivacity and cheerfulness. But when she was found not to meddle in business, though all were pleased with her, yet few came to make their court to her, as few found their account in it.

At the close of March, their Majesties promoted Burnet to the rich see of Salisbury as an acknowledgment for his services. "When Mary did me this valuable service," remarks the partizan prelate, "she told me she hoped that I would set a pattern to others, and would put in practice those *notions* with which I had taken the liberty sometimes to entertain her;"—notions, be it observed, which were so thoroughly distasteful to the English people, that his inaugural pastoral letter, in which he affirmed that William and Mary ruled by right of conquest, was, by order of Parliament, burnt by the common hangman. Although William and Mary had succeeded to the sovereign authority by the consent of a majority of the Peers and the Parliament, several Lords, Spiritual as well as Temporal, refused to take the oath of allegiance to them. The nonjuring prelates were Sancroft, Archbishop of Canterbury, Turner, Bishop of Ely, Ken, of Bath and Wells, White, of Peterborough, Lake, of Chichester, Lloyd, of Norwich, Thomas, of Worcester, and Frampton, of Gloucester. The four last had been imprisoned in the Tower by James, for refusing to publish his declaration for liberty of conscience. The Peers Temporal who refused the oath were the Duke of Newcastle, the Earls of Clarendon, Lichfield, Exeter, Yarmouth, and Stafford, and the Lords Griffin and Stawel. Several hundred of the minor clergy also forsook their livings, rather than break the oath they had sworn to King James II.; and from this period these and all others who were averse to the government of William and Mary, were distinguished by the appellation of non-jurors or non-swearers. Most of these non-jurors rejected the idea of a King *de facto*, as well as all other distinctions and limitations, and declared for the absolute power and divine, hereditary, indefeasible right of sovereigns.

CHAPTER III.

Coronation of William and Mary—They receive the sovereignty of Scotland—William never permits Mary to meet the Parliament—Mary's unpleasant visit to the play—Satire on her and her sister Anne—Quarrels with Anne—Corruption in every department of government—William's popularity declines—He purchases Kensington House—Anecdote of Mr. Carstares—Project to seize James II.

HE eleventh of April was the day appointed for the solemn inauguration of William and Mary. On the morning of that eventful day, whilst their Majesties were robing, previous to setting out for Westminster Hall, they received the unwelcomed intelligence of the landing of James II. in Ireland, and immediately afterwards Lord Nottingham delivered to Mary a letter of remonstrance and malediction from her father. In this letter, terrible in itself, and delivered at a time which rendered its reception doubly appalling, King James informed his daughter that he had attributed her previous unfilial conduct to the necessity she was under of obeying the commands of her too ambitious husband; "but," he added, "it is in your power not to be crowned, and if you dare to encircle your brow with the usurped crown, whilst I and your brother, the Prince of Wales, are living, the curses of an outraged father and the wrath of God, who has commanded obedience to parents, will light upon you and yours to all eternity." Dismayed and irritated by this letter, William declared that the part he had played in the revolution was by the advice and consent of his consort, and therefore she herself, and not he, had brought her father's malediction upon her. "Perhaps so," retorted Mary, who was evidently too hard-hearted to be terrified by the curses of her grossly ill-treated parent; "but remember, if my father regains his authority, my husband may thank himself for letting him go as he did." "When James heard of this unnatural speech," writes the exiled King himself in his Memoirs, "he perceived that his own children had lost all bowels not only of filial affection but of common compassion, and were as ready as the Jewish tribe of old to raise the cry, 'Away with him from the face of the earth!' It was the more grievous, because the hand which gave the blow was most dear to him. Yet Providence gave her some share of disquiet, too; for this news coming just at their coronation, put a damp on those joys which had left no room in her heart for the remembrance of a fond and loving father. Like another Tullia, under the show of sacrificing all to her country's liberty, she truly sacrificed her honour, her duty, and even religion, to drive out a peaceful Tullius, and set up another Tarquin in his place." This startling incident, more resembling a scene in a tragedy than an event of real life, delayed the ceremony of the coronation from eleven in the morning till half-past one at noon.

At ten in the forenoon, the King went by water from Whitehall to Westminster Hall, where he rested in an adjoining apartment, known as the "Prince's chamber." An hour afterwards, the Queen was conveyed thither in her chair, and went direct to the court of wards, where she reposed for awhile. But few Peers and Peeresses were in attendance. "Much of the splendour of the ceremony," remarks Evelyn, "was abated by the absence of divers who should have contributed to it. There were but five bishops and four judges: no more had taken the oaths; several noblemen and great ladies were absent." When due preparations had been made, the Peers and Peeresses proceeded four abreast from the Court of Requests, down the staircase into Westminster Hall, where they took their places, and where their Majesties took their seats on the throne, which was placed under a canopy above the table. At the early part of the ceremony, a strange blunder occurred. When their Majesties, as they knelt by the altar, were about to make their first offering, consisting of twenty guineas, enveloped in silk; the envelope was there, but not the gold. The Grand Chamberlain and the Lord Treasurer looked aghast; they had no money, nor had the King nor the Queen, and a dead pause ensued, till at length Danby drew out the required amount, and put a period to the ridiculous delay. The Bible was presented to their Majesties to kiss, and after the communion service, Burnet, Bishop of Salisbury, preached the sermon, which lasted half an hour; and being a string of satirical, abusive railing against James II. by name, was pronounced excellent. As the Archbishop of Canterbury was a non-juror, the crowning and anointing was performed by Compton, Bishop of London, who, before placing the crowns on their Majesties' heads, administered to them the subjoined oath, which had been especially framed for the occasion, and bound the new sovereigns to maintain the Protestant religion as established by law.

"Will you," demanded the Bishop, in a loud, clear voice, "solemnly promise and swear to govern the people of this kingdom and dominions thereunto belonging, according to the statutes in parliament agreed on, and the laws and customs of the same?"

William and Mary, both holding up their right hands, answered simultaneously, "I solemnly promise so to do."

"Will you," repeated the Bishop, "to your power cause law and justice in mercy to be executed in all your judgments?"

"I will," replied each of the sovereigns.

"Will you," again demanded the Bishop, "to the utmost of your power, maintain the laws of God, the true profession of the gospel, and the Protestant reformed religion as by law established? and will you preserve unto the Bishops and clergy of this realm, and to the churches committed to their charge, all such rights and privileges as by law do or shall appertain to them, or any of them?"

"All this I promise to do," replied William and Mary, both of whom immediately afterwards placed their right hand upon the gospels, and said: "The things which I have herebefore promised I will perform and keep, so help me, God."

Compton anointed William first and Mary afterwards, and crowned them with the same crowns that had encircled the brows of James II. and Maria Beatrix. It was whilst going through this portion of the ceremony, that Mary remarked to her sister, who only took the part of a spectator in the scene, that "a crown, after all, was not so heavy as it appeared." It was past four before the august assemblage sat down to the coronation banquet, and then the non-arrival of Dymock, the royal champion, occasioned a further delay of two hours. At last he entered, made his challenge in the name of our sovereign Lord and Lady, William and Mary, and threw down his gauntlet, which tradition affirms was picked up by an old woman, who left in its place a lady's glove, in which was a written acceptance of the challenge, appointing the hour, and naming Hyde Park as the place of meeting. According to this story, the brave champion of the exiled King kept his appointment, and paced Hyde Park from two to four the next day; when, as no Dymock appeared, he went away, heaping curses on the heads of usurpers and their unprincipled courtiers. The banquet, which was sumptuous, rare, and costly, was not concluded till past eight in the evening, when their Majesties, exhausted by the ceremonies of the day, retired to privacy and rest. Next day, the Commons in a body waited on the King and Queen at the Banqueting-house, Whitehall, to congratulate them on their coronation; and a few days afterwards, William and Mary proceeded to Hampton Court, where they received the congratulations of the ambassadors and other officers of foreign kingdoms and states.

William and Mary received the sovereignty of Scotland without unction or crowning. The Estates, after a stormy debate, voted them King and Queen of the Scots, and deputed the Earl of Argyle, Sir James Montgomery, and Sir James Dalrymple, to present to their Majesties letters from the Estates, the instruments of government, and a list of the grievances they wished to be redressed. These William and Mary received in due form, whilst seated on their throne in the Banqueting-house, after which the Earl of Argyle pronounced aloud, and they each, with their right hand uplifted, simultaneously repeated after him the subjoined coronation oath :—

"We, William and Mary, King and Queen of Scotland, faithfully promise, and swear, by this our solemn oath in the presence of the eternal God, that during the whole course of our life we will serve the eternal God to the utmost of our power according as he has required in his most holy word, revealed and contained in the New and Old Testaments, and according to the same word shall maintain the true religion of Jesus Christ, the preaching of his holy word, and the due and right administration of his sacraments, now received and preached within the realm of Scotland ; and shall abolish and *gain stand* all false religion contrary to the same, and shall rule the people committed to our charge, according to the laudable laws and constitutions received in this realm, no ways repugnant to the said work of the eternal God, and shall preserve to the utmost of our power, to the Kirk of God, and the whole Christian people, true and perfect peace at all time coming. That we shall preserve and keep inviolate the rights and rents, with all just privileges of the crown of Scotland, neither shall we transfer or alienate the same; that we shall forbid and repress in all estates and degrees, *reif* [robbery], oppression, and all kinds of wrong; and we shall command and procure that justice and equity be keeped to all persons without exception, as the Lord and Father of Mercies shall be merciful to us. And we shall be careful to root out all heretics—"

Here William interrupted Argyle, and said, "If this means that I am obliged to become a persecutor, I will not take the oath." The commissioners answered that it meant nothing of the sort; that by the law of Scotland, no man could be persecuted for his private opinions; and even obstinate and convicted heretics could *only* be denounced and outlawed, and their moveable estates confiscated. With this explanation the King expressed himself satisfied, and he and his consort again repeated after Argyle—

"And we shall be careful to root out all heretics, and enemies to the true worship of God, that shall be convicted by the true Kirk of God, of the aforesaid crimes, out of our land and empire of Scotland. And we faithfully affirm the things above written by our solemn oath.

"Under our hand, April 24, 1689."

It was expected that after the coronation, William would take his consort in state to meet the parliament; but the Dutch King loved himself to engross every symbol of sovereignty, and, to the surprise of the court and the nation, Mary was never once permitted to meet the assembled houses. William was evidently ashamed of this conduct; for whenever he met his parliament in the early years of his reign, he went there privately, and closely guarded, by water.

In reward for his services in promoting the revolution, William bestowed on Lord Churchill the title of Earl of Marlborough. But the Earl shortly afterwards learned the unpleasant truth, that the Dutch King despised and neglected him "Treatment," says Lady Marlborough, "which my husband richly deserved, for not knowing how much better he was off before he turned his back upon King James." William once said of Marlborough, "He is a great general, but a vile scoundrel; and although I have profited by his treasons, I abhor the traitor."

In June, William returned from Hampton Court, to discuss in council, at St. James's, the state of affairs in Ireland. Mary, who had accompanied her consort to London, seized the opportunity to gratify her taste for the drama. There was a play, the "Spanish Friar," by Dryden, which had mightily pleased King Charles II., but which, on account of its holding up to ridicule one of the Catholic faith, King James II. had forbid. This play she chose to witness; and a more unfortunate choice could not well have happened; for, instead of telling against her father, as she expected, it abounded with supposed allusions to her own unfilial conduct, which deeply mortified her, and caused a confusion such as perhaps never occurred from a theatrical representation before. "The only day her Majesty gave herself the diversion of a play," wrote the lord chamberlain Nottingham, "the piece performed was the 'Spanish Friar,' the only play forbid by the late King. Some unhappy expressions, amongst which, those that follow put her into the greatest disorder, and frequently forced her to hold up her fan, and often look behind, and call for her palatine and hood, or anything she could think of, whilst those who were in the pit before her [the King's box then was in the centre of the house] constantly turned their heads over their shoulders to see how she bore the application of what was said. In one part of the performance, where the Queen of Arragon is going to church in procession, it was uttered on the stage, 'Very good, she usurps the throne, keeps the old King in prison, and at the same time is praying for a blessing on the army.' Again, one of the actors remarked, ''Tis observed at court who weeps, and who wears black for good King Sancho's death.' And in another speech occurs the subjoined, 'Who is it that can flatter a court like this? Can I soothe tyranny, seem pleased to see my royal master murdered, his crown usurped, a distaff on the throne? What title has this queen, but lawless force? and force must pull her down.' These, and twenty more things were said in the play, which faction applied to the Queen; and though it never could be originally intended, it furnished the town with talk, till something else happened which gave equal occasion of discourse." Her Majesty's desire to frequent the national theatres, induced her to order another play, Sir Robert Howard's cavalier comedy of the "Committee," but her husband prevented her from witnessing the performance; and, proceeds Lord Nottingham, "she amused herself by visiting Mrs. Graden's, Mrs. Ferguson's, and other Indian houses, where they sell fine ribbons, rich head-dresses, and fancy articles, and curiosities. One day she dined at Mrs. Graden's, and the King, when he heard of it, flew in a great rage, and with many oaths told her it was no proper place for her to visit;" indeed, remarks our author, "more was said than was ever heard before, but it was borne like a good wife who leaves all to the direction of her lord, who amuses herself with walking six or seven miles every day, with looking after her buildings, making of fringe, and such like innocent things."

At this period, Mary was addicted to gluttony, and, if her enemies are to be believed, she occasionally indulged in strong potations. She had a tendency to obesity, and whilst the King, who detested the English and their manners, and in his social moments was wont to smoke and drink hollands with his Dutch courtiers with closed doors, was hourly growing leaner, she continued to increase in bulk. The first week in July, her Majesty took up her residence at Hampton Court for the summer. She was present when her sister Anne brought into the world Prince William, an event which took place at Hampton Court on the twenty-fourth of July, and which gave infinite joy to Mary and the partizans of the revolution, who believed, and not without reason, that a Protestant heir to the throne would render the restoration of the Roman Catholic Stuart line next to impossible. Since the accession of William and Mary, the Princess Anne had depended on them for her income. The Commons had voted the considerable sum of £600,000 for their Majesties' civil list, and from out of this Anne was to have been provided. William, however, preferred that she and her husband should remain dependents on him; and when, to free herself from such thraldom, she caused the subject of her income to be mooted in the Commons, the Queen one night took her to task for it, and asked her what was the meaning of those proceedings? Anne answered, "that she heard her friends there wished to make her some settlement." "Friends, indeed!" replied the Queen, hastily. "Pray what friends have you, but the King and me?" However, in the subsequent December, the Commons advised the King to allow the Princess Anne £50,000 out of the civil list, and from this moment commenced a coolness between Mary and the Princess her sister, which eventually ripened into an implacable enmity.

In the winter of 1689-90, the nation loudly clamoured against the reckless extravagance of the government, and the frauds and the peculations of the government servants. The corrupt spirit of the revolution became manifest in its own workings; in one year, the revenue which James had left plus and flourishing, was minus more than three millions. Every one attributed the defeat at Bantry Bay, not to lack of skill or bravery, but to the shameful embezzlement of the funds provided for the victualling and fitting out of Admiral Herbert's squadron. The merchants complained that convoy money was unjustly extorted from them, and yet withal, their merchant-men were plundered by pirates and privateers; whilst in the army, such was the spirit of peculation, to use a mild expression, that the troops sent to drive King James out of Ireland, were supplied with bad food, and improper and insufficient clothing and arms, which, in too many cases, were quite worthless. That patriotic officer, Mr. Harbord, was regularly paid for a regiment, the existence of which was limited to its standard, which he kept in his dressing-room; and both he and General Kirk carried on such a wholesale system of embezzlement, that they dared not audit each other's accounts. Deeply as William deplored the dishonest conduct of his unprincipled partizans, necessity compelled him to pass it over in silence. "It is only such men as these,' he remarked to his favourite, Bentinck, whom he had lately elevated to the earldom of Portland, "who support the revolution; there are thousands of upright, honourable Englishmen, but unfortunately they are not my friends" a conviction teeming with truth, but which did not prevent the ambitious monarch from patronizing that most abominable of perjurers, Titus Oates. The parliament reversed the sentence of Oates, and immediately afterwards William granted him a pension of £520 a-year, and presented him with two rich Church of England benefices:—conduct too scandalous to be overlooked, and which incensed the people against the Dutch King, "whose popularity," remarks Smollett, "had already began visibly to decline." Mary was dissatisfied with William's measures, and a great number even of those who exerted themselves for his elevation, had conceived a disgust from his personal deportment, which was very unsuitable to the manners and disposition of the English people. Instead of mingling with his nobility in social amusements and familiar conversation, he maintained a disagreeable reserve, which had all the air of sullen pride; he seldom or never spoke to his courtiers or attendants; he spent his time chiefly in the closet, retired from all communication, or among his troops, at a camp he had formed at Hounslow, or in the exercise of hunting, to which he was immoderately addicted. This had been prescribed to him by physicians, as necessary to improve his constitution, which was naturally weak, and by practice had become so habitual that he could not lay it aside. His ill health cooperating with his natural aversion to society, produced a peevishness, which could not fail of being displeasing to those who were near his person; this was increased by the disputes in his cabinet, and the opposition of those who were professed enemies to his government, as well as by the alienation of his former friends. As he suffered from asthma, and could not breathe without difficulty in the air of London, he resided chiefly at Hampton Court, and expended considerable sums in beautifying and enlarging that palace. He likewise purchased the house at Kensington, of the Earl of Nottingham; and such profusion, in an expensive war, gave umbrage to the nation generally. Whether he was advised by his councillors, or his own sagacity pointed out the expediency of conforming with the English humour, he now seemed to change his disposition, and in some manner to adopt the manners of his predecessors. In imitation of Charles II., he resorted to the races at Newmarket; he accepted an invitation to visit Cambridge, where he behaved himself with remarkable affability to the members of the university; he afterwards dined with the Lord Mayor of London, accepted the freedom of the city, and condescended so far as to become the sovereign master of the Company of Grocers.

William completed the purchase of Kensington House in the spring of 1690, and he immediately employed Sir Christopher Wren and Nicholas Hawksmoor to convert it into a royal palace. It was during William's residence at Kensington Palace, that the following scene occurred; a scene that does honour to the fidelity of Mr. Carstares, his confidential secretary. His Majesty, who had been rendered suspicious of the Scottish clergy, during the absence of their steady advocate, Mr. Carstares, was induced to issue out an order, that every minister should take the oath of allegiance, and sign an assurance, declaring King William to be King *de jure* as well as *de facto*, before he should be allowed to take his seat in the general assembly. Lord Carmichael, the commissioner sent to Scotland to execute this decree, perceiving the determined spirit of the Presbyterian ministers against this measure, sent dispatches to the King, stating that, if persisted in, it would endanger the peace of that country. Lord Carmichael's despatches arrived at Kensington a few hours before the return of Mr. Carstares, who, on his arrival, found that the courier had been sent back with positive orders to enforce the royal command. He immediately hastened after the messenger, and overtaking him, demanded his despatches in the King's name: when, though late at night, and his Majesty in bed, he requested an audience on a matter of the utmost importance. On entering the royal chamber, he found the King sound asleep, when he fell upon his knees, and gently awoke his Majesty, who with surprise, demanded his business. "Sire," said Mr. Carstares, "I come to solicit my life." "And is it possible," said the King, "that you can commit a crime that should forfeit it?" He acknowledged he had, and showed the despatches he had taken from the messenger. "And have you," demanded his Majesty, sternly looking at him, "have you presumed to countermand my orders?" "It was to *save* one of the pillars of your Majesty's throne," replied the secretary, who was graciously permitted to explain his reasons for an act of such peril; and as the explanation satisfied the King, he ordered Mr. Carstares to throw the despatches into the fire, and prepare fresh instructions, couched in such terms as he deemed advisable, assuring him that he would immediately sign them.

Having resolved to head the army in Ireland in person, William caused an Act of Parliament to be passed, investing Mary with full regnal powers as regent, during his absence. As her Majesty's council of regency, he nominated the Marquis of Carmarthen, formerly Lord Danby, together with the Lords Pembroke, Nottingham, Marlborough, Devonshire, Monmouth, Godolphin, and Admiral Russell and Sir John Lowther. Just previous to his departure occurred the following extraordinary circumstance, which we relate in the words of Bishop Burnet. "The day before the King set out for Ireland," writes the prelate, "he called me into his closet; he seemed to have a great weight upon his spirits, from the state of his affairs, which were then very cloudy. He said, that for his own part, he would either go through with his business or perish in it. He only pitied the poor Queen, the poor Queen! repeating that twice with great tenderness, and wished that those who loved him would wait much on her and assist her. He lamented that the nation was distracted by factions, which the clergy inflamed instead of allaying. He declared that going to war was naturally no unpleasant thing to him, and he was sure he understood that better than how to govern England; adding, that though he had no doubt or mistrust of the cause he went on, yet the going against King James in person was hard upon him, since it would be a vast trouble both to himself, and to the Queen, if he [James] should be either killed or taken prisoner. Then he desired my prayers, and dismissed me, deeply affected with what he had said." A deep affectedness, it may be observed, that was mere sham, or at least transient as an April shower, as will presently be rendered evident. "I had a particular occasion," proceeds Burnet, "to know how tender our sovereign William was of King James's person, having learnt an instance of it from the first hand. A proposition was made to the King that a third-rate ship, well manned by a faithful crew, and commanded by one who had been well with King James, but was such an one as the King might trust, should sail for Dublin and declare for King James. The person who told me this, offered to be the man that should carry the message to King James, for he was (well known) to him, to invite him to come on board, which he seemed to be sure he King James would accept of; and when he was on board, they should sail away with him, and land him either in Spain or Italy, as the King should desire; and should have twenty thousand ponnds to give him, when he should be set ashore. The King thought it was a well-formed design, and likely enough to succeed, but he would not hearken to it—he said he would have no hand in treachery; and King James would certainly carry some of his guards and of his court abroad with him, and probably they would make some opposition, and in the struggle some accident might happen to King James's person, in which he would have no hand. I acquainted the Queen with this, and I saw in her a great tenderness for her father's person, and she was much touched at the answer the King had made."

If the bishop really believed in the sincerity of this pretended kindness of William, the nephew, and this sham filial affection of Mary, the daughter, he was grossly deceived; for the moment his back was turned, their Majesties came to the murderous resolution that his proposition was but a half measure, and immediately executed a warrant, autnorizing Admiral Torrington to entice King James upon his ship, and then seize him, sail with him to Holland, and deliver him up to the tender mercies of his implacable enemies, the Dutch, for them to dispose of as they should think fit.

CHAPTER IV.

William proceeds to Ireland—Mary rules as Queen Regent and Regnant—Quarrels with the Queen Dowager—Arrest of Lord Clarendon—Her regnal difficulties—Defeat of the fleet at Beechy Head—Troubles that followed—Letters on William's wound, and on the Battle of the Boyne—Lord Lincoln—Feud between the Council and the Privy Council—Scotch Jacobite plot—Royal estates in Ireland—Burnet's sermon on the Boyne victory.

ON the fourth of June, William bade adieu to Mary, and set out for Ireland, attended by Prince George of Denmark, the Duke of Ormond, the Earls of Oxford, of Scarborough, of Manchester, and many other persons of distinction. He landed at Belfast on the fourteenth, and during the period that he was successfully battling against James and the Jacobites in Ireland, Mary detailed to him the more important of her sayings and doings in a series of letters, which were found in his strong box at Kensington Palace, after his death. William's letters in reply, have never come to hand, and it is supposed that Mary destroyed them a short while before her decease.

On the nineteenth of June, Mary, on hearing that her royal husband had safely arrived in Ireland, wrote him—"You will be weary of seeing every day a letter from me, it may be; yet being apt to flatter myself, I will hope that you will be as willing to read as I to write. And, indeed, it is the only comfort I have in this world, besides that of trust in God. I cannot thank God enough for your being well past through the dangers of the sea. I beseech him, in his mercy, still to preserve you so, and send us once more a happy meeting upon earth."*

In her next, after detailing how Lord Feversham, chamberlain to the Queen Dowager, Katherine of Braganza, had prevented the prayer ordered to be said throughout England, for the success of her absent lord's arms against King James in Ireland, from being said in the chapel belonging to Katherine of Braganza's dower palace of Somerset House, Mary proceeds—"I was extremely angry, which the privy council saw. I told them I thought there was no more measures to be kept with the Queen Dowager herself, after this, that is, if it were her orders, which no doubt it is. When Lord Feversham heard from Lord Nottingham how annoyed I was at his conduct, he came to my bed-chamber at the hour when there was a great deal of company—I mean just before dinner; he looked as pale as death, and spoke in great disorder. He said he must own it a great fault, since I took it so, but he begged me to believe that it was done, not out of ill-intention, nor by agreement with any one. He assured me the Queen Dowager knew nothing of it; and after declaring that it was a fault, a folly, an indiscretion, or anything I would call it, said, God pardoned sinners when they repented, and so he hoped I would. I told him God saw hearts, and whether their repentance was sincere; which since I could not do, he must not deem it strange if I trusted only to actions; and so I left him. I pity the poor man for being obliged thus to take the Queen Dowager's faults upon him, yet I could not bring myself to forgive him. The Queen Dowager will come here to-day, to see me, but desired an hour when there was least company; so I imagine she will speak something of herself." Katherine of Braganza attended the levee, but instead of speaking something of herself, she, to the mortification of Mary, acted as if

* Our limits preclude us from giving these interesting letters in full. They are published verbatim in Dalrymple's Appendix.

profoundedly ignorant of the offence. "The Queen Dowager has been," Mary remarked before sealing her letter, "but did not stay a moment, or speak two words. I have still the same complaint to make, that I have not time to cry, which would a little ease my heart, but I hope in God I shall have such news from you, as will give me no reason, yet your absence is enough; but since it pleases God, I must have patience. Do but continue to love me, and I can bear all things with ease."

On the French fleet, which had long been expected to invade England, being seen in the channel, Mary wrote, "The news which is come to-night [June twenty-second] of the French fleet being upon the coast, makes it necessary to write to you. I think Lord Torrington [Admiral of the English fleet in the channel] has made no haste, and I cannot tell whether his being sick and staying for Lord Pembroke's regiment will be a sufficient excuse; but I will not take up your time with my reasonings. I shall only tell you I am so little afraid, that I begin to fear that I have not sense enough to apprehend the danger. Just as I was going to bed, Lord Nottingham brought me a letter, of which he is going to give you an account; for my own part, I shall say nothing to it, but that I trust God will preserve us—you where you are, and poor I here."

At this crisis Mary acted with marked energy and decision. She in person reviewed the London militia, caused numbers of the discontented nobles and gentry to be arrested, and banished every Catholic from London and its neighbourhood. On this subject, she, in a letter to King William, dated June the twenty-fourth, remarks, "Since I writ to you about the coming of the French fleet upon the coast, the Lords have been very busy. I shall not give you an account of all things, but only tell you some particular passages One happened to-day at the privy council, where I was, by their advice. When they had resolved to seize on suspected persons, in naming them, Sir H. Capel would have said something for Lord Clarendon, but as It believed it as necessary that he [Lord Clarendon] should be *clapt up* as any, I thought myself obliged to say so. By a letter from Lord Torrington [who then was commanding the fleet off Beachy Head], dated yesterday, I see he thought this day was likely to decide a great deal there. I cannot but be in pain, it may be I do not reason justly on the matter, but I fear, besides disheartening many people, the loss of a battle would be such an encouragement to the disaffected ones, that might put things here into disorder, which, in your absence, would be a terrible thing; but I thank God, I trust in him, and that is really the only consolation I have. I was last night in Hyde Park, for the first time since you went; it swarmed with those who are now ordered to be *clapt up*. Since I have writ this, I was called out to Lord Nottingham, who brought me your dear letter, which is so welcome, that I cannot express it; especially because you pity me, which I like and desire from you, and you only. God be praised that you are so well; I hope in his mercy he will continue it. I have been obliged to write this evening to Schulemberg, to desire him to advance money for the six regiments to march, which they say is absolutely necessary for your service, as well as honour. The Lords of the Treasury have made me pawn my word for it, and to-morrow £20,000 will be paid to him."

The difficulties which beset her Majesty at this period, are rendered painfully apparent in the subjoined epistle, which she addressed from Whitehall, to her absent husband, on the twenty-sixth of June, 1690:—

"By this express I shall write freely, and tell you what great suspicions increase continually of Major Wildman. It would be too long to tell you all the reasons of suspicion, but this one I will give, that since your going from hence, there is not one word come from Scotland, neither from Lord Melville nor Colonel Mackey to Lord Marlborough, which methinks is unaccountable. Lord Nottingham desired I would sign letters to he governors of Berwick and Carlisle, not to let any persons go by who had not a pass; and that they should stop the mails and send word how many were come from thence in this time. This I have done, and the express is to be immediately sent away. I ever fear not doing well, and trust to what nobody says but you, therefore I hope it will have your approbation. Lord Bath is very backward in going down to assume his command, but with much ado he sends his son who only says he stays for a letter of mine, which is signed this morning, to empower him to command at Plymouth in his father's absence, which he tells me you promised before you went; and it is upon your leave Lord Bath pretends to stay here; but I told him I suppose you had not foreseen the French being so near. The Duke of Bolton also told me last night, you had given him leave to raise some horse volunteers, for which he should have had a commission, but that you went away, and therefore he would have me give it; but I put it off, and Lord Marlborough advises me not to give it. Lord President [formerly Lord Danby, now Marquis of Carmarthen] some time since, told me the same thing, but I will not give any positive answer till you send me your directions. I must also inform you of what Lord Nottingham told me yesterday: he says Lord Steward [Devonshire] was very angry at Lord Torrington's deferring the fight, and proposed that somebody should be joined in commission with him. But that the other lords said could not be done, so Lord Monmouth offered to take one whose name I have forgot, he is newly made, I think, commissioner of the navy; and as Lord Nottingham tells me, you had thoughts of having him command the fleet, if Lord Torrington had not this man, Lord Monmouth proposed to take and go together on board Lord Torrington's ship as volunteers, but with a commission about them, to command in case he [Torrington] should be killed. I told Lord Nottingham I was not willing to grant any commission of that nature, not knowing whether you had ever had any thoughts of that kind, so that I thought he was only to be thanked for his offer. I added, that I could not think it proper that he, being one of the nine you had named [as my council] should be sent away. Upon which he (Nottingham) laughed and said, that it was the greatest compliment I could make him (Lord Monmouth) to say I could not make use of his arm, having need of his counsel. I suppose they are not good friends, but I said it as I meant, and besides, to hinder propositions of this kind for Mr. Russell (Admiral Russell); for I see Lord Carmarthen has, upon several occasions, to me alone, mentioned sending Mr. Russell; and I believe it was only to be rid of him; for my part, after what you have told me of all the nine, I should be very sorry to have him from hence. And now I have named Mr. Russell, I must tell you, that at your first going, he did not come to me, nor, I believe, to this hour would have spoken with me, had not I told Lady Russell one day I desired it. When he came, I told him freely that I desired to see him sometimes, for being a stranger to business, I was afraid of being too much led or persuaded by one party. I hope I did not do amiss in this, and, indeed, I saw at that time no body but Lord President Carmarthen, and I was afraid of myself. Lord Carmarthen is upon all occasions afraid of giving me too much trouble, and thinks, by little and little, to do all. Every one sees how little I know of business, and therefore, I believe, will be apt to do as much as they can. Lord Marlborough advised me to resolve to be present as often as possible, out of what intention I cannot judge; but I find that they meet often at the secretary's office, and do not take much pains to give me an account: this I thought fit to tell you. Pray be so kind to answer me as particularly as you can."

Suspicions, doubts, and jealousies, still tormented the Queen and her cabinet. Fearing to risk an engagement with the French, on account of the lamentable state of the fleet under his command, Torrington wrote Mary, that he deemed it advisable to attempt nothing beyond defending the coasts from invasion. This conduct many of the council attributed to disloyalty, and intrigues and stormy debates ensued, the particulars of which Mary forwarded to her wedded partner, in a letter dated June twenty-eighth, and from which we make the subjoined extracts.

"As for Lord Torrington's letter, you will have an account of that, and the answer from Lord Nottingham. I shall tell you, as far as I can judge, what the others did. Lord Carmarthen was with me when Lord Nottingham brought the letter; he was mighty hot upon sending Mr. Russell down to the fleet; but believing that Russell and Torrington were not friends, that Torrington ought not to be provoked, and that Carmarthen's object was to get rid of Russell, I said what I could against it, and found most of the lords of my mind when they met, but Monmouth was not with them. Mr. Russell drew up a sharp letter for us to sign, but it was softened down, and wrote in such terms as you will see; to which all agreed but Lord Devonshire, who said that he believed it very dangerous to trust Lord Torrington with the fate of three kingdoms, and that he was absolutely of opinion that some other should be joined in the commission with him. To which Mr. Russell answered, 'You must send for him prisoner, then;' and all the rest concluded it would create too much disturbance in the sight of the enemy, and would be of dangerous consequence. So the letter was signed, and Lord Nottingham writ another letter, in which he told him our other accounts we have received of the fleets from the Isle of Wight. After I had gone, Lord Monmouth came to the other lords who were still sitting, and offered, if the Admiralty would give him the commission of a captain, to hasten to Portsmouth, fit out the best ship there, and with it join Lord Torrington. Being in a great passion, he swore he would never come back again if they did not fight. By his desire, and the approbation of the lords, Lord Nottingham came to ask my consent. I asked who was there, and finding that two-thirds of the committee were present, so that if put to the vote it would have been carried, and seeing they were as earnest as he for it, I thought I might consent. Indeed, I had a thought which I would not own, though I found some of the lords had the same, about the 'lemon letters,'* which I suppose you have heard of, which come so constantly, and are so very exact; the last of which told even the debates of the committee, as well as if one of the lords themselves had written them. This looks odd, and I believe makes many forward for this expedition; and, for my own part, I believe Lord Monmouth may be best spared of the company.

"Ten at night. Since writing this, there has come much news. As I was going to the cabinet council in the morning, Sir William Lockhart came with a letter from the committee there. Lord Monmouth was there; he made great professions at parting, and desired me to believe there are some great designs."

The Queen's next letter was written immediately after the disastrous defeat of the combined English and Dutch fleets by the French, off Beachy Head. She remarks, "As to the ill success at sea, I am more concerned for the honour of the nation, than for anything else; but I think it has pleased God to punish them justly, for they really *talkt* as if defeat were impossible, which looks too much like trusting in the arm of flesh. I pray God we may no more deserve the punishment, and trust he will do more than we deserve. What Lord Torrington can say for himself, I know not, but I believe he will never be forgiven here: the letters from the fleet before and since the engagement, show sufficiently he was the only man there who had no mind to fight, and his not doing it, was attributed to orders from the council. Those which were sent and obeyed, have had but very ill success, the news of which has come this morning. Lord Monmouth, I am sorry to say, has come back, and in compliance with your orders, Mr. Russell, who had

* Letters written in lemon juice, which detailed the proceedings of William and Mary and their cabinet, and were directed to M. Courtenay, Amsterdam. These letters Monmouth brought every post-day to the Queen, under pretence that his intriguing friend, Major Wildman, had intercepted them. It is generally believed that he himself wrote them, to further his own ambitious projects.

been sent away against my wish, has returned, so that now the nine are together again."

On the third of July, Mary, still addressing her husband on the same subject, wrote—"I and the nine have been troubled to select suitable persons to take charge of the shattered fleet, for it has been resolved that Lord Torrington* shall be disgraced and tried. The post was declined by Lord Monmouth and Mr. Russell, and when I offered it to my Lord Chamberlain and Lord Marlborough, they both assured me they would be laughed at if they interfered in sea matters. I therefore conferred it on my Lords Devonshire and Pembroke, which so annoyed my Lord President, who wished to undertake the commission himself, that I found it expedient to privately assure him that you could not spare him from his post; but he answered he did not look upon himself as so tied. He is also vexed at another affair, which is, that neither Mr. Hampden nor Mr. Pelham will sign the docket for Lady Plymouth's £8000. He complained to me, I promised to ask them about it, which I have done; and both of them asunder, have told me the sum was too great to be spared at present, when money was so much wanted; and in truth, I think them in the right. I hope you will let me know your mind upon it. They say Sir Stephen Fox signed it by surprise, and is of their mind. The only thing I could say to this was, that you had signed the warrant before you went, which I thought was enough. I must also tell you that Lord Shrewsbury [Mary's reputed lover] was at my dinner: I cordially welcomed him. He did not stay long, but was here again at my supper; and, as I thought, took great pains to talk, *which I did to him as formerly, by your directions.*" She then concludes—"I am fully persuaded that God will do some great thing or other, and it may be when human means fail he will show his power. This gives me courage to wait patiently for the result. But what gives me pain, is fear that all that is done may not please you. I am sure my great desire is to act as your second self, but you know I must do what the others think fit. I long to hear from you, for I love you more than my life, and desire only to please you."

On the sixth of July, Mary, on learning that her husband had been wounded in Ireland, wrote to him, "I can never give God thanks enough, as long as I live, for your preservation. I hope in his mercy that this is a sign he preserves you to finish the work he has begun by you; but I hope it may be a warning to you to let you see you are exposed to as many accidents as others; and though it has pleased God to keep you once in so visible a manner, yet you must forgive me if I tell you, that I shall think it a tempting God to venture again without a great necessity. For God's sake, let me beg of you to take more care for the time to come; consider what depends upon your safety; there are so many more important things than myself, that I think I am not worthy naming among them; but it may be, the worst will be over before this time, so that I will say no more."

The news of William's victory over James II., at the signal battle of the Boyne, fought July the first, 1690, filled Mary with ecstasies. In a letter dated Whitehall, July the seventh, she thus addressed her husband—"How to begin this letter I do not know, or however, to render God thanks enough for his mercies; indeed, they are too great, if we look on our deserts; but, as you say, it is his own cause, and since it is for the glory of his great name, we have no reason to fear but he will perfect what he has begun. I am sorry the fleet has done no better, but it is God's providence, and we must not murmur, but wait with patience to see the event. I was yesterday out of my senses with trouble; I am now almost so with joy. I hope in God, by the afternoon, to be in a condition of sense enough to say much more, but for the present I am not."

In the afternoon she resumes—"I am still in such a confusion of thoughts, that

* He was tried and acquitted. The king, however, dismissed him from his service, and would never again admit him into his presence.

I scarcely know what to say; but I hope in God you will now readily consent to what Lord President wrote last night, for methinks there is nothing more for you to do. I must put you in mind of one thing, which is, that you will take care of the Church in Ireland. Everybody agrees that it is the worst in Christendom. There are now bishoprics and other places vacant, and I trust you will fill them with suitable persons. I am very uneasy in one thing, which is, want of somebody to speak my mind freely to: it is a great constraint to think and be silent; and there is so much matter, that I am one of Solomon's fools, who am ready to burst. I believe Lord President and Lord Nottingham agree very well, and Lord Marlborough is always with them. As yet, they (I mean the whole nine) have differed so little, that, to my surprise, it has never come to put anything to the vote. This I attribute to the great danger all have apprehended, which has made them of a mind."

The fact was, they had all played traitor to King James: his return would have proved their ruin, hence their unanimity.

After detailing Lord Monmouth's futile efforts to prejudice her against her friend Lord Nottingham, her Majesty proceeds —"Lord Pembrook I never see but in council. Shrewsbury comes as little as he can, and never to the cabinet council. Devonshire will be a courtier among the ladies; but Lord Nottingham seems to be hearty and sincere in all affairs, although he does not take much pains to persuade me of it, as others do, for he never spoke but once of himself, yet I confess I have a good opinion of him. He brought me your letter yesterday, and I could not hold; so he saw me cry, which I have hindered myself before everybody till then, that it was impossible. And this morning, when I heard the joyful news, I was in pain to know what was become of *the late King* [James II., her father], and durst not ask till Lord Nottingham came, when I did venture to do it, and had the satisfaction to know he was safe. I know I need not beg you to let him be taken care of, for I am confident you will for your own sake; yet add, that to all your kindness, and for my sake, let people know you would have no hurt come to his person. Forgive me this."

In conclusion. Mary remarks—"I long to hear what you will say to the proposition [that the King would immediately return to England] which will be sent to you to-night by the Lords; and I flatter myself mightily, with the hopes to see you, for which I am more impatient than can be expressed, loving you with a passion which cannot but end with my life."

The Earl of Halifax, in a poem on the battle of the Boyne, draws the subjoined not unfaithful sketch of Mary's conduct at this eventful epoch:—

"Who can forget the Queen's auspicious smile?
The pride of the fair sex, the goddess of our Isle;
Who can forget what all admired of late?
Her fears for him, her prudence for the state.
Dissembling cares, she smoothed her looks with grace,
Doubts in her heart, and pleasure in her face;
As danger did approach, her courage rose,
And putting on the King, dismayed his foes.

To return to the Queen's correspondence with her husband: she wrote on the eighth of July, "At last I have obtained what I long wished for in vain, a sight of Lord Lincoln [a nobleman, we may remark parenthetically, who was incited by the cabinet council to harass the council of nine, by whom her Majesty was solely guided]. I met him as I came from prayers, with a hundred people at least after him. I cannot represent to you my surprise at so unexpected, so strange an object, and his words were, if possible, more strange than his acts. He called Lord President by name, and all in general who are in trust, 'rogues,' and told me, I must go back with him to the privy council to hear his complaint, which I think was against Lord Torrington; he talked so like a madman, that I answered him as calmly as I could, looking on him as such, and so with much ado got from him. I shall say no more now, but that I shall live and die entirely yours."

Two days afterwards, her Majesty narrated to the King the troubles in which she was involved by the opposition of the privy council to the council of nine. The Queen, by the King's orders, but rarely attended the privy council, which so enraged that body, that they declared their functions were superseded by the council of nine, and broke out into a state bordering on rebellion. After mentioning that Mr. Russell had been sent down to the fleet, Mary proceeds—"The day I received yours by Mr. Gray, the privy council was called extraordinarily, it being thought fit to formally acquaint them with the news of the victory at the Boyne. Seeing you had left me to the advice of the committee [council] of nine when to attend the privy council, I asked them in the morning if I should go on this occasion, as for my part I thought not. It was decided in the negative; but in the afternoon, when the privy council met, all began to ask if I came. The Lord President said, No; upon which there was great grumbling. Sir R. Howard said he thought it not reasonable that I did not come to privy council. He was seconded by the Duke of Bolton; and Lords Monmouth and Devonshire came to me in my closet, and requested me to go with them to privy council, to appease the storm. I will not trouble you with what they said, but they were very pressing. I was surprised, and answered them at first civilly, but being much pressed, I grew peevish, and told them I thought it a proud fancy of some of the privy council, which I did not feel myself bound to humour. I had declared in the morning that I would not come, and if I complied now, I should in the end be sent for whenever anybody had a mind to it. But all I could say would not satisfy them, and had not Lord Nottingham come in, I believe they would not have left me so soon This was the same day Lord Lincoln was here, as I wrote you on the eighth; and he sat in the gallery, crying aloud 'that five or six lords shut me up, and would let nobody else come near me,' yet never asked it all the time. Lord Nottingham will give you an account of the Lord Mayor's being called next day to the privy council, [to appease the discontents of that body, Mary was compelled to call them together, and preside over their deliberations in person] where I was; but I must observe, that he came with his answer ready wrote, and pulled out his paper and read it. Upon which many of those who came with him, looked upon one another as amazed; and the more because the Lord President did not desire it till Friday." This is one of the first instances of a public functionary bringing his speech in his pocket, ready written; and the novel circumstance so alarmed the Queen, that she attributed it to treachery on the part of the mal-content privy council, whom she suspected of plotting to overturn the government.

At this period a formidable Jacobite plot was hatching in Scotland; but before it came to maturity, the leaders, Lords Annandale and Breadalbane, confessed the whole to their majesties and betrayed their colleagues; one of whom, Lord Ross, several of the Privy Council desired to protect. The Queen thus mentions the circumstance*—"Another thing happened that I must tell your Majesty: Lord Nottingham had secured Lord Rosse, and now desired the Privy Council that he might be sent to the Tower, as well as many other Jacobites. All consented. Duke of Bolton asked why? Lord Nottingham replied, 'there were informations against him, and more, his own letters to Sir J. Cochrane;' upon which all said a warrant should be drawn. But when it came to be signed, Duke of Bolton would not; and hindered Lord Devon by a whisper, and his son by a nod. Lord Montague would not sign it either; if this be usual, I cannot tell, but methinks it ought not to be so."

In the subsequent week, Mary wrote her husband:—"You will excuse me from answering your letter I received yes-

* On the fourteenth of July Queen Mary issued proclamations for the apprehension of the Earls of Lichfield, Aylesbury, and Castlemain; the Lords Montgomery, Preston, and Bellasis; Sir Edward Hales, Sir Robert Hamilton and several others mostly officers. Pepys, the author of the "Diary," had been arrested on the twenty-fifth of June, upon a charge of giving information to the French of the state of the English navy.

terday morning, when you know I have been this morning to Hampton Court, where I must tell you all things are going on very slowly for want of money* and Portland stone. Sir Charles Littleton has offered to resign his commission. I have accepted it, and am glad of it, for reasons too long to tell now. Pray send word who shall have the appointment, for it is judged necessary to be filled up as soon as may be." In another letter the Queen says, "All my fear is, the French ships which are going to St. George's Channel, and are already at Kinsale; but I hope the express, which goes this evening to Sir Cloudesley Shovel, will reach him time enough to prevent any surprise. I am the most impatient creature in the world for an answer about your coming, which I hope may be a good one." I have been also desired to beg you not to be too quick in parting with the confiscated estates [they were the private inheritance of her father, and William III. bestowed them on his mistress, Elizabeth Villiers], but consider whether you will not keep some for public schools to instruct the poor I risk. For my part, I must need say, that I think you would do very well, if you would consider what care can be taken of the poor souls there; and, indeed, if you would give me leave, I must tell you I think this wonderful deliverance and success you have had, should oblige you to think upon doing what you can for the advancement of true religion and promoting the gospel. On Monday next I go to Hyde Park to review the militia—you may be sure I go against my will. I will say no more at present, but that the Bishop of Salisbury [Burnet the historian] made a *long thundering sermon* [on the Boyne victory] this morning, which he has brought me, and requested me to print; which I could not refuse, although I should not have ordered it, for reasons which I told him. I am extremely anxious to hear from you; but above all, I hope I shall not meet with a disappointment of your coming, for in that case I don't know what I should do; my desire of seeing you is equal to my love, which cannot end but with my life."

* The Queen had used her utmost endeavours to supply William with money while in Ireland, even to pawning many of her jewels.

CHAPTER V.

Cabinet factions—Mary quarrels with the Admiralty—Appointment of Russell and others as Admirals of the fleet—Kensington Palace—Passage of the Shannon—Mary intercedes for Mr. Hamilton—Examines Jacobite traitors—Her Dutch bias—Deplores the loss of her husband's cannon—Dialogue with Russell—Family gossip—Tender affection for her husband—Dreads his going to Flanders—He returns to England—Embarks for the Hague—Proceedings of the Jacobites—Nevill Payne put to the torture.

AS the battle of the Boyne had annihilated the probability of James the Second's restoration, Mary's councillors, no longer united by a fear of her father's return, broke out into a state of fierce party strife, which drove her Majesty almost beside herself. "I have at last seen the Council in a great heat," she writes her husband on the twenty-eighth of July, "but shall stay till I see you, to tell you my mind upon it. Lord Lincoln was with me for more than an hour, reforming the fleet, correcting abuses, and not shy of naming persons; he talked so much like a madman, and made me the *extravagantest* compliments in the world. He used an expression I have heard often within these few days, which is, that I have the power in my hand, and they wonder I do not make use of it, and why should I stay for your return, and whether it is well for me to lose time by writing you word is doubted, that is, when they must stay till an answer can come. I shall tell you more of this when I see you, or can write you a longer letter, for I have taken the vapours and dare not to-night." It certainly does honour to Mary as a consort, that she turned a deaf ear to the entreaties of the powerful party who urged her to acts of independent sovereignty. Strange it is, that a base, heartless daughter, should prove a gentle, loving, obedient wife, yet such is the case with Mary the Second; a Queen who, to her father, was one of the worst of offsprings, to her husband the best of wives.

At the commencement of August, the Councils were at issue respecting the appointment of an admiral to command the fleet; the King, and, of course, also the Queen, wished to confer the honour upon Mr. Russell, but on account of the late naval defeats, he refused to accept it, unless two others shared the responsibility with him; the one Lord Shrewsbury, the other an experienced naval officer. Their Majesties raised no powerful objection to Lord Shrewsbury, but they insisted on Sir Richard Haddock, a gentleman hated by Russell, being the third admiral. Russell resisted, and the feuds which thereby ensued, Mary thus describes to her absent lord:—"The commissioners of the Admiralty were sent for, and Lord President Carmarthen told them, that Russell and Haddock, in conjunction with a nobleman, should have the command of the fleet. Sir Thomas Lee grew pale as death, and told me that the custom was for they, the commissioners of the Admiralty, to recommend, and to answer for the persons, since they were to give them the commissions, and might be called to account in Parliament. I shall not repeat all that was said. Lord President argued with them. At last Sir Thomas Lee said plainly, 'Haddock they did not like.' He added, 'I might give a commission, but they could not.' When I saw he insisted on their privilege, I said, 'I perceive then, that the King hath given away his own power, and could not make an admiral which the Admiralty did not like.' Sir Thomas Lee replied: 'No, no more he can't.' I was ready to say, 'Then the King should give the commission to such as would not dispute with him;' but I did not, though I was heartily angry with him. Lord President, after more discourse, desired them to retire. They next resolutely refused to sign the commission. I asked Lord President 'what answer was to be sent?' he was very angry, and talked at a great rate; but I stopped him, and told him, 'I was angry enough, and desired him not to be too much so, for I did not believe it a proper time.' He said, 'The best answer that he could give from me was, that they, (the commissioners of the Admiralty,) would do well to consider it.' I desired he would add: 'That I could not change my mind,' if it was proper to say so much. He said, 'it was rather too little.' I saw Mr. Russell this morning, and found him much out of humour; he excused the conduct of Sir Thomas Lee, and, endeavouring to talk it over, said: 'That Haddock was not acceptable to them, because they believed Lord Nottingham had recommended him, and they did not like that.' I saw he shifted off signing the commission; and as there was company by, I had no opportunity of saying more to him, only he pressed naming Shrewsbury for the third admiral of the fleet, as the best means to allay these disagreements. This afternoon Lord Marlborough came to me about the same thing, and I told him why I should be unwilling to name Shrewsbury myself, for I thought it would not be proper for me by any means to name a person who had quitted office just upon your going away, though I was persuaded you would trust him; yet, for me to take upon myself so to name him, without being assured of your approbation, I thought not proper. I pray God send you here quickly, for I see all breaking out into flames. Devonshire was with me this afternoon from Sir Thomas Lee, to excuse himself to me. He said, the reason was, because he saw Haddock's appointment was a business between two or three, a concerted thing, and that made him he could not consent. I told Devonshire, he himself could have assured Sir

Thomas Lee, it was your own orders in your letter to me. At which he shaked his head. I asked 'if he, or Sir Thomas Lee, did not believe me?' He said, 'Sir Thomas Lee thought that Haddock was imposed on the King.' 'I said I did not believe that was so easy.' 'I mean,' said Devonshire, 'recommended by persons they don't much like.' 'Indeed, my lord, if they only dislike Haddock because he is recommended by such as they don't approve, it will only confirm me in the belief that he is a fit man, since they can make no other objection against him.' 'I confess,' said I, 'my lord, I was very angry at what Sir Thomas Lee said yesterday, but this is to make me more so; since I see it is not reason, but passion makes Sir Thomas Lee speak thus.' Upon which, I and Devonshire fell into discourse of the feuds in Council, which we both lamented; and I think we were both angry, though with one another. He complained that people were too much believed that ought not to be so, and we could not agree. If I have been too angry, I am sorry for it. I fancy I am not easily provoked, but I think I had reason, if I may say so. I think people should not be humoured to this degree."

"One thing more," proceeds the Queen, "I much desire to know positively, which is about Kensington; whether you will go there, though my chamber is not ready. Your own apartment, Lord Portland's, Mr. Overkirk's, and Lady Darby's, are done, but mine impossible to be used, and nobody else's lodgings ready. The air there is now free from smoke, but your closet as yet smells of paint, for which I will ask pardon when I see you. This is the true state of your house at Kensington; but if you will sleep only there, for I suppose business will keep you at Whitehall during the day, pray let me know. You may be sure I shall be willing to suffer any inconvenience for the sake of your dear company. I hope this long letter will meet you so near, that you may bring your answer; if not, if you love me, either write me a particular answer yourself, or let Lord Portland do it for you. You see the necessity of it, for the public; do a little, also, for my private satisfaction, who loves you much more than my own life."

In an epistle dated August nine, Mary, resuming her narrative of incidents, writes her husband: "You will not wonder that I did not write last night, when you know that at noon I received yours by Mr. Butler, whose face I shall love to see ever hereafter, since he has come twice with such good news. I have now another — a very strong reason to be glad of your coming, and that is the divisions which, to my thinking, increase here daily. The business of the commission is again put off by Mr. Russell, who persists in excusing Sir T. Lee; how the matter will end, God knows. I went last night to Kensington, and will go again by and by. They promise me all shall be ready by Tuesday next, that is the night of Mr. Butler's reckoning, that with a fair wind you may be here; though I think by your dear letter it is possible you may come a day sooner. At most, if you lie at Whitehall two nights, the third you may, if it please God, be at Kensington. I will do my endeavour, that it may be sooner, but one night, I reckon, you will be content to lie at Whitehall. I wrote to you in my last, how I thought you might shift at Kensington without my chamber, but I have thought since to set up a bed—which is already ordered—in the Council Chamber, and that I can dress me in Lord Portland's, and use his closet. M. Neinburg is gone to get ready other rooms for him; thus I think we may shift for a fortnight, in which time I hope my own chamber will be ready, they promise it sooner. This letter, I hope will meet you at Chester, and I have one thing to beg, which is that, if it be possible, I may come and meet you on the road, for I do so long to see you, that I am sure had you as much mind to see your poor wife again, you would propose it; but do as you please, I will say no more, but that I love you so much, it cannot increase, else I am sure it would."

Mary evidently penned the above letter in the hope of beholding her absent husband before the lapse of another week. This hope was, however, disappointed. In Ireland, success had turned in favour of the Catholic party. The Jacobite Colonel Sarsfield obstinately and successfully defended Limerick. William was forced to raise the siege; and when, at length, he resolved to return to England, the victorious fleets of France rode triumphantly in the English and in St. George's Channels, and compelled him to defer it from week to week, greatly to the disappointment of her Majesty, who, in her next epistle, dated August the second, remarks, "Unless I could express the joy I had at the thoughts of your coming, it will be vain to undertake telling you of the disappointment it is to me, your not coming so soon. I am grieved to think that your dear person may be exposed at the passage of the Shannon, as it was at that of the Boyne: this is what goes to my heart; but yet I see the reasons for it so good, that I will not murmur, for certainly your glory would be the greater to terminate the war this summer, and the people here will be much better pleased than if they must furnish next year for the same thing again. Since it has pleased God so wonderfully to preserve you all your life, and so miraculously, now I need not doubt but he will still preserve you; yet, let me beg of you not to expose yourself unnecessarily; that will be too much tempting that Providence which I hope will still watch over you. Mr. Russell is gone down to the fleet last Thursday, to hasten as much as may be all things there, and will be back on Monday, when there is a great council appointed. I doubt not but this commission will find many obstacles; and this naming Killigrew, among such as do not like him, will be called in question, as well as the naming of Ashby and Haddock, and I shall hear again that it is a thing agreed on amongst two or three."

King William took the same view that Mary had done of the insolent conduct of Sir Thomas Lee. His Majesty justified her displeasure, and she in reply wrote him on the fifth of August:—"Last night I received yours of the third of July, and with great satisfaction. Your approving of my anger is a great ease to me, and I hope may make things go on the better, if it be possible, though there are great pains taken to hinder the persons named from serving at all, or from agreeing, but I hope to little purpose. Lord Nottingham will give you an account of all things, and of some letters which, by great luck, are fallen into our hands. I have been to Kensington: it is ready; had you come to-night, as I flattered myself you would have done, you could have lain there, that is to say in the Council Chamber, and there I fear you must lie when you do come, which God grant may be soon. I must needs tell you upon the subject, that when it first became known you intended to come back, it was said: 'What! leave Ireland unconquered—the work unfinished?' Now, upon your not coming, it is wondered whose counsel this is, and why you leave us to ourselves in danger. Thus people are never satisfied; but I must not begin upon the subject, which would fill volumes, and as much as I was prepared, surprises me beyond expression. I am very impatient to hear again if you are over the Shannon; that passage frightens me. I pray God in his mercy keep you, and send us a happy meeting here on earth, before we meet in heaven."

In her letter of August the ninth, Mary remarks:—"This passage of the Shannon runs much on my mind, and gives me no quiet night nor day. I have a million of fears, which are caused by that which you cannot be angry at; and if I were less sensible I should hate myself, though I wish I were not so *fear full*, and yet one can hardly go without the other, but it is not reasonable I should torment you with any of this. The Earl of Devonshire desires me to let you know he has had a letter from Madame de Grammont, about her brother, Mr. Hamilton; they earnestly desire he may be exchanged for Lord Mountjoy.* I told

* Miss Hamilton was the wife of that Count de Grammont, whose scandalous memoirs of the Court of Charles II. add more notoriety than lustre to his name. Mr. Hamilton was her brother; he fought for King James, and had been made prisoner by William at the battle of the Boyne. Lord Mountjoy was considered the head of the

Devonshire that I knew nothing of Hamilton's faults, which I perceive he apprehends the Parliament will take into consideration, if Hamilton be not out of their power, but that upon his (Devonshire's) earnest desire, I would let you know it. I would have had Devonshire write it you himself, but he begs me to do it. As for Lord Mountjoy, I hope you will consider if anything can be done for him. I can never forget that I promised his son's wife to speak to you, and she really died of grief, which makes me pity her case; his family is in a miserable way, and I am daily solicited from his eldest daughter about him. If you would let Lord Portland give me some answer to this I should be glad, for I cannot wonder at people desiring an answer, though I am tormented myself."*

In her next letter, Mary remarked:—"Lord Steward [Devonshire] was with me this afternoon, and I had a long conversation with him, which it will be worth your while knowing when you come, but he has made me promise to write you word some part of it, which is, that he begs you to consider if you will not have a new Parliament, for this he is sure will do no good; this, he says, is his opinion. I see it is a thing they are mightily set upon. Lord President, methinks, has very good arguments to try the present Parliament first, but of all this you will judge best when you come. I have had this evening Lord Annandale, who is to tell all, and then I am to procure a pardon from you; but I think I shall not be so easily deceived by him, as I fear Lord Melville has been by Sir James Montgomery; but these are things to talk of when you come back, which I pray God may be very soon."

The Lords Annnadale, Breadalbane, Ross, and others, had originally espoused the Orange cause, but being dissatisfied with the reward they received for their services, they joined the plot against the government of William and Mary; this plot had been disorganised in the previous year by the death of Dundee, and now, to save their heads, these unprincipled nobles turned informers against their associates, with the understanding that they were to confess everything, receive a free pardon, and not be confronted with their victims.

In an epistle addressed to her husband, on the thirteenth of August, Mary proceeds: — "The commissioners of the Admiralty have resolved to come to me to-morrow with some names for flags. Mr. Russell recommends Churchill and Ellmore, because he says nothing has been done for them, though they were both trusted when you came over, and have been ever very true to your interest. But I think, if it be possible, to let them alone till you come, though Mr. Russell seems to think it cannot be delayed. I shall hear (if it must be so) what the other commissioners think, and do as well as I can."

Three days afterwards, her Majesty, resuming her narrative of incidents, says:—"I think I writ you [King William] word, or should have done, that he (Lord Annandale) sent by his wife to Sir William, that he would surrender himself, if he might be sure not to be made an evidence of; upon which Sir William drew up conditions that he should tell all, and then should be made no evidence, and has my word to get your pardon. I think I writ you this before, but to be short, he is come in, and I have spoke twice with him. Lord Annandale told me, that after the time the papers were burnt (wherewith this ends) Sir James Montgomery proposed sending a second message by the same Simson, but he (Annandale) rejected it as much as he durst, but was afraid to say plainly he would not. So, having a mind to get out of this, he (Annandale) pretended business at his own house in the country; but his coolness made Sir James Montgomery the warmer in it, and he assured him that he would spend his life and fortune in *that interest*" [the interest of Mary's father, James II.].

Protestant party in Ireland; and whilst in France, endeavouring to dissuade James II. from opposing William and Mary in Ireland, Louis XIV. caused him to be seized and shut up in the Bastile.

* This petition, backed by the entreaty of Devonshire and the fair Grammont, had the desired effect, and shortly afterwards Mr. Hamilton was exchanged for Lord Mountjoy.

In continuation of her narrative, Mary says: "Lord Breadalbine came to see Annandale on his way to Chester, where he went to meet you. He told him that Sir J. Montgomery had sent another message to St. Germain's [James II.], but he, Breadalbine. was not engaged in it, and he believed nobody was but Lord Arran, though he could not be positive if Lord Ross were not likewise in. This he told me last night, and desires to be asked more questions, that he may, if possible, remember more. Thus he seems sincere, but, in truth, one scarcely knows in what to believe; but this much is certain, that Lord Ross has not kept his word with me, much less has Sir J. Montgomery with Lord Melville: for he has been in town a week, and I have heard nothing of him, which is a plain breach of the conditions. D'Alonne [Mary's French secretary] is to send Lord Portland, by this post, a copy of a letter from Mr. Priestman, in which you will see what need you have of that Divine protection which has hitherto so watched over you, and which only can make me easy for your dear sake. The same God who has hitherto so preserved you, will, I hope, continue, and grant us a happy meeting here and a blessed one hereafter."

On the nineteenth of August, the Queen again writes:—"Last night I received yours, after I was in bed. I was extremely glad to find by it you had passed the Shannon, but cannot be without fears, since the foe has still an army together, which, though it has once more run away from you, may yet grow desperate for aught I know, and fight at last. These are the things I cannot help fearing, and as long as I have these fears, you may believe I cannot be easy; yet I must look over them, if possible, or presently everybody will think all lost. This is no small part of my penance; but all must be endured as long as please God, and I have still abundant cause to praise him who has given you this new advantage."

How completely Dutch Mary had become since her marriage, is corroborated by the subjoined. "When I writ last," she continues, "I was so full of my Scotch business that I forgot Mr. Harbord; so I must now tell you that Harbord wrote to Sir R. Southwell; but he has a great deal to say; he pleased me extremely to hear how much people love me there. When I think of that, and see what folk do here, it grieves me too much, for Holland has really spoiled me in being so kind to me—that they are so to you, it is no wonder. I wish to God it was the same here: but I ask your pardon for this; if I once begin upon this subject, I can never have done."

Mary next reverts to the solicitations of Marlborough, that his brother, Captain Churchill, who had been expelled from parliament on account of his wholesale peculations, should be pushed over the head of a brave old naval officer, into the important post of Admiral. She herself leant to the appointment, and proceeds: — "Marlborough says, that Lord President may write to you about one Carter. Probably he will, for he tells me he [Carter] is a much older officer, and will quit if others come over his head, and says, all goes by partiality and faction, as, indeed, I think it is but too plain in other things; how it is in this, you will be best able to judge. I could not refuse my Lord Marlborough, nor, indeed, myself the writing you the matter as it is, though he expects I should write in his favour, which, though I would not promise, yet I did make him a sort of compliment *after my fashion*."

The Queen commences her epistle of the twenty-second of August with an allusion to Colonal Sarsfield's successful attack on William's cannon and ammunition before Limerick. A few days previously, a messenger had arrived with the ill tidings, and she now wrote—"I received yours to-day, and am sorry to see the messenger's news confirmed; but it has pleased God to bless you with such a continued success all this while, that it may be necessary to have *some little cross*. I hope in God this will not prove a great one to the main business [the siege of Limerick], though it is a terrible thought to me that your coming is put off again. However, I will say nothing of what my poor heart suffers, but must tell you that I am now in great pain about the naming of the flags. Mr. Russell came to me last night, and said it would now be absolutely necessary. I insisted upon staying till I heard from you. He desired to know if I had any particular reason. I told him, plainly, that since I could not pretend to know myself who were the fittest, it troubled me to see all were not of a mind; that I was told by several persons that there were ancient officers in the fleet [Carter and Davis] who had behaved themselves very well, who would quit if these were preferred; so I desired in this difficulty to stay for your answer. To this, Russell answered with more passion than I ever saw him, 'That Carter and Davis, which he knew Lord President and Lord Nottingham had spoken for, were two pitiful fellows and very mean seamen, and that next summer he would not command the fleet if they had flags.' After a long dispute I have put him off till the last moment comes, when they are to sail. He says, he must mention it to the commissioners, and hear who will speak against it, by which I may judge. I see Marlborough is much set on this matter, as well as Russell. On the other side, Lord President says—'If Churchill have a flag, he will be called the flag by favour, as Marlborough is called the general of favour.' Lord President also says, 'If Churchill have a flag, Carter will quit;' he commends him highly; but I must also tell you, that he (Lord President) is mightily dissatisfied with the business of Kinsale."

Kinsale and Cork still held out for James II., and William accepted Marlborough's offer to reduce, with a re-inforcement of five thousand men, those two places before winter; and the Dutch King himself prepared to sail to England, the moment the victorious French fleet left the passage sufficiently free.

"He does not," proceeds her Majesty, "oppose it, for he says it is your order and must be obeyed; but among other things, he endeavours to frighten me by the danger there is of being so exposed, when the fleet and five thousand men are gone, which he reckons all the force, and tells me how easily it will be then for the French to come with only transport ships, and do what they will. You will have an account from Lord Nottingham of what has been done this day and yesterday. I know you will pity me, and I hope will believe, that had your letter been less kind, I don't know what had become of me. I hear you daily expose yourself to great dangers, which puts me in continual pain. A battle, I fancy, is soon over, but the perpetual shooting you are now in, is an intolerable thing to me. For God's sake, take care of yourself; you owe it to your own country, to this country, and to all in general. I must not name myself, where Church and State are equally concerned, yet I must need say you owe a little care for my sake, who, I am sure, love you more than you can do me; and the little care you take of your dear person I take to be a sign of it; but I must still love you more than life."

On the 26th of August, she wrote to her husband—"I have just written to your aunt, the Princess of Nassau, in answer to one which she wrote to let me know of her daughter being about to marry the Prince of Saxenschnach. I believe you will be glad, for your cousin's sake, that she will be disposed of before her mother dies; and I even heard at the Hague, that this young man was good-natured, which will make him use her well, though she is so much older than he is. I cannot help laughing at this wedding, though my poor heart is ready to break every time I think in what perpetual danger you are. I am in great fear, count the hours and the moments, and have only reason enough to think, so long as I have no letter, all is well. I believe by what you write, you got your cannon on Friday, and then Saturday I suppose you began to use them. Judge then, what cruel thoughts they are to me, to think what you may be exposed to all this while. I never do anything without thinking now, it may be, you are in the greatest danger: and yet I must see company upon my set days: I must play twice a-week, nay, must laugh and talk, though never so much against my will. I believe I dissemble very ill to those who know me, at least it is a great constraint to myself, yet I must endure it. All my motions are so watched, and all I do is so observed, that if I eat less, or speak less, or look more grave, all is lost in the opinion of the world. So that I have this misery added to that of your absence, and my fears for your dear person, that I must *grin when my heart is ready to break*, and talk when it is so oppressed I can scarce breathe. I don't know what I should do, were it not for the grace of God, which supports me. I am sure I have great reason to praise the Lord while I live, for his great mercy that I don't sink under this affliction; nay, that I keep my health; for I can neither eat nor sleep. I go to Kensington as often as I can for air, but then I never can be quite alone, neither can I complain—*that* would be some ease; but I have nobody whose humour and circumstances agree with mine enough to speak my mind freely to. Besides, I must hear of business, which being a thing I am so new in, and so unfit for, does but break my brains the more, and not ease my heart. It is some ease to me to write my pain, some satisfaction to believe you will pity me; it will be yet more when I hear it from yourself in a letter, as I am sure you must, if it be but out of common good-nature, how much more then out of kindness; if you love me as you make me believe, and as I endeavour to deserve a little by that sincere and lasting kindness I have for you.

"But by making excuses, I do but take up your time, and therefore must tell you, that this morning Lord Marlborough* went away; as little reason as I have to care for his wife, yet I must pity her condition, having lain in but eight days; and I have great compassion for wives when their husbands do go to fight." This expression of sympathy for one whose pen forgot not to slander her, does honour to Mary, who proceeds—"I hope the business will succeed; though I find if it do not, those who advised it will have an ill time, all, except Lord Nottingham, being very much against it; Lord President only complying because it is your order, but not liking it, and wondering England should be left so exposed, thinking it too great a hazard. There would be no end, should I tell you all I hear upon this subject; but I thank God I am not afraid, nor do I doubt of the thing, since it is by your order.

"I have always forgot to tell you, that in the Utrecht Courant they have printed a letter of yours to the States of Holland, in which you promise soon to be with them. I cannot tell you how many ill hours I have had about that, in the midst of my joy, when I thought you were coming home, for it troubled me to think you would go over and fight again there. Now my letter is already so long, but it is as if I were bewitched to-night; I cannot end for my life, but will force myself now, beseeching God to bless you, and keep you from all dangers whatsoever; and send us a happy meeting again here upon earth, and at last a joyful and blessed one in heaven, in his good time. Farewell, do but continue to love me, and forgive this

* Marlborough landed near Cork, on the twenty-first of September, and united with the German and Danish troops, whom King William had left under the command of the Duke of Wirtemberg. At this moment he experienced those vexatious squabbles which often arise when high birth and military talents are brought into competition. But by the interposition of Brigadier La Mellonerie, a French refugee, a compromise was effected, and the two generals agreed to exercise the command alternately. The first day Marlborough gave *Wirtemberg* as the word, and the compliment was returned by his colleague. The vigour and enterprising spirit of the British general excited equal surprise and satisfaction during his short stay in Ireland, which did not exceed thirty-seven days. He reduced Cork and Kinsale, straitened the communications of the insurgents with France, and confined them to the province of Ulster, where they could not subsist without the utmost difficulty.

After this short, but brilliant expedition, Marlborough returned with his prisoners to England, in the latter end of October. He was welcomed with the most flattering reception by the King, who said of him—"I know of no man who has served so few campaigns, equally fit for command." The English nation also, long accustomed to see the execution of the most important enterprises confided to foreigners, exulted to find that a native officer had gained more advantages in a single month, than many of the foreign generals in several campaigns. — *Coxe's Life of Marlborough.*

taking up so much of your time by your poor wife, who deserves more pity than ever any creature did, and who loves you a great deal too much for her own ease, though it can't be more than you deserve."

On the fifth of September, 1690, William embarked at Duncannon fort, with his brother-in-law, Prince George of Denmark, and other persons of distinction. The voyage was so prosperous, that the next day he arrived in King's Road, near Bristol. Two days afterwards, the Queen received intelligence of his landing, and immediately dispatched to him the subjoined epistle:—

"Whitehall, September 8th, 1690.

"Lord Winchester wishes to go and meet you; whether I ought to send him out of form sake, I cannot tell; but it may pass for what it ought to the world, and to your dear self at least, I suppose it is indifferent. Nothing can express the impatience I have to see you, nor my joy to think it is so near. I have not slept all this night for it, though I had but five hours' sleep the night before, for a reason I shall tell you. I am now going to Kensington, to put things in order there, and intend to dine there to-morrow, and expect to hear when I shall set out to meet you. I had a compliment last night from the Queen Dowager [Katherine of Braganza], who came to town on Friday. She sent it, I believe, with a better heart because Limerick is not taken; for my part, I don't think of that, nor anything else but you. God send you a good journey home, and make me thankful, as I ought, for all his mercies."

Thus concludes this remarkable correspondence, a correspondence which proves the Queen, with all her faults, to have possessed greater literary and regnal abilities than is generally supposed.

On the ninth of September, Mary, with infinite joy, met her husband at Windsor, whence they proceeded to Hampton Court, and two days afterwards to Kensington Palace, which they made their principal residence till the sixth of the subsequent January, when William embarked for the Hague, and again left Mary to govern, by the assistance of the same council of regency—called by the disaffected, the nine Kings—that had supported her sceptre during William's absence in Ireland. The King did not permit his consort to assist at the solemn opening of parliament, in the autumn of 1690; and the Jacobites celebrated his departure to the Hague, by singing—

"His father he beat at the Boyne;
Let all who can, sing for joy.
He mawled Irish Turk,
With Ginkell and Kirk.
Rare old Willie, cheating Willie,
Willie, the Orange boy!

But now he to Holland is gone,
Let all who can, sing for joy;
He's not left us alone,
For his Queen guards the throne.
Oh, this rare old Willie, cheating Willie,
Willie, the Orange boy!"*

The King embarked for Holland in troublous times; the very day of his departure, Lord Preston and Mr. Ashton were tried for conspiring the restoration of James II. Ashton was condemned and executed, but Preston was pardoned; not, however, at the entreaty of his little daughter, who, it has been asserted, melted the heart of Mary, by observing, whilst gazing on the portrait of James II., in the St. George's Gallery, "Oh, how hard it is, your Majesty, that my father must die for loving your father;" but that others implicated in the plot might be betrayed by his evidence. Several too, were betrayed and cruelly tortured. As an instance of the cruelty resorted to by the executive at this period, we mention the following:—In the summer of 1690, one Nevill Payne, a plebeian Jacobite, had been arrested in Scotland, by the Queen's orders. Now the Queen and her council judged him to be one of the conspirators, and as bribes and entreaties failed, they resolved to force him to turn informer, against his associates. The barbarous means resorted to for this purpose, are thus detailed in an epistle, sent by the Earl of Crafurd, from Edinburgh, to Lord Melville, at the court in London. "Yes-

* Almost the same sentiments as are embodied in this lyric, occur in another Jacobite song of the same period, commencing, "He at the Boyne his father beat."

terday, Nevill Payne was questioned upon some matters of no great moment, and had but *gentle torture* given him. This evening, about six o'clock, we repeated it. We inflicted on both his thumbs and one of his legs, *with all the severity that was consistent with humanity, even to that pitch that we could not have preserved life and gone further;* but without the least success, for his answers to all his interrogations were negatives. Yea, he was so manly and resolute under his sufferings, that such of the council who were not acquainted with all the evidence, were confounded with amazement, and began to give him charity that he might be innocent. It was surprising to me and others that flesh and blood could, without fainting, endure the heavy penance he was in for two hours. Being witness to an act so cross to my natural temper, put my stomach out of tune; but the dangers from such conspirators to the person of our incomparable King, have prevailed over me, in the council's name, to have been the prompter of the executioner to increase the torture to so high a pitch."*

* According to Burnet, he was afterwards brought up to be examined before Parliament; but, in consequence of a threat he sent to some of the lords, especially the Duke of Hamilton, that "he could discover enough to deserve his pardon," which "struck terror into many of them," the enquiry was stifled.

CHAPTER VI.

Mary's proceedings with the Church—Preston conspiracy—King returns from the Hague—Fire at Whitehall—Mary insulted—William embarks for Flanders—Fire at Kensington—Mary beset with difficulties—William returns—Final rupture between Mary and Anne—Disgrace of the Marlboroughs—Glencoe massacre—William again proceeds to Holland—The reins of government consigned to Mary—Her administration beset with difficulties—Naval victory of La Hogue—Admiral Russel refuses a title—William and Archbishop Tillotson never baptized.

FOR more than a year Mary hesitated to take any decisive measures against the nonjuring clergy, in the hope that expediency would ultimately induce them to compromise their principles by taking the oath of allegiance. But, finding her expectation vain, she, on the first of February, formally deprived Sancroft, Archbishop of Canterbury, Ken, Bishop of Bath and Wells, and five other prelates, and four hundred—some estimated seven hundred—divines. Ken, after vainly protesting and then publicly declaring against the legality of the Queen's proceedings, retired from his bishopric, to the home of his hospitable nephew, Isaac Walton, in Salisbury close; but Sancroft declared he had done nothing to merit such treatment, and if her majesty wished for his palace at Lambeth, she must force him out. Accordingly, at the close of May, the Queen sent him notice to quit Lambeth before the expiration of ten days. He disobeyed this mandate, was thrust out of his palace on the twenty-third of June, and afterwards retired to a small estate he possessed in Suffolk—it brought him but fifty pounds a-year—and there he ended his days. The ignorant, warrior-spirited Dr. Compton, Bishop of London, sued the King and Queen to appoint him to the vacant archbishopric; but Dr. Tillotson, who by pecuniary assistance had completed the success of William's previously mentioned experiment in popularity at Canterbury, was marked by His Majesty for high episcopal promotion, and on the thirty-first of May, 1691, Mary nominated him to the primacy. To fill the Deanery of Canterbury, vacated by the elevation of Dr. Tillotson, William, usurping the function of the Chapters in convocation, sent his consort from Holland three names, from which to appoint the one most agreeable to herself. On the list was her faithful old almoner Dr. Hooper, and on him she immediately conferred the appointment. The Orange King, on hearing how Mary had acted, was extremely enraged. His hatred to Dr. Hooper was, he knew, patent to his consort, and he evidently had only placed the name of that divine on the list, to mortify him by her rejection.

Meanwhile the Preston conspiracy, or plots more or less connected with it, occupied the attention of the Queen and her council. She issued a proclamation for the discovery and apprehension of Dr. Turner, the late Bishop of Ely; William Penn, the renowned Quaker; Mr. James Graham, and Lord Dartmouth, as persons implicated in these Jacobite designs. Turner, Penn, and Graham absconded, but Dartmouth was committed to the Tower, on the third of April, 1691, where soon afterwards he died. At this period Lord Clarendon, who the reader will remember had been "clapt up in the Tower" by the Queen, his niece, during William's absence in Ireland, endeavoured to obtain some relaxation of his hard confinement. His more complying brother, Laurence Hyde, and his relative, Lady Katherine Ranelagh, became suitors in his behalf, and about July, 1691, he was liberated from the Tower, but bound to confine himself to his house in the country.

The King returned to England on the third of April, to obtain a further supply of money and troops; and four days before his arrival, the principal part of Whitehall was consumed by fire. The conflagration, occasioned through the negligence of a female servant, burst forth at eight at night, in the Duchess of Portsmouth's apartments, and burned furiously till four the next morning, consuming all the stone gallery and buildings behind it as far as the Thames. The flames reached the Queen's chamber, after her Majesty, unconscious of the danger, had retired to rest; and half asleep and in her night dress, she was dragged forth into St James's park, where the Jacobites Colonel Oglethorpe and Sir John Fenwick encountered her, and with jeers and taunts told her that she was a base, heartless daughter, and that her present distress was but a foretaste of the punishment so justly due to her filial sins.

Early in May, William having obtained a large supply of money and troops, embarked for Holland, to prosecute the war with all possible vigour. On the thirteenth of October, he returned again to England, and had scarcely taken up his residence with Mary, at Kensington Palace, when an alarming fire burst forth there (November the tenth, 1691), which fortunately was extinguished before reaching the royal apartments. William, on his return, severely reproached Mary for appointing Dr. Hooper to the deanery of Canterbury; nor did he afford her a word of condolence for the troubles, anxieties, and difficulties, she had endured in his absence, although she had braved them all with the fortitude, tact, and experience, of a successful ruler. Her correspondence with William this summer we cannot obtain, but certain it is, that corn was at famine prices. The country was weighed down by taxation; from causes which it belongs to history to explain, victory had neither favoured the British army or navy. The Jacobites were busy plotting the restoration of the deposed Stuart sovereign. Marlborough, disgusted that his military achievements in Ireland had not been rewarded with the Order of the Garter, and from other motives, opened a secret correspondence with his late master, James II., to whom "he testified in the most unqualified terms, his contrition for his past conduct, and anxiety to make amends for his defection," offering, at the same time, to bring the Princess Anne back to her filial duty; whilst Mary herself was on terms of ill will with her sister Anne, and without a single friend or object of affection, saving her husband, whose absence and exposure to the toils and dangers of war she hourly mourned. In a letter to Lady Russell, dated July, 1691, she remarks—"You are indeed right in supposing that the life I at present lead is not so fine a thing as many suppose. The continual pain I am in for the King, destroys my happiness; but I perceive one is not ever to live for one's self. I have had many years of ease and content, and was scarcely sensible of my own happiness; but I must be content with what pleases God, and this year I have good reasons to praise him for the successes in Ireland, which have followed so quick one upon another, that I fear some ill from other places. But I pray God, my fears will not be realized, though, by appearances, we must expect but little good either from Flanders or sea." Her Majesty judged aright. In Flanders, thousands of brave soldiers were sacrificed without a single victory of importance being obtained, and only disaster and disgrace attended the navy.

On the twenty-second of October, 1691, the King opened parliament in person; and although Mary had for nearly two years swayed the troublous regnal sceptre in his absence, without once meeting the assembled legislature of the kingdom, he again prevented her from accompanying him on his solemn mission; and in his speeches from the throne, in which he alludes to the successes in Ireland, he never once mentioned her name: an omission, which, whether intentional or accidental, the parliament immediately repaired by presenting addresses to the Queen, acknowledging "her prudent care in the administration of the government during the King's absence." The address of the Lords ran as follows:—

"We, your Majesty's most dutiful and loyal subjects, the Lords spiritual and temporal, in parliament assembled, from a true sense of the quiet and happiness the nation hath enjoyed in your Majesty's administration of government in the King's absence, do hold ourselves obliged to present our most humble acknowledgments to your Majesty, for prudent conduct therein, to the universal satisfaction, as well as the security of the kingdom."

A few weeks after receiving the above congratulatory address, Mary was annoyed by the unavoidable widening of the breach between herself and her sister Anne. On the first of December, 1691, the Princess Anne, influenced by the Duke and by her favourite, the Duchess of Marlborough, addressed a submissive, penitential letter to her father, James II. Long before the letter reached St. Germains, their Majesties were apprised that it was on its way thither. They also knew that Marlborough had taken a similar step; and whether for this or any other more venial sin, the accomplished general, after fulfilling his usual duties as lord of the bed-chamber, on the tenth of January, 1692, received an order from the King, through Lord Nottingham, secretary of state, announcing his dismission from all his offices both civil and military, and prohibiting his appearance at court.* Anne expressed deep sorrow and mortification at the disgrace of her favourite's husband. She and the Duchess of Marlborough vituperated the King and Queen with unmeasured abuse; by the agency of Lady Fitzharding, who was the spy of Elizabeth Villiers in Anne's household, the King was made acquainted with their proceedings a few hours afterwards. Violent altercations ensued between her Majesty and the Princess her sister. Mary threatened to deprive Anne of half her income. Anne knew the threat to be vain, the parliament having secured it to her; and what further irritated the Queen, the princess, on receiving her last payment, settled an annuity of £1000 on the Marlboroughs, and on the subsequent reception day at Kensington, took Lady Marlborough with her to court: a procedure which drew the subjoined epistle from Queen Mary to her sister Anne of Denmark:—

"Kensington, Friday, 5th of February.

"Having something to say to you which I know will not be very pleasing, I choose rather to write it first, being unwilling to surprise you, though I think what I am going to tell you should not, if you give yourself time to think; that never anybody was suffered to live at court in my Lord Marlborough's circumstances. I need not repeat the cause he has given the King to do what he has done, nor his [the King's] unwillingness at all times to come to such extremities, though people do deserve it.

* Evelyn says Lord Marlborough was dismissed from all his employments, military and others, for his faults in excessive taking of bribes, covetousness, and extortion, on all occasions, from his inferior officers.

"I hope you do me the justice to believe it is as much against my will that I now tell you, that, after this, it is very unfit Lady Marlborough should stay with you, since that gives her husband so just a pretence of being where he ought not.

"I think I might have expected you should have spoken to me of it, and the King and I, both believing it, made us stay so long; but seeing you was so far from it, that you brought Lady Marlborough hither last night, makes us resolve to put it off no longer, but tell you she must not stay, and that I have all the reason imaginable to look upon your bringing her as the strangest thing that ever was done. Nor could all my kindness for you (which is ever ready to turn all you do the best way at any other time), have hindered shewing you that moment; but I considered your condition [Anne was within a few weeks of her confinement], and that made me master myself so far as not to take notice of it then.

"But now I must tell you it was very unkind in a sister, would have been very uncivil in an equal, and I need not say I have more to claim, which though my kindness would make me exact, yet when I see the use you make of it, I must tell you, I know what is due to me, and expect to have it from you. 'Tis upon that account, I tell you plainly Lady Marlborough must not continue with you, in the circumstances her Lord is.

"I know this will be uneasy to you, and am sorry for it; and it is very much so to me to say all this to you, for I have all the real kindness imaginable for you as I ever had, so will always do my part to live with you as sister ought: that is not only like so near relations, but like friends, and as such, I did think to write to you. For I would have made myself believe your kindness for her [Lady Marlborough], made you at first forget what you should have for the King and me, and resolved to put you in mind of it myself, neither of us being willing to come to harsher ways.

"But the sight of Lady Marlborough having changed my thoughts, does naturally, and since by that I see how little you seem to consider, what even in common civility you owe us; I have told it you plainly, but withal assure you, that let me have never so much reason to take anything ill of you, my kindness is so great, that I can pass over most things, and live with you as becomes me: and I desire to do so, merely from that motive, for I do love you as a sister, and nothing can make me do otherwise, and that is the reason I choose to write this rather than tell it you, that you may overcome your first thoughts. And when you have well considered, you will find that though the thing be hard (which I again assure you I am sorry for), yet it is not unreasonable, but what has ever been practised, and what you yourself would do were you in my place.

"I will end this, with once more desiring you to consider the matter impartially, and take time for it. I do not desire an answer presently, because I would not have you give a rash one. I shall come to your drawing-room tomorrow before you play, because you know why I cannot make one. At some other time we shall reason the business calmly, which I will willingly do, or anything else that may shew it shall not be my fault if we do not live kindly together. Nor will I ever be other by choice, but your truly loving and affectionate sister, M. R."

The next day Anne wrote the Queen —"You must needs be sensible enough of the kindness I have for my Lady Marlborough, to know that a command from you to part with her, must be the greatest mortification in the world to me. * * * And I must as freely own, that as I think this proceeding can be for no other intent than to give me a very sensible mortification, so there is no misery that I cannot readily resolve to suffer, rather than the thoughts of parting with her."

Mary returned no answer to this letter, and an official order was transmitted by the Lord Chamberlain, enjoining the Duke and the Duchess of Marlborough to remove from the Palace of Whitehall.

This order was the prelude to an utter breach. Anne, disdaining to remain in a place from whence her favourite was excluded, quitted her own apartments—that portion of Whitehall then known as the Cock-pit—and after a temporary stay at Sion House, the seat of the proud Duke of Somerset, established her residence at Berkeley House. She took Lady Marlborough with her, and showered on her all conceivable marks of esteem and affection. Her husband, Prince George of Denmark, accompanied her, and William, annoyed at their conduct, took their guards from them, and deprived them of the honours they had been accustomed to receive at court; and the distance between the royal sisters became such, that the visiting the Princess was deemed a neglect of the Queen's displeasure.

Affairs in Scotland were not progressing very favourably. The Highlanders had taken up arms in favour of King James, and William had issued a proclamation, offering them an indemnification upon their coming on a stated day, and taking the oaths. The Macdonalds of Glencoe had been among the most clamorous and obstinate. Their chief, however, according to Burnet, "went to the governor of Fort William on the last day of December and offered to take the oaths; but he being only a military man, could not tender them to him: the snows were then fallen; so four or five days passed before he could come to a magistrate: he took the oaths in his presence, on the fourth or fifth of January, when, by the strictness of law, he could claim no benefit by it; the matter was signified to the council, and the person received a reprimand for giving him the oaths when the day was passed. This was kept up from the King." At the instigation of the Earl of Breadalbane, who strove to render the King odious to the Highlanders, the Secretary of State, Lord Stair, prevailed upon William to sign the subjoined order for the massacre of the whole clan, which was carried into effect in February, 1692; though not by the Queen's sanction, as some authors assert.

"William R.—As for the M'Donalds of Glencoe, if they can well be distinguished from the rest of the Highlanders, it will be proper, for the vindication of public justice, to *extirpate that set of thieves.* W. R."

A few hours before the massacre, Campbell, of Glenlyon, received the following order for the cold-blooded murder of the Glencoe clan:—

"For their Majesties' service.
"To Captain Campbell.

"Bailderesis, February 12, 1692.

"Sir,—You are hereby ordered to fall upon the rebels, the Macdonalds, of Glencoe, and put all to the sword under seventy. You are to have a special care that the old fox and his sons do, upon no account, escape your hands. You are to secure all the avenues, that no man escape. This you are to put in execution at five of the clock, precisely; and by that time, or very shortly after it, I'll strive to be at you with a stronger party. If I do not come to you at five, you are not to tarry for me, but to fall on. This is by the King's command, for the good and safety of the country, that these miscreants be cut off root and branch. See these be put to execution without fear or favour, else you may expect to be dealt with as one not true to King or government, nor a man fit to carry commission in the King's service. Expecting you will not fail in the fulfilling hereof, as you love yourself, I subscribe this with my hand,

"Robert Duncanson."

These barbarous orders were more than executed. The defenceless clan were unexpectedly attacked before the peep of day. Glencoe, the chief, was shot dead, as he rose from his bed; his wife was stripped and ravished by the soldiers, and expired next morning of horror and grief. In other parts of the vale, men, women, and children, were shot dead, or put to the sword; all who could, escaped to the hills, and were preserved from destruction by a tempest that added to the horrors of the night; and when Colonel Hamilton, with four hundred men, entered the glen at noon to complete the massacre, a childish old man of eighty was the only victim that remained. But rapine and desolation succeeded the carnage. The houses were burnt to the ground, the cattle were destroyed or driven off, and the women were violated, and, together with the children, stripped naked and left to seek the shelter of some far-off friendly habitation, or perish of cold and hunger.

"In 1695, a parliament was held in Scotland," says Burnet. "The massacre in Glencoe made still a great noise, and the King seemed too remiss in inquiring into it; but when it was represented to him, that a session of parliament could not be managed without high notions and complaints of so crying a matter, and that his ministers could not oppose these, without seeming to bring the guilt of that blood, that was so perfidiously shed, both on the King and on themselves: to prevent that, he ordered a commission to be passed under the great seal for a precognition in that matter. This was looked on as an artifice, to cover that transaction by a private inquiry; yet when it was complained of in parliament, not without reflections on the slackness in examining into it, the King's commissioner assured them, that by the King's order, the matter was then under examination, and that it should be reported to the parliament: the inquiry went on.

"The report of the massacre was made in full parliament: by that it appeared, that a black design was laid, not only to cut off the men of Glencoe, but a great many more clans, reckoned to be in all above six thousand persons: the whole was pursued in many letters that were writ with great earnestness, and though the King's orders carried nothing in them that was in any sort blamable; yet the Secretary of State's letters went much farther. So the parliament justified the King's instructions, but voted the execution in Glencoe to have been a barbarous massacre, and that it was pushed on by the Secretary of State's letters, beyond the King's orders: upon that, they voted an address to be made to the King, that he and others concerned in that matter might be proceeded against, according to law: this was carried by a great majority."

On the fifth of March, 1692, the King embarked for Flanders, to prosecute the war there, and again left the Queen to reign alone, in times troublous as formerly. The Princess Anne had written to her father, James II., that she would fly to him the moment he effected a landing in any part of Great Britain. The fleets of France swept the narrow seas in triumph. The leading naval and military commanders were either the known or suspected partizans of the ex-King; the majority of the courtiers were prepared to instantly turn with the tide, should it ebb in favour of James II.; and, in fact, the Jacobites, and the nation generally, fully anticipated the deposition of Mary and her husband, and the restoration of her ill-used father. These alarming dangers and difficulties, enough to appal an ordinary mind, were by the politic, energetic Queen, boldly encountered and successfully overcome. She reviewed in Hyde Park the ten thousand strong trained bands of London and Westminster, destined to defend the metropolis in case of a French invasion. She caused Marlborough to be arrested on the fifth of May; warrants also to be issued against the Earls of Huntingdon and Scarsdale, and Dr. Spratt, Bishop of Rochester, and likewise ordered several other persons into custody, particularly the Lords Middleton, Griffin, and Dunmore, Sir John Fenwick and Colonels Slingsby and Sackville, all of whom were known partizans of James II.

The Jacobite admiral, Russell, her Majesty despatched to sea. He was joined on the eleventh of May by the squadron under Delaval and Carter, and being reinforced by the Dutch fleet, sailed for the French coast on the eighteenth of May, and the next day gained the famous naval victory of La Hogue, over the French; a victory obtained by the valour of the British seamen almost against the will of their commanders.

Russell signified to Tourville, the admiral of the French fleet, 'that if he would slip out under the cover of a dark night, and with King James on board, he should pass unmolested; but if he defied him in open day, he should be compelled to give him battle in earnest.

James II. thought the proposition reasonable, but Tourville declared, as the navy of France had triumphed over that of England, ever since the accession of William III., it would doubtless do so now. He dared the English to fight, and the result was the almost utter destruction of the fleet under his command.

The victory of La Hogue completely annihilated the hopes of the Jacobites, and so delighted Mary, that immediately the English fleet reached Spithead, she ordered gold medals to be presented to the officers, and thirty thousand pounds to be distributed amongst the common sailors. She wished to invest Admiral Russell with a title, but the bluff naval commander refused the proffered honour.

On this subject her Majesty wrote:—"I have seen Mr. Russell this day, and find he is resolved to be Mr. Russell still. I could not press him further on a thing he seemed so little to care for, so there is an end of that matter. Whether the King will think I have done well in this I cannot tell, but it is not my nature to compliment, which always makes me take people at their word."

Shortly afterwards, the admiral's relative, Rachel, Lady Russell, applied to Mary for a place at Court for one of her friends. The Queen, not daring to gratify her wish without William's consent, referred her to the King; but as his Majesty generally sold the Court places, Lady Rachel had recourse to the intercession of Archbishop Tillotson, who answered:

"On Sunday morning, August 1, 1692, I gave yours to the Queen, telling her that I was afraid it came too late. She said, perhaps not. Yesterday, meeting the Queen at a christening, she gave me the enclosed to send to your ladyship, and if you will wink at my vanity, I will tell you how this happened. My lady, Marchioness of Winchester, being lately delivered of a son, spake to the Queen to stand godmother; and the Queen asking, who she thought of for godfather, she said, 'Only the Earl of Bath and whatever others her Majesty might please to name.' They agreed on me, which I doubt not was a gracious contrivance of her Majesty to let the world know that I have her countenance and support. I pray God preserve my good master, William the Third, and grant him children, that I, who am said not to be baptized myself, may have the honour to baptize a Prince of Wales."

The report that neither the King nor Tillotson had ever been baptized, gave rise to the following bitter but truthful epigram:—

"Here lies the widowed Anglican church,
Half buried, half dead, and left in the lurch.
Oh! sick and sorrowful English church,
You weep and wail and sadly search
To hide from the mocking enemy
The utter shame of your misery.
Let not Rome know
The depths of your woe,
By fanatics bit from the land of fogs,
Defiled and choaked by a plague of frogs.
Oh! sorrowing, wretched Anglican church,
Speak not of your head or archbishop,
For that schismatic primate and Hollander King
Are still in want of christening."

CHAPTER VII.

Blood-money—Distillation of spirits—Mutiny act—Return of William to England—Corruption and immorality overspread the kingdom—The King embarks for Ireland—Mary again left to reign solus—William's passion for war—Military and naval disasters—Change of Ministry—Mary scandalized—William resumes the campaign in Flanders—Mary founds Greenwich Hospital—Plots to seize her and restore James II.—The King returns—Opens Parliament—Carmarthen and others impeached for corruption—Death of Sancroft, and of Tillotson—Mary taken ill—She destroys her papers—Her malady proves to be the small-pox—Anne's efforts to become reconciled to her—Her life despaired of—Erysipelas covers her face—She receives the sacrament—Wanders in mind—Dies—Embalmed—Buried

—Wax effigy—Reproving letter she left for the King—James II. informed of her death—His conduct and remarks on it—Sermons, elegies, and epigrams on her departure.

N the thirteenth of September, 1692, Mary, by royal proclamation, offered forty pounds per head for the apprehension and conviction of highwaymen and burglars. This, her greatest error of legislation, was productive of woful results to the people; the reward speedily obtained the appellation of "blood-money," and stimulated gangs of human monsters, known as "thief takers," and even the gaolers themselves, to make a trade of swearing away the lives of, in too many cases, perfectly innocent people, for the sake of the spoil, which, when obtained, they divided amongst themselves at carousals, significantly known as "blood feasts." The writings of Gay, Swift, and Fielding, caused a check to be put to the horrid traffic. But the abominable reward-conviction system was not completely swept away till 1816. Nor was this crime-engendering act of Mary's more injurious than some of the measures which emanated from her husband. To William the people of England are indebted for the Mutiny Bill, with its accompanying anti-national cruelty of the use of the lash in the army, and also for the early encouragement which he strenuously recommended Parliament to afford to the distillation of that mother of sin and woe, ardent spirits.

William, after losing a sharply-contested battle in Flanders, now returned to England. He landed at Yarmouth, on the eighteenth of October, and on the twentieth was met by the Queen at Newhall; and passing with her through the City of London, amidst the acclamations of the citizens, the blaze of bonfires and illuminations, the booming of cannon and other demonstrations of joy at his return, reached Kensington. At eight o'clock the same evening, he received a congratulatory address from the Lord Mayor and Aldermen, with whom he and the Queen dined in public on the tenth of November. The Parliament met six days previously. The House of Lords was deeply infected with discontent, which, in some measure, proceeded from the dissensions between the Queen and her sister Anne. Anne still persisted in retaining her favourite, the Lady Marlborough, and for her obstinacy underwent every mortification that the Court could inflict. Not only was she deprived of her guards, but all honours which had been paid to her rank by the magistrates of Bath, where she sometimes resided, and even by the ministers of the church where she attended divine service, were ordered to be discontinued, by the express command of their Majesties. Her cause was naturally espoused by those noblemen who had adhered to her in her former contest with the King about an independent settlement, and these were now reinforced by all the friends of the Duke of Marlborough, who united by a double tie, resented the disgrace and confinement of that lord; (he had lately been released,) and thought it a duty to support the Princess Anne under a persecution, incurred by an attachment to his wife. As to the people, they were divided into three parties; Williamites, Jacobites, and the discontented Revolutionists: these factions took all opportunities to thwart, to expose, and to ridicule the measures and principles of each other, so that patriotism was laughed out of doors as an hypocritical pretence; public virtue was become the object of ridicule, and the whole kingdom was overspread with immorality and corruption. This contention established a belief that every man consulted his own private interest at the expense of the public; a belief that soon grew into a maxim, universally adopted. The practice of bribing a majority in Parliament had a pernicious influence upon the morals of all ranks of people, from the candidate to the lowest borough elector. The expedient for establishing funds of credit for raising supplies to defray the enormous expenses of Government, threw large premiums and sums of money into the hands of low, sordid usurers, brokers and jobbers, who distinguished themselves by the name of "the monied interest." Intoxicated by this flow of wealth, they affected to rival the luxury and magnificence of their superiors; but being destitute of refined sentiment and taste, they ran into the most absurd and illiberal extravagances. They laid aside all decorum; became licentious, insolent, intemperate, and riotous. Their example was caught by the more vulgar. All principle, and even decency, was gradually banished; talent lay uncultivated, and the land was deluged with a tide of ignorance and profligacy.

William having obtained another large supply of men, money, and war weapons, again embarked for Holland, in March, 1693. The administration was left in the hands of the Queen till the 13th of October, when his Majesty arrived at Kensington. The maintaining a large army in Flanders, where he yearly lost a bloody battle, was the ruling passion of the Orange King. This year he lost the hard-fought battle of Landen;* and under Mary's guidance, the naval war proved truly calamitous. Tourville took revenge for the defeat he had sustained at La Hogue, by destroying twelve English and Dutch men-of-war, and plundering the rich merchant fleet which they were convoying home from the Mediterranean.† Admiral Benbow made an unsuccessful attack on the town of St. Malo; and to add to the troubles, Sir Francis Wheeler returned to England, with his shattered squadron, from an unfortunate expedition in the West Indies. When the King opened parliament on the seventh of November, he expressed his resentment against the authors of the naval disasters, attributed the loss of his own battle to insufficient supplies of money, represented the necessity of increasing the army and the navy, and demanded a suitable supply for these purposes. The people, already groaning under a heavy load of taxation, and appalled at the prospects of an increase of the crushing burden, clamoured louder and louder against the ministers and the court. The Commons made searching inquiry into the cause of the late naval defeats; and the King, unable to check the mutinous clamour of the factious malcontents, threatened to abdicate in favour of Mary, but in the end satisfied himself by changing the administration. The Earl of Shrewsbury was made prime minister, Sunderland was brought into the ministry, Nottingham was dismissed, all the high offices of state were filled by Whig noblemen; and the city of London lieutenancy, and all other commissions over England, were altered in favour of the Whig interest. Mary, it appears, expressed approval of the new ministry, to please her husband—personally she was averse to the change; and the rumour that she entertained a tender penchant for Shrewsbury, is a groundless scandal, first circulated by her dismissed chamberlain, Jack Howe: who also, about the year 1694, spread abroad the idle tale, that if left a widow by the death of William, she would assuredly become the Countess of Shrewsbury.

During her husband's absence in the summer of 1694, Mary had to mourn the complete defeat of the expedition against Brest: a defeat in which General Tollemache and one thousand six hundred English and Dutch soldiers were killed; and which was occasioned by the treachery of Marlborough, who sent intelligence to France of the proposed attack.

This year her Majesty completed her worthy project, of founding the Royal Hospital at Greenwich, as a national asylum for seamen disabled by age, or maimed in the service of their country.

* Sir Charles Sedley, in the following witty epigram, celebrated the disasters of William's two previous campaigns:—

"The author sure, must take great pains,
Who pretends to write his story;
In which of these two last campaigns,
He acquired the greatest glory.
For while that he marched on to fight,
Like hero, nothing fearing;
Namur was taken in his sight,
And Mons within his hearing."

† Twenty-nine merchant vessels were taken, and about fifty destroyed. The loss on this occasion was valued at a million sterling.

Mary resolved that Greenwich palace, which Charles II. had begun to rebuild, and finished one wing, should be converted to this use; and to his honour, the great architect, Sir Christopher Wren, superintended the new buildings for many years without emolument or reward. The letters patent for this grant bear date October the twenty-fifth, 1694. In the following year, William confirmed them, and endowed the hospital with £8,000; a sum, be it observed, not taken out of his private purse, but out of the civil list. An equal amount was at the same time raised by private subscription, and Mary, it appears, although willing and anxious to become a great foundress, had appropriated all her private income to the maintenance of her husband's warfare in Flanders, and had not a penny to bestow on this great charity. Greenwich Hospital consists of four distinct piles of buildings, which are named Charles, William, Mary, and Anne, in honour of their Majesties Charles II., William III., Mary II., and her sister Anne. The royal hospital was first opened in January, 1705, when forty-two seamen were admitted; the number has since been increased to about three thousand, and the out-pensioners are more numerous. A charter was granted to the hospital in 1775; sixpence per month was first contributed by every seaman for its support, and the payment was advanced to one shilling, from June 1795: it now possesses a revenue exceeding £70,000 per annum.

This summer her Majesty's administration was disturbed by the practices, or pretended practices, of the Jacobites. Several gentlemen of Lancashire and Cheshire were prosecuted for taking part in the conspiracy, formed in favour of James II.'s projected invasion from France. Colonel Parker, and one Crosby, were imprisoned, and bills of treason found against them; but Parker escaped from the Tower, and was never retaken, though a reward of £400 was set upon his head. Mary was also in some danger of being seized, and dragged into the presence of her father, at St. Germains, by the device of Sir George Barkly, the Lieutenant-General of her guards, and his acquaintance, Sir John Friend, who plotted to seize the Queen and her husband, and convey them across the channel to James II.; a scheme which, two years afterwards, they matured into a conspiracy to assassinate William II., then a widower, as he returned from hunting at Richmond.

William having concluded this year's campaign in Flanders, landed at Margate on the ninth of November, slept the same night at Canterbury, and the next day was met by the Queen at Rochester, and with her proceeded to Kensington. He opened parliament on the twelfth. The parliament voted thanks to Mary for her wise, energetic administration; brought in the famous act for triennial parliaments: and proceeded to impeach the Marquis of Carmarthen, now Duke of Leeds, Sir John Trevor, Speaker of the Commons, and others, for gross corruption, and receiving and distributing bribes. The enquiries into these gross mal-practices, compromised the character of several of the Queen's household; but death snatched Mary away before these enquiries were terminated, and spared her the pain of witnessing the disgrace of her corrupt ministers.

On the twenty-third of November, 1693, the worthy William Sancroft, late Archbishop of Canterbury, had calmly closed his eyes in death, at his humble residence in Suffolk, and his successor, Archbishop Tillotson, survived him little more than a year. Whilst her Majesty was at Whitehall chapel, on the twenty-fourth of November, 1694, Tillotson, who officiated, was struck with paralysis, and expired a few days afterwards. Their Majesties were greatly affected by the event; and, although they immediately elevated Dr. Tennison to the primateship, the sudden unexpected end of their favourite divine, Tillotson, filled them with awe. Indeed, Mary could not mention the event without weeping; and her health visibly declined. and her spirits sunk. At length, whilst at Kensington, on the nineteenth of December, she fell ill; on the twentieth she became worse, and a presentiment that death was at hand, and the compunctions of a guilty conscience, induced her to sit up the whole night, and burn and destroy all her papers of an important portentous nature. She ended her solitary vigils on that anxious night, by addressing to her husband a letter, respecting his amours with Elizabeth Villiers, which she superscribed, "not to be delivered till after my death," and locked up in her private cabinet. Next day she grew worse. Dr. Ratcliff and Dr. Millington, the most skilful physicians of their day, attended her; but whilst the former erroneously declared that she was sickening for the measles, the latter rightly pronounced her malady to be the small-pox. On Christmas day, unmistakeable symptoms of small-pox presented themselves; and the Princess Anne, who herself was suffering from dropsy, on hearing of the dangerous condition of the Queen, her sister, sent a message—she was not permitted to appear at court—requesting Mary to allow her to wait on her; but her Majesty returned a formal court answer, desiring her to defer the visit. "The day after," writes Burnet, "the King called me into his closet, and gave a free vent to a most tender passion; he burst out into tears; and cried out, that there was no hope of the Queen; and that from being the happiest, he was going to be the miserablest creature upon earth. He, said, 'during the whole course of their marriage he had never known one single fault in her; there was a worth in her that nobody knew besides himself.'" On the twenty-sixth, Anne, if possible to become reconciled to her dying sister, dispatched the Lady Fitzharding to Kensington; this lady broke into the Queen's presence, and in a pathetic appeal, assured her of her sister's deep concern for her condition; but the only reply she could obtain from her dying Majesty, was the cool monosyllable "*Thanks!*" In fact, if the Duchess of Marlborough is to be accredited, Mary was inimical to her sister to the last, and died without seeing her, or even sending a message to her. Burnet, however, states that the Queen "sent a reconciling message to the Princess; and so that breach was made up. It is true," he adds, "that the sisters did not meet; it was thought that might throw the Queen into too great commotion, so it was put off till it was too late."

The Queen's face was covered with erysipelas on the Friday preceding her death. The physicians pronounced her case hopeless, and Archbishop Tennison by consent of the sorrowing King, acquainted her with her danger. She received the archbishop's communication with calmness, and "told him," says Burnet, "to look carefully for a small scrutoire that she made use of, and deliver it to the King [in it was the letter of reproof she had written to his Majesty on the night she destroyed her papers]. Having despatched that care," proceeds Burnet, "she avoided giving herself or her husband the tenderness which a final parting might have raised in them both. She was almost perpetually in prayer. The day before she died, she received the sacrament, all the bishops, who were attending, being admitted to receive it with her. She ordered the archbishop to be reading such passages of Scripture as might fix her attention, and raise her devotion. She then composed herself solemnly to die. She slumbered some time, but said she was not refreshed by it. Once or twice she tried to say something to the King, but was unable to go through with it; several cordials were given to her, but all was ineffectual: she lay silent for some hours, and then her mind wandered, and her thoughts began to break." In this state she lay till about an hour past the midnight of Sunday, December the twenty-eighth, when she breathed her last, in the thirty-third year of her age, and the sixth of her reign.

The King, when informed on the Sunday evening that his consort could not live the night through, fainted and fell to the ground; thrice that day he had swooned, and he became so sad and ill, that it was feared he would not long survive.

The body of the departed Queen was embalmed, and on the fifth of March interred, with royal obsequies, in Westminster Abbey. The members of the House of Commons attended the funeral as mourners. A wax effigy of her Majesty was carried over the coffin in the procession, and, after the interment, deposited in Westminster Abbey. In 1702, the effigy of William III., after being similarly carried at his funeral, was placed by the side of that of his consort. They left no issue, and no monument was raised to their memories. On the day of the Queen's burial, the parish bells throughout England tolled, and a funeral sermon was preached in every parish church, but not universally in her praise, for one Jacobite clergyman took for his text, "Go now, see this accursed woman, and bury her, for she is a King's daughter!"

Tennison delivered Mary's posthumous letter to the King, and at the same time sharply reproved him on the subject of his amours with Elizabeth Villiers. When her father heard that Mary had died without repenting of her unfilial conduct, he was horrified to find "a child he loved so tenderly, persevere even to death, in a state of signal disobedience and disloyalty, and to find ner crimes extolled for virtues by the flatterers around her." He shut himself up, and mourned her loss in private, but would not go into black for her; and by his request, Louis XIV. ordered the court of France not to assume mourning: an order which gave umbrage to several of the French nobility, who claimed kindred with the house of Orange.

Of the odes and elegies written in commendation of Mary II., the best is by the Duke of Devonshire, in which these lines occur—

"Long our divided state
Hung in the balance of a doubtful fate;
When one bright nymph the gathering clouds dispelled,
And all the griefs of Albion healed.
Her the united land obeyed,
She knew her task, and nicely understood
To what intention kings were made,
Not for their own, but for their people's good.
'Twas that prevailing argument alone,
Determined her to fill the vacant throne.
* * * * * * * * *
When waiting only for a wind,
Against our isle the power of France was armed;
Her ruling arts in their true lustre shined,
And winds themselves were by her influence charmed.
Secure and undisturbed, the scene
Of Albion seemed, and like her eyes serene.

Perhaps the most fulsome rhyming effusion to the memory of Queen Mary, is the following by Bishop Burnet; whose funeral sermon on the same subject we pass by as a panegyric at once absurdly partial, weak, worthless, and contemptible:—

"To the state a prudent ruler,
To the Church a nursing mother,
To the King a constant lover,
To the people the best example.
Orthodox in religion,
Moderate in opinion,
Sincere in profession,
Constant in devotion,
Ardent in affection,
A preserver of liberty,
A deliverer from Popery,
A preserver from tyranny,
A preventer of slavery,
A promoter of piety,
A suppressor of immorality,
A pattern of industry,
High in the world,
Low esteem of the world,
Above fear of death,
Sure of eternity.
What was great, good in a Queen,
In her late Majesty was to be seen.
Thoughts to conceive it cannot be express'd,
What was contained in her royal breast.

Numerous other elegies in memory of Mary II. were circulated by the Orange partizans; and her foes, the Jacobites, handed about in the coffee-houses many sarcastic and malicious epigrams, with two of which we close this memoir.

ON THE DEATH OF MARY II.

"The Queen deceased, the King so grieved,
As if the hero died, the woman lived!
Alas! we erred i' the choice of our commanders—
He should have knotted, and she gone to Flanders."

ON THE DEATH OF MARY II. AND MARSHAL LUXEMBOURG.

"Behold, Dutch Prince, here lies the unconquered pair,
Who knew your strength in love, your strength in war.
Unequal match, for both no conquest gains,
No trophy of your love or war remains."

Queen Anne.

ANNE,

Fourth Queen Regnant.

CHAPTER I.

Anne's parentage—Birth—Christening—Education—Early Intimacy with Sarah Jennings—Fondness for card-playing—Introduced to Court—Attends Lord Mayor's feast—Suffers from small-pox—Her favourite married to Churchill, afterwards Lord Marlborough—She is confirmed—Visits her sister Mary, and her father in exile—Unsuccessfully wooed by Prince George of Hanover—Personal charms—Visits her exiled father in Scotland—Clandestinely courted by Sheffield—Married to Prince George of Denmark—Sarah Churchill becomes one of her ladies—Her affection for Sarah, and for her father, who kindly augments her income—Misfortunes as a mother—Extravagance—Birth of her half brother, known as the Pretender—She pronounces him a supposititious child—Conspires with her sister Mary against her father, James the Second—Deserts with her husband to the Prince of Orange, afterwards William the Third.

NNE of YORK, the last Sovereign of the Royal House of Stuart, and a Princess whose reign was brilliant, but whose goodness of heart and Christian excellences have been overrated by general history, was the second daughter and fourth child of James, Duke of York, afterwards James II., by his first wife, Anne Hyde, daughter of Lord Chancellor Clarendon. She was born at St. James's Palace on the sixth of February, 1665, and a few days afterwards was christened according to the rites of the Church of England, in the chapel at St. James's: her godfather was Sheldon, Archbishop of Canterbury; her godmothers were her cousin, the Duchess of Monmouth, and her sister, the Lady Mary of York, afterwards Queen Mary II. of Great Britain.

As mentioned in the preceding memoirs, the sisters, Anne and Mary, passed their early youth together. A propensity to gluttony, which her too-fond mother indulged, laid the royal child, Anne, on the bed of sickness; by the advice of the Duke's physicians, she, in 1669, was sent to France; and such was the effect of change of air and scene, that, after an absence of eight months, she returned in excellent health and spirits. The death of her mother in March, 1674; the little regard paid to her education, the early intimacy which she formed with Sarah Jennings, afterwards Sarah Churchill, Duchess of Marlborough, and her father's conversion to the Catholic faith, and marriage to Maria d'Este, have all been duly mentioned in the first pages of the memoir of Queen Mary II., and therefore need not be repeated in this place.

Like her sister Mary, the Lady Anne became early in life such an inveterate card-player, that she played even on the Sabbath. She was first introduced to court in December, 1674, when she performed in the ballet of "Calista, or the Chaste Nymph;" and in the subsequent year, she accompanied her father and the King and Queen to the Lord Mayor's feast at Guildhall, where, to the delight of the good citizens, she indulged her inordinate love of eating, with the zest of a London alderman. On the 29th of October, 1677, she witnessed the civic procession got up by the citizens of London, in honour of the approaching marriage of Mary of York to William, Prince of Orange; but she was prevented from being present at the nuptials, and from bidding her sister adieu, when that sister embarked with her husband for the Hague, by an alarming attack of the small-pox, which seized her on the thirty-first of October, and confined her to her chamber at St. James's till the first week of December, when, as the danger had passed, and she had already began to recover, the Duke, her father, informed her of the departure and the safe arrival in Holland of her beloved sister Mary. It is supposed that Anne caught the infection when visiting the City; but, however this may have been, a few days after she was attacked, the small-pox burst forth at St. James's as virulent as a plague; and on the day on which thanks were returned to God for her recovery, her governess, Lady Frances Villiers, died of the fatal contagion. On the sixteenth of December, four days after the death of that infant brother, whose short existence had, for a brief period, clouded the regnal prospects of the heiresses of York, Anne, being quite convalescent, attended divine worship at St. James's Chapel; and about the same time the King appointed Lady Clarendon to succeed Frances Villiers as her governess.

In the winter of 1677, Anne's favourite playmate, Sarah Jennings, the beautiful daughter of Mr. Jennings of Sandridge, near St. Alban's, confessed to the Duchess of York, that she had formed a stolen match with the handsome Colonel Churchill, afterwards Duke of Marlborough. The Duchess reconciled Churchill and Sarah to their offended relatives; and shortly afterwards, Sarah, who, although young in years, was wise in world-craft, caused Mrs. Cornwallis, Anne's best-beloved friend, to be driven from St. James's, as a denounced papist, and at once set about obtaining for herself that remarkable ascendancy over the mind of the Lady Anne, which she maintained for so many years, and exercised to so little good purpose.

On Easter Sunday, 1678, Anne having previously been confirmed at Whitehall Chapel, by her preceptor, Henry Compton, Bishop of London, received the sacrament at the chapel of St. James's. The Bishop of Exeter officiated on the occasion, and the Princess so far forgot herself, as to partake three times of the wine; conduct highly censurable, and which astonished and disgusted all who witnessed it.

In October, 1678, Anne and her step-mother, Maria Beatrix, paid a short, but affectionate visit to her sister Mary, the Princess of Orange, at the Hague, the particulars of which have already been detailed in the two preceding memoirs. The Duke of York had been driven to exile in Brussels but a short while, when, by permission of his brother, Charles the Second, his daughter Anne, and his young half-sister, Isabella, were sent to him in the summer of 1679. In the subsequent September, Anne accompanied her exiled father and step-mother on a visit to the Princess of Orange; and at this period the affection subsisting between the Duke of York and his daughters, Anne and Mary, seemed to be sincere, deep rooted, and indissoluble.

"During her residence at Brussels," remarks Harrison, "the Princess Anne had her own Protestant chaplains allowed her, and a place assigned for the exercise of her devotions, according to the Church of England. Nor was she at all importuned to go, or ever went to mass with her father, as I have been assured by her Protestant servants, who attended her there. But the family lived in perfect harmony, as if there had been no religious differences between them; which appears very strange, if His Royal Highness was that zealous, bigotted Prince he is represented to have been. For when could he have had greater opportunities of urging his daughter Anne to embrace the Popish religion, than in a country where that religion was established?"

When James was recalled to England, Anne accompanied him; but she remained in the land of her birth, and resided chiefly at St. James's, whilst her father was forced to take his first journey to Scotland. It was at this period, and whilst the Duke of York was holding his court at Holyrood, that Prince George Lewis of Hanover, afterwards George the First, made his appearance at the Court of St. James's, as a suitor for the hand of the Lady Anne. Charles the Second cordially welcomed him, presented him to the Queen, Katherine of Braganza, and permitted him to kiss the lips of his desired bride. Nevertheless, the suit failed; and, provoking though it be, the cause of the failure remains, to this day, involved in mystery. By some accounts, the royal adventurer was disgusted with the person and deportment of Anne; and the Prince of Orange, who, as the match might possibly shut him out from the succession to the throne of Great Britain, took infinite pains to prevent it, caused the unpleasant intelligence to be imparted to Anne, through the medium of the Villiers' sisterhood; whilst, according to others, equally creditable authorities, Anne was so displeased with the ordinary person, and the rude, awkward manners of the German wooer, that she refused him with disdain. But, doubtful as these statements may be, it is certain that Prince George was suddenly recalled by his father to pay court to his fair cousin, Sophia Dorothea, heiress of Zelle. This lady he espoused on the first of November, 1682. The match proved a truly unhappy one. Under a real or pretended belief that Sophia had violated her marriage vow, Prince George treated her with brutal severity. He caused her to be divorced from him in December, 1694, and from that period to the day of her death, November the thirteenth, 1726, confined her as a state prisoner in the Castle of Ahlden, on the south bank of the Aller. As she never once came to England, and was neither acknowledged by George the First, nor by the nation, as Queen Consort of England; her memoirs will not appear in this work.

The Lady Anne, although not a peerless beauty, possessed considerable personal attractions. She was of middle size, but not so majestic as her sister Mary; and her hair a deep chestnut brown, her complexion sanguine and ruddy. Her face was round, but rather comely than handsome; her features were strong and regular, the only blemish in her face was that of a defluxion, which had affected her eyes when young, and left a contraction in her upper lids, and given a cloudiness to her countenance. Her bones were small, her hands beautiful. She had an excellent ear for music, was a good performer on the guitar; and her voice being strong, clear, flexible, and melodious, she took pleasure in the practice of vocal harmony.

Anne's visit to her father in Scotland, has already been noticed in the memoirs of Maria Beatrix. She returned with him in the summer of 1682, and again took up her residence at St. James's Palace. A few months afterwards, she fell in love with the accomplished and handsome Sheffield, then Earl of Mulgrave, one of the lords of the bedchamber to Charles the Second, and afterwards Duke of Buckingham. This nobleman commemorated her beauty in flowing numbers, and on winning her heart, secretly corresponded with her by letter, and made her an offer of marriage. Sarah Churchill, however, resolved to prevent the match. She purloined two tender epistles, the one from Anne to the Earl, the other from the Earl to Anne, which she placed in the hands of Charles the Second; and the result was, that the Earl was forthwith dispatched on an expedition to Tangiers, in a rotten, leaky vessel, with the view, it has been most absurdly asserted, of disposing of him in the vasty deep; and King Charles and his cabinet provided what they deemed a more suitable suitor for the Lady Anne, in the person of Prince George of Denmark. The Prince was poor, possessed neither extensive influence nor great abilities, but he was a Protestant, and that alone was deemed merit sufficient. He reached London on the nineteenth of July, 1683. Evelyn, who saw him immediately afterwards, noted that he had a blonde Danish countenance, in his manners was heavy and reserved, and spoke French with a bad accent, but was reported to be valiant. Prince George was received with great courtesy by the King, Queen, and the Duke and Duchess of York. He dined with them in public on the day of his arrival in England, and nine days afterwards, it being St. Anne's day, July the twenty-eighth, 1683, was married with royal pomp to the Lady Anne, in the Chapel Royal, at St. James's, by the Bishop of London, at the unusually late hour of ten at night. The bride was given away by her merry uncle, Charles the Second, who delighted in being present at marriages and christenings. The chapel was brilliantly lit up; and as the King, the Queen, the Duke and the Duchess of York, and the leading nobility then in London, were present, the scene was magnificent, dazzling, and joyous. The citizens of London also took their part in the nocturnal festivity. Throughout the metropolis the bells rang all night, bright bonfires blazed at every door, the conduits ran with wine, and showers of fireworks and other popular sports and pastimes were provided for the amusement of the people. Charles Montague, afterwards Earl of Halifax, celebrated the marriage of Anne in a trashy ode. In allusion to the Prince and Princess, he remarks :—

"See, see, how decently the bashful bride
Does bear her conquests; with how little pride
She views that Prince, the captive of her charms,
Who made the north with fear to quake,
And did that powerful empire shake.
Before whose arms, when great Gustavus led,
The frighted Roman eagles fled."

It has been suggested that the father of Anne was against this match; and yet those who put forth this suggestion, at the same time assure us that the King was under the influence of the Duke, his brother. Assertions which contradict each other, without we suppose that the Duke influenced the King in trifles only, and submitted to his will in matters of importance. But, whatever might have been the Duke's private sentiments in regard to the match, the protracted examination of that monster bugbear, the Popish Plot, had at this period thrown the nation into such a state of religious excitement, that, to all appearances, nothing, saving himself embracing the Church of England creed, which his conscience would not permit, could so firmly secure to him his right of succession to the crown of Great Britain, as the marriage of his daughters Mary and Anne to Protestant husbands. Therefore, it is only reasonable to suppose, that the Duke of York made no powerful opposition to the match; especially as he never once urged his Protestant daughter, Anne, to forsake the Church of England for that of Rome.

It was arranged that Prince George of Denmark, who was about fifteen years his bride's senior, should remain in England; and, that Anne and her husband might be enabled to maintain the state and dignity becoming their exalted station, Charles II. settled on her, by Act of Parliament, £20,000 per year, and himself purchased, and gave to her for a residence, the Cockpit, a capacious building, which had formerly been the theatre of Whitehall Palace. Immediately the marriage festivities were terminated, Anne's establishment was appointed by her uncle, King Charles, and Sarah Churchill requested and obtained permission to become one of her ladies. Anne, who made the request to her father, thus announces the circumstances to her favourite and confidant, Mrs. Churchill—"The Duke of York came in just as you were gone, and made no difficulties, but has promised me that

I shall have you, which I assure you is a great joy to me. I should say a great deal for your kindness in offering it, but I am not good at compliments. I will only say, I do take it extreme kindly, and shall be ready at any time to do you all the service that is in my power."

The manner in which Mrs. Churchill contrived to obtain and to retain her influence over the Princess Anne of Denmark, she herself relates, with consummate egotism, in the following words:—

"The beginning of the Princess's kindness for me, had a much earlier date than my entrance into her service. My promotion to this honour was wholly owing to impressions she had before received to my advantage; we had used to play together when she was a child, and she even then expressed a particular fondness for me. This inclination increased with our years. I was often at court, and the Princess always distinguished me by the pleasure she took to honour me preferably to others with her conversation and confidence. In all her parties for amusement I was sure by her choice to be one; and so desirous she became of having me always near her, that upon her marriage with the Prince of Denmark, it was at her own earnest request to her father, I was made one of the ladies of her bedchamber. What conduced to render me the more agreeable to her in this station, was doubtless the dislike she had conceived to most of the other persons about her, and particularly to her first lady of the bedchamber, the Countess of Clarendon, a lady whose discourse and manner—though the princess thought they agreed very well together—could not possibly recommend her to so young a mistress, for she looked like a mad woman, and talked like a scholar. Indeed, her highness's court was throughout so oddly composed, that I think it would be making myself no great compliment if I should say her choosing to spend more of her time with me than with any of her other servants did no discredit to her taste. Be that as it will, it is certain she at length distinguished me by as high, or perhaps a higher place in her favour than any person ever before arrived at, with queen or princess; and if from hence I may draw any glory, it is that I both obtained and held this place without the assistance of flattery, a charm which in truth her inclination for me, together with my unwearied application to serve and amuse her, rendered useless, but which, had it been otherwise, my temper and turn of mind would never have suffered me to employ.

"Young as I was when I first became this high favourite, I laid it down for a maxim that flattery was falsehood to my trust, and ingratitude to my greatest friend, and that I did not deserve so much favour if I could not venture the loss of it by speaking the truth, and by preferring the real interest of my mistress, before the pleasing her fancy in the sacrifice to her passion. From this rule I never swerved; and though my temper and my notions in most things were widely different from those of the Princess, yet, during a long course of years, she was so far from being displeased with me for openly speaking my sentiments, that she sometimes preferred a desire, and even added her command, that it should be always continued, promising never to be offended at it, but to love me the better for my frankness. Favour with a princess upon these terms engaged me to her in the manner that it ought—I mean by a sentiment which I choose to call honour rather than gratitude or duty; because whilst it implies all the justice and affection of these, it seems to express a more disinterested principle of action. For I can truly affirm that I never considered myself on any occasion, where her interest or glory was concerned, nor had I any idea of a misery which I would not have sooner incurred than the inward shame of being conscious of a failure in this respect. The facts themselves which I am going to relate will, in a great degree, evince the truth of what I say; and that the princess was perfectly persuaded of it, is I think sufficiently manifest both from her letters to me, and from that unreserved intimacy of friendship in which we for many years lived together.

"Kings and Princes for the most part imagine they have a dignity peculiar to their birth and station, which ought to raise them above all connexions of friendship with an inferior. Their passion is to be admired and feared; to have subjects awfully obedient, and servants blindly obsequious to their pleasure. Friendship is an offensive word; it imports a kind of equality between the parties, it suggests nothing to the mind of crowns and thrones, high titles, or immense revenues, fountains of honour or fountains of riches, prerogatives which the possessors would have always uppermost in the thoughts of those who are permitted to approach them. The Princess Anne had a different taste. A friend is what she had most coveted, and for the sake of friendship, (a relation which she did not disdain to have with me), she was fond even of that equality which she thought belonged to it. She grew uneasy to be treated by me with the form and ceremony due to her rank, nor could she hear from me the fond words which implied in them distance and superiority. It was this turn of mind which made her one day propose to me, that whenever I should happen to be absent from her, we might in all our letters write to ourselves by feigned names, such as would import nothing of distinction of rank between us. Morley and Freeman were the names her fancy hit upon, and she left me to choose by which of these I would be called. My frank, open temper naturally led me to pitch upon Freeman, and so the Princess took the other; and from this time Mrs. Morley and Mrs. Freeman began to converse as equals, made so by affection and friendship."

This Mrs. Churchill's account of her own open, candid disposition, and her high sense of honour and sincere, disinterested affection and friendship for the Princess Anne, must be received with caution; indeed, it will hereafter be rendered apparent, that Anne possessed no more selfish, intriguing, unprincipled friend than the wife of the great Duke of Marlborough.

At this period, the greatest affection subsisted between Anne and her father and her step-mother. When James II. ascended the throne, he publicly paid to the Princess of Denmark the most marked attention. At his coronation, although her promising condition precluded her from taking part in the ceremony, she witnessed it from an elegant curtained enclosure which was fitted up for her in Westminster Abbey; and her newly-crowned stepmother, Queen Maria Beatrix, before returning in procession to Westminster Hall, crossed over to her, and spent some time in familiar conversation with her. She also accompanied her step-mother, the Queen, to witness the ceremony, when her father, King James II., opened his first parliament. Indeed, James II., who beheld in her the ultimate heiress to his throne, had the paternal weakness to permit her to assume nearly all the external state and homage of a reigning sovereign; a distinction which she afterwards felt no inclination to resign at the birth of her half-brother, the Pretender. Nor was this, the permission to assume the dignity of a queen, the only indulgence that the fond King granted to his youngest daughter. He augmented her and her husband's income to the enormous sum of £32,000 per year (about £65,000 present money). "And yet withal," remarks a cotemporary, "such was the extravagance, such the mismanagement of the household of the Princess Anne, that this sum did not suffice, and the King had more than once to clear off her debts."

Anne as a mother was truly unfortunate; for years after her marriage she experienced hopes of maternity every twelvemonth; yet, to the deep sorrow of herself and her husband, many of her confinements were premature and abortive, and not one of her offsprings lived to maturity. On the twelfth of May, 1684, she brought into the world a still-born daughter; but her next infant, a daughter, born on the second of June, 1685, promised to live, and was christened Mary, after the Princess of Orange, with becoming solemnity, in the chapel at Whitehall. The third daughter of Anne of Denmark first saw the light at Windsor, on the twelfth of May, 1686, proved a fine healthy babe, and was baptized Anna Sophia. The hopes that the little Princesses, Mary and Anne Sophia, gave of reaching maturity speedily vanished. The Princess of Denmark experienced a miscarriage on the twenty-first of January, 1687, and from its effects she had scarcely recovered, when first the little Lady Anne Sophia, and then her sister, the Lady Mary, expired. On the second of February, remarks the Ellis correspondent, "died (of hydrocephalus it is supposed) the Lady Anne Sophia, youngest daughter of the Princess of Denmark, to the great grief of us all. Four days afterwards, the little Lady Mary, who had for weeks been in a consumption, breathed her last, and greatly increased the affliction of Anne." Her husband, Prince George, was at this very time dangerously ill of a fever: "It was a sad sight," writes a contemporary, "to see the Prince and the Princess of Denmark together, hand in hand, the day after the death of their eldest daughter, sometimes weeping, sometimes moaning their bereavement in words; he in bed, she nursing him, as carefully as can be imagined. As soon as he was able, they went to the palace at Richmond, and their two little children were interred in St. George's Chapel, at Windsor."

At the subsequent Christmas, it was found that Anne's debts exceeded her income by £7000. Her uncle, Lawrence Hyde, who was then lord-treasurer, suspected that her funds were being unjustly appropriated by greedy favourites: King James entertained the same suspicion, and hastening into her presence, gently reprimanded her, adding, "I will once more relieve you, but remember in future you must be more exact in your accounts." Anne only answered with tears; but the moment the King was gone, Sarah Churchill, who, hid in a closet, had listened to all that passed between James and his prodigal daughter, came forth with a bounce of the foot, and exclaimed, "Ah, Madam, you may thank your rascally old uncle, Lawrence Hyde, for all this!" But, despite the malice of Anne's favourite, Lord-Treasurer Hyde was a wise and honest financier. However, Anne, who had gambled or given away large sums to the Churchills, was henceforth forced to live within her income, and on this account she and her favourite ever afterwards detested and dreaded the remonstrances of the treasurer of James II.

When it became probable that the Queen, Maria Beatrix, would give birth to an heir to the throne, Anne, in conjunction with her sister Mary, took alarm, and resolved to go to any length rather than relinquish the prospect of one day wearing the crown of Great Britain, and transmitting it to her descendants. Anne's correspondence on this subject with Mary of Orange, has already appeared in the Memoirs of that Princess, and therefore need not be repeated in this place. A short extract from one of these letters will suffice, to show Anne's selfish, unfilial intentions: "If this expected infant," said she, "should prove a son, I for one will believe it to be no other than a supposititious child." In another letter she remarks: "One thing I must say of the Queen (Maria Beatrix), which is, that she is the most hated in the world of all sorts of people; for every body believes that she presses the King to be more violent than he would be of himself, which is not unlikely, for she is a very great bigot in her way. She pretends to have a great deal of kindness for me; but I doubt its reality, for I never see proofs of it, but rather the contrary."

Not satisfied with thus grossly vilifying the Queen, Anne, in another letter addressed at this period to the Princess of Orange, insinuates that the King, her father, is capable of murdering his own children As already shown in the two preceding memoirs, James II. was a most kind and indulgent parent; and yet, such was the ingratitude, such the base-heartedness of his fondly-humoured youngest daughter, that she thus addressed her sister at the Hague: "If King James should desire you and the Prince of Orange to come over to make a visit, I think it will be better to excuse yourselves; for although the King probably has no thought against either of you, yet, since people can say one thing and do another, one cannot help being afraid. Really, if you or the Prince should come,

I should be frightened out of my wits, for fear any harm should happen to either of you."

To avoid being present at the Queen's accouchement, Anne retired to Bath, under pretence that she was herself enceinte, and required to partake of the waters. The unwelcomed brother entered the world on the tenth of June, 1688, and on the eighteenth she, with her characteristic duplicity, wrote to the Princess of Orange—"My dear sister cannot imagine the concern and vexation I have been in, that I should be so unfortunate to be out of town when the Queen was brought to bed, for I shall never now be satisfied whether the child be true or false. It may be it is our brother, but where one believes it, a thousand do not; for my part, except they give me very plain demonstrations (which is almost impossible now), I shall ever be of the number of unbelievers. *I don't find people are at all disheartened, but seem all of a mind, which is a very comfortable thing at such a time as this.*"

In another letter, dated July ninth, Anne writes—"The Prince of Wales has been ill these three or four days; and if he has been so bad as some people say, I believe it will not be long before he is an angel in heaven." At length, after Anne had answered a string of technical questions on the subject from Mary, these two very dutiful and affectionate daughters came to the understanding, that whatever might be done or said in the matter, they would on no account own the infant as their brother.

In September, all London was agitated with reports of the projected invasion by the Prince of Orange; and James' father-in-law, Lord Clarendon, made many, but useless attempts, to awaken Anne's filial feelings. She evaded him as frequently as possible, and when forced to give him audience, made no answer to his intreaties. Anne, under the pretended fear of a miscarriage, refused to be present when evidence was formally taken of the Queen's delivery, and to the council who waited upon her with a copy of the depositions, she replied, "My Lords, this is not necessary, the King's word is more to me than all these depositions;" yet at this very time she was in the daily habit of making the birth of her brother the subject of doubt and sarcasm.

On the third of November, Anne was informed by her father, that the Dutch armament had been seen off Dover. On the fifth William landed, and in a few days noble after noble went over to his standard. On the twelfth, Lord Cornburn, son of the Earl of Clarendon, deserted from James' army, with three regiments of cavalry, and six days afterwards Anne wrote to her brother-in-law, William of Orange, "I hope my husband, the Prince of Denmark, will soon be with you, to let you see his readiness to join with you, who I am sure will do you all the service that lies in his power. He went yesterday with the King towards Salisbury, intending to go from thence to you, as soon as his friends thought it proper. I am not certain if I shall continue here, or remove into the city; that shall depend upon the advice my friends will give me; but wherever I am, I shall be ready to show you how much I am your humble servant."

In accordance with this advice, Prince George of Denmark went over to the enemy on the twenty-fourth, the day after the desertion of Churchill and Grafton, and addressed an apology to the King, in which he declares, "Nothing but the cause of religion is able to tear me from you, whilst the same affectionate desire to serve you continues in me. Could I secure your person, at the hazard of my life, I should think it could not be better employed."

Anne, on learning that her husband, with Churchill and others, had successfully left the camp of her father, sent for the Bishop of London, and arranged with him a plan for her own escape from the Cockpit, at Whitehall. At one o'clock, when all the household were wrapped in sleep, she stole from her chamber with Lady Churchill and Mrs. Berkely, descended a back staircase which had been recently put up for that very purpose, and found, as had been arranged, waiting near the gate, a hackney-coach, in which were the Bishop and the Earl of Dorset. She entered the coach, and the whole party drove to the prelate's house in Aldersgate Street, whence, before the dawn of day, they hastened to Copt Hall, the Earl of Dorset's seat, in Waltham Forest, and after partaking of refreshment there, proceeded to a meeting of the Orange partizans at Northampton. From Northampton, the Princess was escorted through Leicester and Coventry to Warwick; and it was during this journey that, according to Lord Chesterfield, she urged her friends to have an association entered into to massacre all the papists in England, should the Prince of Orange be killed or murdered by any of them. Whether she considered that her father, as the head of the English catholics, would be the first to fall under the vengeance of this extermination association cannot be stated for certainty; but if she did not, her stupidity must at this time have been greater than appears probable; however, we trust, for her soul's sake, the decapitation of her indulgent parent was not her object in being enrolled as the chief of this horrible confederacy. At the Cockpit, Anne's disappearance was not noticed, probably not meant to be noticed, till the morning had far advanced, when her bed-chamber door was burst open, and her domestics, with real or affected despair, hastened to the Queen's apartments and rudely demanded their mistress, whilst a riotous mob assembled outside the palace, vociferating that she had been assassinated or kidnapped by the papists. However, in a short time the tumult was subdued, by the discovery of the subjoined letter, which lay open on the Princess's toilet:—

"The Princess Anne to Queen Maria Beatrix.

"Madam,

"I beg pardon if I am so deeply affected with the surprising news of the Prince [George of Denmark] being gone, as not to be able to see you, but to leave this paper to express my humble duty to the King and yourself, and to let you know that I am gone to absent myself to avoid the King's displeasure, which I am not able to bear, either against the Prince or myself; and I stay at so great a distance, as not to return before I hear the happy news of a reconcilement. And as I am confident the Prince did not leave the King with any other design than to use all possible means for his preservation, so I hope you will do me the justice to believe, that I am not capable of following him for any other end.

"Never was any one in such an unhappy condition, so divided between duty and affection, to a father and a husband; and therefore I know not what to do, but to follow one to preserve the other. I see the general falling-off of the nobility and gentry, *who avow to have no end than to prevail with the King to secure their religion;* which they saw so much in danger by the violent councils of the priests, who, to promote their own religion, did not care to what danger they exposed the King. I am fully persuaded that the Prince of Orange designs the King's safety and preservation, and hope all things may be composed without more bloodshed, by the calling of a parliament. God grant a happy end to these troubles, that the King's reign may be prosperous, and that I may shortly meet you in peace and safety; 'till when, let me beg of you to continue the same favourable opinion that you have hitherto had, of your

"Most obedient daughter and servant,

"Anne."

When we remind the reader, that the dutiful, veracious Anne had eight days previously pledged her word to the Prince of Orange for the defection of her husband, whose desertion she herself had planned and instigated, and that of late she never mentioned her father without slandering him, or magnifying his faults, it will at once appear that the above letter is one tissue of hypocritical pretensions and gross falsehoods, and withal an evidence of the unrighteous disposition of its author.

James II., on hearing of Anne's flight from Whitehall, burst into tears, and exclaimed, "God help me! my very children have forsaken me in my distress." A few days afterwards, Clarendon met

William at Salisbury, in the vain hope of effecting an amicable arrangement between King James and the Orange Prince. He there saw Prince George of Denmark, who told him that Anne's excuse of pregnancy was a falsehood; an assertion which so startled the Earl, that he exclaimed, "Good God, bless us! nothing but lying and dissimulation in the world."

CHAPTER II.

Anne unconcerned for her father's misfortunes—Dissatisfied with the settlement of the succession—Gives birth to Prince William, Duke of Gloucester—Contentions with her sister, Queen Mary—Settlement of her income—Writes a penitential letter to her father—Openly quarrels with William and Mary—Refuses to dismiss Lady Marlborough—Retires from court—Receives a harsh visit from Queen Mary—Breach widened—Her duplicity—Failure of her efforts to become reconciled to her dying sister Mary—Hollow reconciliation with her departed sister's consort, William III.—Her fortune exalted by the death of her sister Mary—Treated by William with marked disrespect—He is forced to recognize her as heir-apparent, and form a separate establishment for her son, the Duke of Gloucester—Precocity and death of Gloucester—William III.'s efforts to exclude her from the succession—She moans the demise of her father—Death of William III.—General mourning—Preparation for war with France and Spain.

NNE, when informed of the final flight of her father, expressed not the least concern, but "called for cards, and was as merry as she used to be." For this unnatural conduct, Clarendon took her to task; "But," he writes, "she was not one jot moved thereby." When the convention declared that the deserted crown of England should be decreed to the Prince and Princess of Orange, and in the event of Mary dying first, without issue, should be retained by William, during his life, Anne repented of the course she had pursued, and being forced to acquiesce in the arrangement, exclaimed, "Oh! fool that I was, to desert a good father in favour of a selfish Prince, who puts by my right with impunity." On the twelfth of February, 1689, Anne and her husband welcomed Mary to England as their Queen, and they were present at the coronation of William and Mary in the subsequent April.

On the twenty-fourth of July, about four in the morning, Anne, to the great joy and satisfaction of their Majesties, and the Orange partizans, gave birth to a son at Hampton Court. "Queen Mary was present the whole time, about three hours, and the King, with most of the persons of quality about the court, came into her royal highness's bedchamber before she was delivered." On the twenty-seventh, the infant was baptized William Henry. The sponsors were the King and Queen, the Marchioness of Halifax, and the King of Denmark; and the same day their Majesties caused him to be proclaimed Duke of Gloucester.

Since the accession of William and Mary, petty bickerings had arisen between Anne and the Queen, respecting the Princess's residences. At this period occurred a more serious difference. "The Princess," remarks Cox, "having announced her acquiescence in the new order of succession, expected that a permanent and independent revenue would have been secured to her for life, as the King had been allowed no less a sum than £600,000 a year for the civil list. Instead, however, of gratifying her expectations, he even showed some reluctance to continue the allowance of £30,000 a year, which she had enjoyed under her father. She was highly incensed at this disappointment, and testified her resolution to appeal to parliament; while the King and Queen were no less offended by her wish to acquire an independent establishment. The subject occasioned the most indecorous altercations between the royal sisters, and became the source of the subsequent quarrel which divided the royal family. Irritated by these disputes, Anne pursued her purpose with redoubled zeal, and her cause was earnestly promoted by the Earl and Countess of Marlborough. Her pretensions were warmly supported by the Tories and disaffected, while the King would rely only on his own personal friends and the zealous Whigs. A considerable majority of the parliament was therefore enlisted on the side of the Princess, and her claims became generally popular among the great body of the nation.

"In this state of the public mind, her friends in the House of Commons proposed to grant her an independent revenue of £70,000 a year. To prevent the decision of the question, the King adjourned the parliament. But the Princess was of too tenacious a character to relinquish her object, particularly as her party was increased by many who were alienated by the reserve of the King. In this crisis lures and threats were alternately held forth to the Countess of Marlborough, with the hope of inducing the Princess to desist through her influence. The Countess continued firm, and the question was revived in the House of Commons soon after the commencement of the session. The court now found that opposition was fruitless. With the consent of both parties, the debate was adjourned; and, in the interval, a compromise was effected, by which an annual allowance of £50,000 was settled in parliament as the civil list of the princess.

"The success of this measure being principally ascribed by Anne to the exertions of the Earl and Countess of Marlborough, contributed still more to endear them to her, while it rendered them in an equal degree obnoxious to the King and Queen. Anne was not tardy in testifying her gratitude for so acceptable a service; and, in an affectionate letter, offered her favourite an additional salary of £1000 a year. The Countess at first declined the generous proposal from motives of delicacy, but her scruples were overruled by the representations of Lord Godolphin."

In October, 1690, Anne of Denmark gave birth to a daughter, who was christened Mary, and died a few hours afterwards. Every year the differences between Anne and her sister Mary became more public, more numerous. Amongst other causes of disaffection, Anne was offended at the rejection of an offer made by the Prince, her husband, in May, 1691, to serve on board the fleet, and still more by the mode in which it was conveyed; she seldom visited the Queen, and when, at the instigation of her favourite, she on the second of August, 1691, earnestly requested the King to confer the order of the garter on Marlborough, although the request was seconded by that of her husband, Prince George of Denmark, their entreaties met with a contemptuous refusal; which so exasperated Marlborough, that he wrote to the exiled James II. at St. Germains, offering him his services, and to bring the Princess Anne back to her filial duty. The expatriated monarch placed no confidence in these professions; but withal, Anne, on the first of December, 1691, wrote a penitential letter to her father, in which she begged of him to accept her proffered duty and submission, assured him she was equally concerned for his misfortunes, and sensible of her own unhappiness; declared she confessed her error, and if wishes could recall the past, had long since redeemed the fault; and in conclusion, expressed a hope, that as she made this open confession, he would receive her humble submission, grant her pardon, and make her compliments to his consort, Maria Beatrix. Long before this letter reached St. Germains, William and Mary learned that such an epistle was on its road. "Such mutual irritation," remarks Cox, "could not long continue without producing an open rupture; accordingly, on the evening of January the ninth, 1692, an indecorous altercation took place between the two royal sisters, and the Queen did not hesitate to threaten the Princess with a reduction of her revenue to one half of the actual amount. Whether Marlborough and his lady were implicated in this uncourtly scene, is uncertain; but he felt the first public effect of the royal displeasure. On the ensuing morning, after fulfilling his usual duties as lord of the bed-chamber, he received an order from the King, through Lord Nottingham, secretary of state, announcing his dismission from all his offices, both civil and military, and prohibiting his appearance at court.

"This affront towards a faithful servant rankled in the mind of the Princess, and a gloomy reserve prevailed in the royal family, which portended a new commotion. At this moment, also, the enemies whom Marlborough had provoked by his remonstrances and sarcasms, omitted no effort to widen the breach. A powerful cabal was formed by the Earl of Portland and the family of Villiers, whose intrigues were rendered more dangerous by their intimate access to the King. To this cabal belonged Lady Fitzharding, a sister of the Countess of Portland, who availed herself of her situation in the household of the Princess, and the confidence of Lady Marlborough, to act as a spy on the conduct of the Princess and her favourite; and to report, in aggravated terms, the indecorous and insulting language which they habitually used in speaking of the King.

"Early in January an anonymous letter was conveyed to the Princess, indicating this cabal, and announcing, that the disgrace of Marlborough would not terminate with his dismission; but that, on the prorogation of Parliament, he would be imprisoned. This correspondent also stated that the tears which she had been seen to shed since the disgrace of Marlborough, had provoked the King and Queen, and that the meeting which he held with Godolphin and Russel on the evening of his dismission, had excited great jealousy at court. It concluded with apprising the Princess that she would be compelled to dismiss Lady Marlborough.

"This informant was not widely mistaken. The Countess, who had absented herself from Court since the disgrace of her lord, was at length persuaded by her friends to attend the Princess at the levée of the Queen, on the fourth of February. Such an imprudent step, which was far from being prompted by motives of respect, was considered as a premeditated insult. On the ensuing morning a harsh letter was conveyed from the Queen, commanding the Princess to dismiss Lady Marlborough without delay.* Instead, however, of complying, she still farther provoked the Queen by a justification of her favourite, and an order was transmitted by the lord chamberlain, enjoining the Countess to remove from the palace of Whitehall. The order was the prelude to an utter breach. Anne, disdaining to remain in a place from whence her friend and confidant was excluded, quitted her own apartments, and after a temporary stay at Sion Hill, the seat of the Duke of Somerset, established her residence at Berkley House. The King, as a mark of ill-will, deprived her and her husband of their guards; and the result was, her carriage was stopped, and she was robbed between Brentford and Sion House, in March, 1692.

"Common resentment and common mortification gave new strength to the romantic affection which subsisted between the Princess and her favourite. To an offer made by the Countess of withdrawing from her service, Anne replied with the most tender expostulations, asseverating that she was not the cause of the rupture which had occurred. In one of her notes she observes, 'I really long to know how my dear Mrs. Freeman got home; and now I have this opportunity of writing, she must give me leave to tell her, if she should ever be so cruel to leave her faithful Mrs. Morley, she will rob her of the joy of her life; for if that day should come, I should never enjoy another happy minute; and I swear to you I would shut myself up and never see a creature.'"

Whilst commenting on these royal quarrels, Burnet remarks, "Upon Marlborough's disgrace, his lady was forbid the court; the Princess would not submit to this; she thought she ought to be allowed to keep what persons she pleased about herself; and when the Queen in-

* See page 837.

sisted on the thing, she retired from the court. There was, no doubt, ill offices done on all hands, as there were some that pressed the Princess to submit to the Queen, as well as others who pressed the Queen to pass it over, but without effect; both had engaged themselves before they had well reflected on the consequences of such a breach. Now the matter went so far, that the Queen ordered, that no public honours should be showed the Princess, besides many other lesser matters, which I unwillingly reflect upon, because I was much troubled to see the Queen carry such a matter so far, and the breach continued to the end of her life. The enemies of the government tried what could be made of this, to create distractions among us; but the Princess gave no encouragement to them. So that this misunderstanding had no other effect, but that it gave enemies much ill-natured joy, and a secret, spiteful diversion."

On the seventeenth of April, 1692, Anne, after a protracted, dangerous labour, was delivered of a son, who was hastily baptized George, and expired shortly afterwards. She dispatched her Dutch maid of honour, Charlotte Beveraart, to impart the sad tidings to the Queen, and Mary visited her; but, instead of offering condolence, rushed into her presence, exclaiming, "As I have condescended to come to you, I expect you will now obey me, and at once dismiss Lady Marlborough." Anne burst into tears, and declared, "That in aught else she would obey her Majesty, but her favourite she could not part with." "Ah," sharply retorted the Queen, "I thought as much;" and with an air of supreme contempt, she instantly rose up and departed, without saying another word. This interview agitated Anne, and threw her into a dangerous fever, from which she had nothing like recovered, when the arrest of Marlborough filled her with fresh terrors, which were augmented by reports, that she herself would shortly be arrested. On this subject she wrote the following letter to Lady Marlborough, who had left Anne, to afford her husband, the Duke, all possible assistance.

"I hear Lord Marlborough is sent to the Tower; and though I am certain they have nothing against him, and expected by your letter it would be so, yet I was struck when I was told it; for methinks it is a dismal thing to have one's friends sent to that place. I have a thousand melancholy thoughts, and cannot help fearing they should hinder you from coming to me; though how they can do that without making you a prisoner, I cannot imagine. I am just told by pretty good hands, that as soon as the wind turns westerly, there will be a guard set upon the Prince and me. If you hear there is any such thing designed, and that 'tis easy to you, pray let me see you before the wind changes; for afterwards one does not know whether they will let one have opportunities of speaking to one another. But let them do what they please, nothing shall ever vex me, so I can have the satisfaction of seeing dear Mrs. Freeman; and I swear I would live on bread and water, between four walls, with her without repining; for as long as you continue kind, nothing can ever be a real mortification to your faithful Mrs. Morley,* who wishes she may never enjoy a moment's happiness, in this world or the next, if ever she proves false to you."

"Whether the hint which the Princess conveys, of a design to place her and her consort under restraint, was an effect of mere rumour; or whether William was unwilling to hazard so decisive a measure, we cannot ascertain. But the Princess suffered no other mortification than the imprisonment of her zealous adherent, and the loss of the honour attached to her high station."

On the twentieth of May Anne wrote to Mary that she had recovered, and was going abroad, but although her duty and inclination urged her to pay an early visit to her Majesty, she feared hard constructions would be put upon her respectful intentions, which would be a great affliction to her, although whatever reason she had in her own mind to complain of harsh treatment, *she would strive*

* The origin of these nomenclatures has already been explained at page 852.

to hide it as much as possible. This letter the Bishop of Worcester conveyed to the Queen, and in a written reply, Mary remarked, "It is not my fault that we live at this distance; I have shown my willingness to do otherwise and will do no more; you know what I require of you; I cannot change my mind, but expect to be complied with; if you don't do this, I can neither show you kindness, nor put any other construction upon your actions than what all the world must do that sees them."

Anne's deceitful policy in writing the above billet to the Queen, she herself unveils in the letter she wrote to her confidant, Lady Marlborough, two days afterwards, in which the following passages occur: "Being now at liberty to go where I please, by the Quen's refusing to see me, I am mightily inclined to go to-morrow after dinner to the Cock-pit, and from thence, privately in a chair, to see you. The Bishop of Worcester brought me the Queen's letter early this morning, and by that letter he said, 'he did not seem so well satisfied with her as he was yesterday.' He has promised to bear me witness, that I have made all the advances that were reasonable, and I confess, I think, the more it is told about, that I would have waited on the Queen, but that she refused me, it is the better, and therefore I will not scruple saying it to anybody, when it comes in my way. Dear Mrs. Freeman, I hope in Christ you will never think more of leaving me, for I would be sacrificed to do you the least service, and nothing but death can ever make me part with you."

Such was the disgraceful duplicity practised by Anne in the spring of 1692; and as the summer advanced, Mary mortified her by announcing that henceforward those lords and ladies who persisted in visiting the Princess of Denmark would not be received at Court; and when she went to Bath, for the benefit of her health, she commanded the mayor and aldermen of that city to pay her neither respect nor ceremony. In revenge, Anne took Marlborough into her household immediately he was released from imprisonment; and although, at the instigation of her Majesty, fresh efforts were made to remove him and his haughty Countess from the presence of the heiress-presumptive of the crown, they signally failed, and Lady Marlborough, who during her husband's incarceration had prudently retired from Berkley House, continued to reside with Anne, as heretofore. When King William returned in September, from the campaign in Flanders, Prince George of Denmark sent him a compliment, as it was called, setting forth "that he and his wife having received many marks of the Queen's displeasure, he scarcely knew whether he should give offence by waiting on his Majesty, as usual." Their Majesties sent no reply to this unsavoury compliment, but the next day they dispatched a verbal command forbidding the text to be placed in Anne's pew in church, as usual; however, Dr. Birch, the clergyman, refused to comply, without a written mandate: this was not sent, and the Princess, greatly to the exultation of herself and her haughty favourite, retained possession of her text, at the newly-built church of St. James's.

From this period, a settled enmity subsisted between the royal sisters: Mary, it is true, took great notice of her nephew, the young Duke of Gloucester, but every kindness showered on the youthful Duke was accompanied by some signal insult to his mother. In December, 1694, when Queen Mary was on her death-bed, Anne made strenuous, but futile efforts to become reconciled to her. The Princess, who at the time was herself suffering from dropsical maladies, which confined her to the house, sent a kind message, imploring her Majesty's permission to wait upon her. This was only answered by the following formal note from Lady Derby, her Majesty's first lady, to the lady of Anne.

"Madam,

"I am commanded by the King and Queen to tell you, they desire you would let the Princess know, they both thank her for sending and desiring to come, but it being thought so necessary to keep the Queen as quiet as possible, hope she will defer it.

"I am, madam, your Ladyship's most humble servant, E. Derby."

"PS. Pray, madam, present my humble duty to the Princess."

"Hitherto," says the Countess of Marlborough, "Lady Derby had behaved with marked insolence to Anne, therefore, the politeness of this postcript made us conclude, more than if the whole College of Physicians had pronounced it, that the Queen's disease was mortal. We could gain no certain intelligence, as there was no regular communication between Kensington Palace and Berkley House, which kept us in horrible snspense." However, two days afterwards, Anne dispatched Lady Fitzharding, who entered Kensington Palace, broke into the presence of the dying Mary, and in a pathetic speech, assured her that the Princess, her sister, was much concerned for her illness, and if allowed the happiness of waiting on her, would, notwithstanding the condition she was in, run any risk for her Majesty's satisfaction. To this appeal the queen coolly answered, "Thanks;" and two days afterwards she died, without seeing, or even expressing a wish to see her sister Anne, who on receiving the mournful tidings, cried like a child.

"The death of the Queen placed William in a new and critical situation. Many had begun to suggest doubts of her right to the crown, and some even argued, that as the Parliament had been summoned in the joint names of the King and Queen, it was dissolved by the death of either. Had the Princess abetted these objections, she might doubtless have created much confusion in the state, and formed a party dangerous to the authority of the King. But instead of testifying the slightest wish to question his right, she made an affectionate appeal to his feelings, in a letter of condolence, expressing extreme concern at having incurred the displeasure of the deceased Queen, and declaring her readiness to wait on him, and give proofs of respect for his person, and zeal for his interest.

"At the moment when this spontaneous overture had produced its effect, Lord Somers, who had long regretted the feuds in the royal family, repaired to the palace of Kensington. He found the King sitting at the end of his closet, in an agony of grief, more acute than seemed consonant to his phlegmatic temper. Absorbed in reflection, William took no notice of the intrusion till Somers himself broke silence, by proposing to terminate the unhappy difference with the Princess. The King replied, 'My lord, do what you will; I can think of no business!' To a repetition of the proposal the same answer was returned. By the agency of Somers an interview was accordingly arranged, in which the King received the Princess with cordiality, and informed her that the palace of St. James's should be appropriated for her future residence." *

The demise of Queen Mary greatly exalted the fortunes of Anne. The Duke of Shrewsbury, in a letter to Admiral Russell, remarks, "Since the death of Queen Mary, and the reconciliation between the Princess Anne and King William, the Court of the Princess is as much crowded as it was before deserted: she has omitted no opportunity to show her zeal for his Majesty and his government, and our friend Marlborough, who has no small credit with her, seems very resolved to contribute to the continuance of this union."

Another noble correspondent remarks, in February, 1695, "Her Royal Highness the Princess of Denmark, and also her husband the Prince, have received visits of condolence for the death of Queen Mary, from all the foreign ambassadors and envoys in London." But withal, Anne continued to carry on a deceptive correspondence with her exiled father, at St. Germains, who fathomed her duplicity, and in his journal remarked, "The Princess Anne, notwithstanding her professions, and late repentance, appears now to be more satisfied that the Prince of Orange (King William) should remain, though he had used her ill, and usurped on her rights, than that her father, who had always cherished her beyond expression, should be restored: but his own children have lost all bowels of compassion and duty for him."

In the autumn of 1695, William, on

* Coxe.

returning from Holland, where he usually passed the summer months, insulted Anne by neglecting to answer her congratulatory address on his military successes in Flanders; (he had taken Namur, and performed other martial exploits;) and treating her with marked disrespect, when she attended his drawing-rooms; conduct which may be accounted for by the fact that the Commons, instigated by the Princess, had forced his Majesty to revoke the unconstitutional grant of the principality of Wales, which he had just previously made to his Dutch favourite Bentinck, and to which Anne believed her beloved son, the Duke of Gloucester, was alone entitled. His Majesty's marked insolence to the apparent successor to his crown, excited against him such audible murmurs from the people, the nobles, and even his own English attendants at Court, that he soon found it expedient to desist from such unpopular proceedings. Accordingly, at the commencement of 1695, he caused all proper respect and ceremony to be paid to the exalted birth and rank of his English sister-in-law, gave her possession of St. James's Palace as a town residence, and Windsor Castle for a summer retreat, and conferred the Order of the Garter on her son, the Duke of Gloucester. Besides making these concessions, the Orange King conciliated the whole of her party, and conferred marks of royal favour on its chief, the Duke of Ormond, and even on several others, who had, he was aware, lately sent proffers of loyalty to James II. "Indeed," remarks Cox, "William seems to have discovered that the extensive correspondence, which in the preceding period of his reign had been maintained with the exiled family, arose, in most instances, rather from fear, selfishness, or ingratitude, than from disaffection; and in proportion as his throne became more stable, his subjects appeared less hesitating in their allegiance. Hence at different times he employed many of those whom he knew to have been implicated in such an intercourse, and found no cause to repent of his confidence. It was probably from the same motive that he at length consigned to Marlborough an employment of the highest trust.

"As it was now deemed proper to form a separate establishment for the young Duke of Gloucester, presumptive heir to the throne, the Princess, his mother was anxious that the charge of his person should be confided to a nobleman so high in her esteem, and so accomplished, as the Earl of Marlborough. Her inclinations were perfectly in unison with the public voice. But the King was at first averse to the appointment, and at one time proposed to fill the offices in the new establishment without consulting her wishes. With a view of excluding Marlborough, he offered the post of governor to the Duke of Shrewsbury, who, from ill health, was then soliciting permission to relinquish the fatiguing office of Secretary of State. The Duke declining the appointment, William remained in suspense, from dislike of Marlborough, and the difficulty of selecting a person who, with equal merit, was less obnoxious. At length his repugnance was overcome by the representations of Lord Sunderland, the suggestions of the new favourite, Lord Albemarle, who had recently supplanted Portland, the recommendation of the Tories, who were rising in influence, and the dread of being obliged to consign the Prince to a nobleman of so froward a temper as Lord Rochester, whose cause was espoused by the violent members of his party. Having taken his resolution, he conferred the office on Marlborough in the most gracious manner; and delivered the young Prince into his care with a compliment of unusual warmth: 'Teach him,' he said, 'to be like yourself, and he will not want accomplishments.'

"The coadjutor of Marlborough in the office of preceptor was the celebrated Dr. Burnet, Bishop of Salisbury, who [although scarcely fitted for the post] was [for the part he had taken in the Revolution] entitled to the confidence of the King. The governor and preceptor indeed differed widely in political principles, for the Bishop was distinguished by his attachment to the Whig cause; but this diversity of sentiment created no discordance in the fulfilment of their important duties. [They made an outward profession of mutual] esteem and respect, and their public connexion became the foundation of a friendship [at least of interests] which lasted through life.

"After making so great a sacrifice in the choice of a governor, William became less scrupulous in inferior regulations. Except the nomination of Burnet, as the preceptor, against the wish of the Princess, who disliked his political principles, the King seems to have left to her, or rather to Marlborough, the selection of the different attendants who were placed about the person of his nephew.

"The very evening of his appointment, Marlborough was restored to his place in the privy council, and to his military rank and employments. In the course of the two succeeding years he was also named one of the lords justices, who were intrusted with the government during the absence of the King.

"The appointment of Bishop Burnet gave great offence to the violent Tories, and they were little more satisfied with that of Marlborough, in whose post they were anxious to place the Earl of Rochester, uncle to the young Prince. But their motion, made in parliament, for an address to remove Bishop Burnet, in consequence of the censure passed by the House of Commons on his Country and Pastoral Letter, which had been ordered to be burnt by the common executioner, was repelled by a great majority.

"Trained up under a governor so accomplished, and under so learned and skilful a preceptor, the young Prince rapidly improved in personal and mental acquirements; and gave the most promising indications of virtues and qualities which were likely to adorn a crown. But like the Marcellus of Rome, he was shown to an anxious country, only to be admired and regretted. In the dawn of youth, amidst the vows and prayers of his destined subjects, he was hurried to a premature grave.

"Lord and Lady Marlborough were at Althorpe when he was first seized; but the progress of the fatal disorder was so rapid, that the afflicted governor arrived at Windsor only in time to receive the dying breath of his royal charge, who expired on the thirtieth of July, 1700, aged eleven years and five days."

The unfortunate young Prince had been delicate from his birth, and suffered from water on the brain. He was an exceedingly precocious child: when seven years old he understood the terms of fortification and navigation, and could marshal a company of boys, who had voluntarily enlisted themselves to attend him. The following is Bishop Kennet's account of his mortal illness:—

"The death of the Duke of Gloucester was in a great measure occasioned by the over-heating of himself in the solemn observance of his birth-day, Wednesday, the twenty-fourth of July, 1700. After the ceremony was over, his highness found himself fatigued and indisposed. The next day he complained of his throat, and of a sickness in his stomach. All Friday he was hot and feverish. On Saturday morning, after being bled, he thought himself a little better; but in the evening, his fever appearing more violent, a blister was applied to him, and other remedies administered. The same day a rash appeared in his skin, which increasing, on Sunday more blisters were laid on; in the afternoon, the fever growing stronger, his highness went into a delirium, which lasted with his life. He passed the night as he did the preceding, in short, broken sleep and incoherent talk. On Monday the blisters having taken effect, and the pulse mending, the physicians that attended him thought it probable his highness might recover; but about eleven at night, he was on the sudden seized with a difficult breathing, and could swallow nothing down, insomuch that he expired before midnight."

The body of the young Prince was solemnly interred on the ninth of August, in Westminster Abbey. The Princess Anne, who a few months previously had brought into the world an infant, that had died shortly after its birth, was now childless; her bereavement she attributed to Providence, as a judgment for her unfilial conduct, and she so wrote to her father, in a sorrowful, penitential letter, detailing the mournful event. Secretly as Anne dispatched this letter, its arrival at St. Germain's became known to William, who was then in Holland, and so exasperated him against her, that he did not choose to reply to the letter which Marlborough dispatched to him, announcing the death of the young Prince, till October, when, without a single expression of condolence or sympathy to the sorrowing parents, he wrote to Marlborough :—"Loo, October the fourth, 1700. I do not think it necessary to employ many words in expressing my surprise and grief at the death of the Duke of Gloucester. It is so great a loss to me, as well as to all England, that it pierces my heart with affliction."

King William returned to England on the eighteenth of October, and the visits he exchanged with the Prince and Princess of Denmark, in the winter of 1700-1, were more formal than friendly. He detested Anne and her husband, and a desire to exclude her from the succession, induced him at this period to renew the offer made at the peace of Ryswick, of adopting James II.'s son, afterwards known as the "Pretender," as his successor. An offer which was firmly rejected, but which at the time became public, caused great excitement amongst the people, and was significantly alluded to in the subjoined Whig effusion, by the venal Tom D'Urfey :—

"Strange news ! strange news ! the Jacks* of the city
Have got," cried Joan, "but we mind not tales ;
That our good King, through wonderful pity,
Will leave his crown to the Prince of Wales,
That peace may be the stronger still,
And that they no longer may rebel."

"Pish ! 'tis a jest!" cried Gillian of Croydon,
Gillian, fair Gillian, bright Gillian of Croydon ;
"Take off your glass!" cries Gillian of Croydon,
"Here's a health to our master's will."

Anne had laid aside her mourning for her only child but a short time, when news of the death of her ill-used father* reached England. Instantly she and her husband resumed their sables; William, also, went into black for his departed uncle ; the Queen Dowager did so likewise; and, in fact, strange as it may seem, the mourning for the exiled James II. became general throughout England. Whether Anne answered the letter from Maria Beatrix, imparting to her her father's forgiveness, blessing, and dying charge, enjoining her to cease injuring her brother—him known in general history as the Pretender—cannot be stated for certainty; although hitherto research has failed to discover any such document.

The next event of importance to Anne was the death of William III. From the day when he heard of the death of James II., William's health rapidly declined. His infirmities were so much increased by anxiety of mind, and embarrassments abroad, that during the summer of 1701 he had repeatedly prognosticated to his friends his approaching dissolution. His death was accelerated by an accidental fall from his horse, Sorrel, at Hampton Court. "Supported by the energy of his mind, his constitution struggled for several weeks against the progress of decay, and his dissolution was suspended by Providence, till he had caused the Parliament to pass an Act of Attainder against the pretended Prince of Wales; followed by another for the abjuration of the pretended Prince, for the secu-

* Jacobites. The above trashy lay was sung to the popular old English tune of "Gillian of Croydon." This Gillian, it is supposed, was a beautiful hostess of Croydon, in the time of Henry VIII.

* In a letter detailing the death of James, and addressed by * * * * to the Rev. Francis Roper, occur the following remarks:—"When he (James II.) was sure and sensible of his condition, he desired and did receive the sacrament. As a preparatory to it, he asked pardon of all whom he might have in any way injured ; at the same time he forgave all the world, the Emperor the P. of O. (William III.), his daughter (the Princess Anne), and every one of his subjects who had designedly contrived and contributed to his harms and misfortunes. You see, Sir, he dyes with the same resignation and tranquillity that he lived. Yet when one looks backe on the misfortunes of this afflicted Prince, his life, and the piety of his death, he can hardly forbeare to thinke that he deserved a more favourable fortune, or refuse him a compassion which may not be safe to expresse here."

rity of his Majesty's person, and the person of the Princess of Denmark, and the succession to the crown in the Protestant line. When the bill of abjuration was presented to William for signature, his hand was too feeble to perform its office, and he stamped his name to it a few hours before he breathed his last." The day before he died, Anne sent a polite message, earnestly entreating to see him; but he sternly answered—"No." And to the Prince of Denmark, who made many attempts to enter his presence, he sent the same rude reply.

He expired in the arms of his page, Sewel, at eight o'clock on the morning of Sunday, the eighth of March, 1702, in the fifty-second year of his age, and the fourteenth of his reign. At midnight, on Sunday, the twelfth of April, his remains were interred with regal, but not imposing obsequies, by the side of his consort, Mary II., in Westminster Abbey.

At this period the Jacobites and the discontented revolutionists were in mourning for James the Second, and the Whigs, in compliance with the Lord Chamberlain's proclamation, went into deep black for William III., which so enraged a rhyming Jacobite, that he wrote—

"In sable weeds your beaux and belles appear,
And cloud the evening beauties of the year.
Mourn on, ye foolish, fashionable things,
Mourn for your own misfortunes—not the King's;
Mourn for the mighty mass of coin misspent,
Most prodigally given, and idly spent;
Mourn for your tapestry, and your statues too,
Our Windsor gutted to adorn his Loo;
Mourn for the mitre, long from Scotland gone,
And much more mourn your union coming on;
Mourn for the ten years' war and dismal weather,
And taxes strung like necklaces together,
On salt, malt, paper, cyder, lights, and leather;
Much for the civil list need not be said,
They truly mourn who are fifteen months unpaid.
Well, then, my friends, since things you see are so,
Let's e'en mourn on; 'twould lessen much our woe,
Had Sorrel stumbled thirteen years ago;
Your sea has oft run purple to the shore,
And Flanders been manured with English gore!"

At the time of William's death, the nation was making preparation for war with France and Spain, a state of things which was thus brought about. On the death of James II., his son's pretensions to the crown of England were supported by Louis XIV., which so exasperated William, that he entered into an alliance with Holland and the Emperor, to cripple the power of France, and to seize upon Spain, and partition it between them; an unjust measure, which was strongly opposed by the parliament of England, and which formed the precedent for the partition of unhappy Poland.

CHAPTER III.

Anne's accession and coronation—She confers favours and high honours on the Marlboroughs and their friends—Declares war against France and Spain—Abolishes the selling of places in the royal household—Establishes "Queen Anne's Bounty"—Makes a progress to Bath—Disguises her revulsion of sentiment towards Lady Marlborough—Confers a dukedom on Marlborough—Secures a permanent revenue on her husband, Prince George of Denmark—Consoles the Duchess of Marlborough on the death of her son—Siege of Bons—The great storm—Bishop Ken—The Archduke Charles visits Anne—She touches for the King's-evil—Birth-day solemnization—Convocation—Occasional conformity bill—Anne enslaved by the Marlboroughs—Returns thanks at St. Paul's for the victory of Blenheim—The Tories offend her by inviting the Electress Sophia to England—She gives her confidence to the Marlborough party and the Whigs.

HROUGHOUT the last night of William's existence, the Princess Anne and her favourite, Lady Marlborough, anxiously awaited at the palace of St. James's the news of the event, which would render the former a queen, and the latter an imperious dictator of England's majesty. Bishop Burnet was the first to bring Anne the news of King William's death; yet, for his officious efforts to gain the advantage over the Earl of Essex, then lord of the bedchamber in waiting, whose proper office it was to communicate the event, " he was turned out of his lodgings at court, and met with several affronts."

On the morning of her accession to the throne, and a bright summer morning it was, Anne held a private levee at St. James's; to this levee the leading courtiers and politicians hastened in crowds; amongst them was Anne's uncle, the unflinching Earl of Clarendon, who, as he refused to swear allegiance to her as his sovereign, and declared that he had only come to talk to her—in fact, to remind her of the promise that she made to her father after the death of her son, that if ever she came to the crown, she would only accept it in trust for her brother, whose restoration she would endeavour by all the means in her power to effect—he was refused admittance to her presence.

Although the day of her Majesty's accession was Sunday, on that day the privy council formally hailed her as their Sovereign; and both houses of parliament met, and after displaying their loyalty in lengthy speeches, they in the evening, and in two separate bodies, presented the Queen with congratulatory addresses. She answered them with remarkable dignity and grace, and about three in the afternoon of this eventful Sunday, was proclaimed Queen of England, Ireland, and *France*, in the cities of London and Westminster, amidst the loud acclamations of the excited populace.

"At the time of the Queen's accession," remarks Coxe, " the doubts she had formerly entertained were suppressed by the change of circumstances, or (what is most in accordance with facts brought to light by modern research) the brilliant prospect which opened to her view. The recent death of her father relieved her from the scruples which (latterly) she had felt at his seclusion; and the disputed legitimacy of her brother, induced her to acquiesce in the arrangements of the legislature; for even if he was not supposititious, she persuaded herself that he was disqualified by his religious principles, and that her assumption of the crown was necessary to secure the existence of the Established Church." "When I saw she had such a partiality to those that I knew to be Jacobites," observes the Countess of Marlborough, "I asked her whether she had a mind to give up her crown? for if it had been her conscience not to wear it, I do solemnly protest I would not have disturbed her, or struggled as I did. But she told me she was not sure that the *Prince of Wales* was her brother, and that it was not practicable for him to come here without ruin to the religion and country."

Her Majesty opened parliament in state on the eleventh of March, and in a speech delivered with a graceful, winning expression, peculiar to herself, observed, "As I know my own heart to be entirely English, I can very sincerely assure you, there is not anything you can expect or desire from me, which I shall not be ready to do for the happiness and prosperity of England; and you shall always find me a strict and religious observer of my word."

Scotland still being a distinct kingdom, Anne was not proclaimed Queen there till the thirteenth of March. She first exercised her regnal authority by nominating her husband, Prince George of Denmark, generalissimo of the army and lord high admiral. Being regarded only as a subject, the Prince continued to occupy a seat in the House of Lords, with precedence before all other peers, in the quality of Duke of Cumberland, a honour and title conferred on him at the coronation of William and Mary.

"Three days after her accession, her Majesty nominated the Duke of Marlborough knight of the garter; and on the ensuing day he was appointed general of the British forces at home and abroad; and shortly afterwards, master of the horse. His countess was also made groom of the stole, mistress of the robes, and keeper of the privy purse."

The Commons settled upon Anne, for life, the like sum which they had granted to his late Majesty, William III.; and on the thirtieth of March she went in state to parliament, to give her assent to this bill, and in a speech from the throne declared, "That she would straiten herself in her own expenses, rather than not contribute all she could to her subjects' ease and relief; and as the revenue would probably fall short of what it formerly produced, she would give directions that £100,000 be applied to the public service, in the present year, out of the revenue they had so unanimously given her." An act of politic generosity, which gave universal satisfaction to the parliament and the nation at large.

In the months of March and April, Anne received visits of condolence on the death of William III., and congratulations on her own accession, from all the ambassadors and envoys in England; and the bishops, the clergy, the city of London, and all the counties, cities, and corporate bodies, presented her addresses on the same subject. The twenty-third of April (being St. George's Day), 1702, was appointed for her Majesty's coronation. At eleven in the morning of that day, Anne, who at the time was disabled from walking, by an attack of gout, went privately in a sedan-chair from St. James's Palace to the Court of Wards, where she remained till the nobles, who took part in the imposing ceremonials, were duly marshalled, when she proceeded in procession to Westminster Hall; and after being robed, took her seat under the canopy, by the side of the table on which the regalia were placed. Immediately these were duly distributed to their appointed bearers, the procession moved forward, through Palace Yard, along by the Broad Sanctuary, and so into the Abbey by the west door. "The Queen," says Boyer, "was carried in an open chair by the Broad Sanctuary, the houses on both sides being crowded with spectators, who made the welkin ring with shouts of joy, as her Majesty passed by." Her train was borne by the Duchess of Somerset, Lady Elizabeth Seymour, Lady Mary Hyde, and Lady Mary Pierrepoint, afterwards the distinguished authoress, Lady Mary Wortley Montague. The ceremonial of the coronation did not materially differ from the precedents previously detailed in this work, and therefore need not be repeated in this place. The primate performed the recognition, by presenting the Queen to the brilliant assembly, and loudly exclaiming, "Sirs, I here present unto you Queen Anne, undoubted Queen of this realm. Whereas, all you that are come this day to do your homage and service, are you willing to do the same?" "God save Queen Anne!" shouted the noble assembly again and again, in reply; and then the trumpets sounded, and the choir chaunted the anthem, commencing, "The Queen shall rejoice in thy strength, O Lord!"

After the sermon, which was preached by the Archbishop of York, Tennison, Archbishop of Canterbury, read the following declaration, which Anne at the same time repeated, and afterwards subscribed: "I, Anne, by the grace of God, Queen of England, Scotland, France, and Ireland, Defender of the Faith, &c.; do solemnly, in the presence of God, profess, testify, and declare, that I do believe, that in the sacrament of the Lord's Supper there is not any transubstantiation of the elements of bread and wine into the body and blood of Christ, at or after the consecration thereof, by any person whatsoever.—Secondly. That the invocation or adoration of the Virgin Mary, or any other saint, and the sacrifice of the mass, as they are now used in the church of Rome, are superstitious and idolatrous.—Thirdly. And I do solemnly, in the presence of God, profess, testify, and declare, that I do make this declaration, and every part thereof, in the plain and ordinary sense of the words read to me, as they are commonly understood by English Protestants, without any evasion, equivocation, or mental reservation whatsoever, and without any dispensation already granted me for this purpose by the Pope, or any other authority or person, or without any hope of such dispensations from any person or authority whatever, or without thinking I am or can be acquitted before God or man, or absolved of this declaration or of any part thereof, although the Pope, or any other person or power whatsoever, should dispense with or annul the same, or declare that it was null and void from the beginning."

When her Majesty had signed this declaration, Tennison, in a loud, clear voice, demanded, "Is your Majesty willing to take the coronation oath?"

"I am willing," responded the Queen.

"Will you solemnly promise and swear to govern the people of this kingdom, and the dominions thereto belonging, according to the statutes of parliament agreed on, and the laws and customs of the same?"

"I solemnly promise so to do."

"Will you, to your power, cause law and justice in mercy to be executed in all your judgments?"

"I will."

"Will you, to the utmost of your power, maintain the laws of God, the true profession of the Gospel, and the Protestant reformed religion, established by law; and will you preserve unto the bishops and clergy of this realm, and to the churches committed to their charge, all such rights and privileges as by law do or shall appertain to them any of them?"

"All this I promise to do."

The Queen then went to the altar, knelt on the steps, and with her right hand upon the great Bible, said, "The things which I have here before promised, I will perform and keep, so help me God."

Having kissed the book, her Majesty returned to her seat, the choir sung "Veni Creator," and the Archbishop solemnly anointed and crowned her; which ceremonies completed, the Archbishop blessed her, in these words :—

"The Lord bless and keep you; the Lord make the light of his countenance to shine upon you, and be gracious to you: the Lord protect you in all your ways, and preserve you from every evil thing: the Lord prosper the works of your own hands upon you: the Lord prosper your handy work."

"Amen!" loudly responded the assembled peers and prelates.

"May all the blessings of heaven and earth plenteously descend upon you: the Lord give you of the dew of heaven and the fatness of the earth, a fruitful country and healthful seasons, a faithful senate, and a quiet empire, wise counsellors, and victorious armies; a loyal nobility, a dutiful gentry, and an honest, peaceable, and obedient commonalty."

To which the assembly responded, "Amen!"

"The Lord preserve your life, and establish your throne, that your reign may be prosperous and your days many; that you may live long in this world, obeyed and honoured and beloved by your people, ever increasing in favour both with God and man, and leave a numerous posterity to rule these kingdoms after you, by succession, in all ages."

"Amen!" was again uttered by the assembled peers and prelates, who then offered their homage, by "seemingly" kissing her Majesty's left cheek, and touching her crown; and as a conclusion to the coronation ceremonies, the final anthem was chaunted, the royal pardon read, the coronation medals distributed, and lastly, the trumpets sounded, and the people, with long and repeated shouts, that made the roof of the Abbey quiver, cried, "Long live Queen Anne! God bless her Majesty!"

After the Queen had been formally divested of her consecrated regalia, and had offered them at the shrine of St. Edward, she assumed her state crown and purple robes, and passing in procession to Westminster Hall, partook of the coronation banquet, which proceeded according to established custom, and was unmarked by any blunder, accident, or misfortune. At half-past eight the banquet terminated; and Anne, exhausted with the duties of the day, privately returned, in a close sedan chair, to St. James's Palace where, immediately she could prevail on her husband, Prince George, to put an end to the carouse in which he and his private friends were indulging, she retired to rest. The coronation gave great satisfaction to the people, who testified their joy by illuminations, ringing of bells, loyal feasts, and drinking bouts, and other entertainments usual on such occasions.

The Countess of Marlborough now ruled as supremely over the Queen as her Majesty did over the people. Amongst other proofs of regard, Anne, recollecting that in their excursions through Windsor Park the Countess had repeatedly admired the situation of the great lodge, seized the earliest opportunity of offering her the rangership, to which that lodge was attached. In one of her familiar notes, after alluding to Lord Portland, who had been ranger under the late King, and detested the Countess, she added, "Mentioning this worthy person puts me in mind to ask dear Mrs. Freeman a question which I would have done some time ago; and that is, if you would have the lodge for your life, because the warrant must be made out accordingly; and anything that is so much satisfaction as this poor place seems to be to you, I would give dear Mrs. Freeman for all her days, which I pray God may be as many and as truly happy as this world can make you." The Countess gratefully accepted this offer, embellished the lodge at a great expense, and it became her favourite residence.

"Similar proofs of favour flowed on those who were connected with Marlborough and his lady by blood or friendship. Lady Harriet Godolphin and Lady Spencer, their two daughters, were nominated ladies of the bedchamber. The Sunderland family also felt the beneficial effects of their powerful interest. At the particular intercession of the Countess, Robert, Earl of Sunderland, obtained the renewal of the annual pension of £2,000, which had been granted him by the late King, together with the payment of the arrears since its suspension. The exertion of the same interest, together with Marlborough's, obtained for Lord Godolphin the title and privileges of lord high treasurer. The principles of Marlborough and Godolphin indirectly influenced the character of the administration formed under their auspices. As they were both moderate Tories, and as the Whig partialities of the Countess were either not yet developed, or not allowed to operate, the Queen was left to consult her own private inclinations and private antipathies in the choice of a ministry, from which the Whigs were mostly excluded. Even the Privy Council was purged of the obnoxious party; for the names of the distinguished Whig leaders, Halifax, Somers, and Orford, found no place in the list announced by the new Sovereign. Not satisfied with monopolising the higher posts of the state and the law, the Tories were anxious to exclude their political antagonists even from the subordinate office of justice of the peace. In this view, however, they were thwarted by the moderate counsels of Marlborough and Godolphin, who would not suffer them to indulge their party antipathies to the full extent.

"As Anne was deeply imbued with the prejudices of the Tories against foreign connexions, and as the natural timidity of her sex inclined her to peace, nothing but the dangers which encompassed her throne could have urged her to adopt the same vigorous policy and the same hostility against France which had marked the reign of her predecessor. Indeed, her situation admitted of neither deliberation nor delay. The power of Louis, which had been rapidly augmented by a long and successful career of violence and craft, had now attained its utmost height. The occupation of the towns and countries on the Upper Rhine opened the way for the invasion of Southern Germany; while the vast preponderance which he had acquired by placing his grandson on the Spanish throne, with the possession of the Netherlands, the Milanese, and other dependencies, rendered him the arbiter of Europe. With such a formidable power to contend against, the Dutch, who yet trembled at the recollection of the recent invasion, and who had purchased the liberation of their captive troops by acknowledging Philip, had no hope of preserving their independence but by the succour and support of England. The Emperor, notwithstanding the temporary success of his arms in Italy, was embarrassed by the rising rebellion in Hungary; and found himself engaged in a contest manifestly unequal, and apparently hopeless, unless he was aided by the maritime powers. The Duke of Savoy, hemmed in by the territories of the Bourbon Princes, was reduced to a state of vassalage under France, and could entertain no hope of deliverance, unless Austria was enabled to extend its acquisitions in Italy.

"Such being the circumstances of those powers, whose position or military force might enable them to make head against the aggressions of France, there seemed little prospect that the states of the Continent would succeed in repelling the common danger. It was obvious that if Louis could even for a short period attach the Dutch to his interest, or render them passive, and paralyse Austria, he would profit by his vast resources and commanding attitude, to restore the dependent family of Stuart to the British throne, and thus secure the only country which could resist his career of ambition. Therefore, on the fourth of May, in conformity with the promise to the States and Austria, a declaration of hostilities was issued against France and Spain; and the oath of abjuration was taken by the members of both Houses, and the name of the Princess Sophia was introduced in the public prayers for the royal family, as next in succession to the crown."

Two of Anne's acts on her accession are highly praiseworthy. She, by order in council, abolished the corrupt practice of selling places in the royal household, and by remitting the first-fruits and tenths of the Church, which she might lawfully have appropriated, established the fund known as "Queen Anne's Bounty," for the augmentation of the livings of the poorer clergy. This summer Prince George suffered severely from asthma, and by the advice of his physicians, her Majesty resolved to accompany him on a progress to Bath. The Queen and Prince set out from Windsor on the twenty-fifth of August; the same evening they reached Oxford, where, after Prince George had been entertained at a sumptuous supper in Christ Church, they rested for the night. The day following, her Majesty visited the University, where she listened with evident satisfaction to a loyal oration delivered by the University orator; was entertained by a concert of music; partook of the banquet provided for the occasion; and graciously accepted the usual presents of a Bible and Prayer-book, and a pair of Woodstock gloves. From Oxford the Queen and Prince took coach to Cirencester, passed the night there, and the next day reached Bath. The road they journeyed along was crowded by spectators, who greeted them with deafening shouts of loyalty, and on nearing Bath, two hundred maidens, attired as Amazons, and armed with bows and arrows, welcomed he Majesty, and escorted her into the city. The royal party visited Bristol, and after a progress in which her Majesty was everywhere received with enthusiastic loyalty, returned to Windsor, and thence, on the fifteenth of October, the Queen and her husband proceeded to London, and took up their abode at the palace of St James's.

"Although the Queen had hitherto concealed the fact, upon her first coming to the throne," remarks Swift, "Lady Marlborough had lost all favour with her." This revulsion in Anne's sentiments towards her "dear Mrs. Freeman," although unknown to Swift, took place about eighteen months before her accession, and was thus occasioned. One day Anne remarked that she had no gloves on, and sent her maid, Mrs. Hill, to fetch them from the table in an adjoining room, where she remembered she had left them. Mrs. Hill obeyed, and on entering the room, found Lady Marlborough there with the very gloves, which she had evidently placed by mistake on her own hands. When apprised of the fact, the haughty countess turned up her nose, and with an air of supreme disdain, exclaimed loud enough

* Coxe.

for Anne to distinctly hear every word, "What, have I that odious woman's gloves on!" Then hastily pulling them off, and dashing them on the floor, proceeded, "Take them away, take them away! for I detest anything that has even touched that disagreeable woman." A gross personal insult, which Anne kept a profound secret, but never forgot nor forgave. Lady Marlborough, not supposing that her too-indulgent mistress had overheard her needlessly-uttered cruel words, was blind to the fact, that her Majesty began her reign with changed feelings towards her. Anne, with a duplicity for which she was remarkable, disguised her sentiments, that, out of gratitude to the Earl of Marlborough, she might gratify his greedy appetite for wealth and titles. With this view, she, on ascending the throne, paid to her supposed favourites greater attentions, and lavished on them more endearing expressions than heretofore; but that her purport was to ultimately put them away, cannot for a moment be doubted.

When the Queen came to St. James's, on the fifteenth of October, she left her haughty favourite at Windsor, and on the twenty-second of October, two days after opening parliament in person, she wrote to the countess: "It is very uneasy to your poor unfortunate faithful *Morley* [Queen Anne], to think that she has so very little in her power to show you how sensible I am of all Lord Marlborough's kindness, especially when he deserves all that a rich crown could give; but since there is nothing else at this time, I hope you will give me leave, as soon as he comes, to make him a duke. I know that my dear *Mrs. Freeman* [Lady Marlborough] does not care for anything of that kind, nor am I satisfied with it, because it does not enough express the value I have for Mrs. Freeman, nor ever can, how passionately I am yours, my dear Mrs. Freeman."

As in this letter no mention is made of an adequate grant to support so high a dignity (an important omission, which it will be seen her Majesty immediately afterwards supplied), the countess wrote in earnest terms to her husband, urging him to decline this accession of honour; but he answered by requesting her to express his heartfelt gratitude to the Queen for her extraordinary kindness to him.

On Lord Mayor's day, her Majesty and the Prince attended the civic banquet, and five days previously Anne wrote to Lady Marlborough: "Since you have staid so long at Windsor, I wish now, for your own sake, that you will stay till after Lord Mayor's day, for if you are in town, you cannot avoid going to the show; and being in the country, is a just excuse, and I think one would be glad of any, to avoid so troublesome a business. I am at this time in great haste, and therefore can say no more to my dear, dear Mrs. Freeman, but that I am most passionately hers."

This was, doubtless, a diplomatic manœuvre of the Queen's, to encourage her own Tory partizans, by the absence on this occasion of her potent Whig favourite, Lady Marlborough, who had already entered the arena of political intrigue, and when her Majesty resolved to create four new peers, all Tories, actually succeeded in procuring the elevation of a fifth, the Whig Mr. Hervey, against the will of the Tories, who at first declined their titles, if a Whig were to be their companion in honour.

Lord Marlborough returned from Holland in November; and the solicitations of the Queen, and the importunities of Lord Godolphin, having vanquished the reluctance of his haughty countess, he was created Marquis of Blandford and Duke of Marlborough, by letters patent, dated the fourteenth of December, 1702. The Queen, fully sensible that his property was insufficient to maintain so high a dignity, sent a message to the House of Commons, stating that she had created him a duke, and conferred on him £5000 per annum out of the post-office for her own life. She concluded with requesting the house to devise a proper mode for settling this grant on himself and his successors to the title. Contrary to her expectation, the proposal occasioned violent debates; and invidious insinuations were thrown out that Marlborough was endeavouring to monopolise the royal favour. Sir Christopher Musgrave, in particular, said, he did not wish to detract from the duke's eminent services, but he must insist that they had been well rewarded. He concluded with expatiating on the profitable employments which he and his family enjoyed. In consequence of the spirit manifested by the Commons, the duke solicited the Queen to recall her message, lest he should be the cause of obstruction to the public service. She accordingly communicated his request to the house, and withdrew her application; but the predominant party did not omit to make a strong remonstrance against the proposed grant, fraught with the most acrimonious reflections on the memory of King William, and on his profusion towards his foreign favourites. This disappointment only rendered the Queen more anxious to display her gratitude and esteem. The very day on which the remonstrance of the Commons was presented, she imparted to the duchess her design of adding £2000 a year out of the privy purse, to the grant of the £5000 already made during her own life, from the revenue of the Post-office. Notwithstanding the earnest solicitations of the Queen, this liberal offer was respectfully but firmly declined. A disinterestedness which would be entitled to high applause, if the duchess had consistently maintained the same spirit; but in a subsequent part of these memoirs, we shall find that on her disgrace she claimed, and received, the whole pension for the preceding nine years.

From gratitude for the kindness of the Queen, Marlborough and his friends zealously exerted themselves in parliament to promote a measure in which she was personally interested. The first wish of Anne on her accession was, to associate her husband in the regal dignity; but her design being overruled, as unconstitutional, she became more anxious to secure to him a permanent revenue. The proposal was communicated to parliament by a message, requesting the settlement of a farther provision on the Prince of Denmark, in case of his survival. Mr. Howe, member for Gloucestershire, a zealous Tory, moved, on the twenty-first of November, for a grant of £100,000 yearly As the Tories, who formed the majority, were decidedly favourable to this measure, no opposition was made to the grant itself; but objections were urged against a clause annexed to the bill, intended to continue to the Prince the offices already conferred on him during the life of the Queen, by exempting him from the effect of that clause in the act of settlement, by which foreigners were forbidden to hold offices of state, on the accession of the Hanover line.

After a trifling debate, the bill passed the Commons, but in the Lords encountered the most violent opposition. The friends of the Queen strenuously exerted themselves, though they did not prevail without extreme difficulty, and by a majority of only one voice. The gratitude of the Queen for the exertions of Marlborough, appears in one of her letters to the Duchess. "I am sure the Prince's bill passing, after so much struggle, is wholly owing to the pains you and Mrs. Freeman have taken, and I ought to say a great deal to both of you, in return; but neither words nor actions can ever express the true sense Mr. Morley [Prince George of Denmark] and I have for your kindness on this and all other occasions, and therefore I will not say any more on this subject, but that, to my last moment, your dear, unfortunate, faithful Morley, will be most passionately and tenderly yours."*

When death snatched away the Duchess of Marlborough's only son, Lord Blandford,† the Queen, with a shudder of horror, remarked to Mrs. Hill, "that the bereavement of the duchess is a just punishment, for the part she took with me in branding my brother, the Chevalier de St. George, as an impostor; for this I lost my promising heir, the Duke of Gloucester; and for this, heaven has deprived her of hers." Indeed, so fully was Anne impressed with this crime-

* Cox, "Life of Marlborough."

† He died of small-pox, on the twentieth of February, 1703, in the seventeenth year of his age.

accusing conviction, that in a letter of condolence to the sorrowing mother, she darkly hints at the subject. These are her words :—

"THE QUEEN TO THE DUCHESS OF MARLBOROUGH.

"*St. James's.*—It would have been a great satisfaction to your poor unfortunate, faithful Morley, if you would have given me leave to come to St. Alban's, *for the unfortunate ought to come to the unfortunate.* But since you will not have me, I must content myself as well as I can, till I have the happiness of seeing you here. I know nothing worth writing; but if I did, I should not trouble you with it, being sure no sort of news can be agreeable to your dear, heavy heart. God Almighty bless and comfort my dear Mrs. Freeman, and be assured, I will live and die sincerely yours."

Throughout the year 1703, the Queen was compelled to occupy much of her valuable time in slavish efforts to satisfy the arrogance and soothe the petulance of the overbearing Duchess. Gladly would England's Queen Regnant have ridded herself of her domestic tyrant, but she now dared not, for the Duchess was the leader of the Whigs; and the Duke, her husband, was carrying on the war on the Continent with a success that put to shame the previous campaigns of King William III.

After Marlborough's successful siege of Bon, in May, 1703, her Majesty wrote to the Duchess—"It is now so late, that I can only thank you for your letter, and congratulate the Duke of Marlborough's being well after the siege of Bon, which is more pleasing news to me than all the conquests he can make. May God Almighty, that has preserved him hitherto through many dangers, continue to do so, and send him safe home to his and my *dear, dear, adored* Mrs. Freeman."

On the sixteenth and seventeenth of November, England was ravaged by that terrible tempest, known in history as the "Great Storm," accompanied by booming thunder, vivid lightning, and floods of rain: the mighty wind stalked like a giant of destruction over the land, marking its track with death and devastation; its power was such, that whole groves of trees were uprooted and torn limb from limb, hundreds of houses and churches were unroofed, in some instances whole families being crushed to death beneath the ruins of their own dwellings; chimneys and church-steeples were levelled with the dust; the leads of many of the sacred edifices in London were rolled up like scrolls; and at London Bridge the Thames was choked up with the wrecks of boats and barges. The devastation on land was immense; the damage in London alone was estimated at £2,000,000 sterling; hundreds of persons were killed, thousands injured, and the loss in cattle was incalculable; in one level alone 15,000 sheep were drowned. But withal in the harbours and at sea, round the south and west coasts, the loss in shipping and lives was still greater. The Eddystone light-house was destroyed; 8000 persons are supposed to have been drowned in the floods of the Thames and the Severn, and in ships blown from their anchors, and never heard of more; and sixteen men-of-war, with 2,000 men, perished within sight of shore; it was on this hurricane-night of the sixteenth of November,—a night

"Wherein the cub-drawn bear would couch;
The lion, and the belly-pinched wolf
Keep their fur dry,"

rather than endure its horrors;—that Dr. Kidder, Bishop of Bath and Wells, and his lady were killed in bed by the falling of a stack of chimneys at the episcopal palace. Mary II. had introduced the dissenter Kidder into this bishopric, immediately after ejecting from it the venerable Bishop Ken; Ken was a nonjuror, so conscientious that at the Revolution he preferred renouncing the wealth and pomp of the world, to taking the new oath, and, laying down his crosier, retired to poverty, but not idleness, for he continued to perform all the spiritual duties of his diocese; and the people of the west almost adored him, because of his noble and courageous resistance of the slaughters of the monster Kirke, in the Monmouth rebellion, when he saved the lives of hundreds. Anne, on her accession, from a desire to be consecrated by Ken, who was deemed the head of the Reformed Church of England, urged him to resume his pastoral staff and revenues; but he refused to take the oath abjuring her brother, known as the Pretender; and now she offered to restore him to his see, without oath being taken, or question asked. This offer infirmity and old age induced him to decline; and at his request, Dr. Hooper, Dean of Canterbury, was inducted into the Archbishopric of Bath and Wells. After suffering from a torturing malady, the gifted, christian-hearted Bishop Ken expired at Longbeat, the rural seat of Lord Weymouth, on the nineteenth of March, 1711. He was buried at daybreak; and at the close of his obsequies the sun rose in golden glory, and that household morning hymn, "Awake my soul, and with the sun," written by Ken, was sweetly carolled by a chorus of children from the village-school, who had followed him to the grave.

Scarcely had the consternation occasioned by the "Great Storm" subsided, when the Archduke Charles, who on the twelfth of September, 1703, had been declared King of Spain by his father the Emperor, and by the King of the Romans, and whose pretensions Anne supported, whilst on his way to take possession of his kingdom, paid a visit to her Majesty, which is thus chronicled in the London Gazette:—

"St. James's, December 31st, 1703.

"The King of Spain arrived at pithead on the twenty-sixth instant, in the afternoon, and had all possible honours paid to him from the fleet and the town. The next day, the Duke of Somerset, master of the horse, waited on his Majesty on shipboard, with a letter and a compliment from the Queen, acquainting him that she was come to Windsor in order to receive the visit that his Majesty had desired to make to her. The next night he lay at Petworth, whither his Royal Highness [Prince George of Denmark] was come to meet him. The twenty-ninth, about seven o'clock in the evening, the King of Spain arrived at Windsor; the Duke of Northumberland, constable of Windsor Castle, the Duke of St. Albans, captain of the band of Pensioners, and the Marquis of Hartington, captain of the Yeomen of the Guards, received him at his alighting out of the coach, and the Earl of Jersey, lord chamberlain of her Majesty's household, lighted him to the stair-head, where the Queen received him; and after he had made his compliments to her Majesty, acknowledging his great obligations to her, for her generous protection and assistance, he led her Majesty into her bed-chamber; and after a short stay there, his Royal Highness [George of Denmark] conducted his Catholic Majesty to the apartment prepared for him. He supped that night with the Queen, who gave his Majesty the right hand at the table (which he with great difficulty admitted), the Prince [George of Denmark] sitting at the end of the table, on the Queen's side. The next day, his Majesty having noticed that the Queen was coming to make him a visit, he met her at her drawing-room-door, endeavouring to have prevented her; but her Majesty went on to his apartments, from whence he led her Majesty to dinner. This afternoon was spent in entertainments of music, and other diversions. After supper, he would not be satisfied till, after great compliments, he had prevailed with the Duchess of Marlborough to give him the napkin, which he held to her Majesty, when she washed. Supper being over, he led her Majesty to her bed-chamber, where, after some stay, he took his leave of her, resolving to depart next morning, which he did accordingly, and his Royal Highness [George of Denmark] attended him to the coach-side, the King not suffering him to go any farther, by reason of his indisposition. His Majesty went to Petworth this evening, designing to be on shipboard at Spithead to-morrow, to which place the Duke of Somerset was commanded by her Majesty to attend him."

King Charles sailed for Portugal on

the fifth of January, but contrary winds drove him back, and prevented him from reaching Lisbon before the twenty-seventh of February.* On the twenty-first of January, Anne made his visit the subject of an express speech to Parliament, and the next day she addressed the following letter to her Admiral, Sir George Rook:—

"St. James's, January 22nd, 1704.

"Your having represented that the King of Spain seemed desirous upon the first turn of the wind to make the best of his way to Lisbon, with such clean ships as shall be in readiness for that service, and this matter requiring the greatest secrecy, I think it proper to give you orders in my own hand, to pay the same obedience to the King of Spain, as to the time and manner of his setting sail, and as to the number of the ships which shall be in readiness to attend him, as you would do to myself.

"I am your very affectionate friend,

To Sir George Rook. ANNE R."

Early in her reign, Anne, to, if possible, increase the importance and sacredness of her royal person, as the anointed Sovereign of England, and heir of the sainted Edward the Confessor, revived the royal gift of healing by touching for the "King's evil." That this touching for the evil might be performed with due solemnity, a service was inserted in the Liturgy, to be used on the occasion; and whenever her Majesty "touched," she was attended by her great officers, and her chaplains officiated. In the newspapers of the day, occur such entries as the following: "Yesterday the Queen was graciously pleased to touch for the King's evil, some particular persons in private." Again, December the nineteenth: "Yesterday, about twelve at noon, her Majesty was pleased to touch, at St. James's, about twenty persons afflicted with the King's evil. The healing service was imposing; it commenced with a collect, and whilst the Queen was laying her hands upon the sick, who were presented to her one by one, the officiating chaplain turned towards her Majesty, and said, 'God give a blessing to this work, and grant, that those sick persons on whom the Queen lays her hands, may recover, through Jesus Christ, our Lord.' At the conclusion, the chaplain, standing with his face towards those that came to be healed, said,

"'The Almighty God, who is a most strong tower to all them that put their trust in him, to whom all things in heaven, in earth, and under the earth, do bow and obey, be now and evermore your defence, and make you know and feel that there is no other name under heaven given to man, in whom, and through whom, you may receive health and salvation, but only the name of our Lord Jesus Christ.—Amen.

"'The grace of our Lord Jesus Christ, and the love of God, and the fellowship of the Holy Ghost, be with us all evermore.—Amen.'"

Her Majesty's birthday, February the sixth, in 1704 fell on Sunday, and was kept on the Monday following, with unusual solemnity and magnificence. On that day, she, by royal message, formally announced to the Commons, her gift of the first fruits and tenths, for the benefit of the poor clergy; and in the evening she held a brilliant Court, when Dryden's play, "All for Love," was performed at St. James's by "the actors, her Majesty's servants, from the two great theatres."

Queen Anne permitted the sittings of the convocation, or spiritual parliament, which William and Mary had so arbitrarily interrupted. The majority in the upper house of convocation were Whig, or Low Church, and recommended moderation towards the Dissenters; whilst those in the lower house were Tory, or High Church, and attached the highest importance to episcopacy. Between these parties, the Queen aimed to maintain a moderating power; but the violence and virulence of their strife gave her great trouble and anxiety, and increased the excitement occasioned by the repeated efforts to pass the bill against occasional conformity; efforts which repeatedly

* The reader may consult our historians for an account of the struggles for the crown of Spain, which followed. Philip finally remained upon his throne, and Charles III. of Spain became Charles VII. of Germany.

succeeded in the House of Commons, but as often failed in the Lords. The Queen, although affecting indifference, was anxious that the bill for preventing occasional conformity should become law. Prince George of Denmark, himself an occasional conformist to the Church of England, voted for it in the first attempt to pass it through the Lords; but that he afterwards remained neuter, is proved by the following letter from the Queen to the Duchess of Marlborough:—

"I give my dear Mrs. Freeman [the Duchess] many thanks for her long letter, and am truly sensible of the sincere kindness you expressed in it; and in return, to ease your mind, I must tell you, that Mr. Bromley will be disappointed if the Prince George of Denmark does not intend to go to the House, when the bill of [against] occasional conformity is brought in. I think him very much in the right, not to vote for it. I shall not have the worse opinion of any of the lords that are for it; for though I should have been glad if it had not been brought into the House of Commons, because I would not have had any pretence for quarrelling, I can't help thinking, now it is as good as passed there, it will be better for the service to have it pass the House of Lords too. I must aver to you, that I never cared to mention anything on this subject to you, because I knew you would not be of my mind; but since you have given me this occasion, I can't forbear saying that I see nothing like persecution in this bill. You may think it is a notion Lord Nottingham has put into my head, but upon my word, it is my own thought * * * * Nothing shall ever alter your poor unfortunate, faithful Morley, who will live and die with all truth and tenderness yours."

It will be observed, that in this letter her Majesty designates herself "your poor unfortunate, faithful Morley;" and unfortunate she indeed was, in having placed herself in the power of the ambitious, selfish, intriguing duchess. Sarah, that she might the more effectually domineer over her mistress and sovereign, resolved to completely surround her with her own party and creatures. The Marlboroughs hated that great leader of the Tories, Anne's uncle, the Earl of Rochester; and to procure his dismissal, the duchess heaped on him a series of insults, and tormented the Queen into ordering him to repair to Ireland, of which country he was lord-lieutenant. This plan succeeded to admiration; at first Rochester boldly refused to quit the political theatre of London, where he was so prominent a figure; and the order being peremptorily repeated, he resigned in disgust, and from this moment became the leader of the discontented Tories, and the principal mover of opposition.

Notwithstanding the disgrace of Rochester, a similar spirit was manifested by the Earl of Nottingham, secretary of state; the Duke of Buckingham, and the Earl of Jersey, who, supported by a strong phalanx in the House of Commons, strenuously opposed Marlborough's foreign policy, and vehemently pronounced against all the principal offices of state being filled by the Marlboroughs, their relations, and nominees. A schism was thus formed in the administration—clashing interests and discordant views embarrassed the measures of government,* and the intriguing duchess "availed herself of the peevish complaints which her husband, who was at the head of the army abroad, incessantly made against the Tories, and revived the unpleasant discussion which had already arisen on this subject with the Queen, by communicating extracts of his letters, accompanied with remarks of the most acrimonious kind. One letter in particular, in which he had announced his wish to resign, was made the subject of such a commentary, and accompanied with the hint of a similar resolution by Lord Godolphin and herself. The effect which these appeals produced on the

* In the early part of 1704, the Earl of Nottingham, after having ineffectually pressed the Queen to discard the Dukes of Somerset and Devonshire, resigned the seals. The Earl of Jersey and Sir Edward Seymour were dismissed; the Earl of Kent, a moderate Whig, was appointed chamberlain; Mr. Harley speaker of the Commons, secretary of state; and Henry St. John, secretary of war.

Queen appears from one of her answers to the duchess.

"*Windsor, Saturday.*—The thoughts that both my dear Mrs. Freeman and Mr. Freeman seem to have of retiring, give me no small uneasiness, and therefore I must say something on that subject. It is no wonder at all that people in your posts should be weary of the world, who are so continually troubled with all the hurry and impertinences of it; but give me leave to say, that you should consider a little your faithful friends and poor country, which must be ruined if ever you put your melancholy thoughts in execution. As for your poor unfortunate, faithful Morley, she could not bear it; for if ever you should forsake me, I would have nothing more to do with the world, but make another abdication; for what is a crown when the support of it is gone? I never will forsake your dear self, Mr. Freeman, nor Mr. Montgomery [Godolphin], but always be your constant and faithful friend; and we four must never part till Death mows us down with his impartial hand."

This letter induced the duchess to believe that but little further exertion was required to gain a complete victory over the political prejudices of her royal mistress. She, therefore, unceasingly tormented her Majesty with eulogies of the Whigs and censures of the Tories (the latter of whom she involved in one common accusation of Jacobitism), till the signal victory of Blenheim turned the balance completely in her favour, and reduced Anne to the pitiable position of a crowned slave.

The moment the victory of Blenheim was won, Marlborough wrote to his duchess the subjoined note, and dispatched his aide-de-camp, Colonel Parke, with it by express:—

"*August* 13, 1704.—I have not time to say more, but to beg you will give my duty to the Queen, and let her know her army has had a glorious victory. M. Tallard and two other generals are in my coach, and I am following the rest. The bearer, my aide-de-camp, Colonel Parke, will give her an account of what has passed. I shall do it in a day or two by another more at large.—MARLBOROUGH."

The duchess, on receiving the note, forwarded it to the Queen, who, in reply, wrote:—

"*Windsor, August* 21.—Since I sent my letter away by the messenger, I have had the happiness of receiving my dear Mrs. Freeman's, by Colonel Parke, with the good news of this glorious victory, which, next to God Almighty, is wholly owing to dear Mr. Freeman, on whose safety I congratulate you with all my soul. May the same Providence that has hitherto preserved, still watch over and send him well home to you. We can never thank God Almighty enough for these great blessings, but must make it our endeavour to deserve them; and I hope he will continue his goodness to us, in delivering us from the attempts of all our other enemies. I have nothing to add at present, but my being sincerely," &c.

The first news of the glorious victory of Blenheim produced an indescribable burst of exultation throughout the whole width and breadth of the British empire. The Queen, accompanied by her husband, Prince George, went in procession to the unfinished cathedral of St. Paul's, to offer up a solemn thanksgiving for the success of her arms; and every class of her Majesty's subjects seemed to vie with each other in expressions of homage to Almighty God, and gratitude to the commander who had been the instrument of the divine favour."

It was in the autumn of this year that Anne, exasperated on ascertaining that Lord Nottingham and his Tory friends had invited the Electress Sophia to visit England, with her grandson, threw herself into the arms of the Marlborough party, who negatived the invitation. In the following note to the duchess she announced her intentions: "I believe dear Mrs. Freeman and I shall not disagree, as we have formerly done, for I am sensible of the service those people [the Whigs] have done me that you have a good opinion of, and will countenance them, and am thoroughly convinced of the malice and insolence of those [the Tories] that you have been always speaking against."

CHAPTER IV.

Anne rewards Marlborough for his military services—Knights the gifted mathematician, Isaac Newton—Her speech to parliament—The Whig junta contemplate altering the Liturgy—They endeavour to assume the disposal of the benefices appertaining to the crown—Anne successfully resists their efforts—Goes in mourning for Katharine of Braganza—Returns thanks at St. Paul's for the victory of Ramilies—Promotes Sunderland to the secretaryship of state—Inducts other of Marlborough's relations and party into office—Marlborough rewarded for his successes—Union of England and Scotland—Continued arrogance of the Duchess Sarah—Rising influence of Mrs. Abigail Hill—Intrigues of Harley—Contention between Anne and the duchess, respecting the influence and marriage of Mrs. Hill to Mr. Masham—Anne opens the first parliament of Great Britain—Grants to the Duchess Sarah the land on which Marlborough House stands—Political struggles—Triumphs of the Whigs—Vain efforts of the Duchess of Marlborough to effect the dismissal of Mrs. Masham—Attempted invasion of Scotland by the Pretender.

N the fourteenth of December, Marlborough, in company with Marshal Tallard and other prisoners of distinction, landed in England, bringing with him the standards and other trophies of his victory. The same morning, the Queen cordially welcomed him at St. James's, and the next day he took his seat in the House of Peers, and was honoured with the congratulatory eulogiums of the Lords and the Commons; in fact, on him was lavished every honour and reward that could be conferred on a subject.

On the third of January, 1705, the trophies of the victories of Blenheim were removed in grand procession from the Tower, where they were first deposited, to Westminster Hall, amidst the thunders of artillery, and the shouts of an exulting multitude—the names of Anne and Marlborough being mingled with the deafening acclamations which burst from all ranks and orders. Anne was now granted permission to heap those riches on the successful commander which a few months before had been withheld by the parliament. The Commons, urged by the national voice, requested her to consider of proper means for perpetuating the memory of the great services performed by the Duke of Marlborough. The Queen, in answer, signified to the Commons, that she was inclined to grant to the Duke and his heirs the honour and manor of Woodstock, with the hundred of Wootton, and requested supplies for clearing off the incumbrances on that domain. Accordingly a bill for the purpose passed both Houses, and received the royal sanction on the fourteenth of March. Not satisfied, however, that the nation alone should testify its gratitude, Anne accompanied the grant with an order to the Board of Works, to erect in Woodstock Park, and at the royal expense, a palace in memory of the victory; and forthwith the ancient towers and bowers of Woodstock were defaced and destroyed, and in their stead the Dutch architect, Vanbrugh, reared that huge, unsightly building known as the Castle of Blenheim, or Blenheim House. The Queen at the same time presented the Duchess of Marlborough with an exquisite miniature of the duke, mounted in gold, set with diamonds and precious stones, and valued at £8000.

In the spring of 1705, the Queen, accompanied by her husband, the Prince of Denmark, made a progress to Newmarket, and afterwards dined by invitation with the University of Cambridge, when she conferred the honour of knighthood on Dr. Ellis, the vice-chancellor; on James Montague, counsel for the university; and on the celebrated mathematical professor, Dr. Isaac Newton.

Although general political history is

foreign to our purpose, it is impossible to illustrate the personal life of Queen Anne, without occasional allusions to the Jacobite Tories, the Hanoverian Tories, the extreme and the moderate Whigs, and other of the parties, whose unprincipled intrigues and cabals form a prominent feature in English history at the period of which we are writing. Urged, nay almost forced, by the intreaties and threats of the Marlboroughs and their friends, Anne, on the eleventh of October, transferred the great seal from Sir Nathan Wright to that unprincipled partizan, Sir William Cowper, and also consented to form her agents of government solely from the ranks of the Whigs and their friends, the dissenters. When her Majesty opened her new parliament, in October, she, in a speech from the throne, after mentioning the war, and the projected union with Scotland, remarked—

"There is another union I think myself obliged to recommend to you, in the most earnest and affectionate manner; I mean an union of minds and affections amongst ourselves: it is that which would, above all things, disappoint and defeat the hopes and designs of our enemies.

"I cannot but with grief observe, there are some amongst us who endeavour to foment animosities; but, I persuade myself, they will be found to be very few, when you appear to assist me in discountenancing and defeating such practices.

"I mention this with a little more warmth, because there have not been wanting some so very malicious, as even in print to suggest the Church of England, as by law established, to be in danger at this time.

"I am willing to hope, not one of my subjects can really entertain a doubt of my affection to the Church, or so much as to suspect that it will not be my chief care to support it, and leave it secure after me; and therefore we may be certain, that they who go about to insinuate things of this nature, must be mine and the kingdom's enemies; and can only mean to cover designs which they dare not publicly own, by endeavouring to distract us with unreasonable and groundless distrusts and jealousies.

"I must be so plain as to tell you, the best proofs we can all give at present, of our zeal for the preservation of the Church, will be to join heartily in prosecuting the war against an enemy, who is certainly engaged to extirpate our religion, as well as to reduce this kingdom to slavery."

This speech was the composition of the deistic-minded Lord-Keeper Cowper, and utterly at variance with the Queen's sentiments. Anne, in common with her subjects, the commonalty of England, truly believed, and with good reason, that at this period the Church of England really was in danger. The Whig junta, Lords Somers, Wharton, Halifax, Orford, and Sunderland, all low churchmen—some, by their own professions, not even Christians—actually contemplated altering the English Liturgy to suit their views. For this purpose, the Lord-Keeper, Cowper, held several conferences with Archbishop Tennison, and that professed enemy of the Church, the Duchess of Marlborough. Fortunately, the measure dropped through a failure, which may probably be attributed to the known sentiments of the people at large, and to the opposition of Anne, who, whatever her failings, was, from the period of her accession, a true friend to the Church of England. In refutation of the assertion of some writers, that neither the Whig junta, nor Tennison, ever contemplated altering the English Liturgy, we may observe that Anne wrote to the Archbishop a letter, desiring him to let her see the alterations proposed to be made in the Common Prayer, previous to his laying them before the Privy Council, and that this letter still exists in the Lambeth Palace Library.

At this period, the Duchess of Marlborough and the state ministers made strenuous efforts to wrest out of the hands of her Majesty the important privilege of disposing of such of the Church dignities and benefices as appertained to the crown. Anne firmly resisted their importunities; and, in retaliation, they propagated a report, "that the Queen, in bestowing the crown-patronage of the Church, was solely influenced by the importunities of the women and the hangers-on at court." In refutation of this scandalous and false charge, Anne wrote to the Duchess of Marlborough that, although the crown-patronage of the Church was a prerogative which she, and she also hoped her successors, would ever maintain, she never had been, nor ever would be, improperly influenced by any one in the disposal of Church livings. She consulted those in office whose counsel ought to be taken, and then acted as she thought best; and if she did not always select the fittest person, the error resulted, not from favouritism, but from the qualifications of the candidates being misrepresented to her, or from some other similar c ause over which she had no control.

"This letter," remarks the Duchess, "was in answer to one I had writ to tell her not to be so long before she disposed of the livings to the clergy, adding, how safely she might put power iuto the hands of such a man as my Lord Cowper."

In February, 1706, the court went into mourning for the Queen-dowager, Katharine of Braganza, consort of Charles II., who had expired in the subsequent December, at Lisbon. This event was followed by the news of the victory of Ramilies, won by Marlborough on the twenty-third of May, 1706; news which at once dispelled from the court every semblance of sable or gloom, and excited in England the greatest enthusiasm. Queen Anne wrote to her successful general, "I want words to express my true sense of the great service you have done to your country, and I hope it will be a means to confirm all good and honest men in their principles, and frighten others from being troublesome."

Addresses poured in from all quarters, and on the twenty-ninth of June, Queen Anne repaired, in solemn procession, to a public thanksgiving in the cathedral of St. Paul's. But amidst all this rejoicing, the Queen was sad at heart. The Marlboroughs still harassed her to accept the services of others, their relations or friends. At length, at the close of the year, and after many shameful threats and upbraidings from the arrogant Duchess, Sarah, her Majesty, to avoid further torments, promoted Marlborough's son-in-law, the Earl of Sunderland, to the Secretaryship of State; a step immediately followed by the creation of several Whig peers; by Sir James Montague, brother of Lord Halifax, being appointed Solicitor-General; by the Lords Stamford and Herbert of Cherbury, with Mr. Pulteney, being constituted Commissioners of Trade; by the chief of the Tories being removed from the Privy Council, and by the administration being formed so completely of Whigs, that only two Tories of note, Harley and St. John, were permitted to remain in office.

At this crisis the Queen suffered intense agony of mind; the Whig junta, with the highly victorious Duke, and the arrogant, tyrannic Duchess of Marlborough at their head, firmly grasped the reins of government, exercised over her an imperious dictatorship, and forced her to acquiesce in all their measures. "I am a crowned slave," she one day remarked, "and only supported in my adversity by the hope that I may shortly be enabled to free myself from the galling thraldom."

On Marlborough's return, after the battle of Ramilies, the parliament, in compliance with the royal will, rewarded his services, by enacting, that his titles and honours should be continued in his posterity, and by settling £5,000 per annum on him and his heirs, for the more honourable support of their dignities.

"Among the papers of the Duchess," remarks Coxe, "we find her thanks to the Queen, written in a cold and formal style, which shows, that either the irritation of their recent dispute was not calmed by this act of munificence, or that the Duchess did not deem herself so much indebted to the friendship of the Sovereign, as to the intercession of her husband.

"'Whether I have or have not the

honour to see your Majesty, I find must always be something which obliges me to return you my humble thanks. The concern I have in the settlement made to Lord Marlborough's family by the act of parliament, makes a necessity of my giving you the trouble of them upon this occasion; and though it is not natural to me to make you so many fine speeches and compliments as some others can do, yet nobody has a heart fuller of the sincerest wishes for your constant happiness and prosperity than your poor forsaken Freeman.

[Indorsed by the Duchess.]

"'This letter to the Queen shows that I did not omit taking any reasonable occasion to please her, even when I saw she was changed to me; for it is certain that she never took any care of me in the settlement; and if I am ever the better for it, it is not owing to her friendship. But whatever the world said of my behaviour to her, I never failed in performing all manner of decencies and faithful services to her, while it was possible for me to do it.'"

Although the crowns of England and Scotland were united by the accession of James VI. of Scotland, as James I. of England, in March, 1603; every effort to unite the legislatures of the two countries had signally failed, till the reign of Anne; when, after considerable opposition, the important measure was passed, and on the first of May, 1707, the union of England and Scotland became a law. When signing the ratification, Anne remarked, "this is the glory of my reign." She then dissolved the Commons, and summoned the first united parliament of Great Britain to meet in the subsequent October, and caused the union to be celebrated, by ordering the first of May to be kept as a day of public festivity and thanksgiving.

It was at this period that a private cabal was forming in the royal household, which widened the breach between Anne and the Duchess Sarah. The particulars of this quarrel we give in the words of Archdeacon Coxe, who, be it understood, is the encomiast as well as historian of the Marlboroughs.

"From the account of the domestic transactions in the preceding year, it appears that the great credit which the Duchess of Marlborough had at first attained with the Queen, had continued to decline. The external appearances of friendship and confidence were still preserved; because the Queen was a perfect mistress of dissimulation, and because the spirit of the Duchess was too lofty, even to suspect that the empire which she possessed over her royal mistress could be undermined. In this she resembled most favourites, who neglect to maintain their power by the means employed to acquire it, and overlook appearances, which seem trifling only to themselves. Nothing, in fact, could perhaps have shaken her interest, but an inferior agent, in whom she placed the most implicit confidence, and on whose situation and abilities she looked down with indifference, if not contempt.

"Averse to the restraint of constant attendance, the Duchess had endeavoured to lighten the fatigues of her envied situation, by placing about the person of her royal mistress, as one of the bed-chamber women, Mrs. Abigail Hill,* an humble relation, whom she

* This Mrs., or, in modern parlance, Miss Hill has already been several times mentioned in these memoirs. The Duchess thus details the relationship in which she stood to her; and the manner in which she became acquainted with the destitute condition of her and her immediate kindred:—"Our grandfather, Sir John Jenyns, had two-and-twenty children, by which means the estate of the family, which was reputed to be about £4000 a year, came to be divided into small parcels. Mrs. Hill had only £500 to her fortune. Her husband lived very well for many years, as I have been told, until, turning projector, he brought ruin upon himself and family. But as this was long before I was born, I never knew there were such people in the world till after the Princess Anne was married, and when she lived at the Cockpit; at which time she came to me, and said, she believed 'that I did not know that I had relations in want,' and she gave me an account of them. When she had finished her story, I answered, 'that indeed I had never heard before of any such relations,' and immediately gave her out of my purse ten guineas for their present relief. Afterwards I sent Mrs. Hill more money, and saw her. She told me that

had rescued from penury, and whose family she had maintained and patronised. Considering this dependant as too lowly in situation, and too confined in abilities * to create jealousy, she little imagined that a person [whom she had snatched from the jaws of poverty,] and who was bound to her by the ties both of gratitude and affinity, would attempt to form an interest against her benefactress. For a time, her cousin answered all her expectations, and seemed a faithful and vigilant observer of the transactions at Court, and the feelings and conduct of the Queen. The Duchess, therefore, relaxed still more in her attendance; and, proud of her husband's splendid services, she gradually became more presumptuous and domineering.

"Mrs. Hill had not, however, long filled her confidential office, before she likewise aspired to a higher degree of consideration; and the state of the cabinet and parties offered a temptation which overcame her sense of gratitude. The violent bickerings which continually arose between the Queen and the Duchess did not escape the vigilant eye of a daily attendant. By the confidential complaints which frequently burst from the Queen, Mrs. Hill found herself growing into consequence; and her rising influence was perceived by the candidates for court favour, almost before it was known to herself.

"Besides that suppleness of temper natural to dependants rising into favour, which formed so advantageous a contrast with the overbearing and provoking conduct of her patroness, the political principles of Mrs. Hill were in unison with those of the Queen. She was deeply imbued with the maxims of the high church party, and was classed among those who were averse to the house of Hanover, if not to the partizans of the Stuarts. Such a congeniality of character and sentiment, joined to the most flattering humility of demeanour, and a watchful observance of her royal mistress's wishes, made a rapid progress in the affections of Anne, whose character was turned to the familiar and romantic friendship which her station forbade, and who at this period peculiarly felt the want of an adviser and confidant.

"The bed-chamber woman found a skilful counsellor and abettor in Secretary Harley, to whom she was related in the same degree by her father as to the Duchess by her mother; and by whom she and her family had been likewise assisted. Their relationship produced intimacy; and in the secret intrigues which Harley was equally meditating against his patrons, he naturally courted the aid of so useful an auxiliary. Mrs. Hill, therefore, was easily estranged from her benefactress, and became the channel of a constant communication between the Queen and the Secretary, more dangerous, as it was less suspected.

"Harley was, perhaps, of all men, the best calculated to win his way through the crooked paths of political intrigue. He had hitherto figured as a Whig or Tory, as it suited his interests, and under the guise of moderation, had gradually acquired a considerable body of adherents, to whom his parliamentary talents gave strength and consistency.

"Knowing the Tory partialities of his royal mistress, her growing aversion to the Duchess, and her anxiety for peace, to free herself from the power of the Whigs, Harley skilfully formed his attacks against the chiefs of the ministry. By the intercourse with the Queen,

her husband was the same relation to Mr. Harley as she was to me, but that he had never done anything for her. I think Mrs. Masham's father and mother did not live long after this. They left four children, two sons and two daughters. The elder daughter (afterwards Mrs. Masham) was a grown woman. I took her to St. Alban's, where she lived with me and my children, and I treated her with as great kindness as if she had been my sister. When an opportunity presented itself, I procured for her, her first appointment, as bed-chamber woman to the Princess Anne."

* Mrs. Hill was a more clever, and a far better woman, in heart and mind, than the Duchess, she, however, being ordinary in person and delicate in constitution.

† The degree of the relationship between Mrs. Hill and Mrs. Harley is involved in mystery: this statement by Coxe differs from that of Lady Marlborough in the preceding note.

which he enjoyed, in virtue of his office, and still more through the channel of Mrs. Hill, he found means to inflame her indignation against the Duchess, to work on that high sense of prerogative, which she had imbibed from her father, and to represent the Treasurer and General as favouring the efforts of the Whigs for engrossing all the offices of State, and reducing her to a degree of dependence unworthy of a Sovereign.* These insinuations were too much in unison with her feelings to fail of the desired effect; and the secret cabals of Harley in the preceding year, had encouraged her to resist the attempts of that party for the appointment of Sunderland. At the same time, the artful Secretary fomented the discontent of the Whigs against Marlborough and Godolphin, by insinuating that the two ministers were lukewarm in their cause, and the only obstacles to their admission into power.

"The confidential friends of the Duchess, among whom was Mr. Maynwaring, had made repeated representations on the rising influence and secret views of Mrs. Hill. But for a considerable time, they remonstrated without effect; for the Duchess was rejoiced at the relief which she had gained from restraint, and could not be convinced of the danger arising from the machinations of her own dependant. At length, the conduct of the Queen, combined with the evident favour of Harley and Mrs. Hill, dissipated the cloud which had hitherto obscured her judgment, and she communicated her apprehensions to Godolphin and the Duke.

"It is, indeed, singular, that the intrigue had escaped the matured sagacity of Godolphin, until it was become notorious; and that Marlborough, to whom the secrets of all the courts in Europe were known, should have been ignorant of a cabal in his own, in which he was so deeply interested. It is still more extraordinary, that after he was acquainted with the influence of the rising favourite, he should think so lightly of its consequences, as to suppose that it might be checked by a mere remonstrance. In reply to the first communication from the Duchess, he says, 'I should think you might speak to her with some caution, which might do good; for she certainly is grateful, and will mind what you say.'*

"In conformity with this advice, the Duchess not only remonstrated with Mrs. Hill, but assailed the Queen with reproaches, and accused her of suffering her political antipathies to be inflamed by the insinuations of a dependant, who conversed only with Jacobites and disaffected Tories. To these accusations, which were urged both in conversation and writing, the Queen replied in a style of affected humility, and real sarcasm, denying with the utmost solemnity the charge advanced against Mrs. Hill.

"'*Friday, Five o'clock, July* 18.—I give my dear Mrs. Freeman many thanks for her letter, which I received this morning, as I must always do, for every thing that comes from her, not doubting but what you say is sincerely meant in kindness to me. But I have so often been unfortunate in what I have said to you, that I think the less I say to your last letter the better; therefore, I shall only, in the first place, beg your pardon once more, for what I said the other day, which I find you take ill, and say something in answer to your explanation of the suspicions you seemed to have, concerning your cousin Hill, who is very far from being an occasion of feeding Mrs. Morley in her passion, as you are pleased to call it; she never meddling with any thing.

"'I believe others that have been in her station in former times have been tattling and very impertinent, but she is not at all of that temper; and as for the

* These facts are usually considered as depending on the authority of the Duchess alone, and, therefore, have been often questioned; but we find them also stated in a letter from Mr. Vernon to the Duke of Shrewsbury, dated the tenth of February, 1708, and even avowed and justified by the Tory advocates of Harley. His insinuations and charges against the Marlborough family, and the measure which he adopted to promote a negotiation for peace, are stated no less strongly by the author of "The other Side of the Question," than by the Duchess herself, p. 324.

* Meldert, June 2, 1707.

company she keeps, it is with her as with most other people—I fancy that their lot in the world makes them move with some, out of civility rather than choice; and I really believe, for one that is so much in the way of company, she has less acquaintance than any one upon earth. I hope, since in some part of your letter you seem to give credit to a thing because I said it was so, you will be as just in what I have said now about Hill; for I would not have any one hardly thought of, by my dear Mrs. Freeman, for your poor unfortunate, but ever faithful Morley's notions or actions.'

"The concealed sarcasm conveyed in this epistle wounded the feelings of the Duchess. She applied to herself the reflection on those who, in a similar situation, 'had been guilty of tattling and impertinence,' and gave utterance to her resentment in a style still more acrimonious than before.

"The doubts of all parties were, however, soon turned into certainty, by the discovery that Mrs. Hill had secretly contracted a marriage with Mr. Masham, whom the Duchess had likewise protected and placed in the royal household. This match, concluded without her privity, and, as she soon afterwards discovered, solemnised in the presence of the Queen and Dr. Arbuthnott, was a thunderstroke of evidence. It proved, not only that Mrs. Masham had forgotten her obligations, but that she possessed the highest degree of confidence. At the moment when this fact transpired, Godolphin also obtained unequivocal proof of Harley's machinations with both Whigs and Tories, and of his private intercourse with Mrs. Masham.

"In this crisis, the Duchess, instead of attempting to conciliate her royal mistress, and to regain her favour by renewing her former attentions, assailed her with bitter reproaches, which were the more provoking, because partly just. On the first intelligence of the marriage, she burst into the royal presence, and expostulated with the Queen, for concealing a secret which nearly regarded her, as a relation. The mortifying replies of the Queen, who warmly vindicated the silence of her favourite, by imputing it to fear of offending, rather inflamed than soothed her resentment; and from this period, their correspondence exhibits a tone of dissembled humility, on the one hand, and on the other a tone of acrimonious reproach. By the interposition of Godolphin, however, Mrs. Masham was induced at length to make an overture of reconciliation; though the interview which ensued showed that the breach was irreparable."

Despite the intreaties and threats of the arrogant duchess, Anne took Mr. and Mrs. Masham with her to the Newmarket October Meeting, and there tarried a month. From Newmarket the royal party progressed to London, and on the sixth of November, 1707, her Majesty, in her speech to the first parliament of Great Britain, observed, "I cannot conclude without recommending to you to confirm and improve the advantages of our happy union, not doubting but at the same time you will have due regard to what shall be found necessary for the public peace throughout the whole island of Great Britain." Little regard, however, was paid to this exhortation. The people of Scotland, now burdened with salt, malt, and other excise duties, beheld the extinction of their parliament with feelings of regret and alarm. They showed unmistakable symptoms of rebellion; invited the Pretender to their shores; loudly petitioned for an immediate repeal of the union; and sung their sorrows in the following and other political ballads:—

"Fareweel to a' our Scottish fame,
Fareweel our ancient glory,
Fareweel e'en to our Scottish name,
Sae famed in martial story.

"Now Sark rins o'er the Solway sands,
And Tweed rins to the ocean,
To mark where England's province stands,
Sic a parcel of rogues in a nation."

At the same time the English evinced jealousy at the Scotch being admitted into their parliament, and for a period, a serious rupture between the united nations appeared inevitable.

In the autumn of 1707, the Queen, after repeated importunities, granted for fifty years that portion of the domain of St. James's on which Marlborough House now stands, to the Duchess Sarah and her heirs. The duchess says, "I had obtained the promise of the Queen, before the death of the Queen-dowager Katharine of Braganza, of the site in St. James's Park upon which my house now stands; the grant was at first but for fifty years, and the building cost between £40,000 and £50,000, of which Queen Anne paid not one shilling, although many angry people believed otherwise."

The people, however, were on this occasion enraged, not at the supposed expenditure of public money in favour of the duchess, but because the oak tree which had sprung from an acorn that Charles II. had plucked from the famous oak which had securely sheltered him at Boscobel, and planted with his own hands, was uprooted, to make room for the foundation of Marlborough House.

On the thirtieth of December, William Gregg, secretary to Mr. Harley, was arrested on a charge of carrying on a treasonable intercourse with the government of France. Gregg was tried at the Old Bailey, and convicted on his own confession. The Whigs strenuously endeavoured to implicate Mr. Harley in the charge against Gregg, and failing this, Marlborough and Godolphin attempted to procure his dismissal, which so enraged the Queen, that she resolved to free herself from the bonds of the Marlborough family junta. Her strength, however, proved unequal to her resolution. Marlborough and Godolphin, after threatening to resign all their appointments, raised a storm, which forced her Majesty to succumb, and Mr. Harley to retire for awhile from her service. Harley retired on the eleventh of February, 1708, and shortly afterwards St. John, Mansell Harcourt, and several others, tendered their resignation. The leaders of this triumphant faction next urged the Commons to petition the Queen to dismiss her new favourite, Mrs. Masham; but the House, to the indignation of the mighty duchess, Sarah, refused so to do.

Just previous to this very proper refusal of the Commons, the duchess resolved, as her husband's threat to relinquish the command of the army, had been followed by the resignation of Harley, by similar means to endeavour to effect the dismissal of her rival in the royal favour. Waiting on her royal mistress, she, after a tirade of reproach and remonstrance, added, "As Lord Marlborough is now about to be forced from your Majesty's service, I cannot, in honour, remain any longer at court." She then expatiated, as usual, on her own services, and on the friendship which the Queen had condescended to entertain for her; and as a recompense, concluded with requesting permission to resign her offices in favour of her two eldest daughters, who from their rank, alliance, and character, were well calculated to merit such a favour.

After listening with seeming embarrassment to this long appeal, the Queen evaded compliance, by affecting much kindness, and repeating, "You and I must never part." The duchess, however, was not diverted from her purpose, and renewed her solicitations, that if circumstances should render her retreat necessary, her Majesty would comply with this request. The Queen, pressed by her importunities, and intimidated by the presence of a person whom she equally feared and disliked, renewed the declaration, "that they should never part." But added, should that even be the case, she would transfer the offices to two of her daughters; and did not hesitate to bind that promise by a solemn asseveration. The duchess took her leave, kissing the Queen's hand; and afterwards Anne yielded to her applications, by confirming in writing the promise which had been verbally given. Still, however, the duchess had reason to feel that her attendance was unwelcome; and on the departure of her husband to the continent, she wrote a letter to Anne, expressing her resolution not to incommode her majesty by her presence, and artfully recalling to recollection the promise which she had before extorted from her.

"March 31.

"MADAM, — Upon Lord Marlborough's going into Holland, I believe your Majesty will neither be surprised nor displeased to hear I am gone into the country, since by your very hard and uncommon usage of me, you have convinced all sorts of people, as well as myself, that nothing would be so uneasy to you as my near attendance. Upon this account, I thought it might not be improper, at my going into the country, to acquaint your Majesty, that even while Lord Marlborough continues in your service, as well as when he finds himself obliged to leave it, if your Majesty thinks fit to dispose of my employments, according to the solemn assurances you have been pleased to give me, you shall meet with all the submission and acknowledgments imaginable."

"It is needless to expatiate on the disgust which this ill-timed application and imprudent impoitunity produced. The Queen and the duchess never met without sullen silence or bitter reproaches; and never wrote without ironical apologies or contemptuous taunts. The effects of these female jars, arising from offended dignity on the one hand, and disappointed ambition on the other, may be traced throughout the series of correspondence, and produced the most sinister effects on the administration of public affairs, by the perplexities into which they perpetually threw both the treasurer and general." *

Since her accession, Anne had secretly cherished feelings of regard towards her half-brother, the Chevalier de St. George; but his attempted invasion of Scotland, in March, 1708, alarmed her, and produced another revulsion in her feelings. She, in her speech to parliament, for the first time, branded him as the "Pretender," and also uttered sentiments favourable to the "Revolution," although in her previous addresses from the throne, she had carefully avoided the use of the word "Revolution."

* Coxe's Marlborough.

CHAPTER V.

Further arrogance of the Duchess of Marlborough—She publicly insults the Queen in St. Paul's—Anne openly quarrels with her—Death of Prince George of Denmark—Temporary reconciliation between the Queen and the Duchess—Artful conduct of the Duchess—Burial of the Queen's Consort—Coalition between the ultra-republican Whigs and the Marlborough faction—Anne long and deeply bewails her husband's death—Attends a thanksgiving at St. Paul's for the victory of Malplaquet—Refuses to constitute Marlborough captain-general for life—Further harassed by the insolence of the Duchess Sarah—Quarrels with Marlborough—Hollow reconciliation—Takes part with Dr. Sacheverell—Attends his trial—Increasing discords between her and the Duchess—Stormy scene between her and the Duchess at their last personal interview.

IN the spring of 1708, Prince George of Denmark suffered intensely from gout and asthma, and in the hope of alleviating his sufferings, the Queen resided with him on the ground-floor at Kensington Palace. He grew worse, and on the approach of summer her Majesty removed with him to Windsor, and took up her residence, not at the castle, the high-up air there being too bleak for his cough, but at the villa she had bought for her own residence, at the period when her sister, the late Queen Mary II., excluded her from court.

The heartless Duchess of Marlborough accuses her of retiring from the bustle of the metropolis, not to nurse and watch over her suffering husband, which, indeed, was her sole object, but to intrigue with the leader of the Tory faction. These are the words of the duchess: "Through the whole summer, after Mr. Harley's dismission, the Queen continued to have secret correspondence with him; and that this might be the better managed, she staid all the sultry season, even when the Prince was panting for breath, in that small house she had formerly purchased at Windsor, which, though as hot as an oven, was then said to be cool; because from the park, such persons as Mrs. Masham had a mind to bring to her Majesty, could be let in privately by the garden."

That the Queen did secretly correspond with Mr. Harley, appears probable; for the spring and summer through she was constantly at variance with the wealth-and-title-grasping Marlborough family junta. She complained that Sunderland repeatedly offered her personal insults, and for a period she was at open war with Halifax, and with her prime minister, Godolphin. The duchess, however, told her to her head, that it was neither wise nor grateful of her to refuse her confidence to the Whigs, or to deny to her highly-successful general, and whoever he might select as his colleagues, the uncontrolled possession of the reins of government. The letter which Marlborough had addressed to his duchess from the battle-field, on the twelfth of July, announcing his victory of Oudenard, and which concluded—"I do, and you must, give thanks to God for his goodness, in protecting and making me the instrument of so much happiness to the *Queen and nation, if she will please to make use of it*," was no sooner received by the haughty Sarah, than she communicated it to the Queen, accompanied with "the severest reflections on the ungrateful return which her Majesty had made to the instrument of such success." She even accused Admiral Churchill of exerting his influence with Prince George of Denmark, and others, against his own brother the duke;* and then inveighed with still greater bitterness against Mrs. Masham. These violent proceedings of the duchess further irritated the wounded feelings of the Queen, and shortly after the victory of Oudenard, their interminable altercations produced an open quarrel.

"The duchess," remarks Coxe, "as mistress of the robes, had arranged the jewels to be worn by the Queen at the solemn Te Deum celebrated on that occasion. The Queen refused to adopt the arrangement; the duchess ascribed her objection to the ill-offices of Mrs. Masham, and reproached her, by letter, for such a proof of unkindness and contempt. She also taunted her royal mistress in the coach, as they passed to the church (St. Paul's Cathedral), and during the service itself, reverting to the subject, she coupled her indiscreet remonstrance with a complaint in the name of the duke, that he no longer enjoyed to the full the royal confidence and favour. As the Queen prepared to reply, the duchess interrupted her, by abruptly bidding her to hold her tongue."

Soon after the ceremony, she sent the Queen a complaining letter from the duke, dated the twenty-third of July,

* She pointedly alluded to the quarrel occasioned by the imprudent loquacity of Admiral Churchill, who, she declared, with a view to mortify the Whigs, had circulated a report that the duke had given a regiment to a Colonel Jones, at the secret instigation of Harley. "He assigned, as his authority, the avowal of Mr. Robert Walpole, then secretary at war, and the confidential agent of the duke in all military affairs. The report, which was communicated to the Queen and Prince by the admiral himself, created the greatest irritation on all sides, and was proved to be false. Mr. Walpole justified himself to his patron, in a letter, printed in the Memoirs of his Life and Administration, vol. xi. p. 9; and in a second letter, dated June 29 (still preserved in the Marlborough Papers), the duke not only condemned the conduct of his brother, but endeavoured to soothe the wounded feelings of Walpole, as well as to exonerate himself from the censure which the report was calculated to excite among the Whigs. The extreme dissatisfaction of all parties is proved by the sensation which an incident so comparatively trifling produced, and evinces the embarrassment which Marlborough encountered from the imprudence of his brother."—*Coxe.*

accompanied with an epistle in a more aggravated style of invective than she had hitherto ventured to employ.

"I cannot help sending your Majesty this letter, to show how exactly Lord Marlborough agrees with me in my opinion, that he has now no interest with you: though when I said so in the church on Thursday (nineteenth of August, 1708), you were pleased to say it was untrue. And yet I think he will be surprised to hear, that when I had taken so much pains to put your jewels in a way that I thought you would like, Mrs. Masham could make you refuse to wear them in so unkind a manner; because that was a power she had not thought fit to exercise before. I will make no reflections upon it; only that I must needs observe, that your Majesty chose a very wrong day to mortify me, when you were just going to return thanks for a victory obtained by Lord Marlborough!"

In answer to this acrimonious effusion, the Queen replied:—

"*Sunday.*—After the commands you gave me on the Thanksgiving-day of not answering you, I should not have troubled you with these lines, but to return the Duke of Marlborough's letter safe into your hands, and for the same reason do not say anything to that, nor to yours, which enclosed it."

The dignity and brevity of this note alarmed the duchess, and drew from her a letter, which, although full of reproaches, concluded with protestations of humility and submission:—

"I should not trouble your Majesty with any answer to your last short letter, but to explain what you seem to mistake in what I said at church. I desired you not to answer me there, for fear of being overheard. And this you interpret, as if I had desired you not to answer me at all, which was far from my intention. For the whole end of my writing to you so often, was to get your answer to several things, in which we differed; that, if I was in the wrong, you might convince me of it, and I should very readily have owned my mistakes. But, since you have not been pleased to show them to me, I flatter myself that I have said several things to you that are unanswerable, and I hope, some time or other, you will find leisure to reflect upon them, and will convince Lord Marlborough, that he is mistaken in thinking that he has no credit with you, by hearkening sometimes to his advice; and then, I hope, you will never more be troubled with disagreeable letters from me; for I should be much better pleased to say and do everything you like. But I should think myself wanting in my duty to you, if I saw you so much in the wrong, as without prejudice or passion, I really think you are, in several particulars I have mentioned, and did not tell you of it; and the rather, because nobody cares to speak out upon so ungrateful a subject. The word 'command,' which you use at the beginning of your letter, is very unfitly supposed to come from me. For though I have always writ to you as a friend, and lived with you as such for so many years, with all the truth, and honesty, and zeal for your service that was possible; yet I shall never forget that I am your subject, nor cease to be a faithful one."

This epistolary wrangle was not long afterwards followed by an interview, in which the duchess set the seal to her indiscretion, by renewing her expostulations on the countenance manifested towards Mr. Harley and Mrs. Masham. The minute of this conversation, of which no trace appears in the "Conduct," is preserved in her hand-writing, and was evidently suppressed on mature reflection. We give this characteristic document without abridgment or alteration.

Heads of the conversation with Mrs. Morley, September 9—20, 1708.

"Nobody trusted or countenanced by her, but who is in some way or other influenced by Mr. Harley.

"Mr. Harley never had a good reputation in the world, but is much worse thought of since he is out of her service, where people were content to suffer him, because he was thought to depend upon Lord Marlborough and lord-treasurer. But since he was tempted by the favour of Abigail to set up for himself, and to betray and ruin those that had brought him into her service, and her service itself also, nobody alive can be more odious than he is, or more contemptible to all parties.

"Why will she not consider fairly and coolly the distinction she makes between some of the Whigs, who did her such real and acceptable service, in the union with Scotland, and in the matter of the invitation, and my Lord Haversham, who, upon both these actions, and many others, talked so insolently and scandalously of her administration, in her own hearing? and yet that man was admitted to her presence with the air of a friend, though he is plainly in another interest, and can never serve her; and the others are kept at the greatest distance, contrary to the advice and opinion of all her servants, whom she has most reason to trust, though they have shown themselves, in her presence also, both able and willing to serve her, and desirous to make her great and happy.

"Even in this last session of parliament, the Tories joined to a man against the council of Scotland, and Mr. Harley himself, underhand; when after all that was over, upon occasion of the late invasion, these men did expose the Tories to all the world, by showing their zeal for her and her government, by strenthening it every way in their power at that time of danger."

In the course of this interview the altercation became so violent, that the high-toned voice of the duchess was heard in the ante-chamber; and when she came out, her eyes were suffused with tears. The Queen was found in a similar state of agitation, by those who first entered the apartment; and we learn from a subsequent letter of the duchess, that she was dismissed with every proof of contempt and indignation.

These fatal contentions could not long be kept a secret from the royal attendants, and the reports which were industriously circulated on the occasion, produced the usual effect attending the decline of court favour. Several of the Whigs began to anticipate this disgrace of their zealous patroness, and treated her with marked coolness and reserve; whilst the Earl of Kent, on being blamed by Mr. Maynwaring for his attentions to Mrs. Masham, answered with an air of pride, "I must behave civilly to all the Queen's servants."

Meanwhile, the health of Prince George of Denmark daily and rapidly declined: towards the close of August, her Majesty accompanied him to Bath, and after a short sojourn there, the royal pair returned, and took up their residence at Kensington. On their return, the Prince exhibited symptoms of convalescence; but these proving fallacious, he breathed his last, at ten o'clock on the morning of the twenty-eighth of October, 1708, in the fifty-fifth year of his age, and the twenty-sixth year of his marriage to Queen Anne. This sorrowful event led to a temporary renewal of the intercourse between the Queen and the Duchess. As the dissolution of the Prince approached, the self-important Duchess addressed to her afflicted mistress, the subjoined offensive epistle.

"*Windsor Lodge, Oct.* 26.—Though the last time I had the honour to wait upon your Majesty, your usage of me was such as was scarce possible for me to imagine, or for any body to believe, yet I cannot hear of so great a misfortune and affliction to you, as the condition in which the Prince is, without coming to pay my duty, in inquiring after your health; and to see, if in any particular whatsoever my service can either be agreeable or useful to you; for which satisfaction, I would do more than I will trouble your Majesty to read at this time."

Scarcely was the letter received by her Majesty, when the bold Duchess, in virtue of her office as mistress of the robes, entered her presence; but the Queen, as might be expected, under the circumstances, received her very coolly, and like a stranger. "Nothing discouraged by the repulse, on the ensuing morning, she again waited on the sorrowing Anne, and was present when the Prince expired; with seeming affection, she removed her weeping mistress from this sad spectacle, and when the other attendants had withdrawn, knelt down and endeavoured to console her. She then, after many urgent, and at first fruitless importunities, obtained her consent to remove her to St. James's. The Queen delivering her watch to the Duchess, told her to retire till the hands pointed to a certain time, and commanded her to send for Mrs. Masham. Annoyed at this mark of preference, the Duchess withdrew, and being too haughty to publish her own decline of influence to the crowd collected in the anti-chamber, neglected to summon the favourite. Having prepared her own coach for the Queen's reception, and desired Mrs. Lowman to make the company fall back whilst the Queen passed, she returned at the appointed hour, announced to the weeping Queen that the carriage was ready, and excused herself for not sending for Mrs. Masham, on the plea "that it might make a disagreable noise when there were bishops and ladies of the bedchamber waiting without, that her Majesty did not want to see:" adding, "your Majesty may send for her at St. James's, when and how you please."

The grief-absorbed Queen acquiesced; but, to the annoyance of the Duchess, Mrs. Hill, the sister of Mrs. Masham, whilst putting on her Majesty's hood, received from her some commission in a whisper; and as Anne passed through the gallery leaning on the arm of the Duchess, who wished it to be supposed that her Majesty had ridden off with her, without so much as thinking of Harley or his relatives, Mrs. Masham herself appeared, accompanied by Dr. Arbuthnot, one of the royal physicians. The Queen spake not, but stepping towards her favourite, "bent down like a sail," and cast on her an earnest look of affection. Immediately after entering the carriage, she requested the Duchess to order the lord treasurer, Godolphin, to examine whether there was room in one of the royal vaults at Westminster to bury the Prince, and leave room for her too; and if not, to select some other place of burial.

"Having escorted her Majesty to St. James's, and induced her to take some refreshment, the Duchess retired, and the lord treasurer was admitted. But the Queen soon followed her to her apartment, and not finding her there, sent a note, which marks her minute attention to all the details of the interment.

"'I scratched twice at dear Mrs. Freeman's door, as soon as lord treasurer went from me, in hopes to have spoke one more word to him before he was gone; but nobody hearing me, I wrote this, not caring to send what I had to say by word of mouth; which was, to desire him, that when he sends his orders to Kensington, he would give directions there may be a great many yeomen of the guards to carry the Prince's dear body, that it may not be let fall, the great stairs being very steep and slippery.'

"In the evening, the Duchess found the Queen at table, and attended by Mrs. Masham, who instantly retired; but she carefully avoided any allusion to the new favourite, and the Queen treated her with marks of renewed regard and familiarity. This was, however, a mere momentary change; for the Duchess observes, that in her subsequent visits, she either found Mrs. Masham with the Queen, or retiring on her entrance, and, indeed, reaped nothing from this sacrifice of her pride, except the mortification of observing the superior favour of her rival, and the decline of her own influence."*

On the eleventh of November, the body of the Queen's consort was removed from Kensington to the Painted Chamber, Westminster, where, having rested in state till the thirteenth, it was on that night buried in the abbey, by torch-light, with imposing funeral rites. Shortly afterwards, the new parliament was opened by commission, and the ultra-republican Whigs, having formed a coalition with the Marlborough faction, were now admitted to office; Lord Pembroke succeeded Prince George of Denmark as lord high admiral; the vice-

* From a narrative of the events which took place on the death of the Prince of Denmark, by the Duchess.

royship of Ireland was transferred to Lord Wharton; the long-contested post of president of the council was conferred on Lord Somers; and to save Godolphin from the consequences of his crime in having corresponded with the court at St. Germains, a general pardon to all such delinquents was published by the Queen, and confirmed by parliament.

Queen Anne, like her sister, although a heartless daughter, was a truly affectionate wife. During the illness of her consort, she sedulously tended him, and did all in her power to alleviate his sufferings; and after his demise, she long and deeply bewailed her bereavement. On the twenty-first of May, 1709, she was too depressed in spirits to prorogue parliament in person; and whilst yet wearing the weeds of widowhood, she was compelled in procession to attend a thanksgiving at St. Paul's, for Marlborough's bloody victory of Malplaquet, the last of the great battles fought in the War of the Succession, and in which, to the deep sorrow of the Queen, 20,000 of her brave subjects were slaughtered. Over-rode, however, as Anne was by the Marlboroughs, she had the courage to refuse acquiescence to the unconstitutional demand which the victorious Duke made on his return from Malplaquet, that she would by letters patent constitute him captain-general *for life;* a refusal in which she was firmly seconded by Lord Chancellor Cowper, and several other noblemen, who previously had never dared to thwart the will of the great general. Piqued at this refusal, the Duke had the audacity and imprudence to write a querulous letter to her Majesty, accusing her of ungrateful disregard of his services, complaining with unmeasured bitterness of the transfer of her affections from the Duchess to Mrs. Masham, and announcing his determination to retire at the end of the war. The bellicose Duchess also continued to carry on an exasperating written and wordy warfare with the harassed Queen. About this time, she requested her Majesty to grant some lodgings recently vacated in the palace of St. James, for the purpose of forming a more commodious entry to her own apartments, claiming a former promise. The Queen, who seemed to have reserved these lodgings for the use of Mrs. Masham's sister, was much embarrassed at this unexpected request, and solemnly denied that she had ever made such a promise. An altercation ensued, in which the Duchess repeated her assertion, and the Queen as positively contradicted it, adding, 'I do not remember that I was ever spoken to for them.' 'But supposing,' replied the Duchess, 'that I am mistaken, surely my request cannot be deemed unreasonable.' The Queen rejoining, 'I have a great many servants of my own, and some of them I must remove;' the Duchess smiled and said, 'Your Majesty then does not reckon Lord Marlborough or me among your servants?' On this the Queen was again embarrassed, and murmuring some unintelligible words, the Duchess observed, 'Some of my friends have pressed me to wait oftener upon your Majesty: I have been compelled, in vindication of my conduct, to relate the usage which I have received from your Majesty; and for this reason I have been under the necessity of repeating, and asserting the truth of what I said, before they could be induced to believe it; and I believe it would be thought still more strange, were I to repeat this conversation, and inform them, that after all Lord Marlborough's services, your Majesty refused to give him a miserable hole, to make a clear entry to his lodgings; I beg, therefore, to know, whether I am at liberty to repeat this to any of my friends.' After some hesitation, and much disorder in her looks, the Queen replied in the affirmative. The Duchess, on retiring, added, 'I hope your Majesty will reflect upon all that has passed;' and, as no reply was given, she abruptly quitted the apartment.*

"Soon after this interview, the Duchess again obtruded herself on the Queen, and solicited her Majesty to inform her what crime she had committed,

* This narrative is taken from an account in the handwriting of the Duchess, and endorsed by her, "An account of a conversation with the Queen, when she refused to give me an inconsiderable lodging to make a clear way to mine."

which had produced so great an alteration in her behaviour. This question drew from her royal mistress a letter, in which she charged her with inveteracy to Mrs. Masham, and with having nothing so much at heart as the ruin of her cousin. After exculpating her from any fault, and imputing their misunderstanding to a discordance in political opinions, she added, 'I do not think it a crime in any one not to be of my mind, or blamable, because you cannot see with my eyes, or hear with my ears.' She concluded, 'It is impossible for you to recover my former kindness, but I shall behave myself to you as the Duke of Marlborough's wife, and as my groom of the stole.'*

"Stung with these unkind expressions, and this proof of further alienation, the discarded favourite had the bold insolence to draw up and send to her royal mistress a copious narrative of the commencement and progress of their connexion, accompanied with extracts from 'The Whole Duty of Man,' on the article of Friendship, and from the directions in the liturgy, prefixed to the communion service, that none could conscientiously partake of the Lord's Supper, unless they were at peace and in charity with all mankind. To this was added, a passage from Bishop Taylor's works on the same subject. In transmitting this insulting paper, she observed, 'If your Majesty will read this narrative of twenty-six years' faithful services, and write only in a few words that you had read them, together with the extracts, and were still of the same opinion as you were when you sent me a very harsh letter, which was the occasion of my troubling you with this narrative, I assure you that I will never trouble you more upon any subject but the business of my office.'

"To this long memorial the Queen briefly replied, that when she had leisure to read all the papers, she would send an answer to them. But she never sent any other answer; and the Duchess, in concluding her relation, observes, 'nor had my papers any apparent effect on her Majesty, except that after my coming to town, as she was passing by me in order to receive the communion, she looked with much good-nature, and very graciously smiled on me. But the smile and pleasant look, I had reason afterwards to think, were given to Bishop Taylor and the Common Prayer-book, and not to me.'*

* Conduct, p. 267.

"This unfortunate breach was speedily followed by the most fatal consequences; for the indignation of the Queen was still further inflamed by the intemperate zeal with which the duchess advocated the cause of the Whigs, and which increased her natural antipathy to a party which she equally feared and detested. Actuated by these feelings, Anne turned with additional confidence to her new favourite, in whom she found a congeniality of political principles, and a suppleness of manners, which formed a striking contrast with the overbearing temper of the duchess. In this state of mind, she listened more and more to the suggestions of Harley, whose intrigues began to acquire consistency, and who had obtained increasing influence by his private cabals."

At this period it became evident to the more discerning, that a political crisis was approaching. Marlborough's efforts to place himself in command for life, impressed the Queen with a belief that he aspired to her throne, and strengthened her resolution to break the chains which bound her to the Marlborough faction. With this view she secretly continued to correspond with Harley, and courted and won the support of all the nobles who were inimical to the Whig faction. She also bestowed the lieutenancy of the Tower, vacated by the death of Lord Essex, on Earl Rivers, without previously consulting the great duke, who she at the same time ordered to confer Lord Essex's regiment on Mrs. Masham's brother, Jack Hill. As both these appointments were usually made at the recommendation of the commander-in-chief, he, instead of complying with the Queen's request, retired in disgust to his lodge at Windsor, on the fifteenth of January, the very day on which a cabi-

* Conduct of the Duchess of Marlborough p. 270.

net council was to be held. The Queen attended the council; but, to the annoyance of the duke and his immediate friends, she took no notice of his absence, and the assembly deliberated, transacted the customary business, and separated, as usual, without one of the members venturing to mention the noteworthy fact of the general not being present.

Violent agitation and busy intrigues ensued; the Whigs and the Marlborough faction generally were not unanimous in their opinion. Marlborough resolved not to continue in the command unless Mrs. Masham was dismissed. a resolution strongly reprobated by several of his friends. However, after an anxious suspense of five days, Anne, whose fears had been greatly excited by the representations of Godolphin, Somers, and other lords, succumbed to the storm, and relinquished her intention of disposing of the regiment to Jack Hill. Marlborough did not enforce his purpose of requiring the removal of Mrs. Masham; and coming to town, was admitted to an audience with the Queen, who, anxious to soothe his resentment, received him with every outward demonstration of kindness and favour. This compromise, however, was productive of no permanent advantage to the Marlboroughs, for the Queen was, in reality, as deeply offended as if the disgrace of her favourite had been enforced, and became more firmly resolved to free herself from the thraldom of the existing ministry the moment an opportunity offered of striking a decisive blow.

Matters were in this state, when the trial of the eloquent high-church orator, Dr. Sacheverell, took place. Sacheverell has been represented in general history as a person possessed of little virtue, learning, or good sense; his powers as an author were certainly inconsiderable, but his sermons and speeches were delivered with overpowering eloquence; in fact, he possessed that rare and commanding gift of rivetting the attention of his hearers, and playing with their passions, as a boy would with a football, when and how he chose. In a sermon which he delivered at St. Paul's, on the fifth of November, on the text, "Perils among false brethren," he revived the obsolete doctrine of passive obedience, reprobated the principles of the revolution, depicted the dangers to which the church was exposed in the strongest colours, loaded the ministers in general with reproach, and especially pointed out Lord Godolphin to public indignation, by the invidious name of Valpone. This sermon lasted three hours, enraptured the audience, was printed with the secret connivance of the Lord Mayor, and gave such umbrage to Godolphin and several of his coadjutors, that it was brought before the cognizance of the legislature, and an impeachment instituted against the preacher. The trial, which commenced on the twenty-seventh of February, 1710, took place in Westminster Hall. The hall was fitted up for the occasion, with a box for the Queen, near the throne; seats for the peers; places for the members of the commons; galleries for ladies and the populace; bar and benches for the prisoner and his counsel; and other conveniences. As the time approached for the trial to commence, the greatest excitement prevailed; the Queen, no longer holding the balance between the great opposing factions, openly took part with Sacheverell, high church and Tory; and although the Whigs were straining every nerve to secure the condemnation of the bold, eloquent preacher, the people clamoured aloud against the whole ministry, declared their Queen was reduced to bondage by a single family, and almost worshipped Sacheverell as a god. In the course of the trial, vast crowds of the people, as well as of the nobility and gentry, attended him daily to Westminster Hall, striving to kiss his hand, and praying for his deliverance; and these same crowds surrounded the Queen, as she was carried each day in her sedan to witness the trial, and made the welkin ring with their reiterated cries of "God bless your Majesty and the Church! we hope that your Majesty is for God and Dr. Sacheverell!" Every day the doctor's popularity increased, the great majority of the nation espoused his cause, the clergy from their pulpits pronounced him the champion of the Church of England, the Queen's chaplains surrounded him at the trial, all London vehemently espoused his cause, and at the highest of the enthusiasm, it was dangerous to go abroad without the oak-leaf, which was considered as the badge of hereditary right, and the metropolis was agitated by riots so fierce and alarming, that order could not be restored without the aid of the military, who actually captured several of the Queen's guards and watermen in the riotous act of leading on the mob to burn and destroy the meeting-houses and residences of the dissenters and others, against whom they levelled their malice. After the trial had lasted three weeks, Sacheverell was found guilty, but received a sentence so mild, that the people and the Tories triumphed as if he had been acquitted, and the ministry was compelled to own a defeat. "Our sentence against Dr. Sacheverell," remarks the treasurer, in a letter dated the twenty-first of March, "is at last dwindled to a suspending him for three years from preaching, which question we carried but by six; and the second, which was for incapacitating him during that time to take any dignity or preferment in the church, was lost by one; the numbers were sixty to fifty-nine. So all this bustle and fatigue ends in no more but a suspension of three years from the pulpit, and burning his sermon at the Old Exchange. The conjunction of the Duke of Somerset and Lord Rivers with the Duke of Argyle, and his brother, the Earl of Ilay, has been the great occasion of this disappointment."*

Whilst the trial was proceeding in Westminster Hall, a scene equally interesting as that in the open court was being performed, in the curtained box from which the Queen and her attendants witnessed the exciting proceedings. This scene is thus described by the Duchess of Marlborough: "I waited on the Queen the first time she went to Dr. Sacheverell's trial, and having stood above two hours, said to the vice-chamberlain, that when the Queen went to any place *incognito* (as she went to the trial, and only looked from behind a curtain), it was always the custom of the ladies to sit down before her; but her Majesty had forgot to speak to us now, and that since the trial was like to continue very long every day, I wished he would put the Queen in mind of it; to which he replied, very naturally, 'Why, madam, should you not speak to the Queen yourself, who are always in waiting?'

"This, I knew, was right, and therefore I went up to the Queen, and, stooping down to her, as she was sitting, to whisper to her, said, 'I believed her Majesty had forgot to order us to sit, as was customary in such cases.' Upon this, she looked, indeed, as if she had forgot, and was sorry for it, and answered, in a very kind, easy way, 'By all means, pray sit;' and before I could go a step from her chair, she called to Mr. Mordaunt, the page of honour, to bring stools, and desire the ladies to sit down, which, accordingly, we did—Lady Scarborough, Lady Burlington, and myself. But as I was to sit nearest to the Queen, I took care to place myself a good distance from her; though it was usual, in such cases, to sit close to her, and sometimes at the basset-table, when she does not appear *incognito*; but in a place of ceremony, the company has sat so near her as scarcely to leave her room to put her hand to her pocket. Besides this, I used a further caution, of showing her all the respect I could in this matter, by drawing a curtain behind me in such a manner, betwixt her and me, as to appear to be, as it were, in a different room from her Majesty. But my Lady Hyde, who stood behind the Queen when I went to speak to her (and who, I observed, with an air of boldness more than good breeding, came up then nearer, to hear what I said), continued to stand still in the same manner, and never came to sit with us the rest of that day, which I then took for nothing more than making

* The Duke of Argyle and the Earl of Ilay pronounced Sacheverell guilty, but voted against the ministry on the subsequent motions, relative to his suspension and disqualification.

a show of more than ordinary favour with the Queen.

"The next day the Duchess of Somerset came to the trial, and before I sat down I turned to her, having always used to show her a great deal of respect, and asked her if her grace would not be pleased to sit; at which she gave a sort of start back, with the appearance of being surprised, as if she thought I had asked a very strange thing, and refused sitting. Upon this, I observed that it was always the custom to sit before the Queen in such cases, and that her Majesty had ordered us to do so the day before; but that her refusing it now, looked as if she thought that we had done something that was not proper. To which she answered, that she did not care to sit, and then went and stood behind the Queen, as Lady Hyde had done the day before, which I took no notice of then, but sat down with Lady Burlington, as we had done before. But when I came to reflect upon what these two ladies had done, I plainly perceived that, in the Duchess of Somerset, especially, this conduct could not be thought to be the effect of humility; but that it must be a stratagem that they had formed in their cabal to flatter the Queen, by paying her more respect, and to make some public noise of this matter that might be to my disadvantage, or disagreeable to me. And this I was still the more confirmed in, because it had been known before that the Duchess of Somerset, who was then with her lord, did act a cunning part between the Duke and Duchess of Marlborough. The Whigs and Tories did not intend to come to the trial. As, therefore, it was my business to keep all things as quiet as possible till the campaign was over, and preserve myself in the meanwhile, if I could, from any possible affront, I resolved to do what I could to disappoint these ladies in their little design; and in order to this, I waited upon the Queen the next morning before she went to the trial, and told her that I had observed the day before that the Duchess of Somerset had refused to sit at the trial, which I did not know the meaning of, since her Majesty was pleased to order it, and that it was nothing more than was agreeable to the constant practice of the court in all such cases; but, however, if it would in any respect be more pleasing to her Majesty that we should stand for the future, I begged she would let me know her mind about it, because I should be very sorry to do any thing that could give her the least dissatisfaction. To this she answered, with more peevishness than was natural to her, in these words: '*If I had not liked you should sit, why should I have ordered it?*'

"This plainly showed that the cabal had been *blowing her up*, but that she could not have us contradict her own orders. What she had now said was a still further confirmation of it, and made it more difficult for the cabal to proceed any further in this matter; and, therefore, the next day the Duchess of Ormond and Lady Fretcheville came to the trial, and, to my great surprise, sat down amongst the rest of us. And thus this matter ended; only that the Duchess of Somerset used some little arts afterwards, which are not worth mentioning, to sweeten me again, and cover her design, which I supposed now she was ashamed of."

The issue of this trial convinced the Queen that the nation was anxious for her to free herself from the bondage in which she was held by the Marlborough family junta and the Whigs; and she and her secret advisers resolved to take instant measures for effecting the greatly-desired change. Meanwhile, another stormy interview took place between the Queen and her haughty discarded favourite, which we give in the words of Coxe, the historian of Marlborough.

"We have already alluded," observes our author, "to the promise which the duchess extorted from the Queen, for the transfer of her offices to the daughters, and her suspicions that it would not be fulfilled. Influenced by repeated importunities, her husband was reluctantly persuaded to solicit the Queen on this delicate subject, and in the last audience before his departure (to open the campaign of 1710), he made two requests to her Majesty: the first, that she would kindly permit the duchess to remain in the country as much as her offices in the household would allow; and the second, that she would accept her resignation in favour of their daughters, at the conclusion of peace, when it was his own intention to retire. To the first request the Queen acceded; and to the second, replied, that she could not think of parting with the duchess, but spoke of the reversion in so favourable a manner, as led him to suppose that it met with her approbation.

" Soon after his departure, however, the duchess found that he had mistaken the Queen's answer; for, on returning her thanks for these kind assurances, her Majesty preserved an obstinate silence, and when pressed to declare whether the duke had rightly understood her meaning, peremptorily replied, ' I desire that I may never be troubled any more on this subject.'

" These repeated intrusions no less perplexed than offended the Queen; and as she was determined to find a pretext for evading this extorted promise, she was doubly anxious to liberate herself from so importunate a visitor. Unfortunately, the indiscretion of the duchess soon afforded such an opportunity.

" While the affairs of the cabinet were involved in mystery, and while rumours of changes in the administration were daily circulated, the friends of the duchess urged her to appear in court, and endeavour to counteract these cabals, by her influence, or, at least, to show by her presence, that her party was not declining in favour. She, however, was too well apprised of the Queen's sentiments, to imagine that her appearance would not be unwelcome, and might expose her to new mortifications. She, therefore, persevered in her resolution to remain in the country, until reports of her indiscretion in speaking disrespectfully of her royal mistress, were industriously circulated. Her indignation being awakened by these imputations, she hastily took the resolution of returning to court, for the sake of vindicating her own character, or, at least, of proving to the public, that her interest was not absolutely lost.

" On the third of April she waited on the Queen, and solicited a private audience, for the purpose of making some important communications before her Majesty quitted London for the summer. The request was, however, received with the most repulsive coldness. She named, in vain, three several hours, in which she knew the Queen was accustomed to be alone, and, at length, was told to present herself at six the ensuing evening, the time which was usually set apart for the royal devotions.

" Unwilling, however, to be importuned with so disagreeable a visitor, the Queen retracted, and not only ordered the duchess to make her communication in writing, but hinted that she might immediately gratify the inclination she had expressed, of returning into the country. Notwithstanding this ungracious repulse, the duchess renewed her solicitations, and declined imparting the subject of her application by letter. The queen, therefore, was obliged to appoint a new time; but before it arrived, again deferred the interview, under the plea of dining at Kensington, and repeated her desire for a written communication. On this second refusal, the duchess wrote a letter, requesting permission to repair to Kensington, and declaring that the information which she was about to afford, related solely to her own vindication, and would neither give rise to any misunderstanding, nor oblige the Queen to make an answer, or admit her oftener than was agreeable.

" On the same day, she went to Kensington, without waiting for a reply. The Queen had just dined, and no one being in waiting to announce her, she asked the page of the back-stairs, if he did not occasionally make a signal at the Queen's door, to apprise her when any person was to be introduced. The page replying in the affirmative, she requested him to make the usual sign, and sat down in the window, as she says, ' like a Scotch lady with a petition, expecting an answer.' After a long interval, which she conjectures was employed in consulting Mrs. Masham, she was admitted.

"On her entrance, the Queen evinced some embarrassment, and said to her, 'I was just going to write to you;' and as the duchess was preparing to speak, interrupted her, by observing, 'Whatever you have to say, you may put it in writing.' The duchess, however, remonstrated against such cruel treatment, and urged the justice of hearing her reply to the calumnies with which she had been assailed. She added, 'There are those about your Majesty, who have charged me with saying things of which I am no more capable than I am of killing my own children; for I seldom mention your Majesty in company, and then always with due respect.' During this address, the Queen contemptuously turned aside, and replied briefly, 'There are many lies told.' The duchess requesting to know the particulars with which she was charged, the Queen alluded to the expression in her letter, that she did not wish for a reply, and several times interrupted her with the exclamation, 'I will give you no answer.' Notwithstanding farther solicitations, she still continued to repeat the same words, adding, at last, 'You desired no answer, and you shall have none.' The duchess proceeding, 'I am confident your Majesty would not treat me with such harshness, if you could believe that my only wish is, to do myself justice, and not to ask a favour;' the Queen moved towards the door, impatiently exclaiming, 'I will quit the room.'

"The duchess followed, and burst into a flood of tears. The Queen appeared to be affected, and the duchess, after a pause, to recover from her emotion, proceeded to recapitulate the reports spread to her disadvantage, and implored her Majesty to state the particulars, without naming the authors. The Queen replied as before, 'You said you desired no answer, and I shall give you none.' The duchess, however, continued her vindication with great warmth and volubility. The Queen heard her sullenly for some minutes, and then rejoined, 'I shall make no answer to anything you say.' Notwithstanding this repulse, the duchess asked, 'Will your Majesty then make me some answer at any other time?' She received only the same reply, and in the agony of indignation, after a second flood of tears, more violent than the former, she said, 'You know, madam, how much I despised my interest, in comparison with your service, and you may be assured that I would never deny anything which I was aware was true, conscious as I am that I have done nothing to displease you.' She could, however, only extort the former reply, 'You desired no answer, and you shall have none.' Perceiving it fruitless to persist, she made her obeisance, and exclaimed with a degree of violence, which she herself does not attempt to justify, 'I am confident you will suffer in this world or the next, for so much inhumanity.' The Queen was roused to indignation by this unpremeditated insult, and replying, 'That is my business,' withdrew to the closet.

"After quitting the royal presence, the duchess sat down in a long gallery to wipe away her tears, and compose her agitation. She then returned to the closet, and scratched at the door; and when the Queen opened it, said, 'As I sat in the gallery, I thought your Majesty would not be easy to see me, when you come to the castle at Windsor, whither I understand you are shortly to remove. Should that be the case, I will refrain from going to the Lodge, that I may not be charged with a want of respect, for omitting to pay my duty to your Majesty when so near.' To this the Queen quickly replied, as if anxious to be freed from her visitor, 'You may, if you please, come to me at the castle: it will give me no uneasiness.'"*

* "This account is drawn from a dialogue which seems to have been written by the duchess soon after the event, endorsed, 'Account of the Conversation with the Queen, Good Friday, 1710:' also from her letter to Mr. Hutchinson. There is a detailed account of this interview in the Conduct, pp. 279—287."

Thus ended this memorable conversation, and from this moment all personal intercourse was broken off between the Queen and her discarded favourite. The duchess, indeed, made an attempt to renew the discussion the following day, by taking an opportunity of forwarding a letter to the Queen from the duke, relative to a supposed plot for assassinating her Majesty. In this she renewed her justification, and complained of the strange usage she had received on the preceding day; but the attempt did not succeed to her wish, for the Queen returned the letter with a line simply acknowleding its reception. The account of this interview was forwarded to the duke, and reached him while he was encamped before Douay; but it was too late to remedy the effects of her indiscretion, and, in his reply, he merely exhorts her to refrain from courting similar mortifications.

"*May* 5.—I have this morning received yours of the seventeenth of April, O.S., from the Lodge, as also the account of what passed between you and the Queen, which is so harsh, that I think you should be persuaded not to expose yourself any more in speaking to her Majesty."

From this time, the duchess became as great an object of disgust and aversion, as she had formerly been of favour and affection; and the anxiety of the Queen to remove from her household so obnoxious an attendant, was one, among many causes, which induced her to accelerate the execution of those meditated changes which had been recommended by her secret advisers.

CHAPTER VI.

Anne's first successful efforts to free herself from the Marlboroughs and the Whigs—Removes Sunderland from office—The Duchess insolently remonstrates thereon—Her reply—The Duchess expostulates—All direct communication between them terminates—The Queen dismisses Godolphin and his Whig coadjutors—Forms a Tory administration—Corresponds with the Duchess through the agency of her physician, Hamilton—Alarmed at the Duchess's threats to publish her letters—Declares cheating is not one of the Duchess's faults—Dismisses the Duchess from her appointments in the royal household—Disposes of her offices to the Duchess of Somerset and Mrs. Masham—Disgraceful conduct of the Duchess—Anne's uncle, Rochester, dies—She corresponds with the Pretender—Break in her constitution—Love of hunting—Takes measures for establishing peace—Violent party feuds—Creates twelve new peers—Dismissal and disgrace of Marlborough—Prince Eugene's visit—Birthday commemoration—Death of Louise Stuart—Anne's declining health—Announces from the throne peace with Spain—Letters to the Princess Sophia and Prince George—Desires the Pretender for her successor—Last speech to parliament—Death of the Electress Sophia—Anne's antipathy to Oxford—She dismisses him—Storms in her council—Carried ill to bed—Her dangerous condition—Suffers mental agonies—Death—George I. proclaimed—Burial—Will—Character.

VAILING herself of the prorogation of parliament, which took place on the fifth of April, of the absence of Marlborough, and of a temporary retirement of Godolphin to Newmarket, Anne, on the thirteenth, caused her lord chamberlain, the Marquis of Kent, for the proffered reward of a dukedom, instantly to relinquish his staff of office, which she forthwith conferred on the Tory Duke of Shrewsbury, and before intelligence of the change could reach her ministers. She next coerced the Duke of Marlborough into making Mr. Masham and Mr.

Hill generals, and took steps for the removal of her detested Secretary of State, Lord Sunderland, from office. Sunderland being son-in-law to Marlborough, every conceivable obstacle was thrust in the way of his removal—but to no purpose. In reply to the entreaties of his friends on his behalf, Anne said, "I have received so many provocations from him, that nothing shall divert me from my purpose of dismissing him." The treasurer, as a last effort, hinted to her Majesty, that if she persisted in her purpose, he feared Marlborough would resign his command, and then he himself must follow his example. This threat, however, fell short of its purpose; the Queen, by letter, on the fourteenth of June, appealed to the patriotism of Godolphin, and announced to him that she had sent for the seals from Lord Sunderland.

Queen Anne to the Earl of Godolphin.

"*Wednesday morning, nine o'clock.*

"I received your letter last night, just as I was going to bed, to which I can say no more than what I did on the subject, in my last, continuing of the same opinion, only that I have no thoughts of taking the Duke of Marlborough from the head of the army, nor, I dare say, any body else. If he and you should do so wrong a thing, at any time, as to desert my service, what confusion might happen might lie at your door, and you alone would be answerable, and nobody else. But I hope you will both consider better of it. Yesterday, in the afternoon, Mr. Secretary Boyle came to me, and I then ordered him to go this morning to Lord Sunderland for the seals, which I think proper to acquaint you with, before you hear it from other hands, and to let you know Lord Dartmouth is the person I intend to give them to, whom I hope you will approve of."

The removal of Marlborough's son-in-law, Sunderland, again excited the ire of the fiery duchess, Sarah, who, disregarding the prudent advice of her husband to avoid intrusion upon her Majesty, either by person or letter, seized the opportunity of addressing to Anne a long and severe remonstrance; in which she deprecated the removal of Sunderland, expatiated on the services of her husband and herself, and to remind her Majesty of her former kindness, and show the change which had taken place, enclosed several of the Queen's affectionate letters to her. She censured the Duke and Duchess of Somerset as the persons causing these changes, and enclosed a confidential letter which the duke a time back had addressed to herself, and in which the Queen was mentioned with but little ceremony. These, and other reproaches, were expressed with a degree of contempt, that even to an equal would have been insulting. But the most biting and offensive portion of the letter was levelled against Mrs. Masham. To this lady she attributed all the mischief which had happened, or was likely to happen; and had the impudence to declare, that a dread of losing this favourite was the motive which had impelled the Queen into the "*ungrateful and impolitic*" conduct she had manifested towards her zealous and faithful servants. She affected to treat with indifference the transfer of the royal favour to such a person; and after declaring with scorn that she would never wish for any address against Mrs. Masham, for the sake of regaining her own influence, she held forth an indirect threat, that the conduct the Queen was pursuing, might produce this very measure, which would not fail to gratify all who loved their country. She concluded by desiring the Queen to return the letter of the Duke of Somerset, which, for nonsense, ingratitude, and good spelling, she considered as worthy of preservation, as a great curiosity, and as being the production of so eminent a politician.

"The Queen made no reply to this effusion till the twelfth of June, the very day preceding the removal of Lord Sunderland. She then reproached the duchess, by letter, for breaking the solemn promise made by herself and the duke, that she would never speak of politics, or even again mention the name of Mrs. Masham, and concluded by observing, 'But I shall trouble you with a very short answer, looking upon it to be a continuation of the ill usage I have so often met with, which shows me very plainly what I am to expect for the future.'

"Shocked at the breach of trust which the duchess had committed, in communicating the confidential letter of the Duke of Somerset, and still more mortified to find that the effusions of her former tenderness had been treasured up by so irritable a woman, Anne added, in a postscript, 'I do not return the letters, knowing they can be of no use to you, but must desire all my strange scrawls may be sent back to me, it being impossible they can now be agreeable to you.'

"Farther reports of her son-in-law's approaching disgrace, joined to the tone of the Queen's letter, drew from the duchess another expostulation in a no less acrimonious style. She testified her surprise at the Queen's short, harsh, and undeserved answer. She justified her own breach of promise in writing on politics and Mrs. Masham, by reminding the Queen, that her Majesty herself had not fulfilled her own promise of reading the narrative which was presented in the preceding October, and giving a precise answer. She vindicated her present interference, on the plea that it was her duty to make every effort to prevent the extremities to which her Majesty was driving the Duke of Marlborough, at the very moment when he was hourly venturing his life for the service. She contended, also, that it was justice to herself to vindicate her own character from the aspersions with which she had been loaded, particularly of attempting to procure the removal of Mrs. Masham; but she again held forth an indirect threat of the dreadful account which the favourite might be required to render for her advice, to ruin a man who had won six pitched battles and ten sieges.

"With regard to the Queen's letters, she stated, that the refusal to return them would induce her to take a little better care of the rest. She expressed, also, surprise that the Queen should retain the letter written by the Duke of Somerset, and declared, that though it had made no impression on her Majesty, she could make other people ashamed for him, by showing it. To prove that she was not herself singular in her opinion of this nobleman, she enclosed several letters, in which, we may suppose, his character was not treated with great respect, particularly one from Lord Rochester, who, she said, could not, in this case, be suspected of partiality. She added, 'My concern for Lord Marlborough's honour and reputation in the world, and the great trouble he expresses on this occasion, brings me to beg of your Majesty, upon my knees, that you would only defer this thing till there is peace, or an end of the campaign; and, after such an expression, your Majesty can have no doubt of my ever entering into any thing that can displease you.'

"To this letter the Queen did not condescend to reply; and with this altercation terminated all direct correspondence between them." *

Her Majesty next resolved to dismiss her treasurer, Godolphin. He guessed her purpose, and after endeavouring to dissuade her from turning her back upon the Whigs and her present ministers, demanded, "Is it the will of your Majesty that I should go on?" [continue in office as Lord Treasurer.]

The Queen replied "Yes;" she looked gloomy, and seemed embarrassed; but Godolphin supposed she meant to abide by that reply; and when the next morning a servant in royal livery left the subjoined note with his porter, he was struck dumb with astonishment.

"*Kensington, August* 7.

"The uneasiness which you have showed for some time has given me very much trouble, though I have borne it; and had your behaviour continued the same it was for a few years after my coming to the crown, I could have no dispute with myself what to do. But the many unkind returns I have received since, especially what you said to me personally before the lords, makes it impossible for me to continue you any longer

* Coxe.

in my service; but I will give you a pension of four thousand a year, and I desire that, instead of bringing the staff to me, you will break it, which, I believe, will be easier to us both."

"On the ensuing morning the Queen briefly announced to the Duke of Marlborough the removal of his friend.

"*Kensington, August* 8.

"My lord treasurer having for some time showed a great deal of uneasiness in my service, and his behaviour not being the same to me as it was formerly, made it impossible for me to let him keep the white staff any longer; and, therefore, I ordered him this morning to break it, which I acquaint you with now, that you may receive this news first from me; and I do assure you I will take care that the army shall want for nothing."

To those who expressed concern at Godolphin's dismissal, the Queen answered, "I am sorry for it, but I can't help it." The removal of the treasurer was speedily followed by the dismission of his son, Lord Rialton, from the office of cofferer of the household, and the treasury was put in commission, at the head of which was Mr. Harley, who, the next day supplanted Mr. Smith in the Chancellorship of the Exchequer, and subsequently was made Lord Treasurer, and created Earl of Oxford and Mortimer. The Queen next resolved to dissolve parliament; and at the instigation of Harley and Shrewsbury, she, in August, withdrew her confidence from the great Whig leader Lord Somers, President of the Council, who, with his colleagues and adherents, forthwith retired from office. On the nineteenth of August, Somers, Devonshire, and Mr. Boyle, resigned, and their respective appointments were filled by the Earl of Rochester, the Duke of Buckingham, and Mr. St. John. The governorship of Ireland was transferred from Lord Wharton to the Duke of Ormond. Lord Orford resigned his commission of the Admiralty, and the presidency of the board was vested in Sir John Leak. Although Harley solicited, and the Queen three times commanded Lord Chancellor Cowper to retain the seals, he resigned, and Sir Thomas Trevor and the Barons Tracy and Scroop were appointed commissioners of the great seal about the same time—Sir Simon Harcourt was made Attorney-General, Lord Keeper, and, finally, Chancellor; and to the annoyance of of Marlborough, her Majesty dismissed Cardonel from the office of Secretary-at-War, and in his room appointed Mr. Granville, afterwards Lord Lansdowne.

"Since the accession of William III.," remarks Coxe, "no change of ministry had ever been carried to such an extent; for before the close of the year, not a single Whig, with the exception of the Dukes of Newcastle and Somerset, retained any office of importance." The parliament was dissolved, and, on the fifteenth of November, the new House of Commons met, and chose for their Speaker the Tory, William Bromley, one of the representatives of the University of Oxford.

Meanwhile the Queen, although she had broken the chains which bound her to the Marlborough family junta and the Whigs, was still harassed by the threats and importunities of the arrogant Duchess Sarah, who now carried on a regular but indirect correspondence with her through the agency of Sir David Hamilton. By the hands of Hamilton, the duchess sent the Queen long narratives of their past transactions, and, in the vain hope of frightening her into consenting to a reconciliation, repeatedly referred to the ill treatment which she considered she had undergone through the influence of Mr. Masham, and threatened to expose to the public eye the tender epistles which her Majesty had addressed to her in the height of affection. Secretary St. John, in a letter to Mr. Drummond, dated November twenty-eight, remarks, "I had almost forgot to tell you an instance of the admirable temper in which the great man [Marlborough] is likely on his return to find his wife. Among other extravagancies, she now declares she will print the Queen's letters; letters writ whilst her Majesty had a good opinion of her, which her violent behaviour since that time has absolutely eradicated."

"In this predicament the Queen was reduced alternately to soothe and threaten her former favourite, and resorted to the intervention of the physician, as well as of other persons, whom she considered as likely to obtain the suppression of these documents. The duchess, however, continued firm, and the fear of driving her to extremities suspended her removal.

"As a last resource, the Duke of Shrewsbury was employed to discover her real intentions, and, if possible, to prevent the threatened publication. He applied to Mr. Maynwaring, and used such arguments and insinuations as his experience in courts suggested. His efforts were not more successful than those before made, for the duchess declined parting with the letters; and, though she professed her aversion to publish such a correspondence, she adroitly threw out hints, that she might be compelled to recur to unpleasant measures, in her own justification, if the ministerial writers were suffered to continue their accusations against her, for peculation and corrupt sale of offices.

"In this struggle between pride, interest, and fear, with the hopes of proving to the public that she was not wholly in disgrace, she wrote a letter to Sir David Hamilton, to be submitted to the Queen, offering to renew her attendance, by assisting in trying on the robes which her Majesty had ordered for some public ceremony. The letter being read to the Queen by her agent, she charged him to prevent the duchess from coming, though not to say that she refused to permit her attendance.

"Hitherto the duchess had acted with no less indiscretion than disrespect, by shocking the political prejudices, insulting the dignity, and wounding the feelings of the Queen. But at the present period she made a new and stronger appeal, which, though objectionable in the mode, was justifiable in the principle. The libellous and scurrilous productions which daily issued from the press under the auspices of the ministry, having exhausted their satire and spleen on the Duke of Marlborough, involved the duchess in accusations which affected her integrity. In one of the *Examiners*, written by Swift, November the twenty-third, 1710, after a variety of insinuations against the peculation and avarice of the duke, a comparison was introduced between the rewards lavished on him, and the recompense conferred on a Roman general, in which the duke's emoluments were estimated in the aggregate at the vast amount of £500,000, and those of a Roman warrior reduced to £994 11*s*. At the end of the same paper an inuendo was introduced, by way of comparison, that the duchess, in the execution of her office during eight years, as mistress of the robes, had also purloined no less than £22,000 a year.

"This slander, though couched in ambiguous terms, was too pointed in its application to be mistaken, either by the public or the party interested. The duchess, therefore, drew up an animated vindication of the duke and of herself, in a private letter to Sir David Hamilton, and sent it with the scurrilous number, to be submitted to her Majesty. The Queen read it over, and, at the conclusion, acknowledged the justice of the vindication by the brief remark, 'Every one knows that cheating is not the Duchess of Marlborough's fault.'"

Such was the critical situation of the duchess, when her husband, returning from his campaign in Holland, reached London, on the twenty-eighth of December, and immediately had several private interviews with her Majesty, in the hope of prevailing on her to permit his fiery wife to retain the golden keys as groom of the stole, mistress of the robes, and privy purse. Anne, however, was too firmly resolved to be moved by his entreaties, and, on the seventeenth of January, 1711, at the last of these interviews, she peremptorily insisted that the golden keys should be delivered to her within three days; and when he on his knees entreated for an interval of a fortnight, she replied by limiting the term to the shorter space of two days, and abruptly terminated the audience.

When Marlborough informed his indignant wife of the Queen's commands, she declared she would never comply

He then commanded her to give him the keys, as he was resolved to return them that very evening. She at first refused; high words ensued, and, in the end, she pitched them at his head, exclaiming, "There, take them, you ass! take them to the odious creature!" He eagerly seized them, and hurrying to St. James's, presented them to her Majesty, who received them with infinite joy, but was so confused, probably at his unexpected appearance, that to his question of what offences had the duchess been guilty, she only faltered out an unintelligible incoherent reply.

Sarah of Marlborough next resolved to claim the £2000 a year which, nine years back, the Queen had offered her, and to carry the whole amount of arrears to her credit. We give the particulars of these proceedings in the words of the duchess, who, after stating that some of her friends persuaded her to make the demand, proceeds: — "Accordingly, I consented that a copy of one of her [the Queen's] own letters, in which she pressed me so much to take that money out of the privy purse, should be shown to her, and that the person that carried it should tell her that I desired to know, before I made up my accounts, whether she still was willing that I should take the money out of the privy purse, as she had desired me in that letter. When this was proposed to her, she blushed and appeared to be very uneasy; but consented that I should do it. Then I sent in my accounts, with that yearly sum charged in them from the time that she had offered it to me. But I still used this further caution of writing at the bottom of the accounts, before I charged the last sum, a copy of the letter I mentioned before, that, when she signed them, she might at the same time attest her own letter, and the offer she had made me of her own accord, and pressed me to take in this manner:—'Pray make no more words about it, and either own or conceal it, as you like best, since I think the richest crown could never repay the services I have received from you.' After this, the Queen kept my accounts almost a fortnight by her, in which time I don't doubt but they were well examined by Abigail and Mr. Harley; but there was no fault which they could pretend to find with them, and they were sent back to me without the least objection being made against them, signed by the Queen's own hand, who had writ under them, that she allowed of them, and was satisfied that they were right. So that the new ministers had nothing left them in this matter but to whisper about the town some scandalous stories of it, and to employ such of their agents as the *Examiner* in propagating them."

Anne, without delay, disposed of the offices held by the Duchess of Marlborough, by making the Duchess of Somerset groom of the stole and mistress of the robes, and transferring the confidential situation of keeper of the privy purse to Mrs. Masham.

On her removal from the royal household, the Duchess of Marlborough relinquished her apartments at St. James's, when, to her own disgrace, and to the indignation of the Queen, she ordered that part of the palace which she had occupied to be ransacked of all the brass locks, the looking-glasses and pictures fixed in the panels of the wainscoting, and the marble chimney-pieces and slabs:—in fact, by her command, the apartments were literally gutted.

The establishment of peace now became the earnest desire of the Queen and her ministers, who, as a preliminary to that important measure, used all possible means to gradually, but surely, mortify and degrade the lately-idolized Duke of Marlborough. It was believed that the war with France would long since have been brought to an honourable termination, but for the avarice and ambition of the great commander; and to convince him that his power and popularity was gone, the House of Commons, influenced by the Queen and her Tory ministry, refused to thank him for his services in Flanders, although he was still permitted to retain his command.

On the second of May, 1711, the Queen's uncle, the Earl of Rochester, died suddenly of apoplexy, and was succeeded as president of the council by the Duke of Buckingham. Rochester believed Anne had no right to the throne, and he joined her ministry in the hope of inducing her to secure the succession to her disinherited brother, the Pretender, with whom she commenced a correspondence, under his auspices. After the demise of Rochester, Buckingham assisted Anne to carry on this correspondence; but as the Pretender firmly refused to renounce the church of Rome for that of England, his exclusion from the throne of Great Britain was inevitable. It was in the summer of this year that the visible break in the constitution of the Queen commenced. A fear lest the Marlborough faction should obtain the majority in parliament, depressed her spirits, and produced hysterical fits; to rally her health, she, about the commencement of July, took up her abode at Windsor, and, although sufficiently restored by the bracing air to frequently enjoy the pleasures of the chase, in the meridian heat of summer,—albeit she hunted in a one-horse chaise, which she drove herself, "furious as Jehu," remarks Swift, "and gaily as the mighty hunter Nimrod"—about the middle of August she was laid up with the gout, which confined her to her bed-chamber for a month.

Meanwhile, the Queen's first efforts to establish peace were revealed sooner than her Majesty or her ministers desired. Prior, the poet, who had been secretly dispatched to France to propose a pacification, was, on his return, seized by the Whig spy Mackey, who held an appointment in the customs, on a frivolous charge, and detained prisoner till his mission became public. Prior's return was speedily followed by the arrival of M. Mesnager and the Abbé Dubois, as secret envoys from the court of France, and on the twenty-seventh of September (O. S.), Anne consented to enter into preliminaries of peace with France. Mesnager was received with distinguished honour by the Queen, who was then at Windsor; he held several strictly private conferences with her, and, says Boyer, "it was confidently reported, that, encouraged by Mr. St. John, he spoke to her in favour of the Chevalier de St. George, whom he called her brother; that her Majesty seemed not displeased with the discourse; and that before he left England, he obtained, by means of Mrs. Masham, a verbal promise, that private instructions should be sent to the British plenipotentiaries, not to insist on the French king's giving up the interest of the chevalier entirely. Moreover, a letter from a good hand in Paris, dated the nineteenth of November (N. S.), imported, 'That upon Mesnager's return thither, he was very sanguine, and affected publicly to affirm, that the peace was as good as concluded; and that, in particular, he laid great emphasis on the advantages granted in favour of the Prince of Wales; which to some people appeared very unlikely, especially when they compared the weight of such an affair with the abilities of Monsieur Mesnager, who was never accounted a great genius.'"

The peace proposals greatly agitated the opposing factions. The violent Tories and Jacobites rose in formidable opposition to Harley and his partizans. Her Majesty, in alarm, invited Lord Somers to confidential audiences, which frightened her ministry into a belief, that the Whigs were winning back the royal confidence, through the agency of the Duchess of Somerset. To preserve their popularity, at the expense of their opponents, the struggling faction filled the newspapers and periodicals with political squibs and lampoons; and the excitement was greatly increased, by the caption of the effigies of the devil, the pope, the pretender, and several cardinals, jesuits, and friars, which had been prepared by the Whigs, to be consigned to the flames, with due solemnity, by the London rabble, on the seventeenth of November, the anniversary of Queen Elizabeth's inauguration.

On the seventh of December Anne opened parliament in person, and in her speech remarked, "I can now tell you, that notwithstanding the arts of those who delight in war, both place and time are appointed for opening the treaty of a general peace. My chief concern is that the Protestant religion, and the laws and liberties of the kingdom may be continued to you, by securing the accession to the crown, as it is limited by parliament, to the house of Hanover." This royal oration occasioned much warm discussion. The people, heartily tired of the war, were anxious for peace, so also were the Commons; but a majority of the Lords were against it, which so alarmed the ministry, that to turn the balance in their favour, they proposed the creation of twelve new peers, a measure at first so strenuously opposed by the Queen and the Duchess of Somerset, that a cry ran through the Harley faction that her Majesty was playing false to them. This, however, was an error; Anne's very natural purport being simply to endeavour, by entreaty and persuasion, to procure the desired majority, before adopting the sweeping proposal of at one stroke elevating twelve commoners to the peerage.

"Among others," says Bishop Burnet, "the Queen spoke to myself; she said, she hoped bishops would not be against peace; I said, a good peace was what we prayed daily for, but the preliminaries offered by France gave no hopes of such an one; and the trusting to the King of France's faith, after all that had passed, would seem a strange thing. She said, we were not to regard the preliminaries; we should have a peace upon such a bottom, that we should not at all rely on the King of France's word; but we ought to suspend our opinions, till she acquainted us with the whole matter. I asked leave to speak my mind plainly; which she granted: I said, any treaty, by which Spain and the West Indies were left to King Philip, must in a little while deliver up all Europe into the hands of France; and, if any such peace should be made, she was betrayed, and we were all ruined; in less than three years' time she would be murdered, and the fires would be again raised in Smithfield; I pursued this long, till I saw she grew uneasy; so I withdrew."

After many private audiences with her nobles, and much wrangling with her ministry, who vainly desired the removal of the Duchess of Somerset from the royal household, Anne succumbed to the wish of her cabinet, and on the twenty-eighth of December, 1711, twelve new Tory peers were created (three peers' sons, and nine commoners), one of whom, Mr. Masham, the husband of the Queen's favourite, was on this occasion raised to the peerage, by the desire of the ministry, and in opposition to the will of Anne.

Meanwhile, the Queen and her ministers resolved on the dismission of Marlborough. The great warrior returned from his annual campaign in November, and after futile efforts to win back the esteem and confidence of his sovereign and his countrymen, was formally dismissed by the Queen from all his appointments, on the last day of the year 1711, and, at the same time, charged by the commissioners of public accounts with unjustly appropriating large sums of money by selling commissions in the army, and by extorting vast bribes and fees from the contractors for the food and clothing of his soldiers. Swift, in a lampoon published at this period, thus addressed the fallen commander:

"So flagrant is thy insolence,
So rich thy breach of trust is,
That longer with thee to dispense,
Were want of power, or want of sense.
Here, Towzer—do him justice."

The dismissal of Marlborough was followed by many other changes. His two daughters, the Countess of Sunderland and the Lady Raitton, relinquished their appointments in the royal bedchamber; the Duke of Ormond was appointed to his office of commander of the forces, and commissioned only to preserve an armed neutrality, till the peace negotiations were settled; Earl Rivers was made master of the ordnance; the Dukes of Northumberland and Beaufort were respectively appointed to the captainships of the royal regiments of horse-guards and of the band of pensioners; the lieutenancy of the Tower was transferred from General Cadogan to Brigadier Hill; the Duke of Somerset was deprived of his appointment of master of the horse; and, in fact, the remnant of the Marlborough ministry was finally dismissed.

Whilst these changes were in progress, the Queen was compelled to give audience to an unwelcomed visitor. On the sixth of January, 1712, Prince Eugene arrived in London, charged with proposals from the new emperor, Charles VI., to Anne, which were calculated to disconcert the schemes of the ministry, and turn the tide of public opinion in favour of the Marlboroughs, the Whigs, and the war. On the evening of the following day, her Majesty, greatly against her will, admitted Eugene to an audience, and after slightly glancing over his papers, remarked, "I am sorry that the state of my health does not permit me to speak with your highness as often as I wish; but," she added (pointing to the treasurer, Harley, and secretary, St. John, who alone were present), "I have ordered these two gentlemen to receive your proposals whenever you think proper."

Shortly afterwards, her Majesty was laid up, with what was said to be a political fit of the gout; she, however, recovered in time to keep the anniversary of her birth-day (sixth of February) with extraordinary pomp and splendour; and although the Marlborough and Whig ladies did their best to mar the pleasures of the day, by absenting themselves from the dazzling scene, and seating themselves in their morning wrappers at a window in St. James's palace, within sight of the whole court; their malice failed of its purpose, and the ardour and brilliancy of the scene was equally remarkable and satisfactory to all present. Prince Eugene, in a "fine suit made up for the occasion," was present at this remarkable birth-day drawing-room, and the Queen presented him with a sword richly set with diamonds, to the value of £4500.

According to some authorities, Eugene, when he found that the Queen and her ministers turned their back on his project for continuing the war, advised Marlborough to suborn the miscreants denominated *Mohocks* to scour the streets at night, and in the midst of the terrors incited by the excesses and cruelties of these Mohocks, to burn the capital, to seize the person of the Queen, to murder Oxford and his associates, and to place the Elector of Hanover on the throne. Coxe pronounces this not a real, but a supposed conspiracy, invented by the Jesuit and Jacobite spy Plunket; but however this may be, the startling tale certainly alarmed the Queen, aggravated her displeasure against Marlborough, and increased her anxiety for the departure of Eugene, and the conclusion of peace. On the seventeenth of March, Eugene, after having a farewell audience of her Majesty, quitted England and returned to Holland, to deplore the failure of his efforts to incite the British Queen and her people to again place their confidence in the Marlboroughs, the Whigs, and the war party.

The death of Anne's half-sister, the Princess Louisa Stuart, at St. Germains, in April, made a deep and mournful impression on her Majesty, and on the nation at large. Had the Pretender died, and the Princess been spared, it was remarked, an end might have been put to all disputes concerning the succession, by the Queen marrying her to a Prince of Hanover. It was also about this time that the following facetious incident occurred. An Irish priest refused to take the oath of abjuration, and when summoned before the magistrates for non-compliance, asked, "Would it not be better to settle all this hubbub, by marrying our gracious Queen to the Pretender?" "Why, man," exclaimed the bench, with consternation, "he is her brother!" "Then if so, your worships, why the divil am I to be sworn to abjure him?" demanded the priest, with a grin of triumph. The magistrates answered not; and the priest on finding that he could gain nothing by farther opposition, upbraided the bench, for not admitting the justness of his reasoning, and with an air of supreme contempt took the required oath.

The Duchess of Marlborough, ever since her final dismission from the royal household, had ceaselessly tormented the Queen with threats of publishing the whole of her letters to her. Harley, now Lord Oxford, at length, hit upon a plan which effectually checked the arrogance of the overbearing, discarded favourite. He procured from Mary Beatrice the treasonable letters which Marlborough had written to James II., at St. Germains, in 1694, betraying to the French the armament dispatched to invest Brest. These letters he privately showed to Marlborough, who, to secure his head, quitted England without delay. Just previously, Marlborough's friend, Godolphin, died, and the disgraced warrior paraded this gloomy event, coupled with what he pleased to designate the ingratitude of his country, as the ostensible cause of his departure. Her Majesty, when informed that he had embarked, remarked, "he had acted wisely in going abroad." Shortly afterwards, the Duchess of Marlborough, who had tarried in England to arrange some private matters, and, if possible, further to aggravate the Queen, proceeded to her husband. But Anne, although free from her presence, continued to be annoyed by her threats to publish their correspondence, threats which she dared not, because she could not perform, at least, whilst the Queen lived, without compromising herself and the Whigs, who were the only friends she could depend upon in England.

At this period several of Anne's ministers, and many of her household and of her friends, were anxious that she should make her brother, "the Pretender," her successor; she herself secretly entertained the same wish, and a revival of the proposition, that Prince George of Hanover should settle in England, increased her abhorrence of the Crown Prince, a circumstance by no means surprising. "For," remarks Lockhart, "when it was first proposed to bring the Elector of Hanover to England, the Whigs dispatched numbers of their emissaries to engage all their friends in the neighbouring counties to be in readiness to show their respect to the first Prince of the royal blood, when he arrived in Britain, by meeting and attending him to London; and they secured a number of reduced officers, who were to be well accoutred in horses and arms, and offer themselves as guard to his person, by which precautions, and the conjunction of their friends in London, they intended that the Prince should pay his respects to the Queen with no less than forty or fifty thousand armed men, the consequence whereof it was very easy to imagine." The cause of the Jacobites, however, received a fatal blow, when, on Sunday, the fifteenth of November, 1712, their powerful partizan, the Duke of Hamilton, was unfairly slain in a duel with the profligate Lord Mohun. At this very time, Hamilton was deeply engaged with the Queen in a scheme for the restoration of the Pretender; and when Anne heard of his death, or, as some writers have it, murder, she, with tears of sorrow, told Mrs. Masham, "that now there was no hope of her brother succeeding to her crown, for she could not trust the delicate arragement to any other nobleman, for fear of treachery."

At the commencement of 1713, Anne beheld with infinite satisfaction the establishment of the long-desired peace, on what she believed to be an equitable and firm basis. The treaty of Utrecht was signed by the plenipotentiaries on the thirtieth of March, 1713. On the third of April it was brought to Whitehall, was ratified four days afterwards, and on the ninth her Majesty opened parliament, and in her speech announced the important fact to the assembled Lords and Commons. By the treaty of Utrecht, Louis XIV. recognised for himself and his successors, the Protestant line of Hanover, and engaged that the Pretender should no longer remain in France; but what was to be done with Anne's unfortunate brother was a difficulty equally perplexing to the English and the French sovereigns, who, after much negotiation, arranged that for the present he should reside within the dominions of the Duke of Lorraine. At this peace France ceded Newfoundland to England; and it is worthy of remark, that of all the European conquests in the reign of Anne, England retains at the present day but Gibraltar, which was taken from Spain by Sir

George Rooke, in July, 1704, and is now deemed impregnable.

In the spring of this year, her Majesty conferred the deanery of St. Patrick's, Dublin, on Dr. Swift. This celebrated wit first earned eminence as a political writer, by extolling the Whigs; but as they neglected him, he turned from them in disgust. In 1710, he was commissioned by the primate of Ireland, to solicit the Queen to exonerate the clergy of Ireland from paying the twentieth parts and first-fruits, which occasioned his introduction to Mr. Harley and the Tories, who received him with open arms, and to whom he, from that time, became a fast friend and steady adherent. He contributed by his pen, in a great degree, to the downfall of the Whig ministry, and supported in the same manner the measures of the four last years of Queen Anne. In 1712, the ministry endeavoured to procure his elevation to the see of Hereford; but the deistical tendency of his polemic writings, and the lack of truth and moral principle in his political and miscellaneous works, so horrified the Queen, that she refused to make him a bishop; and yet, singular to relate, a brief while afterwards she willingly inducted him into the deanery of St. Patrick.

Meanwhile, the Queen's health gradually declined, she grew every day more unwieldy, "and," remarks Swift, "the gout and other disorders so increased on her, that those at court might have fixed the period of her life, without pretending to prophecy." She took no exercise, ate and drank to excess, was harassed in mind by the political feuds in her cabinet and household, and, what further hastened her demise, was one day prompted by her conscience to name the Pretender her successor, and the next day driven by her fears to proscribe him for the heir of Hanover. In fact, on this point she remained from the period of which we are writing, till her dissolution, in a state of agonising indecision. In June, the House of Lords suspecting the Queen's partiality to her unfortunate brother, voted an address, requesting her to procure the removal of the Pretender from Lorraine. Her Majesty answered:

"I take kindly your address, and your thanks for what I have done to establish the Protestant succession. I shall repeat my instances to have that person removed; and I promise myself you will concur with me, that if we could cure our animosities and divisions at home, it would be the most effectual method to secure the Protestant succession."

Dissatisfied with this reply, the Lords voted a second address, in which, "after returning thanks for the reply of the Queen to the preceding address, they expressed their surprise that her instances had not been effectual, and concluded with assurances of supporting her Majesty in a demand so necessary for her own honour and safety, and for the present and future peace and quiet of her people.

"The Queen, giving no answer to this second address, on the first of July, General Stanhope made a similar motion in the House of Commons, in still stronger terms, designating the Pretender as the person who, in defiance of her Majesty's most undoubted title to the crown, and the settlement to the illustrious house of Hanover, had assumed the title of King of these realms. To this address the Queen briefly replied, that she thanked them for it, and would give directions according as they desired.

"On the seventh of July, the public thanksgiving for the peace was celebrated at St. Paul's, attended with the usual state, except the presence of her Majesty, who, from indisposition, could not assist at the solemnity. On the sixteenth of July, the Queen prorogued the parliament in person, to the eighth of August, and it was on that day dissolved.

On the twenty-third of December her Majesty gave orders that the dower, which during her reign had been withheld from her step-mother, the Queen-dowager, Maria Beatrix, should forthwith be paid; and immediately after doing this tardy act of justice to the widow of James II., she was seized with an inflammatory fever which threatened to put a period to her existence. The particulars of this illness are fully detailed by Dr. Shadwell, one of the Queen's physicians, in a letter to the Duke of Shrewsbury:

"On Wednesday, the twenty-third of December, her Majesty was very uneasy all night with the gout in her foot. The next morning it went entirely off, and she said she was well. But, about one o'clock that day, she complained of a pain in the upper part of her leg, and was seized with a violent shivering, which lasted above two hours. Extreme heat followed, with intense thirst, great anxiety, restlessness, and inquietude. The pulse was full, hard, and quick; which continuing, the next day I very much pressed bleeding, urging, it would probably carry off a good part of the fever, and bring a fit of the gout; but it was not agreed to; and these symptoms continuing till Saturday morning, when her Majesty fell asleep, waked refreshed, and on Sunday morning there was a perfect intermission of the symptoms; but the pulse, in my opinion, was not quiet. The next night, about twelve, she was attacked with an exacerbation of the fever, which lasted all the Monday till midnight. Most of the Queen's physicians, judging her distemper to be an ague, proposed and pressed the giving her the Jesuits' bark; but though I warmly opposed this, yet the physician who watched that night gave it, saying, 'he found the pulse calm.' No exacerbation appeared after this: but, nevertheless, I declared I did not like the pulse. That there was no perfect intermission of the fever; but that the pulse was at work, to separate the morbific matter into the gout, or some worse shape. The pains of the leg increasing, till three or four doses of the bark were given, I laid a stress upon having that part examined; but the other physicians called it a fit of the gout. I answered, it could not properly be called so in the muscles; and being of opinion that this was an inflammatory fever from the translation of the gout, and not a common ague, or intermitting fever; and finding that, after thirty-nine hours' continuance, there was a perfect remission, but no intermission, I made a prognostic, that, unless the feverish matter were separated and thrown off into a smart fit of the gout, a worse symptom might happen; as its falling into the leg, and fixing into an erysipelous tumour. This opinion was justified by a severe fit of the gout that came upon her Majesty a few days after, carried off the great danger, and gave some hopes of her entire recovery."

Whilst Anne lay in this alarming condition, it was reported, and very generally believed, that she was dead; and both the Jacobites and the Whigs had the imprudence to express unbounded joy at the event; the one in the hope of the restoration of the Pretender, the other in anticipation of the accession of the house of Hanover; conduct which filled the Queen with alarm, and impressed her with a belief, that, in the event of either her brother or the Hanoverian heir landing in England, her deposition, and perhaps decapitation, would take place.

On the sixteenth of February, 1714, the Queen being sufficiently recovered, returned from Windsor to Hampton Court, and the next day to St. James's; but, on account of her indisposition, the new parliament was opened by commission on the eighteenth of February. On the second of March, her Majesty was carried in a sedan to the House of Peers, and announced to the assembled Lords and Commons, that the treaty of peace between Great Britain and Spain had been ratified. She also observed, that designing men had maliciously insinuated that the Protestant succession in the House of Hanover was in danger under her government; but that those who endeavoured to distract the minds of men with imaginary dangers, can only mean to disturb the public tranquillity for no other purpose but that of bringing real mischief upon us. She said, after all she had done to secure the religion and liberties of the people, she could not mention such proceedings without some degree of warmth, and she hoped her parliament would agree with her, that attempts to weaken her authority, or to render the possession of the crown uneasy to her, could never be proper means to strengthen the Protestant succession. Affectionate addresses of thanks were voted without opposition by the Lords and the Commons; but as both the houses were divided into numerous opposing factions, who each voted as suited their own particular interest or view, their proceedings were singularly clashing and contradictory. At one time they voted the Protestant succession not to be in danger; at another its perilous state was proved by the repeated motions for the removal of the Pretender from Lorraine. This proceeding, and a renewal of the proposition for the residence of the Electoral Prince in England, terrified the Queen into addressing the subjoined remonstrance to her aged kinswoman, the Princess Sophia, Dowager Electress of Brunswick.

"*St. James's, May* 19, 1714.

"MADAM, SISTER, AUNT,

"Since the right of succession to my kingdom has been declared to belong to you and your family, there have always been disaffected persons, who, by particular views of their own interest, have entered into measures to fix a prince of your blood in my dominions, even whilst I am yet living. I never thought, till now, that this project would have gone so far, as to have made the least impression on your mind. But, as I have lately perceived by public rumours, which are industriously spread, that your electoral highness is come into this sentiment, it is of importance, with respect to the succession of your family, that I should tell you such a proceeding will infallibly draw along with it some consequences that will be dangerous to that succession itself, which is not secure any other ways, than as the prince, who actually wears the crown, maintains her authority and prerogative. There are here (such is our misfortune) a great many people seditiously disposed. So I leave you to judge what tumults they may be able to raise, if they should have a pretext to begin a commotion. I persuade myself, therefore, you will never consent that the least thing should be done that may disturb the repose of me or my subjects.

"Open yourself to me with the same freedom I do to you, and propose whatever you think may contribute to the security of the succession; I will come into it with zeal, provided that it do not derogate from my dignity, which I am resolved to maintain. I am, with a great deal of affection, &c."

The Queen, at the same time, wrote as follows to the grandson of the electress, the Duke of Cambridge, afterwards George II.

"*St. James's, May* 19, 1714.

"COUSIN,

"An accident, which has happened in my Lord Paget's family, having hindered him from setting forward so soon as he thought to have done, I cannot deter any longer letting you know my thoughts with respect to the design you have of coming into my kingdoms. As the opening of this matter ought to have been first to me, so I expected you would not have given ear to it without knowing my thoughts about it. However, this is what I owe to my own dignity, the friendship I have for you and the electoral house to which you belong, and the true desire I have that it may succeed to my kingdoms. And this requires of me, that I should tell you, that nothing can be more dangerous to the tranquillity of my dominions, and the right of succession in your line, and consequently more disagreeable to me, than such a proceeding at this juncture.

"I am,

"With a great deal of friendship,

"Your very affectionate cousin,

"ANNE R."

A few weeks after dispatching these remonstrances to her kindred of Hanover, Anne startled her ministers, and disappointed the hopes of the Jacobites, by, of her own self, and without previously consulting a soul, commanding a proclamation to be issued, offering a reward of £5000 for the apprehension of the Pretender, dead or alive, should he land in Great Britain or Ireland.

This proclamation was issued on the twenty-third of June, and the Commons voted a further reward of £100,000 for the same important service. The proscription of the exiled Stuart, by the evident desire of his own sister, overjoyed the Hanoverian partizans; but their triumph was cut short by another amazing change in the conduct of the Queen. That staunch and powerful Jacobite, the Earl of Marr, was, on his marriage, presented to Anne, and she not only received him graciously, but afterwards made him one of her ministers. Thus it was, that the hopes and fears of the great opposing parties, the Hanoverians and the Jacobites, were alternately raised and depressed by the vacillations of her Majesty, whose real purpose was to prevent either the Crown Prince or the Pretender from visiting England during her life-time, and, if possible, to leave her crown to her exiled brother. How powerful the Jacobites were at this period, and what a probability there was of their cause succeeding, may be gleaned from the subjoined words, addressed at the time of which we are writing, by their avowed enemy, the Duchess of Marlborough, to Mrs. Clayton.

"I have it from too good hands, that as soon as the emperor can be forced into a peace, the Prince of Wales is to come into England; and 'tis said in France that the Queen will consent to it. Perhaps she is not yet acquainted with that part of it. But, however, when the things are prepared for it, there can be no great difficulty in that, nor no great matter whether the Queen likes it or not. Perhaps the King of France may be strong enough to place him upon the throne without the consent of England; but if they take another way to do it, by parliament, to be sure there will be acts passed to quiet people, and to assure them that all things shall remain as they are; and is it more ridiculous to believe we shall be safe under the power of the King of France, and a Roman Catholic prince to govern under him, than what the majority of England have already done?

"I was never much concerned for the disappointment of the honest people [the Jacobites] concerning the words changed in the address for the proclamation, if the Prince of Wales landed; and, by a letter I had lately, I am yet more confirmed that I was in the right. For it appears to me, that the great struggle the ministers made to have that matter left to her Majesty's own time, and then the Queen answering that she did not think it necessary, must needs help to convince men, that can yet be in doubt of the mysterious designs, which is certainly the chief thing; for when the prince does really land, whatever the proclamations are of either side, those that conquer will do as they please; and, therefore, I think the first thing is, to make people see their danger all the ways that can be imagined."

Meanwhile, the Queen's health remained precarious; she was continually being confined to her bed-chamber with the gout and other maladies; and so completely had she relinquished all exercise or bodily exertion, that to save the trouble of walking up and down stairs, she was raised and lowered in a chair, by means of ropes and pulleys, after the fashion adopted by her bloated predecessor, Henry VIII., in his declining days. Nevertheless, she continued to frequently witness, from her private box, the discussions in parliament. This she did, with a view to preserve something like order amongst her combative senators, who this session terrified her by railing for and against the Hanoverian and the Stuart succession, with all the extreme malice of envenomed party hatred.

On the seventh of July, and in the midst of these political feuds, her Majesty went in state to the House of Lords, and prorogued parliament to the tenth of August. In her speech—the last she ever made to parliament—she, after the usual thanks for the supplies, concluded, in a tone which betrayed her deep displeasure at the intended residence of the electoral prince in England.

"My chief concern is, to preserve to you and to your posterity our holy religion, and the liberty of my subjects, and to secure the present and future tranquillity of my kingdoms. But I must tell you plainly, that these desirable ends can never be obtained, unless you bring the same dispositions on your parts; unless all groundless jealousies, which create and foment divisions amongst you, be laid aside; and unless you show the same regard for my prerogative, and for the honour of my government, as I have always expressed for the rights of my people."

At this period, Baron Bothmar, envoy extraordinary from the Elector of Hanover, arrived in England with the sad news of the sudden death of the Electress Sophia. The intelligence created a great sensation, and Anne and her court assumed the garb of mourning, and the name of the Elector was substituted for that of his mother, Sophia, in the liturgy of the church of England, as heir to the throne. The circumstances of Sophia's death are thus detailed in a letter from Mr. Molyneux to the Duke of Marlborough:

"*Hanover, June*, 1714.

"Not an hour after post, I went to Hernhausen, the country-house of the court, and there the first thing I heard was, that the good old electress was just dying in one of the public walks. I ran up there, and found her just expiring in the arms of the poor electoral princess, and amidst the tears of a great many of her servants, who endeavoured in vain to help her. I can give you no account of her illness, but that I believe the chagrin of those villanous letters* I sent you last post, has been in a great measure the cause of it. The Rheingravine, who has been with her these fifteen years, has told me she never knew any thing make so deep an impression on her as the affair of the prince's journey, which I am sure she had to the last degree at heart; and she has done me the honour to tell me so twenty times. In the midst of this concern, those letters arrived, and those I verily believe have broke her heart, and brought her with sorrow to the grave. The letters were delivered on Wednesday at noon. That evening, when I came to court, she was at cards, but was so full of these letters, that she got up and ordered me to follow her into the garden, where she gave them to me to read, and walked, and spoke a great deal in relation to them. I believe she walked three hours that night. The next morning she was out of order; but, in the morning of Friday, she told me she was very well, but seemed very chagrined. She was dressed, and dined with the elector as usual. About four she sent me to town, for some letters, and then she was still perfectly well. She worked and talked very heartily in the Orangerie. After that, and about six, she went out to walk in the gardens, and was still very well. A shower of rain came, and as she was walking pretty fast, to get to shelter, they told her she walked a little too fast. She answered, 'I believe I do,' and dropped down in saying those words, which were her last. They raised her up, chafed her with spirits, tried to bleed her; but it was all in vain, and when I came up to her, she was as dead as if she had been four days so. No princess ever died more regretted, and I infinitely pity those servants who have known her a long time, when I, that have had the honour to be known to her but a month, can scarce refrain from tears in relating this."

Shortly after the rising of parliament, the ministerial discord burst into an open rupture. The lord-treasurer, Harley, Earl of Oxford, who corresponded at the same time with the dethroned family and with the house of Hanover, had offended the Queen and Mrs. Masham, by clandestinely thwarting their efforts for the restoration of the Pretender. Oxford was considered as the prime minister, and enjoying the sole confidence of the Queen; but the secretary of state, St. John, Lord Bolingbroke, by superior tact and address, and by a steady adherence to the Jacobite cause, speedily won from him the royal confidence, and a violent party feud ensued between Oxford and Bolingbroke, and their adherents. Early in July, Mrs. Masham told Oxford that her Ma-

* Anne's previously quoted letters, dated May nineteenth, 1714.

jesty wished him to resign; but, as he refused to do so, the Queen, after complaining to the council that he often entered her presence drunk, and otherwise misbehaved himself, told them, "she was resolved to take the white staff out of his hands." Accordingly, on the morning of the twenty-seventh of July, she, by letter, requested his resignation; he had an interview with her the same morning; in the afternoon made his arrangements, and in the evening, after, in her presence, violently quarrelling with Bolingbroke and Mrs. Masham, and telling them that they had rogued him, but he would be revenged, and leave some people as low as he found them, formally surrendered the white staff into her hands. The same evening a cabinet council was held, when it was agreed that the treasury should be put in commission, at the head of which was to be placed Sir William Wyndham, who had just been made chancellor of the exchequer; but on account of the violent dissensions between the Jacobite members of the council and those who took part with Oxford, the other four members of the commission could not be determined on, and at two in the morning the stormy scene was brought to an abrupt termination, by her Majesty sinking to the floor in a swoon. She was immediately carried to bed, where the night through she did nothing but weep and bewail the feuds in her council, which she said had so upset her that she should never survive it. The council again met the next day (Wednesday), and was again abruptly terminated by the serious illness of the Queen. Anne again passed a restless night, and the next day Mrs. Danvers, on entering her chamber, was surprised to find her—instead of, as she had expected, in bed—standing before the clock, intently gazing at it.

"Does your Majesty see anything extraordinary in the clock?" demanded the lady of the bed-chamber.

The Queen made no reply, but turning her head, cast her eyes on the attendant with an horrific, death-like stare. Lady Danvers' shrieks of alarm brought instant assistance, and her Majesty was carried to her bed, more dead than alive. The physicians pronounced that the agitation of her mind had suddenly checked the imposthume on her leg, and caused her constitutional gout to fly to her brain; and believing she suffered from apoplexy, they immediately bled her. This restored her to consciousness; but about nine in the evening she sunk into a lethargy, and for more than an hour continued speechless and motionless. It was judged that she was dying, and about two in the morning of the 30th of July she was cupped, which somewhat relieved her; still she enjoyed no sound sleep, and continuously murmured, "Oh, my brother! my poor brother! Alas, alas! I have wronged him! Oh! what will become of my poor brother?"

At half-past eight she suffered a severe relapse, combined with unmistakeable symptoms of indigestion, when it was deemed advisable to make her danger public, and her physicians, Drs. Arbuthnot, Hamilton, Shadwell, Mead, Hans Sloane, and Lawrence, advised that she should lose ten ounces of blood from the arm; which proving but a transient relief, she at ten the same morning was seized with excruciating pains in the head, which deprived her of reason, and induced her attendants to again believe that she was dying; indeed, Dr. Mead, who, be it observed, was a staunch Whig, predicted that she "could not last more than another hour." The Duchess of Ormond, one of the ladies of the bedchamber then in waiting, instantly dispatched this intelligence to her husband, who was then with the council, assembled at the Cockpit.

The news was swiftly spread abroad. The privy council immediately repaired to Kensington, and there resumed their sitting. In the midst of their discussions, the Whig Dukes of Argyle and Somerset suddenly entered the council-chamber, and declared they had come to offer their assistance in the present crisis. In the pause of surprise that ensued, the Duke of Shrewsbury rose and thanked them for their kind offer. Somers and other Whig lords repaired to Kensington the same afternoon; Bolingbroke and his partizans were terrified into silence; and from that moment the Whigs carried all their own way.

When a deputation of the council waited upon her Majesty, and recommended the Duke of Shrewsbury to fill the post of lord-treasurer, she, with a faint, faltering voice, answered, "I approve of the choice;" and placing the white staff in the Duke's hands, bade him use it for the good of her people.

Shortly afterwards, she relapsed into a delirious agony, in which she continuously cried out, "Oh! my brother, my poor brother; oh! save my brother;" in fact, the wrongs she had done her brother weighed heavy on her heart, and added the pangs of agonizing compunction to the anguish of death. "Oh! my poor brother—save my brother!" she unceasingly reiterated, till every sense failed, and her pulse ceased to beat; then it was that her physicians unanimously pronounced her case hopeless, and those of the council who were in her bedchamber withdrew, and left Robinson, Bishop of London, to pray by her side. But, alas! the precious moments had been allowed to slip by; the slowly-dying Queen had lost all consciousness, and the loud, long, and earnest prayers of the bishop, fell dead upon her ever-palsied ears.

At one in the noon, and six in the evening of Saturday, she slightly rallied, but each time only for a short while; and after lingering the night through in a death-like lethargy, she ceased to breathe at seven in the morning of Sunday, the first of August, 1714, in the fiftieth year of her age, and the thirteenth of her reign.

Meanwhile, the council had taken all the needful measures to secure the Hanoverian succession, and the death of Queen Anne was followed by the immediate proclamation of the Elector of Hanover, by the title of George the First. Lady Mary Wortley Montague thus describes this ceremony, as it was performed at York: "I went this day to see the King proclaimed, which done, the archbishop walking next the lord-mayor, and all the country gentlemen following, with greater crowds of people than I believed to be in York, vast acclamations, and the appearance of a general satisfaction; the Pretender afterwards dragged about the streets, and burned; ringing of bells, bonfires, and illuminations, the mob crying, 'Liberty and property!' and 'Long live King George!'"

The remains of Queen Anne laid in state at Kensington Palace till the twenty-first of August, when they were removed to the Prince's-chamber, and on the night of Tuesday, the twenty-fourth, interred by torch-light in Westminster Abbey, with great solemnity. "There had been a new vault made on the south side, and towards the east end of Henry the Seventh's chapel," observes a contemporary, "in which lie the bodies of Charles the Second, of William the Third, of Mary and Prince George of Denmark; and here, also, were deposited the remains of the good Queen Anne, the last of the Stuart sovereigns; and there being no more room left, the vault was closed up with brick-work."

No monument nor tablet marks the burial-place of Queen Anne; but her wax effigy, carried at her funeral, is still preserved in Westminster Abbey; and her statue, sculptured by Bird, and erected in the west area of St. Paul's Cathedral, facing Ludgate Hill, in the autumn of 1708, is still in good preservation.

Queen Anne made a will, but death seized her before she signed it, "which," remarks Swift, "was a matter of little moment, as the time had long gone by for particular regard to be paid to the wills of sovereigns." Partial party historians have painted the character of Queen Anne in very opposite colours. Some of the Tory writers have lauded her as the best, the most virtuous of women, and the greatest of England's sovereigns; whilst those who devoted their pen to the Whig and the Hanoverian cause, have, with equal injustice, attributed to her almost every conceivable vice, and scarcely allowed to her a redeeming virtue. The truth is, her conduct, whilst Princess, towards her father, her step-mother, and her brother, was base in the extreme; but as a wife, she was all that could be desired. Her regnal career was decidedly successful; and with advancing years her affections warmed, and she became upright in intention, sincere in friendship, so mild and merciful, that throughout her reign, no subject's blood was shed for treason, and, through her intercession, many unfortunates were saved from the scaffold; so charitable, that her privy purse was facetiously styled, "the national poor-box;" and so laudable, that whether under the influence of Whig or Tory, she could boast of a boundless and irresistible popularity; in fact, the people sincerely loved her, and never spoke of her but as THE GOOD QUEEN ANNE, an epithet by which they fondly remembered her throughout the two subsequent reigns.

CAROLINE OF BRANDENBURG ANSPACH,

Queen of George the Second.

CHAPTER I.

Caroline's birth—Parentage—Education—Talents and accomplishments—Marriage to George Augustus, afterwards King of England—Birth of her son, Frederick, and of the Princesses, Anne, Amelia, and Caroline—Her father-in-law ascends the throne of Great Britain as George I.—George Augustus created Prince of Wales—Caroline comes to England—The coronation—The City of London entertainment—Party contention—Birth of a dead son—Birth and death of Prince George—Quarrel between the Prince and the King—Caroline and her husband retire from St. James's—Their court at Richmond—They and their friends are forbidden the court—Mrs. Clayton and Mrs. Howard—Caroline's influence over her husband—Birth of the Duke of Cumberland—Inoculation of the Princesses Amelia and Caroline—Birth of the Princesses Mary and Louisa.

AROLINE WILHELMINA DOROTHEA, of Brandenburg Anspach, the first of those German princesses who, for more than a century, shared the throne of England with the illustrious House of Hanover, was born on the twenty-third of September, 1683. When but a young child, she had the misfortune to lose her father, John Frederick, Margrave of Brandenburg Anspach; and shortly afterwards, on the marriage of her mother, Eleanor Erdmuth Louisa, daughter of John George, Duke of Sax-Eisenach, she left the court of her step-father for that of her guardian, that Elector of Prussia, who, in 1701, raised the duchy, over which he bore sway, to a kingdom, and assumed the crown as Frederick I. A contemporary, after observing that the young Caroline was carefully educated under the immediate superintendence of the judicious, well-disposed Sophia Charlotte, consort of Frederick I. of Prussia, observes, "She grew up a princess of extraordinary parts and accomplishments; she had a ready and quick apprehension; a lively and strong imagination, with a large compass of thought. She excelled in conversational powers; was by nature vivacious, mirthful, and humourous; and being skilled in several languages, invariably expressed her ideas in words and sentences the most apt, forcible, graceful, and elegant. She loved a repartee, was happy in making one herself, and hearing it from others; and, as the talent was rendered inoffensive by an amiable, cheerful disposition, which may not inaptly be styled one of the ornaments of virtue, she was (without respect to the dignity of her rank)

the life of every company—the delight of every person who had the honour to approach, or be approached by her. Her memory was excellent; her discernment of personal character and ability, remarkable; and her historical and genealogical learning, considerable. She was an excellent judge of books; well skilled in politics and polemics; and although more partial to philosophy and philosophers than to any other pursuit or persons, was neither pedantic, grave, nor vain of her superior gifts and acquirements."

Such was Caroline of Anspach, when, in the bloom of youthful womanhood, she, after refusing, on the score of religion, the hand of the popish king, Charles II. of Spain, accepted the suit of, and was married to, the protestant George Augustus, Electoral Prince of Hanover, and son of George Louis, the first English sovereign of that august house. The marriage was celebrated with becoming pomp, on the twenty-second of August, 1704, at Hanover; where, on the twentieth of January, 1706, Caroline gave birth to Prince Frederick Louis, afterwards Prince of Wales, and father of George III. Anne of York, then Queen of England, by a special ambassador, formally complimented the electoral prince and princess on the birth of their heir, and shortly afterwards she invested the former with the order of the garter, and raised him to the English peerage, under the title of Duke of Cambridge. These, and other marks of distinction, conferred by the Queen of England upon the illustrious House of Hanover, were received by the elector [afterwards George I.] with a coolness bordering on aversion; but the proud old dowager Electress Sophia was so charmed by them, and so ambitious to grasp at the honours in store for herself or her heirs, that she declared, if she could only live to have inscribed on her tomb, Sophia, Queen of Great Britain and Ireland, she would willingly die the moment afterwards. "But," remarks Coxe, "the electoral prince partook neither of the eagerness of his grandmother to anticipate her expected honours [honours which we have seen, in the previous memoir, snatched from her vision by the hand of death], nor of the stern contempt with which his father regarded the established forms of princely intercourse. On the contrary, he seized every occasion to manifest his respect to Queen Anne, and his regard to the nation over whom he was destined to reign as George II.; but he was too confined, both in means and influence, to be an object of attention to any of the parties who then were striving to ingratiate themselves with the future sovereign."

Whilst in Hanover, Caroline of Anspach became the mother of three princesses: Anne, Princess of Orange, born October the twenty-second, 1709; Amelia Sophia, born May the thirtieth, 1711; and Caroline Elizabeth, born May the thirty-first, 1713. We have seen, in the preceding memoir, that Queen Anne, in her declining days, entertained a marked aversion to the electoral family, which was increased by the summon of the electoral prince, as a peer of the British realm, to his seat in the House of Lords. This summons, however, had scarcely reached Hanover, when Queen Anne breathed her last, and the elector succeeded to the throne of Great Britain and Ireland, by the title of George I. The new King, of course, came to England with all convenient speed; his son, the electoral prince, accompanied him, and a few weeks after their arrival at Greenwich (August the seventeenth), was formally created Prince of Wales. The Princess of Wales—as, from this time, to the accession of her husband, Caroline of Anspach was called—remained at Hanover, till news arrived of the landing in England of her husband and his father. "When," remarks Tindal, "on the ninth of October (N. S.), her two eldest daughters, Anne and Amelia, (the youngest, Caroline, being left at Hanover on account of indisposition), were sent forward to journey by easy stages to the Hague. Three days afterwards she herself set out, and, attended by the Countess of Pickenburg, arrived at the Hague on the seventeenth, with the two eldest princesses, her daughters. The following morning she received the compliments of the States General; in the afternoon she and her suite took a drive in the Voorhout, and in the evening she held a drawing-room, which was thronged by persons of distinction. The next day she received visits from the French ambassador and other foreign ministers; and, on the twentieth, the Earl of Berkeley, who, with Sir John Walter of the green cloth, had left the squadron of men-of-war at Helvoet Sluys, with orders for the yachts to sail up to Rotterdam, having informed her that the wind was favourable, she, with her daughters, went on board a Dutch yacht, accompanied by the Earls of Albemarle and Strafford, the Count and Countess of Harran, the Princes of Anhault and Hesse, and other persons of distinction. At Rotterdam, mother and daughters embarked on board the English yacht, Mary, and after a pleasant voyage, they and their suite landed at Margate, on the eleventh of October (O. S.), and the next day proceeded to Rochester, where they were met by the Prince of Wales, accompanied by the Dukes of Somerset and Argyle; the Earl of Bridgewater, lord chamberlain to their royal highnesses; and the Countesses of Dorset and Berkeley, who had been named two of the ladies of the bed-chamber." On the thirteenth, their highnesses, in a coach and six, followed by another coach, in which were their daughters, passed through the city of London to St. James's, where they took up their abode. Caroline and her husband were present at the coronation, which was solemnized with the usual pomp and ceremony at Westminster, on the twentieth of October; three days afterwards, they, with their royal father, the King, were sumptuously entertained in the Guildhall by the Lord Mayor and corporation of London, and, on the twenty-sixth of May, 1715, their beloved little daughter, Caroline, arrived in London, and took up her residence with them at St. James's.

The pertinacious partiality of the King for the Whigs, and the greediness and censurable harshness of that party now that they commanded a not very great majority in parliament, raised throughout most parts of the kingdom murmurs of discontent, which were followed by riots, and, in the end, by a formidable Jacobite rebellion, in which blood was spilt on both sides; the government, however, came off victor, and after crushing the rebellion, punished the rebels with unsparing severity and cruelty. But with these matters we have not to do, saving so far as they affected the subject of this memoir, her husband, or progeny. Oxford took part in the Jacobite rising, and the university, in revenge for the impeachment of the Duke of Ormond, which deprived him of his chancellorship, and in defiance of the King, who had put the Prince of Wales in nomination for the office, chose Ormond's brother, Lord Arran, as their future chancellor. But, as if to counterbalance this galling rejection from Oxford, "the university of Dublin unanimously elected his Highness, the Prince, for their chancellor."

On the sixteenth of February, 1715, the Prince also acted as Regent, by the title of Guardian of the Kingdom, and his Majesty's Lieutenant, during the King's first visit to Hanover, from July, 1716, to the subsequent January; and Walpole assures us, that in the performance of those regnal duties, he displayed a fondness for playing king, which so excited the anger and jealousy of his sire, that he was never again entrusted with the high office. It was during this visit to Hanover, that the King invested the Prince of Wales's son, Prince Frederick, with the order of the garter.

In the autumn of 1716, the life of Caroline was endangered by a protracted and mis-managed labour, followed by the birth of a dead son. "The good Princess," writes Bishop Kenneth to Mr. Blackwell, "had the symptoms of labour on Sunday evening, and it is thought might have been safely delivered of a living son that night, or any time before Tuesday morning, if Sir David Hamilton or Dr. Chamberlayne, who attended without, might have been admitted to her; but the Hanover midwife kept up the aversion of the princess to have any man about her, and so notwithstanding the importunity of the English ladies, and the declared advice of the lords of the council, she continued in pains till between one and two on the morning of Friday, November the ninth, 1716, when, the midwife alone delivered her of a dead male child, wounded in the head. She has since been extremely weak, and subject to continual faintings, and 'tis said all things are not after the manner of women in that condition; but the last account is more comfortable. 'Tis said her Royal Highness is somewhat better, and if this night pass well over, there will be great hopes of her doing well."*

Caroline, although greatly weakened, speedily recovered, and on the twenty-fourth of November, the bishop again wrote to Mr. Blackwell: "The Princess is in a very safe condition; the long-depending labour, and the loss of a fine prince upon it, made a great ruffle at court. The persisting of the midwife that she wanted no other help, has put the English ladies out of all good opinion of her; and the unwillingness of Sir David Hamilton to interpose without express command, brought on him severe expostulations and rebukes from the women, and particularly from good Mrs. Wake. He is most concerned, that the archbishop, in tenderness to the Princess, should tell him that he neglected his duty to the public."†

The next accouchement proved more favourable. "Your physician, Sir David Hamilton," observes the above quoted contemporary to his friend, Mr. Blackwell, "has very much improved his interest at court, upon the occasion of the good Princess's delivery of a son [on the third of November, 1717]; for though he did not assist in the immediate moments, yet, by the ignorance or humour of the same midwife, her Royal Highness was so slow and so far gone into convulsive faintings, that there was great danger of her life and the child, if Sir David had not prescribed some medicines that brought on a speedy, safe delivery." The prince was christened George William, at St. James's, by the Archbishop of Canterbury, and he died on the subsequent February, and was privately buried in Westminster Abbey. This christening led to the outbreak of a quarrel, which had long been brewing, between the father and grandfather.

"The Prince of Wales," observes Walpole, "had intended his uncle, the Duke of York, to be co-godfather with the King; but, to his indignation, the King named that, to him, hateful noble, the Duke of Newcastle, for the second sponsor, and would hear of no other. The christening took place, as usual, in the Prince's chamber; but no sooner had the archbishop closed the ceremony, than the Prince, crossing the foot of the bed, stepped up to the Duke of Newcastle, and holding up his hand and forefinger, in a menacing attitude, said, 'You are a rascal! but I shall find you;' meaning, in broken English, 'I shall find a time to be revenged.' The King was so provoked at this outrage in his presence, that he pretended to understand it as a challenge, and the Prince was actually put under arrest! The arrest was soon taken off; but at night the Prince and Princess were ordered to quit St. James's Palace;" and, leaving behind them three daughters, who continued to reside with the King till his death, they retired to the house of the Prince's chamberlain, the Earl of Grantham; and at the commencement of 1717, the Prince purchased Leicester House, where they immediately established their London court, whilst at Richmond Lodge they enjoyed all the sweets and beauties of the country. "At this period," remarks the Right Honourable John Wilson Croker, "Pope and his literary friends were in great favour at this young court, of which, in addition to the handsome and clever Princess herself, Mrs. Howard, Mrs. Selwyn, Miss How, Miss Bellenden, and Miss Lapell, with Lords Chesterfield, Bathurst, Scarborough, and Hervey, were the chief ornaments. Above all, for beauty and wit, were Miss Bellenden and Miss Lepell, who seem to have treated Pope, and been in return treated by him, with a familiarity that appears strange in our

* M.S. Lansd. 1013, fol. 202.

† Ibid, 1011, fol. 208.

more decorous days. These young ladies, probably, considered him as no more than what Aaron Hill described him:—

> 'Tuneful Alexis on the Thames' fair side,
> The ladies' *plaything*, and the Muses' pride.'"

The court of the Prince and Princess of Wales was more gay and brilliant, and although far from moral, in the present acceptation of the word, not near so licentious as that at St. James's, where the King, who had divorced and imprisoned his unfortunate wife, Sophia Dorothea, in the castle of Ahlden, in the German dukedom of Zell, maintained some half-dozen German and English mistresses. Perhaps his Majesty was annoyed at his son outliving him; but, whatever might have been the cause, he precluded from his court all peers, peeresses, and persons of distinction, who visited 'the monster and his she-devil,' as he very kindly designated his son and daughter-in-law, and he never again became reconciled to them.

This ill-will, however, detracted but little from their enjoyments. The Prince from inclination, the Princess from policy, presided over an almost daily round of pleasures during the lifetime of George I. They held drawing-rooms every morning, gave a ball and evening party twice a week, and were frequent visitors to the play, the opera. and other public entertainments. But withal, it was said, that Caroline was under the influence of Mrs. Clayton, and that George Augustus was completely swayed by his mistress, Mrs. Howard, two ladies who were bed-chamber women to the Princess, but whose influence was less than it was supposed to be.

The character of Mrs. Clayton has been variously drawn; Lord Hervey, who knew her intimately, says, "she had really a warm, honest, noble, generous, friendly heart; she took pleasure in doing good, and frequently used her influence at court in favour of those who had never solicited it, and could never repay her; in fact, in these matters, she reversed the maxims of courtiers generally, and rather considered who wanted *her*, than whom *she* wanted." *

Walpole describes her as "an absurd, pompous simpleton;" and, as evidence that she was shamefully corrupt and brazen-faced, observes, "she had received a pair of diamond earrings as a bribe, for procuring a considerable post in Caroline's household; and, decked with these jewels, paid a visit to old Sarah, Duchess of Marlborough, who, as soon as she was gone, said, 'What an impudent creature, to come here with a bribe in her ears!' 'Madam,' replied Lady Mary Wortley Montague, who was present, 'how should people know where wine is sold, unless a bush is hung out?'" If this anecdote be true, Lord Hervey's portraiture of Mrs. Clayton is certainly overdrawn.

Mrs. Howard we may pity, but not praise; she had the misfortune to marry, when very young, Mr. Howard, "a wrong-headed, ill-tempered, obstinate, drunken, extravagant, brutal, younger brother of the Earl of Suffolk's family." She was married in Queen Anne's time; and poverty, or perhaps ambition, drove her and her husband to seek their fortunes at the rising court at Hanover. She there fascinated Prince George Augustus, and when George I. ascended the throne of England, she was appointed bed-chamber woman to the Princess Caroline; she next separated from her profligate husband, and became the acknowledged leman of the Prince of Wales; but over him she, nor any other woman, saving his consort, ever obtained any very considerable influence. Between her and Mrs. Clayton there always existed a bitter enmity, the result of the one being attached to the Prince, the other to the Princess; "each was jealous of the other's interest, and each over-rated it;" but the last fact was not proved till the accession of George II., when it became apparent that the mistress of the *Prince* had as little influence over the King, as the favourite of the

* Lord Hervey's Memoirs, a work to which we refer the reader for more ample details of the court and cabinet of George II. and his consort.

Princess had over the Queen. The truth was, that George Augustus thought it great and grand to keep a mistress, and appear not to be led by his wife; whilst the, perhaps, more ambitious than affectionate Caroline, who completely ruled him in everything, to retain her political and domestic sway, artfully winked at his connubial infidelity, retained Mrs. Howard in her service without a murmur, and, that she might herself have leisure to attend to subjects of superior import and questions of state policy, permitted Mrs. Clayton to act as her representative in matters of minor significance.

On the fifteenth of April, 1721, the Princess Caroline was safely delivered, at Leicester House, of a son, who, in after years, as Duke of Cumberland, mercilessly slaughtered the Scots Jacobites at Culloden. This royal infant was on the second of May christened William Augustus, the sponsors being the King and Queen of Prussia, and the Duke of York, respectively represented by the Earl of Grantham, the Duchess of Dorset, and Lord Lumley.

At this period, Lady Mary Wortley Montague introduced inoculation to England from Turkey, and Dr. Mead, by command of Prince George Augustus, tested its efficacy upon several condemned criminals. The experiment succeeded to admiration, and the doctor was permitted in the subsequent April to inoculate the Prince's two daughters, Amelia and Caroline, whose speedy recovery was followed by the inoculation of several of the young nobility; but withal, public prejudice for years afterwards denounced the practice as dangerous, and even sinful. Dr. Mead was ultimately appointed physician in ordinary to the Prince of Wales.

On the twenty-second of February, 1723, the family of George Augustus and Caroline was increased by the birth of the Princess Mary; and on the seventh of December, 1724, their last-born child, the Princess Louisa, first saw the light at Leicester House.

CHAPTER II.

Accession of George II. and Caroline—The Walpole ministry retained—The King and Queen's revenues—George II. destroys his father's will—Coronation—The Queen and Walpole rule the nation—Prince Frederick created Prince of Wales—His parents hate him—Caroline and the Dissenters—She takes Lord Stair to task—The Excise bill—Marriage of the Princess Royal to the Prince of Orange—Retirement from court of the Lady Suffolk.

N the eleventh of June, 1727, George the First, whilst on his road to Hanover, suddenly expired at Osnaburg. The premier, Sir Robert Walpole, was the first to carry this by no means disagreeable tidings to the Prince, now George II., and his consort; the former of whom willingly accepted his homage; but in reply to his question as to who should compose his Majesty's speech, gave him to understand that his services as prime minister would no longer be required, by politely referring him to Sir Spencer Compton, who was at the time speaker of the House of Commons, treasurer to the Prince, and paymaster to the army. Sir Robert was neither surprised nor disconcerted by this cool reception; he knew that the King hated him, and the Queen despised him, because, in his coarse way, he had called her a "fat bitch," when she was Princess of Wales; but, like ministers in more modern times, he clung tenaciously to office, and when the thick-headed Sir Spencer proposed that her Majesty's jointure should be £60,000 per year, he instantly offered to increase it to £100,000, together with Somerset House and Richmond Lodge; and, furthermore, undertook to procure for her a present income of £50,000 per year, being just £10,000 more than Sir Spencer had proposed. This significant bribe won for the briber the good-will of the Queen, and, through her, that of her consort. Compton was made a peer, and shelved; and Sir Robert, now premier, not only prevailed upon the willing Commons to make the abovementioned grants to the Queen, but also persuaded that honourable assembly to vote the King the whole produce of the civil list, about £830,000 a year, whilst the income of his father, George I., amounted to only £700,000. The Queen did not wait for these measures being carried out, to publicly evince the favour in which she held Sir Robert and his family. The first few days of her accession as Queen Consort, she was occupied with her husband in receiving compliments and condolences from the prelates, lords, ambassadors, and other functionaries; "and on this occasion," says Horace Walpole, "my mother (Sir Spencer's designation, and not its evaporation, being known) could not make her way between the scornful backs and elbows of her late devotees, nor could approach nearer to the Queen than the third or fourth row; but no sooner was she descried by her Majesty, than the Queen cried aloud, 'There, I am sure I see a friend!' The torrent divided, and shrunk to either side; 'and as I came away,' said my mother, 'I might have walked over their heads if I had pleased.'"

The King, as well as his consort, was so charmed by Walpole's having procured him an unexpectedly large revenue, that, although in his father's reign he had called that minister "rogue and rascal!" and his brother Horace "scoundrel and fool!" he already gave him his confidence, and the whole of the Walpole ministry, including those nobles the Duke of Newcastle and Lord Townsend, whom the King, as Prince, had heartily hated and despised, were, with only two exceptions, retained in office. These exceptions were, Sir Robert's son-in-law, Lord Malpas, who was unceremoniously ejected from the mastership of the robes, the day after the King's accession, and Sir William Young, "Thinking Young," as the King used to designate him, who was turned out of the treasury; but even these statesmen, to use Lord Hervey's sentiment, "only dived to come up again fresh as ever."

Our first two Hanoverian Kings paid but little regard to the testamentary documents of their departed relatives. The last will of the unfortunate Sophia Dorothea, and that of her aged father, the Duke of Zell, were both destroyed by George I.; and when, at the council-board, Dr. Wark, Archbishop of Canterbury, and one of the executors of the late King, placed that monarch's will in the hands of George II., the new King, instead of gratifying the expectant council by unsealing it and reading it aloud, very coolly put it into his pocket, and walked out of the chamber. It was immediately afterwards rumoured, and generally believed, that George II. had burned his father's will; and as that will has never since been heard of, it is but natural to conclude that the rumour was not groundless. The two duplicates of this will, which George I. had placed in the hands of two German princes, were, for certain fees and rewards, also given up and destroyed, and, in the end, the matter was compromised, by the payment of various sums to the King of Prussia, the Duchess of Kendal, and some other of the reported legatees, who threatened actions at law.

In October, the royal coronation was solemnized at Westminster Abbey, with extraordinary pomp, and the usual ceremonies. On this occasion of gay, gorgeous display, the King was attired in every conceivable "badge and trapping of royalty," and the dress of the Queen was equally magnificent. She wore a rich pearl necklace, the only one of Queen Anne's jewels which George I. had not distributed amongst his German favourites; and, remarks Lord Hervey, "besides her own jewels, which were numerous and valuable, she had on her head and shoulders all the pearls she could borrow of the ladies of quality at one end of the town, and on her petticoat all the diamonds she could hire of the Jews and jewellers at the other; so that the appearance and the truth of her finery were a mixture of magnificence and manners not unlike the *éclat* of royalty in many other particulars, when it comes to be nicely examined, and its sources traced to what money hires, or flattery lends."

That the Queen, whilst affecting to be led by the will of her husband, really ruled him, and that Walpole ruled the nation through the Queen, now became evident to every one save the King himself, who, poor silly mortal as he must have been, so little dreamed that his clever consort seriously interfered with public matters, or influenced him by her counsel, that to those about him he perpetually repeated, "she never meddles with business;" and to show how independent he believed himself to be, he "one day," says Lord Hervey, "remarked, Charles I. was governed by his wife, Charles II. by his mistress, King James by his priests, King William by his men, Queen Anne by her favourite woman, his father by anybody who could get at him;" and then, with an air of triumph, he exclaimed, "and who do they say governs now?" The courtiers present replied, as all good courtiers would have done, with a compliment; but shortly afterwards, a wit, with more rudeness, but greater truth, wrote—

"You may strut, dapper George, but 'twill all be in vain,
You know 'tis Queen Caroline, not you, that reign;
You govern no more than Don Philip of Spain.
Then if you would have us fall down and adore you,
Lock up your fat spouse, as your dad did before you."

For their son, Prince Frederick, neither George nor Caroline had much affection. They, not without some reason, pronounced him selfish, wayward, and vicious; and, to avoid the annoyance of his presence, they forced him to reside at Hanover, till the parliament and the people began to murmur at his absence; when, with an ill grace, the King called him to England. He arrived on the fourth of December, 1728, and shortly afterwards was created Prince of Wales, and sworn of the privy council. But the meeting between the Prince and his parents produced no happy result. The sire refused to pay the debts which the son had contracted during his residence abroad; and the son retaliated by throwing himself into the arms of the opposition, and it soon became apparent, that Prince Frederick was the most malicious and hated personal and political enemy of George II., his consort, and the court. When Gay's Beggar's Opera was found to annoy their Majesties and the ministers, the Prince secretly encouraged its performance, and he even privately countenanced the Duchess of Queensbury in her patronage of Gay, and in her insulting efforts at court to procure subscribers for the publication of that author's harmless, but prohibited opera of Polly. This unfilial conduct further aggravated George and Caroline against their heir; and when the King proceeded on his visit to Hanover, on the seventeenth of May, 1729, he, to the deep mortification of the Prince, named the Queen sole regent during his absence.

In the summer of 1730, occurred one of the many instances of Caroline's political influence. The dissenters, especially the Presbyterians, took advantage of the approaching dissolution of parliament, to demand the repeal of the Corporation and Test Acts. The government could not afford to lose the votes of these dissenters at the forthcoming general election; but to grant their request, reasonable as ministers admitted it to be, was to give mortal offence to the churchmen, whose votes the crown was equally anxious to retain. Under these circumstances, Sir Robert Walpole resolved, if possible, to prevail upon the dissenters to defer their request to a more convenient opportunity, and fixed upon Hoadly, Bishop of Salisbury, to carry out his project; but, as he himself had ill-used the bishop in matters of preferment, and felt ashamed to ask a favour of him, the Queen sent for Hoadly to Kensington, and by flattering compliments and skilful reasoning, cajoled him, not out of his opinions, for he honestly told Caroline that whenever the repeal was brought forward he should support it with all his interest;

but into consenting to urge the dissenters, for the present, to withhold their petition. Immediately after this interview, it was rumoured abroad that the Queen had bribed the prelate to desert the cause of the dissenters. Hoadly, in alarm for his reputation, called upon Walpole, and endeavoured to draw from him a promise, that if the claims of the dissenters were deferred till the meeting of the new parliament, the court would then support them; but Sir Robert, whilst admitting the reasonableness of the demand, adroitly avoided making such a promise, and subsequently Hoadly had several conferences with the Queen on the subject, with no better satisfaction to either party.

The question now began to wear a serious aspect. The dissenters organized an agitation throughout the country, with a central committee in London; and their efforts would doubtless have been crowned with success, but for the venality of some of their leaders, and the tact of the premier. "The *honest* gentlemen who composed this London committee of dissenters," says Lord Hervey, "were all monied men of the city, and scriveners, who were absolutely dependent on Sir Robert, and chosen by his contrivance, and acted only as he guided."

This committee, for appearance sake, transacted all their business with the utmost gravity and seeming formality. They had a solemn meeting with the administration, at which Sir Robert Walpole repeated "most of the things he had before said to the Bishop of Salisbury." The speaker was "explicit on the inexpediency of bringing the petition before parliament." "My lord president looked wise, was dull, took snuff, and said nothing. Lord Harrington took the same silent, passive part; and the Lord Chancellor and the Duke of Newcastle had done better had they followed that example too; but both spoke very plentifully, and were both equally unintelligible; the one from having lost his understanding, and the other from never having had any."*

* Lord Hervey.

After this meeting, the hypocritical committee terminated the farce by coming to a resolution, "That if a petition was to be preferred to parliament in their favour, that there was no prospect of success." This result well pleased the Queen and her minister, but many of the dissenters believed that their cause had been betrayed by their delegates, and poor Bishop Hoadly had the misfortune to offend both parties; the dissenters thought he had supported their cause too little, the court thought he had supported it too much.

The year 1733 affords a farther illustration of the power and political influence of Queen Caroline. When the excitement occasioned by Sir Robert Walpole's excise scheme was at its height, those peers who took advantage of the circumstance to further their own personal interests, delegated Lord Stair to wait on the Queen at Kensington, and remonstrate with her on the subject; but the Scottish laird proved no match for her Majesty, and forgetting alike himself and his subject, he launched out a tirade of personal invectives against Walpole, whom he denounced as an ill-doing tyrant, who was alike hated and dreaded by the nobles, the clergy, the city of London, and many of his own followers, and who disposed of offices to the Campbells, which in justice should have been given to him, Stair. The Queen listened to him with patience, and then, with mingled sarcasm, irony, and cutting contempt, told him in reply, that in supporting the peerage bill he had betrayed the interests of his constituents, and turned traitor to his country. "Talk not therefore to me of patriotism," she proceeded, "nor of your conscience, or I shall faint. Who taught you to play this part I know not, but your politics are those of the 'Craftsman,' and your sentiments, or rather professions, you get from my Lord Bolingbroke and my Lord Carteret, whom you may tell if you think fit, that I have long known to be two as worthless men of parts as any in this country, and whom I have not only been often told are two of the greatest liars and knaves in any country, but whom my own observation and experience have found so."*

The chap-fallen Scottish laird admitted his defeat, by requesting her Majesty to keep "the particulars of this conference secret, which she promised to do on her part, so long as he did so on his." But he immediately afterwards bragged to Lord Carteret, "that he had staggered her;" and Carteret, in a speech in the Lords, on the army supplies, observed, when Cardinal Mazarin was ruling and oppressing France, one of the greatest men of the time sought an audience of the Queen, and in that interview told her to her face, "that she was maintaining a man at the helm of affairs, who should be rowing in the galleys." This speech, reported by Lord Hervey to the Queen, convinced her that Lord Stair had revealed what he had requested her to keep secret, and therefore she "out with it all" to Lord Hervey, from whose Memoirs those particulars are gleaned.

Perhaps no stronger proof exists that Sir Robert Walpole really was the Queen's minister, than the following. When the clamour against the excise bill, both in the parliament and throughout the country, had risen to a dangerous height, Sir Robert told not the King, but the Queen, that to appease the nation, either the bill must be dropped, or its projector must quit office. "For himself," he observed [we quote verbatim from Lord Hervey], "he was so far from desiring to be *in* her Majesty's service, if she thought it was not *for* her service, that he should lay down and retire with all the satisfaction in the world; and if her Majesty thought it for the advantage of the King's affairs, or that it would facilitate in any manner the King's business in parliament, that he was ready that very night to quit, and should never impute his disgrace to her Majesty's want of kindness towards him, but merely to his own ill fortune. The Queen, in reply, told him, that she would not be so mean, so cowardly, and so ungrateful as to accept his resignation; and she prevailed on the King to express himself on the subject in similar words to the premier."

A few days afterwards, the Queen, when informed that Sir Robert was in a majority of seventeen only, burst into tears, and exclaimed, "It is over, we must give way." The King, if less depressed, was equally disappointed and annoyed at the failure; and when Lord Hervey repeated to him the names of some of those who had swelled the opposition, he thus commented on each name. Lord James Cavendish — "*a fool.*" Lord Charles Cavendish—"*he is half mad.*" Sir William Lowther—"*a whimsical fellow.*" Sir Thomas Prendergast — "*an Irish blockhead.*" Lord Tyrconnel—"*a puppy that never votes twice together on the same side.*" The London populace also made their angry comments on the proceedings at court. Besides burning the effigy of Sir Robert Walpole, with that of a fat woman, meant for the Queen, they conducted themselves in a riotous manner, and assailed the members of parliament who voted for the bill, with groans, hisses, and cries of "No slavery! no excise! no wooden shoes!" It was generally imagined that if Walpole fell, the Queen's power would then cease; but this was an erroneous supposition. "The future ministry," says Lord Hervey, "would certainly have been of her nomination in case of a change, as much as the present, and if they had subsisted as much at her devotion; for had she found them less so, their reign would not have been long." However, her Majesty resolved that the ministry should not be changed; and as a last resource, in the present case, to save them, if possible, from being defeated, she "closeted and schooled" the Bishop of Salisbury. Hoadly promised all that he could, consistently with his principles: but it was now too late for him to act; victory declared in favour of the opposition, and the unwilling Walpole was forced to withdraw his favourite excise bill.

In the meantime, the long-desired marriage of the Princess Royal engaged

* Hervey's Memoirs, where the interview is more fully detailed.

the serious thoughts of their Majesties. The Princess was in her twenty-fourth year, and still a sighing maiden. She was ambitious to be a queen; mad to be a wife. Louis XV. had refused to share his crown with her, on the score of religion, he being catholic, she protestant; and as no better offer presented itself, she resolved to marry the dwarfish, deformed Prince of Orange, who in age was her junior by about two years. For this purpose a treaty was forthwith entered into, and the parliament voted the Princess a dower of £80,000. The Prince arrived on the seventh of November, and took up his residence at Somerset House. Neither the King nor the Queen paid him much honour—in fact, they were not sanguine for the match. Caroline called him the "hideous animal;" and when, on the day of his arrival, Lord Hervey told her "he fancied the Princess must be in a good deal of anxiety, the Queen told him he was extremely mistaken, that she was in her own apartment at her harpsichord, with some of the opera people, and that she had been as easy all that afternoon as he had ever seen her in her life. 'For my part,'" continued her Majesty, "'I never said the least word to encourage her to this marriage, or to dissuade her from it; the King left her, too, absolutely at liberty to accept or reject it; but as she thought the King looked upon it as a proper match, and one which, if she could bear his person, he should not dislike, she said she was resolved, if it were a monkey, she would marry him."*

To this last remark, a modern author, by a stretch of imagination, has made the King's answer what he probably thought—"Then have your way; you will find monkey enough, I promise you." She did have her way, but not so soon as had been expected.

On the day previous to that appointed for the marriage, the Prince fell sick of fever, and neither physic, physicians, skill, nor the invigorating waters of Bath could fully re-establish his health till the subsequent spring, when, in the evening of the fourteenth of March, 1734, the marriage was solemnized with great pomp in the French chapel adjoining St. James's. A sumptuous supper followed; and some time after the midnight hour had chimed, the illustrious pair were put to bed, when the whole court were, according to custom, admitted to see them in their night dresses. As soon afterwards as circumstances admitted, the Prince of Orange was naturalized by act of parliament, and £5000 a year was settled on his bride. Those matters arranged, they, towards the close of April, "embarked at Greenwich for Holland." The parting, as such partings generally are, was sorrowful. All her Highness's brothers and sisters, saving the Prince of Wales, who was not present, were bathed in tears. "Her father wept piteously, gave her a thousand kisses, but not the worth of a guinea; her mother never ceased crying for three whole days; and yet, three weeks afterwards, her Highness was as much forgotten as if she had been buried as many years."* She, however, had not forgotten her English home; and in the following July, she, to the surprise and indignation of the King, and to the no very great joy of the Queen, found her way back to St. James's, in the hope of lying-in there; and it was not till the subsequent November, and after "much ado," that she could be prevailed upon to relinquish her purpose, and retrace her steps to the Hague.

Both Caroline and George were glad to get her gone, for just then the King had quarrelled with his favourite, Lady Suffolk, formerly Mrs. Howard; and this event, and the conduct of Prince Frederick, engrossed all the attention they could give to domestic matters. Lady Suffolk had long endured many petty annoyances from the Queen; she was fast losing her beauty, her hearing, and her sweetness, or rather easy pliancy of temper; the King had grown tired of her, he ceased to visit her in the evening as was his wont, and she, perceiving that the "spell was broken"—her influence gone—threw up her appointment as mistress of the robes, to

* Lord Hervey's Memoirs.

* Lord Hervey.

which the more virtuous Countess of Tankerville succeeded, and retiring from court, married the Honourable George Berkeley, a personal and political friend of Mr. Pulteney. Her retirement is thus mentioned by the Duke of Newcastle in a letter to Mr. Walpole, who at that time was in the country.

"November 13, 1734.—You will see by the newspapers that Lady Suffolk has left the court. The particulars that I had from the Queen are, that last week she acquainted the Queen with her design, putting it upon the King's unkind usage of her.* The Queen ordered her to stay a week, which she did; but last Monday had another audience, complained again of her unkind treatment from the King, was very civil to the Queen, and went that night to her brother's house in St. James's Square."†

On her departure, the Princess Royal remarked to Lord Hervey, "I wish with all my heart the King would take somebody else, that mamma might be a little relieved from the ennui of seeing him for ever in her room!" An extraordinary sentiment for a newly-married royal daughter to utter in reference to her parents; and as that daughter was considered an unquestionably virtuous Princess, an uncontrovertible evidence of the immorality of the times.

* This statement seems strange, and might be questioned, was it not verified by Lord Hervey, who says, Lady Suffolk, on this occasion, expressed herself to the Queen in something like the following words: "Madam, your husband being weary of me, I cannot possibly stay in your house or your service any longer."

† Coxe.

CHAPTER III.

Malicious conduct of the King and Queen towards their heir—Count de Roncey and his sister—Caroline's love of power and politics—Scotch election petition—The King and his new mistress, Madam Walmoden—Caroline encourages her husband's amours—The King's opinion of England and the English—His ill-humour—Home-scene at the royal palace—Marriage of the Prince of Wales—The Mortmain and Quaker relief bills—King again with Madam Walmoden at Hanover—Tumults and riots—Caroline's extraordinary correspondence with the King—The King's return delayed—Effects of the delay—Storms—Alarms for his safety—His arrival—Caroline's secret malady—Increase of the Prince of Wales's income moved in Parliament—Porteus' rioters punished—Caroline's coarse remarks on Horace Walpole.

ROM the middle of October to the close of November, the Queen was confined to her chamber with illness, which was probably aggravated by the unfilial conduct of the Prince of Wales, who, bad as he was, was certainly to be pitied, for his parents hated him, his sisters betrayed him, his brother was exalted above him, and his friends made a party-tool of him. To him, Caroline was indeed a harsh mother. She advised the King not to allow him a permanent income. "He costs the King £50,000 a year, which, till he is married, I am sure is allowance sufficient for him," said the more politic than affectionate Queen. The Prince at this time was in debt; and when, at an audience which the King granted him, he requested permission to serve a campaign on the Rhine, and asked for an augmentation of his income; the King made no answer to the first request, and only gave hopes that the second might be granted, if he behaved better to the Queen in future. But this he was not likely to do, whilst such scenes as the following were enacted. When Lord Hervey, after paying a farewell visit to the Princess of Orange on the morning she set out for the Hague, returned to the palace at Kensington, he found the Queen and the Princess Caroline together, drinking chocolate, weeping and sobbing aloud, at the departure of the Princess Anne; and scarcely had he succeeded in turning the current of their thoughts into a less melancholy channel, when the gallery-door opened, and the Queen exclaimed, "What! the King here already?" When, however, it proved to be the Prince of Wales, she, "detesting the exchange of the son for the daughter, burst out anew into tears, and cried out, 'Oh! my God, this is too much.*'" Fortunately for her overstrained nerves, the King did arrive very soon afterwards, and seeing, without seeming to see, the Prince of Wales, walked up to the Queen, and led her out to walk. "Whenever," observes Lord Hervey, "the Prince [of Wales] was in a room with the King, it put one in mind of the stories one has heard of ghosts that appear to part of the company, and are invisible to the rest; and in this manner, wherever the Prince stood, though the King passed him ever so often, or ever so near, it always seemed as if the King thought the place the Prince filled a void." The Prince conducted himself with as great, or even greater impropriety towards his parents, and thus a reconciliation was rendered morally impossible.

At this period Count de Roncy, created Earl of Lifford, in Ireland, and his sister Charlotte, governess of their Majesties' younger children, two French Protestant refugees, who had no source of subsistence saving the scanty charity of the court, nightly in the country, and thrice a week in town, "were alone,'" says Lord Hervey, "with the King and Queen for an hour or two before they went to bed, during which time the King walked about, and talked to the brother of armies, or to the sister of genealogies, whilst the Queen knitted and yawned, till from yawning she came to nodding, and from nodding to snoring."

This ill-paid pair were viewed in the light of court-drudges, but they certainly led a more easy and independent life than the Queen, who, says Lord Hervey, "was at least seven or eight hours *tête-à-tete* with the King every day, generally saying what she did not think, assenting to what she did not believe, praising what she did not approve, and forced, like a spider, to spin out of her own bowels all the conversation with which the fly was taken." But to this, and to much more, the proud Queen willingly submitted, for the sake of exercising uncontrolled political power, and of having it said that she completely ruled her obstinately firm husband, and that the country was governed not by him, but by her. To this love of power Caroline was a willing slave; but, spite the assertions of her detractors to the contrary, her regnal talents were considerable, and her application to political matters was untiring. Thus, when at the commencement of 1735, on the morning before the Scotch Election petition—a measure brought forward by the opposition, with prospects of success, but which was decided in favour of ministers—was to be presented to parliament, "the Queen was so anxious to know what was said, thought, done, or expected on this occasion, that she sent for Lord Hervey, whilst she was in bed; and because it was contrary to the queenly etiquette to admit a man to her bedside, whilst she was in it, she kept him talking on one side of the door which opened just upon her bed, whilst she conversed with him on the other, for two hours together, and then sent him to the King's side [of the palace, where his Majesty's separate apartments were], to repeat to his Majesty all he had repeated to her.†"

Again, on the fifth of June, 1735, the King set out on a visit to Hanover, and whilst he was there, basking in the deceptive sunshine of pleasure and illicit love, the Queen, as Regent, in conjunction with Sir Robert Walpole, the premier, ruled the nation with laudable ability and success. Caroline viewed her husband's departure with pleasure,

* Hervey's Memoirs.

† Lord Hervey.

for it freed her during his absence from the trouble of ruling through him, and from the annoyance of his almost unbearable petulancy. But her pride was wounded by intelligence which he forwarded to her shortly after his arrival, and from which she learned that he had found a new mistress in Madame Walmoden, a young married German lady, who deserted her husband for the King, and, after the Queen's death, was created Countess of Yarmouth. Lord Hervey, after asserting that the pride of the Queen was much more hurt than her affections on this occasion, proceeds—"It is certain, too, that from the very beginning of this new engagement, the King acquainted the Queen, by letter, of every step he took in it, of the growth of his passion, the progress of his applications, and their success—of every word as well as every action that passed; so minute a description of her person, that had the Queen been a painter, she might have drawn her rival's picture at six hundred miles' distance; he added, too, the account of his buying her, and what he gave her, which, considering the rank of the purchaser, and the merits of the purchase, as he set them forth, I think he had no great reason to brag of, when the first price, according to his report, was only 1000 ducats, a much greater proof of his economy than his passion." To these, and other equally-indelicate epistles from her profligate husband, Caroline returned equally indelicate answers, actually encouraging him in his amours. That such extraordinary confidences could have been, seems strange, yet so it was; and the fact has been put beyond doubt, by the concurrent testimony of Lord Hervey, Horace Walpole, and Lord Chancellor King, the latter of whom observes, "that Sir Robert Walpole assured him that the King [during this visit to Hanover] constantly wrote to her [Majesty] long letters of two or three sheets, being generally of all his actions, what he did every day, even to minute things, and particularly of his amours, what women he admired * * * * and that the Queen, to continue him in a disposition to do what she desired, returned as long letters, and approved even of his amours, not scrupling to say that she was but one woman, and an old woman, and that he might love more and younger women * * * *, by which perfect subserviency to his will, she effected whatever she desired, without which it was impossible to keep him within bounds." *

This new amour caused the King to leave his beloved Hanover with feelings of more than ordinary regret; and when he reached Kensington, on Sunday, the twenty-sixth of October, he was in a most abominable temper, which was aggravated by an attack of a painful disease,† brought on by hasty travelling. As he alighted from his coach, he permitted the Queen to "glue her lips to his hands"—a honour he only granted when she had been acting as Regent—but at the presentation which took place immediately afterwards, "he had only ill-words for the company, and black looks and frowns for the Queen." Nothing, he declared, ever was, would, or could be done as it should be by the English; in fact, England was a pandemonium, Hanover a paradise. Just after giving utterance to these unpatriotic sentiments, and, indeed, by unceremoniously cursing the islands over which he reigned, and the Queen to boot, he noticed, that in his absence, the Queen had had several worthless paintings removed from the drawing-rooms at Kensington, and replaced by masterpieces of art, when, pointing to the latter, he exclaimed, "I will have these silly daubs removed, and my old pictures restored." Lord Hervey begged that the two Vandykes, which had been substituted for the two sign-posts done by nobody knows who, might remain. "As you please about that," answered the King; "but for the picture with the dirty frame over the door, and the three nasty little children, I will have them taken away, and the old ones restored." "And would your Majesty have the gigantic fat Venus restored too?" observed Lord Hervey, from whose

* Lord Campbell's Lives of the Chancellors, vol. iv. p. 633.

† The piles.

Memoirs this dialogue is extracted. "Yes, my lord," rejoined the King, "I am not so nice as your lordship; I like my fat Venus better than anything you have given me instead of her." Lord Hervey thought, though he did not dare to say, that if his Majesty had liked his *fat Venus* as well as he used to do, there would have been none of these disputations. The King's ill-humour continued, and the next morning, at breakfast time, "He snubbed the Queen, who was drinking chocolate, for being always stuffing; the Princess Amelia for not hearing him; the Princess Caroline for being grown fat; the Duke of Cumberland for standing awkwardly; Lord Hervey for not knowing what relation the Prince of Stultzbach was to the Elector Palatine; and then carried the Queen to walk, to be re-snubbed in the garden."* Sir Robert Walpole told the Queen, that he believed her husband's ill-humour proceeded from weariness of her person; he assured her she was no longer young enough to hold him by the charms of her fading beauty, and that, if she would retain her influence, she must herself select for him such favourites as were too weak, or too well-intentioned, to deprive her of her power—a most ingracious piece of advice, but to which, it is said that Caroline listened with great good humour.

As evidence that Walpole had good reason for supposing that the King had left his heart with Madame Walmoden at Hanover, we cite the subjoined interesting home scenes, condensed from Lord Hervey's Memoirs, a work to which we refer the reader for more ample details.

"About nine o'clock every night the King used to return to the Queen's apartments from that of his daughter, where, from the time of Lady Suffolk's disgrace, he used to pass those evenings he did not go to the opera or play at quadrille; constraining, then tiring himself, and talking a little indecently to Lady Deloraine, who was always of the party. At his return to the Queen's side, the Queen used often to send for Lord Hervey to entertain them till they retired, which was generally at eleven. One evening, among the rest, as soon as Lord Hervey came into the room—the Queen was knitting—the King walking backwards and forwards, jocosely attacked him upon an answer just published to a book of his friend, Bishop Hoadley, 'On the Sacrament.' The King grew warm, and spoke sharply against the bishop, whom he designated 'a canting hypocritical knave, to be crying, *The kingdom of Christ is not of this world*, at the same time, that he [the bishop], as Christ's ambassador, was in the receipt of £6000 or £7000 a year.' Lord Hervey, in order to turn the conversation [which we have not the space to detail], told the King that he had that very day been with Wilcocks, Bishop of Rochester, a prelate, who, he felt assured, would never disturb his Majesty's government with writing, and who had that day showed him the restored old bronze gates to Henry VII.'s chapel. Whilst Lord Hervey was minutely describing and praising these gates to the Queen, who was pleased with the description, the King abruptly stopped the conversation, by sharply remarking, 'My lord, you are always putting some of these fine things into the Queen's head, and then I am to be plagued with a thousand plans and workmen.' Then, turning to the Queen, he said, 'I suppose I shall see a pair of these gates to *Merlin's Cave*,* to complete your nonsense there.' The Queen answered, with a smile, 'Merlin's Cave is complete already, and I hear the Craftsman has abused it.'

"'I am very glad of it,' interrupted the King; 'you deserve to be abused for such childish, silly stuff, and it is the first time I ever knew the scoundrel in the right.'

"The Queen bit her lips, and, to change the topic of conversation, expressed disapprobation at the expensive custom of giving money to the servants of the house in the country at which one pays a visit; and observed, that she had found it a pretty considerable ex-

* Hervey's Memoirs, vol. ii. p. 35.

* The Queen's grotto in Richmond gardens, and so called from a statue of Merlin erected thereon.

pense this summer to visit her friends even in town.

"'That is your fault,' angrily remarked the King; 'for my father, when he went to people's houses in town, never was fool enough to give away his money.'

"'I have only done what Lord Grantham assured me was customary,' pleaded the Queen, who began to perceive that her efforts to lull her husband's churlish anger had failed.

"'And a pretty director Lord Grantham is,' growled out the King; 'but then, you are always asking some fool or other what you are to do; and only a fool would ask another fool's advice.'

"Here Lord Hervey observed, 'that liberality would always be expected from her Majesty when she honoured any of her subjects by visiting them at their houses.'

"'Then,' said the King, 'she may stay at home as I do. You do not see me running into every puppy's house to see his new chairs and stools, nor is it for you,' said he, addressing the Queen, 'to be running your nose everywhere, and trotting about the town to every fellow that will give you some bread and butter, like an old goat that loves to go abroad, no matter where, or whether it be proper or no.' The Queen coloured, and knotted a good deal faster during this speech than she did before, whilst the tears came into her eyes, but she said not one word.

"Lord Hervey perceiving her embarrassment, and with the view of diverting the King's wrath from her, chimed in, 'that the Queen loved pictures, and the only way to see private collections was to visit people's houses.'

"'And what matter whether she sees a collection or not?' said the King; 'besides, if she does thus satisfy her curiosity, the obligation is equal, for she obliges the people whose houses she honours with her presence; and furthermore, suppose she had a curiosity to see a tavern, would it be fit for her to satisfy it?—and yet the innkeeper would be very glad to see her.'

"'If the innkeepers,' replied Lord Hervey, 'were used to be well received by her Majesty in her palace, I should think the Queen's seeing them at their own houses no additional scandal.' The King perceiving this answer to be unanswerable, turned to the Queen, and vehemently poured out an unintelligible torrent of abuse in German, to which the Queen made no reply, but knotted on till she tangled her thread, then snuffed the candles that stood on the table before her, and snuffed one of them out, upon which, the King in English began a new dissertation upon her Majesty, and took her awkwardness for his text."

Lady Suffolk observes, that "scenes such as the above were of frequent occurrence; and that the Queen, at such times, keenly as she felt the sting, always endeavoured—generally successfully—to assume an appearance of ease and indifference; and when, occasionally, the tears could no longer be constrained, she, to hide them, would pretend to smile, and then burst out into a fit of laughter, but which was more hysterical than joyous."*

The marriage of the Prince of Wales was a subject which Caroline had for some time contemplated. The Prince had scandalized the name of royalty by improper intimacies with Miss Vane,† Lady Archibald Hamilton, and other noble born, but bad women; and when, in 1735, he threatened his parents with a parliamentary address to the throne on the subject of his "marriage and settlement, the Queen, after much coaxing, prevailed on the King, through her, by a formal message, to inform the heir-apparent, that 'he intended to marry him forthwith to any lady he chose to select for his bride.' But Prince Frederick was prevented, by the artifice of Sir Robert Walpole, from making the proposed choice; and the King having failed in a

* Inedited letter of Lady Suffolk to Mr. Berkeley.

† Miss Vane was maid of honour to the Queen. In 1732, she gave birth to an illegitimate son, christened Fitz-Frederick Vane, and although this infant, doubtless, owed its existence to the Prince of Wales, the Prince, Lord Hervey, and the first Lord Harrington, have each been pointed to as its father; and, according to Horace Walpole, they each claimed the child as their own.

negotiation for his alliance with a Princess of Prussia, next proposed, by the Queen's advice, to marry him to Augusta, Princess of Saxe Gotha. Neither the Prince nor the Princess's parents objected to the match; the preliminaries were arranged without difficulty; the bride arrived at Greenwich on Sunday, the twenty-fifth of April, and, on the subsequent Tuesday, she proceeded to St. James's, where, in the evening, the marriage was solemnized in the chapel by the Bishop of London, the joining of hands being announced by the firing of the park and the tower guns. At the supper, which was served up a little after ten, the bride wore robes of "silver stuff with a coronet on her head, and a train supported by four dukes' daughters and two earls." She sat on the left of the Queen, and the Princesses Amelia and Caroline sat on the left of her; Prince Frederick sat on the King's right, and the Duke, his brother, sat next to him. About twelve followed a ceremony which has very properly gone into disuse. Immediately after the bride had retired to her bedchamber, the bridegroom proceeded to his dressing-room, "where the duke undressed him, and the King did him the honour to put on his shirt. The bride was undresssed by the princesses, and being in bed, in a rich undress, his Majesty came into the room, and the Prince following soon after in a night-gown made of silver stuff and cap of the finest lace; the *quality* were admitted to see the bride and bridegroom sitting up in bed, surrounded by all the royal family." *

On this occasion, numerous congratulatory addresses and poems were presented to their Majesties and the newly-married pair; and Mr. Pitt, in a speech in the Commons, spoke so favourably of the Prince, that ever afterwards the King hated and the Queen despised him.

Meanwhile, the measures brought before parliament, were a source of anxiety to her Majesty. The dissenters brought in their long-threatened bill for the repeal of the Corporation and Test Acts. This, the Commons, to the gratification of the court and church, negatived; but a bill to amend the Mortmain acts, and another to render more easy the payment of tithes by quakers, they sent to the Lords, who, to the disappointment of the Queen and the court, only passed the former; the quakers' bill, as it was called, being lost by a majority of two, through the bishops and the lawyers, whose pecuniary interests it threatened, combining against it. This conduct of the bishops so incensed the King, that he called them "a parcel of black, canting rascals." The Queen also vented her wrath against the offending diocesans, by telling them to their heads that they were "all a set of fools." She, however, had the wisdom to avoid giving them mortal offence, and to advise the King not to drive them to desperation. But, to this prudent counsel, George, it is said, made answer, "I am sick to death of all this foolish stuff, and wish, with all my heart, that the devil may take all the bishops, and the devil take your minister, and the devil take the parliament, and the devil take the whole island, provided I can get out of it and go to Hanover."*

The fact was, that when last in Hanover, he had promised Madame Walmoden to again see her in May, 1736; and true to his word, he named the Queen regent in his absence, and, on the twenty-second of that month, the day after the prorogation of parliament, set out for the electorate. The day before his departure, he sent a message to the Prince, that "wherever the Queen-regent resided, there would be apartments for him and his princess." This measure Frederick very justly complained against, as being adopted with a view to make prisoners of him and his bride during the King's absence, and to deprive them of the power of holding a separate court. He resolved to disobey the arbitrary mandate; and when the Queen removed to Richmond, his Princess feigned illness, and this illness he pleaded as an excuse for not following her. He was also annoyed beyond measure at the Queen being regent; and when Caroline opened

* Extract quoted from the "Gentleman's Magazine" for April, 1736, by the editor of Lord Hervey's Memoirs.

* Lord Hervey's Memoirs, vol. ii. p. 100.

her commission, which she made a rule of doing immediately she heard that the King had reached Hanover, he contrived to arrive at Kensington just after the council had terminated its sitting.

During the absence of his Majesty in 1736, the whole kingdom was disturbed by tumults and riots. There were corn riots in the west, to oppose the exportation of corn; riots in Spitalfields, against the employment of Irishmen as weavers; anti-turnpike riots in the country; gin riots in the metropolis, because the people resolved, spite of the Act just previously passed to the contrary, to get intoxicated on "the mountain dew," where, when, and how they chose; and the whole coast was infested with daring bands of smugglers, whom the people, in defiance of the authorities, encouraged in their lawless traffic, and bold, and too frequently murderous, encounters with the revenue officers. As may be supposed, sedition also stalked abroad, and the rioters, whatever their prime object, generally concluded by "cursing the Germans, reviling the King and Queen, and huzzaing for James III."* The most dreadful of these riots took place at Edinburgh, and was occasioned by the people's sympathy for a desperate, but heroic, smuggler, who was hanged for his crimes. At the execution the mob pelted the soldiers, who, by command of their officer, Captain Porteus, fired, and killed several innocent persons. For this, Porteus was tried and convicted of murder; but the Queen reprieved him, which so exasperated the populace, that they rose in riot, set fire to the prison, and taking Porteus out, hanged him, and heartily cursed the Queen, who was so enraged by the intelligence, that she declared General Moyle, who commanded the troops in Scotland, deserved to be shot by order of the court-martial, for not endeavouring to suppress the riot, and that every one of the rioters deserved to be hanged.

When the Queen wrote to her husband the particulars of these riots, he observed: "Ah, if half the English were hanged, the other half would learn to behave themselves; but the laws there are so loose, that the rogues look at the gallows and laugh at it."* As heretofore, Caroline maintained a continuous correspondence with the truant King; and even to *her* the task of daily writing long, affectionate letters to a husband who, by his own confession, had crossed the sea to, at least for a season, bestow his love on another, must have been bitter and galling. She, however, exhibited neither jealousy nor displeasure till the King's return was protracted beyond the usual period, and then Sir Robert Walpole found it advisable to give her, what he most inappropriately designated "a little wholesome advice," which was neither more nor less than to write to the royal profligate, intreating him to bring Madame Walmoden to England with him, and promising to treat the mistress with all conceivable kindness. The thoughts of penning this extraordinary epistle made her weep; but she wrote it, and, to the minister's surprise, sent it too. George, in reply, thanked Caroline for her kindness; and after, in language more elegant than truthful, expressing an earnest desire to imitate the goodness and virtue he so admired in her, desired that the lodgings formerly occupied by Lady Suffolk might be prepared for Madame Walmoden. The Queen wrote that the lodgings should be prepared; but about this time the King was annoyed by a supposed intrigue between Madame Walmoden and Monsieur Schulemberg. The gardener one night found a ladder placed suspiciously against Madame's bedchamber window, and on searching the garden discovered Monsieur behind some bushes. The affair created considerable excitement; and the King, who was very anxious to acquit his mistress of the charge, wrote the particulars to the Queen, "asking her as he would have done a man friend, what she thought of the business; saying, perhaps his passion

* Lord Hervey.

* This exclamation I am indebted for to the kindness of the late learned Dr. Lingard. The Doctor's authority I have forgotten; but, as Lord Hervey attributes almost the same disgraceful sentiments to George II. (Memoirs, vol. ii. p. 144), its authenticity need not be doubted.

for Madame Walmoden might make him see it in a partial light for her, and desiring the Queen, before sending her answer, to consult Sir Robert Walpole, in the matter, who understood such affairs better than she did."*

In the meantime the Prince and Princess of Wales inflicted a multitude of petty annoyances on the Queen; and Caroline lost no opportunity of returning the compliment. The people paid little regard to these royal peccadilloes, but they loudly murmured at the King's protracted absence, and satirized his fondness for Hanover and Hanoverian mistresses. On the gate of St. James's Palace a pasquinade to this effect was posted: "Lost or strayed out of this house a man who has left a wife and six children on the parish; whoever will give any tidings of him to the churchwardens of St. James's parish, so as he may be got again, shall receive *four shillings and sixpence* reward. N.B. This reward will not be increased, nobody judging him to deserve a *crown*." But what produced the greatest sport was an old hack, lame, lean, and blind, with a worn-out saddle and pillion on his back, which some wag had turned loose in the city, with an inscription on his forehead, which stated that no one was to stop him, as he was the King of Hanover's equipage, going to fetch his Majesty and his * * * * * to England."*

At length the King announced his return from Hanover, and vessels were sent to escort him to England. He left his beloved mistress and electorate with regret, and on the eleventh of December, 1736, reached Helvoetsluys. But the wind, which had been calm and favourable, suddenly veered round, and a violent storm arose, and prevented him from embarking. Day followed day, and still the hurricane raged. In England all was excitement and anxiety; no tidings arrived of the royal voyager; and at length a report prevailed that the whole fleet had sunk in the stormy waters· and the Queen, Sir Robert Walpole, and the court party began to feel more uneasiness than they felt inclined to express, as, to their perhaps jaundiced eyes, Prince Frederick already had began to assume the airs of kingship, and to court popularity. This latter fact, if fact it be, so irritated the Queen, that she remarked to Lord Hervey: "My God! popularity always makes me sick; but *Fritz's* popularity makes me vomit * * Did you observe the air with which he came into my drawing-room in the morning? I swear, his behaviour shocked me so prodigiously, that I could hardly bring myself to speak to him when he was with me; afterwards, I felt something here in my throat that swelled and half choked me."* But amidst these alarms, forebodings, and expectations, in which the people joined—some hoping for the best, and many heartily wishing the King and all regality at the bottom of the sea—a courier, who had successfully braved the tempest, arrived at St. James's with a letter from his Majesty to the Queen, informing her that he neither had embarked, nor would attempt it till a fair wind set in. A gleam of fine weather followed, just sufficient to excite a belief that the King had sailed, when again the wind veered round and a tempest burst forth and raged with indescribable fury. Many that had previously hoped, now gave up the King for lost; and the alarm which the Queen could no longer conceal, was increased by several of the ships which had left Helvoetsluys finding their way into various harbours in a dreadfully wrecked condition, and bringing only the miserable tidings that his Majesty had embarked, but the storm had shattered the fleet, and possibly the royal yacht had returned to Helvoetsluys. The King had so returned in safety; and as his own impatience had induced him to insist on Sir Charles Wager, who commanded the fleet, putting to sea against his will, he now, that he had experienced something of the horrors and dangers of a tempest, waited till Sir Charles pronounced the weather sufficiently favourable, when he again embarked, and after a rough passage landed at Lowestoff, and arrived at St. James's on the

* Lord Hervey, vol. ii. p. 127.

† Ibid. vol. ii. p. 191.

* Lord Hervey, vol. ii. p. 210.

fifteenth of January, 1737, in excellent spirits and pleasant mood, but suffering from a bad cold. To the Queen he was all affability, smiles, and affection; he told Sir Robert Walpole that she was the best, most affectionate of wives, and he seemed to have already forgotten Madame Walmoden; but his cold growing worse, he was prevented from opening the parliament in person. Walpole thought his condition dangerous; but this was not the case, and he slowly recovered.

At this same period the Queen was also unwell; she was suffering from a malady with which she had been afflicted ever since 1724, and which she kept so secret, that it was only known to the King, her German nurse, and one other person, and rightly guessed at by Sir Robert Walpole. She was ruptured; but her illness did not prevent her from, so far as circumstances permitted, transacting the business and performing the public ceremonials of the sovereign. The first annoyance she experienced after her husband's return was from the Princess of Wales, who requested permission to make Mrs. Townshend her bed-chamber woman, a request previously refused by the King. This annoyance was followed by a more serious one: Prince Frederick had long been dissatisfied, because out of a Civil List of £800,000 he had received but £50,000, whilst his father, when Prince of Wales, had £100,000 out of a Civil List of £700,000. To this circumstance he permitted his friends to call the attention of parliament, in the hope of obtaining an increase of income. Before the motion was made in the Commons, Sir Robert Walpole, if possible, to avert the storm, entreated their Majesties to send a message to the Prince in the King's name, informing him that his sire intended to settle on him the £50,000 a year, which he now received at the King's pleasure, and also to settle a jointure on the Princess. To this measure George and Caroline reluctantly assented, and the lords of the council made the proposal in form to the Prince, who returned a verbal answer, which the lords thus rendered in writing, and delivered to the King: "That his Royal Highness desired the lords to lay him at his Majesty's feet, and to assure his Majesty that he had, and ever should retain, the utmost duty for his royal person; that his Royal Highness was very thankful for any instance of his Majesty's goodness to him or the Princess, and particularly for his Majesty's intention of settling a jointure upon his Royal Highness; and that as to the message, the affair was now out of his hands, and therefore he could give no answer to it." After which his Royal Highness used many dutiful expressions towards his Majesty, and then added, "Indeed, my lords, it is in other hands; I am sorry for it," or to that effect. This reply irritated the King, and exasperated the Queen beyond measure; she sharply rated Walpole for having counselled the making an offer which she had foretold would be scornfully rejected; and whilst the question was being warmly discussed in the Commons, she repeatedly called the Prince a "bullying fool," and "the most hardened of all liars;" and when the motion for the address was lost by a majority of thirty, she was overjoyed, and told Lord Hervey that the victory had cost the King but £900, £500 to one man and £400 to another.* Caroline thought that this defeat would dishearten the Prince and his party, and prevent the same motion from being mooted in the Lords: but she was mistaken; the motion was made in the Upper House, but on a division, it was lost by a majority of 103 to 40.

This session the attention of parliament was directed to two other measures, in which the Queen took great interest —the Porteus riots and Sir J. Bernard's proposition for the reduction of the interest on the national debt from four to three per cent. On the first of these subjects Caroline expressed a belief that Porteus had been murdered, and a wish that only those should be punished who had taken part in the crime. She was annoyed at the Scotch judges being compelled to come to London to appear at the bar of the House of Lords; and after they had returned to Scotland, she

* Hervey's Memoirs, vol. ii. p. 280.

told Lord Hervey she should be glad to know the truth, but believed she could never come at it, whether the Scotch judges had been really to blame or not in the trial of Captain Porteus; "for between you and the Bishop of Salisbury," said she, "who each of you convince me by turns, I am as much in the dark as if I knew nothing at all in the matter; he comes and tells me they are all black as devils, you, that they are white as snow, and whoever speaks last I believe. * * * Therefore, since the more I hear the more I am puzzled, I am resolved I will hear no more about it; but let them be in the right or the wrong, I own to you I am glad they are gone."

The bill for the punishment of the magistrates and city of Edinburgh, on account of the murder of Captain Porteus, in its progress through parliament, was shorn of its most vengeful features; and when at length it passed and received the royal assent, it consisted of but two articles, the one imposing a fine of £2000 sterling on the city of Edinburgh, the other depriving the city provost, Alexander Wilson, of his office, and incapacitating him from ever again holding a government appointment. "The fine," says Lord Hervey, "was to give the cook-maid, widow of Captain Porteus, and make her, with most unconjugal joy, bless the hour in which her husband was hanged." *

It was through the exertions of Sir R. Walpole that the bill for the reduction of the interest on the national debt was thrown out by the Commons. To this bill the Queen was heartily opposed; and Horace Walpole, the brother of the premier, by frequently speaking in favour of it, so offended her, that she called him "an opinionative fool," and expressed a personal repugnance to him in language the lowest and coarsest. "She used," says Lord Hervey, "to complain of his silly laugh hurting her ears, and his dirty, sweaty body offending her nose, as if she had never had the two senses of hearing and smelling, in all her acquaintance with poor Horace, till he had talked of three per cent. Sometimes she used to cough and pretend to retch, as if she was ready to vomit with talking of his dirt, and would often bid Lord Hervey open the window to purify the room of the stink Horace had left behind him, and call the pages to burn sweets to get it out of the hangings; she told Lord Hervey, too, she believed Horace had a hand in the 'Craftsman;' for that once, wearied in disputing on this three per cent. affair, he had more than hinted to her that he guessed her reason for being so zealous against this scheme, was her having money herself in the stocks." *

The above is but one of the many instances on record of the coarseness in which the refined Queen too often indulged. The picture is grimy, but truthful; and from it it is our painful duty to turn to one which presents her Majesty in the still more unfavourable light of a hateful, revengeful mother.

* Lord Hervey's Memoirs, where the matter is more fully and graphically detailed.

* Lord Hervey's Memoirs, vol. ii. p. 333.

CHAPTER IV.

Extraordinary conduct of the Royal Family—The Prince of Wales keeps secret the pregnancy of his Princess—Hurries her from Hampton Court to St. James's, where she is taken in labour—She gives birth to a Princess—Indignity of the King and Queen—Night visit of Caroline to St. James's—King's angry message to the Prince—The Prince's reply—Their Majesties refuse to grant him an interview—He further irritates them—His daughter christened—He and his Princess are turned out of St. James's—Further and more angry correspondence on the subject—The Prince, Princess, and their friends forbidden the court.

RINCE FREDERICK'S efforts to obtain through parliament that revenue to which he very naturally considered himself justly entitled, infuriated his mother and his sister Caroline against him. "A hundred times a day," observes Lord Hervey, "they wished he might drop down dead of an apoplexy. The Queen cursed the hour of his birth, and the Princess Caroline declared she begrudged him every hour he continued to breathe, called him 'the greatest liar that ever spoke,' and declared that 'he was a nauseous beast, who loved nothing but money and his own nauseous self,' and who would not hesitate 'to put one arm about anybody's neck to kiss them, and then stab them with another.' The King treated him with silent contempt, and called him 'a silly, insolent, undutiful puppy and rascal.'"* This vindictive spite in due time produced its fruits; it irritated the Prince, and induced him to pursue a similar but less ferocious line of conduct towards his parents. His princess was *enceinte;* the Queen anxiously wished to be present at the birth, and he resolved to disappoint her. He did not make the expected event known to their Majesties till within a month of its anticipated occurrence, when, in a letter dated July the fifth, 1737, he officially announced it to the Queen, on the authority of Dr. Hollings and Mrs. Cannon, a midwife. Caroline disbelieved the announcement, and at once closely—too closely, even, for a mother-in-law—questioned the well-schooled Princess on the subject, from whom she could elicit no other reply to her many queries than "I don't know." The court was then sojourning at Hampton Court, and the Queen, who believed her hated Fritz capable of attempting to palm upon his family and the nation a supposititious child, wished that a command should be sent for the expected birth to take place at Hampton Court, that she might be present; but, through the negligence of Sir Robert Walpole, this order was never sent. These suspicions, which were made no secret of, doubly annoyed the Prince. Twice when the Princess was attacked with indisposition he removed her to St. James's, and each time returned with her in disappointment to Hampton Court. This was kept secret from the Queen; and on the evening of Sunday, the thirty-first of July, the Princess, after having dined in public with their Majesties, was taken seriously ill. Instantly a coach was prepared, and into it the suffering Princess, spite her tears and entreaties to be permitted to remain in quiet where she was, was "lugged" by Dunoyer, the dancing-master, and Bloodworth, the equerry. The Prince, after enjoining such of his household as remained at Hampton Court to strict silence, himself got into the coach, and was followed by Lady Archibald Hamilton and two of the Princess's dressers; whilst Vreid, who, besides valet-de-chambre, was surgeon and man-midwife, mounted the box, and Bloodworth and two or three others got up behind. They drove furiously to St. James's, the Princess all the time suffering intense agony. At the palace no-

* Lord Hervey's Memoirs, vol. ii. p. 255.

thing was prepared for them; even for sheets, tablecloths had to be substituted: however, after a great deal of bustle and confusion, matters were arranged in something like order, and at a quarter to eleven, and in the presence of Lord President Wilmington and Lord Privy Seal Godolphin—the other lords of the council could not, or would not, attend—the Princess gave birth to a daughter, described by Lord Hervey as "a little rat of a girl, about the size of a large tooth-pick case," but who grew up a handsome woman, and became the mother of that unfortunate Queen, Caroline of Brunswick, consort of George IV.

At Hampton Court, their Majesties, expecting nothing unusual, retired to rest at eleven. At half-past one Mrs. Tichburne entered the Queen's bed-chamber, when Caroline waking up, exclaimed: "Is the house on fire?"

"No," replied the bed-chamber woman; "but a courier has just brought intelligence that the Princess of Wales is about to become a mother."

"Good heavens!" cried the Queen, "my night-gown; I'll go to her this moment."

"Your night-gown! madam," replied Mrs. Tichburne; "aye, and your coaches too; the Princess is at St. James's."

This announcement doubly astonished the Queen; and when it was imparted to the King, he flew into a rage, and angrily observed to the Queen, "You see now, with all your wisdom, how they have outwitted you. This is all your fault. *There is a false child will be put upon you;* and how will you answer it to all your children? This has been fine care and fine management; for your son William, he is mightily obliged to you; and for Anne, I hope she will come over and scold you herself; I am sure you deserve anything she can say to you."

The Queen made no reply; but sending for the Duke of Grafton and Lord Hervey to accompany her, immediately set out from the palace, accompanied by the two princesses her daughters, two ladies, and three noblemen. They reached St. James's at four in the morning, and as they proceeded up-stairs, Lord Hervey invited the Queen to take refreshments with him in his apartments: she consented, and, with a wink, whispered, "you need not fear my tasting anything on this side of the house." As she approached the Prince's apartments he met her, and after saluting her in the German fashion, detailed to her the particulars of the flight and birth; to him she was cold and haughty, but to the Princess she spoke and behaved with the greatest affection and tenderness; and taking the child in her arms, she kissed it, and exclaimed: "May the good God bless you, poor little creature! you have arrived in a disagreeable world."

After scolding Lady Hamilton for assisting the "young fools" in their peril-fraught flight, she told the Prince, whose gossip annoyed her—he forged lies faster than smiths forged nails, she afterwards observed—to go to bed; and having made assurances of her affectionate regard to the Princess, descended the stairs, and crossed the court to Lord Hervey's lodgings; where, whilst sipping chocolate, she called her son Fritz an insolent, impertinent fool, for receiving them all as if nothing had happened, and they were the best friends in the world; and expressed a firm conviction that the "poor, little she-mouse" of a child really was the Princess's; although had it been a "brave, fat, jolly boy, she should not have been cured of her suspicions." Nay, she observed with warmth, "I should have gone about the Prince's apartment like a mad woman, played the devil, and insisted on knowing what chairman's brat he had bought." Sir Robert Walpole now arrived; and after the chocolate drinking party had alternately laughed and railed at the folly and imprudent conduct of the Prince and the to-be-pitied Princess of Wales, the Queen remarked with an air of self-consolation, "Well, though one does not care a farthing for them, the giving oneself all this trouble is a good grimace for the public; and the more impertinences they do, and the more civilities we show, the more we shall be thought in the right, and they in the wrong, when we bring it to an open quarrel."* The royal party left St. James's shortly after day-break, and at eight in the morning the Queen reached Hampton Court. She found the King in anxious suspense, and on her relating to him all that had passed in this romance of real life, he fell into a fury of paternal rage. and with his usual vehemence heartily execrated his hated son. The rage subsided, he held a conference with the Queen and Sir Robert Walpole on the subject; and the result was, Lord Essex was despatched with the following message from his Majesty to the Prince on the third of August.

"The King has commanded me to acquaint your Royal Highness that his Majesty most heartily rejoices at the safe delivery of the Princess; but that your carrying away her Royal Highness from Hampton Court, the then residence of the King, the Queen, and the royal family, under the pains and certain indication of immediate labour, to the imminent danger and hazard both of the Princess and her child; and after sufficient warnings for a week before to have made the necessary preparations for this happy event without acquainting his Majesty or the Queen with the circumstances the Princess was in, or giving them the least notice of your departure, is looked upon by the King to be such a deliberate indignity offered to himself and to the Queen, that he has commanded me to acquaint your Royal Highness that he resents it to the highest degree."

This message surprised the Prince; who, in reply, expressed astonishment at the anger of his sire, and sorrow for having giving him offence; and in the evening sent the subjoined epistles to his royal parents by Lord Jersey, his lord-in-waiting.

"*St. James's, August* 3, 1737.

"SIR,

"It is with all the mortification imaginable that I see by the message my Lord Essex has brought me, that my coming to town with the Princess has had the misfortune to displease your Majesty. Permit me, sir, to represent to you, that in the pressing situation I was in on Sunday, without a midwife or any assistance, it was impossible for me to delay one moment, otherwise I should not have failed to have come myself to acquaint your Majesty with it; besides which, the greatest expedition in the world could never have brought Mrs. Cannon in less than two or three hours after the birth of the child. As the Princess had had the cholic for some days, Mrs. Cannon, Dr. Hollings, and Dr. Broxholme, who were often consulted, all assured me she was not yet so near her time, of which opinion these two physicians still were on Sunday at noon; but in case she had pains different from the cholic that a cordial should be given her, and that she should be brought to town as soon as possible. This advice I followed in every point: and am very much concerned that a case should happen in which my tenderness for the Princess might seem one moment to remove what is otherwise first in my thoughts—the desire of shewing my devotion to your Majesty. Besides this, if I may take the liberty to say so, the Princess desired me so earnestly at that time to carry her to London, where all assistance was nearer at hand, that I could not resist it; for I could never have forgiven myself if, in consequence of my refusal, any accident had happened to her. I hope all this will move your Majesty; and that you will give me leave to lay myself at your feet to-morrow at your levee, which I should not have failed to have done last Monday, if the Queen had not ordered me to defer it till this day; the only thing that has hindered me to-day, is the fear I have had, since I have seen my Lord Essex, of displeasing your Majesty in case I should come into your presence before I took the liberty to explain to you, with all submission, the true and only motive of the step with which you seem offended.

"I am, with the greatest respect imaginable, sir, your Majesty's most humble and most obedient son, servant, and subject, FREDERICK."

* The above scenes are chiefly compiled and closely condensed from Lord Hervey's interesting Memoirs, to which the reader is referred for more ample details.

"*St. James's, August* 3, 1737.

"MADAM,

"You cannot imagine how much the message my Lord Essex brought me has afflicted me. I flattered myself, that the reasons I took to give your Majesty, when you had the goodness to come and see the Princess, would have justified my departure from Hampton Court to the King. I have taken the liberty to recapitulate those reasons in the letter I have done myself the honour to write to him upon the subject; flattering myself your Majesty will be so good to lend them your assistance.

"I am, with great respect, madam, your most humble and most obedient son and servant,

"FREDERICK."

The self-defending, excusing, instead of crime-acknowledging, pardon-begging tone of these letters, further aggravated their Majesties against their hated son: instead of a written answer, the King sent by Lord Jersey a verbal reply, that he could not see the Prince, and the Queen also, by a verbal message, expressed sorrow that the Prince, by his own misconduct, had deprived her of the power of effectually interceding for him with the King.

Next day the Prince again wrote to the King only, as follows:—

"SIR,

"Will you permit me to lay at your feet my grief for the refusal I received last night, to make my court to you today? I cannot express how much I suffer from being deprived of that honour, and seeing myself out of your Majesty's favour; if anything would comfort me in that misfortune, it would be the innocence of my intentions, which I beg your Majesty to believe can never be to offend you. I do not take the liberty to recapitulate the reasons which induced me to leave Hampton Court so suddenly; but I flatter myself that your Majesty will more easily grant me that pardon which I ask, when you reflect on the condition in which I found myself with the poor Princess, at a time when it was not fit for me to delay a moment. I take the liberty then, most earnestly to conjure your Majesty to restore me to your favour. and to permit me to make my court to you to morrow, at your levee, till which time I cannot be easy.

"I am, with all the respect imaginable, sir, your Majesty's most humble and most obedient son, servant, and subject, FREDERICK."

After reading this letter, the King dispatched Lord Essex to inform Lord Carnarvon, the bearer, that as its purport was the same as that of the night previously, the answer would also be the same; namely, that his Majesty would not see the Prince. But presently Lord Essex returned, and stated that Lord Carnarvon wished to have the reply in writing; and placing the pen and ink before his Majesty, asked if he should call one of the ministers? when the Queen, who was present, immediately exclaimed, "For what! to give an answer to *Fritz?* Does the King want a minister to tell him what answer he likes to give to his son, or to call a council for such a letter, like an affair *d'état?*" And then, addressing the King, she proceeded, "*But I suppose, sir, you will not write to your son; and I have already told Lord Essex that I believe he would trouble you upon this subject to very little purpose.*" "Accordingly," observes Lord Hervey, from whose Memoirs the above is extracted, "the King being thoroughly, by this hint, apprised of what he was to have a mind to, told Lord Essex he should give no other answer than what he had given already, and in no other manner."

This family feud now became, if possible, more fierce and undignified than heretofore. The Queen declared, that "it was high time his Royal Highness was well lashed;" and his sister Caroline sent to him the very acceptable message that, "in her opinion, he and all those about him, saving the Princess, his wife, deserved to be hanged."

Meanwhile, the Prince, although keeping a cooler temper than his parents, conducted himself in a manner by no means agreeable to them. He endeavoured to win popularity at the expense of his royal father. The Queen he always spoke of, and wrote to, simply as "madam" and "you," but never as "your Majesty;" and when Caroline, with her two eldest daughters, visited the Princess of Wales, the ninth day after her accouchement, he went no further than the Princess's bed-chamber door to receive her, and never once spoke to her during her stay; but when she departed, he gracefully led her to the coach door, and "to make the mob believe he was never wanting in any respect, he kneeled down in the dirty street and kissed her hand. As soon as this operation was over, he put her Majesty into the coach, and then returned to the steps of his own door, leaving his sisters to get through the dirt and the mob by themselves as they could; nor did there come to the Queen any messages, either from the Prince or Princess, to thank her afterwards for the trouble she had taken, or for the honour she had done them on this visit."*

On the twentieth of August, the King, at Hampton Court, sent the subjoined message to the Prince at St. James's, by Lord Dunmore, his Majesty's lord in waiting.

"It being now near three weeks since the Princess was brought to bed, his Majesty hopes there can be no inconvenience to the Princess, if Monday, the twenty-ninth instant, be appointed for baptizing the Princess, his granddaughter; and having determined that his Majesty, the Queen, and the Duchess-dowager of Sax-Gotha shall be godfather and godmothers, he will send his lord chamberlain to represent himself, and the Queen's lady of the bed-chamber to stand for the Duchess-dowager of Sax-Gotha, and the King will send to the Archbishop of Canterbury to attend and to perform the ceremony."

To this message, the Prince, in reply, sent the two following letters by Lord Carnarvon the same evening.

"*St. James's, August* 20, 1737.

"Sir,

"The Princess and I take the liberty to thank your Majesty most humbly for the honour you intend to do our daughter in standing god-father to her; the orders my Lord Dunmore has brought shall be punctually executed. I should thing myself very happy, if, upon that occasion, I might take the liberty to come and throw myself at your feet; nothing could prevent me but the prohibition I have received from your Majesty; to be deprived of your favour, is the thing in the world the most mortifying to me, who not only respect you, but, if I may make use of that expression, most tenderly love you; will you permit me once again, humbly to beseech you to pardon a fault in which, at least, the intention had no share, and to permit me again to make my court to you at your levees? I take the liberty to conjure you to grant this request, as a thing that will restore my quiet.

"I am, with all possible submission, sir, your Majesty's most humble and most obedient son, subject, and servant,

"Frederick."

"*St. James's, August* 20, 1737.

"Madam,

"Permit me to thank you most humbly for the honour you think fit to do the Princess and me in being godmother to our daughter. I have taken the liberty to return the King my thanks in writing. I have added. likewise, the grief for the situation I am in. I beseech you, once again, madam, to assist me with your good offices, which can never be employed for your son in a more essential point than in restoring him to his father's favour.

"I am, with all possible respect, madam, your most humble and most obedient son and servant,

"Frederick."

On the twenty-ninth of August, the Prince of Wales's daughter was christened Augusta; the Duke of Grafton and the Ladies Burlington and Torrington standing proxies for the King, Queen, and the Duchess-dowager of Sax Gotha: immediately afterwards, the Prince, merely for annoyance sake, declared that she should be called not the Princess, but *the lady* Augusta, according to the old English fashion, and styled her Royal Highness, although his sisters were not so styled till after the accession of their father.

* Lord Hervey, vol. ii. p. 409.

The day after the christening, the Prince sent Lord North to Hampton Court with the subjoined letters to their Majesties:—

"*St. James's, August* 30, 1737.

"SIR,

"It is with all possible respect, that I take the liberty to thank your Majesty once more for the honour you have thought fit to do the Princess and me, in being godfather to our daughter; I cannot let this opportunity pass, without repeating my petition for that pardon which I have so often asked. I should be glad to find words that could soften the paternal heart of your Majesty; if there were any that could stronger mark my grief and my respect, I assure your Majesty I would make use of them; there remains, then, nothing more for me to say, but to conjure you once again to re-establish me in your favour, and to assure you that nothing in the world shall change the tender respect I owe you, being, with great submission,

"Sir, your Majesty's most humble and most obedient son, subject, and servant, FREDERICK."

"*St. James's, August* 30, 1737.

"MADAM,

"I think it my duty to thank you once more, most humbly, for the honour you have done the Princess and me, in being godmother to our daughter. I am extremely mortified that the King's prohibition hinders me from doing it by word of mouth. Nothing else should stop me. I flatter myself, that the continuation of your good offices, joined to the letter I have done myself the honour to write to the King on that subject, will procure me that permission, and that I shall soon have the satisfaction to appear before you again.

"I am, with all imaginable respect, Madam, your most humble and most obedient son and servant,

"FREDERICK."

With the tone of these letters their Majesties were so little satisfied, that they resolved to turn the Prince out of St. James's, without further delay. Accordingly, the following official message was prepared, and on Saturday, the tenth of September, conveyed from Hampton Court by the Dukes of Grafton and Richmond and Lord Pembroke to the Prince at St. James's:—

"GEORGE R.

"The professions you have lately made in your letters of your peculiar regard to me, are so contradictory to all your actions, that I cannot suffer myself to be imposed on by them.

"You know very well, you did not give the intimation to me or to the Queen that the Princess was with child, or breeding, until within less than a month of the birth of the young Princess. You removed the Princess twice in the week immediately preceding the day of her delivery from the place of my residence, in expectation, as you have voluntarily declared, of her labour; and both times, upon your return, you industriously concealed from the knowledge of me and the Queen every circumstance relating to this important affair: and you at last, without giving any notice to me or to the Queen, precipitately hurried the Princess from Hampton Court, in a condition not to be named. After having thus, in execution of your determined measures, exposed both the Princess and her child to the greatest perils, you now plead surprise and tenderness for the Princess, as the only motives that occasioned these repeated indignities offered to me, and to the Queen, your mother.

"This extravagant and undutiful behaviour, in so essential a point as the birth of an heir to my crown, is such an evidence of your premeditated defiance of me, and such a contempt of my authority, and of the natural right belonging to your parents, as cannot be excused, by the pretended innocence of your intentions, nor palliated or disguised by specious words only; but the whole tenor of your conduct, for a considerable time, is so entirely void of real duty to me, that I have long had reason to be highly offended with you, and until you withdraw your regard and confidence from those by whose instigation and advice you are directed and encouraged in your unwarrantable behaviour to me and to the Queen, and until you return to your duty, you shall not reside in my palace, which I will not suffer to be made the resort of them, who, under the appearance of an attachment to you, foment the division which you have made in my family, and thereby weaken the common interest of the whole in this situation. I will receive no reply but when your actions manifest a just sense of your duty and submission, that may induce me to pardon what at present I must justly resent.

"In the meantime, it is my pleasure that you leave St. James's with all your family when it can be done without prejudice or inconvenience to the Princess. I shall leave to the Princess the care of my granddaughter until a proper time calls upon me to consider of her education.

"(*Signed*) G. R."

Whilst this humiliating message was being read to him, the Prince became agitated and distressed, and before dismissing the bearers thereof, he begged them "to present his duty to the King, and say he was very sorry for what had happened."* The next morning, at breakfast, the Queen *wished to God that she might never see him again.* And she had her wish: the last meeting on earth of the estranged royal mother and son, was on the previous ninth of August, when the Prince, by kneeling down in the dirt, and kissing her Majesty's hand, in the presence of the assembled populace at the gate of St. James's, as he led her to her coach, caused her indignation to shrink into supreme contempt. The King spoke with equal harshness against his "puppy of a son." "He has too little sense," remarked the royal, but stern, unforgiving parent, "to feel his present degradation, and, as he only listens to boobies, fools, and madmen, those about him are not likely to lay his case before his eyes in its true colours." His Majesty then described the Prince's household in anything but flattering terms: Lord Carnarvon he designated a half-witted coxcomb; Lord Townshend a wrong-headed booby; Lord North a poor creature; Lord Baltimore a mad, unprincipled fellow; and young Lumley a strutting puppy.

On the twelfth of September, the Prince and Princess, together with their daughter and their whole household, removed from St James's to Kew; they were not allowed to take a particle of the furniture with them; and when it was suggested that they should be permitted to take the chests and other articles of necessity, as they could not carry away their clothes like dirty linen in a basket, the King sharply answered, "Why not? a basket is quite good enough for them." The Queen pretended to wish that this permission should be granted to them; "but," observes Lord Hervey, "the King's perseverance in being against it, is a full proof that she was against it too." On reaching Kew, the Prince sent for Lord Carteret, Sir William Windham, and Mr. Poulteney; and the King, when informed of this fact, observed to Lord Hervey, "Ah! they will soon be tired of the puppy; for, besides a scoundrel, he is such a fool, that he will talk more fiddle-faddle to them in a day than any old woman talks in a week."

The Prince, at this period, wished to address another letter to the Queen, but as correspondence with his parents was interdicted, he caused Lord Baltimore to write as follows to Lord Grantham:

"*London, Sept.* 13, 1737.

"My Lord,

"I have in my hands a letter from his Royal Highness to the Queen, which I am commanded to give or transmit to your Lordship; and as I am afraid it might be improper for me to wait on you at Hampton Court, I beg you will be so good as to let me know how and in what manner I may deliver or send it to you. If I may presume to judge of my royal master's sentiments, he does not conceive himself precluded by the King's messages from taking this the only means of endeavouring, as far as he is able, to remove his Majesty's displeasure.

"I am your Lordship's very humble servant,

"Baltimore."

* Lord Hervey.

To the above Lord Grantham replied by the following letter, drawn up by Sir Robert Walpole, at the Queen's command.

"*Hampton Court, Sept.* 15, 1737.

"MY LORD,

"I have laid your lordship's letter before the Queen, who has commanded me to return your lordship the following answer:

"The Queen is very sorry that the Prince's behaviour has given the King such just cause of offence, but thinks herself constrained, by the King's last message to the Prince, from receiving any application from the Prince upon that subject.

"I am, my lord, your lordship's, &c.,

"GRANTHAM."

Before this answer reached Kew, the Princess's vice-chamberlain, Sir William Irby, brought the following undated letter from the Princess to the King to Lord Pembroke, who delivered it to his Majesty on the morning of the fifteenth of September.

"SIR,

"It is with all possible respect that I take the liberty to thank your Majesty most humbly for the honour you were pleased to do me in being godfather to my daughter. I should not have failed to come myself and pay my duty to you at Hampton Court, to thank you by word of mouth: but as I have at present the misfortune to be debarred that honour, I hope your Majesty will not be displeased that I take the liberty of doing it in writing. It is a great aggravation of my sorrow upon this occasion, to find that by the Prince's tenderness for me I am the innocent cause of his disgrace; and I flatter myself if I had had leave to throw myself at your Majesty's feet, I could have explained the Prince's conduct in a manner that would have softened your Majesty's resentment. How much am I to be pitied, sir, that an incident so grateful to me and at the same time so agreeable to the public, should unfortunately become the unhappy cause of a division in the family. I shall trouble your Majesty no further than to assure you that as it is to you I owe all my happiness, so to you I flatter myself, that I shall likewise soon owe the quiet of my life.

"I am, with all the respect imaginable, sir, your Majesty's most humble and most obedient daughter,

"AUGUSTA."

This letter his Majesty, by the advice of Sir Robert Walpole, thus answered on the eighteenth of September:

"I am sorry, madam, that anything should happen to give you the least uneasiness; it is a misfortune to you, but not owing to me, that you are involved in the consequences of your husband's inexcusable conduct. I pity you to see you first exposed to the utmost danger in the execution of his designs, and then made the plea for a series of repeated indignities offered to me. I wish some insinuations in your letter had been omitted, which, however, I do not impute to you, as I am convinced it is not from you they proceed.

"G. R."

On the morning of Sunday, September eighteen, and whilst the above was on its road to Kew, Sir William Irby arrived at Hampton Court with the subjoined letter from the Princess to the Queen.

"*Kew, Sept.* 17, 1733.

"MADAM,

"I take the liberty most humbly to thank your Majesty for the honour you did me in coming twice to see me, and also for having been pleased to be godmother to my daughter. I am extremely mortified that I could not do it in person, as I certainly should have done if the King's orders had not put it out of my power. I am extremely concerned at the manner in which the conduct of the Prince has been represented to your Majesty, and especially in the article relating to our two journeys from Hampton Court to London the week before I was brought to bed. I can venture to assure your Majesty that the physicians and the midwife were then of opinion that I should not lie-in before the month of September, and that the pain I complained of was only the cholic; and indeed, Madam, is it credible that if I had gone twice to London with the design and expectation of being brought to bed, I should have returned to Hampton Court? I flatter myself that time and your Majesty's good offices will procure a happy change to the present situation of affairs, which must affect me so much more sensibly, as I look upon myself to be the innocent cause of it.

"I am, with all imaginable respect, Madam, your most humble and most obedient daughter and servant,

"AUGUSTA."

This epistle gave more offence to their Majesties than any of the Princess's previous correspondence; and when shown to Sir Robert Walpole, he declared that he detected "You lie! you lie! you lie! from one end of it to the other." The Queen's anger was heightened by it having been reported to her that the Prince had just previously boasted that when he became King, and his mother Queen Dowager (an event which it appears he made certain of), he would fleece, flay, and mince her; his sister Emily he would imprison; and he would leave the Princess Caroline to starve. "His two youngest sisters," observed the enraged Queen, "he did not deign to mention; but of his brother, the Duke of Cumberland, he spoke with great affectation of kindness, and offered to relinquish his right to the succession of Hanover in his favour for £50,000 a year; an offer," said Caroline, "which does not astonish me, for I always believed that the poor-spirited, avaricious monster would sell not only his reversion in the electorate, but even in this kingdom, if the Pretender would give him five or six hundred thousand pounds in present; but, thank God! he has neither right nor power to sell his family, though his folly and knavery may sometimes distress them." *

The merits, or rather demerits, of the last-quoted offending missive from the Princess were warmly discussed by the King, Queen, Lord Hervey, and Sir Robert Walpole; and after the letter in question had been denounced as "a most abominable piece of impudence," and the Queen had declared it impossible to have the lie given one without returning it, even though the Prince was the real offender, and "the Princess only the involuntary vehicle," the subjoined reply was concocted and written and sent by the Queen to the Princess:

"*Hampton Court, Sept.* 20, 1737.

"I am very glad, my dear Princess, to hear you are perfectly recovered of your lying-in. You may assure yourself, as you have never offended either the King or me, I shall never fail to give you every mark of my regard and affection. I think it would be unbecoming either of us to enter into a discussion of the unhappy division between the King and my son; and when you are truly informed of the several declarations that have been made relating to your journey from Hampton Court, by whom and to whom they were made, you will be convinced that the conduct of your husband has no way been misrepresented. I hope time and due consideration will bring my son to a just sense of his duty to his father, which will be the only means of procuring that happy change which you cannot more sincerely wish than I do.

"CAROLINE."

The Prince being denied the court, now made Carlton House, in Pall Mall, his London residence; and when he was turned out of St. James's, their Majesties caused an order to be issued, prohibiting persons of rank and birth from paying their court to him or his to-be-pitied Princess; but as this order was daily infringed, the lord chamberlain, by their Majesties' commands, issued the subjoined:—

"His Majesty having been informed that due regard has not been paid to his order of the eleventh of September, 1737, has thought fit to declare that no person whatsoever who shall go to pay their court to their Royal Highnesses the Prince and Princess of Wales, shall be admitted into his Majesty's presence at any of his royal palaces.

(*Signed*) "GRAFTON."

* Lords Hervey, Chesterfield, and others.

CHAPTER V.

Caroline declares that she will never cease to hate her son Frederick—She becomes seriously ill—Desires not to see the Prince—Her secret malady too late discovered to her medical attendants—Parting interviews—She rallies—The Archbishop of Canterbury attends her without administering the sacrament—Bright picture of her character—The King's brutality and tenderness to her—The closing scene—Her death—The King's affection for her—Burial—Epitaph—The King remains a widower—Birth of George III.—Reconciliation between the King and the Prince—The feud again rages fiercely—Death and burial of the Prince—Jacobite epitaph—Regency bill—George II.'s death—Bequeathments—Burial.

UEEN CAROLINE persevered equally with her consort, the King, in punishing and execrating her despised son. At this period, when the Prince had been made to suffer for his rash disobedience, and when her Majesty might, with good grace and credit to her maternal feelings, have extended to him the hand of reconciliation, she remarked to Lord Hervey—we quote verbatim from his lordship's interesting diary—"My dear lord, I will give it you, under my hand, if you are in any fear of my relapsing, that my dear first-born is the greatest ass, and the greatest liar, and the greatest *canaille*, and the greatest beast in the whole world, and that I most heartily wish he was out of it."

This most unnatural wish Caroline did not live to see fulfilled. Her own end was fast approaching. She had long been in a declining state of health, and twice during the summer had suffered from unusually severe attacks of her secret malady; but she was not seized with her mortal illness till Wednesday, the ninth of November, on which day a powerful dose of Daffy's elixir, administered by Dr. Tessier, failed to remove the distressing symptoms under which she laboured, and before noon she took to her bed. But her resolution to avoid an appearance of being ill being great, she rose in the afternoon to preside at the Wednesday drawing-room. She had been in the drawing-room but a short while, when Lord Hervey advised her to retire. She told him she really was too fatigued to entertain the company; and as soon as the King, who then was discussing the merits of the Dragon of Wantley, a new operatic extravaganza, written by Carey, and cleverly set to music by Lampe, was at leisure, he was apprised of her condition, and withdrew; "telling her," says Lord Hervey, "as he went by, that she had overlooked the Duchess of Norfolk. The Queen apologised to the duchess, who was the last person she spoke to in public, and then retired and went immediately to bed, where she grew worse every moment." In the evening, cordials were administered, but without producing the desired effect; and the night through, "the King, greatly to the inconvenience of himself and the Queen, lay on his consort's bed in his night-gown." Early the next morning her Majesty was bled, by order of Dr. Broxholm; but as no symptoms of amendment were visible, the aid of Sir Hans Sloane and Dr. Hulse were called in, and by their advice blisters were applied to the legs, a remedy for which both the King and Queen entertained great aversion.

On the eleventh Lord North arrived at St. James's, with a message from the Prince of Wales, expressive of filial affection, and requesting permission to see his sorely-sick mother. The King, on receiving this message, with demoniac rage, flung at his hypocritical son every curse, denunciation, and evil wish that his imagination could invent, or his foul tongue utter; and then calming down, he ordered Lord Hervey to write, and, in the presence of witnesses, read the following answer to the Prince's messenger:—

"I have acquainted the King with the message sent to Lady Pembroke, and his Majesty has ordered me to say, that in the present situation and circumstances, his Majesty does not think fit that the Prince should see the Queen, and therefore expects he should not come to St. James's."

"In the afternoon," observes Lord Hervey, "the Queen said to the King, 'she wondered *the Griff* (the nick-name of the Prince) had not sent to ask to see her, yet it would be so like one of his *paroîtres;* but (she proceeded), sooner or later, I am sure we shall be plagued with some message of that sort, because he will think it will have a good air in the world to ask to see me, and perhaps hopes I shall be fool enough to let him come and give him the pleasure of seeing my last breath go out of my body, by which means he would have the joy of knowing I was dead five minutes sooner than he could know it in Pall Mall.'"

The King then bade her not be under any apprehensions of a trouble of this kind, for that he had already taken care to prevent it; and then related to her every circumstance of the message he had received, and the answer he had returned by Lord Hervey. The King told the Queen, too, that if she had the least mind to see her son, he had no objection to it, and begged her to do just what she liked.

"'I am so far,' said the Queen, 'from desiring to see him, that nothing but your absolute commands shall make me consent to it. For what should I see him? for him to tell me a hundred lies, and to give myself, at this time, a great deal of trouble to no purpose. If anything I could say to him would alter his behaviour, I would see him with all my heart, but I know that is impossible. Whatever advice I gave him, he would thank me for, blubber like a calf all the while I was speaking, and swear to follow my directions, and would laugh at me the moment he was out of the room, and do just the contrary of what I bade him the moment I was dead. And therefore, if I should grow worse, and be weak enough to talk of seeing him, I beg you, sir, to conclude that I doat or rave.'"

On the twelfth (Saturday), the King whispered to the Queen, that he intended to name to her medical attendants the malady from which she was suffering. She entreated him, in the name of heaven, not to do so; but when next a violent paroxysm of pain came on, Ranby, the surgeon, by his Majesty's orders, approached her, and although she directed his attention to her chest as the source of suffering, he skilfully slipped his hand to the affected part, kept it there till he had satisfied himself, and walking up to the King, by the fire-place, spoke to him in a whisper. Starting suddenly up in bed, Caroline fixed her eyes upon Ranby with a glassy stare, and vehemently exclaimed, "You blockhead! you are telling the King I have a rupture;" and on the surgeon asuring her that such was the case, and not a moment's time was to be lost, the discovery caused her to weep, the only tears she was known to shed during her trying illness. The eminent surgeons, Shipton and Bussier, were now called in, and an operation with the knife was proposed, but ultimately it was agreed to endeavour to reduce the tumour by means less violent. The treatment was painful, but the Queen bore it with fortitude. Her daughter, Caroline, who had affectionately and assiduously watched and nursed her, became, this same Saturday afternoon, herself so unwell, that Ranby bled her. She was advised to retire to her apartments, but refused so to do, and at night she slept on a couch in a chamber adjoining that in which her mortally-ill mother lay. Lord Hervey also, worn out with watching, lay on a mattrass on the floor, at the foot of her couch; the King went to bed, and the Princess Emily sat up with the Queen.

On Sunday, the surgeons pronounced that the wound which caused the Queen's sufferings had begun to mortify, and, as a consequence, death must speedily ensue. "This terrible and dreaded intelligence" was imparted to all, and the Queen herself was the least disconcerted or distressed by it. She took leave of the King and her children—the detested *Fritz* and the Princess of Orange excepted—with solemn resignation. To her favourite son, the Duke of Cumberland, she gave wholesome advice. After recommending him to be as a prop to his father in his old age, she enjoined him not to mortify his brother, the Prince, but simply to endeavour to outshine him by superior merit. To the Princess Caroline, she consigned the care of the younger Princesses, Louisa and Mary. She had little to say to the Princess Amelia; and she expressed a desire not to see her daughter Anne, Princess of Orange, who accordingly was excluded from her presence. Her parting interview with the King was serious, but singular. Taking a ruby ring off her finger, and placing it on the finger of the King, "she said," observes Lord Hervey, "'This is the last thing I have to give you; naked I came to you, and naked I go from you. I had everything I ever possessed from you, and to you whatever I have I return. My will you will find a short one; I give all I have to you.'" She then enjoined the King to marry again after her death; upon which, he burst into a flood of tears, and sobbing aloud between each word, stammered out, "No, I will then have mistresses."

"Ah, mon Dieu!" replied the Queen, "the one need not prevent the other."

"I know," observes Lord Hervey, "this episode will hardly be credited, but it is literally true."*

This strange scene concluded, Caroline fell into a profound sleep; and the King, believing she was dying, remained by her side, and repeatedly kissed her, and muttered: "'It is over, she will suffer no more.' But, to his agreeable astonishment, she awoke again greatly refreshed, and after declaring that her nasty heart would not break yet, she expressed a conviction that she should linger on till the Wednesday."* "She was born," she said, "on a Wednesday, married on a Wednesday, gave birth to her first child on a Wednesday, heard the first intelligence of the late King's death on a Wednesday, was crowned on a Wednesday, and she believed that she should die on a Wednesday." Caroline had expressed indifference as to holding a parting interview with Sir Robert Walpole; but when the great man was ushered into her presence, she addressed him in these words—"My good Sir Robert, you see me in a very indifferent situation. I have nothing to say to you but to recommend the King, my children, and the kingdom to your care." This recommendation alarmed the minister, who feared it would bring down the King's envy and ill-will upon him. These fears, however, proved groundless; and after the Queen's death, the King's regard for Sir Robert increased, as it seemed, for her sake. When the surgeons again dressed her Majesty's wounds on Sunday, they declared that the mortification had not spread, and gave faint hopes of her recovery. The truth was, they had mistaken inflammation for mortification; and now, in their eagerness to repair their error, they held out hopes of recovery, which proved transitory. Caroline continued to grow worse, but she submitted to painful operations with extraordinary fortitude and resignation; and when the tortures of the knife or the probe did occasionally extort from her an involuntary groan, she invariably apologized to the surgeons, and bade them to do their duty without heeding her silly complaints.

On Wednesday a murmur ran through the city and the court that the dying Queen had not yet made her peace with God. And Sir Robert Walpole, rather than offend popular prejudice, recommended that Dr. Potter, Archbishop of Canterbury, should be sent for. "This farce must be played, Madam," he observed to the Princess Amelia, "and the archbishop will act it very well. You may bid him be as short as you will. It will do the Queen no hurt, no more than any good; and it will satisfy all

* Lord Hervey, vol. ii. p. 516.

* Lord Hervey, vol. ii. p. 516.

the wise and good fools who will call us all atheists if we don't pretend to be as great fools as they are."* Accordingly, Dr. Potter was commanded to attend her Majesty mornings and evenings. She received the primate with pleasure, although she liked him not, and paid devout attention to his prayers and exhortations, but refused to receive the sacrament. This refusal, it is supposed, was occasioned by her firm determination not to become reconciled to her hated son *Fritz*, who, it must be observed, in palliation of this unmaternal conduct of the dying Queen, she herself knew was at this very time anxiously watching to exult over her death, and who, in his impatience to receive the awful tidings, was heard to exclaim: "Well, we shall have good news soon; she can't hold out much longer." What a fearful, unchristian, family picture is this; and yet the Queen is said to have died "in a manner worthy of a christian." And furthermore, the author of an essay on her character, published in 1738, asserts, that when the hopes and fears of this world were at an end, she frequently declared "That she had made it the business of her life to discharge her duty to God and man in the best manner she was able; that, as she had no heavy burden upon her conscience, she hoped God would pardon her infirmities and accept of the sincerity of her endeavours, which were always intended to promote the king's honour and the prosperity of the kingdom; that she was a hearty well-wisher to the liberties of the nation; that if she had been mistaken in any part of her conduct, it was from an error of her judgment, not her will; that she could not charge herself with a thought of having unjustly given an hour's pain to any one person in the world; and that she had studied all the means that were in her power of contributing to the happiness of the royal family, and strengthening the common interest of all who wished well to the King's government."† It was generally believed that she was extremely pious, and partial to the study of divinity; but this belief was occasioned by a partiality which she evinced through life for theological controversy, and by her having, since 1736, occasionally amused herself, during breakfast, by reading "Butler's Analogy of Religion to Human Nature," a book of which Hoadly, Bishop of Winchester, remarked, that to only look at it gave him the head-ache.

* Lord Hervey, vol. ii. p. 527.

† An Essay towards the Character of her late Majesty, Caroline, &c., p. 34.

The King now began to exhibit a most unseemly mixture of brutality and tenderness towards his dying consort. To his children and his friends he lauded her as being "the best wife, the best mother, the best companion, the best friend, and the best woman that ever was born."* Her head, heart, temper, were also of the best, he said; and in her was blended all the softness and delicacy of woman, with the courage and intellectual powers of man, whilst, extraordinary as it may appear, he with the same breath, and with all seeming sincerity and seriousness, declared, that "if she had not been his wife, he would rather have had her for his mistress than any other woman upon earth." Such was the theme which now, it appeared, wholly absorbed the thoughts of the King, and on which he was almost unceasingly expatiating at great length; and yet so inconstant was his temper, so habitually brutal his manners, that at this same period he scarcely once entered the presence of his beloved Caroline—he doubtless loved her as well as such a husband could love a wife—without snapping and growling as though he hated her. When pain had rendered her restless, and she desired to sleep, he peevishly remarked, "How the devil should you sleep, when you will never lie still a moment! You are always moving about—nobody can sleep in that manner; and that is always your way; you never take the proper method to get what you want, and then you wonder you have it not."† Another time, when he noticed that she was vacantly gazing with glassy eyes at the window, he snappishly remarked to her, "What

* Hervey's Memoirs.

† Hervey's Memoirs.

the deuce are you staring at now? Why do you fix your eyes in that fashion? Why, you look like a calf with his throat cut." These, and many other equally uncouth remarks, the petulant King meant for tokens of affection, and in most instances they were received as such by the mortally-sick Queen.

Thus matters proceeded; the King alternately snubbing and eulogizing his death-stricken consort, and the Princess Amelia, annoyed at her father mingling, as he did, much of self-laudation with his praise of her mother, calling him a tiresome fool, liar, and coward, whose stories made her sick. The Queen still grew worse and worse, and on Sunday, the twentieth, she felt that her end was drawing nigh, and demanded of Tessier, her physician, "How long can this last?" "Your Majesty will soon be eased of your pain," was the reply. "The sooner the better," she remarked; and then prayed aloud extemporaneously, and with a flow of eloquence which fully demonstrated the power and vigour of her mind, and astonished all present. But the last period of this melancholy scene was yet to come; about ten in the evening, when her speech began to falter, and she was thought to be expiring, she summoned all her strength, all the powers of her departing spirit, to assist her for one glorious moment, that she might die in a manner becoming a great Queen. She requested to be raised up in bed, and as she grew faint, by her own desire was twice sprinkled with water. She desired all present to kneel and pray for her; and whilst prayers were being read, she murmured, "Louder yet, louder, that I may hear." And after the Lord's Prayer was concluded, in which she joined as well as her failing strength permitted, she, with eyes fixed and dim, and with a voice more sepulchral than earthly, uttered a protracted so—o—o! calmly waved her hand in token of farewell to those around her, and tranquilly laying down, expired just as the clock struck eleven. The Princess Caroline held a looking-glass to her lips, and finding it not the least sullied by breath, exclaimed, "'Tis over," and immediately ceased to weep. The King repeatedly kissed the face and hands of the lifeless clay, and then retired to rest; but a superstitious dread of apparitions, ghosts, and witches prevented him from sleeping alone; as on that night, and every succeeding night for several weeks afterwards, he caused one of his pages to sleep in the same room with him.

The King felt deeply the loss of his consort. During her illness, harsh as his conduct had been, he had assiduously watched by her bed-side, and taken but little food or rest. He incessantly wept for several days after her death, and when the first overpowering emotions of grief had passed away, he took to recounting her history, mingled with that of his own, from the hour he was first acquainted with her to the day of her death. Whilst the big tears rolled down his cheeks, he would again and again enumerate her virtues and charms, and attribute to her person all that was beautiful and captivating, and to her mind and heart all that was excellent, great, good, and holy; but his grief, like his general conduct, was singular, and Lord Hervey assures us that "any unexpected event, if in the least degree ludicrous, would be sure to cause him, in the midst of his tears, to burst into a roar of loud laughter." Nevertheless, few royal widowers have felt the loss of a wife more keenly than did George II.; with a flood of tears he told Walpole that Caroline had been more than his right hand to him; and now that she was gone, he knew not what to do, or which way to turn himself. Some time afterwards, early one morning, before rising, he remarked to Baron Brinkman, one of his German attendants, "I hear you have a portrait of my wife, which she gave you, and which is a better likeness than any in my possession; bring it to me." It was brought; the King gazed at it, seemed greatly affected, and after a brief pause said, "It is very like her; put it upon the chair at the foot of my bed, and leave it till I ring." Two hours afterwards, the baron was summoned; and the King, with eyes swollen with weeping, looked at him, and pointing to the portrait, exclaimed, "Take it away, take it away; I never yet saw the woman worthy to buckle her shoe."

The remains of Queen Caroline were interred, with imposing obsequies, on the seventeenth of December, in a new vault in Henry the Eighth's chapel, in Westminster Abbey, where the King, by his own orders, was afterwards buried by her side. The procession set out from the Prince's chamber adjoining the House of Lords. The coffin was richly ornamented, and the pall was supported by the Dukes of Richmond, Montague, Argyle, Buccleugh, St. Alban's, and Kent, six in all. The Princess Amelia, and not the King, was chief mourner. She was supported by two dukes; two duchesses, assisted by Lord Robert Montague, bore her train, and six duchesses and ten countesses acted as her assistants. The Rev. Dr. Wilcox, Bishop of Rochester and Dean of Westminster, read the burial service. The choir, to the number of one hundred and forty performers, chaunted "the ways of Zion do mourn," an anthem set to music by the great composer Handel for the occasion, and Garter King-at-Arms proclaimed her Majesty's style and titles as follows: "Thus it has pleased Almighty God to take out of this transitory life, to his divine mercy, the late most high, most mighty, and most excellent Princess Caroline, by the grace of God, Queen Consort of the most high, most mighty, and most excellent monarch George II., by the grace of God, King of Great Britain, France, and Ireland, defender of the faith, whom God bless and preserve with long life, health, and honour, and all worldly happiness."

Many epitaphs and political eulogies were written to the memory of the consort of George II. Of these we select the subjoined stanzas, which possess the double merit of elegance and brevity:

"How soon frail royalty is o'er,
  That fame deluded monarchs trust;
To-day their greatness we adore,
  To-morrow trample on their dust.

How near oblivion to renown,
  The end of glory to its bloom;
The altar where she took her crown,
  Close to the spot that boasts her tomb.

Thus state and majesty are lost,
  And death recruits its empty urns;
Thus the vain pomp, the mighty boast,
  To silence and the shade returns."

After the death of Queen Caroline, the King did not again marry, but he acted as he had said he would—he kept mistresses in a manner more openly than heretofore. The feud continued to rage between the monarch and his heir, Prince Frederick; and when, on the fourth of June, 1738, the latter became the father of a son, who was christened George, and ultimately ascended the throne of Britain, by the title of George III., the former, so far as circumstances permitted, avoided all notice or mention of the fact. The Prince, however, by a coalition of his own partisans and the country party, became the leader of a powerful opposition, who, at the commencement of 1742, succeeded in driving from office Queen Caroline's minister, Sir Robert Walpole, a measure followed by the accomplishment of what at the time was called a reconciliation between the King and the Prince. "On Thursday night," writes Horace Walpole, in a letter dated February the eighteenth, 1742, "Mr. Pultney went to the Prince, and without the knowledge of Argyle, et cetera, prevailed on him to write to the King. He was so long determining, that it was eleven at night before the King received his letter. Yesterday morning the Prince, attended by two of his lords, two grooms of the bedchamber, and Lord Scarborough, his treasurer, went to the King's levee. The King said, 'How does the Princess do? I hope she is well.' The Prince kissed his hand, and this was all. He returned to Carlton House, whither crowds went to him. He spoke to the Duke of Newcastle and Mr. Pelham, but would not to the three dukes, Richmond, Grafton, and Marlborough. At night the royal family were all at the Duchess of Norfolk's, and the streets were illuminated and bonfired." This reconciliation brought to the Prince an addition to his income of £50,000 a year, the restoration of his guards, and other important favours. But withal, it proved, as Walpole now Earl of Oxford, prophecied, "a mere sham, of short duration." Towards the

Prince the King gradually became more and more cool and insolent, the Prince conducted himself with equal impropriety towards the King, and in 1747, he and his party joined the opposition, with a firm determination not to again desert them.

The feud between the two first personages in the realm now became a matter of party strife, and continued to grow fiercer and fiercer till death snatched the Prince from the scene of contention. This event took place on the twentieth of March, 1751, and is thus mentioned by Horace Walpole: "The Prince died last night, between nine and ten. * * * He had a pleurisy, and was recovering. Last Thursday was senate; he went to attend the King's passing some bills in the House of Lords, and from thence to Carlton House, very hot when he unrobed, put on a light unaired frock and waistcoat, went to Kew, walked for several hours in the gardens there, though it was a bitter day, came home tired, and lay down for three hours upon a couch in a very cold room in Carlton House, that opens into the garden. Lord Egmont told him how dangerous it was, but the Prince did not mind him. My father once said to this King (George II.) when he was ill and royally untractable, 'Sir, do you know what your father died of? Of thinking he could not die.' In short, the Prince relapsed that night; he has had three physicians ever since, and has never been supposed out of danger till yesterday. A thrush had appeared, and for the two or three last evenings he had dangerous suppressions of breath. However, his family thought him so well yesterday, that there were cards in his outward room. Between nine and ten he was seized with a violent fit of coughing. * * * Hawking, the surgeon who attended him, had occasion to go out of the room, and said, 'There is something I don't like.' The cough continued; the Prince laid his hand upon his stomach, and said, 'Oh, this is death!' The person who held him up felt him shiver, and cried out, 'The Prince is gone!' The Princess, who was at the foot of the bed, snatched up a candle, but before she got to the head of the bed he was dead. Lord North was immediately sent to the King, who was looking over the table where the Princess Emily, the Duchess of Dorset, and the Duke of Grafton were playing. He was extremely surprised, and said, 'Why, they told me he was better.' He bade Lord North tell the Princess he would do everything she could desire, and has this morning sent her a very kind message. He is extremely shocked, but no pity is too much for the Princess; she has eight children, and is seven months gone with another. She bears her affliction with great courage and sense. They asked her if the body was to be opened; she replied, 'What the King pleased.'"

On the thirteenth of April the Prince was buried in Henry the Seventh's chapel, Westminster Abbey, with becoming ceremony, but with only a small show of respect from the court and leading nobility.

"The most extraordinary of the reflections on his death," says Horace Walpole, "were set forth in a sermon at Mayfair Chapel. 'He had no great parts,' observed the preacher, 'but he had great virtues; indeed, they degenerated into vices. He was very generous, but I hear his generosity has ruined a great many people; and then his condescension was such, that he kept very bad company." But great as his failings or his vices may have been, in one respect he outshone his boorish, illiterate father; he was a most distinguished patron of authors, artists, philosophers, and statesmen. Of the verses poured out upon his death, the following Jacobite epitaph became the most popular:

"Here lies Fred,
Who was alive and is dead.
Had it been his father,
I had much rather.
Had it been his brother,
Still better than another.
Had it been his sister,
No one would have missed her.
Had it been the whole generation,
Still better for the nation;
But since 'tis only Fred,
Who was alive and is dead,
There is no more to be said."

Prince George, afterwards George III., when informed of his father's death, "turned pale, and laid his hand on his breast." Upon which Ayscough, his tutor, remarked, "I am afraid, sir, you are not well."

"I feel something here," replied the young Prince, pressing his hand to his breast more firmly; "I feel something here, just as I did when I saw the two workmen fall off the scaffold at Kew."

The fact was, he felt distressing grief, but was at a loss for words to describe the choking, depressing sensation. A few days after the burial of his father, he was formally created Prince of Wales—the order of the Garter had been previously conferred on him—and before the summer had passed away, an act was passed, settling the regency of the kingdom on the Princess, his mother, in case the crown devolved to him before he was of age. This bill was, however, rendered needless by the King, gouty and infirm as he was, living on till the year 1760, when, on the twenty-fifth of October, he was, in a manner, suddenly and unexpectedly seized with the agonies of death. He had risen as usual, drank his chocolate, called his page, and inquired about the wind, as if anxious for the arrival of the foreign mails. He then said he would take a walk in the garden, and the page left the room, but immediately afterwards heard the sound of a heavy fall, and hastily returning, found the King lying on the floor with a deep gash on his right temple and cheek, cut, it was supposed, by the edge of a bureau, against which he fell. The death-stricken monarch looked up into the face of the page, gasped out, "Call Amelia!" and then, with a rattling gurgle in the throat, expired. The attendants placed the body upon the bed, and the moment afterwards the Princess, who had been sent for hurriedly, entered the apartment, rushed to the bed-side, and being purblind and hard of hearing, leaned over it in the belief that her father was speaking to her in a low voice. When she found that he was to all appearances dead, the colour left her cheeks, her lips quivered, and tears gushed from her eyes. But with great presence of mind she despatched one messenger for medical aid, and another to the Prince of Wales, at Kew. The surgeons and physicians instantly arrived, and endeavoured to bleed the body, but without effect; the right ventricle of the heart was ruptured, and George II. had died, like his bitterly-hated son, Prince Frederick, without priestly aid or religious consolation.

Horace Walpole thus alludes to the death and bequeathments of George II.

"I am not gone to Houghton, you see; my Lord Oxford is come to town, and I have persuaded him to stay and perform decencies. King George II. is dead, richer than Sir Robert Brown, though perhaps not so rich as my Lord Hardwicke. He has left £50,000 between the Duke, Emily, and Mary: the Duke has given up his share. To Lady Yarmouth, a cabinet with the contents; they call it £11,000. By a German deed he gives the Duke to the value of £180,000, placed on mortgages not immediately recoverable. He had once given him twice as much more, then revoked it, and at last excused the revocation on pretence of the expenses of the war, but owns he was the best son that ever lived, and had never offended him—a pretty strong comment on the affair of Closterseven. He gives him, besides, all his jewels in England, but had removed all his best to Hanover, which he makes crown jewels; and his successor residuary legatee. The Duke, too, has some uncounted cabinets. My Lady Suffolk has given me a particular of his jewels, which plainly amount to £150,000. It happened oddly to my Lady Suffolk, two days before he died she went to make a visit at Kensington: not knowing of the review, she found herself hemmed in by coaches, and was close to him whom she had not seen for so many years, and to my Lady Yarmouth, but they did not know her; it struck her, and made her very sensible to his death."

The remains of George II., who expired at the age of seventy-seven, were interred in Henry VII.'s Chapel, Westminster Abbey, by the side of his consort, Queen Caroline, on the eleventh of November, 1760. The funeral is thus graphically described by Horace Walpole:—

"Do you know I had the curiosity to go to the burying t'other night? I had never seen a royal funeral; nay, I walked as a rag of quality, which I fancied would be, and so it was, the easiest way of seeing it. It is absolutely a noble sight; the Prince's chamber hung with purple and a quantity of silver lamps, the coffin under a canopy of purple velvet, and six vast chandeliers of silver on high stands, had a very good effect. The ambassador from Tripoli and his son were carried to see that chamber. The procession through a line of foot guards, every seventh man bearing a torch, the horse guards lining the outsides, their officers with drawn sabres and crape sashes, on horseback, the drums muffled, the fifes, bells tolling, and minute-guns — all this was very solemn; but the charm was the entrance of the abbey, where we were received by the dean and chapter in rich robes, the choir and alms-men bearing torches, the whole abbey so illuminated, that one saw it to better advantage than by day, the tombs, long aisles, and fretted roof, all appearing distinctly and with the happiest *chiaro-scuro*; there wanted nothing but incense, and little chapels here and there, with priests saying mass for the repose of the defunct; yet one could not complain of its not being catholic enough. I had been in dread of being coupled with some boy of ten years old; but the heralds were not very accurate, and I walked with George Grenville, taller and older, to keep me in countenance. When we came to the Chapel of Henry VII., all solemnity and decorum ceased, no order was observed, people sat or stood where they could or would, the yeomen of the guard were crying out for help, oppressed by the immense weight of the coffin. The bishop read sadly, and blundered in the prayers; the fine chapter —'Man that is born of woman,' was chaunted, not read, and the anthem, besides being immeasurably tedious, would have served as well for a nuptial. The real serious part was the figure of the Duke of Cumberland, heightened by a thousand melancholy circumstances; he had a dark-brown Adonis and a cloak of black cloth, with a train of five yards. Attending the funeral could not be pleasant; his leg extremely bad, yet forced to stand upon it near two hours, his face bloated and distorted with his late paralytic stroke, which has affected, too, one of his eyes, and placed over the mouth of the vault into which, in all probability, he must so soon descend—think how unpleasant a situation!—he bore it all with a firm and unaffected countenance. This grave scene was fully contrasted by the burlesque Duke of Newcastle; he fell into a fit of crying the moment he came into the chapel, and flung himself back into a stall, the archbishop hovering over him with a smelling-bottle; but in two minutes his curiosity got the better of his hypocrisy, and he ran about the chapel with his glass to spy who was or was not there, spying with one hand and mopping his eyes with the other; then returned the fear of catching cold, and the Duke of Cumberland, who was sinking with heat, felt himself weighed down, and turning round, found it was the Duke of Newcastle standing upon his train, to avoid the chill of the marble. It was very theatric to look down into the vault where the coffins lay, attended by mourners with lights. Clavering, the groom of the bedchamber, refused to sit up with the body, and was dismissed by the King's order."

Such was the funeral of George II., a King whose abilities were scarcely above mediocrity, whose reign was decidedly prosperous, and whose death, observes Walpole, "was most felicitous to himself, being without a pang, without tasting a reverse, and when his sight and hearing were so nearly extinguished, that any prolongation could but have swelled to calamities."

Queen Charlotte.

CHARLOTTE OF MECKLENBURG-STRELITZ,

Queen of George the Third.

HAPTER I.

Sophia Charlotte—Parentage—Birth—Education—Infancy and girlhood—Incidents which led to her marriage—Marriage treaty concluded—Journey to England—Arrival at St. James's—Marriage to George III.—Singular address—Visit to Drury Lane Theatre—Her personal appearance and manners—Household established—Coronation—Visit to Covent Garden Theatre, and to the City of London on Lord Mayor's Day—Parliamentary settlement of her dower—Buckingham House purchased for her—Birth-day commemoration.

OPHIA CHARLOTTE—or Charlotte, as she was more commonly designated--consort of George III., was the fifth child and youngest daughter of Charles Lewis Frederick, Duke of Mirow, and his Duchess, Albertina Elizabeth, daughter of Ernest Frederick, Duke of Saxe-Hildburghausen. Her father was the second son of the Duke of Mecklenburg-Strelitz, a dukedom to which her eldest brother ultimately succeeded. She first saw the light at the ducal palace of Mirow, on the sixteenth of May, 1744, and was christened with the rites of the Lutheran church. Her amiable and accomplished mother paid great attention to her education, and appointed as governess to her and to her sister, Christina Sophia Albertina, who was born on the sixth of December, 1735, Mademoiselle Seltzer, a lady noble born, highly accomplished, erudite, and endowed with superior educational talents. In 1751, her father died, when the family removed from Mirow to Strelitz, and the poetess, Madame de Grabow was appointed to assist in the education of the two princesses. Shortly afterwards, these instructresses were succeeded in their office by Dr. Gentzner, under whose able tuition the Princess Charlotte successfully studied the languages and literature of Germany, France, and Italy; but, unfortunately, as neither the governesses nor the tutor had the slightest knowledge of English, the pupil was not taught the tongue of that nation over which she was destined, in womanhood, to bear sway as the Queen-consort of George III. The Princess was also well grounded in history, geography, natural and revealed religion, and the general principles of the arts and sciences, whilst, as accomplishments, she successfully practised drawing, vocal and instrumental music, dancing, needle-work, lace-making, and embroidery.

If Fénelon, an eye-witness, is to be accredited, the court at Strelitz, at this period, was a matchless model of social contentment, unity, felicity, and morality. He says—

"They have no ambition here but that of serving their prince and country; they idle not away their time, but act with the utmost diligence in their respective departments; they behave with a just dignity and decorum, avoiding the extremes of meanness and pride; they are content with their paternal fortunes, which set them above the inordinate desire of riches; they are open and sincere, which renders them lovers of truth; they have no occasion to cringe to a prince whose aversion is flattery; they have the highest ideas of honour, and, consequently, are true to their engagements; they have an inviolable regard for all civil duties; they have a love for their prince, on account of his virtues, and esteem him for his capacity. To conclude, it may be truly said, that instead of encouraging the ridicule of virtue, this court is a pattern of morality and religion, a school of probity and honour, a seminary of politeness, and, in fine, the seat of every social virtue. This is no exaggeration, but a fair portrait. The court of Strelitz, indeed, is not very numerous, but it is one of the most regular and most agreeable of any in the whole empire. No private family is governed with more order, and, perhaps, no prince is served by abler officers, and with greater diligence and affection."

"Well it would have been," remarks a learned author, "if this state of things had been permanent;" but, unfortunately, the peaceful little court at Strelitz was doomed to learn, by bitter experience, how short-lived human felicity usually is. The disastrous "Seven Years' War," which broke out in 1756, and spread desolation over Germany, was felt with peculiar severity throughout the duchy of Mecklenburg. The whole territory was taken possession of as a military station by Frederick the Great, King of Prussia, whose troops committed atrocities disgraceful to civilized soldiers. The Princess Charlotte felt deeply for the sufferings of the people amongst whom she was born; and amidst the exultation produced by the King of Prussia's victory over the Austrians at Torgau, on the eleventh of November, 1760, she addressed the following impressive appeal to the Prussian monarch:—

"May it please your Majesty,

"I scarcely know whether I should congratulate or condole with you on your late victory, since that same success which has crowned you with laurels has overspread Mecklenburg with desolation. I am aware, sir, that in this age of vicious refinement it is deemed scarcely becoming of my sex to feel for one's bleeding country, to lament the horrors of war, or to pray for the return of peace. I know you may deem it more properly my province to study domestic matters and the arts of pleasing; but, unbecoming in me though it may be, I cannot resist the desire of interceding for this unhappy people.

"But a short while ago this territory wore the most promising aspect: the land was tilled, the peasants happy, the towns rich and prosperous; but now, alas, how changed the picture! I am not apt at description, nor can my fancy heighten the horrors of the scene around me—a scene at which conquerors themselves would surely weep. The whole country—my dear country—lies one frightful waste. The husbandmen and shepherds, unable to longer continue their employments, have turned soldiers themselves, and help to ravage the soil they formerly tilled—to destroy the flocks and herds they formerly tended. The towns are deserted by all, saving a few old men, women, children, and maimed and invalided warriors. The alternate insolence of each of the opposing armies, as they happen to advance or retreat, is intolerable. No pen can express the confusion which even those calling themselves our friends excite; and as to redress, those from whom we might reasonably expect it, almost daily oppress us with new calamities. Therefore, sir, it is from your justice that we hope for relief; to you whose humanity stoops to the meanest petition, whose power is capable of repressing the greatest injustice, the famishing women and children of Mecklenburg appeal for succour and redress."

On the twenty-fifth of October, 1760, the Prince of Wales, who was yet unmarried, and had but just completed his twenty-second year, succeeded to the throne of his grandfather, by the title of George III., King of Great Britain and Ireland, &c.; and shortly afterwards, a copy of the above letter falling into his hands, he exclaimed to Lord Hertford, "This is the lady whom I shall select for my consort: here are lasting beauties, on which the man who has any mind may feast and not be satisfied. If the disposition of the Princess but equals her refined sense, I shall be the happiest man, as I hope, with my people's concurrence, to be the greatest monarch in Europe."

Not a moment was to be lost, and General Græme, a Scotchman, who previously had been dispatched with the utmost secresy to the courts of Germany to discover a suitable consort for his Majesty, and had made choice of Charlotte, was employed to pay another secret visit to the court at Strelitz. He met with a favourable reception; and on his return to England, and whilst the court and the nation were being amused with the rumours that the King was about to form a matrimonial alliance either with a princess of the House of Brandenburgh, with one of his own subjects—either Lady Sarah Lennox, or Hannah Lightfoot, to the latter of whom a report prevailed that he had been married a few years previously—or with some other royal or noble-born damsel, his Majesty, in an extraordinary council, convened on the eighth of July, 1761, made the following declaration:—

"Having nothing so much at heart as to procure the welfare and happiness of my people, and to render the same stable and permanent to posterity, I have ever since my accession to the throne turned my thoughts towards the choice of a princess for my consort; and I now, with great satisfaction, acquaint you that, after the fullest information and mature deliberation, I am come to a resolution to demand in marriage the Princess Charlotte of Mecklenburg-Strelitz, a princess distinguished by every eminent virtue and amiable endowment, whose illustrious line has constantly shown the firmest zeal for the Protestant religion, and a particular attachment to my family. I have judged proper to communicate to you these my intentions, in order that you may be fully apprised of a matter so highly important to me and to my kingdoms, and which I persuade myself will be most acceptable to all my loving subjects."

Although the council was taken by surprise, this declaration was published in the Gazette the same evening, accompanied by an order for the coronation to be solemnized on the twenty-second of September. The Earl of Harcourt, as ambassador extraordinary, accompanied by General Græme, as the confidential agent, sailed from Harwich on the eighth of August, arrived at Strelitz on the fourteenth, and the next morning formally demanded the Princess Charlotte in marriage for the King, his master. The same day, the marriage-treaty was signed, and her Royal Highness, after receiving the compliments of the states of the duchy, partook of a sumptuous banquet, given in honour of the occasion. At this banquet she sat at a separate table, with her sister, Christina, and her grand-aunt, the Princess of Schwartzburg. The Earl of Harcourt, and several nobles and ladies of his suite, dined with the Duke of Mecklenburg in the grand saloon, and in two other apartments four tables were served, with upwards of one hundred and sixty choice and delicate dishes. During the banquet the guns fired, in the evening the castle and the town were illuminated, and the next day was devoted to festivity and rejoicing.

Sorrow and joy, however, are common companions, and the bride elect parted in tears from her relations and friends. She commenced her journey on the seventeenth of August, and the honours paid to her on this occasion by the inhabitants of the old town of Strelitz, are thus mentioned by M. Tangatz, who himself witnessed the pleasing scene.

"On a plain, at no considerable distance from the ducal palace, was erected a superb triumphal arch, decorated with natural foliage and festoons, and surmounted with two globes, exhibiting the conquests of England, and over which were the arms of Great Britain and Mecklenburg united; close to the arch, on a platform, were drawn up the town militia under arms. On either side of the front of the arch were bowers and tents, where the numerous spectators might obtain refreshments. On each side, within the arch, stood six young maidens, clothed in white, and each bearing a wreath of myrtle in her hand. The procession, conducted by a captain of Mecklenburg horse, was headed by Marshal Zesterflesh, with two running footmen; then came in coaches and six, his Highness, the Duke, with his brother, Prince Charles, attended by running footmen and horse-guards; and as they passed through the arch, the burghers saluted them with their arms, colours, and music. After the march of the horse, came, in a coach of state and six, the bride elect, with her sister, and the Countess of Cocceius. Beneath the arch her Highness paused, whilst the burgomaster, Tangatz, addressed her in the name of the corporation and citizens, and each of the maidens recited to her congratulatory verses, and flung myrtle-wreaths into her coach. These addresses concluded, she expressed her satisfaction in the most gracious terms; and proceeding onward, was followed by twelve horse-guards, an empty coach, and then, in a coach and six, the Earl of Harcourt, who paused to view the arch, and presented each of the maidens with a ducat. After the Earl, the rear of the procession was brought up by Councillor Hardenburg, from Hanover, followed by about thirty coaches."

In this order the royal train proceeded to Mirow, where Charlotte bade an affecting farewell to her sister, and, with a heart more sad than joyous, hastened on her journey. Proceeding through Perleburgh and Letzen, she, on the twentieth, reached Ghorde; and having twice dined there in public, crossed a branch of the Elbe, and dined in a grand tent on the river's bank on the twenty-second; and the same evening entered Strade in public procession, amidst the booming of cannon, the ringing of bells, and the blaze of a general illumination. The streets through which she passed were lined with the burgesses under arms, and adorned with triumphal arches, and congratulatory verses were presented to her by the principal ladies of the town. The next day, Sunday, she passed at Buxtelhude, where, having courteously received an address from the members of the Hamburg Company, she, on the following morning, embarked on board the yacht Charlotte, amidst the acclamations of the assembled populace; and accompanied by her brother, Prince Charles, by the Duchesses of Ancaster and Hamilton, and by the Earl of Harcourt and Lord Anson. Immediately the Princess embarked, the whole squadron destined to escort her to England, fired a salute; but adverse winds prevented the yacht from weighing anchor till the next day, the twenty-fifth, when the Royal Charlotte got under sail, put Prince Charles on shore the next morning at Cuxhaven; and on the twenty-eighth, although the weather was wild and stormy, the whole squadron put to sea. As the King was anxious that the ceremony of the nuptials should precede that of the coronation, there was not a moment to lose, and Lord Anson made every exertion to speedily reach the Nore; but the wind blew against him with such violence, that it was only after a ten days' voyage, and twice sighting Falmouth Head, and each time being driven to sea again with considerable damage and danger, that he at last entered the road of Harwich, on the evening of Sunday, September the sixth. Her Highness, storm-tossed as she had been, had enjoyed excellent health and spirits throughout the voyage; and, as no preparations had been made at Harwich for her arrival, she remained on board the yacht till three P.M. the next day. In the interval, her route was settled, and instructions received as to the manner of her proceeding to St. James's. On landing, she was received by the mayor and aldermen of Harwich, in their usual formalities. The same afternoon, she entered Colchester, and after partaking of tea at the house of Mr. Enew, and receiving a box of eringo root — a presentation always made to any of the royal family who honoured Colchester with a visit — proceeded to Lord Abercorn's, at Witham, where she arrived at a quarter-past seven, and passed the night. A little after twelve, the next morning, the King's servants met her at Romford, at the house of Mr. Dalton, a wine merchant, where they served her with coffee; after which, the young Queen, as the bride-elect was now considered, attired entirely in the English fashion, entered the King's coach, accompanied by the Duchesses of Ancaster and Hamilton. The attendants of her Majesty were in three other coaches. They proceeded at a rather slow pace, that the populace, who had assembled to obtain a glimpse of their new queen, might gratify their curiosity. Passing through Stratford-le-Bow, Mile End, and Hackney, they wended their way up Old Street to the City Road, across Islington, along the New Road, into Hyde Park, down Constitution Hill, into St. James's Park, and thence to the garden gate of the palace, where her Highness was handed out of her carriage by the Duke of Devonshire, as lord chamberlain, and received by the Duke of York. His Majesty met her in the garden, and as she was about to drop on her knees, and pay him obeisance, affectionately raised her up, saluted her, and then led her into the palace, and introduced her to the Princess-dowager of Wales, and a select assembly of the royal family and the nobility. After dinner, the bride's-maids and court were introduced to her, and she gratified the assembled populace by making her appearance in the gallery, and at the windows of the palace.

About eight in the evening, first the Princess, and then his Majesty, proceeded, in grand procession, to the chapel-royal, where they were united in holy matrimony by Dr. Secker, Archbishop of Canterbury. The Duke of Cumberland gave away the bride; and immediately their Majesties joined hands, the Park and Tower guns were fired. After the ceremony, the King and Queen occupied on one side of the altar, two tate chairss, under a canopy: the Princess-dowager of Wales sat facing them, in a similar chair of state on the opposite side; the other branches of the royal family occupied stools, and for the peers, peeresses, bishops, and foreign ministers, were provided benches. Dr. Boyce's anthem, "The King shall rejoice in thy strength, oh Lord!" was sung by the choir; after which, the procession returned to St. James's, and there was a public drawing-room, but no persons were presented. At the conclusion of the ceremony, the Park and the Tower guns were fired; the bells were rung; all London was brilliantly illuminated, and the inhabitants devoted the night to festivity and rejoicing.

On the following day, Wednesday, the ninth, a grand levee and drawing-room was held at St. James's, "when," says Horace Walpole, "everybody was presented to the royal bride, [and all the ladies of the court kissed her hand]; but she spoke to nobody, as she could not know a soul. She was very civil, and not disconcerted. Her French is tolerable; she exchanged much, both of that and German, with the King, the Duke, and the Duke of York. The King looked very handsome, and talked to her continually, and with great good humour. It does not promise as if they two would be the two most unhappy persons in England from this event."

At this levee her Majesty's ten bride's-maids appeared, in white lustring dresses, ornamented with silver trimmings and costly jewels, and the same night there was a grand ball, which was opened by the Duke of York and the Princess Augusta. Levees were also held at court on the subsequent Thursday, Friday, and Sunday; and on the Saturday, the King gratified her Majesty by taking her to Richmond Palace to dine.

On Monday, September the fourteenth, the lord mayor, aldermen, and common council of London, presented addresses of congratulation to their Majesties, on the subject of their marriage; and shortly afterwards, the universities, and most of the towns, counties, and corporate bodies followed the loyal example of London.

But the most singular and amusing of these addresses, was the subjoined :—

"To the Queen's most excellent Majesty,

"The humble address of the ladies of the borough of St. Albans, in the county of Hertford.

"MAY IT PLEASE YOUR MAJESTY,

"We, your Majesty's most dutiful and affectionate subjects, being *by custom* precluded from being named in the address of the mayor and corporation of this place, beg leave to approach your Majesty with the warmest congratulations of your happy nuptials.

"Formed by nature [?], and improved by the completest education, you were selected by the best of kings, to add the only happiness that was wanting to his Majesty in the world.

"As subjects are greatly influenced by the example of their sovereign, we have the greatest reason to hope that the matrimonial state will be duly honoured by your Majesty's dutiful subjects cheerfully following the royal example—an example too much wanted in this degenerate age—wherein that happy state is made the object of ridicule instead of respect, by too many of vain, giddy, and dissipated minds. If the riches of a nation consists in its populousness, this happy country will, in that respect, too soon become poor, whilst the lawful means to continue posterity are either shackled by the restraint of mistaken laws, or despised by those who regard none.

"But as every virtuous and commendable action is encouraged by your royal consort's and your own noble sentiments and conduct, we hope this example will be duly followed by your Majesty's loyal subjects.

"That you may long remain a pattern of conjugal fidelity and happiness, and see a numerous offspring grow up as tender plants under your maternal influence, to be a blessing to their royal parents and to this nation, are the sincere and ardent wishes of your Majesty's most dutiful and devoted subjects,

"THE LADIES OF ST. ALBANS."

On the fourteenth of September their Majesties went in the evening to Drury Lane Theatre, to witness the "Rehearsal." The Queen, who had never before beheld a dramatic entertainment, was highly delighted with the performance; but, unfortunately, the crowd at the doors of the theatre was such, that many persons were injured, and a girl was trampled to death.

So soon as the marriage was solemnized, the King, by an order in council, commanded, that in the prayers for the royal family, his consort's name, as Queen of England, should be placed immediately after his own, and before that of his mother, the Princess-dowager of Wales; an order which the clergy cheerfully and promptly obeyed.

The rejoicings occasioned by the royal marriage were not confined to the metropolis; throughout the whole British empire, even to the remotest villages, a similar spirit of gladness and loyalty was manifested, and many trashy poems were written, commemorative of the auspicious event. Of these vapid, but loyal and patriotic lyrics, the subjoined, by the Honourable John Gray, from the Cambridge Collection, may perhaps be considered the best :—

"While o'er Germania's ravaged plains
Stern Desolation ruthless reigns;
While as she darts her redd'ning eye,
Death gives his keenest shafts to fly,
The gift of plenty and repose,
Safe on her cliffs, Britannia knows;
Her valleys spread their verdant vest,
Her fields in richest robes are drest.
No hostile hoof her laurel'd walks invades,
Or frights their sisters from their peaceful shades.

"I see the god whom Venus bore
To Bacchus, on Illissus' shore.
In yellow folds his mantle plays,
His torch sends forth a brighter blaze.
He waves his hand: I feel, he cries,
Such transport in my bosom rise,
As when I wreathed the myrtle twine,
To bind the brows of Caroline,
Or when the Clifden's bowers to Frederic's arms,
I give the treasure of Augusta's charms.

"Ye nymphs who arts of conquest try,
Who bend the neck, who roll the eye,
See Charlotte win that grace and ease,
And please without a wish to please.
Ye purple tyrants, slaves to love,
From fair to fair, who sated rove,
What is the boast of beauty, say?
That spark Time's wing soon wafts away.
Go, from a British monarch learn to place
Your bliss on virtue's adamantine base.

"Hail! happy union, the presage
Of glories down from age to age;
Yes, as through time I dart my sight,
Successive Georges spring to light.
Patriots, by lessons and by laws,
To aid expiring freedom's cause;
Warriors, by many a daring blow,
To check each vain, presumptuous foe;
Till vaunting Gaul a mighty power shall own,
And Spain's proud genius bow to Brunswick's throne."

Her Majesty, who at this period had just entered her eighteenth year, although not an absolute beauty, was decidedly prepossessing in appearance, and engaging in manners. In figure she was rather small, but proportionate; with a round, fair face; soft, blue, expressive eyes; a diminutive and curled-up nose; a rather large mouth; rosy lips; white, regular teeth; auburn hair; small, delicate hands; a fair and sweetly chiseled neck; and in port graceful and queenly. Her household was established with every regard to liberality and splendour; all her German attendants were dismissed except Madame Schwellenburg, and one or two other less significant persons; and it is worthy of remark, that between the Queen and her attendants there speedily sprang up an attachment so sincere and lasting, that, of those who entered her establishment, few retired from it but at the bidding of death; and although, during the long reign of George III., the kingdom was occasionally agitated by the rage of faction, neither party strife nor political animosity ever disturbed the domestic tranquillity of the Queen and her household.

The twenty-second of September was appointed for the royal coronation. At nine in the morning on that eventful day, their Majesties went in their chairs from St. James's, through the park, to Westminster Hall when the King reposed in the Court of Wards, and the Queen in the Black Rod's chamber, till the processional was arranged. The Queen then took her seat in the Hall, under a canopy on the left of the King, whilst the regalia were ceremonously delivered to the nobles appointed to carry them; after which the royal pair proceeded, in grand procession, to Westminster Abbey. The way, which was boarded and covered with blue cloth, was strewn with flowers; and, to enliven the scene, drums beat, trumpets sounded, and loyal anthems were chaunted by a choir of vocalists, who marched in the procession. As they entered the Abbey by the west door, the choir chaunted the anthem from the 122nd psalm, "I was glad when they said unto me, Let us go into the house of the Lord." The recognition, anointing, crowning, enthroning, and homage were performed according to established usage, and therefore need not be detailed in this place. Dr. Drummond, Bishop of Salisbury, preached the sermon from the 1st of Kings, chap. x. ver. 9:—"Blessed be the Lord thy God, which delighteth in thee, to set thee on the throne of Israel: because the Lord loved Israel for ever, therefore made he thee king, to do judgment and justice." A text which was a sermon in itself. This pulpit oration was eloquent, and to the purpose, but short; and after the King had been anointed and crowned, the like services were performed to the Queen, by the Archbishop of Canterbury. Between the performance of the ceremonies the choir sung "Veni Creator," the anthems "The king shall rejoice in thy strength, O Lord," and "The fool hath said in his heart, there is no God;" and the "Te Deum." After the crowning, their Majesties received the sacrament, when the King took off his crown, and, although no precedent existed of this act of humility at a coronation, insisted on laying it aside. During the administration, the Queen also wished to lay her crown aside, but as it was so fastened, to keep it from falling, that it could not be removed without the assistance of her dressers, this was dispensed with, and the Queen wore her crown, not, she observed, as a symbol of royalty, but simply as part of her dress. Their Majesties next retired to St. Edward's chapel, and after changing their crowns and robes, returned in grand procession to Westminster Hall, where they partook of a sumptuous banquet. The ceremonies at this banquet were regulated in everything by ancient custom. At ten at night the entertainment concluded; their Majesties and their noble company retired, and immediately afterwards the populace were permitted to rush into the Hall and carry away every article that was moveable.

Of the remarkable incidents which occurred at this coronation, Horace Walpole has left the subjoined particulars. To the Honourable Henry Seymour Conway he writes:—"The coronation is over; 'tis even a more gorgeous sight than I imagine. I saw the procession in the Hall, but the return was in the dark. In the morning they had forgot the sword of state, the chairs for the King and Queen, and their canopies. They used the Lord Mayor's sword for the first, and made the last in the Hall, so they did not set forth till noon; and then, by a childish compliment to the King, reserved the illumination of the Hall till his entry, by which means they arrived like a funeral, nothing being discernable but the plumes of the knights of the Bath, which seemed the hearse. Of all the incidents of the day, the most diverting was what happened to the Queen. She had a retiring chamber, with *all* conveniences, prepared behind the altar. She went thither; and in the *most convenient* what found she but the *Duke of Newcastle.*" In another letter he observes: "The Earl [of Talbot, who brought up the first course at the banquet] piqued himself on backing his horse down the Hall, and not turning its rump towards the King; but he had taken such pains to dress it to that duty, that it entered backwards, and at his retreat the spectators clapped —a terrible indecorum, but suitable to such Bartholomew-fair doings'.' In other letters he remarks—"Some of the peeresses were dressed over-night, slept in arm-chairs, and were waked if they tumbled their head-dresses; and thousands of the spectators took their places at midnight. It was indeed a brave sight. The multitudes, balconies, guards, and processions, made Palace-yard the liveliest spectacle in the world. The Hall, when once illuminated, was noble, but they suffered the whole parade to return into it in the dark, that his Majesty might be surprised with the quickness with which the sconces catched fire. The champion acted well; the other paladins had neither the grace nor alertness of Rinaldo. Lord Effingham and the Duke of Bedford were but untoward knights-errant; and Lord Talbot had not much more dignity than the figure of General Monk, in the Abbey The habit of peers is unbecoming in the last degree; but the peeresses made amends for all defects. * * * Lady Harrington was noble at a distance, and so covered with diamonds, that you would have thought she had hid somebody or the other, like Falstaff, 'rob me the exchequer.' Lady Spencer and Lady Bolingbroke were not the worst figures there. The Duchess of Ancaster marched alone after the Queen with much majesty; and there were two more Scotch peeresses that pleased everybody —Lady Sunderland and Lady Dunmore. *Per contra* were Lady P., who had put a wig on; and old E., who had scratched hers off. Well, it was all delightful, but not half so charming as its being over. The gabble one heard about it for six weeks before, and the fatigue of the day, could not well be compensated by a mere puppet-show; for puppet-show it was, though it cost a million."

Another eye-witness, after describing the gorgeousness of the scene, the solemnity of the ceremonies, the sumptuousness of the banquet, observes, "During the dinner it was pleasant to see the stratagems made use of by the company in the galleries to come in for a snack of the good things below. The ladies clubbed their handkerchiefs to be tied together to draw up a chicken, or bottle of wine. Some had been so provident as to bring baskets with them, which were let down like the prisoners' boxes at Ludgate, on the gate-house, with a

Pray remember the poor. I must also tell you that in returning to Westminster Hall the great diamond fell out of the King's crown, but was immediately found, and restored; and that several coronation medals in silver were thrown among the populace at the return of the procession; and also some of gold were thrown amongst the peeresses in the Abbey, just after the King was crowned; but they thought it below their dignity to pick them up."

The coronation, which was not damped by a single accident that it was possible for human forethought to prevent, was celebrated all over the kingdom by the firing of cannon, ringing of bells, illuminations, and the most extravagant demonstrations of joy. One black spot upon this otherwise sunny picture must, however, for truth's sake, be recorded. Whilst the crowns were being placed on the heads of the sovereigns, a press-gang, too powerful to be resisted, was let loose upon the multitude, and after murderous encounters, captured some fifty loyal subjects, who were immediately packed off like condemned culprits to serve on board the royal navy, whilst in their absence their wives and children were left to starve, or to steal, and be hanged; such was the state of society, such the law of the good old days of George III.—But to return to the Queen. The third evening after the coronation, their Majesties and the royal families visited Covent Garden Theatre. On this occasion two magnificent boxes were fitted up—the one for the King and Queen, and the other for the Princess-dowager of Wales—at a cost of £700. The piece chosen for representation was "the Beggar's Opera;" and the performance so pleased the Queen, that she signified her intention of visiting Covent Garden once a week, and the other houses as often as circumstances permitted; which, of course, rendered the drama and opera more fashionable than ever, and filled the theatres to overflowing.

In compliance with established custom, the King, Queen, and royal family, were invited to the civic feast on the ninth of November, 1762. In magnificence the spectacle approached that of the coronation; the whole line from St. James's to Guildhall was thronged with spectators. About twelve at noon their Majesties, with the royal family, and their suites, proceeded from St. James's, not to Guildhall, but to a house opposite Bow church, in Cheapside, then the residence of Mr. Barclay, a silk mercer, and quaker, and the ancestor to the head of the firm of Barclay and Perkins, the brewers; where they tarried to see the civic procession, which was as gorgeous as money and tinselled pageantry could make it. The procession passed, the royal party proceeded to Guildhall, where, after they had partaken of the costly feast, and the usual loyal and patriotic toasts had been drank, a grand ball was opened, with a minuet by the Duke of York and the lady mayoress. During the ball the King and Queen remained seated under a canopy of state; and the entertainment (with which their Majesties expressed themselves highly gratified) did not terminate till an hour after midnight. A fortnight after this entertainment, their Majesties, in compliance with the request of the lord mayor and corporation of London, ordered their portraits to be taken, and placed in the Guildhall.

About the middle of November, a patent passed the privy seal, appropriating £40,000 a year for the civil list, for the support of the Queen's household; and, in compliance with the royal will, an Act of Parliament was passed, settling on her Majesty a dowry, the same as that of the late Queen Caroline, namely, £100,000 a year, with Somerset House, and the old park and lodge at Richmond, annexed. This Act received the royal assent on the second of December, and a fortnight afterwards the King purchased Buckingham House, as the domestic residence of his beloved consort, to whom he presented it—whence it was called the Queen's House—and upon whom, fourteen years afterwards, the parliament settled it, in exchange for her right to Somerset House, which was forthwith converted into public offices. As the birthdays of the sovereign and his consort came within a few weeks of each other—the former on the fourth of June, the latter on the sixteenth of May—it was announced, by royal command, that, for the benefit of trade and manufactures, that of the Queen would always be celebrated on the eighteenth of January. Accordingly her Majesty's first birthday celebration in England took place on the eighteenth of January, 1762, with all befitting state and splendour. It, however, was not numerously attended; in fact, the young nobility were miserably disappointed with the new court; pleasure and gaiety, which they had fondly hoped would alone reign there, were scarcely admitted within the royal palaces. Their Majesties gave supperless parties, were parsimonious to a fault, and observed a routine so strict, regular, moral, and devoid of excitement, display, or extravagance, that the votaries of fashion gave the name of Holyrood House to the Queen's residence, and murmured aloud against the pride and poverty of German connexions.

CHAPTER II.

Birth and christening of the Prince of Wales—Institution of Knights of the Garter—Royal visit to Eton College—Peace concluded—Miss Chudleigh's fête—King's birthday celebration—Birth of the Duke of York—Marriage of the King's sister Augusta to the Prince of Brunswick—Queen patronises her foreign relations—Her benevolence to unfortunate Germans—Patronage of various laudable institutions—King's illness—Recovery—Regency Bill—Birthday celebrated—Birth of the Duke of Clarence—Disloyal address—Death of the King's brothers, the Duke of Cumberland and Prince Frederick—Marriage of the King's sister Matilda to the King of Denmark—Birth of the Princess Royal—Death of the King's brother the Duke of York—Birth of the Duke of Kent—Order on Court mournings—Death of the King's sister Louisa—The King of Denmark's visit—Birth of the Princess Augusta Sophia—Royal juvenile drawing-rooms—The Queen's political influence—Birth of the Princess Elizabeth—Visit of the King's mother to Germany—Governors and tutors of the princes.

HE Queen, shortly after her marriage, proved *enceinte;* and at length, about two in the morning on the twelfth of August, 1762, and whilst at St. James's Palace, where she had resolved to lay in, she became unwell. Immediately the Princess Dowager of Wales was fetched, and at five, orders were dispatched commanding the instant attendance of the ladies of the bed-chamber, the maids of honour, and the great officers of state. All the lords and state officers, except the Archbishop of Canterbury, who alone was admitted into the lying-in-chamber, remained in an adjoining room. Dr. William Hunter was in waiting, but he did not officiate; and at twenty-four minutes past seven, Mrs. Draper safely delivered her Majesty of a Prince. Intelligence of this happy event was immediately dispatched to the King, who rewarded the messenger with £500, and hastening to his consort, tenderly saluted her, and fondly kissed and caressed their infant heir. The glad tidings was made public by the firing of the Tower guns, and the ringing of the church bells. Just after this important accession to the royal family was announced, the treasures—estimated at a million sterling—of the ship Hermione, a Spanish prize captured by two English frigates near Cape St. Vincent, passed St. James's in a long train of waggons, when his Majesty and the nobility present appeared at the palace windows, and joined heartily in the acclamations of the populace In a letter, dated August the twentieth, 1762, Mr. Symmers writes to Andrew Mitchell, Esq.:—

"As I presumed the notification of so great and joyful an event for Great Britain as that of the birth of a Prince of Wales would of course immediately be made to all our foreign ministers, I have not till now taken occasion to wish you joy on the happy occasion. He is a charming little creature. Mrs. Symmers and I, along with some other company, had the honour and pleasure of seeing him to-day. Sure, if ever the birth of a Prince was ushered in with favourable omens, his is. He is born at a time when the glory of the British arms is at a higher pitch than ever it was known to be before. He had not been come into the world above an hour, when near a million of treasure, taken from the enemy, passed in a procession of twenty loaded waggons before his windows; and before he was six days old, an account comes of one of the most important victories that has been obtained during the war—that of the Havannah." *

The royal babe was born Electoral Prince of Brunswick Lunenburg, Duke of Cornwall and Rothsay, Earl of Carrick, Baron of Renfrew, Lord of the Isles, and Great Steward of Scotland. On the seventeenth he was formally created Prince of Wales and Earl of Chester, and in 1820 he succeeded to the crown of his father by the title of George IV. By an order of council the Archbishop of Canterbury prepared a thanksgiving for her Majesty's safe delivery, which was offered up in every church throughout the British dominions and the name of the Prince of Wales was inserted in the prayers for the royal family in the Book of Common Prayer. On the eighth of September, the anniversary of the royal marriage, the Prince was christened George Augustus Frederick, by the Archbishop of Canterbury, in the great Council Chamber. The and sponsors were the Duke of Cumberland, the reigning Duke of Mecklenburg-Strelitz, represented by the Duke of Devonshire, and the Princess Dowager of Wales. This solemnity was celebrated with but little pomp, and without the presence of her Majesty. Before the Prince was twelve days old, it was announced that, for the gratification of the public, his Royal Highness was to be seen at St. James's, between the hours of one and three, on drawing-room days; and such was the number of ladies admitted to behold the royal babe and taste the Queen's cake and caudle, that the daily expense for cake alone was estimated at forty pounds.

On the thirteenth of September her Majesty was churched with the usual ceremonies in the Chapel Royal; and eight days afterwards she accompanied the King to Windsor, to be present at the grand installation of Prince William and the Earl of Bute, as Knights of the Garter. The spectacle was highly imposing. The great hall, in which their Majesties, the royal family, and the knights partook of a sumptuous dinner, presented a magnificent appearance; and the display of splendour, elegance, and beauty at the ball in the evening was at once dazzling and enchanting. The dress worn by the Queen on this occasion was of surpassing richness: the stomacher alone was studded with £50,000 worth of jewels, and a single one of these diamonds was valued at £10,000. Their Majesties returned to St. James's on the twenty-fifth, and on their way they paid a visit to Eton College. The birth of the heir-apparent greatly increased their popularity, and congratulatory addresses were presented to them by the bishops, by the City of London, the two Universities, and other corporate and influential bodies, whilst in the newspapers and magazines appeared trashy odes and sonnets, addressed to the King and Queen and infant heir. The bathos in the conclusion of one of these ludicrous effusions is remarkable—

"Back from their spheres the planets have been hurled,
To mark Prince George's entrance on a wondering world;
Descending gods were happy when he smiled,
And thronged with pride to sugar-sop the child."

* Ellis's Royal Letters.

The seven years' destructive war, in which the half of Europe had been in arms against England and Prussia, was, to the extreme gratification of the Queen, brought to a termination in February, 1763; when, on the tenth, peace was concluded at Versailles between Great Britain, France, and Spain, and, five days afterwards, at Hubertsberg, between Austria and Prussia. In England the peace was extremely unpopular; but the Queen, as an expression of thankfulness for the delivery of the land of her birth from oppression and misery, presented a handsome donation to the Asylum for Female Orphans, and afterwards established an institution in Bedfordshire, in which, at her own sole cost, fifty girls, the daughters of naval officers, and another fifty, the daughters of military officers, who had fallen in the late war, were liberally provided for, and instructed in every necessary art and polite accomplishment.

As before remarked, the Queen's real birthday was not kept in England; but this year Miss Chudleigh, maid of honour to the Princess Dowager, complimented her Majesty, on her natal day, by giving a grand *fête* in celebration of the peace. After the magnificent ball and a grand display of fireworks, "a large scene," observes Horace Walpole, "was lighted in the court, representing their Majesties, on each side of which were six obelisks painted with emblems (for the royal family) and illuminated. * * * The lady of the house made many apologies for the poorness of the performance; but it really was fine and pretty. Behind the house was a cenotaph for the Princess Elizabeth, a kind of illuminated candle, the motto, 'All honours the dead can receive.' This burying ground was a strange codicil to a festival, and, what was still more strange, about one in the morning this sarcophagus burst out into crackers and guns."

At this period the disposition of the people to rush into civil war, on account of the peace, greatly depressed the spirits of the King, and, to alleviate his cares, the Queen surprised him with an unexpected entertainment in celebration of his birthday. Their Majesties, who then resided at Buckingham House, proceeded to St. James's on the fourth of June, where the Queen, by tender stratagems, detained her consort whilst the needful preparations for the entertainment were made with all haste and secrecy. The King returned to Buckingham House at ten in the evening on the sixth, when, on the Queen leading him to the window that looked into the grounds, to his surprise and joy, he beheld a superb temple and bridge, with a painting of himself, giving peace to the world, the whole being brilliantly illuminated, and with an orchestra of fifty eminent musical performers ranged along the front of the temple. This magical scene formed part of a *fête*, to which were invited most of the royal family, and a select party of the nobility.

This year, August again proved propitious to their Majesties, by the birth of another Prince (afterwards Duke of York). On the sixteenth, about ten in the morning, the Queen was safely delivered at Buckingham House, the Princess Dowager of Wales being present, and several lords of the council in waiting. On the fourteenth of September the infant was christened Frederick, with much ceremony, by the Archbishop of Canterbury, in the great Council Chamber at St. James's, and in the presence of their Majesties, the royal family, and a brilliant assemblage of the nobility. Two days afterwards, the Queen returned with her children to Buckingham House, which now became the London residence of their Majesties, St. James's Palace being only used for public occasions.

On the twelfth of January, 1764, the hereditary Prince of Brunswick landed in England, and four days afterwards, he was married to the King's sister, the Princess Augusta, by the Archbishop of Canterbury. This marriage gave extraordinary brilliancy to the celebration of her Majesty's birthday, and for more than a week the court did nothing but dance at balls, attend *fêtes*, and pay visits to the theatres and the opera. The Prince and Princess of Brunswick set out for the continent on the twenty-sixth; and shortly afterwards, the Queen, who, under the able tuition of Dr. Majendie, assisted by the readings of the

King, became a tolerable mistress of the English language, presented his Majesty with the subjoined verses, which have been attributed to her own royal pen, in an elegant embroidered valentine, worked by her own hands:

"Gentle is my Damon, engaging his air,
His face, like the morn, is both ruddy and fair;
Soft love sits enthroned in the beam of his eyes,
He's manly, yet tender—he's fond, and yet wise.

He's ever good-humoured, he's generous and gay,
His presence can always drive sorrow away;
No vanity sways him, no folly is seen,
But open his temper, and noble his mien.

By virtue illumined his actions appear,
His passions are calm and his reason is clear;
An affable sweetness attends on his speech;
He's willing to learn, though he's able to teach.

He has promised to love me, his word I'll believe,
For his heart is too honest to let him deceive;
Then blame me, ye fair ones, if justly you can,
Since the picture I've drawn is exactly the man."

Expedient as her Majesty found it to refrain from patronizing foreigners, this year, through her influence, the order of the Garter was conferred on her brother, the reigning Duke of Mecklenburg-Strelitz; the governorship of Zell was bestowed on her brother, Prince Charles; and a commission in the Hanoverian service was given to her younger brother, Prince George, whilst she herself made costly presents to several of her German relations and friends. This summer the two Princes caught the hooping-cough; the symptoms at first were severe, but afterwards they progressed favourably, and were sufficiently recovered by the twelfth of August to give a grand juvenile ball to the youthful nobility at Richmond Lodge.

Towards the close of 1764, her Majesty made benevolent exertion on behalf of six hundred poor Germans, natives of Bavaria and Wurtzburg, who had left their homes under a pledge of being conveyed to St. John's Island, near the mouth of the St. Lawrence, in North America, at the expense of a speculator, who, being unable to complete his engagement, had brought them to the shores of England, and then deserted them. Shortly afterwards, the Queen, to alleviate the distresses of the weavers in Spitalfields, laid aside all foreign silks, and wore only those of British manufacture; a laudable example, which all the loyal ladies of Great Britain immediately followed. This same principle of benevolence induced her Majesty to extend her patronage to the Lying-in Hospital, to the Magdalen charity, to Sunday schools, and other laudable institutions, and also to encourage to the utmost of her ability the arts and manufactures of the kingdom.

In the spring of 1765, an affection of the brain confined the King to his chamber for about a month. Throughout this trying period her Majesty, although far advanced in pregnancy, affectionately tended and nursed her afflicted husband; and to keep the matter secret, and to avoid alarming the already greatly-excited nation, she caused assurances of his speedy recovery to be published in the newspapers, and held drawing rooms, and went in state to the Chapel Royal as usual. At length, his Majesty was pronounced convalescent, and on the twenty-second of April he proceeded in procession to the House of Lords, where, in a speech from the throne, after alluding to his regard for the welfare of the kingdom, his late indisposition, and the tender age of his offspring, he concluded, "I take the earliest opportunity of meeting you here, and of recommending to your most serious deliberation the making such provision as would be necessary, in case any of my children should succeed to the throne before they shall respectively attain the age of eighteen years. To this end, I propose to your consideration whether, under the circumstances, it will not be expedient to vest in me the power of appointing, from time to time, by instruments in writing under my sign manual, either the Queen or any other person of my royal family usually residing in Great Britain, to be the guardian of the person of such successor, and the regent of these kingdoms, until such successor shall attain the age of eighteen years; subject to the like restrictions and regulations as are specified and contained in an act passed upon a similar occasion in the twenty-fourth year of the reign of the late King, my royal grandfather: the regent so appointed to be assisted by a council composed of the several persons who, by reason of their dignities and offices, are constituted members of the council established by that act, together with those whom you may think proper to leave to my nomination."

This speech was immediately answered by a joint address from both houses; but such was the spirit of opposition and faction on this occasion, that the bill met with strenuous opposition in the Commons, and at last was passed in a form approved by the ministry, but repugnant to the feelings of the King. During the debate, many personal reflections were made upon the Princess Dowager, whom public scandal accused of granting improper liberties to Lord Bute; but against the Queen, who wisely stood aloof from all political intrigue, not a word was said by either party. The bill received the royal assent on the fifteenth of May, and was followed by a complete change in the ministry.

This year the King's birth-day was kept with extraordinary splendour; the court was attended by a numerous and brilliant assemblage, who, in compliance with royal orders, appeared in dresses entirely of British manufacture. One of the ladies, the Countess of Northumberland, wore jewels valued at £150,000; another, a peerless beauty, in an elegant painted silk dress, attracted such general admiration, that the Queen, it is said, composed and addressed to her the subjoined lines:—

"Stella's gay robe with so much art was framed,
That Flora the invention might have claimed.
So fair was Stella's face, so bright her eyes,
She seemed that goddess in a sweet disguise."

The birth-day of Prince Frederick was also, this year, kept with extraordinary splendour, in commemoration of his having just previously been elected to the episcopal principality of Osnaburg; and six days afterwards, August twenty-first, at four in the morning, her Majesty was safely delivered of a Prince at Buckingham House—an event made public by the firing of the Tower guns, and illuminations at night. On the eighteenth of September, the royal infant was christened William Henry, by the Archbishop of Canterbury, at St. James's, in the presence of their Majesties, the royal family, and a brilliant assembly of the nobility and foreign ministers. The sponsors were the Duke of Gloucester, Prince Henry Frederick, and the Princess of Brunswick. The Prince was afterwards created Duke of Clarence, and ultimately succeeded to the throne as William IV.

At this period the proceedings against Mr. Wilkes, the unpopularity of Lord Bute, the weight of taxation, and the stagnation of trade and commerce, had so fully destroyed the popularity of the ministers, that the city of London, in an address to the King, after congratulating him on the increase of the royal family, had the boldness to assure his Majesty that, "from a zealous attachment to his royal house, and the true honour and dignity of his crown, *whenever a happy establishment of public measures should present a favourable occasion*, they would be ready to exert their utmost abilities in support of such wise measures as apparently tended to render his Majesty's reign happy and glorious." This address was, of course, received with great coolness, and it rather injured than benefited the cause it was meant to serve.

The Queen, shortly after recovering from her lying-in, had to mourn the death of two of the royal family: the Duke of Cumberland, the last-born son of King George II., and the hero of the successes and excesses at Culloden, expired suddenly on the thirty-first of October; and on the twenty-ninth of the subsequent December, the King's youngest brother, Prince Frederick William, breathed his last, in the sixteenth year of his age, after a severe lingering illness. The remains of this short-lived prince and his uncle were solemnly interred in the royal vault in Henry VII.'s Chapel, in Westminster Abbey. Their Majesties deeply mourned these melancholy events, "the court put on its sables," and the celebration of the Queen's birth-day was postponed to the twentieth of February, 1766.

At this period the Prince of Wales and the Bishop of Osnaburg were inoculated, by Pennel Hawkins, surgeon extraordinary to the King, in the presence of their Majesties, at Buckingham House; an example which, although it failed to entirely dispel the prejudices then generally entertained against inoculation, was, nevertheless, a commendable effort to lead the way to the only true mode of exterminating that fearful scourge, the small-pox.

It was in the autumn of this year that the King's unfortunate sister, Caroline Matilda, was married at St. James's; the Duke of York, her brother, stood proxy for the Danish King, Christian VII., her husband, and the next morning she proceeded on her journey to Denmark. Shortly after her arrival there, the court at Copenhagen was disturbed by an event which to this day remains involved in mystery. Count Struenzee, a German physician, who had been raised to the highest offices in the state, having rendered himself obnoxious by his extensive plans of reform, was accused of intriguing with the young Queen Matilda. His enemies, aided by the powerful influence of the Queen-dowager of Denmark, and her son, Prince Frederick, procured his immediate execution; and the Queen herself would have shared the like fate, but for the British minister, through whose interposition she was permitted to retire to Zell, where she died of a broken heart, on the tenth of May, 1775, in the twenty-fourth year of her age.

On the twenty-ninth of September the Queen gave birth to a daughter, who, a month afterwards, was christened Charlotte Augusta Matilda, by the Archbishop of Canterbury, the sponsors being the King and Queen of Denmark, by proxy, and the Princess Louisa Anne, in person. In September, 1767, their Majesties experienced a domestic affliction in the death of the King's brother, the Duke of York; he died of a malignant fever at Monaco; and scarcely had they received the mournful intelligence, when the Queen was again brought to bed. The infant entered the world at noon, on the second of November, at Buckingham House, proved a healthy boy, and, on the thirteenth, was ceremoniously christened Edward; the sponsors being the Prince of Brunswick, Prince Charles of Mecklenburg-Strelitz, and the Landgravine of Hesse Cassel, respectively represented by the Earls of Hertford and Huntingdon, and the Duchess of Hamilton. The Prince was afterwards created Duke of Kent, and ultimately became the father of our present sovereign, Queen Victoria, whom God preserve. The remains of the Duke of York were brought to England, and, on the third of November, solemnly interred in the Chapel of Henry VII., in Westminster Abbey. Seven days afterwards, the city of London sent up to the throne a most respectful and loyal address, on the recent birth and death in the royal family; which his Majesty graciously received, and, in reply, after thanking them for their expressions of loyalty and condolence, observed—"The religion and liberties of my people have always been, and ever shall be, the constant objects of my care and attention, and I shall esteem it one of my first duties to instil the same principles into those who may succeed me."

The court went into deep mourning for the Duke of York; but, on the twelfth of January, the King, in compliance with the wish expressed in addresses presented to the throne by the manufacturers and traders of London, the weavers of Spitalfields, and others, commanded that in future the period for the ceremonial of court mourning should be reduced to one half what it had previously been—a measure so gratifying to the manufacturing and trading communities, and to the weavers of Spitalfields especially, that the latter went in procession to St. James's, and presented a loyal address of thanks to the King, Queen, and royal family, for their generous patronage and encouragement of the wrought silks of British manufacture.

In the spring of 1768, death again

visited the royal family. The King's sister, Louisa Anne, fell into a rapid consumption, which, to the deep sorrow of the whole family, carried her off in the twentieth year of her age. She expired on the thirteenth of May, and, on the twenty-second, was privately interred in the royal vault in Westminster Abbey.

Three months afterwards, the King of Denmark paid a rather protracted visit to England. "He arrived on Thursday" [August the eighth], says Horace Walpole, "and supped and lay at St. James's yesterday evening (the twelfth); he was at the Queen's and Carlton House, and, at night, at Lady Hertford's assembly. He is small, pale, and delicate, in features resembles George II., acts the king exceedingly, struts in the circle like a cock sparrow, and does the honours of himself very civilly."

During his sojourn in England he visited Cambridge, Oxford, York, and other places, dined in public with the lord mayor and aldermen of London, was entertained by their Majesties with a grand ball and supper at Buckingham House, and himself gave a magnificent masked ball at the Opera House, which was attended by the nobility and the royal family, but to which the King went only privately, and sat in an enclosed box, where he could see and not be seen, and from which the Queen, who disapproved of such entertainments, entirely absented herself. His Danish Majesty embarked for Calais on the thirteenth of October; and, on the eighth of November, the royal family was increased by the birth of a princess, who, a month afterwards, was christened Augusta Sophia.

The twenty-fifth of October, 1769, was remarkable for an infantile drawing-room, which, it has been asserted, the Queen caused the Prince of Wales and the Princess Royal to hold, with no other view than that of turning the current of public opinion into the peaceful channel from which it had been diverted by faction. Certainly, at this period, the tyrannic, unconstitutional proceedings of ministers had aroused the indignation of the people to the highest degree, and endangered the safety of the throne; still it cannot, for a moment, be supposed that either the Queen, King, or court ever expected to overcome these serious political evils by infantile drawing-rooms, which the great mass of the people either passed over with indifference, or held up to scorn. But whatever her Majesty's motives might have been, at the first of these drawing-rooms the Prince of Wales appeared dressed in scarlet and gold, with the insignia of the order of the Garter; the Bishop of Osnaburg wore blue and gold, with the insignia of the order of the Thistle; Prince William was attired in a Roman toga; and the Princess Royal presented herself in a rich muslin frock. With the appearance and behaviour of the royal children, the noble company present (especially the ladies) expressed themselves highly delighted: but, shortly afterwards, when the Prince of Wales gave a ball and supper at Buckingham House, the populace broke into the court-yard, and so alarmed the company by their riotous threats and acts, that a stop was put to these expensive displays of juvenile royalty.

Some writers have asserted that the Queen's political influence was considerable; but that this was not the case, at least up to this period, we have the evidence of Lord Chesterfield, who, in one of his letters, remarks—"Her Majesty is a good woman, a good wife, a tender mother, and an unmeddling Queen. The King loves her as a woman, but I verily believe has not spoken one word to her about politics."

On the twenty-second of May, 1770, the Queen gave birth to the Princess Elizabeth; and being, on this account, unable to take part in the subsequent public celebration of her consort's birthday, she on that day, June the fourth, presented to him the subjoined stanzas, which were partly, some say wholly, composed by herself.

"When monarchs give a grace to fate,
And rise as princes should;
Less highly born than truly great,
Less dignified than good;

"What joy the natal day can bring,
From whence our hopes began;
Which gave the nation such a king,
And being such a man.

"The sacred source of endless power,
Delighted sees him born;
And kindly marks the circling hour
That spoke him into morn.

"Beholds him with the kindest eye
Which goodness can bestow;
And shows a brighter crown on high
Than e'er he wore below."

On the eighth of June, the Princess-dowager of Wales, goaded by insult and terrified by the dismal aspect of the times, embarked with a princely retinue for Germany, with the intention of ending her days at Zell; but for some reason, nowhere clearly explained, she altered her mind, and returned to England on the twenty-seventh of October.

Their Majesties directed much of their attention to the education of their children; who, on being emancipated from the nursery and superintendence of Lady Charlotte Finch, were placed under the care of Dr. Majendie, till the spring of 1771, when a separate establishment was formed for the Prince of Wales at Buckingham House, and about the same time the royal children were placed under the governorship and tuition of the Earl of Holderness, Lord Bruce, Mr. de Salzes, a native of Switzerland, and Mr. Markham.

CHAPTER III.

Birth of the Duke of Cumberland—Royal Marriage Act—Death of the King's mother—Birth of the Duke of Sussex—Dr. Beattie's interview with their Majesties—Private life of the royal family at Kew—Births of the Duke of Cambridge and the Princess Mary—Change in the Prince of Wales's household—The Perreaus and Dr. Dodd—Birth of the Princess Sophia—The war—Royal progress—Parliamentary grants to the royal family—Royal visit to the Bishop of Winchester—Birth of Prince Octavius—Prince William sent to sea—Queen's benevolence—Visit to the Duchess-dowager of Portland—Poetical eulogium.

ON the fifth of June the Queen gave birth to a prince, christened Ernest Augustus, who afterwards was created Duke of Cumberland, and, in 1837, succeeded to the kingdom of Hanover. The recent marriages of the then Duke of Cumberland with Mrs. Horton, and of the Duke of Gloucester to the Countess of Waldegrave, both scandalized and exasperated their Majesties to that degree, that the King, in order to prevent such unions in future, caused to be passed, in the first session of parliament, in 1772, that impolitic, arbitrary measure, known as the Royal Marriage Act; in consequence of which, none of the descendants of George II. can lawfully marry, without the consent of the sovereign, before the age of twenty-five, nor at and after that age, without the consent of either the sovereign or the parliament. This act has certainly proved highly injurious to the august line which it was intended by its originator to preserve; nor did it pass without a violent opposition in both houses. "The descendants of George II." observed the opposing peers, "may, in time, comprehend a very numerous description of people, and it would be an intolerable grievance, that the marriages of so many subjects, dispersed amongst the various ranks of civil life, should be subject to the restraints of this act. It seems indecent to the royal family, to suppose that they arrive later at the age of discretion than others, and absurd to allow them to be capable of governing a kingdom at an age when they are not to be trusted in the choice of a wife. It seems to be a mere act of power, having neither the force nor obligation of law, and contrary to the inherent rights of human nature, to disable a man from contracting a marriage, perhaps for life; and it is pregnant with civil discord and confusion, as having a natural tendency, at some future period, to produce a disputed title to the crown — and all this, for ends wholly disproportionate to such extraordinary efforts; as the main purposes of the bill might have been answered without creating that perpetuity of restraint, which we think ourselves in conscience bound to oppose." In the Commons it was urged, that such a measure would hurry the bachelor princes of the royal family into libertinism and other vices, and thus increase the evil it was intended to remedy. But this, and other equally sound arguments, proved futile; the act was carried by a majority of fifty votes, and immediately afterwards passed into a law.

On the eighth of February, 1772, his Majesty's mother, the Princess-dowager of Wales, after a lingering illness, expired, in the fifty-fourth year of her age, at Carlton House, in Pall Mall. When she lay on the bed of death, both the King and Queen visited her daily, and by every attainable means endeavoured to alleviate her sufferings; her loss they deeply deplored, and by their express command her remains were interred by the side of her beloved husband in Westminster Abbey, with great funeral pomp, on the eighteenth of February. In early life the Princess was esteemed by the British public, but after the accession of George III., the influence which she possessed, and as it was supposed, exercised over the mind of the King, her son, to the injury of the nation, caused her to be held up to public scorn and persecution. But reprehensible in this respect as probably was her conduct—for she had been educated in the despotic courts of Germany, and believed in the infallibility of royalty—they who best knew her have pronounced her to be highly virtuous and well-intentioned Bishop Newton, her chaplain, observes, "The sums which she expended in private charity and pensions amounted to £10,000 a year, and the merits of her charities were greatly enhanced by their secrecy. Several families who were relieved by her, did not so much as know who was their benefactor till her death, when the current of her bounty ceased to flow. The calmness and composure of her death, were further proofs and attestations of the goodness of her life. She died as she had lived, beloved and honoured most by those who knew her:" and we may add, that after her husband's death, she paid off his debts out of her jointure—an act, considering the circumstances and the times, for which alone the nation should reverence her memory.

On the twenty-seventh of January, 1773, her Majesty was delivered at Buckingham House of a prince, who, on the twenty-fifth of the subsequent month, was christened Augustus Frederick, at St. James's, and afterwards created Duke of Sussex. It was at this period that their Majesties, in order to lead a life as retired and tranquil as possible, resolved upon making the palace at Kew their principal residence, and about the same time Carlton House was fitted up for the chief abode of their elder sons.

Some idea of their sentiments on religion and morality may be gleaned from the following account of the interview they granted Dr. Beattie, on the twenty-fourth of August, 1773:—

"At twelve," observes Dr. Beattie, in his diary, "I and Dr. Majendie went by appointment to the King's house at Kew. We were received in the most gracious manner by both their Majesties. I had the honour of a conversation with them, nobody else being present but Dr. Majendie, for upwards of an hour, on a great variety of topics, in which both the King and Queen joined, with a degree of cheerfulness, affability, and ease that was to me surprising, and soon dissipated the embarrassment which I felt at the beginning of the conference." After detailing the royal encomiums on his writings, particularly his "Essay on Truth," the doctor proceeds: "We had much conversation on moral subjects, from which both their Majesties let it appear, that they were warm friends to Christianity, and so little inclined to infidelity, that they could hardly believe that any right-thinking man could really be an atheist, unless he could bring himself to believe that he had made himself. Both the King and Queen highly commended the quakers; after which, I was asked many questions about the Scots university, the revenues of the Scots clergy, their mode of praying and preaching, the length of our vacation at Aberdeen, and the closeness of our attendance during winter; the number of students that attended my lectures; my mode of lecturing, whether from notes or completely written lectures; about Mr. Hume, and Dr. Robertson, and Lord Kinnoul, and the Archbishop of York, &c. His Majesty, after asking what I thought of Lord Dartmouth, observed, 'They say that he is an enthusiast, but surely he says nothing on the subject of religion, but what every Christian may, and ought to say.' He asked whether I did not think the English language now on the decline. I answered in the affirmative; and the King agreed, and named the Spectator as one of the best standards of the language. Dr. Majendie mentioned Dr. Oswald's 'Appeal to Common Sense on behalf of Religion,' with commendation. I praised it too, and the Queen took down the same, with a view to send for it. We discussed many other topics, for the conversation lasted upwards of an hour. The Queen bore a large share in it. Both the King and her Majesty showed a great deal of good sense, acuteness, and knowledge, as well as of good nature and affability. At last the King took out his watch, which Dr. Majendie and I took as a signal to withdraw, which we accordingly did immediately. At parting, the King assured me that he should always be glad of an opportunity to show the good opinion he had of me. The Queen sat all the while, and the King stood, sometimes walking about a little. Her Majesty speaks the English language with surprising elegance, and little or nothing of a foreign accent. There is something wonderfully captivating in her manner; so that if she were only of the rank of a private gentlewoman, one could not help taking notice of her as one of the most agreeable women in the world. Her face is much more pleasing than any of her pictures, and in the expression of her eyes, and in her smile, there is something peculiarly engaging."

That the private life of George and Charlotte was remarkably simple, regular, and methodic, we have the evidence of an eye-witness, who, writing about this time, observes:—

"At six in the morning their Majesties rise, and the two succeeding hours they enjoy wholly as their own. At eight the Prince of Wales, the Bishop of Osnaburg [Duke of York], the Princess Royal, and the Princes William and Edward are brought to breakfast with their royal parents. At nine the younger children attend to lisp or smile their good morrows; and whilst the elder Princes are away at mental tasks or bodily exercises, the little ones and their nurses pass the morning in the garden. The King and Queen frequently amuse themselves with sitting in the room whilst the children dine; and once a week the whole family make a holiday at Richmond Gardens, where, in the cottage there erected from her own design, the Queen busily plies her needle, whilst the King reads aloud to her, from Shakspeare or some other favourite author; and whatever charms ambition or folly may conceive to avail so exalted a station, it is neither on the throne nor in the drawing-room, in the splendour or the toys of sovereignty, that they place their felicity. It is in social and domestic gratification, in breathing the free air, admiring the works of nature, tasting and encouraging the elegancies of art, and in living without dissipation. In the evening, all the children pay their duty at Kew House before they retire to bed; after which, the King reads to her Majesty, and having closed the day with a joint act of devotion, they retire to rest. This is the order of each revolving day, with such exceptions as are unavoidable in their high station. The sovereign is the father of his family; not a grievance reaches his knowledge that remains unredressed, nor a character of merit or ingenuity disregarded; his private conduct, therefore, is as exemplary as it is amiable."

Another sketch, by Mr. Young, represents the Prince of Wales, when about twelve years old, and his brother Frederick, occupied harmlessly and healthfully it is true, but in a manner more befitting young husbandmen than the scions of the royal house of Hanover.

"A spot of ground," says Mr. Young, "in the garden at Kew, was dug by his Royal Highness the Prince of Wales, and his brother the Duke of York, who sowed it with wheat, attended the growth of their little crop, weeded, reaped, and harvested it solely by themselves. They thrashed out the corn and separated it from the chaff, and at this period of their labour were brought to reflect, from their own experience, on the various labours and attention of the husbandman and farmer. The Princes not only raised their own crop, but they also ground it, and having parted the bran from the meal, attended to the whole process of making it into bread, which it may well be imagined was eaten with no singular relish. The King and Queen ate of this philosophical repast, and beheld with pleasure the very amusements of their children rendered the source of useful knowledge."

From this period till the summer of 1776, we have nothing of importance to chronicle, saving the birth of two royal children, Prince Adolphus Frederick, afterwards Duke of Cambridge, who first saw the light at the Queen's house, on the twenty-fourth of February, 1774, and the Princess Mary, now Duchess of Gloucester, and sole survivor of the family, who entered the world, at the same royal palace, on the twenty-fifth of April, 1776. Shortly after this last event, an important change was made in the household of the Prince of Wales. Lord Bruce was succeeded as governor by the Duke of Montague; and Dr. Markham, Bishop of Chester as preceptor, by Dr. Hurd; and that neither Lord Bruce nor Dr. Markham might take offence at the change, the former was elevated to the earldom of Aylesbury, and the latter to the see of York. When this last promotion was made, the pious Dr. Porteus, who enjoyed the Queen's confidence and patronage, was at her Majesty's particular recommendation elevated to the see of Chester.

At the commencement of this year, the wife of Robert Perreau, in person, petitioned the Queen to intercede in behalf of her husband, who, together with his brother, Daniel Perreau, had been found guilty of forgery, a crime then punished with death. Her Majesty gave the petition to the King; but as one of the Perreaus could not be pardoned without the other, whose guilt had been rendered manifest to the council, the King signed the death warrants, and the unfortunate brothers were executed at Tyburn. In the subsequent summer, Queen Charlotte was again deeply distressed by a similar application from the wife of a more exalted, more unfortunate culprit, the ill-starred Dr. Dodd. The reverend Doctor had been found guilty of forging a bond in the name of Lord Chesterfield for £4200. The singularity of his case excited the sympathy of all classes, and strenuous exertions were made to procure his pardon. Amongst the many petitions imploring that, at least, his life might be spared, was one to the throne by the City of London, followed by another signed by 20,000 of the inhabitants of Westminster, and one to the Queen by the Magdalen Society. The Queen supported the prayer of these petitions with all her influence; but when the case was brought before the council, Lord Mansfield remarked to the King, "If your Majesty pardon Dr. Dodd, you will have murdered the Perreaus;" and accordingly the reverend culprit was hanged, on the twenty-seventh of June, 1777.

On the fourth of November, 1777, their Majesties' fifth daughter, the Princess Sophia, was born; and shortly afterwards, the contest which had been raging for three years between Great

Britain and her revolting colonies in America was brought nearer home, by what might be called the suicidal conduct of the court of Versailles. On the sixth of February, 1778, France acknowledged the independence of the United States of America; and immediately afterwards England declared war against France. The Queen, deeply as she deplored the necessity for war, denounced the American republicans as rebels and atheists, and declared that, by supporting their cause, the King of France and his ministers had committed a grand blunder. On the third of May she accompanied his Majesty to review the fleet at Portsmouth, where they were received by all ranks with enthusiastic demonstrations of loyalty and joy; and with him she made two more progresses in the autumn: one, at the close of September to inspect the camp in the neighbourhood of Winchester; the other for the King to review the troops at Coxheath. in Kent. Throughout these progresses her Majesty let no opportunity of doing good slip by; by her kindness and courtesy, she endeared herself to the gentry, citizens, and yeomen, and by leaving munificent sums as alms for the poor in the parishes through which she passed, won for herself the affection of the peasants and labourers.

In April, 1778, the parliament, in compliance with the royal will, passed an act, enabling the King to settle an annuity of £60,000 on the six younger Princes; £50,000 on the five Princesses; and £12,000 on the son and daughter of the Duke of Gloucester; but the former of these annuities were not to take effect till the demise of the King, nor the latter till the death of the Duke of Gloucester.

It was this year that their Majesties, with several of their children, honoured Dr. Thomas, Bishop of Winchester, formerly preceptor to the King, with the visit mentioned in the subjoined letter from the bishop's niece, Mrs. Chapone, to Mr. Burrows, dated the twentieth of August, 1778:—

"Mr. Buller went to Windsor on Saturday; saw the King, who inquired much about the bishop, and hearing that he would be eighty-two next Monday, 'Then,' said the King, 'I will go and wish him joy.' 'And I,' said the Queen, 'will go too.' Mr. Buller then dropt a hint of the additional pleasure it would give the bishop if he could see the Princes. 'That,' said the King, 'requires contrivance; but if I can manage it, we will all go.'" On the Monday following, the royal party, consisting of their Majesties, the Prince of Wales, Duke of York, Duke of Clarence, the Princess Royal, and Princess Augusta, visited the bishop. "The King," continues Mrs. Chapone, "sent the Princes to pay their compliments to Mrs. Chapone; himself, he said, was an old acquaintance. Whilst the Princes were speaking to me, Mr. Arnold, the subpreceptor, said, 'These gentlemen are well acquainted with a certain ode prefixed to Mrs. Carter's Epictetus, if you know anything of it.' Afterwards, the King came and spoke to us, and the Queen led the Princess Royal to me, saying, 'This is a young lady, who, I hope, has much profited by your instructions. She has read your Letters on the Improvement of the Mind more than once, and will read them often; and the Princess assented to the praise which followed, with a very modest air. I was pleased with all the Princes, but particularly with Prince William, who is little of his age, but so sensible and engaging, that he won the bishop's heart, to whom he particularly attached himself, and would stay with him while all the rest ran about the house. His conversation was surprisingly manly and clever for his age; yet, with the young Bullers, he was quite a boy, and said to John Buller, by way of encouraging him to talk, 'Come, we are both boys, you know.' All of them showed affectionate respect to the bishop; the Prince of Wales pressed his hand so hard that he hurt it."

On the twenty-third of February, 1779, her Majesty gave birth to another Prince, who, being the eighth son, was, on the twenty-third of the following month, christened Octavius. Shortly after this event, the King resolved that Prince William, afterwards King William IV., should become a sailor. The Queen remonstrated against exposing her youthful son to the perils of the deep, and the hardships and dangers of war. The Prince himself felt no inclination to descend from the dazzling height of royalty, to fill a subordinate post in the navy, at a time, too, when England was engaged in a fierce struggle with two powerful foes. But the remonstrance and entreaty of the mother and son made no impression on the obstinately firm monarch, and, on the eighteenth of June, 1779, Prince William was rated as a midshipman on board the Prince George, of ninety-four guns. That he might not play, but act the sailor, his court dresses were laid aside for the equipments of an ordinary midshipman; and, on the evening before going on board, the King presented him with a Bible, and in a sensible address, too lengthy for these pages, exhorted him to fill his new peril-fraught office with diligence, bravery, generosity, kind forbearance, and, above all, obedience to his superiors. His mother parted from him in tears, and his first conduct as a sailor, proved that he had not forgotten his father's counsels. When introduced into the midshipman's cabin, his companions were puzzled how to address him; they knew he was the King's son, but as a brother middy they deemed him their equal, and one of them boldly asked him by what name he was rated in the ship's books. 'I am entered as Prince William Henry,' he replied, with unaffected affability; 'but my father's name is Guelph, and as I am only a sailor amongst you, I will thank you to call me simply William Guelph.'"

This year the destruction of the Quebec frigate, Captain Farmer, which was blown up in the bravely-contested action off Brest, when all on board, save seventeen persons, perished, so deeply affected the Queen, that she procured a pension of £800 a year for the captain's widow and family; obtained a lieutenant's commission for Mr. Moor, the master's mate, who, although wounded, was picked up alive; and otherwise provided for the rest of the survivors. But these and other laudable acts of benevolence, did not prevent the tongue of slander from accusing her Majesty of *excessive* penuriousness and uncharitableness; an accusation which, did the assigned limits of this memoir permit, might be fully disproved, by adducing the many authentically-recorded instances of her sympathy for the distressed and unfortunate, her alms to the poor and afflicted. It was these acts of munificence, her many virtues, and the encouragement she afforded to all that tended to the religious, moral, social, and commercial advancement of the nation at large, that won for her the esteem of every one who really knew her. In works of benevolence she expended about £5000 a year; and although she made no pretensions to extraordinary literary attainments, she did not overlook the merits of Madame d'Arblay, Mrs. Hannah More, Mrs. Trimmer, Charlotte Smith, and other fair literary stars of her era. One of these ladies, the accomplished Mrs. Delany, who was honoured with especial marks of her royal favour, at this period resided on terms of intimate friendship with the Duchess-dowager of Portland, at Bulstrode; and in an interesting letter to the Honourable Mr. Hamilton, dated January twenty-eighth, 1779, she thus details a visit which the royal family paid to her friend, the duchess:— *

"What a task you have set me, my dear friend! I can no more tell the particulars of all the honours I received last autumn from the King and Queen and eight of their royal progeny, than I can remember last year's clouds — a simile, by-the-bye, ill adapted to the grace and benignity of their manners, that gave a lustre even to Bulstrode, superior as it is to most places. I had formed to myself a very different idea of such visitors, and wished the day over; but their affability and good humour left me no room for anything but admiration and respect; for, with the most obliging condescension, there was no want of proper dignity to keep the balance even. They were delighted with the place, but, above all, with the mistress of it, whose sweetness of manners

* Correspondence of Mrs. Delany with Mr. Francis Hamilton.

and knowledge of propriety engage all ranks. To give you a just notion of the entertainments, you should have a plan of the house, that I might lead you through the apartments; but imagine everything that is elegant and delightful, and you will do more justice to the place and entertainments than I can by my description.

"The royal family, ten in all, came at twelve o'clock. The King drove the Queen in an open chaise, with a pair of white horses. The Prince of Wales and Prince Frederick rode on horseback, all with proper attendants, but no guards; Princess Royal and Lady Weymouth in a post-chaise; Princess Augusta, Princess Elizabeth, Prince Adolphus, and Lady Charlotte Finch, in a coach; Prince William, Prince Edward, Duke of Montague, and Bishop of Litchfield, in a coach; another coach full of attendant gentlemen, amongst the number Mr. Smelt, whose character sets him above most men, and does great honour to the King, who calls him his friend, and has drawn him out of his solitude (the life he had chosen) to enjoy his conversation every leisure moment. These, with all their attendants in rank and file, made a splendid figure as they drove through the park and round the court up to the house. The day was as brilliant as could be wished—the twelfth of August, the Prince of Wales's birthday. The Queen was in a hat and in an Italian nightgown of purple lustring, trimmed with silver gauze. She is graceful and genteel; the dignity and sweetness of her manner, the perfect propriety of everything she says or does, satisfies everybody she honours with her distinction so much, that beauty is by no means wanting to make her perfectly agreeable; and though age and long retirement from court made me feel timid in my being called to make my appearance, I soon found myself perfectly at ease, for the King's condescension and good humour took off all awe but what one must have for so respectable a character, severely tried by his enemies at home as well as abroad. The three Princesses were all in frocks, the King and all the men were in an uniform, blue and gold. They walked through the great apartments, and attentively observed everything, the pictures in particular. I kept back in the drawing-room, and took that opportunity of sitting down, when the Princess Royal returned to me, and said the Queen missed me in the train. I immediately obeyed the summons with my best alacrity. Her Majesty met me half-way, and seeing me hasten my steps, called out to me, 'Though I desired you to come, I did not desire you to run and fatigue yourself.'

"They all returned to the great drawing-room, where there were only two arm chairs placed in the middle of the room for the King and Queen. The King placed the Duchess-dowager of Portland in his chair, and walked about admiring the beauties of the place. Breakfast was offered all, prepared in the long gallery. The King and all his royal children and the rest of the train chose to go to the gallery, where the well-furnished tables were set: one with tea, coffee, and chocolate; another, with other proper accommodation of eatables, rolls, cakes, &c.; another table with fruits and ices, in the utmost perfection, which, with a magical touch, had succeeded a cold repast. The Queen remained in the drawing-room, and the Duchess-dowager brought her a dish of tea on a waiter, which was what she chose. After she had drank her tea, she would not return the cup to the Duchess, but got up and would carry it into the gallery herself, and was much pleased to see with what elegance every thing was prepared. The delightful appearance they all made, and the satisfaction all expressed, rewarded the attention and politeness of the Duchess of Portland, who is never so happy as when she gratifies those she esteems worthy of the favour. The young Royals seemed quite at home, from the eldest to the youngest, and to inherit the gracious manners of their parents. The King desired me to show the Queen one of my books of plants; she seated herself in the gallery at a table, and the books laid before her. I kept my distance till she called me to ask some question about the mosaic paper-work; and as I stood before her Majesty, the King set a chair behind me. I turned with some confusion and hesitation on receiving so great an honour, when the Queen said, 'Mrs. Delany, sit down, sit down; it is not every lady that has a chair brought her by a king;' so I obeyed. Amongst many genuine things, the Queen asked me, 'Why I was not with the Duchess when she came, for I might be sure she would ask for me?' I felt flattered, acknowledged the distinction, and said I was particularly happy at that time to pay my duty to her Majesty, as it gave me an opportunity of seeing so many of the royal family. 'O, but,' says her Majesty, 'you have not seen *all* my children yet;' upon which the King came up, and observed to the Queen, 'You may put Mrs. Delany in the way of doing that, by naming a day for her to drink tea at Windsor Castle.' The Duchess of Portland was consulted, and the next day fixed upon, as the Duchess had appointed the end of the week for going to Weymouth.

"We went at seven, the hour appointed; were ushered into a long room with great bay windows, where were all the Princesses and younger Princes, with their attendants, and passed on to the bed-chamber, where the Queen stood in the middle of the room with Lady Weymouth and Lady Charlotte Finch; the King and the elder Princes had walked out. When the Queen took her seat and the ladies their places, she ordered a chair to be set for me, opposite to where she sat. At eight the King, &c. came into the room. It was the hour the King, Queen, and eleven of the Princes and Princesses walked on the terrace; they apologized, but said the crowd expected them. When they returned, we were summoned into the next room to tea, and the royals began a ball, and danced two country dances, to the music of French horns, bassoons, and hautboys, which were the same that played on the terrace whilst their Majesties walked there. But the ball was terminated abruptly by the King, who said to the Prince of Wales, he was sure, when he considered how great an effort it must be to play that kind of music so long a time together, that he would not continue their dancing, but that the Queen and the rest of the company were going to the Queen's house, where they should resume their dancing, and have proper music."

In 1779, appeared a rhyming dialogue, in the form of a burlesque satire on the Queen, and which, in reality, is a skilfully-sketched portraiture of the pleasing side of her Majesty's character. The bard, after eulogizing the King, makes his querist observe—

"I own your satire just and keen,
Proceed and satirise the Queen."

To which the poet replies—

"With all my heart. The Queen, they say
Attends her nursery every day,
And like a common mother shares
In all her infants' little cares—
What vulgar, unassuming scene
For George's wife and Britain's Queen.
'Tis whispered also at the Palace,
(I hope 'tis but the voice of malice)
That (tell it not in foreign lands)
She works with her own royal hands,
And that our Sovereign's sometimes seen
In vest embroidered by his Queen.
This might a courtly fashion be,
In days of old Andromache,
But modern ladies, trust my words,
Seldom sew tunics for their lords.
What secret next, must I unfold?—
She hates, I'm confidently told—
She hates the manners of the times,
And all our fashionable crimes,
And fondly wishes to restore
The golden age and days of yore,
When silly simple women thought
A breach of chastity a fault—
Esteemed those modest things, divorces,
The very worst of human curses,
And deemed assemblies, cards, and dice,
The spring of every sort of vice.
Romantic notion, all the fair
At such absurdities must stare,
And, spite of all her pains, will still
Love routs, adultery, and quadrille."

"Well! is that all you find to blame,
Sir critic, in the royal dame?"

"All I could find to blame? No, truly.
The longest day in June and July
Would fail me ere I could express
The half of Charlotte's blemishes.
Those foolish and old-fashion ways
Of keeping holy sabbath days—
That affectation to appear
At church, the word of God to hear—
That poor-like plainness in her dress,
So void of noble tawdriness—
That affability and ease,
Which can her menial servants please,

But which incredibly demean
The state and grandeur of a queen.
These and a thousand things beside
I could discover and deride ;
But here's enough —another day
I may perhaps renew my lay.

Are you content ?"

"Not quite, unless
You put your satire to the press ;
For sure a satire in this mode
Is equal to a birthday ode."

CHAPTER IV.

London riots—Birth and death of Prince Alfred—Peace—Loss of America—Death of Prince Octavius—Birth of the Princess Amelia—Commemoration of Handel—A royal concert—Death of Prince George of Mecklenburg-Strelitz—Private life of the Royal Family—Installation of Knights of the Garter—King's Birthday—Disgraceful conduct of the elder Princes—The King stabbed at by Margaret Nicholson—Royal visit to Nuneham, Oxford, and Blenheim—Visit to Whitbread's Brewery—The Prince of Wales' debts and difficulties—Progress to Cheltenham and its neighbourhood—The King's mental illness—Parliamentary discussions on the Regency—Sorrow, care, and fortitude of the Queen—The King's recovery—Unfilial conduct of the Prince of Wales and the Duke of York—Queen's drawing-room—Visit to Covent Garden Theatre—Public thanksgiving for his Majesty's recovery—Queen's birthday—Progress to Weymouth—Marriage of the Duke of York—Calamitous visit to the Haymarket Theatre—Unceremonious gala—War—Royal progress—Deaths of the Queen's brother Frederick, and of her sister Christina of Mecklenburg—Marriages of the Duke of Sussex, and of the Prince of Wales—Attempts on the King's life—Birth of the Princess Charlotte.

AT this period the King and Queen passed much of their time at Windsor, where a residence near to the Castle wall was built at the express desire of her Majesty, and called "the Queen's Lodge at Windsor." But it so happened that their Majesties were at Buckingham House when those fearful riots burst forth, which in June, 1780, threatened London with destruction; and although several of the nobles and ladies of the court were terrified into hurrying into the country with their jewels and other valuables, neither the King nor the Queen—and her Majesty was *enceinte*—would stir from the metropolis till order was restored, when they proceeded to Windsor Lodge, where, on the twenty-second of September, the Queen was delivered of her last-born son, Alfred, who, eighteen months afterwards, expired, and was privately interred in the royal vault in Westminster Abbey.

In December, Prince William returned in safety from the fleet, which, however, he shortly afterwards joined, and proceeded with to America, where he passed the winter of 1781-2. This same month, Prince Frederick departed for Germany, where he remained for several years, to complete his military studies; and on the first of January, 1781, the Prince of Wales was declared to be of age, and received the congratulations of the court on the occasion. From this period we have no remarkable event to record in the personal history of Queen Charlotte, saving the celebration, this year, of her own and her eldest son's birth-days, with extraordinary splendour, and the death of her sister Sophia, in the summer of the subsequent year, till 1783, when, on the twentieth of January, preliminaries of peace were signed between Great Britain, France, and Spain—a truce, which afterwards terminated by a treaty of peace, was entered into with Holland—and the independence of America was acknowledged. The loss of America—an event deeply deplored by the King, and, as such, a source of pain to his affectionate consort—was shortly afterwards followed by a demise in the royal family, which overwhelmed their Majesties with sorrow. Prince Octavius fell ill of the small-pox; the malady proved mortal; he died at Kew, on the third of May, and, a week afterwards, was buried by the side of his brother Alfred, in Westminster Abbey. This catastrophe laid the Queen on the bed of sickness; and scarcely was she restored to convalescence, when her last-born child, the Princess Amelia, first saw the light, on the eighth of August, 1783, at Buckingham House.

In the spring of the subsequent year, the first grand festival in commemoration of Handel took place in Westminster Abbey, under the especial patronage of their Majesties, who, accompanied by Prince Edward, the Princess Royal, and the Princesses Augusta, Elizabeth, and Sophia, attended the performance, which, as a spectacle, was magnificent—as a concert, sublime beyond description. The next day the performance was resumed at the Pantheon, and a week afterwards, that *chef-d'œuvre* of the great composer, Handel, "The Messiah," was performed before their Majesties in Westminster Abbey. Both the King and the Queen took great interest in this musical commemoration, and on it they lavished the highest encomiums; nor is this surprising, as the performance was surpassingly grand. The Queen had a taste for oratorios, and the King professed to be a musical connoisseur, played the bass-viol, and, with that instrument, frequently took part in the performance of symphonies and other instrumental part music.

An amusing anecdote of one of these royal concerts went the round of the papers of the day. The party composed a quintett under the direction of the King himself, who, whilst he sawed away at the bass-viol, had no idea that it was possible to surpass him or the sounds he produced. The Princess of Wales presided at the harpsichord, the Duke of Newcastle played the first violin, the Duke of Devonshire, the tenor, and the facetious Philip Dormer, the flute. It so happened that the King had his own notions of time and tune; and as his Majesty performed for his own amusement only, and possibly with the idea of gaining some instruction, he never scrupled to go over a passage two or three times, or to take any liberties, or to make any blunders that seemed good to him, without consulting, or in any way warning the rest of the orchestra; it was, therefore, necessary for every member of it, whilst giving his eyes to his own music, to give his ears to the King's, and as rapidly as possible to follow the direction and eccentricities of the royal performer. On the present occasion it became evident, however, that this concert was going wrong; but the most acute of these select amateurs could not imagine where they were in error. The royal bass-viol was proceeding on its course as sedately as the march of an elephant; the violin looked in vain, backwards and forwards, for several bars, to see where he could glide in, but could discover nothing resembling what he heard; the tenor, knowing there was a difficult passage just passed over, and being well aware of the royal practice with regard to such, boldly went back and repeated it; the harpsichord, believing the time had been altered from fast to slow, slackened its pace; and the flute, entertaining a different opinion, went away at double speed. Such a strange medley was never heard before: nevertheless, the King was seen leaning forward, with his eyes fixed on the music, working away with the royal elbow, evidently too absorbed in his own performance to heed the confusion that distracted the audience, and made the other musicians feel extremely uncomfortable. It was not etiquette to notice the King's mistakes, or the youthful maids of honour would have laughed outright. The Duke of Newcastle, a studious courtier, knew not what to do: he played a few notes here and there, whispered to the Duke of Devonshire, nudged Philip Dormer, whose blowing had become desperate, he glanced at the look of the Princess without obtaining any clue to the cause of the inextricable disorder; but still he plied on, knowing that matters could not be worse than they were. The King at last brought up the party "all standing," as the sailors say, by coming suddenly and unexpectedly to the end of his symphony. The Princess, who alone dared to speak, discovered that his Majesty had turned over two leaves at once; the monarch, with the utmost composure, turned back to the part which had not been played, and, without uttering a syllable, set to work, rasping away, followed by the other musicians, who this time were in at the death, with tolerable exactitude.

On the sixth of November, 1785, the Queen's brother, Prince George of Mecklenburg, died; and, in consequence, the British court went into mourning, and the commemoration of her Majesty's natal day was put off to the ninth of February, when it was celebrated with unusual splendour. The interesting letters of Mrs. Delany, written solely for private information, and intended by the authoress to be impartial and truthful sketches, besides other valuable information, afford the subjoined pleasing details of the domestic life of the Queen and her beloved spouse at this period :—

"On Thursday, the ninth of May, I received a note from Lady Weymouth, to tell me the Queen invited me to her Majesty's house to hear Mrs. Siddons read 'The Provoked Husband.' You may believe I obeyed the summons, and was much entertained. It was very desirable to me, as I had no other opportunity of hearing or seeing Mrs. Siddons; and she fully answered my expectations—her person and manners perfectly agreed. I was received in the great drawing-room by the King and Queen, their daughters, and Prince Edward. Besides the royal family, there were only the Duchess-dowager of Portland and her daughter, Lady Weymouth, and her beautiful granddaughter, Lady Aylesford, Lord and Lady Harcourt, Lady Charlotte Finch, Duke of Montague, and the gentlemen attendant on the King. Mrs. Siddons read standing, and behaved with great propriety. After she was dismissed, their Majesties detained the company some time, to talk over what had passed, which was not the least agreeable part of the entertainment."

In another letter, the same accomplished correspondent observes :—"I have been several evenings at the Queen's lodge, with no other company but their Majesties' own most lovely family. They sit round a large table, on which are books, work, pencils, and paper. The Queen has the goodness to make me sit down next to her, and delights me with her conversation, which is informing, elegant, and pleasing beyond description; whilst the younger part of the family are drawing, working, et cetera, the beautiful babe, Princess Amelia, bearing her part in the entertainment, sometimes in one of her sister's laps, sometimes playing with the King on the carpet, which altogether exhibits such a delightful scene as would require an Addison's pen or a Vandyke's pencil to do justice to it. In the next room is the band of music, who play from eight to ten. The King generally directs them what pieces of music to play—chiefly Handel's."

On the twenty-seventh of April, 1786, their Majesties stood sponsors to Lord Salisbury's daughter, Georgiana Charlotta, to whom they presented a superb salver, weighing one hundred and twenty ounces. In June, another grand musical festival, in commemoration of Handel, was held at Westminster Abbey, which they honoured with their presence; and, on the third of the same month, their royal sons, the Princes Edward, Ernest Augustus, Augustus Frederick, and Adolphus Frederick, were, together with the Landgrave of Hesse Cassel and several nobles, installed Knights of the Garter. On the anniversary of the King's birth-day, which this year was kept with great splendour, the Queen wore a royal purple robe, covered over with rich Brussels lace, and the magnificence of her appearance was heightened by a bouquet composed solely of the valuable diamonds which the King had just previously received as a present from the Nizam of the Deccan in India.

The intemperance, immorality, extravagance, and gambling propensities of the elder Princes had long been a source of affliction to their royal parents; and at this period the Prince of Wales found himself overwhelmed with pecuniary difficulties. His debts, including £24,000 for completing Carlton House, amounted to £250,000; and as his mother frowned upon his profligateness and prodigality, and his father would neither countenance nor assist him, he resorted to the expedient of reducing his household from £25,000 to £5000 a-year; but with what good effect will hereafter be shown.

On the second of August, Margaret Nicholson made an unsuccessful attempt to stab the King, as he was stepping out of his chariot at the garden-entrance to St. James's. On this occasion the Queen was saved all unnecessary emotion by the judicious forethought of the Spanish Ambassador, who, the moment the assassin was seized, posted to Windsor, and by keeping her Majesty in deep conversation, prevented her from hearing the alarming report till the King arrived, and told it her with his own lips. "The knife," said the fortunate monarch, "slightly cut my waistcoat, and luckily, very luckily it was that it went no farther, for there was nothing beneath but a little linen and a great deal of fat." The Queen's consternation was great, and for a long time afterwards she felt uneasy whenever her husband was present in London.

On the sixteenth of the same month, his Majesty, the Queen, and several of the Princesses, paid a friendly visit to the Harcourt family, at Nuneham, whence they proceeded to Oxford, where they viewed the colleges and halls, and the King received two addresses—one from the University, and the other from the Corporation. From Oxford the royal party returned to Nuneham, and the following morning they honoured the Duke of Marlborough with a visit, at Blenheim, where, after surveying the palace, they drove round its demesne, formerly the royal park of Woodstock.

In the autumn of this year, the royal family experienced a domestic affliction in the death of the Princess Amelia, the last surviving issue of George II. and his Queen, Caroline. The Princess had lived a life of celibacy, and for years had retired from the bustle of the court. After a protracted illness, she breathed her last on the twenty-sixth of October, in the eighty-fifth year of her age. Her remains were interred, with private obsequies, in Henry VII.'s Chapel, in Westminster Abbey, on the evening of the eleventh of November.

On the twenty-sixth of May, 1787, their Majesties, and three of the Princesses, and their suite, visited Messrs. Whitbread's extensive brewery, in Chiswell Street. They were ceremoniously received by the proprietor and his daughter; and after examining the steam-engine and the store, the Queen and the Princesses amused themselves by going into the great vat or store cistern, which, when full, contained four thousand barrels of beer. They next proceeded to the cooperage, where Mr. Whitbread was assailed with so many questions from the King, that, remarks Peter Pindar in his satirical account of this visit—

"The brewer exclaimed, May I be cursed !
If I know which to answer first."

The royal party, after carefully viewing the whole of the premises, and partaking of a cold collation in the dwelling-house, expressed themselves highly gratified, and departed.

The situation of the Prince of Wales was, at this period, highly singular and critical. The prejudice which the nation generally entertained against him on account of his licentiousness and prodigality, was increased by a report—which, indeed, was true—that he had contracted a secret marriage with Mrs. Fitzherbert, a lady beautiful and accomplished, but of the Roman Catholic religion. These unfavourable circumstances alarmed many of his creditors; and their persecuting clamours, and the impossibility of satisfying their claims with his present limited income, induced the Prince, in the spring of this year, to consent to a proposal for laying the state of his affairs before parliament. Accordingly his friends brought the matter before the Commons, when a warm debate ensued; but before the House could come to a vote on the subject, Mr. Pitt, by desire of the King, met the Prince, and informed him, that if the intended motion were withdrawn, everything might be settled to his Royal

Highness's satisfaction; this being acceded to, the King directed £10,000 a year to be added to the allowance of the Prince of Wales, out of the Civil List; and the Commons, in compliance with a royal message, voted an address, requesting his Majesty to direct the sum of £162,000 to be paid out of the Civil List, for the discharge of the Prince's debts; and the further sum of £20,000 to complete the repairs of Carlton House. At the same time the King sent for the Prince. granted him forgiveness, and introduced him to his royal mother and sisters. The Prince immediately afterwards increased his household to its former magnificence, and by again pursuing a heedless, profligate course, in which the elder of his brothers shared largely, again became overwhelmed with pecuniary difficulties; and to increase his income, and discharge his debts, he resorted to means the most dishonourable and the most criminal that can well be imagined.

In the summer of 1788, the King experienced symptoms of indisposition, for which his physicians recommended a course of the mineral waters at Cheltenham; accordingly Bayshill Lodge, Cheltenham, was taken for their Majesties, who, with the three eldest Princesses, proceeded thither on the twelfth of July. During their sojourn at this favourite resort of fashionable invalids and idlers, the royal party amused themselves, and gratified the inhabitants of the neighbourhood, by making excursions to the most noteworthy places in the vicinity. They conferred the honour of a royal visit on Tewkesbury, Cirencester, the cities of Gloucester and Worcester, Hartlebury Castle the episcopal palace of Bishop Hurd, Pauswick, Stroud, and other palaces and places of historic interest. At Worcester, they paid a formal visit to the corporation at the town hall, and attended the performances of the three choirs of Hereford, Gloucester, and Worcester. Throughout these excursions, they were everywhere received with fervent demonstrations of loyalty; and their condescension and affability were praiseworthy and remarkable. The King took no guards with him; and he and the Queen frequently walked about Cheltenham and its neighbourhood, accompanied by only two or three of their suite, and attended by crowds of people.

On the fifteenth of August, the royal party returned to Windsor. The King was in excellent spirits. His health appeared established; but shortly afterwards he was attacked with bilious fever, and other maladies, and by the end of October it could no longer be concealed that a mental derangement had taken place, which rendered him quite incapable of attending to public business. The advice of the most skilful physicians was taken, and they gave it as their opinion, that his Majesty, although at present decidedly insane, would recover at some future period. Under these circumstances, both the ministers and the parliament turned their attention to the establishment of a regent. Mr. Pitt urged that the supreme power should be vested in the Queen, whilst Mr. Fox declared, that it belonged, of right, to the Prince of Wales: every possible stratagem was resorted to, to induce her Majesty to take part in this party agitation—for such it really was; but the sorrowing Queen, who, at this time, was wholly occupied in endeavours to restore her beloved consort to reason and health, for a time resisted every attempt to engage her in political contests; and declared, that for herself, she only required permission to watch over her afflicted husband. However, in a short while, the unfilial conduct of her two eldest sons became unbearable, and she ceased to remain neutral, gave her sanction and support to the proceedings of the ministers; and wrote a letter to the Prince of Wales, charging him with "designs to take advantage of the weak state of the King to get possession of his treasures, and to change the whole face of things." Matters were in this state when the parliament resolved that, during the mental illness of the King, the royal power should be invested in the Prince of Wales, as regent; and that the care of his Majesty should be committed to the Queen, who should nominate all persons to the offices in the household. A Bill to this effect passed the Commons on the twelfth of February; but whilst it was under discussion in the Lords, the King was declared to be convalescent; for nearly three weeks afterwards all parliamentary business was suspended; and on the twenty-seventh, the further progress of the Bill was stopped by an announcement of the perfect recovery of his Majesty. An announcement hailed with enthusiastic joy by the nation; and followed, on the second of March, by an order for the discontinuance of the prayer for the King's recovery, and for the offering up of a thanksgiving for his restoration to health, in all churches and chapels.

The King, on his recovery, attended divine service at Kew, and with the Queen, and the three elder Princesses, received the sacrament. The happy event was celebrated in London, Edinburgh, and other places, with illuminations, ringing of bells, and the usual demonstrations of loyal joy; and the parliament, the city of London, and the corporate bodies generally, presented congratulatory addresses to both their Majesties, which, of course, were received very graciously. But whilst the people rejoiced at the recovery of the sovereign, his nearest heirs were loth to acknowledge the fact. The Duke of York had strenuously supported the Prince of Wales in his endeavours to seize the legal power from the hand of the invalided King; and indeed, in his conduct at this period, he proved himself of the two, perhaps, the worst son. Here is Lord Bulkeley's picture of him just previous to this illness of his father:—

"The Duke of York talks both ways, and I think will end in opposition. His conduct is as bad as possible; he plays very deep, and loses; and his company is thought *mauvais ton*. I am told, that the King and Queen begin now to feel how much sharper than a serpent's tooth it is to have an ingrate child. When the Duke of York is completely 'done up' in the public opinion, I should not be surprised if the Prince of Wales assumed a different style of behaviour. Indeed, I am told that he already affects to see that his brother's style is too bad."*

The first interview these filial sons, the Prince of Wales, and his brother of York, had with their sire after his recovery, is thus described by Lord Grenville:—"The two Princes were at Kew yesterday, and saw the King in the Queen's apartment; she was present the whole time, a precaution for which, God knows, there was but too much reason. They kept him waiting a considerable time before they arrived; and after they left him, drove immediately to Mrs. Armstead's, in Park Street, in hopes of finding Mr. Fox there, to give him an account of what had passed. He not being in town, they amused themselves yesterday evening with spreading about a report, that the King was still out of his mind; and with quoting phrases of his, to which they gave that turn. It is certainly a decent and becoming thing, that when all the King's physicians, all his attendants, and his two principal ministers, agree in pronouncing him well, his two sons should deny it. And the reflection, that the Prince of Wales was to have had the government, and the Duke of York the command of the army, during his illness, makes this representation of his actual state, when coming from them, more peculiarly proper and edifying. I bless God that it is some time before these matured and ripened virtues will be visited upon us in the form of a government."†

On the twenty-sixth of March, the Queen held a brilliant drawing-room, on which occasion she treated with marked coolness several of the time-serving courtiers who, during the King's indisposition, had advocated vesting the whole regal power, without restrictions of any kind, in the Prince of Wales, as regent. A week afterwards, she gave a grand concert and supper to a select company of nobles and ladies, known as the King's friends; and on the fifteenth of April, her Majesty, with the Princesses Augusta and Elizabeth, visited

* Memoirs of the Court and Cabinet of George III., by the Duke of Buckingham.

† Ibid.

Covent Garden Theatre for the first time since the recovery of her consort, when such was the enthusiastic loyalty displayed by the audience, who, upstanding, and uncovered, sang, "God save the King!" no less than six times in the course of the evening; that at the commencement of the performance her Majesty, and, indeed, the whole house, even to the performers, were much affected, and burst into tears. The King's religious feelings prevented him from being present on this occasion—he had resolved that his first public appearance after his recovery should be to offer up a solemn thanksgiving; accordingly, on the twenty-third of April, about ten in the morning, his Majesty, accompanied by the Queen and royal family, and attended by both houses of parliament, the great officers of state, the judges, and other officers, proceeded in grand procession to St. Paul's Cathedral. At Temple Bar, the corporation joined the cavalcade, which was closed by a troop of horse-guards. In the Cathedral the scene was splendid, the music sublime, the service deeply impressive. Psalms, and choruses to anthems, were chaunted by six thousand charity children; and the sermon, which was neither an eulogy in praise of royalty, nor a political or party oration, was preached by the Bishop of London, from Psalm xxvii. 16—"Oh, tarry thou the Lord's leisure; be strong, and he shall comfort thine heart; and put thou thy trust in the Lord." After the sermon, an anthem was sung; and as their Majesties were about to depart, the charity children sung the 104th Psalm, with impressive effect. The royal party returned with the same state to Buckingham House, where they arrived at about half-past three. The route they took was lined with thousands of spectators, who, as they passed and repassed, greeted them with deafening acclamations of loyalty.

The conduct of the three elder Princes, on this solemn occasion, was highly disgraceful. In the Cathedral they talked aloud during the service, and, out of doors, took means to raise a riot in favour of the Prince of Wales. In fact, to repeat the sentiment of Lord Bulkeley, the King's mind was torn to pieces by the disgraceful conduct of his sons; the breach between his Majesty and the Prince of Wales was too wide to be filled up, and, under the mask of attention to their royal parents, they outraged and insulted them in every way they could devise.

This same day, her Majesty caused eighty of the Sunday School children at Windsor to be completely clothed, and the mayor and corporation proceeded with them in procession to divine service. Numerous other entertainments were also given, in celebration of the King's recovery, throughout the British dominions, and even in Germany. Of these, the three most splended were a fête given by the Queen and the Princess Royal, on the first of May; a grand entertainment given by the French ambassador to the royal family and nobility, at his house in Portman Square; and a gala still more magnificent and brilliant, given by the Spanish ambassador to the Queen and about two thousand royal and noble personages, at Ranelagh. This year, his Majesty's birth-day was kept at St. James's, with regal magnificence, when the drawing-room was thronged with visitors; but on account of the shock occasioned by the duel just previously fought between the Duke of York and Colonel Lennox, the King himself was absent, and the whole burden of the ceremonials was borne by the Queen.

To invigorate his Majesty's constitution after the severe blow it had sustained, change of air and a course of sea-bathing were recommended. Weymouth was chosen for this purpose, and thither their Majesties, with the three elder Princesses and their suite, proceeded, and, on the thirtieth of June, took up their abode at the Duke of Gloucester's lodge. The royal party, during their residence at Weymouth, chiefly occupied themselves by making short aquatic trips, paying visits to the remarkable places in the neighbourhood, occasionally going to the theatre, giving audience to the neighbouring nobility and gentry, and walking on the esplanade or the sands, with only a few attendants, and followed by crowds of respectful loyal subjects. On this occasion their Majesties honoured with their presence Exeter, Plymouth, Mount Edgecombe, Milton Abbey; Mariston, the seat of Mr. Heywood; Sherborne Castle, the seat of Lord Digby; Saltrum, the seat of Lord Barrington; Lulworth Castle, the seat of Mr. Weld, brother to Mrs. Fitzherbert, and a Roman Catholic, and other note-worthy places, but which the assigned limits of this memoir prevents us from even mentioning.

The royal party left Weymouth on the fourteenth of September, the same evening reached Longleat, the seat of the Marquis of Bath, and after spending a day there, proceeded onward to Tottenham Park, the seat of Lord Aylesbury, where they rested till the eighteenth, on which day they again set forth, and the same afternoon reached the Queen's Lodge at Windsor, in excellent health and spirits.

This trip so charmed the King and Queen, that, in the subsequent year, they again proceeded to Weymouth, and passed a week there, from the third to the tenth of September. Shortly after their return, the Duke of York married the Princess Frederica Ulrica Catherine, eldest daughter of Frederick the Great, King of Prussia. After the marriage had been solemnized with becoming magnificence, at Berlin, on the first of October, the royal pair set out for England, and owing to the delays and insults they were forced to endure from the partizans of the French revolution in their progress from Brussels to Calais, they did not reach Dover till the twenty-first. They landed the same day, reached York House on the twenty-second, and, on the evening of the twenty-third, were married according to the rites of the Church of England, by the Archbishop of Canterbury, assisted by the Bishop of London, at the Queen's house, and in the presence of their Majesties, the royal family, and the lord chancellor, who signed the marriage certificate. On account of this marriage, the Duke's income was raised to £35,000 a-year, and a dowry of £30,000 per annum was settled on the Duchess, who was a really virtuous, gentle, and accomplished princess.

On the fourth of January, 1792, their Majesties, with the Duke and Duchess of York, Prince William (who, on the nineteenth of May, 1789, had been created Duke of Clarence), and six of the Princesses, visited the Haymarket Theatre, to witness the fourth performance of the ballad opera of "Cymon," when, sad to relate, the rush at the pit door was so violent, that one person was trampled to death, and several others were injured.

Two years afterwards, there occurred, at this same theatre, another accident, occasioned by similar circumstances, and which was so appalling, that their Majesties resolved never again to visit that place of amusement. This catastrophe happened on the third of February, 1794, when a visit from the royal family drew such crowds to the house, that in their endeavours to enter the pit, the foremost in the crowd fell down, and others, driven forward by the resistless press from behind, were forced either to trample over them, or themselves fall and be trampled over. A dreadful scene of death, terror, and confusion ensued; and, when something like order was restored, it was found that fifteen persons had been crushed to death, and twenty others injured so severely, that several of them survived only a few hours.

As the formal court balls and galas fatigued the king, without affording him pleasure, the Queen gave, at Windsor, on the tenth of January, a grand ball and supper, such as she knew would afford real gratification to her beloved spouse. This unceremonious gala was heartily enjoyed by the King, and formed a striking contrast to the formal ceremonious celebration of her Majesty's birth-day, which took place a few days afterwards, and was the most full, brilliant, and splendid court since the Queen's coronation.

At this period a dread that the republicanism of France would sweep monarchy from the face of Europe, impelled the ministry into a war in defence of ancient institutions. Already were the moral as well as the political effects of the Gaulish struggle for freedom, and that alluring impossibility, equality, being felt to an alarming degree throughout the British empire; and but for the fortitude of the sovereign and the energy and decision of ministers, the French reign of terror might have crossed the Channel, and marked its horrors in the annals of Britain in letters of blood.

On the first of February, 1793, the French convention declared war against England; and, twenty-five days afterwards, three battalions of guards, destined for foreign service, commenced their march from St. James's Park, and, at their departure, were reviewed before the King, Queen, and royal family, who took leave of them with the kindest expressions of regard and encouragement.

In the subsequent June, when Lord Howe arrived at Spithead, with the ships he had captured at the defeat of the French fleet off Ushant, their Majesties, with other branches of the royal family, to invigorate the patriotism and loyalty of the nation, paid a formal visit to the fleet, at Portsmouth; when they went on board the Queen Charlotte, and, as a mark of royal approbation, the King, with his own hands, presented a superb diamond-hilted sword to Lord Howe, and made honorary presents to several other of the naval officers.

On Friday, the King held a grand levee, at which all ranks of officers were admitted. On Saturday, the royal party witnessed the launching of the Prince of Wales, a fine war-ship of ninety-eight guns, and afterwards sailed up the harbour and inspected the fleet and the naval trophies of Lord Howe's victory. On Monday, they sailed for Southampton, where they landed in the afternoon, and, entering their carriages, proceeded direct to Windsor. There the Queen received the mournful intelligence of the death of her brother, Adolphus Frederick, Duke of Mecklenburg-Strelitz, and shortly afterwards news arrived of the demise of her sister, Christina.

This year, too, the marriage of the Duke of Sussex to Lady Augusta Murray, first at Rome and then in England, was a source of sorrow and annoyance to her Majesty. This marriage had been solemnized without the King's consent, and in open violation of the Royal Marriage Act. On the third of August, 1794, it was pronounced invalid by the Ecclesiastical Court, and Lady Augusta immediately separated from her husband. Of the two children, the fruit of this union, the daughter still survives, the wife of the late Lord Truro, formerly Mr. Serjeant Wylde. After the death of Lady Augusta, the Duke of Sussex married Lady Cecilia Letitia Underwood, who now survives him as Duchess of Inverness.

At this period the armies of the French republic were everywhere successful. Holland was conquered under favour of the patriotic party, and, in consequence, the Stadtholder sought an asylum in England. On the twenty-sixth of January, 1795, he arrived in London, with his family and suite. Their Majesties cordially welcomed him, ordered Hampton Court to be fitted up for his residence, and, on the nineteenth of May, the Queen did him the honour to have a fair held in the Dutch style, at Frogmore, to which his Highness and his family, together with many of the nobility, were invited.

Her Majesty was present at the unfortunate marriage of the Prince of Wales to the Princess Caroline of Brunswick; and shortly afterwards, the bold ultra-democratic expressions which the parliamentary debates on the debts of the heir-apparent, combined with the success of the French revolution, emboldened the press and the republican party to indulge in, caused the Queen serious alarm. The King endeavoured to dispel her fears, and, at the close of the summer, conducted her to Weymouth; but in October, the threatening aspect of public affairs drew their Majesties to the metropolis, that the parliament might assemble at an unusually early period; and as the King was proceeding to open the session, an immense throng surrounded his carriage, clamorously vociferating, "Peace!" "Bread!" "No King!" whilst stones were thrown at the coach; and, on passing through Palace Yard, a bullet, fired, it was supposed, from an air gun, broke one of the coach windows. On his Majesty's return to St. James's, these outrages were repeated; and as he proceeded from thence to Buckingham House, the royal carriage was again surrounded, stones thrown at it, and at one time several persons made a rush, exclaiming, "Down with the King!" "Drag him out!" However, at this perilous moment, the loyal Mr. Bedingfield flew to the assistance of his Majesty, and after knocking down several of the assailants, drew a pistol from his pocket, and thus kept back the riotous mob.

Throughout these trying scenes the grossly-insulted monarch preserved great coolness. But the news so terrified the Queen and the Princesses, that it was with difficulty he could prevail upon them to accompany him on the following evening to Covent Garden Theatre, where, to their infinite satisfaction, they were received by a crowded house with enthusiastic demonstrations of loyalty, "God save the King!" being thrice sung with encores during the evening. Both houses of parliament expressed great indignation at the late outrages, and numerous loyal addresses on the subject were presented to his Majesty by the City of London and other corporate bodies, whilst a bill was passed for the more effectually preventing seditious meetings and assemblies. Yet, withal, the rebellious spirits abroad daily grew in force and daring, and again royalty was outraged on the first of February, 1796. On that day, as the royal family were returning from Drury Lane Theatre, a stone was flung into the carriage, which struck the Queen on the cheek, and then fell into Lady Harrington's lap. In this case, as in that of the previous insults offered to his Majesty, the offenders were never brought to justice, although £1000 were offered for their detection.

On the seventh of January, 1796, a daughter was born to the heir-apparent. Her Majesty was not present at the accouchement, but at the christening she stood as one of the sponsors, and gave the name of Charlotte Augusta to the royal infant. This event was followed by the separation of the parents, who had been linked together by worldly policy, and whose repugnance to each other eventually settled down into implacable hatred. This separation of the Prince and Princess of Wales was a cause of sorrow and domestic trouble to their Majesties. The King, it is said, took a favourable, the Queen an unfavourable view of the Princess's character and conduct; more than once words ran high between them on this subject, and her Majesty's maternal feelings blinded her to the fact, that she overlooked the failings of her son, the Prince of Wales, and was strongly prejudiced against his consort, the Princess Caroline.

CHAPTER V.

Gloomy aspect of the times—Death of Madame Schwellenburgen—Marriage of the Princess Royal—Mutiny at Portsmouth and the Nore—Naval victories—Fête by the Queen at Frogmore—Volunteers—Attempt at the theatre to assassinate the King—Entertainment at Frogmore—Progress to Weymouth—Christmas festivity—Union with Ireland—Catholic question—Resignation of Pitt—The King again suffers from a maniac malady—Recovers—Peace followed by a renewal of war—Loss of Hanover—Review of Volunteers—Presentation of colours—Their Majesties' birth-days—Aquatic fête at Weymouth—Mr. Pitt again minister—Royal entertainment at Windsor — Installation of knights of the garter — German operetta—Visit to Chelsea Hospital—Death of the Duke of Gloucester, brother to the King—The naval victory of Trafalgar—The Queen's conduct to the Princess of

Wales—Home scenes at Windsor—The Duke of York and Colonel Wardle—Jubilee on the King's entering the fiftieth year of his reign.

HE year 1797 opened to her Majesty with a gloomy aspect; her faithful servant, Madame Schwellenburgen, mistress of the robes, died suddenly on the seventh of March, and on the eighteenth of May, the Princess Royal was, to the sorrow of her mother, the Queen, united in marriage to Frederick William, hereditary prince of Wirtemburg Stutgardt, who was a widower, and whose former wife, it was said, had, by his sanction, been confined in a prison in Russia, and there murdered. As to public affairs, they, at the commencement of the year, presented a prospect truly alarming. The war was proving ruinous and unfortunate; national credit seemed to be destroyed, and Ireland was ripe for rebellion. Disaffection was on the increase in England, and whilst a foreign invasion impended, a serious mutiny broke out in the channel fleet, which was followed by one still more alarming at the Nore. But, withal, the year closed more brilliantly than might have been expected. The mutiny of the seamen was suppressed; the alarm occasioned by the stoppage of cash payments at the Bank had speedily subsided; public confidence was restored; the Lords St. Vincent and Duncan had respectively defeated the Spanish and the Dutch fleets; and, on the nineteenth of December, a proclamation was issued for a public thanksgiving for our great naval victories, which was celebrated with the usual solemnities—the King, Queen, and royal family repairing to St. Paul's Cathedral in the same state, and amidst the same acclamations, as upon similar occasions.

In the following autumn, whilst their Majesties and the Princesses were on their annual visit to their favourite watering-place, Weymouth, intelligence arrived of Admiral Nelson's naval victory over the French at the Nile: a victory so splendid and decisive, that the news threw the whole nation into a fervour of enthusiastic loyalty and patriotism. The guns fired; the bells rang; London and all the chief towns throughout the kingdom were illuminated; a liberal subscription was made for the brave fellows who fell in the action; Admiral Nelson was created a baron, with a pension of £2,000 a year, and the twenty-eighth of September was observed as a day of solemn thanksgiving.

On the eighth of March, 1799, her Majesty gave an entertainment at her now favourite residence, Frogmore, to commemorate the recovery of the Princess Amelia, who for some time had been seriously indisposed. To this gala only those known as the King's friends were invited: the supper was superb; the ball select, but brilliant; the scene imposing, gladsome, and exhilarating. The Queen gave this fête with a willing and a joyous heart; but her next entertainment, the ball and supper, on the sixteenth of May, to which, besides about two hundred of the leading nobility, the Princess of Wales was invited, and which was intended as a prelude to the recall of that Princess to court, was given against her inclination, and with no other view than to gratify the desire of her beloved consort.

This year his Majesty paid remarkable attention to the associations of volunteers in the metropolis and the adjacent counties. On his birth-day he reviewed upwards of eight thousand of these loyal troops in Hyde Park, and in the presence of all the beauty and fashion of London, who greeted him on his arrival and departure with deafening exclamations of loyalty. The Queen and the Princesses, accompanied by the Countess of Harrington and Lady Mary Stanhope, witnessed the imposing scene from the house of Lady Holdernesse, and from that of Lord Cathcart; and when the vast assemblage made the welkin ring with loyal shouts, tears of gratitude moistened the cheeks of their Majesties and their beloved daughters. On the twenty-first of this month, between eight and nine in the morning, his Majesty, mounted on a white charger, set out from Buckingham House, to visit and inspect the different volunteer corps of the metropolis at their several stations. After passing over Westminster Bridge by the obelisk to Blackfriars, and thence to the Artillery Ground, he proceeded to the residence of the Lord Chancellor in Guildford Street, where, with the Queen and the Princess, who had awaited his arrival, he partook of a cold collation. Immediately afterwards, he mounted his charger, and proceeding to the Foundling Hospital, reviewed the several corps collected there; and then, with the Queen and the royal family, entered the chapel, where the children entertained them by singing a hymn, and "God save the King!"—Two more of these note-worthy military spectacles occurred this summer. On the fourth of July, his Majesty, in the presence of the Queen, reviewed the Surrey volunteers on Wimbledon Common; and on the first of August, the volunteer associations of Kent passed under his inspection in the Moat Park, the seat of the Earl of Romney, near Maidstone. At this latter spectacle, the Queen and the Princesses were present; and after the review, the royal family and the nobility partook of a sumptuous banquet in marquees erected on the lawn; whilst at tables, all of which were in view of the royal tent, upwards of six thousand volunteers sat down to a dinner consisting of every delicacy of the season.

The fifteenth of May, 1800, proved a most eventful day in the life of George III. In the morning, whilst his Majesty was inspecting the grenadiers' battalion of the guards in Hyde Park, and during the firing from centre to flank, a shot, from an undiscovered hand, was fired, which wounded a spectator, who stood only a few yards from the King. The same evening, the royal family visited Drury Lane Theatre, and as his Majesty entered the box, and was in the act of bowing to the audience, a pistol was fired at him by a person in the pit: the house was immediately in an uproar, and cries of "Seize him!" burst from every part of the theatre. The King, apparently not the least disconcerted, came nearly to the front of the box; at that moment the Queen entered, and inquired the cause of the confusion. The King waved his hand for her to keep back, and replied, "Only a squib, a squib; they are firing squibs for diversion." After the assassin had been seized, the Queen came forward, and in great agitation, curtsied. The Princesses, on learning what had happened, fainted away; and on recovering, they and the Queen urged his Majesty to return home; but he answered, "No, no, be calm; we will sit the performance out, for the danger is now over." They did so, greatly to the gratification of the audience; and at the end of the farce, "God save the King!" was sung, with the following additional verse, which had been written impromptu, and which was heartily encored by the whole house.

"From every latent foe,
From the assassin's blow,
God save the King!
O'er him thine arm extend,
For Britain's sake defend
Our father, prince, and friend,
God save the King!

The unhappy offender proved to be James Hatfield, an old soldier, who had served under the Duke of York on the continent, and had since become a lunatic. He was confined during the remainder of his life in Bethlehem Hospital.

On returning to the palace, the King, after bidding the Queen good night, observed, "I believe I shall sleep soundly; and my prayer is, that the poor prisoner who committed the rash assault upon me, may rest as calmly as I shall this night."

The next morning, the royal Dukes and the Prince of Wales, with an affectation of gratitude for their sire's preservation, which, at least, some of them scarcely could have felt, hastened to Buckingham House and took breakfast with the King, Queen, and the Princesses; after which a levee was held, which was crowded by a brilliant assemblage, who congratulated their Majesties on the King's escape.

The Queen was present when the King reviewed the Hertford Volunteers in the Marquis of Salisbury's demesne, at Hatfield, on the twelfth of June; and two days afterwards, she gave, in Frogmore Gardens, a grand open-air entertainment, which, in its general features, bore a striking resemblance to the popular Tivoli or Cremorne galas of the present day.—This summer their Majesties and the royal family made their accustomed annual progress to Weymouth, and after passing the time there, as usual, in bathing and excursions, returned, in October, to Windsor, where, on Christmas-day, the Queen provided a dinner for sixty of the poor, and an evening entertainment for the children of the inhabitants of the neighbourhood.

The legislative union with Ireland, a measure lauded by the Queen as the glory of her husband's reign, took effect on the first of January, 1801, when a royal proclamation announced the regal style and title as "George III., by the grace of God, of the United Kingdom of Great Britain and Ireland, King, Defender of the Faith." The King approved of the union, but resolutely rejected Mr. Pitt's propositions relative to Catholic emancipation; and in consequence, that gifted statesman, after being minister for more than seventeen years, resigned, and was succeeded by Mr. Addington, who had won the gratitude of her Majesty in the following singular manner: — In February, the King, whose mind had been greatly excited by the agitation in favour of Catholic emancipation and by the resignation of Mr. Pitt, was attacked with an illness resembling his former maniac malady, and which rendered him restless to that degree, that the medicines administered failed to produce repose. In this emergency, the anxious Queen, at the recommendation of Mr. Addington, caused a pillow of hops, in the stead of down, to be placed under the head of her suffering husband; who, to her infinite joy, from that moment began to recover, and on the twelfth of March was declared convalescent. From this circumstance Mr. Addington's political opponents sarcastically named him Dr. Addington.

The King, having purchased the former residence of the Duke of Gloucester at Weymouth, proceeded thither with the Queen at the close of June. This season their Majesties returned from Weymouth early in October, when the Queen took up her residence at Frogmore, where, at the close of the year, she entertained a select circle of friends with a grand gala.

With the spring of 1802, came the blessings of peace. The treaty of Amiens was signed on the twenty-fifth of March, but as it did not eradicate distrust, the elements of new strife speedily received ample support; and before the palm of peace had been planted a twelvemonth, it was torn up by a new war, which proved lasting and devastating, and at the very onset of which the French made themselves masters of Hanover, and collected an immense flotilla at Boulogne, for the purpose of invading England. The loss of Hanover greatly mortified the King and the Queen; but the threatened invasion gave such a vigorous impetus to patriotism, as to materially strengthen the hands of the government, and to afford their Majesties some consolation for the loss of the German electorate. The volunteers again flew to arms; and on the twenty-sixth of October the King reviewed upwards of 12,000 of these patriotic and loyal citizens, in the presence of the Queen, the royal family, the exiled princes of France, with their train, a brilliant assemblage of the nobility, and about 200,000 of the people. This grand military spectacle took place in Hyde Park, and, two days afterwards, was succeeded by the review of the Westminster, Lambeth, and Surrey volunteers, another and an equally interesting display of citizen soldiership, patriotism, and loyalty.

On the fourth of January, 1804, a superb regimental standard, the work of the hands of her Majesty and the Princesses, was presented by Lady Harrington, on behalf of her Majesty, to the Queen's Royal Volunteers at Ranelagh, with great pomp and ceremony. The Queen's birthday was this year kept with becoming magnificence, but the King was prevented from being present by an attack of indisposition which, by the middle of the subsequent month, assumed an aspect so alarming, that public prayers were offered up in all churches and chapels throughout the kingdom for his recovery. By the end of the month, however, the progressive amendment of the royal sufferer was reported; and, to the joy of his anxious consort and to all loyal subjects, he was pronounced convalescent at the close of March; and on the ninth, tenth, and eleventh of May, he rode with the Queen and Princesses through several of the streets of London.

At the close of August their Majesties went to Weymouth, where, on the twenty-ninth of September, in honour of the birthday of the Duchess of Wirtemberg, a grand aquatic fête was given to them on board the royal yachts. To this entertainment about two hundred and sixty of the nobility were invited. A Dutch fair was held after dinner, and the whole concluded with an interlude played by the principal performers from the London theatres.

On the second of November their Majesties returned to Windsor; and on the twelfth the King and the Prince of Wales, between whom the breach had been further widened by the royal sire refusing to appoint his heir-apparent to a post of active service in the army, had an interview at Kew, which, although friendly, disappointed the hopes of the Queen and the nation, by proving but a hollow reconciliation.

The year 1805 brought with it no cessation of arms. The ambitious Napoleon, who in the previous December had been crowned Emperor of France, aimed at nothing short of universal monarchy; and England, to oppose his designs, for a second time committed the helm of state to the vigorous guidance of Mr. Pitt. But although the land bristled with arms, and all other sounds were stifled or swallowed up by the hoarse note of war, the national spirit was not damped; and a brilliancy was imparted to the court at the commencement of the year, by a magnificent entertainment given by their Majesties at Windsor Castle, to upwards of four hundred of the nobility and world of fashion, and which consisted of a grand ball, music, cards and supper, and was succeeded on the subsequent day, the twenty-sixth of February, by a grand public breakfast, given by the Queen at Frogmore. As the spring advanced, the gaiety of the court was enhanced by one of those splendid festivals, a grand installation of the Knights of the Garter, which took place at Windsor Castle on the twenty-third of April, in the presence of the Queen, the Princesses, and a select company of the nobility. The summer, too, brought with it a series of royal entertainments; but their Majesties' domestic felicity was embittered with unfortunate differences which existed between the Prince and Princess of Wales, and the very serious charges brought against the latter.

This year, the Queen's real birthday, the ninth of May, was kept at Windsor Castle with great splendour; and on the eleventh her Majesty gave a comic German operatic entertainment in the outbuilding called the Barn, in her demesne at Frogmore, the characters being sustained by two German boys and two German girls, whose facetious acting delighted their Majesties, and produced roars of laughter from the noble spectators. On the twentieth of June, the Queen accompanied her beloved consort and the Princes and Princesses on a visit to Chelsea Hospital; and the royal party, after going over every part of that noble institution, were conducted by the Duke of York to view the Military Asylum, of which his Royal Highness was the founder and patron.

The annual royal visit to Weymouth took place this year; but the pleasure of the trip was diminished by the death of his Majesty's brother, the Duke of Gloucester, who expired on the twenty-fifth of August, in the sixty-second year of his age, and was interred with great funeral pomp in St. George's Chapel, Windsor.

Scarcely had the royal family returned from Weymouth, when news of the important naval victory of Trafalgar arrived; and their Majesties, in common with their subjects, whilst exulting over the signal triumph, deeply bemoaned the death of the hero Nelson, who in the early part of the action received a wound of which he expired about an hour afterwards.* Nelson's last signal, on going into the engagement was, "England expects every man to do his duty;" and we may, spite of alarmists and panic-mongers, confidently rely, that this signal, flying from the mast-heads of the English battle line in any future contest, will be followed by a hurricane of fire that shall wither up the mightiest force which the banded despots of the world could hope to array against the last bulwark of the liberties of Europe.

In the summer of 1806, the King's eye-sight, which had been slowly, but gradually failing, became dim, almost to blindness; and, in consequence, he could no longer attend the levees, and the fatigue of the drawing-room on his birth-day devolved wholly upon the Queen.

The investigation of the moral conduct of the Princess of Wales by an appointed committee, and her exclusion from court at this period, was a cause of intense public excitement. The Queen was accused of taking part in the persecution of the Princess; and although this charge was groundless, her Majesty certainly took umbrage at the conduct of her unhappy daughter-in-law; and in consenting to her re-admission to court, sacrificed her own inclination to the laudable desire of keeping the King's mind in a tranquil state.

At the close of this year her Majesty's troubles were increased, by her native country, the Duchy of Mecklenburg, falling a prey to the victorious French, who committed dreadful ravages throughout the whole duchy, and would not permit her to relieve the distresses of the unfortunate inhabitants.

In July, 1807, the aged Duchess of Brunswick—sister to George III., and mother of the Princess of Wales—whose family had been ruined by the successes of the French in Germany, arrived in England, a widowed exile, and was received by the King, the Queen, and the royal family, with becoming kindness and respect.

At this period their Majesties resided principally at Windsor, in comparative retirement; the infirmities of age prevented them from taking any very prominent part in public matters; but that senility had neither rendered them inactive, petulant, nor misanthropic, is evident from the subjoined trustworthy sketch of the private life of the royal family at Windsor at this period :—

"The King's mode of living is not quite so abstemious. He sleeps on the north side of the castle, next the terrace, in a roomy apartment, not carpeted, on the ground floor. The room is neatly furnished, partly in a modern style, under the tasteful direction of the Princess Elizabeth. The king's private dining-room, and the apartments *en suite*, appropriated to his Majesty's use, are all on the same side of the castle.

"The Queen and the Princesses occupy the eastern wing. When the King rises, which is generally about half-past seven, he proceeds immediately to the Queen's saloon, where his Majesty is met by one of the Princesses, generally either Augusta, Sophia, or Amelia; for each in turn attend their revered parent. From thence, the sovereign and his daughter, attended by the lady in waiting, proceed to the chapel in the castle, wherein divine service is performed either by the dean or sub-dean; the ceremony occupies about an hour. Thus the time passes till about nine, when the King, instead of proceeding to his own apartment, and breakfasting alone, now takes that meal with the Queen and the five Princesses. The table is always set out in the Queen's noble breakfasting-room, which has been recently decorated with very elegant modern hangings; and since the late improvements by Mr. Wyatt, commands a most delightful and extensive prospect of the little park. The breakfast does not occupy half an hour. The King and Queen sit at the head of the table, and the Princesses according to seniority. Etiquette in every other respect is strictly adhered to.

"After breakfast the, King generally

* Neither the King nor the Queen greatly respected Nelson, but they knew his worth as a naval warrior; and it was not the death of the man, but the loss of the hero, that they moaned.

rides out on horseback, attended by his equerries. Three of the Princesses, namely, Augusta, Sophia, and Amelia, are usually of the party. When the weather is unfavourable, the King retires to his favourite sitting-room, and sends for Generals Fitzroy or Manners, to play at chess with him. His Majesty, who knows the game well, is highly pleased when he beats the former, that gentleman being an excellent player.

"The King dines regularly at two, the Queen and Princesses at four. His Majesty visits and takes a glass of wine with them at five. After this period public business is frequently transacted by the King in his own study, wherein he is attended by his private secretary, Colonel Taylor. The evening is as usual passed at cards in the Queen's drawing-room, where three tables are set out. To these parties many of the principal nobility, and others residing in the neighbourhood, are invited. When the castle clock strikes ten, the visitors retire. The supper is set out; but that is a mere matter of form, and of which none of the family partake. These illustrious personages retire at eleven, to rest for the night. The journal of one day is the history of a whole year."

In the spring of 1809 their Majesties learned with sorrow, that charges of a serious nature had been brought against the Duke of York, by one Colonel Wardle, in the House of Commons. These charges, whether well or ill founded, were negatived by a majority of the Commons; but so fully accredited by the people, that in the end, the Duke, as an act of expediency, resigned his appointment as commander-in-chief, and was succeeded in that office by General Sir David Dundas.

This is not the only instance of the people making their voice heard in the present reign; but, although they occasionally opposed the measures of government, or even clamoured aloud against the King, the Queen, or their family, a new opportunity of testing the nation's loyalty invariably united all ranks and parties on the side of the sovereign and the constitution; and never, perhaps, was loyalty less equivocally manifested throughout the kingdom than on the twenty-fifth of October, 1809, when his Majesty entered the fiftieth year of his reign; and which was celebrated as a national jubilee and thanksgiving. On this auspicious day, the performance of divine service in the churches was succeeded by extraordinary festivities and illuminations; all business was laid aside; the whole nation dedicated the day to rejoicing, and the Queen gave a grand entertainment at Frogmore. What, however, is more worthy of record, throughout the empire the hungry were fed, the naked were clothed, schools and hospitals were endowed and founded; and the King, as an act of grace, pardoned all deserters, both military and naval; discharged all debtors confined for debts due to the crown, and granted an amnesty to all military delinquents.

CHAPTER VI.

Death of the Princess Amelia—Permanent insanity of the King—Queen appointed guardian of the King's person—Prince of Wales appointed Regent—Assassination of Mr. Perceval—Progress of the King's malady—Temporary overthrow of Napoleon—Peace—Visit from royal and noble foreigners—Princess of Wales excluded from the Queen's drawing-rooms—She departs the kingdom—Anecdote of the King—National jubilee—Return, and final fall of Napoleon—Peace firmly established—Marriage of the Duke of Cumberland and of the Princess Charlotte—Queen attends Ascot races—Marriage of her daughter Mary—Death of her brother, the Duke of Mecklenburg—She suffers from a spactic affection—Visits Bath—Death of the Princess Charlotte—Marriage of the Princess Elizabeth—Parliamentary grant to the royal dukes—Queen's last drawing-room; last appearance in public; last illness—She witnesses the marriages of the Dukes of Cambridge, Kent, and Clarence—Grows worse, and dies—Her conduct as a mother canvassed—Burial—Will—Death and burial of George III.—Final remarks.

ITH the year 1810 came to the King, Queen, and their court, prospects of felicity, which speedily proved fallacious; the Queen's birthday was kept with great splendour, but their Majesties' youngest daughter, the Princess Amelia, who was naturally delicate, and had long suffered from a painful malady, was attacked with symptoms of an alarming nature at the commencement of the year; grew worse as the summer advanced; and after much suffering, breathed her last, about noon, on the second of November, in the twenty-eighth year of her age. The King sedulously attended his dying and, perhaps, best-beloved daughter; whose last act of filial tenderness, was to place on his finger a ring containing a lock of her own hair; and whilst looking into his afflicted countenance, to articulate, with moving emphasis, "Dear father, remember me!"

Peter Pindar, the bitter satirist of George III. and his court, commemorated this touching scene in the subjoined lines, which, spite the paradox, bear witness to the at least seeming loyalty, and to the tender, pathetic powers of this gifted, but too exclusively wealth-seeking poet:—

"With all the virtues blest, and every grace
To charm the world and dignify her race;
Life's taper losing fast its feeble fire,
The fair Amelia thus bespoke her sire:—

"'Faint on the bed of sickness lying,
My spirit from its mansion flying;
Not long the light these languid eyes will see:
My friend, my father, and my king,
Oh! wear a daughter's mournful ring.
Receive the token, and remember me!'"

The remains of her Royal Highness, who was beloved by all who knew her, were privately interred on the fourteenth of November, in St. George's Chapel, Windsor, by torch-light. The Prince of Wales, and the Dukes of York and Clarence, attended the funeral, and were deeply affected during the performance of the last sad rites of humanity.

In the commencement of October, his Majesty's health and spirits had been visibly on the decline; and the perplexed state of public affairs, followed by the afflicting scene of the ring, a scene for which he had received no previous preparation, overpowered him with grief, and completing the work which disease had began, brought on a permanent return of that mental malady, with which he had formerly been only temporarily afflicted. He was incapable of business early in November; grew worse in December; and in consequence, the ministers in parliament proposed to appoint the Prince of Wales, under certain restrictions, Regent; and to commit the guardianship of the King's person, and control of the household, to the Queen and a council appointed for that purpose. To this measure, with some slight modifications, both houses, after violent opposition, agreed; and to their address, requesting her to undertake the duties assigned to her in the Regency Bill, her Majesty answered:—

"My Lords and Gentlemen,

"That sense of duty and gratitude to the King, and of obligation to this country, which induced me, in 1789, readily to promise my most earnest attention to the anxious and momentous trust at that time intended to be reposed in me by parliament, is strengthened, if possible, by the uninterrupted enjoyment of those blessings which I have continued to experience under the protection of his Majesty since that period; and I should be wanting in all my duties if I hesitated to accept the sacred trust which is now offered to me. The assistance, in point of council and advice, which the wisdom of parliament proposes to provide for me, will make me undertake the charge with greater hopes that I may be able satisfactorily to fulfil the important duties which it must impose upon me. Of the nature and importance of that charge, I cannot but be duly sensible, involving, as it does, everything that is valuable to myself, as well as the highest interests of a people endeared to me by so many ties and considerations; but by nothing so strongly as by their steady and affectionate attachment to the best of kings."

The Prince of Wales was sworn in before the privy council as Regent of the kingdom, on the fifth of February, 1811. Shortly afterwards, the King, who was confined in Windsor Castle, became more tranquil and collected; his physicians entertained hopes of his recovery; and by the middle of May he was so far restored to the possession of his faculties, that he inquired into the state of public affairs; on the nineteenth, proceeded to the Queen's apartments, and congratulated her on the return of her birthday; and the next day, attended by two equerries, and accompanied by the Princesses Augusta and Sophia, took a short ride out on horseback; but, to the deep sorrow of the Queen, and, in fact, of the whole nation, about six weeks afterwards, he suffered a severe relapse; and his mind became a dead blank, never again to be reinstated in its functions.

At the commencement of 1812, the parliament, after a vigorous resistance from the opposition, voted an addition of £10,000 a-year to her Majesty's income, to meet her extraordinary expenses; and shortly afterwards, the untimely death of Mr. Perceval, by assassination, in the lobby of the House of Commons, drew forth a strong expression of sympathy from both the Queen and the Regent. In the changes of administration which followed this calamitous event, Lord Sidmouth was appointed secretary of state, the Earl of Harrowby, lord president of the council; and Mr. Vansittart, chancellor of the exchequer.

Meanwhile, the King became totally blind, extremely deaf, and, towards the close of the year, suffered from frequent and violent paroxysms of delirium. But his system withstood the shock, and, the next year, he settled down into a state of gentle, harmless insanity. His general health continued good; but such was the deranged state of his mental faculties, that, to his attendants, it is said, he several times observed, "I must have a new suit of clothes; and I will have them black, in memory of George III."

Whilst thus overwhelmed with domestic affliction, the Queen had the gratification to find that the heroic efforts of the nation,. and its allies, to free Europe from the grasp of the too-aspiring Napoleon, were being crowned with success. The allied Sovereigns entered Paris on the thirty-first of March, 1814. Napoleon was deposed, and embarked for Elba on the twenty-eight of April. Louis XVIII. quitted his asylum in England, and, entering Paris on the third of May, took possession of the throne of his ancestors; and, on the thirtieth of May, peace was signed between England and France. This sudden and unlooked-for overthrow of the colossal power that recently had hurled defiance at the whole civilized world, was hailed with extravagant demonstrations of joy, in which the Queen heartily joined.

The Emperor of Russia, the King of Prussia, and other royal and noble foreigners, paid a visit to the English court, and were entertained with regal magnificence. The Queen honoured these august visitors by holding two grand drawing-rooms during their stay; but from these drawing-rooms she, in compliance with the expressed will of the Regent, excluded the Princess of Wales—an unpleasant proceeding, which was followed by an equally unpleasant correspondence, that was laid before the House of Commons, who, after a warm discussion, voted her Highness an annuity of £50,000; but she refused to accept more than £35,000, and shortly afterwards withdrew in disgust to the continent.

Although a confirmed lunatic, the King had occasional lucid intervals, but of only short duration. One day, during the visit of the illustrious foreigners, a deceptive promise of amelioration in his gloomy condition manifested itself, and the Queen visited him. She found him seated at a harpsichord, singing a hymn; he noticed her not, and, on concluding the solemn strain, he fell on his knees, and prayed aloud for his consort, his children, his people, and, finally, that the Almighty would either restore him to reason, or give him resignation to patiently bear the heavy affliction under which he laboured. This act of devotion concluded, he rose up, burst into tears, and the next minute was a raving maniac.

On the first of August, the day of the national jubilee festival in commemoration of the peace, and of the centenary of the accession of the House of Hanover, her Majesty gave a splendid dinner to the Regent and two hundred and fifty distinguished personages. The success of the Allies, and the restoration of peace, was to the Queen and to the nation a source of extreme gratification. But whilst the powers of Europe were devising measures to render the peace permanent, Napoleon again returned to France, the flame of war again blazed out, and a fearful struggle ensued, which, however, after a short space, terminated in the final fall of the heroic man of fate, after the memorable battle of Waterloo, and the establishment of a lasting peace, for which a solemn thanksgiving was offered up, on the eighteenth of January, 1816.

Meanwhile the Duke of Cumberland was married to the Princess of Solms-Braunfels, daughter of the reigning Duke of Mecklenburg-Strelitz, in the church of Strelitz, on the twenty-ninth of May, 1815, and at Carlton House, in conformity to the Royal Marriage Act, on the twenty-ninth of August. As the Queen opposed this match, on account of the King having previously disapproved of it, she refused either to receive the Duchess at Court, or to honour the nuptials with her presence; and, in reply to remonstrances and importunities on the subject, declared that "she could not think of taking advantage of the King's unconscious state to do that which she would not venture to do in opposition to his will and judgment."

At the commencement of 1816, the Queen, with the Princesses her daughters, and her granddaughter, the Princess Charlotte, paid a short visit to the Regent, at his marine palace, the Pavilion, at Brighton. Her Majesty had for years taken great interest in the Princess Charlotte; for her better education, she prevailed upon Mrs. Hannah More to produce that excellent work, entitled "Hints towards forming the Character of a Young Princess;" and when Prince Leopold of Saxe-Coburg arrived in England, in February, 1816, she expressed to him her approbation of his intended union with her royal granddaughter, entertained him at a grand fête, at Frogmore, on the twenty-sixth of April; and was present when the Princess Charlotte was married to him, with regal pomp, by the Archbishop of Canterbury, at Carlton House, on the second of May.

A fortnight afterwards, her Majesty held, at Buckingham House, a grand drawing-room, which, on account of the presence of the newly-wedded royal pair, was crowded to suffocation; and, as if to defy the infirmities of age, or, as some writers have it, that she might not be accused of neglecting to patronize a popular amusement, the Queen, this season, accompanied by the Princesses, publicly attended the races at Ascot. The spectacle entertained her: but she experienced far greater pleasure on the twenty-second of the following month, when, in the presence of herself and a numerous assemblage of the royal family and the nobility, the Princess Mary was married to the Duke of Gloucester, in the grand saloon at Buckingham House.

The melancholy tidings of the sudden death of the Queen's brother, the Grand Duke Charles of Mecklenburg-Strelitz, on the sixth of November, followed by the outrage offered to the Regent, in his return from opening the parliament, on the twenty-eighth of January, 1817, depressed her Majesty's spirits, visibly affected her health, and hastened the appearance of a spastic affection, which, on the night of the twenty-second of April, attacked her with such violence, that her physicians deemed it expedient to publish the subjoined bulletin:—"The Queen has had a cold, attended by some fever and pain in the side. Her Majesty found the pain severe in the night, but it is much abated this morning."

The Queen rapidly improved, and on the twenty-sixth, her convalescence was officially announced. But, withal, her health continued indifferent; although present with the Princesses and the Regent at a most brilliant Montem, or Etonian procession, on the twenty-seventh of May. On the third of November, however, accompanied by the Duke of Clarence and the Princess Elizabeth, she visited Bath, in the hope, if not of recovery of health—at least, of an alleviation of pain.

On the Thursday, a loyal address was presented to her by the Corporation, and, about four o'clock, arrived a dispatch from Lord Sidmouth, announcing that the Princess Charlotte had been delivered of a still-born male child, "but that her Royal Highness was doing extremely well." The news was afflicting, but, at six, the Queen sat down to dinner with her usual company of fourteen persons. During the dinner, she was surprised at General Taylor being privately called out of the room; but she expressed no concern till the Countess of Ilchester withdrew from the table in the same abrupt manner, when the truth flashed across her mind, and suddenly exclaiming, "I know what it is!" she fell to the ground in a fit. On recovering, she was informed that the Princess, after a protracted and painful labour, had expired at Claremont, on the sixth of November. Her distress could only be equalled by that of the Prince Regent, and of the nation at large. She returned, on Saturday, to Windsor Castle, and there, with the Princesses, remained in seclusion and sorrow till the funeral, which was solemnized on the eighteenth, with great pomp, at St. George's Chapel, Windsor.

Her Majesty again proceeded to Bath, at the end of November; and although, under the circumstances, no radical benefit from the mineral waters could have been expected, she returned to Windsor, apparently recruited in strength, and, on the twenty-sixth of February, 1818, held a drawing-room at Buckingham House, where, shortly afterwards (on the seventh of April), the Princess Elizabeth was married to the Prince of Hesse Homburg, in the presence of her Majesty and a numerous assemblage of the royal family, and various persons of distinction—a match evidently most desirable for the German potentate, whose whole revenue, it was said, did not exceed £3000.

At this period, the three royal Dukes of Clarence, Kent, and Cambridge, were about to enter into the holy estate of matrimony; a circumstance which induced the Regent to take necessary steps for the augmentation of the incomes of each of his royal brothers, except the Duke of Sussex. Lord Castlereagh proposed that a bonus of one year's income should be given to each of the Princes, and that their incomes should be raised—the Duke of Clarence's by £22,000 a year, and the Dukes of Kent, Cumberland, and Cambridge, by £12,000 a year each. This proposition, however, met with such strenuous opposition in the Commons, that the minister found it expedient to reduce the grants to £10,000 to the Duke of Clarence, and £6,000 a year to the three junior dukes. The sum named for the junior dukes was carried by a small majority; but on a division of 193 to 184, the grant proposed for the Duke of Clarence was reduced to £6,000, the same as that of his brothers, and the allowance to the Duke of Cumberland was negatived by a majority of 143 to 136. The resistance of the Commons deeply irritated the Regent, and so chagrined the Queen, that to Lord Castlereagh she observed, "Really, the house ought to be reprimanded, and that, too, from the throne, for its disloyalty and meanness."

Her Majesty's life was now fast drawing to a close; her last drawing-room she held on the twenty-third of April, and her last appearance in public was made about a week afterwards, when, in what is termed "half state," she proceeded to the Mansion House, to afford her patronage to the national schools of the metropolis. In this transit through the City, the mob, impressed with the conviction that the Queen hated their too-fondly idolized favourite, the Princess of Wales, greeted her with such an alarming and continuous volley of disloyal hissings, hootings, and groanings, that she became unwell, and afterwards, whilst dining at the Duke of York's, suffered a sudden and violent spastic attack, in consequence of which she was confined to her chamber till the close of May, when she recovered sufficiently to witness the remarriage of the Duke of Cambridge to the Princess of Hesse Cassel—a solemnity performed according to the rites of the Church of England at Buckingham House, on the first of June.

Spite a naturally sound and vigorous constitution, and the skilful efforts of her medical attendants, the disorder under which her Majesty laboured, slowly but visibly increased—the anasarcous symptoms which had long been visible, became so unequivocally marked, as to afford no hope of recovery. To, if possible, reduce the virulence of the malady by change of air, and with the view of at least spending her last moments under the same roof with her afflicted husband, who, although blind, deaf, and insane, continued to enjoy good health; she resolved to proceed to Kew, and thence to Windsor. The journey from Buckingham House to Kew was accomplished with great suffering, and the progress to Windsor was delayed, till it was found to be quite impossible to remove the royal sufferer, whose anxiety to again behold her beloved consort beguiled her into entertaining fallacious hopes of at least a partial recovery.

On the seventh of July, an attempt to take carriage airing brought on a violent relapse; but her Majesty so far recovered by the thirteenth, as to be able, on that day, to witness the nuptials of the Dukes of Kent and Clarence, who were respectively married to the Princesses Victoria of Saxe Coburg, and Adelaide of Saxe Meiningen, in the drawing room at Kew, according to the rites of the Church of England, and in conformity with the "Royal Marriage Act."

From this period to the nineteenth of October, her Majesty suffered from frequent paroxysms—spastic and anasarcous. Only during the first fortnights in August and in October, did the malady sufficiently subside to permit of her being occasionally wheeled in an easy chair from out the bed-chamber into an adjoining room; and on the night of Monday, the nineteenth of October, she suffered a severe relapse, attended with fever, violent spastic pangs, a hectic cough, and a restlessness which exhausted her strength, destroyed her appetite, and deprived her of sleep. The virulence of these symptoms continued, with only slight alternations, till the Thursday noon, when the paroxysms abated, and were succeeded by a lethargic repose, from which her Majesty awoke only to endure, if possible, more excruciating repetitions of the previous life-wearying pangs. In this state of extreme suffering, her Majesty lay till the last flickering spark of life was extinguished. The trial was severe, but she bore it without a complaining murmur. On the fourteenth, by scarification at both ancles, a considerable quantity of water was discharged, which afforded her some relief, but mortification ensued; and after completing her will, she, at twenty minutes past one, on the afternoon of the seventeenth, calmly expired in the arms of the Regent, and the presence of the Duke of York, the Duchess of Gloucester, and the Princess Augusta, at her favourite palace at Kew. The absence of the other Princes and Princesses from the death-bed of their mother, gave rise to a belief—we think unfounded—that as a parent, the Queen had neither acted wisely, well, nor affectionately.

Upon this subject, a contemporary,* after observing that the Duke of Cumberland was out of the question, says, "The inflexible, but well-meant determination of the Queen, to stigmatize her niece

* The Times newspaper.

by shutting the doors of the royal palace against her, may excuse strong feelings of estrangement or resentment on the part of the Duchess and her kindred; but that the Dukes of Clarence, Kent, and Cambridge, at the same time, should have quitted, as if by signal, their parent's death-bed, is a circumstance which in lower life would have at least astonished the community. The departure of the Princess Elizabeth, the Queen's favourite daughter, who married and took leave of her in the midst of that illness which was pronounced must shortly bring her to the grave, may, perhaps, have been owing to the express injunctions of her Majesty [there had been a difference between the royal mother and daughter, but they became reconciled before the latter left the kingdom]. The Duke of Gloucester stands in a more remote degree of relationship—Prince Leopold more distant still—but they all quitted the scene of suffering, at a period when its fatal termination could not be doubted; and as these have departed, it is no less apparent to common observers, that the Queen of Wirtemburg [Charlotte Augusta, eldest daughter of George and Charlotte] might have approached the bed of a dying mother, from whom, by the usual lot of princes, she has been so long separated, as that her royal parent has not accepted from her the performance of that painful duty."

The same journal further remarks, "That her Majesty's voluntary tastes were not exactly those which had been inferred from the habits of her matrimonial life, may be conjectured from the revolution which they seemed to undergo soon after the period when her royal husband ceased to exercise the supreme authority in this realm. At that period a transition was observed from grave to gay. The sober dignity, the chastened grandeur, the national character of the English court seemed to vanish with the afflicted sovereign. A new species of grandeur now succeeded, in which there was more of the exterior of royalty, and less of its becoming spirit. A long series of what was meant to be festivities, crowded balls, and elaborate suppers, glittering pomp, gaudy and gorgeous, yet fluttering decoration; reckless, capricious, yet never-ending profusion; all the apparatus of common place magnificence were introduced with the Regency, and countenanced, or apparently not discountenanced, by the Queen."

The journalist, in this paragraph, draws a wrong inference. That with the Regency was introduced at court a change from sober gravity to gaudy gaiety and glittering pomp, is an undisputed fact; but that the Queen did not discountenance the change, is as great an error as ever newspaper editor committed. A noble lord, now living, whose statement may be relied on, but whose name we have not the authority to mention, has assured us, that, on this occasion, her Majesty did send for the Regent, and sharply reproved him for not walking in the footsteps of his father; but that, after listening to his mother's lecture with evident impatience, this very *dutiful* son, with an angry air and tone which almost terrified the old Queen into hysterics, answered, "How dare you to question my conduct? I am as good as king, and, by G—d! if you again attempt to oppose my will, you will draw down upon you the wrath of him who is, in everything but name, your sovereign."

Queen Charlotte died in the seventy-fifth year of her age, and the fifty-eighth year of her marriage. Her remains lay in state at Kew with but little pomp, and for only six hours, on the first of December, and the next day they were interred in the royal mausoleum constructed by order of George III., beneath St. George's chapel, at Windsor. The funeral was public and pompous, but the attendance of peers and peeresses was remarkably thin, and the procession was too military in its character to be deemed appropriate.

The following is a copy of her Majesty's will.

"This is the last will and testament of me, Charlotte, Queen of the United Kingdom of Great Britain and Ireland.

"I direct all my debts, the probate of my will, and testamentary legacies, to be paid out of my personal property, or out of the value arising from the sale of the personals, if there should not, at the period of my death, be a sufficient sum in my treasury to provide for such legacies and annuities.

"My property consists of a real estate in New Windsor, called the Lower Lodge, and of personals of various descriptions, those of chief value being the jewels in the care and custody of ( ), or deposited ( ).

"These jewels are classed as follows:

"First, Those which the King bought for £50,000, and gave to me.

"Secondly, Those presented to me by the Nabob of Arcot.

"Thirdly, Those purchased by myself at various periods, or being presents made to me on birthdays and other occasions.

"In the event of the King, my husband, surviving me, and if it shall please the Almighty to relieve him from the dreadful malady with which he is at present afflicted; I give and bequeath to him the jewels which his Majesty purchased for the sum of £50,000, and gave to me as beforesaid; but if the King should not survive me, or if he should unfortunately not, previously to his death, be restored to a sound state of mind, then, and in that case only, I give and bequeath the said jewels to the House of Hanover, to be settled upon it, and considered as an heirloom in the direct line of succession of that House, as established by the laws and constitution of the House of Hanover.

"My eldest daughter, the Queen-Dowager of Wirtemburg, having been so long established in Germany, and being amply provided for in all respects, I give and bequeath the jewels received from the Nabob of Arcot to my four remaining daughters, or to the survivors or survivor, in case either, or any of them, should die before me; and I direct that these jewels shall be sold, and that the produce, subject to the charge and exceptions provided for in the first item in this my last will and testament, shall be divided among them my said four remaining daughters, share and share alike.

"I give and bequeath my remaining jewels to my four younger daughters aforesaid, or, in the event of either or any of them dying before me, to the survivors, to be divided in equal shares between them, according to a valuation to be made under the direction of my executors, to be hereafter named.

"The house and garden at Frogmore, and the Shawe estate, having been granted by act of Parliament of 1807 to my executors, administrators, and assigns for the term of ninety-nine years, if I and my four daughters residing in England should so long live, I conceive that these estates being so vested in me, I may dispose of them by will or by any other deed in writing, and in any manner I may think proper; I therefore give and bequeath my right and property in the lease and grant of the aforesaid estates of Frogmore and Shawe, with the several buildings thereon, to my eldest unmarried daughter, Augusta Sophia; but as the expense of keeping it up may prove too considerable for her means, it is my earnest desire and wish, and my will and pleasure, that the possession of the said house and buildings and estate should in that case revert to the crown, and that a due and sufficient compensation should be made to my said daughter Augusta Sophia, for the value of the lease and of the right and property arising from the parliamentary grant and from this my disposal of this property. It is also my earnest desire and hope, that in the valuation of such right and property, due attention may be paid to the improved state of the house and grounds and of the estates, and to their value as now established. In this expression of my wish and desire as to the disposal of the house and grounds at Frogmore, and of the Shawe estate, I am anxious that it should be clearly understood that my object is, that my daughter Augusta should receive in money the full value of that property, estimated according to my lease of it and the parliamentary grant, and with a due consideration to the improvements made, whether it shall please my beloved son the Prince Regent to reserve the possession of the said house and grounds and estate as an appendage to Windsor Castle, or to authorize any other disposal of them; and provided also, that the arrangement by which the payment of the amount of such valuation is secured to my said daughter Augusta Sophia, shall preclude any appropriation of the said house and grounds and estate, which shall be directed or authorized towards giving due and sufficient effect to this my last will in respect to the same.

"I further give and bequeath the fixtures, the articles of common household furniture, and the live and dead stock within the said house at Frogmore, or on the said estates, to my said daughter Augusta Sophia.

"I give and bequeath my real estate in New Windsor, purchased of the late Duke of St. Alban's, as specified in the abstract of deeds annexed to this my last will and testament, now commonly called the Lower Lodge, and its appendages and appurtenances, to my youngest daughter, Sophia.

"I give and bequeath my books, plate, house linen, china, pictures, drawings, prints, all articles of ornamental furniture, and all other valuables and personals, to be divided in equal shares according to a distribution and valuation to be made under the direction of my executors, among my four younger daughters aforesaid, saving and excepting such articles as shall be specified hereinafter, or in a codicil to this my last will and testament, or in a list annexed to it.

"Having brought from Mecklenberg various property as specified in the list No. I. annexed to this my last will and testament, it is my last will and pleasure that such property should revert to the House of Mecklenburg-Strelitz, and I direct that it shall be sent back to the senior branch of that house.

"I give and bequeath, as specified in the list No. II., annexed to this my last will and testament, to be paid out of the value of my personal property within six months after my death.

"I nominate and appoint Charles George Lord Arden and M. Gen. Herbert Taylor to be trustees of the property herein bequeathed to my daughters Elizabeth and Mary, which property is hereby left to them, independent of any husband they have or may have, for their sole benefit and use, and for which their receipt shall be a full discharge to the said trustees.

"I nominate and appoint Charles George Lord Arden and M. Gen. Herbert Taylor to be executors to this my will, and I do hereby declare this to be my last will and testament.

"In witness thereof, I, the said Charlotte, Queen of the United Kingdoms of Great Britain and Ireland, have to this my last will and testament set my hand and seal this sixteenth day of November, in the year of our Lord 1818.

"Signed, CHARLOTTE R. (seal).

"Sealed, published, and declared by the said Charlotte, Queen of the United Kingdoms of Great Britain and Ireland, as and for her last will and testament, in the presence of us, who in her presence and at her desire, and in the presence of each other, have hereunto subscribed our names; as witness hereof,

"H. TAYLOR,
"F. R. MILMAN,
"HENRY HALFORD."

The blanks in the will were, it is said, occasioned by her Majesty being unable at the time to recollect where or in whose hands the property referred to was placed; and it was ascertained that neither the list of property stated to be annexed to the will under the mark No. I., nor the list of bequests marked No. II. were so annexed; and the executors, after a diligent but unsuccessful search for such lists, took oath at Doctors' Commons, that they believed her Majesty had never prepared any, although she had signified to Herbert Taylor her intention so to do. The personal property was sworn to as being under £140,000. In compliance with the Queen's verbally-expressed intentions, a superb set of garnets were presented as a legacy to the Queen of Wirtemburg, and the whole of her Majesty's highly valuable wardrobe was given to her chief dresser, Madame Beckendorff.

On the demise of the Queen, the Duke of York accepted the office of custos of his insane father's person. The people did not object to the appointment; but when it was found that for performing this little more than act of filial duty the Duke was to receive £10,000 a year, they expressed astonishment and bitter indignation. The services of the well-paid royal guardian were, however, needed but for a comparatively brief period. The poor decrepid old king, now dead to all around him, and unconscious to all affairs of state, unable even to comprehend that his consort had been borne to the tomb, and existing only in a world of his own—a world of gentle, of loving spirits and imaginary angels, with whom alone he conversed—gradually became helpless as an infant, and at length, on the twenty-ninth of January, 1820, just a week after the death of his son, the Duke of Kent, he sunk calmly and unconsciously into the arms of death, in the eighty-second year of his age and the sixtieth of his reign. His remains were interred with great funeral pomp by the side of his Queen in St. George's Chapel, Windsor, on the seventeenth of February.

Of the numerous family of George and Charlotte, four became sovereigns: George and William, successive Kings of England; Ernest, King of Hanover; and Charlotte, Queen of Wirtemburg. The married daughters died childless. Of the married sons, only three left left legitimate issue. The King of Hanover, a son, who succeeded him in 1851; the Duke of Kent, a daughter, our present sovereign, whom God preserve; and the Duke of Cambridge, a son, the present Duke of Cambridge, and two daughters, Augusta, Grand Duchess of Mecklenburg-Strelitz, and the Princess Mary of Cambridge, not yet married. Thus the numerous children of Queen Charlotte, all of whom, saving the fourth daughter, the venerable Duchess of Gloucester, have followed their parents to the tomb, have left behind them but five representatives. The third generation, however, promises to be much more moral, intellectual, and liberal-minded than the first, and far more numerous than the second generation.

CAROLINE OF BRUNSWICK,

Queen of George the Fourth.

CHAPTER I.

Caroline's parentage—Birth—Education—Girlhood—Offers of marriage declined—Pecuniary embarrassment of George, Prince of Wales, afterwards George IV.—To procure a parliamentary settlement of his debts, he resolves to marry Caroline—The marriage agreed upon—Caroline's journey to England—Disappointing interview with the Prince—Marriage—Bride and bridegroom's quarrel—Settlement of the Prince's debts—The Princess's name inserted in the Liturgy—Caroline neglected by her husband—Treated with coolness by Queen Charlotte—Gives birth to the Princess Charlotte—Is separated from her husband—Retires to Montague House, Blackheath—Her revenue—Engaging manners of her daughter.

HE unfortunate Caroline Amelia Elizabeth, daughter of Charles William Ferdinand, Duke of Brunswick Wolfenbuttle, and his consort, the Princess Augusta, of England, was born on the seventeenth of May, 1768. She was the second child of a family of six; her only sister, Charlotte, entered the world in December, 1764; and her brothers, Charles, George, William, and Leopold, were respectively born in 1767-9, 1771 and 1772. But little attention was paid to her education, and she grew up a forward, sharp-witted, warm-hearted, hasty, self-willed, indiscreet maiden. She was a clever pianist, an excellent vocalist, an expert manufacturer of toys and trinkets; a fearless, giddy romp; a brilliant conversationalist; and a sayer of dashing repartees and witticisms: but many of her remarks were censurably free and unbecoming; she was pert, froward, self-sufficient to a fault, and, unfortunately, almost a stranger to the true principles of religion and morality. Whilst but yet on the threshold of womanhood, she received and promptly declined offers of marriage from Prince George of Darmstadt, from the Prince of Orange, and other distinguished suitors; and then she had the misfortune to fix her affections on a handsome young German prince, whom she could not marry: but about this period she was invited by the Court of Britain to enter into the estate of matrimony with the heir-apparent, George, Prince of Wales—a tempting invitation, which her father prompted—by some accounts, forced—her to accept.

All that is known of the circumstances which led to the marriage of the Princess Caroline, may be thus briefly narrated:—The Prince of Wales had for years been running a round of profligacy and crime; the Royal Marriage Act prevented him from lawfully marrying whom he chose; and this fact he made an excuse for forming immoral connexions with Perdita Robinson, Mrs. Fitzherbert, whom he illegally married, the Countess of Jersey, Mrs. Crouch, and many other frail ladies. He was also a great gambler and spendthrift. The parliament paid his debts without much ado in 1787; but seven years afterwards, when overwhelming pecuniary embarrassments compelled him to again apply to his father for assistance, that assistance was only promised on condition of his marrying according to the will of his royal parent. To this condition the Prince agreed; and the King immediately fixed upon Caroline of Brunswick, as a suitable partner for his profligate heir. Into making this unfortunate choice, George III., it is said, was deceived by the *couleur de rose* report of the Duke of York, who, just previously, had passed some time at the ducal court of Brunswick, in the society of the talented and well-meaning, but highly indiscreet Caroline; and of whose character he had formed a most flattering, but, in many respects, erroneous opinion.

In November, 1794, Lord Malmesbury was dispatched to the court of Brunswick, to settle the marriage preliminaries, marry the Princess by proxy, and bring her to England. On his arrival, he was heartily welcomed by Caroline, her parents, and their court. He found the Princess to be prepossessing in appearance, but dirty in habits; and in manners and morals exceedingly deficient. He also found that her father openly kept a mistress; that her mother was wanting in mind and principle; and that one-half of the court drank, and that they and the other half were neither cleanly in habits, elegant in manners, nor chaste in conversation. He foresaw that the marriage would be likely to bring misery to the bride and bridegroom; but as his instructions were imperative, and as Major Hislop, who arrived on the third of December, with a portrait of the Prince—in return for that of the Princess, which had previously been sent to England—brought a dispatch, commanding him to hasten his return to England with the much-wished-for bride; he caused the marriage to be performed by proxy on the eighth of December; and after the event had been celebrated with all imaginary festivity and hilarity, he, on the twenty-ninth of the same month, set out with his precious charge *en route* for England.

From kindred and associates Caroline parted as royal young ladies always do part from their parents and friends, when about proceeding to the home of a husband whom they neither love nor know—with an abundance of tears, regrets, fears, and hopes. She set out on her journey, attended by her mother and a splendid retinue; and she treated with the most marked respect and veneration Lord Malmesbury, who, as well as proxy-lover, played mentor to her; and took every opportunity to store her mind with wise counsel, by which she promised to profit, but which she forgot immediately on landing in England.

The journey was tedious and peril-fraught. England and Holland were at war with France; and the various features which this war assumed, at one time impelled the royal travellers onward, and at another forced them to hastily retrace their path to the town they had last left, and change their route; whilst their discomfiture was increased by the weather being bitterly cold. After an unavoidable detention at Osnaburg, which they had reached with difficulty, they again set forth, and on the twenty-fourth of January, 1795, entered Hanover, where they tarried till the twenty-fourth of March. During this sojourn, Lord Malmesbury had two long and serious conversations with the Princess Caroline—one on the toilette and cleanliness; the other on delicacy of speaking. His remark made a temporary impression. "But," he writes, "on these, as on all other subjects, I had too many opportunities to observe that her heart is very, *very* light, unsusceptible of strong or lasting feeling."*

At Hanover the mother parted from the bride, who, with Mrs. Harcourt, Mrs. Aston, Mrs. St. Leger, Lord Malmesbury, and her suite, arrived at Stade, on the twenty-seventh of March, embarked the next day on board the Jupiter, a fifty-gun ship, and, guarded by a

* Lord Malmesbury's Diary.

British fleet, put to sea. After a tolerably fair voyage, the Jupiter reached the Nore, on the evening of Friday, the third of April, and the next day anchored off Gravesend, whence, on the following morning, the Princess went on board one of the royal yachts, and ascended the Thames to Greenwich Hospital, where she landed at mid-day, amidst the deafening huzzas of thousands of spectators.

The governor of the hospital received her with all possible respect; to her chagrin, however, the carriages from court did not arrive till an hour afterwards, and then not the bridegroom, but Lady Jersey, one of his mistresses, came, with a retinue of nobles and ladies, to welcome her to London. After Lady Jersey had sneered at her dress, and robed her in elegant white satin, with a superb turban cap, also of satin, ornamented with a plume of white feathers, in imitation of the Prince of Wales' crest, and studded with diamonds—a present from the Prince—she again proceeded forward, escorted by the Prince's regiment of Light Dragoons; and, a little before three in the afternoon, alighted at St. James's, and was introduced into the apartments prepared for her reception, looking into Cleveland Row. Immediately her arrival was formally announced, the Prince of Wales paid her a visit, which Lord Malmesbury thus details in his Diary :—

"I, according to the established etiquette, introduced (no one else being in the room) the Princess Caroline to him. She very properly, in consequence of my saying to her it was the right mode of proceeding, attempted to kneel to him. He raised her (gracefully enough), and embraced her, said barely one word, turned round, retired to a distant part of the apartment, and calling me to him, said, 'Harris, I am not well; pray get me a glass of brandy.' I said, 'Sir, had you not better have a glass of water?' Upon which he, much out of humour, said, with an oath, 'No, I will go directly to the Queen.' And away he went. The Princess, left during this short moment alone, was in a state of astonishment; and on my joining her, said in French, 'My God! is that the Prince? He is large, coarse, and by no means so fine as his portrait.'" In fact, bride and bridegroom were both disappointed with each other's manners and appearance; and before many days had elapsed, this disappointment was succeeded by a fixed disgust, at least, on the part of the latter, who, to drown his trouble, had recourse to the bottle.

On the evening of the eighth of April, the unfortunate marriage was celebrated with great pomp and splendour in the chapel-royal of St. James's, by the Archbishop of Canterbury. The procession proceeded from the state drawing-rooms to the chapel, with a sombre solemnity more befitting a funeral than a wedding. The King, who, together with the Queen, took part in the ceremony, gave the bride away with a heartiness which cheered her drooping spirits, and shed a gleam of sunshine over the otherwise gloomy scene. The bridegroom was too inebriated to stand, and whilst kneeling at the altar, during the progress of the solemn service, glared wildly around him, and rose up, with the seeming intention of rushing from his compulsory fate. The archbishop paused; when the King, with becoming presence of mind, stepped forward, and with a whisper, prevailed upon the Prince to again kneel till the service, which linked together in matrimony two unloving hearts, was brought to a not very happy conclusion. After the procession had returned to the palace, the King and Queen held a brilliant drawing-room, which was followed by a sumptuous supper in the Queen's palace, whence, at midnight, the bridegroom and bride retired to Carlton House, snapping and snarling at each other by the way like two angry dogs. "Judge," observed Caroline to one of her attendants some time afterwards, "what it is to have a drunken husband on one's wedding day; and one who passes the greater part of his bridal night under the fire-grate where he fell, and where I left him. If any one say to me at dis moment, Will you pass your life over again or be killed? I would choose death; for you know, sooner or later, we must all die, but to live a life of wretchedness twice over, oh! mine G—d! no, never."* Such was the unhappy marriage of George and Caroline; a marriage celebrated by booming of guns, illuminations, and ringing of bells, and hailed by all ranks and orders of British subjects with unbounded enthusiasm.

The Prince and Princess were felicitated on their union by addresses from the city of London and other places; but to these the Prince, at least, paid but little regard. His debts amounted to the enormous sum of £619,570, and their liquidation was the almost sole object of his attention. Mr. Pitt brought this subject before parliament; and the Commons and Lords, after much warm discussion, agreed to settle upon the Prince £125,000 per annum, together with the revenue of the Duchy of Cornwall, estimated at £13,000; and granted the Princess a jointure of £80,000 a year; but out of the Prince's revenue, the annual sum of £73,000 was to be appropaiated for the settlement of his debts within the period of nine years, under the direction of parliamentary commissioners; a measure which, as George had married for the sole purpose of having his debts cleared off at once, was declared, both by him and his brothers, to be a gross violation of compact; and, moreover, was followed by disgraceful parliamentary debates, which more fully proved to the unfortunate Princess the real purpose for which she had been made a wife.

Meanwhile the newly-married pair, accompanied by all the royal family, visited Covent Garden Theatre; and the name of the Princess was introduced in the prayer for the royal family in the liturgy of the Church of England. But the Prince made evident the line of conduct he intended to pursue as a husband, by taking the Princess on a visit to the King and Queen at Windsor, and also taking with him his mistress, Lady Jersey. Galled by this mark of conjugal contempt, the ill-fated bride wept and stormed, but entreaties and threats were alike vain; the Queen, and nearly the whole of the royal family, saving the King, treated her with marked coolness; and her ill-doing husband shut her up in the Pavilion, at Brighton, whilst he, in London, was enjoying the society of Mrs. Fitzherbert, to whom, some time previously, he had been privately married—a secret which at this period Caroline had the extreme mortification to discover. However, the Princess, as before stated, was herself far from faultless. A packet of letters in which she had unwisely spoken ill of the Queen, and which the Rev. Dr. Randolph was to have delivered to her relations and friends in Brunswick, never reached their destination; and by some mysterious means they fell into the hands of the Queen, who opened them, read them—an unwarrantable liberty, by the by—and ever afterwards treated her indiscreet daughter-in-law with coldness and contempt.

Thus stood matters when Caroline gave birth to the Princess Charlotte. This event took place between nine and ten o'clock in the morning of the seventh of January, 1796, in the presence of the Duke of Gloucester, (brother to the King,) the Archbishop of Canterbury, the Lord Chancellor, the Lord President of the Council, the Lord Chamberlain, the ladies of her Highness's bedchamber, and other lords and ladies. The addresses of congratulation to the Prince and his parents were numerous; but the Prince refused to receive that of the City of London in public, under a plea that the inadequacy of his establishment, which the necessity of paying off his debts had impelled him to reduce, prevented him from giving a formal reception with the dignity befitting his exalted station: a plea which so offended the members of the Corporation, that they refused to depart from the customary form, and the address was never presented.

The Prince, indeed, was neither a "happy father" nor a "loving husband," and he had no wish to be congratulated as such, at the period when he was seriously contemplating a separation from his so-called "beloved consort." He deputed

* Diary, illustrative of the Court, &c. of George IV.

Lady Cholmondeley to inform the Princess that he desired to be separated from her; Caroline requested his desire in writing, and also wished it to be understood that, if the proposed separation was effected, the former intimacy should not, under any circumstances, be renewed. Immediately afterwards, Caroline received the subjoined letter:—

"MADAM,

"As Lord Cholmondeley informs me that you wish I would define in writing the terms upon which we are to live, I shall endeavour to explain myself upon that head, with as much clearness, and with as much propriety, as the nature of the subject will admit. Our inclinations are not in our power, nor should either of us be held answerable to the other, because nature has not made us suitable to each other. Tranquil and comfortable society is, however, in our power; let our intercourse, therefore, be restricted to that, and I will distinctly subscribe to the conditions which you required through Lady Cholmondeley, that even in the event of any accident happening to my daughter—which I trust Providence in its mercy will avert —I shall not infringe the terms of the restriction by proposing at any period a connection of a more particular nature. I shall now finally close this disagreeable correspondence, trusting that, as we have completely explained ourselves to each other, the rest of our lives will be passed in uninterrupted tranquillity.

"I am, Madam,
"With great truth,
"Very sincerely yours,
"GEORGE, P."

To the above epistle, Caroline replied by a letter in French, of which the subjoined is a translation:—

"The avowal of your conversation with Lord Cholmondeley neither surprises nor offends me; it merely confirms what you have tacitly intimated for this twelvemonth; but, after this, it would be a want of delicacy, or rather an unworthy meanness, in me, were I to complain of those conditions which you impose upon yourself.

"I should have returned no answer to your letter, if it had not been conceived in terms to make it doubtful whether this arrangement proceeds from you or from me; and you are aware that the credit of it belongs to you alone. The letter which you announce to me as the last, obliges me to communicate to the King, as to my sovereign and my father, both your avowal and my answer. You will find enclosed the copy of my letter to the King: I apprize you of it, that I may not incur the slightest reproach of duplicity from you. As I have at this moment no protector but his Majesty, I refer myself solely to him upon this subject; and if my conduct meet his approbation, I shall be in some degree consoled. I retain every sentiment of gratitude for the situation in which I find myself, as Princess of Wales, enabled by your means to indulge in the free exercise of a virtue dear to my heart—I mean charity. It will be my duty likewise to act upon another motive—that of giving an example of patience and resignation under every trial. Do me the justice to believe that I shall never cease to pray for your happiness, and to be

"Your much devoted
"CAROLINE."

Shortly after the receipt of the previously-quoted letter from the Prince, Caroline was finally, but not formally, separated from her persecuting husband. She retired to Charlton, near Woolwich, but shortly afterwards was appointed Ranger of Greenwich Park, and took up her abode at Montague House, Blackheath, where, without a court, and with but few attendants, she passed a life of mingled mirth and sadness. After a period, her revenue was settled at about £20,000 per annum, towards which the Prince contributed £12,000. Upon this income she lived in comparative content, and directed her attention to gardening, the education of poor children, and other laudable objects; but, being naturally indiscreet, she unwisely indulged in the games of blind-man's-buff, hunt the slipper, and other romping sports and pastimes.

Caroline had resided at Blackheath but a short while, when her daughter Charlotte was removed to Shrewsbury House, near Shooter's Hill, and permitted an interview with her but once a-week.

In August, 1801, Dr. Porteus, Bishop of London, paid the young Princess Charlotte a visit, and was so charmed by her manners, that he thus mentioned the interview in his diary:—"She [the Princess] is a most captivating and engaging child. . . . She repeated to me several hymns with great correctness and propriety; and on being told, when she went to Southend, in Essex (as she afterwards did, for the benefit of sea-bathing), she would then be in my diocese, she fell down on her knees and asked my blessing."

CHAPTER II.

Caroline becomes intimate with Sir John and Lady Douglas—Adopts the infant boy Austin—Breaks off her intimacy with the Douglases—Serious charges brought against her by Lady Douglas—The Delicate Investigation—She refutes the charges of her calumniators—Is acquitted of gross wrong, but reprimanded for levity—Her husband prevails on the King to put off her reception at court—Publication of "THE BOOK"*—Caroline at length received at court—Her last personal interview with her husband—Her widowed mother flies to England—Pecuniary embarrassment—Formal separation from her husband.*

N November, 1801, Caroline had the misfortune to form a very intimate acquaintance with her neighbours, Sir John and Lady Douglas, by the latter of whom the singular commencement of this acquaintance is thus mentioned:—

"In the month of November, when the ground was covered with snow, as I was sitting in my parlour, which commanded a view of the heath, I saw, to my surprise, the Princess of Wales, elegantly dressed in a lilac satin pelisse, primrose-coloured half-boots, and a small lilac satin travelling-cap, faced with sable, and a lady pacing up and down before the house, and sometimes stopping, as if desirous of opening the gate in the iron-railing to come in. At first I had no conception that her Royal Highness really wished to come in, but must have mistaken the house for another person's, for I had never been made known to her, and I did not know that she knew where I lived. I stood at the window, looking at her, and as she looked very much, from respect curtsied (as I understood was customary); to my astonishment she returned my curtsey by a familiar nod, and stopped. Old Lady Stuart, a West Indian lady who lived in my immediate neighbourhood, and who was in the habit of coming in to see me, was in the room, and said, 'You should go out; her Royal Highness wants to come in out of the snow.'

"Upon this I went out, and she came immediately to me and said, 'I believe you are Lady Douglas, and you have a beautiful child; I should like to see it.' I answered her that I was Lady Douglas. Her Royal Highness then said, 'I should like of all things to see your child.' I answered, I was very sorry I could not have the honour of presenting my little girl to her, as I and my family were spending the cold weather in town, and I was only come to pass an hour or two upon the Heath. I held open the gate, and the Princess of Wales and her lady, Miss Heyman (I believe), walked in and sat down, and stayed about an hour, laughing very much at Lady Stuart, who, being a singular character, talked all kind of nonsense."

When the intimacy, thus commenced between Caroline and Lady Douglas, had ripened into familiar friendship, the former, for some strange, unaccountable reason, took under her own especial charge and keeping a young infant, who was proved to have been born of Mrs. Austin, the wife of a poor dockyard labourer, in Brownlow Street Hospital, on the eleventh of July, 1802. Some time afterwards, the Princess, on being cautioned that Lady Douglas was a "dangerous character," broke off the intimacy, and declined to explain her reasons for so doing. The Douglases, annoyed at this treatment, and at having received anonymous letters, and a disgusting drawing, of which they expressed a belief that Caroline was the authoress, so contrived, that these and other matters were brought to the knowledge of the Dukes of Kent and Sussex, the latter of whom carried the information to the Prince of Wales, at whose request Lady Douglas made a long and most indelicate statement, to the effect that Caroline was low, coarse, and immoral in language, manners, and conduct; that she had indulged in illicit amours; that she was the mother of the child, Austin; and that she had endeavoured to corrupt the morality of Lady Douglas, and otherwise conducted herself in a manner most unbecoming and wicked. The formal attestation of this startling statement was followed by the examination of witnesses before a commission.

On the eleventh of January, 1806, William Cole, formerly page to the Princess, asserted that some years previously "*he had seen* Mr. Canning several times *alone* with her Royal Highness for an hour together," and that he was dismissed from Montague House, because, in 1802, the conduct between her Royal Highness and Sir Sidney Smith had one day startled him into giving a "significant look at the gentleman." He added, that since his dismission, Fanny Lloyd had assured him, there were "delightful things amongst them," and that her Royal Highness was guilty of gross improprieties with Captain Manby.

In conclusion, he detailed conduct equally disgraceful which he had witnessed himself, he said, between Caroline and "Sir Thomas Lawrence the painter."—Robert Bidgood, who had been twenty-three years in the service of the Prince, and seven years in that of the Princess, gave evidence against his royal mistress which will not bear to be repeated. It was him who swore, that one day he saw, by the reflection of a mirror, "Captain Manby kiss the lips of the Princess, who shed tears when the captain left her." Several of Caroline's female servants went even further than Bidgood in their evidence against her, and the consequence was, that on the twenty-ninth of May, 1806, the King issued his warrant, directing Lords Erskine, Spencer, Granville, and Ellenborough, to examine into the truth of these startling assertions, and report the result to his Majesty. The witnesses underwent a searching examination upon oath before these commissioners, and their statements frequently differed from their previous depositions. However, after a lengthened investigation, the commissioners brought their by no means agreeable labours to a close, and drew up the subjoined report:—

"May it please your Majesty,

"Your Majesty having been graciously pleased by an instrument under your Majesty's royal sign manual, a copy of which is annexed to this report, to authorise, empower, and direct us to inquire into the truth of certain written declarations touching the conduct of her Royal Highness the Princess of Wales, an abstract of which had been laid before your Majesty; and to examine upon oath such persons as we should see fit, touching and concerning the same, and to report to your Majesty the result of such examinations: we have, in dutiful obedience to your Majesty's commands, proceeded to examine the several witnesses, the copies of whose depositions we have hereunto annexed; and in further execution of the said commands, we now most respectfully submit to your Majesty the report of the examinations as it has appeared to us. But we beg leave at the same time humbly to refer your Majesty for more complete information to the examinations themselves, in order to correct any error of judgment in which we may have unintentionally fallen, with respect to any part of this business. On a reference to the above-mentioned declarations, as the necessary foundation of all our proceedings, we found that they consisted in certain statements which had been laid before his Royal Highness the Prince of Wales, respecting the conduct of her Royal Highness the Princess of Wales; that these statements not only imputed to her Royal Highness great impropriety and indecency of behaviour, but expressly asserted, partly on the ground of certain alleged declarations from the Princess's own mouth, and partly on the personal observations of the informants, the following most important facts, viz.—That her Royal Highness had been pregnant in the year 1802, in consequence of an illicit intercourse, and that she had in the same year been secretly delivered of a male child, which child had ever since that period been brought up by her Royal Highness in her own house, and under her immediate inspection.

"These allegations thus made, had, as we found, been followed by declarations from other persons, who had not indeed spoken to the important facts of the pregnancy or delivery of her Royal Highness, but had stated other particulars in themselves extremely suspicious, and still more so when connected with the assertions already mentioned. In the very painful situation in which his Royal Highness was placed by the communications, we learnt that his Royal Highness had adopted the only course which could, in our judgment, with propriety be followed: when informations such as these had been confidently alleged, and particularly detailed, and had been in some degree supported by collateral evidence, applying to other points of the same nature, (though going to far less extent), one line could only be pursued. Every sentiment of duty to your Majesty, and of concern for the public welfare, required that these particulars should not be withheld from your Majesty, to whom more particularly belonged the cognizance of a matter of state, so nearly touching the honour of your Majesty's royal family, *and by possibility affecting the succession of your Majesty's crown.* Your Majesty had been pleased on your part to view the subject in the same light. Considering it as a matter which in every respect demanded the most immediate investigation, your Majesty had thought fit to commit into our hands the duty of ascertaining, in the first instance, what degree of credit was due to the informations, and thereby enabling your Majesty to decide what further conduct to adopt concerning them. On this review, therefore, of the matters thus alleged, and of the course hitherto pursued upon them, we deemed it proper, in the first place, to examine those persons in whose declarations the occasion for this inquiry had originated; because if they, on being examined on oath, had retracted or varied their assertions, all necessity of further investigation might possibly have been precluded. We accordingly first examined on oath the principal informants, Sir John Douglas and Charlotte his wife, who both positively swore, the former to his having observed the fact of the pregnancy of her Royal Highness, and the latter to all the important particulars contained in her former declarations, and above referred to. Their examinations are annexed to this report, and are circumstantial and positive. The most material of those allegations, into the truth of which we have been directed to inquire, being thus far supported by the oath of the parties from whom they had proceeded, we then felt it to be our duty to follow up the inquiry, by the examination of such other persons as we judged the best able to afford us information as to the facts in question. We thought it beyond all doubt, that, in the course of inquiry, many particulars must be learnt which would be necessarily conclusive on the truth or falsehood of these declarations, so many persons must have been witnesses to the appearance of an actual existing pregnancy, also many circumstances must have been attendant upon a real delivery, and difficulties so numerous and insurmountable must have been involved in any attempt to account for the infant in question, as the child of another woman, if it had been in fact the child of the Princess, that we entertained a full and confident expectation of arriving at complete proof, either in the affirmative or negative, on this part of the subject.

"This expectation was not disappointed. We are happy to declare our perfect conviction that there is no foundation whatever for believing that the child now with the Princess of Wales is the child of her Royal Highness, or that she was delivered of any child in the year 1802; nor has anything appeared to us which would warrant the belief that she was pregnant in that year, or at any period within the compass of our inquiries. The identity of the child now with the Princess, its parents, age, the place of its birth, the time and circumstances of its being taken under her Royal Highness's protection, are all established by such a concurrence both of positive and circumstantial evidence, as can in our judgment leave no question on this part of the subject. That child was beyond all doubt born in Brownlow Street Hospital, on the eleventh day of July, 1802, of the body of Sophia Austin, and was first brought to the Princess's house in the month of November following. Neither should we be more warranted in expressing any doubt respecting the alleged pregnancy of the Princess, as stated in the original declaration, a fact so fully contradicted, and by so many witnesses, to whom, if true, it must, in various ways be known, that we cannot think it entitled to the smallest credit. The testimonies on these two points are contained in the annexed depositions and letters. We have not partially abstracted them in this report, lest by any unintentional omission we might weaken their effect; but we humbly offer to your Majesty this our clear and unanimous judgment upon them, formed upon full deliberation, and pronounced without hesitation, on the result of the whole inquiry. We do not, however, feel ourselves at liberty, much as we should wish it, to close our report here. Besides the allegation of the pregnancy and delivery of the Princess, those declarations, on the whole of which your Majesty has been pleased to command us to inquire and report, contain, as we have already remarked, other particulars respecting her Royal Highness, such as must, especially considering her exalted rank and station, necessarily give occasion to very unfavourable interpretations. From the various depositions and proofs annexed to this Report, particularly from the examinations of Robert Bidgood, William Cole, Francis Lloyd, and Mrs. Lisle, your Majesty will perceive that several strong circumstances of this description have been positively sworn to by witnesses, who cannot, in our judgment, be suspected of any unfavourable bias, and whose veracity in this respect we have seen no ground to question.

"On the precise bearing and effects of the facts thus appearing, it is not for us to decide; these we submit to your Majesty's wisdom; but we conceive it to be our duty to report on this part of the inquiry, as distinctly as on the former facts, that, as on the one hand, the facts of pregnancy and delivery are to our minds satisfactorily disproved; so, on the other hand, we think that the circumstances to which we now refer, particularly those stated to have passed between her Royal Highness and Captain Manby, must be credited until they shall receive some decisive contradiction; and, if true, are justly entitled to the most serious consideration. We cannot close this Report without humbly assuring your Majesty, that it was on every account our anxious wish to have executed this delicate trust with as little publicity as the nature of the case would possibly allow; and we entreat your Majesty's permission to express our full persuasion, that, if this wish has been disappointed, the failure is not imputable to anything unnecessarily said or done by us; all which is most humbly submitted to your Majesty.

"Erskine.
"Spencer.
"Grenville.
"Ellenborough."

This Report, dated the fourteenth of July, 1806, and accompanied by the several depositions, was immediately presented to his Majesty; but nearly a month elapsed before Caroline received a copy of it, and then the depositions and other important matter were kept from her till the commencement of September; in fact, she was not permitted to meet her accusers face to face, nor even made acquainted with the nature of their evidence against her till some time afterwards. During this painful period, although acquitted of the grosser charge, she was held to have been guilty of immorality, both by the report of the commissioners and by the declared conviction of her husband, his friends, and party.

She was commanded not to enter the royal presence until she had proved herself, in legal language, *not guilty;* and being thus excluded from court on account of alleged crimes, to disprove which no opportunity had been permitted her, Mr. Perceval (one of her many talented friends), in a most able appeal to the King in her behalf, denied the charges brought against her, pointed out discrepancies in the evidence of the witnesses, proved her to be a most hardly-used Princess, and implored for her the favour and protection of his Majesty.

In this memorial, which is far too lengthy to be inserted in these pages, Caroline observes, "With respect to the fact of Sir Sidney Smith visiting frequently at Montague House, both with Sir John and Lady Douglas and without them; with respect to his being frequently there at luncheon, dinner, and supper, and staying with the rest of the company till twelve o'clock, or even sometimes later; if these are some of the facts 'which must give occasion to unfavourable interpretations, and must be credited till contradicted,' they are facts which I never can contradict, for they are perfectly true. And I trust it will imply the confession of no guilt to admit that Sir Sidney Smith's conversation, his account of the various and extraordinary events and heroic achievements in which he has been concerned, amused and interested me, and the circumstance of his living so much with his friends, Sir John and Lady Douglas, in my neighbourhood on Blackheath, gave the opportunity of increasing his acquaintance with me. * * * As for the circumstance of my permitting him to be in the room alone with me—if suffering a man to be so alone is evidence of guilt from whence the commissioners can draw any unfavourable inference—I must leave them to draw it; for I cannot deny that it has happened, and happened frequently, not only with Sir Sidney Smith, but with many other gentlemen who have visited me; tradesmen who have come to receive my orders, masters whom I have had to instruct me in painting, in music, in English, &c., that I have received them without any one being by; in short, I trust I am not confessing a crime, for unquestionably it is a truth that I never had any idea that there was anything wrong or objectionable in thus seeing men in the morning; and I confidently believe your Majesty will see nothing in it from which any guilt can be inferred; I feel certain that there is nothing wrong in the thing itself. * * * * But whatever character may belong to this practice, it is not a practice which commenced after my leaving Carlton House. While there, and from my first arrival in this country, I was accustomed, with the knowledge of his Royal Highness the Prince of Wales, and without his ever having hinted to me the slightest disapprobation, to receive lessons from various masters for my amusement and improvement. I was attended by them frequently from twelve to five in the afternoon—Mr. Attwood for music, Mr. Geffadiere for English, Mr. Turnerelli for painting, Mr. Tutvye for imitating marble, Mr. Elwes for the harp. I saw them all alone, and, indeed, if I were to see them at all, I could do no otherwise than see them alone. * * * * However, if in the opinions and fashions of this country there should be more impropriety ascribed to this practice than it ever entered into my mind to conceive, I hope your Majesty and every candid mind will make some allowance for the different notions which my foreign education and habits may have given me."

This memorial was accompanied by the duly-attested depositions of several respectable witnesses, who bore evidence to the innocence of the Princess. The gifted artist, Sir Thomas Lawrence, in refutation of Cole's allegation, that whilst painting the portrait of the Princess, he was often alone with her late at night, under circumstances extremely suspicious; solemnly swore that he was never alone with her but once for a short time, to answer an insignificant question when he was about to retire with the rest of the company, and that nothing ever passed between her Royal Highness and himself which he could have the least objection for all the world to have seen and heard. Captain Manby, in answer to the assertion by Bidgood, that he had seen him kiss the Princess from the reflection of a mirror, deposed, "I do solemnly and upon oath declare, that it is a vile and wicked invention, wholly and absolutely false; that it is impossible he ever could have seen in the reflection of any glass any such thing, as I never, upon any occasion or in any situation, ever had the presumption to salute her Royal Highness in any such manner, or to take any such liberties, or offer any such insult to her person." To Bidgood's assertion, "that he and other of the servants suspected that the captain slept in the house," Captain Manby replied—"I solemnly swear that such suspicion is wholly unfounded, and that I never did sleep in any house occupied by or belonging to the Princess of Wales, and that nothing ever passed between myself and the Princess of Wales that I should have been in any degree unwilling that all the world should have seen." Much other evidence was also adduced in refutation of the accusatory depositions of Caroline's female servants, and in fact the innocence of the persecuted Princess was as fully proved as it was possible to prove the innocence of a woman unjustly accused of crimes under such extraordinary circumstances.

The above memorial and depositions were addressed to the King, on the second of October, 1806; and nine weeks elapsed without Caroline receiving any communication on the subject, excepting a letter from the lord chamberlain, stating that his Majesty had read the memorial and depositions, and ordered them to be laid before the commissioners. In a letter addressed to the King, on the eighth of December, she very naturally complained of the prejudice to her honour occasioned by this delay. The world, in total ignorance of the real state of the facts, began to infer her guilt from it. She felt herself sinking in the estimation both of the English nation and of what remained to her of her own family, into a state in which her honour appeared equivocal, and her virtue was suspected; a state intolerable to a mind conscious of its purity and innocence. From this unhappy condition she humbly entreated his Majesty to perceive that she could have no hope of being restored until the King's favourable opinion should be notified to the world, by his receiving her again into the royal presence, or until the full disclosure of the facts shall expose the malice of her accusers, and do away every possible ground for unfavourable inference and conjecture. Caroline then proceeded to remind the King, that the anniversary of his consort's birth-day was drawing near, when an occasion would be offered for assembling the royal family; and that should his Majesty's answer be delayed beyond that period, the world would infallibly conclude, that the answer to the report of the Commissioners had proved altogether unsatisfactory, and that she had been deemed guilty of the really infamous charges brought against her. "I, therefore," she remarks in conclusion, "take this liberty of throwing myself again at your Majesty's feet, and entreating and imploring your Majesty's goodness and justice and pity for my miseries, which this delay so severely aggravates; and in justice to my innocence and character, to urge the commissioners to an early communication of their advice."

To the above letter Caroline received no reply till the last week in January, 1807, when, through the lord chancellor, she was officially informed, that his Majesty deemed her innocent of the infamous charges of adultery and treason brought against her by the perjured Lady Douglas; but that there appeared many circumstances of conduct which could not be regarded by him without serious concern; and which suggested the expression of a desire and expectation, that such a line of conduct might, in future, be observed by her Royal Highness as would fully justify those marks of paternal regard and affection which his Majesty had always wished to show to every member of the royal family. It must be admitted, that there was much necessity for this reproof; Caroline was coarse and vulgar in conversation and manners, indiscreet in the choice of friends, and unwisely disobedient, provoking, and defiant as a wife; but if she was weak and faulty, the Prince of Wales was all this, and much more to boot. In fact, "the first gentleman in Europe" was a licentious lewdster, a notorious adulterer, and a selfish, heartless, persecuting husband. He resolved that the persecution of the grossly injured Princess should not terminate with the "delicate investigation," as the above proceedings were designated; and on learning that the King had made known to the suppliant Caroline his intention to fix an early day for receiving her at Court, he declared that he intended to institute further proceedings against her; and, in consequence, she received a note, dated Wednesday, February the 10th, informing her, that the King "considered it incumbent upon him to defer naming a day to the Princess of Wales until the further result of the Prince's intentions should have been made known to him."

Driven to desperation by a prospect of the further continuance of this heartless persecution, the unhappy Princess consented with reluctance to the publication of THE BOOK,* as it was entitled, in which was detailed at length the whole particulars of the "delicate investigation;" and she continued to address pathetic appeals to the old, enfeebled King, who now was too blind to read them, and almost too decayed in intellect to understand them. However, in March, the Grenville administration was succeeded by that of the Portland; and the new ministry, of which Mr. Perceval was the recognized leader, being the Princess's friends, they, on the twenty-second of April, advised his Majesty "that the two main charges alleged against her Royal Highness the Princess of Wales are completely disproved . . . and that all other particulars of conduct brought in accusation against her Royal Highness, to which the character of criminality can be ascribed, are satisfactorily contradicted; or rest upon evidence of such a nature, and which was given under such circumstances as render it, in the judgment of your Majesty's confidential servants, undeserving of credit." . . . . Therefore, "that it is essentially necessary, in justice to her Royal Highness, and for the honour and interest of your Majesty's illustrious family, that her Royal Highness the Princess of Wales should be admitted with as little delay as possible into your Majesty's royal presence, and that she should be received in a manner due to her rank and station in your Majesty's court and family."

Accordingly, apartments in Kensington palace were assigned to Caroline, who, in May, was presented at a drawing-room, held by the Queen, the King being too imbecile to attend. The welcome she received from her Majesty and the royal family was, as had been anticipated, cold and formal. On the King's birth-day, in the following month, she again attended the drawing-room, was received by the Queen as before; and for the last time encountered, and for a few brief moments conversed with, the Prince, her husband.

The battle of Jena, in which Caroline's sincerely beloved father fell, mortally wounded by a bullet, was followed by the immediate occupation of Brunswick by the French, and by the flight

* THE BOOK was prepared for publication by Caroline's political friend, Mr. Perceval, who, to the surprise of the public, after it had been printed, and a few copies got abroad, suppressed it, was made Chancellor of the Exchequer, and turning his back upon the Princess, became a warm partizan of the Prince of Wales, and so continued to the day of his death.

of her widowed mother to England, in the summer of 1807. For a period, the lonely mother and the deserted daughter occupied the same hearth, and mutually commiserated each other's helpless condition. In 1809, pecuniary embarrassment compelled the Princess to apply to the government for assistance; the subject was warmly discussed in parliament; her debts amounted to about £50,000, and ultimately the Prince consented to himself clear them off, to the amount of £49,000; her income was settled at £22,000; a controlling treasurer was appointed to prevent the recurrence of similar difficulties; and the ill-matched royal husband and wife signed a formal deed of separation.

CHAPTER III.

Caroline's husband created Regent—He further obstructs her communication with her daughter—Her domestic life, follies, and frivolities—Report of further unpleasant proceedings against her—She writes to the Regent on the subject—He refuses to reply—She publishes the letter—The Privy Council justify the conduct of the Regent—She addresses the House of Commons on the subject—They debate thereon—Motion in her favour lost—She meets her daughter in the highways—Death of her mother—Visit of the great Continental Sovereigns—She is precluded from Court—Angry correspondence on the subject—Her revenue increased.

N 1810, the King became permanently insane; and at the commencement of the following year, the Prince of Wales was created Regent. The elevation of her husband was, however, productive of no pleasant results to Caroline; who, from this time forward, found that every imaginable obstruction was thrown in the way of her holding personal, or even written, communications with her daughter, the Princess Charlotte. Nevertheless, life still passed on with her as merrily, if not as happily, as with mankind in general. Shocked by the eccentricity of her conduct, the number of her noble friends gradually diminished; and with her usual lack of judgment, she filled their places in her social circle by meanly-born persons; and what was infinitely worse, sometimes by low-minded, ill-doing profligates. She delighted to take part in romantic adventures and exciting scenes; disguised as a citizen's wife, she would mingle with the people in the parks, or other public places, and learn what the popular sentiment was in regard to herself. Her grandest parties she gave on Sundays; and round her dinner table might frequently be seen a motley group of lords, ladies, authors, artists, poets, players, politicians, fiddlers, dancing-masters, and even roués, and other worse characters.

Thus Caroline lived on; indulging, to use expressions of the mildest, in follies and frivolities, which, for a woman in her peculiar situation, were highly unbecoming. Her friends in the House of Commons continued to exert themselves in her behalf. They again drew from their opponents an admission that she was not guilty of the more serious charges brought against her by Lady Douglas. Others of her so-called friends kept her in a state of excitement, by publishing statements which, however well they might serve the cause of party faction, sometimes did injury to that of Caroline. They very justly denounced the needlessly stringent restrictions which kept the Princess and her daughter apart, as arbitrary and unjust; and on account of these restrictions, and a report that further unpleasant proceedings were about to be instituted against her, Caroline addressed a sealed letter to the Prince Regent, and transmitted it by Lady Charlotte Campbell, through the Earl of Liverpool and Lord Chancellor Eldon. It was returned next day unopened. Three days afterwards, it was again enclosed to their lordships, and again returned as before. The Princess, irritated, but not cowed, for a third time dispatched it, with a request that their lordships would make known its contents to his Royal Highness; and at length an answer arrived, that the Prince Regent had read the letter, but declined replying to it.

Stung by this contemptuous treatment, Caroline, without regard to the advisability of the course, immediately published the letter, of which the subjoined is a copy, in the *Morning Chronicle* newspaper.

"SIR,

"It is with great reluctance that I presume to obtrude myself upon your Royal Highness, and to solicit your attention to matters which may, at first, appear rather of a personal than a public nature. If I could think them so—if they related merely to myself—I should abstain from a proceeding which might give uneasiness, or interrupt the more weighty occupations of your Royal Highness's time; I should continue, in silence and retirement, to lead the life which has been prescribed to me, and console myself for the loss of that society, and those domestic comforts to which I have so long been a stranger, by the reflection that it has been deemed proper I should be afflicted without any fault of my own—and that your Royal Highness knows it.

"But, sir, there are considerations of a higher nature than any regard to my own happiness, which render this address a duty both to myself and my daughter. May I venture to say—a duty also to my husband and the people committed to his care? There is a point beyond which a guiltless woman cannot with safety carry her forbearance. If her honour is invaded, the defence of her reputation is no longer a matter of choice; and it signifies not whether the attack be made openly, manfully, and directly—or by secret insinuation; and by holding such conduct towards her as countenances all the suspicions that malice can suggest. If these ought to be the feelings of every woman in England, who is conscious that she deserves no reproach, your Royal Highness has too sound a judgment, and too nice a sense of honour, not to perceive how much more justly they belong to the mother of your daughter—the mother of her who is destined, I trust, at a very distant period, to reign over the British empire.

"It may be known to your Royal Highness, that, during the continuance of the restrictions upon your royal authority, I purposely refrained from making any representations which might then augment the painful difficulties of your exalted station. At the expiration of the restrictions, I still was inclined to delay taking this step, in the hope that I might owe the redress I sought to your gracious and unsolicited condescension. I have waited in the fond indulgence of this expectation, until, to my inexpressible mortification, I find that my unwillingness to complain has only produced fresh grounds of complaint; and I am at length compelled either to abandon all regard for the two dearests objects which I possess on earth—mine own honour, and my beloved child—or to throw myself at the feet of your Royal Highness, the natural protector of both.

"I presume, sir, to represent to your Royal Highness, that the separation, which every succeeding month is making wider, of the mother and daughter, is equally injurious to my character and to her education: I say nothing of the deep wounds which so cruel an arrangement inflicts upon my feelings, although I would fain hope that few persons will be found of a disposition to think lightly of these. To see myself cut off from one of the very few domestic enjoyments left me—certainly the only one upon which I set any value—the society of my child, involves me in such misery, as I well know your Royal Highness could never inflict upon me, if you were aware of its bitterness. Our intercourse has been gradually diminished. A single interview weekly seemed sufficiently hard allowance for a mother's affection; that, however, was reduced to our meeting once a fortnight; and I now learn that even this most rigorous interdiction is to be still more rigidly enforced.

"But while I do not venture to intrude my feelings as a mother upon your Royal Highness's notice, I must be allowed to say, that in the eyes of an observing and jealous world, this separation of a daughter from her mother will only admit of one construction—a construction fatal to a mother's reputation. Your Royal Highness will also pardon me for adding, that there is no less inconsistency than injustice in this treatment. He who dares advise your Royal Highness to overlook the evidence of my innocence, and disregard the sentence of complete acquittal which it produced — or is wicked and false enough still to whisper suspicions in your ear, betrays his duty to you, sir, to your daughter, and to your people, if he counsels you to permit a day to pass without a farther investigation of my conduct. I know that no such calumniator will venture to recommend a measure which must speedily end in his utter confusion. Then let me implore you to reflect on the situation in which I am placed; without the shadow of a charge against me — without even an accuser — after an inquiry that led to my ample vindication—yet treated as if I were still more culpable than the perjuries of my *suborned traducers* represented me, and held up to the world as a mother who may not enjoy the society of her only child.

"The feelings, sir, which are natural to my unexampled situation, might justify me in the gracious judgment of your Royal Highness, had I no other motives for addressing you but such as relate to myself. But I will not disguise from your Royal Highness what I cannot for a moment conceal from myself, that the serious, and it soon may be, the irreparable injury which my daughter sustains from the plan at present pursued, has done more in overcoming my reluctance to intrude upon your Royal Highness than any sufferings of my own could accomplish; and if, for her sake, I presume to call away your Royal Highness's attention from the other cares of your exalted station, I feel confident I am not claiming it for a matter of inferior importance either to yourself or your people.

"The powers with which the constitution of these realms vests your Royal Highness, in the regulation of the royal family, I know, because I am so advised, are ample and unquestionable. My appeal, sir, is made to your excellent sense and liberality of mind in the exercise of those powers; and I willingly hope that your own paternal feelings will lead you to excuse the anxiety of mine, for impelling me to represent the unhappy consequences which the present system must entail upon our beloved child.

"Is it possible, sir, that any one can have attempted to persuade your Royal Highness, that her character will not be injured by the perpetual violence offered to her strongest affections—the studied care taken to estrange her from my society, and even to interrupt all communication between us? That her love for me, with whom, by his Majesty's wise and gracious arrangements, she passed the years of her childhood, never can be extinguished, I well know; and the knowledge of it forms the greatest blessing of my existence. But let me implore your Royal Highness to reflect how inevitably all attempts to abate this attachment, by forcibly separating us, if they succeed, must injure my child's principles — if they fail, must destroy her happiness.

"The plan of excluding my daughter from all intercourse with the world, appears to my humble judgment peculiarly unfortunate. She, who is destined to be the sovereign of this great country, enjoys none of those advantages of society which are deemed necessary for imparting a knowledge of mankind to persons who have infinitely less occasion to learn that important lesson; and it may so happen, by a chance, which, I trust, is very remote, that she should be called upon to exercise the powers of the crown, with an experience of the world more confined than that of the most private individual. To the extraordinary talents with which she is blessed, and which accompany a disposition as singularly amiable, frank, and decided, I willingly trust much; but beyond a certain point the greatest natural endowments cannot struggle against the disadvantages of circumstances and situation. It is my earnest prayer, for her own sake as well as her country's, that your Royal Highness may be induced to pause before this point be reached.

"Those who have advised you, sir, to delay so long the period of my daughter's commencing her intercourse with the world, and for that purpose to make Windsor her residence, appear not to have regarded the interruptions to her education which this arrangement occasions; both by the impossibility of obtaining the attendance of proper teachers, and the time unavoidably consumed in the frequent journeys to town, which she must make, unless she is to be secluded from all intercourse, even with your Royal Highness and the rest of the royal family. To the same unfortunate counsels I ascribe a circumstance, in every way so distressing both to my parental and religious feelings, that my daughter has never yet enjoyed the benefit of confirmation, although above a year older than the age at which all the other branches of the royal family have partaken of that solemnity. May I earnestly conjure you, sir, to hear my entreaties upon this serious matter, even if you should listen to other advisers on things of less near concernment to the welfare of our child?

"The pain with which I have at length formed the resolution of addressing myself to your Royal Highness is such as I should in vain attempt to express. If I could adequately describe it, you might be enabled, sir, to estimate the strength of the motives which have made me submit to it. They are the most powerful feelings of affection, and the deepest impressions of duty towards your Royal Highness, my beloved child, and the country, which I devoutly hope she may be preserved to govern, and to show, by a new example, the liberal affection of a free and generous people to a virtuous and constitutional monarch.

"I am, sir, with profound respect, and an attachment which nothing can alter,

"Your Royal Highness's
"Most devoted and most affectionate
"Consort, cousin, and subject,
"CAROLINE LOUISA."

"*Montague House*, 14*th Jan.* 1813."

The appearance of the above letter in the public papers astounded the government. The privy council were immediately assembled; and they reported to the Regent, that, having read the letter lately published by the Princess of Wales, and examined all the documents relative to the inquiry instituted into her conduct in 1806, they were of opinion that the intercourse between the Princess of Wales and the Princess Charlotte should continue to be subject to regulation and restraint; and they further felt it their duty to declare that, as the words *suborned traducers*, in Caroline's letter, might, by misconstruction, be supposed to have reference to the conduct of his Royal Highness, that the documents laid before them afforded ample proof that there was not the slightest foundation for such an aspersion.

This report Caroline received as a further attack upon her character; and, with the determination to resent the insult by an appeal to the Parliament, she addressed a letter to the Lord Chancellor, and another to the Speaker of the Commons. The former letter was withheld from the House of Peers, but the latter, of which the subjoined is a copy, was read by the Speaker to the assembled Commons, on the second of March.

"*Montague House, March* 1.

"The Princess of Wales informs Mr. Speaker that she has received from Lord Viscount Sidmouth a copy of a report, made to his Royal Highness the Prince Regent by certain members of his Majesty's Privy Council, to whom it appears that his Royal Highness was advised to refer certain documents and evidence, regarding the character and conduct of the Princess of Wales. This report is of such a nature that her Royal Highness is persuaded that no person can read it without considering it to contain aspersions on her character, though its vagueness renders it impossible to be precisely understood, or to know exactly with what she is charged.

"The Princess of Wales feels conscious of her innocence; and considers it due to herself, to the two illustrious houses with which she is connected by blood and marriage, and to the people of this country, in which she holds such a distinguished rank, not to acquiesce for a moment in the reflections which have been cast upon her honour. The Princess of Wales has not been permitted to know on what evidence this report has been founded, nor has she had any opportunity of being heard in her own defence. What she knew on the subject was only from common rumour, until she received the report; nor does she know whether it proceeded from persons acting together as a body, to whom she could make her appeal, or only as individuals. Her Royal Highness throws herself upon the wisdom and justice of parliament, and desires the fullest investigation of her conduct during the time that she has resided in this country. She fears no scrutiny, provided she be tried by impartial judges, in a fair and open manner, consistent with the laws of the land. Her Royal Highness wishes to be treated as innocent, or to be proved guilty. She desires Mr. Speaker to communicate this letter to the honourable the House of Commons."

The reading of this letter was followed by a warm debate, on a motion for the production of all the papers relative to the differences between the Regent and the Princess, including the documents of the "delicate investigation." The motion was lost, but Mr. Whitbread drew from Lord Castlereagh an admission that Caroline was innocent of the more serious of the charges brought against her; and also an assertion, which was a disgrace to the government, that a desire to avoid bringing matters of such delicacy before the world had prevented ministers from proceeding against the base Sir John and Lady Douglas. Meanwhile, Caroline was somewhat damaged in reputation by the publication of the "Spirit of the Book," and further annoyed by being forbidden to call at Warwick House, to see her daughter. She, however, spirited woman as she was, declared that no one could prevent her from meeting the Princess Charlotte on the highway; and so the mother and daughter frequently met, to the annoyance of Queen Charlotte and the extreme mortification of the Regent.

The remainder of 1813, and more than half of the subsequent year, Caroline passed in comparative retirement. On the death of her aged mother, the Duchess of Brunswick, in March, 1813, she was gratified by the Regent permitting the Princess Charlotte to pay her a visit of condolence. But, when the great potentates of Europe visited London, in the summer of 1814, Caroline suffered further indignities. The Prince Regent notified that he had determined never again to meet her, either in private or public, and, in consequence, she was excluded from the two drawing-rooms which the Queen held in honour of the foreign sovereigns, and neither invited to the civic feast nor to the other banquets and courtly scenes at which these monarchs and their princely suites were entertained; in fact, she was shut out from the court; and, to please her persecuting husband, the foreign sovereigns passed her dwelling without even condescending to pay her a visit of courtesy. Caroline did not brook these insults in silence: she appealed, by letter, to the Queen and to the Regent, and unable thus to obtain her end, she sent to the House of Commons copies of this correspondence—from which the subjoined letters are extracted—with expressions of her belief that the Prince Regent's determination never more to meet her, was fraught with danger to the security of the succession, and to the domestic peace of the kingdom.

"*Windsor Castle, May* 23, 1814.

"The Queen considers it to be her duty to lose no time in acquainting the Princess of Wales, that she has received a communication from her son, the Prince Regent, in which he states that her Majesty's intention of holding two drawing-rooms in the ensuing month having been notified to the public, he must declare, that he considers that his own presence at her court cannot be dispensed with; and that he desires it to be understood, for reasons of which he alone can be the judge, to be his fixed and unalterable determination, not to meet the Princess of Wales upon any occasion, either in public or private.

"The Queen is thus placed under the painful necessity of intimating to the Princess of Wales, the impossibility of her Majesty's receiving her Royal Highness at the drawing-rooms.

"Charlotte R."

The answer:

"*Connaught House, May* 24, 1814.

"Madam,

"I have received the letter which your Majesty has done me the honour to address to me, prohibiting my appearance at the public drawing-rooms, which will be held by your Majesty in the ensuing month, with great surprise and regret.

"I will not presume to discuss with your Majesty, topics which must be as painful to your Majesty as to myself.

"Your Majesty is well acquainted with the affectionate regard with which the King was so kind as to honour me up to the period of his Majesty's indisposition; which no one of his Majesty's subjects has so much cause to lament as myself;—and that his Majesty was graciously pleased to bestow upon me the most unequivocal and gratifying proof of his attachment and approbation, by his public reception of me at his court, at a season of severe and unmerited affliction, when his protection was most necessary to me. There I have since, uninterruptedly, paid my respects to your Majesty. I am now without appeal, or protector; but I cannot so far forget my duty to the King, and to myself, as to surrender my right to appear at any public drawing-room, to be held by your Majesty.

"That I may not, however, add to the difficulty and uneasiness of your Majesty's situation, I yield, in the present instance, to the will of his Royal Highness the Prince Regent, announced to me by your Majesty, and shall not present myself at the drawing-rooms of next month.

"It would be presumptuous in me to attempt to inquire of your Majesty, the reasons of his Royal Highness the Prince Regent for this harsh proceeding, of which his Royal Highness can alone be the judge. I am unconscious of offence; and in that reflection, I must endeavour to find consolation for all the mortifications I experience; even for this, the last, the most unexpected, and the most severe;—the prohibition given to me alone to appear before your Majesty, to offer my congratulations upon the happy termination of those calamities with which Europe has been so long afflicted, in the presence of the illustrious personages, who will, in all probability, be assembled at your Majesty's court, with whom I am so closely connected by birth and marriage.

"I beseech your Majesty to do me an act of justice, to which, in the present circumstances, your Majesty is the only person competent,—by acquainting those illustrious strangers with the motives of personal consideration towards your Majesty, which alone induce me to abstain from the exercise of my right to appear before your Majesty: and that I do now, as I have done at all times, defy the malice of my enemies to fix upon me the shadow of any one imputation, which could render me unworthy of their society and regard.

"Your Majesty will, I am sure, not be displeased that I should relieve myself from a suspicion of disrespect towards your Majesty, by making public the cause of my absence from court, at a time when the duties of my station would otherwise peculiarly demand my attendance.

"I have the honour to be your Majesty's most obedient daughter-in-law and servant, Caroline P."

The Queen in return:

"*Windsor Castle, May* 25, 1814.

"The Queen has received, this afternoon, the Princess of Wales's letter of yesterday, in reply to the communication which she was desired by the Prince Regent to make to her; and she is sensible of the disposition expressed by her Royal Highness, not to discuss with her topics which must be painful to both.

"The Queen considers it incumbent upon her to send a copy of the Princess of Wales's letter to the Prince Regent; and her Majesty could have felt no hesitation in communicating to the illusrioust strangers, who may possibly be present at her court, the circumstances which will prevent the Princess of Wales from appearing there, if her Royal Highness had not rendered a compliance with her wish, to this effect, unnecessary, by intimating her intention of making public the cause of her absence.

"CHARLOTTE R."

The Princess of Wales returned:

'*Connaught Place, May* 26, 1814.

"The Princess of Wales has the honour to acknowledge the receipt of a note from the Queen, dated yesterday; and begs permission to return her best thanks to her Majesty, for her gracious condescension, in the willingness expressed by her Majesty, to have communicated to the illustrious strangers, who will, in all probability, be present at her Majesty's court, the reasons which have induced her Royal Highness not to be present.

"Such communication, as it appears to her Royal Highness, cannot be less necessary, on account of any publicity which it may be in the power of her Royal Highness to give to her motives; and the Princess of Wales, therefore, entreats the active good offices of her Majesty, upon an occasion which the Princess of Wales feels it so essential to her, that she should not be misunderstood. CAROLINE P."

The Queen's answer:

"*Windsor Castle, May* 27, 1814.

"The Queen cannot omit to acknowledge the receipt of the Princess of Wales's note of yesterday, although it does not appear to her Majesty to require any other reply than that conveyed to her Royal Highness's preceding letter.

"CHARLOTTE R."

This correspondence led to the following letter to the Prince:

"*Connaught-House, May* 26, 1814.

"SIR,

"I am once more reluctantly compelled to address your Royal Highness; and I enclose, for your inspection, copies of a note which I have had the honour to receive from the Queen, and of the answer which I have thought it my duty to return to her Majesty. It would be in vain for me to inquire into the reasons of the alarming declaration made by your Royal Highness, that you have taken the fixed and unalterable determination never to meet me upon any occasion, either in public or private. Of these your Royal Highness is pleased to state yourself to be the only judge. You will perceive, by my answer to her Majesty, that I have only been restrained by motives of personal consideration towards her Majesty, from exercising my right of appearing before her Majesty at the public drawing-rooms, to be held in the ensuing month.

"But, sir, lest it should be, by possibility, supposed that the words of your Royal Highness can convey any insinuation from which I shrink, I am bound to demand of your Royal Highness, what circumstances can justify the proceedings you have thus thought fit to adopt.

"I owe it to myself, to my daughter, and to the nation, to which I am deeply indebted for the vindication of my honour, to remind your Royal Highness, of what you know,—that, after open persecution, and mysterious inquiries upon undefined charges, the malice of my enemies fell entirely upon themselves; and that I was restored by the King, with the advice of his ministers, to the full enjoyment of my rank in his court, upon my complete acquittal. Since his Majesty's lamented illness, I have demanded, in the face of parliament and the country, to be proved guilty, or to be treated as innocent. I have been declared innocent. I will not submit to be treated as guilty.

"Sir, your Royal Highness may possibly refuse to read this letter; but the world must know that I have written it, and they will see my real motives for foregoing, in this instance, the rights of my rank. Occasions however, may, arise (one, I trust, is far distant), when I must appear in public, and your Royal Highness must be present also. Can your Royal Highness have contemplated the full extent of your declaration? Has your Royal Highness forgotten the approaching marriage of your daughter, and the possibility of our coronation? I waive my rights in a case where I am not absolutely bound to assert them, in order to relieve the Queen, as far as I can, from the painful situation in which she is placed by your Royal Highness, not from any consciousness of blame, not from any doubt of the existence of those rights, or of my own worthiness to enjoy them.

"Sir, the time you have selected for this proceeding is calculated to make it peculiarly galling. Many illustrious strangers are already arrived in England; amongst whom, as I am informed, the illustrious heir of the house of Orange, who has announced himself to me as my future son-in-law; from their society I am unjustly excluded. Others are expected, of equal rank to your own, to rejoice with your Royal Highness on the peace of Europe. My daughter will, for the first time, appear in the splendour and publicity becoming the approaching nuptials of the presumptive heiress of this empire. This season your Royal Highness has chosen for treating me with fresh and unprovoked indignity; and, of all his Majesty's subjects, I alone am prevented by your Royal Highness from appearing in my place to partake of the general joy; and am deprived of the indulgence in those feelings of pride and affection, permitted to every mother but me.

"I am, Sir,
"Your Royal Highness's faithful wife,
"Caroline P."

The communication of these letters brought on an animated debate in the Commons, and as Caroline was again suffering from pecuniary embarrassment, Lord Castlereagh endeavoured to bribe her into silence by proposing to increase her income to £50,000 a year; but, with laudable self-denial, she, in consideration of the heavy burdens that pressed on the nation, relinquished £15,000 of the sum, and the Commons fixed her annual revenue at £35,000. At the same time Mr. Whitbread observed in the Commons, "The Princess, I know, will scorn to barter her rights or silence for money. However, if the House will make her Royal Highness an adequate provision, I shall rejoice in it as a testimony of its approbation; but the grant shall not silence me, if, upon any future occasion, I shall think the Princess aggrieved."

CHAPTER IV.

Proposed marriage of the Princess Charlotte to the Prince of Orange broken off—Unsuccessful flight of the Princess Charlotte to the home of her mother—Caroline resolves to go abroad—Her letters on the subject—Journey to Brunswick—Suite—Sojourn at Geneva—Unbecoming conduct—Takes Bergami into her service—Travels in Italy—Further improprieties—Purchases the Villa d'Este—Constitutes Bergami her chief chamberlain—Her English friends desert her—She surrounds herself with Italians—Her proceedings secretly watched and reported to her husband by the "Milan Commission"—Her extraordinary conduct—Travels in the East.

T the close of 1813, the Prince of Orange came to England with the intention of marrying the Princess Charlotte. The Prince Regent and the Queen were favourable to the match; and as the spring advanced, the speedy solemnization of the marriage was fully anticipated by the public. But in this they were disappointed—the lady objected to the wooer; it was with marked reluctance that she, to please her sire, granted him several interviews, and permitted him to hand her from her carriage; and when he, in unmistakable language, assured her that if united to him she must reside in Holland, and not think of receiving the visits of the Princess of Wales at his palace, she with indignity declared, that "she would on no account abandon her persecuted mother," and immediately broke off the match.

The Regent had set his heart on this union; and its failure, combined with a knowledge that the Princess Charlotte had latterly contrived to maintain an epistolary correspondence with her mother, irritated him into a resolution of changing her residence, and surrounding her with a new suite of attendants and servants. Without previous intimation, he secured Cranbourne Lodge as her new abode; and on the morning of the twelfth of July, 1814, accompanied by her new household, proceeded to her then residence, Warwick House, and after telling her that her establishment in that residence was dismissed, commanded her to immediately depart with her new suite to Carlton House, and thence to Cranbourne Lodge. She expressed surprise; but a promise of willing compliance obtained for her a quarter of an hour's respite, to make ready for the unexpected change. The Regent, not suspecting his daughter's intentions, retired; and the next moment the adventure-loving Charlotte slipped out at a back door, and hastening down Cockspur Street into the Haymarket, entered a hackney coach there, and was driven to Connaught House, the residence of her mother, who was then on her way from Blackheath to London, and who, on receiving intelligence of her daughter's flight, very wisely hastened to both houses of parliament in search of Mr. Whitbread and Earl Grey, neither of whom, as it happened, were in attendance. Caroline, on reaching Connaught House, found Miss Elphinston, Mr. Brougham, and other of her and her daughter's friends already arrived there. Mr. Brougham, as law adviser to the Princess of Wales, explained that the "King or the Regent had the absolute power to dispose of the persons of all the royal family during their minority, and therefore advised that the Princess Charlotte should immediately return to the home provided for her by her sire." Caroline, pleased as she was by this display of her daughter's filial affection, also prudently urged her to bow to the harsh will of the Regent; and as Lord Chancellor Eldon and her uncles, the Dukes of York and Sussex, the former of whom had in the meantime arrived with a message to her from her father, and the lords of the council likewise joined in this advice, and promised that she should not be harshly treated on her return, she reluctantly submitted, and about four in the morning returned with the Duke of York to Warwick House, whence a few days afterwards, she was removed to Cranbourne Lodge, where she was forced to live a secluded life, and debarred of even the hope of again corresponding with her mother.

Before the public excitement occasioned by the unsuccessful flight of the royal heiress of England had subsided, Caroline, whose cause the nation at large fervently espoused, astonished all classes and parties, by avowing her intention to immediately depart the kingdom. The reasons assigned for this unwise resolution are thus stated in the subjoined letter from the Princess of Wales to Lord Liverpool:—

"*Connaught House, July 25th*, 1814.

"The Princess of Wales requests Lord Liverpool to lay before the Prince Regent the contents of this letter.

"Actuated by the most urgent motive, that of restoring tranquillity to the Prince Regent, as well as to secure the peace of mind of which she has been for so many years deprived, the Princess of Wales, after mature reflection, has resolved to return to the continent. This resolution ought not to surprise the ministers of the Prince Regent, considering the trouble and disagreeable experience of the Princess for so long a time; and still more, after the indignity and mortification to which she has been exposed, by being withheld from receiving her nearest relations, and the most intimate friends of the late Duke of Brunswick, her illustrious father.

"The Princess is extremely anxious that the Prince Regent should be informed of the motives, and clearly comprehend the tenor of her past conduct as politically exhibited. In exacting a justification from this noble nation—her sole protection since the unfortunate indisposition of the King—she is to be understood as solicitous only to maintain her rights and her honour, which are dearer to her than life itself.

"The Princess of Wales would have undertaken her projected tour long before, if she had not been prevented by the breaking off in the projected marriage of the Princess Charlotte with the Prince of Orange. She could not resolve to leave her daughter without protection, at a period so critical. The Prince Regent having planned to settle the new-married couple at the Hague, the Princess Charlotte on that account principally declined the match. Unwilling to prove any obstacle to future arrangements favourable to the happiness of her daughter, the Princess of Wales has at length resolved to return to Brunswick, her native country. She may afterwards travel into Italy and Greece, where she may probably be able to select an agreeable abode, and live in it for some years. The Princess flatters herself that the Prince Regent will have no objection to this design.

"The Princess of Wales requests Lord Liverpool to represent to the Prince Regent that she resigns Montague House, and the title of Ranger of Greenwich Park, in favour of her daughter, as also the house bequeathed to the Princess of Wales by her mother. The Princess of Wales hopes the Prince Regent will comply with these requests, the last that her Royal Highness intends to offer.

"The Princess embraces this opportunity to explain the motives which have induced her to decline the grant of £50,000 a year, voted to her by the nation in parliament. She expresses her lively acknowledgment to this great people for the readiness to make her so liberal a pension during her life; but she has only taken £35,000, because, as the gift was intended to support her in her proper rank, and to enable her to hold a court as became the wife of the Prince Regent, the receipt of it would interfere with her views of travelling, and her purpose to quit England for a season. Such is the substance of her present communication to Lord Liverpool, which the Princess would have made before, but for the fear of producing new debates in parliament. She has, therefore, awaited the rising of that august body, and is now about to depart for Worthing, to embark, not intending to return previously to London.

"The Princess of Wales is happy to assure Lord Liverpool, that she will ever be ardently solicitous for the prosperity and glory of this generous nation."

The Prince Regent was not displeased with this communication; and, three days afterwards, Lord Liverpool addressed to Caroline the following favourable reply:—

"*July 28th*, 1814.

"Lord Liverpool has had the honour to receive the letter of her Royal Highness. Having acquainted the Prince Regent with its contents, he has ordered him to state that his Royal Highness can have no objection to the design she has intimated, of returning to her native country, to visit her brother the Duke of Brunswick, assuring her that the Prince Regent will never throw any obstacle in the way of the present or future intentions of her Royal Highness as to the place where she may wish to reside.

"The Prince Regent leaves it entirely to the liberty of her Royal Highness to exercise her own discretion as to her abode in this country or on the continent, as it may be convenient to her.

"Lord Liverpool is also commanded, on the part of the Prince Regent, to inform her Royal Highness, that he will not throw any obstacles in the way of the arrangements of her Royal Highness, whatever they may be, respecting the rest of the private property of her Royal Highness. But that, for reasons rather too long to explain, the Prince Regent will not permit the Princess Charlotte to be Ranger of Greenwich Park, nor occupy any of the houses at Blackheath, which the Princess of Wales has hitherto occupied.

"Lord Liverpool has also been enjoined, on the part of the Prince Regent, before he closes the letter which he has the honour to send to her Royal Highness, to inform her, in relation to the two articles which her Royal Highness has inserted in her letter concerning the rupture of the marriage of the Princess Charlotte with the Hereditary Prince of Orange, as well as to the reasons for which the allied sovereigns did not, previously to their departure from England, pay their visits to her Royal Highness, that, as to the first article, Lord Liverpool is commanded by the Prince Regent to inform her Royal Highness, that the Prince Regent is not persuaded that the private considerations of the circumstances in which the Princess of Wales is placed, can have been an obstruction to the marriage of the Princess Charlotte. As to the second article, Lord Liverpool is also enjoined, on the part of the Prince Regent, to inform her Royal Highness that the Prince Regent never opposed himself to the allied sovereigns making a visit to the Princess of Wales during their stay in England.

"Lord Liverpool has the honour to be, with profound esteem and consideration, respondent to her Royal Highness.

"P.S. The Prince Regent can make no difficulties on the subject of the directions which the Princess has the intention of giving as to the house at Blackheath; neither will the Prince Regent oppose her Royal Highness retaining the rooms in Kensington Palace, in the same manner as she possessed them while in London, for the convenience of herself and her suite."

On the twenty-fifth of July, Caroline also addressed the subjoined epistle to Mr. Whitbread, the leader of her party in the House of Commons, to Mr. Brougham, her legal adviser, and to her other political and partizan friends:

"The Princess of Wales has the pleasure to inform, and frankly to avow to Mr. Whitbread, that she is about to take the most important step in her life. She has embraced the resolution of quitting this country for a time; and has written to Lord Liverpool to inform the Prince Regent immediately with her intention. The Princess encloses a copy of this letter to Mr. Whitbread, to make him and his friends understand the plan of conduct which she has adopted.

"The Princess is so fully persuaded

of the well-known integrity of Mr. Whitbread and Mr. Brougham, that she cannot doubt but they would have proposed such a step, if motives of delicacy had not prevented them. The Princess is deeply penetrated with gratitude for the attentions which they have shown her, at all times and on all occasions. This kindness on their part has withheld her from asking their advice on the present occasion; in every other instance, she assures them, she has always followed the suggestions of her advisers and friends, and conformed to their superior intelligence.

"Her conscience tells her, that her conduct is worthy of her character and of her sentiments, and will always remain so. She has had sufficient leisure to reflect maturely before she adopted her present resolution. People who know not the character of the Princess, may be disposed to believe that she has been induced to adopt this measure in a moment of ill-humour; but she takes the Almighty to witness, that she has been intending to travel ever since 1806, although reasons too long for explanation have prevented her. No person possessed of pride and feeling, could endure to be degraded below her rank in this kingdom, as Princess of Wales, or even as a simple individual, bear to be so hated by its ruler, as to be debarred from his presence both public and private. The Princess of Wales knows not how to support so much debasement and mortification. She cannot allow herself to be treated as a culprit by the Prince and his family, while her innocence has been acknowledged by ministers and by parliament, after an investigation which has done away the accusations of traitors and enemies.

"The Princess having obtained this public satisfaction, cannot in conscience remain a burden to her friends any longer. Events are continually occurring, which oblige her zealous and generous advocates to step forward in her defence.

"The Princess of Wales is deeply penetrated with the generosity of this brave nation, which, after having taken so lively an interest in her misfortunes, and in her afflicting condition, so willingly affords to her the means of living peaceably in future. She hopes that her gratitude, which will only cease with her existence, will be one day renewed in the Princess Charlotte, and that her daughter will give proofs of it by her zeal for the glory and happiness of this kingdom; by defending the rights of her people; and proving by her conduct, that great and powerful as she may be, she will not tyrannise over any one, merely because they have not the good fortune to please her.

"The Princess of Wales would probably not have departed so soon, had not the marriage of the Princess Charlotte with the Prince of Orange been broken off at her own instance. Dear as her daughter is to her, she could not resolve to leave her without protection in a situation so critical. The Princess, aware that the match was ardently desired by the people, wished neither to impede the happiness of the nation, nor that of her daughter. On this account she is solicitous to depart at once, for it is pitiable to see a child rendered on all occasions a source of dispute between her parents.

"The Princess of Wales is assured that in future the Princess Charlotte will be more happy and tranquil; and she is led to make this sacrifice, that if she remains some time longer unmarried, there may be fewer obstacles to her appearance in public. Her father, the Prince Regent, may thus choose the most suitable of her nearest relations to introduce her into society, that she may enjoy the pleasures congenial to her age, and become acquainted with the character of the most distinguished persons in the nation, of which knowledge she has hitherto been deprived.

"The Princess Charlotte will the less feel the privation of her mother's society, as she has not had it for the two last years. During that time, five or six months in succession have passed away without the mother being allowed to see her daughter. She has even been refused the consolation of receiving any of her letters, and thus her regret at leaving her is lessened; for although living in the same capital, they were not allowed to speak, even when they met in their airings. Her daughter's coachman was forbidden to stop, and directed to act as if he knew not the carriage of the Princess of Wales. Thus to quit her will be but the grief of a day, whilst to remain were only to continue the sorrows of both mother and child. The Princess cannot rest in a situation so unfortunate for herself, and so uneasy to others, and is sure that Mr. Whitbread and his friends will be affected by these considerations; that their sentiments will accord with her own, and that they will approve of her resolution.

"The Princess, before she ends this long letter, is solicitous to explain to her advisers the most urgent reason for her quitting England, and to show them that delicacy has obliged her to put herself under the protection of this great and generous nation, having no other refuge since the indisposition of the King. How much it has cost her to make public this declaration—that is to say, that his Royal Highness has been strangely biassed and imposed upon by false accusers and enemies to her honour.

"That which renders her situation still more embarrassing, is, that this generous nation has shown more devotion towards herself than to its ruler, who ought to be the blessing and glory of his people. The Princess hopes, that when she has quitted England, the Prince Regent will make public his conviction, that her conduct and character have not merited reproach; and thereby regain that popularity which is due to him, and to which his many excellent qualities entitle him in other respects.

"The Princess of Wales most devoutly assures Mr. Whitbread and his friends of the immutable sentiments of lively gratitude and perfect esteem towards them, which shall have the same ending with her existence only."

The publication of the above correspondence excited for Caroline a fresh outbreak of public sympathy—greater perhaps than would have happened had the fact been generally known, that all the Princess's letters which we have quoted relative to her conduct and to the ill treatment she was forced to endure as a wife, were written with the expressed intention of being published, and not by herself, but usually by her political friends or legal advisers.

After taking, by permission of the Regent, a hasty farewell of her daughter, Caroline proceeded to Worthing, with the intention of there embarking. She took the boy Austin with her; had conspicuously placed amongst her luggage a large tin case, on which was painted in white letters, on a black ground, "Her Royal Highness the Princess of Wales, to be always with her;" and for several days lingered on the shore bewailing her misfortunes; but after having, by these and other means, excited public sympathy and curiosity to the highest pitch, she pretended that it would be dangerous to pass through the crowd then collecting, and privately proceeding to South Lancing, about two miles distance, was there driven to the beach in a "small pony cart," and entering a barge, was thence conveyed on board the Janson frigate, Captain King, on the ninth of August. Whilst proceeding in the barge to the frigate, she continually kissed her hand in token of farewell to the crowd collected on the beach, who returned the compliment; the men by uncovering their heads, the ladies by waving their handkerchiefs.

On quitting the shore of England, she wept till she fainted; but her spirits speedily recovered their wonted buoyancy. On the twelfth of August, the Regent's birth-day, the Janson, whilst passing the Texel, fired a salute, by her desire, it is said, in honour of the anniversary; and after dinner she drank health, prosperity, and glory to his Royal Highness the Regent, with a heartiness that might have deceived the most incredulous into a belief that she was of wives the most loving and beloved. After a favourable voyage, Caroline left the Janson, and assuming the appellation of Countess of Wolffenbuttel, passed through Hamburgh to Brunswick, where she was cordially welcomed both by her brother, the unfortunate Duke of Brunswick, who fell at Quatre Bras in 1815, and by the people.

At this period, the Ladies Charlotte Lindsey and Elizabeth Forbes were her maids of honour; Mr. St. Leger, Sir William Gell, and the Hon. Keppel Craven, were her chamberlains; Dr. Holland was her physician, and Captain Hesse was her equerry; but before she left Brunswick, where she tarried but a few weeks, Mr. St. Leger resigned his office, and not many days afterwards Lady Charlotte Lindsey followed his example. From Brunswick Caroline travelled, under the assumed title of Countess of Cornwall, through Germany to Switzerland. She made a short sojourn at Geneva, and there passed much of her time in the company and companionship of Louisa Maria, consort of Napoleon, the ex-emperor of France, whose sense of propriety she shocked by appearing before her one night at a dress ball, in an unbecoming costume, under the assumed character of Venus.

On the eighth of October, 1814, Caroline entered the city of Milan. Her appearance there excited great curiosity and interest, but her conduct failed to win for her the respect of those whose esteem a discreet princess would have most prized. Here it was that the aspect of her household began to change from English to foreign, and that she appointed as one of her couriers the celebrated Italian, Bartholomew Bergami, a pale-visaged, long-whiskered, but, withal, a fine handsome personage, who, although poor, bore the imposing title of baron; was said to be a knight of Malta; had served in the *etat-major* of the troops commanded by Lieutenant-General Count Pino, and ultimately became the most esteemed and favoured of Caroline's suite.

From Milan the giddy Countess of Cornwall, as Caroline persisted in styling herself, proceeded forward, through Rome to Naples, where she paid an ostentatious visit to the then Neapolitan King, Joachim Murat, who received her with equal ostentation, and whose bust she afterwards crowned with laurel at a masked ball, where, accompanied by Bergami, she sustained several characters, including those of a Turkish peasant and the Genius of History, in a manner, it is said, neither becoming a princess nor a mother. Her life at this period was a giddy round of pleasure and gaiety. She almost daily took part in a ball, masquerade, festival, or fête. The English suite counselled her to pursue a course of life more quiet and unexceptionable; but their advice was not followed, and they one by one all relinquished their posts, some to afterwards rejoin her, others to never more see her face.

At this period she purchased the pretty Villa d' Este on the lake of Como, and with her usual indiscretion—to use a mild expression—elevated Bergami to the dignity of her chief chamberlain, permitted him to a seat at her own table, and conferred on him favours which, by the aid of a little exaggeration on the part of her enemies were made to grime her character with infamy. On finding that her English court were fast deserting her, and that all application to friends in England to fill the places of these deserters were met by refusals, she appointed Italians to the vacant posts, till at length her whole suite became Italian, and few English ladies or nobles paid her even the trifling honour of a complimentary visit.

Meanwhile, her hating husband in England was informed of the ill character she left behind her in her wanderings; and although his own moral conduct was of the grossest kind, he resolved that at least his wife should not be permitted to infringe the laws of propriety and decorum with impunity. The Duke of Cumberland reported to him that, when in Brussels, he had heard through White, the servant of Mr. Burrell, who had accompanied the Princess in several of her Italian excursions, that her conduct at Milan had been infamous; and upon this report the famous "Milan Commission" was established, with all possible secrecy, to watch and investigate her conduct. Caroline heard of their doings, denounced them, and justly so, as a set of spies; but instead of being more circumspect in her behaviour, foolishly acted as though she wished to court infamy, declaring that nothing pleased her so well as to perplex and mortify her annoying husband.

Of Caroline's further wanderings but little need be said. In 1816 she went to Jericho, both in fact and in the popular sense of the expression. She set out in January: spent a month at Tunis; at Athens generously liberated three hundred imprisoned debtors; was at Constantinople in June; a month afterwards pitched her tent amidst the ruins of Ephesus; thence wandered on to Acre, passed through Jaffa to Jerusalem, when she visited the "Holy Places," and after there instituting the chivalric order of St. Caroline—a saint not to be found in the calendar, but that to her was of no consequence—and of this new order creating Bartholomew Bergami grand master, and her *protégé*, young Austin, a knight, she and her suite, seated on asses, set off to Jericho. But scarcely had they reached there, when the fierceness of the heat drove them back to Jaffa, where they embarked and proceeded by sea to Syracuse, whence they sailed to Rome, and after a brief stay in the "Eternal City," returned in safety to the Princess's Italian home on the Lake of Como.

CHAPTER V.

Caroline visits Vienna—Sojourns at Trieste—Watched closely by spies—Marriage and death of her daughter—Death of George III.—Accession of her husband by the title of George IV.—She is Queen Consort—The name omitted in the Liturgy—She resolves to come to England—The King offers her a princely revenue to reside on the Continent, and relinquish her queenly rights and title—She rejects the offer, and comes to England—The King institutes proceedings against her—Vain efforts to effect an amicable arrangement—The Reports of the Milan Commission examined by a secret committee of the Peers—Bill of Pains and Penalties brought into the House of Peers against Caroline—The House consents to hear her counsel—Her letter to the King on the subject—Trial—She attends the House whilst the bill is in progress—Overcome by the appearance of Majocchi—Evidence of witnesses—The defence—The bill relinquished by the government—Joy of the nation, sorrow of Caroline—She goes in state to St. Paul's—Numerous addresses presented to her—Claims a right to be crowned with the King—The right negatived—She protests against the decision—Is refused admittance to the coronation—The refusal breaks her heart—Visits Drury Lane Theatre—Death—Riots at her funeral procession—Body conveyed to Brunswick, and buried in the cathedral of St. Blaize.

IN 1819, Caroline paid a visit to Vienna, but meeting with only cool, contemptuous treatment in the Austrian capital, she hastily withdrew to Trieste, and there sojourned long enough to win for herself an ill name. Throughout her wanderings she was closely watched and dodged by spies employed by the agents sent out from England for that purpose; and she herself, weak Princess as she was, knew this to be the case, and yet gave them ample occasion to report, as they did, most unfavourably of her conduct and character. During her wanderings, her daughter had, in compliance with her will, which in this instance did not run counter to that of her husband's, married Prince Leopold, and the news of the marriage gave her joy; but when, seven months afterwards, the Princess Charlotte died in giving birth to a still-born infant, the mournful intelligence overwhelmed her with sorrow. In 1820, the tidings of the death of George III., an event which made her Queen Consort of Great Britain, similarly affected her: she declared that in him she had lost more than a father; and as her name was intentionally omitted in the new prayer for the royal family in the Liturgy, and as further charges of misconduct were whispered against her, she resolutely resolved immediately to return to England, and throw herself on the generosity of that nation over whom she fondly hoped to bear sway as the consort of George IV. This resolution equally surprised her British friends and foes, as it was understood that in the year previously an arrangement had been effected by which she had agreed that in the event of the Regent becoming King, she would remain abroad and relinquish her title as Queen, so long as the income settled upon her by parliament was regularly transmitted to her.

After travelling through part of Italy and France with tedious slowness and difficulty, the result of the French monarch having commanded that no official attention was to be paid her, the Queen—for such we must now designate Caroline—arrived at St. Omer's on the first of June, and there met Mr. Brougham, one of her legal advisers, and Lord Hutchinson, the latter of whom submitted to her from the ministry a proposal—at first verbal, but as she refused to so receive it, afterwards in writing—to the purport that his Majesty would settle upon her £50,000 a year, on condition that she should remain abroad and never again visit any part of the British dominions, and that she should relinquish the title of Queen of England, and use no other title belonging to the royal family of Britain; but that if this proposal was not accepted, all compromise would be refused, and immediately she landed in England proceedings would be instituted against her. These terms she rejected with indignation, and immediately proceeding with Alderman Wood, Lady Anne Hamilton, and one or two other attendants to Calais, there discharged her Italian household, and embarked with her little suite on board the Prince Leopold sailing packet, which, with the royal standard floating in mid-air, the only regal honour paid to her, voyaged in safety across the channel to Dover, where her Majesty was received with all conceivable demonstrations of sympathy and loyalty. Caroline made no stay at Dover, but hurrying through the welcoming throngs that lined the road whither she went, pressed forward to London, where she arrived in the afternoon of June the sixth; and as Lord Liverpool had not even answered her letter requesting that the government would provide a suitable habitation for her, she took up her residence at the house of Alderman Wood, in South Audley Street.

The same day, Lord Liverpool appeared in the House of Peers, and Lord Castlereagh in that of the Commons, each with a green bag, containing, it was supposed, reports upon her Majesty's conduct. During her absence from England, each delivered a message from the King to the assembled Houses, to the effect that the Queen, having returned to England, his Majesty deemed it necessary to communicate to them certain papers relative to her conduct, and which he recommended to their immediate serious attention. The ministers made this communication to parliament with evident reluctance. They declared that "the King felt a most anxious desire to avert, by all the means in his power, a necessity as painful to the people as to his own feelings." Caroline's parliamentary friends, dreading lest some of the charges against her might be substantiated, evinced a desire to avoid the opening of "that fatal green bag," as it was designated by Mr. Wilberforce; whilst the highly moral and decorous, afraid of disclosures on both sides, were anxious that almost any course should be adopted rather than such a banquet of scandal should be served up to the nation. However, on the first of June, Mr. Brougham acquainted the Commons with her Majesty's reasons for returning to England, and her willingness to meet her accusers, and submit her conduct to the most searching investigation. In the House of Peers Lord Liverpool moved for the appointment of a *secret* committee to examine the reports relative to the malpractices of the Queen whilst abroad, referred to in the King's message, and Lord Castlereagh made a similar motion in the Commons; but the appointment of the committee was adjourned, in the hope that an amicable arrangement would be effected.

Pending this adjournment, the Duke of Wellington and Lord Castlereagh, on the part of the ministry, and Mr. Brougham and Mr. Denman, on the part of the Queen, met; but after much discussion, failed to effect an adjustment. In fact, the proposition of the Duke and Lord Castlereagh was preposterous; they offered to her Majesty a revenue of £50,000 a year, in the hope that this princely bribe would induce her to relinquish her title, rights, and privilege as Queen, and reside abroad, with the brand of infamy upon her character; terms which were a disgrace to the ministry, and which both the Queen and her legal advisers rejected with scorn. Caroline did not object to reside abroad, but she insisted on being acknowledged as Queen of Britain, by her name appearing in the liturgy, or by an equivalent, which would have the effect of protecting her against the unfavourable inference to which she might be liable, in leaving the country under the peculiar circumstance in which she was placed; and the great majority of the people supported her against the ministers in this demand. All efforts to accomplish a private arrangement having failed, Mr. Wilberforce was made the agent of the strongest party in the Commons, and he moved an address of the House, praying the Queen to succumb; but the majority in favour of the motion was small, one hundred and twenty-four voted against it; and when the address was presented to her Majesty, she replied, that "she could not consent to the sacrifice of any essential privilege, nor withdraw her appeal to those principles of public justice, which are alike the safeguard of the highest and humblest in the realm."

All hope of an amicable adjustment being thus crushed, the secret committee of the House of Peers proceeded to inspect the documents contained in the greatly-dreaded "green bag" on the twenty-eighth of June; and six days afterwards, they reported that the documents laid before them, charged the Queen with a continued series of unbecoming and disgraceful acts, which deeply affected the honour and dignity of the crown, and the reputation of her Majesty; and, therefore, they recommended that these charges should be made the subject of a solemn legislative inquiry. Next day, Lord Darce presented a petition from the Queen to the assembled peers, praying that her counsel might be forthwith heard at the bar of the House. The prayer of this petition was rejected; and immediately Lord Liverpool brought in his Bill of Pains and Penalties, charging the Queen with "an adulterous connection with Bartholomew Bergami, whom she had originally engaged in her service in a menial capacity, and with afterwards procuring for, and conferring upon, the said Bergami, orders of knighthood and titles of honour; and with conducting herself towards the said Bergami with indecent and offensive familiarity and freedom: and, therefore, praying the House to enact that she should be deprived of the rank and title of Queen, and that the marriage between her and the King should be dissolved." The day following, another petition was presented from the Queen, again desiring that her counsel might be heard, and this prayer was granted; but as it was generally understood, that the Bill of Pains and Penalties was meant to intimidate the Queen into consenting to a compliance; to allow time for this object, it was arranged that the next stage of the bill should not be taken till the seventeenth of August. Meanwhile, a copy of the Bill was presented to her Majesty, by Sir Thomas Tyrwhitt; and Lord Erskine moved that the House of Peers should forward to the Queen a list of the witnesses against her. This motion being negatived, he, on the twenty-fourth, presented a petition from Caroline, requesting a specification of the time and places, when and where, she had committed the gross acts imputed to her. This request was also refused; and on the seventh of August, Caroline addressed a long letter to the King. From this letter, which was written especially for the public eye, and not by, but for, the Queen, we make the subjoined forcible extracts:

"As long as the protecting hand of

your late ever-beloved, ever-lamented, father, was held over me, I was safe; but the melancholy event which deprived the nation of the active exertions of its virtuous King, bereft me of friend and protector, and of all hope of future tranquillity and safety. To calumniate your innocent wife was now the shortest road to royal favour; and to betray her, was to lay the sure foundation of boundless riches and titles of honour. . . . . Your court became much less a scene of polished manners and refined intercourse than of low intrigue and scurrility. Spies, bacchanalians, tale-bearers, and foul conspirators, swarmed in these palaces, which had before been the resort of sobriety, virtue, and honour. To enumerate all the various privations and mortifications which I had to endure, all the insults which were wantonly heaped upon me from the day of your elevation to the Regency to that of my departure for the Continent, would be to describe every species of personal offence that can be offered to, and every pain, short of bodily violence, that can be inflicted on, any human being. Bereft of parent, brother, and father-in-law, and having my husband for my deadliest foe—seeing those who have promised me support bought by rewards to be amongst my enemies—restrained from accusing my foes in the face of the world, out of regard to the character of the father of my child, and from a desire to prevent her happiness from being disturbed—shunned from motives of selfishness by those who were my natural associates—living in obscurity whilst I ought to have been the centre of all that was splendid; thus humbled, I had one consolation left, the love of my dear and only child. But, more inhuman than the slave-dealer, your Majesty tore my child from me, deprived me of the power of being at hand to succour her, took from me the possibility of hearing her last prayers for her mother; and when you saw me bereft, forlorn, broken-hearted, chose that moment of woe for redoubling your persecutions. Let the world pass its judgment on the constituting of a commission in a foreign country, consisting of inquisitors, spies, and informers, to discover, collect, and arrange matters of accusation against your wife, without any complaint having been communicated to her. Let the world judge of the employment of ambassadors in such a business, and of the enlisting of foreign courts in the enterprise; but on the measures which have been adopted to give final effect to those preliminary proceedings, it is for me to speak, it is for me to remonstrate with your Majesty, it is for me to protest, it is for me to apprize you of my determination to demand not to be subjected to sentence by the parliament passed in the shape of *a law*, but to a trial in a court where the jurors are taken impartially from amongst the people, and where the proceedings are open and fair. Such a trial I court; and to no other will I willingly submit. If your Majesty persevere in the present proceeding, I shall, even in the Houses of Parliament, face my accusers; but I shall regard any division they may make against me as not in the smallest degree reflecting on my honour; and I will not, except compelled by actual force, submit to any sentence which shall not be pronounced by a *court of justice.*"

This too truthful, but too malicious-toned epistle, thus concludes: "Having left me nothing but my innocence, you would now, by a mockery of justice, deprive me even of the reputation of possessing that. The poisoned bowl and the poniard are means more manly than perjured witnesses and partial tribunals; and they are less cruel, inasmuch as life is less valuable than honour. If my life would have satisfied your Majesty, you should have had it on the condition of giving me a place in the same tomb with my child; but since you would send me dishonoured to the grave, I will resist the attempt with all the means that it shall please God to give me."

The publication of this irritating letter proved of no service to the Queen, beyond that of keeping alive the popular ferment in her favour. In the language of the law, she "took nothing by her motion;" but though, on the seventeenth of August, the "Queen's trial"—as the future proceedings in the House of Peers against Caroline was designated—commenced, the Ministry allowed the Queen every facility of legal talents and pecuniary aid for her defence. Lord, then plain Mr., Brougham was her Attorney-General, Mr. Denman was her Solicitor-General, and the other counsel were Dr. Lushington, Mr. Williams, Thomas Wild, and N. C. Tindal, all eminent members of the legal profession. At this period, Lord Liverpool privately expressed a hope that the Queen would give way—but he was mistaken. Caroline's popularity at this period was great; numerous popular addresses were presented to her, riots occurred in her favour, and the Italian witnesses against her, on landing at Dover, were roughly handled by a mob of her partizans, composed chiefly of women. She, relying on this popularity, stood firm to her purpose, and daily appeared, throughout the period of her trial, in the House of Peers, where accommodation befitting a Queen-consort was provided her.

At this period, her Majesty resided at Brandenburgh House, Hammersmith, and at a mansion in St. James's Square, next door to the residence of her persecutor in the Commons, Lord Castlereagh; and her progresses from, sometimes one, sometimes both of these mansions, to the House, were witnessed by immense crowds of democrats or radicals—as they were then designated—who vociferously shouted, "The Queen! The Queen! God save the Queen!" and insulted every passer-by, who would not join in their cry.

Although the "Queen's trial" commenced on the seventeenth of August, on which day Caroline, for the first time, attended the House, and was treated by the Peers as the Queen-consort of the realm, nothing of im~ortance was done till two days afterwards, when the attorney-general opened the case for the crown. The examination of witnesses commenced on the twenty-first, but as much of their evidence was of a peculiar nature, it, for decency's sake, will be passed over. The first witness called was the notorious *Non mi ricordo* (I don't remember) Theodore Majocchi; and the moment he entered, the Queen, overcome by the appearance against her of one who owed her a deep debt of gratitude, passionately exclaimed, "Oh, traditoro!" (oh, traitor!)—and hurrying out of the House, returned to her home in a state of intense mental agitation.

According to what was considered the most reliable portion of Majocchi's evidence, Bergami attended Caroline in the bath (but she wore a bathing-dress at these times), and, in the hot climate of the east, he slept under the same tent in which she slept, on board of one of the vessels in which they sailed; but the tent, on these occasions, was always partially open. The other portions of Majocchi's evidence produced but little impression. He appeared to "speak by rote," and not from recollection. "Besides," remarks the writer of a letter in the Diary illustrative of the Court, &c., of George IV., "besides, I do think he was a knowing rogue, who *forgot* to remember many things which, perhaps, might have changed the hue of his insinuations. I do not say that what he did say was not sufficient to induce a strong suspicion of guilt itself in the members of an English society, but this is the very thing complained of. The Queen was in *foreign* society, in peculiar circumstances, and yet our state Solomons judge of her conduct as if she had been among the English."

The other witnesses against Caroline—captains, boatmen, tradesmen, mechanics, labourers, chambermaids, and others, many with long aliases to their names—all swore to her having acted with impropriety, at inns, on board ship, and in other places; and if the evidence of some of them is to be accredited, she was really guilty of the crimes imputed to her by the crown.

On the seventh of September, the case against the Queen closed on the part of the attorney-general, and the further proceedings were adjourned till the third of October, on which day Mr. Brougham opened the defence of the Queen, in an eloquent and powerful speech. Mr. Williams next commented with great force and boldness on the evidence of her Majesty's accusers, and numerous witnesses were called in the Queen's behalf, whose sworn testimony, in some instances, was in complete contradiction to that of the crown witnesses —in fact, gross perjury there must have been on one side or the other, or, perhaps, on both. The evidence for the Queen, however, proved of a character so favourable, that ministers seriously contemplated relinquishing the bill.

On the twenty-third of October, the witnesses on her Majesty's behalf having all been examined, Mr. Denman summed up for the defence in a long, luminous, energetic speech, and, on the following day, Dr. Lushington closed the defence with an able address, embracing a variety of topics but slightly noticed by the preceding advocates. The attorney and the solicitor-general closed the case by skilful replies, and the debates on the evidence commenced on the second of November and continued till the sixth, when the second reading of the bill was carried by 123 to 95.

The next day Caroline signed a protest against this decision of the assembled peers, and whilst doing so, exclaimed aloud, "There, Caroline is Queen in spite of you!" The smallness of the majority in favour of the second reading of the bill, twenty-eight, further alarmed ministers; but, after consultation, they again resolved not to abandon the bill, and the House went into committee on the divorce clause. Several of the bishops and temporal peers had expressed their determination of voting against the bill if this clause was not cut out of it; and, in consequence, Caroline's supporters, to increase the number of their votes at the third reading, now voted for this clause, and caused its retention to be carried by a large majority. The manœuvre, for such it really was, succeeded admirably. Upon the division on the third reading of the bill, which took place on the tenth of November, there appeared 108 for it and 99 against it, being only a majority of nine—exactly the number of cabinet peers—and, in consequence, Lord Liverpool remarked, "that, in the present feeling of the country, and with a division of sentiment in the House so nearly balanced, he felt it to be the duty of himself and his colleagues not to proceed further with the bill; he moved, therefore, that the question, 'that the bill do pass,' should not be put till that day six months."

This abandonment of the Bill of Pains and Penalties was received with considerable cheering by the House, and celebrated in the metropolis and other places by the ringing of bells, illuminations, and other tokens of public joy.

But whilst the people rejoiced at the victory they had achieved, Caroline was suffering unspeakable anguish. She felt that the verdict of the peers, although carried by only a small majority, had condemned her, and, whether guilty or not, branded on her character the indelible mark of infamy. In the height of her grief, she exclaimed, with bitterness, "The victory is not for me, but for the nation. Oh, mine God! the ministry, although forced to withdraw the dreadful bill against me, first triumphed by carrying it. They say I am guilty, but they let me off to please the sovereign people. Oh, d—n! d—n!" She, however, speedily rallied from this mood of gloom and grief, and boldly demanded of the premier a residence befitting her rank and dignity. This demand was politely refused, and immediately she again claimed to have her name inserted in the liturgy, and to receive the revenue of a queen consort. Next she resolved to publicly return thanks at St. Paul's for the failure of the ministerial efforts to crush her. She appointed the twenty-ninth of November for this object, due notice of which was given to the proper officials of St. Paul's; but the holy men of that cathedral, influenced by authority of the highest, resolved to make no change in the ordinary service; and, but for the efforts of the Corporation of London, not the smallest preparations would have been made for her reception. At the appointed time, Caroline set out, with her very slender suite, from Brandenburgh House, and, on the route to the cathedral, her procession was gradually swollen by the addition of numbers of her parliamentary and public friends and supporters. All London was abroad; the "City companies" were marshalled out to do her honour, and, contrary to the expressed opinion of the cathedral functionaries, the multitude, who welcomed her with hearty shouts and huzzas, conducted themselves in a manner becoming the solemn occasion. Thus triumphantly Caroline proceeded to St. Paul's, where the ordinary service was performed in her presence. But the officiating clergy neither offered up any especial thanksgiving in her name, nor even in the general thanksgiving prayer read the paragraph—"particularly to those who desire now to offer up their praises and thanksgiving for thy late mercies vouchsafed unto them." In fact, they showed by their conduct that they wished it to be understood that the Queen had no business to make a public offering of gratitude to God for her narrow escape from the snares laid for her by her enemies.

In this and the subsequent month, Caroline was literally inundated with congratulatory addresses, for the most part presented by bodies of artizans in procession; and the revolutionary tone of some of these addresses rather injured than benefitted the cause they were meant to serve.

As the annual income voted by the parliament to Caroline, as Princess of Wales, ceased on the death of George III., the King, when he opened the parliamentary sessions, in January, 1821, recommended to the House of Commons that a revenue, as a separate maintenance, should be settled upon her Majesty. The proud Queen at first refused to accept of any pecuniary allowance until her name was inserted in the liturgy; but as on this point the government made a firm stand, and obtained a vote against her in both houses of parliament, whilst she herself was fast sinking into the depth of poverty, she, to the disappointment of many of her friends, gave way, and an annuity of £50,000 a year was settled upon her.

The royal inauguration next became the all-absorbing topic. In May, it was determined that the King's coronation should be solemnized during the parliamentary recess; and immediately this determination became known to the Queen, she further exasperated her husband against her by claiming a right to be crowned with him as Queen Consort. Lord Liverpool wrote her that his Majesty had resolved that she should take no part in the coronation ceremonial; but she persevered in her efforts to obtain what she knew would never be granted; and on the fourth of July the privy council sat at the Cockpit, Whitehall, to hear counsel in support of her claim. Messrs. Brougham and Denman spoke in her behalf at great length. They exerted their utmost to persuade their hearers that Caroline, as Queen Consort, could demand to be crowned with her husband; but both the attorney and the solicitor-general fully demonstrated the fallacy of their arguments; and the lords of the council, after long and solemn deliberation, decided that "the Queens Consort of this realm are not entitled of right to be crowned at any time;" a decision which the King was pleased to approve, and which was formally communicated to the Queen.

Although foiled, Caroline was not silenced; she demanded of Lord Sidmouth that suitable accommodation might be provided for her at the forthcoming coronation, as she had resolved to be present at that ceremony. In a letter insulting to her dignity, Lord Sidmouth replied, that the King had resolved that her request should not be granted. She then wrote to the same purport to the Duke of Norfolk, as Earl Marshal of England, and he forwarded her letter to Lord Howard of Effingham, the appointed "acting Earl Marshal" at the coronation, who, with expressions of regret, assured her Majesty that "under existing circumstances it was impossible for him to have the honour of obeying her commands." That no stone might be left unturned, the foolishly-persevering Queen next caused it to be notified to the Archbishop of Canterbury that she desired to be crowned at Westminster at an early day after the inauguration of the King, and before the fittings and appointments for that ceremonial had been taken down. The primate replied, that being the King's servant, it was his duty to only obey the commands of his royal master on the subject in question; and immediately afterwards the Queen published a long and spirited protest against the decision of the privy council. This protest, which was addressed to the King, and was too crowded with harsh threats, remonstrances, and revilings to serve any purpose beyond that of further protracting the public excitement, was drawn up by Caroline's legal adviser, who hoped that as her dignity had now been sufficiently vindicated, she would not hazard any further steps in the matter. In fact, this, it is said, was Mr. Brougham's advice to her; but to such advice she turned a deaf ear.

The coronation, one of the most splendid on record, was to be solemnized on the nineteenth of July; and about half-past five on the morning of that day, her Majesty, accompanied by Lord and Lady Hood and Lady Anne Hamilton, proceeded in her state carriage, drawn by six horses, through St. James's Park to Westminster. On her way she was loudly greeted with the cry of "The Queen! the Queen for ever!" mingled, however, with occasional hisses. At Westminster Hall gate her Majesty alighted, and, accompanied by Ladies Hood and Hamilton, and leaning on the arm of Lord Hood, proceeded to the door leading to the Speaker's house, when the mistake being discovered, she turned round, and followed by a multitude of people, who were anxious to witness the result, ascended to the platform, along which persons with peers' tickets passed into the abbey. Here their tickets were demanded by an officer in command of the soldiery drawn across the platform; but Lord Hood declared that he had authority to be there, and presenting a paper to the officer, satisfied him, and the Queen and her attendants were suffered to pass on. After more blundering, the way being led by a posse of constables and the mob to the passage leading to the kitchen, Caroline and her suite at last reached the Abbey entrance at Poet's Corner, where Lord Hood demanded admission for the Queen. The door-keeper declared that his instructions were to admit no one without a peer's ticket.

"Did you ever hear of a Queen being asked for a ticket before?" demanded Lord Hood. "This is your Queen."

"My orders," replied the door-keeper, "are general, and without any exceptions; I have never been in a similar situation before, and can say nothing as to the propriety or impropriety of refusing her Majesty admission."

"I present to you your Queen," rejoined Lord Hood, with warmth; "do you refuse her admission?"

"Yes, I am your Queen, and wish to be admitted," joined in the degraded Caroline.

"My orders are imperative," repeated the door-keeper, "and therefore, however willing to oblige her Majesty, I dare not suffer her to pass without a ticket."

At this moment Lord Hood exclaimed, "I have a ticket!" and on producing it, the door-keeper observed that it would admit but one individual. Caroline felt half inclined to enter alone, but as the door-keeper declared that no preparations had been made for her reception, she, half laughing, half crying, with mortification, resolved to return to her carriage. At this moment some one in the door-way burst into a loud derisive laugh, which drew from Lord Hood the observation, that in such a place he expected to meet with decorous conduct, and not insult toward a sovereign. Caroline had not proceeded many paces, when she passed through a bevy of noble ladies, who were going to the Abbey with tickets, but who took not the slightest notice of her. She was followed from the platform by a crowd, of whom some praised and others blamed her conduct. On entering her carriage, she was greeted from the windows and balconies by hisses and cries of "Shame! shame! off! off!" but, as before, the excited mob cheered her with unbounded enthusiasm.

On returning home, Caroline, with a flood of tears, bitterly bewailed this the greatest of her humiliations. She felt that her degradation was now sealed, and the mortification killed her. Her health, which for some time had been declining, from this hour rapidly gave way.

Eleven days after admittance to the coronation had been rudely refused her, she visited Drury Lane Theatre, but was too ill to sit out the performance. This was her last appearance in public: on the second of August a bulletin, issued by her medical attendant, announced that she was suffering from a dangerous internal malady; other bulletins proclaimed the fact that she grew worse and worse, and it soon became evident that her dissolution was at hand. She herself from the first pronounced her illness mortal. She repeatedly expressed a wish to die; and having signed her will, ordered her diary to be burned, and spoken kindly and charitably of every one, she calmly expired at half-past ten in the morning, on the seventh of August, surrounded by Lord and Lady Hood and Lady Anne Hamilton, whilst near at hand were her legal advisers and medical attendants, with Alderman Wood and one of his sons. She died in the fifty-fourth year of her age, a martyr to her own folly and to the harsh persecutions of her unprincipled husband, who, because he hated her, strained every nerve to punish her presumed violation of the marriage vow, whilst he claimed imputation for being himself a most unclean, vicious adulterer.

Caroline bequeathed nearly the whole of her property to her protége, William Austin, who survived her but a short while; and she also willed that, three days after her death, her body, which was not to be opened, was to be conveyed to Brunswick, and there buried; and that on her coffin was to be inscribed, "To the memory of Caroline of Brunswick, the injured Queen of England." Her executors were Dr. Lushington and Mr. Wilde; and the government offended both them and the public by undertaking the funeral arrangements, and resolving that the procession should not pass through the city.

A harsh correspondence took place between the ministers and the Queen's friends as to when and how the royal corpse should be conveyed to Brunswick. The lord mayor and corporation of London expressed an earnest wish to join the funeral *cortège* in its passage through the city; but to all inquiries and entreaties on the subject, the government returned one stereotyped reply—their arrangements had been made in compliance with the King's wish, and were irrevocable.

Accordingly, on the fourteenth of August, her Majesty's remains were conveyed, with but little funeral pomp, and a military escort, from Brandenburgh House, Hammersmith, where had been held the ceremony of lying in state, with the intention of proceeding by Bayswater, the New Road, and Islington, to Romford, and thence by the direct road to Harwich, the port of embarkation. But the people declared that they, and not the King (as had been announced), would have to pay the funeral charges; and with a determination that their expressed will for the procession to pass through the city should be complied with, they collected in vast crowds. The morning was murky and stormy; rain poured down in torrents, and inundated the streets with mud; but, spite rain, mud, and military escort, the multitude, with wild hurrahs, demonstrated their gigantic power by constructing a barricade at Church Street, Kensington, which forced the procession to proceed in the direct route to the city. The Life Guards and Sir R. Baker, the chief police magistrate at Bow Street, speedily arrived, with the intention of dispersing the determined mob—but this they found to be impossible; and when, in compliance with orders in the meantime received from the government, they endeavoured to conduct the procession through the Kensington gate of Hyde Park into the Edgeware Road, the people took forcible possession of the gate, closed and barricaded it, and with tumultuous shouts of victory, again forced the authorities to proceed with the coffin in the required direction. But again ministers despatched an imperative order to Sir R. Baker to conduct the procession through the Park by some one of the roads into the Edgeware Road. Strenuous efforts were made to carry out this order. At first every avenue was effectually blocked up by the people, who loudly shouted, "The city! the city!" Speedily the struggle became fiercer; stones and sticks were resorted to, the line of procession was broken, and whilst the combatants were fighting for the mastery at Park Lane, Mr. Bailey, the undertaker, seized a favourable moment to rush with the coffin through the gate into the Park. The military followed, and the authorities conducted the procession across the Park to Cumberland Gate; but here, again, the excited multitude had collected in a dense mass. They held the gate, and hooted and pelted at the military, till at last the irritated Life Guards fired and killed two men and wounded several others. The people, after flinging a shower of stones thick as hail at the soldiery, now gave way, and the procession pushed hurriedly forward past the wounded in triumph, and shaped their course into and along the New Road. But the multitude, now joined by several of the mourners, who had left the procession to take part in the perilous contest, suddenly rushed forward, and at Tottenham Court Road tore up the stones, and effectually blocked up every street saving those which led to the city; and towards the city the procession was forced to proceed, amidst deafening shouts of popular triumph and execration. To turn in any other direction was found to be impossible; every street and alley leading into the suburbs was effectually barricaded; and thus the procession was driven forward, spite the efforts of its conductors, along Tottenham Court Road and down Drury Lane into the Strand.

The people now felt that victory was theirs; and when at length the royal remains were carried under Temple Bar, they rent the air with loud, long, and deafening shouts of triumph. At Temple Bar the lord mayor and aldermen joined the procession, and they proceeded with it to Whitechapel, the eastern limit of the city. Thus the people, although repeatedly beaten back, and once repulsed with loss of life, finally triumphed. The authorities, at the risk of inciting a revolution, held out to the last; they yielded only to sheer force; and yet a month afterwards Sir R. Baker was deprived of his office, and Major-General Sir Robert Wilson was dismissed his Majesty's service.

From Whitechapel, London, the mourners, Mr. Austin, Lord and Lady Hood, Lady Anne Hamilton, Count Vassali, and Dr. and Mrs. Lushington, followed the royal remains to Harwich. From this port the Pioneer schooner proceeded with the corpse of the lamented Caroline of Brunswick to Cuxhaven, whence it was conveyed up the Elbe and the Schwinde to Stade, from which place it was carried with due respect to Brunswick, and there, on the twenty-fourth of August, interred, with solemn funeral rites, in the cathedral of St. Blaize, in the vault where rest the remains of her heroic father and brother, the former of whom fell at Jena, the latter at Quatre Bras.

ADELAIDE OF SAXE-MEININGEN,

Queen of William the Fourth.

CHAPTER I

Parentage—Birth—Disposition—Father dies—Arrival in England—Marriage to the Duke of Clarence—Journey to Hanover—Daughter born prematurely—The infant dies—Tour to Saxe-Meiningen—Journey to England—Miscarriage—Residence at Walmer Castle, at St. James's, and at Bushy—Daughter Elizabeth born—Dies—Indisposition occasioned by the bereavement—More tours on the Continent—Residence at Bushy—Domestic life—Income increased on the death of the Duke of York—Accession of her husband—Career as Queen of Britain commences—Coronation—First introduction in public as Queen—Popularity—Appointment to the rangership of Bushy Park—Kindness to the natural children of the King her husband—Character assailed—Popularity declines—Regency Act—Conduct to the Princess Victoria—Mother dies—Husband, William IV., becomes unwell—Dies.

DELAIDE AMELIA LOUISA THERESA, one of the most virtuous and well-intentioned of the Queens-Consort of England, was the daughter of George Frederick Charles, Duke of Saxe-Coburg Meiningen, and his duchess, Louisa Eleanora, daughter of Christian Albert Louis, Prince of Hohenloe Langenburg. She first saw the light on the thirteenth of August, 1792, and was the first born of a family of three. Her sister, Ida, was born in 1794, and in 1816, married Bernard, son of the Archduke Charles of Saxe-Weimar-Eisenach, by whom she had issue. Her brother, Bernard Henry, who eventually succeeded to his father's dukedom, entered the world in 1800, and married Mary, daughter of Prince William of Hesse Cassel. From earliest girlhood, Adelaide, in disposition and habits, was remarkably sedate, thoughtful, and retired. She found no charm in the gaieties of courtly life; her studies she pursued with commendable diligence; her leisure hours were passed in simple, cheerful, innocent amusements; and she let no opportunity of doing good slip by. Her father died in 1813, and left the guardianship of his children to the Duchess-dowager, as Regent. And to this Duchess, who was a most affectionate mother, and a wise, erudite, and accomplished instructor, Adelaide was indebted for those moral, liberal, charitable principles, which rendered her, in womanhood, a worthy pattern of domestic piety and private charity, and a brilliant ornament to that throne which she shared with her husband, the Reformer, King William IV.

In 1817, the much-lamented Princess Charlotte died; and influenced by this event, and by a desire to increase their revenues, the Princes of the blood-royal of England resolved to enter into the holy estate of matrimony. The Duke of Clarence chose for his bride the Princess Adelaide; and in April, 1818, ministers formally announced his intentions to parliament, and moved that his income be augmented by an addition of not less than £10,000 a year; but in the Commons, on the motion of Mr. Sumner, who complained of the Duke's being in debt, the addition was reduced to £6000 a year. The Duke of Clarence, annoyed at this reduction, declared that such a paltry increase of revenue would not enable him to maintain an establishment suitable to his dignity, if he entered the married state. He even caused Lord Castlereagh to announce to the Commons that the negotiation for the marriage was at an end. But shorly afterwards he found it expedient to accept the parliamentary grant, and resume the correspondence for his marriage with the subject of this memoir. Circumstances, however, prevented him from then going to Germany, and the Duchess-dowager of Saxe-Meiningen having brought her daughter, the Princess Adelaide, to England, the marriage was solemnized at Kew, on the eleventh of July, 1818. The Duke and Duchess of Kent were at the same time re-married, according to the rites of the church of England. The Prince-Regent gave away both the brides, and the Archbishop of Canterbury performed the ceremony. Queen Charlotte attended the solemnization of the nuptials; but the fatal illness, from which she then was suffering, forced her to retire immediately after she had bestowed her blessing on the two royal brothers and their brides. At five, the whole party sat down to a sumptuous dinner; and a few days afterwards, the Duke and Duchess of Clarence took leave of the royal family and proceeded to Hanover, where they resided till the spring of 1819. Their sojourn at Hanover was shortened by an event which put the life of her Royal Highness in great jeopadry. On the twenty-ninth of March, 1819, Adelaide gave premature birth to a daughter, who lived only a few hours, and was interred in the royal vault, at Hanover. Her illness was protracted; and when sufficiently recovered, change of air being recommended, she proceeded to Meiningen, in Saxony, her native place; visiting Göttingen, Hesse, Phillipsthal, and other places, *en route.*

"The joy of the people of Saxony," observes a popular author, "on again beholding their beloved Princess, knew no bounds; and from the moment she entered the precincts of the Duchy, she was met and welcomed by the vassals of her brother, and escorted in triumph for a distance of nearly thirty miles to the capital, where holiday was kept for a month. The royal Duke, too, by his kind and condescending manner, and devoted attention to his amiable consort, soon won the hearts of the people of Meiningen, and became as popular as one of their own princes. After a residence of six weeks in the castle, the court removed to Liebenstein, a celebrated bathing-place, where, by the aid of its mineral springs, in the course of the summer the Duchess recovered her health."

In October, 1819, the royal pair set out for England. On the way nothing remarkable occurred till they reached Dunkirk, when the Duchess had the misfortune to miscarry. Again her illness was severe; but when sufficiently recovered, she, with her consort, embarked in the Royal Sovereign yacht, and landed safely at Dover. Her Royal Highness being yet too weak to proceed to London, and recommended by her medical advisers to sojourn for a period on the sea coast, the Duke, on the invitation of the Earl of Liverpool, then Warden of the Cinque Ports, proceeded with her to Walmer Castle, whence, after a residence of six weeks, she was enabled to accompany him to St. James's. Immediately Bushy, which was undergoing repairs, was rendered fit for their reception, the royal pair proceeded thither; and for a period, this pleasingly-situated rural mansion became their chief residence.

On the tenth of December, 1820, her Royal Highness gave birth to a princess; an event thus mentioned by Lord Chancellor Eldon in a letter to his daughter, the Hon. Mrs. E. Banks:

"I had not mentioned to you that I was the only cabinet minister and councillor who was in time to attend the Duchess of Clarence on Sunday evening, when she brought into the world a presumptive heiress to the crown; who has since been christened by the name of Elizabeth Georgiana. I hope the bairn will live: it came a little too early, and is a very small one at present, but the doctors seem to think it will thrive, and to the ears of your humble servant it appears to be noisy enough to show it has great strength. Nobody in the room at its birth but the doctors, the nurse, and chancellor."*

As predicted by the chancellor, the royal bairn, although small, proved, to all appearance, strong and healthy. The fond parents anxiously hoped that their infant would reach maturity, and succeed to the throne of Britain; but when scarcely three months old, the Princess bitterly disappointed those hopes, by rather suddenly dying, from introsusception of the bowels. The calm resignation of the bereaved parents in this moment of severe trial, and their humble submission to the Divine will, is described by one of their household as "one of those scenes which give dignity to rank, and impress deeply upon the mind the truth and value of the christian faith." But however truthful this description may be, certain it is, that the bereavement proved a severe affliction to the Duchess, and brought on a dangerous indisposition, from which she only recovered after several months of severe suffering.

On the thirteenth of June, 1822, the Duke and Duchess of Clarence again embarked for the Continent. They sailed in the Royal Sovereign yacht to Antwerp, and thence proceeded to Ghent, where they were sumptuously entertained by the Duke of Saxe Weimar. From Ghent they journeyed on through Coblentz; passed some time at Niewied, with Prince Maximilian; paid a visit to the Landgrave and Landgravine of Hesse Homburg, at Frankfort; and on the fourteenth of July, met the reigning Duke of Saxe-Meiningen, at Nalda. Throughout the tour they were everywhere received with the greatest possible distinction; and after some time pleasantly passed at the welcoming little court of Saxe-Meiningen, they proceeded from Heidelberg, through Brussels and Ghent, to Antwerp; and thence voyaged to England in the Royal Sovereign. In 1825, and in 1826, the Duke and Duchess again made similar tours on the Continent. These travels being terminated in the latter year, they came to reside permanently at Bushy.

Dr. Beattie, private physician to the Duke, thus describes the domestic life of their Royal Highnesses at this period:—

"To his illustrious partner, whose many and exalted virtues his Royal Highness so duly appreciates, no man can possibly evince more delicate and uniform attentions. There is not, perhaps, at the present day two personages of similar station in whom the virtues of domestic life are more pleasingly exemplified. With those excellent qualities of mind and heart, so eminently possessed by the Royal Duchess, it is not surprising that her Royal Highness should have won, and should retain, the esteem and affection of her illustrious consort. His mind is fully alive to their vital importance as regards his present happiness, and to the influence they must exercise over his future prospects."

The death of the Duke of York, on the fifth of January, 1827, made the Duke of Clarence heir-presumptive to the throne; and on the sixteenth of February, in pursuance of a message from his Majesty (George IV.), both houses of parliament agreed to a grant of £6000 a year, as a jointure for the

* Life of Lord Chancellor Eldon, by Horace Twiss.

Duchess of Clarence, and £3000 a year to the Duke, which, with £3000 a year to which he was entitled on the death of the Duke of York, made an increase to his income of £12,000 a year. From this period, the biography of the Princess Adelaide presents scarcely a scene of a stirring or an eventful character. She continued to walk in the paths of virtue, and to pursue the ways of peace and charity; and, as is usual with the virtuous and sedate, her life was unchequered by thrilling incidents or passion-exciting circumstances.

On the death of George IV.—June the twenty-sixth, 1830—her beloved consort ascended the throne, by the title of William IV., and she became Queen-consort.

The coronation of King William IV. and Queen Adelaide did not take place till the eighth of September, 1831. His Majesty, it is said, wished to pass over the pageant altogether; but the Duke of Wellington thwarted the royal wish, by moving the subject in the House of Peers. Although it may be questioned whether William did or did not desire to be crowned, certain it is that only the usual and indispensable inauguration ceremonies were performed in Westminster Abbey by the Archbishop of Canterbury; and that the frugal King caused all needless display of pomp and magnificence to be suppressed. There was no grand banquet, and the sight-seeing world was further disappointed by there being no royal procession, saving a meagre one from St. James's Palace to the Abbey. In the evening, however, the metropolis was brilliantly illuminated, the theatres, Vauxhall Gardens, and other places of amusement, were thrown open to the public gratuitously, and a grand display of fireworks in Hyde Park attracted thousands of spectators. The coronation was followed by a grand dinner, at which the King, having given the toast, "The land we live in," remarked, "that he was much gratified at the events of the day, but he did not at all agree with those who considered such a ceremony indispensable, for that the compact between the prince and the people was as binding on his mind before as after; and that no member of the House of Brunswick could forget the conditions on which he held the crown." From some cause, which time only can truthfully reveal, both the Duchess of Kent and her beloved daughter, the Princess Victoria, were absent from the ceremony.

The Princess Adelaide was first introduced in public as Queen on the seventeenth of July, 1830. On that day, a deputation from the University of Oxford, and another from that of Cambridge, presented congratulatory addresses to her consort; and immediately after they had been permitted the honour of kissing hands, the King, to their agreeable surprise, desired them to remain till they had been introduced to the Queen, who, without delay, came forward and gave them a most gracious reception.

The popularity enjoyed by Adelaide whilst Duchess of Clarence, was greatly increased on her elevation to the crown matrimonial. Her means of doing good were enlarged, and these means she employed in a manner most able and worthy. After tarrying a short while at Windsor Castle, their Majesties proceeded to the Pavilion at Brighton, for the benefit of the sea air; and whilst sojourning there, the King made frequent excursions in the neighbourhood: one of these excursions was to Lewes, where the King was presented with an address, and entertained at a banquet. On the health of himself and his consort being drank, the King replied in a lengthy but neat speech, from which the subjoined is extracted:—

"There is, gentlemen, one point which I have passed over, but of which it was my intention to have taken notice. You have drank the health of her Majesty the Queen, and, in returning you my thanks, I meant to have done the same on her part also. Among the many favourable circumstances under which Providence has called me to ascend the throne of this country, there is none for which I feel more grateful, upon which I set a higher value, than that it had previously been my happy fortune to be married to an individual so excellent in every amiable and good feeling. In this country, character finds its way forth into the world, and is always known. I have no doubt, therefore, that you are already well aware of what I would say; but I must take the opportunity of speaking what I am most sincerely convinced of, that her Majesty, who sits before you, possesses every estimable quality calculated to give worth and lustre to her exalted station. Of this I am satisfied, also, that a great share of that good and kind feeling which has been so largely manifested towards me since I have occupied the throne, has not only been due to her estimable qualities, but has strictly and truly been exhibited and paid on account of that sense which is entertained of them." This speech made a deep impression on the company, and the Queen was sensibly moved by the manner in which her consort alluded to his domestic happiness.

At this period, the King bestowed the rangership of Bushy Park upon the Queen for life, thereby indicating, it was presumed, that Bushy should become her Majesty's future residence, in case of her surviving him: indeed, Adelaide, from her long residence there, had previously expressed a strong attachment to the place.

To the natural children of her husband, Adelaide, from the hour of her marriage, had evinced the greatest kindness, and now that she was Queen, that kindness, if possible, increased. "They were all retained in the closest intimacy with her court. She witnessed, with pleasure, their being ennobled, and she felt delighted in beholding the King distributing all the private fortune he could command amongst them."

As a full detail of Adelaide's career as Queen-consort would be dry and uninteresting, only a few of the leading events will be noticed. Her time she passed in the society of the King and her royal relations, with the former of whom she appeared on almost every public occasion; and her popularity being great, she was usually received at these times with enthusiastic welcomes. But, many as were her virtues, extensive as was her popularity, she had numerous political enemies. The ultra-liberals accused her of exercising undue influence over the mind of her loving husband in public matters, and they denounced her as being at most but a lukewarm friend to reform advancement and the principles of popular government. It was asserted that she lent private support to the opponents of the Reform Bill; and the unexpected break-up of the Melbourne ministry in November, 1834, and the restoration of the Tories to office, were attributed to her sole influence. This latter incident, the secret history of which has not yet been fully revealed, and which created a political excitement only less intense than that occasioned by the passing of the Reform Bill, was not even known to the Queen till after it had been made public. The misstatement was immediately contradicted; but, withal, it greatly damaged her popularity, and created a feeling against her in the minds of the people generally, too permanent to be fully effaced during her lifetime. She herself felt that her character had been unjustly assailed; and when, on the anniversary of the King's birth-day, in 1835, the bishops presented their customary addresses, the Queen, in performing her part of the ceremony, concluded her reply to the loyal prelates in the following significant words:—"My lords, I am particularly obliged to you for this declaration of attachment at this period, when I am most cruelly and undeservedly insulted and calumniated on many occasions."

At the commencement of the reign of William IV., an act was passed, setting forth that, in case of a posthumous child by the Queen, her Majesty should be guardian during its minority; and that, in the event of the King's demise without legitimate issue, and before the Princess Victoria—the heir-presumptive —was of age, the Duchess of Kent should be Regent during the minority of the Princess, her daughter. This act, it was said, gave umbrage to the Queen: there was no chance of her again becoming a mother; and as there *was* a chance of her outliving the King, her husband, who might perhaps die before the Princess Victoria *was* of age, she felt hurt that parliament had not declared her, in that case, to be Regent. She, however, took pleasure in treating and regarding the Princess Victoria as the heiress to the throne of Great Britain; and one of her last acts, as Queen-consort, was the giving an extremely magnificent ball at St. James's palace, on the twenty-fifth of May, 1837, in commemoration of the Princess Victoria attaining her eighteenth year—the age when it became lawfully eligible for her to at once ascend the throne on the demise of William IV.

The spring of 1837 brought trouble to the Queen. Her venerated mother, whose health had been declining for several months, expired on the twenty-ninth of April, at the age of sixty-eight. The distressing intelligence, although not altogether unexpected, proved a severe shock to her Majesty, who had scarcely recovered from the bereavement, when the health of her beloved consort, William IV., gave way; and it soon became evident that he, too, would shortly be gathered to his fathers. The good old king's health had been gradually breaking ever since the commencement of the year; as the summer advanced, he grew weaker and weaker; and in June the public were apprized of his dangerous condition, by the publication of bulletins. He bore his sufferings with christian fortitude and resignation, retained his consciousness almost to the last moment of his existence, and with unfeigned gratitude repeatedly expressed, to use his very words, "Thanks! a thousand thanks!" at the untiring attentions which he received from those around him. On Sunday, the eighteenth of June, he received the sacrament from the hand of the Archbishop of Canterbury; and on the twenty-sixth he breathed his last, as his arm rested on Queen Adelaide's shoulder, and his faithful partner's hand supported his breast, a position which her Majesty had maintained for upwards of an hour previous to the fatal event.

The Queen's attention to her dying consort had been close, constant, and assiduous; for twelve days she had remained in the sick chamber, administering comfort and consolation; and throughout that period she did not once take off her clothes—an affectionate discharge of her conjugal duties deserving of the highest commendation, and which may be worthily imitated, but can scarcely be surpassed, by the best, most patient, and affectionate of wives. The melancholy bereavement produced a depression of spirits and a corresponding decline of health, from which the Queen-dowager did not recover till some time afterwards; nevertheless, she was present in one of the royal closets during the funeral service, when the remains of her husband were interred, with imposing obsequies, in St. George's Chapel, Windsor, on the eighth of July.

CHAPTER II.

Adelaide's enormous dower as Queen-dowager—Residence at St. Leonards-at-Sea—And at Malta—Tours in England—Abode at Sudbury—Visit to Queen Victoria—Residence at Canford House, and at Witley Court—Private charity—Home at Cassiobury—Visit to Germany—Abode at Bentley Priory—Fatal illness—Death—Burial—Character—Acts of munificence.

FTER the death of King William IV., the Queen-dowager Adelaide received the enormous sum of £100,000 a year, together with Bushy and Marlborough House, for residences—an extravagant dower, which parliament settled upon her for life, in August, 1831; and to which the nation willingly assented, as one of the bribes for the passing of the Reform Bill—a measure which the people had a just right to demand, and which a truly wise and liberal aristocracy would have ceded to the nation years previously. The subsequent autumn and winter Adelaide passed at St. Leonards-on-Sea. In October, 1838, she, by the advice of her medical attendants, proceeded to Malta; and was there received with unfeigned demonstrations of enthusiastic joy by the populace, and with every possible mark of distinction by the authorities.

"At this period the want of church accommodation was much complained of at Malta by the British residents there—amounting to about two thousand—whilst the only means provided was the government palace chapel, which only afforded three hundred sittings. The Queen-dowager, on being informed of this spiritual destitution, resolved to supply the want by the erection of a new church. The first stone was laid by her Majesty on the twentieth of March, 1839; and the sacred edifice was completed at a cost of £15,000, exceeding by one-third the amount of her Majesty's original grant. The dimensions of this church exceed those of any of the modern churches in London; the length of the area being one hundred and ten feet; breadth, sixty-seven feet; and height, forty-five feet. The front of the edifice, facing north-east, has an Ionic portico, with a bas-relief of St. Paul casting the viper off his hand into the fire immediately after his shipwreck (Acts xxviii. 3). The wings have a statue of St. Peter and St. Paul; and the tower and steeple are one hundred and thirty feet high, terminating with a cross."

Queen-dowager Adelaide returned to England in May, 1839; and in the subsequent autumn, she, for change of air and scene, visited the Earl of Denbigh, at Nuneham Paddock; the Earl of Howe, at Gospall Hall; the Earl of Warwick, at Warwick Castle; Sir Robert Peel, at Drayton Manor; and the Duke of Rutland, at Belvoir Castle; and in November, returned to London, and there passed the winter. In the following summer, her Majesty set out on an excursion to the lakes of Cumberland, visiting, on her way, the Earl of Brownlow, at Belton House, near Grantham; and the Earl of Harewood, at Harewood House, near Leeds. After making the tour of the Lakes, she paid a short visit to the Earl of Shrewsbury, at Alton Tower; and thence, after a progress to Matlock, proceeded to view Lord Vernon's seat of Sudbury Hall, which she engaged as her winter residence. Adelaide took up her abode at Sudbury, on the twenty-eighth of September. In November, she came to London to congratulate Queen Victoria (whom God preserve) on the birth-day of the Princess-Royal. The visit was a short one; and Adelaide hastened back to Sudbury, and there continued to reside till the commencement of the subsequent spring. But again, at the close of autumn in 1841, she proceeded to Sudbury to pass the winter; and whilst residing there, her health so completely gave way, that for a period her life was despaired of. She, however, recovered, and in the winter of 1842, took up her residence at Canford House, the seat of Lord De Mauley, in Dorsetshire, whence, in the spring, she proceeded to Marlborough House, and there resided for some time. In August, 1843, she took Lord Ward's seat of Witley Court, near Worcester, for three years; and during her residence in this commodious sylvan mansion her health never once gave way. Here it was that the Queen-dowager performed those numerous acts of private charity and munificence, which won for her the high esteem and grateful remembrance of the inhabitants of Worcestershire. In September, 1846, the Queen-dowager proceeded to Cassiobury, the seat of the Earl of Essex, near Watford, which splendid seat she took for a short period, and where the Queen and Prince Albert honoured her with their company for three days. In the subsequent June, Adelaide embarked at Ramsgate for Ostend; and after making a delightful tour in Germany, returned to England in August. Throughout this "progress" she was everywhere enthusiastically welcomed by the populace, and received by the authorities with all the honours due to her exalted rank and eminent private virtues. Still her Majesty continued to travel, in the hope of strengthening her naturally delicate constitution. Accompanied by their Serene Highnesses the Duchess Ida, Prince Edward, and the Princess of Saxe-Weimar, she, in October, 1847, embarked on board the *Howe* war ship, of one hundred and twenty guns, at Portsmouth, for Madeira, and on the way thither put in at the Tagus, and paid a complimentary visit to the Queen and Prince-consort of Portugal. In March, 1848, Adelaide embarked for England. After a prosperous voyage, she reached Spithead, on the second of April; the same day visited the Queen and Prince Albert at Osborne, slept that night on board the *Howe*, and the next day proceeded to London.

In the autumn of 1848, the Queen-dowager took Bentley Priory, the seat of the Marquis of Abercorn, near Stanmore; and there passed the following winter, but without adding vigour to her weakly constitution. As the spring of 1849 approached, her health became alarmingly delicate, and incipient symptoms of dropsy presented themselves. Her physicians exercised all conceivable care and discretion, with the view of combating the disease and fortifying the failing strength of the royal patient against any crisis that might occur. A change to the sea-air being deemed advisable, the Queen-dowager, on the twenty-eighth of May, proceeded to Worthing; but as her health continued to decline, after a fortnight's residence there she removed to Tunbridge Wells, where the Queen and Prince Albert paid her a visit. Towards the close of June, the Queen-dowager returned to her residence in Bushy Park, in a very unsatisfactory condition. Her constitution was evidently breaking; and now change of air no longer proved, as it always had done previously, in the slightest degree beneficial. Her Majesty and her household removed from Bushy to Bentley Priory, on the first of September; and meantime, her relatives in Germany, having been apprized of her declining condition, the Duke and Duchess of Saxe-Meiningen, and the Princess Mary, arrived from the Continent on the fourth of September, and were followed by the Prince-hereditary. Their serene highnesses remained on a visit to the Queen-dowager till the twentieth of September, and on the twenty-ninth of the same month, the Duchess Ida of Saxe-Weimar, and the Princesses Anne and Amelia, arrived, and by their presence afforded great consolation to the royal sufferer, who, notwithstanding her increasing weakness, was enabled to take frequent carriage airings up to the sixth of October, which was the last day she was enabled to enjoy out-door exercise. She then took to her chamber, and from that period her health rapidly declined. On the twelfth of October, the Queen and Prince Albert, on their return from Osborne, visited their illustrious relative, who, in the same week, received visits from the Duchess of Kent, the Duke and Duchess of Cambridge, the Duchess of Gloucester, and the hereditary Grand Duke and Grand Duchess of Mecklenburg-Strelitz. On the eighteenth of October, the Bishop of London attended at the Priory, and by Adelaide's own express desire, administered the Holy Sacrament to her.

The Queen and Prince Albert paid their last visit to their illustrious relative on the twenty-second of October, before leaving for Osborne; and shortly afterwards the Duchess of Kent twice visited the dying Queen. On Friday, the thirty-first of October, the condition of the royal sufferer excited the greatest alarm. On the afternoon of that day a distressing change took place, and her immediate relatives were hastily summoned to her chamber. She, however, rallied, and the next morning was apparently more cheerful; but the same day, at seven in the evening, another serious change took place, which denoted, beyond doubt, the approach of death. From this time her Majesty never rallied, but passed from life in a calm slumber, after a feeble cough, which occasioned the bursting of one of the vessels of the lungs. Their Serene Highnesses the Duchess Ida of Saxe Weimar, the Princes Edward and Gustave, and the Princesses Anne and Amelia, were present at the dissolution of their illustrious relative. The Earl and Countess Howe, Sir David Davis, the Rev. Canon Wood, the Rev. G. P. Hudson, Sir Andrew Barnard, Colonel and Mrs. Cornwall, and Miss Hudson, were also in attendance.

On the demise of her Majesty, the subjoined bulletin was issued by her physicians:—

"*The Priory, Dec. 2nd*, 1849.

"Her Majesty the Queen-dowager expired at seven minutes before two o'clock on Sunday morning, the second of December, without any apparent suffering, and retaining her composure of mind to the last.

"David Davis, M.D.
"Richard Bright, M.D."

At a later hour, a London Gazette extraordinary was published, containing the melancholy announcement in the following words:

"*Whitehall, Dec. 2nd*, 1849.

"This morning, at seven minutes before two o'clock, her Majesty the Queen-dowager departed this life, at Stanmore Priory, to the great grief of her Majesty and of all the royal family, after a painful and protracted illness, which she bore with exemplary patience. The loss of this most excellent Princess will be deeply mourned by all classes of her Majesty's subjects, to whom her many eminent virtues rendered her the object of universal esteem and affection."

Captain Bedford, gentleman usher to the departed Queen-dowager Adelaide, conveyed the mournful intelligence of her Majesty's demise to London with all possible speed. Expresses were hastily forwarded to the Queen and Prince Albert, to the Duchess of Kent, and to the Duke and Duchess of Cambridge, with intelligence of the mournful event; tidings of which were also communicated on Sunday forenoon to Sir George Grey, her Majesty's principal secretary of state for the home department, and to the lord mayor. The great bell of St. Paul's cathedral, as is customary on the demise of a member of the royal family, tolled, soon after the news was received in the city of London. A deep gloom was cast over the village of Stanmore from the mournful death of Queen Adelaide, whose liberal charities to the poor of the district, as well as her naturally unostentatious deportment, had rendered her deeply beloved by all classes of the inhabitants.

The funeral of Queen-dowager Adelaide was, in compliance with her own expressed desire, conducted with but little "pomp of the dead," or "pageantry of state." The ceremony of "lying in state" was altogether dispensed with, as also was the process of embalming the royal remains; and, contrary to the usual custom, the obsequies were performed at mid-day instead of after sunset by torch-light. The funeral took place on Thursday, the thirteenth of December. At eight in the morning the royal remains were removed from Bentley Priory for interment in the royal mausoleum in St. George's Chapel, Windsor. The procession was unostentatious; and, with the exception of a strong detachment of Life Guards, there was nothing beyond the ordinary display observable at the funeral of a private individual. The coffin, or rather the outer coffin—for there were three of them in all—was of Spanish mahogany, covered with rich crimson silk velvet; a double row of gold nails formed the outline, and the compartments were shaped by a triple row of smaller gold nails. The sides were relieved by massive gold handles, and the corners were of the same, ornamented by an engraved crown. The lid, in its upper compartments, had a large raised regal crown, and in its lower division a reversed torch and an extinct serpent. The plate bore the inscription—

Depositum
Serenissimæ Principessæ
ADELAIDE
Reginæ Dotariæ
Obiit Die Decembris
Anno Domini MDCCCXLIX.
Ætatis Suæ LVIII.

The procession proceeded with befitting solemnity through Ruisslip, Uxbridge, and Slough; and upon arriving at the south porch of St. George's Chapel, Windsor, the royal body was received at the door by the Archbishop of Canterbury and the canons of Windsor, and placed upon the platform. The crown of the departed Queen, with its cushion, was deposited on the coffin, and the procession then moved into the choir in the following order:—

The Canons of Windsor.
Garter.
The Lord Chamberlain of her Majesty's Household.

	Supporters of the pall.	THE BODY,	Supporters of the pall.	
Five Sailors.	Lord Byron. Lord Frederick Fitzclarence. And the Earl of Sheffield.	covered with a black velvet pall, adorned with escutcheons of her late Majesty's Arms.	Lord Adolphus Fitzclarence. Viscount Barrington. And the Marquis of Ormonde.	Five Sailors.

The chief mourner the Duchess of Norfolk, veiled, attended by Lady Cowper.
His Royal Highness Prince George.
His Serene Highness Prince Edward of Saxe Weimar.
His Serene Highness Prince Gustave of Saxe Weimar.
Master of the Horse to her late Majesty.
Lord Chamberlain to her late Majesty.
Vice Chamberlain to her late Majesty.
Ladies of the Bedchamber to her late Majesty.
Maids of Honour to her late Majesty.
Women of the Bedchamber to her late Majesty.
Clerk Marshal to her late Majesty.
Equerries to her late Majesty.
Chaplains to her late Majesty.
Physicians to her late Majesty.
Surgeons to her late Majesty.
Gentlemen Ushers to her late Majesty.
Dressers and Wardrobe Maid to her late Majesty.
Service page to her late Majesty.

On entering the choir, the chief mourner took her seat at the head of the coffin, the lord chamberlain of the departed Queen took his place at the feet, the vice-chamberlain standing near his lordship, and the other persons composing the procession arranged themselves behind the chief mourner, and on either side of the chapel. The Archbishop of Canterbury performed the service; and after he had read the lesson, the fifteenth chapter of the First Epistle to the Corinthians, from the twentieth verse to the end, the pall was withdrawn; and whilst the anthem, "When the ear heard her, then it blessed her," was being sung, the coffin was gradually lowered into the vault. When the archbishop had read the last collect and pronounced the benediction, garter king of arms, standing near the grave, pronounced the style of the departed Queen as follows: "Thus it hath pleased Almighty God to take out of this transitory life into His divine mercy, the late most high, most mighty, and most excellent Princess Adelaide, the Queen-dowager, relict of his Majesty King William IV., uncle to her most excellent Majesty Victoria, by the grace of God, of the United Kingdom of Great Britain, Queen Defender of the Faith, whom God bless and preserve with long life, health, honour, and all worldly happiness." The lord chamberlain and vice-chamberlain of the departed Queen-dowager Adelaide then stepped to the mouth of the tomb, and amidst profound silence broke their staves of office, and kneeling, deposited them on the coffin in the royal vault.

Thus ended the obsequies of the last Queen-dowager of England. There were present at the solemn ceremony Prince Albert, the Duke and Duchess of Cambridge, the Duchess of Kent, the Duke of

Saxe-Weimar, the Princesses Anne and Amelia of Saxe-Weimar, the Dukes of Wellington and of Norfolk, the Marquises of Lansdowne and of Abercorn, Lord John Russell, and other noble and illustrious personages.

The character of Queen Adelaide was pre-eminently distinguished by piety, liberality, unbounded charity, and benevolent sympathy. By her munificence the previously-mentioned church at Malta was built and endowed, as also was the Naval Asylum at Penge, for the widows of commanders, lieutenants, masters, and pursers in the Royal Navy. She likewise was a liberal contributor to the Society for the Propagation of the Gospel in Foreign Parts, the Colonial Bishopric Fund, the Church Missionary Society, the Sons of the Clergy, the Emigrants' Episcopal Fund, the fund for the erection of churches in Nova Scotia, Newfoundland, Cape Town, the Australian, and other British Colonies; the National Society, the London Diocesan Board of Education, the Ragged Schools, the Christian Knowledge Society, the Metropolis Church Fund, the Church Building Society, and to numerous other societies, institutions, and funds established for the religious, moral, and social advancement of mankind. According to the "Times," it was also the practice of Queen Adelaide "to subscribe largely to all the charities in every place where she happened, even for a time, to reside, especially to those of the parish of St. Martin, in which her London residence was situated." Her efforts in the furtherance of art, science, and literature were considerable; and in her choice of artists, sculptors, and architects, and in the commissions which she so liberally gave to painters, sculptors, and others, she exercised remarkable taste and discrimination.

Such was Adelaide of Saxe-Meiningen, a queen of inestimable piety, gentleness, and beneficence, and whose loss was felt and deeply lamented by all classes throughout the kingdom.

THE END.

MISCELLANEOUS—Continued.

Atlas. Appletons' Modern Atlas of the Earth, on 34 Maps. Colored. Royal 8vo. Half bound, 3 50

—— **Cornell's New General Atlas.** 1 handsome vol. 4to..... 1 00

Attache (The) in Madrid; or Sketches of the Court of Isabella II. 1 vol. 12mo..... 1 00

Baldwin's Flush Times in Mississippi and Alabama. 12mo. Illustrated............... 1 25

———— **Party Leaders.** 12mo. ....Cloth, 1 00

Barker (Jacob) Incidents in the Life of. 8vo. 2 portraits. Cloth, 1 00

Barth's Travels in Africa. (in press.)......................

Bartlett. Personal Narrative of Explorations in Texas, New Mexico, California, &c. &c. Maps and Illustrations. 2 vols. 8vo....................... 4 00

Bartlett. The same, in half calf extra 7 00

———— The same, in full calf extra 8 00

———— The same, cheap edition, in 1 vol., bound.................. 3 50

Basil. A Story of Modern Life. By W. Wilkie Collins. 12mo. ....Cloth, 75

Benton's Thirty Years' View; or a History of the Working of the American Government for thirty years, from 1820 to 1850. 2 very large vols., 8vo. pp. 1527, well printed,
Cloth, 5 00
Sheep, 6 00
In half calf or half mor., 7 00
In full calf, 8 00

Abridgment of the Debates of Congress, from 1789 to 1856. From Gales and Seaton's Annals of Congress; from their Register of Debates; and from the Official Reported Debates, by John C. Rives. By the Author of "The "Thirty Years' View." Vol. I. (to be in 15) preparing. Price per vol. 3 00

Beyminstre. By the author of "Lena." 1 vol. (in press)........

Bridgman's, The Pilgrims of Boston and their Descendants. 1 large vol., 8vo.....Cloth, 3 00

Butler's Philosophy of the Weather, and a Guide to its Changes. 12mo..........Cloth 1 00

Brace's Fawn of the Pale Faces. 12mo.............Cloth, 75

Brownell's Poems. 12mo. Boards, 75

———— **Ephemeron; a Poem.** 12mo............Paper, 25

Bryant's Poems. New edition, revised throughout. 2 vols. 12mo.
Cloth, 2 00
Extra cloth, gilt edges, 2 50
Morocco, antique or extra 6 00
Half morocco, gilt, 4 00
Half calf, antique or extra, 4 00
Full calf, antique or extra, 5 00
" In 1 vol. 18mo.....Cloth, 63
Gilt edges, 75
Antique morocco, 2 00

Bryant's What I Saw in California. With Map. 12mo..... 1 25

Burnett's Notes on the North-Western Territory. 8vo. Cloth, 2 00

Burton's Encyclopædia of Wit and Humour. Illustrated. 1 large vol. 8vo. (In press.)......

Calhoun (J. C.) The Works of (now first collected). 6 vols. 8vo. per vol......................... 2 00

———— Sold separately:
Vol. 1. ON GOVERNMENT.
2. REPORTS & LETTERS.
3, 4. SPEECHES.
5, 6. REPORTS & LETTERS.
Or, sets in 6 vols. half calf, 20 00
" " " full calf, 24 00

www.ingramcontent.com/pod-product-compliance
Lightning Source LLC
LaVergne TN
LVHW021259110826
845150LV00003B/432

* 9 7 8 1 4 2 5 5 6 0 8 2 9 *